THE

WORKS

OF

JEREMY BENTHAM

PUBLISHED UNDER THE SUPERINTENDENCE OF
HIS EXECUTOR,

John Bowring

Volume 6

Elibron Classics
www.elibron.com

Elibron Classics series.

ISBN 1-4021-6388-6 (paperback)
ISBN 1-4212-8079-5 (hardcover)

This Elibron Classics Replica Edition is an unabridged facsimile of the edition published in 1843 by William Tait, Edinburgh; Simpkin, Marshall, & Co., London.

THE

WORKS

OF

JEREMY BENTHAM,

PUBLISHED UNDER THE SUPERINTENDENCE OF
HIS EXECUTOR,

JOHN BOWRING.

VOLUME VI.

EDINBURGH:
WILLIAM TAIT, 107, PRINCES STREET;
SIMPKIN, MARSHALL, & CO., LONDON.
MDCCCXLIII.

INTRODUCTORY VIEW

OF

THE RATIONALE OF EVIDENCE;

FOR THE USE OF

NON-LAWYERS AS WELL AS LAWYERS.

BY JEREMY BENTHAM,
OF LINCOLN'S INN, ESQ.

CONTENTS.

CHAPTER I.
Title-page Justified.

§ 1. Persons for whose use — Non-lawyers as well as Lawyers, ... *page* 5
2. Rationale — propriety of the appellative, ib.

CHAPTER II.
Relation of Law to Happiness — of Procedure to the main body of the Law — of Evidence to Procedure.

1. Relation of Law to Happiness — of Judicature, *i. e.* Judicial Procedure, to Law, ... 7
2. Relation of Evidence to Judicature, . ib.

CHAPTER III.
Ends of Justice on the Occasion of Judicature.

1. True or proper ends of Judicature, . 8
2. False, but actual ends of Judicature, 10

CHAPTER IV.
Duties of the Legislator in Relation to Evidence.

1. List of these Duties, ... 12
2. Regard paid to these Duties in English practice, ... 13

CHAPTER V.
Probative Force — whence measured — how increased — how diminished.

1. Whence measured — Standard quantity, 14
2. Sources of Increase, ... ib.
3. Source of Diminution, ... 15

CHAPTER VI.
Degrees of Persuasion—thence of Probative Force — How expressible, . 16

CHAPTER VII.
Causes of Trustworthiness and Untrustworthiness in Testimony — thence of Belief and Unbelief.

1. Connexion between Trustworthiness and Belief, ... 17
2. Intellectual Causes, ... 18
3. Moral Causes in general — viz. the several Sanctions, ... ib.
4. The Physical Sanction, ... 19
5. The Popular or Moral Sanction, . . ib.
6. The Political, including the Legal Sanction, ... 20
7. The Religious Sanction, ... ib.

CHAPTER VIII.
Of the Securities for Trustworthiness in Evidence.

1. Qualities desirable in Evidence, . . 21
2. Instruments of Security, for securing to Evidence those Qualities, ... 22
3. Punishment, ... ib.
4. Judge and Co. — False Evidence rendered by them dispunishable, where profitable to themselves — Mendacity Licence, ... ib.
5. Shame, ... 24
6. Interrogation — including Counter-Interrogation, ... ib
§ 7. Counter-Evidence — Admission given to it, ... *page* 25
8. Writing, ... ib.
9. Publicity, to most purposes and on most occasions, ... 26
10. Privacy, to some purposes and on some occasions, ... 27

CHAPTER IX.
False Securities for Trustworthiness in Evidence— Oaths and Exclusions.

1. Ceremony of an Oath — a False Security for Trustworthiness, ... 28
2. Exclusion of Evidence — a False Security against Deception, ... 29

CHAPTER X.
Of the reception and extraction of Evidence, viz. with the help of the above Securities.

1. Oral Interrogation — Minutation or Notation — Recordation or Registration, . 30
2. Extraction should not be severed from Decision, ... 31
3. Epistolary Interrogation, ... 32
4. Modes of Interrogation principally in use, 33
5. Oral or Epistolary Mode — which to employ? . . . . ib.
6. Cross-examination — Anglicé and Romano-Anglicé, ... ib.
7. Confrontation and Repetition Romanicé, 34

CHAPTER XI.
Collection of Evidence — English Practice.

1. Natural Procedure, — Fit modes — Parliamentary and Jury Trial, &c., . . ib.
2. Unfit employed, to the exclusion of the above fit modes, ... 36
3. Deposition, Romano Anglicé — its inaptitude, ... ib.
4. Affidavit Evidence — its inaptitude, . . 37
5. English Judges — conscious of the Unfitness of their own Practice, . . . 40
6. Source of the unfit Modes — Sinister Interest, ... 42

CHAPTER XII.
Of Circumstantial Evidence.

1. Extent and Use of this Inquiry, . . 44
2. Facts, principal, evidentiary, probative, disaffirmative, infirmative, ... ib.
3. Principal fact, Delinquency; — evidentiary facts, inculpative and disculpative, ib.
4. Conversion of Inculpative Acts into separate Offences, ... 45
5. Principal, any physical fact, — disprobative fact, physical improbability: — or improbability physical — its operation in the character of counter-evidence, ib.
6. Principal, any psychological fact; — disprobative fact, — psychological impossibility, ... 47
7. In a train, principal, any prior act; — probative, any posterior, ... ib.
8. In a train, principal, any posterior act, probative, any prior, ... 48
9. Principal fact, spuriousness or unfairness; — probative fact, non-observance of formalities, ... ib.

§ 10. In litigation, principal fact want of merits; probative fact, discontinuance of procedure — its fallaciousness, . *page* 49
11. Probative force of circumstantial evidence, no fit subject for general rules, 50
12. Inferences of Judge-made Law, . . 53

CHAPTER XIII.
Of Make-shift Evidence.

1. Unoriginal Make-shift Evidence, . . 57
2. Extrajudicially written, Make-shift Evidence, ... ib.
3. Modifications of unoriginal Evidence, 59
4. Points of Infirmity common to Make-shift Evidence, ... ib.
5. Facienda by the Legislator in regard to Make-shift Evidence, ... ib.
6. English Practice in regard to Make-shift Evidence, ... 60

CHAPTER XIV.
Of Preappointed Evidence.

1. Its Nature and Origin, ... ib.
2. Uses of Preappointed Evidence, antilitigious, and statistic, ... 61
3. Legislator's Duties in relation to it, . 62
4. Subject-matters of Preappointed Evidence, ... ib.
5. Legally operative Facts, considered as subject-matters of preappointed Evidence, ... 63
6. Contracts and Instruments of Contract — Formalities, their use, ... 64
7. Contracts continued — Formalities, Means of enforcing Observance, . . ib.
8. Of Wills, ... 66

CHAPTER XV.
Difference between Preappointed and Unpreappointed Evidence.

1. The Difference developed, ... 68
2. Inconsistency and Confusion: *Anglicè*, for want of a right conception of it, . 70

CHAPTER XVI.
Preappointed Official Evidence.

1. Transactions of offices at large, considered as subjects of Preappointed Evidence, ... 72
2. Transactions of Judicial Offices, . . . 76
3. Of Laws considered as constituting the matter of Preappointed Evidence, . 77
4. Of Debates in Legislative and other Political Assemblies, in which Law is made, ... 78

CHAPTER XVII.
Extempore Recordation, how applicable to legally operative facts at large.

1. Demand for Recordation thus applied, 79
2. Principle on which a supply for this demand may be grounded, ... 81
3. Precedents from English and French Law, ... 82

CHAPTER XVIII.
Of Derivative, including Transcriptions, Recordation, wherein of Registration.

1. Derivative Recordation or Registration, its uses, ... 83
2. To what Instruments applicable, . . ib.
3. The obligation of Registering, how enforceable, ... 84
§ 4. The Function, by whom performable, *p.* 84
5. Quantity of Matter to be entered in the Registry, ... 85
6. Means of securing Transcripts against Error, ... ib.
7. Registrar's Duty in respect of Registration, ... ib.

CHAPTER XIX.
Exclusion of Evidence — General Considerations.

1. Modes of Exclusion, positive and negative, ... 86
2. Mischiefs liable to result from Exclusion put on Evidence, ... ib.
3. Principles respecting the Exclusion of Evidence, ... 88
4. Causes for which Exclusion is always proper, ... 89

CHAPTER XX.
Exclusion continued—Causes for which it is proper or not according to circumstances,

1. Avoidance of Delay, ... 90
2. Avoidance of Vexation at large, — Vexation, its modifications, ... 92
3. Vexation — in what cases a proper cause of Exclusion, ... 94
4. Avoidance of Vexation by Disclosure, 95
5. Evidence that ought not to be admitted — Disclosure of Catholic Confession, 98
6. Evidence that ought to be exacted, — Clients' Communication, ... 99
7. Avoidance of Expense, ... 101
8. How to minimize Evil in all these cases, 102
9. English Practice in relation to the above Evils, ... 103

CHAPTER XXI.
Exclusion continued — causes for which it cannot be proper.

1. Avoidance of Deception: viz. 1. through Imbecility, ... 105
2. Through Interest; viz. Sinister Interest, ib.
3. Through Improbity — including Religious Persuasion, ... 106
4. Avoidance of Vexation by Self-Inculpation, ... ib.

CHAPTER XXII.
Exclusions by English and other Laws — Analytic and Synoptic Sketches.

1. Undisguised Exclusions, ... 110
2. Disguised Exclusions, ... 113
3. Table of grounds of Exclusion, extracted from various Codes, . . . 116

CHAPTER XXIII.
Safeguards against suspicious Evidence: including Instructions concerning the weighing of Evidence.

1. Demand presented for such Safeguards, by the fear of change in case of the abolition of exclusions, ... 116
2. First Safeguard — Declaration of Credence from the Exhibitant, . . . 117
3. Second Safeguard—Code of instructions concerning the weighing of Evidence, 118
4. Third Safeguard—Recordation of cases where suspicious evidence has been received, ... 119

CHAPTER XXIV.

Authentication and Deauthentication, as applied to Preappointed and other written Evidence.

§ 1. Subject-matters of Authentication and Deauthentication, ... page 119
2. Proper course where Genuineness is unsuspected, ... 120
3. Course remaining where Suspicion has been declared, ... 121
4. Advantages from the here proposed, compared with the established course, 122
5. English Practice. — Case 1. Authenticative testimony of Parties excluded, 123
6. English Practice. — Case 2. Authenticative Testimony of non-attesting Witnesses excluded, ... 125
7. English Practice. — Case 3. Admission given to Instruments without Authentication, ... 126
8. English Practice.—Case 4. Shifts where the Script is in the power of the adversary, ... 127

CHAPTER XXV.

Exclusion and Nullification applied to contractual matter, in so far as writing has been omitted to be employed in giving expression to it.

1. Relation of this to preceding topics, viz. Preappointed Evidence, Exclusion, Authentication. &c., ... 128
2.—Case 1. Writing not employed: object of the exclusion, preventing or frustrating spurious Contracts orally expressed, ... 129
3. Impropriety of the Exclusion, &c. in this case, ... ib.
4. — Case 2. Writing employed: object, preventing or frustrating spurious orally-expressed alteration, . . . 132
5. Greater impropriety of the exclusion in this case, ... 133

CHAPTER XXVI.

Of the Exclusion and Nullification of Contractual Matter, informally though scriptitiously expressed, in a transaction which has been the subject of matter formally expressed, 134

CHAPTER XXVII.

Imprisonment for Debt: — Disguised Exclusion of Evidence involved in it.

1. Course prescribed in relation to this head, by Natural Procedure, . . . 135
2. Course actually pursued in relation to this head, by English Technical Procedure: — groundlessness and needlessness of the infliction in this case, ib.

CHAPTER XXVIII.

Of the burthen of Proof: on whom shall it lie? — (a question produced by undue exclusion of evidence.)

1. Answer to the question, on the ground of Natural Procedure, ... 136
2. Practice of the English Equity Courts, in relation to this head, ... 137
3. Practice of the English Common Law Courts in relation to this head, . . 138

CHAPTER XXIX.

Evidence considered in its relation to this or that fact in particular — why discarded from this work, . . page 139

CHAPTER XXX.

Evidence in relation to particular facts and pleadings under Technical Procedure, ... 141

CHAPTER XXXI.

False Theory of Evidence (Gilbert's) — its foundation: — precedence given to written before unwritten.

§ 1. Errors of this Theory — their efficient cause, ... 143
2. Errors of this Theory—their final cause, 144

CHAPTER XXXII.

Liberalists and Rigorists — Parties belligerent in the field of Jurisprudence, and in particular of Evidence, 145

CHAPTER XXXIII.

Conclusion, ... 148

APPENDIX A.

Cautionary Instructions respecting Evidence, for the use of Judges.

CH. I. Propriety of Cautionary Instructions, in preference to unbending Rules, 151
II. Considerations proper to be borne in mind in judging of the weight of Evidence, ... 153
III. Considerations respecting the effect of Interest in general upon Evidence, 155
IV. Considerations respecting the effect of pecuniary Interest upon Evidence, 156
V. Situations, ... 160
VI. Make-shift Evidence, ... 164
VII. Scale of Trustworthiness, ... 167
VIII. Best Evidence, what? 168
IX. English Law Scale of Trustworthiness, 175

APPENDIX B.

Of Imprisonment for Debt.

§ I. Its inaptitude as an Instrument of Compulsion, ... 176
II. Its inaptitude, applied as it is as an Instrument of Punishment, . . 177
III. Its needlessness demonstrated by experience, ... ib.
IV. End, or final cause of the institution —Judge and Co.'s sinister interest, 178
V. Means employed — Mendacity and Usurpation, ... ib.
VI. Affidavit previous to Arrest — its unfitness, ... 179
VII. Consequence of the Exclusion thus put upon Evidence, ... ib.
VIII. Advocates for the abolition of Imprisonment for Debt — their Errors, 180
IX. Scotch Law — Cessio Bonorum, its inadequacy, ... 181
X. Agenda — course proper to be taken on the occasion of Insolvency, . . 182

APPENDIX C.

False Theory of Evidence (Gilbert's) . 183

AN

INTRODUCTORY VIEW

OF THE

RATIONALE OF EVIDENCE.

CHAPTER I.

TITLE-PAGE JUSTIFIED.

§ 1. *Persons for whose use — Non-Lawyers as well as Lawyers.*

THE extent — the almost boundless expanse of the subject, — the variety of the matters touched upon, — the novelty of the points of view in which many — perhaps most of them — not to say all of them, will be found presented, — the unavoidably consequent novelty of not a few of the terms which it had been found necessary to employ, — all these things considered, it seemed to the author, that a general, and, how slightly soever, yet all-embracing outline, abstracted, and, like "*a panorama explanation,*" detached from the work at large, for the purpose of preparing the eye for the contents of the more fully-delineated scene, might not be without its use.

Should this be among the instances in which the Greek adage concerning books is destined to find its exemplification, the lighter burthen may at any rate do service, by saving the hand which takes it up, from the heavier load which is yet to come.

The field of evidence is no other than the field of knowledge. On that field, the researches, the result of which form the matter of the present work, extend not, it is true, beyond the case in which evidence is capable of being operative to a *legal purpose.* But forasmuch as on the whole field of human knowledge there is scarcely a conceivable spot from which evidence may not on one account or another be called for to a legal purpose* — hence it is, that, in effect, the portion cut off from the field of research by this limitation, will be found to be neither very considerable, nor altogether determinate.

Proportioned to the extent of that field will be the number of persons, to whom, in the character of *readers,* independently of any such misfortune as that of feeling themselves stretched on the rack in the character of *litigants,* it may happen to find in the work, matter on some account or other not altogether devoid of interest: and in proportion as this supposition comes to be realized, a justification will be afforded to the words, by which, in the title-page, *non-lawyers* are spoken of as persons to whose use, as well as that of lawyers, it may be found applicable.

§ 2. *Rationale — propriety of the appellative.*

The justification of the clause, "*for the use of non-lawyers,*" having been thus attempted, the word *rationale,* in the clause "rationale of evidence," remains to be justified.

To whomsoever, with other than a professional eye, it can have happened to take up a book on the subject of evidence, be the book what it may, it can scarcely have been long, before he saw more or less reason to suspect that in the formation of the mass of rules of which he found it composed, the share taken by that faculty, which, when applied to other subjects, goes by the name of reason, must have been small indeed. Towards any determinate *end,* good or bad, unless it were the increase of power and profit to the framers — scarcely any symptom of regard: arbitrary will — disguised, or not disguised, by this or that technical figure of speech, the sole, as well as the ever active efficient cause of everything that has been done: — such is the spectacle that will have presented itself to his view.

In matters of law — in matters of legislation at least — reason is an instrument by which *means* are employed and directed to the at-

* Examples of cases, in which facts, that to a first view might not seem of a nature to come under legal cognizance, have been taken, or may at any time be taken, for the subjects of legally delivered evidence: 1. On the occasion of a dispute concerning the value of *things*, or of the services of *persons* employed in the character of *instruments*, facts belonging to any branch of art, or even of science.

2. Facts relative to the authorship of *inventions*, the commercial benefit of which has for a time been legally secured to the inventor by a patent,

3. By means of a *wager*, the existence, actual or even probable, of any supposed matter of fact whatever, actual or conceivable, may, if desirable, be taken for the subject of legally delivered evidence.

tainment of an *end*. Of legislation the proper end may, it is hoped, without much presumption, be stated as being, — not but there are those who will deny it, — in every community, *the creation and preservation of the greatest happiness to the greatest number* — or, in one word, *happiness:* a *false* end, the creation and preservation of the greatest quantity of happiness to a few, to the prejudice, and in diminution of the happiness of the greatest number: — to a few, and those few naturally and usually the possessors of the several powers of government, with their official subordinates, and their other associates and connexions: — and this, in proportion as the machinery of government is looked into, will almost everywhere be seen to be the end, principally at least, if not exclusively, aimed at and pursued.

As to the faculty called *will*, its act, *volition*, has on each occasion, for its causes, *interests*, acting in the character of *motives*. In what way these springs of action, with as little assistance as perhaps in any instance was ever received or looked for from the faculty of *reason*, give existence everywhere to the law of evidence, and more particularly to the law of English evidence, is among those questions, the answers to which will in some shape or other, it is supposed, be found as occasion serves, presenting themselves to the reader in his progress through the work.

Knowledge of the proper *remedies* is seldom to be obtained without knowledge of the *mischief*;—for the purpose of remedy, knowledge of the *effect* is seldom sufficient without knowledge of the *cause*.

To the *non-lawyer*, or as in lawyers' language he is called, the *unlearned reader*, not only in respect of perspicuity, but in respect of that sort of satisfaction which is afforded by the observation of practical use, under each head, a delineation more or less particular, of the state of the law *as it is*, would naturally have been in no small degree acceptable;* but with the design of the present sketch, any such illustration would have been altogether incompatible. If the contents of two large quartos could have been compressed into three or four hundred octavo pages, doubtless so much the better; but if they could, the difference would have been so much surplusage. What has all along been within the bounds of possibility, at least whether within or not within the bounds of the author's ability, has been to *excite* curiosity: what could only here and there be so much as attempted, has been in some degree to satisfy it.

Remedy supposes mischief. Rules are seldom laid down, but with a view more or less distinct to antecedent transgressions: and, not only upon the *rules* that will here be seen suggested, but upon the state of the law which during the framing of them was in view, the observation may, for the use of the unlearned reader, afford some light. Accordingly, as often as upon the view of this or that suggestion, the propriety of it may happen to present itself, as being so completely obvious and indisputable as to reflect upon it the imputation of nugatoriness and uselessness, the danger of error will not be great, if his conclusion be— that this dictate of the plainest common-sense stands, in a great part, if not in the whole of its extent, contravened by the practice of English judges.

Thus, if in what *ought* to be done, a man reads what *has not* been done, and in what *ought not* to be done, what *has* been done, the text itself, may, with the assistance of this short hint, perform the office of a comment.

Should any such question be asked, as how it can have happened that, in the sight of the legislator, in almost everything they did, men thus called, and thus chosen, kept doing that which was evil, the answer, true or not true, will at least be found simple and intelligible. What they did was evil, because to do otherwise than evil, both *will* and *ability* were always wanting: *will* was wanting, because *interest* was wanting: *ability* was wanting, because *will* was.

Of this opposition between what might seem *duty* on the one hand, and *interest* coupled with power on the other, the *causes*, as well as the *existence*, have been shown already in another work: and to everything that, in the course of the present pages, will be seen indicated in relation to established practice, these observations, short as they are, may afford a clue.

Thus, and thus alone, may be accounted for, — accounted for in crowds, — phenomena which otherwise would have been plainly unaccountable.

When thistles only are sown, grapes ought not to be expected.

As in every other part of the field, so in this: — of that rule of action, on the state of which, everything that is valuable to man is in so high a degree dependent, very different is the representation that would assuredly have been most agreeable to the feelings of the generality of those who live under it, and of none in a higher degree than of him, on whom the task of giving the picture, which is here given of it, has devolved. Unfortunately, by certificates of health, neither in the body natural, nor yet in the body politic, are disorders to be cured.

* For the instruction of the non-lawyer, including the law-student, if any such there be, who being engaged in the study of *law as it is*, has nerves to endure a sight, or so much as a prospect, so unwelcome as that of *law as it ought to be* — in other words, who, his prosperity depending upon the depravity of the system, can endure the contemplation of anything tending to a cure, I would venture to recommend the perusal *pari passu* of Peake's compendium of the law of evidence.

By means of the relation, the all-regulating relation, constantly and comprehensively kept in view; viz. the relation of *means* to *end*, the aim has all along been to give to the branch of legislation here in question the form of *an art*, and in respect of comprehensiveness as well as precision, the form (but if possible without the repulsiveness) of a science.

CHAPTER II.

RELATION OF LAW TO HAPPINESS — OF PROCEDURE TO THE MAIN BODY OF THE LAW — OF EVIDENCE TO PROCEDURE.

§ 1. *Relation of Law to Happiness — of Judicature*, i. e. *Judicial Procedure, to Law.*

THE *adjective* branch of law, or *law of procedure*, and therein the *law of evidence*, has everywhere for its object, at least ought to have, the giving effect throughout to the several regulations and arrangements of which the *substantive branch* or *main body* of the law is composed.

As to the main or substantive branch, it has for its *ultimate* fruits happiness and unhappiness, in infinitely diversified and ever-changing proportions; but, in the meantime, for its *immediate* fruits, it has those fictitious indeed, but indispensably employed, creatures of imagination and language, viz. *rights* and *obligations*: *rights* its sweet fruits, pregnant with whatever is good, whether in the shape of security or pleasure: *obligations* its *bitter* fruits, evil in themselves, good in so far as they are the indispensable instruments of all created good, being necessary as well to the creation, as to the preservation, of all law-created *rights*.

Vain would be the attempt to impose *obligations* — *legal obligations*: — vain, therefore, the attempt to give effect to *rights* — to *legal rights* — unless, in a state of constant preparation to give execution to the will of the sovereign in this behalf, there existed a mass of physical force, superior to all resistance, which in the ordinary state of political society could be likely in any case to be opposed by private hands; and to which, accordingly, whether by reflection, or by habit and imitation, the members of the community at large were in a state of constant disposition to pay, if not an active, at least a passive and unresisting obedience.

This disposable force — the sort of person or character to whose disposition it stands committed — is that which stands expressed by one common abstract denomination, as employed in the singular number, viz. *the judge*: *the judge*, including in that one word all persons — all the individuals — to whom, on any given occasion, for the purpose in question, any portion of that force happens to be intrusted.

It is therefore by means, and in respect of the efficient *service* of this exalted functionary rendered immediately to the sovereign in his quality of legislator, but through him and in ultimate result to the community at large, that *execution* and *effect* — *occasionally* execution, and thus *constantly* effect — are given to those *expressions* — those *evidences* — those *repositories* — those *vehicles* — of the sovereign's will, which are spoken of under the name of *laws*.

§ 2. *Relation of Evidence to Judicature.*

Be the law or portion of law what it may, antecedently to execution — if not in form, at any rate in effect — if not expressed in words, declared at any rate by actions — comes *decision*: judicial decision, — in official language called sometimes *judgment*, sometimes *decree*, sometimes — itself or its difficultly distinguishable consequences — by various other names, such as *rule*, *order*, *writ*, *precept*, *mandate*, and the like.

In every instance in which, expressly or virtually, judgment is thus pronounced, two propositions are expressly or virtually delivered; viz. a proposition concerning the state of the *law*, and a proposition concerning the state of certain matters of *fact* — of matters of fact which belong to the case, and to which the law that belongs to the case is considered as applying itself. On the subject of the state of the law, the proposition has for its ground, in the case of *written*, i. e. *statute* law, the very words of the law; of that portion of the law, which on the occasion in question is in question: — in the case of *unwritten* law, a sort of law, of the essence of which it is, not to have any determinate set of words really belonging to it, the supposed purport of some portion of written law, which on the occasion in question is feigned or imagined for the purpose.

Thus much as to law: — in relation to matter of *fact*, the decision has for its ground the evidence* by which term is on every occasion understood some *other* matter of fact, which on that same occasion is presented to the mind or sense of the judge, for the purpose of producing in his mind a persuasion assertive of the existence or non-existence of a matter of fact first mentioned, which is always some *individual* matter of fact supposed to be of that *sort*, which on the occasion in question the legislator is supposed to have had in view.

Matters of fact being in such or such a

* Judgment, 1. *Ex visu judicis*, or from view; 2. From the supposed *notoriety* of the fact; 3. From the judge's *private* knowledge; 4. From the supposed *improbability* of the alleged fact; 5. Judgment by *default*, or from *non-observance of formalities*. In all these several cases the ground of the judgment will be seen to be reducible to the notion of evidence.

state, — such and such (says the legislator) shall be the state of *right* and thence of *obligation:* — he who is in such or such a situation comprehended in that state, *shall have a right to receive upon demand, such or such a service at the hands of the judge.* Placing himself in the plaintiff's side, "I am in such a situation," says a man, addressing himself to the judge — "I am in such a situation — it is therefore now your duty to render me that service."

Thus, on each occasion on which a *suit* is instituted — a judicial *demand* preferred, — a *service* of a nature adapted to the nature of the demand — a service always of the *positive* cast — is by the *plaintiff* called for at the hands of the judge. At the same time, if the demand be contested — the *suit defended,* — a service of an opposite nature—a service of the *negative* cast — is called for on the part of the *defendant:* — a service which consists in the *non*-imposition of those obligations — those burthensome obligations — obligations to act, to forbear, to suffer, — the imposition of which would be necessary to the rendering to the plaintiff the service, be it what it may, which is prayed for on his side.

Meantime, to constitute a foundation for this right, so far as depends upon the matter of fact, there can be nothing but the *evidence:* — for the reception of which, to the purpose of rendering, in conformity to the will declared as above by the legislator, either the positive service prayed on the plaintiff's side, or the opposite and negative service prayed on the defendant's side, according as the plaintiff is or is not in the situation in which he says he is, the judicatory cannot but lie equally open on both sides.

In this state of things, if on the ground of matter of *fact* it happen to the plaintiff to fail — to fail of making out his right to the service prayed for — he at the same time having that right, — it may be in one or other of three ways, and it cannot be in any ulterior way: — 1. Evidence necessary and sufficient to the formation of the ground in question is *not forthcoming;* 2. Forthcoming and standing alone, *i. e.* without counter-evidence on the defendant's side, it fails of obtaining the necessary *credence;* 3. On defendant's side, *counter-evidence* — evidence, the belief of which is incompatible with the belief of that which is adduced on the plaintiff's side, obtains *stronger* credence. But by the supposition, the plaintiff has really a right to the service which he demands: — this being the case, what follows by the same supposition is — that in the evidence adduced on the part of the defendant, there is something of *incorrectness*, or partially-operating *incompleteness* — something, at any rate, which thereby has produced a deceptious effect on the judgment of the judge.

CHAPTER III.

ENDS OF JUSTICE ON THE OCCASION OF JUDICATURE.*

§ 1. *True or proper ends of Judicature.*

THE aggregate of the objects thus meant to be designated, being *the standard of reference*, to which, through the whole course of this work, every other object will be referred — the *test* by which everything will be tried — everything that is approved of, approved; — everything that is condemned, condemned; — it seemed necessary, thus, at the very outset, to bring together, under one view, a list of those same objects, placed in such sort, that, as well each by itself, as their mutual relations and dependencies being clearly understood, may on each succeeding occasion be present, or capable of being readily presented to the mind.

Of the ends of judicature, were there none of them but what were capable of being presented in a *positive* or *affirmative* shape, the list might be very short.

I. In case of *wrong* supposed to have already been committed: —

1. Application of the matter of *satisfaction where* due, — and in the *shape* in which it is due.

2. Where on the score of *punishment* ulterior suffering† is supposed necessary, application of such suffering *where* due, and in the *shape* in which it is due.

II. In the case where no wrong is supposed to have been committed, but, at the hands of the judge, a *service*, consisting generally in the conferring of some *new right*‡ on the plaintiff or demandant, is demanded.

---

* For shortness, say at pleasure, either the *ends of judicature*, or the *ends of justice.* Taken by itself, and without the limitation thus applied, the expression *ends of justice*, besides that the import of it is multifarious and indeterminate in the extreme, is one for which there will scarcely be any particular demand to the purpose of the present work.

Let *utility* be the leading word, that word translated immediately into *good* and *evil*, and those again into *pain* and *pleasure*, the question will be all along concerning human *feelings*, and their causes. Let *justice* be the leading word, the question will be no other than concerning the meaning of that word, and for the solution of it, no less a task than that of hunting out the different occasions on which it has been employed, or would be necessary.

† *Ulterior suffering.* — From the rendering to one person *satisfaction* at the expense of another, suffering, on the part of this other, will, in every case, be found inseparable.

‡ *New right.*] When upon the sale of a mass of property, to a share in which he is entitled by will, for example, or as a creditor to a person insolvent—a person receives, in virtue of the decision of a judge, the sum of money representative of the net amount of that share, the rights included in the property of the money constitute a mass

3. *Collation of right* where due, and in the *shape* in which it is due.

4. *Reddition of judicial service* at large* where due, and in the shape in which it is due.

Thus short and simple might be the list of the ends of judicature, were there none but such as are of the *positive* cast, such as are the above, to call upon the legislator for his regard.

But for the accomplishment of those positive ends—for the production of good in those positive shapes—let any course be taken—even the best imaginable—*evil* in various shapes is still liable to be produced:—and of this evil, so many shapes as there may be any use in distinguishing, so many negative ends or objects may be assigned as possessing, on the occasion of judicature, a demand for attention and pursuit on the part of the judge:—the *good*, that the production of it may, as far as possible, be accomplished;—the *evil*, that the production of it may, as far as possible, be prevented.

Of these *negative* ends of judicature, the description cannot in any other way be given than by giving a list of the several *evils*, by the prevention or avoidance of which, in so far as possible, these several ends are proportionably accomplished. Of these evils, the list may stand as follows, viz.—

I. Referable to the *penal* and the *non-penal*† departments of the field of law taken together, *directly-resulting evils* incident to judicature—*i. e.* evils resulting in a *direct* way from misapplication of the power of judicature:—

1. Non-application of the matter of *satisfaction* where due.

2. Application of the matter of satisfaction (though it be where due) in a *shape*‡ not due.

3. Application of the matter of satisfaction where *not* due.

4. Non-application of the matter of *punishment* where due.

5. Application of the matter of *punishment* (though it be where due) in a *shape* not due.

6. Application of the matter of punishment where *not* due.

7. Non-collation of *right* where due.

8. Collation of right in a *shape* not due.

9. Collation of right where *not* due.

10. Non-reddition of *judicial service* (at large) ‖ where due.

11. Reddition of judicial service in a *shape* not due.

12. Reddition of judicial service where *not* due.

---

of new rights conferred upon him by the judge. Till the decision of the judge pronouncing what is thus made due is made known, and (the time allotted for the payment being elapsed) the money has remained unpaid, there is no wrong done by anybody—no right violated: the right which the party in question had till then, was not an already formed right to any specific sum of money, but a right to such sum, as on the ground in question should come to be adjudicated by the judge; including an antecedent right to the correspondent *service* at the hands of the judge, viz. the service rendered by the collation of the mass of rights, included in the right of recovering the money as above.

* *Judicial service at large.*] Cases are not altogether wanting, in which, otherwise than by *collation* of any *new right*, *service* is *rendered* by the *decision* and consequent *order* of a judge.—Example:—1. Removal of a mere *physical* impediment to the enjoyment of a man's personal liberty, or any part of his property;—a wrong-placed gate—a noisome manufactory, &c.—anything coming under the denomination of a *nuisance*.

2. In every case in which *satisfaction* is administered, in so far as it is of the *vindictive* kind, it is applied by the simple application of *punishment*, and without the creation of any new right.

So multifarious, so ill defined, so fugitive, so intertwined one with another, and as yet so imperfectly distinguished and explained, are the fictitious entities called *rights*, that, on such a subject, in such a place as the present, to afford anything like complete satisfaction, is plainly impossible. The anatomy of rights has never yet found a professor to explain it.

† Commonly called *civil*. But when employed as an adjunct to the word *law*, the word *civil* is moreover employed to signify *non-constitutional*, or *non-political*, or *non-military*, or *non-ecclesiastical* law: as also to designate *Rome-bred* law, and in *Rome-bred* law itself, it is used as synonymous to *non-canon* law. A word which is used promiscuously in so many different senses, all of them on occasions on which they require to be distinguished from each other, is incapable of answering the purposes of him who wishes to understand, or of him who wishes to be understood.

‡ *In a shape not due.*] Where, being applied where due, the matter of satisfaction is applied in *a shape not due*, the evil includes in it, by implication, another evil, an evil of an opposite description, viz. *non*-application of the object in question in its *due* shape. But as in the case of a pecuniary account, with errors in it on both sides,—the effect of this reduplication is—not to increase, but to compensate for and diminish the effect of the error which stands expressed:—thus it is in regard to satisfaction;—and so it is where *punishment* is to be applied, where *rights* are to be conferred, or where other judicial services are to be rendered, as below.

Under *shape* may be included *quantity*, *quality*, *place*, *time*: under *undue shape*, undue in point of quantity, undue in point of quality, and so forth.

Suppose the error to be in point of *quantity*—in this case, so far as quantity alone is concerned, (the application of the object in a quantity *not* due, including in it the *non*-application of it in the quantity that is due,) the undue *suffering* to one party, the undue *advantage* to the other party, cannot either of them amount to anything more than the difference.

‖ *Service at large.*] i. e. otherwise than by *collation* of a *right*, which, as above, is the most frequently exemplified, though not the only shape in which judicial service, not consisting in the application either of satisfaction for wrong, or of punishment, is rendered.

If the error be only in respect of *quality*, the *quantity* being exactly what is due, the evil (it may occur) may be but imaginary. The answer is — if it be the evil of the first order, and nothing farther, that is looked for; — yes; viz. that which has for its seat the *feelings* of the *parties* on either side, or on both sides: notwithstanding the error, quantity — of suffering on the one side, of enjoyment on the other — being by the supposition the same as if there had been no such error. But, however it may be in the case of *satisfaction*, in the case of *punishment*, if as by the supposition there be an error in respect of *quality*, the effects of that error will render themselves sensible, by the production of evil of the *second* order, *i. e.* the people at large will, in some shape or other, viz. *danger* or *alarm*, or both, be sufferers from it. Of the importance of *quality* in punishment, and of the distinction between *first* and *second* orders as applied to *evil* and to *good*, views have been given in other places.*

Referable still to the same two departments, follow in the list of evils incident to judicature, such as may be termed *collaterally resulting* — evils resulting in a collateral way from the misapplication of the powers of judicature: —

1. *Delay*, where, and in so far as, unnecessary or preponderant.†

2. *Vexation*, where, and in so far as, unnecessary or preponderant.

3. Expense, where, and in so far as, unnecessary or preponderant.‡

In the word *misdecision*, we have a general term, under which any decision, under and by virtue of which any of the above-mentioned evils, mentioned as correspondent, and opposite to the *direct negative* ends of judicature, are considered as produced.*

Given the *ends of justice* on the occasion of judicature, given in the same degree of detail are the *duties of the judge*.

If, as it has been endeavoured to be made, this analysis be found all-comprehensive, every imaginable breach of duty commissible on the part of a judge, as such, will be found referable to one or more of the heads contained in it.

§ 2. *False, but actual ends of Judicature.*

The objects hitherto brought to view, under the name of the *ends of judicature*, are those which seemed the *proper*, or, in one sense of the word *true*, the true ends of judicature.

Opposite to these ends stand those which, it should seem, may without impropriety be termed the *improper* ends, or, in one sense of the word *false*, the *false*: — in England, at least, these, alas! will be found to *have* always *been* — not to say *to be* — the *actual* ends.

In England, in the early ages of the constitution, reckoning from the Norman conquest, the one all-embracing false *end* may be stated as having for its correspondent *interest*, private and personal, the sinister interest of the monarch: his sinister interest, in the several shapes in which the sinister interest of a public man is capable of displaying itself, viz. those of which the objects are, respectively, *money*, *power*, *reputation* (*reputation*,

---

* See Introduction to Morals, &c. Ch. XII. p. 69; and Principles of Penal Law, Part II. Book I. Ch. II. p. 395.

† *Unnecessary or preponderant.*] See, in Scotch Reform, (Delay and Complication Tables) a detailed explanation and exemplification of this *triad* of judicial evils, a view of their relations and bearings to each other; and of the effect of the terms *unnecessary* and *preponderant* as respectively applied to them. See likewise below, the chapter on *Exclusion*, § 2.

‡ Follows a list of certain evils referable to the constitutional department. To these, there not being any need of reference for the purpose, or on the occasion of the present work, the text might (it was thought) be exonerated from them without loss: —

1. On the part of judges, ***insubordination:*** including on the part of any judicatory, non-observance of the ordinances of the legislator, and on the part of a *subordinate* judicatory, non-observance of the orders of its super-ordinate.

2. *Usurpation of jurisdiction:* viz. on the part of any judicatory: whether to the prejudice of the authority of the legislator alone, or to the prejudice of the authority of any judicatory, super-ordinate, co-ordinate, or subordinate.

3. *Ununiformity in judicature:* viz. whether as between system and system of procedure, or under the same or different systems, by difference as between decision and decision in the same case, viz. in the same individual case, or in two individual cases of exactly the same sort.

Important as they are, these ends are but of the *second* order: for, for argument sake (though the fact is so much otherwise,) suppose that none of these *other* evils which belong to the non-penal and penal departments ever have place, *these* are but *nominal* not *real* evils.

* The evils just termed *collaterally resulting*, viz. unnecessary or preponderant delay, vexation and expense, — is it not by *decision* (it may be asked) that these evils also are produced? — and such *decision*, is it not *misdecision* likewise?

Answer — In so far as they are produced under and by virtue of the established and undisputed course of the judicial procedure, and accordingly without *contestation*, they are produced without express decision, and thence in so far without *mis-decision*.

If, in relation to any one of these topics, matter of dispute happen to take place, — in this case, a demand for decision, and along with it room for *misdecision*, does indeed take place. But in this case, any such dispute is in effect a separate suit, or cause, and if, on the subject of it, misdecision takes place, it will be found, it is supposed, clothed in one or more of the twelve forms, and referable to one or more of the twelve heads above mentioned.

when operating upon an extensive scale, called *fame*,) constantly ease, and occasionally *vengeance*.*

To the sinister interest of the monarch, the indolence and imbecility incident to that situation, joined to the necessary industry and comparative mental vigour of his instruments and substitutes, *the judges*, substituted by degrees, and in a principal degree, the sinister interests of these his subordinates:—the seat of the sinister interest thus gradually shifting, the *shapes* in which it operated still the same.

Among the *false* ends, the above may be termed the *direct* ends of judicature. Relation had to these, the name of *collateral* ends may be given to those which correspond with the sinister interests of those other members of the governing body who, in the character of *sinecurists*, or *over-paid placemen*, or holders of *needless* places or otherwise, have, for the benefit of their support, been suffered without repugnance to come in for shares in the profits of high-seated and irresistible depredation:—fruits of scientifically and diligently cultivated delay, vexation, and expense.

Among these, a place of pre-eminence is due to the *man of finance*, who—from taxes, whether under the name of *taxes*, or under the name of *fees*, imposed upon justice (*i. e.* from the sale of that commodity to all those who *have* wherewithal to pay for it, coupled with the denial of it to all who have not,) over and above any part of the produce which, on any such false pretence as that of official labour performed, he may have contrived to put into his own pocket, or that of this or that more or less near connexion—derives that comparative *ease* which, from a hundredth part of the same suffering, inflicted upon an equal number of patients, capable of making their cries heard in concert, might receive intolerable disturbance.†

In the fabrication of *priest-made religion*, even in its most pernicious forms, the predominance of sinister interest would scarcely be found more incontestable than it may be seen to be in *judge-made law*—seen even in the picture given of it by Blackstone—seen notwithstanding all his varnishes.

For the sake of emolument and advantage in other shapes extractible out of the expense, to manufacture on every occasion, in the greatest endurable quantity, the inseparably-interwoven tissue of abuses—*viz.* unnecessary delay, vexation, and expense—may be seen throughout to have been the only real object of solicitude. Fortunately, in pursuit of the only real object, it was not possible to proceed without the appearance, nor even altogether without the reality of justice; and to the necessity thus produced may, without much danger of error, be ascribed what little of justice may be found perceptible in the result.

Bearing in mind thus much, the reader, learned or unlearned, will find himself in a condition to account for the several phenomena of actual law, as they present themelves to view: if, on the contrary, the burthen be felt too heavy for endurance, everything he sees will be an effect without a cause.

As human nature is constituted, the preservation of the individual and of the species depending upon the ascendency universally maintained (here and there an extraordinary case excepted) by *self-regarding* over *social interests*; so in judicature, as in every other department of government, the preference has of course been all along given to the *false ends*, in their competition with the *true*: the false ends, as above described, having all along been pursued, as far as the craft or indifference of the monarch, and the blindness or patience of the people, would permit: the true pursued so far, and so far only, as *reality* appeared necessary to the keeping up of *appearance*.

Read the history of the Council of Trent, as written by Paul Sarpi. Observe by what springs of action each result was produced: believe the actors themselves, by piety—everything by pure piety: believe the historian, by everything *but* piety.

Such as was the share which *piety* had in the production of that portion of ecclesiastical law which received its establishment from the council of Trent, such, or thereabouts, may be seen to have been the share which *the love of justice* had in the production of that part of the rule of action which, instead of *the* legislator, has had *judges* for its authors; particularly that part which is composed of the law of *procedure*, and in the law of procedure, that which is composed of the law of evidence.

Of the present sketch, few, perhaps, are the pages that may not be seen to add, more or less, to the proof of that instructive truth.

* Possible, and, if possible, not inconvenient, names of the respective interests taken from their respective symbols:—interest of the *purse*, the *sceptre*, the *trumpet*, the *pillow*, and,—if critic gall can keep itself in—the *gall bladder*. For the corresponding *pleasures*, *pains*, and motives, see Table of Springs of Action, Vol. I. p. 195.

† For the matchless mischief of this species of tax, see *Protest against Law Taxes*. As to the monarch (I mean of present time,) setting aside his share in the benefit of the vast common fund, which, even without hands to apply it, operates through the medium of hope and fear, in so commodious a manner, and so extensively efficient a degree, in the character of *matter of corruption*, the pittance which has been left to his personal share is scarcely worth mentioning. Strained through a number of intermediate sponges, it drops into the privy purse, to the amount of no more than £5000 or £6000 a-year, under the name of *green wax*.[a]

[a] Finance Reports, 1797–8, or 1806–7.

But in the chapter on *Exclusion*, the section which speaks of that operation, as performed on the ground of a supposed danger of deception, will perhaps be found to comprehend within the smallest compass, the greatest quantity of such matter as concurs in giving probability to that inference.

CHAPTER IV.

DUTIES OF THE LEGISLATOR IN RELATION TO EVIDENCE.

§ .. *List of these Duties.*

AFTER what has been said of the relation of judicature to law, and of evidence to judicature, the duties of the legislator, in relation to evidence, will, it is supposed, be found comprisable under the six following heads — under each of which follow a few words of explanation, together with a brief intimation of the sort of regard paid to these duties in English practice. For giving expression to them, the imperative mood has been suggested by grammatical convenience: —

1. For the support of every *right conferred*, of every obligation imposed by you, do whatsoever is in your power towards the securing existence, and thereafter *forthcomingness** to whatsoever evidence may be necessary: — saving on each individual occasion all due regard to the collateral ends of judicature,† as above indicated.

2. *Avoid* putting an exclusion upon evidence on every occasion on which exclusion of evidence is improper; — as it will be shown to be in every case, except those in which it is called for by a due regard ‡ to the collateral ends of judicature.

3. Put an exclusion* upon evidence on every occasion on which exclusion is *proper*; — as it will be shown to be, on every occasion on which it is called for by a due regard to the collateral ends of judicature.

4. So order matters, as far as may be, that on each individual occasion, whatsoever evidence comes to have been received, shall not, in respect of the degree of persuasion produced by it in the mind of the judge, operate with an effect *greater*† than its due effect.

5. Nor less† than its due effect.

6. So order matters, that saving always the regard due to the collateral ends of justice, each article of evidence *shall*, to the mind of the judge, present itself in its *best* shape: ‡ —

---

* *The securing forthcomingness.*] Physical compulsion — application of the matter of punishment — application of the matter of reward — such are the means by which, whether it be for the purpose of *evidence*, or for the purpose of *justiciability* (including what in technical language is called execution) — whether it be on the part of *things* or *persons* — forthcomingness is effected. But to the subject of procedure — not to the subject of evidence, belong the operations which have for their objects the production of these several effects. In a work on the law of evidence, these effects are in general supposed to be already accomplished: the evidence or the person or thing in which it has its source, is already *forthcoming*, and waits for nothing but the order of the judge. The only case in which evidence is here taken up at any antecedent period, is that which affords room for the sort of evidence brought to view at the end of this list, under the appellation of *pre-appointed* evidence.

† *Collateral ends,*] viz. prevention, or avoidance of the evils of *delay*, *vexation*, and *expense*, in so far as unnecessary or *preponderant*.

‡ *Due regard.*] The *regard* here spoken of as *due*, consists in neither more or less than the observance of the simple and most unexceptionable rule — *produce not a greater evil* in preference *to a less*. For the application of this rule to the subject of evidence, see the chapter on *Exclusion*.

* *Exclusion.*] On the occasion in question, if the article of evidence in question be not forthcoming, *forbearance* to cause it to be forthcoming is, in a sort of *negative* way, putting an exclusion upon it: — exclusion in a *positive* way is — where the evidence, although it were tendered, would not be received.

† *Greater than its due effect; — less than its due effect.*] Among mankind at large, the general propensity is — to give to evidence too much rather than too little credence. Although deception may in either case be alike the consequence, yet to prevent too *great* credence is, in a manner, except where religion has been concerned, the only object of the two, on which, on the part of government, any care has been employed. For this purpose, the only course that has been taken is *exclusion*: — for fear of deception, exclusion put upon all such evidence, in the instance of which it has been apprehended that, if received, too great credence would be bestowed upon it, and thereby *deception*, deception put by it upon the judge would be the consequence.

Avoidance of deception by evidence being the *end*, *exclusion* of evidence will here be represented as in *no* case proper and conducive: *instruction*, viz. as from the legislator to the judge, as being in *every* case proper and conducive, and the only sort of application that in the nature of the case *can* be conducive to that end.

‡ *Best shape.*] In some instances, evidence is not to be had but in its *own shape*, and, as it were, ready made; so that all that the judge has to do with it is to *receive* it. — Examples: — 1. *Memorandums* made for private use; 2. *Letters*, after or before transmission; 3. *Things* in general, in the character of sources of *real* evidence — a modification of *circumstantial* evidence.

In other instances, the judge has to *extract* it himself, or at any rate, finds nothing to hinder him from extracting it: in which case, the *shape* in which it will present itself depends upon himself: *interrogation* being the chief instrument employed in the extraction of it. According to the circumstances in which it is *received* or *extracted*, great is the variety of *shapes* of which it will be found susceptible.

Before the art of writing came into use, personal testimony, delivered or extracted *viva voce* in the presence of the judge, presented the only shape in which personal evidence could make its appearance. Since that period, *pre-appointed* meaning, by its *best shape*, that in which it is least likely to be productive of deception — to operate with an effect *greater*, or with an effect *less* than what is due.

7. By arrangements of a general complexion, taken beforehand, do what the nature of the case admits of, not only towards securing in each instance, as above, the *forthcomingness* of such necessary evidence as may happen to have been brought by other causes into existence, but also towards securing *existence* to such necessary lots of evidence.

N. B. Evidence brought into existence by the operation of the sort of providence thus indicated, will herein be designated by the appellation of *pre-appointed* evidence.

§ 2. *Regard paid to these Duties in English Practice.*

Such, in as far as the view here taken of the subject may be found correct, being the list of the *duties* or *tasks* proper to be performed by the *legislator* — understand always, by the *sovereign* in his character of legislator — in the field of evidence, a brief intimation of the sort and degree of regard, which, it is supposed, will be found to have been paid in English practice to these duties, may even, in this early stage of the inquiry, be not altogether without its use.

As to the sovereign, considered in his character of legislator, on English ground in particular, in relation to the whole extent of this part of the field of action, the most supine neglect will, on his part, be everywhere but too discernible: arrangements, on which justice is so completely dependent, left, almost without exception, to be made by sinister interest, and interest-begotten prejudice, in the person of the judge: — of the judge who, in this as in all other parts of the field of law, pretending to *find* already made whatsoever he makes, makes and mars exactly what he pleases. If here and there, to this or that arrangement the touch of the legislative sceptre may be seen applied, it is, in every instance, by the hand of the judge that the instrument has been guided, no symptoms of thinking being anywhere perceptible, on the part of that which *should* have been, and is spoken of as if it *were*, the all-directing mind.

1. Under the head of *forthcomingness*, as above explained, the system of arrangements provided have, in proportion as they have been looked into, been found in a deplorable degree scanty, inapposite, inconsistent, and inadequate. But the system of *procedure* — judicial procedure at large — being the system to which arrangements of this description properly belong, it can only be in an *incidental* way that any such deficiencies can meet the eye, in the course of the present work.

2. In regard to the system of exclusion, pursued to so prodigious an extent, and with not less prodigious inconsistency, if the observations that will be brought to view are found just, it will be seen to be groundless and pernicious, to an extent little short of that to which it has been applied.

3. In regard to the applying the exclusion, on any such ground as that of preponderant inconvenience, in the shape of *delay*, *vexation*, and expense — thereby embracing the lesser evil in preference to the greater — of any such application of human prudence, scarcely an idea will be to be found: — cases of vexation to a small extent only excepted — cases in which, to the greater part of that small extent, the supposed vexation will be found to be purely imaginary, not having any existence independent of that which is inseparably attached to such infliction, as in the name of *punishment* or *satisfaction* (*obligation* of rendering satisfaction,) cannot but be assumed to be *due*.

4 & 5. In regard to the affording assistance and guidance to the judge, in forming his estimate of the *probative force* of evidence, so that in each instance the effect produced by it in the way of *persuasion* on the mind, may be neither greater nor less than what is its due, this whole quarter of the field will be found a complete blank. Nothing was done, or so much as thought of being done, but by the operation of *will*: — nothing by assistance afforded to *intelligence*. Instead of *instruction*, *exclusion* employed as above.

6. In regard to *shape*, putting aside the best, which, as having been originally the only shape, is the most obvious* as well as the simplest shape, — by an abuse of the art of *writing*, it has been the art and care of the English judge to give (as will be seen) to evidence, in so far as hath lain in his power, the two most deceptious, and in every respect the worst shapes † that could be given to it: in doing which, his own sinister interest has (it will be seen) in various shapes been promoted, while the interests of the public, in respect of truth, morality, and justice, have thereby been sacrificed: nor in this case, on the part of the legislator, have the transgressions of the judge been merely the result of blind confidence reposed in that subordinate; — the sinister interests of *the leaders in legislation* having on this ground interwoven themselves with, and given effect to, the sinister interests of the judge.

evidence (of which immediately) has presented another sort of evidence, which, as will be seen, received its shape from the hand of the legislator, or during his sleep, from the hand of the judge.

* *Most obvious.*] Viz. examination *viva voce*, as before *juries* — before *justices* of the peace — before *committees* of the legislature.

† *Worst shapes.*] Affidavit evidence, written deposition, taken as in *equity court*, *ecclesiastical* court, and *admiralty* court practice.

7. Under the head of *pre-appointed* evidence, it will be seen how badly *individual prudence* has, on this part of the field, been seconded and supported by *legislative providence*.

By general rules, which he has seen and suffered to be deduced from practice — from judicial practice — the legislator breeding and nourishing in every bosom the expectation of seeing his enforcing sanction applied to contracts of all sorts — to agreements and conveyances, — while the judge, by unpre-announced and unforseeable exceptions, without reason, and without end, has been violating the engagements taken by these same rules; the legislator looking on, and, by his perpetual connivance, making himself a perpetual accomplice in this perpetual breach of faith.*

CHAPTER V.

PROBATIVE FORCE — WHENCE MEASURED — HOW INCREASED — HOW DIMINISHED.

§ 1. *Whence measured — Standard quantity.*

IN regard to evidence, such as hath just been seen, being the legislator's duties, and amongst them, the doing what depends upon his *power*, including in this case in a more especial manner, his *wisdom*—towards preventing evidence from operating, in any case, either with *greater* or with *less* effect than is its due, hence it is that, — as in the instance of any *one* article of evidence it is an object (how difficultly-soever attainable,) highly desirable, to know what degree of probative force is the due of that one article of evidence, — so (what may be found not quite so difficult,) as between *two* articles of evidence, exhibited on the opposite sides of the cause, *which* it is that ought to be considered as possessed of the greatest degree of probative force. This being the case, a preliminary point, alike necessary to either purpose, will be seen to be the fixing upon some describable quantity of *probative force* capable of being referred to in the character of a *standard quantity*, from which, in every case, as well *increase* as *diminution*—*diminution* as *increase*, may be capable of being measured. If, in this as in so many other instances, the nature of the case admits of little precision, — if, in this as in so many other instances, ignorance and weakness are the lot of human nature, — it is not the less needful to us to make ourselves as well acquainted as possible with the *nature* and *degree* of that ignorance and weakness.

To this standard, then, will the reference be made, as often as, by the operation of this or that circumstance in the character of a *cause*, either *superiority* or *inferiority*, in the probative force of this or that article of evidence, is considered as being produced.

For this standard of reference, take, for example, a portion of discourse, *orally* delivered in the hearing of one or more persons; — a portion of discourse, by which a person, whose reputation in respect of trustworthiness, as applied to the purpose in question, is, in all points, upon the ordinary medium, or *average* level: or rather (what comes to the same thing, and presents a sort of condition, the fulfilment of which is much more easily ascertained,) whose character is *not known:* this person, let him assert or declare himself to have been, at a time and place individually described, a percipient witness of the existence of the matter of fact in question; it being such, that, of the existence and nature of it, every person of sound mind is qualified to obtain adequately strong and distinct *perceptions*, form an adequately correct *judgment*, and retain an adequately correct and complete *remembrance*.

In this standard lot of evidence, as thus described, two particular circumstances, in the character of potential causes of increase or diminution of probative force, will require to be noted; viz. 1. The *source from* which the *evidence* — the information — springs, and is delivered; and, 2. The *shape* in which it is delivered.

In relation to the source, again, two particulars may be observed; viz. 1. The *nature* or *quality* of it, as delivered in to the judge or other person for whose use it is destined; 2. The *propinquity* or *nearness* of it in relation to *the seat of perception;* viz. of those perceptions, the existence of which is asserted by it.

§ 2. *Sources of Increase.*

As to increase and superiority, consider now by what means it is, that, to the standard degree of probative force, as thus described, any addition can be made.

1. In regard to the *quality* of the source, one means by which probative force is capable of being added to it is—by substituting to a declaration of this *unknown* person, a declaration to the same effect, made by a person *selected* * for this purpose, in contemplation, and under

* *Breach of faith.*] *Question*—where is the breach of faith? It is from *judicial practice* alone (there being no *statute law* on the subject) that the general rule, *contracts will be enforced*, can have been formed: and by the same practice by which this general *rule* is indicated, so are the *exceptions*.—*Answer*. By its extreme simplicity the general rule takes hold of and fixes itself in every mind: — by their incongruity, unconnectedness, inconsistency, variety, and multitude, — and by the obscurity of the language in which they are expressed — the exceptions are rendered — to lawyers difficultly and imperfectly cognoscible — to non-lawyers, utterly uncognoscible.

* *Selected.*] Hence one advantage derivable from the employment of that species of evidence which has been designated *pre-appointed* evidence.

the persuasion of a superior degree of relative trustworthiness as existing in his instance. 2. Another obvious, and much less questionable mode is—by adding to the number of the persons, in whose declarations, in relation to the supposed matter of fact, an exact coincidence has manifested itself. 3. In respect of *propinquity* with relation to the source of perception, if the *narrating* witness, as above described, was himself the *percipient* witness, to whose senses the perceptions in question manifested themselves, probative force admits not, it is manifest, any *increase*.

Decrease, on the other hand, it will be found to admit of, and to any imaginable degree; viz. in the case where the matter of fact, the perception of which is thus expressed, is, by the person by whom it is expressed, stated as having been perceived — not by himself, the *narrating* witness, but by some *other* person or persons, on whose credit the existence of the supposed matter of fact is thus averred.

Thus much concerning the *source* of the evidence or information.

As to the *shape*;—of the shape in which the standard lot of evidence, as above described, is supposed to have made its appearance, what is plain enough is, that it is not only the natural shape, but the *only* natural shape. But by means of a variety of additaments — instruments — operations — states of things — arrangements,—of which, under the collective name of *securities* for trustworthiness—*securities* against *deceptious incorrectness* and *incompleteness* in evidence, particular mention will be made, whatsoever probative force belongs to the information in this its natural and primitive shape will presently be seen to have received additions, the importance of which will not be found to be open to dispute.

§ 3. *Source of Diminution.*

As to what concerns the source, and in particular the *quality* of that source, what is manifest enough is—that by any circumstance by which the trustworthiness of the person in question is diminished, the *probative force* of the evidence deduced from that *source*, or passing through that *channel*, will be proportionally reduced. Of the causes of trustworthiness and untrustworthiness† in testimony, a view is given under the head so denominated.

As to *remoteness* from the source of narration — from the supposed *seat* of perception — in the character of a quality, by which, in proportion to the degree of it, a correspondent defalcation cannot but be made from the probative force of the evidence so circumstanced, it has already been brought to view.

As to the *shape*; — of the circumstances, upon which the inferiority or superiority of an article of evidence in this particular depends, intimation has just been given. By any addition made, of any of them, to the standard species of evidence, the trustworthiness of the article has already been spoken of as receiving a correspondent addition and increase.

But, admitting such to be their virtue and effect, it will follow that, except in so far as it may happen that the application of them stands prohibited by preponderant inconvenience, in the shape of *delay*, *vexation*, and *expense*, the whole aggregate of these securities should, in every instance, be employed to bear upon the evidence. This being supposed, the absence or non-application of any of them may, with reference to the article of evidence in question, be considered as operative of a defalcation made from the due and proper quantity of its probative force, and thence as a cause of comparative untrustworthiness, if not on the part of the person in question, at any rate on the part of his evidence.

One cause of diminution of probative force — one cause of inferiority in point of probative force, as between evidence and evidence, remains to be noted.

As yet, for simplicity's sake, the matter of fact deposed to, as above, has been tacitly supposed to be the very matter of fact in question, whatever it be.

But, independently of human testimony, between matters of fact themselves, such is found to be the connexion, that by the existence, no matter how established, of one or two connected facts, a persuasion, more or less strong, is produced, of the existence of the others: — the fact, of the existence of which the persuasion is thus produced, call it the *principal* fact; the fact by which such persuasion is produced, call it the *evidentiary* fact.

Considered as tending to produce a per-

* *Person or persons.*] Between this supposed *percipient*, and the *deposing* or *narrating* witness, any number of supposed percipient and narrating witnesses may, it is obvious, have been interposed. Concerning the diminution thus effected in the degree of probative force, see Chapter XIII. *Of Makeshift Evidence.*

† *Untrustworthiness.*] These will, in every instance, be found to consist in some infirmity, relative and comparative, in the state or condition of the mental or psychological faculties, and qualities, intellectual or moral, of the supposed percipient and narrating witness or witnesses. — It is for the purpose of bringing to view the aggregate of these several securities, that the word *shape* is here employed. Any infirmity — any inferiority — which, on any occasion, may be perceptible in the *shape* of the evidence will, accordingly have for its cause, if not the inapplicability, at least the non-application, of some one or more of the articles, of which the list of those securities will, as above, be seen to be composed.

suasion of the existence of any fact viewed in the character of a *principal* fact as thus explained, any other fact, thus operating in the character of an *evidentiary* fact, may accordingly be termed, as in common parlance, as well as technical language it actually is termed, an article of *circumstantial evidence:* and in contradistinction to such circumstantial evidence, whatsoever be the particular matter of fact in question, any article of evidence, considered as applying to it immediately, and not through the medium of any other matter of fact, is technically as well as familiarly, as above,* termed an article of direct evidence.

Of the *measure* of *probative force* in evidence, the description will be found to be different in the case of *direct,* which, in respect of the source from whence it issues, is always *personal* evidence, as compared with *circumstantial,* which, although to a certain extent, and in particular in the instance of *deportment,* it may, in respect of its source, be considered as *personal*—will, moreover, to a considerable extent, in respect of its having its source in the state of *things* as contradistinguished from *persons,* be found to belong to the category of *real* evidence.

In the case of *direct* personal evidence, supposing, on the part of the matter of fact affirmed, nothing of improbability, either on a *physical* or a psychological score, nor any weakness in the force of the persuasion expressed in and by his testimony, its probative force has for its measure the trustworthiness of the affirmant: in the case of *circumstantial* evidence, the existence of the evidentiary fact being, either by the perception obtained of it by the perceptive faculty of the judge himself, or by unquestioned extraneous testimony, placed effectually out of dispute, probative force may be said to depend altogether upon the *closeness of the connexion,*† between the *principal* matter of fact, and the matter of fact which is considered as *evidentiary* of it.

As in the case of *direct* evidence, its probative force will, as already intimated, be found to be rendered less and less, by and in proportion to the number of *media* through which it has passed, or is supposed to have passed, so will it be seen to be in the case of *circumstantial* evidence.

* Concerning circumstantial evidence, see the chapter so entitled, viz. ch. 12.

† *Closeness of connexion.*] Not that this expression is exclusively applicable to the case of *circumstantial* evidence; since in the case of *direct personal,* i. e. *testimonial* evidence, it may be said (it should seem,) without impropriety, that the measure of its probative force is *the closeness of the connexion* between the existence of the matter of fact affirmed by the individual in question, in the character of the *principal* matter of fact, and the *fact of its having been by him affirmed* in the character of an *evidentiary* fact with relation to that *principal* fact.

Between each pair of facts, the closeness of connexion being supposed in each instance the same, then, if so it be, that matter of fact A is not evidentiary of matter of fact C, but through the medium of matter of fact B (A being evidentiary of B, and B of C,) it follows, that the probative force with which A is evidentiary of C, will be but half as great as that with which A is evidentiary of B, or that with which B is evidentiary of C.

Of the above-mentioned securities for trustworthiness, a summary view will presently be given, as well as of what appears to be the mode of applying them with most advantage to this their purpose. But previously, it has been found necessary to speak of the mode of giving *expression* to the different *degrees* of which probative force is susceptible, and thereafter to present a summary view of the objects already mentioned under the denomination of *causes of trustworthiness and untrustworthiness.*

CHAPTER VI.

DEGREES OF PERSUASION — THENCE OF PROBATIVE FORCE — HOW EXPRESSIBLE.

On the occasion, and for the purpose of *decision*—and for that same purpose, on the occasion of *deposition*—the degrees of which persuasion is susceptible, in what manner shall they find expression? In answer to this question, in the arithmetical language of the doctrine of chances, mathematical science affords an established, and hence an obvious mode. Unfortunately, correct as this mode is—and in truth the only correct mode of which the nature of the case admits—it will presently be seen to be altogether inapplicable to any judicial purpose. On the affirmative, as well as on the disaffirmative side, in the mathematical scale of probability, the degrees *rise* above, as well as sink below one another, on a scale to which there are no assignable limits. But, on whatsoever grounds formed, a scale, with at least a *fixed top* belonging to it, if not with a *fixed bottom,* is absolutely necessary to every legal purpose. In every case, on one or other side, a degree high enough to warrant decision on that side is the one thing needful.

In the case of affirmance, for any expression indicative of any degree *above* that necessary degree, there cannot be any use: on the other hand, for expressions indicative of degrees of persuasion *below* that degree, real and substantial uses, it will be seen, may be found.

In a many-seated judicatory, the different votes are frequently the result of degrees of persuasion widely different. Were matters so arranged, as that these degrees could, each of them, find an adequate mode of expression,—

in such case, what might every now and then happen is — that a decision which, upon the present plan, is, by a small majority, pronounced in favour of the affirmative side, would on that plan be pronounced in favour of the disaffirmative side, and *vice versa*.

In the case of a judicial decision — whatsoever were the degree of force pitched upon as sufficient, and at the same time necessary, to give to it its legal effect — from the allowing a man to place the declared force of his persuasion at a degree as much *below* that standard as he pleased, no inconvenience could possibly ensue. On the other hand, if for giving to it a degree of force *above* the standard, an equal latitude were allowed, no sooner were passion, in any degree, to enter upon the scene, than an *auction* would commence; and to the *biddings*, forasmuch as there would be nothing to pay, there would be no end.

When anything that bears the name of *power* is in question, be the nature of it what it may, no great danger is incurred by allowing a man to give to it as *little* effect as he pleases; — allow him to give as *great* an effect to it as he pleases, the consequences need not be mentioned.

Even when the judicatory has in it but a single seat, — even in this case, with a view to appeal, a scale of this sort might be not altogether without its use. Not unfrequently, in the mind of the judge, so confessedly near to an equilibrium are the contending forces, that nothing but the necessity of deciding would have determined him to decide on the side chosen by him, rather than on the other side.

In any such case, were the real degree of persuasion suffered to find its adequate expression, appeal, where proper, would frequently find not only better encouragement, but more substantial ground, than in the established mode, in which the only degree of persuasion allowed to be declared, is that to which the *highest* degree of practical effect is attached.

In the procedure of ancient Rome, judicial practice received a refinement, which has found few or none to copy it. The judge, on whose mind the grounds on both sides operated with equal weight, insomuch that, consistently with *veracity*, he could not say that the scale of his judgment had turned on either side, nor, consistently with *probity*, give the effect of a vote to either side, found in an appropriate form the means of preserving in unsullied purity those virtues, the extirpation of which has, with such conspicuous industry, and with proportionate success and profit, been laboured at by English judges. *Non liquet: — just grounds of decision being wanting to me, I will not decide.* No perjury here! — no torture! Destitute of such necessary instruments, how could justice do her work?

To the witness's box this same mode of expression would not be found less capable of being applied, than to the bench: but in the case of the witness, for simplicity's sake, suppose but one witness, and in the breast of that witness let trustworthiness be entire. On the part of the judge, the force of persuasion will, on this supposition, be the exact copy of that of the witness, and the same *numbers* will give the *expression* of it. But taking the public mind at its present state of culture, the debasement of the soil having been the only object of such labour as by the official husbandman has been as yet bestowed upon it, the refinement, appearing in this case still greater than in the other, could do no otherwise than expect a proportionable resistance.

Of the particular plan of expression which, to the purpose in question, would be necessary, the development must be confined to the body of the work. Lawyers of the *Roman* school — lawyers of the *English* school — it will there be seen into what awkward shifts — into what inadequate and uncharacteristic modes of expression they were driven — driven by their endeavours to give expression to *degrees of probability*, without having recourse to *numbers*.

CHAPTER VII.

CAUSES OF TRUSTWORTHINESS AND UNTRUSTWORTHINESS IN TESTIMONY — THENCE OF BELIEF AND UNBELIEF.

§ 1. *Connexion between Trustworthiness and Belief.*

To form any substantially grounded estimate of the *probative force* of testimonial evidence, it will be necessary to take a view, on the one hand, of the causes of *correctness* and *completeness* — in other words, of *trustworthiness*;* on the other hand, of deceptious incorrectness

* *Trustworthiness.*] *Trustworthiness* and *probative force* — between these two expressions the relation is intimate, but the coincidence is not complete: in a considerable part of its extent, *probative force* will be found to outstretch *trustworthiness.*

Probative force is alike applicable to direct and to circumstantial evidence; — and in the case of circumstantial evidence, trustworthiness is out of the question: circumstantial evidence having for its sources *things* as well as *persons*: and when a person is the source of it, the probative force of it has no dependence whatsoever on his trustworthiness; circumstantial evidence, and that of the most instructive kind, being (as will be seen) afforded, in cases where the highest degree of untrustworthiness is a matter of the fullest assurance.

Nor even in the case of *direct personal* evidence is the coincidence complete. Even in this case, *trust-worthiness* may be at the highest pitch, and at the same time *probative force* to

and incompleteness — in other words, of *untrustworthiness*, in human discourse. Of these causes, the clearer our conception is, the more distinct and correct will be our estimate of that force: and to these causes, and to the conception, more or less accurate, which in each instance it happens to us to form in relation to them, — to these sources it is, that we must look for the only intelligible and practically useful account, that can be given of the foundation of *affirmative* and *disaffirmative* persuasion, — of belief and unbelief.

Of trustworthiness, and of untrustworthiness, the causes are to be looked for, partly in the state of the *mental faculties*, intellectual and moral, of the individual, partly in the state of the *external circumstances*, to the operation of which it happens to those faculties to stand exposed.

§ 2. *Intellectual Causes.*

Of the intellectual faculties, in so far as they are in a state adapted to the purpose of testimonial discourse, *i. e.* to the giving relative *correctness* and *completeness* to the statement in the delivery of which they have borne a part, nothing in particular will be to be said. But by any of those *infirmities*, to which they are respectively subject, any statement which they have borne a part in the delivery of, is liable to be rendered in a greater or less degree deceptiously incorrect or incomplete: hence the necessity of observing the lines of separation by which they stand distinguished from each other, and, in the character of causes of misreport, noting the weaknesses of which they are respectively susceptible.

Simple perception, *attention*, *judgment*, *memory*, — by these terms may be brought to view the *sources*, as by expression the *vehicle*, of discourse at large, — and thence of testimonial discourse. As it is to these that we are to look for the intellectual causes of *correctness* and *completeness* in testimony, in so far as it is in a correct and complete state; so likewise of its *incorrectness* or *incompleteness*, in so far as it is in an incorrect or incomplete state. As to the *imagination*, contributing nothing to correctness, or, in so far as it is distinct from *memory*, to *completeness*, so it is that upon testimony it can scarcely operate in any other character, than that of a cause of *incorrectness* or *incompleteness*, more particularly and obviously of *incorrectness*. Acting under the orders of the *will*, and directing its exertions to a particular end, it becomes *invention*: taking for its end *deception*, and that deception being *pernicious*, the *will* its director, operating under the impulse or attraction of *sinister* interest — (that is, as will be seen, of any *interest* or motive acting in that sinister *direction*)—it becomes *mendacity*.

Perception, by its *faintness*, or *indistinctness*, — *attention*, by its *absence*, or its *weakness*, — *judgment*, by its errors, of which the *faintness* of the *perception*, and the *absence* or *faintness* of the *attention*, are among the causes, — *memory* by its *absence*, its *faintness*, or its *indistinctness*, — thus it is, that these *faculties*, these fictitious psychological entities, are liable to become each of them occasionally a cause of the undesirable effect: and, as it is by *expression* alone that the state of the narrator's mind is communicated to, and impressed upon the intellectual faculties of the judge, there is scarcely a modification, or instance, of incorrectness or incompleteness, capable of being produced by an infirmity in any of those *sources*, that is not capable of being produced by an infirmity in this *vehicle*.

To develope, and exemplify the modes and causes of the mischief as above indicated, and at the same time to endeavour to bring to view such feeble, and unhappily but too precarious remedies, as the nature of the case admits of, forms in the body of the work the task of a chapter allotted to that purpose.

§ 3. *Moral Causes in general — viz. the several Sanctions.*

As to *moral* causes, — not only incorrectness and incompleteness in testimony, but (what seems almost to have escaped notice) correctness and completeness, owe their existence to *good* and *evil* — to *pleasure* and *pain* — in *experience* or in *prospect*, existing in the mind in the shape of *interests*, and, in so far

any degree weak: viz. where, on the part of the deponent in question, *intensity of persuasion* (judging from the expression given to it by him) is in that same degree weak.

In the case of *direct* evidence, declared by two witnesses, both being *percipient* witnesses, the degree of *trustworthiness* being supposed the same, to render the degree of *probative force* exactly the same, two ulterior points of coincidence must have place:—1. Intensity of persuasion, as evidenced by intensity of averment, must, as above, be the same; and, 2. In regard to *counter-evidence* (under which head will be seen to be included *improbability*,) there must be either none in either case, or the same, *i. e.* operating with the same degree of probative force in both cases.

Between *degree of probative force* on the part of the evidence (the whole mass of evidence being taken together,) and *intensity of persuasion* on the part of the judge, the coincidence seems to be complete: and this, whether the question be concerning what *is*, or concerning what *ought to be*. To say that the probative force of the evidence *is* at such or such a degree, is to say that, in the bosom of the judge, intensity of persuasion *is* at that degree: to say that such a degree of probative force is *properly belonging* to the mass of evidence in question, is to say that, upon the receipt of that same mass of evidence, the same degree of intensity of persuasion is the degree which is *fit and proper* to have place in the bosom of the judge.

as yet but in *prospect*, operating in the shape of *hope* and *fear*, in the character of *motives*.*

Veracity, therefore, not less than *mendacity*, is the result of *interest*: and, in so far as depends upon the *will*, it depends, in each instance, upon the effect of the conflict between two opposite groupes of contending interests, which of them shall be the result.

Collectively taken and ranged into groups, and deduced each group from a particular *source*, and thereupon considered in the character of causes of human *action* in general, and of *discourse*, including testimonial discourse in particular, these modifications of pleasure and pain, experienced or expected, have elsewhere been brought to view under the name of *sanctions*.†

So far as they are considered as the result of causes purely physical, the action of other rational agents from without not having any share in the production of them, they are referable to a sanction which may be termed the *physical*, the *purely physical*, sanction: — in so far as they are expected at the hands of rational agents, they have been referred to one or other of three sanctions: — 1. The *popular* or *moral sanction*; 2. The *political*, including the *legal* sanction; 3. The *religious* or *supernatural* sanction. To the popular or moral sanction it is that they may be referred, in so far as the pleasures or pains in question are considered as about to result, or liable eventually to result, from the good or ill *offices*, and thence from the good or ill *will*, thence again from the good or ill *opinion*, of other human beings: viz. in virtue of whatsoever portion of liberty to this effect may have been left to them, by the state and condition of the *law*.

To the *legal*, or (to take it in its full extent) the *political* sanction, they may be referred, in so far as they are considered as about to result, or liable to result, from the exercise of the powers of government, whether in the track of the legislative, the judicial, or the administrative department. To the *religious* or *supernatural* they may be referred, in so far as they are considered as about or liable to result from the exercise of the powers of government, by the almighty hand of a supernatural and invisible being, in the present life, or in a life to come.

§ 4. *The Physical Sanction.*

I. In general, it costs less *labour* to *report* a matter of fact, with its circumstances, as presented by the *memory*, than, at a moment's warning, to *invent*, in a train of a given length, circumstances, which, without being true, shall, to the very end, be taken for such. So far as this observation agrees with the nature of the case, so far may the *physical* sanction be said to operate in restraint of deceptious incorrectness and incompleteness.

At the same time, if it be in strict form and high degree that correctness and completeness are required, neither is the labour of the *memory* altogether free from uneasiness: a labour which is the greater, the more distant in point of time the matters of fact were, and at the time of perception the less impressive, especially if, of the first impression, the recollection have not, in the meantime, been refreshed by intervening interests: and here again we see the physical sanction operating— operating, but now in the character of a cause — not of correctness and completeness, but of incorrectness and incompleteness.

In the uncertainty on which side this purely physical sanction will operate with greatest force, and in the comparative weakness with which it operates with a preponderant force in favour of correctness and completeness, may be seen the demand which has place for the operation of the several other sanctions that have just been mentioned — sanctions to which, in contradistinction to it, may be given the common denomination of *rationally-operating* ones, inasmuch as in their respective operations the *reason* — the judicial faculty— cannot but have been made to bear a part.

§ 5. *Popular or Moral Sanction.*

II. In the second place, comes under review—the *popular* or *moral* sanction.

As to the *direction* in which, on the field of evidence, it operates, the *restraint* which, generally speaking, it applies to deceptious incorrectness and incompleteness is obvious, and furnishes the matter of the general rule.

Unhappily, out of this rule, ere it can in every part have been reduced within the limits of exact truth, exceptions, and to no inconsiderable an extent, must be cut out of it. Follows a brief indication of the groups in which they will be found arranged: —

1. Cases where, by contending interests or prejudices, a sort of schism, more or less permanent, is produced, in the aggregate force of this sanction, form one class of these exceptions.

2. Another class is composed of those in which, by the misapplied influence of the political sanction, — *i. e.* of the constituted authorities, at whose disposal that influence is placed — instead of being applied to the *restriction*, the force, not only of the *political*, but thereby even of the *popular* sanction, is applied to the *encouragement* and *increase* of deceptious incorrectness and incompleteness, and *that*, as there will be occasion moreover to mention under the next head, in its most vicious and pernicious form — mendacity.‡

* See Table of Springs of Action, Vol. I. p. 195.

† See Introduction to Morals and Legislation, Vol. I. Ch. III. p. 14.

‡ *Mendacity*.] Lest the general rule, as above indicated, should stand chargeable with incor-

On one and the same occasion, and even in the instance of the same individual, in case of delinquency on his part, the force of the popular sanction may be seen acting in opposite directions at once, — urging him on in or towards the path of mendacity on the one hand — pulling him back from it on the other. In this conflict, which, then, will prevail? — the mendacity-promoting, or the mendacity-restraining force? The act in question being an immoral act, and by the popular or moral sanction reprobated as such, brings shame upon him who is understood to be guilty of it: and the individual in question being by the supposition actually guilty of it, if, on being interrogated, he speak the truth, and thereby confesses himself guilty of it, he thereby subjects himself, with more or less probability, to *punishment*, and at the same time with certainty to *shame*. If, on the other hand, his answers to the interrogatories are in any respect that which, to afford him any chance of safety, they must be, materially false, no sooner does detection follow (nor can he ever see that instant, in the next to which it may not follow) than his lot becomes, in this case also, the same. To note the *existence* of this conflict, is all that belongs to the present purpose: as to the *result* of it, obviously enough it will on each individual occasion depend on the preponderance, as between the aggregate force of the motives operating on the one side, and the aggregate force of the motives operating on the other side.

rectness, for want of another defalcation, — a defalcation, the need of which is indicated, — not as in those cases, by circumstances of a local and temporary complexion, but by the universally prevailing and unalterable nature of things, mention could not here be altogether refused to that class of cases, narrow as the description of it is, on which the substitution of falsehood to truth being, by the principle of *probity* (taken in that largest sense in which that of *humanity* is included in it) not merely *allowed* but *prescribed*, is by mankind in general, in their character of administrators of the force of the popular or moral sanction, exempted in their view from that censure which attaches upon it in other cases. For examples, the cases of a *madman*, or a *malefactor*, requiring information for purposes of mischief, will supersede the need of any other. Neither in the shape of *veracity*, nor in any other shape, *virtue*, — nor in the shape of *mendacity*, nor in any other shape, *vice*, — being of any importance but with reference to *utility*, — to *universal* utility, — let *falsehood*, as in the rare cases above mentioned, be necessary to the *prevention of mischief*, falsehood, instead of a *crime*, becomes a *duty*. But, upon examination, not inconsiderable would the ground be seen to be in extent, on which, while in respect of *probity*, *i. e.* regard for *others* — duty towards *others* — departure from the line of truth may be matter of indifference, yet by the rule of *prudence*, *i. e.* by *self-regard*, it would be seen to be rigourously proscribed.

Thus much as to *direction*. As to *force*, to the obvious and but too indisputable insufficiency of this sanction, in cases where mendacity-promoting interests are in a condition to act with those degrees of force which are but too commonly exemplified, is referable that demand, of which the existence is so universally acknowledged, for the more steady as well as impressive force of the political sanction: especially in that regulated and conspicuous form, in which it is made to operate in the hand of the judge.

§ 6. *The Political, including the Legal Sanction.*

III. In the third place, comes the political or legal sanction.

Follows a list of the topics which, in relation to this sanction, and its applicability and application in restraint of deceptious incorrectness and incompleteness, will come under review: —

1. Cases or points, in relation to which, in restraint of deceptious incorrectness and incompleteness, in judicially delivered testimony, this sanction is in its nature capable of being made to operate with a degree of efficiency superior to that of the popular or moral sanction.

2. Cases or points, in relation to which, in restraint of mendacity, the force of the popular sanction being divided against itself, as above, the force of the legal sanction is wont to be made to operate with a degree of *uniformity* greater than that which the force of the *popular* sanction operates with, in these same cases.

3. Occasions on which, it being radically inapplicable to this purpose, the legal finds itself obliged to resign its task to the force of the moral and religious sanctions.*

4. Occasions on which, under and by virtue of English law, its operation is rendered habitually adverse to truth, habitually subservient to mendacity, and upon an all-comprehensive scale, actually, and to a great extent purposely, productive of that most pernicious and all-infecting vice.

§ 7. *The Religious Sanction.*

IV. In the fourth and last place, comes the religious sanction.

Under every religion, what is but natural is — that to every important purpose, whether it be from legal operation, or from any other

* Examples: — Among psychological matters of fact, in many instances, *motives* and thence *dispositions*, especially where, in the situation of the individual in question, motives more than one are assignable, any one of which might have been sufficient to the production of the effect. In regard to another class of psychological facts, viz. *intentions*, the legal sanction is sufficiently well qualified to take cognizance of them, and, on all sorts of occasions, actually does.

source, that the importance of the purpose is derived, the religious sanction should, with its whole force, be made to operate in restraint of mendacity:—in restraint of deceptious incorrectness and incompleteness. The influence of a master on the minds of his disciples—the power of a leader over the conduct of his followers—depends upon the correctness and completeness of the judgment he is enabled to form, as to what their conduct on every occasion material to his purpose eventually *will be;* and thence, upon the correctness and completeness of such information as he can obtain, as to what their conduct and mode of being *is* and *has been:*—their *mode of being*, in every imaginable point, not excepting their most secret thoughts, intentions, affections, and opinions.

In the religion of *Moses*, and in the religion of *Jesus*, the energy, as well as steadiness, with which the force of the religious sanction is applied to this purpose, are observable in a pre-eminent and conspicuous degree.*

CHAPTER VIII.

OF THE SECURITIES FOR TRUSTWORTHINESS IN EVIDENCE.

§ 1. *Qualities desirable in Evidence.*

1. QUALITIES desirable in an article of evidence:—these, for distinction sake, may be termed the *internal* securities for trustworthiness in evidence.

2. Instruments—operations—states of things—arrangements, legislative and judicial, which have presented themselves as conducive to the investing of the subject in question with these desirable qualities:—these may be termed the *external* securities for trustworthiness in evidence.

Correctness and completeness—by these two already so often mentioned appellatives, are presented two qualities, obviously desirable, both of them, in every article of evidence—each of them for its own sake, and without need of having its utility enhanced by subserviency to any other quality;—unless, for the expression of that desirable quality, to which they are both subservient, some such term as *undeceptiousness* were provided and employed. *Correctness* and *completeness*—call them accordingly qualities of the first order—primary qualities—qualities intrinsically—on an intrinsic account—on their own account—desirable.

Of these important and desirable qualities, a perfectly correct conception will scarcely, however, be formed, unless their respective opposites, incorrectness and incompleteness, be taken into account, and their import limited by an *adjunct* bearing reference to these opposities.

This adjunct is *deceptious*.

In a statement or narration, delivered by any person, on any occasion, in relation to any matter of fact, particulars may have had place in any number, which, though altogether *true* in themselves, may be equally *immaterial* in relation to the question, whatever it be, which happens to be on the carpet.—So many as there are of these *immaterial* or *irrelevant* particulars, so many are there, in respect of which it may happen, that neither incompleteness, *i. e.* partial omission, nor *incorrectness, i. e.* misrepresentation, shall, with reference to the matter in question, be productive of any deceptious effects.

By *correctness*, therefore, must, on this occasion, be understood—not *absolute*, but *relative* correctness;—by *completeness*, not *absolute*, but *relative* completeness:—in other words, by *correctness*, that and that alone, which has for its opposite, *deceptious incorrectness*—by completeness, that, and that alone, which has for its opposite, *deceptious incompleteness;*—incompleteness, in that case, and in that case alone, where, in relation to the matter of fact in question, deception is amongst the effects which it has a tendency to produce.

Taking the above for the qualities desirable on their own account, the following are the *secondary* qualities, which present themselves as desirable, on account of those same primary qualities, viz. in the character of means subservient to the purpose of securing to the article of evidence in question, the possession of those same primary qualities.

To save the critic ear from excruciation, to the abstract substantive let us substitute the concrete adjective. By one or other of the following epithets may be expressed, it is supposed, all the qualities which, in the character of secondary qualities, can contribute to invest an article of evidence with either of these primary ones:—1. *Veracious;* 2. *Particularized;* 3. *Distinct;* 4. *Interrogated, i. e.* extracted, and thence completed, and if need be corrected, and explained, by interrogation; 5. *Permanent, i. e.* consigned to, and expressed by those permanent characters, of which written language affords the most convenient as well as familiar example; 6. *Unpremeditated*, in so far as a design of *falsehood* might receive assistance from premeditation; 7. *Recollected*, in so far as recollectedness may be necessary to *truth, i. e.* to

* In the instance of the Hindoo religion, a very remarkable set of exceptions will be brought to view: but by the licence granted to mendacity in these excepted cases, no defalcation, materially prejudicial to the interests, is made (it will be seen) from the influence and power of the leading classes.

Concerning the perversion made of the force of the religious by the political sanction, by means of the ceremony called *an oath*, see the ensuing chapter.

relative correctness and completeness; 8. *Not assisted by undue suggestion, i. e.* by suggestion by which falsehood would be more likely to be served than truth; 9. *Assisted by due suggestion, i. e.* by suggestion by which truth would be more likely to be served than falsehood.

§ 2. *Instruments of Security, for securing to Evidence those Qualities.*

The following are the heads, under which every instrument, capable of serving in that character with advantage, will, it is supposed, be found reducible:—

1. Punishment.
2. Shame.
3. Interrogation (including counter-interrogation.)
4. Counter-evidence—admission given to it.
5. Writing — use made of it for giving permanence, &c. to evidence.
6. Publicity — to most purposes, and on most occasions.
7. Privacy—to some purposes, and on some occasions.

Under each of these heads, follow a few words of explanation:—

§ 3. *Punishment.*

Of the force of the political sanction, considered as applicable in the character of a source of security against deceptious incorrectness and incompleteness in evidence, mention has been made above. Punishment is, to every eye, the most extensively applicable, and in general the most efficient, shape, in which, to this as well as other purposes, that force can be applied.

Quantity — quality — in this place, under neither of these predicaments, need anything be said: on both of them, though without any special reference to evidence, consideration has already been bestowed in other places.* Remains as the only topic, for consideration of which any special demand presents itself in this place, that of the extent proper to be given to the use of this instrument, in its application to the purpose here in view.

Mendacity being but an instrument in the hand of delinquency — an instrument applicable to the purpose of giving birth, through delinquency, to mischief in all its shapes, — co-extensive surely with the mischief producible by mendacity ought to be the application of punishment, in so far as punishment is, with preponderant advantage, applicable to the prevention of it.

In the track of judicial procedure in particular, co-extensive with the application and applicability of that instrument of mischief, ought to be the application of this remedy.

* See Introduction to Morals and Legislation, and Rationale of Punishment.

§4. *Judge and Co.—False Evidence rendered by them dispunishable, where profitable to themselves.—Mendacity Licence.*

Thus much as to *propriety*:—for *practice*, learned ingenuity has discovered and pursued a more convenient course.

Under the English, not to speak of other systems of technical procedure, by means of the command, so easily, when indirectly, exercised by *power* over *language*, an expedient was found for rendering mendacity punishable or unpunishable at pleasure. In the person of a party litigant, or a witness, when it was to be rendered *punishable*, the allegation or statement was called *evidence*; and to mark it as such, a particular *ceremony* — the ceremony of an *oath* — was made to accompany the delivery of it. When it was to be rendered *dispunishable*, it was *not* to be called *evidence*:—it was to be called *pleading* — *pleadings* — anything but *evidence*; — and the *ceremony* was to be carefully kept from touching it.

At this time of day, few tasks would naturally be more difficult, than that of satisfying the English lawyer, that *pleadings* not upon oath — that anything, in a word, which in legal use has been carefully and customarily distinguished from evidence, can with propriety be termed *evidence*. But though, thanks to his ingenuity, so it is that pleadings, — all pleadings at least, — are not evidence in *name*, yet so it is, that everything that goes by the name of *pleading* is evidence in effect. All testimonial *evidence* is *statement* — *narration* — *assertion*: — everything that goes by the name of *pleadings* is so too. Of *evidence*, the use and the sole use, is to command decision:—by *pleadings*, decision is commanded, and in cases to a vast extent and in continual recurrence, and with a degree of *certainty* altogether denied to *evidence*.

To the purpose of imposing on the adverse party the obligation of going on with the suit, the contents of every instrument included under the name of *pleadings*, how replete soever with manifest falsehood, are taken for true, and as such, without the *name*, have the effect of evidence. The effect (it may be said) is but provisional: but definitively, to the purpose of giving to the suit a termination favourable to the party by whom the instrument is exhibited, — to the purpose of producing a decision — a decision as favourable to him as could be produced by anything to which the name of *evidence* has been left, — to the purpose of producing the selfsame decision, which, by evidence, supposing it believed, would be produced, — it has the effect — not simply of evidence, but of *conclusive* evidence: — the party who fails to meet the instrument in question, by that instrument which at the next step, on the other side, ought, in the appointed course to follow it, loses his cause.

Of this eventually conclusive evidence, the power, it may be said, cannot be great: since, by so proper and simple an operation as that of exhibiting the corresponding counter-instrument, the party to whose prejudice the conclusion would operate gets rid of it. Simple enough, — Yes: but instances are but too abundant, in which the operation, simple as it is, is impracticable — foreknown to be impracticable. To the performance of the operation, money is necessary: and on that side, money being by the other side known not to be forthcoming, what is thereby known is, that the exhibition of the counter-instrument is not practicable. It is accordingly because foreknown to be impracticable, that the operation is thus called for: for which purpose, falsehood, the most barefaced falsehood, is admitted to serve, admitted by those judges to whom its quality is no secret: — admitted with exactly the same composure as if it were known to be the strictest truth.

Thus it is, that, under favour of the mendacity thus established, every man who, being to a degree opulent, has, or desires to take, for his adversary, a man to a certain degree less opulent, has it in his power, whether on the plaintiff's side, or on the defendant's side, to give to his judicially delivered allegations, by what name soever denominated — *pleadings* or any other — the effect of *evidence:* the effect not only of evidence, but of *conclusive* evidence.

And thus it is, that by the forbearance — the astute forbearance — to give, to the security afforded by punishment, the extent necessary to justice, mendacity is generated and cherished—injustice through misdecision produced: — the evils opposite to the *direct* ends of justice, produced, by means of the evils opposite to the *collateral* ends of justice.

Among lawyers, and more especially among English lawyers, so commodiously, and thence so universally, is *custom* accepted as an adequate substitute for *reason* — so unprecedented is it for a man to trouble himself with any such thought, as in regard to any of the established torments, out of which his comforts are extracted, what in point of utility and justice may have been the ground for the establishing of them, — or so much as, whether they have, or ever had, any such ground at all, — that at the first mention, a question to any such effect will be apt to present itself to them, as no less novel, than idle and absurd. But concerning *judgment by default*, and everything that is equivalent to it* — be it in a House of Commons, — be it in a House of Lords, — or be it in any other place, — should any such misfortune happen to him, as to feel himself under a necessity of finding something in the character of a reason to give, in answer to the question — why it is that *judgment by default* is made to follow upon default,—his reason would be this or nothing, viz. that in this case, on the defaulting side, *want of merits* is inferred; and not only so, but that it is from the allegations contained in the instrument last delivered on the other side — it is from that, and nothing else, that the inference is deduced.

At the same time, that which, be he who he may, is well known to him — or at least, but for his own wilful default, would be known to him—that which he has always in his hands the means of knowing — means beyond comparison more ready than any which are possessed by the vast multitude, who, at the instance of his tongue, and by the power of his hand, are so incessantly and remorselessly punished — punished for not knowing that which it has so diligently and effectually been rendered impossible they should know, is — that, in the case of an average individual, the chances *against* the truth of the conclusion, thus built and acted upon, are many to *one*.

To be assured of this, all that a man has to do, is — on the one side of the account, to look at the average, or even at the minimum amount of the costs on *both sides*, which, on each side, a party subjects himself to the eventual burthen of, — or though it were at those on one side only: — on the other side of the account, at the annual amount of what an average individual of the labouring class (beyond all comparison the most numerous class) — or even though it were an average individual of the aggregate of all classes, the very highest not excluded—has for the whole of his possible expenditure. This comparison made, then it is that any man may see, whether, by forbearance to *go on* with an existing suit, at any stage, on *either* side, whether on the *plaintiff's* side, by forbearing to *commence* a suit,—any preponderant probability may be afforded, of what is called a *want of merits*.

Of two all-pervading masses of instances, in which, throughout the whole system of technical judicature, conclusions having been built, are continually acted upon by men, to whom, one and all, the *premises* on which those conclusions are built, and thence the conclusions themselves, are, or without their own wilful default, would be known to be, false, — this is the first, for the mention of

* *Equivalent to it.*] Examples: — In common-law practice, *judgment as in case of a non-suit:* in equity practice, taking of the bill *pro confesso*, in what is called *contempt;* for when, by the ruin of his fortunes, and consequent inability to pay the appointed price for a chance of justice, a man has been reduced to the lowest pitch of humiliation, *contempt*, the offspring of *pride*, is imputed to him: and it is for his *pride* that he is punished: — punished, by being excluded from that chance.

which the occasion has here happened to present itself.

Under the head of *non-observance of formalities*, a failure, considered as being, or at least, dealt with as if it were *evidence* — evidence conclusively probative of unfairness on the part of a contract, or spuriousness on the part of an instrument of contract — under this other head, mention of another instance will come to be made, in the chapter on *Pre-appointed Evidence*.

Nullification — to which belong conjugates and quasi conjugates, much too abundant to be here collected, — *null, void, bad, quash, set aside,* and so forth — *nullification* is the name given to the factitious engine of iniquity, by which the sort of effect here spoken of is, in both instances, produced. Instruments and operations of judicial *procedure* — *contracts* and *instruments of contract* — whatsoever has been the *subject* to which it has been applied, *lawyer's profit* is what the machinery will be found to have had exclusively for its *object* — *lawyer-craft* for its inventor and constructor — iniquity and misery for its *effects*.

By encouragement as well as impunity thus given to mendacity, if it be on the plaintiff's side, the number of suits is made to receive that addition, which is brought to it by those in which the dishonesty — the *mala fides*, as the phrase is — is on the plaintiff's side: by the like boon bestowed on the defendant's side, the like addition is made to the number of those to which *continuance* is given by dishonesty on the defendant's side.

See more to this purpose under the head of *Oath*.

On all these occasions, partner and accomplice in the fraud on one side of the cause, in the oppression on the other, the judge, as well as his collaborators, extract emolument out of the mendacity thus produced under the name of *pleadings*, — the mendacious evidence thus suborned is all in writing, — and the mass of writing is a mine of fees.*

§ 5. *Shame.*

By *punishment*, one part of the force of the *political* sanction is employed; by *shame*, viz. that which a man is exposed to by detection, or even by suspicion, the corresponding part of the force of the *popular* or *moral* sanction is employed.

In respect of the *extent* to which they are respectively applicable, compared with punishment, shame has the advantage. For the application of it, much less evidence being necessary, mendacity thus experiences restraint in cases in which it would otherwise experience none.† Whether it shall in a greater degree be exposed to shame than punishment, depends, however, in a more direct way upon the *individual* circumstances, than upon the *species* of the case.

Taken by itself, and without punishment, or legal power in any other shape, for its support, the insufficiency of shame, to this as well as other purposes, is, however, but too manifest.

In cases where the profit of delinquency rises to a certain height, the inadequacy of shame needs no words to prove it. Though in the case of shame less evidence be necessary than in the case of punishment, yet as neither in the case of shame, any more than in the case of punishment, can the principle of restraint operate, but in proportion to the apparent probability of the transpiration of evidence, — thus it is, that in this, as in other instances, on the will of those at whose disposal punishment — legal punishment — is placed, it depends, in a great degree, to keep delinquency out of the reach of shame, viz. by refusing, or stifling, that legal inquiry without which the evidence cannot be made to transpire.

Applying, with that exception, to all sorts of *cases*, shame, when alone, does not, however, apply to all sorts of *persons*. Of the few, a great proportion are too *high* to be reached by it: of the *many*, a great proportion are too *low*.

By a situation by which, in this case, a man is placed above punishment, he is thus but too effectually, as we have just been seeing, placed, moreover, above shame. Under the name of *perjury*, mendacity is covered, not only with punishment, but with infamy: under the names of *fiction* and *practice*, it is covered, not only with reward, but with honour. Shame touches not that mendacity, the seat of which is either at the *bar* or on the *bench*.

§ 6. *Interrogation — including Counter-Interrogation.*

In this may be seen the operation which, under some circumstances, is necessary even to the *existence* of the evidence, and in all cases, eventually, if not absolutely necessary to its security against deceptious incorrect-

* To quote or refer to the instances in which profit-yielding mendacity is thus generated, would be to quote or refer to the whole contents of the several law-books, in which, under the name of *books of practice*, for the use and benefit of the members of the profession, the course of judicial procedure is delineated.

† In the courts of *natural procedure*, recently established in *Denmark*, under the name of *reconciliation courts*, shame is, or at any rate, originally was, the sole cause of restraint, to the action of which testimonial mendacity was subjected: neither *punishment* nor oath were there employed: and the success has been such, as to have reduced to a small fraction the antecedently customary number of causes instituted in the courts of *technical procedure*.

ness, as well as against deceptious incompleteness.

Note, that a mass of testimony, spontaneously delivered, being supposed incomplete, thereupon, if, to interrogation asking whether it be complete, the answer be in the affirmative, incompleteness becomes *incorrectness.*

On whom — by whom — shall the operation be performable?

1. On whom? — that is, on what person? —the only proper answer seems to be, on every person, from whom, in the situation of *examinee*, information for any purpose of justice may with reason be expected; — let this situation, as more particularly described, be on the *plaintiff's* side of the cause, on the *defendant's* side of the cause, or in the witness's box. Applied to the case of a *malâ fide examinee*, the utility, not to say the necessity, of the operation is manifest: applied to the case of a *bonâ fide* examinee, its utility will be found to stand on ground no less clear; and in practice, it has been less narrowed.

By what hand shall this instrument of elucidation be applicable? Prejudice apart — prejudice derived from primeval barbarism and unreflecting practice — the answer seems not difficult:—Subject only to the necessarily controuling hand of the judge, from every hand from which, in this shape, any useful suggestion can with reason be expected. Not to speak of the judge, whether *principal* and *permanent*,* or *assistant* and *occasional*,† — from the hand of a *party* by whom the evidence was called for — from the hand of *another* party on the *same* side of the cause — from the hand of the party on the *opposite* side, or if on that side there be divers parties, from the hand of *each one* of those parties — from the hand of a *witness* or *co-witness* called on the opposite side — from the professional *assistants* or *substitutes* of the parties in all these several situations — why not even from an *amicus curiæ?*

Interrogation undequaque is the adjunct by which interrogation may be expressed, when the light which it is so well suited to afford is let in from all quarters, from which, to the purpose here in question, light can reasonably be expected: and, due allowance made for special reasons to the contrary in special cases, *interrogation undequaque* may, it should seem, be stated as the mode prescribed by reason and justice.

Meantime, by whomsoever applied, cases are not altogether wanting, in which, whether *physically* or no, this security, important as it is, will be seen to be *prudentially* inapplicable: in the shape of delay, vexation, and expense, preponderant inconvenience presents a class of occasional exceptions, the propriety of which is obvious.

Meantime, as to what concerns vexation and expense, a cause of this nature may exist at one time, cease to exist at another: and the cause ceasing, so may the effect.

Cross-examination is a mode of interrogation familiar to every English ear: but under this same name, operations importantly different in nature and efficacy are confounded and disguised.

In all cases, it has for its opposite *examination in chief.* Interrogation performed upon an extraneous witness, at the instance of that one of the parties by whom his appearance in the character of a witness was called for — or, if his appearance was called for on both sides, at the instance of him by whom his actual deposition was first called for,—interrogation thus performed, being interrogation *in chief*; *cross-examination* is interrogation at the instance of a party whose station is on the opposite side of the cause. Cross-examination being thus described, it will immediately be seen to be but an incompletely extensive, and upon reflection, it is supposed, an inadequate application of the principle of *undequaque* interrogation, as above explained. In English practice, *English-bred* procedure has its cross-examination;—*Rome-bred*, to which belongs *equity* procedure, a cross-examination of its own, and that a very different one. Hence ambiguity and confusion, the clearing up of which must for the moment wait — wait for matter which, in the next chapter, will present itself under its proper head.

§ 7. *Counter-Evidence—Admission given to it.*

In relation to any supposed matter of fact, evidence being delivered on one side of a cause, *counter-evidence* is any evidence delivered in relation to the same supposed matter of fact on *the other* side: if more parties than two with conflicting interests, on *any other* side.

Besides the influence exercised by counter-evidence when delivered, the expectation of it will naturally operate with more or less force, through the medium of fear of punishment and shame, as a security against *temerarious* as well as *mendacious* statement; thence against deceptious *incorrectness* and *incompleteness* on the other side.

Note, that as often as, to any article of evidence, the name and effect of *conclusive* — as in the phrase *conclusive evidence* — is given, an exclusion is thereby put, in the lump, upon all counter-evidence not already received, and upon *the effect* of all counter-evidence received or not received. With what propriety, will be seen in an ensuing chapter.

§ 8. *Writing.*

In its application to this purpose as to other purposes, *writing*, like most other efficient and

* Viz. the judge so called.
† Viz. a juryman.

powerful instruments, is capable of being made productive of the most beneficial, and, at the same time, of the most pernicious effect.

To maximize use—to minimize abuse,—such here, as elsewhere, ought to be the object of the legislator.

In what way, from this instrument, evidence may be made, in the most effectual manner, to receive not only *permanence*, but *distinctness* and *recollectedness*, will be seen more particularly as we advance. Moreover where, by distance, the collection of evidence in the *oral* mode is rendered either *physically* or *prudentially* impracticable, to this instrument it is that it must be indebted, not only for *perfection* but for *existence*.

As to the evil effects of which it is liable to be made productive, one comprehensive lot of them has been already brought to view. Of the ways in which English judges have contrived to derive emolument and power from mendacity, a glimpse has just been given: in all these cases, the mendacity has had writing, not only for its *vehicle*, but for its actual and probably for its necessary and indispensable instrument. *Vivâ voce* lies could not be *taxed* like written ones.

In this way, the evil, of which the abuse is most directly and certainly productive, is that which stands correspondent and opposite to the *collateral* ends of justice, viz. the evil composed of *delay*, *vexation*, and *expense*.

But on either side of the cause, by stripping the party of the *power*, or even of the *will*, to maintain his right, this same instrument, through the medium of the collateral ends of justice, is continually felt striking and with fatal effects, against the *direct* ends.

Of writing is composed — if not the whole, a part at least of the ticket, which every man has to purchase, who puts into, or is forced into, the lottery of the law. On either side, he to whom the purchase *is* physically — *is* or is thought *to be* prudentially — impracticable, loses his right, and the loss has *misdecision* for its immediate cause.

In the following instances, the evil is that which stands immediately correspondent and opposite to the *direct* ends of justice:—

1. It will be seen how, by keeping the deponent out of the reach of those means of elucidation — prompt and immediate elucidation — which apply to the case of orally-delivered testimony, *writing* is capable of being made an instrument of *indistinctness* in testimony, producing that frequently deceptious effect to any amount.

2. By the time which the use of it necessarily demands, it affords room for mendacity-serving invention to do its work.

3. Keeping the deponent out of the reach of all mendacity-restraining eyes, it affords room and opportunity for the receipt of mendacity-serving suggestions from all quarters.

True it is that, in some degree, these evils receive a compensation from the room which, at the same time, is left for reflection to other persons, who, lest the mendacity, if credited, should be productive of its intended fruit, viz. *misdecision*, stand engaged, by interest or by duty, to apply their exertions to the exposure of it.

But, of the compensation, it will be seen that it is scarcely adequate; and, be that as it may, that it may be had without the inconvenience.

For a brief indication of the means whereby the *maximization* of the *use* may be conjoined with the *minimization* of the *abuse*, the following hints, loose as they are, must yet, for the present, serve:—

1. Writing having, for its necessary accompaniments, delay, vexation, and expense, — never employ it but for a determinate purpose.

2. Never employ it, but in so far as it promises to be preventive of preponderant evil — viz. in the shape of misdecision; — viz. either on the occasion of the suit or cause in hand, or on the occasion of future contingent suits or causes: or in the way of recordation to a statistic purpose, for legislative use.

3. For *distinctness*, let it be cast into articles or paragraphs, short and numbered.

4. For prevention of mendacity-promoting *invention* and *suggestion*, first receive the testimony in the *orally-delivered* mode; then, for recollectedness, receive it in the *scriptitious* mode.

5. To give *permanence to orally-delivered* evidence, by *minutation* and *recordation* convert it into *scriptitious*.

§ 9. *Publicity, to most purposes, and on most occasions.*

Publicity and *privacy* are antagonising qualities: from *privacy*, in so far as it obtains, *publicity* receives its limits: considered as the effect of *design*, *privacy* takes the name of *secresy*.

As to publicity, — *conceivable* publicity has no other bounds than that by which the total number of human beings is circumscribed.

In regard to judicial instruments and operations in general, and in regard to evidence and the delivery of evidence in particular, both publicity and privacy, over and above those uses by which they are numbered among the securities against deceptious incorrectness and incompleteness in evidence, have other uses, which are referable to the ends of justice: — but those other uses, some of which will presently be brought to view, have no direct bearing on the present purpose.*

* In the Wesminster-Hall courts — in those chief seats of English judicature, — of the smallness of the apartment, — of the small room it affords, by the large proportion necessarily occupied

Uses of Publicity in relation to Evidence.

1. Of publicity applied to all those instruments and operations without distinction, one capital and all-comprehensive use consists in the operation it has in the way of restraint upon misdecision, and against injustice in all its other shapes, on the part of the judge: by it, in character of a safeguard, the force of the *popular* or *moral* sanction is brought to bear upon his conduct in a direct way: and moreover, in a less direct way, viz. by its helping to furnish eventually-convicting evidence, the force of the *legal* sanction; and in so far as, in the exercise of his authority, it lies in the way of the judge to restrain or to promote deceptious incorrectness and incompleteness in evidence, in so far does publicity operate in the character of a security for correctness and completeness.

2. By publicity, in proportion to the extent of it, the mendacity and temerity-restraining force of the *popular* or *moral* sanction is brought to bear directly upon the evidence.

3. In cases in which, by ignorance of the demand for it, or by sinister interest, in the shape of consciousness of delinquency or any other shape, *forthcomingness* of evidence is obstructed—in such cases, in proportion as the proceedings receive publicity, the probability of obtaining evidence receives increase.

Means of effecting Publicity in relation to Evidence.

In the case of *orally-delivered* evidence, the means of publicity depend upon—1. The *size* of the theatre of justice; 2. The *accommodation* which it affords to spectators and auditors; and 3. The facility with which they obtain *admittance*.

In the case of *written* evidence, whether ready *written* or *minuted* down from orally-delivered discourse, it depends upon the application made of the *press* to this purpose, and upon the *extent* to which its productions so applied are disseminated.

In the case of *orally-delivered* evidence, in so far as depends upon the *size* and other circumstances belonging to the theatre of justice, publicity depends altogether upon *government*:—upon the mode in which application is made of its powers to this purpose. In the giving publicity to written evidence shall government be active, or content itself with being passive? *Answer*—As far as, on the part of individuals, adequate *interest* and adequate *means* are found united, a purely passive may be the best part for government:—so far as, on the part of individuals, it happens to either of those requisites to be deficient, in so far it lies with government to supply the deficiency, regard being always had to expense in the character of a preponderant inconvenience: whether it be so or not, will depend upon the importance of the cause.

In so far as, in relation to evidence, publicity is necessary to justice, it is so no less before than after litigation commenced, and to this purpose the distinction between *actual* and *potential* publicity should be kept in mind.

This distinction applies in a more especial manner to *official* evidence: documents indicative of the transactions of public offices. In whatsoever office *ultimately-potential* publicity is from any part of the proceeding banished, in so far despotism is established. But to *ultimately-potential* to substitute *actual* publicity throughout, would, over and above special inconvenience by disclosure—(an inconvenience varying according to the nature of the business,) be productive of such inconvenience, as, in the shape of vexation and expense alone, would of itself be found preponderant.

Of official evidence, more may be seen in the chapter on Pre-appointed Evidence.

§ 10. *Privacy, to some purposes, and on some occasions.*

Of the circumstances by which, in regard to legal evidence, a demand for privacy—understand always relative and provisional privacy—may on one account or other be created, a general intimation may be conveyed by a few words.

I. Purposes bearing relation to evidence, and subservient to the direct ends of judicature:—

1. Prevention of mendacity-serving information:—the architectural arrangements of, as well as the course of proceeding in, the theatre of justice, so ordered, that the testimony, delivering and just delivered, by one witness, may be kept secret from another.

2. Prevention of those reticences, and consequent defalcations from the *completeness* of a mass of testimony, which, in some cases, are apt to be produced by extreme timidity, on the part of a deponent whose trust-worthiness stands clear of suspicion: especially pre-

by the immediate actors in the drama, and by such other members of the profession as are in attendance—of all these causes taken together, such is the effect, that, with the exception of a very small proportion of those members of the public at large, who, had they the *means*, would not want *motives* for attendance, *publicity is excluded*:—excluded, not indeed by *legal* laws, but by instruments of somewhat stronger mould,—by *physical* ones.

On the occasion of those architectural improvements which have been sometimes talked of, the provision made, in relation to the points brought to view in the text, will, in the breasts of the directors, afford in no inconsiderable degree, a *test* and a *measure* of the regard entertained for the ends of justice.

vention of defalcation from the completeness of disclosure, where, in resentment of disclosure, special injury is apprehended from the unjust resentment of this or that particular individual.

II. Purposes bearing relation to evidence, and subservient to the collateral ends of judicature: —

3. Prevention of disclosures injurious to the *pecuniary* reputation of individuals, especially of suitors.

4. Prevention of disclosures injurious to the *moral* reputation of individuals, and the peace of families.

III. Purposes regarding the ends of judicature, but not through the particular medium of evidence: —

1. Securing the peace of the judicatory, and the person of the judge, against casual violation. Power to the judge, on any particular occasion, but for that time only, to apply, to the *number* of the spectators, for special cause assigned, any such *limits* as shall be deemed necessary to this purpose.

2. Prevention of any disclosures that threaten to be subservient to *non-forthcomingness* on the part of persons or things, on whose part forthcomingness is necessary to justice, whether to the purpose of *justiciability*, or to the purpose of evidence.*

Publicity being among the natural instruments of justice, — *secresy*, unless under particular limitation, one of the most mischievously efficient instruments of despotism, — hence an obvious memento, on no occasion to give to *privacy* any extent beyond what the particular nature of the occasion absolutely requires.†

Attached to every *great* theatre of justice should be a *little* theatre. Leaving the auditory in the great theatre undisturbed — (not driven out like cattle, as in a division in the House of Commons) — as often as any special demand for privacy happens to present itself, (for example, where, for relief to an unoffending party or witness from an impending burthen, pecuniary circumstances are to be inquired into,) let the judge, taking with him such persons, the propriety of whose presence is indicated by a compromise between the antagonizing principles, shift the scene for the occasion into the little theatre.

* Example:—Temporary relative privacy, necessary to conceal, from a delinquent, evidence, by which he would receive warning to withdraw himself or his effects out of the reach of justice.

† In the metropolis, in examinations taken in criminal cases by police magistrates, privacy is occasionally given, and *that* avowedly, to this or that part of the inquiry: and this secret mode, — not being employed otherwise than sparingly, and for special and visible cause, nor even thus being other than provisional and capable of being eventually succeeded by complete publicity coextensive with the privacy,—justice seems to have everything to gain, nothing to lose by the temperament.

CHAPTER IX.

FALSE SECURITIES FOR TRUSTWORTHINESS IN EVIDENCE — OATHS AND EXCLUSIONS.

§ 1. *Ceremony of an Oath — a False Security for Trustworthiness.*

Securities against mendacity brought to view — securities in such numbers and variety — and no mention yet of oaths — no mention of that sacred instrument, which, in the general estimation of mankind, occupies the highest place on the list of these securities, and has so frequently been employed, not only in preference to, but to the exclusion of, all those others.

That by the omission here spoken of, an emotion of surprise should be produced, cannot itself be matter of much surprise. In the character of an instrument actually and generally thus employed, the title of this ceremony to a place upon the list of these securities, admits not of dispute. But, in the character of an instrument fit to be so employed, the more closely it is looked into, the more plainly, it is supposed, will its unfitness to be so employed be recognised.

Exhibited in detail, and with a degree of particularity in any degree corresponding to the importance of the subject, the consideration by which the condemnation here in question was produced, would have given too long an interruption to the thread of the inquiry, and run into a degree of extension altogether disproportionate. Not requiring to be taken into consideration on the occasion, or for the purpose, of anything that follows, the matter belonging to that head is here omitted.‡

Meantime, of the considerations by which so important a conclusion was produced, some intimation, how slight and general soever, may in this place be not altogether without its use.

The following are the propositions by which they may stand expressed. For the present, they may be considered as so many positions set down for proof: —

1. That, in the very essence of this instrument, a rash and grossly incongruous supposition is involved; viz. that, for the purpose of eventual punishment, and thence for the purpose of dominion, applicable to any end in view at pleasure, the power of the Almighty lies at all times at the disposal — at the absolute disposal, of any the most worthless of human kind.

2. That, by the religion of Jesus, in so far as the precepts ascribed to Jesus are to be

‡ It will be found in the tract entitled "Swear not all," in vol. V. of this collection.

admitted as containing the expression of it, the application of any such instrument to any such purpose as the one here in question stands prohibited; prohibited in the plainest and most pointed terms:* and that for any exception which a man may feel himself disposed to cut out of that prohibition, imagination is the only warrant that can be found.

3. That, by the articles expressive of the particular tenets of that modification of the religion of Jesus which is established in England, the use of it, though declared *allowable*, is not on any occasion *enjoined*.†

4. That, to any such good purpose as that in question, its efficiency will, if attentively examined, be found to amount to nothing: inasmuch as, in every case in which this supposed security presents itself to view as if operating with effect, other instruments, of which, in the character in question, the efficiency is altogether out of dispute, — two other instruments, viz. *punishment* and *shame*, may be seen, one or both of them, operating on the occasion in question, in that same direction, and to that same end: — and that, when these instruments are both of them out of the question, — have not either of them, any place, — mendacity, any application made of this instrument, notwithstanding, is altogether without restraint: — and if called for by any exciting motive, takes place accordingly: — and to this purpose, *university oaths* and *custom-house oaths* are brought to view.

5. That, of its inutility in the character in question, a continual and unquestionable, but tacit and virtual, recognition is made, in and by the practice of both houses of parliament: inasmuch as, by the House of Commons, operations, of incomparably greater importance than any to which the sanction of an oath is ever applied, viz. measures of legislation — in a word, *laws* of all sorts — are continually established on the ground of evidence obtained without any assistance from this instrument.

6. That, while to *good* purposes it is thus inefficient, to *bad* purposes, vast and indefinite in extent, variety, and importance, it has been, is, and threatens to continue to be, but too efficient: for that the instrument being in its nature alike applicable on every imaginable occasion, — viz. not only on those occasions on which the oath has been distinguished by the name of an *assertory* oath, but on those on which it retains the name of a *promissory* oath, — whatsoever pernicious effects it is found pregnant with in the latter of these two characters, will be attached to it, inseparably attached to it, in whichsoever of the two it be employed.

7. That, in the character *here* in question, viz. that of an *assertory* oath, it has already been seen to be a main, an indispensable instrument, in the organization of the system of *mendacity licences* above mentioned.

8. That, in this same character, it has, in a variety of ways, the effect of obstructing the action and weakening the efficiency of the laws.

9. That, in a sort of ambiguous or mixed character, composed of that of the *assertory*, and that of the *promissory* oath, it has the effect of bewildering the conceptions, corrupting the morals, and enslaving the consciences of men in the situation of *jurymen*: contributing, in conjunction with other instruments, to the converting them into puppets in the hands of *judges*.

10. That, in the character of a *promissory oath at large*, it is employed, and but too naturally, and with but too much frequency and success, in giving union, force, and effect, to the mischievous enterprises of criminal and lawless conspirators.

11. That, in this same character of a *promissory* oath, in the mouth of an English monarch, it is but too well adapted to the affording pretence and encouragement to misrule by abuse of prerogative: and on this occasion, the application made of it on and by the *coronation oath* is brought to view.

12. That, in those seats of superior education, in which the characters of a considerable proportion of the future rulers of the community are formed, the use that has been made, and continues to be made, of this instrument, is such, as to have introduced distortion into the intellectual, as well as corruption into the moral part, of the mental frame: and on this occasion, a fundamental error in morals and legislation — an error respecting the use and application of punishment — forced by an irresistible pressure into the mind in that tender and yielding state of its growth, is brought to view.

13. That, on any of the occasions, on which, to the purpose of judicature, it is employed in the character of an *assertory* oath, there exists not any real need of it: — for that its place may be supplied, and with great advantage, by other and unexceptionable arrangements: of which arrangements an indication is accordingly brought to view.

§ 2. *Exclusion of Evidence — a False Security against Deception.*

In the character of a security against deception, *putting exclusion upon evidence* is a practice, which appears to have as yet been everywhere in use: and in the boundless field of evidence, vast in the aggregate, — prodigiously diversified in respect of the seat of the particular spots, — is the extent that would be found occupied by this mode of

* Matt. v. 34—"Swear not at all"

† Article 39—"We judge that the Christian religion doth not prohibit, but that a man may swear when the magistrate requireth."

husbandry, even in those regions, whichsoever they may be, in which the use made of it has been least extensive.

"So universally as this sort of arrangement has been received in the character of a security against deception, is not then its title to that character," says somebody, "a good one? If *exclusion* put upon false evidence be not a security against *deception* by false evidence, what else can be? In comparison of this, how precarious is the effect of all those other securities put together! Can a man have been deceived by evidence which has never been so much as present to his mind?"

No, certainly: and so it is, that if no evidence at all were on any occasion admitted, deception by evidence could not on any occasion be produced.

But deception may be, and is produced, — deception and thence misdecision, — not only *by* evidence, but for *want* of evidence: produced, viz. by false or otherwise fallacious evidence on the other side: or by causing not to be believed, the existence of a really existing fact, the existence of which, had the evidence been admitted, would have been believed.

Moreover, if, on the part of the judge, *deception* be pernicious, it is so only in so far as it is productive of *misdecision:* and if misdecision itself be pernicious, it is so no otherwise than in so far as it is productive of *injustice: injustice,* viz. of that sort which stands opposite to the *direct* ends of justice, as above explained.

If *misdecision* be one cause by which injustice is produced, *non-demand* is another. When a man is well assured that the evidence, without which the justice of his demand cannot be made appear, will not, if presented, be admitted, — in such case, be his demand ever so just, and the loss of the object of it ever so fatal to him, he forbears, if he be well advised, to present it.

By non-demand and misdecision taken together, that of the practice of putting exclusion upon evidence, the *effect* is much more frequently to *produce* than to *prevent* injustice, — so much so, that it would be a prodigious benefit to justice, if exclusion of evidence were, in so far as it takes this for its ground, itself for ever, and in every instance, excluded, — is a persuasion, entertained after little less than fifty years of consideration, on grounds of which a slight outline will be given in the present abstract, the filling it up being reserved for the body of the work.

"But *trustworthiness* — (it may be asked) why speak here of trustworthiness? By whom can any such conception have been entertained, as that exclusion of evidence can operate as a security for the trustworthiness of evidence? as a security for its title to credence, any more than for its actually obtaining credence?"

No, certainly: not for the trustworthiness of the particular lot of evidence to which, in the instance in question, the exclusion is applied: for, by the exclusion put upon it, its untrustworthiness is always affirmed: — not for the trustworthiness of that one lot; but however for the trustworthiness of the whole remaining mass, of which that lot, had it obtained admittance, would have made a part: if so it be, that after the exclusion of whatever articles have been excluded, there *be* remaining any others to which admittance has not been refused.

CHAPTER X.

OF THE RECEPTION AND EXTRACTION OF EVIDENCE, *viz.* WITH THE HELP OF THE ABOVE SECURITIES.

§ 1. *Oral Interrogation — Minutation or Notation — Recordation or Registration.*

Reception and *extraction* — under these two words may be included all the several modes in which, and operations by which, an article of evidence can make its way, and present itself to the faculties of the judge.

If, on the delivery and *reception* of the article of evidence, not only the person by whom it is delivered, but the judge by whom, or under whose direction, it is received, and everybody else, is, with the exception of the acts just mentioned, purely passive, — *reception* presents itself as being in that case the proper term.

If, for the purpose of producing or promoting the delivery, any operation be performed, that operation will be found to be an act of *interrogation;* and, in so far as any evidentiary discourse, that follows in the form of a *response,* is considered as the fruit or result produced by the operation, the operation may be termed *extraction,* and the evidence thus obtained may be said to be *extracted.*

Of *reception* as applied to evidence — of an operation so eminently simple, — little, it is obvious, can naturally require to be said. On the subject of *extraction* — a business of no slight complexity and difficulty — no inconsiderable part of the work will unavoidably be expended.*

By interrogation in the *oral* form, by interrogation in the *epistolary* form, or by any such mixture of the two as by incidental convenience may happen to have been indicated, — by any of these three means — in any of these three modes, may evidence be extracted. In the body of the work, how to employ each to the best advantage, will be found a principal subject of inquiry, in the book of which this chapter bears the title.

Answers, impromptuary — called forth without *time* allowed for mendacity-assist-

* Book III.

ing invention or recollection — questions put *singly*—questions deduced from and *grounded on the answers*, — from these circumstances, which attach themselves as of course to the *oral* mode, the efficacy of that mode of *extraction*, and, except in particular circumstances, its superiority over the *epistolary* mode, will be deduced: its superiority, viz. with reference to the *direct* ends of judicature, over and above its more manifest superiority with relation to the *collateral* ends of judicature, — viz. avoidance of delay, *vexation, and expense.*

Of the advantages deducible from this mode of extraction, a part, which in some cases will be in no inconsiderable degree pregnant with instruction, will in effect be lost, if the judge by whom, on the matter of fact, the decision is to be pronounced, be not *present* on the occasion; himself a percipient witness of the *deportment* of the person from whose lips the verbal information is extracted: — deportment, that mode of expression and source of instruction, by which, on the theatre of amusement, without any aid from words, whatever is meant to be communicated is not unfrequently expressed.

Notes or *memorandums* in writing, in any and what cases — on any and what *conditions* — by any and what *persons* — shall they be consultable, under examination? Interrogation of a *suggestive* nature — in any and what cases — by or from any and what *persons* — shall it be allowed? *Discreditive* interrogation — interrogation, the effect of which may be to reflect discredit on the examinee — to fix a stain, or cast a shadow of doubt upon his reputation for probity, and thereby diminish the apparent trustworthiness — the probative force — of his testimony, shall it, in any and what cases, be allowed? In the body of the work, to all these several questions, answers are endeavoured to be provided.

Be the evidence thus extracted what it may, it would lose much of its eventual use, and of any decision grounded on it, the chance of its being conformable to justice would be very precarious, — if, in the article of *permanence*, in the event of its being, in the opinion of a party on either side, worth the trouble and expense, it were not capable of being put upon the footing of ready-written evidence.

Hence comes the demand for *registration* or *recordation*; — the two words being considered as synonymous, and taken in the large and simple sense thus indicated, — and not perplexed and narrowed by technical restrictions.

Hence again, on the present occasion, the demand for minutation or notation, — on the present occasion, the necessarily attendant operation by which the matter for registration must be supplied.

To the judge, for the purpose of occasional recollection, — *against* the judge, in the case of incidental misconduct, or misdecision, if accompanied with blame, — both ways, to and for the benefit of the parties on both sides of the suit in hand, and more especially to the party on that side which is most in the right, — in some cases, to the parties eventually concerned in *future* contingent suits, in which it may happen to the same matter of fact to come, any part of it, into question, — to parties to whom, but for the evidence thus preserved, it might happen to find themselves under the necessity of endeavouring to establish this same matter of fact, and to that purpose to engage in a contest which by this means is prevented, — lastly, to the *legislator*, in respect of the grounds, on which, in case of admittance given, as hereinafter proposed, to suspicious evidence, he may, by observation taken of its nature and result, feel himself disposed and authorized to give confirmation to any rules, to which in this behalf he may have thought fit to give a provisional acceptance, or to substitute other rules in their stead; — in all these ways, the transformation of *oral* into *written* evidence will be seen to have, in cases to an indefinite extent, its use. *Notation*, or say *minutation*, — followed by *recordation*, or say *registration*, — are the operations by which this transformation is effected.

In what *cases* shall these operations be performed? — by what *person* or *persons*, and in what *mode?* Such are the questions for which, under this head, answers are, in the body of the work, endeavoured to be provided.

§ 2. *Extraction should not be severed from Decision.*

Superintending, at the very time of extraction, the extraction of the evidence which is to form the ground of the decision, — and forming the decision which has that evidence for its ground, — between these two operations so intimate is the connexion, that without considerable danger of misdecision they cannot (reason may have already been seen to suspect) be severed and allotted to different minds. The one is no less essentially a judicial function than the other. By any deficiency, in respect either of skill or probity, on the part of him by whom the *grounds* for the decision have been *formed*, the most consummate measure of both these qualifications in the breast of him by whom, on these same grounds, the *decision is pronounced*, may have no better effect than that of rendering misdecision the more sure; and whoever is not fit to be intrusted with the *definitive* function, it seems not easy to conceive how he should be fit to be intrusted with that which, in the way that has just been seen, is *preparatory* to it

When the judge, by whom a decision on the evidence is pronounced, was not present at the extraction of it, the loss of the information afforded by *deportment* creates a deficiency, the value of which presents, as already intimated, a consideration, to the force of which, no preponderant force, it should seem, can be opposed.

When the judicatory, being a *many*-seated (as a mathematician would say, a poly-hedrous) judicatory, one judge, who, alone or with others, had been employed in the business of receipt and extraction, is, in conjunction with those, if any, and with others in additional numbers, employed in the forming the decision, — it may be a question whether, under this palliative, the mischief of the severance be diminished or increased. Adding to a judge, whose means of judging are superior, a number of others, with equal power, whose means are inferior, is an arrangement which, upon the face of it, presents no very great probability of superior rectitude.*

In the case of *appeal*, if on the question of fact appeal be allowed, this disadvantage must be submitted to: and under whatsoever forms, and by whatsoever names, an appeal on the question of fact is carried on, whatsoever advantages may be found attached to it, will have this disadvantage to contend with.

Of a severance, upon the very face of it so unnatural, the not very deep-seated causes will be pointed out: and it will be seen how far they are from coinciding or being consistent with any sincere regard for the interests of truth and justice.

In judicial procedure, everything having for its author the man of law — everything, on this as on other occasions, under favour of the darkness of the age, had everywhere, of course, for its chief, not to say its sole object, in as far as circumstances admitted, the convenience — the advantage in every shape — of the man of law.

To this cause may be referred, without difficulty, so many pernicious applications as in this field may be seen made of the principle of *the division of labour;* — that genial principle, the fertility of which is, in the field of political economy, so salutary.

Beneath, as well as *on*, the bench, in each offset, into which by division the *polypus* — not to say the *leach* — has contrived to multiply himself, behold at the same time a *screen*, by which the light of true information is shut out, — a discolouring medium, by which false light is let in, — and a sponge, by which the substance of the litigants is absorbed.

The judge, decomposing himself into the evidence-collecting and the deciding judge:— the agent of the party, into the attorney and the advocate: — each of these again into a cluster of sub-offsets, the more numerous, the more favourable to *misrepresentation*,* — to its consequence, *misdecision*, — to the boundless increase of factitious and needless *delay*, *vexation*, and *expense*.

Immediately under the bench, the scribe has decomposed himself, or rather has been decomposed by his master the judge, into a similar cluster of the like offsets, that in each of them the master may find an additional sponge. By the whole tribe together, as much as possible done of that by which fees are collected; as little as possible, — and little indeed that is! — of that by which the purposes of justice — the true ends of judicature — are served.†

§ 3. *Epistolary Interrogation.*

In certain cases, the employment of the written, viz. the *epistolary*, mode of extracting evidence becomes matter of necessity or convenience: — what (it will be asked) is the description of these cases? For furnishing an answer expressed in general terms, two classes of cases may be brought to view: 1. Where, by the nature of the case, for the formation of such answers as shall be necessary to the correctness and completeness of the mass of evidence, a greater length of time employed in recollection and consideration is necessary, than is compatible with the operation of extraction, when performed in the oral mode; 2. Where, by the remoteness of the abode of the examinee from the seat of judicial inquiry, the employment of the oral mode is

* Under Rome-bred procedure, in the French edition of it, in the deciding judicatory, the judge by whom the mass of evidence had been received and extracted, was called the Juge-Rapporteur: — and so in other countries in which Rome-bred procedure is principally employed.

The turning over to a clerk's clerk, examining each witness in a *tête-à-tête*, — the formation of those grounds, on which, in all the parade of publicity, the decision pronounced by the head of the law is to be determined, is among those exemplifications of interested negligence, which were reserved for English judicature.

By the arrangement by which he is thus laid under the happy impossibility of judging well, the purse of this or that other great dignitary is, as usual, swelled.

In other countries, in those judicatories in which the same mode of extraction, viz. the Roman mode, is pursued, not only is the functionary, by whom the evidence is extracted, a judge of the same class, denomination, and rank, — and at other times employed in public in the same occupations as those are, by whom the decision which is to be pronounced on the ground of the evidence thus collected is to be formed, — but in that judge, improbity finds a constantly present check, imbecility a constantly present support, in the person of *an attendant scribe.*

† For examples of a sort of matter which might with advantage be consigned to remembrance, and is not, see Chaper XXIII. *Safeguards, &c.*

rendered either physically or prudentially impracticable.

For the better securing the efficiency of the interrogative process when carried on in this mode, two arrangements, in the character of *sub-securities*, will be brought to view: for the sense of *responsibility*, responses (as under natural procedure) in the *first person*, not (as under *technical* procedure) in the *third*;—for *distinctness* and *facility of reference*, thence also for responsibility, paragraphs, *limited in length and numbered*.

Of these practical arrangements, the rationale is particularly developed in detail: and if such as is supposed be the demand for them, notwithstanding the security afforded by an instrument so powerful as the practice of interrogation is under whatsoever disadvantages applied,—much greater must it be in the case, in which the declaration is delivered without the benefit of any such security, as in the case of a *bill* in equity,—an *answer* in equity,—a paper of *special pleading* at common law,—or an affidavit.

§ 4. *Modes of Interrogation principally in use.*

The *form* of the discourse, viz. *oral* or *scriptitious*,—the constitution of the *judicature*,—and the distinction, such as it is, between *publicity* and *privacy* :—out of these three circumstances put together, five distinguishable, and alike established modes of *examination* or *interrogation* may be seen composed :—1. The oral mode, *per partes, coram judice et assessoribus publice* ;* 2. The *epistolary* mode *per partes* ;† 3. The oral mode, *in secreto per judicem delegatum* ;‡ 4. The oral mode, *in secreto per judices utrinque electos* ;‖ 4. The oral mode, *per judicem publice*.¶—Of these several modes, the comparative subserviency to the purposes of justice is in the body of the work endeavoured to be brought to view.

Browbeating—I mean the species of professional or rather official insolence and oppression (I say official, for the advocate cannot offend unreproved, but he has the judge for his accomplice)—browbeating presents an objection, which by practitioners under the *secret* mode has been urged§ against the first of these modes, and with but too much justice, if, as it seems to be tacitly assumed, the abuse were an irremediable one. A remedy, if not absolutely sanative, palliative at least, will be found suggested.

* As in jury trial. † As by a bill in equity.

‡ As in the court of chancery's examiner's office, in town causes.

‖ As under the commissions issued by the court of chancery, for taking evidence in country causes.

¶ As on examination taken by a justice of peace.

§ Brown, I. 479.

§ 5. *Oral or Epistolary mode—which to employ?*

By the oral mode in its best form, or by the epistolary mode in its best form,—by which, in any given case, will, upon the whole, be rendered service the most profitable to the purposes of justice? The answer has been seen already, and has an unavoidable dependence on the individualizing circumstances of each individual case. Among the cases—(extensive the collection of them will be seen to be)—in which a conflict is apt to take place between the *direct* and the *collateral* ends of judicature, this will be seen to be one. In many instances, where for *rectitude of decision* the oral mode might be preferable, for avoidance of *delay*, *vexation*, and *expense*, attached to personal attendance, the epistolary mode may be the only mode *prudentially*, in others the only mode *physically* practicable. In other cases, where, for assistance to the *oral*, the *epistolary* mode, or *vice versa*, might not be altogether without its use, the additional load of delay, vexation, and expense, that might be found inseparable from it, might recommend the sacrifice of it.

The proposed examinee,—in what quarter is his station in the theatre of justice?—on the *defendant's* side, on the *plaintiff's* side, or in the *witness's* box? Correspondent to these differences in position, different answers may be found best adapted, upon the whole, to the purposes of justice.

Epistolarily extracted,—shall it, in any, and what cases, be deemed sufficient, without *orally-extracted* evidence? In the first instance and *provisionally*, the answer will be seen to depend, as above, upon the particular circumstances of the individual case. But, in ultimate resort, the conflict between affirmance and disaffirmance still remaining, no decision that is to be immediately definitive, will, it is believed, be found sufficiently grounded, that has not for its warrant an examination, *coram judice, et partibus*, face to face.*

§ 6. *Cross-examination—Anglicé, and Romano-Anglicé.*

Under the general head of *interrogation*, *cross-examination* has been mentioned as a term pregnant with confusion: for an attempt to dispel that confusion, matters are now ripe.

Cross-examination being performed, as above, in the only genuine and rational—in the *English-bred* mode,—the questions put on one side have in part, for their ground, the answers given to the questions put on the other:—performed in the *Rome-bred* mode,

* Thus, after an *answer* put in upon oath to a *bill* in equity, the contest is liable to conclude (though by a separate cause) with jury-trial, on an indictment for perjury. Add to this the more frequent case of an *issue*.

the questions are all framed, by a person, from whom all questions on the other side, consequently all errors of which they can be productive, are kept avowedly and anxiously concealed.

In *Rome-bred* procedure, the process of extraction, for how many days or weeks continued, being kept involved in impenetrable darkness, what the nature and effect of cross-examination thus performed is, may be a secret, — not only to the non-lawyer, but even among lawyers, to any except those whose particular branch of experience has initiated them into the mysteries of that antique and adscititious system of procedure.

§ 7. *Confrontation and Repetition Romanicé.*

In *Rome-bred* procedure, two courses or stages of proceeding, — the one *confrontation*, the other *re-examination*, Romano-Gallicé *recolement*, — *Romano-Scoticé repetition*, — *Romano-Anglo-Ecclesiasticé*, also *repetition*,* — both of them, in *name* at least, and in the character of distinct processes, and causes of proceeding, in *substance* alike unknown in English-bred procedure, occupy each of them a conspicuous place.

If so it be, that on a question of fact, in all *places*, and at all *times*, not to speak of all *causes*, the means and modes of forming a just ground for decision cannot but be much the same, — how comes it, that two operations, to which, under the governments of civilized countries in general, modern as well as ancient, so much importance has been attached, should be in a manner unknown to English practice?

On the continent, both *confrontation*, and the examination called *recolement* and repetition, are confined to penal cases of the higher order. By confrontation, the system of dark seclusion being, for this purpose, and *pro tanto*, subjected to a partial and momentary relaxation, supposed co-delinquents, with or without the addition of unsuspected witnesses, are brought together, and set to ply each other with mutual interrogations:—scene, the darkness of the judicial closet, — under the inspection of the judge — with or without his scribe, — at any rate, with no other check upon him than what may be supposed to be applied by the presence of that more or less dependent subordinate. Establishing the *identity* of the supposed delinquent, and promoting the *disclosure* of all relevant matters of fact, are the objects which *confrontation* is stated as having in view.

Securing correctness and completeness against misrecollection on the part of the examinee, — securing his freedom against seduction, whether in the form of intimidation or enticement, considered as capable of being administered to him by the judge, — securing the authenticity of the minutes against misrepresentation at the hands of the judge, — such are the purposes, to which the system of regulations relative to these objects appears, how unsuccessfully soever, to have been directed.

Between these two operations, thus upon the face of them so dissimilar, so close however is the analogy imagined and ascribed to them, that, under the *Romano-Gallic* procedure, cases are laid down, in which *confrontation* is to find in *repetition* a declaredly adequate substitute.

In the case of *confrontation*, the *scantiness* of its application, — as if there were any sort of case in which light from all quarters were less conducive to rectitude of decision than another, — in the case of *repetition* as well as confrontation, their conjunct *insufficiency* to every useful purpose, in comparison of the security afforded by publicity and open doors, will be held up to view.

Under the English mode, without the name and form, *jury-trial*, whether preceded or not by the preliminary examinations performed by a magistrate, gives in part the effect, and by a slight extension of the right of interrogation might be made to give the whole, of the effect of *confrontation*. In regard to *repetition*, preceded by that same preliminary examination, it gives actually part of the good effect, and might easily be made to give the whole of the good effect, so vainly aimed at by repetition when performed in the close mode.†

* Brown, I. 479.

† Viz. by *undequaque* interrogation, if substituted to the incomplete mode in use.

CHAPTER XI.

COLLECTION OF EVIDENCE — ENGLISH PRACTICE.

§ 1. *Natural Procedure, — Fit Modes — Parliamentary and Jury Trial, &c.*

"Video meliora proboque, deteriora sequor."
The best they know and praise, — the worst pursue.

NEVER was trite adage more fully exemplified, never more completely verified — verified in those high situations in which it is least excusable.

Of the system best adapted to the collecting of evidence, though the several leading features, with their respective uses and excellences, may never yet have been distinctly and completely brought to view, of this best system, — the only one that ever could really have had for its object the discovering of truth, and administering of uncorrupt justice, there is no secret: no secret can there ever have been, to any of those by whom, to the extent of their power, the two worst modes that could be found have all along, as will be seen, been employed in preference.

This consciousness will be placed in broad daylight, before this chapter is at its close.

On this occasion, for giving ideas of perfection carried into practice, two modes of extraction require to be presented to view on the same line; viz. the mode pursued in *parliamentary committees*, and the mode pursued in *jury-trial:*—presented, not now it is true, as standing as yet, either of them, on the very summit of the scale of perfection, or at least jury-trial,—but as capable, when put together, of enabling the mind to form an idea of it:—the parliamentary mode as being nearest to perfection,—the jury mode as being the most familiar to the public mind.

On this same occasion, be it observed, the *composition of the judicatory* is a subject that should be kept completely out of view. How important soever,—in itself, and with reference to the ultimate result of the inquiry,—yet, with reference to the subject here in question, viz. the mode of receipt and extraction, it is a matter comparatively foreign and irrelevant.

At the time when the system of jury-trial was first formed, not only was *printing* altogether unknown, but even *writing*, the great source of complication, was, except in the instance of here and there an instrument of primary importance, public and private together, scarcely in use. The ignorant simplicity of the age, while it insured a proportionable degree of simplicity to all subjects of discussion, insured at the same time a correspondent degree of simplicity, precipitancy, and imperfection, to the course pursued in examining into the grounds and merits of all subjects of dispute. Slight was the degree of complication, or even of estimated difficulty and importance, that sufficed to give, to a legal knot, the character of a Gordian one:—and in that case, for the cutting of it, in some instances an assertion of the party, conceived in the most general terms, with the ceremony of an oath for sanctionment, and a general attestation of character for corroboration,—in others, a mutual attempt to murder, called *an appeal to heaven*, was received in preference to, and to the exclusion of, all other evidence.

In jury-trial, the grand features of excellence are—interrogation *by parties* on both sides—examination *vivâ voce*—consequent exclusion, to a considerable degree, of the faculties of mendacious *invention* and *suggestion*—these, together with the *publicity* given to that part of the system of procedure. Of these,—in contradistinction to *epistolary statement*, and *written* depositions, consisting of statements minuted down in the shape of answers to preconcerted and written interrogatories,—*vivâ voce* deposition was the necessary result of the rudeness and ignorance of the age: while, in contradistinction to interrogation by the judge alone,—interrogation performed by persons interested on both sides, as well as by the judge,—this, and the publicity of the inquiry, was, with or without any adequate or clear conception of use and subserviency to truth and justice, the natural, if not the necessary, result or accompaniment of what there was of *popularity* in the constitution of the judicatory:—a jury being a sort of *select committee*, gradually and silently substituted to the whole body of the freeholders,—to the whole mass of that portion of the people whose feelings and interests were alone, in those days, considered as having any claim to notice.

In the mode of *extraction* then and thus pursued, the great defect was and is—the want of *time* for occasional *recollection*, and eventually necessary *ulterior investigation*,* and consequently the non-employment of *writing*, in the character of an instrument for exhibiting, correcting, completing, and preserving, the result of those instructive operations.

In the system of parliamentary procedure—parliamentary-committee-procedure—this deficiency, fatal to the purpose of inquiries, applied to such subjects, and directed to such objects, as it could not but have been,—has long since, and continues to be, effectually supplied. This modern mode of procedure, not having taken its commencement till the art of writing had come pretty generally into use,—till, in the character of instruments of investigation and dispute, the productions of that mind-exalting art had become abundant and generally diffused,—and (as will be seen a little further on) no sinister interest having place, powerful enough to overrule, in this, as in the other case it has done, the dictates of truth and justice,—the consequence has been that degree of comparative perfection, the fruits of which have been so copiously reaped, while, for want of motives and occasions for holding it up to view, the thing itself has been so little noticed.

In the mode of collecting evidence pursued in the courts of summary procedure in general, and in particular in the summarily pro-

* It is by this deficiency, that, in cases attended with a certain degree of complication,—cases of *account*, for example—jury-trial has been found to be absolutely unfit for use:—instances to a great extent, and of capital importance, absolutely incapable of being applied to the purposes for which it continues to be in outward show employed, and declared to be in use. In these cases, no decision being really produced by it, the party who is in the right, is made to suffer the whole of the burthen, without the possibility of reaping any benefit from it. Thus is the *serpent* substituted for the *fish*, and in the hands of Judge and Co. employed as an instrument of deceit and depredation, in a manner that has been particularized and proved in another place. See *Scotch Reform*.

ceeding judicatories of *justices of the peace*, as well as in the small-debt courts called *courts of conscience*, there exists nothing to hinder the combination of those several features of perfection: — nor, under favour of the auspicious absence of all technical bars, does any reason present itself for supposing, that in such desirable combinations they are not actually and generally employed. But as in these comparatively simple cases, any comparatively considerable demand for recollection, investigation and reference to, and selection from, written documents, will not frequently present itself, so, in both these instances, concerning the mode of procedure thus pursued, so little is the notice that has been generally taken, and so slender is the utmost account that is anywhere to be found of it in print, — that, on the present occasion, what mention is made of them has principally for its object the showing, that, while so richly deserving as they are, not only to be brought to view — but held up exclusively for imitation, they have not on the present occasion been overlooked.

§ 2. *Unfit employed, to the exclusion of the above fit modes.*

In relation to the modes of collecting evidence, employed, to the exclusion of the jury-trial mode, by English judges, if ever the time should come, in which, to the good people of England, justice and injustice should cease to be matters of indifference, the following propositions will not perhaps be deemed altogether undeserving of their notice.

1. That the only forms in which, in so far as they have found themselves at liberty, English judges have received those communications, to which, with the *effect*, they have given the *name* of *evidence*, are depositions and affidavits.

Depositions, being composed of testimony collected in the Rome-bred mode, viz. in secret, under the sanction of an oath, by the nominee of a judge, or by the nominees of the parties on both sides, in answer to strings of questions, prepared on behalf of the parties, and thus reduced to a written form, to which the deponents are made respectively to annex their signatures and *affidavits* of ready-written statements delivered under the same sanction, but without being subjected to interrogation.

2. That these modes are both of them repugnant to every one of the true ends of judicature, conducive to deception, and thence to misdecision — conducive to needless delay, vexation, and expense.

3. That of the unfitness of these modes of proceeding, those by whom they were introduced, — those by whom they are continued, — and those by whom they have been upholden, — have all been, and without exception are, fully and undeniably conscious: — and that in the whole profession, unless among the professors of Rome-bred law any exception should be to be found, there exists not so much as the pretence of doubt.

4. That the modes of judicial proceeding thus known to be repugnant to truth and justice, have always been, and continue to be in a pre-eminent degree, subservient to the private and sinister interest of those by whom they were introduced, — of those by whom they continue to be practised, — and of those by whom they continue to be upholden.

§ 3. *Deposition, Romano-Anglicé — its Inaptitude.*

In comparison of the jury-trial mode, more particularly if, when occasion requires, improved by minutation and recordation, and by opportunity of amendment, — the following may be stated as the features of inaptitude observable in the Rome-bred deposition mode.

I. Deception favoured; viz. by exclusion of portions of the testimony, extractible from one and the same examinee: —

1. The adverse party not being apprised of the answers that will be given by the examinee to the questions put to him by the party by whom his testimony is called for, nor so much as what those questions themselves will be, — no effectual counter-interrogation — no *cross-examination* in the ordinary sense of the word — has place: so that, from this defect, were it the only one, deceptious incompleteness and incorrectness, and consequent deception and misdecision, may be stated as the natural and ever probable result.

II. Deception favoured; viz. by weakening the restraint put upon mendacity and temerity by the sense of responsibility: —

2. If, as in the open mode, and in ordinary conversation, the deponent were, from first to last, made to speak in his own person, — if the words exhibited as *his* had been the very words that had been in the first instance employed by himself for giving expression to his own recollections or pretended recollections, — if, in a word, the discourse, to which he is made to annex his signature as being *his*, were his own, — were originally and without variation his own, — the sense of responsibility, which to the form of speech in question attaches itself in a degree so much more acute than to any other, would in some degree operate as a check upon mendacity and temerity, — as a security against deceptious incorrectness and incompleteness.

As if to deprive truth and justice of the benefit of this security, the discourse, which in answer to the questions that had been propounded, had been delivered by the deponent himself, is in this mode set aside, — another discourse, framed, not to say *invented*, by the examiner, is substituted, — and it is to this discourse, thus framed by another person, that the deponent is made to annex that signature, by which he certifies it to be his.*

III. Deception favoured;—viz. by exclusion put upon the entire testimony of witnesses in any number.

3. In the open mode, by the evidence produced in the first instance, and afterwards by the publicity given to the whole case, it will frequently happen—and especially in cases, in the nature of which it is to afford a copious fund of evidence, among which those of the greatest importance are apt to find themselves—that ulterior sources of evidence will be indicated, and on a subsequent occasion, the evidence from these sources obtained. Of the *close* mode, the exclusion of all casual and supplemental evidence not only is the natural and frequent result, but has been a professed object.†

IV. Deception favoured;—viz. by clouds of irrelevant or needless matter introduced.

4. In the *open* mode, viz. in the way of *vivâ voce* examination performed in public—performed by advocates, in the presence of managing agents on both sides, with or without that of parties,—it will frequently happen, that by a short statement made by a witness antecedently examined, ulterior evidence, which to an unlimited amount would otherwise have been adduced, being plainly rendered unnecessary, is saved. In the *close mode*, all such casual lights being shut out, the consequence is—that lest any possible advantage should be lost, whatsoever evidence presents a possibility of proving serviceable to the party, is by each party irrevocably and irreducibly extracted. Moreover, questions and answers being in this mode all committed to writing,—and the string of questions that shall be put to the witness pre-appointed,—hence needless delay, vexation, and expense.

V. Delay, vexation, and expense produced,—cause, lawyer's sinister interest.

5. Of all the functionaries, public as well as private, employed in the collection of evidence in this *close and written mode*, there is not perhaps one who has not an interest in giving unnecessary increase to the expense of it, and consequently to the delay subservient, and the vexation concomitant, to that expense:—nor any one who does not find it more or less in his power to promote that sinister interest.

VI. Delay, &c. produced:—cause, financier's sinister interest.

6. The *man of finance*, seeing a source from which money is extractible, and without that disturbance to his own case, which is the natural result, where the persons on whom the burthen rests are in a condition to combine their exertions for the purpose of opposition and remonstrance,—the man of finance, observing in that denial of justice with which the great majority of the people are thus afflicted, a sure, yet little-noticed, means of enabling the class, to which he and the circle in which he moves belong, to keep in a state of irremediable oppression the inferior classes,—makes the most of the opportunity thus afforded of distressing the distressed, and instead of affording relief against licensed oppression and depredation, which he sees exercised by others, stretches forth his hand to aggravate it.

In the *open mode*, *sound* not being taxable as *writing* is, the afflicted escape thus from his inexorable hand. They are saved from his inhumanity by his impotence.

§ 4. *Affidavit Evidence*—*its Inaptitude.*

Comparison made with the open and oral interrogation mode,—comparison even made with the close interrogation mode, as above,—the following may be stated as the features of inaptitude, that have place in the uninterrogated—the *affidavit* mode.‡

1. Not being accompanied by any evidence extracted from the same source, either by counter-interrogation, or so much as by primary interrogation, it lies thereby under a preponderant probability of being incorrect as well as incomplete, and thereby deceptious,

* When the art of writing was in a manner confined to priests and lawyers, and among non-lawyers ignorance was so gross and general, as, on an occasion thus solemn and thus formidable, scarcely to admit of any approach to correct and instructive statement, without tutorage,—it was natural enough, that the individual from whom the information came, and who, in writing at least, was not able to give his own account of it, should, instead of being himself the *speaker*, be *spoken of*, viz. by the man in authority, by whom in this learned form the information was delivered.

Not but that, in this way, instead of the more trustworthy shape of immediate testimony, the information presented itself, to the eyes and ears of several persons at least, in the less trustworthy shape of *hearsay* evidence,—hearsay evidence, repeated in writing by a person, himself unapparent and unknown. But in those days, distinctions thus refined would attract little notice.

† The reason on which this exclusion is grounded, is such as, of itself, affords an indication of the state of moral depravation, to which such a system of judicature is calculated to give birth and continuance. The assumption is,—that if the facts which a man wanted to have proved were known, for the proof of them, evidence in an unlimited quantity might always, or generally, be obtainable.

Of the *true* evidence in existence, the quantity is in every case a limited quantity: and by the *exclusion* of an undeterminate and unknown portion of it, what additional probability of correctness and *completeness* could a man hope to give to the aggregate mass of evidence?

‡ *Deposition* is delivery of affidavit evidence:—what shall delivery of oral evidence be called? *Testification*? from to testify?—or might not *testification* be employed as a generic term, including *viva voce* testification and deposition.

— even where nothing of *mala fides* — of intention or wish to give rise to deception — has place.

2. From the same cause, in case of *mala fides*, the probability of mendacity in the texture of such evidence, and of deception as the fruit of it, cannot but receive great and indisputable increase.

In this respect, bad as the close interrogation mode has been seen to be, this uninterrogated mode is seen to be still worse. In *that* mode, truth is deprived of the benefit of such questions as would not have been put, had it not happened to them to be suggested by answers to antecedent questions: — in *this* mode, not so much as one question can be put.

3. By a *malâ fide* deponent, *time*, in any quantity which depends upon his own will, is in this mode applied to the purpose of mendacious invention: — *time*, without any stint at all, in the case of such affidavits, as being delivered in the first instance, and having found no other affidavits to which they are called upon to make answer, may be termed initiative affidavits — time always relatively ample, for making answer, and organizing safe mendacity and evasion, in the case where, being thus preceded by affidavits on the other side, they may be termed *responsive* affidavits.

4. By the *malâ fide* deponent, the like facility is possessed, for receiving and communicating mendacity-serving information and suggestion: and *that* as well from professional advisers, as from such other persons, whose wishes and exertions are, by personal interest, by sympathy, or by antipathy, engaged on the same side.

5. In the case of *deposition* evidence, it has been seen how far the statement, to which the deponent is made to annex his signature, is from exhibiting a true and genuine impression of his mind. In the case of *affidavit* evidence, it is still farther from exhibiting any such desirable result.

In the case of the *deposition*; questions put to the deponent being the instruments constantly employed for the extraction of evidence, so it is, that (unless in the case of that sort of suggestion, the utterance of which would on the part of the examining functionary be an act of transgression and malpractice) before any words are found for the deponent, it is left to him to find words for himself: and thereupon it is, that, when the substituted words, which are presented to him for his adoption, have been committed to writing, should the deviation be such as to present to his mind the idea of a material misrepresentation, the recollection of his own words — the recollected sound of his own voice — helps to point his attention to the error, and affords an additional chance for the correction of it.

In the case of an *affidavit*, even this check, inadequate as it is, is wanting. The attorney gets up the story, — dresses it in such colours as appear most advantageous for his client's interest (not forgetting his own) — represents to him what turn given to the phrase will be best suited to the purpose, — and should the complexion of it be in a greater or less degree more favourable than the correct truth would have been, it is then left to the discernment of the client — the unpractised and naturally awe-struck and bewildered client — to discover all along what necessary demand there may be for correction, — and to his probity and activity, working against the bias of his interest, to apply it.

6. In the *affidavit* mode, matter and expression both being, as above, altogether at the choice of the deponent, with his professional adviser and assistant, the consequence is — that in the case of *mala fides*, every advantage is enjoyed, which is derivable from the faculty of producing by means of vague generalities, out of the reach of being, as in the open and interrogated mode, reduced by apt interrogation to particularity, — of producing, viz. in the texture of the several declarations and allegations, whatsoever modes and degrees of indistinctness, obscurity, and ambiguity, are found most convenient: — this, in each distinguishable part taken separately: — and moreover, by studied disorder and confusion in the arrangement of the parts, every serviceable addition to indistinctness, obscurity, ambiguity, evasiveness, and deceptiousness, in the composition of the whole.*

7. In the close Rome-bred mode, the case where, as above, the questions, which the examining judge is required to put, being on each side prepared by a professional scribe,

* To no inconsiderable extent, after all that can be done to narrow the application of it, true it is, that admission to evidence in this shape cannot (it will on reflection appear manifest) be refused: for example, on *ex parte* applications; and on applications to which, supposing the facts to be as stated, there cannot be any reasonable ground for apprehending objection on the other side. But a rule which presents itself as being capable of being without danger established in the character of an inviolable one, is, — that no such evidence shall in any case be received, without being eventually subjectible to *counter-interrogation*: — and *that* sooner or later, in the oral form.

Under the existing practice, no such counter-interrogation being in any case admitted, the consequence is, — that against mendacity in and by affidavit evidence, there exists not any other remedy than a prosecution for perjury. But, even in this case, the party prosecuted is not allowed to be interrogated; — the testimony of another person opposed to his is not of itself deemed sufficient to warrant conviction; — and where conviction *does* take place, punishment with lawyer's profit takes place of that *prevention*, which *without* expense of punishment might in the other case have been the result. Here, then, under the mask of tenderness, is needless rigour, — and that rigour ineffectual: — here, as elsewhere, such are the tender mercies of the man of law.

and (so it has happened) distinguished from one another by *numbers*, some sort and degree of separateness and distinctness has by this means been in *that* instance given to the responses, of which the mass of evidence extracted from each such examinee is composed: — some sort of preservative, more or less efficient, provided against confusion, designed or undesigned.

In the case of the mass of evidence, delivered in and by the *affidavit* of each deponent, the same principle of *distinctness*, or at least of *distinguishableness*, might be employed with equal ease. But, with the exception of the *bonâ fide suitor*, or — where the cause happens to be such as affords them on both sides — suitors, — none of the persons, professional or official, on whom the quality of the composition depends, having anything to gain by the distinctness of it — many of them always by the indistinctness, — no wonder that this mode has obtained (the wonder would have been had it *not* obtained) the favour so exclusively bestowed upon it.

8. In the *deposition* mode (understand all along under English Rome-bred procedure,) — in the case where the individual, on whom the operation of collecting his testimony is proposed to be performed, is a party, and *that* a party defendant — (not where he is a party *plaintiff*, for in that case pretence and occasion is made for an additional suit) — a *party*, and not an extraneous *witness*, — his submission to the operation is, with perfect propriety, made, as it could not but be made, matter of *obligation:* and the coercive arm of the law is employed to give effect to it.

In the *affidavit* mode, neither is the individual, from whom testimony in this shape is derived, compelled to answer questions — (if he *were*, his testimony, it will be seen, would not be delivered in the shape in which by the supposition it is here delivered,) — nor is any individual, either in the character of a party, or in the character of an extraneous witness, compellable, in any case, to deliver any testimony in this shape.

The consequence is — that while, by the interest he has in the cause, a party stands on either side engaged to deliver his testimony, in so far as admission will be given to it, a *witness* who is not a party, stands in this respect altogether free.

Mark here the inconsistency and caprice. Where the shape in which the testimony, if delivered, must and will be delivered, is the interrogated shape, the good shape, — there the testimony of an *extraneous witness* is compelled, while, on the ground either of fear of deception, or fear of vexation, the testimony of a *party*, so far from being compelled, is excluded: at the same time, where, as here, the shape given to the testimony is the uninterrogated, the bad shape, — here, though no person's testimony is compelled, every person's is admitted. So the shape in which he presents his testimony be this shape, no person is excluded — every person is admitted, no questions asked. A further consequence is — that, naturally and necessarily, like an election vote, an affidavit is an object of solicitation: nor in this shape is testimony ever delivered, without bearing, on the face of it, presumption more or less strong, of partiality in favour of the party under whose banner it presents itself. And, in addition to the advantage which, as hath been seen elsewhere, is given by a mass of expense, tolerable to one alone of two litigants, here may be seen another advantage given to the overbearing depredator, or to the oppressor by irresistible power and influence. Not having for its excuse the plea of legal obligation, an affidavit, made in favour of one side, is, as towards the other, an act of hostility, and as such a cause of apprehended vengeance.

9. When it is in any less untrustworthy and deceptious shape that the evidence is received, great (great as in due time will be seen) is the anxiety manifested, — on the one hand, under the apprehension of giving birth to *deception*, by testimony *consonant* to the wishes of the examinee — on the other hand, under fear of giving birth to *vexation*, by testimony *repugnant* to his wishes.

Thus scrupulous is the anxiety displayed, where the shape, in which the testimony presents itself, is that which possesses the highest claim to confidence. On the other hand, no sooner does it change to that which, in the degree that has just been seen, is untrustworthy and favourable to the purpose of deception, than all those scruples vanish. Not by *interest* in any shape, not by *improbity* in any shape, not even by recorded *perjury*, is a man excluded from delivering his testimony — if this, the most deceptious of all shapes, be the shape in which it is clothed: — nor, on the other hand, when, by a hostile affidavit, called upon to defend himself against or submit to, the threatened burthen — even though it be a penal one — will the severity of any vexation, to which it may be the effect of compliance to subject him, serve as a plea to save him from it.

10. Upon evidence in a shape thus completely unfit to be admitted in any contested cause, is decision grounded, where the question is (for such are the questions entertained and decided upon) whether one and the same matter of fact *shall*, or shall *not*, be inquired into, by means of evidence delivered in its best shape — in the jury-trial shape: and again* after a decision grounded on evidence

* *And again.*] viz. after conviction on an information, or an indictment, under the name of affidavits in *aggravation*, or in *extenuation*, antecedently to judgment or sentence.

collected in that *best* of shapes, — even then, on the ground of evidence received in this *worst* of shapes, is the decision which should have been grounded on that well-shaped evidence avowedly modified, — and thereupon, frequently, on this worst of possible grounds (that of naked and unsanctioned assertion excepted) — frequently, on the score of a fresh, though no otherwise proved offence,— is delinquency pronounced, and additional punishment inflicted.

§ 5. *English Judges — conscious of the Unfitness of their own Practice.*

As to the question — whether, of the only shapes in which they have suffered, or will suffer, the evidence to come before them, the unfitness, as here brought to view, can ever have been a secret to those arbiters of human destiny, — the answer might, without other documents, and without danger of error, be left to the plainest dictates of common sense.

In the situation of those judges whose seat is in the *ecclesiastical* and *admiralty courts*, it might, for anything that appears, be possible to pretend ignorance of the unfitness of the evidence, in the only form in which they receive it: — by this bye portion of the hierarchy, such ignorance might possibly be pretended, without receiving contradiction and confutation from their own lips or their own practice.

In the situation of those whose seat is in a court calling itself a *court of equity*, this is *not* possible: of this impossibility, a sufficient intimation is conveyed by the single word *issue*, in the phrase, *to direct an issue.*

The chancellor *directs an issue — to be tried:* — that is, directs a question of fact to be tried by evidence collected in the open mode, in the way of jury-trial: in about one cause out of fifty, this mode of collecting the evidence is employed, — employed in that one cause, and for what reason? For the same reason which, if true, passes the most just and decided condemnation on the course (what that course is, has just been seen) which is pursued — so inexorably pursued — in the other forty-nine.

Where was ever that cause, for the trying of which that Rome-bred mode was a fit mode? Not anywhere. Why then is not *an issue* directed in every case? The grievance — would it not at this price be removed? On the contrary, it would be aggravated. An additional load of factitious and needless delay, vexation, and expense — (for there would be no *substitution* — it would be all addition;) with an additional load of recorded lies to befoul the case — (stories about a pretended wager, and so forth) — to heap confusion upon confusion, and to multiply by forty-nine the insults at present offered to morality and justice.

Moreover, not only in the Lord High Chancellor's Equity court does the chancellor, but in the Exchequer do the judges of that honourable court, when so it pleases them, direct *an issue*—but in this case to be tried before one of themselves: for this is an amphibious judicatory;—it has an equity side in it, and a common-law side; each judge is composed of two discordant halves; each half is persuaded — constantly persuaded, (and was ever persuasion more just?) of the unfitness of the course pursued by the other: the judgments pronounced, or about to be pronounced, by the common-law half, the equity half *(pulveris non exigui jactu)* is ever ready to stop or to overrule: the mode of collecting evidence employed by the equity half being, to its own perfect conviction, not calculated for the discovery of truth — calculated for nothing but the oppressing the subject with an intolerable load of factitious delay, vexation, and expense —it stops upon occasion, its own snail's pace *(moyennant finance)* and for a time turns over the business to the common-law half, adding always to, instead of ever subtracting from, the load of manufactured delay, vexation, and expense.

All this while, what to a chancellor, paradoxical as it may seem, is not impossible, is — the admitting into his presence, and interrogating with his own lips, the individual — be he party, be he witness — from whom the information is required:—nor to this purpose, strange again as it may seem, is it necessary that twelve unlearned men should be sitting by, shut up in a box called a *jury-box*. The assertion is positive: — and for the truth of it, the appeal is made — not to common sense — not to any such pretendedly despised and secretly feared and hated arbiter — but to precedent: — to that almighty and ever adored viceroy over common sense and common honesty in a lawyer's breast: — Yes — to precedent: for, besides that, of old time, even chancellors were neither deaf nor blind to suitors, a comparatively recent instance, — in which, seeing no other mode of settling the business, a chancellor, in a fit of delirium or self-forgetfulness, betrayed the cause of equity, and with his own noble and learned lips put a question to a party or a witness, — is actually to be met with in the books.

So much for the *close* and *badly* interrogated mode: a word or two at present as to the use of the *affidavit mode*, — the *altogether* uninterrogated mode — the use made of it, and at the sametime the opinion entertained of it.

Throughout the whole expanse of technical procedure — those spots excepted, on which, in a period of inscrutable darkness, causes at present inscrutable gave to jury-trial a hold too firm to be loosened, and those on which antique priestcraft succeeded in planting the

Rome-bred mode; throughout the whole of this vast wilderness, — in the *common*-law courts — in the *equity* courts — in the *ecclesiastical* courts — in the *admiralty* courts,* — this worst of all shapes is the only shape in which, for any purpose, on any occasion, for the determination of any question of fact, testimony will be received by any English judge.

Be it in a separate cause — be it on the occasion of an incidental application made in the course of a cause which receives its main and ultimate decision on the ground of other evidence, — (what matters it?) — not to speak of causes termed *criminal*, — it is on the ground of evidence received in no other shape than

* In the Prize and Admiralty judicatory of the *American United States*, the *Rome*-bred mode of collecting evidence was at the first sitting of the first congress abrogated, and the jury-trial mode — say rather the *natural procedure* mode — for it is without a jury, — substituted to it. — (Acts of the American States, I. 120, 121, 134, anno 1795.)

Here, again, in proof of *possibility*, will *fact* be admitted? If in England this is impossible, in America how comes it to be fact? For explanation may the following observations serve? — In America, there is no fee-gathering judicatory: — No *prize-court* judge, with an income of from £6,524 a-year,[a] to as much more as by extension of war it can be made to produce, extracted out of human suffering, in 65 days sitting, out of the 365, through that one channel, — besides what, in 19 other days,[b] is drawn by the right honourable pluralist, through other similar channels, while justice is delayed in this: —

No over-paid and double feed-attorney forced by the judge into the confidence of unwilling clients, exacting fees on both sides,[c] and, under the name of king's proctor, drawing from that same impure source £10,722 a-year with its indefinite increase[d]: —

No over-paid placeman and pluralist, under the name of *King's Advocate*, extracting from it a mass of emolument, the undisclosed amount of which may in some measure be guessed at by the magnitude of that which is attached to that other office, which is so much inferior to it in dignity: —

No sinecurist, under the name of *marshal*, drawing from £4,210 (the amount in 1797,) to whatsoever greater sum it may have amounted to by this time — (27th Report of the Finance Committee of 1797–8, p. 257.) —

No bedchamber-haunting sinecurist, drawing from the same blood-stained source from £20,357 (the amount as per account before anno 1810,) to spend or hoard, *plus* £26,017 to dispose of in sub-clerkships or sub-sinecures: — the suitors being kept out of their money, while £7,800 a-year, in part of the £20,357 a-year, was squeezed out of it. (First Report of the House of Commons' Sinecure Committee, p. 45. Date of the order for printing, 20th June 1810.)

Men, to whom it belongs to determine between war and peace, engaged in support of war by masses of emolument, the gift and receipt of which have all the character of bribery, except the punishment and the shame; — bounties given by them to one another and to themselves; — bounties so vast in the amount — bribes so vast in the receipt; — and still is it to be a question, whence it is that, unless to recommence immediately, wars never cease? But peace, — to make peace — does it not require two parties? Undoubtedly: what *may* therefore, or may *not* be in their power, is — to put an end to the war: — what at all times *is* in their power *is* — to put an end to the sinister interest.

Of the emolument thus reaped from that continuance of war, and increased by every extension given to it, suppose a part, though it were but a tenth part, or a twentieth part, received from the hand of this or that foreign power, which at the time happened to have an interest in the continuance of that scourge, — Russia or Sweden for example, — suppose any such incident to transpire — what an outcry! And were the law suffered to take its effect (which in that case, at the charge of such great characters, in such high situations, in all probability it would not,) how penal the consequence! But the value of money, or the force with which it operates in the character of a sinister motive — in the character of a cause of mischief — is it diminished by the absence of whatever danger would, in another case, be attached to the receipt of it?

Giving commencement or continuance to war is not the only effect produced or producible, in relation to that scourge, by the preference given to procedure in an unfit shape, and evidence in an unfit shape, over procedure and evidence in a fit shape. Another effect is — giving increase to the miseries of war, by delivering into the hands of the enemy, to an unlimited amount, vessels and their cargoes, for want of that protection of which, by the factitious uncertainty, delay, vexation, and expense, manufactured by this unfit mode of carrying on procedure and collecting evidence, they are deprived. By several examples of proctor's bills, and the observations for which they afforded matter, this effect has been brought to view in Cobbett's Political Register for 5th August 1809. Where the enemy's privateer or other ship of war is to a certain degree small, it becomes clear, that in consequence of the uncertainty of success in the suit necessary for condemnation, coupled with the certainty of the expense, the capturing of it would be an operation, not reconcilable to the rules of human prudence. And so in the case of an enemy's vessel of the mercantile class. Thus it is, that our own shores are so frequently lined with the enemy's vessels of war, and the enemy's shores with his own vessels of the mercantile class, navigating, in effect, under the protection of the noble and right honourable and honourable and learned gentlemen above mentioned.

Thus it is, that in the *Prize-court*, the *enemy* receives the same sort of protection and encouragement, as in *Equity* and the *Lords* (not to speak of common law) the *malâ fide* suitor: — and from the operation of the same causes.

[a] The amount, as per third Report of the House of Commons Committee on Public Expenditure, p. 297. Date of order for printing, 29th June 1808.

[b] Employed in the Consistory Court. This account of the days of sitting was extracted from the official books of the year 1810.

[c] Commons Debate, No. 18.

[d] Third Report, as above, p. 303.

this, that questions, and that to a value to which there are no limits, receive their decision, — questions to a number exceeding (but it belongs only to parliamentary inquiry to say in what proportion) the number of those that receive their decision on the ground of evidence collected either in the only good, or in the other bad shape.

In a bankruptcy cause — in that sort of cause, in which hundreds of thousands, not to say millions, are to receive distribution from the noble and learned hand, if the application wear the form of a *petition*, *affidavit* evidence, and no other, is the ground, on which all questions of fact belonging to it are decided. Is it that of this shape, any more than of the secretly-received *deposition* shape, the unfitness is a secret to the "great character" by whom it is employed? No: for here, too, where truth has been thought worth coming at, *issues* have been directed.*

On any of these occasions, while a well-connected string of perjuries is in reading, if so it should happen, that a person by whom it could be proved to be what it is being in court at the time, under the very eye of the judge, he were to offer himself, or be offered to be examined, would he be heard? Not he indeed: — any more than, in a libel cause, in the character of a party defendant, a man who after feeing, in the character of an advocate, a bottle companion of the judge, and finding his cause betrayed, should, instead of feeing other such defenders, in a number to which there are no limits, presume, in contempt of judge-made law, to open his own mouth in his own defence.

§ 6. *Source of the unfit Modes — Sinister Interest.*

As to the interest — the private and sinister interest — by which the feet of these rulers have thus perseveringly been confined to paths so plainly opposite to those of truth and justice, the different shapes, in which in their situation it may be seen to operate, have already been sketched out: — sketched out, in the little work, to which there has been such frequent occasion to make reference.† In the whole sphere of action of an English judge, can that particle of space be found, in which his interest is not in a state of opposition to his duty? — a particle, in which that opposition may not be seen to triumph? — *Emolument*, *power*, *ease*: — interest of the *purse*, interest of the *sceptre*, interest of the *pillow*: all these together form but a part of the whole number of shapes, in which, by the sacrifice thus made of the interests of the many, in the character of suitors, — (those included, who, having need to become, are, at the same time, by the expenses debarred from the possibility of becoming suitors) are sacrificed to those of the exalted and pampered few. Of the emolument thus gained by the wilful substitution of evidence in the two worst shapes to the same evidence in the best shape, an account may be collected from the particulars brought to view by the several *committees on finance*: always remembering that, in point of effect, between what a man has in pocket, and what he has in patronage, there exists not any essential difference.‡

By what is received in the shape of *power* — power of pursuing without restraint the dictates of sympathy, antipathy, or caprice — by advantage in this shape, though not susceptible of being expressed in pounds, shillings, and pence, the impression made on the mind is not the less sensible, nor the less operative.

In the shape of *ease* — that negative, indeed, but not the less efficient, principle of action, so powerful, yet so little heeded — in the shape of *ease*, the profit gained by the substitution of deceptious to instructive evi-

* Written in January 1812. Since that time, this subject appears to have received considerable elucidation, from a conversation, of which the following is the report, given in the Morning Chronicle of the 30th of July 1812: —

"*House of Lords*, *July* 29, 1812.

"Respecting the inclosure affidavit bill, the Lord Chancellor observed, that it required further consideration. If its object were merely to register affidavits to facilitate the proof of hand-writing relative to inclosure bills, there could be little objection to it; but if it were intended that these affidavits were to serve as proofs of the facts stated in them, their Lordships would no doubt pause a good while, before they sanctioned a proceeding by which they would give up the most effectual test of truth as to the allegations in a private bill, — the examination of witnesses *vivâ voce* upon oath; there being no doubt that were it not for that examination upon oath before their Lordships' committees, private bills might frequently operate the greatest injustice towards individuals."

Extracts from the "Report from the committee" (of the House of Commons) appointed to inquire into the "causes that retard the decision of suits in the High Court of Chancery." Date of the order for printing, 18th June 1811: —

Page 35. — "Account of the Receipts of the Lord Chancellor, continued from the 5th April 1810 to the 5th April 1811: — At the bankrupt office, £4,946 : 14 : 8." At the bankrupt office; that is, for hearing and determining causes upon evidence never presented in any other than the affidavit shape, of which the effects are above described.

Morning Chronicle, *December* 8, 1812. — "*House of Lords*, *December* 7. — Lord Redesdale observed . . . . that with respect to the bankrupt cases which came before the Lord Chancellor, many of them were of more importance to the country, especially in a commercial point of view, than any that were decided in any other court."

† Scotch Reform. ‡ Ibid. Letter I.

dence, is too great and too various, to admit of any tolerably adequate description, within the limits prescribed by the design of the present sketch. Strained through learned and ever obsequious lips, the information, though always more or less false and delusive, comes purified from everything that could render it offensive, perfumed at the same time by clouds of appropriate incense: — everything that is squalid, rough, and vulgar, being, at the same time, and by the same means, kept from obtruding itself upon learned and reverend eyes. Of the wretches out of whose torments the comforts of the wearer of purple and fine linen are extracted, the torments are kept from presenting themselves to his reverend eyes, the cries and just reproaches from wounding his reverend ears: in a word, everything that is at once pleasing and delusive is let in — everything that is displeasing and instructive shut out, and kept at a distance. Of the miseries of which he is the well paid author, he escapes from the reproach, because though in his situation ignorance, — non-observance, — anything short of the fullest knowledge — is impossible, yet, not being sure to see them, he stands clear from the imputation of having given birth to them — clear and spotless in the awe-struck eyes of the ever-admiring and ever-deluded multitude.

The favourite shape — the *deposition* shape — which, in so far as they have found themselves at liberty, English judges, borrowing it from the Roman school, have taken upon them to give to evidence — is it really in a correspondent degree favourable to the discovery and display of truth? Confine it not, then, within the narrow sphere of equity — extend the benefit of it to the whole country — apply it to inquiries carried on for a *legislative* purpose — introduce it into the *House of Commons*.

Conceive now, in that source and seat of inquisitorial scrutiny, evidence wanted for the detection of a peculating or enemy-pensioned minister: — conceive thereupon, instead of the *there* so happily and unavoidably established efficient mode, that mode of inquiry employed, which, as it were in derision, is called *equity:* — conceive, under the name of a *bill*, a volume of notorious lies delivered in, with three or four months time for a *first answer*, and, after *exceptions* taken of course, two or three months for a *second* — then *amendments* made to the bill, with more such delays, and more succeeding *answers*, — then a *cross bill* filed on the other side, and a *second* such cause thus mounted on the shoulders of the *first* — then volumes heaped upon volumes of *depositions* — then, after years thus employed, a *decree* obtained, by which nothing is decided — then the whole matter, and everything that has been made to grow out of it, sent to be investigated in the hermetically-sealed closet of a sort of under-judge called a *Master* — with days of attendance, separated from each other by days or weeks — length of attendance each day, nominally an hour, really half or a quarter of the time — a clerk furnishing examination and decision, the Master auspices — the judge paid for *three* attendances, and bestowing one — (for the statute which transports men for obtaining money on false pretences does not extend to judges) — the party whose interest and purpose is served by delay, attending or not attending, according as by attendance or non-attendance that interest and that purpose are best served, — then, in the course of a few more years thus employed, out of a dozen or two of parties, one carried off by death, and then another, — and upon each death another bill to be filed, and the same or a similar course of retardation to be run.

Conceive this to be the course — the only course — appointed (*practised* it could not be) for coming at the truth in the House of Commons: — conceive this, and let any experienced equity draughtsman say how long before the first *answer* had been completed, the House would have found itself made into a barrack for the troops of Bonaparte.*

All this while, the mode best suited to the coming at truth through evidence, does it really change its nature, according as the person who is, or pretends to be, in search of it sits with a gown or without a gown, in one part of Westminster Hall or in another? If so, then, but then only, so it is, that the mode by which, if pursued in a committee-room, the whole country would be involved in prompt and universal ruin, — that this one of the only two modes of inquiry employed by English judges, when they have had their choice, may *really* be well adapted, and by its employers may really have been *thought* to be well adapted, to the purposes for which it is professed to be employed — the purposes designated by the sacred names of *equity* and *justice*.†

* The fatal billet by which the Duke of York was fixt — fixt in the course of an hour or two, by a sudden order from the House of Commons, — say that a *bill in equity* could have been and had been filed for the *discovery* of it? To this hour the cause would have remained unconcluded, and, on the part of the defendant, years before any mandate for the production of it had reached his hands, nothing but insanity could have saved it from the all-protecting and all-tranquillizing flames.

† Confined, as in respect of *persons* it is, to *defendants in equity*, and at the same time, in respect of the mode of enunciation, to *writing* — the form given to the instrument called in equity procedure *an answer*, was not on this occasion thought worth erecting into a separate and independent mode.

CHAPTER XII.

OF CIRCUMSTANTIAL EVIDENCE.

§ 1. *Extent and Use of this Inquiry.*

To present an all-comprehensive, or so much as any considerably-extensive view of circumstantial evidence, even when narrowed by the sort of limitation applied to it by the words *to a legal purpose,* is an undertaking which, at first view, may be apt to appear impracticable. It may, moreover, be not altogether unapt to appear *useless*—void of practical use.

The matter of fact which, with relation to the other matter of fact in question, considered in the character of a *principal* fact, is proposed by you as *evidentiary* of it, is it so in reality? It will present itself as such of itself,—it may be said:—your instruction is therefore of no use. Does it fail of presenting itself in that character? Neither in this case can your presenting it as such be of any considerable use.

1. As to *all-comprehensiveness*—as to the giving to the view in question this degree of *completeness,* the task, if it be within the range of human power, is not, at any rate, at present at least, within the power of the individual by whom this attempt is made: the advance capable of being made towards it may, however, upon examination, be found less inconsiderable, perhaps, than what upon a first glance might have been expected.

2. As to *utility*—of a review of this sort, the utility, if any it have, will show itself in the one or other of two opposite ways:—1. If the matter of fact in question be true, in *causing,* or contributing to cause it, to be believed; 2. If not true, in *preventing,* or contributing to prevent it, from being believed.

In both ways, the subject has presented itself as being open to observations, capable of being conducive to the desirable effect:—

1. In the case where the matter of fact is *true,* instances will be adduced of facts in the character of *principal* facts, to which will respectively be found applicable *evidentiary* facts, in classes so ample in extent, and of which the probative force seems to have been subjected to so little scrutiny, that any observations, by which any assistance may be afforded towards the making a correct estimate of it, can scarcely be ill-bestowed.

In some of these instances, circumstantial evidence of the most instructive nature has been found involved in that system of *exclusion,* of which the folly, and rashness, and iniquity, will be held up to view: and if, in these instances as in so many others, the exclusion should be found indefensible, the more important and instructive the lights of which justice is thus deprived are seen to be, the stronger the ground that will thus have been made for amendment in this line.

2. So, on the other hand, in the case where the matter of fact in question is *untrue,* instances will be adduced of classes of *principal* facts, to which will respectively be found applicable classes of *evidentiary* facts, of a *disaffirmatively probative,* or say *disprobative* tendency:—facts of such a nature, that, for want of due attention to them, supposed facts, which, as above, are untrue, are (it will be seen) liable, at any time, to be believed;—thereby gaining a credence which is not their due. If, by the indication of any such disprobative fact, so it should happen that, in any number of instances, *deception* and consequent *misdecision* should come to be prevented, the greater the number of these instances, the greater in this case will be the utility of the observations by which mischief, in this shape, will thus have been averted.

§ 2. *Facts principal, evidentiary, probative, disaffirmative, infirmative.*

Considered with a view to these opposite effects, facts operating in the character of articles of circumstantial evidence, may be divided into two classes. To those, the effect or tendency of which is to gain credence for the principal fact in question, may be preserved the appellation of *positive* or *probative evidentiary facts;* or say simply, *evidentiary* facts as above. As to a fact of the *other* class, it supposes the existence of some other fact in the character of a *probative evidentiary* fact; and the effect or tendency of it is—to *weaken* the probative force, on the magnitude of which the intensity of the persuasion produced by it depends:—call it therefore, with reference to such probative force, an *infirmative* fact.

Between the principal fact and the assumed evidentiary fact, is the connexion an immediate one? To form it, can no other fact or facts be found, the intervention of which, as of so many links between the two extreme links of a chain, is necessary? If yes, then so many as can be distinguished of these intermediate links, so many are the probative facts, of each of which the probative force is liable to be opposed and weakened by a separate set of infirmative—of *disprobative* facts.

In this case, the probative force of circumstantial evidence is diminished, in the same way as that of direct testimony will presently be seen to be, by the interposition of one or more supposed intermediate reporters beween the supposed *quondam percipient* and the *now deponent* witness, as in the case of *hearsay* evidence.

§ 3. *Principal fact, Delinquency;—evidentiary facts, inculpative and disculpative.*

By one single word, viz. *delinquency,* is brought to view a class of facts so ample, as to cover by its extent, one of the great departments, viz. the *penal*, into which the whole field of law and legislation is divided.

Taking this for the principal fact, viz. delinquency in any shape — offence — transgression (viz. against the law) in any shape — we see at a glance how extensive, and, at the same time, how important, an object of research is afforded by the aggregate of any such discoverable and expressible matters of fact, as can be seen to bear to it respectively the relation of *probative*, and *disprobative* or say *infirmative*, facts, — or, to employ the narrower and more opposite denominations, by which in this case they may be characterized, — *inculpative* and *disculpative*; — such* as are inculpative having for their tendency, the causing the defendant to be considered as *guilty*, such as are disculpative, as *not guilty*, in relation to the same forbidden act, considered in the character of the *principal fact*, of whatsoever nature in other respects it may happen to it to be.

Of the chief species of facts which have been in use to be contemplated in the character of *criminative* facts, a list has on this occasion been collected, containing somewhat about a score:† and along with each such criminative fact, will be given a list of such other facts, as presented themselves as bearing relation to it in the character of *infirmative* facts.

The very idea here expressed by the term *infirmative* including *disculpative* facts, being in the character of a general idea commensurate in its extent with that of an inculpative fact, is as yet a novel one, — no wonder if, for want of sending their minds in quest of facts of this description, law-writers of the highest name should have given as *conclusive* of delinquency, facts which, when the infirmative facts that bear upon the case are brought to view, will be seen to be far indeed from warranting any such conclusion.

Instances will moreover be produced, in which, upon the mere ground of this or that single fact, considered in the light of an *inculpative* fact, the legislator, acting in such his character, has required conviction to take place, in a case, in which the existence of one or more species of facts, operating in the character of *infirmative*, and thence of *disculpative* facts, has nothing in it but what is conformable to every day's experience.

§ 4. *Conversion of Inculpative Acts into separate Offences.*

As, for the prevention of mischief, in whatever shape it is capable of assuming, the legislator, proceeding with due caution, may find sufficient warrant for putting upon the list of prohibited acts, any sort of act that presents itself as having, in a preponderant degree, that tendency, — and this absolutely, and without reference or regard to any other sort of act; — so may he for putting upon that same list any sort of act, under the notion of its being an inculpative circumstance, evidentiary of delinquency in this or that substantive and independent shape. Nor is it to be denied but that this, if any, is of the number of ways in which the field of punishment may be, and has been, made to receive so many beneficial extensions, and the progress of delinquency so many additional impediments and checks.‡

But, to preserve an arrangement of this sort from rendering itself injurious to convenience and repugnant to justice, two precautionary conditions are necessary to be fulfilled: 1. That, if not by the very nature of the case, at any rate by positive institution, in so far as depends upon the legislator, the existence of the prohibition be effectually presented to the mind of every individual on whom it is imposed; 2. That the matter of fact, on which, with reference to the individual placed in the circumstances in question, the character of a conclusively inculpative fact is thus bestowed, be not one the existence of which, by blameless ignorance, or any other cause, it may have been put out of his power to prevent. Of neither of these conditions will the fulfilment be found altogether so consistent as could be wished. Particulars will find their place in the body of the work.

§ 5. *Principal, any physical fact, — disprobative fact, physical improbability: — or improbability physical — its operation in the character of counter-evidence.*

Wide as is the extent of the principal fact above mentioned, viz. delinquency — an extent which knows no other limits than those of the entire field of penal law, — still wider in extent is that principal fact, which is liable to find opposed to it, in the character of a *disprobative* fact, the circumstance of *improbability*.

---

* In the case when the delinquency is considered as rising to *criminality* (not that between this superior part, and the inferior part or parts of the scale, any precise line has ever been attempted to be drawn,) *inculpative* facts might be termed *criminative*; — *disculpative*, with less felicity, *disincriminative*, not *discriminative*, *that* being already appropriated to a very different purpose.

† Under this head, the *Austrian* criminal code, established during the reign of *Maria Theresa*, was found to afford considerable assistance. Understand, so far as concerns *criminative* facts; for as to *infirmative* facts, here as elsewhere all was blank.

By several English trials, and in particular by that of Captain Donnellan for murder by poison, and that of *John Hill*, better known by the name of *Jack the Painter*, the list has been augmented, and illustrative exemplifications afforded.

‡ See Principles of Penal Law, Part III. Ch. XV.

Not to speak of the whole field of legal judicature — the field which in every part of its extent lies open to the application of the disprobative fact now upon the carpet, terminates there and there only, where existence, or if absolute precision be desired, where *humanly perceptible existence* terminates.

When the degree of improbability is meant to be represented as a very high one, in that case, for the sake of impressiveness, to the word *improbability*, the word *impossibility* is, in a loose way of speaking, apt to be substituted: *impossibility*, the predication of which would, in relation to any conceivable matter, if performed seriously, and meant to be taken strictly, be found to involve, on the part of him by whom the word is thus employed, an assumption of *omniscience*.

When attentively examined, even the term *improbability* will be found not to have for its representative any *real* and *distinct* quality actually inherent in, and belonging to, the facts themselves, but a *fictitious* quality, attributed to them for the convenience of discourse: — a quality, having nothing of reality connected with it, but the *persuasion* — (the act of the judicial faculty) — the persuasion as it has place in the mind of him, by whom, for the more convenient expression of it, or for the more effectual spreading of the like persuasion, the fictitious quality in question is thus attributed to, and spoken of as if it were a quality of, the fact itself.

Of this persuasion, if the cause be looked for, it will be found to consist in neither more nor less than the opinion entertained by the individual in question — either on the ground of his own reflection, or on the ground of the opinions or the supposed opinions of others, — that the supposed fact in question would, on the supposition of its being real, be in a state of *disconformity* to what is looked upon as the established mode of being, and course of nature.

In the midst of this darkness, in the hope of infusing into it some faint lights, and for the purpose of affording, in the present state of comparative inexperience and correspondent ignorance (on the part of the age in general, and of the individual in particular,) what, in the language of Sir Humphry Davy, may be called *a resting-place for the fancy*, — an attempt is here made, to find ground of distinction, and correspondent form of expression, for three modes or gradations of this disconformity: disconformity *in toto*;* — disconformity in respect of *degree* or *quality*;† — and disconformity in *species*: ‡ disconformity *in toto*, importing some mode of being, which, supposing it realized, would be a violation of some one or other of *the laws of nature*: those metaphorical and fictitious laws, of which an exposition, supposed to be in some respects new, though not in any respect in opposition to generally received conceptions and opinions, will in the body of the work be attempted.

Be the fact what it may, between its existence and non-existence (*time* and *place* given) there is no medium: and thence it is that, ascribed to facts themselves, *probability* and *improbability*, with their infinity of degrees, are mere figments of the imagination: of the *imagination*, not to say of the *tongue*. But, of *persuasive force*, and *persuasion* its effect, — *negative* as well as *positive*, *disaffirmative* as well as *affirmative*, the number of degrees is truly infinite: — the number of degrees of this cause and this effect, — and thereby of *probability* and its contrary, — in the only sense in which these terms are the representatives of anything that is true.

Thus it is that *probability* and *improbability* are neither of them anything more than relative: neither of them being anything but with relation to the person in whose mind they serve to represent the mode and degree of persuasion which therein has place, in relation to the fact to which they are respectively applied. Thence it is, that, though the same fact is never, at the same *time* and in the same *place*, in itself both *true* and *false*, instances are, however, in continual occurrence, in which the same fact is both *probable* and *improbable*: probable to Titius, improbable to Sempronius. Thus it is, that, even to the best informed mind, so many facts are *improbable*, and taken for *false*, — so many falsely imagined facts *probable*, and taken for *true*.

Probability is conformity, improbability disconformity, to the supposed general and ordinary course of nature: — *i. e.* to the conceptions entertained concerning that course by him by whom the opinion expressed by these words repectively is pronounced.

Thus it is, that, in proportion to the ignorance of the individual, or the age, — *i. e.* to its non-acquaintance with the general and or-

* *Examples*: — Under the name of a *witch*, a woman mounting aloft in the air, without any other help than that of a broomstick: — a man who has forced himself into a quart bottle.

Laws of nature violated: — 1. The universal law of attraction violated, without adequate assistance from any of those minor forces, such as magnetism, gaseous repulsion, or elasticity, &c. which by antagonizing with it, give to the objects which surround us, the situation and condition made known to us by experience; 2. In the case of the human species, the laws of the animal economy.

† *Examples*: — Men (say) above nine feet in height, under the name of *giants*; 2. Men (say) above 200 years of age.

‡ *Examples*: — 1. Serpents with wings, under the name of *dragons*; 2. Men with wings, under the name of *angels*; — mermaids, — men with fishes' tails instead of legs and thighs.

dinary course of nature — is the facility — in proportion to the knowledge, the difficulty, — with which facts are regarded as probable and true.

From the case in which, a matter of fact being in question, the existence of it is regarded as being, in one or other of the above ways, disconformable to the established course of nature, and on that account more or less improbable, — it may be matter of practical use and importance to distinguish the case of a *self-contradictory proposition*, or *contradiction in terms*: a case in which, though to appearance the existence alone of some matter of fact is asserted, and *that* matter of fact upon the face of it an improbable one, in reality no conceivable matter of fact is discoverable, of which the existence and nothing but the existence is affirmed; — but one and the same matter of fact, — perhaps improbable, perhaps so far from improbable as to be proved by continual and univeral experience, is, under favour of a diversity in the form of expression — in the assemblage of words employed in the two cases — asserted, — in the same breath asserted, — to exist and not to exist.

The *verbal impossibility* (for in this sense, though in this sense alone, is the assertion of impossibility compatible with a due and duly-acknowledged sense of human weakness) — the verbal impossibility of the truth of a statement of this self-contradictory complexion — neither prevents it from being said to be, nor even from really being, the subject of a sort of credence. Be it what it may, hope and fear suffice to account for its being said to be so.

§ 6. *Principal, any psychological fact; — disprobative fact, — psychological impossibility.*

In the case of *disconformity*, the established cause in question may be — either that course of events and state of things which is purely physical, or that state of things and course of events, of which the scene lies in the human mind. Improbability is accordingly distinguishable into *physical* and *psychological*. The course of psychological existence being, in so prominent a degree, less uniform than that of purely material nature (in insanity, the uniformity being liable to vanish altogether,) hence it is, that, in the character of an article of disprobative circumstantial evidence, the force of psychological improbability — though so continually, and irreproachably, and unavoidably, in conjunction with other evidences, or even singly, taken for the ground of the most important practical conclusions, — is, generally speaking, in comparison of physical improbability, but feeble.

When the principal supposed fact consists of *delinquency* in any shape, — in this case, *character* or *reputation*, *station in life*, *degree of atrocity* ascribed to the supposed offence, have been commonly considered as presenting so many instances or causes of psychological improbability, and thence so many articles of circumstantial evidence, applicable in disproof of the supposed fact; viz. in so far as, on the part of the individual in question, delinquency, in the shape in question, is considered as included in it. Of these several articles of circumstantial evidence, the disprobative force is taken for the subject of examination in the body of the work.

§ 7. *In a train, principal, any prior act; — probative, any posterior.*

In a series of acts, following one another in pursuit of a more or less customarily entertained and regularly pursued design, — by the undisputed existence of a consequent article, in a series of this sort, what probability is afforded of the performance of the first article of the whole series? — and so in regard to the several intermediate articles? — *Priora quatenus signata* posterioribus? or, Posteriora *quatenus signa priorum?*

In a case of this sort, the degree of probative force with which the existence of the *antecedent* article is probabilized by that of the *consequent*, will depend (it is evident) upon the regularity with which, according to the experienced and sufficiently notified course of human practice, the several articles in the series have succeeded one another; or rather, to speak more pointedly, according to the regularity with which an article, of the species or description of the individual consequent article in question, has been preceded by an article of the species of the *antecedent* article in question.

On this occasion, the series of actions by which the most impressive, as well as important, illustration may (it should seem) be afforded, is that of which the course of judicial procedure is composed. Let the *consequent* in question be the last, or among the last, of the constantly necessary articles, if such there be, in such a series,* in either of these cases, the probative force, — with which the existence of the antecedent, in the character of the principal fact, is probabilized by that of the consequent, in the character of an evidentiary fact, — will to any eye, in any the slightest degree conversant with the course of legal procedure, be apt to present itself as little less strong than that with which the existence of past infancy is probabilized by present old age.

But, as from one place to another there are frequently different roads, so also between the first and the last stage of a course of ju-

* Consequent, for example, in common-law language, the *judgment*; in equity-law language, the *decree*: — antecedent, (the first, or among the first) — in common-law language, the *writ* or the *declaration*; in equity-law language, the *bill*.

dicial procedure. And by this circumstance (it is easy to see,) that the degree of probative force with which the existence of an ordinarily *antecedent* fact is probabilized by the existence of an ordinarily *consequent* fact, will be liable to be in a greater or less degree diminished, according to the nature of the case.

§ 8. *In a train, principal, any posterior act; probative, any prior.*

E conversò in a series of the same sort, or in the same individual series by the existence of an antecedent, what probability is afforded of the existence of a consequent article? In this case, the probative force and correspondent probability will present itself immediately as sunk to a much lower degree in the scale. Be the course of action what it may, — lawful or unlawful, — by *consummate* acts *inchoate* are rendered much more probable than by inchoate, consummate.

In every series of this sort, suppose the articles as they occur entered upon a *register*, and that register kept with the regularity of which a document of this sort is susceptible, and which the importance of it demands, the indications afforded by it to this purpose would, on being presented, in numbers, afford to judicial decision a still more substantial basis, than, in the case of *maritime insurance*, is afforded by the list of *arrivals*, compared with the list of *policies*.

In the English law report-books, cases exemplificative of this reversed series are to be found in no inconsiderable number: but, of any instance of recourse made to any such numeral and mathematical ground of decision, no expectation would be very abundantly satisfied, nor (it should seem) very naturally entertained.

In a case of this sort, on what ground then is it that the decision has been formed?

The question is easily proposed, — the answer not altogether so easily returned.

§ 9. *Principal fact, spuriousness, or unfairness; — probative fact, non-observance of formalities.*

On the part of any written instrument, purporting to be designed to give expression to a contract (taken in the largest sense of the word *contract*,) to an *agreement*, a conveyance, or a last will, — principal fact, either *unauthenticity* or *unfairness;* evidentiary fact — fact regarded as conclusively probative of unauthenticity or unfairness — *non-observance of formalities.* In point of reason and justice, on this ground, and no other, stand the host of *nullifications*, so plentifully poured down upon, and with so little or such ill-directed thought applied to those bonds of society by learned hands:—how weak that ground,—how strong the force of the considerations, which in the character of *infirmative* facts, rise up in opposition to the inference deduced from it, — as questions which will be brought to view under another head.*

Laying aside a species of indication thus unconclusive, on the part of a written document of any kind,—what other facts does the nature of the case afford, capable of operating in the character of evidentiary facts, disprobative of its authenticity? and in particular, in the case of an instrument purporting upon the face of it to be, or exhibited as being, of an *ancient date?* To afford assistance towards the finding answers in every case to these questions, is in the body of the work the business of one or two parts of a short book.†

Non-observance of formalities being thus spoken of in the character of a circumstance taken as evidentiary of *unfairness* on the part of a contract, or of *spuriousness* on the part of an instrument purporting to exhibit the expression of a contract,—continual error would be apt to be the result, if for the prevention of it, apt warning — distinct and timely warning — were not afforded.

What is here meant is — that where, on the alleged ground of non-observance of this or that formality, the instrument has been pronounced (as the language is) *null and void*,— the judicial service being thereupon refused, the rendering of which is, on the part of the judge, necessary to the giving to the instrument the legal effect which it is seen to aim at, — an opinion, ascribing either *unfairness* to the *contract*, or *spuriousness* to the instrument, was either the reason or the pretence; — was either professed and entertained accordingly, or if not actually entertained, at least, upon occasion, professed to be entertained. But that, in every instance in which such opinion has been thus professed — impliedly at least professed, it has been really entertained, is itself an opinion the assertion of which, if sincere, will not be found consistent with the plainest common sense: inasmuch as in such an opinion would in many instances be included, the belief of a self-contradictory proposition; such as, that one and the same contract was throughout fair and unfair—one and the same instrument throughout genuine and spurious.‡

In saying, that non-observance of this or that formality is, by this or that judge, regarded or treated as evidence, and *that* conclusive of unfairness or spuriousness on the part of the instrument in question, all therefore that is here meant to be expressed is —

* See Chapter XIV. *Pre-appointed Evidence:* Ch. XIX. XX. and XXI. *Exclusion*, &c.

† Book of Authentications and De-authentications, infra Ch. XXIV.

‡ *Example:* — One and the same testament, *void* as to estate called *real* estate — *valid* as to estate called *personal* estate.

that, if on his refusal to give effect to it, he were to be pressed for a justification — for such an one as, with reference to the ends of justice, should be a rational, and to an unlaw-learned and uncorrupted mind an intelligible one, — of this sort is the best or only justification, which he would find himself able to give: in the giving of which justification, sincerity on his part might in some instances be morally possible, but in other instances would be morally impossible.

I speak here of the judge or judges by whom, in the first instance, decisions of the nature here in question have on such grounds been pronounced. But (says a well-known French proverb) *Ce n'est que le premier pas qui coute:* and in no other line of action, perhaps, has the truth of the observation received such ample exemplification as in judicature. Where, under the name of deference to authority, or under any other name, the adoption of opinions, without examination and upon trust, is made matter of merit, any one opinion is just as easily adopted as any other: the highest wisdom takes a pride in sinking itself to the level of the lowest folly: and now it is that self-contradictory propositions obtain credence, and *that* not merely with as little difficulty, but even with less difficulty (it will be seen) than is experienced by propositions less directly and palpably repugnant to reason and common sense.

Concerning the justice of the reasoning, by which *unfairness* or *spuriousness* is inferred from *non-observance of formalities*, more will come to be said under the head of *Pre-appointed Evidence.**

But according to the intimation, the occasion for which has been so frequent, the truth of the matter is — and by every eye that has nerves to endure the spectacle will be seen to be — that at any rate in the earlier ages of judicature, the *ends* above described under the appellation of the *false ends*, have, to English judges, been the main, not to say the sole objects of pursuit: — the *true ends*, at best but secondary ones: — that for their assistance in that main pursuit, instruments of iniquity, in great variety and abundance, were invented and put to use:† — and that of these instruments, the one here in question, viz. *nullification*, was one of the most extensively operative, as well as of the most efficient and safe.

§ 10. *In litigation, principal fact want of merits; probative fact, discontinuance of procedure — its fallaciousness.*

In every ordinarily and completely constituted and furnished judicatory,‡ every suit or cause has at least two sides, viz. the plaintiff's and the defendant's: and if so it be that the number of sides in it is greater than two, the cause, being in this case a complex one, is capable of being resolved into a determinate number of simple causes, each having its two sides and no more.

In the language of *natural* procedure, on the plaintiff's side, discontinuance is *non-suit* — on the defendant's, *non-defence:* — in the language of English technical procedure, the place of these two terms is filled by a multifarious vocabulary not wholly different, for which whoever has patience enough may see the books.

Under the technical system, be the side which it may, discontinuance on that side is regarded, or professed to be regarded, as proof — and that conclusive — of want of merits; that is, here, as before, that course is taken which, — to render it reconcilable, if reconcilable it were with justice, — would require a conclusion to that effect to have been formed.

Of the conclusion in this case, the rashness, if it were an honest one — *i. e.* if such were the opinion really entertained — would be much more egregious than in the instance last mentioned; viz. in which, on the ground of failure in the observance of this or that formality, a contract is convicted of *unfairness*, or an *instrument of contract* of *spuriousness.* Population of England, say ten millions: number of persons capable of carrying on a suit or cause to a conclusion, in the least expensive Westminster-Hall court, on the least expensive plan, not so great as half a million. Accordingly, to the defendant, twenty to one but pecuniary power of continuance may be wanting from the very first: and, as above, frequently will it be so to the plaintiff. As he cannot be such but by his own act, it will not be so at the first: but by accident it may be rendered so at any succeeding stage.

Principal fact here, want of merits: pretended *probative* fact, discontinuance: infir-

* See Chap. XIV. Section 6.

† *Exceptions:* — 1. Court of Claims: — Judicatory having cognizance of claims made by individuals on the public. *Example:* — For claims made by the American loyalists on the score of their losses by the war which ended in the independence of the United States. The suit here is unilateral: sole party, the claimant, *i. e.* the plaintiff: the function of *defendant* being placed in the same hands as that of *judge*, — consolidated with that of *judge*.

2. *Audit Courts:* — Judicatories established for exacting repayment, or proof of discharge, from receivers of public money. Suit, here again unilateral: function of *plaintiff*, in the same hands with that of *judge:* as under the system of procedure styled *inquisitorial*, pursued frequently in penal causes in German judicatories.

In both instances, for the purpose of responsibility, might it not be an improvement, if some official person were to be charged with the functions of the suitor, on the side on which the station of the suitor is vacant?

‡ See note † in previous column.

mative fact, — by the greatly preponderant probability of which the conclusion is rendered erroneous, and the pretence false, — want of pecuniary power of continuance.

When a discontinuance, as above, takes place, would you really wish to know what it has had for its real cause? — consciousness of want of merits? — want of pecuniary power? — or what else? The mode of obtaining from the suitor this information and *that*, without putting your reasoning powers to rack, can no more be a secret to you, than if, instead of being your suitor, he were your servant or your son. In an ordinary case, *ears* and *tongue* alone (or rather *ears* alone — for of his own accord, if you would but hear him, he would be ready enough to inform you) would be needful to you: or, in an extraordinary case, for epistolary communication, *eyes*.

But no: — whatsoever is necessary to render it possible for you to do justice, your great object is — not to *know* it, but to *avoid* knowing it: such knowledge would be unprofitable: such ignorance has been made profitable: — darkness of course is more pleasant to you than light. See further — as you will, if you cannot avoid seeing — the chapters on the exclusions put on evidence, and in particular, that on the exclusion put in the case of *imprisonment for debt*.

§ 11. *Probative force of circumstantial evidence, no fit subject for general rules.*

Under the English constitution, in one knows not exactly what dark age, a species of judicatory developed itself, in which, in so far as the distinction found hands capable of delineating it, the matter to be decided upon was divided into two portions, on one whereof, as often as it presented itself in a state of separation from the other portion, the persons to decide were a *permanently* established *judge*, or *bench of judges:* while on the other, the persons to decide were, under the name *jurors*, or *jurymen*, a number of persons, originally indeterminate, in most instances fixed at twelve, serving in the character of occasional judges, the authority of each set confined to one individual suit or cause.

To the jurisdiction of the permanent, or official judge — the only sort of *judge* called by that commanding name — was understood to belong, in so far as the separation happened to be made, every decision, the terms of which would be expressive of a *general rule* — of that sort of *proposition* which by logicians has been distinguished by the appellation of a *general* one.

To the authority of the above-mentioned occasional or ephemeral body of judges called *jurors*, was understood to belong the decision on whatsoever matter came to be subjected to their cognizance, by and under the authority of their learned and authoritative directors — the judges that stood distinguished by the name of *judges*.

Having constructed this *palladium* — as it has been so often called — of the constitution, viz. *the jury-box*, — the same combination of undiscernible causes left, above and in contact with this palladium, a set of men, whose obvious interest, and consequently whose endeavour it has been, to weaken and undermine it.

From the very first — and, as will be seen, not altogether without just cause, — they took upon themselves — these experienced and learned judges — to determine what *evidence* should, and what should *not*, be presented to the cognizance of these their unexperienced and unlearned assessors: — but the *evidence* once presented to them, by these unexperienced and unlearned assessors it was, that the *judgment* on it was to be formed and pronounced.

Once presented to them? Good. But this or that lot of evidence, suppose it not presented to them by these their directors — what *then* became of it? *Answer* — It was decided — and with it commonly the fate of the whole cause determined — by these their directors themselves: with what consistency, as well as with what fruit, will be seen as we advance.

All evidence is either *direct* or *circumstantial* evidence. From any evidence that comes under the denomination of *direct*, it appears not that, on any occasion, they have as yet taken upon themselves to deduce the inference. On the contrary, — so abundant are the instances in which, speaking of evidence in general, the acknowledgment has been made to juries, that to them, and them alone, it belongs to say what credit is due to the evidence, whatsoever it has been, that they have been permitted to hear, and thereupon to deduce the inference from it, — that the reproach of usurpation is universally beholden ready to fall, in the character of an inevitable punishment, on the head of every judge, who should take upon him to attempt the depriving them of this function — this inestimable right — without which their office would be no better than a pernicious sinecure. In regard to *circumstantial* evidence, the question has never yet been stated — nor, if it were, does it seem possible to find any rational answers to it — why, in this instance any more than in that other, any attempt should be made to take the decision out of these popular hands, by which, in the sort of compound judicatory in question, without a shadow of objection, and amidst universal plaudits, every question, in so far as it turns upon *direct* evidence, is determined.

Out of these same hands, then, has any attempt been ever made to take the charge of drawing the inference from *circumstantial* evidence? — avowedly, in the lump, that is, in all cases, and under that name: No: on the contrary, there being few causes in which the nature of the case does not present the two species of evidence in a state of the most intimate union, so it is, that the *circumstantial* evidence is judged of by them, as of course, along with the *direct;* — nor, for any such purpose as that of dividing the cognizance between *the jury-box* and *the bench*, is any distinction made.

At the same time, so it is, that as often as evidence of the *circumstantial* kind has presented itself, the business of drawing the inference from it has, as often as such has been his pleasure, been, by the judge, taken out of the hands of the jury, and under the name of *matter of law*, taken into his own hands; and this with such effect, as, in and by so doing, to determine the fate of the suit or cause.

Between the cases in which the drawing the inference from circumstantial evidence is *proper* to be left to the jury, and the cases in which it is *proper* for it, thus to be taken out of their hands by the judge, — has any line been ever attempted to be drawn? Not any. Propriety out of the question, *could* any line be drawn, distinguishing with any tolerable clearness the cases in which *the one* course *has been* taken, from the cases in which *the other* course has been taken, in actual practice? Impossible. What then is the result? That in this, as in so many other cases, *arbitrary will* — to say no worse — has been the only guide.

By this sort of assumption, what have been the effects produced on the administration of justice?

1. In each cause taken by itself, has the probability of right decision received any increase? — does any sufficient reason appear for concluding that the inference thus drawn by the judge, was more rational than that which, in that same case, would have been drawn by the jury? On the contrary, when the inferences thus drawn come to be looked at, so flagrant will their absurdity and folly be frequently — not to say, most frequently — seen to be, as to preclude the idea that any inference so absurd and foolish could have been drawn by any understanding, not corrupted by that species of half-absurdity, half-nonsense, which among lawyers has received the name of *science:* and it is under the assurance, that under the guidance of common sense no such inference would be drawn by the twelve unlearned men whom he has to deal with, that the judge has thus taken the business upon himself. Under that assurance? Yes: — and for that very reason: for on the supposition of an expectation on his part, that the inference, and from the inference the decision formed by them, would have been the same as that which it was his desire to see formed: *use* there would be none, even with reference to his own purposes, in thus taking it out of their hands. — *Mischief the first* — Producing misdecision in each particular cause, on the occasion of which the assumption in question has been made — the incongruous power exercised.

2. As often as they have been uttered, these assumptions, along with the other acts and discourses emaning from the same learned sources, have been liable to be recorded:* and recorded they have been, in but too many instances: and in this shape, not inconsiderable has been the addition made to the chaos of jurisprudential science.

Ill-grounded with reference to the particular individual case which respectively gave birth to them, these assumptions have, if possible, been still worse grounded with reference to those other suits or causes, to the decision of which, when thus recorded, they have been applied without reserve. With neither of the two facts of which the circumstantial evidence in question is composed, could they ever have had any sort of connexion: they have thus been converted, each of them, into a mine of false inferences, and erroneous decisions. — *Mischief the second* — Contributing to the composition of an aggregate mass of delusive and pernicious error, under the name of science.

3. By the whole amount of it, the power thus exercised has been a usurpation upon the acknowledged right of juries. By the whole amount of it, it has operated in diminution of that security which is sought for at the hands of juries. By the whole amount of it, it is a violation of that principal support of the constitution so universally acknowledged to be a fundamental one. — *Mischief the third* — Mischief done to the constitution by violation of the acknowledged rights of juries.

Of the circumstances capable of operating in proof of delinquency, any of them taken singly may be far from being of itself sufficient to warrant a conclusion in affirmance of any inculpative suspicion. At the same time, put but a number of them together, the proof shall be so satisfactory as not to leave room for doubt as to any practical purpose. Instances might perhaps even be found, in which, for the production of sufficient assurance to a duly cautious mind, so small a number as two would appear sufficient. In the several instances in which conviction has taken place on the sole ground of circumstantial, without any assistance from direct evidence, a number considerably greater than two would, it is supposed, be found upon examination to have concurred.

In the cases in which English judges have

* In the printed books of reports.

taken upon them to form conclusions respecting matters of fact, on the ground of circumstantial evidence, it will be found that in every instance it has been on the ground of some one single fact considered in the character of an evidentiary fact; — upon no more than one article of circumstantial evidence that the conclusion has been formed.

It is possible, that in the instance of the individual suit or cause, on the occasion of which, on the single ground in question, a decision has been pronounced, such decision was not chargeable with injustice. Why? Because, though in the formation of that decision, the one circumstance in question was the only circumstance expressly brought to view and mention,—yet it may have happened that the case afforded other evidences, by each of which a part more or less considerable was borne in the formation of the decision so pronounced.

So much for what is possible; — what is certain is, that in every rule by which expression is given in general terms to a conclusion thus formed, all these corroborating circumstances, if any such there were, will be excluded. What is the consequence? That though, on the occasion on which the rule was formed, misdecision did not take place, yet the rule once formed remains and continues operating in the character of a perennial source of deceptious inferences; — in a word, of error and injustice.

Of the conclusion drawn from a fact considered in the character of an article of circumstantial evidence, the effect, if it be by a jury that the conclusion is drawn, never goes beyond the individual suit or cause which has given birth to it. All the other evidence which the suit or cause happens to afford, coming along with it, under their observation, and contributing to the formation of the conclusion, nothing hinders but that, applied as it is to the individual principal fact which alone is in question, the conclusion thus formed may, in each such suit, be right and well grounded.

Drawn by a judge, it most frequently happens that a conclusion conceived in the same terms will be productive of error and false judgment. Why? Because when drawn by a hand so situated, it swells itself out, and constitutes itself into a general rule — and will be thereafter applied to cases in indefinite numbers, and rendered productive of the sort of results just mentioned.

When the conclusion has been drawn by the jury, of the infirmative facts, by which, supposing them to have had place, its probative force would have been weakened or destroyed, none, it may be presumed, have been proved, none so much as probabilized.

In the several cases in which the general rule, containing the expression of the conclusion so drawn as above, will come to be applied by successive judges; whatsoever infirmative facts the case admits of, may have had place in any number: yet of none of them can the existence be brought to view; for the inference, as drawn, is regularly all-comprehensive; nor can any hand but that of a judge presume to narrow it.

Of the conclusion drawn by a jury, the mischief, if it be erroneous, and thence mischievous, goes not beyond that individual case: — Of the same conclusion drawn by a judge, the mischievousness, except in so far as it may happen to it to receive correction from an exceptive rule, operating in contradiction to the former conclusion, comprises a course of error and mischief to the very end of the system.

When fact A is considered as circumstantial evidence of fact B, the inference being made by a judge or bench of judges, and an account of it finds its way into a published law-book, general words being employed in the account given of it; the character in which it is presented, is of course that of a general rule laid down for the avowed purpose of its serving for determination of the decisions to be pronounced in all subsequent similar cases; that is, in each individual case in which for the description of the individual principal fact, and the individual evidentiary fact, which in such individual case, are respectively in question, the same general terms are respectively capable of being employed.

Applied to any such subsequent individual fact, the inference thus made, as described by the general rule formed as above, may have been represented either as absolutely conclusive, or as only *primâ facie* conclusive, or in other words, conclusive *nisi*: — as *primâ facie* conclusive, and no otherwise, if in the enunciation of it, an indication is made of this or that species of fact, as being, in the character of an infirmative fact, capable of annulling the inference, and thus preventing the principal fact in question, if not from obtaining credence altogether, from obtaining credence from the sole probative force of that evidentiary fact.

In a theoretical view, and for the purpose of affording the clearer conception of the sort of matter of which jurisprudential law is made, this distinction may have its use. But in practice it can scarcely be said to be exemplified, and has little or no influence. For among the prerogatives of an English judge, is that of taking a distinction whenever he pleases — taking a distinction, and thereby applying a *limitation*, or, what is the same thing, an exception to the general rule whereby to the purpose of the individual case in question, and so to the purpose of each succeeding individual case as it presents itself, the substance of the rule is picked out of it, and the rule left in the state of an empty husk.

If, then, the general rule happen to be to the taste of him to whom in that character it is presented, he simply pronounces it conclusive, and thereupon conforms to it; if not, he pronounces it conclusive *primâ facie* only, and taking his distinction, leaves the rule inoperative, and for that time sets it aside.

If the effect of the rule be to establish a fact in the character of circumstantial or presumptive evidence of a principal fact, the distinction will be taken by setting up, in the character of an infirmative fact, destructive of the probative force of the evidentiary fact, another individual fact presented at that same time, whether to his senses by testimony, or to his mind by imagination: — Yes, by imagination, for to warrant a man in dissenting from the conclusion indicated by an article of circumstantial evidence, it is not necessary that the possible fact by which the probative or disprobative force of the evidentiary fact is considered as destroyed, should have been proved.

Whether, therefore, the evidence be simply termed conclusive, or said to be conclusive *nisi* (or in whatever other words the distinction may stand expressed,) it comes in a manner of course to the same thing. By the reporter of the anterior case, let it have been simply styled conclusive — the judge, if it be not his pleasure to conform to the rule, will set up against it some fact, actual or hypothetical, in the character of an infirmative fact: let it have been reported as conclusive *primâ facie* only, or conclusive *nisi*, if, in the individual case before him, it be his pleasure to consider it as simply conclusive, he will say as much, refusing to receive, on the individual occasion in question, in the character of an infirmative fact, any individual fact which happens to have been proved, or brought to view as capable of having taken place.

Such is the state of things — such the despotism produced by taking out of the hands of jurors the function of deciding on the question of fact, in so far as the allegation concerning it is considered as proved, disproved, or not proved, by circumstantial evidence. And in this sample may be seen the whole substance of that false science of which the chaos called *jurisprudential law* is composed.

Along with *direct*, had the function of deciding upon circumstantial evidence been left to jurors inviolate, there would, so far as concerns the question of fact, have been no such sham learning — no such despotism; — no such distinction, as that between evidence simply and absolutely conclusive and evidence conclusive *nisi* or *primâ facie*, would have had place. On each occasion, after hearing whatsoever evidence, direct or circumstantial, could be produced, in the character of evidence probative or disprobative of the fact in question, in the character of the principal fact, the existence of such principal fact would—viz. by the jury—have been affirmed or disaffirmed. In a word, no instance would have had existence, of that sort of general rule, by which, as above, it has been rendered it is hoped pretty apparent, that much mischief has been done, and that no good ever has been, or ever could be done.

§ 12. *Inferences of Judge-made Law.*

Sample 1. Legitimacy from Husband's Non-Expatriation.

Two rules not altogether unconnected with each other; — the one imagined for the purpose of comparison — the other actually expressed in English judge-made law, may here serve for illustration: —

1. Principal fact, sexual intercourse; evidentiary fact, parturition; — the inference deemed absolutely conclusive.

This may be set down as one of the few imaginable instances in which a general rule pronouncing one species of fact conclusive with regard to the existence or non-existence of another species of fact, is not in danger of doing mischief; viz. by leading judges into decision manifestly ill grounded. But of what possible use can such a rule be? Where is the judge, where is the jury, who, but for the instruction afforded by this rule, would be in danger of mistake?

Of this kind is every judge-made rule of circumstantial evidence which is not in its tendency in a preponderant degree deceptious and pernicious.

2. Principal fact, the husband is the father of the child of a married woman: evidentiary fact, abode of the husband and wife, during some part of the period of gestation, in some part of the island of Great Britain. Inference deemed absolutely conclusive;—so conclusive that no evidence tending to the contrary persuasion shall be received.*

Here we have an example of a rule of circumstantial evidence, which at one time at least was received as an established rule of English law. True it is, that after having continued in force many hundred years, this rule was reversed.† But by the same authority by which the good old rule was reversed, the reversal itself may be reversed at any time. At any rate, as an example, it is as good as ever it was.

The absurdity of the rule is almost too palpable to admit of illustration. During the whole length of time in question, the husband may have been bed-ridden in the last stage of caducity at the northern extremity of Scot-

* See Co. Litt. 244; Bl. Com. I. 445.

† Com. Str. 925, 1076; B. R. H. 379.

land; the wife living in adultery at the southern extremity of Cornwall. Yet the husband was the father of the child of the wife, said the wisdom of these sages.

This law — for such it was in effect — this law, it is almost superfluous to say, is upon the face of it an insult to common honesty, as well as common sense. The object of it, if it had any, could not have been any other than the encouragement of adultery, by casting upon the injured husband the burthen of maintaining the spurious issue. On this supposition, it was a law made by the common-lawyers, to make business for themselves and another set of lawyers — the civilians, the practisers in the spiritual courts.

But in its origin, suppose it to have had any the least show of reason, it must have been in some such way as follows: — On the occasion or cause which gave birth to this general rule, so it was, that though, during the time in question, the ordinary abodes of the husband and the wife were at a considerable distance from each other, yet, for anything that appeared to the contrary, access and intercourse might have taken place.

For justifying the decision which, on the occasion of the individual suit or cause in question, it was determined to pronounce, a general rule was, as usual, deemed necessary to be stated as already in existence — in reality, to be made.

Coupled with the reasoning on which it may thus have been grounded, it may have been expressed in words to some such effect as follows: — "When, in the case of husband and wife, access has not been impossible, it is better to presume it to have had place, than by means of any direct testimony to attempt to scrutinize into the question, since, if the parties have lived in a certain space, within a certain distance of each other, no man can say that no intercourse can by possibility have taken place. But where shall the limits of this space be found? The island, within which the jurdisdiction of Westminster Hall has its geographical field, is surrounded by the sea: let this island be the space; the sea will then be the limits drawn by nature: suppose the sea divided into four portions, and speak of the four seas, season the rule with Latin, say *quatuor maria*, and who is there that shall gainsay it."

Here, then, we have the general rule, and now for the application: —

In cause A, as above, reason more or less there may have been for supposing it possible that between the parties in question, intercourse did take place. Comes now cause B, on the occasion of which it becomes manifest, that within the time in question no such intercourse did actually take place: none perhaps could by any possibility have taken place. No matter: a rule has been made — a rule of law concerning evidence, by which this question has been determined. "We are ready to prove," say the counsel for the husband, "that the husband was never, during any time at which the child could have been begotten, within fifty miles of the wife." — "Nay," say the counsel on the other side, "this is what you cannot be permitted to prove, for the law in its wisdom has decided the matter against you; you and we were within *quatuor maria* all the time, and therefore you are the father of the child."

Between the individual principal fact in question in cause B, and the individual fact or mass of facts taken from cause A and applied to cause B to be employed in it, in the character of an evidentiary fact probative of the said principal fact there is not by the supposition any sort of connexion whatsoever.

Evidentiary fact A took place at the beginning of sixteenth century—principal fact B not till the eighteenth century. No matter: borrowed from cause A, fact A is taken, and in the character of an evidentiary fact applied to the fact in question, in the character of a principal fact, on the occasion of cause B; and of this evidentiary fact, the probative force is deemed conclusive. In the cause which was decided, anno 1510, it was not proved that John Stiles could not have had access to his wife, Mary Stiles, so as to be the father of her son William: therefore, in the cause that now comes to be decided, anno 1790, it ought to be considered as proved that Nicholas Nokes is the father of Nathaniel, the son of his wife Elizabeth Nokes. Such is the logic, as often as, for determining a question of fact on the ground of circumstantial evidence, recourse is had to a general rule.

Had admission been given to the evidence belonging to the cause, the impossibility of any such *genesis* would have been proved by circumstances in abundance; but to save the trouble of hearing evidence, or for some other purpose, the law has laid down a rule, in virtue of which, as often as it is applied for determining whether, in the case in question, the fact which is in question did or did not take place, the evidence to be admitted and considered is not any evidence which this individual cause actually affords; but the imagined evidence which is supposed to have been afforded in and by this or that other cause which had nothing to do with it.

Upon the ground of some imagined evidence, supposed to have been delivered, relative to some one fact, in a case which has nothing to do with it, is the case in question determined, to the exclusion of all such evidence as properly belongs to it. Such has been the wisdom of those sages, as often as, for fear of that deception to which simple men in the situation of jurors are exposed, it has pleased them to take the business of determining a question of fact out of those inexperienced hands:—"Judging from evidence, simple men as you are, you would be misled by it;—to save you from error, we," say these sages, "will take the question into our own hands, and decide it for you without evidence."*

Sample 2. Malice from Homicide—Murder from Malice.

To any man, without any such wish, has it been your misfortune to have been the cause of death? To save to the jury the trouble of inquiring under what circumstances, and the danger of being deceived by evidence, the judge, if such be his pleasure, will find you guilty of murder, and so order matters that you shall be hanged for it. If on your part there has been *malice*, your doom is predetermined: *murder* has been your *crime*—*death* will be your punishment. Would the jury, had the inference been left to them, have found in your bosom any such thing as malice? This is of the number of those things which they are not to be trusted with.—This or that judge, who has been dead these two or three hundred years, knows more of the matter than they;—and by implying malice in your bosom, he who knows nothing about you or your case, he it is who has saved them the trouble of thinking whether any such thing as *malice*, whatever be meant by the word, had in your case any existence.

But what is meant by it? The same thing that is meant by so many other words, such as *felony*, *felonious intent*, and so forth: on the part of those sages, a disposition, they cannot tell, or care not to tell why, to cause you to be hanged:—to be hanged as well as all such other persons to whom it shall happen to be in your case;—in plain English, in whose instance, it may happen to any successor of these sages to be disposed to have them hanged. Such is the safety of the subject, under the dominion of what, in contradistinction to *statute*, is called *common* law.

And thus most conveniently open to despotism is the field, where, in the text of the law, real or supposed, there is an expression which should have been indicative of the matter of fact, or of a portion of the matter of fact, of such a texture as to indicate, so extreme is its generality, nobody can exactly say what. Such is the case with the word *malice* in the essential phrase, *of malice aforethought*:—in the original Latin *ex malitiâ præcognitâ*:—in the tenor of the established instrument of accusation, the *indictment*, as it is called.

In every mouth but a lawyer's, *malice* means neither more nor less than a particular modification of *ill-will*; in a lawyer's, on the present occasion and for the present purpose, for no better reason than because *malice* is, by substitution of an *English* to a Latin termination, derived from *malitia*, and *malitia* is derived from *malus*—by which in Latin is denoted everything that is thought or pretended to be thought bad—it is made to denote anything, for which, in the character of a bad thing, he feels himself disposed to put a man to death.

Of malice, according to the indictment, the supposed existence was necessary. But in proof of this essential matter of fact, according to the doctrine of some reverend and learned person who wanted to destroy a man, of whom, in the eyes of a jury, it would, it was feared, not appear fit that he should be destroyed, it was not necessary that any probability should be presented by evidence. Presuming is shorter than proving:—power more pleasant than impotence: and so, because it had not been *proved* to the jury, it was *presumed* by the judge.

"Killing (in the words of Gilbert) is so bad a thing,—so ill-natured and bloody an action,† that it is to be *presumed* to be malicious;" that is, all *killing* is to be *presumed* to be murder, and punished, on the supposition of its being murder,—punished as murder. In this case, the physical matter of fact is by the supposition out of the question, as well as the share which the defendant had in the production of it: in this same case, who does not see that of the existence of the psychological matter of fact, the state of the mind, the supposition is not less uniform? But to save trouble, and to save the risk of an unacceptable verdict, especially when innocence happens to be manifest, this, instead of being proved to, and *found* by, the jury, is, on the mere ground of the physical fact, to be *presumed* by the judge.

All this while, in a case in which it is his pleasure to reduce the punishment, and for that purpose call the offence *manslaughter*, the physical fact has been exactly the same—the share which by his physical organs the defendant has had in the production of it exactly the same—and yet the psychological fact is not thus presumed from it.

Thus, then, stands the matter:—When it is his pleasure the defendant should be destroyed, the judge draws the inference, and calls the offence *murder*: when it is his pleasure the man should not be destroyed, he leaves the inference undrawn, and calls the

* All this while, Common Sense has been bursting with impatience. "The man and wife themselves have probably some knowledge how the case was. Why not ask them? why prefer vague conjecture?" "No (says Common Law:) *that* would be against our rules:—what in your eyes is the best evidence, in our eyes is no evidence at all." But this belongs to the topic of Exclusions, of which further in its place.

† On Evidence, p. 234.

offence *manslaughter*. But in his zeal to destroy somebody, who, though the jury would have thought otherwise, it must be *presumed* deserved to be destroyed, Gilbert, who on this occasion is the representative and mouthpiece of the learned tribe, forgets that there was any such distinct thing as *manslaughter*, and that, according to the account thus given of the matter by himself, *murder* and *manslaughter* are exactly the same thing.

Note here, that as above, when *malice means* anything in particular, *i. e.* in the sense in which it is used in every other mouth than a lawyer's, it means *ill-will*—ill-will towards him who is the intended object of it, and is intended to be made the sufferer by it. Note at the same time, that in a case which is but too frequently exemplified, as towards the person who has been not only the eventual, but the intended sufferer, there has not existed in the breast of the author of the death any such emotion or affection as that of ill-will. This is where the object which the crime has for its purpose to procure is the gratification looked for in any shape or from any other source than the contemplation of the suffering produced in the breast of the party injured. Such is the case where death is produced by assault, made in prosecution of a plan of forcible depredation; for example, in a house* or on the highway.

Such is, in even a more particular degree, the case, where the murder has had for its object the acquisition of the matter of wealth in any shape — in the way of succession, as in the instance of the parricide committed at Reading in 1752, on the person of her father, by Mary Blandy. In the breast of that not altogether ill-educated female, the unvaried tenderness of her father had not failed altogether to keep alive, even to the last, some sparks, however faint, of a correspondent affection; but by the violence of her passion for her lover, by whose instigation she committed the crime, the gentler affection had been subdued. In neither of these cases was the crime-producing interest, the interest of the gall-bladder in one of them, it was the interest of the purse; in the other, the interest of the sexual appetite.

Now these cases in which, law jargon apart, there existed not the least spark of any such affection as *malice*, are precisely the cases in which the mischief of murder rises to the highest point of the scale. Why? Because these are both of them of the number of the cases in which, in respect of probability, the danger of becoming sufferers by the sinister operation of the interest in question in the character of a *motive*, is in the apprehension of persons in general apt to rise to the highest pitch. In both cases, of the aggregate mischief of the offence, that part which has been distinguished under the name of the mischief of the second order, —*i. e.* the *general* part of the mischief, and which, in respect of extent, measured by the number of the persons exposed to it, is to that of the mischief of the first order, *i. e.* the particular part of the mischief, comparatively speaking, as infinity to one;—is far greater in those cases where, ordinarily, and properly speaking, there is no malice, than when, in the same sense, in the breast of the offender, the offence has had malice for its sole cause.

Putting together these two cases, viz. this relative to murder and malice, the other relative to legitimacy on the part of the child of a married woman — the one belonging to the penal, the other to the non-penal division of the field of law — each of them in its department a case of considerable importance; some conception may be formed of the process by which the rule of action is formed, when the hands by which it is formed are those of a judge, or bench of judges, acting as such; and of the shape in which it is produced, in so far as a nonentity is susceptible of shape.

In neither case any such conception manifested, as that law is or ought to be an instrument employed towards a determinate end — or at least, that if it be, the greatest happiness of the greatest number is that end. If it had any such end, then and then alone would come the inquiry, what were the operations employed in the character of means with reference to that end, and in what respects, they were respectively conducive or non-conducive to it. But in the present instance, no such end being perceptible, all inquiries in relation to means are manifestly inapplicable.

Such as are these two samples, together with the others which occur here and there in the course of this work, such it may, without danger of the imputation of injustice, be said is judge-made law throughout. In each case, by some view suggested by that particular case (never by any such general view as that of picking out grosser from less gross specimens of absurdity) has the selection been made. In addition to its absurdity, it would be found throughout (not from beginning to end, for it has neither) a tissue of inconsistencies; and in this respect, as Ovid would have said, it is consistent.

Such is the nature, such the result of law, *i. e.* the imaginary thing to which is given the force of law, penal or non-penal, when tumbled out by judicature, substituting itself to legislation, or overruling legislation: the mode employed, that mode in which the unalterable nature of things places the work, in whatsoever hands, under the impossibility of being done well. Matter of law made after

* For example, the murders at Wapping in 1812.

the fact, after the fashion of *ex-post facto law*, — made under the quibbling pretence of being declared. Matter of fact decided upon by abuse of words; — decided upon without evidence, or by this or that scrap of evidence caught up blindfold from some anterior case, known or unknown, and applied to facts of which those, whose testimony it was, could have had no knowledge. Legislator's power exercised without authority;—judicial power exercised in the teeth of principle; — the sceptre filched from the king in parliament, and the balance wrested from the hands of juries.

Thus much as to substance: as to language, in jurisprudence and legislation, things are no more capable of being by anybody shown to be what they are in and by that part of the English language which has been poisoned by the mouths or the pens of English lawyers, than in chemistry they could ever be by Sir Humphrey Davy, if he were confined to the language employed by those who in former times occupied the place of chemists, the united brotherhood of impostors and dupes called alchemists.

CHAPTER XIII.

OF MAKE-SHIFT EVIDENCE.

§ 1. *Unoriginal Make-shift Evidence.*

OF the several modifications of evidence which are here brought to view in conjunction, under the common appellation of *make-shift* evidence, the common characteristic is — the circumstance of their being in a greater or less degree untried by those tests which have already been brought to view under the name of *securities*,—securities against deceptious incorrectness and incompleteness:— untried by those securities in general; — but, in particular, by *interrogation*, considered as combined with those co-securities, and furnished with those sub-securities on which, in a greater or less degree, its efficiency may have been already seen to depend.

In some cases, the person by whose lips or whose hand the discourse assertive of the matters of fact in question is presented to the ear or to the eye of the judge, is not the individual to whose perceptive faculty these supposed matters of fact are so much as supposed to have presented themselves.

In these cases, by the very nature of the case, so long as the evidence continues in this case, the grand security afforded by interrogation is incapable of being applied to it.

Of this class of cases, *hearsay* evidence presents the only primeval, and at the same time the most simple and familiar example; especially when, as in the most simple and obvious cases which that appellation is qualified to express, *oral* is as well the form *actually* assumed by the actual discourse of the deposing witness, as the form *supposed* to have been assumed by the *supposed* discourse of the supposed percipient witness.

A modification, in modern times, not much less familiar, and perhaps still more simple, is that which may be presented to view by the appellation *transcriptious* evidence. But though in this case, as well as in the other there are at least two sources of information which, by and in proportion to their number (each being exposed to its own causes of deceptious incorrectness and incompleteness, and neither affording, by any additional information, any increase to the probative force of the other,) render the probability of deceptious incorrectness and incompleteness at least twice as great as if there were but one. At the same time, what is little less obvious is, that in the case of transcriptious evidence, the increase given to the probability of incorrectness and incompleteness, is in general beyond comparison less than in the case of *hearsay* evidence.

In the case of hearsay evidence, the information, supposing it orally delivered by a percipient witness, finds an additional intellect, which has to occupy itself, not only about the *tenor*, but about the *purport* of it, and in which it has, as it were, to be remoulded and recast: — and in which, as well as in that of the supposed percipient witness, it finds itself exposed to all those causes of deceptious incorrectness and incompleteness, which, under the appellation of intellectual causes, have already been brought to view.

To the case of transcriptious evidence, scarcely in any degree have these causes any application: — with the *tenor* alone, as exhibited by the visible signs, has the copyist, unless by accident, any concern; — with the *purport*, except in case of doubt, for the purpose of determining his conception in relation to the tenor — he has none.

In the case of hearsay evidence, commonly the individuality of the supposed percipient witness, and at any rate the *form* in which the discourse expressive of his supposed perceptions is supposed to have been conceived, are given and determinate; since if it were not, no regard would be bestowed upon it: in the case of *transcriptious* evidence, considered simply as such, these particulars may be still to seek. A consequence is — that any of those circumstances by which, in respect of trustworthiness and probative force, evidence is raised above, as well as any of those by which it is sunk below, the ordinary level, may indifferently be found in it.

§ 2. *Extrajudicially written, Make-shift Evidence.*

In the class of cases here in question, there exists not, in the nature of the case, anything by which the discourse which presents itself to the judges, or, to speak more precisely, the person whose discourse it is, is rendered incapable of being subjected to the action of those purifying tests; but only, it has happened that he has not been subjected to any of those tests: — the case being, that at the time of the formation, *i. e.* the writing of this discourse (it being by the supposition a portion of written discourse,) there existed not any external hand in a situation to subject him in respect of it to the action of those tests.

The signs in which the information in question stands expressed, were formed (such at least is the supposition) *not* for the purpose of being employed to the judicial purpose to which it happens to them to be employed, — or at any rate, not to the purpose of the particular suit, but to some other purpose: in whatsoever state, with a view to that other purpose, they were brought into existence, in that same state having been found, and having, on the occasion in question, been deemed applicable in the character of evidence to the service of justice, in that same state they are pressed, as it were, into that service.

The following are the modifications of extra-judicially written evidence: —

1. Casually-written scripts (including memorandums and miscellaneous letters.)
2. Evidence *preappointed ex parte* (including mercantile account books and letters.)
3. These, together with evidence which, having been regularly received or extracted *aliâ in causâ* on the occasion and for the purpose of another cause or suit, — may be termed *adscititious*, or borrowed evidence.

First modification of extra-judicially written evidence — casually written evidence.

Without much violence, either under the head of a *memorandum* or that of a *letter*, may everything that is written be comprised.

Designed for the use of the writer and no other person, it is a memorandum: communicated to any other person, or designed to be read by any other person, it becomes in effect a letter or epistle: published or designed for general publication, a literary work, which is in effect a letter addressed to the world at large.

It may happen, that the operation of the head has been the work of one person, the operation of the hand that of another; as in the case of dictation to a scribe. Anomalies of this kind will come under notice in another place.

Second modification of extra-judicially written evidence — *ex parte* preappointed evidence.

To the head of make-shift evidence, preappointed *ex parte*, may be referred any such statement as, though in the nature of it it can scarcely but have been intended to have eventually, in the character of evidence, at least as between some parties, a legal operation, yet, in respect of the sinister interest, under the influence of which it is brought into existence, joined to the circumstance of its not being subjected to the tutelary action of the securities for correctness and completeness, wears upon the face of it a suspicious aspect, and cannot without manifest impropriety be considered as standing, in point of probative force, on a level with ordinary judicial evidence. Of this species of evidence, the sub-modification most in use is composed of mercantile books of account, together with such letters as belong to mercantile correspondence.

Agreeing in respect of design and preparation—agreeing therefore in their nature (were it not for the circumstance expressed by the adjunct *ex parte*) — with the extensive and highly diversified class of evidence, which under the denomination of *preappointed* evidence will come next to be considered, they will be seen rather to contrast than assimilate with it, when compared with it, in respect of probative force: in the scale of probative force, the station of preappointed evidence at large being *above*, that of evidence preappointed *ex parte*, *below* the level of ordinary evidence. Why? Because, in the case of preappointed evidence at large, the statement stands clear of the sinister action of self-regarding interest, or if exposed to the action of that powerful cause of deceptious incorrectness and incompleteness has for its security against these imperfections the eventually controuling action of the several antagonizing interests on which the evidence is in a way to operate.

Third and last modification of extra-judicially written evidence — *adscititious* evidence. Judicial with reference to the cases from which it is borrowed, evidence of this description, is extra-judicial with reference only to the cases *in* and *for* which, on the occasion in question, it is borrowed. Parties the same or different; — judicatory the same or of a different country: — if it be of a different country, of a country dependent or independent of our own — amicable with relation to it, or hostile. In the judicatory, if different, the mode of receiving or extracting the evidence the same, or different — by any of these varieties may the nature and probative force of adscititious evidence be diversified.

In point of trustworthiness and probative force, the case in which adscititious evidence comes nearest to evidence received and extracted in the very cause in question, is—where not only the *judicatory* but the *parties* were the same. But even here, though the diversity be least, the coincidence is not complete. Opportunity of interrogation—say even *undequaque* interrogation — the same; parties to avail themselves of it, even these the same: still, if the purpose were in any respect different, the course taken in and by the interrogation may nevertheless be, in a more or less material degree, different from what it is necessary it should be, ere it can exhibit such a picture of the transaction in question as, with reference to the purpose now in hand, shall be a correct and complete one: by this difference, slight as it may be, supposing fresh interrogation neither physically nor prudentially impracticable, a demand, and that a sufficient one, for that operation, may accordingly be produced.

How should it not? If, even in the very cause in hand, after the interrogations which have been propounded, and the answers which have been extracted in consequence, there be reason to think, that by fresh interrogation a matter of fact, capable of demonstrating the propriety of reversing or modifying the existing decision, may be brought to light, it can scarcely be said that such interrogation ought not to be admitted: — and if in that case justice may require the admission of it, *à fortiori* may it in any case of adscititious evidence.

The more trustworthy the shape is in which the adscititious evidence has been received or extracted, — the less; the less trustworthy the shape,—the greater will be any abatement that may be to be considered as being made, in the trustworthiness and probative force of this relatively extra-judicial, when compared with ordinary judicial evidence.

From the number of the *changes* capable of being *rung* upon the several sources of diversification above mentioned, an idea may be formed of the amplitude of the scale that would be necessary to comprehend all the several gradations of which, in the several different cases, its trustworthiness and probative force might be found susceptible.

§ 3. *Modifications of unoriginal Evidence.*

In the case of *unoriginal* evidence, when the imperfection of the evidence has for its cause the want of originality, or (say) unimmediateness, — setting aside the case of characteristic fraud (of which presently,) in which the whole body of it together is substituted, by or under the direction, or for the sake, or in favour of the party by whom it is produced and exhibited to the judge,—*media* of transmission may, in any number, have intervened between the original statement made by the *percipient* (for in this case, by the supposition, the case really presents a *percipient*) and *deposing* witness. So many as there have been of these *media*, so many different sources (it is obvious) there have been of actual, and — blameable or no — at any rate of more or less probably deceptious incorrectness and incompleteness.

Intervening media, say in any number more than one: in that case by supposing, in the instance of one or more of these intermediate channels, the discourse to have been expressed in the oral form, and again, in one or more, in the already written form, — sub-modifications, in an indefinite multitude, none of them incapable of being realized, may be conceived and denominated. To give descriptions of, and denomination for them, in so far as such an operation presented a prospect of being of use with a view to practice — either to judicial or to legislative practice — is of the number of the tasks, the performance of which will in the body of the work be found attempted.*

§ 4. *Points of Infirmity common to Make-shift Evidence.*

Agreeing in this characteristic property, viz. that of their being all of them destitute of the benefit of the salutary scrutiny so often mentioned, the species of evidence included under these two general heads will moreover be seen to agree in two other properties, which find in that infirmity their common cause; with peculiar degree of facility they give admission to two distinguishable causes of deceptious incorrectness and incompleteness, viz. *unintentional error*, and *fraudulent contrivance*.

As to this contrivance, the capacity of being taken for the instrument of it being inherent in the very essence of unscrutinizable evidence, it may, with relation to all evidence, for the designation of which the term *make-shift* evidence has herein been employed, — unoriginal evidence, and extrajudicially written evidence included, — be termed the *characteristic fraud*.

In all these several cases, the characteristic fraud will be found comprisable under one and the same description: for some sinister purpose, whether immediately his own or that of another person, confiding in the nature of the species of evidence by which the information in question, to how great a degree soever deceptiously incorrect and incomplete, will, by the non-application of the requisite judicial securities, stand exempted from the actions of those tests of truth, a man frames on that ground a body or article of deceptious information, adapted to the nature of the occasion, as well as to that of the dishonest purpose.

§ 5. *Facienda by the Legislator in regard to Make-shift Evidence.*

In relation to all these modifications of defectively-constituted evidence, of the course that has presented itself as proper to be taken by the legislator, intimation has in general

* Book VI.

terms been already given:—so far as *prudentially* as well as *physically* practicable to add or substitute to the defectively-framed evidence, evidence drawn from the same original source or supposed source, but, by the application of the requisite securities, so moulded as no longer to labour under the same defects.

So far as practicability in either of these its modes is wanting, — insomuch that, from the original source in question, evidence in any less defective state is not to be obtained, — to do the next best thing in his power — leaving the judge in possession of the evidence, such as it is, — let the legislator do what depends upon his own exertions towards guarding the judge from that deception the danger of which is let in by it: —laying aside for a moment his *power*, let him employ his *wisdom*, whatsoever it be, in the endeavour to hold up to view, in the form of *instructions*, a light to lighten the understanding, and at the same time to serve as a safeguard to the probity of the judge.

As on the several other occasions, so on this, a set of INSTRUCTIONS adapted to this purpose will be found in their appropriate place in the body of the work.*

Of the cause of such *unblameable*, or at any rate *non-fraudulent* incorrectness and incompleteness, of which the defectively-constituted evidence is in these its several shapes respectively susceptible, — to give the requisite intimation, as well as to bring to view and lay open the *characteristic fraud* in the several shapes which, in the case of these several modifications of make-shift evidence, it will have to assume, will be sure to form a principal part of the business of these *instructions*.

§ 6. *English Practice in regard to Make-shift Evidence.*

As on the several other occasions, so on this, to confront with, and throw light upon the picture thus given, of what presents itself as the *proper* practice, adapted to the nature of the case, sketches will here and there be given, of what, under English law more particularly, appears to have been, in relation to this head, the *actual* practice.

From one and the same original source, evidence admitted in less trustworthy shapes not admitted in the most trustworthy shapes; — admission given to broken hints, refused to explanations; — *ignes-fatui* let in, while sunbeams are excluded; — gnats strained at, while camels are swallowed: — such, under this head, is the scene — such is the system of practice which there will be occasion to bring to view.

Of the exclusions put as above, the impropriety must wait for its exposure till the time comes for the chapter allowed to that subject. Against the instances of admission considered by themselves, nothing might perhaps here be to be said; but when these admissions are coupled and confronted with the exclusions put upon evidence in its best shape from the same source, the inconsistency and impropriety of the practice may perhaps be thought already proved, if it should be found to agree with the description given of it.

* See Book X., and also Appendix A.

CHAPTER XIV.

OF PREAPPOINTED EVIDENCE.

§ 1. *Its Nature and Origin.*

BY the term preappointed evidence, may be understood any evidence whatsoever, considered in so far as provision is made for the creation or preservation of it, antecedently to the existence of any right or obligation for the support of which it may happen to serve, or to the manifestation of any individual occasion for the production of it.

Recordation or registration are names by which may be designated, any act which has for its object the creation or preservation of preappointed evidence.

Rights being beneficial things — sources of *good* to those whose rights they are — sources of every benefit which it is in the power of man to grant or to secure, — thence it is, that of such evidence on which, as on their indispensable foundation, all rights rest, the creation and preservation are operations in every instance prescribed by the same imperious considerations as those by which men's attention is directed to the obtainment and preservation of those rights themselves.

In so far as the subject-matter of the right, or rather of the aggregate cluster of rights, by which *the property* of a thing is composed, is of a *moveable* nature, especially if it be of the number of those things which are not put to use but in proportion as they are destroyed,* the collection of circumstances of which that most variably and mysteriously constituted, howsoever familiar relation called *possession*, is composed, presents in itself, generally speaking, evidence sufficient for the preservation as well as establishment of these rights.

Differently circumstanced the case in this respect is, where the right has, for its subject-matter, either an immoveable portion of the planetary mass, on some part or other of which all human beings find their place — or this or that particular kind of service which, in virtue of some particular relation, one human being finds himself under the obligation of rendering to another:—in both these cases,

* *Examples* — Meat and drink, &c., and in general such other things as are most indispensably necessary to the continuance of man's existence.

to ascertain, and upon all occasions to make known, the existence of the right in question, requires the aid of some permanent sign, or assemblage of signs, in the shape and character of *evidence*.

When as yet the art of writing was unknown, or not sufficiently in use to be generally applicable to this purpose, feeble and inadequate were the contrivances, — the instruments, or operations, — devised and employed for this purpose: but when this invaluable art was once invented, serving in the character of preappointed evidence, as it was among the most important uses in which it could be employed, so it was among the first in which it actually was employed.

A person, and at first view, even the only person, on whom the care of providing and preserving the evidence necessary to the support of a right naturally devolves, is of course the person to whom the right belongs; — but by the concurrent operation of a variety of circumstances, other persons, it will be seen, are brought upon the stage in great variety, by whom the task of making this provision is necessarily either shared with the person so situated, or even taken altogether out of his hands: to him, if considered by himself, the operation being rendered either physically or (what comes in effect to the same thing) prudentially impracticable:—1. By immaturity of age he may be rendered as yet incapable of any such charge; 2. At the time when the provision requires to be made, he may even be not as yet in existence;* 3. In the right in question, persons, in any number, may have a joint and equally valuable interest, the value of which would, however, in the instance of any one of them, be outweighed and destroyed by the burthen of the task, were he the only person charged with it.†

Another circumstance there is, which would of itself be sufficient to prevent the charge of providing evidence of a right, from resting exclusively on the possessor of that same right, whosoever he may be. The person on whom rests principally the charge, as of giving effect to the right itself, so accordingly of giving correspondent effect to whatsoever evidence may happen to be provided for the support of that same right, is — not the possessor of the right — not any such feeble operator, but the *sovereign* himself — the person or persons by whose hands, to this and the several other public purposes, the whole power of the state is exercised—the *sovereign* by authority of the whole community—and by authority from him, though in all ordinary cases without need of recurrence to any special decision on his part, his subordinate the judge.

But on these two persons, in due subordination the one to the other, it depends — not only to what rights, but, for the support of those rights, to what evidence they will lend this sanction—and, as well on the occasion of these rights, as on the occasion of that evidence, on what *conditions* it shall be lent.

* *Example* — All rights that are acquired by birth.

† *Example* — Corporate rights.

§ 2. *Uses of Preappointed Evidence, anti-litigious, and statistic.*

Of the uses to which, in the form and character of preappointed evidence, evidence may be put — of the services which, in that form and character, it may be made to render, — it may not be amiss to present in this place a comprehensive view.

Uses and corresponding services of the first order; — Uses and services of the second order. To effects, good and bad, resulting from human agency, clothed or unclothed with authority, the principle of division thus brought to view has been employed elsewhere,‡ nor, if useful there, will it be less so here.

Uses and services of *the first order*, — those by which the parties — the known and assignable parties — to the individual transaction in question, or other individual transactions specially connected with it, are served.

Uses of *the second order*, —those by means of which, on future contingent occasions, in respect of future contingent transactions, following one another in a series without end, it may happen to the at present unknown and unassignable parties to these same future transactions respectively, to be served and benefited.

Uses and services of the *first* order may again be distinguished into *litigious* and *anti-litigious:* litigious, rendered on the occasion of an existing suit or cause; viz. by contributing to give effect to the rights and obligations which come in question in and on the occasion of that cause: — anti-litigious, — services which, though unseen, and even in a certain sense unfelt, are but the more useful, rendered as they are, by nipping in the bud the suits, which, but for the evidence thus expressed and perpetuated, might have sprung up: giving, without ulterior expense, full effect to those rights and obligations to which, in case of actual litigation, effect can neither be given nor sought for, but out of the fire of that furnace.

Uses and services of the *second* order, — to this head may be referred those which may be termed *statistic:* services performed by furnishing to the legislator whatsoever information he may stand in need of, for the purpose of judging, from time to time, whether, on those parts of the field of legislation to which the information in question is applicable, anything yet remains to be done of those things, which for the improvement of man's condition

‡ Introduction to Morals and Legislation.

in the community in question, the nature of things admits of.

In other words, it is by helping to form, on the ground of experience, a basis for legislative arrangements, including as well those which at the time in question happen to be actually in force, as any which may happen hereafter to be established.

Such are the parties concerned, and such the distinctions respecting them, in so far as the faculty considered is the *sensitive* faculty — the faculty in and by means of which man *enjoys* and suffers.

If the sorts of persons to whom, in respect of the *active* part of their frame, the information applies, be considered, and the persons in consequence of whose agency, positive or negative, the enjoyment or suffering in question, as above mentioned, may take place, — they will be found to be two sorts of official persons, viz. *judges* and legislators: the judge as being he by whom, in case of litigation, effect will be given or refused to the rights and obligations of which the evidence in question constitutes, or has been alleged to constitute, the basis: — he to whom, on the other hand, should the anti-litigious tendency of this mass of information ripen into effect, the labour of hearing and determining will be saved: — the legislator, as being the official person, to whose intellectual faculties such services will be rendered, as the body of evidence of which the article in question forms part and parcel, is qualified for rendering, in virtue of its above-mentioned statistic uses; and to whose active faculties the community will be indebted for whatever benefit it may happen, in virtue of its sensitive faculties, to receive from such arrangements, present and future, of which the evidence in question may contribute to form the basis as above.

RECAPITULATION.

Uses and corresponding services applying to the sensitive faculties, viz. of the members of the community considered in the aggregate, uses and services of the first order, and ditto of the second order — Uses and services of the first order, *litigious*, rendered on the occasion of litigation; — *anti-litigious*, rendered by the prevention of litigation.

Uses and corresponding services applying to the active faculties, viz. of persons in official situations, acting as trustees for themselves and the rest of the community, — uses and services to the judge — *judicial* uses: — Uses to the legislator — *statistic* uses.

Such are the *uses* to which evidence, considered as produced in the form and character of preappointed evidence, is capable of being put; such the service capable of being derived from it.

§ 3. *Legislator's Duties in relation to it.*

Be the evidence in question — the preappointed evidence — what it may, to provide for the *existence* of it, — to provide for its subserviency in the highest practicable degree, to the purpose with reference to which it may be of use, under one or other of these two heads the whole duty of the legislator may, it is supposed, be ranged.

Under the last-mentioned of these heads may be considered as included, the obviously proper and unexceptionable condition, that in each instance, the advantage derivable from the evidence shall be such as to afford a reasonable promise of being found preponderant over the expense and vexation attendant on the creation and preservation of it.

Subject to this condition, what may be considered, perhaps, as forming the subject of a separate head of duty, is, the looking out for all occasions on which the creation and preservation of preappointed evidence promises to be in this sense productive of a net balance on the side of advantage: —

1. Subject-matters of preappointed evidence.

2. In relation to each such subject-matter, means applicable to the purpose of rendering the evidence subservient to the several uses to which it is applicable. To one or other of these two heads may be found referable whatsoever ulterior indications will here be to be given of the matters of detail, which in the body of the work will be found under this same head of preappointed evidence.

§ 4. *Subject-matters of preappointed Evidence.*

1. Legally operative facts; 2. Contracts;*

* Under the denomination of a contract, to some eyes a will (a last will) may perhaps not appear comprisable; to others, not even a conveyance. But unless this word contract be accepted for the designation of a *legally operating disposition*, no less exceptionable *single worded* appellative, one may venture to say, being to be found, we shall be reduced to the employing on every occasion the complex and unwieldy, as well as novel appellative just mentioned.

On this subject, the indistinctness of existing language — the natural and almost necessary result of confusedness of conception — opposes to the communication of all instructive truth, a perpetually recurring and most distressing obstacle.

In the language of the English school as delivered by Blackstone — of the English school, derived, in this quarter of the field, in part but not altogether from that of the Roman — under the term *contract*, are included, in all cases, agreements, and in some, but not in all cases, conveyances. Applied to a house, for example — *sale* is a *conveyance*, not a *contract*. Applied to a horse, it is a *contract*, not a *conveyance*.

But considering that for the designation of all *legally operative dispositions* relative to property (right to *human service* in all shapes, being included under the denomination of property,) some single-worded appellative is, in respect of clear conception and clear description, indispensably necessary; and considering that under the term CONTRACT, conveyance is in

3. Transactions of offices belonging to the judicial department; 4. Transactions of offices belonging to the administrative department; 5. Laws and transactions of offices belonging to the legislative department; 6. Registration applied to transcripts; 7. Registration applied to evidence of authorship. To one or other of these subordinate heads may be referred whatsoever observations there may be occasion to bring forward in relation to the subject-matters of preappointed evidence.

In the description of the operations to be performed, viz. by the creation and preservation of preappointed evidence — there will be found a material difference, according as the subject-matter of it is *evanescent* or *permanent:* — evanescent, in which case are all human *actions*, as well as all other *events;* permanent, in which case are all written *instruments* — all instruments to which any portions of written discourse, or any other visible marks employed for the communication of ideas, are consigned.

In the case of events, or other *evanescent* modes of being, all that the nature of the case allows to be done in the way of preappointed evidence, is — to create and preserve the indications of their existence, including their material circumstances: in the case of a permanent instrument as above, there exists, in the character of a subject-matter capable of recordation, in the first place, the fact of its being brought into existence; in the next place, the tenor or purport of its *contents*.

Correspondent to this difference in the nature of the subject-matter will be seen to be the differences observable in the *operations* that will require to be performed on, or in relation to it.

§ 5. *Legally operative Facts, considered as subject-matters of preappointed Evidence.*

1. Legally operative — to which may be added, or statistically useful — facts. To one or other of two heads — viz. genealogical facts and miscellaneous facts, be their diversity what it may, they will all of them be found referable.

To the head of genealogical facts may be referred, deaths, births, and marriages.

As to marriage, besides its being, in so far as by the act of celebration it is placed, like death and birth, upon a footing with genealogical facts, — by this act a species of contract is entered into — and that the most important of all contracts: considered in this point of view, it will find its place under the head of contracts, as below.

Of legally operative or statistically useful facts of a miscellaneous nature, a sample of considerable amplitude and variety will be found in the note.*

---

some cases as above comprehended, and that under the term *conveyance* wills are also included; it has been thought fit here to venture upon the application of it in such sense as to include along with *agreements*, *instruments of conveyance* of all sorts, and among them *wills*.

* Of the matters of fact to the recordation of which, for judicial purposes, as above described, the care of the legislator may with more or less use and advantage be directed, the following may serve as a pretty ample specimen: —

I. Facts of a nature to be regularly recurring: facts belonging each of them to a species, individuals of which are sure to be continually taking place:

1. Genealogical facts: 1. Deaths; 2. Births; 3. Marriages.
2. Arrivals at majority.
3. Declarations of insanity.
4. Declarations of dissolution of marriage, by any other cause than death.
5. Entrance into apprenticeship.
6. Dissolution of apprenticeship, by any other cause than death or expiration.
7. Entrance into partnership.
8. Dissolution of partnership, by whatever cause.
9. Entrance into official situation.
10. Exit from official situation, from whatever cause.

II. Facts having relation to Contracts.

1. Entrance into contracts: the fact of the entrance into, making of, or joining in the contract in each case.
2. Dissolution or modifications applied to contracts so entered into or made.

N. B. — The fact of the entrance into a contract of this or that sort, is, like these other facts, among the subject-matters of original recordation or registration. The contract itself, as expressed by a written instrument, is the subject of transcriptious registration.[a]

III. Facts of casual or incidental recurrence. These will generally be of a disastrous nature: and the main use capable of being derived from the registration of them, is by learning what can be learned of their causes, thereby either to reduce the number of casualties themselves, or the amount of mischief of which they are productive. Examples:

1. Deaths, in the production of which there appears ground for suspecting that culpable agency may have had a share.
2. Wrong; of which, whether to persons or things, the consequences are by permanence, or extent, or otherwise, rendered of a serious nature; — such as cases of mutilation, destruction, or forcible deterioration of houses and other works, public or private.
3. Calamities; such as inundation, conflagration, contagious disease, famine, or dearth.

---

[a] In England, out of twenty marriages registered, not so much as one perhaps that affords a marriage-settlement to register: nor is that subjected to registration but in two or three counties. Where there is no marriage-settlement, the terms of the contract are settled by the law: say rather, should be; for where are they to be found? what and where are the terms of which they are composed?

Births, marriages, and deaths, such (need it be said,) had the interest of justice been the objects, would have been the facts consigned to remembrance: unhappily, instead of these, the sinister interests of a church party militant and triumphant, having been the objects, the consequence has been, that to births, marriages, and deaths, have been substituted church-of-England baptism, church-of-England marriages, church-of-England burials. Of the great national family, members in countless numbers excluded from the benefit of such remembrance, as if those and those alone, whose lot had subjected them to the prejudices of a prevailing domineering party, were fit to be born, to marry, or to die.*

§ 6. *Contracts, and Instruments of Contract—Formalities, their use.*

Institution of apposite formalities; — provision made for the observance of these formalities: to one or other of these two heads will (it is supposed) be found referable whatsoever expedients may have been employed, or may be found capable of being employed with advantage, to the purpose of rendering preappointed evidence, in its application to contracts, subservient in the utmost possible degree to its appropriate uses.

It may here be asked, what are the objects to which the observances thus exacted require to be directed?

To this it may be answered — 1. Securing the intended effect to such contracts as are not unfair: and thence to such instruments of contract as (the contracts themselves not being unfair) are genuine: genuine, that is, neither in the whole nor in any part spurious. 2. Preventing the formation or the effect of— at any rate, the intended effect of — such contracts as are unfair. Preventing the formation, or at any rate the intended undue effect of such instruments of contract as are in the whole or in any part spurious.

Meantime, how far, and for what reason is it desirable, that the formation or intended effect of an unfair contract, — that the formation or intended effect of a spurious instrument of contract — should be prevented? Answer—according to the principle of utility, so far and so far only as the giving to it such its intended effect would to a preponderant amount be productive of mischievous consequences — for this reason, and for this reason only, that to such preponderant amount it would be productive of such consequences.

Under all systems of law, in so far as the principle of utility has been taken for the guide, *unfairness* on the part of the contract itself — *spuriousness* on the part of an alleged instrument of contract — have been regarded as conclusive evidence of such preponderant mischievousness. Regarded, and assuredly by no means without reason: always understood, that if, in any case, and in any particular, either in the instance of an unfair contract, or in the instance of a spurious instrument of contract, in the event of its being carried into effect, the balance would, upon the whole — the aggregate interest of the whole community being taken into the account — be on the side—not of mischief, but of advantage; this being supposed, no sufficient reason for refusing to give effect to it would have place: on the contrary, the reason for giving effect to it would, by the supposition, predominate or stand alone.

As to mischievousness, it is, however, only in so far as unfairness and spuriousness are considered as sufficient evidences of it, that, in the case of a contract, the consideration of it belongs to the present purpose. *Formalities* in some shape or other being scarcely so much as in idea altogether separable from the idea of a contract, hence it is, that the consideration of contracts, considered as subject-matters of recordation, involves in it of necessity the consideration of formalities: and it is only to the prevention of unfairness and spuriousness, and thence, and thus far only, to the prevention of mischievous effects, considered as liable to take their rise in contracts, that *formalities*, in so far as in the institution of them the principle of utility has been taken for the guide, have been directed.

A contract may be termed *unfair*, in so far at it is the result of force or fraud: to the head of force may be referred not only physical force, but mental or (say) *psychological* force, viz. intimidation: to the head of *frauds*, not only fraudulent *discourse* or *deportment*, but fraudulent *reticence*.

To point out by what obstacles, in use or not yet in use, unfairness and spuriousness may with least inconvenience and greatest promise of success be opposed, is of the number of the tasks, the execution of which will be found attempted in the body of the work.

§ 7. *Contracts continued—Formalities, Means of enforcing Observance.*

Formalities of any given description being appointed, for securing observance to them, two appropriate species of instruments, natural and technical, present themselves. The instrument which in this case may be characterized by the epithet natural, is suspicion: that suspicion of unfairness or spuriousness which the non-observance of any such formalities, the observance of which presented itself as prescribed, or, though it were but recommended by the sanction of public authority, would, supposing them adequately notified, so naturally, not to say so necessarily, excite.

For designating the natural instrument for securing observance to the formalities at-

* This absurdity has been put an end to by the registration acts 6 & 7 W. IV. c. 85 and 86.

tached to contracts, we have the word *suspicion:* for the technical instrument, one other word suffices, viz. *nullification.*

As to nullification, if it were possible seriously to consider the use made of this device as having ever had justice for its object, it would be on the ground already indicated, viz. that of a persuasion inferring *unfairness*, or spuriousness, from the non-observance of this or that one of a set of formalities that had been imposed. But, as to any such persuasion, be it or be it not entertained by men at large, it is certain that cases are not wanting in which it cannot have been entertained by those men of law, by whose power or influence on the alleged ground of the non-observance of this or that formality the contract in question has been rescinded. Why? Because, for the non-observance of that formality (in regard to which, effectual care had been taken to keep it from the knowledge perhaps of all mankind — at any rate, of the vast majority of those who were doomed to sufferance in the event of their not knowing it,) the self-same instrument, the same last will, must, upon this supposition, be deemed to have been either unfair or spurious, and at the same time neither unfair nor spurious:— neither unfair nor spurious as to the bequest of a horse; unfair or spurious as to a bequest of the field in which it feeds.

All this while, in this same case of a last will, under the notion of *favour*, the observance of these formalities has, in the instances where the testator is a person of this or that description, been dispensed with: as if it were a favour done to a man to enable an impostor to dispose of his property in his name! — as if the exception could be beneficial, unless the rule were mischievous!*

Useless or unjust in every case — either the one or the other—such is the only alternative useless, when there exists adequate reason for imputing unfairness or spuriousness; repugnant to justice, where no such reason is to be found.

In every such act of nullification, an act of perfidy and treachery is involved. That which men in general are suffered to understand,— that which no man can avoid understanding, viz. that in virtue of a general rule or habit, a contract, on the supposition of its not containing matter particularly objectionable, will eventually, at the hands of the judge, receive the force of law,—that which is kept all along hidden in the breast of the judge, is—that on this or that one of a string of pretences of which there is no end, and of which the party cannot by any possibility have any knowledge, until, to his dismay and destruction, it is brought forth out of that its hiding-place, by a decree framed for the purpose, by and for the profit of the judge, the faith thus plighted by the sovereign will be broken at pleasure.

To make men suffer for not knowing, and to keep them from the possibility of knowing, are operations that have all along gone hand in hand — that have all along been pursued with equal solicitude and success — by the manufacturers of unwritten, alias *judge-made* law. Of whatsoever goes by the name of *unwritten law*, it is the essence to be uncognoscible.

In a sort of paper, of which, under the general name of promulgation-paper, mention has been made in another work, instruments of contract would find, each of them, in a margin of letter-press, either *in terminis* or in the way of reference—either at length, or in abridgment, as circumstances might admit and require — a designation of every portion of the matter of law that would be found to bear upon a contract of the sort of those, to the reception of which the sort of paper in question stood allotted.

Thus much for notification. Unfortunately, as it is with everything else, so it is with a law: — before it can be made known, it must have been brought into existence.†

* Applied whether to instruments of contract, or to instruments and operations of judicial procedure (for, in both these wide extending departments of the field of law, this engine of iniquity is played off with the most pernicious wantonness,) the principle and practice of nullification may be seen involving in its texture two abominations, viz. *ex post facto* law and vicarious punishment, each of them in the utmost possible degree hostile to the ends of justice. For non-observance of an article of imaginary law, which not having been so much as imagined by the pseudo legislator (I mean the judge who in this way takes upon him the exercise of legislative power,) could still less have been present to the mind of the subject who is thus dealt with. In the first place, suffering, having the effect of punishment, is produced where no possibility of avoiding it had been allowed; — in the next place, the person on whom it is inflicted is not the law adviser, whose fault, had there been any, the non-observance would have been, — but the client so advised.

Had the principle of nullification been anything better than a disguised instrument of corruption and depredation in the hands that worked with it, two conditions would uniformly have been attached to the application of it: 1. Observance in the power of the individual on whom the burthen of the formality is imposed; 2. Obligation of observance, and penal consequence of non-observance, adequately notified: — Existence of adequate power; existence of necessary knowledge.

† To exemplify the use of this promulgation-paper, take, for example, that species of contract which has place in the case of *marriage*. In the character of an instrument provided for the giving expression to this most important of all contracts, what is it that the law has furnished? A mass of vague generalities, from which everything capable of affording to the parties any useful information, applicable to the direction of their conduct in the state into which they are about to enter, are carefully, and as if it were religiously

§ 8. *Of Wills.*

Wills, in the largest sense of the word contract — a particular species of contract — require, in several respects, a particular consideration.

That, of the allowance so generally, though not universally, given to dispositions of this description,* the effects are upon the whole beneficial to society, is a position which, however true and important, belongs not properly to the subject of this work.

That, in regard to this species of disposition, the powers of creation and alteration should, at least as to a considerable portion of his property, be not only imparted to the proprietor, but continued to him to the last moment of his life, is at the same time a position not altogether foreign to the subject of this work. Why? Because, according as it *is* or *is not* thus continued, difference in respect of the formalities will necessarily have place.

By the law of Scotland, what are there called *death-bed wills* (of which sort are the English wills) are not allowed.† A *will* is thereby put upon the footing of an ordinary deed — of what, in the language of English law, would be called a deed — a revocable deed of settlement.

Deprived of the power of making a deathbed will, a man is left exposed to ill-usage — unpunishable ill-usage — at the hands of those in whose favour a registered deed of settlement has been made; — he is at the same time deprived of the benefit of employing this power in the purchase of human service in a variety of shapes, on any of which the preservation of life may depend.

excluded: religiously, as if nothing could be made sacred to religion without being rendered useless to justice.

On the promulgation-paper, with the addition of a few forms of interrogation, by the answers to which the legal aptitude or inaptitude of the parties for the state in question might be established, we might find a useful addition at least, if not a substitute, for the present marriage-rite, in an account of the duties arising from this state, if the Median and Persian laws of a church, which, though not infallible, is incapable of being either instructed or deceived, allowed a substitute.

In this case we have an example, in which, for the securing of veracity to the evidence so extracted, nullification might be employed without imputation or danger of injustice. By the prospect of nullification, supposing detection in any degree probable, mendacity on one side at least would be deprived of its object and its use. Those inconveniences would be seen impending, in the avoidance of which, the contract finds its only use and end.

* Viz. dispositions so ordered as not to take effect till after the death of the disposer, and in the meantime revocable at pleasure.

† The law of Scotland only gives the heir-at-law a right to set aside a deed affecting the *real property* to his prejudice, if executed on his deathbed. — *Ed.*

From these, with or without the addition of other considerations, a conclusion is drawn in favour of the allowance given to *death-bed* wills.

On an occasion on which a man may by infirmity be placed in a state of such absolute dependence on those by whom the access to his person may, at their pleasure, be unavoidably engrossed, the importance, and at the same time difficulty, of preserving freedom to the exercise of this power, is not unobvious. Subservient to this object will be found (it is supposed) the following rule: — Whatsoever formalities are appointed for deeds, — for instruments of contract at large, — let the departure from them be as undiscernible as possible in the case of wills: to the end that when a man is executing a *will*, it may not be known but that it is some *deed* or other which, were he to survive, would still be necessary to the ordering of his affairs.

Accordingly—for example, in respect of the *number* of attesting witnesses required for an instrument executed in regular form—let the *number* be the same in one case as the other.

On this momentous occasion, amidst a confederacy of interested witnesses, circumstances may throw in a man's way an opportunity for obtaining one faithful assistant, without more, or by stealth two assistants, one after another, though not at the same time. For this reason, on the part of attesting witnesses, let conjunct presence be *recommended*, rather than *required*.‡

To the case of *wills*, applies, in a more especial manner, the above-mentioned principle, which recommends the giving to the non-observance of formalities the effect of a ground of *suspicion* only, and not of peremptory nullification.

On this principle is grounded the distinction between what may be termed a *regular* will, and what may be termed a *will of necessity*.

A *regular will* will be that, in the framing and execution of which, all the desirable, and thence authentically recommended formalities, have been observed. A will in which any of those formalities has failed of being observed, will, if deemed fair and genuine, be deemed such in the character of *a will of necessity;* non-observance, in so far as it has

‡ Under English law, to a *deed* at large, no attesting witness is requisite; two is the number customarily employed.

In a *will*, for dispositions made of what is called *personal estate*, no witness at all has been rendered necessary: for dispositions made of what is called *real estate*, three witnesses have been made necessary.[a]

N. B. Between personal and real, the distinction is verbal only; since, in either way, an interest of the same value in the same subject-matter may be created and conferred.

[a] Two witnesses are now made necessary in both cases, by the statute of wills, 1 Vic. ch. 26, § 9.

place, being considered as having had for its cause, either want of power to comply with the formalities, or want of knowledge of the existence of the provision of law, by which the observance stands recommended.

Should the day ever arrive, in which the peace, security, and comfort of individuals and families, will have been taken for the objects to which, in this part of the field of law, the labours of the legislator have been directed — should he ever desire that law may be employed in any better character than that of a snare, in which the prey may be caught by and for the benefit of the fowler, then, for the first time, it will have occurred to that trustee of the people, that to call in *wisdom* to the aid of *power*, is neither beneath his dignity, nor foreign to his duty.

In addition to the display of the *imperative* dispositions of the law, the margin or back of the *promulgation-paper* designed for wills will in that case contain a set of *mementos* and *instructions* from the legislator to testators.

For conveying a general conception of the nature of the contents, the following examples may serve:—

1. A view of the different *exigences*, by which a demand for the exercise of this power will be apt to be created. These exigences will have their rise, partly in the nature and situation of a man's property; partly in the situation and condition of life of those who, on the occasion in question, may in general custom, or particular circumstances, find a more or less natural and reasonable ground, for the expectation of being admitted to share in it. This for the guidance of a *first will*.

2. A view of the *alterations*, the propriety of which may come to be indicated by the changes liable to take place in the condition of individuals and families. In the testator's own instance, — marriage, for example, or widowhood: in the instance of the natural objects of his care, birth, marriage, or death: in regard to the general mass of his property, considerable increase or diminution in the qualities or the subject-matters of it — change, for example, from moveable to immoveable, or *vice versa*.

3. In respect of *formalities*, indicative of those which, in the character of safeguards against *unfairness* and *spuriousness*, have been thought fit to be *recommended:* warning that, from the omission, or material misapplication of them in any instance, suspicion will be apt to arise.

4. For the more effectual security in respect of apt and adequate *expression*, recommendation to call in some fit person in the character of a notary: if pecuniary circumstances admit, a professional assistant: if not, under the denomination of *an honorary notary*, a neighbouring magistrate, clergyman, or schoolmaster.

5. Indication, of the natural security for, and pledge of *fairness* as well as *genuineness* afforded by *autography*.* Recommendation to employ it, unless prevented by want of skill, power, or opportunity. Instructions how to perform it in such manner as to maximize the difficulty of successful falsification, and afford reason for concluding that it has not been attempted.

6. To the designation of the *time* recommendation to add that of the place at which the instrument is attested, or the places, if more than one, at which so many successive acts of writing have been performed: the place, viz. the very house, according to a mode of designation exhibited for the purpose. By the designation of the place, a security is afforded not only against unfairness and spuriousness, but, in the case of a fair and genuine *will*, a clew for the eventual tracing out of attesting witnesses.

7. Suggestions respecting the choice of attesting witnesses. Instructions respecting the mode to be employed for the designation of each person, with a view to the facility of his eventual forthcomingness while living, and when dead, the facility of establishing the fact of his death.

8. Instructions for questions to be put, and other suggestions to be made, by the notary, professional or honorary, with a view to *prudential* and *provident* disposition, as well as fairness and genuineness.

9. Obligation on the notary, professional or honorary, to annex his name, in such his character, adding to it an adequate designation of his condition in life, and abode. By this, salutary responsibility would be fixed; which at present, unless by accident, has no place. *N.B.* The use of this formality is not confined to *wills:* it has place alike, it will be seen, in the case of *deeds*.

For any provision respecting *orally*-delivered wills, — as the art of writing spreads, there will be less and less use: but that they will ever be altogether out of use, is more than the legislator could at present, if ever, with propriety, take upon himself to conclude.†

* In the language of French law, *testament olographe* is a *will* written *the whole* of it by the testator's own hand.

† In what is called the *statute of frauds* — (a denomination not altogether inappropriate) — a desire is expressed that wills delivered, or supposed to have been delivered, in this evanescent form, should be committed to writing; and to give effect to what is desired, here as elsewhere, *nullification*, the favourite engine, is employed. In regard to fairness and genuineness — more particularly genuineness, — what in this case is the security afforded, what the provision made? Not any: no: — whatever title the instrument may have to these qualities, is left to the joint charge of fraud and fortune.[a] Should

[a] A paper writing purporting to exhibit, in tenor

CHAPTER XV.

DIFFERENCE BETWEEN PREAPPOINTED AND UNPREAPPOINTED EVIDENCE.

§ 1. *The Difference developed.*

IN the case of preappointed evidence, —as also with a view to preappointed evidence in the case of evidence not preappointed but judicially delivered,—language has obtained, which having been produced by indistinct or erroneous conception, has in its turn, as will always be the case, served as an instrument for the preservation of the confusion or error in which it took its rise.

In the endeavour to substitute, on this part of the field of law, distinct expression and conception to indistinct — correct to incorrect, a few lines, or even a few pages, may not, it is hoped, be altogether misemployed.

Since writing has come into general use, all evidence to which the epithet preappointed is applicable is scriptitious:* — but it is not all scriptitious evidence that comes under the denomination of preappointed.

The use of preappointed scriptitious evidence is, to be in readiness to be eventually applied to a judicial purpose: and thereby (in case of a suit or cause with relation to which the matter of it may be capable of being employed in the character of evidence) to be employed accordingly on the occasion of such suit or cause: — this is its judicial use; or, what is much better, by presenting beforehand, to the view of all parties concerned, what, in the event of the institution of any such suit or cause, will be the result of it, — to prevent the commencement of a series of operations both vexatious and undesirable.

In every case in which, on the occasion of a suit at law, in the character of judicially delivered evidence, destined to serve, or help to serve, as a ground for the judgment or decision expected to be pronounced, any article of preappointed evidence is employed: the moment at which this instrument is brought for the first time into existence, is of course, and of necessity, anterior to the moment at which it is thus delivered and exhibited.

Of evidence constructed in this shape, the use, or at least one great use, depends upon this anteriority in point of time; that is, to speak more precisely, the utility of it, is, *cæteris paribus*, inversely as the distance between the point of time at which the perception in question took place, and the point of time at which it happens to it to be thus recorded: *cæteris paribus*, the possibility of incorrectness and incompleteness on the part of the picture presented of any perception or set of perceptions by the memory, being directly as the length of time between the instant of perception, and the instant of the formation of such picture.

On whatsoever occasion, therefore, an article of preappointed evidence is exhibited in the character of an article of judicially-delivered and received evidence, so it is that, as to what concerns those perceptions which it is employed to commemorate, the distance between the instant of perception and the instant of scription will be less than the distance between the instant of perception and the instant of exhibition, as above.

This being the case, generally speaking, the time or date of preappointed evidence will be anterior to the time or date of judicially-delivered evidence; that is, in the instance of every article of preappointed evidence exhibited in the character of judicially-delivered evidence, its formation will be earlier than its exhibition in that same character.

But if the date of the instant of judicial delivery of an article of evidence, in one suit or cause, be compared with the date of the instant of scription in the case of an article of preappointed evidence in another cause —

Should it ever be thought proper to take the business out of such hands, this seems to be among the occasions on which, by the ministry of the *honorary* sort of *notary* as above described, acting under directions and instructions from the legislator, and under the check of a certain degree of publicity in the character of *evidence-educting* judge, no inconsiderable service might thus, it is supposed, be rendered to truth, probity, and justice.

* Of the species of official person, styled *a remembrancer*, the denomination seems to have reference to a state of things, in which a demand for remembrance was presented by legally operative matter, in a quantity greater than that which the obtainable quantity of scriptitious talent was adequate to the recordation of.

The national official establishment contains an official person thus denominated, viz. the Remembrancer of the Exchequer; the official establishment of the metropolis another. In both instances, the office is of such very remote antiquity, that the origin of it seems to have been lost in the depths of time.

---

tenor or in substance, certain supposed orally-delivered death-bed dispositions, supposed to have been made by a person whose death took place (say) within the time limited by the law: — this instrument, with or without a signature recognising it as having been penned by the individual whose signature it is, is produced by somebody — by anybody. At what *time*, in what *place*, at *whose instance*, was it thus penned?—in the presence of any and what other person or persons were the particulars delivered by the supposed testator? Is this the only instrument which in this same character has been drawn up? By different persons may not different ones have been drawn up?—by different persons, or even at different times by the same person, according as, in the character of a bidder, one supposed legatee or another has been looked to as likely to afford the most advantageous terms? So many inlets to fraud, and not so much as the slightest fence attempted to be set up by the wisdom of the law!

and in both instances the instant of perception be taken for the point up to which you measure, — what may very well happen is — that, in the case of the judicially-delivered evidence, the interval shall be shorter than in the case of the pre-appointed evidence; — in the case of the preappointed evidence, the interval shall be longer than in the case of the judicially-delivered evidence.

In regard to scripts, there are some cases in which the length of time between the moment of perception and the moment of scription, may be considered as equal to 0: there are others in which it is capable of running out to an indefinite magnitude.

Cases in which it is equal to 0, in which the moment of perception and the moment of scription, or commemorative recordation, coincide, are the following: —

1. Among instruments of contract, all diversilateral ones. For, considering that the transaction is not regarded as perfected till the moment of the act of *recognition*, in the inexpressive language of English law, *delivery*, this is the moment at which not merely the expression thus given to the concurrent and united will of the several parties, but even the ultimate formation of the perception or psychological act so denominated, may be considered as having place.

2. Among instruments of contract, the particular species of instrument called a last will or testament.

In so far as the hand by which it was written happens to have been a hand other than that of the disposing party, the testator — the time of recognition presents a point of time no less determinate than in the last-mentioned case. In so far as it is the hand of the testator himself, supposing it known at what precise point of time the part in question was written, the time of recognition would in this case be as determinate as in the other case. But when, the instrument being as above autographous throughout, bearing no date, or being written different parts of it at different times, bearing dates in numbers smaller than the number of those times, — thus far, to the length of the interval in question there are no determinate limits.

In this respect, the sort of evidence for the designation of which the term *ex parte* preappointed evidence has above been employed, stands next to preappointed in respect of exactness and constancy of coincidence. Between these two, the line of separation is not indeed in every part a very clear one: in particular, in the case of that branch of *ex parte* preappointed evidence which consists of mercantile correspondence. To a bill of exchange or a promissory-note of hand, though both but unilateral, the appellation of an article of preappointed evidence can no more be refused than to a common bond for the payment of money, which itself is but unilateral: and between an order for the payment of money, such as is a bill of exchange or a draft upon a banker, and an order for the delivery of goods addressed and sent in the form of a letter by one mercantile man to another, the difference is not always a very explicit one. The person to whom it is addressed, — does he or does he not stand bound to compliance? On this point it is that the question seems to turn: and this is a matter concerning which it will not, in every case, be found easy to speak with any well-grounded assurance.

In the case of preappointed evidence, and that of an obligatory nature, whether mutually appointed or but *ex parte*, it is to the obligatory matter that the observation respecting the exact coincidence between the moment of perception or conception, and the moment of expression (in the case of expression in the scriptitious mode, the moment of scription,) is to be confined. In various sorts of instruments of contract — in various sorts of deeds, are commonly contained matters of recital — *recitals*, as the term is, viz. statements made of facts of various kinds, the recollection and consideration of which contributed, in the character of matter of inducement, towards giving birth to the will or act of power which, by the expression given to it in and by the discourse composing the matter of the instrument, is put in exercise. Every one of those facts must, to some person or persons, — parties to the instrument, strangers to the instrument, or of both descriptions — at one time or other have been the subject of perception — of perception entertained at a determinate moment: but, between that anterior moment and the moment of expression, the moment of scription, or more correctly, the moment of recognition, the moment in which the act of recognition was performed, the distance may have been of any length not greater than that of the field of history.

As to scripts at large, generally speaking, they will not afford any such exact coincidence: whether they do or not, will, at any rate, be matter of accident.

In the article of trustworthiness, or probative force, with relation to the matters of fact which they are respectively employed to commemorate, we see at present the superiority possessed by pre-appointed scriptitious evidence when judicially delivered in the character of judicial evidence, over judicially-delivered scriptitious evidence of every other description, for the fixation and conservation of which no such salutary instrument has been employed.

In the case of a diversilateral contract, and instrument of contract, there is, in the first place, the mutuality of declaration, the concurrence of persons acting under the influence of opposite interests in the expression given to, and the averment made of the same matter of fact, present in the most intimate manner to the perceptive faculties of each. In the next place, the coincidence (in point of time) between the moment of perception and the moment of enunciation, the discourse enunciated being at the same time committed to writing—this moment is that at which that operation is performed, by which the perception is placed, perhaps for ever, out of the reach of oblivion and misrepresentation. In the case of the unilateral contract and instrument, the source of superiority is confined to this last-mentioned circumstance.

§ 2. *Inconsistency and Confusion:* Anglicè *for want of a right conception of it.*

In the language in use among English lawyers, no such distinction is made as that between preappointed and other scriptitious evidence; — a mass of information brought into existence without a suit, without a view to any determinate suit — a mass of information brought into existence by a suit, and for the mere purpose of that suit; — both are spoken of without distinction, both are confounded under the common appellation of written evidence.

An instrument of contract, a deed, is written evidence: a mass of writing, in and by which expression is given to statements made by a man on a judicial occasion, in the character of a deposing witness, is written evidence.

Not that, in this last case, it is, in every one of the shapes in which it is capable of being presented, and is wont to be presented, denominated written evidence.

1. Delivered *ex interrogatu, uno flatu;*— in the epistolary form, at a distance from the interrogator, in the form of an uninterrupted string of statements, made in reply to an uninterrupted string of interrogations scriptitiously expressed and sent off in a mass; — delivered, in a word, in the form of the instrument called an answer to a bill in equity, it is written evidence.

2. Delivered in like manner *uno flatu*, but *absque interrogatu;* — delivered, in a word, in the affidavit shape, it is still written evidence.

3. Delivered in the shape of a succession of answers orally delivered in reply to a succession of interrogations administered in like manner by a present interrogator in the character of an evidence-collecting judge, these interrogations having been, at some indefinitely much anterior point of time, by the hand of a professional penman, scriptitiously expressed and formed into one unbroken mass, and by the hand, or under the eye of the evidence-collecting judge, the several responses committed to writing, and ranged each of them under the head of the interrogatory by which it was called forth; — delivered, in a word, in the shape of a mass of depositions exhibited on the occasion of, and in the course of a suit in equity, it is again, it is still, written evidence.

4. Delivered in the shape of a succession of answers orally delivered, in reply to a succession of interrogations administered in like manner, by this or that present interrogator in any one of a variety of characters, to which this power is imparted, — party, or advocate on one side; — party or advocate on the other side;—permanent judge, styled judge; — this or that one of a body of ephemeral judges styled jurymen; — the interrogatories extemporaneously uttered; — the responses uttered in like manner;—collected, and in a much more perfect state of correctness and completeness than in the last-mentioned case; — committed to writing by some note-taker or note-takers, employing or not employing the means of promptness of fixation, and thence of correctness and completeness afforded by the art of short-hand; it is not in this case, if the name of it be taken from these lawyers, written evidence; it is, in contradistinction to written, styled by them *parole* evidence, which is as much as to say, orally delivered evidence.

In cases to a vast extent, if in the form of what is called written evidence, expression has been given to an instrument of contract, — what is called parole evidence is not admitted in alteration, or so much as in explanation of it.

In cases to another great extent, a contract by howsoever great a number of witnesses proveable, is not so much as allowed to be valid, except in so far as, for the expression of it, a written instrument is employed constituting an article of evidence of that sort which is ranked under the head of written evidence.

At the same time, in this same scientific language, not only an answer to a bill in equity, but a mass of equity depositions, and even a mass of evidence in the affidavit shape, are so many articles of written evidence. According to the arrangement indicated by this nomenclature, — at least where the existence and particulars of a contract are the matter of fact in question, — the probative force of parole evidence, *i. e.* for example, testimony extemporaneously extracted, in an open judicatory, by the contending parties on both sides, or their advocates, by means of interrogation and counter-interrogation, should be inferior, not only to an answer in equity, and a mass of equity depositions, but even to a mass of evidence in the affidavit shape, and that to such a degree, as that, where it is supposed that evidence in either or any one of those three shapes is to be had, it is not on any terms fit to be admitted.

In comparison of, or in company with, what in these three forms is called written evidence, what is called parole evidence is so untrustworthy, that in lieu of, or in company with, these species of evidence respectively, it ought not (where these several evidences have for their subject-matter respectively, the sort of subject-matter here in question, viz. the existence or contents of a contract) to be so much as admitted: while, on almost every other occasion, by the universal acknowledgment of all lawyers, unless the ecclesiastical school afford an exception, those three species of what is called written evidence are, in point of probative force, decidedly inferior to the species of evidence called parole evidence.

By Gilbert, some time Lord Chief-baron, in his work on evidence, all evidence being divided into *written* and *unwritten*, an order of precedency in the line of trustworthiness is established; and to all that is *written*, above all that is unwritten, the upper hand is assigned. According to this order of things, such is its clearness and consistency, to the testimony of a given person, received in any of the three comparatively untrustworthy modes and shapes above mentioned, viz. *answer*, *deposition*, and even *affidavit*, the *precedence*, and along with it the *preference*, is given, over the testimony of the same person, extracted in the most trustworthy of all modes and shapes, interrogation checked by counter-interrogation, both administered *vivâ voce*, and employed in the extraction of impromptuary answers. These responses—does it happen to them to be committed to writing, and set down word for word as they came forth? No matter: *written* they *may be* in an *unlearned* sense — *written* they are not in a *learned* and *legal* sense: they belong not to the class of evidence to the designation of which the appellation of *written* has been consecrated and confined by learned and reverend hands.

Dissatisfied with *answers* — sensible of the comparative unfitness of evidence in this shape, to the purpose of depicturing the transaction in question by any representation to which, with any tolerably well-grounded confidence, the associated attributes of correctness and completeness can be applied—the learned manufacturer of equity, sitting in the character of Lord High Chancellor, *directs an issue*.

Dissatisfied with *depositions* — and with at least equal reason — sitting as the same High Chancellor, he again *directs an issue*. Dissatisfied with *affidavit evidence* — and with so much greater reason — sitting in his character of judge in matters of bankruptcy, and in that character receiving petitions and deciding upon them on no other ground than that of evidence delivered in this most untrustworthy, this most palpaply unfit shape, on every disputed occasion, he once more *directs an issue; i. e.* directs that the question of fact shall, under the direction of a judge, be decided upon by a jury, in the course of a fresh suit, a suit at common-law, which, conscious of his inability of coming at that truth on which the justice of all his acts and doings so indispensably depends, he forces those whose misfortune it is to be forced to come to him for what he calls relief, to commence and drag one another through the delays and justice-killing forms of.

Feeling every day the inferiority and unfitness of that which, from the grand masters of this branch of science, he has learnt to call the *superior* evidence; — dissatisfied on this and that particular, as if there existed an occasion on which he ought to be satisfied with this essentially unsatisfactory evidence, at an expense to the parties, at the thoughts of which he himself is continually acknowledging himself to be terrified, he calls for that which, in spite of learned theory, he has found by constant experience to be in practice and reality the superior evidence.

In the case of contracts in general, whether diversilateral or unilateral, the promptitude or freshness of the act of commemoration—of the act by which the existence and particulars of the contract are placed out of the reach of oblivion and misrepresentation; and in the case of diversilateral contracts, the mutuality of the recognition — the ground afforded for the persuasion that the correctness and completeness of the picture given of the transaction by each, has been acknowledged by the others — these are the circumstances by which the preference given by these lawyers to what they have called written evidence (viz. in the case when so it is that they have bestowed upon it this preference) can alone, in so far as it has been given by them, be justified: these are the grounds on which, in so far as reason has had any share in the production of it, it appears really to have been built by them.

Of what has here been distinguished by the name of preappointed evidence, these are the characteristic properties; but of the various species of which is composed the heterogeneous mass of evidence which by them has been lumped together and confounded under the common appellation of written evidence, these are not the common properties: expressed at some undistinguished point of time or other, by the characters of which a mass of writing is composed,—this is the only property appertaining in common to their written evidence: and this is a property by which no species of evidence whatever is capable of being distinguished, since there exists not any individual article of evidence whatsoever, in which it may not happen to it to be found.

CHAPTER XVI.

PREAPPOINTED OFFICIAL EVIDENCE.

§ 1. *Transactions of offices at large, considered as subjects of Preappointed Evidence.*

EVERY office, in which written documents of any kind are kept, is a *repository*, and with few or no exceptions, more or less a *source* of preappointed evidence. In that character, service in some shape or other was in such situations rendered to the ends of government, while the art of applying permanent signs to the giving expression to ideas was most rare; and since the art of multiplying those signs in so indefinite a degree by the operations of the press has come into use, the field of preappointed evidence has thus received a degree of expansibility to which there are no bounds.

In this way, whatsoever is produced, is always so much better than nothing. But in the doing of it, — for the doing of it as correctly, completely, and usefully as possible, four points require to be attended to: —

1. What the *uses* are to which such evidence as may be found derivable from these sources may be capable of being rendered subservient; 2. On what principles a just *estimate* may be formed of its *trustworthiness* and *probative* force; 3. By what means its trustworthiness may be most effectually perfected and secured; 4. By what means, in so far as it is useful, and its uses not outweighed by preponderant inconvenience, the quantity of it may be most extensively increased.

I. Uses of official evidence. Direct and collateral; — under one or other of these two heads, may be placed, it is supposed whatever uses such evidence can be made subservient to.

To the head of its *direct* uses, may be referred all such as either the chief manager or managers in the office itself that is in question, or any persons that have dealings with it, whether in the character of private individuals, or in the character of public functionaries belonging to any other offices, standing whether in a superordinate, co-ordinate, or subordinate capacity, in relation to it, may in the course of those dealings be enabled to derive from it.

To the head of *collateral* uses, may be referred, in the first place, the *judicial* uses, viz. any which, on the occasion of a cause or suit, it may be found applicable to in the hands of a judge, acting as such. In the next place, the *statistic* uses, — such uses as it may be found applicable to in the hands of the legislator, acting as such; and which, under this same name, have been already mentioned.

To the head of its *judicial* uses, besides such as are casual and miscellaneous, may be referred, that of affording eventual documents for the *eventual indication*, demonstration, and thence, in a more or less considerable degree, the actual prevention of any such transgressions, of which the office itself is, by the nature of the business carried on in it, rendered liable to become *the source*, or at least *the scene*.

2. Trustworthiness of official evidence, how to estimate. For the purpose of forming, on any occasion, an estimate of the trustworthiness of official evidence, the following considerations may perhaps be found not altogether without use: —

Pre-eminent responsibility — viz. in what may be termed the beneficial* sense of the word *responsibility* — pre-eminent responsibility and *presumable impartiality, i. e.* exemption from the action of sinister interest: — these, with or without the addition of presumable superordinary moral and intellectual culture, may be mentioned as being, in a situation of the sort in question, the principal efficient causes of *pre-eminent testimonial trustworthiness.*

Such being, in the sort of situation in question, the causes from the operation of which testimonial trustworthiness may naturally be expected to receive increase, neither should those circumstances, if any such there be, which present themselves as operating in relation to that quality, in the character of *drawbacks*, be overlooked.

Whilst, in the beneficial sense of the word, responsibility, as above, in the sort of elevated situation in question, is naturally raised more or less *above* the ordinary pitch, in the *burthensome* sense by which alone it operates as a security for such trustworthiness, it is apt to be depressed *below* the ordinary pitch. Though in the situation in question a man has more to lose, he is less in danger of being made to lose: *magnitude* of eventual suffering is *increased*, *probability* is *diminished.*

By the extensiveness, by the intricacy, by the scientific nature of the business — by all or any of these causes, if there be delinquency to any extent, *detection*, to any such effect as that of producing general notoriety and consequent disrepute and *exposure*, may to any degree be rendered difficult and improbable,

* *Beneficial*, viz. the sense in which a man is considered as furnished and endowed with a correspondent quantity of the *matter of good*, and in respect thereof rendered *capable* of being, by means of eventual privation, subjected to a quantity of punishment greater than that to which a man less favoured by fortune stands exposed. By the *burthensome* sense of the same word, may be understood the sense in which, whether by the provision actually made in the way of punishment, or other burthensome obligation, or by the eventual probability of detection, a man is considered as being, with reference to this or that other person, or to persons in general, more likely to be subjected to any such burthen.

while in that same situation, if it be in a certain mode and degree elevated, exposure may take place, and still neither punishment, nor so much as disrepute, follow.

Junction of the official person in question with a set of colleagues, in the form of a *bench*, a *board*, an *assembly*, a *body corporate*. In this case, the above three drawbacks operating in the same or different degrees of force, may all of them be found combined. By the consolidated power and influence of the whole body, each member is secured from punishment; — by multiplicity and privacy, each is even screened from shame — shame not seeing which to fix upon.

By the irresponsibility of the superior officers on the bench, or at the board, joined to the abstruseness of the matter and the non-publicity of the facts, in like manner in the situation of individual and subordinate officers under the bench or the board, falsity being screened from detection, thence from punishment and from disrepute, the untrustworthiness incident to the superordinate situation may thus extend itself to the subordinate functionary, who, being supposed to be sufficiently well looked after by his superiors, is the less looked after by the public eye.

Of the pitch to which, by the operation of the above-mentioned causes, testimonial untrustworthiness, in the case of an official body, is capable of being screwed up, the evidentiary instruments of which, under the technical system of procedure, the great judicatures are the sources, afford an example no less melancholy than instructive.

In no instance, perhaps, in the compass of the same quantity of testimonial discourse, is mendacity found in so large a proportion as in that sort of composition, which, under the name of a record, on the occasion of every suit at common law, is, or at least ought to be made up, and that under the direction of English judges. Undistinguishable from the flood of mendacity and nonsense in which it is drowned, what little of truth there is in it, serves rather to increase than diminish the deceptious quality of the whole mass. Whilst sinister interest has made up the false tale, and irresistible power has pronounced it superior to contradiction,* effrontery has not scrupled to ascribe to it a degree of infallibility* vying with that which, under the gloom of more mysterious terms, has been claimed by falsehood and nonsense on other ground, and in other shapes.

In few, assuredly, if in any instances, can mendacity have been employed to more pernicious purposes, — if so it be, that to depredation, to denial of justice, to oppression, to confederacy with dishonesty on both sides of the cause — confederacy not the less efficient for being so successfully disguised — all practised by dint of irresistible judicial power — the epithet *pernicious* may without impropriety be applied.

By the indignation of that public at whose expense it has been practised, immorality in so galling a shape should naturally, it may have been expected, have been long ago driven off the stage. But, the only situation from which any peep behind the curtain is obtainable, having naturally and constantly been filled up by interested supporters, and the unlearned spectators having been to such a degree deluded as to have been made to look upon the vice as being subservient or even necessary to justice,—hence it is, that instead of *reproach*, the immorality has ever hitherto been, and need little fear the not continuing to be, covered with applause.

If in no other sort of official situation the same causes of irresponsibility, as opposed to responsibility in the burthensome sense, and thence of testimonial untrustworthiness, are to be seen combined and operating with such mighty force; yet in many another official situation, howsoever in *degree* the effect may be inferior, in *specie* it can scarcely fail to be the same.

Sinister interest absent — thence impartiality perfect, — intellectual qualification competent — the information drawn immediately from the *source*, *i. e.* from the very seat of perception, and by the united power of the several securities for correctness and completeness extracted in the best shape, — these are so many requisites, the concurrence of which is necessary to the composition of a certain degree of testimonial trustworthiness out of office, it will scarcely be less necessary in office.

In the case of official evidence, so far as concerns that occasional use (which has above been distinguished by the name of the judicial,) not merely an ordinary, but rather a superordinary degree of testimonial trustworthiness, is, it must be acknowledged, the natural state of things. But, though most frequently, it cannot with any reason be expected to have place in every instance: and the error would be a mischievous one, if because, in ninety-nine instances, the application of those securities be *not* necessary to justice, in the hundredth, in which it *is* necessary, it were to stand prohibited.

The official recordator or deponent, has he anything to gain by misrepresentation? If yes, then so it is, that for the reason above brought to view, his statement is less trustworthy than that of an individual not in office, whose character is unknown.

So far as concerns official transgression in every shape, on the part of any official person belonging to the office, — so far, in the character of evidence, whether for the use of

* Gilbert on Evidence.

the administration-in-chief, or for the use of the judge, an official instrument or entry seems less likely to be impartial, and in so far less trustworthy, than a statement made by a person at large.

3. *Trustworthiness in official evidence — how to secure it.* — Included in the faculty of making the most effectual provision, in the best manner, for securing, in an official as in any other situation, the quality of trustworthiness to evidence, is that of forming a just estimate of the degree of trustworthiness actually appertaining to any given lot or article of such evidence.

In the following practical rules, an attempt is made to compass both those objects — the one of them through the other: —

Rule 1. In official as in other evidence, look out for the causes of inferiority or infirmity that apply, as above, to evidence at large; — viz. 1. Whether the matter of fact attested be not the principal matter of fact itself, but another considered as evidentiary of it; — in other words, the evidence not *direct* but *circumstantial;* 2. If the information there given be not original, note in this case, as well the nature and position as the number of the *media* interposed; 3. If original, note if not scrutinized or not interrogated; 4. Observe the trustworthiness of the witness or witnesses in question, viz. whether supposed percipient, directly reporting, or intermediately reporting, also if such trustworthiness be diminished, viz. by sinister interest, or by intellectual inaptitude absolute or relative.

Rule 2. If among the facts spoken to by the document, there be any, by the belief or disbelief of which, the interest of him under whose direction it is written may in any way be affected, — in this case, so far as depends upon impartiality, superiority of trustworthiness has no place, — inferiority rather.

Rule 3. On a judicial occasion, for avoidance of delay, vexation, and expense, official ready-written evidence may, though unsanctioned and uninterrogated, — or even a sufficiently authenticated transcript of it, — be in general received in that state; which is as much as to say, it may be considered as possessing the sort and degree of provisional trustworthiness sufficient for that purpose.

Rule 4. But if, on any of the grounds above mentioned, reason appear for suspecting it of deceptious incorrectness or incompleteness, the corresponding securities employed in other cases for perfecting and securing testimonial trustworthiness, ought not to be withholden in this case.

Rule 5. On the part of any party interested, the declaration of a desire to cause application to be made of those securities to the article of official evidence in question, ought to be considered as sufficient proof of the justness as well as of the existence of such suspicion; nor, except on the distinctly alleged ground of preponderant delay, vexation, and expense, ought it to be in the power of the judge to refuse it.

Rule 6. Although the trustworthiness of the individual in question be at the highest pitch, yet, for the purpose of relative completeness as well as correctness, interrogation may be not the less necessary.

Rule 7. Though in the case of this or that sort of official document, the information furnished by it be in a greater or less proportion constantly false, yet by such falsity, the utility of it in the character of evidence will not be destroyed, if by application of the appropriate instruments of extraction, true information be obtainable by means of it: — just as, from the mouth of a necessarily mendaciously disposed examinee, — for example, in a criminal cause, a guilty defendant, — false information assists often in leading to the discovery of true.

Rule 8. For the use of the administrator-in-chief and the legislator, for securing the correctness and completeness of the statements relative to matters of fact, look out on each occasion for percipient witnesses in competent and convenient number, and by them or one of them let their names in that character be written upon the face of the document: if in the character of supervisors the names of any other persons, not being percipient witnesses, be inscribed, let them in like manner be inscribed by the parties themselves, distinguishing the character in which such their attestation is subjoined.

Rule 9. In the case of a transcript, in a determinate place at the bottom of each page, let the scribe write his name, with the year, month, and day, and the word *scripsit,* or some word of the like import, at the end of it; and so if to the same page there be more dates or more scribes than one.

By this means, each scribe will be rendered responsible for the correctness of his script, and the quantity of service rendered by each will, upon occasion, be exactly visible.

Rule 10. In cases where, on a particular occasion, order for the writing of a script is given by this or that official person in particular; for fixing the responsibility upon that person, it may be of use that a designation of the person by whose order it was written should moreover be subjoined.

Rule 11. When, in case of error, correction is applied, let it be performed in such manner that the state of the script antecedently to the correction may still appear: — viz. in the case of omission, insert the omitted word in a place over the line, with a mark underneath: in case of redundancy, mark the redundancy by cancelling the word, but so as not to obliterate it: and in like manner, let substitution be performed by the cancelling of the one word, and the insertion of the other, as above.

In this way, without a direct and discoverable forgery, no alteration will be capable of being made to an unknown effect on an unknown occasion, by an unknown hand.

If the securing to evidence in general, in the most effectual manner, and in the highest practicable degree, the desirable properties of correctness and completeness, be a fit object of the legislator's care, — so in particular will it be in the case of official evidence — in the case of all such evidence of which in any line of public office official situation is either the repository or the source.

For securing correctness and completeness, or in one word, *trustworthiness*, to evidence in this instance, what then shall be the means employed in this case? The same as are employed in the instance of other evidence.

But official evidence, being the evidence of official men, has, in official men, found the persons by whom the task of adjusting the course to be taken in relation to it has been executed: and with them the main object has naturally been rather to cause it to be regarded as invested in the highest degree with the respectable qualities in question, than to cause it to be really possessed of them.

Accordingly, though in the character of original information, in addition to what has been said, and what remains to be said under this head in relation to evidence at large, anything that could be said in relation to official evidence in particular, might, not without reason, be regarded as repetition and superfluity; yet in the way of memento, at any rate, if such as has just been intimated be the natural propensity to turn aside from it, it may not be altogether without its use.

Between evidence at large, and official evidence, one material distinction requires in this place to be held up to notice. In the case of evidence at large, the public functionary for whose use — and, in this case, for whose use alone — it requires to be collected, is the judge; the use made of it by the judge is not merely the principal use, but the only use to which, except in the collateral way above spoken of, it is applicable.

In the case of official evidence, on the contrary, whatever use may come to be made of it by the judge is but occasional, accidental, collateral. The person, from its reference to whose service it derives its most direct, most important, and only constant use, is the chief ruler of the department or combination of offices in question.

In this case, and in this situation, the mass of evidence habitually furnished by any such office is neither more nor less than the produce of the system of *book-keeping* pursued in that same office.

This being the case, what are the ends to which a system of that sort, considered in the most general point of view, and with reference to offices in general, ought to be directed?

Upon a second glance, this question will be seen naturally to divide itself into two branches:—

1. What is the general description of the operations themselves, that in the situation in question are habitually carried on?

2. What are the means proper to be employed for furnishing at all times a correct and complete conception of what has been the nature and character of those operations?

1. Answer — to the first of these two questions. In each department, and each office of that department, the system of operations carried on ought to be such as promises to be conducive in the highest degree to the end or purpose for which the department or office was instituted, and from which is derived the warrant for the expense charged on the public by and for its maintenance and support.

2. Answer — to the second of these two questions. In each department, and in each office, the mode of book-keeping pursued should be such as is in the highest degree subservient to the following ends or purposes, viz. —

1. To afford, by permanent documents, for the use of all persons having need to be made acquainted with the business carried on in the office, as clear a conception as possible of the several operations actually performed in that same office.

2. To present to view, in as clear and instructive a manner as possible, the relation which, in the way of subserviency, each such operation bears to the common end or purpose of the office, including, on the one hand, the nature and value of the service rendered by it; on the other hand, the labour and expense by which that service is purchased.

3. As to what concerns the persons whose labour is employed in the performance of the several operations, — to present to view, in like manner, a conception of the manner and proportion in which their respective labours, supposing them applied in the manner and quantity expected and required by the rules and constitution of the office, contribute to the rendering of that aggregate mass of service; also, a conception of the degree of punctuality with which such their respective duties are fulfilled; — or, to speak more precisely, of the quantity by which their respective labours respectively fall short of the quantity so expected and required.

In a word: — 1. The merit and demerit of the system; 2. The merit and demerit of the several persons employed in the execution of it. Such, considered in the most general point of view, are the objects, to the display of which the system of book-keeping pursued in each department or office ought to be directed.

Considered upon the general principles of reason, so plainly obvious may these suggestions be apt to appear, that the number of them may be esteemed superfluous. Yes,—if they were as generally conformed to, as when considered in this point of view they appear obvious.

Unfortunately, their obviousness is not more conspicuous than, upon an inquiry into the actual state of things, the neglect of them will be found.

On every such occasion, custom, not rea[illegible] the standard referred to; by conformity or disconformity to which, the propriety of every act and operation is judged of and measured.

Why? Because by every deviation from custom—by every deviation by which the improvement of the business, and the more perfect fulfilment of the public end and purpose of the office is aimed at, the private and personal interest of a proportion, more or less considerable, of the persons belonging to the office, is injured: for even if, by the improvement or supposed improvement, no emolument lawful or unlawful, avowed or unavowed, would be taken from them or any of them, additional labour in some shape or other cannot fail to be imposed.

§ 2. *Transactions of Judicial Offices.*

Beside that which offices in general afford, judicial offices afford evidence of a sort peculiar to themselves.

That which, in a judicial office, is viewed *ab extra* under the name of evidence, is *ordinary*, not *preappointed* evidence. Of that which in this place calls for consideration under the name of *judicial official evidence*, or more shortly *judicial evidence*, that alone is *preappointed*, of which the office is not only the repository, but the source.

Instruments and *entries:* to one or other of these two heads will (it is supposed) be found referable the several constituent parts of the aggregate mass of this species of official evidence:—written instruments delivered in, and minutes or entries made of the several operations performed:—performed by the several actors in the judicial drama.

That which an instrument necessarily records and shows, is its own tenor, the date of it included:—those things which it does not of itself record,—are, the *fact* of its being delivered in, the *date* of the delivery, together with such other operations as may happen to be performed in relation to it.

From one and the same article of judicial official evidence may result, to so many different descriptions of persons, so many different uses:—I. To parties and their representatives, in respect of the suit on hand: of this sort are the uses which, in the present instance, fall under the denomination of the *direct uses:*—II. To persons at large, in respect of any future contingent suits, to the purpose of which, the same facts, or any of them, may require to be established: these may be considered as forming one branch of the *collateral uses:*—III. To the legislator, in the character of an eventual component part of that fund of information, the use of which is to serve as a basis for any such ulterior regulations, as from time to time may in his view promise to be conducive to the ends of justice:—and here may be seen another of the collateral uses of this species of evidence, viz. *statistic uses.*

I.—1. To form the ground for ulterior operations on the same or the opposite side;—2. To show whether the instrument or operation itself were proper or no, *i. e.* has been conformable to such rules as have been laid down for the composition or performance of it; 3. In case of impropriety, to afford a ground for the application of the matter of satisfaction or of punishment, or of both, according to the exigency of the case. Under this head seem cognizable the purposes to which, in the suit in question, the recordation of the instrument or operation promises to be necessary or subservient.

II. With regard to the future contingent suits of future contingent litigants, the best effect plainly is the prevention of their existence; the next best, the prevention as well of misdecision on the occasion of them, as of this or that avoidable portion of delay and vexation or expense to which they might otherwise have given rise.

Under the natural, under the tutelary system of procedure, the radical operation which at or near the outset, except in any such particular circumstances as may have rendered it physically or prudentially impracticable, will fall to be recorded, will of course be the appearance of both or all the parties, face to face, in the presence of the judge: thereupon the decision itself, viz. the final decision, or the circumstances which, creating a demand for delay, prevented for that time such decision from being pronounced.

Under the technical, under the predatory system—under the system which has had for its object and effect a too successfully disguised despotism, and under favour of it that aggregate of overpaid places and sinecures—that excessive and misapplied mass of emolument, of which the particulars, the services and the shapes, have elsewhere been displayed under this system of regulated pillage,* the

* 27th and 28th Finance Reports, 1787-8.

performance of that essential operation having, in pursuit of those sinister objects, been universally eluded, the ulterior operations to be recorded have been all such as, for the profit extracted from and by reasons of the delay, vexation, and expense, pretences have been found for necessitating — a series to the intricacy and perplexity of which there is no end.

III. Statistic uses — Uses to the legislator. — Neither have these been altogether overlooked. A synoptic sketch of them has been prepared. But of any suggestions to the legislator, the practical use depends upon the existence of a legislator—a legislator disposed to put them to use. And while by the blindness or patience of the uncorrupted portion of the people, the legislator is suffered to continue to take for the sole object of his labours on this part of the field of law, the preservation of those abuses, in the profit of which he has secured to himself so large a share, the indication of these uses may with little practical loss wait for a period much more remote than the completion of any such work as the present.

Meantime, in a succeeding chapter of this Introduction, a slight exemplification of them may be found.*

§ 3. *Of Laws considered as constituting the matter of Preappointed Evidence.*

Of laws, under any such heads as *registration formalities, genuineness, fairness,*—so far as by fairness is meant freedom from external violence, — nothing need here be said; — nothing that could be said would here be in its place: but under the head designated by the words *existence, knowledge of the inducements to observance, knowledge of the particulars to be observed,* thence, in a word, *possibility of observance,* analogy and consistency concur in forbidding, even in this abridgment, an altogether unbroken silence.

When, in token of adoption, and for the purpose of his being subjected to the obligations created by it, an instrument of *contract* is made to receive the signature of a party to it, unfairness, and not without reason, is apt to be imputed to the transaction, if adequate means of making himself at all times acquainted with the particulars of the obligations thus imposed upon him, had not been put into his hands. But if, in this case, by means of an act of adoption thus signified by the respective parties, the particular rules contained in and expressed by the individual instrument in question, acquire on this occasion, and now for the first time with reference to these particular parties and their legally connected representatives and other relatives, the force of law; — at that same time the general rules of law, under and by virtue of which, in consequence of the particular engagement thus entered into, the fate of the parties will be disposed of, and on which the whole of that engagement will have to depend, — must already be in possession of that same eventually binding force.

Be it an expression of private will, be it an expression of sovereign will, be it a discourse of any other kind,—for making himself more or less acquainted with their contents, a man has but two ways — to read them with his own eyes, to hear them with his own ears.

For reading or hearing read the *particular* rules just mentioned, possibility is *not* wanting: words have been found for the expression of them; these words exist, and existing, want nothing but to be read. For reading or being read those *general* rules, on which the effect of those particular rules so completely depends, possibility *is* wanting: words for the expression of them do *not exist:* words for the expression of them have been, and will continue to be, anxiously kept from existing: and words that exist not cannot be read.

In any domestic or private situation, in any other situation how public soever, of command, to the man who should expect to see his will conformed to, — to any such man, were he backward in giving expression to it, much more if, leaving it purposely unexpressed, he were to make effective provision for securing the infliction of suffering, under or without the name of punishment, — on every occasion on which such industriously concealed will failed of being conformed to, to any such man, not merely would wisdom be thought wanting, but sanity itself would be a questionable possession.

To the extent of a vast and indefinite portion of the field of law, so far from giving expression to his will in England, not to speak of other countries, the sovereign has not so much as set himself to form a will. But, instead of forming a will, and giving expression to it, what has he done? He has abandoned this part of his duty to a set of men, to whom, in the character and under the name of judges, his negligence, or his craft has left the power of doing what little is in such hands possible to be done towards supplying this deficiency — towards making amends for this failure. To these substitutes for executing this task with any tolerable degree of beneficial effect every requisite is, and ever must be, wanting—adequate knowledge, adequate motives, adequate power, — everything. The power, whatsoever it be, which by them is exercised, is power exercised, not as power exercised by the legislator is, over men and things in classes, but over individuals: over individuals, and in that form of tyranny which, with the character of tyranny stamped on the face of

* Chap. XXIII. *Safeguards.*

it, has become proverbial under the name of *ex post facto* law. Those general rules, from which alone it would have been in men's power to receive notice and to take warning, it being out of the power of these pseudo legislators to give birth to; every step taken by them in this course is marked by unlooked for suffering—suffering in some shape or other inflicted upon individuals to whom the means of escape have been denied:—every step they take is followed, if not by the exclamations, by the pangs of the afflicted, whose peace and comfort are thus offered up in sacrifice to high-seated and hard-hearted indolence.

In comparison of what it would be, if this first duty of the sovereign were not, by this grossest and most wide-stretching of all neglects, kept in a state of constant violation, the condition in which society is thus left, is as yet but a state of anarchy.

Till the collections of published histories of decisions, and thence of cases liable to call for decision, had attained a certain degree of copiousness and extent, the legislator (true it is) was not as yet furnished with the stock of materials necessary for such his work, — matters, in a word, were not ripe for it. But so long as this symptom of immaturity shall continue, government itself cannot as yet, with propriety, be said to be of full age: — the period of complete civilization cannot be said to be as yet arrived.

In the histories of future ages, that period will be dated — from what event? From the extirpation of the last remnant of that most voluminous and proportionably mischievous nonentity, which, with such perfect propriety in one sense, with such flagrant impropriety in another sense, calls itself *unwritten law.*

§ 4. *Of Debates in Legislative and other Political Assemblies in which Law is made.*

Of the subjects which present a demand for contemporaneous recordation, and which as yet have not received it at all, or if at all, no otherwise than from precariously existing instruments, and in a more or less imperfect state, it would be too much on the present occasion to attempt giving anything like a complete list.

By the all-comprehensiveness of their extent, two sets of legally operative facts, however, seem on the present occasion to present a claim for consideration, such as, even in a work having for its subject evidence considered in its most general point of view, cannot consistently remain altogether unsatisfied. These are—

1. Transactions of those assemblies, of the manifestation of whose will, law in the state of statute law is composed.

2. Transactions of those persons and assemblies, of the manifestation or supposed manifestation of whose will, the ideally existing, but too really governing, nonentity called common law is composed.

In regard to both these important collections of legally operative facts, three observations present themselves: —

1. That, of these several collections of facts, as correct and complete a representation as the nature of the case admits, ought regularly to be framed and published.

2. That no such representation is actually made.

3. That representations, more or less incorrect and incomplete, are habitually suffered to be framed and published, and are habitually, *i. e.* frequently, though not regularly, framed and published accordingly.

Such being the matter of fact, thereupon come two altogether natural, and in no small degree interesting questions: —

1. How happens it, that no system of correct and complete, and thence undeceptive, representation has hitherto been established?

2. How happens it, that the system or practice of incorrect and incomplete, and thence deceptive, representation has now for a considerable length of time had place?

For these two questions, separate as they are in themselves, one and the same answer may serve: that answer being applicable with little variation to both cases.

Under all governments, the external operations of the governors have been carried on under, have been determined by, the internal and conjoint operation of two antagonizing interests: — a public interest coincident with the interest of the governed, and a separate and comparatively private interest of their own, acting in opposition to that public one.

The conduct of each member of the governing body will, on each occasion, be determined by that one of the two, on which the circumstances of the time and the idiosyncrasy of the individual, taken together, have concurred in bestowing the greatest degree of operative force.

In general, in the state of things in England in respect of government, while the private and personal interest of the members is still far from being brought so near to a coincidence with their public interest, that is, with their duty, as it might be,—in case of conflict, real or apparent, between the two, except in so far as an exception is made by a time of great public danger, the private and separate interest is that which, in the bosom of each individual, will find itself in greatest force, and it is by this that his public conduct will be determined.*

* If, for example, the commencement or continuance of a war being the question upon the carpet, if, upon his calculation, a hundred a-year during the continuance of the war, or for ever, will be the amount of the contribution which according to his calculation he will have to pay,

Under a despotic government, this ascendency of separate over common, of private over public interest, finds nothing to counteract it: under a mixed government it finds a controverting power, an antagonizing and controuling principle, in the spirit of the people, operating with a force depending jointly on the share possessed by them in the government, and the degree of cultivation acquired by the public mind.

Under the English constitution, in so far as legislation and the exercise of supreme power is concerned, the governing body has two branches.

In each of them, except in so far as by correct and complete representation, reputation, and through reputation power, appears likely to be preserved or gained, it is the interest of each member that from correct and complete representation his speech and his vote should (as often, and in so far as it is likely to present itself to the public eye, as having been dictated by sinister interest as above described) stand as effectually protected and screened as possible.

In this view, the most favourable of all possible arrangments is that in which, being buried in utter and impenetrable darkness, as under the constitution of Venice, no representation at all is ever given of his discourse. From that point of perfection, the arrangement in relation to this head degenerates and falls off by numerous but difficultly distinguishable degrees, till it has sunk to that state of things in which, everything being represented exactly as it happened, every man (for in a political and deliberating assembly the only works are words) every man is by every other man judged of by his works.

At present, though in point of right, in so far as right is capable of being created by usage acting in opposition to manifest general interest, under the semblance and cloak of a representative body, of the members of which all are pretended to be, and some are really, deputed by the people they are said to represent, the country is governed by an oligarchy, in a proportion sufficient, could they agree among themselves, to substitute for the present constitution of England, the quondam constitution of Venice; — yet, on the othe hand, in point of prudence, things are come to that pass, that so to order matters, as that, of the discourses there held, no representation at all shall transpire is, generally speaking, reputed either physically, or if not physically, prudentially at least, impracticable.

This point being given up, what remains is, so to order matters as that such representations as transpire should be, if not as far from being actually correct and complete, yet as far from being capable of being fixed upon and referred to as being correct and complete, as possible.

To the members individually, from this state of things results this manifest and great advantage of the discourses respectively delivered by them: whatsoever parts are found or expected by them to be productive of general disapprobation, may be, howsoever falsely (falsehood being by this means protected from complete disproof,) denied and disowned; while, on the other hand, whatsoever is found or expected to be productive of a contrary effect, is capable of being pourtrayed, not simply in its own proper colours, but in others as highly flattering as ingenuity can produce.

(and if in his calculation not only the amount of his own share in the burthen, but the interest which in the way of sympathy he takes in the amount of such part of the burthen as will have to be borne by his private and particular connexions of all sorts be taken into the account,) if his expected profit by the war be equal to 0, and no particular gust of passion intervene, to drive him from the pursuit of what appears to be his lasting interest upon the whole, — he will be against the war, and what influence it may happen to him to possess, will be exerted on that side. But if, while to the amount of £100 a-year loss by war is calculated upon as probable, profit to the amount of £1000 a-year, accompanied by equal or correspondent probability, presents itself as about to be secured to him by the operation of the same cause, — the man being an average man, not particularly known to you, — no consideration can warrant, nor can anything but mere mental weakness produce in you any such expectation as that peace will find in him a real advocate, or that whether he himself be or be not aware of what passes within him, his conduct will have for its determining cause, anything but the balance of profit and loss above brought to view.

CHAPTER XVII.

EXTEMPORE RECORDATION, HOW APPLICABLE TO LEGALLY OPERATIVE FACTS AT LARGE.

§ 1. *Demand for Recordation thus applied.*

OBLIVION and misrepresentation are the disorders to which the matter of discourse stands exposed; against which the art of writing, and that alone, is capable of applying a specific remedy.

Take any fact whatsoever, — suppose it to be of the number of those to which the law (which, for the purpose of the argument, must itself be supposed to be of the number of those, of the knowledge of which the tendency is, upon the whole, of the beneficial cast) has given a capacity of legal operation, as above described, — misrepresentation and oblivion are *accidents* against which, by the supposition, it is desirable that the fact should be secured, viz. for and during the length of time, whatsoever it be, during which it is desirable that such capacity of legal operation should continue: since it is only in so far as these accidents are arrested, that the intended operation of the fact can continue to have place.

In so far as (in the nature of it) to the several parties, or to any of the parties whose interests are in any way liable to be affected, and by them known to be liable to be affected by its legal operation, the fact is, in the nature of it, an object of previous expectation, a natural as well as possible attendant circumstance is — that by the joint care of the whole number of persons, or at any rate of a part of that number, the arrangements, whatsoever they may be, which, in the state of society in question, are in use to be taken for the prevention of those accidents, will be made.

Thus it is, accordingly, in that case which, among those which present a demand for preappointed evidence, has already been mentioned as the case of principal importance, viz. the case where the matter of fact thus requiring to be observed is the existence of a legal contract, of a certain purport and tenor, made on a certain occasion, in virtue and execution of a legal power possessed by a person or persons certain to that effect. Whatsoever, on an occasion of that sort, is about to pass, being, if not by all parties eventually about to possess, by all parties actually possessing, in conjunction with apposite power, an immediate and determinate interest in the result intended, and in consequence foreseen and looked for,—what is natural and usual is, that the customary and appropriate arrangements adapted to the purpose of fixation and conservation as above, should accordingly with joint concurrence be made.

But among the facts which eventually become possessed of a legally operative virtue, there exist many in number, and in the aggregate stretching to an unlimited extent, in respect of which any such regular and universally agreed sort of provision as is here in question, is either in the nature of the case impracticable, or in point of fact has never hitherto been made. Here, then, in the field of duty, may be seen another path presenting itself to the view of a provident and diligent legislator.

Upon the degree of success with which the application of the instrument of fixation in question has (in the case of a legally operative fact of any kind) been attended, the result of the operation of that fact is not less completely, and still more immediately dependent, than upon the nature of the fact itself. In so far as the state of the case is such, that in the provision made for this most important collateral operation, so it is, that among the persons jointly but oppositely interested in the seeing it made, it happens to any one or more not to have actually taken a part in the making of those arrangements, in the instance of every such person in whose instance such circumstance has failed to have place, a possible cause of partiality, and thence of deceptious and injurious incorrectness and incompleteness in regard to the representation given of the matter of fact in question, cannot, it must be acknowledged, but have place.

Here, then, is one cause of misrepresentation and consequent deception, to the operation of which every system of arrangements that can be devised for extemporaneous recordation, cannot but remain exposed.

But if, for the securing of so important a result, no means at all be employed, the consequence is, that the fact will remain exposed to every possible cause of misrepresentation, including the particular cause just mentioned, viz. not only oblivion, but misrepresentation, in so far as it is to so high a degree apt to have place, in cases where design has had no part in the production of it.

The consequence being, that for the extemporaneous recordation of miscellaneous and casual legally operative facts, any system of recordation is better than no system at all: and thereupon what remains for consideration is — by what sort of shape a system of arrangements, having this object in view, may be most effectually adapted to its proper ends.

Even under the existing system of exclusion, the particular cases of exclusion contained in it excepted, no man, how great soever may be in reality his trustworthiness, is either excluded or exempted from officiating, when the time comes, in the character of a deposing witness. There is no man, therefore, in whose instance, at the very moment, or as near as possible to the very moment of perception, it is not manifestly of use, that in so far as prudentially as well as physically it may happen to be practicable, it will not be, for the purposes of truth and justice, desirable that this specific against misrepresentation as well as oblivion shall be employed.

Suppose the security in question not applied, the testimony of the individual in whose person, in the character of a percipient witness, the capacity has place, of furnishing direct evidence of the fact, in the character of deposing witness, continues, down to the very instant of deposition, exposed, and without any more safeguard at one time than another, to the influence of whatsoever causes of seduction, and consequent deceptious incorrectness and incompleteness, the situation and interior character of the witness stands exposed. Suppose this security applied, and the representation thus given of the fact exempt in any given degree from deceptious incorrectness and incompleteness, then, and in this case, from the moment the memorandum in question has been placed out of his power, any sinister interest by which he might be prompted to give any such subsequent representation of the matter as should in any degree be, in point of correctness and completeness, inferior to such antecedent representation, would find in it a manifestly formidable and probably victorious body of counter-evidence.

§ 2. *Principle on which a supply for this demand may be grounded.*

Happily, on this occasion, the legislator, if prepossession and bad habit will suffer him to avail himself of the means which offer themselves to his hands, will find his endeavours not ill seconded by the nature of the case.

Of every man by whom, with a view to any judicial purpose whatever, a mass of evidence is prepared, it is, or at least is thought by him to be, for his interest that such evidence should obtain credence: for without such persuasion the act thus performed by him would be without a motive—an effect without a cause.

The probability which the mass of evidence in question has of obtaining credence will be as the apparent and supposed trustworthiness of the person of whose testimony it is composed. Whosoever, therefore, is the sort of person who, by the person by or on whose account the evidence in question is in contemplation to be exhibited, is considered as likely to possess, in the scale of imputed trustworthiness, the highest place in the opinion of the judge, — he is the official person who, by the intended witness in question, supposing him to be known for such, is most likely to be employed.

These observations premised, taking therefore under review a number of official persons of different descriptions, such as in the existing state of society in question it happens to the official establishment to afford, let the legislator, in the instrument designed for the notification of his will in relation to this subject, set them down in an order declared by him to be the order of preference. This done, whosoever, without more vexation and expense, has it in his power to obtain this service of the official person whose name stands highest upon the list, will not, without some special reason or motive to the contrary, address himself to any person whose name stands lower upon that same list.

For the function of casual recorder (for by that name, it should seem, it may not unaptly be designated,) a justice of the peace, a member of the governing body in any corporate town, a minister of the established church — a minister of any dissenting congregation — a member of the financial establishment,—in a word, any person holding an office of any kind under the crown — a person exercising any branch of the medical profession — a person belonging to the profession of the law, in the character of either barrister, attorney, or student:—these may serve as examples of classes of persons, who, in respect of probable trustworthiness, intellectual aptitude, and aptitude on a moral account, consideration of pecuniary responsibility included, might in the list of the law be proposed for choice.

On this, as on all other occasions, substituting to the principle of nullification the principle of declaration of suspicion, the legislator may declare, that if of two persons, both open to a party's choice, the one who is manifestly the most fit be set aside, the one least fit employed in his stead, in the undue preference thus given, a natural and justifiable cause of suspicion will be observable: whilst in the mind of him, whosoever he may be, to whom, on the occasion in which the preappointed evidence thus recorded is produced, it happens to officiate in the character of judge, its probative force will naturally and properly undergo a proportionable diminution.

By persons in any number, none of whom have been the objects of such choice, should the same functions be undertaken and performed, no inconvenience, no confusion, no difficulty, will ensue. Under the principle of nullification, yes; — difficulties innumerable, infinite, and each of them insuperable: of all these extemporaneous registers, all but one would be to be pronounced void; one, and one alone, good: which shall it be?

By the law as it stands at present, of these persons, they being by the supposition all of them percipient witnesses — there is not one, how little soever trustworthy, who would not, in the event of litigation, be liable to be called upon to testify in the character of a deposing witness: but with this check upon intentional, as well as support against unintentional incorrectness and deceptious incompleteness (or in a word against misrepresentation,) be his trustworthiness ever so low in the scale, there is not one of them whose trustworthiness would not by this security be raised to a higher level than what it would otherwise occupy.

No doubt but that, under this arrangement, and notwithstanding this arrangement — say even in consequence of this arrangement — so it might be, that on this or that occasion, for this or that purpose, in the shape in question, the sort of preappointed evidence in question might be fabricated. But what if it were? Being by the supposition false, and in point of intention of a deceptious tendency, the being an object of suspicion is a lot from which it would never find so much as a possibility of escape. Any plan of intended deceit,—where, then, is the advantage which, from the proposed arrangement in question, it would be possible for it to receive? Suppose no such means of fixation in existence; without it, the length of time during which a plan of fabrication may carry on its operation free from suspicion, is the whole time that intervenes between the moment at which the matter of fact has place, and the moment at which, if at all, it is taken for the subject-matter of judicial deposition: suppose the plan in question established, no sooner is the simple fact, viz. that by the person or persons in question, in relation to the transaction in question, at the place and time in question, — a minute has been made, than in the breast of all persons, to whom it happens to possess or take any interest in the affair, suspicion springs up, and all scrutiny that could be wished for, with all its force.

At the same time it may be observed, that if any such article of fabricated pre-appointed evidence were not communicated to the parties interested in it, at or near to the time at which the event to which it purported to relate took place, it would scarcely have the least chance of being received as evidence.

§ 3. *Precedents from English and French Law.*

In the English code, by several statutes of old date, in some cases of delinquency, the disorder being of the chronical cast,* power is given to a justice of the peace to repair to the spot, and taking his observation of what passes, to commit to writing the discourse expressive of such observations; and to this written expression so given to such discourse, the statute gives the name and effect of a *record*.

Of the principle here in question, a sort of exemplification, such as it is, may be seen in those antique, but not altogether ill-imagined laws. But of the boundless ocean of possible legally operative facts, the provision thus made amounts not, in comparison with the whole of that boundless ocean, to more than one drop.

Under French law, before the revolution, this same practice, or, as it might be said, this same principle, had received a very wide extension.† Wheresoever, in the case of any species of transaction, lawful or unlawful, a judicatory could be assigned, under the cognizance of which, the nature of the fact considered, it might be reasonably expected to come, in general a judge belonging to that same judicatory—in particular cases an official person of a different description—had by some statute or other been designated, whose duty it had been made to repair to the scene of action, and there upon the very spot to make a sort of statement, or record or report, of whatsoever material facts presented themselves to his senses in the character of a percipient witness.

A record of this kind was termed a procès-verbal, — *verbaliser* was the verb by which the act of making it was designated. In the character, as was sufficiently manifest, of a security against misrepresentation, as well intended and studied, as casual and unintended, such was the importance attached to the circumstance of promptitude, that by a general rule it was provided that every such statement should, from beginning to end, be committed to writing upon the spot.

Such was the rule; though for enforcing it the punishment employed was, as usual in such cases of official delinquency, of the *misseated* kind. The sort of punishment distinguished by the term nullification: the official person the offender, the person punished, not he but this or that individual by whom the offence could neither be committed, nor could have been prevented.

In all these instances, as, time and place being considered, might well be expected, power has gone much beyond the mark, at least beyond the mark which, in the above suggestion, has been stated as the proper one.

In the oldest of the two English instances, a single justice of the peace, to the function of witness percipient, and thence deposing witness as therein appointed, is made to add that of judge, sole judge; and from the judgment so passed by him, no appeal is allowed.

In the next, still the same accomplished despotism: only, instead of its being given in an entire state to one, it is divided among three.‡

Under French law, in several of the instances, those of tax-gatherers in the number, the sort of preappointed evidence thus framed was required to be received in the character of conclusive evidence. In this way, saving possible contestation between A and B, which of them should be considered the one true man, the power of the judge was, though in a disguised state, and under another name,—and but the more effectually for being disguised,—bestowed upon the witness himself.

By application to a court of equity, you in certain cases have an examination of witnesses *in perpetuam rei memoriam*.

By this instrument, in so far as the use of it extends (for the not giving to it a wider field of action has been an oversight,) the purposes of the inventors are served with the usual fidelity: those of justice, and whoever has need of justice, with the usual faithless-

* Forcible Entry: — Statutes 15 R. II. c. 2: 8 H. VI. c. 9.
Riot: — 13 H. IV. c. 7; 15 R. II. c. 2; and others passed in amendment of these two original ones.
To this *authority*, both statutes add powers of much greater importance: one of them, that of punishing the alleged offenders in pursuance of a judgment, from which no appeal is allowed. — On this head a few more words presently.

† Dict. portatif de Jurisprudence. Paris 1763. Tit. Procès-Verbal.

‡ Two justices of the peace at least, and the sheriff.

ness. In regard to the field of action, its limits are the same as those of a court of equity. Whatsoever may be the limits of a court of equity? No; not exactly so, not quite so extensive: — file your bill, and one of these days, and in your own particular case, some day or other, you will know, or you will not know, what they are. Delinquency, at any rate, delinquency is not included in them in any: say rather — for this is always safest — is included in them, if at all, scarcely in any of its shapes.

Be the purpose what it may, to this purpose, says the Practical Register in Chancery, a book in its day of high authority, no witnesses shall be examined but the aged or impotent. By this time, very likely it may be in some cases* otherwise; but in so far as it is so still, note the result. A remedy allowed, and the application of it confined to a state of things in which, upon the face of it, the probability is, that the purpose will not be answered by it.

If he be not impotent (whatever may be here meant by impotence,) the person must be aged: — would you know whether your wished-for witness be sufficiently aged? If you have a few hundred pounds more than you know what to do with, file your bill; and if you should happen to outlive the suit, you may perhaps know. Would you wish to know before your money is spent? Apply to the nearest astrologer: for five shillings he will give you as well-grounded an assurance as it is possible for any learned adviser to give you, for as many guineas.

Wheresoever quantity is concerned, it is among the properties of judge-made law — equity shape, as well as common-law shape — to be incapable of drawing lines; *i. e.* in other words, of serving in any person's case in the character of a guide — of guide to that action of which it calls itself the rule. This happy incapacity is interwoven in its very essence: and in this, which is but one out of several circumstances, any one of which would suffice for rendering it radically incapable of answering its intended purpose, may be seen one of the attributes by which it is rendered so lovely in the eyes of its professors, and so oppressive to all those upon whom application is made of it.

CHAPTER XVIII.

OF DERIVATIVE, INCLUDING TRANSCRIPTIOUS, RECORDATION, WHEREIN OF REGISTRATION.

§ 1. *Derivative Recordation or Registration, its uses.*

A CONTRACT (suppose) is entered into, — an agreement — a conveyance — a last will made, — the dispositions of which it is to consist settled, — the words expressive of those dispositions committed to writing: — the operation of writing finished, the paper, parchment, or other *substratum*, on which the written characters stand expressed, becomes thereby *an instrument of contract.* This done, by this same operation, a *sort of* RECORDATION, which may be termed *original* recordation, is performed. Grounded on this, deduced from this, any act of recordation or registration (for the terms are synonymous, or nearly so) may, with reference to it, be termed *derivative;* — and, in so far as the words of the original are copied without variation, *transcriptious:* as to the uses of this operation, considered in a general point of view, it will be seen that they bear a necessary reference to the different descriptions of persons, in favour of whom, or at the charge of whom, the operation, and its product, may be attended with effect.

1. To *parties* and their *representatives*, it may be of use, for security against any of those accidents to which, in private hands, it is the destiny of such originals to be exposed.

2. To *third persons*, the principal use is *as against* parties and their representatives; the third persons in question standing, or having it in contemplation to stand, in the relation of creditors or purchasers to one or more of the parties.

To an extent more or less considerable, the ground of pecuniary credit being necessarily composed of the style and mode of living, and apparent habitual expenditure of the party to whom credit is given, the use here is — to preserve creditors from those frauds and disappointments which have place when the property to which they trusted is clandestinely dissipated, or without equivalent transferred to other hands.

Not to speak of those *financial* uses, which, in so copious a stream, have under all governments been derived from this source, — in the character of *collateral* uses; those above mentioned, under the appellation of *statistic*, are too obvious to require in this place any further notice.

§ 2. *To what Instruments applicable.*

To what instruments is this process applicable? Understand always with preponderant advantage. *Answer:* To all in general, saving exceptions grounded on special reasons.

And those reasons, — what are they? — *Answer:* Delay, vexation, and expense. On this, as on so many other occasions, by these instructive words the instrument is presented, by which, and by which alone, the line can ever with propriety be drawn between what is useful, considered with reference to a particular purpose, and what is useful upon the whole.

* 3. P. Williams 77.

On the one hand, the services capable of being rendered to justice by this operation being understood; — on the other hand, the mass of collateral inconvenience, of which delay, vexation, and expense, are the component elements, being also understood: — which of the two quantities is to be deemed preponderant? Under the head of *delay* may be considered, either the mere consumption and loss of time (which, however, in the case of a person depending, as do the bulk of mankind, for subsistence on some profit-seeking occupation, is equivalent to expense,) or inconvenience in the same shape, with the addition of any such losses and disadvantageous incidents (including loss of opportunities of positive gain,) as may be liable to take place within the compass of that same portion of time.

To the head of *vexation*, inconvenience in those same shapes may, with still more direct and obvious propriety, be referred, if the effect alone being considered, the circumstance of *time*, considered in the character of the *cause*, be laid out of the account. So far as it comes under this description, the vexation liable to be found included among the results of the operation in question, may be termed *vexation at large*.

Vexation, in a shape in which it may be distinguished by the appellation of *special* vexation, is that which, in the sort of case in question, is liable to be produced by *disclosure:* disclosure of the pecuniary and other domestic and private concerns of the parties interested.

As affording an instance, in which, partly in respect of *delay*, partly in respect of *vexation at large*, the inconvenience resulting from the operation in question seems to be in a pre-eminent degree likely to be found preponderant, three species of contracts may here be brought to view: — *draughts on bankers*, *bills of exchange*, and *circulating promissory-notes*.

As affording an instance in which, in the shape of *special vexation*, the sort of *disclosure* inseparable from the operation is liable to be productive of inconvenience, and that inconvenience to be, or at least to be thought to be, preponderant, the case of *last wills* may, in like manner, be brought to view.

§ 3. *The obligation of Registering, how enforceable?*

Where the performance of this operation is thought fit to be rendered obligatory — as, saving exceptions such as the above, in all cases where, for want of it, creditors or purchasers are liable to be defrauded, it surely ought to be; — by what means shall the fulfilment of the obligation be provided for? — and, in particular, shall *nullification* be of the number of these means?

Here, as elsewhere, the answer will depend partly upon the facility given to the operation, partly upon the certainty of the obligation being present to the mind — to the minds of those on whom, in case of non-fulfilment, the burthen of the suffering which results or is made to result as a consequence from such failure, comes to be imposed.

Sometimes improbity, more frequently indolence, perhaps indolence or negligence, are the obstacles which the obligation will have to contend with.

Employing punishment to surmount the obstacle, common honesty, under the guidance of common sense, naturally would apply the remedy to the person of that individual, and that individual alone, in whose transgression the mischief found its cause. Different, far different, has been the course taken by English lawyers. The transgression (it is manifest) is the transgression of the professional agent, manager, and adviser: leaving him untouched, nullification, instead of that, casts the punishment in every case upon some individual or other in the character of a client — upon him in whose instance ignorance and guiltlessness are always natural, ignorance, generally invincible and unavoidable—upon him, or his still more helpless representatives.

Not that even upon the transgressing law-adviser the punishment would be just, unless the directions were so clear, that without improbity or culpable negligence on his part, transgression could not have place. But, if the directions be not intelligible, or not so much as communicated to the professedly learned few, how should they be known to the ignorant and helpless multitude?

§ 4. *The Function, by whom performable.*

If in England, as before the revolution in France, the professional agent, manager, and adviser, were, under the name of *the notary*, considered upon the footing of a public officer, his office might of itself with great facility be rendered, to the purpose of all instruments in which he was concerned, a sort of register-office; — in that case, and for that purpose, appropriate forms of book-keeping might by law be prescribed to him, with apt penalties in case of non-observance. Transmitted from these dispersed and occasionally ambulatory offices, to a fixed central one, duplicates would at the same time serve to secure compliance to the regulations, and minister to the general statistic purposes.

In proportion as the law of contracts was rendered determinate, intelligible, and clear, parties would be enabled, and naturally disposed to exempt themselves from the expenses of calling in, as at present, the assistance of a *professional* notary, or the humiliation of begging that of an honorary one. But if among the instructions contained in the printed border of the promulgation-paper, on which the contract is here supposed to be written, the non-appearance of the name of a notary on the face of an instrument were set down as a cause of *suspicion*, the custom of taking the benefit of such assistance would scarcely, in that case, be expected to lose anything of that constancy which belongs to it at present.

And surely, if by fixation and simplification of the service, as above proposed, the quantum of the remuneration were confined within the bounds of that moderation, of which, in the nature of the case, it is not unsusceptible, the expense, considering the degree of security that might be attached to it, is such as need not be grudged.

§ 5. *Quantity of Matter to be entered in the Registry.*

Of the matter of each such instrument, what portion shall be subjected to this process? Here again, for the answer, recourse must be had to the so often mentioned triad. But for that cluster of opposing considerasions, — the whole; — these considerations taken into the account, such parts as are called for with a predominant energy by the respective uses above indicated.

Meantime, in and by this answer, on the part of an instrument of the kind in question, the supposition of the existence of distinguishable parts is involved. Unfortunately, any more than a mathematical point, a chaos has no parts. To be in respect of, and to the extent of, such and such of its parts, subjected to registration, an instrument must in its form be composed of parts capable of being distinguished, denominated, and numbered: but, in the compound of mendacity, surplusage, and misrepresented truths, in which, in an instrument of contract in the English style, the small proportion of efficient matter, to keep it from being intelligible to those whose everything depends upon its being understood, is dissolved and drowned, effectual care has been taken that there shall be no parts.

§ 6. *Means of securing Transcripts against Error.*

To possess so much as a single transcript exempt from the possibility of error, is a blessing which not many centuries ago would have been pronounced fabulous. Means of realizing this prodigy to any extent have now, for some years, been in familiar use. In three perfectly distinct modes has modern ingenuity furnished the means of producing this desirable effect.*

If in the article of dispatch the advantage should in the instance of these ingenious inventions, any or all of them, be found to fall short in any degree of what at first view might have been expected, the advantage in respect of authenticity and security surely is of that sort from which no defalcation can be to be apprehended from any the severest scrutiny.

This is not the place for any such thing as an exposition in detail of the facilities that might thus be afforded to the business of derivative registration; — moderate is the share of reflection that would suffice, it is supposed, to render it superfluous.

§ 7. *Registrar's duty in respect of Registration.*

In so far as the interest of creditors is concerned, the extent given to the application of this instrument of security will depend upon, and be in proportion to, the degree of probity that has place in that governing body, on which the condition of the aggregate mass of the community, on this and so many other particulars, depends.

Unfortunately, in this country it has been found composed in no small proportion — and that (strange to think) upon trial actually a preponderant one — of men in whose eyes the *faculty* at least, if not the *art*, of carrying on the operation of swindling with effect and impunity, upon a large scale, was too valuable to be parted with.

Under the English law of property, for the joint convenience of the members of the predatory profession, and of the fraudulently disposed individuals of the higher orders, so happily are matters disposed, that, on condition of giving to his property a certain shape, — on condition of laying out the profits of dishonesty in the purchase, for example, of land,† or even keeping his property in that shape, — a man finds himself, to an unlimited amount, empowered by law to cheat his creditors: — By rich men calling themselves Christians, with the countenance and protection of men of law calling themselves Christians, jewels of gold and silver are borrowed, and Christians are legally and regularly spoiled without redress.

Not many years ago, the question was fairly put. Noble lords and honourable gentlemen — shall they, as well as trading men, continue in possession of the means of cheating their creditors? The answer was: Trading men, no: — but in the hands of noble lords and honourable gentlemen, the power of cheating — the *jus fraudandi* — was a privilege too valuable to be parted with.†

* 1. Multiplication by impression from writing.
2. By and during the act of writing, multiplication by pens moved at the same time, by the same hand: —
3. During the act of writing, by one and the same pen, communicating the impression at the same time to different strata of paper, one under another.

† By 3 and 4 William IV. c. 104, freehold and copyhold lands are now made liable, in courts of equity, to simple contract debts, after specialty debts are paid.

By any system of registration, in proportion to the extent given to it, the swindling licence thus established and confirmed would, it is manifest, be proportionally trenched upon and infringed. Under the principles, the triumph of which was on that occasion displayed, it may be imagined what sort of reception a plan of general registration would have met with.

CHAPTER XIX.

EXCLUSION OF EVIDENCE. — GENERAL CONSIDERATIONS.

§ 1. *Modes of Exclusion, positive and negative.*

SHALL it be admitted? — shall it be excluded? Be the supposed article of evidence what it may, these more especially under the practice at present established, will naturally be the first questions that will present themselves in relation to it.

If admitted, then come those other questions which have formed the subjects of consideration in the preceding parts of this work.

If excluded, then come two other questions —two all-comprehensive questions — viz. In what *cases?* — and, in the several cases, for what causes?

Modes of exclusion — what are the different *modes* or *means*, in or by which the effect thus denominated is capable of being produced? Answer: Two: and, from each other they may stand distinguished by the adjuncts, *positive* and *negative:* —

1. In the positive mode, the exclusion may be said to be produced when, though it were proffered, the evidence would not be suffered to be delivered.

2. In the negative mode, the effect of exclusion may be said to be produced, in so far as the means necessary to the obtainment of it are, either purposely or by negligence, omitted to be employed.

As to the cases in which, whether by or without design, the negative mode of exclusion has place, these may, if not all of them, at any rate the most prominent among them, be comprehended under the term *non-compulsion.*

The case being such, that in the character of a deposing witness, the services of the individual in question, if rendered, would or might have been conducive to the proof or disproof of some matter of fact which is in question, and thereby to the forming, in relation to such matter of fact, a right persuasion and consequent decision on the part of the judge, and that, in and by the application of compulsory means, those services would or might have been rendered, but for want of them have not been rendered, — the employment of such means has by the judge been, or if applied for would have been purposely forborne.

Of this description is that which forms at least the most prominent case of negative exclusion; and which, at any rate, under the head of exclusion, there will in the course of this work be the most frequent occasion to bring to view.

§ 2. *Mischiefs liable to result from Exclusion put on Evidence.*

In every case that can be imagined — on every supposition that can be framed, whether the exclusion be or be not upon the whole conducive to the ends of justice, a distinct view of the mischiefs of which it is liable to be productive, cannot be without its use.

That by exclusion put upon evidence, mischief is not incapable of being produced, will not to any person be matter of doubt: the exclusion of all evidence would be the exclusion of all justice.

An article of evidence being given, the nature of the mischief resulting from the exclusion of it will be found to depend upon and be varied by the following circumstances: —

1. In relation to the matter of fact in question, the *cause* or *suit*, does it or does it not furnish other evidence of a nature to operate in favour of the same side?

2. The side from which the support, that would have been given to it by the evidence thus taken away—is it the plaintiff's side of the cause, or the defendant's?

3. The cause, is it of a penal or a non-penal nature?

By the changes of which these three causes of variation are susceptible, the variations of which the nature of the mischief is susceptible will stand expressed in the eight following cases: —

Case first: —1. The excluded evidence the only evidence on that side.

2. Side deprived of the support, the *plaintiff's* or prosecutor's.

3. Nature of the suit *penal.* Mischievous result, a virtual licence to commit crimes and transgressions of all sorts, in the presence, as well as upon the persons, of all such individuals to whom the cause of exclusion applies.*

* It is thus that, in the West India colonies, a freeman, on condition of concealing the enormity from other freemen — a concealment to which in general nothing more than common discretion was necessary — could enjoy the benefit, such as it was, of committing at pleasure all manner of enormities, short of murder, on the bodies of all persons in a state of slavery; that is, of all those of whom the great majority of the whole population is composed. In some places, by the substitution of a small fine to all other punishment, the licence to add or substitute murder to every other injury is completed.

What is at the same time manifest is, that by the same exclusion, the same danger is, in appearance at least, extended to freemen likewise. But that for the protection of freemen, the effect

Case second: — 1. Excluded evidence, as before, the only evidence on that side.

2. Side deprived of the support, the *plaintiff's* as before. Nature of the suit, now *non-penal.* Mischievous result, a virtual licence to every man to frustrate every other of all rights, for the giving effect to which the aid of the judge is necessary: — a licence granted in violation of the general engagement taken by the sovereign, in virtue and by means of the several articles or rules of substantive law, by which those rights were respectively created and conferred.

Case third: — 1. Excluded evidence, as before, the only evidence on that side.

2. Side deprived of the support, now the defendant's.

3. Nature of the suit, now again *penal.* Mischievous result, a power, — though, when exercised, not quite so sure in its operation as in the two former cases, — a power to every one who, to the purpose in question, is disposed to act, or willing and able to engage any other person to act for him in the character of a mendacious and falsely criminative or inculpative witness, to cause innocent persons in any number to be convicted of, and be punished as for crimes or other transgressions, of any sort and in any number, at his pleasure.

The mischievous power not quite so sure in its operation in this case as in the two former. Why? Because, whereas in those cases, for the production of the mischievous effect, a mere negative state of things suffices, viz. the non-appearance of a witness; in this case a positive cause, viz. the operation of some person in the character of a witness is necessary; — in which case, by means of counter-interrogation, with the benefit of such other of the securities against deceptious incorrectness and incompleteness as operate in conjunction with it, detection will always be more or less liable to be produced, and thus the intended mischievous effect of the mendacity, and of the exclusion put upon the evidence that would have been opposed to it, destroyed.

Case fourth: — 1. Excluded evidence, as before, the only evidence on that side.

2. Side deprived of the support, now again *the* defendant's.

3. Nature of the suit, now *non-penal.* Mischievous result, a power, though under the same limitation as in the former case, to subject persons in any number to be unexpectedly loaded with undue and burthensome, so they be not penal obligations, to any amount and extent, including, in the case of each such person, the loss of everything he has; and this, so far as concerns such things as are in their nature transferable, to the profit *pro tanto* of any person by whom this mischievous power is exercised.

Cases 5, 6, 7, and 8: — The same as cases 1, 2, 3, and 4 respectively, except that the excluded evidence is not the only evidence on that side.

In all these several cases, the probability of the mischief which the exclusion tends to produce is of course less than in the corresponding former cases, diminishing in proportion to the number of witnesses whose testimony, not being comprehended in any principle of exclusion, is accordingly admitted.

On the other hand, in all these several cases, in whatever proportion the probability and danger of mischief, in any of those its forms, is diminished, in that same proportion, on the supposition that, from the admission of the excluded evidence, preponderant danger of deception, and thence of misdecision, would have been produced, is the amount of such danger, and thence the utility of any such exclusion, diminished likewise.

Upon the whole, the result is — that the effect, or tendency at least, of exclusion put upon evidence, is — to give encouragement and increased probability to criminality, and delinquency, and transgression, and wrong, in every imaginable shape: and thereby, except in so far as any specific and adequate countervailing benefit can be seen to be produced by it, to give increase as well as birth to human suffering, in almost every imaginable shape.

On this subject, that which, in the course of the succeeding pages, will, it is supposed, be made sufficiently apparent, is — 1. That, in the shape of delay, vexation, and expense, cases may have place, in which, by means of exclusion of evidence, mischief to a greater amount than what is produced by exclusion put upon that same evidence, may be saved.

2. But that, in the shape of mischief producible by misdecision through the medium of deceptious evidence, no saving in the way of mischief can in any case be reasonably expected to be made by exclusion put upon evidence: for that, in every case by exclusion, misdecision for want of evidence is more likely to be produced, than by admission, misdecision through deception and by means of evidence.*

of the evidence-excluding law should, in some way or other, be upon occasion counteracted and done away, is as natural as that, for the protection of slaves, it should not be counteracted, but left to take its course.

* *N. B.* Another cause, by which mischief in all these varieties is produced, is composed of the mass of *factitious delay, vexation, and expense,* and in particular the expense by means of which, under *judge-made* law, for the sake of the profit extractible out of the expense, justice has, to all who are not able to bear the expense, been denied, while to all others it has been *sold.* The

§ 3. *Principles respecting the Exclusion of Evidence.*

The mischiefs liable to be produced by the exclusion of evidence have been brought to view. These notwithstanding, cases will be brought to view, for which exclusion, it is believed, will in some instances be found to be proper; viz. as being subservient, upon the whole, to the proper ends of justice, on the occasion of judicature. But if in these cases proper it be, it is because the exclusion, it will be found, is a necessary result of certain measures which will be seen to be indispensably prescribed by a regard for certain of those ends, viz. those collateral ends, which are so unfortunately liable to be found acting in the character of antagonists to the direct ends.

Not that in these, any more than in any other cases, — taken by itself, the exclusion of material evidence is a desirable result, — a result *in itself* subservient to any of the ends of justice; but that, in the cases here in question, it is an effect of which, though in itself evil, the production is necessary to the exclusion of some evil of still superior magnitude.

In itself, and abstraction made of its consequences, exclusion of evidence is as far from being proper as infliction of punishment is: but forasmuch as for the exclusion of still greater evil, evils under the name of punishment, to so unhappily ample an extent, not only may be, but must be produced, so for the like cause, though to a much narrower extent, evil by exclusion of evidence not only may be, but in some cases ought to be.

On the occasion of the receipt of evidence, as on any other occasion, the following rules will, it is hoped, be found neither altogether devoid of practical use, nor in any respect open to dispute: —

1. Produce not a greater evil in pursuit of the means of excluding a lesser evil.

2. Exclude not a greater good in pursuit of the means of obtaining a lesser good.

3. Produce not any preponderant evil in pursuit of the means of obtaining any good.

4. Exclude not a preponderant good in pursuit of the means of excluding any evil.

difference is — that of the injustice of which *exclusion* put upon evidence is the instrument, the burthen falls upon all without distinction, rich and poor alike: — whereas, from the burthen the injustice of which *factitious expense* is the instrument, the rich, to the amount of a comparatively small part of the whole population, stand in part exempted, viz. to the amount of the difference between what is produced by the absolute *denial*, and what is produced by the *sale* of justice.

Of the nature, amount, and causes of such factitious delay, vexation, and expense, an explanation in some detail may be seen in *Scotch Reform*, particularly Letter I.

These rules being taken for a standard and a guide — for a standard of reference, and for a guide to practice — are any cases to be found (it may be asked,) in which exclusion put upon this or that article of evidence would be conducive upon the whole to the ends of justice? *Answer:* Yes; beyond doubt there are. *Question:* What are these cases? *Answer:* All such cases in which, in a quantity preponderant over that which would be produced by such exclusion, a mass of evil, composed of any of the evils in the avoidance of which the ends of justice respectively consist, would be produced by admission given to that same article of evidence.

Of which soever of these evils, viz. misdecision on the one hand, — delay, vexation, and expense on the other — in the whole, or in part, — the apprehended disease consists; — in either case, in so far as *admission* given to evidence is the cause of the disease, exclusion put upon that same evidence operates, of course, in the character of a remedy; and in so far as delay, vexation, and expense, is the disease, it is the only remedy.

But in relation to those two different species of disease, its efficacy exhibits a difference, which in respect of its practical importance will be seen to have the highest claim to notice.

Misdecision is an evil, for the prevention of which, in favour of either side of the cause, by the application of the exclusion in question in the character of a remedy, no chance (it will be seen) can ever be obtained without producing in all cases a greater chance, in some cases a certainty, of producing that same disease, to the prejudice of the opposite side of that same case.

On the other hand, against delay, vexation, and expense, in so far as produced by the exhibition of evidence, exclusion put upon that same evidence is a complete and sovereign remedy. Against misdecision to the prejudice of one side, exclusion of evidence cannot be employed without producing a greater probability of it to the prejudice of the other side: — against delay, vexation, and expense, to the prejudice of either side, it may be employed — not indeed always without producing a greater or less probability of misdecision, but always, unless by some extraordinary accident, without producing any chance at all of preponderant, or so much as any additional evil in the shape of delay, vexation, and expense, to the prejudice of either side.

To the distinction that is thus pointed out, the circumstance that gives importance is this. In the *pharmacy* of the man of law, especially under English law, it is in the character of a remedy against misdecision that this species of purge has been almost exclusively employed; — and in this character prodigious is the extent in which it will be seen to have been employed:—against delay, vexation, and expense — diseases to which, in so much *superior*, not to say in an *exclusive* degree, it will be seen to be applicable with advantage — in this character, scarcely any application, it will be seen, has been made of it.

§ 4. *Causes for which Exclusion is always proper.*

This being premised, for the purpose of the question, — in what cases and for what causes *is* or may the exclusion of evidence be proper — in what cases and for what causes improper,—a primary distinction that will require to be made, is — that between such evidence as is either *irrelevant* or *superfluous* on the one hand, and such as is neither irrelevant nor superfluous on the other.

As to *irrelevancy*: — Of a portion of discourse tendered in the character of evidence, to say that it is *irrelevant*, is as much as to say that, with relation to the fact in question, it is *not* evidence; —it does not possess the character and qualities of evidence. But inasmuch as it not only is, by the party who tenders it, brought forward in that character (for this it is by the supposition,) but until it have been more or less examined into, may, upon the face of it, be not altogether unapt to wear in appearance that same character,— an appellation of some sort or other will still be necessary to distinguish it from any such matter as has no pretension at all to the character of evidence: and to this purpose, the word *evidence* itself is rendered competent, when the adjunct *irrelevant* is added to it.

As to *superfluity*:—Of a portion of discourse tendered in the character of evidence, to say that it is *superfluous*, is as much as to say (supposing it admitted,) not indeed that it is not evidence, but (what comes to the same thing) that, if added to that mass of other evidence with relation to which it is considered as superfluous, so it is that, under the existing circumstances, it would not be itself capable of producing, or contributing anything to the production of, the effect of evidence. Thus, though evidence may be *superfluous* without being irrelevant, it cannot be *irrelevant* without being *superfluous*: and thus, under the more extensive denomination of *superfluous*, *irrelevant* evidence may occasionally be included.

In respect of the nature of the mischief to which it is their tendency to give birth, the two qualities, *irrelevancy* and *superfluity*, stand in some respects upon the same — in other respects, upon a somewhat different, footing. Of the several evils correspondent and opposite to the several ends of justice, there is not one to which irrelevancy is not capable of giving existence. On the mind of the judge, in the first place, *perplexity* and *hesitation*: thence, to the parties, but more particularly to the party in the right, delay, vexation, and expense: — delay, vexation, and expense, after the production of the superfluous evidence, viz. while the time of the judge is occupied by the consideration of it.

Of this mass of evil, though the maximum may be very considerable, the minimum may be next to nothing: — but a mass, the quantity of which will be always more or less considerable, is that which has been generated by and during the production of the irrelevant evidence. Thus much as to delay, vexation, and expense. But in the mind of the judge, by irrelevancy in the evidence, not only perplexity and hesitation, but deception, and thence misdecision, are capable of being produced.

When, without being *irrelevant*, the evidence is but *superfluous*, in this case, so far as concerns the delay, vexation, and expense, incident to the task of production, quantity for quantity, it stands upon the same footing as so much irrelevant evidence: and so, perhaps, as to what concerns vexation on the part of the judge. But as to delay resulting from perplexity, and danger of misdecision through deception, — of the evils liable to be produced by *irrelevant*, these seem scarcely liable to be produced by merely *superfluous* evidence.

By accident there is scarcely any sort of evidence to which it may not happen to be superfluous: but a species of evidence, of which, except in particular circumstances, it is of the essence so to be, is that particular modification of unoriginal make-shift evidence which has above been brought to view under the name of hearsay evidence.

The following are the particular circumstances just spoken of, by which that species of information, which, generally speaking, will be superfluous and useless, is capable of being rendered serviceable. One is — the non-existence, or non-obtainability, physical or prudential, of all evidence of a more trustworthy complexion from the same source; viz. in case of hearsay evidence in general, the non-existence of that original evidence in which it had its source: — in the case of hearsay evidence of a more distant remove from the original, the non-existence of non-original evidence of a *less* distant *remove*.

The other accidental circumstance by which hearsay evidence is capable of being taken out of that state of superfluousness and uselessness which is most natural to it, is where evidence supposed to be derived from the same original source, and from a station nearer to that source, having been delivered, the supposed derivative evidence is called forth, and made to serve in the character of a test of correctness and completeness, and thereby as a security against deceptious incorrectness and incompleteness, on the part of that same anterior, or supposed anterior, evidence.

The account given of the transaction in question, by him who now in relation to it appears in the character of a *deposing* witness, and who, in relation to this same transaction, was at the time, if this his account be true, a percipient witness,—is it consistent with all such other accounts as it has happened to him to give of that same transaction at any other times? On the one hand, the pertinency of this sort of question— on the other hand, the needfulness of hearsay evidence, as presenting the only sort of information by which an answer can be given to it, — are points not only manifest to reason, but recognised in judicial practice.

The other distinct modification of unoriginal or derivative evidence, is *transcriptious* evidence. Exists there a case in which, to the purpose of a question concerning the genuineness of a supposed original written instrument, it is in the nature of a supposed or acknowledged transcript to be capable of being rendered serviceable? *Answer:* Yes; — for example, where, in relation to the supposed original, a suspicion has place, that, subsequently to the making of the transcript, it has been falsified. But, in comparison of the number of instances in which the demand for *hearsay* evidence on this ground is wont to present itself, that of the instances in which the demand for *transcriptious* evidence on this same ground can be expected to present itself, will of course be extremely rare.

Note, that in the case of *hearsay* evidence, the supposition of two different narrators, two different memories, — two distinct but sinister sources of deceptious incorrectness and incompleteness,—is necessarily involved: — not so in the case of *transcriptious* evidence.

CHAPTER XX.

EXCLUSION CONTINUED—CAUSES FOR WHICH IT IS PROPER OR NOT, ACCORDING TO CIRCUMSTANCES.

§ 1. *Avoidance of Delay.*

FOR the purpose of making it the more distinctly apparent, in what manner exclusion of evidence may be rendered conducive to the ends of justice upon the whole, by and in respect of its subserviency to the collateral ends of justice, — viz. avoidance of preponderantly mischievous delay, vexation, or expense, — and this even in the case where the excluded evidence is neither *irrevelant* nor *superfluous*, it may be of use to bring to view, under one or more of these heads, a case or two in which this conduciveness and subserviency will be manifest.

Case I. Where exclusion of evidence may be rendered conducive upon the whole to the ends of justice, by the subserviency of such exclusion to the avoidance of preponderantly mischievous delay.

In a country in which, in such abundance, the legal ties that connect man with man are spread over the whole surface of the polished portion of the globe, no determinate limits can be set to the *length of time* that may have elapsed, before this or that article of evidence which, in the suit in question, may be necessary to right decision, can be obtained: — no determinate limits, not even on the supposition, that for receiving and extracting evidence from parts of the earth not subject to the authority of the judicatory in question, those operations, which the nature of the case requires as well as indicates, but which are as yet so new, or at best so imperfectly known to English practice, were set on foot, and, upon an all-comprehensive scale, regularly employed.

But in this, as in every case, if the length of delay necessary for the production of the evidence in question be not allowed, — to refuse such allowance is in effect to put an exclusion — a negative exclusion at least — upon the evidence.

Such exclusion — is there a case in which, in this state of things, it could be proper? *Answer:* Yes; — for, on the other hand, in the same individual case, what may also happen is — that, while an article of evidence necessary to justice on one side of the cause is waited for, another article, not less necessary to justice on the other side, may perish, and cease for ever to be obtainable.

Not that, if evidence B be in the meantime obtainable, it ought to be suffered to remain unobtained, for no other reason than that evidence A cannot as yet be obtained.

But still, in the same individual case, another circumstance, not incapable of having place, is — that while the decision is thus delayed *for want* of an article of *evidence*, which a defendant, truly or falsely — and if falsely, — blameably or unblameably — has alleged himself able to procure, — that in this same case, the plaintiff, if found to be fully entitled to the object of his demand, will be found to have suffered, for want of it, and thereby for want of the decision which should have put him in possession of it, such damage as will be irreparable.

In this case, as in so many others, the only choice open to the legislator and the judge, is a choice of evils: — all that is left to them is to reduce to its least dimensions that mass of evil which it is not in their power wholly to exclude.

In this view, the temperament indicated by the nature of the case seems to be to this effect: — In the first instance, let the judge have power to pronounce, in favour of the plaintiff, a decision without waiting for the distant evidence: — but this decision, let it be, not ultimate and immutable, but reversible or modifiable, in the event of the production of the evidence in question, within a time, in the first instance limited, and thereafter enlargeable, or not enlargeable: — the plaintiff, before he is put in possession, finding adequate security for eventual restitution.

By a decision pronounced under these circumstances, without waiting for an article of evidence, by which, had it been forthcoming, a sufficient demand for a different, or even opposite decision, might have been produced, a negative indeed, but not the less effective exclusion, we see, is put upon the distant, and for the present unobtainable, evidence: an exclusion, viz. to the purpose of the decision in question:—but because, for the avoidance of the evil of which the delay necessary to the production of it would have been productive, it is excluded to the purpose of *that* decision,—it follows not but, that whensoever it is really forthcoming, it may thereupon be admitted, and such fresh decision pronounced as may be required by the aggregate body of evidence, composed of the original mass with the addition of this supplemental article.

On the same principles, though with differences in the mode of application corresponding to the change of situation, a temperament directed to the same ends might be applied to the case, where the side, on which the demand exists for the distant evidence, is the plaintiff's side.

In what multitude and variety might not facilities be afforded to justice — facilities not less obvious than hitherto unexampled — should the *proper* ever take place of the *actual* ends of judicature.

All this while, what is not to be denied is, that if the word evidence be taken in its largest sense, no service can ever be rendered to justice by deciding without evidence. In respect of the question of fact, for anything that he does, or can propose to himself to do, no reason can the judge ever find, other than what is composed of evidence. On this occasion, as on every other, if so it be that what he does is right, inasmuch as while for avoidance of delay he decides against the side from which, at the end of the delay, evidence might be expected, he renders this decision ultimately defeasible, — defeasible on the actual exhibition of the so-expected evidence, —if in so doing, what he does is right, it can only be, because for the so doing he finds even then a sufficient ground and warrant in evidence.

But the case is — that here the evidence is evidence of a particular sort of fact, and in that sense so far is evidence of a peculiar sort. The fact here, is not the fact actually and immediately in question in the cause, but another fact, which howsoever connected with it, is perfectly distinct from it, viz. the *existence* of evidence — of evidence to the effect in question, relative to that same fact. The evidence on which is grounded the decision pronounced for want of the *expected* evidence, is simply *evidence:* the evidence on the ground of which, by another though simultaneous decision, that first decision is rendered defeasible on production of the expected evidence, may be termed *evidence of the second order*, or *evidence of evidence.*

In English practice, an application for putting off a cause on the allegation of the absence of a material witness,—which ought to be, and probably always is, coupled with that of his expected forthcomingness within a length of time, more or less precisely indicated,—is a frequently exemplified instance of that incidental and interlocutory sort of cause which is made to spring up within the principal and parent cause: — and, as already noted, it is by affidavit evidence—by evidence delivered in a shape in which it is not fit to form a ground for decision in any the slightest contested question, —that this incidental cause, on which the fate of the principal cause so frequently depends, and with it the question between opulence and want, between life perhaps and death, is decided.

And the delay which in these cases, and for these reasons, is either denied or granted, what is it? Of what length is it? Not the length which justice requires, viz. the shortest time within which, without preponderant inconvenience, the forthcomingness of the evidence can be obtained, but one or other only of those outrageous lengths, in which alone, according to circumstances which have nothing to do with justice, that commodity is cut out in the great shops which sell it; viz. not in lengths of so many days, or of so many hours, but in lengths of a quarter of a year, of half a year, or of a year, — never less than a quarter of a year, according to the distance of the place in which the question is to be tried, from the chief seat of the system of misrule called government.*

* Such is the effect, or at least one of the effects, of that master invention of the demon of chicane, composed of *terms* and *circuits;* that system of cool atrocity, the maintenance of which might of itself, on the part of all those by whom the real effects of it are understood, suffice for a perpetual refutation of all pretension to any such feeling as a sincere regard for justice; — that abomination to which the duped and misguided people are so well reconciled — reconciled by the same causes by which they have been reconciled to sinecures, to deodands, to sweeping forfeitures, to corruption of blood, to imprisonment for debt, to punishment for opinion — to capital punishment — were so once to trial by red-hot ploughshares, and trial, by duelling,—and, no less than the people of Mexico and Otaheite, would have been to human sacrifices, had the blood of human victims been

§ 2. *Avoidance of Vexation at large — Vexation, its modifications.*

To the purpose here in question, vexation, considered as liable to be produced by the exhibition of evidence, may be distinguished into vexation at large, and vexation by disclosure: — and under the former of these two heads may be included every species of vexation that is not comprehended under the other. Follows in the present section what concerns vexation *at large*.

1. Judges; 2. Subordinate judicial officers; 3. Jurymen, viz. on the occasions in which these temporary assessors to the professional and permanent species of judges are admitted; 4. Agents of the parties, such as counsel and attorneys of all classes and denominations; 5. Parties to the cause; 6. Witnesses, viz. extraneous witnesses, including all such *examinees* as are not parties; 7. Persons at large. Under one or other of these denominations may be comprised the various descriptions of persons, in whose breasts the search for *vexation at large*, considered as liable to be produced by the receipt or extraction of evidence, and thence capable of being *pro tanto* saved and avoided by the exclusion of such evidence, requires to be made.

1. In the situation of the judge, vexation from the source in question may be considered in the first place *in itself*, *i. e.* in so far as the seat of it is confined to the bosom of the judge: in the next place, *in its consequences*, viz. in so far as it is liable to be followed by consequences prejudicial to other persons, such as the parties in the cause in question, or persons at large in the character of litigants, actual or eventual, in other suits or causes.

In the breast of the judge — in proportion to the quantity of the evidence, even when relevant, — but in a greater proportion where irrelevant perplexity is liable to be produced: —by perplexity, hesitation and danger of misconception; — by hesitation, delay, viz. of decision; — by danger of misconception, danger of misdecision. Of vexation derived from this source, and having its seat in the breast of a person in this situation, such are the derivative or consequential mischiefs.

worth as much as their money to the tribes of priests and lawyers.

At the first institution of circuits, no shorter length was to be had than seven years: and under this mode of dealing, so delighted was the inventor[a] with the invention, that the only symptoms of sensibility exhibited from the beginning of his work to the end of it, are those which are called forth by the thoughts of this offspring of the union of genius with public virtue. And of this invention, what is the date? Not anterior to the flood, but so long posterior to it as the days Henry the Second of England.

[a] Glanville.

By delay of decision, evil, in a mass proportioned to the length of the delay, is produced: — in the first place, to the prejudice of the parties on one or both sides of the suit or cause in question; in the next place, to the prejudice of such individuals as are, or are about to be, parties in other suits or causes: in each of which the decision experiences a fresh retardation from every retardation that comes to have been experienced by this or any other antecedent suit or cause.

When the evidence is either irrelevant or superfluous, this vexation and this delay, and this danger of misdecision, are so much uncompensated evil: — when the evidence is neither irrelevant nor superfluous, but material and necessary, this vexation and this delay are still each of them, by the whole amount of it, so much evil: which evil has, by the supposition, its compensation; but that compensation may be adequate, *i. e.* preponderant, or not adequate.*

2. In the case of a *subordinate officer of justice*, the consequential mischief is in its nature and extent the same as in the case of the judge: between the one situation and the other, the principal as well as most prominent difference being — that what is done by the *subordinate*, is liable to be reversed or modified by his *superordinate*.

3. The case of the juryman may be apt to present itself as being in this respect not naturally different from that of the judge: the functions, exercised by the particular species of judge thus denominated, being, to the extent of his authority, the same as those of the judge at large, to whom, in customary language, the appellation is exclusively appropriated.

But the difference is this — and it is of no slight moment. In regard to *delay* by means of that part of the mechanism of the jury-box, by which the utmost quantity of evidence, that any suit or cause is capable of affording, is compressed within a limited space of time, the maximum of which is the same, whether the time necessary to the delivery of it be one hour or one hundred, — that part of the consequential mischief which consists of mere delay is thus reduced to an amount comparatively inconsiderable.

On the other hand, in regard to misdecision — an evil of which, in that particular situation, a mass of evidence, when disproportionately large, is, through the medium of *perplexity*, in a particular degree liable to be productive, — the mischief here in question, viz. the consequential mischief of the vexation liable to be produced by the exhibition of evidence — is here at its maximum: — the capacity of forming a right decision, thence the quantity of knowledge derived from ex-

* It is always adequate in the case of the judge.

perience and degree of skill derived from habit, thence again, in so far as depends on the state of the intellectual faculties, probability of rectitude of decision, — being, in the case of these unexperienced or little-experienced functionaries, less than in that of the more experienced one, while the time allowed for the operation is, in the case of the less experienced operator, compressed and limited as above, instead of being left in that unlimited state, in which, for his own accommodation, the more experienced and skilful operator has taken care to keep it.

4. In the situation of a professional agent of one of the parties, vexation considered as liable to be attendant on the exhibition of evidence is still susceptible of the same distinctions and the same consequences: — the chief difference being that which regards the description of the sort of person on whom the mischief falls.

In the situation of the judge, in so far as, through the medium of perplexity, vexation derived from such a source is liable to be productive of misdecision, the party who is in the right, and he alone, is the party liable, or, when the question concerns *degree*, the party in the highest degree liable to receive prejudice from it: whereas, in the situation of the professional agent of the party, that party whose agent the professional man in question is, is the party who, if not as at first sight it might seem exclusively, is at any rate, in by far the highest degree, liable, and apt to be the sufferer, by such mischief, of which it happens to it to be productive.

5. By every article of evidence exhibited, be it *personal oral*, be it *personal written*, be it *real*, favourable to the party exhibiting it or unfavourable, vexation more or less considerable to the party by whom it is sought out, procured, and exhibited, is of course produced: — vexation, viz. in so far as the labour thus employed is his own. But, in so far as that labour is turned over to a professional agent, such agent receiving as usual, at the charge of the principal, remuneration for it, and that in a pecuniary shape, the evil becomes in the person of the principal commuted, being transformed into expense.

Be it vexation, be it expense, evil thus producible by the exhibition of an article of evidence can never, in so far as it is confined to the breast of the party who tenders it, form a just ground for the exclusion of it: the evil being, in the estimation of the sole, or at least the most competent judge, preponderantly compensated, viz. by the advantage expected by him to be derived from it.

6. To an individual in the situation of a witness, from the exhibition of his testimony, a mass of attendant vexation is inseparable, and that vexation susceptible of almost boundless variety and magnitude, not to speak of *expense*, an evil which belongs to another head, and is of a nature to be susceptible of a compensation, which, being in the same shape as the damage, is capable of being rendered completely adequate to it: *consumption of time* is an evil, to the magnitude of which, regard being had to the infinite variety of which its casual consequences are susceptible, there are no determinate limits; and the nature of which, it not being like pecuniary damage susceptible of compensation in its own shape, puts an absolute negative upon all assurance of adequateness on the part of whatsoever compensation may come to be applied to it, — whether in the pecuniary or in any other shape.

Journeys to and from the theatre of justice — *attendance* thereat, and *demurrage*; — such are the standing items of vexation, which in the case of a witness delivering his testimony in the judicatory in question in the oral mode, may be considered as included in, or superadded to that which stands expressed by the words *consumption of time*.

These,—though, especially where the geographical field of jurisdiction is of small extent, they may frequently, all of them put together be of small importance, — form so many constant items: and in England, where so it happens, that during the length of time in question, the residence of the individual in question is not within the limits of the kingdom, they constitute all together in practice as in justice a ground sometimes for delay, sometimes for definitive exclusion, according to the circumstances of the case. And to these *standing* causes or elements of vexation are liable to be added casual ones, resulting from the particular situation of the individual witness, altogether indefinite in number and importance.

In regard to parties, in so far as, at his own instance, or at the instance of an adverse party, the testimony of a *party* comes to be received or extracted, he is, by such receipt or extraction, placed in the predicament of a witness.

But, by the union of the two characters in his one person, instead of being increased, the vexation of which the delivery of his evidence is the cause, is diminished: his labour in hunting himself out, and corresponding with himself, cannot be great; and in respect of journeys and so forth, as above, the two masses of vexation are consolidated.

7. As to *persons at large*, if to any person, by the receipt or extraction of evidence, how material soever to the suit or cause, vexation in any shape should be liable to be produced, quantity for quantity, evil in this shape, and threatening to fall upon this extraneous quarter, has, in proportion to its quantity, as just a claim to be taken into account, as if it fell in any of the shapes, or in any of the quar-

ters, above mentioned. But, except in the shape of vexation, by disclosure — of which presently under a separate head,—it appears not how, in any such extraneous quarter, unless in this or that state of things too accidental to admit of any common description, any such vexation should have place.

§ 3. *Vexation — in what cases a proper cause of Exclusion.*

On these, as on all other occasions, vexation, being so much evil, ought of course to be avoided and excluded, except in so far as, if admitted, it will find a preponderant compensation, in the shape of some greater evil excluded, or some more than equivalent good produced. If, by the exclusion of the article of evidence in question, so it be that the vexation in question will be prevented, the evil produced by such exclusion being not only less than the evil of the vexation, but less than any other evil by the production of which the vexation would be prevented, — on this supposition the exclusion of the evidence is proper; otherwise, not.

When the evidence is either *irrelevant* or *superfluous*, then, forasmuch as by the supposition whatsoever evil would be attendant on the exhibition of the evidence, would bring with it no good capable of operating as a compensation for it, the propriety of putting an exclusion upon the evidence stands above dispute.

When the evidence is neither irrelevant nor superfluous, but material and necessary, in these cases — an exclusion cannot be put upon it, but that by such exclusion evil is introduced; viz. a certainty, or a probability more or less considerable, of injustice by misdecision, to the prejudice of that side of the cause, in favour of which the evidence, had it been admitted, would have operated.

1. In the situation of judge, so far as the evil of vexation is, on this occasion, confined to that which has its seat in the feelings of that one individual, no case can present itself, in which, by any vexation capable of being inflicted on him by the exhibition of material evidence, any sufficient ground can be found for the putting an exclusion upon that same evidence.

If it be with his own consent that he was placed in that commanding situation, whatsoever be the advantages, natural and factitious, by which that consent was determined and produced, in these advantages, all such vexation has found its compensation,* and that by the supposition a preponderant one.

But in England, the too narrow circle excepted, within which the only system of procedure compatible with justice — viz. the natural system,—has been suffered to continue unexcluded, the system actually established having had the judges for its authors, has, on every occasion, and in every shape, had the accommodation of those its authors for its main object, thence it is that evidence in its best shape, being at the same time productive of less profit and more vexation to the judge than in the unfit shapes in which alone it is received, stands excluded in the manner shown on a former occasion,† in so far as it has been in their power to exclude it, in the lump.

2. The same considerations, in so far as concerns the impropriety of putting an exclusion upon material evidence, on no other ground than that of the vexation or trouble liable to be produced by it to the functionary whose duty it is to extract or receive it, apply alike, it will be seen, to the case of the subordinate minister of justice.

3. Under English and English-bred law, the juryman being, as above, a species of judge, the same considerations should naturally be found applicable to his case. But by the tissue of incongruities and inconsistencies in which, by primeval barbarism, this species of judicature is enveloped, every application of human reason to the subject is in a manner ‡ repelled and put aside.

4. In the case of the professional agent of the party, the nature of the relation between him and his employer, *i. e.* the compensation which, for whatever vexation the agent as

* See note ‡ next page.

† See Chap. XI.

‡ The judge so called is, by the compensation afforded him for the vexation attached to his office, placed in a state of opulence. The common juryman, taken by compulsion from a situation frequently but little above indigence, is subjected to vexation the same in kind, and severer in degree, without any compensation. The special juryman, distinguished from the common juryman by nothing but a superiority, but that a very marked one — a superiority which places him above the habit as well as the need of drawing upon his time for his subsistence, — is left at liberty to serve or not to serve, and when it pleases him to serve, receives a real compensation for an imaginary damage.

At the same time, to the quantity of vexation which, in each suit or cause taken by itself, the juryman is capable of being subjected to, a limit is, in the instances of both classes of jurymen, applied, viz. by the above-mentioned mechanical expedient of confining the mass of evidence to the quantity capable of being delivered within the compass of a single sitting. By this contrivance, in an unknown proportion of the whole number of causes, an unknown proportion of the quantity of evidence that, under a system adapted to the ends of justice, would have been delivered, is squeezed out and excluded: and thus it is, that by exclusion of evidence, the prisoner in the jury-box, after vexation has been heaped upon him with the one hand, is let out from under it with the other, — but not till after the load thus heaped upon him has swollen to such bulk as to become physically insupportable.

such is subjected to, he receives of course, excludes all demand for exclusion of evidence on this score.

5. In the case of the *witness*, the magnitude of the vexation, combined with the impracticability of making amends for it by an adequate compensation, has very frequently, as above mentioned, the effect of putting not only a temporary, but a definitive exclusion, upon the evidence which it would have been in his power to afford. This exclusion is of the negative cast above mentioned: having for its cause the non-performance of the operations necessary to the extraction of the evidence.

This omission is referable in part to the imperfections of the system; and in so far, the exclusion cannot but be pronounced improper: on the other part, to the obstacles opposed by the nature of the case; and in so far as on that account, *proper:* those obstacles being either physically or prudentially insurmountable: prudentially, when, if they were surmounted, the mass of vexation thereby produced would be so heavy, that the suffering to the proposed witness, by means of his attendance, would be greater than the suffering to the party, by reason of the non-attendance of such witness, although the loss of a just demand, or the failure of a just defence, were to be the certain consequence.

As to the imperfections of the system, howsoever on this as on other occasions they may be found to have had, for their principal cause, the operation of an *active* sinister interest, they would be found at the same time owing in no inconsiderable degree to the *absence* of that active zeal for the service of justice which a system directed to the ends of justice would have inspired: — to carelessness — to indifference — in a word, to the love of ease. Observe now the fruit of sinister interest in this shape.

It is only in so far as the attendance of the proposed witness at the judicatory in question has place, the spot which at the time in question would otherwise have been the chosen place of his residence, being more or less remote from it, that the vexation produced by journeys to and fro, attendance and demurrage, has place. In the character of a ground of exclusion, this vexation would be removable by either of two expedients: — viz. 1. Examination in the oral mode by a judicatory *ad hoc;* viz. whether of the number of the permanent judicatories already established on the spot, or by a special commission issued from the judicatory in question for this individual purpose: — 2. Examination in the epistolary mode; — or if confined to that class of cases in which the security afforded for correctness and completeness by counter-interrogation is not necessary, the uninterrogated or spontaneous deposition mode, as exemplified in the case of affidavit evidence, might in that state of things be employed.

Of all these three modes, there is not one (it has been seen) but what is perfectly familiar to English practice, though, by that practice, with but few exceptions, — excluded from this state of things in which they would have necessity for their sanction, — confined to a state of things in which that sanction does not apply to it.

From a common-law court, a special commission for taking the examination of a witness at any part of the globe, is not without example. But on what condition? That the party, to whose disservice the testimony is to operate, consent to it. Thence comes one or other of two evils: either the remedy is left unapplied, in the case where the party against whom the evidence is wanted is a *malâ fide* litigant, conscious of being in the wrong, and accordingly determined to take advantage of every incident foreign to the merits, which can contribute to his success, — that is, in the case in which the demand for it is most urgent and most frequent; — or the judge employs some indirect expedient for extorting a forced consent, thereby obtaining a plea, and making a precedent, for the extension of that arbitrary power, the perpetual increase of which is among the sure effects, as it has been among the constant objects, of judge-made law.

An acknowledgment that must here be made is — that, on the part of the judge, the existence of effectual jurisdiction, in relation to the individual and the purpose in question, is not so *certain* when applied to a man in the situation of an extraneous *witness*, as when applied to a man in the situation of *party* litigant in the suit or cause. In the case of a party litigant, the interest, whatever it may be, that he has in the suit or cause, suffices, to a *certainty*, to give to the hand of justice a hold, the strength of which is proportioned to the value of that interest: while, in the case of an extraneous witness, there being no such interest, — in this case, whether to the purpose in question the hand of justice have or have not any such hold upon him, is matter of *accident*. But in this, as in every other case, the existence of this or that state of things in which the remedy is not applicable, affords not any reason why, in any instance in which it is applicable, it should not be applied.

§ 4. *Avoidance of Vexation by Disclosure.*

In regard to vexation by *disclosure*, one very simple consideration will suffice to show how necessary it is that it be admitted, in the character of a ground capable of being found sufficient to warrant the putting an exclusion upon an article of evidence.

But for this, it would be in the power of any *two* persons at any rate—for example, by means of a wager—not to say in the power of any *one* person, to force disclosures, pregnant with mischief in any degree to the public or to individuals: — disclosures of which the subject might be a fact of any sort at their pleasure: — with the most disastrous effect — investigations which public peace, not less than private delicacy, would forbid, would continually be made by the most indelicate hands.

So far as concerns the public, scarcely a day passes, but, in one or other of the two legislative assemblies, information called for on one side of the House is on this ground refused on the other, and by the majority of the House the refusal sanctioned. That, in out too many of the instances in which refusal takes place, no preponderant mischief would by concession have been produced, the refusal having self-conscious misconduct for its cause, cannot, so long as the conduct of public men remains short of perfection, admit of doubt; since wheresoever misconduct has any shape and place, all evidence, by which such misconduct might be brought to light, will of course, in so far as the power of refusal is in the hands of any person who, in the character of party to such misconduct, or that of third person acting under the influence of undue sympathy towards any such party, be refused: — but what will always be above doubt is, that there will have been other instances in which the mischief from disclosure would have been preponderant, and accordingly by official duty the refusal not only permitted, but commanded.

Parties litigant — extraneous witnesses — individuals at large—and the public at large; — such are the different descriptions of persons on this occasion it may be of use to keep in view.

Vexation by disclosure, — in what cases shall it, in what shall it not, be considered as forming an adequate ground for putting an exclusion upon evidence? Towards furnishing an answer to this question, the following rules, as far as they go, may perhaps be found to be not altogether without their use: —

1. Except as hereinafter excepted (viz. by Rule 6th,) so long as, with relation to the transgression which is directly in question, the article of evidence called for is not either irrelevant or superfluous in such case, although among the consequences or tendencies of the evidence or disclosure thus called for should be that of subjecting or exposing, either the examinee himself or any other person, to legal punishment, whether on the score of the transgression in question, or on the score of any other transgression which is not the direct subject of the inquiry, be that punishment what it may, the vexation produced by it ought not to be considered as constituting a sufficient, or in any degree proper ground, for putting an exclusion upon such evidence.

Reason. For, in the necessarily implied opinion of the sovereign, by whom the penal law creative of the transgression in question is upholden, whatsoever vexation is liable to result from the application of the punishment in question, in execution of the law in question, will receive its compensation: — its compensation, and that a preponderant one; viz. in respect of the evil which it is the object of the law thus to produce. Party litigant — extraneous witness — and individual at large; — to all these several situations, this rule seems to apply with equal justice.

2. Vexation, composed merely of the burthen of satisfaction as for wrong, ought not to be considered as constituting any sufficient ground for the exclusion of the evidence by which an individual would be subjected or exposed to it.

Reason. The same, *mutatis mutandis,* as in the preceding case.

3. Vexation, consisting merely of the loss and sensation of regret incident to the legal obligation of surrendering or failing to obtain a valuable object, which belongs of right to another party, — or of rendering a burthensome service, which in any other shape is by law due to such other party, ought not to be considered as constituting a sufficient ground for exclusion, as above.

Reason. The same, *mutatis mutandis,* as above.

4. Whatsoever disclosure, in consideration of the vexation which might result from it to an individual in the situation of *principal, i. e.* person interested on his own account, ought not to be extracted from the breast of the individual himself, ought not to be extracted from the breast of any person to whom it has happened to receive information of it by means of any situation of trust possessed by him in the character of trustee in relation to such principal.*

* Note, that to the situation of party litigant, and that of extraneous witness, the means of compulsion adapted to the extraction of testimony, are by the nature of things rendered altogether different. To the situation of extraneous witness, that is, of a person who has no such interest in the cause as gives the hand of justice (as above) a hold upon him, some extraneous instrument of compulsion — such, for instance, as coercive imprisonment, is necessary. On the other hand, in the situation of party litigant, the interest a man has in the cause is, in the hand of the judge, an instrument sufficient for the purpose. From pertinacious non-responsion after pertinent interrogation, want of merits is the inference which, on the occasion of any private inquiry, is drawn of course by common sense: and the same on the occasion of legal inquiry would have been the inference drawn by common law, if by common law, common sense, in conjunction with common

Reason. For, the disclosure being the same, the vexation produced by it will not be materially different, whatsoever be the *source* from which the disclosure may happen to have been extracted.

5. But where the principal himself ought not to stand exempted from the obligation of making the disclosure, neither should any trustee of his be, on his behalf, so exempted.*

Reason. For, to the principal, the vexation will not be greater if the breast from which the disclosure is extracted be that of another person, than if it were his own: and if no adequate ground for the exclusion can be formed by the vexation produced by the disclosure in the breast of the individual whose interest in the matter is of the self-regarding kind, still less can it be formed by that sympathetic species of vexation which on such an account is unfit to be considered as forming a separate item, as being liable to be produced, as it were by contagion, in the breasts of a number of persons, and thence, in a quantity altogether indefinite, in the case of each individual

honesty had been taken for its guides. From non-responsion, and that which is equivalent to it, the inference is, on either side, want of merits: the principal fact probabilized, want of merits: evidentiary fact, non-responsion, false or evasive responsion. *In penali*, on the defendant's side, fact probabilized delinquency, viz. in the shape specified in the charge: from false responsion, or evasive inference, the same: of this circumstantial evidence, the probative force is not indeed absolutely conclusive, being liable to be weakened by possible infirmative circumstances (see the chapter on Circumstantial Evidence.) It is, however, much more so than many an article of circumstantial evidence, which, in present practice, is in use to be acted upon as conclusive.

* For avoidance of needless hardship by disclosure, the nature of things admits of a variety of expedients, which, in a system directed really to the ends of justice, and founded in a regard to human feelings, would be adopted with alacrity; but which, under a system directed to such opposite ends, and under the dominion of such opposite affections, will of course be treated with affected scorn as visionary and ridiculous.

The mischief to be guarded against, suppose it to have its source in the apprehended and unpunishable resentment of this or that individual in relation to whom, by some domestic or other intimate connexion, the party has been placed in a state of dependence, more or less strict and irresistible: — father, guardian (the party being of full age, or under age,) husband, expected husband or wife, father or guardian of ditto, patron, official superior, principal customer in the way of trade, and so forth.

1. By the principle of occasional privacy (as explained Chapter VIII. § 10,) much might be done towards the avoidance of mischief in this shape. The witness examined by the judge, in his adjoining *privy-chamber* — with or without the presence of persons named for the purpose, one by the party on each side, with the approbation of the judge, and bound by a solemn promise want of secresy.

2. The objectionable testimony in question not to be called for, but in case of necessity, *i. e.* for of other sufficient evidence.

3. Power to the judge, to exact or refuse to exact, to admit or refuse to admit, the objectionable testimony, according to the judgment formed by him on the question, whether by admission or exclusion the greater evil would be produced: such opinion to be supported by special reasons, to be thereupon entered in a book, to be kept for such purpose: a *secret register*, not accessible but to particular persons and for particular purposes.

4. Power to the judge, if, in his declared opinion, the importance of the matter in question be sufficient to warrant such an expedient, to convene the individual, whose apprehended resentment constitutes the objection — to convene him for the purpose of reconciling him, by proper representations, to the inquiry the necessity of which is imposed by the exigences of justice.

Other temperaments directed to the same objects—amongst them, regulations having in view the prevention of the abuses to which the powers in question stand exposed — might here have been brought to view: but in so contracted a sketch as the present, too much space will already be thought to have been bestowed upon an object so anomalous and so hopeless.

Operations of so domestic a cast will be immediately seen to be not compatible with the system of technical procedure, nor therefore with that mode of jury-trial which it involves.

A system of which they formed a part could be no other than a modification of the system of natural procedure, such as that brought to view in another work (*Scotch Reform*,) under which, in non-penal cases in general, and perhaps, to a certain extent, as at present under justice-of-peace law in the lighter and less important penal cases, without the forms, and consequently without the *delay*, *vexation*, and *expense*, to which, under the existing system, may be added the *precipation*, inseparably or otherwise attached to jury-trial, the suit or cause might be tried and receive its decision *in the first instance* from a single judge, with or without un-lawlearned assessors, two or some such small number, changing like jurymen, and of the class of jurymen; — jury-trial not to be resorted to, but in so far as demanded by a party in the way of appeal, as at present in the case of new trial: causes too complicated to receive a well grounded decision in the compass of a single sitting, being as there mentioned, decomposed and resolved into separate issues triable by separate juries.

Against discretionary power, when proposed to be given to a judge by law, and limited by the same law, meaning always real law, — against power to the exercise of which all eyes would be directed by the very law by which it would be conferred, the eye of public jealousy is apt enough, frequently more than enough, to put itself upon the alert. Towards power almost infinitely more extensive and exposed to abuse, so it have been assumed and exercised without law, — such as is all power exercised in the haze of common, *alias* unwritten law — especially if the abuse be in a particular degree inveterate, no such guardian eye can be prevailed upon to open itself.

Under judge-made law, all judicial power is arbitrary — essentially and irremediably arbitrary. Where there is no fixed standard, on whom can aberration justly be chargeable? When there is nothing *to err from*, how can aberration ever have place?

in whose breast is produced any particle of vexation of the self-regarding kind.

6. On the ground of apprehended mischief to the public, the judges ought to be not only authorized, but required, to apply to the demanded disclosure, absolutely or provisionally, exclusion or modification, according to the exigency of the case: declaring at the same time, in what particular shape it is that the mischief is apprehended; and if it be to the prejudice of the business of any particular official department, making communication of the matter to the chief of such department, giving at the same time notice to the parties of the communication so made, and appointing a day on which, on failure of sufficient cause shown for non-disclosure, disclosure shall be exigible.

7. There are certain transgressions, the nature of which is such, that the evil which they are liable to produce is produced wholly or principally by disclosure. If on either side, on the occasion of a suit or cause, penal or non-penal, having a different object, evidence be called for, of which, if delivered, the effect may be to expose any person, party or not party to the suit or cause, to the suspicion of having been concerned in a transgression of this description, it ought to be in the option of the judge to exact the delivery of such evidence, to permit it simply without exacting it, or to prohibit and prevent the delivery of it; pursuing that one of those courses which in his judgment promises upon the whole to be productive of the least balance on the side of evil, or the greatest on the side of good.

On any such occasion, for striking a balance such as above mentioned, the following are the items that seem most material to be kept in view in the taking of the account: —

Item 1. The nature and magnitude of the *evil*, for the *avoidance* of which — or (what is the same thing in other words) of the *good*, for the production of which the evidence in question is demanded: the evil, for example, subjection to undue punishment — subjection to an undue burthensome obligation, on the score of satisfaction as for wrong; — subjection to an undue burthensome obligation on any other score; — undue loss of any valuable possession, or of any valuable service due at the charge of this or that individual: — the good — viz. by the application of punishment where due — by the administration of satisfaction as for wrong, at the charge of the wrong-doer — and so forth, as above.

Item 2. The probability of the evil apprehended, in the event of an exclusion put upon the proposed article of evidence. The greater the probability, that without the proposed article of evidence, the effect proposed from it will be produced by other means — *i. e.* the less the need there is of it, to the purpose of producing that effect, — the less the advantage is, which, in case of its being delivered, there will be to set against the evil attached to the disclosure.

Item 3. The magnitude of the evil producible by the disclosure.

Item 4. The probability or improbability, that if not by the proposed evidence, the disclosure will be brought about by some other means.

To *probability* substitute *certainty*, the evil chargeable on the delivery of the evidence in question vanishes.

8. On the score of an offence of a purely public nature, unaccompanied with suffering inflicted on any assignable individual, punishment may with less inconvenience be, in any given individual instance, remitted, than satisfaction as for wrong done to an assignable individual refused.

Reason. For if the offence be but rarely repeated—the more rarely, the less is the need of punishment for the prevention of it: on the other hand, if frequently — the more frequently repeated, the more frequently will the opportunity occur of inflicting punishment in respect of it, without need of producing, in addition to such punishment, the casual and extraordinary evil here in question — viz. the vexation producible by disclosure.

§ 5. *Evidence that ought not to be admitted— Disclosure of Catholic Confession.*

Question. On the occasion, or for the purpose of a suit or cause, penal or non-penal, ought a priest to be compellable or receivable to reveal any communication made to him as such in the way of confession, according to the rites of the Catholic or any other church or religious persuasion?

Answer. Neither compellable nor receivable.

Reasons. — 1. In any law or mode of procedure, rendering such information compellable or receivable, would be included the effect of a penal law, prohibiting, in relation to the most important cases in general, and all criminal cases in particular, the exercise of the religious function in question: — a penal law, having for its penalty the punishment or burthensome obligation, whatsoever it might be, to which, by the testimony of the priest, the individual confessing, or any other individual, would be liable to be subjected.

In whatsoever suit or cause, penal or non-penal, it were proposed to make a religionist of the persuasion in question defendant, it would become a matter of course for the plaintiff or prosecutor, under the direction or by the instrumentality of his law adviser, to look out for the priest to whom the proposed defendant was in the habit of resorting for this purpose, and to summon him to appear as a witness.

A regulation to any such effect would therefore be a virtual proscription of the exercise of the Catholic religion.

2. In compensation for the evil of this tyranny, no good would in any shape be produced.

To the public at large, in respect of the interest it has in giving execution and effect to the aggregate body of the laws — in a word, to the ends of justice, so far from being conducive, an obligation to this effect would be purely adverse. In relation to the most mischievous crimes, for example, the effect of the institution in question, in so far as it has any, is much the more sincerely and uniformly, not only preventive, but compensative, than the effect aimed at by the laws for the sake of which, if at all, the proscription of it would be called for.

1. It is in regard to the contingent future *preventive*, in so far as, by means of the intercourse in question, any such impression as *repentance* and *reformation* is produced.

2. It may, even in a more determinate way, have, and doubtless ever and anon has had, the happy effect of exercising a preventive influence. Suppose that, by this means, on the part of a penitent of his, the existence of this or that particular mischievous habit or propensity has come to the knowledge of the spiritual guide, various are the ways in which, without exposing the penitent to discovery, measures may be employed for the prevention of the impending mischief.

3. Of this spiritual guide and comforter, the influence will naturally, be it what it may, in proportion as circumstances indicate a probability of success, be applied, not only to the prevention of future transgressions, but the disposing of the penitent to make reparation for mischief done by misdeeds already perpetrated.*

Crimes of sectarian fanaticism apart, by this time nearly, if not altogether, out of date, in no respect or degree can this sort of power be conducive to the taking anything away from the usefully-preventive, or in any other way remedial operation of the political or legal sanction. But if by means of the power of absolution, which is considered as attached to the exercise of this religious function, the usefully-preventive influence of the religious sanction be, in that class of religionists, upon the whole rendered less than 0 — a proposition the truth of which will, by the consideration just brought to view, be at least rendered dubious — then the diminution is an inconvenience inseparable from the Catholic religion, and not removable but by the extirpation of it.

§ 6. *Evidence that ought to be exacted,— Clients' Communication.*

Question. A lawyer — ought he to be compellable or receivable to disclose a matter of fact, the disclosure of which would be disserviceable to a client of his, in respect of a suit or cause, non-penal or penal, in which such client is party, plaintiff, or defendant?

Answer. Yes: compellable at any rate; if not when uncalled for receivable. For what reason ought he to be exempted? — from an obligation to that effect, what is the real evil capable of taking place? None whatever: unless, in a penal case, the subjecting a man to punishment where due, — in a non-penal case, the subjecting a man to the obligation of rendering the service demanded where due, or compensation, or both, be to be placed to the account of evil: — placed on this occasion, while they are not on any others.

The considerations which forbid the compelling or admitting the Catholic confessor to disclose misdeeds revealed to him in confession, have just been brought to view: — neither these nor any other considerations of a like tendency, will be found to have any application to the lawyer's case.

To the non-transgressor — to the innocent and honest client — no such exemption can be of any the smallest use. By the supposition, not having done anything wrong, nothing wrong will he have to confess.

The criminal,— the wrong-doer,— to these and these alone, the man of law himself excepted, can an exemption of this sort be of any use.

To the Catholic priest and confessor, it

* In the case of mischievous criminality, the duty of compensation and the use of the confessional in promoting the fulfilment of it, has, among Catholics, been a known subject of consideration and publication. A treatise, *Sur la Restitution*, by La Placelle, is a work the title of which cannot be altogether unknown even among Protestants.

To this purpose, let the actual effect produced by Catholicism be ever so small, it can scarcely be much smaller than the utmost effect aimed at by English judge-made law; and in particular, that part of it, which being the product of the most unexperienced and barbarous ages, is so piously held to view as a standard to which the rule of action in a riper and milder state of society ought for ever to be kept conformable. In so far as that branch of the law finds the means of execution, when the criminal has been consigned to legal slaughter, what property he has, instead of remaining for the subsistence of his innocent family, or being applied to the purpose of affording compensation to the injured as well as innocent victim or victims of his crime, is seized and made a prey of, nominally to the benefit of the monarch alone, really to the joint benefit of the monarch and the ever-industrious manufacturers of his prerogative.

With this "vicarious satisfaction," the morality of Blackstone has declared itself perfectly well satisfied. The satisfaction of the learned panegyrist would probably not have been quite so cordial, had the principle of vicarious application extended itself to lawyers' salaries and fees.

is matter of universally understood and acknowledged duty to do what depends upon him, as above mentioned, towards the lessening the number of mischievous acts in general, and lessening the amount of the mischief produced by such as have been committed; and that towards so salutary an end, more or less, how much soever less than could be wished, is constantly done, can scarcely be doubted.

By the lawyer, in his character of counsel or attorney for the criminal or self-conscious wrong-doer, so far from being ever exercised, no such salutary influence is ever so much as pretended to be exercised, or anything done towards the exercise of it.

On the contrary, in relation to a transgression of any description — say for example a felony — the part taken by a lawyer in the character of counsel for the defendant, is exactly the part which is taken by an accessary after the fact to that same felony, with no other difference than that between ignorance and danger on the one part, and knowledge, skill, and security, on the other.

In the situation of judge, the man of law (I speak more especially of English practice) manufactures flaws and loop-holes for malefactors and wrong-doers to creep out at:* — in the situation of counsel for the criminal or wrong-doing defendant, (not to speak of wrong-doing and unjustly demanding plaintiff,) he lets out to the malefactor and wrong-doer his best endeavours, to the purpose of enabling him to make his advantage of the assistance and encouragement thus provided and held out to him by his confederate on the bench.

It is a maxim among the brotherhood — a maxim not only acted upon but avowed, as often as under favour of opportunity, acquiescence can be hoped for — that *right* and *wrong* are creatures of their creation, and of which the existence is at all times dependent upon their pleasure; that, in so far as practised or encouraged by a judge, vice becomes virtue — in so far as punished or vituperated by him, virtue becomes vice.

It is in virtue and under favour of this maxim, that, under the name of *fictions*, falsehoods, in comparison of which the worst of those which in vulgar language receive the name of *lies*, are current: liberty-oppressing and money-catching falsehoods — falsehoods by these same arbiters of human destiny themselves committed, rewarded, and more than encouraged,—compelled; were, as Blackstone himself found himself everywhere obliged to confess, employed throughout as materials in the foundation of the system of procedure in particular, and in general in the whole fabric of judge-made law, *alias* common, *alias* unwritten law.

It is in virtue and under favour of this same maxim, that, for the benefit of Self and Co. they have licensed Co. to render to malefactors that sort of support and encouragement for the rendering of which, those to whom they have not communicated the licence are, under the name of *accessaries after the fact*, dealt with by them as felons.†

* Flaws, viz. by means of the principle of *nullification*, and other *devices*.

† "Call upon a man — of all men, call upon a man of law — to break his trust?" cries the man of law. Yes, surely: and why? Because the same considerations of general utility and justice, which in other cases call upon the ministers of justice to compel the observance of a trust, call upon him in this case to compel the breach of it: the breach — or if instead of the cooler word *breach*, the more impassioned word *betraying* or *violation* be employed in preference, the state of the case will not be altered.

A *trust* is but a species of *contract*. Be the contract what it may, from an arrangement of law authorizing or enjoining the breach of it, what is the consequence apprehended? On each individual occasion, one or other of two consequences it must be, viz. that either the contract will not be entered into, or if entered into, it will be broken. But if the effect of the contract, as often as it has any, be of a nature mischievous to the community, productive of a balance on the side of evil, — that these consequences, the one or the other of them, should on every occasion take place, is exactly the result, the happening of which will be the wish of every man, in whose scale of importance the welfare of the community in question, the greatest happiness of the greatest number of its members — occupies a higher place, than that of a wrong-doer and his hired accomplice.

An act which in itself — which in its own nature — is prejudicial to society, is it in the power of two men, by agreeing to join in the performance of it — of any two men, so as one of them be a lawyer — to render it innoxious and justifiable?

What is desirable is, that by honest men of all descriptions, honest and preponderantly beneficial contracts of all descriptions should be observed, performed, and carried into effect. Does it follow, that between dishonest men of all descriptions, and their respective confederates and coadjutors, hired from this or that one of the several houses of call in the neighbourhood of Temple-Bar, to contracts having for their object the giving success to dishonest acts, and security to the actors, the like force and effect should, as far as depends upon law and judicature, be secured? In the case of an honest engagement, it is by the observance of it — in the case of a dishonest and pernicious engagement, it is by the breach of it — that the community is served.

In a case of felony — in a case of swindling or smuggling — in a case of criminality or of transgression in any other mischievous shape, — it is not contended that, between accessary and accessary *before* the fact, engagements, having for their object either the effectuation of the distinct purpose, or the safety of the transaction, should be kept: — then why as between accessary and accessary after the fact?

Mischievous contracts ought not to be formed: and were it only to the end that in other instances they *may* not be formed,—in those in which they have been formed, they ought not to be ––

§ 7. *Avoidance of Expense.*

Cases where exclusion of evidence may be required, by the subserviency of such exclusion to the avoidance of preponderantly mischievous expense.

Of this class of cases, an exemplification, though under another head, has been already given. In case of compensation, vexation to A becomes expense to B, at whose charge the compensation is afforded. But in this case, the effect of the compensation is — to take away the need, and thence the propriety, of putting an exclusion upon the evidence, even supposing that, but for the compensation, the propriety of such exclusion would have been ever so clear and incontestable.

But, by whatsoever cause produced (compensation for vexation, or any other,) in what cases, if in any, shall *expense* attached to the exhibition of evidence — expense in its own shape — be considered as constituting a proper ground for the exclusion of it?

Of the general principle from which, in every case, an answer to this question may be deduced, sufficient explanation, it is supposed, has been given above.

For conveying a conception, however slight of the difficulties with which this spot in the field of procedure is incumbered, a reference, however short, to existing practice, seems scarcely to be dispensed with.

Under English judge-made law, for getting through these, as well as so many other difficulties, a very simple rule suffices: — *right to justice depends upon opulence.* The law is a lottery: have you money enough for a ticket? Down with your money and take your chance. Does money run short with you? Lie still and be ruined. It was not for you that justice, or, what is the same thing, that judge-made law was made.

On the mere tender of a sum of money *adequate* (*i. e.* that shall eventually be deemed adequate) to the expected expense, be his testimony relevant to the matter in issue or not, every man is bound to attendance: without such adequate tender, no man is bound to attendance.

Where needless and uncompensated, the vexation imposed — where necessary to justice, and thereby the vexation compensated, the service not exacted — such, on this part of the field, are the evils produced by judge-made law.

From the further end of the kingdom a man may be called away from his business, and kept from it days or weeks: for his expense, he receives a compensation, adequate or inadequate: for his loss of time — a loss in which pecuniary loss, the equivalent of expense to an indefinite amount, may have been involved — no compensation does he receive whatever.

Watching his opportunity, it is in the power of any man buying at the justice-shop an instrument called a *subpœnâ*, and paying moreover to the proposed witness any sum of money of the sufficiency of which he is assured, to inflict injury to an unlimited amount on any other man in whose suffering he beholds a source of sinister enjoyment.

Such is the mischief to which the hand of venal justice lends itself, by exacting labour in this shape, where it ought not to be exacted.

On the other hand, let the need of it be ever so urgent — let the consequences of its being withholden be ever so ruinous — let the vexation attached to the rendering of it be to the proposed witness ever so slight and inconsiderable, — no money, no evidence.

Money at stake upon the cause, say £4000

---

formed, — they ought not to be suffered to be performed.

A trust is a sort or species of *contract*: — and who is the sort of man who, for the furtherance of his own sinister interest, at the expense of every honest interest, calls for a blind and indiscriminating observance of this pernicious contract? Who but that very sort of man, who, for the furtherance of the same sinister interest — with the principle of nullification in his hand — that instrument of his own manufacture, by a touch of which not only all private engagements, but all public engagements — in a word, all laws, are broken and bereft of all their efficacy at his pleasure, — breaks and annihilates any the most beneficial engagements without remorse.

With a view to, and for the sole purpose of the general good, to the prejudice of that particular and sinister interest of his own, he will not hear of the annulment of a contract: — when, without so much as the pretence of good, general or particular, on the mere ground of this or that quibble — this or that palpably absurd or mendacious assemblage of words in his mouth, on grounds confessedly, or rather professedly, foreign and irrelevant to the merits — for non-compliance with this or that condition, never announced, and by the most sagacious discernment and ingenuity incapable of being anticipated — for non-performance of this or that condition, the performance of which he has taken care shall be impossible, he destroys whatsoever contract comes in his way at pleasure.

Note also, that the same sinister interest which for the benefit of his own trade engaged the man of law to secure to himself so convenient an exemption, engaged him, by means of the same uncontrouled power, to secure to himself the monopoly of it. The medical practitioner, to whose healing art a malefactor, wounded in the prosecution of his enterprise, has had recourse for relief, and who by his lips is called upon to help to destroy the life which his hand had saved: — the trust reposed in the exerciser of this pain-assuaging and life-preserving art — of whose labours good in the purest shape is the unvarying object, is this purely virtuous and beneficial trust secured likewise from disclosure? Not it indeed: — any more than that of the *banker*, or the exerciser of any other honest trade or profession by which service without fraud or hypocrisy is in any shape performed.

advance necessary to defray the proposed witness's expense, say £5;—rather than the rich man should suffer a loss of £5, upon the poor man a loss is imposed of £4000.

Of the mass of mischief capable of issuing from this source, under the complication of uncertainties under which business of this sort labours, a portion more or less considerable must, it cannot but be acknowledged, remain always unavoidable.

But in comparison of that, the source of which may be seen in the imperfections of the system, the part which has its source in the inexorable and incorrigible nature of things will be found inconsiderable.

By those timely explanations, the need of which there has been such perpetual occasion to bring to view,—difficulty in this, as in so many other shapes, would, by far the largest portion of it be cleared up—evil in these, as in so many other shapes, by far the largest portion of it dispelled. No such explanations have place—no such explanations ever can take place. Effectual care has been taken that no such explanations ever shall take place:—and why? Lest in these same shapes, *evil* to *suitors*, and thence *good* in the shape of profit, power, and ease to Judge and Co., should be dispelled.*

* "To enable a man to produce his witnesses before a jury," says Mr. Peake,—(but how is it where there is no jury?)—"in cases," continues he, "where they will not voluntarily appear in his behalf," (add—or it is apprehended may not,) "the law," continues he, "has provided a compulsory remedy by the writ of *sub-pœnâ*."—"The service of the writ of *sub-pœnâ* is made," he goes on to say, "by delivering a copy to the witness, and showing him the original, at the same time tendering a *reasonable* sum of money for his expenses, *according to his station in life;* and, if after this he neglect to attend, he will be liable either to an attachment, to an action at the common law for damages, or to an action on the statute of 5 Hen. c. 9. for the penalty of £10; and the further recompence given by that statute at the election of the party injured by his negligence."

Thus far the learned expositor. Of all these several optional consequences, or any one of them, on the occasion in question, in and by the message by which a man's attendance is commanded, is any the least intimation given to him whatever?—but instead of it, what he is threatened with is—the payment of a sum, the same in all cases (£100,) for which in no known instance was a man ever called upon: a prophecy so sure to be mendacious, that by the learned expositor, in his list of remedies, no mention, it may be seen, is made of it. Here then, as usual, may be seen English judges, in habitual solemnity, declaring themselves "witnesses" to a downright lie, and that capable of being a most pernicious one. For suppose that, at the expense of £100, by withholding this service when due, a man saw an assurance of reaping, in the shape of money, vengeance, or any other shape, an advantage more than equivalent to that expense, what the judge by this message gives him to understand is,—that such is the opportunity which the law, in its wisdom, has put into his hands.

Exists there that malefactor, be he ever so vile, by whom, were credence given to his word, an honest man would be so likely—not to say so certain—to be deceived, as by the purest of English judges, expressing himself deliberately and solemnly—sometimes under his own hand, sometimes by the hands of his appointed instruments, sometimes telling the lie in his own name, sometimes representing the king as telling it, and himself as witnessing it.

On a charge of murdering his father, or cutting a piece of cloth into smaller pieces, suppose a man hanged for want of the exculpation which a man who should have been witness would have afforded:—who in this case gets the promised "damages?" As soon would they be got by the man's ghost, as by his widow or his orphans. Such from beginning to end—if under the pressure of necessity the terms may be applied to a nonentity which has neither—such, from the beginning to the end of its fictitious texture, is the providence of judge-made law: and under such providence reigns a rule, sacred among lawyers and lawyer-led legislators, consigning to infamy with the word *theorist* upon his forehead, the man who shall dare to propose any such dangerous innovation as that of applying a remedy in any shape, to mischief in any shape, before it has been proved to have already taken place.

8. *How to minimize Evil in all these cases.*

Of the course necessary to be taken for this purpose, an indication has, in general terms, been already given—(see § 3.) The first thing to be done, is to reduce to its minimum the whole mass of the delay, vexation, and expense necessary to the production of each such portion of the proffered or supposed obtainable evidence, as shall be pronounced neither *irrelevant* nor *superfluous*. This done, as to any portion the exhibition of which appears to be unavoidably attended with a mass of evil in the shape of delay, vexation, and expense, such as threatens to outweigh any evil of which, in respect of danger of misdecision, for example, the exclusion of that same portion of evidence would be productive, then it is that, as to any such portion, a determination is to be taken, whether, upon the whole, it is by admission or by exclusion that the most effectual provision would be made for the fulfilment of the ends of justice.

But as to both these points, what, upon the bare mention of it, can scarcely fail to render itself manifest to an unprejudiced mind is—that, to the purpose of any individual cause, no well grounded or rational determination can ever be taken but upon a distinct and comhensive view of the particular circumstances of the individual case. What are the indivividual facts that require proof?—in relation to each such fact, what are the articles of evidence that are expected?—and in relation to each such article of expected evidence, what are the source or sources from whence it is expected?

What, at the same time, will be no less manifest is — that by no other means can these individual circumstances be ascertained, either with anything near the security against deceptious incorrectness and incompleteness, or with nearly so little delay, vexation, and expense,* as by means of those *mutual explanations* which take place with such perfect facility and effect, wheresoever at the outset of the cause, the parties are brought together face to face in the presence of the judge: in which confrontation is included and implied, not only spontaneous deposition on both sides, but interrogation *ex adverso*, and, upon occasion, even interrogations *undequàque*, as in a former chapter explained.

In a subsequent chapter, on the occasion of a particular species of fact, viz. the genuineness or spuriousness of a proffered legal instrument, an exemplification will be given of the service which, by such timely opportunities of mutual explanation, would, throughout the whole field of judicature, be rendered to the ends and interests of justice.

Relevant, or irrelevant? — not superfluous, or superfluous? On questions such as these, the power of deciding may to some eyes present itself as exposed in no inconsiderable degree to abuse. It will, however, be found not to be so in a greater degree than many others of the powers inseparably involved in the general power of judicature; and in particular that of determining, in each individual instance, whether, as just mentioned, the degree of collateral inconvenience — of delay, vexation, and expense incident to admission, shall or shall not be regarded as sufficient to render exclusion preferable.

As to these powers, particularly in the case of irrelevancy or superfluousness, were they in ever so much greater a degree exposed to abuse, they would not be the less necessary: since, but for the safeguard they afford, cases would not be wanting in which, by the force of overbearing opulence, the merits of the cause, as well as the substance of the less opulent party, might be overwhelmed and drowned—drowned in an ocean of delay, vexation, and expense.†

By the timely explanations just spoken of, all unnecessary evil incident to the production of evidence would be prevented; as in every corner of the field of judicature, fortunate enough not be polluted by the claw of the technical harpy, it is prevented of course.

Articles of evidence, of which, upon explanation, it were seen and acknowledged that they would be either *irrelevant* or *superfluous*, would be discarded, — discarded before an atom of that delay, that vexation, or that expense, which would have attended the production of them, had been produced.

When, of two objectionable articles of evidence appertaining to the same fact—the one requiring but a small mass of delay, vexation, and expense—the other, a mass of those same evils in any amount larger, expectation is entertained that the least burthensome may suffice to command the decision, this least burthensome will be the mass to be produced in the first instance; eventual liberty being reserved for the production of the more burthensome mass, should the other be found insufficient.

§ 9. *English Practice in relation to the above Evils.*

By the explanations just spoken of, the above several evils would for the greatest part be excluded. But out of these same evils, and in a mass proportioned to the aggregate mass of those same evils, does the profit of Judge and Co. increase. It is therefore the interest of Judge and Co., that — not the evils themselves, but the explanations by which they would be excluded, should be excluded: — and excluded they are accordingly: and of such exclusion a cornucopiæ of those same evils is the result: for the box of Pandora is the cornucopiæ of the man of law.

Under the impossibility of determining beforehand, in relation to this or that article from which advantage is looked for, whether it will be deemed relevant and admitted, or irrelevant and excluded,—in relation to this or that article, whether after the production of what other article there may be of the same tendency, a demand for it will be found existing, or whether it will not be found superfluous, — every particle of information that presents any the smallest chance of proving serviceable and admissible is anxiously looked

* Except always the comparatively rare case, in which, for a time or for ever, such confrontation is either *physically* or *prudentially* impracticable: in which case, oral examination finds a necessary substitute, temporary or definitive, in the *epistolary* mode.

† In the idea of excluding a mass of evidence on the ground of irrelevancy, a sort of apparent self-contradiction may be apt to present itself;— for, "How can you tell what it is," it may be asked, "till you have either read or heard it?" But relevancy will, it is believed, be found to regard the relation between fact and fact, rather than that between fact and evidence — rather than the relation between a given matter of fact, and evidence *directly* probative of that matter of fact: — to reject evidence on the score of irrelevancy, will accordingly in general be, to say — *this fact*, the existence of which you require to be admitted to prove, viz. in the character of an evidentiary fact or circumstance probative of the principal fact in question, has not, supposing it proved, any connexion with it, sufficiently close and strong to compensate the mass of delay, vexation, and expense, that would be inseparable from the production of it: — therefore it shall not be produced.

out for, hunted out, and, at an expense to which there are no limits but those of the pecuniary faculties of the party and the estimated importance of the cause, dragged to the scene of action: and thus the pecuniary faculties of the parties at least, if not the theatre of justice, are oppressed by a load composed of irrelevant or superfluous, or irrelevant and superfluous evidence.

Of this aggregate mass of evidence — this or that item — necessary and proper, irrelevant or superfluous,—cannot (suppose it found or apprehended) be obtained within the regularly allotted time; — thus comes more delay, and by need of application for this extra time — and application made accordingly — and opposed or not opposed, — more expense.

"How many witnesses have you to examine?" So many. "How many hours, think you, may the examination of them, with your speech upon it, take up?" So many. "Oh, then; trying the cause now will be impossible." Thence comes one or other of two jobs — *a remanet*, or a *reference:* — a *remanet*, with fresh fees for the counsel already employed: — or a *reference*, with fees *de die in diem* as above, for others of the same robe, one or more, in the character of judges.

Thus in one cause: — while, in another cause, by economy or by pecuniary inability, this or that article of evidence, which on the trial is discovered and pronounced to be indispensable, is kept back: consequence, if it be on the plaintiff's side that the deficiency has place, a nonsuit.

If on the defendant's side, so much the better: because, in that case, under the name of *motion for a new trial*, comes a second for trying whether there shall be a third; — and thereupon, by the blessing of God, that third: — whereas, in the case of the *non-suit*, *two* is the number of blessings to the enjoyment of which, in the first instance at least, the piety of the long robe is limited.

Till a quarter of a year, or half a year, or a whole year, after the discovery has been made, no misconception shall be set right, no error corrected, no omission supplied, no obscurity or ambiguity cleared up — till a quarter, or half a year, or a whole year, according to the distance from the seat of government — behold in this state of things one of the laws virtually included in the institution of *terms and circuits:* and this too under a system, under which, in virtue of the principle of nullification, errors are imputed to a man *ad libitum*—errors for which, if not finally debarred of his right, he is thus, in his painful pilgrimage for the attainment of it, thrown back, for having omitted to interpret, or failed in his interpretation of, this or that dream that never had been communicated, if as yet it had been so much as dreamt.

And merely because they are told so — told so by a set of men whose profession it is to deceive everybody, and whose interest it is to deceive *them*,—still, and in this nineteenth century, the good people of England are weak enough to conceive it possible, that a system, with two such features in it as the above causeless delay established by law, and nullification for causes foreign to the merits — (two such features out of twenty such that have elsewhere* been brought to view)—could have really had for its object the furtherance of the ends of justice.

Of these two features, one alone, viz. that of religiously-established delay, suffices of itself, in the eye of an English lawyer, to render the very idea of employing exclusion of evidence provisionally, in the character of a remedy against delay, not merely odious, but ridiculous, and scarcely intelligible. That the quantity of delay established should be reducible to anything less than at least ninety times as great as it need be, and elsewhere is, — is a state of things, to the conception of which, even in the way of fiction, familiar as fiction is to him, his mind knows not how to fashion itself.

Under the common-law, the jury-trial system, all these gordian-knots are cut through at a stroke. A mass of evidence, to the quantity of which, and consequently to the length of *time* necessary to the exhibition of which, there are no determinable limits, is undertaken to be forced into the compass of a single sitting. The consequence is,—that, in no small proportion of the whole number, causes are, of necessity, badly tried, and, in another not inconsiderable proportion, they are not tried at all. In these last cases, the cause is sent off, as above, to *reference:* and thus it is that, at *common law*, the trial of matters of fact makes a *job* for the benefit of barristers, fee'd in the character of judges, *quoad hoc* in the character of *referees*, or *arbitrators;* — as *in equity*, for the benefit of the sort of subordinate judges called *masters:* both receiving payment, in such a mode as puts their interest in a state of the most point-blank opposition to their duty: — payment, viz. in proportion to the quantity of delay, vexation, and expense, to which they have given existence—both operating in that secresy by which every desirable facility is afforded to the sacrifice to which the interests of justice have been doomed.

By way of prelude to this scene of pillage, the parties, without any of the *benefit* of jury-trial, have had the whole of the *expense:* and thus it is, that the more completely incompetent it is to its professed and pretended objects, the more indefatigable are the eulogies of which this mode of judicature may for ever

* Scotch Reform.

be assured, at the hands of the only class of persons who can so much as pretend to have anything like a distinct and adequate comprehension of it.

In relation to this subject, anything in the way of detail would here be not only misplaced, but needless: in another work,* indication, and in considerable detail, has been given, not only of the *mischief*, but of the remedy — the only sort of remedy which the nature of the case admits of.

CHAPTER XXI.

EXCLUSION CONTINUED—CAUSES FOR WHICH IT CANNOT BE PROPER.

§ 1 *Avoidance of Deception: viz.* 1. *through Imbecility.*

A CLASS of cases in which (as there has already been more than one occasion incidentally to observe,) exclusion of evidence cannot (it will be seen) be in any instance *proper*, that is, subservient to the ends of justice upon the whole, is that in which it has for its sole ground or cause, a regard for the direct ends of justice, viz. the desire of preventing misdecision, in respect of the question of fact — and thence of preventing deception, deception by the operation of the evidence, against which, in the character of a safeguard, the exclusion of it is proposed. Say for shortness, exclusion *on the score or ground of deception*;—or, exclusion *for fear of deception.*

Imbecility, interest, improbity, viz. on the part of the individual whose testimony is in question: to one or other of these heads will, it is supposed, be found reducible every plea for exclusion, in the case where it has danger of deception for its ground.

As for *imbecility*—intellectual infirmity—were it not for the purpose of showing that it has not been overlooked, it would, in so abridged a sketch as the present, be scarcely worth mentioning. In the body of the work, it will be brought upon the carpet, and with it the imbecility displayed upon the subject by English judges, who are not the less good witnesses.

Mental derangement, non-age, superannuation: these three words may suffice to bring to view its modes, — its modes as deduced from its causes. As to trustworthiness, it depends in this case altogether upon degree: depending upon *degree*, it depends upon *idiosyncrasy:* and of idiosyncrasy, examination, which cannot be without admission, presents the only test.

§ 2. *Through Interest; viz. Sinister Interest.*

1. Of *interest*, it may perhaps by this time be suspected at least, that no proper cause of exclusion will be found capable of being deduced from it.

If by *interest*, a proper ground for exclusion were afforded, all evidence that has the human breast for its source, would be to be excluded: all *personal* evidence; and along with it, all justice.

2. Of interest it has been shown (Ch. VII.) that but for its influence, no evidence at all would ever be produced: that if it be by interest that all mendacious incorrectness and incompleteness is produced, so it is by interest that all security against deceptious, — against mendacious, as well as against temerarious incorrectness and incompleteness, — is produced.

3. From interest, it is only through the medium of incorrectness or incompleteness that deception can be produced. From interest, the worst that is apprehended as the immediate effect of it — the effect of it on the testimony of the witness, is falsehood; *i. e.* material incorrectness or incompleteness. Now from such falsehood, no evil effect — to the purpose of the individual occasion at least, is produced, but in so far as deception is produced. But of falsehood, even of meditated falsehood, deception is no necessary or constant consequence; and in so far as antecedently to decision it is detected, instruction, — and in so far, not *misdecision*, but *right decision*, is the natural fruit of it.

4. In the case of mendacity-prompting interest, — in proportion as its mendacity-prompting influence is obvious, — obvious to all mankind, exactly in that same proportion is it unlikely to prove deceptious.

5. A *pecuniary* shape, is that shape in which its mendacity, and temerity-promoting influence is most plainly and most universally obvious. It is in this shape, and scarcely, if at all, in any other, that *interest* has been taken for a ground of exclusion by the founders of the English law of evidence. Love of *power*, — regard for *reputation*, — *sensual appetite*, — *sympathy*, — *antipathy*, — in none of all these shapes, single or in combination — no, not though all were combined together, — is any influence, worth the employing of this their universal remedy for guarding against it, attributed to interest, by these sages. Such is the truth, such the depth, of their system of psychological dynamics; — love of money is the only love which in their theory has any force.

6. In the ordinary concerns of life, business in general is undertaken and carried on, in part or even wholly, on the ground of information from persons, in whose breasts, not only interest, but interest in a pecuniary shape, is acting, and that with no less force than what it would, on a judicial occasion, be acting with within the breast of a witness or party, and without that restraint which, in

* Scotch Reform.

the case of judicial testimony, is applied by the fear of punishment and public shame. Under these circumstances, deception is, it is true, but too common; yet, in comparison of undeceived judgment, rightly deduced from statements true or false, or partly in the one case, and partly in the other, the case of deception is still comparatively but a rare one. Deception as often as it occurs—deception, as being a case comparatively extraordinary, is sure to attract notice:—right judgment, being the ordinary case, passes unobserved, and no account is taken of it.

The giving admission to what is called interested evidence (as if there were any evidence that were not in some way or other under the influence of interest,) is therefore not a rash projected experiment that remains to be tried:—it is a course of experience that has been carrying on, and with success, as long, and to as great an extent, as human life itself.

§ 3. *Through Improbity — including Religious Persuasion.*

In the order of consideration after interest comes improbity. Why? Because it is only through the medium of interest, that, in the case of improbity, danger of deceptious incorrectness or incompleteness can be produced. Exposed to shame at any rate, and to punishment, unless in this respect, in manner before mentioned (Chap. IX. *Oath*,) the legislator has been unobservant of his duty, the testimony of the most profligate man will not be any more likely to turn aside into the path of *mendacity*,—no, nor even into the less crooked path of *temerity*—than that of the most virtuous, unless led into it by the promoting influence of interest—of interest in some sinistrously-directed shape.

To the head of exclusion on the score of *improbity*, belongs exclusion on the score of *religious persuasion*—persuasion on the subject of religion. Not that to persuasion, howsoever erroneous, nor even how mischievous soever the error resulting from it,—not that even to such persuasion, supposing it sincere, any such imputation could consistently with justice be attached, but that such is the imputation which in fact men are but too generally found in such cases to attach to it.

Concerning *atheism*, it can scarcely fail of being acknowledged as soon as mentioned, that the mode of persuasion indicated by it is of that sort which cannot ever be proved upon a man but by means of veracity on his part—and that to a degree of which, even among Christians, the extreme rarity is proved by experience, unhappily but too incontestibly:—veracity in circumstances in which, in case of mendacity, detection is impossible. For in such security rests every false declaration of internal persuasion, of the falsity of which no special indication can be given by any special external sign or act.

As to *cacotheism*, it is an appellative, which by any person to whom the grammatical import of it is known, cannot be refused to any religious persuasion, in so far as to the Almighty are ascribed by it any such qualities as those of malevolence and maleficence. But such unhappily are his attributes in the eyes of religionists in general: malevolent in description, he is benevolent only in name. But surely, consistently either with moral justice or grammatical propriety, not even on the ground of any such persuasion, how pernicious soever in its effects, can any such imputation as that of improbity be attached—that imputation, which, on the ground of simple non-belief as above, as if in revenge for contradiction, men in general are so forward to attach.

§ 4. *Avoidance of Vexation by Self-Inculpation.**

In the last preceding chapter, in the case of a conflict betwixt any one and any other of the ends of justice—say the direct and collateral—the comparative magnitude of the good and evil in question were held up to view, as constituting the proper criterion by which, in every such case, the choice should be determined. The principle itself will scarcely be regarded as subject to error: in the application of it, should any error ever be suspected, it is in the mode of application, if anywhere, never in the *principle* itself, that the cause of the error will be found:—on one side or other, for example, some *item* left out of the account: on one side or the other, to this or that item, such a quantity ascribed, as turns out to be more or less above, or more or less below, the truth.

In the case of a penal law, for example, the vexation which, in a given individual instance, would, by the execution of it, be unavoidably produced in the breast of an unoffending third person,—would the evil of it be greater than that which, in the same individual instance, would result from impu-

* *Self-inculpation*, on this occasion *self-accusation*, is the term that has been generally employed: *nemo tenetur seipsum accusare.* This, however, is not the term suited to the occasion. *Accusation* implies *spontaneity*: but where a question has been put, the act of answering to it is not *spontaneous*. Ill adapted to the purposes of correct expression, the term was not the worse adapted, but the better adapted, to the deception that was intended.

To inculpate a man, is to assert or to show that his conduct has been blameable: by the man himself, in certain cases, after a question put to him, this may be as effectually shown by silence as by discourse: but in any case, to say of *silence* that it is *self-accusation*, is plainly a figure of speech, and, if employed in argument, a rhetorician's trick.

nity on the part of an offender? If yes — then, rather than the vexation should be produced, the impunity ought to be suffered to take place. By impunity given to an offender, the ends of justice contravened are indeed the *direct* ends; by *vexation*, inflicted on that same occasion, the ends of justice contravened are but the *collateral* ends. True: but the question of real importance, the question on which depends the propriety or impropriety of the choice is — not that of which *words*, but that of which sensations, are the subject; viz. as between two lots of good or evil, which is the greatest, which the least.

Laying out of the case all danger to innocent third persons, confine now the evil to the offending breast. No evil here of that sort which stands opposed to the *direct* ends of justice: as little — for let that too be part of the supposition — any evil of that sort which stands opposed to the *collateral* ends of justice: no evil but that of the punishment, and, by the supposition, that punishment not falling but where it is due. But in this case, though of punishment there be not any but what is due, of *vexation* there is not less in this case than in the other. *Punishment* itself is in itself neither more nor less than *vexation* — vexation inflicted on purpose, and for a particular purpose. But because there exists not that punishment, to which, as often as it is inflicted, the name of *vexation* may not also, and without impropriety, be applied, does it follow that punishment ought not in any case to be inflicted? Extravagance such as this has never yet been exemplified.

Not only is punishment vexation—vexation at the time of its being inflicted, but to the individual on whom, in the event of its being inflicted, it will be applied, all inquiry tending to such infliction is already productive of vexation. But, from this, does it follow that no such inquiry ought in any case to be made? In the scale of extravagance, let the supposed notion just mentioned stand ever so high, this can scarcely be placed below it.

Among the singularities of English law, and (note well) of *judge-made law* — for under *legislators' law*, it will be seen, the case is different — may, however, be seen a rule, composed of this very extravagance. To a defendant in a *penal* cause, not to speak at present of *non-penal* ones, be the cause what it may, no question, from the answer to which, supposing him guilty, the discovery of his guilt may be facilitated, ought judicially to be put: — if put, he is not bound to answer: — nor, from his silence, should any such inference as it is impossible for common sense to avoid deducing, be deduced by law. And thus it is, that an exclusion is put upon one of the most instructive species of circumstantial evidence.

But it is in the practice under this rule that anything like consistency is no more to be found, than in the practice under any other rule belonging to the law of evidence — not to speak of any other part of the mass of judge-made law. But whatsoever be the deduction that may here be found to have been made by inconsistency, what remains will present but too much matter for regret to every eye, to which, by sinister interest, the spectacle of human suffering has not been rendered an object of satisfaction or indifference.

In proportion as absurdity is gross and palpable, the imputation of *trifling* is a reproach to which it exposes every observation that can be employed in the manifestation of it.

In the course of those which follow, not a step can be taken but this imputation must be encountered. But so replete with mischief, and at the same time so deplorably strong and inveterate, is the prejudice in which this rule is grounded — so completely under the direction of interested lawyer-craft have barbarity and absurdity succeeded in passing themselves upon the public mind for humanity and wisdom — that few occasions, it is supposed, would be to be found, in which any such peril could be encountered for a worthier cause.

1. Be the defendant ever so guilty, the only ultimate evil that can befal him, whatsoever be the evidence by which his guilt is manifested, is that of the suffering, to which, on the score of *punishment*, it may happen to the question so addressed to him, to be contributory. But if, for forbidding such questions, so it be, that the danger of this evil constitutes a sufficient reason, where the individual to whom the questions are addressed is the defendant himself, so must it in the instance of every other individual that can be mentioned: an equally sufficient reason must it afford for prohibiting all questions of that tendency, to whatever other individual it may happen to them to be addressed: — in other words, for offering impunity to every delinquent whatsoever.

2. Different, in this respect, might be the case, if, in the first place, so it were that, on the part of men in general, when under prosecution with a view to punishment, there existed any such propensity as that of subjecting themselves to the punishment, when, in truth, they are innocent; if, moreover, in the next place, such were the strength of that propensity, as to render the danger of a man's being made to suffer such undue punishment by means of testimony given by him against himself, greater than by testimony given against him by other persons at large: all such included, as by injury supposed to have been received from him, or on any other score have been placed in the number of his particular enemies. But if in human nature there be really any such self-hostile propensity,

no traces of it seem as yet to have come to light.

3. In the character of a separate suffering, resulting from the particular mode in which, in this case, the evidence is obtained, — *vexation, hardship, suffering* — everything of this sort is altogether imaginary. The suffering consists in the punishment. The punishment being given, is it in the nature of man, that to him who is to suffer it, whether the evidence, by means of which the suffering is produced, be obtained from this source, or any other source, in this *shape* or in any other shape, it should make any the smallest sensible difference? Before the affirmative be asserted, first let some one man be found who, having his choice, rather than be made to pay £5 by means of this sort of evidence, the fact of the delinquency being in both cases rendered equally manifest, and equally notorious, would put his hand into his pocket, and pay down £6.

4. Those who are free from guilt, — is it possible that these should have been the persons for whose protection the rule was intended? They are exactly the very persons, and the only persons, to whom it cannot ever be of any use. Take any such person, for example: by the supposition he is free from guilt: but by the same supposition he is suspected. This being the case, the suspicion of which he is the object, it is surely his interest — if he be of sound mind, it is no less surely his wish — to remove: it is accordingly as well his wish as his interest that all such explanations as can contribute to that removal, and such, in particular, as afford the best chance for it, should be afforded. But from what other quarter can any explanations be expected, of which there can be so good a chance — if chance be here the proper term — of their being directed to that end?

5. All *other* evidence — all evidence *except* the testimony of the defendant himself — that would have been the evidence, to which to have applied the exclusion, supposing the eyes on which it depended open to this one object, shut against every other. But by such a substitution, supposing it practicable, neither the interests, nor consequently the purposes, of the contrivers of this rule, would (as will be seen presently) have been served.

6. If the saving a guilty defendant from the hardship of observing that the evidence by which his delinquency is exposed and his punishment produced, had been extracted from his own bosom, — if this be the object, in pursuit of which the exclusion was established, this object is after all not compassed. For not only is any letter or memorandum, which to the effect in question he has been deemed to have written, read against him, but any oral discourse, which to that same effect he is reported to have uttered, is delivered in evidence against him, delivered in his hearing, and without scruple or reserve. In its purest and most perfect state, in its acknowledged best state, — it is only in that state that evidence from this source finds the technical door so inexorably shut against it. Yet open this shut door is to evidence from this very source, when once it has been strained through other lips, and by that means reduced to the universally acknowledged inferior shape and condition of hearsay evidence.

7. Of the exclusion in the one instance, coupled with the admission in the other instance, what is the effect of the rule, as towards the only person for whose sake, if for anybody's, it professes to have been established?

For want of such explanations, as very frequently are neither obtained nor obtainable from any other mouth—explanations of which, if true, the effect might have been to substitute exculpation to conviction, — a lighter at least, to a deeper shade of delinquency,—conclusions to any degree dangerous to him are liable to be drawn from such casually written or hearsay evidence: and explanations to any such effect are not received from him in the character of evidence.

8. Of the exclusion thus put upon *first-hand* evidence, while admission is given to *second-hand* evidence, behold in one view the consequences: —

1. Whatsoever be the purpose in question, to that same purpose the information thus received is almost sure to be incomplete — deceptiously incomplete: for in relation to the matter of fact in question, whatsoever, if anything, it be, that on the extrajudicial occasion was said by the party in question, it is only so much as the deposing witness is at the same time able and willing to recollect, that is thus brought forth in evidence.

2. Of the remainder, which is not altogether suppressed, the account thus given may, by want of recollection, by negligence, or by improbity, have been rendered in any degree incorrect.

3. By the party himself, the incompleteness might be completed — the incorrectness corrected. No such completion—no such correction, is permitted.

4. From the substitution of such almost necessarily incomplete to less incomplete, of such naturally incorrect to less incorrect evidence, the only means of completing the incompleteness and correcting the incorrectness being at the same time excluded, the innocent are injured, as well as the guilty served.

9. In those situations, and on those occasions, in which the existence of real tenderness for the feelings of the individual concerned, as well as of the desire of coming at the truth,

are most indubitable, no such determination against drawing information from the most instructive source — no such predilection for second-hand, to the exclusion of first-hand evidence, is ever to be found.

In the case of a servant, or a child, if any instance of supposed misbehaviour is to be inquired into, where is the master of the family, where is the schoolmaster, where is the father, where is the mistress, where is the mother, weak enough to take for the model of his or her conduct, in this particular, the practice of English judges?

10. In the case of those higher classes of offences which have received the name of *felonies*, this rule of spurious law has for centuries been acting in the teeth of the only genuine law.

By two successive statutes of Philip and Mary (1 & 2, c. 13; 2 & 3, c. 10,) in case of suspicion of felony, the justice or justices of the peace before whom the suspected person is brought, are required "*to take the examination of such persons*," as well as "*the information of those who bring him.*" Examination? — concerning what? "*Concerning the fact and circumstances thereof*," says the statute, — viz. of the supposed felony. To what end? To the end that, in case of delinquency, such answers as shall have been then extracted may, along with the other evidence, contribute to his conviction, says the statute; — for this it is, "*or as much thereof as shall be material to prove the felony*," that is required to be "*put in writing*," and "*certified*," and so forth.

It is in virtue of these two statutes, that those *examinations* are taken, which are so constantly taken in every case of felony: and, if not for the purpose of eventually contributing to conviction, for what other useful purpose could any such inquiry be made, or have been ordained to be made?

Unfortunately for justice and good government, to offences below the rank of felony this did not extend, nor has the principle of it been extended. True it is, that in so far as in point of mischievousness those offences which in point of punishment fall short of being equal to felonies, the demand for such evidence falls short of being so imperious as it is in the case of felonies: but in the same proportion does the objection, — which on whatever score, and under whatever name—*hardship*, *severity*, *vexation*, *injustice*, *danger*, or *nuisance*, or whatever else the word may be, capable of being urged against the inquiry so directed, — fall short, in point of strength, of being equal to what it is in the case to which, by and under the only genuine sort of law, this most unobjectionable course for coming at the truth is ordained and pursued — pursued, viz. either in reality or in appearance, as is most agreeable to the worthy gentlemen, on whom in each individual instance it depends.

11. Yes: as is most agreeable. For in the class of cases in question, in which are comprised the most highly penal, capital cases included, by the exclusion put by judge-made law upon such evidence, coupled with the admission given to it as above by legislators' law, a disguised and despotic power of pardon has been virtually placed in the hands of those magistrates. Wishing to do justice, the magistrate conducts the examination according to the intention of the legislature: — wishing to show undue favour, and at the same time make a display of clemency and legal science, he takes his stand on judge-made law, and warns the criminal against suffering the language of self-accusation to issue from his lips.

12. In the case where the punishment would be no other than pecuniary, the inconsistency of the practice with itself affords the most conclusive proof of absurdity, that it is in the power of absurdity to receive. If the case be called penal, under the name of *punishment*, five shillings cannot be taken out of a man's pocket by evidence extracted immediately out of his breast, through the medium either of his lips or his hand. If the case be called *civil*, money to any amount — money, or money's worth, to the amount of his whole property, be that property ever so vast, may be taken out of his pocket, by evidence extracted — not indeed through the medium of his lips, but — what in respect of the enormity of the expense is to him far worse — through the medium of his hand; — and this is among the cases in which, to perform the extraction, *judge-made law* takes the name of *equity*.

13. The class of malefactors, to which this article of judge-made law is, perhaps, most continually favourable, are those whose situation in respect of power and opulence exempts them, in the pursuit of sinister interest, from the necessity of engaging in any of those dangerous paths by which men are exposed to the hazard of being subjected to such preliminary examinations: those whose crimes, being committed on a large scale, and consisting in peculation or in abuse of public power, in some well disguised and protected shape, receive at the hands of kindred iniquity every practicable facility and indulgence: and in this effect and tendency, coupled with the contribution made by it towards the aggregate mass of disguised despotism vested in judicial hands, may be seen at least probable cause, if not of the creation, of the ever tender care bestowed upon the preservation of it.

CHAPTER XXII.

EXCLUSIONS BY ENGLISH AND OTHER LAWS—ANALYTIC AND SYNOPTIC SKETCHES.

§ 1. *Undisguised Exclusions.*

OF the two most permanent and most comprehensive grounds and cases of exclusion, a view, howsoever abridged, has been already given a detailed view will be seen to occupy the extent of not less than a volume in the body of the work.* But even in this place, to leave in the state of a mere blank space, so important a compartment in the field of actual jurisprudence, was not to be endured: — an analytic sketch, howsoever meagre and compressed, seemed preferable to total silence.

Undisguised and *disguised:* by these two words, expression may be given to the first and most comprehensive distinction that requires to be brought to view.

Undisguised the exclusion may be termed, when, and in so far as, both the *fact* of the exclusion — the fact that upon a species of evidence of such or such a description an exclusion has been put, and the consideration on which, in the character of grounds or reasons, that exclusion has been, or upon occasion would be justified, seem out of doubt: —*disguised* it may be termed, when, and in so far as, either that fact or those reasons appear more or less unobvious and difficult to be discerned or ascertained.

Indirect — undiscriminating — limping — undiscernible — blind — wanton : by these several adjuncts — sometimes one, sometimes two or more of them together, the exclusion will, it is supposed, be found not unjustly characterizable, in most, if not all of the cases, in which it will appear susceptible of the more comprehensive appellation of *disguised.*

When the exclusion presents itself as having been the result of a view taken of some one or more apprehended inconveniences, considered in the character of grounds or justificative causes, serving as warrants for the exercise of such an act of power, the act of exclusion, as well as the consideration or considerations on which it was grounded, will concur in entitling it to the appellation of undisguised: — and here, although the ground itself should in the balance of reason be found deficient, still it is to *thought* itself, not to the mere absence of it, that the exclusion will appear referable.

On a simple ground, or on a complex ground: by these two words, viz. *simple* and *complex*, may be characterized the distinction which takes for its subject the cases in which the exclusion is undisguised: — simple, when *one* circumstance and no more presents itself as the ground on which the exclusion was built: — complex, where several such grounds present themselves.

Take, in the first place, the case where the ground of exclusion is simple. In this as in other cases, the ends of justice which, if any, have been had in view, will have been either the *direct* ends, or the *collateral* ends: — the *direct* ends, viz. prevention of *misdecision,* in the several forms of which it is susceptible: — the *collateral* ends, *i. e.* prevention of unnecessary *delay, vexation,* and *expense.*

Misdecision, in so far as produced by evidence, is produced through the medium of *deception:* deception, *i. e.* erroneous judgment, produced by it in the mind of the judge.

On the part of an article of evidence, whatsoever circumstance tends to diminish its justly probative force—this same circumstance, in proportion as the judge fails of being adequately apprized of such its tendency, tends to produce deception in the mind of the judge. On this consideration, every such circumstance has been already stated as constituting a proper ground for *suspicion,* though, for the reasons that have been given, not a proper ground for *exclusion.*

In English practice, any such cause of inferiority, how minute soever, is to a large extent considered and employed as a proper ground for exclusion: but with a degree of inconsistency, of which intimation has been already given : — such being the effect, which, in cases where the force of the cause is at its *minimum,* has been deduced from it, while in cases in which that force is at its *maximum,* this same effect has not been deduced.

Such, so far as concerns exclusion of evidence, is the complexion exhibited by English practice, when viewed in a mass, and when, and as the cases successively present themselves, groupe after groupe. In particular groupes, this complexion will not be seen to exhibit any considerable change.

In regard to *collateral* inconvenience, in all its three several forms as above, it has been stated as capable of constituting a proper ground of exclusion: the propriety depending, on each individual occasion, upon the proportion between the two evils — viz. the evil to be apprehended in case of *exclusion,* and the evil to be apprehended in case of admission. At the same time, *temperaments* have been brought to view, having for their object the exclusion of evil from both those sources, the complete exclusion of it, or, at any rate, the reduction of it to the least dimensions of which it is susceptible.

In English practice, in the shape of *delay* or *expense,* such *collateral* inconvenience appears scarcely to have been taken into account. In the shape of *vexation* it has been employed in the character of a ground of ex-

* Viz. in the original edition.

clusion, but with a degree of *inconsistency*, of which intimation has also been given above.

Let us consider, in the first place, the distinctions which present themselves in the case where the evil, by the apprehension of which the exclusion was produced, has been *misdecision*, viz. through deception.

The fact, to which the article of evidence in question immediately applies, may be either the fact itself which is in question, — say as before, the principal fact, — or some other matter of fact, which, in relation to it, is considered as *evidentiary*,—say as before, the *evidentiary* fact, — viz. either *probative* or *disprobative*. In the former case, the evidence is said to be *direct*: in the latter case is all *circumstantial* evidence, as above.

In its very nature, circumstantial evidence, viz. any single article taken by itself, has already been stated as being generally inferior in probative force to direct, (though not so in disprobative,) and in so far, as being comparatively speaking a proper object of suspicion, but in no instance as involving in its nature a proper ground for exclusion.

In English practice, circumstantial evidence, as such, is not in general considered as doomed to exclusion: but, in cases to a considerable extent, it will be found to be so; as will be seen more particularly in the *body* of the work.

Take now the case in which the evidence is *direct*. *Source* and *shape*: in these two, may be seen the characteristic terms by which the two branches produced by the next division, will stand expressed.

If, in respect of probative force, weakness be on any specific ground imputed to the evidence, the object pointed to as the *seat* of the weakness will either be in the *source* from whence — *i. e.* the person from whom— the evidence is immediately derived, or the *shape* in which it is received or extracted from him.

If, as above, it be in the person — *i. e.* of the proposed deposing witness — it will be either in his *relative position*, relation being had to the *means of information* afforded by it, or in the personal character and qualities attributed to him.

As to his means of information, it will have been presented to him either *ab intra*, by *internal cognizance*, — or *ab extra*, by external report: in the former case, it is afforded to him by the perceptions presented to him by his own senses or intellectual faculties; in the other case, by the supposed perceptions of some other person or persons as reported to him by such other person or persons. In so far as the former is the case, it is only to his own personal character and qualities as above, that any such imputation as above can point itself: in the other case, whatsoever be the personal character and qualities ascribed to such his informant or informants, the testimony delivered by him will, by at least one degree of distance, be removed from the seat or supposed seat of perception: and by such remoteness, how entire soever be the trustworthiness of the several supposed informants, — by such remoteness, in proportion to the number of degrees by which as above it is increased, will in every case be presented an incontestable cause of weakness, or diminution of justly probative force.

In so far as the alleged cause of weakness lies in the supposed character and qualities either of the deposing witness, the supposed percipient witness, or of any supposed intermediate reporting witness or witnesses — the alleged seat of such weakness lies in the supposed *nature* of the source from which, or of this or that one or more of the channels through which it is supposed to have passed. In the other case, it lies in the remoteness of the information from its supposed source.

State of the *intellectual* department — state of the *moral* department, of the man's mind: such are the terms by which the two branches produced by the next division may stand expressed.

Imbecility independently of age, imbecility by reason of age — such is the distinction that has place when the disorder in question, viz. apprehended untrustworthiness, has for its seat the intellectual department as above.

Having its *source* in the circumstance of *age*, imbecility will have for its *efficient cause* either *deficiency* or *excess*: — deficiency, viz. in the case of non-age; — excess as in the case of caducity, or say more expressively, *antiquation*.

If the disorder have the *moral* deportment for its seat, it can have no other than *sinister interest* for its efficient cause — sinister interest, *i. e.* as above, interest in any *shape* acting in the sinister direction here in question; viz. a direction in which its *tendency* is to produce deceptious incorrectness or incompleteness in the evidence.

Actual *exposure* to the operation of sinister interest in this or that particular shape— more than ordinary *sensibility* to the action of that stimulant: to one or other of these circumstances will the disorder in question be referable, in so far as, having its *seat* in the *moral* department of the human frame, it has for its *efficient cause, sinister interest*, as above.

Actual exposure to the action of *sinister* interest in the case of him who, with reference to the matter in question, is, in the language of English law, said simply *to have an interest*, or to be, if a witness, an *interested witness*.

To the purpose here in question, more than ordinary sensibility to the action of sinister interest is expressible in and by one word — *improbity*.

If the positions hereinabove endeavoured to be established be conformable to reason, *suspicion*, and no more than *suspicion*, is the proper practical inference deducible from any such disorder, actual or presumable, in the frame of mind of the proposed witness, and that whether the intellectual or the moral department be the seat of it.

Not only in England, but in other countries, and probably without exception in all other countries, either by statute or by judge-made law, have causes of exclusion been deduced from all these several sources: but with a degree of inconsistency, the complete development of which would require volumes.

Period of supposed *perception*, and period of *deposition:* by the state of things that has had place in one or other or both of these two periods, it is, that the *shape* in which the evidence presents itself is determined; and to one or other of which any intrinsic weakness that can be found imputable to it will be to be referred.

In so far as the period of *perception* is the time to which the weakness is referred, the imputation will have for its ground the absence of some one or more of those accompaniments which, in the case of preappointed evidence, have already been brought to view under the appellation of *formalities:* — in so far as the period of *deposition* is the time to which the untrustworthiness imputed to it is referred, the imputation will have for its ground the absence of some one or more of those accompaniments which have already been brought to view under the appellation of *securities* — securities for trustworthiness, securities against deceptious incompleteness and incorrectness.

As to *formalities*, the state of things which admits them is confined to that which admits of *preappointed* evidence: a case in which, the fact in question being foreseen, provision is made beforehand for the preservation of the means of proving it.

Of the accompaniments which, in the character of *formalities*, presented themselves as promising to be in the most advantageous way conducive to that proposed end, a general idea has hereinabove been given: — *suspicion*, not *exclusion*, has on *that* same occasion been mentioned as the practical inference, and the only practical inference proper to be deduced from any incorrectness or incompleteness, with which the best of such of them, as on any given occasion happens to have been employed, may be found chargeable.

In the state and condition of English law, statute and common law together, notice of the tissue of inconsistencies observable under this head has been already given. In the way of real law, — in the way of prospective law, — no tolerably complete system of formalities ever appointed: — in the way of judge-made law, — in the way of *ex-post-facto* law, — here and there, this or that formality set up in the character of one that ought to be observed: — from the non-observance of this never-notified formality, exclusion sometimes deduced, sometimes not: — practical inference, always *exclusion*, if anything; simple *suspicion*, never.

Prescribed or not prescribed by the law, the securities termed *formalities* — the securities for the eventual forthcomingness of adequate evidence — are capable — such is their nature — of existing and being employed, without having been called into existence by the law. The securities termed as above *securities* — the securities against deceptious incorrectness and incompleteness in the evidence when produced — are, almost without exception, creatures of law, depending upon the law for their existence.

As to these last-mentioned securities, if the positions herein endeavoured to be established be conformable to reason, in so far as practicable, — prudential as well as physical practicability taken into the account, — to a proposed article of evidence not yet brought into existence, they ought, all of them, to be applied: as also, upon occasion, to an article of evidence already in existence, such, if any, as have not as yet been applied to it; and from the absence, coupled with the inapplicability of all or any of them, *suspicion*, but not exclusion, ought to be, and that uniformly, the principal inference.

In the course taken under this head by English law — understand judge-made law — for in this part, as almost in every other part of the field of evidence, it is to the judicial authority that the framing the rule of action has been almost entirely abandoned by the legislative — the features of inconsistency have already been shown to be still broader, perhaps, than in any other. The accompaniments best adapted to this purpose have been fully understood; and on these occasions — *i. e.* on the occasion of those modes of trial in which the mode of procedure has not been capable of being shaped altogether according to the interest and pleasure of the judges — the absence of any of them has been laid hold of as a ground of exclusion; and exclusion — inexorable exclusion — in some instances has been put upon the evidence accordingly; while, on other occasions, viz. on the occasions of those modes of trial, the framing of which has been the work of the uncontrouled authority of the judges — on those occasions, all these securities have been excluded, — that inadequate portion of them excepted, which has been wrapped up in, and disguised and enfeebled by the ceremony of an oath: — and thus, as far as circumstances permitted, the door has been shut against evidence in its most trustworthy shape, opened to it in no shape but the most deceptious that could be given to it.

Remains the class of cases, in which, for the designation of the ground on which the exclusion appears to have been built, the term *complex* was employed. Fear of the evils opposed to the *direct* ends of judicature, fear of the evils opposed to the collateral ends of judicature, or one of them; in other words, desire, real or pretended, of avoiding to produce *misdecision* through the medium of *deception* — desire, real or pretended, of avoiding to produce, in this or that particular shape, *vexation*: such were the two grounds, with a view to which the word complex was employed.

The individual in question, a party to the suit or cause — a party, whether plaintiff or defendant; — the individual in question, connected by the matrimonial tie, with a party in the cause, bearing towards him or her, the relation of wife or husband: —

By these two more particular cases, the class of cases here in question are, if not absolutely exhausted, at any rate extensively exemplified.

From neither of these grounds, saving the comparatively narrow exceptions already indicated, if the positions hereinabove endeavoured to be established be conformable to reason, on neither of them, nor, for the same reasons, from both of them put together, can any proper cause of exclusion be deduced.

Under English practice, inconsistency may be seen triumphant here as elsewhere: exclusion abundant, but far from constant:—where it has place,—what the ground of it has been, — what the mischief meant to be avoided — whether one alone of the two mischiefs in question, or both, is not always clearly discernible: — to an ample, though not everywhere easily definable extent, the front-door has been shut against the evidence, but a side-door opened to it:—fact in question the same, — state of interests the same — the same in quantity, in quality, or in both — no matter, so the *name* given to the species of *suit* or cause be different: — since thus, besides the general benefit of *uncertainty*, and thence of obscurity and confusion, — two or more suits or causes have not unfrequently been manufactured out of one.

In the case where the term *negative* applies to it, the exclusion has for its efficient cause the non-application of some legal instrument necessary to the obtainment of the evidence.

On the part of a proposed witness, antecedent and introductory to the act of *deposition*, may be seen a multifarious and complex train of acts — all of them, for the purpose in question, sufficiently brought together by one word, forthcomingness.

Correspondent to these two modes of being on the part of the proposed *witness*, are so many modes of *negative* exclusion on the part of the *law*: non-provision of the powers, and other means necessary to the production of *deposition*, on the part of the proposed witness, supposing him in a state of forthcomingness; — non-provision of the powers and means, one or more or all of them, necessary to insure his being found in that state.

When, and in so far as it is left to a man's option, whether, on the occasion in question, he will or will not appear and act in the character of a witness, — in this case, in the *positive* sense, exclusion is *not* put, but in the *negative* sense, exclusion *is* put, upon evidence.

In the present work, what in relation to this head is contended for is, that,—due provision, excepted in this as in all other instances, for the case of preponderant inconvenience in the shape of *delay*, *vexation*, and *expense*, more particularly in the shape of vexation, — to render or not to render to justice, service in this shape ought not to be left to the option of the individual: — in other words, that *negative* exclusion is not proper, but where *positive* exclusion is so too: — for that of such option the tendency is to stock the judicatory with partial, and in that respect less trustworthy witnesses: and more particularly to render testimony, and thence decision dependent upon money or power — upon overbearing and oppressively aristocratical influence.

As to *actual* law: under this head, as under so many other heads, judge-made law may be seen exhibiting its usual inconsistencies as well as its usual imperfection and deficiency: in regard to forthcomingness, to no small extent the necessary means not applicable, because not created: — in other instances, though created, not suffered to be applied.

In particular, as to optionality, when the only shape in which evidence is admitted is that favourite shape which is the worst of all shapes in which the information admitted receives the name of *evidence* — viz. affidavit evidence, — deposition or non-deposition left completely at the option of the proposed witness: — thereby the probability of *misdecision*, viz. through the medium of deceptiously incorrect and incomplete evidence, screwed up to its *maximum* — say, in one word, *maximized*.

§ 2. *Disguised Exclusions.*

So much for the cases where the fact of the exclusion, the evidence it applies to, and the ground which, in point of utility, real, or supposed, it proceeds upon, all lie open to view. Come now the cases in which, wrapt in some disguise, these same objects shrink from observation. Thick is now the darkness that covers the face of the jurisprudential deep.

Analysis is here at a stand. Directed by her best guide, pursuing here and there such faint lights as offer themselves, enumeration enters upon her task, without any assurance of its completion.

1. Cases where the exclusion is effected by limits set to the quantity of evidence that shall be allowed to be extracted or received: for example, to the number of the witnesses who, in the case in question, or in relation to the fact in question, shall be heard: much as if a similar limitation were set to the number of sheets of paper on which the depositions shall have been entered, or to the bulk or length of the aggregate mass. Spanish, not English, is the system of law from which the idea of this species of exclusion has been derived. Vexation on the part of the judge, thence perplexity, thence misdecision — or delay, vexation, and expense — or both, appear to have been the evils the avoidance of which was contemplated here.

In this case, the object hid from sight is — not the fact of the exclusion, but the particular nature of the evidence to which it applies.

2. Cases where the exclusion is effected by limits set *to the length of time* during which evidence shall be received: thence excluding in the lump whatsoever is over and above the quantity that can be received within the length of time thus limited.

To this head belongs the exclusion put, under English law in jury-trial, by the practice which confines the quantity to that which can be received on the compass of a single sitting: in particular, when justice travels post, as on the circuits. Of the evidence thus excluded, the nature is wrapt in impenetrable darkness. Even the fact of the exclusion seems to have been a secret to the people at large. In the instance last mentioned, the exclusion will be readily enough acknowledged to be absurd, being outlandish, and having nothing to do with jury-trial:— in this latter instance, it is as it should be, being English, and connected with jury-trial, and thereby with liberty.

Such is the justification which the man of law has in store for it, should eyes ever be opened, and complaint made of it — made by any of the thousands who, under and by virtue of it, are wronged and plundered.

Want of reflection seems to have here been the cause — if not of the mischievous arrangement itself, at any rate of the patience of the people under it — if not of the creation of the abuse, at any rate of the preservation of it. On these occasions, and in this manner, evidence continues to be excluded from the judicatory, because reason continues to be excluded from the throne, custom and prejudice having usurped its place.

3. Cases where, before the body of evidence which the fact happens to have afforded has been collected, or otherwise disposed of, such evidence as has been already collected is kept concealed. Of such concealment, one effect, and that a declaredly intended effect, is — to put an exclusion upon all such other evidence, in regard to which, but for such concealment, either *the need* of it, or *the means* of procuring it, would or might have been indicated.

In this instance, the exclusion is a natural, and seems to have been a constant accompaniment of the Rome-bred mode of collecting evidence,—viz. extraction *per judicem ad hoc, in secreto judicis, partibus non præsentibus* — and from the Roman school, adopted and employed in the English edition of Rome-bred procedure, as employed in the *equity*, the ecclesiastical, and the admiralty judicatories.

In this class of cases, the disguise is still thicker than in the class last mentioned: the mode of exclusion still more indirect.

The evil, the contemplation of which appears to have furnished, in this instance, not only a *pretence*, but in some measure a reason, is — the immensity of the mass of collateral inconvenience — of delay, vexation, and expense — to which the evidence thus excluded might perhaps have given birth: but to whatsoever evidence may come thus to be excluded, the reason cannot apply without having in the first place, and with equal justice, been applied to whatsoever has been, and is predestined to be, admitted.

Here, as elsewhere, the mischief has for its cause — the exclusion put by technical procedure upon those timely explanations between the parties in the presence of the judge, to which there has been such frequent occasion to make reference, and which, under the natural system of procedure, take place of course.

4. Cases where, to this or that species of evidence, are given, if by any general rule, the denomination and effect of *conclusive* evidence. The effect is to exclude in the lump all evidence whatsoever, that could have been brought on the other side.

This conclusive and exclusive evidence,— is it of the nature of *direct* evidence? Infallibility and impeccability are the attributes ascribed to the witness. Is it of the nature of *circumstantial* evidence? Between the principal and the evidentiary fact in question, a connexion is supposed, so close and intimate, that, in the whole storehouse of nature, no species of fact has place, by which, in the character of an *infirmative* fact, a severance between them is capable of being made. Cases of this sort are at any rate extremely rare: and if so it be, that of any such infirmative fact no instance exists, the advantage reaped from the exclusion of such non-existent evidence cannot be very considerable.

Either inoperative or deceptious, — in the first case useless, in the latter case pernicious, — such is the character of any such general rule.*

5. Cases where, for the proof of this or that particular species of fact, this or that particular instrument, document, or other species or article of evidence, is pronounced indispensably requisite. The effect is — to put an exclusion upon all other evidence, in relation to the fact in question, on the same side.

In the last preceding case, the evidence excluded was—all evidence on the opposite side. Counterparts, or companions, as it were, to each other — and not ill-matched — are these two cases.

Of this species of exclusion, the most important exemplification is that which is afforded by the rules that have taken place, respecting the evidence required in proof of the genuineness of an instrument of contract —say a *deed* or a *will*. To the examination of this particular sort of case, the next succeeding chapter has been appropriated.

* *Evidence conclusive—presumption in law.* To the eye of unsophisticated common sense, one and the same fact, and that the only fact of which these phrases are ever really conclusive — and of that, as often as they occur, they may well be taken for *conclusive*, — is the presumption, foolish or dishonest, of the man of law.

Between the principal fact and the evidentiary fact in question, can any room be found for any *infirmative* fact or facts? The inference is liable to prove false; the rule by which it is rendered *peremptory* is pregnant with deception. Can no such room be found?—the rule which makes the inference peremptory is needless: no danger is there that an inference to the effect in question will fail of being made.

Whichever be the mode of trial, viz. with or without jury, in which a conclusion is thus blindly drawn, the effect of it is to pronounce, on the subject of the individual fact in question, judgments grounded upon other individual facts that are irrelevant to it — inferences drawn from other facts, that, individually taken, have nothing to do with it.

Such is the mischief when the case in which the blind conclusion is employed is an equity-law case, an ecclesiastical-law case, or an admiralty-law case. Is it a common-law case? It is then by a jury that the question should have been tried. To the other mischiefs, add now that of taking the question of fact out of the hands in which in form and pretension it is reposed — out of the hands in which constitutional principles have reposed it,— out of those only proper hands — into improper hands, — the hands of the judge or judges. Behold in both cases, folly: in the last case, fraud and usurpation.

On a trial for a criminal offence, amongst others murder: in this and that case the law presumes malice. Of the presumption in this case, what is the plain English? That, fearing that by a jury the man would be acquitted, the determination of the judge is, that he shall be convicted.

6. Cases in which, to one and the same fact, witnesses, in a *number* greater than one, are pronounced indispensably requisite. The effect is—in relation to the fact in question, to exclude the testimony of every witness who does not bring another in his hand, giving the same account of the matter that he does.

7. Cases in which, antecedently to a man's being admitted to deliver his testimony, it is made necessary that he should join in the performance of this or that formality, expressive of this or that particular persuasion on the subject of religion: such as the *ceremony* of *an oath*. The effect is — to put an exclusion upon the testimony of every person who will not join in such formality.

The ground of exclusion is, in this case, the man's repugnance to mendacity: for, if he have no such repugnance, there is nothing to hinder his saying what is thus endeavoured to be put into his mouth to say. The man thus excluded is a man who, in demonstration of his repugnance to mendacity, has given a proof, beyond what any man whose testimony is admitted, can ever give.

If, for such refusal, no mode of penal compulsion be appointed, the consequence is — that, to avoid delivering any article of evidence, which it is not agreeable to him to deliver, a man has no more to do than to aggregate himself to any such oath-refusing sect.

If, for such refusal, a mode of penal compulsion be appointed and applied, here is *persecution* on a religious ground, and the severer the punishment which the man endures, the stronger is that repugnancy to mendacity, of which the endurance is conclusive evidence.

8. Cases where the exclusion has for its efficient cause, the rule of which the leading terms are, the words *best evidence*. for example, *the law requires the best evidence which is to be had.*

In this case, the ground or pretence of exclusion is obvious enough: fear of *misdecision* through *deception*. Not equally so the *fact of the exclusion*, or the *nature of the evidence* to which it is applied or applicable.

Question 1: What is the best evidence? — True answer: Whatever evidence we have thought fit, on the occasion in question, to admit, *in preference* to, — meaning thereby, when such is our phrase, to the exclusion of,— every other.

Question 2: The evidence which you thus prefer, why do you thus prefer it? Answer: Because it is the best evidence.

Even where the evidence in question may with propriety be termed *the best evidence*, *i. e.* where it is of that sort, supposing the *sort* determined, of which, *source*, *shape*, and everything else that is material, taken together — the probative force is greater than of any other, — from no such relative and comparative goodness can any rational cause be deduced for putting an exclusion upon any other evidence. This best evidence, suppose it encountered and shaken, or in danger of being encountered or shaken by counter evidence, or counter interrogation on the other side, — the support, whatever it may be, if any, that might be afforded by other evidence on the same side, ought it to be refused?

§ 3. *Table of grounds of Exclusion, extracted from various Codes.*

Whether compared with one another, or with the ends of justice, the various circumstances which, by or under the laws of different nations, have been taken for grounds of exclusion, present a curious, nor altogether uninstructive spectacle. A dozen or so is the number of the bodies of law, from which matter of this sort having been collected, in the body of the work will be seen condensed into a synoptic table.*

Two contrasted subjects of observation will naturally be presented by it to view: — on the one hand, the universality of the practice, and, so far, of the adoption and application made of the *principle;* together with the amplitude of the *extent* to which, in the code of each nation, it has been carried: — on the other hand, the extreme *diversity* of the *mode* as expressed in the list of particular circumstances, to which in one code this effect has been given, compared with the list of them to which it has been given in the several other codes;—to which, had the sources been accessible, might have been added, in so far as the matter stood on the ground of statute law, at different periods, the diversity of the enactments; in so far as it stood upon the ground of *judge-made* or *bookmaker-made* law, the inconsistency of the authorities: — not to speak of the uncertainty, in many cases, whether it was in the character of a cause of exclusion, or only in that of a ground of *suspicion*, that the circumstance was considered.

As to the extent, if the several grounds of exclusion exhibited by the several codes, were put together, and made into one mass, the proscription would be found to have spread itself over the whole species, and thus not to have left so much as a single witness for the service of justice.

In some of these pictures,—for example, that which takes for its scene quondam France, and that which takes for its scene quondam Scotland, — one half of the species — the whole of the female sex, may be seen cast out at one stroke.†

From the universal reception and employment given to the exclusionary principle, an argument, not altogether destitute of plausibility, will be liable to be deduced: but to this argument in the character of sources of counter-argument, two circumstances may already have presented themselves. In the first place, the extreme diversity of the *modes* in which the application has been made of the principle, — the diversity real, the identity but nominal: — in the next place, *the sinister interest*, in which, it being in some instances best served by exclusion, in other instances by admission, the two modes of dealing, how opposite soever in themselves, would so easily find their common root.

CHAPTER XXIII.

SAFEGUARDS AGAINST SUSPICIOUS EVIDENCE: INCLUDING INSTRUCTIONS CONCERNING THE WEIGHING OF EVIDENCE.

§ 1. *Demand presented for such Safeguards, by the fear of change in case of the abolition of Exclusions.*

THROUGHOUT the whole texture of this work one practical conclusion is continually presenting itself: *for fear of deception exclude not any evidence.*

How incontestable soever may be the propriety, such at the same time is the novelty of this recommendation, that, for obviating the reluctance which, in spite of reason, habit and imagination are on every such occasion so sure to produce, no safeguards which the

---

* 1. Roman civil law. 2. Roman canon law. 3. French law. 4. Spanish law. 5. Portuguese law. 6. Hungarian law. 7. Austrian law. 8. Russian law. 9. Polish law. 10. Danish law. 11. Swedish law. 12. Scottish law.

As to English law, on any such enterprise as that of exhibiting in a tabular form the state of it in relation to this subject, several circumstances concurred in putting an unavoidable negative. These were—1. The great variety of the circumstances presented to view by it in this character. 2. In many instances, the extreme uncertainty whether on any future occasion they would respectively be considered as productive of this effect. 3. The multiplicity of the instances in which the exclusion was liable to be evaded; the same evidence which in one mode of procedure is excluded, being in another mode admitted.

† In some cases, by accident, or by the very nature of the case, an ample stock of principal witnesses will have been afforded. In a case of this sort, with or without sufficient reason, to save time, trouble, and perplexity, the judge, it may have happened, selected some to the exclusion of the rest. Noting the general ground of the exclusion without noting the superabundance in which it had its particular cause, the reporter may, for want of the proper distinction, have set down the ground of exclusion absolutely and simply, as applying to persons of the description in question, as well when the fact had not had any other principal witnesses, as when it had had them in superabundance

nature of the case presents as capable of being opposed to apprehended mischief, seem much in danger of being regarded as superfluous.

In this character, three proposed arrangements will here be brought to view: —

I. *Declaration of credence* on the part of the exhibitant.

II. Code of instructions, as from the legislator to the judge, concerning the weighing of evidence.

III. Appropriate recordation;—viz. recordation of the cases in which suspicious evidence — evidence characterized by any cause of infirmity — has been exhibited — with the result, *i. e.* the decision that has ensued, and thence the credence or discredence which was produced by it: viz. in so far as, from the nature of the aggregate body, of which the particular article of evidence in question, in a case where it is not the only evidence, forms a part, any decided and well-grounded inference can be deduced.

§ 2. *First Safeguard — Declaration of Credence from the Exhibitant.*

Of the sort of safeguard here in question, one exemplification or application has already been brought to view, viz. the *declaration of credence* proposed to be made by the party exhibitant, in the case of exhibition, made of a script in the character of an article of written evidence.

Of a declaration to this effect, the subject-matter there in question extended not beyond the *genuineness* of the script; but the principle there brought to view will be found susceptible of an application somewhat more extensive.

Among the objects and effects of the technical system, has been seen to be the giving to improbity, and thence to its principal instrument, fraud, every possible advantage: and, in particular, the providing for it a lurking place, where it may do its work in safety, secure not only against *punishment* so called, but against *detection*, and thereby against *shame:* to fraud in a *negative* shape thus securing, and without danger, that benefit which, at the hazard of so much danger, is sought for by fraud in its *positive* shape: — to fraudulent reticience, the benefit which, on other occasions, cannot be put in for, but under the perils which attach upon fraudulent mendacity.

Of the natural system the object is, and in proportion as it prevails, the effect will ever be, to divest improbity and fraud of this, as well as so many other subterfuges: to force improbity either to give up its purpose altogether, or to give to its instruments its more odious as well as only punishable shape: to compel fraud to divest itself of the veil of reticience, and to stand forth in the stark nakedness of positive mendacity.

For effecting this exposure, nature has offered to justice the efficient instrument so often brought to view, viz. interrogation: especially extemporaneous *vivâ voce* interrogation.

At every meeting of the parties *coram judice*, this instrument, in the instances that have been already brought to view, has been seen applying itself as of course: no mind so rude and uncultivated as not to be able, with more or less facility, to apply it: none so inexperienced and helpless as not to be disposed and ready to apply it.

But in that most efficient of its forms which has just been brought to view, the application of this instrument supposes mutual *presence:* existence of at least three persons in the presence of each other, viz. the *two parties* and the judge.

At the same time, as there has been such frequent occasion to observe, cases are not wanting, in which, either physically or prudentially speaking, such tripartite presence is impracticable: and from the existence of this state of things, results the need of a succedaneum to such *vivâ voce* interrogation, viz. interrogation in the *epistolary* form: — or what may perhaps in some instances be made to perform the like office, and at any rate with less delay, vexation, and expense, uninterrogated declaration in the terms of a preappointed *formulary.*

If it be fixed by a preappointed formulary, a declaration of this sort is not, however, by any means exempt from danger. The danger is — lest, by inappropriate penmanship, a man whose mind it finds in a state of probity and sincerity should be forced by it, not merely into insincerity, but into mendacity, as it were in his own defence: thus becoming productive of the very evil against which it is employed in the character of a remedy.*

To testimony of the ordinary stamp, about to be delivered by a person in the character of a witness, it will scarcely be found applicable. Generally speaking, except in the case of preappointed evidence, the persons to

* When, to enable a man to entitle himself to *right* in any shape, or (to speak still more generally) to *advantage* in any shape, any such declaration is exacted from him as without danger of discovery may in any respect be false—falsehood, and upon a scale to which there are no bounds, is sure to be the result: — *falsehood*, of which the legislator who exacts or permits the exaction of any such declaration, is the *suborner*. In this case, the right — the advantage — is a *bounty* upon insincerity—upon positive mendacity; and the hand of the sovereign is the hand which offers it.

It is in this way that, by the hand of tyranny, religion has, to so prodigious an extent, and with such disastrous success, been employed in the extirpation of morality, by the culture of mendacity and insincerity — instruments of immorality — instruments of criminality in all its shapes.

whose service, in the character of witnesses, a man finds himself obliged to have recourse, are not of his choice:—1. The character and disposition of the witness may be dishonest and mendacious, and the party know nothing about the matter; —2. It may be not only mendacious, but even known by himself to be hostile to himself, and he not the less obliged to have recourse to it; —3. Mendacious to any degree, it may still throw upon the subject such instructive lights as could not be had from any other source; for when recognised for what it is, falsehood itself becomes a guide to truth; and the grounds on which the probity and veracity of a proposed witness are suspected, may be sufficient to warrant the suspicion while retained by the party in his own breast, without being sufficient to warrant the divulgation of them, and thereby the imprinting on the character of the witness the stain of infamy, which, at the same time may be altogether undeserved.

On the technical theory, according to which, as above, the person of whose testimony a party happens to stand in need is to be considered as his *own* creature — the work of his own hand—it belongs not to you "*to discredit your own witness;*" that is, when you find him mendacious, to use any endeavours to cause him to be regarded as such — any more than it belongs to a workman to discredit his own work.

If to the lot of the inventor of that maxim it had fallen to pen a declaration of credence to be made by a party exhibitant, and to be applied to the testimony of the witness produced by him, — what would have been the effect of it on the shape that would have been given to it by the learned pen? In the instance of every witness, except the comparatively few of whose probity the party happened to stand well assured, he would have found himself compelled to deprive himself of the benefit of their testimony, or else to purchase it by a lie.

So much for orally and other judicially delivered evidence. In the case of written, viz. already written evidence, in addition to the *genuineness* of the script exhibited by him, if there be any other matter of fact to which a *declaration of credence*, to be delivered by the party exhibitant, according to a preappointed formulary, be safely applicable, it will be, in the case of an instrument of contract, the *fairness* of the contract.

Perhaps also, in some cases, where in and by the script in question, this or that matter of fact is averred or assumed by a statement of which, by the exhibition of the script in the character of evidence, he seeks to avail himself, an additional subject of his declaration of credence may be the verity of the whole, or of this or that part of the contents of the so-exhibited script.

With these observations, the applicability of a declaration of credence — understand always *according to a preappointed formulary* — may be left, till the time shall come for putting the instrument to the test by the application of it to this or that particular case.

But let it not be forgotten, that the declaration of credence to which the above-mentioned objections apply, is only of that sort which would be consigned to a preappointed formulary. Extracted by interrogation, the declaration is not the less a declaration of credence: and in this shape it may be rendered obtainable, without any of that danger to which, as above, it would, in the case of a preappointed formulary, stand exposed.

Correspondent in some sort to the declaration of credence as above described, on the part of a party exhibitant, is, on the other part, the *declaration of discredence* which, by the relation it bears in the way of opposition to the other, seems sufficiently explained: it is a sort of counter security, that presents itself as requisite to be given, in return for and in consideration of the other.

The object of the one is to prevent dishonest and insincere *exhibition:* of the other, to prevent dishonest and insincere contestation; — that sort of contestation, by which, under the encouragement given by the technical system, a party in whose mind no doubt respecting the verity, or as the case may be, the genuineness of this or that article of evidence which is ready to be exhibited on the other side,—or in case of an instrument of contract, the fairness of the contract,—requires the proof of it, partly for the purpose of oppression, viz. by means of the delay, vexation, and expense, partly for the chance of succeeding by *misdecision;* by misdecision, the looked-for result of accident, by which the forthcomingness, or the authentication of the articles of evidence in question, may be prevented: and the perpetually recurring result of that system under which, from the non-observance of some unpreappointed and *ex post facto* established condition, on grounds frequently not so much as pretended to have any relation to the merits of the cause, a pretence for refusing to the plaintiff the promised service, is, at the suggestion of a dishonest defendant's law-assistants, extracted by the judge at pleasure.

§ 3. *Second Safeguard — Code of instructions concerning the weighing of Evidence.*

By the article thus denominated, is meant to be presented to view, a body of *instructions* sanctioned by the *legislator*, and by him addressed to the judge, to serve him for his guidance.

In the character of a preservative against deception, in place of *exclusion*, *suspicion* has, in the course of this work, been all along brought to view.

In the several instances in which, under the present system, on the ground of untrustworthiness, and for fear of deception, exclusion is, with any appearance of reasonable cause, howsoever inadequate, put upon this or that article of evidence, the main object and use of such a code will be to direct the eye of suspicion upon the evidence, by indication of the circumstances by which, in the character of causes of comparative untrustworthiness, the demand for suspicion, and thence for circumspection and scrutiny, is produced.

Of the system of instructions in question, this, however, though the main object, and the only object which on the present occasion and to the present purpose comes directly in view, will not by any means be the only object, the only business, or the only use. Taken all together, the object of such a system will be, to present to, and keep under the eye of the judge, under the head of each species of evidence, a sort of table of the circumstances by which the probative force of it seems liable to be influenced.

For the construction of such an instrument of security, fortunately the hand of power—of public power—is not altogether necessary. An instrument of this sort, put together, in a form however imperfect, out of such materials as honest diligence unarmed with power could command, forms accordingly part of the matter contained in the body of this work.*

Of the circumstances which, with so blind a precipitancy, have by temerity or dishonesty been taken for grounds of exclusion, many will naturally be found to serve in the character of grounds of suspicion,—but, even in that character, not all of them.

Of instructions, furnished as here by an uncommissioned hand, *one advantage* is—that under so powerful a check as that which will be so sure to be opposed to them by adverse authority, exerted by sinister interest and intrenched in prejudice, they are in little danger of operating with greater force than is their strictest due:—a disadvantage is, that over whatever part of the field the iron hand of exclusion stretches, the voice of instruction, for any effect it can produce, is powerless, and might as well not be lifted up.

§ 4. *Third Safeguard—Recordation of cases where suspicious evidence has been received.*

By the substitution of the system of instruction to the system of exclusion, could any real fear of prevalent deception and consequent misdecision be produced? By the testimony of experience, as recorded under a set of appropriate heads in the official books, all such fears might effectually be dispelled.

1. Causes in the year so many;—2. Whereof, causes in which, to suspicious evidence, of such and such species, distinguishing each species, admission had been given, so many;—3. Among which, the instances in which the result had been in favour of the suspicious evidence, are so many;—4. In the number of those in which the result was in favour of the side on which the suspicious evidence was admitted, would be seen the maximum of the mischief, if any, that could have been thus produced by the abolition of the exclusionary system: I say, *if any;* for, on the occasion of any given suit or cause, it is only from the view of the whole body of evidence, and not from the mere circumstance of admission given in each individual instance to suspicious evidence, coupled with that of a decision pronounced in favour of that side, that any just ground could be made for any such inference as that deception, misdecision, and thence mischief, had in that cause been the result.

In regard to scripts in general, and instruments of contract in particular, it has been stated as a matter of general notoriety, that in comparison of the whole number exhibited, the number of those of which the genuineness has been matter of real distrust or doubt, and as such has been rendered the subject-matter of contestation, is small in the extreme.

Of the here proposed system of recordation, one effect would be the exhibiting the exact number of, and thence the exact proportion between, these two aggregates: and so, in the case of those instruments of contract, in the instance of which the *fairness* of the contract itself,—of the engagement entered into, or the disposition made—became a subject of contestation.

In the same way, in the list of contested instruments would be noted and preserved the difference between the number of those in which, to appearance, the prescribed *formalities* had been observed, and the number of those in which, in that respect, failure was in any shape visible; notice being likewise, in each instance, taken of the particular shape or shapes in which the failure had presented itself.

CHAPTER XXIV.

AUTHENTICATION AND DEAUTHENTICATION, AS APPLIED TO PREAPPOINTED AND OTHER WRITTEN EVIDENCE.

§ 1. *Subject-matters of Authentication and Deauthentication.*

THREE main species or parcels have again and again been mentioned, as comprising together the whole possible matter of evidence—*real*, *oral*, and *written*. The same term, *authentication*, may be employed with reference to

* See also Appendix A.

each of them: but the import of it in the three cases differs to a certain degree, according to the different natures of the subject-matter to which it is respectively applied.

1. In the case of *real* evidence, to authenticate the evidence is to establish the identity of the body (whatever it be) which is the source of the evidence, — the body, the appearances of which constitute the evidence, — together with the authenticity of those appearances: to make it appear, to the satisfaction of the judge, that the body exhibiting certain appearances at the time of its being produced in court, or subjected to the examination of a scientific witness (acting on that occasion in the character of a subordinate and deputed judge,) is the same body as that by which the evidentiary appearances were exhibited in the first instance; and that the appearances exhibited by it at the two points of time, and during the intervening interval, are the natural consequences of the principal fact, and have not been either fabricated or materially altered, either by design or negligence.

2. In the case of *personal oral* evidence, to authenticate the evidence is to establish the identity of the person who, in the character of a deposing witness, is subjected to oral examination, — who, in the character of a deposing witness, is admitted to give his testimony in the presence of the judge, — 1. That he who speaks of himself as being such or such a person, is really that person; 2. That the person who, at the time in question, in presence of the judge, speaks of himself as having been present on a certain past occasion, on which a person known by a certain name was actually present, is that same person: — whether, on the occasion in hand, he call himself or is called, by the same, or by a different name.

3. In the case of *written* evidence, to establish the genuineness of the document is to make it appear, to the satisfaction of the judge, that the document exhibited as containing the discourse expressed by a certain person on a certain occasion, does really contain the discourse of that same person; and (where the occasion is material) that this discourse did really issue from him on that same occasion.

Correspondent to the respective natures of the respective species of evidence, will be the several courses requisite and proper to be taken for establishing their authenticity.

1. The case of *real* evidence admits of safe custody: — an expedient that applies not at all, or not with equally and uniformly unexceptionable propriety, in either of the other cases. For this purpose, a particular sort of person is not unfrequently appointed by law, in contemplation of his presumed trustworthiness with reference to this purpose. He takes charge of the article, keeps it in his possession till the time comes for its being produced in the character of evidence before the judge; and it is partly by the fact of his having thus kept it in his custody, partly by the testimony he gives, or is considered as giving, of its having been so kept without any fallacious alteration, that its authenticity is established.

2. The case of *personal oral* evidence — that is, of a person appearing before the judge to give his testimony — admits not of any appropriate mode of authentication. His being the same person as he who (commonly under the same name) is stated by him as having been present on the occasion in question — been present in the character of a percipient witness — is included of course in the testimony he gives. The fact of his identity (if there be any doubt about it) will, like any other matter of fact, be to be proved or disproved, as the case may be, by such evidence of any kind or kinds as the occasion furnishes.

3. It is in the case of *written* evidence that the business of authentication admits of the greatest diversity, and demands a proportionable degree of attention. The different modes of authentication may be divided into direct and circumstantial; — but for a detail of the different species of evidence requisite, and of the relative trustworthiness of each, reference must be made to the body of the work.

In questions relative to authenticity, the affirmative proposition is, except in here and there an extraordinary instance, the true one: — but since instances of this extraordinary description are unhappily found to exist, hence an operation opposite to authentication comes sometimes to be performed. Correspondent, in good measure, to the list of modes of authentication, will consequently be the list of modes of *deauthentication*. For the variations and additions, reference must be made, as above, to the body of the work.

§ 2. *Proper course where Genuineness is unsuspected.*

Such being the subject-matters of authentication and deauthentication; next comes the inquiry, what is the proper course to be pursued upon any given occasion.

Here a distinction must be taken, in the first instance, between provisional and definitive authentication.

By provisional, I mean that evidence which may be received as sufficient for the authentication of the article in question, provided that no suspicion of its authenticity be expressed on the other side. By definitive, I mean that which, if satisfactory in itself, shall be deemed sufficient proof of the authenticity of the instrument, notwithstanding all protestations and contestations on the other side.

For the purpose of provisional authentication (that is, in all ordinary cases,) that mode of authentication will be the most eligible, which in each instance can be employed with least vexation, expense, and delay. But should the authenticity of the document be disputed on the other side, — in a word, should it be accused of forgery, — in such case, the subordinate consideration referring to these collateral inconveniences must give way to the superior consideration referring to the direct justice of the case: — always supposed, that the imputation of forgery may not be allowed to be made through wantonness, much less in the express view of giving birth to those collateral inconveniences; and that accordingly, in the case of *malâ fides* or temerity, the burden of the inconvenience may rest ultimately on the head of the party to whose misconduct it owed its birth.

If the mode of authentication, which is not needful but in case of contestation, be regularly employed where there is no contestation, where no doubt of the authenticity of the document is really entertained; and if, between the two modes of authentication necessary in the two cases, there be, upon an average, any considerable difference in respect of vexation, expense, or delay; — the aggregate mischief unnecessarily produced in those three shapes must be prodigious indeed. Among the writings of all sorts which come to be exhibited in a court of judicature in the character of evidence, if there be one out of a thousand in respect to which any such suspicion as that of forgery is really entertained, the proportion would prove much larger than I should expect to find it. Upon this supposition, in nine hundred and ninety-nine instances out of every thousand, this mass of inconvenience will be created without necessity or use, if in pursuit of a phantastic idea of regularity, the employment of the definitive mode of authentication be insisted on, to the exclusion of the provisional mode — the most convenient, *i. e.* least vexatious, expensive, and dilatory mode, which might so unexceptionably have supplied its place. This oppressive plan of authentication we shall find established in English jurisprudence.

In the adjustment of the modes of authentication to be established in regard to written evidence, the leading points or ends require to be kept in view: — on the one hand, satisfaction in respect of trustworthiness — on the other hand, avoidance of delay, vexation, and expense, the three inseparable modifications of collateral inconvenience.

Of these two ends, this first mentioned, being the main and principal end, has in general been pursued with a degree of preference, which would have been very proper, but that the sacrifices that have been made to it, at the expense of the triple collateral ends, have been inordinate, and much beyond anything which good economy in this respect would be found to authorize.

The supposition upon which judges and legislators have proceeded, in the fixation of the modes of authentication which have been prescribed, has been that of a universal and constant disposition on the part of all suitors to commit forgery: — or if that supposition have not, in every instance, been actually entertained, it is the only one on which the modes prescribed are capable of being justified — the only one by which the price paid in the shape of delay, vexation, and expense, for the supposed advantage in the shape of satisfaction in respect of trustworthiness, would not be recognised to be excessive and oppressive. If among a thousand cases in which the legal *effect* of a piece of written evidence is in dispute, there be not so much as one in which the *authenticity* of it is a matter of real doubt on the part of the suitor against whom it is produced, — it is only in the one case where it is matter of real doubt, that the price paid for authentication in the shape of delay, vexation, and expense, or all together, need be so considerable as to be worth counting. Under the existing system, there is scarcely a cause in which it is not considerable, and in many a cause it would be found to be seriously oppressive.

Thus it happens, that for one grain of mischief produced, or that would or could be produced, by fraud in the shape of *forgery*, a thousand, ten thousand, are produced by fraud in the shape of *chicane*: of chicane, produced partly by the enmity of suitors, partly by the rapacity of agents, abetted by that of the subordinate officers of justice; both passions protected and encouraged and engendered by judges and legislators. Familiarized with the spectacle of continual misery, generated according to rule and custom, and therefore on their parts without blame; the reduction of the mischief to its minimum — the reduction of it so much as within narrower bounds, never presents itself to them as worth regarding. Like so many other processes, which go on as it were of themselves, according to pre-established and never-considered rules, the authentication of evidence is considered as a sort of mechanical operation, the pathological effects of which have no claim upon them for so much as a thought. Whence all this composure? For the observance of the established rules, the man in office is responsible: — for the propriety of these rules, for their subservience to the ends of justice, he is not responsible.

§ 3. *Course remaining where Suspicion has been declared.*

To attempt in this place to combat the triple-headed monster of delay, vexation, and expense, by any proposed regulation of detail, would be to touch upon the topic of procedure: a general observation or two may serve to indicate the course. Authentication in the ultimate, and what may be styled the adverse mode, ought, instead of being the routine of practice, to be the *dernier resort*, the extraordinary resource. The process of authentication should be carried on, not at the time of trial, but between party and party at a preliminary meeting, either in the presence of the judge, or before some inferior minister of justice, whose time can best be spared.

The party who has a document to produce, produces it in the first instance to the adverse party, who either admits the authenticity of it, or declares his intention to contest it. If he admit it, he marks it as admitted. If he choose to contest it, he has a right to do so, but he uses it at his peril; at the peril of simple costs in case of simple temerity; at the peril of extra costs in case of *mala fides*. The end in view is, in every instance, to save the suitors from the delay, vexation, and expense of adverse authentication, in so far as these several inconveniences are avoidable. The means to be employed in the prosecution of that end, is the making such arrangements as shall render it the indisputable interest of every individual concerned, each in their several stations—(parties, agents of parties, officers of justice of all classes)—to abstain from giving birth to these several inconveniences any further than as they are necessary.

The virtual penalty inflicted on this occasion by imposition of costs with the above views, should not depend on the ultimate decision of the cause, but should be inflicted *pro unaquâque vice*, for each act of authentication unnecessarily performed. Otherwise, to the enmity of a suitor, who was persuaded of his having the law on his side, the proposed remedy would apply no check. The principle would remain unapplied, unless to each particular act of vexation, its own particular penalty stood opposed.

To rash, as well as to *malâ fide* contestation, various are the other checks that might be, and if the ends of justice were the objects, naturally would be applied. If, for example, by the production of a source of evidence, the needfulness of which (after the mutual explanations in question) appeared more or less doubtful to the judge, delay and expense to a certain amount would manifestly be necessitated; — not only would eventual compensation for the damage by such delay be secured; as well as the expense attendant on the production of the evidence in question cast upon the party by whom the production of it was thus insisted on; — but if, by the exhibition of this evidence, a demand for counter-evidence to be exhibited by the adverse party were produced, the expense of such counter-evidence might provisionally be charged in the first instance, upon the party thus insisting; rather than that by such means it should be in his power to oppress his adversary, by exhausting his means of maintaining his post in the field of litigation — his means of pursuing, in the character of plaintiff, his own claim, or repelling, in the character of defendant, that of the party on the other side.

In some cases, for the purpose of provisional authentication, instead of the executed, or rather say *recognised* instrument, a *transcript* or an *archetypal draught** may be employed; — and by this means, useless delay, vexation, and expense may be avoided.

Of the actual execution, and thence of the genuineness, of the proper instrument — so likewise of the correctness and completeness of the succedaneous script; even in case of contestation or doubt, — for saving of delay, vexation, and expense, evidence less conclusively probative than for the purpose of a definitive decision might be necessary, might for the purpose of a *provisional* decision be received on either side.

Even if contested, a script which is authentic *ab intrà* (*i. e.* which on the face of it presents the signature of the apparent author affixed to it for the evident purpose of authentication) need not be authenticated *ab extrà* in the first instance. Why? Because, unless it be supposed to be tainted with forgery, its authenticity cannot appear dubious. But delinquency ought not in any case to be presumed without special ground; much less delinquency of so high a cast.†

Inability to affect the authentication of a script, on or before a certain day, need not, ought not, to be rendered so much as a cause of delay, much less of ultimate miscarriage. A decision, in all other respects ultimate, might be made provisional, dependent upon the subsequent authentication of the instrument on or before a day to be named: nor need even that nomination be so inexorably peremptory, as to allow accident, much less fraud, to triumph over justice.

§ 4. *Advantages from the here proposed, compared with the established course.*

In all these cases, the advantage and propriety of giving provisional admission and effect to such succedaneous evidence as above, depends upon the relative quantity of the inconvenience saved by it in the shape of delay, vexation, and expense. But, let it not be forgotten, that to this quantity there are no limits other than those of the earth's circumference.

---

* *Archetypal*, i. e. the corrected and settled draught from which the instrument itself was transcribed, and which served as an *archetype* or *original* to it.

† In Scotland, a deed executed according to certain forms is presumed genuine, until its spuriousness be proved in a separate action by the person impugning it.—*Ed.*

Note, moreover, that so far as concerns *written* evidence (including the fact of its *genuineness* and the nature of its contents,) the savings capable of being made in case of contestation would, the whole mass of them put together, be inconsiderable in comparison of that which, in the case of the supposed proper script upon a call made by the party exhibitant, would have place by reason of admission without contestation as above.

To these savings in the shape of delay, vexation, and expense, may be added a saving that in the account of an honest man will not be regarded as fit to be neglected — a saving in the article of improbity: improbity on the part of the parties and their professional advisers, — improbity on the part of the judges, — improbity on the part of the *custos morum*, — improbity on the part of the keeper of the royal conscience.

In the ordinary intercourse of life, a man to whom it has happened to deny his own hand-writing is pointed at as a man of lost character; and to such a degree lost, that, to a person to whom the like loss is not a matter of indifference, it may be scarcely safe to associate with him.

On what ground is it that, for such a mode of conduct, a man is thus consigned to infamy? On this, or on none, viz. that in this way he was knowingly and wilfully guilty of falsehood: — wilful and deliberate falsehood for the purpose of injustice.

The man by whom his adversary in litigation is loaded with the delay, vexation, and expense of proving (as well as exposed to the peril of not being able, after all, in the teeth of so many opposing quirks, to prove at any expense) the genuineness of a document, of which there exists no real doubt; — literally speaking, and to outside appearance, this man does *not* commit the falsehood that would have been committed, had the question, "*Is the genuineness of this document matter of doubt to you?*" been put, and answered in the affirmative. The falsehood is not committed: — but what is committed is an injustice; — an injustice which, in point of mischievousness, is exactly upon a level with such falsehood: the injustice, in which such falsehood would have found its sole object, and its sole advantage.

The falsehood has not been committed: — but *why* has it not? Only because the judges (in whom the practice in this behalf has found its creators and preservers) have taken such good and effectual care to secure, to every dishonest man who in this way finds his account in making himself their instrument, the *benefit* of such falsehood; without that *risk* which, had the eventual necessity of it been left subsisting, would have constituted the expense of it.

In so far as concerns justice and veracity, there are two codes of morality that in this country have currency and influence; — viz. that of the public at large, and that of Westminster Hall. In no two countries, can the complexion of their respective legal codes be easily more opposite, than that of those two moral codes, which have currency, not only in the same country, but in the same societies: — and if so it be, that, in the public at large, the system of morals that has place in practice is upon the whole honest and pure; — it is so, not in proportion as the morality of Westminster Hall (of which so many samples have already been, and so many more will be exhibited) is revered and conformed to, but in proportion as it is abhorred. So far as concerns love of truth and justice, the greatest, but at the same time the most hopeless improvement would be, the raising of the mind of a thorough-paced English lawyer, on a bench or under a bench, to a level with that of an average man taken at random, whose mind had not, for professional views and purposes, been poisoned with the study of the law: — as, on the other hand, in point of sound understanding and true wisdom, the raising the same sort of mind to a level with that of a man of competent education, of the nature of that to which the term *liberal* is commonly applied.

Yes: — it is from novels such as Maria Edgeworth's, that virtues such as the love of justice and veracity, — it is from the benches, the bars, the offices, the desks, in and about Westminster Hall, that the hatred of these virtues, and the love of the opposite vices, — is imbibed. — But that which to Maria Edgeworth was not known, or by Maria Edgeworth was not dared to be revealed, is the genealogy of her *Lawyer Case*: that that very ingenious and industrious gentleman had for his elder brother the Honourable Charles Case, barrister-at law, M. P. in the lower house; and both of them for their father, the Right Honourable the Lord Chief-Justice Case, Christopher Baron Casington, in the upper: — and that it was only by executing the powers given or preserved to him, and earning the rewards offered and so well secured to him, by his noble and learned father, that the younger son became what he was.

How long, for the self-same wickedness, shall the inferiors in power and opulence — the inferiors, who are but instruments, — be execrated, and the superiors, who are the authors of it, adored? Attorneys, solicitors, — were they makers of common-law? — were they the makers of the technical system of procedure? — were they the makers of the law of evidence?

§ 5. *English Practice. — Case 1. Authenticative Testimony of Parties excluded.*

The distinction between *provisional* and *definitive* authentication is unknown to English law. In all cases alike, it insists upon having the authentication performed in the same mode: — without allowing of any exceptions on the score of vexation, expense, or delay. It presumes all mankind to be forgers; — and where there is forgery, affords no facilities for the detection of it. It guards against deception where there is none to guard against; and where deception is at work, interdicting the interrogation of the suspected person, it interdicts the most efficient means of scrutiny.

Previous meeting between the parties, for the purpose of ascertaining whether any and what documents presented by one party are contested by the other, there is none: — disputed or not, the authenticity of every document must be *proved*.

True it is, that for saving of delay, vexation, and expense, sometimes it does happen, that on one or both sides the genuineness of this or that instrument of contract or other script (or, as it may happen, of all the scripts meant to be exhibited) is admitted. But it is only in so far as on both sides, or (if it be an equity suit or cause) on all sides, and that to an indefinite number, all persons concerned, law advisers as well as suitors, are honest, — and not only *negatively* honest, but completely and *actively* and zealously honest, — that any such admission, with the consequent savings, can have place.

In regard to the species of fact here in question, as in regard to every other, the most satisfactory, and on every account beyond comparison the most eligible, evidence (need it again be said?) is that of the parties; — viz. in relation to each fact, that one of the parties against whom it makes.

By the exclusion put upon the preliminary meeting, this evidence stands excluded, from the commencement of the cause. And when, at the end of half a year, or a whole year, or some number of years, from the day of the commencement, that inquiry which ought to have begun, and in most instances would have been concluded on that same day, is under the name of *the trial* suffered to take place,—upon this same best evidence is an exclusion again put, by means of another exclusionary rule.

In the eye of common sense, this is the best evidence possible: in the eye of the law, it is no evidence at all; therefore not the *best* evidence. For on this part of the field, when exclusion is the object, out of the word *best*, is formed the basis of the pretence.

Always excepted (I mean from the exclusionary rule) the case where an extra price, and that a most enormous one, is paid for opening the door to that which otherwise would be the excluded evidence; — viz. at the equity shop, and elsewhere. By the immeasurable and profitable addition thus made to vexation and expense together, coupled with the comparative badness of the shape in which the evidence is extracted, the objection which would have been so peremptory, is now removed.

Rather than give admission to that best and most satisfactory of all evidence, no evidence so loose and unsatisfactory, but that admission will be given to it: — in the case of an instrument of contract, for example, proof (*i. e.* what is called proof, viz. mere circumstantial evidence) of the genuineness of a couple of words, purporting to be the name of an attesting witness. Look at these words, viz. *John Smith*. Did you ever know any person who ever bore that name? Yes. Did you ever see him write, or receive letters, which you understood to have been written by his hand? Yes. Judging from these opportunities, do you believe these words to have been written by him? Yes.

True it is, that, when no better is to be had, the exigence of the case necessitates the reception of this loose, this circumstantial evidence. But when the case affords not only direct evidence, but the most trustworthy of all direct evidence,—to exclude that best evidence, and admit this loose evidence instead of it — how inexplicable the folly, were it not for the sinister interest that lurks at the bottom of it!

Wounded by the rule itself, justice is again wounded by the evasions of the rule.

1. Three obligors jointly bound in a bond. Proof by extraneous witnesses (it must be supposed) being somehow or other unobtainable, one of the obligors is called to prove the execution of it. But for this purpose, he must have been left out of the action, and the recourse against him lost. Just as it happens in penal cases, where one of two malefactors is let off, that his testimony may be employable against the other.

2. If a subscribing witness is become infamous, — on producing his conviction, his hand may be proved as if he were dead. Here inferior evidence is let in, to the exclusion of the best: — circumstantial, to the exclusion of direct. So much for security against deception. Moreover, the conviction must be produced: — a lumbering record, lugged in at a heavy and unnecessary expense, to prove a fact in itself notorious, and capable of being sufficiently proved by less expensive means; and which, after all, cannot be sufficiently proved by this means. John Brown was convicted: — true, but how does the dead parchment prove that it was the same John Brown?

3. So, when an attesting witness being the only surviving witness, had become interested,* without any prejudice to his character, his hand was allowed to be proved by somebody else, on the presumption that he himself would have denied it. Pre-established

* Comyns, 106.

rules apart, the experiment might have been tried, at least, and if he had perjured himself, then might it have been time enough to encounter the perjury by other evidence.

§ 6. *English Practice.* — *Case 2. Authenticative Testimony of non-attesting Witnesses excluded.*

Witnesses to the number of half-a-dozen, or half-a-score, all of them unexceptionable, are ready to be produced; each of them ready to say, "I saw the several parties attaching their respective signatures to this instrument, saying (each of them) *I deliver* this as my act and deed."

Quibbleton, counsel for the defendant, addressing himself to the first of these witnesses —"What is your name?"

Answer — "John Stiles."

Quibbleton —"My Lord, here is the deed: two (your lordship sees) and but two attesting witnesses; — neither of them is named John Stiles."

Judge — "Set aside this witness."

Half-a-dozen, or half-a-score, all of undisputed character, all ready to speak to this plain fact, and not one of them permitted. Why not permitted? *Answer:* Because, in the first place, if permitted, they would all of them perjure themselves; they would all of them, in spite of counsels' cross-examination and judges' direction, obtain credence. Two persuasions these, neither of them (it is true) avowed, because, when absurdity or improbity enter upon the stage, they do not, either of them, present themselves stark naked. But to give to the exclusion so much as the colour of being conducive to the ends of justice, these persuasions must both of them be entertained; or, at any rate, of the matters of fact respectively predicated by them, the *certainty*, or (to speak with a degree of correctness new as yet to lawyers' language) the *preponderant probability* must be assumed.

But supposing these persuasions entertained, on what ground is it that they must have been entertained? On this ground, and no other, viz. that the names of these persons are not to be found upon the face of the instrument, in the character of attesting witnesses.

Exists there, then, any article of law, by which it is required (on pain of nullity, or any other pain,) that upon the face of every deed of the sort in question (wills being out of the question,) there shall be visible the names of two persons in the character of attesting witnesses? No: — neither of any article of real (*i. e.* legislative) law, nor so much as any rule delivered in the shape of judge-made law.

On what ground, then, stands the rejection? *Answer:* On this ground, viz. that when the name of a person, purporting to have been written by him in the character of an attesting witness, is visible on the face of the instrument, — the testimony of any number of persons who (if they are to be believed) *actually* saw what it is there *declared* that this man saw, is not, with relation to the fact in question, *the best evidence.*

Non-lawyer: What! — the evidence being *good* enough to produce a complete (or at least preponderant) persuasion; — in this case, by the mere circumstance of its not being the very best imaginable (admitting, for argument's sake, that it is not the very best,) by this one circumstance, is any sufficient ground afforded for shutting out this evidence, when there is no other? — and when, in consequence, if this be shut out, the party who has right on his side must lose his cause?

Lawyer: Oh! but where, there being upon the face of the deed an attesting witness, he is not produced, but instead of him others are produced, whose names are not upon the deed: here is an *omission;* from which we draw a conclusion: — and the conclusion is, that, had the attesting witness been produced, his testimony would have been against the genuineness of the deed.

Non-lawyer: And on this conclusion it is that you build the two other necessary conclusions, viz. that the non-attesting witnesses, being all of them so many intended perjurers, would all of them have affirmed the genuineness of the deed, the fact being otherwise, and thus falsely affirming it would have gained credence!

With submission, suppositions of a contrary tendency might be raised in any number, any one of them less improbable than the above.

Independently of regulation — positive and effectually notified regulation — it is difficult to say what there is that should determine the choice of the party in favour of a supposed *attesting,* to the exclusion of (or even in preference to) a *non-attesting,* but by him equally known to have been a *percipient* witness. True it is, that, by the signature of the attesting witness, proof is so far given, that in relation to the transaction in question he was a percipient witness. Yes; — but is it a proof that no other person was? — a proof too, which by those who know that the contrary is true, is to be regarded as a convincing one?

The attesting witness would cost (suppose) so much money to produce: the non-attesting witness may be had for a few shillings less. This, in the eye of a *considerate,* and, especially in the eye of a *poor* man, honestly advised, should suffice to give the preference to the non-attesting witness. The attesting witness would, after all expenses paid him, suffer inconvenience (suppose) from the attendance: — the non-attesting witness would not suffer any inconvenience: — this, in the eye of a *humane* and considerate man, would suffice for securing the like preference.

Oh! but we have a rule about the *best evidence*, viz. that in no case shall any evidence be received but the very best evidence which the nature of the case admits of.

Preciously instructive rule! *We receive no evidence but what we receive:* — for anything more precise, or intelligible, or wise, or honest than this, will not be found in it.

No evidence do we ever receive other than the *best* evidence. And what is the best evidence? *Answer:* It is, on each occasion, that which we receive as such.

They know not themselves what their own rules are. Strange indeed it would be if they did: for that which has no existence, how is it to be known to anybody? They know not themselves what their own rules are: they resolve that every other man shall know them; — that is, without the possibility of knowing them, shall, as often as occasion offers, be punished for not knowing them.

Nemo tenetur ad impossibilia, says another of their maxims. But in any one of their maxims, so sure as there is anything good, so sure is practice opposite.

Once more: Partly upon the *source*, partly upon the *shape*, depends the goodness of an article of evidence. As to the shape: — in so far as depends upon themselves, in none but the very worst shape (come it from what source it will) do they receive any evidence: — and so it be in this worst shape, no source so impure but that from that bad source they are ever ready to receive it. Yet such is their delicacy, that (as if for evidence, as for meat, there were a market at which, with money in his hand, a man may pick and choose) none, forsooth, will they put up with, but the very best of evidence.

§ 7. *English Practice. — Case 3. Admission given to Instruments without Authentication.*

By the man of law, wherever you see a gnat strained at, on a second glance make sure of seeing a camel taken up and swallowed.

Behold an instrument, for the authentication of which, to-day, a whole score of witnesses, who (every one of them, if they are to be believed) were percipient witnesses of the execution of it (they not being attesting witnesses) will not suffice: it is accordingly dealt with as if it were forged. Wait till tomorrow; this spurious deed becomes genuine: and so plainly genuine, that for the proof of its genuineness no evidence is required.

This metamorphosis, by what was it effected? *Answer:* By time. Yesterday, the script wanted a day of being thirty years old: to-day, the thirty years are fulfilled.

This admission has neither quite so much absurdity in it, nor quite so much mischievousness, as the exclusions. The instrument, if it be not what it purports to be, is a forgery. Forgery, a flagitious and pernicious crime, is not to be presumed. Independently of particular argumentative grounds, the odds against the fact, as testified by experience, are prodigious: — for every forged instrument, you have genuine ones by thousands.

Not but that to this crime (by the exclusion put upon the interrogated testimony of the party by whom, or in whose behalf, the instrument is produced) every encouragement has been given, which it has been in the power of Judge and Co. to give to it. Suppose the party to have forged it: he puts it silently into the hands of his lawyer, and it is the lawyer's business to fight it up. At the lawyer's elbow, if so it please him, sits the forger. There he may sit till he is tired, for he is in no danger; the law has taken him under her care: not a single question can be put to him.

Convenient as this law is to every criminal, to an honest man it may happen but too frequently to be laid by it under an embarrassment, out of which it seems not altogether easy to say how he is to be delivered.

The instrument purporting upon the face of it to be thirty years old or more: this antiquity, coupled with *possession* (*i. e.* with the relation borne to the suit or cause, or to the fact in question, by the individual in whose possession it has been,) is accepted as evidence sufficient for the authentication of it. But the individual (suppose) in whose possession it is, is the plaintiff; — and for the whole of the time that has elapsed since the execution of it, or for a part, more or less considerable, of that length of time, he has kept it locked up in his strong box: not having in all that time shown it (because in all that time no occasion has called upon him to show it) to any person who is without interest in the suit or cause. By whose testimony, then, is the custody of it to be proved? By *his*, the plaintiff's? Oh no: that would be contrary to the inviolable rule. But if not by *his* testimony, it cannot — by the very supposition it cannot — be proved by that of any one else.

Yes: if he had had information, timely information, of the existence of this rule of law; for in that case he might have got this or that uninterested person to look at it. But if any such information had reached his mind, the care and pains taken by Judge and Co. for so many centuries to keep it out of his reach would have been frustrated. By keeping them from receiving existence in and from any determinate form of words, care has been taken — very effectual care — that neither by non-lawyers, nor by lawyers themselves, shall any of these portions of imaginary law be laid hold of by *inspection*. By their uniform repugnance to every conclusion that would be drawn by common sense, care not less effectual has been taken that they shall never have been laid hold of by *inference* or *conjecture*.

If, in this case, the exemption granted from the obligation of authenticating the document by evidence *ab extrà* be proper, it can only be because, in the other cases, the obligation is itself improper, being needless. Forgery is not the crime of any particular point of time; — whatever be the probability of it at this present day, it was not less on this day thirty years. A deed purporting to have been fairly executed thirty years ago, may have been forged or falsified at any subsequent point of time. Forged writings, of an apparent date two hundred years anterior to their real date, forged writings ascribed to Shakespear,* have been known to deceive the very elect among English lawyers.

§ 8. *English Practice.—Case* 4. *Shifts where the Script is in the power of the adversary.*

The hostility of the technical system to the ends of justice — the consciousness of that hostility on the part of those who, while they are acting under it, are profiting by it, — the violation at the same time so continually offered by themselves to the very principles to which by themselves the highest importance is attached, — all this may be seen exemplified in a case which shall now be brought to view.

When the article of written evidence which the party in question stands in need of, happens to be in the hands of a party on the other side; — when an instrument which a plaintiff (for example) stands in need of, happens to be in the possession of the defendant; — the sort of shift that has been made is truly curious.

Under a rational system of procedure, the course is plain and easy; — the evidence acted upon is of the best kind imaginable. Both parties being together in the presence of the judge, the plaintiff says to the defendant — "To make out my case, I have need of such or such an instrument" (describing it:) "you have it, have the goodness to produce it." "Yes," says the defendant (unless his plan be to perjure himself,) "and here it is:" or — "I have it not with me at present — but on such a day and hour as it shall please the judge to appoint, I will bring it hither, or send it to you at your house, or give you access to it in mine."

Under the technical system, no such meeting being to be had, no such question can at any such meeting be put. But, at the trial (viz. under the *common-law*, alias *non-equity* system, of which jury-trial makes a part,) at the trial, that is, after half-a-year's or a year's, or more than a year's factitious delay, with its vexation and expense; then it is, that, for the first time, a chance for procuring the production of a necessary instrument may be obtained.

Though either for any such purpose, or for any other, neither to the party on either side, nor to any agent of his, can anything in the shape of a question be put *vivâ voce* by a party or agent on the other side, — the question (for example) *the instrument* (describing it,) *have you it or no?* — yet under the name of a *notice*, a sort of requisition in writing calling upon him to exhibit it, may be, and every now and then is, delivered. Of this notice to exhibit the instrument, what is the effect? — that the defendant is under any obligation to exhibit it? No such thing. To produce any such effect would require nothing less than a suit in equity; whereupon the instrument would be exhibited or not: and if exhibited, not till the end of the greatest number of years to which the defendant (having an adequate interest) had found it in his power to put off the exhibition of it. To have enabled the party thus far to have obtained justice without aid from equity, would have been robbing the Lord Chancellor and the Master of the Rolls, and the swarm of subordinates, of whose fees the patronage part of their emolument is composed.

What, then, is the effect? *Answer*: That after this notice, if that best evidence which is asked for be not obtainable, — not obtainable only because those on whom it depends do not choose that it should be obtained, — what is deemed the next best evidence that happens to be in the plaintiff's possession is admitted: and on this occasion no evidence is too loose to be admitted.

After such notice given, one succedaneum that has been admitted is a supposed transcript: — "*an examined copy*," are the words. — Another is, "*parol evidence of the contents.*"

In the midst of all this laxity, observe and admire the strictness: — "In case it be a copy that is offered, it must first be proved that the original, of which it purports to be a copy, was a genuine instrument." So much the more business for the benefit of the man of law: — so much the more chance of failure, for the benefit and encouragement of the wrong-doer.

But suppose no such copy producible, — the best and only evidence which it is in the plaintiff's power to produce, being as above, "parol evidence of the contents," *i. e.* some account given of the supposed instrument, by a person into whose hands, by some accident or other opportunity of bestowing upon it a perusal more or less adequate, — of throwing over it a glance more or less correct and complete, — it has happened to find its way.

This casual reporter, — for his report to

* See the controversy between Mr. Malone and Mr. Chalmers.

be received, is it necessary that he (or, in his stead, the party by whom he is called in) should have established in due form the genuineness of the instrument, which, for ever so short a time, chance had thus thrown into his hands?

In this one point may be seen a mine, a rich mine, of future cases.

Behold now another mine. The two sorts of make-shift evidence thus brought to view in the case of a deed,—viz. a *supposed transcript* (copy examined or not examined,) and *parol evidence of supposed contents,* — shall they apply, and under any and what modifications, to any and what other sort of scripts?

Delight paints itself on the countenance of the man of law, at the thoughts of such a mine of non-suits, and to the lawyer at any rate, if not to the client and suitor, of agreeable surprises.

Good all this, as far as it goes; when so it is that a man's good fortune has put into his hands any such make-shift evidence. But if not, what in that case becomes of the notice? In that case, the wrongdoer triumphs: the party who is in the right loses his right, whatever it may be; and so the matter ends.

Did but the judge deign to admit, at the outset, into his presence, the persons whose properties and liberties he has contrived, with so little trouble, to dispose of, — whatsoever were the instrument wanted, if it were not found in *one* of two hands in which it was expected to be found, it would be in *another:* every instrument that was necessary to justice would be ferreted out; as it actually is, in the case where, justice being necessary to his own personal protection as well as that of the public, it has been the pleasure of the man of law that the necessary instruments should be made forthcoming,—viz. in the preparatory examinations taken, as in a case of murder, robbery, or other felony, by a justice of the peace. No loophole (or at least not so many loopholes) would then be left for the wrongdoer to creep out of; thus foiling for a time, or for ever, the party whom he has wronged.

But, under the technical system, this business of *notices* affords to the wrong-doer an inexhaustible fund of chances: in this lottery, a *nonsuit* (the produce of which is an additional suit) constitutes the prize, in which Judge and Co., with their *protegés* and partners, the wrong-doers, are sharers.

In one sample more, read at once the nature of judge-made law in general, and therein read the technical system of procedure; and therein, again, the law of evidence in particular.

When the script you want is in possession of your adversary, you have seen already what the succedaneum is, and what sort of chance there is of its being obtainable.

When the script is in possession of a person capable of being a witness (a non-litigant witness,)—for the purpose of having it exhibited, you serve him with a writ called a *subpœna duces tecum,* by which he is ordered to attend, and bring with him the script. If he obey, it is well:—if he obey, that is, if so it be that he not only attend, but bring it. But, what if he come without it? To this hour it is not settled what is to be done with him,* nor how the script is to be got at, and applied in the character of evidence. At any rate, to the party who, being in the right, has need of the evidence, the cause is lost for that time:—saved to him, or not saved, the liberty of trying a new one.

CHAPTER XXV.

EXCLUSION AND NULLIFICATION APPLIED TO CONTRACTUAL MATTER, IN SO FAR AS WRITING HAS BEEN OMITTED TO BE EMPLOYED IN GIVING EXPRESSION TO IT.

§ 1. *Relation of this to preceding topics, viz. Preappointed Evidence, Exclusion, Authentication, &c.*

Remains for consideration one head of practice, in the examination of which four several topics, which have already, each of them, received a separate consideration, viz. preappointed evidence, exclusion, and nullification, authentication and deauthentication, will require to be brought under review together.

To the purpose of evidence — on all occasions, and in each of the two periods or stages of its existence, viz. the period of perception, and the period of narration or statement, on a judicial occasion, or for a judicial purpose — the utility of written, say scriptitiously expressed discourse, in contradistinction to orally expressed discourse, has already on several occasions been brought to view.*

Impressed, or pretending to be impressed, with a general sense of the extreme utility of that master art, and, in particular, in respect of the application it is susceptible of to so important and all-comprehensive a subject as that of legally operative evidence — impressed perhaps with at least a due sense of this public and social use of it, and certainly not insensible to the more private benefit derivable by men of their own order in the character of professors of it, in its application to the profit-yielding sort of purposes here in question, men of law have, in England as elsewhere, applied their power to the purpose of compelling men, on the occasion of their several

* The object of the exclusion put upon orally expressed matter, is that writing may be employed: therefore it is that to the sort of contract in question, whatever it may be, in case writing be not employed in it, the nullification is applied —applied, viz. by means of the exclusion put upon the only evidence by which the contents of it can be brought to view, or the existence of it proved.

legal transactions — their agreements — the dispositions made by them of their property — to have recourse to it.

Their power has been accordingly applied: and in what way? On this and that occasion, if by the party or parties in question, for the giving expression to contractual matter of any kind, as above designated, orally expressed, in contradistinction to scriptitiously expressed discourse, has been employed, they have taken upon them to put an exclusion upon whatsoever evidence might be necessary or conducive to the establishment of such contract — upon all evidence, in so far as applied to the proof of such discourse, *i. e.* to the fact of its having been holden, and consequently to the statement of its contents.

Of this exclusion, what has been the consequence? — 1. Every contract, or mass of contractual matter, upon the evidence of which such exclusion has been put, has been thereby nullified: — nullified — and on what ground? On the ground that contractual matter, the genuineness of which has no other proof than the sort of evidence thus excluded, ought to be considered not as genuine, but as spurious.

Here, then, by the want of that formality, viz. *writing*, which is of the essence of preappointed evidence, and of more value than all other possible formalities put together, an exclusion is put upon evidence; and by means of such exclusion, matter of a contractual nature is considered as deauthenticated; and thereby the contract — be the expression judicially declared to have been given to it ever so genuine — nullified.

Disguised, is the class to which the sort of exclusion here applied seems referable. For the deception, the apprehension of which has been the source or efficient cause of the precaution thus taken, has had for its ground not any quality ascribed to this or that class of witnesses — for the exclusion applies alike to all witnesses — but the consideration of the infirmity of the vehicle, viz. orally expressed discourse, employed in the conveyance of it.

In regard to the exclusion here in question, one observation that will be apt enough to present itself is — that the ground, on which in point of reason and utility it rests, is much stronger than in any of those cases which have been brought already under review.

This being acknowledged, still it will appear that the ground, how much soever less weak in this than in those other cases, wants much of being strong enough to support the structure that has been built upon it.

§ 2. — *Case* 1. *Writing not employed: object of the exclusion, preventing or frustrating spurious Contracts orally expressed.*

The exclusion which, in this way, has been put upon orally expressed contractual matter, in favour of scriptitiously expressed contractual matter, has been put upon it in two very distinct cases: —

1. Where, in relation to the same transaction, no scriptitiously expressed contractual matter is forthcoming: in which case, the exclusion may be said to be *absolute*.

2. Where, in relation to that same transaction, scriptitiously expressed matter having been brought into existence, is forthcoming and exhibited: in this case, the exclusion may be said to be limited — limited, viz. to the case in which, in relation to the same transaction, contractual matter scriptitiously expressed makes its appearance.

In these two cases, the propriety of the nullifying exclusion will be seen to stand on grounds considerably different.

In the first place, presents itself as being the most simple, the case in which the exclusion is, in the sense just explained, *absolute*.

§ 3. *Impropriety of the Exclusion, &c. in this case.*

In the character of an objection to the exclusionary system, one observation presents itself *in limine*. Writing, in its application to the preservation of evidence, — writing, the art of writing, is, comparatively speaking, of modern date. When as yet it was unknown, not only a man's property, liberty, reputation, and condition in life, but his very life, was disposed of on the mere ground of orally expressed evidence. What! — every judicial act by which, at the stage of society anterior to that in which writing came into common use any of those possessions were disposed of, was it an unjust act? — the evidence on which it was grounded, was it in every instance spurious or false?

This consideration, were even this the only one, might of itself suffice to dispose a man to pause before he acceded to the propriety of the application so lightly made of the evidence-excluding principle on this as well as so many other occasions.

Against the employment of so harsh an instrument, the same objections, which apply in every other occasion, will be found to apply in this; whilst, in the character of a highly advantageous substitute to so harsh an instrument, still the same succedaneum presents itself; viz. declaration of suspicion, notified by effective promulgation.

Of the lightness, not to say the absolute nothingness of the mischief, by the apprehension of which this weapon of defence — this instrument of supposed security — was put into the hand of the man of power, still the same evidence, still the same demonstration afforded by experience. I mean the experience afforded by the inconsistency by which the practice under this head has been marked; viz. the inconsistency between the application made of the instrument in some cases, and the refusal to make application of it in other cases.

The object of apprehension, the fraud apprehended, is the employing of false testimony to the setting up as genuine, and really entered into by the parties in question, this or that matter of contract, which, though pretended to have been agreed upon by them, was not really agreed upon by them.

But on this, as on other occasions, what is manifest is — that if, antecedently to regulation, fraud to any given amount or effect be capable of being with equal facility operated with success, in each one, say of half-a-dozen shapes, — then so it is, that, by regulation which, how effectual soever in preventing the commission of the fraud in four of the shapes, leaves it in the remaining two no less practicable than before, the quantity of fraud commissible is not really diminished, nor is any real advantage gained: — instead of its being dried up, all that can have been done with the current is to turn it out of this or that one into this or that other channel.

By this inconsistency, whatsoever may be the supposition concerning the *veracity* of an indeterminate and consequently unknown witness, the course taken by this exclusionary policy is rendered equally indefensible: — veracious, a man ought not to be excluded when he is excluded: mendacious, he ought not, upon the principles of the system, to be admitted when he is admitted.

Another circumstance that ought naturally to operate with considerable effect as a sedative against all apprehensions of considerable public mischief by fraud in this shape, if the supposed security afforded by the nullifying exclusion were taken away, is this, — viz. that all along, how slight soever the orally delivered testimony by which the imputation has been supported, the imputation of fraud has all along been considered sufficient to deauthenticate and destroy the effect of the most formally as well as scriptitiously expressed instrument of contract.

True it is, that of the mischief to which men are thus exposed by means of mendacious orally-delivered evidence, the extent is not so great under the exclusion put upon evidence of orally-expressed contractual matter as in the other case, — the extent is not in a manner unlimited, as in the other case: inasmuch as the persons exposed to suffer by mendacious evidence, by which fraud is falsely imputed to this or that one of a number of persons concerned together as parties to a contract, — that contract being of the number of those which have found their expression in the form of a written instrument, — are such and such only to whom it has happened to have been engaged in some contract or other so expressed.

But how far soever from being equal to the unlimited number above mentioned, so great is the number of persons who, having been actually engaged in a scriptitiously expressed contract of this or that nature, have thereby stood exposed to become sufferers by the sort of fraud which consists in the seeking to nullify the genuine written expression of a *bonâ fide* contract by means of the imputation of fraud cast upon this or that one of the parties engaged in it, that by the continuance which, without complaint or objection, has for so many centuries been given to a practice under which credence is given to the orally-expressed evidence of perhaps no more than a single witness, in opposition to scriptitiously expressed preappointed evidence concerning that same transaction, no slight presumption seems to be afforded, that the amount of any mischief that can have been produced by orally-expressed mendacious evidence, delivered without the check afforded by a scriptitious instrument of contract relative to the same transaction, in support of a falsely-particled orally-expressed contract, cannot have been very considerable.

In all the cases in which, under the notion of saving a jury from being deceived by false evidence, and the individual from being made a sufferer by it, an exclusion in the character of an extraordinary safeguard is thus put upon evidence, safeguards of the ordinary kind may exist in any number, and in any degree of force; — in every instance counter-interrogation, to wit, applied to each mendacious witness, and as it may happen, counter-evidence from the mouth of whatsoever number of honest witnesses the individual case in question may happen to afford; while, from the fraud which, upon invitation even by the law, is committed by those who plead the law against a contract which, though in this secret way nullified by the law, was really entered into, there exists no possible means of escape: if so the case be but of the number of those to which the exclusion extends, so sure as is the fraud attempted, so sure is it committed.

In favour of the exclusionary and nullification system, as applied to evidence in support of supposed orally expressed contracts, an argument has been produced and fabricated out of that other application of the exclusionary system, by which, in jury-trial in the common-law courts, an exclusion is put upon the testimony of parties on both sides of the cause.

Suppose an altogether imaginary contract, supposed to have been entered into between two parties between whom no such transaction ever passed — and this is the case in which, in respect of the number of persons threatened by it, the danger assumes the most formidable aspect; — in the conflict that would take place between testimony and testimony in the presence of the judge, with what advantage would not the injured party have to contend against his mendacious adversary!—with all that advantage which self-conscious truth and innocence have over self-conscious mendacity and guilt.

But this is among the means of detection, by which the technical system has taken care that its most profitable servant and best customer, the mendacious depredator — the depredator whose instrument of depredation is composed of fraud, shall not be embarrassed and annoyed.

Pernicious in the extreme is the spectacle where insincerity and improbity are universally and indubitably seen to be crowned with success, and that success is with equal invariability and certainty seen to have had for its cause, the encouragement given to those vices by the law itself.

Under the system of exclusion and nullification, in its application to orally-expressed contractual matter — this unseemly state of things may be exhibited in a variety of ways: —

1. Of the expression given to the orally-expressed contractual matter, there may have been percipient witnesses in any number, all perfectly agreeing in the account given by them of the transaction, and each of these giving to his statement any degree of publicity that may be imagined.

2. When, by the assistance of the law, a man whom it has found or made dishonest, thus gets rid of his engagement, not only is this corruptive quality of the law known to the man himself, in whose hands it has been an instrument of iniquity, but by extrajudicial discourses of his, whether of a *confessional* or a *jactantial* nature, it may happen to it to be rendered notorious to other persons in any number: yet all this while, the law being peremptory, the notoriety of the fraud will not detract anything from its nullifying force. And in the sight of everybody there remains the law, at all times, and on any number of occasions, able and ready to give to the like fraud the like existence, and to secure the like success.

Under the system of declaration of suspicion, no such corruption, no such pernicious notoriety, can have place. Notwithstanding the warning given by it, suppose a plan of predatory mendacity, such as the statute professes to prevent, formed and executed with success; with success, the jury being deceived by it: no such general disastrous expectation is produced here. *One* jury has been thus deceived; but it follows not that any other will be: whereas, by the nullifying law, the judge, though not deceived, is, in the eyes of all, seen to be not only authorized but forced to act, and ever more to act, as he would do if he were deceived.

The facility afforded for the admission of truth under the exclusionary system, — compare it with the facility afforded by the warning system.

Under the warning system, notwithstanding the warning, each article of evidence on the one side, as on the other, is left capable of being estimated at its exact worth,—left to operate with its proper degree of probative force: and this on both sides. Under the nullification system, by means of exclusion,—under the exclusionary system, be the number of evidences on that side, and the aggregate of the probative force, ever so great, — they are, in every case alike, divested of the whole of it — stript of their whole value: the whole body of it is smothered and suppressed.

From the exclusionary system, and in particular in its application to the present case, whatsoever utility can be expected, depends altogether upon the notoriety of the regulation made by it — upon the efficiency of the measures, if any, taken for the purpose of causing it to be present to the several minds on which the effect aimed at by it is to be produced. Whatsoever good it has any chance of doing, is in proportion as it is known: in proportion to the number of instances in which, on the occasion in question, it is present to the mind on which it is designed, or pretended to be designed, to operate. Of the mischief which it is so much more assured of doing, the quantity runs in proportion to the number of instances in which, on the occasion in question, it fails of being present to the mind on which it is designed, or pretended to be designed, to operate.

Of the authors of the technical system, of which the evidence-excluding system makes so essential a part, it being the interest that the good should be at its minimum, and the evil at its maximum, such accordingly has been the result.

Upon a state of things so unexampled, and as yet so hopeless, as that of a tolerably efficient system of promulgation, the efficiency of the warning system, in the character of a preservative against deception from the source here in question, has no such strict dependence. No doubt but that the thing to be desired in the first place is, that no such attempt should be made: no vexation of that sort which, even in the least vexatious mode possible, it is impossible that litigation should not produce: no expense in the article of money on either side — no expense in the articles of probity and veracity on one side — should be incurred to ensure the accomplishment of this object. But in the next place, to whatsoever attempts of the sort in question it may happen to be made, the thing to be desired is, that they may be frustrated: and to this purpose, even the monitory observation, without any antecedent promulgation — the monitory observation from the mouth of the judge, or though it were but from the mouth of the party interested, especially on the supposition of its having received the sanction of the law, and been adopted into the text of the law, may suffice.

Compared with the system of exclusion and nullification, the system of warning presents another great advantage: the utility and even the innoxiousness of the system of exclusion and nullification is completely dependent on the skill of the legislative draughtsman — on the correctness, completeness, and clearness of the description which he has given of the cases to which it has been his meaning that the exclusion should apply, and of the cases to which it has been his meaning that it should not apply.

Of any failure in this respect, the natural consequence will be, that even should it have been his sincere intention and endeavour to do nothing but good, the result of these endeavours may be productive of nothing but evil: of the entrance left open to fraud at some other hole while one hole is stopped up, the effect will be, that the fraud which he has it in view to exclude will not be diminished: and thus, of the sort of fraud to which in the very nature of the case no such exclusion can avoid giving encouragement and existence, the mischief will stand uncompensated, constituting the only fruit of which this policy is productive.

And such, accordingly, has been the product of that work, the which, under the name of the statute of frauds, is said to have had for its efficient cause the united wisdom of the most eminent lawyers of that time, including the twelve judges.

To the system of effective promulgation and declaration of suspicion, no such nice workmanship is necessary. For it to produce not only all the effect which it is capable of producing, but all the effect which is desirable, nothing more is necessary than on each occasion the pointing the attention of those, to whom it belongs to judge, to a plain suggestion of common sense, deduced from experience, — in a word, to those very considerations, in which, though so unhappily applied, the system of exclusion and nullification took its rise: — to a plain suggestion of common sense, leaving the application of it to be governed, as in each individual case it ought to be governed, by the peculiar circumstances of each individual case.

§ 4. — *Case 2. Writing employed: object, preventing or frustrating spurious orally-expressed alteration.*

Comes now the case in which the application of the nullifying exclusion put upon orally-expressed contractual matter, in favour of scriptitiously-expressed contractual matter, is limited: limited, viz. to the case by which, in relation to the same transaction, contractual matter scriptitiously expressed makes its appearance.

In this case, matter of either description may, in its relation to matter of the other nature and quantity, be considered entitled to the appellation of principal matter, leaving thus, for the distinctive appellation of the other, the epithet *accessory.*

At the same time, considering the obvious advantage with which the use of writing is in this as in so many other cases attended, — to the scriptitious matter, if the case afford any, will the epithet *principal* be in general found to be with greatest propriety applicable.

In this case, *the contract* is the appellation by which the aggregate quantity of scriptitiously expressed matter, or if it consist of scripts more than one, the principal script, will naturally be designated. In this case, *accessory contractual matter* will be the denomination expressive of the sort of relation which the orally-expressed contractual matter bears to the other.

And here at the same time it appears how inadequate the existing nomenclature is to the exigency of the case, and why it is, that, for the purpose of comprehending at the same time whatsoever matter is considered as principal, and whatsoever matter is considered as accessory, the term contractual matter has been employed.

Placed upon this footing, the practical question here to be considered is — a contract scriptitiously expressed: in other words, an instrument of contract being forthcoming, shall or shall not an exclusion be put upon evidence, the effect of which is to assert the existence and exhibit the supposed contents of contractual matter orally expressed, supposed to have been agreed upon in relation to the same transaction between the same parties? and thereupon to constitute so much accessory matter applicable in explanation or alteration of such principal matter?

If admission be given to the supposed accessory matter orally expressed, a supposition virtually included in such admission is — that without the addition of the orally expressed matter, the statement and representation given by the scriptitiously expressed matter, and in particular by the instrument of contract, is incomplete.

But note, that in this same case, if the existence of such supposed orally expressed contractual matter be considered as established, and the purport of it sufficiently ascertained, the consequence is, that without it, the expression given to the contract by the scriptitious matter alone cannot but be considered as incomplete, and in proportion to the nature and importance of the deficiency, deceptious.

§ 5. *Greater impropriety of the Exclusion in this case.*

Whatsoever considerations have been seen pleading against the nullifying exclusion in the preceding case, will be seen pleading against it in this case: pleading against it, but with augmented force.

1. In the first place, of the apprehended mischief to which the exclusion has been applied in the character of a remedy, the extent is in that case beyond comparison greater than in the present: in that case unlimited, in the present case limited.

Among persons capable of contracting in the way in question, there exists not any person against whom pretended contracts may not to any amount be by possibility set up, supported by mendacious evidence, and who is not consequently exposed to be made a sufferer to an unlimited amount by fraud in that shape: whereas in the present case, the persons exposed to be made sufferers by fraud in the shape here in question, are, by the supposition, such and such only to whom it has happened to have been engaged in a contract of some sort or other scriptitiously expressed.

2. In the next place, supposing evidence of the supposed orally expressed matter admitted, the danger — *i. e.* the probability of the mischief in question, wants much of being as great in this as in that other case.

The circumstance to which this diminution of probability is owing is this, viz. —

In the present case, by the supposition, by the parties in question, in the course and for the purpose of the transaction in question, writing has been actually employed. Out of this established fact arises a material inference, an apparent probability, that the importance of this mode of expression to the purpose of giving to the contractual matter in question a determinate, permanent, and invariable existence, was by these same parties understood. But, admitting this mode of expression to be understood by them to be the fittest and most eligible mode, it is inconsistent — it is in a high degree improbable—that in the course of the same transaction the same parties should, even for the explanation, much more for the alteration of the matter expressed in this most trustworthy mode, apply other matter, expressed no otherwise than in that other and least trustworthy mode.

Here then, as often as, in the sort of case in question, by orally or otherwise expressed direct evidence, the existence of orally expressed contractual matter, agreed upon at the time in question by the parties in question, is affirmed, so it is that this direct evidence finds itself encountered by an article of circumstantial evidence, to the effect above described: — *principal fact* evidenced or probabilized, spuriousness of the supposed orally expressed matter; — correspondent *evidentiary fact*, improbability — psychological improbability — improbability, viz. that under a persuasion of the superior eligibility of the scriptitious mode of expression, the oral mode should by all parties have been employed: employed, and if for the purpose not of mere *explanation*, but *alteration*, employed for the purpose of its operating *pro tanto* in contradiction of matter expressed in a mode, of the superior trustworthiness of which there is room to suppose, as above, that on the occasion of this same transaction, they themselves were duly sensible.

Such is the consideration on which all direct evidence, true or false, exhibited in proof of supposed orally-expressed contractual matter, supposed to have been grafted in the character of accessory matter upon principal matter scriptitiously expressed, finds a constantly attendant article of counter-evidence.

Such at the same time is the consideration in which the judicatory, to which the evidence is exhibited, finds a natural and constant warning, putting it upon its guard against all deception, to which in such case it can stand exposed to be subjected to by false evidence.

And though, together with whatsoever matter of law happens to bear upon the species of contract in question, the factitious warning supposed to be expressed and notified by the legislator can never receive a too universal and universally efficient notification, yet the more powerful is the operation of the natural warning thus afforded by the nature of the case, the less is the need of the artificial warning, the less the inconvenience liable to result from any deficiency in the effective notification given to it.

And what is the consideration which it may be the expectation of the legislator to find already present in case of litigation, — present to the mind of the judges, and which, for the prevention of litigation, it is or ought to be his design and object to impress beforehand, — to impress at the time of entering into the contract, and giving to it its expression, — on the minds of the parties? It is no other than the very consideration which, in the minds of the authors of the exclusionary and nullifying law, or rule of law, — supposing their intention upright and sincere, — must, in the character of efficient or productive motive, have given birth to the measure by which the nullifying exclusion was thus applied.

To evidence assertive of the existence, and stating the alleged contents of an instrument of contract, therein and thereupon asserted to have been destroyed, admission has been given without scruple, and thereupon credence bestowed upon it, upon the testimony of a single witness. Comparatively speaking, in a case in which no such instrument ever was in existence, how easily and safely might not a false tale, assertive of its existence, be fabricated; — how much more difficultly and perilously, where, operating in the character of a check upon any such falsely asserted accessory matter, declared to have been orally expressed, there exists principal matter, in a scriptitious form, — in the form of an instrument of contract, of which the genuineness is out of dispute!

CHAPTER XXVI.

OF THE EXCLUSION AND NULLIFICATION OF CONTRACTUAL MATTER, INFORMALLY THOUGH SCRIPTITIOUSLY EXPRESSED, IN A TRANSACTION WHICH HAS BEEN THE SUBJECT OF MATTER FORMALLY EXPRESSED.

Of the two cases already brought to view, the reason, such as it is, that pleads in behalf of the exclusion, has been seen to grow fainter in the second, than it was in the first. In the present case, it will be seen vanishing altogether.

In both these cases, the *generation* of fraud, and that under auspices under which success cannot possibly fail to attend it, was what the exclusion was seen to have for its certain consequence. On the other hand, the *prevention* or frustration of fraud, and that in a case in which it would not otherwise have been frustrated, may possibly, in here and there an instance, have been among the effects of it, more particularly in the first of these two cases.

In the present case, the produce of the exclusion will be seen to be pure unmixed evil: — fraud, even successful fraud, may be, and probably is, generated by it; none can be prevented by it.

Of any accessory formalities, which in addition to the only essential and fundamental formality, consisting in the use of that master art by which determinateness and permanence is given to the matter of human discourse, have ever as yet been employed in the most formal instruments, — of any such accessory formalities, such as signing and sealing by the *parties*, signing and sealing by attesting *witnesses*, the only real use is to establish the genuineness of all such scripts, be they what they may, as in the course of the measures taken for giving expression to the intention of the parties, happen to have been employed. But, on the occasion on which the question has been — whether, in *addition* to, and in *explanation* or *alteration* of, such contractual matter as has received expression in and from a *formal instrument*, other matter which has received its expression no otherwise than in and from an informal script, shall be received, the *genuineness* of the matter contained in the *script* has always been out of dispute.

Among the fruits of this policy, in addition to fraud, as above, two others, viz. depredation and oppression — injuries both of them alike unpunishable and irresistible — being committed, not against law, but with the assistance and by the power of the law, come now to be brought to view.

By the technical system of procedure, a sort of *imperium in imperio*, a graduated system of tyranny, has, as there has been such frequent occasion to show, been organized and established.

Under English law, not to speak of other systems, the sort of commodity called *justice* is not only sold, but being like gunpowder and spirits made of different degrees of strength, is sold at different prices, suited to the pockets of so many different classes of customers. On a lower shelf stands *common-law justice;* — and above it, on a higher shelf, the sort which is of a superior degree of strength — *equity-court justice.* The *hundreds*, who alone can come up to the price of *equity-court justice*, tyrannize over the thousands who cannot come up to the price of anything above common-law-court justice; while those who, though unable to pay equity-court price, are yet able to pay common-law-court price, have on their part the satisfaction of retaliating upon the millions to whom, — with the exception of that sort by which men are either hanged or transported, or fined, or with or without pillory* imprisoned, — everything denied that ever bore the name of *justice.*

Generally speaking, of the complication produced by the grafting of informally though scriptitiously-expressed contractual matter upon the matter of a formal instrument of contract, the effect is to transfer the cognizance of the dispute, if on both sides there be money enough to feed it, from a *common-law court* to an *equity court.*

If the ground of your claim be comprised within the compass of a single instrument of contract, such as *an agreement*, or *a lease* to a tenant, you may, unless it be the pleasure of your antagonist to carry up the cause into a court of equity, obtain a decision upon it at the hands of a court of common law.

But if, in addition to the one formally expressed instrument of contract, so it be that, in an informal shape, contractual matter relative to the same transaction has been consigned to some informal script — say *a couple of letters*, say a *minute of agreement* — not even will the consent of your antagonist avail to keep you out of a court of equity. For amongst so many quirks and quibbles of the growth of the common-law courts, one is, that you cannot ground an action upon two instruments at once. And thus it is that the common-law

---

* By 7 & 8 Will. IV. c. 23, the pillory is now abolished. — *Ed.*

system, being in such sort put together, that without assistance from some other quarter, it was impossible that society itself should be kept together, another system, under the name of *Equity*, was by necessity suffered to be imported in ecclesiastical bottoms, to apply a palliative to some of the most intolerable of its imperfections, to entangle with it, to obstruct it, to be obstructed by it, and to overrule it.

As to the case of *wills*, it has been already glanced at:—glanced at in a former chapter, in which it has been shown how, according to the technical form given to the description of the subject-matter disposed of, the self-same instrument of disposition, to the perfect and universal satisfaction of all lawyers for this century and a half past, is pronounced genuine and spurious at the same time.

Referred to in and by a formally expressed will and testament, and not otherwise, a script of any kind, deemed to bear application to the matter of it, is, in a court of temporal learning, genuine, and forms part of it; if not so referred to, spurious:—in a court of spiritual learning, the same script, referred to or not referred to, is genuine, and, of the expression given by the testator to the will declared by him concerning the posthumous disposition of his property, is as true a portion as any the most formal part of it.

On this most productive of all subject-matters, not only have *spiritual* courts a different mode of going to work, as compared with temporal courts, but so among these temporal courts, have equity courts as compared with common-law courts: that so, under favour of the maximum of confusion and uncertainty created and preserved, the maximum of oppression for the benefit of the *rich* among *non-lawyers*, and the maximum of depredation for the benefit of lawyers, may be for ever more and without ceasing exercised.

CHAPTER XXVII.

IMPRISONMENT FOR DEBT:—DISGUISED EXCLUSION OF EVIDENCE INVOLVED IN IT.

§ 1. *Course prescribed, in relation to this head, by Natural Procedure.*

FOLLOW in relation, to this head what present themselves as the proper subjects of inquiry:—

1. To the alleged creditor, by the alleged debtor, to the amount in question or to any other amount, and in the case of mutual accounts upon a balance, is a debt due?—is there any, and what, reason for supposing, that upon inquiry any such debt will be found to be due?

2. If due, in the possession or in the power,—at the command—of the debtor, is there in existence property, or other lawful means of compensation in any shape, to the amount of the debt, or any part of that amount?

3. Over and above the alleged debtor in question, are there any, and what person or persons, who jointly with him, in any and what proportion, or in his default, absolutely or eventually stand bound for the discharge of it?

4. To the alleged debtor in question, on the occasion of the contracting of the debt, or in respect of the non-discharge of it, is blame in any and what shape imputable?

5. If yes, in what shape? In the shape of fraud or rashness, or negligence;—and in each case, is any and what circumstance of aggravation on the one hand—of extenuation on the other hand, to be found attaching upon the offence?

6. In addition to the alleged creditor at whose instance, on the occasion in question, the demand is made, exist there any other and what persons, who on any and what score respectively, upon the effects of the alleged debtor have any such claim, as by satisfaction administered to the demand made on the present occasion, would to any and what amount be prejudiced?

Such are the points, or at least among the points, in relation to which, had justice been the object and humanity the guide, evidence would have been thought fit to be heard, or if not heard, at any rate in the best producible shape received and read:—heard or read, as the case may be, before any such sufferings as those which are attendant on imprisonment or local confinement had either definitively or provisionally, in execution or on mesne process, as the phrase is, been inflicted.

Evidence received?—from whom?—and in what shape? Answered a thousand and a thousand times over:—from the parties at the initiative meeting in the presence of the judge—in the orally expressed shape,—subject to interrogation,—unless in so far as personal appearance is by accident rendered on either side physically or prudentially impracticable.

Forewarned, an insolvent debtor might withdraw his person or his effects out of the track of justice:—suspicion to this effect declared, at the plaintiff creditor's peril, on record, no reason why, with the secresy and suddenness that have place at present, the debtor should not be arrested, provided always, that instead of jail or spunging-house, he be brought immediately into the presence of the judge, there to undergo examination, as above.

§ 2. *Course actually pursued in relation to this head, by English Technical Procedure:—groundlessness and needlessness of the infliction in this case.*

Above we see *what ought to be*:—now as

to what is. — Under technical procedure — under Westminster-Hall procedure, on scarcely any of these points is evidence in any shape at any time received: on almost all of these points, evidence in all shapes stands at all times excluded.

Look to the efficient cause, and no further: in all this nothing will be seen but that sort of error which, throughout the greater part of this work, has been seen exercising its baneful rule — exclusion of evidence.

Include in your view the consequences and the final cause, the author's end in view, and the means — everything will be seen by which the heart or the head of a man is most disgraced.

1. For consigning a man to imprisonment definitively till the debt is discharged — that is, bating the accident of insolvent acts, or release given by the injured creditor, to the end of life — in the ordinary course, viz. the common-law course of procedure, all that is required is, direct proof of the debt, — or what is considered as an equivalent, in the character of circumstantial evidence of it, and that conclusive, — inability to defray the charges of defence.

2. For consigning a man to imprisonment provisionally, viz. on mesne process, till he find responsible persons who engage, in the event of a judgment in affirmance of the debt, either to discharge the debt themselves, or deliver up his body to the definitive imprisonment — to imprisonment, viz. in a common goal, or if he able and willing to bear the extra expense, to a place of less incommodious confinement, commonly called a *spunging-house*, till the reign of George II., nothing more was necessary than repairing to one of the *justice-shops (officinæ justitiæ*, as in lawyers' Latin they have been called,) in which the liberty of the subject was and continues to be sold at a fixed price, by and for the benefit of the judges; — going to one of these shops, and paying to the agent of the judge the price of the lying instrument, by which authority for the exercise of this act of oppression was and is conferred.

At present, the matter stands not exactly upon this footing. Anno 1725, at the end of a term of oppression of several hundred years continuance, without so much as the faintest colour of justice (after the degree of opposition that may be imagined,) what was pretended to be a remedy was applied.

Antecedently to arrest, as a condition precedent to the issuing the warrant for arrestation, an affidavit was required to be exhibited by the plaintiff creditor — an affidavit in which the existence of a debt not less than to a certain amount, as due to him from the alleged debtor, was asserted, but in the most general terms, without any the slightest indication given of the ground of the demand — without any such assertion as that that or any other amount was due upon the balance, or that for the vexation, inconvenience, and expense to which the alleged debtor was thus subjected, there existed any such reason as that which would be afforded by his probable insolvency, coupled with his eventual nonforthcomingness for the purpose of definitive imprisonment, as above.

The matter of fact deposed to, insufficient to warrant the suffering inflicted; — the sole source of the evidence the most untrustworthy of all sources, — the party testifying in his own cause, without the check of counter-evidence — that evidence received in the most untrustworthy of all shapes, viz. the affidavit shape; — to the purpose in question, this evidence taken for conclusive; — all counter-evidence excluded; — the party defendant condemned to this inconvenience, vexation, and expense, unseen and unheard: — such was the arrangement which, when applied to the abomination above described, a lawyer-led legislature was weak or wicked enough to present to the people in the character of a remedy.

CHAPTER XXVIII.

OF THE BURTHEN OF PROOF: ON WHOM SHALL IT LIE? — *(a question produced by undue exclusion of evidence.)*

§ 1. *Answer to the question, on the ground of Natural Procedure.*

THE obligation of adducing proof, on whom — *i. e.* on which of two contending parties — shall it on each occasion be imposed? In this may be seen a question, the answer to which is, under the *technical* system of procedure, encompassed with endless difficulties.

On the ground of natural justice, which is the only justice — under the reign of natural procedure, nothing can be more simple — nothing can be more easy.

On that one of the parties, says the answer, let the obligation be, in each individual instance, imposed, by whom, in that instance, if fulfilled, the fulfilment of it will be attended with least inconvenience; — inconvenience meaning always delay, vexation, and expense.

But how and when can it be known which that party is? *Answer:* Under technical procedure, never: — care, as hath been seen, — effectual care — has ever been taken that it shall not be.

Under natural procedure, along with so many other points that may require to be ascertained, it becomes ascertained — ascertained of course — at the initial meeting of the parties *coram judice*.

Nay: — but by the party by whom the allegation is made, by him it is that the truth of it ought to be proved. Such is the aphorism which on this occasion commonly, and not unnaturally or unplausibly, presents itself.

But, besides that it is in the technical, rather than in the natural system, that it would be found to have its root, and that accordingly the collateral ends of justice, viz. avoidance of unnecessary delay, vexation, and expense, are altogether disregarded by it,—so it is, that as statutes have been drawn up, the application of it has been found embarrassed by knots more easily cut than untied.*

Under the *natural* system, *allegation* is itself proof:—at least, in so far as in relation to the *principal* matter of fact in question, or any matter of fact that is considered as evidentiary of it, the *party alleging* alleges himself to have been a *percipient* witness.

At the same time, generally speaking, it is not so good proof—proof to such a degree trustworthy—as an allegation to the same effect would be, if made by an extraneous witness.

Much less is it as good proof, as an allegation, made to the same effect, by the *adverse* party—by the party to whose interest it is adverse. In his mouth, if his evidence be to the same effect, no allegation respecting perception can be necessary;—declaration of persuasion—*i. e.* admission, in which declaration of persuasion is included—of persuasion, how slight soever, so it be on that side, is sufficient.

In this point of view, the opposite to the aphorism in question, has therefore more of truth in it than the aphorism itself. Supposing the matter in question to have fallen within the cognizance of the adverse party,—of the party adverse to him by whom the allegation is made—the mouth of such adverse party is the properest out of which proof of it can come:—the mouth out of which it will come in the most satisfactory shape:—the proof may in that case be considered as conclusive.

In another point of view, true it is, that the author of the allegation is the party on whom it is *incumbent* that *proof* of it shall have been exhibited, or rather that *evidence* shall have been bestowed upon it. Incumbent?—upon that party, in what sense incumbent? In this sense, viz. that if such evidence fail to be bestowed, he it is by whom the evil consequences of such failure will be felt.

On this occasion, the *plaintiff's* side of the cause is the side which is naturally the first, if not the only one, that presents itself to view. Why? Because, on the plaintiff's side, if his be the side that prevails, there must, in every instance, have been something that has been regarded as having been proved:—whereas to the *defendant* it may happen, not only to contend, but to contend with success, when and although on *his* side nothing has been proved, or so much as been attempted to be proved:—nothing alleged but the opposite of some proposition that has been alleged on the plaintiff's side. For on the side of the *defendant*, such is the state of the case, where, on the side of the *plaintiff*, the *allegation*, together with whatsoever *other* proof, if any, it has found for its support, has failed to obtain credence.

§ 2. *Practice of the English Equity Courts in relation to this head.*

Among the artifices of the technical system, has been the keeping the means of obtaining proof—the means of securing the forthcomingness, whether of persons or things, for the purpose of evidence, in a state of the most perfect imperfection possible. In this policy, two advantages have been sought for and obtained:—in the first place, the uncertainty whether the proof necessary to success will after all be found obtainable—that uncertainty, in which the worst cause need never despair to find more or less of encouragement and incitement to perseverance: in the next place, the plunder collectable and collected in the course of the slow and expensive steps made requisite to be taken for the obtainment of the proof, in a track, every inch of which is kept as open as possible to dispute.

In a court of equity, for example, the evidence which, under natural procedure, you might at the first meeting get from your adversary, without a farthing's worth of expense, in a couple of minutes,—you obtain, if fortune be in your favour, at the end of as many years, and at the expense of as many hundreds of pounds:—the noble, and learned, and pious, and indefatigable keeper of the king's conscience, with eyes lifted up to heaven, lips invoking that God to whom he is soon to render his account, right hand upon "the sacred tabernacle of truth his breast," self-chained all the while to the judgment seat, like the pillar-saint to his pillar, and denying himself his natural rest, to expedite you:—musing ever and anon, with a mixture of pity and astonishment, on the unhappy condition of those barbarian regions, which, not only on the continent of Europe, but even in this our island, it is said, are to be found, to which the blessings which it is the province of a

* In the English books of practice, matter relative to the *onus probandi* is here and there to be found, but no chapter or section is to be found with any such title at the head of it. It is, however, a sort of matter which on one occasion or other is not unfrequently coming into view.

In Peake on Evidence, matter relative to this head is to be found in Part I. Ch. 1. intituled, "*Of the General Rules of Evidence*,"—and in Part II. Ch. V. intituled, "*Of the Evidence in Actions on Statutes.*"

court of equity to dispense, are unknown, — so completely unknown, that not so much as the name of it is to be found in their language.

Here there may be seen a scantling of that state of things, in and by virtue of which a question naturally of such subordinate importance, and so easily settled, as that concerning the *onus probandi*, has been converted into a question of cardinal importance, on which it may often happen, that the fate of the cause, and of the parties in respect of it, may have to hinge.

§ 3. *Practice of the English Common-Law Courts in relation to this head.*

Thus much as to equity procedure: observe now how the matter stands, at the stage of jury-trial, at common law.

At the trial, sits the plaintiff in one part of the court, and the defendant in the same or another. In this supposition, there is nothing of extravagance — nothing but what is every now and then realized. For the purpose of Judge and Co., had it been necessary that, in the physical sense of the word exclusion, an exclusion should have been put upon the parties in that case, that in that or in any other sense, an exclusion would long ago have been put upon them, need not be doubted — an exclusion with the same right, and the same reason, and the same facility, as that with which, so far as concerns testimony, an exclusion in cases and on pretences such as have been seen, has been put upon extraneous witnesses. But so long as, figuratively speaking, he is in the presence of judge and jury, no suitor is suffered to come into or remain in court, without a gag in his mouth, — so long as, literally speaking, a suitor on one side is not only not compelled, but not permitted to give answer to so much as a single question put to him by a suitor on the other, the doors of the judicatory remain as yet unclosed against those to whom what is called *justice* is administered: — and while his ruin is decreeing (for, without exaggeration, the loss of any single trial, such is the expense of it, would to any one of a vast majority of the whole number of the people, be absolute ruin,) while this is passing, the man who has right on his side may, if so it be that his conception can comprehend the explanation given him of the jargon that passes in his hearing, have the satisfaction of hearing with his own ears the proximate cause of the ruin to which, with so deliberate a solemnity and regularity, he is doomed.

Be this as it may, within a yard or two of the plaintiff (to resume the case,) sits the defendant. At this stage at last, if by half a year, or a whole year, or more than a year, spent in doing nothing but fee-gathering, the rapacity of Judge and Co. could be satiated, at this last, or almost last stage, if the plaintiff being allowed to put a question or two to the defendant, so it were that the defendant were on pain of loss of his cause obliged to answer him, that evidence, which at the very outset of the cause might have been, would now at last be, *extracted*, or, according to circumstances, at least indicated.

As it is, no such question being to be put, the consequence is, — that if so it be that it being determined that it is on the plaintiff the burthen of proof lies, no other than that which is thus refused to him being at the moment within his reach — a *nonsuit*, or, according to circumstances, a *verdict* against him, is the consequence.

If it be the defendant who finds himself in the like disastrous situation, the defendant's not being the situation in which a nonsuit can be suffered, an adverse verdict is the least misfortune by which he can be affected.

If, having right on your side, you have a verdict against you, — a misfortune which, on the part of your law advisers, any supposed breach of a rule, never declared or so much as made, may on the occasion of any suit or cause at any time bring down upon you, — then so it is, that for ultimate success your only chance depends upon a motion for a new trial; that is, a second trial in the worst mode imaginable, in order to know whether a third trial in the same less bad mode as the first shall take place.

If, instead of having a verdict against you, it be your good or ill fortune to receive the indulgence of a nonsuit, the consequence is — that on condition of retreading a certain number of useless and expensive steps, a quarter of a year, or half a year, or a whole year afterwards, according to the latitude of the scene of action—according as it is to the south or to the north—a second trial, though not in this case under the name of a new trial, is at your command.

In this statement may be seen the effect of the question, the curious and learned question concerning the *onus probandi*, and the use of it to those for whose profit the delay, vexation, and expense, have been manufactured: — of this question, as of questions in abundance of the like nice and curious frame, and amongst others, questions concerning evidence, — see many of the preceding chapters and the succeeding one.

Such are the questions on which, after arguments addressed to the judge alone, the jury remaining in the state of puppets, so large a part of the time which ought to be employed, in arguments on which the jury, with assistance only from the judge, should decide, is consumed.

Of the immense heap of pestilential matter of which the chaos called jurisprudence is composed, no inconsiderable proportion is composed of cases which, under the primitive system of personal appearance, could not have had existence.

Such, for example, are those which belong to the question concerning the *onus probandi.**

On this head, as on so many others here touched upon,—justice, genuine justice allows but of one general rule: — the burthen of proof, lay it in each individual case upon that one of the parties on whom it will sit lightest: a point which cannot be ascertained but by the explanations above mentioned.

Look to the books, and here, as elsewhere, instead of clear rules, such as the nature of things forbids to be established by anything but statute law, you have darkness palpable and visible.

The affirmative is that which shall be proved: — plausible enough; — but affirmative or negative depends not merely on the nature of the fact, but also on the structure of the language employed in the description of it. After, and notwithstanding this rule, come exceptions: and who shall assign an end, — among lawyers, who would wish to assign an end,—to the string of exceptions?

In the *onus probandi* may be seen one of those innumerable gulphs into which many fortunes are destined to be thrown, but which no number of fortunes will fill up.

An offence is created, and in the creation of it, in relation to that offence in the character of causes of justification or exemption, a number of circumstances are established. On the part of the plaintiff, the existence of the act of delinquency is of course to be proved: — but of the several circumstances, any one of which suffices to exempt a man from the penalty,—to entitle the plaintiff to the service he demands at the hands of the judge, shall it be necessary for him to prove the non-existence respectively?—or shall the proof of the act in question suffice, unless on the part of the defendant the existence of one or more of them be proved?

Having to his own satisfaction sufficient assurance, that on the part of him whom he is prosecuting, no one of all the appointed causes of justification or exemption has existence, so sure as the confrontation had place, being assured of finding in the answer, or even the silence of the defendant, sufficient proof, — he would exempt himself in the first instance, and ultimately the defendant, from the expense attendant on the proof, supposing it possible, of all those negatives. But the lawyers, with whose interest security on the part of suitors and clients is incompatible, have taken care that there shall not be any such assurance. In the darkness in which he is left to grope his way, the plaintiff, under the guidance of a professional adviser, whose profit increases with the burthen, under the impossibility of learning an opinion and a will which he to whom it belongs to form it has not yet formed, loads himself, if he be able, with the whole of the vexation and expense of which it is supposed that by any possibility it can happen to it to be pronounced necessary. If, sinking under the burthen, he fail in his conjecture concerning that which it has been rendered impossible for him to know, be the justice of his case ever so clear, he loses it.

It is the interest of the fraternity, that the traps thus laid on the plaintiff's side for catching plaintiffs should be multiplied to infinity, that, on the defendant's side, a man, be the badness of his cause ever so clear, may be encouraged to defend himself: accordingly, it was a maxim of Lord Chancellor Rosslyn, that no cause ought ever to be given up as desperate.

But men are thus discouraged from commencing a cause: and unless a cause be begun, how can it be continued? No such thing: if, setting aside the traps, the plaintiff's cause be good, he is assured that it is good: — but nothing is said of the traps — they do not come till afterwards.

A legislative draughtsman who understood his business, would, in penning the substantive part of a new law, make due provision for the solution of these difficulties in procedure: — but as the system is constituted, it is not the interest of any legislative draughtsman to understand the business: — and if he did understand the business, what he would understand still better is, — that so long as the reproach of incapacity can be avoided, it is his interest to multiply and not to diminish the number of all such difficulties. Nor, after all, does the nature of the mischief admit of anything like a co-extensive remedy, other than the restoration of that feature of primitive justice — confrontation of the parties at the outset *coram judice* — which a man at the head of the law, had he as many hands as Briareus, would cut them all off sooner than he would co-operate in, or even be a witness to the restoration of.

* See Peake, p. 272.

CHAPTER XXIX.

EVIDENCE CONSIDERED IN ITS RELATION TO THIS OR THAT FACT IN PARTICULAR—WHY DISCARDED FROM THIS WORK.

CONSIDERED in its relation to this or that particular matter of fact,—whether it be individual fact or species of fact,—evidence, it will upon review be manifest, has not been comprised in the field of inquiry marked out in and for the present work.

On further consideration, a proposition for which the assent of the reader may not unreasonably be expected, seems to be, that when considered in any such narrow point of view, the consideration belongs not properly —notwithstanding the apparent contradiction in terms — to any work, purporting on the face of it and by the title of it, to be a work on evidence — or even, to come home to the point, a work having for its object the law of evidence.

On every occasion on which any matter of fact comes in question, so does whatsoever evidence is considered as bearing relation to it: so, therefore, does evidence considered in its relation to that same matter of fact.

But from this circumstance, no occasion has ever yet been taken to consider every work in which matters of fact are brought in question as a work on evidence: — to consider the word evidence as constituting of itself a proper title to such work, or as fit so much as to constitute an elementary portion of any such title.

If so, not only all political history, but all religious history, all natural history, and even all natural philosophy, all physics, including all mathematics — for mathematical propositions, in so far as they have any truth, are but physical propositions of the utmost amplitude — would present each a title to a place in a work on evidence. True (it may perhaps be said,) if evidence, without any word of limitation disjunctive of the class of facts which were meant to be the subject of it, were the appellative in question. But prefix to it any such word as legal—or say, law of evidence—it will thereby be understood at once, that facts susceptible of a legal operation — facts capable of producing legal effects, are the only sorts of facts with relation to which, in a work so entitled, evidence is about to be considered.

Admitted: but, on the other hand, what has already been shown is, that there is scarcely that imaginable species of fact, to which it may not happen to be comprised within the class of legally operative facts.

All this while, a consideration that can scarcely fail to have already presented itself to the mind of every professional reader, is, that of the matter of this or that book, purporting by its title to be a book on the law of evidence, a full moiety is of such a description, that what is there spoken of under the name of evidence, bears in every instance relation to this or that particular fact; and, at the same time, that no mention of such matter or reference to it is included in anything, that in treating of the subject of evidence in general has in the course of the present work been brought to view.

Matter of this sort, it may be asked, — in a book purporting by its title to be a work on the law of evidence, — has there been any impropriety in the insertion of it? — to go further, had no mention been made of such matter in a book thus entitled, — could it have been regarded otherwise than as incomplete?

In justice, the answer, it should seem, cannot be otherwise than in the negative — and the reason is — that where, in so far as the evidence in question is in its application limited not only to such facts as come ordinarily under the appellation of *legally operative* facts, but to the dispositions that appear as yet to have been made by the law, as it now stands, in relation to such facts, the space within which the matter of such a work is capable of being compressed will be seen to be altogether of very moderate extent; so moderate, that if, in a work professing to be an all-comprehensive one on the subject of evidence, matter of this description were omitted, the work, especially when considered with relation to the sort of information requisite for the purpose of the professional reader, might justly be taxed with being incomplete.

But in a work designed for the use of professional men, while thus, for the sake of completeness, the title to admission presented by matter of this sort cannot but be confessed, — at the same time, for the sake of clearness and correctness of conception, neither can the demand which appears to present itself for a clear and strong line of distinction between the two divisions, in themselves so dissimilar, of a subject, which by its customary denomination is declared in both cases to be the same, be looked upon, it should seem, as fit to be left unsatisfied.

In Peake's Treatise on the Law of Evidence, this line has accordingly been drawn; and in that work, as it should seem, for the first time — for neither in the work of Lord Chief-Baron Gilbert on Evidence alone, nor in the work of Mr. Justice Buller on the Law of Evidence considered in the law of *nisi prius! (nisi prius!* what an appellative)— in neither of these masses of technical jargon is any trace of it to be found.

By Mr. Peake, in whose useful compendium, wretched as it is in its own nature, the matter appears to much greater advantage than in either of these others, so strongly, prominently, and decidedly drawn has been this line, that before that part, which in no other than a practical and incidental point of view belongs as above to the subject of evidence, had at all been touched upon by him, that part in which, if the view here given of it be correct, the whole of the matter that, strictly speaking, belongs to the subject of evidence is contained, had for some time been published.

"Evidence in general, as regulated by the pleadings and other proceedings in a cause," is the title employed by the learned author in designation of the matter comprised in the second part of his work. Whether by that title, or by the title prefixed to the present chapter, the clearest and most correct notion will be given of this part of the subject matter of the law of evidence as it stands in highest English practice, is more than I can take upon me to say. On the present occasion, the reason of the preference given to it, for the purpose of this work, is, that in and by it, is rendered more distinctly present the consideration by which the exclusion of it from the present work was determined; — for setting aside all reference to the pleadings and other proceedings belonging to this or that technical system of procedure, the circumstance of the reference all along made to particular facts considered in the character of facts, exercising their legally operative force on such or such particular occasions — on the occasion, and in support of or opposition to such or such particular demands, would have sufficed to insure the exclusion of all matter of this description from the pale of the present work.

Suppose that instead of the law of England, the law of any other country, Scotland (suppose) or France, had been the system of actual law taken in the course of the present work as the standard of reference. The evidence, in so far as regulated by the pleadings and other proceedings in a cause would in that case have assuredly been found to wear a very different aspect from that which it does under the law of England: yet whatsoever matter is here omitted out of a work, looking throughout the whole course of it, as does the present, principally though not exclusively to the law of England, would equally have been excluded from this work, had the system of actual law principally regarded in it, been either of those two other systems.

CHAPTER XXX.

EVIDENCE IN RELATION TO PARTICULAR FACTS AND PLEADINGS UNDER TECHNICAL PROCEDURE.

"Of evidence in general, as regulated by the pleadings and other proceedings in a cause." Such is the title which, in the most comprehensive as well as instructive of all works, that under the English system of technical procedure have as yet appeared on the subject of evidence, stands prefixed to the second and rather more copious of the two parts between which the matter of it is divided.

Such is the description therein given of the sort of matter which, for the reasons that have just been given it has been thought proper to discard out of this work, in which everything belonging to *evidence in general*, was meant and endeavoured to be brought under review.

In the instance of the present work, for the omission of all such particular matter, the reasons above assigned will, it is supposed, not be found insufficient.

In the instance of that professional and learned work, the necessity of giving insertion to all such particulars as are there inserted, appears upon the face of the description given of it as above.

Of the sort of matter thus dicarded, considering that its title to be considered as matter belonging to the subject of a book on the law of evidence cannot be wholly set aside, it may be some satisfaction to the reader, especially to the professional reader, to see some account given — some conception, how general and loose soever afforded, on the principles corresponding to the principles adopted in the course of the present work.

In the form of opinions and propositions, some of the most striking conclusions shall accordingly, in this place, be briefly brought to view: —

1. Of this matter of detail, a great part is of such a nature as, under a system properly constituted and consistently conformed to, would never have found a place in any work on the law of evidence: it either would not have found under any title a place in any book of law, or if under any title, not under any such title as that of evidence.

2. Of the matter contained in this book, which has any reference to the subject of evidence, the whole is furnished by no other sorts of suits or causes, than those in the course of which jury-trial has place.

3. On these occasions, in so far as the question discussed is a question relating to evidence, it is a question concerning circumstantial evidence; — *i. e.* whether, in relation to a fact of such or such a description, considered in the character of a principal fact, a fact of this or that other description shall, in the character of an evidentiary fact, be admitted, and if admitted, be considered as conclusive.

4. The decisions on any such question reported,—the instances in which any question of any such nature has been suffered to be discussed, are so many instances of usurpation recorded: — of usurpation made by the judges upon the constitutionally proper, and never directly contested, however continually and covertly invaded province of the jury, in their quality of judges of the matter of fact.

With few, if any, exceptions, the matter contained in that volume would be found referable to one or other of the heads following: —

1. A matter belonging to the substantive branch of law, viz. some point which exists in the shape of real, *i. e.* statute law.

2. A question concerning the import and effect to be given to this or that clause, in this or that instrument of contract in common use: an instrument the terms of which constitute, as between all persons interested in it, so much of the matter of statute law.

In both these instances, on one side or the other, this or that portion of discourse is proposed as proper to be applied to the text of the statute, in such manner as to operate in explanation, or, in some way or other, under the notion of explanation, in alteration of it: — in alteration; viz. by producing the effect producible by addition to, or defalcation from, or substitution in relation to such or such portion of the matter contained in it.

3. A question belonging to the same branch of law, but to some part of it which has no other than an imaginary existence, being of the nature of jurisprudential, *alias* judge-made, *alias* unwritten, *alias* common law.

4. A question belonging to the law of procedure:—of which sort is every question concerning the *onus probandi* as above described, and any question concerning the sort of evidence requisite for the support of an allegation made to this or that particular effect, in and by this or that one of the written instruments in which are contained the pleadings in the cause.

5. A question concerning circumstantial evidence, *i. e.* whether, in relation to this or that particular fact in the character of a principal fact, such or such matter of fact shall or shall not be admitted in the character of an evidentiary fact. If admitted, the evidence afforded by it is generally considered as *conclusive*.

In every one of these instances, the deplorable state of the law, considered in any such character as a rule of action, having for its end and object the welfare of the individuals whose fate is governed by it, may be seen exemplified.

1. As to statute law: — what there is of it, is a mere shapeless mass; bulky in its form, and at the same time scanty in its matter: — consisting of no more than a collection of disjointed materials, laid in patches upon a groundwork consisting of imaginary law; — of law, the words, and consequently the substance and import of which, are left to be on each occasion shot at by imagination and conjecture.

Supposing the whole to possess the form and extent required, digested in some such way as every work is which is really intended to be understood, under a connected assemblage of titles and sub-titles, — on this supposition, as often as for the purpose of receiving explanation, or, under the notion of explanation, alteration at the hand of the judicial authority, the words of such explanation or alteration, instead of being either left to drop into oblivion, or settled between a self-appointed note-taker and the bookseller, his customer or employer, would, at the requisition of the legislature, be settled, and applied to the text, in the manner of amendments made at present to a bill, by the judge or judges by whom the decision was pronounced; and being notified to the two Houses of Parliament, might then, from the tacit and implied consent of the two authorities, receive that binding force which at present they receive at the hands of the two estates, viz. the note-taker and bookseller, as above.

2. As to jurisprudential, *alias* judge-made law, *alias* common-law:—neither on this nor on any other occasion, can it without risk of producing misconception be brought to view, if brought to view in any other light, than that of, — from beginning to end a monstrous system of absurdity and imposture, of which it is impossible for any man to speak properly without self-contradiction, or an enlightened lover of mankind to think of without melancholy or without shame.

On no occasion whatsoever, can any portion of it be spoken of without being spoken of as having such or such an assemblage of determinate words belonging to it. But in no part of it has it any such determinate words belonging to it. By the individual who, on any occasion or for any purpose, has need to speak of it—client, suitor, attorney, advocate, judge — to the minutest fragment which on that occasion happens to come in question, a set of words are assigned at a venture, — one advocate on one side saying that such and such ought to be the assemblage of words — the advocate on the other side, such and such other words, — one judge, in like manner, one set — another judge the same or another set, — no such advocate, nor any such judge, for five minutes together, after the time of their dropping out of his mouth, troubling himself to remember what they were; — the note-taker, if any such self-appointed officer happen to be present, neglecting or noticing them, conceiving them aright, or misconceiving them,—setting down upon his paper those same words, or any others, as it may happen, and so forwarding them or not forwarding them to the bookseller or the printer.

And thus it is that on the present, as on every other occasion, a nominal existence is given to the portion in question of the non-entity to the designation of which the sacred name of law is prostituted, and which, for the affliction of mankind, has been endowed with the force of law, — that ideally existing, yet but too really acting power, by which the purposes of oppression and extortion and depredation, and, in every other assignable shape, injustice, are so correctly and admirably fulfilled; while, to every honest and useful purpose, it possesses that sort of efficiency which from a non-entity ought in reason to be expected.

3. As to the law of procedure, in whatsoever shape it happens, in the part in question, to be existing, — whether in the real shape of statute, or the imaginary shape: — of the matter referable to this head, a large exemplification is afforded by that in relation to which the question is, on which of the two contending parties the *onus probandi*,—the obligation of exhibiting proof, — shall be imposed.

CHAPTER XXXI.

FALSE THEORY OF EVIDENCE (GILBERT'S*)— ITS FOUNDATION:—PRECEDENCE GIVEN TO WRITTEN BEFORE UNWRITTEN.

§ 1. *Errors of this Theory—their efficient cause.*

BY inapposite arrangement, how vast is the mischief—by apposite arrangement, how great the service — that may be rendered to useful science!

From incorrect or incomplete conception in the first place, from incorrect judgment in the next place, inappropriate nomenclature, and the classification which is included (for in proportion to the extent of the collection of things which it is employed to designate, nomenclature is classification,) receive their existence: and, once established, give permanence to the same undesirable result from which they received existence.

In the books of English lawyers, when the topic of evidence comes upon the carpet, and in particular in those books of which evidence constitutes the sole topic, the first division made of the subject is the division of evidence into written and unwritten: — written occupying the first place:— and of the nature of this sort of evidence, description being given, such as it is, before anything is said on the subject of unwritten evidence.

For the mass to which the appellation of unwritten is allotted, is reserved everything which in the course of this work has been said on the subject of trustworthiness and untrustworthiness, including whatsoever has been done and established in the way of exclusion — that field on which the fraternity of lawyers has, so much at its ease, and with such demonstrations of vigour and delight, been seen disporting itself.

The wise and the foolish, the just and the unjust, the interested and the uninterested, the man of untainted and the man of tainted character, — thus various are the descriptions of persons out of whose mouth it may happen to evidence to have issued, according to a discovery which is made — at what period? by and not before the time at which everything has been said which required to be said on the subject of written evidence.

Of the persons from whose minds evidence not committed to writing, or whatsoever else is meant to be distinguished by the word *unwritten*, has been delivered, — such and such are the different characters and descriptions. Be it so: — such, in consideration of these several characters, is the disposition that has been made by English law in relation to their respective testimonies. Alas! it is but too true.

But the persons from whose minds the sort of evidence called written is delivered, what sort of persons are they? — their evidence, is it not susceptible of trustworthiness and untrustworthiness? — their character and dispositions — of wisdom and weakness, of probity and improbity? — their respective situations, are they not respectively capable of standing, unreached by, or exposed to, the action of sinister interest?

Or is it that the beings, of whose evidence written evidence is composed, are one class of beings — those of whose evidence unwritten evidence is composed, another and a different class of beings; — the authors of written evidence, as the place allotted to them imports, being creatures of a superior class, the authors of unwritten evidence of an inferior class?

By a conception implying a judgment passed on the affirmative side of the above question, does the first step taken in this line of arrangement appear to have been determined: — and of this first step such was the importance, and such the delight with which it was accompanied, that by this first step all those that followed it were determined; and whither they led—into what a labyrinth of error and absurdity the mind by which this course was thus pursued would be conducted—was a consideration for which no sort of attention had been reserved.

In the demesne of written evidence, the first field you come to is that in which the produce has the lords of this vineyard themselves for its authors; viz. that sort of written evidence, that super-sacred sort of evidence, distinguished by the appellation of a *record*.

Of this super-sacred and super-human class of persons, one attribute is the being exempt from all human weakness. In the king, whom the pious commentator Blackstone has pourtrayed in such glowing colours as supreme, all-perfect, immortal, and omnipresent, they behold their God: in themselves the most perfect, the most exalted, and the most justly exalted of his creatures. From this perfection on the part of the workman, follows the perfection of the work: — falsehood is a property of which no assertion flowing from such a source is susceptible. False to any degree in itself, by passing through such a medium, the assertion, whatsoever it be, is

* For account of the manner in which Lord Chief-Baron Gilbert has treated the subject of Evidence, see Appendix C.

rendered true. Truth and falsehood, and by their means, right and wrong follow "the finger of the law." Falsehood, if not, literally and strictly speaking, converted into truth, is acted upon, treated, and in every respect acted upon as if it were: — it gives rise to action on the part of the authors of all justice, and by their irresistible hand it is protected from that contradiction which it might otherwise be exposed to suffer at the hands of the profane.

Of those truths which it is the function of mathematical science to usher into the world, it is a common property not to be susceptible of contradiction: *demonstration* is the appellation given to that species of discourse by which a truth of this class is shown to be what it is: a diagram is a sort of figure or picture of graphical exhibition, of visible sign, or figured representation, which, for the purpose of giving facility to such demonstration, is employed by that branch of mathematical science in which the circumstance of figure is taken into account.

According to the definition given of it by Lord Chief-Baron Gilbert, a record is accordingly a diagram for the demonstration of right. The problem proposed by him to himself was — to prove all English judges, whose station is in Westminster Hall, to be infallible. Such as has here been seen is the medium of proof—such the demonstration: never was Q. E. D. written with more perfect satisfaction by the master geometrician, or received with more perfect acquiescence and admiration by his pupils.

And this diagram for the demonstration of right, what is it? The constantly filled receptacle of falsehoods, not only among the most pernicious, but among the most notorious that the repositories of profane discourse, taking the world throughout, was ever known to furnish—falsehoods which, though acted on as if they were truths, are not altogether without exultation recognised in their character of falsehoods, and under the name of fictions, confessed and delineated by Blackstone.

Of the principle of arrangement here in question, such has been the object in view— such in too great a degree the effect: to procure for the most degrading vice a species of adoration beyond what could ever be due, if bestowed upon the sublimest virtue.

In a preceding part of this work, the suggestion has been already hazarded, that official persons in general, and judicial persons in particular, are but men, made of the same mould as other men: men in whose instance, for the purpose of evidence and judicature, as for other purposes, trustworthiness is to be examined into by the same lights, and determined by the same tests, as in the instance of men of lower degree, or of no degree at all.

Whether for the formation of a right judgment on a subject of this kind, the course pointed out by the suggestion so hazarded as above, or that which has been taken by the demonstration just reported, be the more promising, is among the questions on which it will rest with the reader to decide.

To some readers, the notion by which fallibility is ascribed to the only class of persons, of secular persons at least, from whose pens, not to speak of tongues, falsehood in a larger proportion than truth, and never without yielding profit in return, is wont to flow, will be apt to appear *speculative* — an epithet in use among official persons for the condemnation of whatsoever proposition is too adverse to private interest not to be hated, and at the same time too manifestly true to be denied.

From this highest level in the scale of authority and excellence and correspondent trustworthiness, Gilbert descends successively to what he calls the inferior degrees; viz. public written evidence of an inferior nature to matter of record, private written evidence, and unwritten evidence.

§ 2. *Errors of this Theory—their final cause.*

Demand is the parent of supply. Of the reputation of trustworthiness, of verity and veracity, the value is felt and recognised by the most stupid. Puffed off by them upon mankind as true, it was their interest that this compost of lies should be taken and accepted as true, the more thoroughly and palpably it was seen and felt by them to be tainted with the opposite vice.

Throw the business into confusion — was the order which, in a moment of agony, the vexation under which he had had to struggle extorted from a distinguished servant of the public, whose services have been so universally felt, and with the help of lawyer's quibbles, and the barbarism, and proportion-confounding law of forfeiture, so perfidiously and ungenerously rejected.

To throw and keep in confusion had been the line of policy pursued by his crafty opponents, who, with so much power to act, had little need to speak or write, and who, if they did speak, were too powerful or too fortunate to be betrayed.

To keep the whole subject involved for ever in confusion, the very thickest confusion that can be manufactured, has been the line of policy so diligently and successfully pursued by the fraternity of lawyers throughout the whole field of law; — throughout the whole of that vast field, and nowhere with more success than in this most important and commanding part of it.

For the creation and preservation of confusion, what more effectual instrument could be chosen, than a system of classification and correspondent nomenclature, in which a subject was undertaken to be taught before any of its properties had been brought to view; — parts and particulars, of the most opposite nature and tendency being lumped together and perpetually confounded under one name, whilst the same things were introduced under two different names?

Fortunate is the man in whose favour art and nature, exertion and carelessness, ingenuity and stupidity, concur and conspire towards the production of the same results!

In this part as in others of the field of law, thus happy has been the situation and position of the fraternity of lawyers. In default of opposite interest, imbecility would of itself have sufficed to fill the paths of law and legislation with weeds and thorns; and of the facility thus afforded by nature, every advantage has been taken that could be taken by the most consummate art: — such being the direction given to everything to which any such appellation as industry, or diligence, or art, or labour, or ingenuity, can be applied; and by these means have non-lawyers been rendered unable in general to unravel the mysteries in which Judge and Co. have involved all legal proceedings, under cover of which they have with so much success pursued their own peculiar and sinister interests.

CHAPTER XXXII.

LIBERALISTS AND RIGORISTS — PARTIES BELLIGERENT IN THE FIELD OF JURISPRUDENCE, AND IN PARTICULAR OF EVIDENCE.

As formerly, under the Roman law, there were the Proculian and Sabinian sects, — so, under English law, judges and law-writers may be considered as divided into *Liberalists* and *Rigorists:* not that between the two sects there is any gulph fixed, but that from either the one to the other an individual may pass, and back again at any time, as often as it happens to him to find it convenient. Praise in one shape or the other he is equally sure of, which soever side he takes: his only difficulty is, on any given occasion to choose between the two shapes, in which of them on that occasion it shall be served up.

The law of evidence, as has been seen, is almost exclusively composed of exclusionary rules; and these rules, as already there has at least been seen reason to suspect, almost exclusively absurd and mischievous. Being thus absurd and mischievous, sufficient reason for the infringement of them can never be wanting: — being at the same time acknowledged rules, over and over again acted upon and conformed to, as little can abundantly sufficient reason ever be wanting for conforming to them: and as often as it is found more agreeable or convenient to conform to the rule than to break it, the chains by which the reverend and learned person feels himself bound to the observance of it, are adamantine chains.

Lord Mansfield, in his day, used to be considered as the great champion and leader of the liberalists:—Lord Camden, his rival and bitter enemy, of the rigorists.

In a fit of courage, Lord Mansfield ventured to give the Bar to understand, that the decisions of his predecessors were apt to be very absurd, and very unfit to set the rule to future ones: — which, when compared with so many rules of statute law, was altogether true, but compared with the absence of all rules, altogether false.

"We do not sit here," says he,* "to take our rules of evidence from Siderfin or Kelk:" — in plain English, when so it happens that a rule laid down by a predecessor of mine in office is not to my taste, I will not hold myself bound by it. At the sight of this flourish, down falls upon the knees of his heart the author of that useful work on evidence, by whom so much labour has been saved to the author of this work, and acknowledges the mind of the judge in question, for one of those "great minds" who exercise the right of thinking for themselves, before they assent to the authority of others.

On another occasion, "The absurdity of Lord Lincoln's case," says the same great mind, "is shocking; but it is now law." — What was the plain English here? That on this occasion he had no particular wish to pronounce a decision repugnant to the rule deducible from that case. Here, then, may be seen the liberalist and the rigorist under one hood: tribute of admiration and applause belonging to both characters received into one box. Speaking with the liberalist, he acted with the rigorist.

Between the first Lord Mansfield and the first Lord Camden — at least as towards the first Lord Mansfield in the breast of the first Lord Camden — there existed not only a rivalry, but a sort of hostility, which, among the partisans and admirers of the "indiscriminate defence of right and wrong," attracted in its day a measure of attention, scarcely inferior to that which, at a later period, has been bestowed upon the contests of Crib and Molyneux by the amateurs of pugilism: — and in the titled pair of boxers, the regard for the welfare of mankind, and for unsophisticated justice, might, without flattery, be stated as not being, *primâ facie,* inferior to what it may reasonably be supposed to be in the untitled ones.

By the accidents of the war of party, the junior of them had been placed on the side which had found its account in taking a line of conduct less unfavourable to the interests

* Blackstone, I. 366.

of the great community than that which, by so many motions of course, had been travelled in by the other.

In the course of the contest, the word *discretion*, being on every occasion employed by every judge, had probably enough been employed by the Lord Chief-Justice of the King's Bench: — and by that noble and learned person, on that occasion as on others, *discretion* had probably been spoken of as a sort of faculty or mental qualification, which, in the execution of his office, it might not be altogether improper for a man in the situation and character of a judge to be provided with and to exercise. Not a syllable more was then and there wanting to satisfy the learned and right honourable the Lord Chief-Justice of the Common Bench — then not as yet a Lord of Parliament — that *discretion* was not only a bad quality, but a quality at least, if by an oblique cast it could be stuck upon the sleeve of the Lord Chief-Justice of the Upper Bench, odious: odious, if not absolutely and to everybody without exception, at any rate to every man whom it found disposed to hate Lord Mansfield for doing what he did, whatever that might be.

"The discretion of a judge," says he, in his Genuine Argument,* bawling out all the way to the eye in capitals — "the discretion of a judge is the law of tyrants; it is always unknown: it is different in different men; it is casual, and depends upon constitution, temper, and passion. In the best, it is oftentimes caprice; in the worst, it is every folly and passion to which human nature is liable."

Till this time, discretion had passed, if not for an heroic virtue, at any rate for an innocent and not altogether useless quality: nor, in the situation of a judge, not to speak of inferior ones, would it have been pleasant to a man to be thought altogether destitute of it.

From that time, by the worshippers at least of the first Lord Camden, it has on all proper occasions been deemed and taken to be that bad thing which he discovered it to be: and indefatigable was the applause which the discovery had been worth to him in his time.

Now suppose two professors of the art of venal eloquence — one paid for being a *liberalist*, the other for being a *rigorist*. Out comes the one with the vapouring about *Siderfin* and *Kelk:* out comes the other with the invective against *discretion:* to which of them will the laurel be due? Judgment-seat the jury-box, gifts of nature equal: Answer — To him who with most fruit has sitten at the feet of Siddons. Judgment-seat the bench: Answer — Who dare!

The curious thing is, that the dart thus aimed at the enemy goes through and through the very heart of their common mother, *Common Law* herself. What, in the way of insinuation, was predicated of, and meant to be deemed and taken to be peculiar to the works of that one of her children, would, upon the strictest examination, be found to be with the strictest truth predicable, and, if she should so long live, will continue for ever predicable, of herself and all her works. The picture is drawn in lively colours, and, to render it a most correct likeness, needs no other change than of the name — for *discretion of a judge*, read *common law*.

Behold here, then, the great, the important difference—that between common and statute law. As to the demirep's two fighting children, of whom the Tory was the better tempered and the better bred, the difference was never to an honest man worth thinking about. "It was casual, and depended upon situation." Had Murray been a Rigorist, Pratt would have been a Liberalist: had Murray been a Whig, Pratt would have been a Tory: The difference? It was between Bavius and Mævius. Both were enemies, as every admirer of common, in contradistinction to statute law, is, and ever will be, — both alike sworn enemies to security in society, to certainty in law.

By such "exercise," as has been seen — by such "exercise of the right of thinking for themselves," not to speak of others — by such a course it is, that, "rejecting those cases which were not supported by principles, that great judge established a system (as it seemed to the learned author above mentioned) for his successors to follow: and competence and credibility," continues he, "so frequently confounded together, are now accurately defined and well understood."

A system for his successors to follow? — What system? — a system of doing what they pleased? This, as has been seen, was the system not only taken up, but avowed by this great judge; and if, what we are to understand from the learned institutionalist be, that this was the system which it was the design of the great judge should be followed by his successors, and that, whether it were or no, it is the system that has been followed by those same successors, these are propositions from which it may be neither necessary, nor upon any good grounds an easy task to dissent.

Competency and credibility, so frequently confounded together, are now accurately defined and well understood. Of these three propositions, the first is altogether above dispute: to the two others, or either of them, the assent given cannot be altogether so clear of reserve. Frequency of confusion; — admitted: — accuracy of definition; — doubtful: — goodness of intellection; — doubtful likewise.

That minds are not wanting by which they

* 4to. Printed for Wilkie 1771.

are well enough understood, may very well be: but as to any definitions that have been given, whether by that great judge or any other, whether it be by means of, or in spite of such definitions, that the act of intellection has taken place, may be not altogether free from doubts.

Yes: if even now so it be that the matter in question be understood, it is not by means, but in spite of, any discourse of which the words competence and credibility, as opposed to each other, are the leading terms, that the intellection must take place: for seldom have any words that have been employed with reference to the purpose for which they were employed, if clear conception be that purpose, been so incompetent as are these two words, of the use of which, confusion having been the object, confusion has so successfully been the effect.

On each occasion, nothing can be more simple than has been the question, when expressed in that simple language, which is adapted to the expression of it. Tender has been made of a person in the character of a deposing witness. *Question:* Shall he be, or shall he not be, admitted? *Admit or not admit,* would have been the simple, the proper language, or, still shorter than not admit, —*exclude.* What is called for is a plain act of will: — but in technical procedure, will is never either so safe or so powerful as when it is in disguise: those adventurous persons, whose exploits gave a subject and occasion to the act called the Black Act — those are the public men whose line of policy, those great men, who conduct and act under the technical system, find so much convenience in pursuing.

To exclude or not to exclude, is the determination which the judge has come to in his own mind: such is the result of his will: required to find a cloak for it? To do this, a discovery is made of two qualities — competence and credibility—in the character of properties inherent in the nature of the testimony itself, — the testimony which, if admission were given to the witness, he would give. To admit him? Is that your determination? You say he is a competent witness: — he belongs to that class of persons to whose testimony the property of competency appertains: — and he being admitted and quietly stationed in the witness' box, then comes the question of credibility — a question on which the determination cannot be given till after his testimony has been heard and produced, whatsoever impression it may be found calculated to produce.

To exclude him? Is that your determination? Without suffering him to open his mouth to say anything, at least anything that is to the purpose, you turn him about, and observing how in regard to externals he is circumstanced, you pronounce the word *incompetent;* — the man, you say, is an incompetent witness; — his testimony, of which you know nothing not having heard it,—whatsoever, if it were suffered to be heard, it would be, — is incompetent evidence.

Two lawyers, or sets of lawyers, having each of them been employed in drawing an act of parliament, — say for shortness, two lawyers, neither of them knowing what they meant,—employed in the description of a witness, one of them the word competent, the other the word credible. Placed where they are, both of these epithets were words of surplusage; neither of them had any distinct meaning attached to it; each of them was much worse than useless.

Credibility, employed on such an occasion, or on any occasion, to designate a property as belonging to a witness,—nothing can be more idle. Credibility is capacity of being believed. Being convicted on the oath of a credible witness — where is the possible witness that is not credible? Where is the witness whose testimony, if it find men who believe it, is not capable of being believed, is not actually believed: — of this word credible, what is the design? To prevent men from believing testimony which cannot by possibility be believed? — or to prevent men from believing testimony which ought not to be believed? Is this the use expected from the word? But if so, in what way is it expected to be productive of or contributory to that effect?

Equally incapable of serving any useful purpose, is the other word competency when so placed. Competent testimony — what is it, if anything, but testimony which ought to be received — which ought not to be excluded?

At no time can there have existed any lawyer in whose mind the faculty of clear conception can have been so completely destroyed as to have been incapable of learning so plain a matter of fact; a subject of such continual experience as that, while in some cases testimony is admitted, in others it is excluded: and that in each case, for determining which shall be a man's lot, ill observed, as well as ill deserving to be observed, as they are, there have always been a set of rules.

Now then, in putting before the expression *witness* the adjunct competent, what, if he had had any beyond the making up the customary mass of surplusage, could have been his meaning? Was it that in the instance of a witness to whose testimony it should happen on any such occasion as that in question to be tendered, application should be made of these rules? Their not being applied was a misfortune, which he could not have had any ground for apprehending, neither had any such obscure and inexpressive word as the word competent any tendency to prevent it. Was it that of these rules, on the particular occasion in question, application should not be made? Still less by the insertion of the word in question, could any such design be promoted: on the contrary, it could not but be counteracted.

Taken by themselves (can it be necessary to observe?) neither in the one word nor in the other is there any meaning, applicable to any such purpose as that of the dispute on the occasion of which they are employed: viz. on the occasion of the individual suit in hand, whether, in the character of a proposed witness, the individual person in question should be admitted or excluded.

To any such purpose, *definition* therefore is an operation of which they are not either of them susceptible. So far as concerns this purpose, everything depends on the sentences, the entire sentences, in which they are respectively employed: — and of these sentences no mention has been ever made.

In regard to these much celebrated words, what upon the whole is the result? That they are both of them words to which, on the occasion in which they were employed, in the minds of the persons by whom they were employed no distinct meanings were annexed: that, employed where and as they have been employed, they have been words without meaning — words, consequently, from which no just conclusions would ever be drawn, by which no light can be reflected on that subject or any other; — that in the character of words significant of so many different attributes of testimony, or of evidence in any other shape, they are not fit to be employed; — that they never have been, nor ever can be accurately defined; — that they never have been, nor ever can be well understood.

What, then, have they been? This is what they have been: Portions of rubbish picked up from the lay-stall upon which they had been shot down; picked up, and by imposture converted into masks for arbitrary power to disguise itself in; designed originally for, and made up into masks, but in the course of a pancratium which had place between two heroes of the technico-jurisprudential school, taken up by each of the combatants, and employed instead of brickbats, to pelt his adversary with.

Of the same convenient character there are two maxims, by which, on all points open to litigation, what is done or proposed to be done, be it what it may, may be defended. The one is *stare decisis*, the other is *malus usus abolendus est*. These are for use under jurisprudential, *alias* common law, at the bar or on the bench.

In a legislative assembly, instead of *stare decisis*, an Englishman has *nolumus leges Anglicæ mutare;* and to the remembrance of these words, the assistance of Von Feinagle is not necessary: but so soon as they are uttered, the hearer may be assured, that what is proposed to be changed is so execrably absurd and mischievous, that but for these four words, there could not be found a one word to say for it.

CHAPTER XXXIII.

CONCLUSION.

According to Blackstone and the rest of the fraternity, such is the excellence of the English common law, no right is without its remedy. The proposition is true: but what it announces is not a matter of fact, but a relation between the signification of two words. The law gives no right without giving a remedy. How so? Because where it gives no remedy, it gives in effect no right. In any other than this quibbling sense, nothing can be more deplorably, more grossly false. To the great body of the people, the whole mass of right is without remedy. Selling justice to the favoured few, denying it to the many, the system gives rights in outward show, takes them away in effect; gives rights by what it says, takes them away by what it does.

In this state of things, such sort of security as under it men enjoy, they are indebted for, in a great degree, to that morality which, in spite of what has been done by lawyers to corrupt them, still remains in the hearts of the people; in a less degree, to what the law is supposed to be; and least of all, to what it really is.

Of the king it is said, and truly, that he can do no wrong; and the despotism that would be created by the irresponsibility involved in the enigma, is checked in some degree by his personal impotence.

Under unwritten law, in a much more simple sense might it be said of a judge, that he can do no wrong. Why? Because, be the thing in itself ever so wrong, it is converted into right, it becomes right of course, in the powerful and irresponsible hand by which it is done.

A part of the penal branch of the law excepted, the law a man lives under in this country is neither more nor less than *le droit du plus fort*, the law of the strongest: — not indeed of the strongest hand, but what comes to much the same thing, the law of the strongest purse.

In this may be seen the cause of one part of the never-ceasing chorus of praises, in which the cries of the afflicted and oppressed are continually drowned; — semi-chorus of lawyers, whose rapacity is served by the oppression — full chorus by the purse-proud non-lawyers, whose pride and tyranny are upheld by it.

Where in one sort of court it costs a man

from £50 to £100 — in another sort of court from £100 to £500 — to purchase any the smallest chance for relief,—with as much expense again, in case of that failure which any one of a thousand well prepared accidents may bring down upon the clearest right—when no man can be permitted either to speak a word for himself or to put a word to his adversary,—what is it that can be done by the most consummate probity, wisdom, active talent, and eloquence, all united in the cause of justice, towards substituting justice to injustice?

Propose that the parties to a suit shall, in all possible cases meet at its commencement, in the presence of the judge, there to give each to the other all such explanations respecting the matters in dispute between them as may respectively be required. By a professional lawyer, these explanations will without hesitation be pronounced impossible. Impossible? Why? Impossible, since they would be inconsistent with that which with him constitutes the standard of right and wrong—the practice of the judicatures in which his emoluments have their source.

Impossible? The country is not yet so unfortunate, but that the mode of procedure which is thus so glibly pronounced impossible, actually has place, and to a greater extent by far, reckoning the number of causes heard and determined within a given length of time, than that only one, to which, according to his metaphysics, the attribute of possibility can be applied. But these causes, being all of them barren of fees, are left of course out of his account, as not being worth including in it.

Impossible? Yes: while in the courts of technical procedure those objects continue to be exclusively pursued, which, from the earliest times of which mention is to be found in history, have ever as yet been pursued, to the exclusion of the only legitimate ends of judicature so often mentioned. But that any such system of corruption and depredation should be an everlasting one, is a notion too degrading to human understanding to be seriously embraced.

The insincerity which it is the object of the arrangements proposed in the foregoing work to prevent, being one among those modifications of improbity, to which it has been among the objects and effects of the technical system to give the utmost possible extent, and to screw up to the highest pitch, any such arrangements will, when proposed, of course be among the objects of horror to a lawyer, with whose sinister interest in all its shapes the perpetuation of that system is entwined.

On the Sunday, he lifts up his eyes to heaven, while those texts are read in which insincerity in all its shapes is held up to view as the object of divine indignation and vengeance.

On the Monday, in the morning he enters the judicatory, and in a speech in which insincerity in all its unpunishable and licensed modes is practised with a degree of energy corresponding with the professional infamy that would attach upon any instance of failure or forbearance, he makes his practical comment upon these sacred texts.

In the afternoon, he enters the theatre of legislation, and denouncing to legislative vengeance the detected conspiracy against everything in the country that is great and good, brands with the associated appellations of Atheism, Utopianism, and Jacobinism, whatsoever wish may be entertained of substituting in any the smallest portion of the field of law, the system of common sense and common honesty, to the system of learned and established absurdity and wickedness.

Atheism, Utopianism, and Jacobinism? — and on what grounds? Atheism, for the endeavour to give a little more effect than hitherto to those sacred denunciations, which in grimace and pantomime he professes to adore: Utopianism, for the endeavour to give a consistent extension to that system of simplicity and justice by which a great majority of causes in number, though not in value, are even now determined: Jacobinism, for the endeavour to give to property, and everything that is dear to men, that security the existence of which is at present no better than a cruelly devised fable.

Yes: — the truth is above dispute, that it is only by a rare accident — and that accident consisting in casting upon the shoulders of the unsuccessful party a burthen artificially excessive, — it is only in that rare case that complete justice, or anything like complete justice, in any one case that ever came before any of the courts in Westminster Hall was, is, or ever can be done.

It is only in that rare case, that after what is called justice has been done to the successful party, he is put into a plight anything near so good as that which he would have been in had the injustice not been committed: — and even in that rare case, the suffering inflicted upon the unsuccessful party being excessive, and by the amount of the difference unjust, the consequence is, that in no one case whatsoever, is that which with so much pomp and pretension is administered under the name of justice, exempt from the well deserved imputation of injustice.

By the hands of these ministers of justice, assisted by that of the minister of finance, the certainty of being able to reduce to utter ruin — if money be not wanting to you, and unless his circumstances have raised him to a level far above that of the vast majority of the people — the man whom you wish to injure — this is the only certainty which, under the technical system of procedure—this is the only certainty which, under the existing system, belongs to law.

A country which endures this, couches under a barefaced tyranny — under a system in which real despotism is screened and aggravated by a show of limitation.

That a system of judicatures, in which never to see or hear the parties is a first principle with the judge,— that such a system of judicature should ever have really had for its objects the real ends of justice, is a delusion than which a grosser was never imposed upon the mental weakness of mankind.

A judge mean to do justice to men whom he will not suffer to come into his sight! In the way of hearsay,—through the medium of a set of representatives, a set of agents whose interest is to misrepresent everything, — to hear everything that relates to the parties without hearing anything from the parties themselves: a man who should really suppose that this is the way to come at the real truth of any case, would be about as rational as a painter, who, having to paint a female portrait, should insist upon taking his idea of her countenance exclusively from the report of a rival beauty, insisting upon it, that if he were ever to see the lady, the portrait would be spoilt.

That if for portraits thus painted from description, better prices were to be had than for portraits painted as the fashion now is, from view, — painters would not be found, and in any numbers, who would be ready to swear, and after a century or two to believe, that it is impossible that a painter who suffers himself to see the original should ever paint a likeness, — is a supposition repugnant to all experience.

Upon the strength of authority, even without pay, self-commendatory propositions find extensive credence: and in the notion thus ascribed to painters, whatsoever there may be of absurdity, self-contradiction there is none.

In some countries, no medical practitioner can ever see his female patient: — in this country, the judge who has robes on, will never see his suitors. The cause is different; but in both cases the felicity of the result is much the same. Justice is about as well served in the one case, as health is in the other; — though perhaps, upon a thorough scrutiny, it would turn out that health could with less detriment lose the benefit of such an interview than justice.

The circumstances by which the practice of the Westminster-Hall courts has been throughout placed in a state of opposition to the ends — in a state of repugnancy to the plainest dictates of justice, — have already in a previous work* been brought to view: and so have the causes in which that opposition and that repugnancy took their rise.

To the correctness of those statements in all the time which has elapsed, from all the multitude of speaking tongues and writing pens, all engaged by interest in every imaginable shape, to controvert everything that with the slightest prospect of success could be controverted, not a tittle of objection has ever ventured to present itself to the public eye.

In that work, it was shown that the whole system of Westminster-Hall proceedings is one great mass of all-comprehensive and remediless injustice: yet propose any the least assuagement, — two things, amongst twenty others, suffice to stop it: the expulsion of the parties from the presence of the judge, and the enormous load of factitious expense which presses on even the cheapest suit: — propose a complete and perfect change, — that real should take the place of factitious law, and natural of technical procedure—and the more clearly beneficial the change shall be seen to be, the more vehemently will it be declared to be pernicious,— the more intensely its approach is apprehended, the more vehemently will it be declared impossible.

Substituting salaries for fees will take away a part, but it will take away no more than a part of the causes which arm judges against justice. It will remove in whole or in part sinister interest in one shape; but besides a swarm of other sinister interests, it will leave interest-begotten prejudices in full force. It will leave the system itself untouched, and with all its vice in full vigour: that system under which it would be impossible to the most consummate wisdom and talent, united to the most consummate probity, to administer anything better or other than injustice.

Yet the prophecy shall be hazarded, that sooner or later, and perhaps before the present generation be altogether passed away, even in the great judicatories now so uselessly crowded into one place, judicature will have for its objects, as in a so much greater number of judicatories it happily already has, the ends of JUSTICE.

* See *Scotch Reform*, first published 1806.

APPENDIX A.

CAUTIONARY INSTRUCTIONS RESPECTING EVIDENCE,

FOR

THE USE OF JUDGES.

CHAPTER I.

PROPRIETY OF CAUTIONARY INSTRUCTIONS, IN PREFERENCE TO UNBENDING RULES.

It has been already shown at length, how fallacious in their tendency, how unfavourable to the interests of truth and justice, with a very few exceptions, the objections commonly made to this or that species of evidence are in general, when the practical result is the shutting a peremptory door against the reception of this or that species of evidence: — or, in the language of English lawyers, where they are considered as constituting peremptory objections to the competency of the evidence. Pernicious, however, as well as ill grounded, as with a very few exceptions they appear to be, in that character — in the character of objections to the credibility or rather to the credit of the evidence, — there are few of them from which information, rational and serviceable information, may not be derived.

Many and many are the occasions on which; of the same proposition of which, in the character of an obligatory rule, the effect cannot but be pernicious, — the effect in the character of a memento would be useful as well as unexceptionable.

Unfortunately, in legislation as in administration, in the senate as in the closet, the exercise of will is easy; — it is the exercise of the understanding that gives trouble.

Though seated in the centre of information — of that privileged sanctuary through which alone lies the road to the pinnacle of wisdom, — though possessing among themselves a share, amounting in some instances even to a monopoly of the efficient causes of wisdom — the rulers of the world have in general been as sparing of their lessons, as they have been liberal of their commands. As to the reputation of wisdom, it is among the appendages of power; and in proportion as men are secure of possessing it, whether they deserve it or no, they are free from anxiety on the score of their not being thought deserving of it.

In the character of a memento, the tendency of a proposition relative to the credit due to a piece of evidence will, in almost every instance, be conducive to rectitude of decision — conducive to the main end of justice: while, in the character of an obligatory rule, of a ground of peremptory exclusion, the effect of a proposition, the same in other respects, will in most instances be pernicious — productive of hardship and injustice, and of that sense of general insecurity of which every instance of injustice, in proportion as it appears to be what it is, is naturally productive.

Of a rule of the monitory kind producing that effect, and that alone, which in each individual instance presents itself to the mind of him to whom it belongs to judge, as suited to the nature of the case, the effect is in each instance purely good, conducive to the ends of justice: — of a rule to the same purport in other respects, but possessing and exercising obligatory force, the effect is in every instance either pernicious or unnecessary; — unnecessary, where in the character of a rule of unobligatory instruction it would have had its influence and guided the current of persuasion — the course of decision; — pernicious, where leaving the judgment unsatisfied, it drags the will by force into a decision condemned and protested against by the judgment.

The amount of the deduction which reason presents as the proper one to be made from the persuasive force of the piece of evidence in question, on the score of the objection made to it, is susceptible of all manner of degrees or modifications in point of quantity. The rule which converts a ground of deduction — a cause of doubt — into an efficient cause of peremptory exclusion, gives to that force, which is thus susceptible of an infinity of degrees, the effect which cannot belong to it with propriety on any other supposition than that of its existing at one and the same invariable degree in every instance.

Though addressed professedly only to judges, instructions, if published, as of course, if sanctioned, they would be, are in effect addressed to all the world. In effect, they are consequently addressed as well to parties as to their advocates. But under the established systems, — even under the system established in England, — it is not every party that has an advocate, since it is not every party that has wherewithal to pay one. Instances are, the common run of trials for predatory offences of indigence, and the petty offences of various sorts, the cognizance of which is given to single magistrates.

As to parties: — on this subject there cannot be an instruction given, of which, if it be of any use, and susceptible of any application, it will not happen to one or other of the parties to be concerned, in point of interest, to claim the benefit of it. But among suitors, especially among suitors too indigent in circumstances to have it in their power to purchase the services of professional assistants, there will naturally be many, not to say a large majority, who, by want of general instruction and mental culture, will be disqualified for turning to account instructions to this effect, or any instructions that could be given them on the subject of evidence by any general rule of law.

It cannot therefore in any case happen but that the care of attending to them and carrying them into effect, in each case for the benefit of the party interested, must rest in some degree upon the judge:—and accordingly they cannot but be considered as addressed to the judges, not in words only, but in design and effect.

Addressed nominally to judges only, but virtually to all ranks without distinction — addressed to them, and received by them, according to the measures of their several capacities and opportunities, they will have a further effect beyond that which they claim in words. By putting the reader upon his guard against those frauds, the exposure to which constitutes so many causes or modes of infirmity in the respective corresponding species of inferior evidence, a natural effect of them will be to prevent the fraud itself, by impressing the persuasion that the effect of this warning given against it will have been to render the attempt perilous, and success hopeless.

In this point of view, a code of instructions to judges respecting the weight of evidence, being in effect a warning against those particular modifications of fraud of which a court of justice is the theatre, constitutes an application of a principle already held up to view: a principle by which, as a means of preventing frauds at large, a system of instructions laying open such frauds as shall have been brought to light by experience, is recommended as one of the instruments by which, in the way of indirect legislation, the legislator has it in his power to ward off crimes.*

In the way of instruction, as contradistinct to regulation, the legislator cannot do harm— he cannot but do good. Harm he cannot do: no, not even should the instruction he gives (unsupposable as the case is) be all of it erroneous and false. Being false, it may prove deceptious, and in so far mischievous. True: but instruction is here considered in contradistinction to—in exclusion of—coercive regulation. Leaving it to the judge to make such use of the instruction as he thinks best — none at all if it appear erroneous, it leaves his will free to profit by such better lights as his own experience and understanding furnish. What if, instead of confining himself to the giving instruction, the legislator had drawn the inference in every case, and converted his erroneous but uncompulsory instructions into compulsory commands?

But the case is scarcely conceivable — certainly not at all probable — in which, by operating in the line of instruction, the legislator can fail of doing good.

The judge, attending to the subject of evidence — to the cases that come before him on that ground, as to any others — no otherwise than as he is called upon to attend to it by this or that individual cause, — his views are naturally limited to the particular and comparatively narrow line on which he is thus called upon to act. The knowledge of the legislator is, or at least might be and ought to be, the aggregate knowledge of the whole state — not to say of the whole world. From each one of the judges subject to his authority, he has it in his power to command the whole result of his opinions and reflections on this as on every other line of action within the limits of his office. The chance which he possesses, or at least is enabled to possess, of procuring for himself correct information, is to the chance possessed by any single judge, as the whole number of the judges is to one.

Not only is it in the power of the legislator, as such, to raise the quantity and value of the accessible mass of information in this line to its maximum, but it is in the power of any and every private and uncommissioned individual, according to the measure of his opportunities and his faculties, to render to mankind the same sort of service, — provided always that the hand of the judge be on each occasion left unfettered, and free to turn to its use the information thus supplied.

The contents of this book are an attempt to render, according to the faculties of the author, this sort of service. Should it be found to bear the test of examination, it may serve as a nucleus to which the mass of desirable information, accumulated by the experience of successive ages, may, as it were by crystallization, aggregate itself.

On the other hand, by way of imperation and coercion, no good can be done — harm cannot but be done: — by coercion imposed upon the judge, the probability of right decision—of decision in conformity to the truth in each instance — cannot be increased, cannot but be diminished.

* See Vol. I. p. 567. *Uses to be drawn from the Power of Instruction.*

CHAPTER II.

CONSIDERATIONS PROPER TO BE BORNE IN MIND IN JUDGING OF THE WEIGHT OF EVIDENCE.

1st *Cause of Suspicion.—Improbability of the fact deposed to.*

THE improbability of a fact in itself, may be considered as a sort of counter testimony—a sort of *circumstantial* evidence, operating in contradiction to any *direct* evidence by which the fact in question would otherwise be considered as proved.

The improbability of a fact may rise to such a degree as to render it absolutely incredible—incapable of being proved to the satisfaction of him who thinks of it, if not by any evidence, at least by any such evidence as is actually adduced in proof of it.

If the inference drawn from the improbability of the fact, viz. that it is not true, be just—*i. e.* if notwithstanding the testimony by which the existence of it is asserted, it really did not exist,—the fault must lie either in the inferences deduced from the testimony, or in the testimony itself. If the testimony itself be to such a degree positive as to assert the existence of the matter of fact in question in direct terms, then the fault cannot be in the inference deduced from the testimony, but must be in the testimony itself. The testimony must either be incomplete or false, or both: though if, as above, it be to a certain degree positive, there may be no room for charging it with being incomplete; and if the fact so asserted be false, the testimony by which the existence of it is asserted, must necessarily be, in some circumstance or other, false. But as an assertion made by a man may be false without his being conscious of its being so, such falsity is not of itself proof of perjury.

When a fact is considered as being to such a degree improbable as not to be capable of being proved by any quantity even of the best evidence, it is commonly termed impossible.

Improbability or impossibility, is either physical, that is natural, or moral. A fact may be said to be physically improbable, when it is considered as being inconsistent with the established and known order of things—with any of those rules and propositions which have been deduced from the general observation of mankind, and are termed laws of nature: such as, for instance, that which asserts as a known matter of fact, the weight or gravity of all the bodies that we see in, upon, or near to this earth; that property, whereby, if a man jump up from the surface of the earth, he feels himself drawn down again.

A fact is said to be morally improbable, when it is considered as being inconsistent with the known course of human conduct. This species of improbability is confined to such facts as have their place in the human mind: such as the entertaining of such and such perceptions, conceptions, intentions, wishes; the being animated by such and such motives, under the existing circumstances of the case.

The degree of distrust produced in the mind of a judge by the improbability of the alleged fact, when that improbability is of the physical kind, as above, will depend upon the confidence he has in his own knowledge respecting the powers and order of nature so far as the particular fact in question is concerned. If he have any doubt, he will do well to have recourse to scientific evidence—to call in the opinion of such persons as, by their professional situation or reputation, are pointed out to him as being particularly well informed in relation to matters of that sort.

Thus suppose, upon the testimony of two witnesses, a demand made upon a man for money in satisfaction for damage done to a garden by the fall of the first inhabited air-balloon that ever rose: and from reflection on the weight of bodies, suppose the judge to have been inclined to disbelieve the testimony, on the ground of the apparent improbability of the fact. In such case, he would have done well to call in the opinion of some lecturer or lecturers on natural philosophy; and accordingly, supposing him so to have done, he would have learned from them that there was really no inconsistency between what he had always observed and heard concerning the heaviness of bodies in general, and what the witnesses had been deposing concerning the extraordinary lightness of the particular body so raised.

Concerning moral improbability, as above described, every man acting in the situation of a judge will naturally consider himself as competent to pronounce. A man on these occasions looks into his own mind, and asks, as it were of himself, whether it be probable or possible, that in the circumstances in which the person in question is stated by the evidence as entertaining such and such perceptions, conceptions, intentions, wishes, and the like, it could have happened in such circumstances to himself to have entertained any such perceptions, conceptions, intentions, wishes, and the like.

Moral improbability of the fact is a sort of evidence upon which conviction or acquittal turns, in most cases of delinquency, especially when against the defendant there is no other than circumstantial evidence. It is seldom that a man can be deemed guilty, unless his intentions be taken into the account; and when he avers his intentions to have been innocent, it is not possible to prove their having been guilty, otherwise than by the moral improbability of their having been otherwise. When Captain Donellan was convicted of murder by the poisoning of Sir Theodosius Boughton, one of the principal circumstances against him, was his anxiety to have the cup immediately rinsed out. On any other supposition than that of the cup's containing a poison by which the fatal symptoms were produced, this anxiety and the expression given to it were looked upon as acts without a motive. Should I in that situation have entertained any such anxiety if I had not been guilty? If in that situation I had been guilty, could I have avoided entertaining the like anxiety, although I should hardly have been so incautious thus to betray it? Such were the questions which, in the situation of the jury by whom he was convicted, every man who joined in the conviction, or approved of it, could not but have put to himself.

2*d Cause of Suspicion.—Interest.*—The testimony of the witness liable to be drawn aside from the line of truth, by the influence of some seducing motive.

There are as many species of interests as there are species of motives:—there are as many species of motives as there are distinguishable sorts of pains and pleasures.

Whatever, on each given occasion, be the complexion of a man's conduct,—lawful or unlawful, commendable or discommendable, beneficial to society or prejudicial,—it is always the result of the action of some motive or motives, or of the difference in point of force between two lots of contending motives;—an action without a motive is an effect without a cause.

Among motives, there are some, the action of which tends in the main, all the world over, or at least in every civilized community, though in different communities with exceptions more or less considerable, to keep men's conduct within the pale of probity, of which a main branch is the line of truth.

These are—1. The motives created by the rewards and punishments administered by the law of the state; 2. The motives depending on good and evil reputation, from whence flow respectively the spontaneous good and ill offices of mankind; 3. The motives created by the affection of benevolence, whether its object be more or less extensive—a man's family, his friends at large, his province, his country, or mankind; 4. The motives created by religion. In consideration of their most usual tendency (though there is not one of them which by means of some error or other has not been productive of actions pernicious to mankind, and in particular has not drawn aside man's testimony from the line of truth,)—all these together may be comprised under the common appellation of tutelary or guardian motives.

All motives whatever, not excepting even the motives termed, in consideration of their regular and ordinary tendency, guardian motives, are liable to act in the character of *seducing* motives on all occasions, and in particular on those occasions where a man is called upon for his testimony by the voice of justice, and thereupon to draw aside the tenor of his testimony from the line of truth.

There are some motives or interests which are most apt to be productive of this sinister effect, and of the sinister tendency of which, on those occasions, it behoves the judge to be more particularly upon his guard; in so much, as the more strongly the situation of a witness exposes him to be acted upon by any one or more of these motives respectively, in such sort that, by swerving from the line of truth, he might procure to himself the gratification of the appetite or passion corresponding to such sinister seducing interest or motive, the stronger the suspicion and distrust with which his testimony will naturally and not improperly be regarded. Not that by any means it follows, that because a man is exposed to temptation, therefore, spite of the utmost efforts of the guardian motives, he will on every occasion yield to it:—but thus much, and thus much only, is the proper practical inference, that the stronger the action of the sinister interests on the part of the witness, the more vigilant ought to be the scrutiny on the part of the judge.

These interests or motives are as follows:—

1. Pecuniary interest:—to which belong the motives created by the desire for *money;* that is, including all things that are to be bought for money.

2. Enmity:—to this passion belongs the motive which, when excited by injury, real or imagined, is termed *revenge.* So, even although there be not so much as an imagination of injury, an uneasiness regarded as having the person or conduct of a particular individual for its cause, will be productive of that same passion, which when in the character of a motive it acts upon the will and influences human conduct, is called revenge.

3. Love of Power:—desire of acquiring or preserving power of any kind;—fear of losing it.

4. Desire of gaining or preserving the protection or patronage, the good will and good offices of a particular individual, in the character of a master, patron, or useful friend.

5. Love:—*i. e.* personal attachment in the case where connected with sexual attraction.

6. Personal attachment; or friendship towards an individual:—the principle by which an individual is led to regard the interests of a friend in the same manner as his own, and to be actuated by them in the same

manner and direction as if they were his own, whatsoever difference there may be in the degree of force.

7. Family attachment:—the principle by which a man is led to adopt as his own, the interests of his family,—a circle which may be more or less wide in its extent, and in which exceptions in any number may be included.

8. Party attachment.

9. Self-preservation:—a motive, in the object of which, if taken in its largest sense, are included all pains and dangers, and thence even losses and disappointments of all sorts;—and which, when the danger apprehended is the loss of life (a loss in which the loss of whatever pleasures a man could hope for is involved,) is termed danger of the loss of life. In so far as the pains in question may have legal punishment for their source, the fear of punishments of all sorts is included within the compass of this motive.

10. Love of ease; or aversion to labour; *i. e.* to the pains which result as the natural accompaniments of labour, when considered apart from the pleasures and sources of pleasure which in the several cases it looks to for its reward.

CHAPTER III.

CONSIDERATIONS RESPECTING THE EFFECTS OF INTEREST IN GENERAL UPON EVIDENCE.

1. THERE is scarcely one occasion on which, scarcely a species of suit in which, it may not happen to a man to be acted upon at the same time by any number of motives, as above exhibited—by any number of different sorts of interests, besides the guardian motives, the force of which acts in general on the side of truth: and these sinister interests may be acting all of them on the same side, or some on one side, some on another.

2. The efficiency of a motive depends, not upon the species to which it belongs, but on the strength with which it happens to act in each individual instance. There is scarcely a species of motive which is not capable of acting with any degree of force, from the lowest to the highest, or not much short of the highest.

3. A man's own testimony, given in his own cause, is of all evidence the most, and most properly, exposed to suspicion, where the tendency of it is in favour of that cause:—it is of all evidence the least exposed to suspicion, when the tendency of it is in disfavour of that cause.

4. But even in this case, it cannot be relied upon with perfect safety. In a penal case, a man may by his testimony subject himself to conviction and punishment as for a certain offence, in the hope of avoiding some greater evil; for example, prosecution, and thence conviction and punishment, for some more severely punishable offence. In a non-penal case, a man may, for the advantage of others, with or without collusion, institute a cause for the very purpose of betraying it.

5. Setting aside the indirect counter-evidence that may be opposed to a man's testimony by the improbability of the fact he deposes to,—it is more easy to disbelieve him where, on the supposition of incorrectness on the part of his evidence, such falsity cannot but have been accompanied with that criminal consciousness which converts it into mendacity, than when it may be accounted for on the supposition of simple incorrectness:—because, in the first case, it cannot have happened but that the mind of the witness must have been subjected to the action of some sinister interest or interests, acting in sufficient force to overcome the united resistance of the whole phalanx of guardian interests.

6. In England, scarcely any crime is so common as that of exculpative perjury;—scarcely any so rare as that of criminative perjury:—especially in the case of the most highly punished species of crimes. The reason is, that in the former case, humanity, *i. e.* sympathy towards the individual over whose head the rod of punishment hangs suspended, is an interest that acts in opposition to the guardian interests:—in the latter case, its force is exerted on the other side.

7. Among professional depredators, the propensity to exculpative perjury is strengthened by the concurrence of other interests. Not only each gang of specially connected depredators, but the whole class, and, as it were, community of depredators taken together, form, as it were, a particular community of itself, which, like other particular communities, lawful and unlawful, honourable and dishonourable, such as that of divines, lawyers, merchants, &c. has its *esprit de corps*, its corporate affections, and other interests. Being a community within a community, it has accordingly a popular sanction, a public opinion of its own, distinct from, and in this instance opposed to, the public opinion of the great community, the public at large. This, therefore, is one of the cases in which the force of the popular sanction is divided against itself, and in which that division which is likely to be strongest is on the side opposed to justice.*

8. Among such professional depredators as are either connected and united into gangs by special compact and habits of co-operation, or though it be only by an acquaintance with the particulars of each other's crimes, the propensity to exculpative perjury is still further

* See Letters to Lord Pelham, and Collins on New South Wales.

strengthened by the influence of the principle of self-preservation. When a member of any such gang comes to be convicted, a natural and frequent result is a disclosure, more or less complete, of the particulars of his former delinquencies, including an indication of the share borne in them by his associates: among the fruits of which indications, is the apprehension of those associates, and the obtaining of evidence sufficient to bring them to punishment.

9. Against criminative perjury, so powerful, so efficacious, is the action of the guardian interests, that, in the character of seductive interests, two of the most powerful motives, viz. love of life, and pecuniary interest—one acting in the greatest possible force, the other acting with more than ordinary force — are scarcely ever known to produce it. Pardon, together with pecuniary reward in masses from £10 up to £1000, are the expedients continually resorted to, in English practice, for the obtaining from an accomplice the necessary mass of evidence, in the case of capital, that is, first-rate crimes. All this while, where self-preservation is out of the question, pecuniary interest, though in a magnitude ever so trifling, and though it be of that comparatively weaker sort which is created by the desire of gain, and not of that stronger sort which is created by the apprehension of loss, is under the same system made to operate as a ground of peremptory exclusion, preventing the testimony from being so much as heard: — and this, too, let the pecuniary interest at stake, and consequently the damage to the party suffering by the perjury, supposing it to take place, be ever so trifling. Pecuniary interest, acting upon the witness by itself, is thus made to shut the door against his testimony: pecuniary interest, when reinforced by another interest infinitely more powerful, acting on the same side, — by an interest which includes all others put together, — no longer shuts the door against, but throws it wide open to the same testimony. All the while, this apparently irresistible invitation to perjury has scarcely ever been productive of its natural, and to appearance unavoidable effect. The reason is nowhere to be found in the joint influence of the two concurring causes, but in the particular difficulty of carrying into effect a plan of perjury in this particular case — a cause which belongs not to the present purpose: the other is the joint influence of the interest of humanity, seconded and supported by a narrow and spurious sort of honour, or regard for a portion of the mass of popular opinion, as above explained. But the force of the action of a principle of humanity, in a case where the tendency of it is to cause one man to save another from a mass of suffering — from a mass of punishment — will naturally be, *cæteris paribus*, directly as the magnitude of that punishment. Hence, although the force of the motive acting in a sinister direction —viz. self-preservation — is also in this case, by the supposition, as the magnitude of that same punishment, yet such is the force of the principle of humanity, seconded as above, that it almost always gets the better of the sinister interest of the same kind, even when that sinister interest has the allied force of pecuniary interest for its support.

CHAPTER IV.

CONSIDERATIONS RESPECTING THE EFFECT OF PECUNIARY INTEREST UPON EVIDENCE.

1. THE value at stake being given, as also the sensibility of the individual to a gain or loss to that amount, as deducible from the state of his pecuniary circumstances in other respects, a man's testimony is more exposed to just suspicion in the case where he is a party to the suit, than where he is not a party: — as also more where he is plaintiff, than where he is defendant. For a man who is not a party to the suit, that is, has no actual interest of the pecuniary kind in the success of that side in favour of which his testimony tends — can in general gain no advantage — can gain no thanks from the party in whose favour, if the testimony be wilfully false, and at the same time successful, the falsehood operates, unless the party be privy to the falsehood, and in some sort a partaker in the guilt. False evidence, therefore, in this case requires two to be concerned in it: — whereas when the party concerned is the witness, it requires but one.

2. In the situation of a defendant, false evidence in a cause relative to money is not so dangerous in its tendency, viz. in the way of example, on the side of the defendant as on the side of the plaintiff. The reason is, that in the character of a defendant, as such, a man has not in his own power the means of increasing the number of his suits at pleasure: on each occasion, whether the suit to which he is party take place, depends directly at least, not upon himself, but upon another person, the plaintiff. By his falsehood, the utmost he can hope to do, is to exonerate himself from the single particular obligation which another person, in the character of plaintiff, seeks to impose upon him: — in the character of defendant, so long as he confines himself to that character, it is not in his power to impose any sort of obligation upon anybody by any succeeding falsehoods, whatever his success may have been in the first.

On the contrary, if on the part of a plaintiff coming forward as witness in his own cause, false testimony obtain credit, and the fraud is thus crowned with success (though the mischief of the first order — the mischief produced by the falsehood in the individual case in question—be no greater in this case than in either of the others,) the mischief of the second order, the mischief in the way of danger and alarm, is much greater: since, in the character of plaintiff, the number of causes it may happen to a man to be concerned in depends altogether upon his own will and pleasure.

If the matter in dispute be, or be alleged to be, equally within the cognizance of the plaintiff and the defendant, whatever illusion the testimony of the plaintiff might have been in danger of producing will have the testimony of the defendant to counteract it: if, in this case, testimony be in any part opposed to testimony, on which side soever truth is, that side cannot but be supposed to possess a natural advantage.

If the testimony given by the plaintiff in his own behalf find opposed to it the testimony of an apparently uninterested witness, truth must be very apparently on the side of the party witness, if the persuasion produced by it be an overmatch for the prepossession which evidence so circumstanced can scarcely fail to excite.

If on the side of the plaintiff there be, besides his own testimony, that of a non-litigant witness, truth and justice have everything to gain by the examination of the plaintiff himself, and nothing to lose by it. Suppose the testimony on this side correct and true, the confirmation given to the statement of the uninterested witness by that of the party cannot but add more or less to the satisfaction of the judge. Suppose the testimony mendacious, the chance of a contradiction between the two conspirators is a chance over and above what the case would have afforded had the testimony of the plaintiff been excluded.

The case in which the testimony of a plaintiff in support of his own demand, supposing the testimony wilfully false, appears to have the fairest chance, is where, upon the face of it, the fact not having come under the cognizance either of the defendant, or of anybody else but the plaintiff, the supposed false testimony of the plaintiff has neither the testimony of the defendant nor any other testimony to contradict it. But in this case it is provided, that though by the supposition the defendant has it not in his power to give any specific testimony, whereby the force of the plaintiff's testimony may be combated, — yet it should be matter of obligation as well as right on the part of the defendant, after hearing the plaintiff's testimony, to declare whether he himself gives credit to it — whether he decidedly believe it — decidedly disbelieve it — or remain in doubt. If he believe it, so may the judge with still less difficulty; — if he be in doubt, doubt from such a quarter may in the mind of the judge afford some confirmation of the plaintiff's testimony. If the defendant, decidedly and firmly, can take upon him to say that he disbelieve it, and no confirmation come in aid of it from any other source, personal evidence or real, direct or circumstantial, there seems little likelihood that the judge should suffer his decision to be governed by such scanty and suspicious evidence. To testimony thus circumstanced, it will oftener happen to be disbelieved when true, than to be believed when untrue.

The force with which a sinister interest of the pecuniary class acts upon the mind may be the same, whether it be certain or contingent—acting on both sides, or acting on one side—acting upon the witness singly, or acting upon him as one of a body of men anyhow composed, — a private partnership, a joint-stock company, a set of persons taxed in conjunction for certain purposes, such as the parishioners of the same parish. In these several cases, the interest in question is but the fraction of an interest: — but a fraction of one sum may be equal to the whole of another.

The prospect which an only son has of succeeding to the estate of his father, the estate not being settled upon the son, is but a contingency: but between the force of an interest created by such a prospect, and the force of an interest created by an estate to the same amount settled upon the son, it cannot reasonably be supposed that in effect there should be any material difference. In the money market, interests called contingencies have their price as well as those which are called certainties.

If by a decision in favour of the plaintiff a witness would gain twenty pounds, while by a decision in favour of the defendant he would gain but ten pounds, the force of the interest by which his testimony is drawn to the side of the plaintiff is equal to a force of ten pounds.

If upon the decision in the cause on which the testimony of a witness is to be given, a joint-stock company, with a million for its capital, in which he has a thousandth share, has at stake a sum of ten thousand pounds, the force of the interest by which his testimony is drawn to the side of the company is equal to a force of ten pounds.

Of a quantity of pecuniary interest represented by any given sum (say £100,) the force will be in a prodigious degree different, according as the result of the decision to the witness will be gain or loss to the amount of that same sum. The suffering produced to a man by a loss to any given amount, is much more than equal to the enjoyment that would be produced by gain to that same amount. If a man who has £400 gain £200, his fortune after the increase is to his fortune before the increase, but as 6 to 4. If a man who has £600 lose £200, his fortune after the loss is to his fortune before the loss, but as 4 to 6. If a man who has £400 gain another £400, his condition after the increase is not very high: — if a man who has £400 lose the £400, his condition after the loss is as low as it ever can be. When a man who had originally £400 receives a gain of £400, his fortune is still capable of receiving accession upon accession without end: but when a man whose original fortune was £400 has lost £400, there is no room for any further losses.

A pecuniary interest to act in the character of a cause of falsehood upon the mind of the witness, and thence upon the testimony he exhibits, must be in existence at the very time in which he is occupied in the delivery of such testimony: — the good or evil dependent on the decision for which his evidence is to furnish or help to furnish a ground, must be still in prospect and not in possession at the time. Whether at the time at which the fact in question presented itself, or is supposed to have presented itself to his cognizance, the interest were or were not then in existence, makes to this purpose no material difference. Although the interest were in existence, and his affections consequently exposed to the action of it at the time, yet if at the time of giving his testimony that interest be no longer in existence, its action on his affections is at an end — his testimony is no longer exposed to be influenced by it. Although at the time when the fact presented itself to his cognizance, the interest were not then in existence, nor his affections accordingly exposed to the action of it, yet if at the time of giving his testimony the interest be in existence, and his affections exposed accordingly to the action of it, his testimony is as much or nearly as much exposed to be influenced by it, as if it had already been in existence at the time when the fact presented itself to his cognizance.

Where, by the rules of law, pecuniary interest would operate in the way of exclusion — and to get rid of the objection, and render the witness admissible, expedients have been employed for extinguishing the interest, and thereby neutralizing, as it were, the mind of the witness, by causing it no longer to be exposed to be acted upon, as supposed, by any such sinister force, — so far as consists in the opening of a source of information which would otherwise have been sealed up, and thereby preventing the undue decision or denial of justice that for want of such information might have taken place, the practice undeniably appears to be useful and desirable, and conducive to the purposes of justice. But if on any occasion the effect of it be, as it naturally enough will be, to withdraw the testimony in question altogether from suspicion, and cause it to be regarded as no longer subject to the action of any sinister interest, in this respect the tendency of the operation is fallacious.

Interest in the present instance—pecuniary interest — is created either by hope of gain or fear of loss.

Hope of gain is the most common case, — the witness, for example, to a will, having a legacy depending on the validity of the will.

In this case, two expedients have presented themselves for the clearing away of the interest: — 1. One is, the putting the witness in possession of the expected good, the legacy. In this case, he has no longer anything to gain by the confirmation of the will: and is in consequence *reputed* clear from the action of any sinister interest. 2. Another is the engaging him to give up his right to receive the expected good, the legacy. In this case, he has no longer any assistance to hope for from the law towards the obtainment of the expected good, the legacy: — and in this case also, is in consequence *reputed* clear from the action of any sinister interest. In this case, the provision of the law would be but incomplete, nor would it extend to all the cases which the expedient was intended to embrace, if the extirpation of the interest depended upon the acceptance of the offer made by the witness to get rid of it. The mere offer has accordingly been deemed sufficient, whether accepted or not accepted: — care being taken to enact, that after an offer to this effect, whether the offer be accepted or not accepted, his right to compel the payment of the money or money's worth shall be equally at an end.

If, however, it be really supposed, that by any such mechanical process the mind of man can really be cleared of interest, or that the security for truth, for the absence of incorrectness and mendacity, is after the performance of any such ceremony in any considerable degree greater than before, the supposition will upon examination be found delusive. Against simple incorrectness it will be found of little or no use. Against mendacity — against wilful perjury, — it will be found of no use at all.

Mendacity — wilful perjury — out of the question, any departure from the line of perfect correctness, of absolute truth, can have no other cause than that of bias. Whatever deviation from that line may take place in his testimony, the witness himself is not sensible of any such deviation: if he be, so far as he is, so far is his testimony mendacious, and himself a perjurer. In this case, whatever may have been the state of his mental faculties in relation to the facts in question, — his perception — his judgment — his memory, before the operation, it does not seem natural, that by the operation any very determinate or natural alteration should be produced.

But, suppose the bias previously existing

and in action, and suppose the legal process to have cleared away this sinister interest, this cause of aberration, from the line of truth, — there remains another, which it is not in the nature of it to clear away, and of which the action will naturally be more powerful than that of the bias itself. This is his regard for his own character, — for his own reputation in respect of veracity, — his sensibility to the pains of the moral sanction. Before the time and occasion for the performance of this legal ceremony can have taken place, he will almost always have given his statement of the affair: — it is from this statement alone that in general the party who has an interest in the restoration of the testimony can obtain that information from which his inducement to put in practice the expedient for the clearing away the objection was derived. But having once given his account of the matter, the witness is concerned, in point of reputation, to abide by it: were he to depart from it in any considerable degree, what he has to lose by such departure is so much of his reputation as is at stake: what he has to gain by such departure is nothing at all. But as it is with mechanical, so is it with human action: to command it, any the least particle of force is sufficient, so long as there is nothing to oppose it on the other side.

In the case of mendacity, the notion of the supposed extirpation of the sinister interest will be found equally delusive. Whatever interest it was that gave birth to the mendacious design, that interest will not be found to have undergone from the process any material change. It will be found, either that the selfsame interest will be found still to continue, or that another interest, or group of interests, equally efficient, have been substituted in the room of it: and, at any rate, the interest that respects reputation will be found to apply alike to this case as well as to the other. Saving the extraordinary and not to be looked for case of unbought and thankless perjury, for the benefit of somebody else, mendacity, on the part of a non-party witness, all profit-seeking mendacity,—supposes conspiracy, all conspiracy supposes confidence. But whatever be the ground or cause of confidence, it is not in the power of any such mechanical process as that in question to destroy the confidence, or take away the inducements, whatever they may have been, that led to the performance of the criminal engagement. After the operation, and so far in consequence of it, it may happen to the conspirators to deceive one another; but so it equally might, had no such operation been performed. Moreover, so long as the conspiracy, and the confidence which is connected with and necessary to give birth to it, lasts, the employment of these expedients will be among the necessary, or at least the natural fruits of it. If without the employment of one or other of these expedients, the law excludes the testimony in question, the employment of one of these expedients is necessary to the purpose of the conspiracy. If, although the testimony be admitted, the trustworthiness of the witness be looked upon as increased by the extinguishment of the interest, the expedient of the apparent extinguishment of the interest is a measure that may be regarded as the natural fruit of the conspiracy, though not absolutely a necessary one.

In the above considerations, the efficient cause of the interest is supposed to be the expectation of gain, and not the apprehension of loss. Such in fact accordingly is the most common case: — because the acquisition at stake being most commonly not yet in possession of either: both have something to gain by the event of the suit, neither have anything to lose. The opposite case, however, is not impossible, even on this side — the plaintiff's side — of the cause. For if the gain to be made by the false witness be not too great for the pocket of the suborning plaintiff, it may happen that the witness takes his payment in the first instance, under the condition of returning it should the decision be adverse: — and in this case, the efficient cause of the interest takes the shape of the apprehension of loss.

But there remains yet another case that may happen; viz. that the side which gives birth to the mendacious conspiracy is the defendant's side: — in this case, the property at stake is already in the hands of one of the conspirators—the principal in the business,— and the fund being already in hand, there will be no more difficulty, but rather less, in paying him before the termination of the suit than afterwards.

One case indeed there is, in which the effect of the process may be to produce a confidence which is not unmerited. This is where a witness to the transaction, being entitled to an emolument arising out of it — say as before a witness to a will entitled to a legacy given by the will — comes forward of his own accord, and gives up his own just claim, lest other claims — claims of more importance, and which he knows to be just — should be defeated.

But, in the first place, if the man of probity in question think fit to make this sacrifice of his own to other interests (understand pecuniary interests,) he is at equal liberty so to do without any detersive process, as under and in consequence of it. The interest in question, if it be not rendered by the law a ground of exclusion, is at any rate rendered by the nature of men and things in a certain degree a ground of suspicion: — if impelled by the same honourable motives in this case as in the other, he choose not only to gain admittance for his testimony, but in this way to augment its force, there is nothing to prevent him.

In the next place, what in this case is the effect of the operation in question upon the whole body of rights at stake taken together? If it confirm one set of rights, it destroys another: — if it confirm the rights of a man or set of men taken without distinction, it destroys the rights of a man, who by his generosity has been manifested to be a man of superior probity and desert.

In this case, then, it has no other effect than what deserves to be regretted. And upon the whole, if it really clear away any interest at all, it does not clear away any sinister interest; if it clear away interest in any case, it is in such cases, and such cases only, in which that interest had no sinister influence. Its effects, therefore, upon the whole, are reducible to these two: either to the prejudice of a man of extraordinary probity, it deprives a man of his rights without any benefit to truth and justice; or in favour of a witness of ordinary mould is productive of an ill grounded confidence—producing in favour of the testimony so vamped up, a degree of confidence beyond any that properly belongs to it.

CHAPTER V.

SITUATIONS.

To the different situations, relations, and conditions in life — public and private, political and domestic — several different sorts of interests either singly or forming different compounds, are apt to be attached.

1. A certain species and degree of interest may be produced, and is very commonly produced, by the relation between customer and dealer. The action of that interest will be more or less strong, according as the dealings are more or less extensive, more or less regular and established, down to purely casual. Let them be extensive to a certain degree, regular to a certain degree,—and neither of them an uncommon degree—the profit to the dealer may in the way of interest operate as a sort of annuity, subject to increase or decrease with the prosperity of the customer, and thereby dependent on the event of the cause.

If, as a cause or consequence of this relation in the way of pecuniary interest, a relation of friendship, sympathy, and good will, more or less warm, should happen to have taken place, here are two distinguishable species of interest combined in one.

2. The relation between protector and protegé,* between a person seeking advancement in any line, and a person supposed to be able and willing to promote his advancement in that same line, is a relation of much the same nature in this respect as that between dealer and customer; though the ground of expectation not being so open to sense and distinct observation as in the other case, the nature and strength of the interest does not so distinctly exhibit itself to view. It is in nature and degree of course as diversified, in the first place, as the aggregate group of profit-seeking occupations; — as diversified, in the next place, as the ways in which in each occupation it may be in the way of one man to serve and help another, are diversified.

Here, as in the case of the relation between dealer and customer, the relation of sympathy and good will — with the interest created by that relation — is at any rate a very frequent accompaniment to the purely pecuniary relation; — though owing to the tyranny, to the imputation of which one side of the relation, and the insensibility and ingratitude, to the imputation of which the other side is obnoxious, not a necessary and inseparable one.

3. Another interest of the same kind in both respects, is that which attaches to the relation between master and servant: meaning hired servant. So long as it subsists — unless where the determination of it is decided upon — desire of retaining, apprehension of losing, pecuniary advantage, will be certain accompaniments; sympathy and good will on the part of the servant as toward the master, a natural accompaniment, though unhappily not an inseparable one. The interest, simple or compound, produced by it — the magnitude of the interest, will in both branches of it be susceptible of an indefinite multitude of degrees, according to the relative magnitude of the emolument, multiplied by the probable duration of it, as deducible from the past duration or from other circumstances. It will be influenced by the nature of the service, whether domestic or in any line of profit-seeking occupation: by the rank of the servant in the service, in the case of a service comprehending different ranks.

4. In the interest which attaches to the relation between master and bond-servant, including that between master and apprentice (of which last, the apprentice is the species which makes the greatest figure,) the interest which attaches includes the interest which attaches to the relation between master and hired servant, with the addition of all the hopes and all the fears of which the coercive power attached to the superior condition cannot but be productive. So far as fears are concerned, the additional interest with which this relation is pregnant, may be referred to

* The French word *protégé* is nearly adopted into the English language. There was the most urgent want of it. The word patron, which used to serve for protector, has no correlative to it: *client*, the correlative to *patronus* in the language of ancient Rome, is not so in that of England.

the head of self-preservation; viz. as against the punishments which at all times, and on all occasions, howsoever moderated by law, or morality, or humanity, it is in the power of such master to inflict.

5. In the interest, which in the instance of the child attaches to the relation between parent and child, are included all the interests which attach to the relation between master and apprentice, but all of them naturally existing and acting in much greater force. To these are added, as peculiar to this relation in contradistinction to the other, the two additional interests created by family attachment, and the hopes and fears attached to the prospect of succession, *i. e.* to the prospect of succeeding to the property, or to a share in the property of the parent, on the occasion of his decease.

6. The interest, which in the instance of the parent attaches to the same relation, contains but one or two of the elementary interests of which the compound interest in the last preceding case is composed — a spice of sympathy and good will, heightened by a spice of family attachment. Yet in so much higher a degree do these efficient causes of partiality exist in this case than in the other, that the inferiority in number is commonly more than compensated for by the superiority of force. Though in point of mere self-regarding pecuniary interest, the profit or loss redounding indirectly to the child from profit or loss accruing to the parent, is much more determinate than the profit or loss redounding indirectly to the parent from profit or loss accruing to the child, yet such, it is generally understood, is the superiority of partiality created in the latter case from natural affection, — from the emotion of sympathy and good will, created and kept up by the view of the physical relation, — that as far as bias is concerned, the testimony of the parent is full as liable to be warped in favour of the cause of the child, as the testimony of the child in favour of the cause of the parent. So fallacious would be the result, if interests were to be merely counted, without being duly weighed.

Yet according to the rules of judging established among lawyers — I mean English lawyers — the partiality of the father or mother to the child is too slight to furnish a ground for the exclusion of their testimony: — while in the estimation of the same sages, the partiality created by the expectation of a sixpence is so irresistibly powerful, that no testimony exposed to so dangerous a cause of seduction, ought so much as to be heard. What would be the reflection of a mother, if, when clasping her child to her bosom in a fit of maternal fondness, she were to be informed that she did not care sixpence for her darling, and that this had been settled of thought and study, from an opinion derived at a vast expense from the experience of ages by the sages of the law?

To the Chinese, who, without his understanding any more of the country and its inhabitants, should hear speak of a nation in which this strength of parental affection was so perfect a secret to the mandarins who governed it, an easy mode of solving the enigma would present itself. "I see how it is in that country," he would say to himself: "eunuchs are there the only lawyers." He would little suspect the real truth of the case, which is, that in every lawyer there are two men — the man of flesh and blood, subsisting such as nature formed him, and the man of law, such as he has been formed by a set of scientific rules; that the man of flesh and blood may in point of intelligence be below, or upon, or about the common level as it may happen; but that the man of law is to be found constantly at a prodigious degree below it — has at a prodigious expense of thought and study succeeded in fixing himself at an unfathomable depth below it. That between these two men, though inclosed in the same wrapper, there is no more communication than between the outer and inner surfaces of a Leyden phial; and that the weakest of them all is never so unwise in his own generation, as to govern himself in the management of his own concerns by the rules by which he has been pleased to guide himself in the disposal of other people's.

7. A group of interests the same in species as those which, on the part of the child, are produced by the relation between parent and child, will on the same part be produced by the relation subsisting between the child and any of those other kindred, who after the decease of the parent, or even during his lifetime, may be considered as a sort of substitutes or representatives of the parent — the grandfather and grandmother, the uncle or aunt, the elder brother or sister, and so on. To each of these relationships a group of interests is attached, and therefore, of causes of partiality, the same in species as those which attach in the relationship between parent and child, varying only in degree. As far as can be determined by general rules, the interest will naturally be regarded as less and less strong, — the cause of partiality consequently less and less powerful, the more remote the relationship, the farther off the superior relation who represents the parent is removed in the line of natural relationship from the person he thus represents. This criterion, however, which in the character ot a general criterion is no otherwise good than inasmuch as the nature of things does not afford a better, is liable in each particular instance to be rendered incorrect, and if blindly adopted, fallacious, by an endless variety of causes.

Between the vice-parent and the vice-child (if the expressions may be allowed,) the connexion will be stronger after the decease of the parent than during his life. Why? Because the frequency of the occasions which the junior relation may have for the protective services of the senior relative will naturally be increased by the removal of him to whose protection recourse would naturally have been had in the first instance.

Identity of sex is another circumstance by which the justness of any inference deduced from the mere circumstance of priority in the line of relationship would be liable to be disturbed. Age in the instance of both parties, but especially in that of the junior relation, the child, is another. Both parents dead, the child in infancy, the services of a grandmother on either side may for a time be more immediately useful, whatever be the sex of the child, than those of a grandfather. As the child advances in that career in which the difference between sex and sex grows every day wider, the services of a grandparent of its own sex will be more and more valuable, in comparison of those of the opposite sex. But by the infinite diversity of varieties of which the interior circumstances of families are susceptible in respect of occupation, habits of life, pecuniary wants and pecuniary means, the operation of even these causes of disturbance is susceptible of a vast variety of other disturbances.

If in the instance of any such senior relation, the legal power annexed to the condition of guardian should have come to be superadded to the natural bond of attachment and partiality constituted by natural relationship, an attachment which otherwise would have been the weaker, may, in virtue of this reinforcement, become the stronger. Invested thus with the authority of a father, an uncle may be a person of more importance in the eyes of a niece, than even her grandmother on either side; the aunt to her niece, or even her nephew, than a grandfather on either side; — and so on without end.

Even in the case of that source of inference, the conclusion derivable from it may be disturbed by the circumstance of place of abode. If the house of the guardian relative be the abode of the ward, then this cause of disturbance has no place. But if the ward have for his or her ordinary abode, the house of some other near relative, while the personal intercourse with the guardian relation is unfrequent, or altogether wanting, the truth of any inference pronouncing superior strength of partiality from the mere circumstance of guardianship, must be manifestly precarious.

Even of the merely casual relation or connexion between the person whose testimony is called for, and the person on whose behalf it is called for—even of so slight, flimsy, and fugitive a connexion as it might seem to be, the influence, in the character of an efficient cause of partiality and bias, has in experience been observed to be far from inconsiderable.

This interest appears in species to be much the same as that which in the case of a more permanent connexion engages the affections, and good wishes, and partialities of the *protector* on the side of the *protégé*. It is composed of the love of reputation, of the love of power, and of an emotion which grows out of the love of power— sympathy towards the individual who gives occasion for the exercise of it. The service which the party stands in need of at the hands of the witness is a service of more or less importance, according to the importance of the interest at stake upon the event of the suit; at any rate, of no inconsiderable importance. In the case of an individual belonging to the inferior classes, that is, in the case of the great majority of the whole number of individuals in every community, a service of this sort is of such importance as to raise the importance of him who is called upon to render it, in his own eyes: — on an important theatre, he becomes an actor in a scene of real life; — in the party who invokes his assistance he beholds a sort of expectant dependent, whose fate hangs in some sort upon his service; — and in a case where corruption and criminal consciousness are out of the question, he finds his character held up in the circle of his acquaintance in a favourable and honourable point of view, by the certificate of veracity implicitly contained in the demand thus made upon him for the exercise of that virtue.*

---

* In the language of the English law, a witness whose good wishes are looked upon as being in favour of the party by whom his testimony is called for, is called a willing witness: one whose wishes are looked upon as being adverse to that side, an unwilling witness.

Addressing myself once to a friend whose experience was such as in the case in question was calculated to stamp a particular value on his estimate, I asked him what, if he were obliged to assign a proportion, would be the proportion he should name as between the number of willing and the number of unwilling witnesses. After due reflection, the answer was, the proportion of 30 to 1. The conjecture of another was 20 to 1.

It would, however, be a great mistake, if the magnitude of this ratio were to be imputed to no other causes than those mentioned in the text. Three or four other causes require to be taken into the account: one of these universal and perpetual in its operation; the other arising more particularly out of the actual state of the English law: —

1. Among the several indications which have been mentioned, though far from being the only one, as leading to the discovery of evidence, one is the information expressly given, or free conversation used on the subject, by the percipient

Thus much for the case where the group of naturally associated interests are supposed to be all active, and all clubbing their respective influences in the character of causes of partiality, on the same side. But all families are liable to become theatres of dissension; and by every instance of dissension, one or more of these naturally-associated and conjunctly-acting interests may come to be thrown out of the group.

The inference from connexion, natural or civil, permanent or casual, to partiality, will appear still more plainly to be in fault, where the circle of the same family includes both parties in the cause. The affections, and thence the testimony of a witness, may in this case be drawn toward the side of the plaintiff by one species of interest — towards that of the defendant by another; towards the one by pecuniary interest — towards the other by sympathy and good will: or even to each by an interest of the same species, and in a degree altogether indeterminate in either case: — to each by expectation of pecuniary benefit, to a value on one side, or on both, altogether unsusceptible of liquidation.

A consideration in all these cases, manifest even to the most superficial glance, is — how inconsiderable and infallibly inefficient a cause of bias and partiality the assurance of this or that certain but limited sum, expectant upon the event of a cause, upon the determination of it in favour of this or that one of the parties, say the plaintiff, must frequently be, in comparison of the opposite interest created by the apprehension of forfeiting the good will of the other party in the same cause, when upon that good will depends a train of services, till then counted upon as certain, to a value some number of times greater than that of the money to be gained. A point sufficiently manifest in this case is, that if presumption of partiality, as deduced from interest, even pecuniary interest (were there no other species of interest,) were a proper ground, not merely for directing a watchful eye upon the testimony of a witness, but for shutting the door against it altogether, it is rather on the side of the defendant than on the side of the plaintiff, that testimony so circumstanced should be forbidden to be produced.

All things considered, it will be found, that from the countenance of a man, and the tone and turn of his answers, indications much more instructive will generally be obtainable in regard to the state of his affections, considered as liable to operate on his evidence as a cause of bias, than from any such superficial marks as can be afforded by any exterior re-

---

witness himself. In this case, the actual and direct information spontaneously given is a scarcely ever failing indication of good will already entertained by the informant towards the party to whom the information is thus voluntarily communicated. Even where no such direct and purposed communication takes place, but the information comes round to the party through a course in some measure accidental, by repetition of the casual conversation of the witness in which it originates, the freedom and publicity of the discourse is at least a mark of the absence of ill will; — inasmuch as, in case of a disposition of that adverse kind, strict silence would be prescribed by it, and every word that could be expected to transpire would be an act exercised in opposition to the supposed wish and purpose.

2. Another cause is, that so far as a man has his choice of witnesses, — and that, of the persons who are pointed out to him by their respective opportunities as likely to have obtained such perceptions as, with relation to the facts in question, have rendered them percipient witnesses, — such and such alone will naturally be called upon by him to come forward in the character of deposing witnesses as he expects to find well disposed, or at least not ill disposed to his side of the cause. But so long as they are not ill disposed, if, before they are thus called upon, they were but neutral, the tendency of the cause already above noticed is, as is there observed, to render them favourable, to range their wishes and partialities on his side.

3. The case is the same, so far as the choice of witnesses results from the choice of facts. Among the evidentiary facts which the cause furnishes, such and such alone will naturally be endeavoured to be established, the evidence of which presents itself to a man as likely to operate in favour of the principal fact which the nature of his claim engages him to establish. If in this way this or that fact appear to make against him, he will turn aside from it, and leave to the other side the bringing forward that fact, with the evidence by which it would be established.

4. A cause particularly connected with the actual state of English jurisprudence, is the want of the means of commanding the testimony of unwilling witnesses, of witnesses whose possession of the required facts is inferred from their situation at the time in question; in a word, from any other source than information furnished directly or indirectly from themselves. The effect of this deficiency will be most readily and clearly perceived, by the observation of those cases to which it does not extend. On the occasion of those preliminary examinations which have place in the case of prosecutions for such crimes as have been raised by the law to the rank of felonies, evidence of all sorts is brought forward as fast as the lights afforded by one witness serve to indicate the further lights that may be expected from another: and the testimony of witnesses, whose evidence being of the hearsay kind, could not with propriety be received into the mass of evidence on which the grounds of the decision are composed, may yet, in the character of indicative evidence, serve to bring to light the testimony of immediate witnesses, who being ill disposed to that side of the cause which stood in need of their assistance, would not have come forward of themselves, nor would have been brought forward at all, but for the indication so obtained.

But the greater the number of unwilling witnesses which are by the above or any other cause excluded, the greater of course must be the number of willing witnesses, in proportion to the whole number brought forward and examined.

lation or connexion, domestic or civil, natural or acquired, with all the interests attached: and that, although the influence of these exterior influencing circumstances ought never to be overlooked, yet neither ought it ever to be implicitly relied upon as an indication capable of superseding the demand for looking out for such ulterior lights as may be deducible from the particular circumstances of each individual cause.

CHAPTER VI.

MAKESHIFT EVIDENCE.

§ 1. *Casually written Evidence.*

1. Where, by a party standing in the same situation in point of interest, as the deceased* author of a casually written discourse — a letter or memorandum, a statement supposed to be applicable to the question of fact upon the carpet, — any such letter or memorandum is produced, the first care of the judge ought to be, to put himself upon his guard against the characteristic fraud to which this species of evidence is exposed. He will inquire and consider whether it be or be not likely, that under the individual circumstances of the case, in the view of compassing an object which could not be compassed till after his death — such as the advantage of an individual or class of persons dear to him, or the detriment of an individual or class of persons odious to him, the author of the paper should have set himself to fabricate false evidence — evidence of the falsity of which he himself was conscious — in consideration of the security which the hand of death would by that time have afforded him against shame and reproach, as well as against legal punishment.

2. If, under the individual circumstances of the case, mendacity does not appear probable, the next point for the consideration of the judge is — how far it may be probable that, under the same circumstances, incorrectness and so far falsity on the part of the statement, might be produced by the effect of bias.

3. If the correctness of the statement do not appear to have been impaired either in the way of mendacity or by bias, another point for his consideration will be — whether the amplitude of the statement may not have been narrowed to the prejudice of either party by omissions, designed or undesigned.

4. To assist his judgment on the above points, the judge will take into consideration the relation of the writer in question to the cause upon the carpet; viz. whether, had he been alive, he would have been a party to it, sole or in conjunction with other parties: and if not, whether, with reference to him or them who at that time could have been parties, or with reference to those who at the time of the cause upon the carpet are now parties, he would have been in any of the situations, as above enumerated, to which different interests liable to act in the character of sinister interests are naturally attached.

5. He will moreover consider, not who was the writer, but who was the author, — not whose hand the writing is, but whose discourse it is, — of whose mind the statement it contains is the expression. A written discourse may be the discourse of a person other than he by whose hand it was written, — either as being a transcript, a discourse transcribed mediately or immediately from an original writing — from a writing of which the writer was the author, — or as having been written from dictation, *i. e.* from the words as spoken, or from memory.

6. If the plea assigned for the exhibition of the written casual evidence in question — the letter or memorandum — be, not death of the author, but peregrination, the danger of the characteristic fraud will here likewise require to be considered: whether the memorandum or letter obtained from the individual in question were not obtained from him, either in the expectation of his quitting the country of his own accord, or in consequence of a plan for engaging him to quit it after the furnishing of this evidence, or even in pursuance of an agreement already entered into with him for that purpose.

7. The case may be, that the letter or memorandum in question was not penned till after the commencement of the suit in the course of which the question arises, whether such letter or memorandum shall be received in the character of evidence. In this case, the judge may require the party by whom it is tendered to join with the adverse party in taking measures for the subjecting the testimony in question to the truth-insuring process, in its several features of oral examination — judicial scrutiny by the judge, cross-examination by the adverse party or his agent — or such of them as the system of procedure established in the foreign country in question will admit of. And as a means of engaging him to this concurrence, will be the rendering the accomplishment of the process in question a condition *sine qua non* of the admission of this lot of evidence.

8. In the same way, provision may be made by the judge for giving trustworthiness to a lot of written casual evidence, already in existence before the commencement of the suit. In both cases, the lot of evidence in question, whether the substance of it be or be not admitted in conclusion into the mass of ultimate

* *Deceased.*] For so long as he is living, the fraud cannot, upon the principles of this work, take place: the success of it being rendered hopeless by the examination of the person in question *vivâ voce* upon oath.

evidence, serves in the character of indicative evidence.

9. If through poverty, the party by whom the written casual evidence is adduced be unable to join in the measures requisite for subjecting it in the foreign country to the proper examination, it will rest with the judge whether to exclude it, or to receive it into the mass of ultimate evidence. But if the party by whom it is opposed offer to defray the costs of such examination at his own expense, such offer ought to be accepted, subject to the measures necessary to be taken to prevent the other party from being definitively a sufferer by the delay, especially if it appear that the desire of the undue advantage to be gained by delay is the motive, or among the motives, by which such offer has been produced.

10. Supposing the law on this behalf to be as above, and to be generally known and understood, — the less the expense of examination *in partibus externis*, the less the probable expense of such examination, the less the probability of the characteristic fraud, in so far as concerns the party being at the expense of making it worth the witness' while to quit his country for the purpose of fabricating such evidence. For, supposing that expense incurred, the design which on this supposition gave birth to the fraud is frustrated. There remains the possible case — that, knowing the witness to be about to go abroad on another account, the party may, without the need of any such expense as above, have engaged him to furnish the makeshift evidence in question, taking his chance for the effect to be produced by it.

§ 2. *Hearsay Evidence.*

Hearsay evidence, *i. e.* oral evidence of oral evidence: — oral evidence sanctioned, scrutinized, and cross-examined, of oral evidence not sanctioned, not scrutinized, nor cross-examined.

1. In the case of hearsay evidence, against the characteristic fraud, the same vigilant precautions will be requisite on the part of the judge as in the case of written casual evidence. To this danger is moreover added that of unintentional incorrectness in the statement given by the deposing witness of the discourse supposed to have been uttered in his presence by the supposed percipient witness.

2. In the case of hearsay evidence of more than one remove, the judge will of course resort at once to the supposed percipient witness; — the attention of the judge, and through him of the parties, will of course be directed at once to the supposed percipient witness. Should he be at home and forthcoming, the occasion for applying to any intermediately reporting witness or witnesses will of course cease: should he be in foreign parts, everything that relates to the provisional admission of his evidence, and to the purification of it, applies to this case, in the same manner as to that, where, between the deposing witness and the supposed percipient witness, there is no supposition of any intermediate pen or tongue.

§ 3. *Evidence extracted in a mode other than the most advantageous.*

In this head of instruction, an apparent inconsistency will be apt to present itself at first view. It represents the legislator as surveying his own work, acknowledging its imperfections, and suffering them to continue unamended. Such and such are the different modes of extracting evidence that have been in use: of these, one only is properly adapted to what ought to be its purpose: as for the others, they are more and more unfit, in proportion as they recede from this only proper one. All these unfit ones I continue, notwithstanding their unfitness; and so doing, I now, instead of correcting the evil, proceed to apprise you of it, and put you upon your guard against their respective unfitness, and of the several degrees and causes of it.

Upon a closer inspection, the inconsistency would be found partly real and partly only apparent:—

1. In the first place, to abolish a few ill-grounded rules on the subject of evidence, is one thing: to reform the whole system of procedure, is another thing. The former task would be comparatively short and easy; the other, at best long and difficult. The former task might be accomplished long before the other, or though the other were never to be accomplished.

2. In the next place, although a thorough reform were to be accomplished, and the imperfect modes of extracting evidence were all, as far even as the nature of things permitted, all of them to give way to the only perfect one, still the reform would operate no otherwise than *in futuro*; — the masses of evidence that had been collected in the several imperfect modes would nevertheless remain such as they were: they could not be regenerated and collected anew according to the perfect mode.

3. In the third place, there are several cases in which, after everything that has been done in the way of reform, after the powers of reformation have been exhausted, the judge is obliged to take up with evidence extracted in a comparatively imperfect and disadvantageous mode: — in which the evidence, such as it is, must continue to be employed by the judge, it not lying within the power of the legislator to cause it to be extracted in any less disadvantageous mode. For example, evidence extracted *causâ aliâ*, and the witness dead.

1. First case of suspicious evidence,*—the suspicion arising from its having been extracted in the course of another cause, between other parties.

The ground of infirmity here arises from this circumstanee, viz. that the party against whom the testimony is produced had no opportunity of encountering it by other evidence.

This ground will be stronger or weaker according to several circumstances: —

It may be that the party, against whom the evidence was produced in the prior cause had exactly the same interest, or what comes to the same thing, an interest equally strong, to do what was in his power to encounter it, as the party against whom it is produced in the case upon the carpet. And though the stakes should not be so great, yet if in the prior cause the interest were adequate and the means adequate, *i. e.* if in the joint considerations of delay, vexation, and expense, there were nothing that was of a nature capable of deterring or disabling the party from encountering the evidence, — from producing the counter-evidence,—the witnesses whether to the same fact or to the ulterior fact, necessary to the purpose in this, — though the interest itself were less strong, the effect of it upon the conduct of the party in question, and thence upon the fate of the cause, would not in general be naturally different.

In this case, the only infirmity attending the extraneous evidence with reference to the purpose of the principal suit, is what results from this circumstance, viz. that a man cannot in general have the same confidence in the exertions of another as he has in his own. To the party it will accordingly be apt to appear, that if in the prior cause the encountering of the evidence had fallen to his share, instead of that of the actual party in that cause—viz. the party against whom it was produced in that cause—his exertions might have been attended with more success. At any rate, such is the observation which he will naturally be disposed to bring forward as an argument against the competency of the credit of the extraneous evidence. But what weight is due to the observation will rest with the judge of fact to determine, consideration had of the individual circumstances of the principal case.

In this case, the supposition is, that in the principal case the means of encountering the extraneous evidence had been carried off by death, or what is tantamount to death: for if not, the case affords no reason why the evidence should not be permitted to be encountered: just as it might have been encountered, if exhibited in the principal cause in the first instance, without having ever been exhibited in any prior cause.

The present case, being the case in which the objection against the lot of evidence in question is confined to the want of opportunity for its being encountered by other evidence, by the party against whom it is now produced, supposes it free from every other objection — from every other infirmity — and therefore extracted in the best manner, with the benefit of opportunity of cross-examination consequently included.

In this case, the circumstance which principally requires the attention of the judge is the danger of *collusion*. A case that may happen, and that has sometimes happened, is — that by procurement or otherwise, by collusion with one of the parties to the principal cause, a prior cause has been exhibited for the express purpose of establishing as true, a statement which in reality was not true, and which would have been proved not to be true, had the evidence which the case afforded been adduced. Take, for example, the case of a marriage, a will, or any other contract. Validating facts really took place, and these are accordingly proved by testimony which has nothing of untruth in it. But by other testimony, invalidating facts* would also have been proved: — by which invalidating facts, the testimony in favour of the validating facts might have been encountered, and the effect of it destroyed. This counter-testimony being kept back, and kept back on purpose, the consequence is, that unless an opportunity be afforded of letting in the counter-evidence — the invalidating evidence — the marriage, the will, the contract, which was really invalid, must be deemed valid, and in that respect injustice be done.

Such collusion will not be very apt to take place, unless it be in contemplation of an act of unwariness, real or supposed, on the part of the law, in rendering evidence thus exhibited in a prior cause between one set of parties absolutely conclusive in a posterior cause between other parties, the faculty of encountering it not being allowed. Since in this case, so long as the percipient witness by whose testimony the fallacious testimony may be encountered and corrected, is neither dead nor tantamount to dead, such collusion would not attain its end. It is not, however, impossible, inasmueh as if the only witness or witnesses by whose testimony the fallacy could be dispelled appear likely to be short-lived, the fallacy may in that event be incapable of being dispelled, and success may crown the collusive and dishonest enterprise.

In the case of a plan of fraud of this description, it is but natural that the party to whose prejudice it would redound, should himself be aware of it: but be this as it may, it is the duty of the judge to be upon his guard against it, and act accordingly.

* No other cause is discussed in the MSS.

* For example — force, intoxication, or permanent insanity.

CHAPTER VII.

SCALE OF TRUSTWORTHINESS.

FOR the purpose of displaying the several modifications of which evidence is susceptible, the simplest and most instructive course that can be pursued is — to take in hand, in the first instance, employing it as a standard of comparison, by reference to which all the other modifications may be explained, that one of the whole number which upon scrutiny, and even upon the first view of it, may be termed the *best*.

This being premised — it will be in consequence of some determinate features of infirmity different in the case of every such species, that each of them will fail of coinciding with that one of them all which is the *best*.

What, then, is the best species of evidence — what is that species which, in speaking of evidence in general, we have in view, when, to distinguish it from all others, we apply to it the epithet expressive of the highest degree of value with reference to use? To characterize it, in the first place, by the effect of which it is productive in the way of use, — it is that species of evidence which, in virtue of the natural constitution of the human mind, as certified by general experience, is productive of the strongest and most determinate degree of persuasion on the part of the mind to which it is presented.

How then shall we recognise, and distinguish by inherent and fixed marks — by marks that do not wait to be imprinted by experience, that species which by the light of experience has been shown to be the best, the most persuasive — and not only at the outset the most persuasive, but at the longrun the most instructive — the least apt to give birth to erroneous decisions — to wrong conclusions?

Happily, the species which, when considered with reference to its effects, may be pronounced the safest as well as strongest — in one word, the *best* — is at once the most simple in its description, and that which presents itself the most frequently in practice: and this not only in the practice of a civilized state of society, but in a still more eminent degree in the original, which is as much as to say, the rudest state.

For the comprehension of the best species of evidence when contemplated in this general and preliminary point of view, a few matters of fact of general notoriety will require to be brought forward, in a station correspondent to that in which mathematicians bring to view their *postulates*: —

1. The first is — that concerning the fact itself, of which it is inquired whether it be true or no — whether the act, for example, of which it has been alleged that at a certain time and place it was done, whether it was done or no — a statement given by any person affirming his having been an eye-witness of that fact, will be more persuasive, and less in danger of proving fallacious, than a statement by the same person affirming his having been an eye-witness of some other fact, from the existence of which the existence of the fact in question is thereupon to be inferred. In other words, and shorter — direct evidence is better than circumstantial — circumstantial is inferior to direct evidence.

2. Another is — that concerning any fact whatever, a statement given by any person thereby declaring himself to have been an eye-witness of that fact will be more persuasive, and in less danger of being fallacious, than a statement given by the same person declaring himself to have been an ear-witness of a discourse held by another person, whereby that other person declared himself to have been an eye-witness of that same fact.

In other words, and shorter, — the evidence of an eye-witness, or other immediate and percipient witness, is better than hearsay evidence — hearsay evidence is inferior to the evidence of an eye-witness or other percipient and immediate witness.

3. A third is — that where a statement of any kind, made by any person, whether in the character of a witness or in any other character, is committed to writing, the writing itself to which such statement is so committed in the first instance, will in the character of a true and correct representation of such statement, be less in danger of being fallacious, and will as such be in general more satisfactory and persuasive, than any other writing purporting to be or designed to be a transcript of such original writing, and thereby to exhibit in the same order the same words: and this whether such transcript had for the penner thereof another person different from the penner of the original writing, or even though it were the same person writing at another time.

In other words, and shorter, — in the case of written evidence, a transcript is inferior to an original.

4. A fourth is — that all evidence is liable to produce deception, in virtue of certain causes of untrustworthiness to the operation of which it is exposed according to the sources from whence the evidence proceeds: — if that source be an object belonging to the class of things, *i. e.* to any other class than that which is composed of declarations or statements made by persons, then by a false colour assumed by or given to the appearance of such evidentiary things: — if that source be a declaration or statement made by a *person*, then by the action of some cause of aberration by which, no matter at present from what cause — say, for example, the influence

of some sinister motive — the declaration or statement given by such person has been made to deviate from the line of truth.

In other words, and shorter, — all evidence is liable to be rendered false by the action of some cause or causes of deception or untrustworthiness.

5. The fifth is — that for diminishing the danger to which as above all evidence stands exposed, viz. the danger of producing deception in the minds of those to whom it belongs to judge, various expedients have been devised—say, for example, examination performed in some established mode under the eye of the judge — all or most of which are more or less employed under the system or judicial procedure in all civilized countries.

In other words, for diminishing the influence of the causes of deception or untrustworthiness in evidence, the influence of certain powers and operations is more or less relied on, and employed and endeavoured to be turned to account, in the character of securities against deception in evidence, or say securities for trustworthiness in evidence: — whence it follows, that in proportion as the efficacy of the securities thus employed corresponds to the intention with which they are employed, any article of evidence in relation to which no use or less use is made of the aggregate force of these securities, will be inferior to an article of the same sort, in relation to which that aggregate force is made the most of.

If, again, the process by which the force of these securities against deception is applied to a lot of evidence be termed scrutinizing, or say scrutinization, proportion to the same effect may be expressed in terms still more concise by saying — evidence altogether unscrutinized, or less perfectly scrutinized, will be inferior to the same evidence more perfectly scrutinized.

Thus far as to such species or lots of evidence as, being compared one with another, are capable of coming into competition. But between two large divisions which include the whole possible extent of the field of evidence, no competition, no choice, can take place. These are the divisions respectively denoted by the terms *personal* and *real* evidence.

By personal evidence, I understand all such evidence as consists of discourse or language of any kind, uttered by any being belonging to the class of persons, — uttered by him, and containing or professing to contain any perception derived, or professed by him to have been derived by him from any matter of fact.

By real evidence, I understand all such evidence as is not comprised under the description of personal evidence: all evidence not consisting of a discourse held, or purporting to have been held, by a being belonging to the class of persons.

CHAPTER VIII.

BEST EVIDENCE, WHAT?

The most advantageous mode of extracting and shaping evidence having been discussed as in the preceding chapter, we are now in some measure prepared for entering upon the question—What is the best evidence? Of the several species of evidence before enumerated, which is the best? *Answer*, in general terms, that which is most conducive to the ends of justice, to rectitude of decision in the first place — to rectitude of decision exclusively, — except in the cases, if such there be, where undue decision or non-decision would be a less evil than the expense or other vexation which might be the necessary attendant on the obtainment of the evidence by which rectitude of decision would be insured.

Another question: — To what purpose the inquiry what is the best species of evidence? Can any mass of evidence be in any case too great?—in any case, can the grounds in which the persuasion of the judge reposes itself be too solid? Suppose two pieces of evidence of different degrees of goodness,—can the superior goodness of the one, afford a reasonable ground for putting an exclusion upon the other? Gold is more valuable than silver: but was that ever a reason to a man for refusing a mass of silver, when he could have it gratis?

On this occasion, one broad line of distinction presents itself in the first instance. In one class of cases, it depends upon the legislator whether the evidence exhibited shall be of one or the other of the two opposite and contrasted species: — in the other class of cases, the species are such as they are; and the choice as between one species or the other of the pair, is beyond the sphere of the legislator's influence.

In the former class of cases, the evidence as between species and species is the same in substance, and it rests with the legislator to make his option as between shape and shape. In this class of cases, the practical use of the inquiry, which is the best evidence, is clear beyond dispute.

In the other class of cases the question still presents itself, to what purpose seek to ascertain which of the two contrasted species is preferable? The answer is,—the practical use, if any, will depend upon the question, whether the two contrasted species are in conjunction with or in opposition to each other: proposed to be exhibited on the same side of the cause, the one or the other; or on the opposite sides?

If on the same side, to what practical use can the determination tend, supposing it to be determined that the one sort is preferable to the other? To this and this alone:—

viz. that in case of superfluity, the inferior sort rather than the superior shall be unexhibited.

If on different sides, to this and this alone — viz. that if on the one side all the evidence exhibited be of the one sort, on the other side all the evidence exhibited be of the other sort, the persuasion should place itself, as of course, on that side which has the superior sort of evidence for its support.

Thus much appears plain and unexceptionable; but a circumstance not to be neglected is, that with a view to practice, the question of superiority as between evidence and evidence lies ultimately — not between one species of evidence and another, but between one individual lot of evidence and another. If in this view the superiority as between sort and sort be worth inquiring about, it is only with reference to and as a means of coming at the solution of the ultimate question, as between individual and individual. From the determination that the first of two contrasted species was preferable to the second, no absolute conclusion could follow as to the superiority possessed by an individual lot belonging to one species in comparison with an individual lot belonging to the other species, on any other supposition than that the least persuasive individual lot of the superior species is in every instance more persuasive than the most persuasive individual lot of the other species. To judge whether this superiority in comparison of species over species be thus uniform and all-extensive, is a question the answer to which must wait, till the time come for bringing the several pairs of contrasted species under review with reference to this purpose.

The examination, to be complete and completely satisfactory, will of course require to be carried through every species of evidence; that is, through every two sorts of evidence which are capable of being distinguished from one another for this purpose; and at any rate, through the several sorts of evidence which have been already indicated.

Let us begin with the class of cases first described. It is that topic of the two which will be most productive of satisfaction — the only one that will be found productive of any very considerable practical use; — unless it be that of serving more effectually to guard the legislature against those illusions — the result of partial and hasty views — by which whole species of evidence have been marked out for inexorable exclusion.

I. First class of cases: — the case in which the question is between shape and shape (and the choice of the shape depends altogether upon the legislator) affords the following pairs of contrasted species: —

1. Scrutinized evidence, and unscrutinized evidence: and in the former case, more perfectly scrutinized, and less perfectly scrutinized.

2. Written and oral: or, to put the distinction upon its proper and clearer footing, evidence expressed by permanent signs, and evidence expressed by evanescent signs.

3. In the case of written evidence — original and unoriginal: that is, in this case autographic, and transcriptious.

I. *Comparison the first — Scrutinized with unscrutinized; and more perfectly with less perfectly scrutinized.*

The catalogue of scrutative arrangements has already been brought to view: they are comprised in the mode of proceeding to be pursued in the examination of witnesses: — 1. Questions in a series — successive, not simultaneous; that invention, mendacious invention, may have the less light to work by; — 2. Answers extemporaneous, and thence unpremeditated and uninstructed; — 3. Questions not immutably prearranged, but each succeeding question grounded on, and thence guided by the answer to the question last preceding; — 4. Depositions of each preceding deponent kept concealed from each succeeding deponent: that memory, and not mendacious instruction, any more than mendacious invention, may be the guide; — 5. Cross-examination; *i. e.* the testimony which has been extracted by questions put by the party at whose instance the witness is produced, checked and completed by questions propounded on the other side; — 6. Confrontation upon occasion as necessary between deponent and deponent; for example, non-litigant witness and defendant; that personal identity may be the more satisfactorily established; — 7. Re-examination of a deponent upon occasion; that other depositions given on a preceding examination may be corrected by lights collected as well from the depositions of precedently examined deponents, when communicated to him, as from his own maturer recollections; — 8. Publication; certain, or more or less probable, and consequently expectation entertained by each deponent of the publicity of his depositions; and thence an increased chance for the ultimate detection of any errors on his part, designed or undesigned.

If the above arrangements, each of them without exception, have their use, in how high a degree must a lot or an article of evidence that for the depuration and completion of it has had the benefit of their united influence, be superior to one which has not had the benefit of any part of that influence! But moreover, if there be not one of them that in the state of things to which it applies has not its use, it will follow, that by any one of them that can be added, the superiority of the security for the correctness and veracity of the evidence will be increased; by every one omitted, it will be decreased.

II. *Comparison the second — Written Evidence, with oral; or, more expressively and properly, Evidence expressed by permanent signs, — with Evidence expressed by evanescent signs.*

If permanence on the part of the character by which a body or an article of evidence is expressed, be necessary to the prevention of subsequent deperition and misrepresentation, as well as for the diffusion of it, upon occasion, with whatever degree of publicity the case may require, it will be evident in how important a degree the written, say rather the permanent form, must be superior to the unwritten, say rather the evanescent.

Establishment — the practice established under both systems, the Roman and the English — will here be apt to suggest another comparison: — oral scrutinized — say completely scrutinized in the best manner; with written unscrutinized, for such in fact is the distinction, the comparison, the option, that blindness and neglect have established and brought to view in the practice of both systems: and which, it may accordingly be asked is preferable, or superior to the other?

I answer — The comparison, in a practical view, is altogether needless. No body of evidence — not any the minutest article of personal evidence — is what it ought to be, unless it be scrutinized, completely scrutinized, in the best and completest manner, and moreover in the written form, at the same time. Between the properties of purity and completeness on the one hand, and permanence on the other, there is not the smallest degree of natural repugnancy. In the best mode, or rather only tolerable mode, of extraction, that which is in use in England in the trial by jury, these properties are actually combined. Each article of evidence — each answer, as fast as it is drawn through the scrutative tests — is laid hold of and rendered permanent by writing.

In Romano-Gallic jurisprudence and legislation, the question is not only started, but decided without doubt or exception; written evidence, the best without dispute. *Preuve par écrit, preuve littérale*, is the perfection of evidence: — *preuve testimoniale*, called also *preuve orale*, is but a makeshift. What is this preeminently superior species of evidence? It is a species of evidence uncompleted, unpurified by any of the scrutative operations: — what is the other, so decidedly inferior, the makeshift sort of evidence? It is the only one of the two that has been subjected to the salutary action of any of these tests, — one that, though not to all, has been subjected to most of them — to all of them, cross-examination excepted (meaning cross-examination by questions propounded by the adverse party:) nor even is that excepted in all cases — viz. in penal cases instituted in prosecution of the most highly penal classes of offences.

And in what ratio is the superiority of such written evidence, in comparison with such oral testimony? On the ground of reason, the question is palpably an absurd one: — the answer is impossible. On the ground of establishment, the answer is plain and clear: — exactly in the ratio of two to one. In a certain class of cases, indeed, oral is thrown out altogether, — it being in those cases good for nothing. In another class of cases, it is however admitted; but where it is admitted, it is inferior to the other, and in that same ratio. How so? Because, in the case of oral testimony, where that species of evidence is admitted to form a ground for a decision, there must be the testimony of two witnesses to warrant a decision: — whereas, in the case of written testimony, where that species of evidence is to be had, the testimony of a single witness serves. Absurdity the first: — to pretend to require the evidence of two witnesses as a necessary ground of persuasion. Absurdity the second: — to accept at the same time of the testimony of a single witness as equivalent. Absurdity the third: — to prefer to almost completely scrutinized evidence, evidence altogether unscrutinized, merely because the signs by which it was expressed at the first moment of exhibition were of the permanent kind, instead of the evanescent. Absurdity the fourth: — to reject this double portion of scrutinized evidence, when half the quantity of unscrutinized evidence is admitted and treated as conclusive. Observe all the while, that the evidence thus styled unwritten is at the time at which the decision comes to be pronounced, just as effectually written as that by which the name of written is monopolized: — the only difference is, that the so-called unwritten, is not written till it has been improved by the action of the meliorative and completive tests. It is true, that in some cases the written evidence will be fresher in the memory than the oral, as in the case of preappointed evidence: but the preference extends much beyond these cases.

And is the procedure of the Romano-Gallic system so completely absurd, then, as it here stands represented? Not exactly so, — not quite so absurd in substance as in appearance. The sort of evidence here in view, under the name of written evidence, is in most cases preappointed, and in some even official evidence: and that it is in the nature of preappointed evidence in general, and more particularly of official evidence, to command a more uniform degree of confidence, to generate a more uniform degree of persuasion than casual evidence, has been already submitted, and will be made more particularly apparent in its place.

Where, then, lies the true comparison? — where the real distinction? Not between written evidence and unwritten, but between preappointed evidence and casual: for though both should be written, or both for ever unwritten, the ground of preference would be the same.

Barring criminal falsification, written evidence, being permanent, expresses itself as itself at all times. Of oral evidence, the identity vanishes as soon as it is exhibited. The next moment it, or rather what professes to be it, is no longer original evidence, but unoriginal, hearsay evidence. Its identity is still questionable, though, when exhibited a second time, it is exhibited by the same mouth.

Written evidence — evidence by permanent signs — may pass through a hundred hands, each taking transcript of it,—each successive transcript taken, not from the original, but from the last preceding transcript: it might in this way pass through a hundred hands, and still in substance — nay even in words — be exactly the same evidence. What would have become of a piece of oral evidence of the same tenor, after it had passed in this same way, each time at the distance of a few days, or though it were but a few hours or minutes, through a hundred mouths?

Suppose in both cases the piece of evidence in question — oral in one case, written in the other — to be brought into existence on any occasion but a judicial occasion, — in any place but a court of justice. On this supposition, the oral evidence, whenever the substance or alleged substance of it comes to be exhibited in a court of justice, cannot exhibit itself but through the medium of another mouth, or at least a separate narrative from the same mouth, and therefore, in the first case, stands upon a footing nowise different, and in the other case but little different, from that of unoriginal hearsay evidence.

In these circumstances may be seen just grounds for preferring written to oral evidence: but these are not the grounds upon which that preference is founded in the cases above referred to.

Comparison the third — Original with transcriptitious Evidence.

The superiority of the former is altogether out of doubt. In the case of transcriptitious evidence, the maximum of ideal perfection would be equality with respect to the original; and at this absolutely highest pitch it will seldom happen to it to stand in the opinion of a judge. Intentional and fraudulent departure on the part of the transcriber will always present a possible cause of departure: — unintentional incorrectness, the result of human infirmity, presents such a cause, the efficiency of which, cannot in any ordinary instance, be regarded as being in a considerable degree improbable. By successive revisals, or even by a single revisal, security may be carried to a degree sufficient for practice even in the most important cases: but mathematically and strictly speaking, absolute equality with the original is a limit towards which a transcript may be ever rising higher and higher, but up to which it can never rise.

From the above three comparisons, the answer to the question, What is the best evidence?—meaning, what is the best of all possible forms in which a mass of evidence given in substance can be presented?—may, it should seem, be exhibited in these words: —The best form to which the testimony of a given person can be consigned is — that in which, being scrutinized in the completest manner, it is in the course of the scrutiny put into the form of a written instrument: whereupon, as often as occasion shall present itself for the taking it into consideration for any judicial purpose, it is the original instrument in question, and not a transcript of it, that is so employed.

From the opinion formed — from even the demonstration obtained of the superiority as between species and species of evidence, the practical conduct proper to be observed by the legislator does not however follow with any such degree of uniformity as at first sight might be supposed: — not even in this class of cases, in which the choice may at first sight appear so completely dependent on the will of the legislator: —

1. In the first place, though in general, and taking together the whole aggregate of individual cases, it depends for the most part upon the legislator, whether to have the evidence in the superior or the inferior shape, yet that is by no means the case in each individual instance. Owing to different causes that will presently be more particularly brought to view—as death — infirmity of mind or body, curable or incurable — unavoidable absence, for example of persons—deperition or displacement of papers,—this or that piece of evidence may not be obtainable in the superior form, and yet may be obtainable in some inferior form. Comes then the question — shall the evidence be employed in the inferior form in which it is obtainable, or shall it be set aside and rejected altogether?

2. In the next place, what in this point of view is the best evidence, may not in every point of view be the most eligible. Rectitude of decision being the main and direct object in view of this and every branch of procedure is the only object to which the inquiry has principally and constantly been directed. But this, though the principal object, is but one of a number of objects, none of which ought for a moment to be lost sight of. Avoidance of the several collateral inconveniences—delay, vexation, and

expense,—in these several collateral inconveniences the legislator may observe so many collateral objects, so connected with the main end that, for the avoidance of these, considerable sacrifices of the main object will in many instances be required. Of such or such a description is the best evidence which the case admits of; but to exhibit that best evidence may in this or that case be an operation attended with such a degree of delay, vexation, expense—any or all of these inconveniences—that the difference in point of superiority, between the best when charged with them, and the next best when clear of them, may not be worth the purchase.

In the effect of the docimastic process upon these two different species of evidence, a very considerable effect will readily be perceived. Parol evidence, brought into existence as it is under the influence and by the very operation of the docimastic process, is converted into written evidence—not the whole together, but in parts and gradually as it comes into existence as the words make their way out of the deponent's mouth.

When a piece of written evidence is subjected to the docimastic process, the result is,—not the original document—the piece of written evidence alone,—but a sort of compound mass, of which the written document forms the basis; the remainder being a mass of parol evidence reduced to writing in its nascent state, and superadded to the original piece of written evidence. The man whose discourse the writing is, is subject to examination *vivâ voce*, and his answers taken down and put into writing as they issue from his lips: the original writing remains as a standard of comparison for the result of this extemporaneous examination, each serving as a test by the help of which the truth of the other is tried and judged of.

In this view of the matter, a mass of evidence collected upon the best principles, and hereby put into the best shape, will unite three characteristic advantageous properties:—1. Originality,—(original writing being preferred to copies;—and in oral evidence, the narrative of the observing witness himself, to the narration given by one whose information is derived solely from a former narration given by an observing witness speaking out of court;)—2. *Triedness*, if the term may be allowed;—3. Permanence;—be it oral, be it written, be it in which of the two shapes it will,—at the moment of its first coming into existence, the evidence itself will of course be regarded as preferable to any supposed repetition made of either the purport or the supposed tenor of it:—from the action of the docimastic process, it will receive *triedness*:—from the written instrument to which it is consigned, it will derive at the instant of its appearance, *permanence*.

II. Second class of cases:—in each, a pair of contrasted species of evidence, where the distinction turns, not upon the form or mode of exhibition—a circumstance variable at the command of the legislator,—but upon substance—upon the unchangeable nature of the evidence itself.

Comparison the first.—Evidence at first hand with hearsay evidence.—The superiority of first hand evidence over hearsay evidence, even of the first remove, and *à fortiori* of every ulterior remove, stands upon ground of the same sort with the superiority of original over transcriptitious evidence in the particular case of written evidence—upon ground of the same sort, but upon much clearer and stronger ground. Mendacity apart, in the case of transcriptitious evidence, the only efficient cause of aberration to the action of which it is exposed, is a deficiency of attention:—in the case of hearsay evidence, the same cause operates with augmented force, with the addition of another very powerful cause—failure in point of memory; a cause the force of which goes on increasing *ad infinitum* with the distance in point of time between the hearing of the supposed extrajudicial statement or narrative, and the supposed repetition made or said to be made of it for the purpose of justice.

Thus much upon the ground of simple incorrectness,—a ground which of itself is amply sufficient to warrant the decided and invariable superiority of first hand over the best possible modification of hearsay evidence.

On the ground of mendacity and fraud, the persuasive force of hearsay evidence stands exposed to further defalcations.

The choice as between evidence at first hand, and hearsay evidence, depends (it may be objected) upon the legislator in this case, as well as in the three former ones:—for where the percipient witness is forthcoming, it depends upon the legislator either to insist upon his coming forward in the character of a deposing witness, or to accept of his testimony, *i. e.* of what passes for his testimony, through the medium of another person, who in such case takes upon himself the function of a deposing witness. Thus much cannot be disputed:—but in this case the question turns not upon the form, but upon the very substance of the evidence. The question is not, in what form the testimony of a given witness shall be exhibited, but whether, in a case where the testimony of a single witness would be the best, it shall be excluded in this way by the interposition of a second witness.

Where the case affords first-hand evidence, the legislator, if he think fit, may permit or order it to be converted into hearsay evidence. But it will often happen that a lot of evidence—a statement or narrative—is not to be had in any other shape than that of hearsay evidence — the percipient witness not being forthcoming. In these cases, it does not depend upon the legislator to have it converted into first-hand evidence. He must admit it in this shape, or not have it at all.

On another ground — an additional and perfectly distinct ground — the inferiority of hearsay evidence, in comparison of first-hand evidence, has already been established. In all hearsay evidence, in respect of the supposed original, the essential and vital part of it, it is completely and necessarily unscrutinized. It is the essence of hearsay evidence to contain two essentially distinct narrations or statements of the same fact or supposed fact: — the one a narrative or statement indubitably given, the deposition given by the deposing witness; — the other, a narrative or statement said by him to have been given: — the narrative or statement said to have been given at the prior point of time in question, in the other place in question, by the alleged percipient or intermediate witness. The narrative or statement given by the deposing witness may be scrutinized or unscrutinized: — if scrutinized, more or less completely scrutinized; — but the supposed narrative or statement alleged by the deposing witness to have been given by the supposed extrajudicial witness, whether percipient or intermediate, can never be subjected to any the slightest degree of scrutiny.

Comparison the second—Preappointed evidence with casual evidence. — Here, as in some of the preceding cases, the superiority is written upon the face of the very terms themselves. Preappointed evidence is picked evidence: casual evidence is evidence taken as it comes.

Comparison the third—Official with unofficial preappointed evidence. — Subordinate to the distinction between preappointed and casual evidence, is that which applies to preappointed — the distinction between official and unofficial evidence.

Here also the superiority, at least in all ordinary cases, is written in characters not unconspicuous. Unofficial preappointed evidence is evidence picked by individual parties, or perhaps by only one of two contending parties: — official evidence is evidence picked by the legislator, and under him by the administrator, or even by the judge.

Comparison the fourth — In the case of casual evidence, personal with personal—the evidence of a person of one description, with the evidence of a person of another description.

To this head may be referred the numerous causes of exclusion with which the English as well as the Roman law teems in such abundance.

The impossibility of establishing, on the ground of any superiority as between species and species of personal evidence, any determinate superiority as between individual and individual witness — much more to such a degree as to build, either upon the ground of certain falsity or inutility, a peremptory exclusion — has been already more than once indicated, and some foundation at least laid for the establishment of it. Whether the danger of simple incorrectness or bias or mendacity be considered, the degree of credibility is, in the instance of every species of witness that can be described, susceptible, of almost any degree of persuasive force, from the lowest to almost the highest: to the very highest in most cases — to the very lowest in all cases.

On the ground of simple incorrectness, it has been seen that the force of the several causes of aberration from the truth is variable *ad infinitum*.

So far as mendacity is concerned, it has been seen that veracity or mendacity depends upon the preponderance, as between the several causes of veracity and mendacity, — causes of and obstacles to veracity, — motives acting in the character of tutelary motives — motives acting in the character and direction of seductive motives; — and that the force of all these various elementary and antagonizing circumstances is in each instance susceptible of variation in an indefinite degree; — and that, of the actual degree of force with which they actually operate in each individual instance, it is impossible that any tolerably accurate estimate can be made by any human eye.

Yet from an observation made of the exposure of the mind in question to the action of some one motive acting in the character and direction of a seductive motive, not legislators only, but even judges, have of their own authority taken upon them to shut the door of justice against witnesses in crowds in a vast variety of instances; and thus acting — with the most self-satisfied confidence—with an acquaintance with the anatomy of the human mind below that of babes and sucklings, in the degree in which deliberate error is more remote from truth than simple ignorance.

Comparison the fifth — Personal with real evidence. From a comparison between these two species of evidence, little practical use can be derived. They can never come in competition with each other: and it is seldom that either can supersede the other. Supposing them on opposite sides from the mere statement that on the one side the evidence is of the real kind, on the other side of the personal kind, it is impossible to say with reason which preponderates. Real evidence without personal, is scarcely susceptible of being so perfectly satisfactory as personal is without real, or indeed of being sufficiently satisfactory to afford a reasonable ground for decision of itself. Conception being assumed for the purpose of persuasion, personal evidence may by the number of witnesses be strengthened to such a degree as to render real evidence superfluous: — whereas in some cases (for example, in cases of disputes concerning *boundaries*,) the matter of fact in question is not capable of being so much as conceived without the help of real evidence.

By real evidence, even where the nature of the case does not render it absolutely indispensable — where sophistication, fabrication, and alteration, are out of the question — a degree of satisfaction may in some cases be afforded, beyond any that can be afforded by any admissible quantity of personal evidence.

Suppose evidence of both these descriptions forthcoming on one and the same side, it is impossible to conclude, from the mere contemplation of the specific difference, that either is superfluous: — in this or that particular individual case, it may happen that the real evidence which the case affords may be rendered superfluous by the body of personal evidence: but so may any one part of the body of personal evidence by the rest.*

If evidence be viewed by other eyes than those of the judge, as is very commonly the case, at least in English judicature, it is a sort of real evidence at second hand — a sort of composite evidence — supposed real evidence exhibiting itself through the medium of personal evidence.

Comparison the sixth — Direct with circumstantial evidence.

Here, likewise, the title to superiority will appear almost as soon as the import of the denominations is apprehended. Direct evidence is evidence of the fact itself — evidence from whatever sources drawn, and in whatever shape exhibited. Circumstantial evidence is evidence not so much as tending to produce any degree of persuasion in regard to the existence of the principal fact, any otherwise than in so far as it tends to give birth to a like persuasion in respect of the evidentiary fact. For a persuasion of, to be altogether equivalent to a demonstration of, the principal fact, the connexion between the one and the other must be absolutely an inseparable one: and the instances in which so perfectly close a connexion is discernible will in practice be extremely rare. In point of persuasive force, circumstantial evidence, circumstanced in the same way in all other respects, cannot at any rate rise higher than to an equality with direct evidence: it will very seldom rise so high: and it may fall short of rising to the same height, by any distance on a scale, to the length of which no limits can be assigned.

Not but that circumstantial evidence will in most, if not all cases, be a very desirable addition and corroboration to a mass or lot of direct evidence.

Not but that circumstantial evidence may even suffice to produce the degree of persuasion requisite even for causes of the highest importance — for causes in which even life is at stake. Accordingly, under the English law, though perhaps not under the Roman, capital sentences have been pronounced and executed upon the single ground of circumstantial evidence, without a particle of direct evidence.

It is commonly obtainable with greater facility, in greater quantity, and of a quality less open to suspicion than in the case of direct evidence. It is less easily concealed or suppressed, and more frequently obtainable from less exceptionable, or altogether unexceptionable witnesses.

Written extrajudicial Evidence.

In speaking of the several contrasted and respectively commensurable species of evidence opposed to each other in pairs, it will be necessary to comprehend in the same view the anomalous incommensurable species of evidence, with which no other can be found to contend or match: — I mean that of which some description has already been given under the name of written extrajudicial, and which is also supposed to be unofficial, and in every respect unpreappointed, evidence.

The evidence before spoken of, as well

* Cases, it is true, are not wanting, in which a degree of satisfaction will be afforded by real evidence, beyond the highest that can be afforded by any quantity, at least any admissible quantity, of personal evidence. Among the sources of real evidence, is the relation of *cause* and *effect*; and between cause and effect (meaning species of cause and species of effect,) the connexion is in many instances, especially in physical agency, closer by a great deal, and less frequently broken by a great deal, than the connexion, between the fact of the exhibition of this or that lot of human testimony, and the truth of that testimony, *i. e.* its complete exemption as well from incorrectness as from mendacity. By the existence of a piece of handwriting, the existence of a writer is proved with more complete persuasion than by the testimony of any number of witnesses; though not necessarily with equal certainty the existence of this or that individual in the character of the author of that individual piece of writing: — by the existence of a piece of painting or sculpture, the existence of a painter or sculptor: and though in these last instances, the imitative operativeness of nature may have gone farther than could have been supposed, yet there are lengths up to which, were it to be affirmed to have been stretched, the *evidentia rei*, even at second hand, and though only reported through the medium of personal evidence, would probably be thought to oppose a more powerful mass of counter-evidence than could be overcome by any admissible number of witnesses.[a]

[a] Case of the supposed natural head of Louis XVI. to be raffled for, for a subscription of £10,000. — *See Mon. Mag. June* 1, 1803, p. 442.

under the name of written as under the name of oral, has been supposed to owe its birth as well as its exhibition to the creative powers of judicature. Even in the case of hearsay evidence, though this could not be affirmed of the supposed narrative or statement of the supposed percipient or any intermediate witness, it is not the less true of the immediate evidence — the evidence of the deposing witness.

Looking a little more closely at this anomalous, but very frequently recurring species of evidence, we shall find it to be analogous in its essential properties to the evidence of a percipient or pretended percipient witness: — the difference is — that it is fixed by virtue of writing, and introduced to the notice of the judge, without the intervention of any person in the character of a deposing witness; that sort of deposition excepted, which consists in the mere act of authentication — the act by which it is presented as being the discourse of such or such an individual, for whose discourse it is intended to pass. To determine the persuasive force possessed by the species of evidence thus denominated, it will be necessary to have examined the nature of hearsay evidence. For it is only by making the analysis, and as it were the decomposition of hearsay evidence, that a correct and clear conception of its nature can be obtained. We shall find it consisting of the first of the two distinct members, of which members at the least, every distinct article of hearsay evidence essentially consists, — I mean the supposed evidence of the supposed percipient, or extrajudicially narrating witness, — but in a fixed and thereby improved state, into which it is put by being consigned to permanent signs. Accordingly, like that frustrum of a piece of hearsay evidence, we shall find it incapable of being subjected to the action of the depurative and completive processes so often mentioned. You might cross-examine the writer if you had him before you, but the writing itself is incapable of being cross-examined.

CHAPTER IX.

ENGLISH LAW SCALE OF TRUSTWORTHINESS.

ENGLISH lawyers on their parts have their scale of trustworthiness in evidence. It consists of two degrees: — the *best* evidence, and whatever is not the best. For they speak of the best evidence: and in the form of a rule they have a proposition, of which the best evidence is the subject: — "You must give the best evidence that the nature of the *thing* is capable of."* By this description, all evidence but regular evidence extracted in the best mode, in a case where preappointed evidence is out of the question, would be excluded: — all testimony but regular testimony extracted in the mode of jury trial — all makeshift evidence at any rate, not to speak of circumstantial evidence, or any other evidence exhibited by affidavit, or in the way of equity justice.

This description being plainly incompetent, and perceived to be so, the expression has been interpreted by another; that is, translated into a different one: — "You must not exhibit any evidence that supposes evidence of a better sort in your own power."

One example, and one only, is given by Buller, of the application of this rule: and previously to the giving of this example, the rule itself is taken in hand, and explained in such sort as to be nearly explained away and modified in such a manner as to convey a meaning altogether different from that which, without the explanation, it would have brought to view: — "The true meaning of this rule," he says, "is, that no such evidence shall be brought, that *ex naturâ rei* supposes a still greater evidence behind, or in the party's possession or power." As to the example, it is that of a man's offering a *copy* of a deed or will, where he ought to produce the original: — and the case in which he ought to produce it is immediately explained to be any case except where he "proves the original deed or will to be in the hands of the adverse party, or to be destroyed without his default."

To judge of this rule by this example (and no other example is given of it, or referred to by it,) it amounts to neither more nor less than this — viz. that in written evidence, and in particular in written preappointed evidence, an original is preferable to a transcript: and of these two articles, and these alone, is the scale of trustworthiness of evidence, as given by Judge Buller, composed, with the work of Chief-Baron Gilbert for his oracle and his theme. And such is the produce of the wisdom accumulated during so many centuries, ending with the present time, by the didactic writers on this subject!

* Buller, pp. 225, 277. Gilbert, pp. 6, 7, 41 84, 85.

APPENDIX B.

OF IMPRISONMENT FOR DEBT.

SECTION I.

ITS INAPTITUDE AS AN INSTRUMENT OF COMPULSION.

In the case of debt, imprisonment, if in any character, can only be justifiable in the character either of an instrument of punishment or of an instrument of compulsion.

In the character of an instrument of compulsion, suffering being an unavoidable attendant, not only of the use of this instrument, but of compulsion itself by whatsoever means produced, it cannot be justified if it be either groundless, or needless, or inoperative, and thence useless.

In the particular circumstances of the individual case, has the application proposed to be made of it a just ground?—is it necessary to the accomplishment of the proposed object?—does it upon the face of it bear a promise to be effectual?

Unless, in relation to every one of these points, the judge have antecedently taken the requisite measures for satisfying his judgment and framing a decision accordingly, such measures not being either physically or prudentially impracticable, the application which by his authority, order, or permission, is made of this afflictive instrument, is unjust and indefensible.

For obtaining any such satisfaction, there exists but one possible means, and that is—receiving evidence: and in this case as in so many others, the testimony of the party himself is not only the best evidence, but to such a degree the best evidence, that without it, all other possible evidence put together which the world is capable of furnishing, may be pronounced insufficient.

In the sort of case in question, it has been and continues to be the interest of the judge to refuse ever to give admission to evidence either to this or so much as to any sort of evidence in general, and in particular in this best and on all occasions indispensable shape. Accordingly, in relation to no one of those several heads will any judge ever give admission to this best and most indispensable sort, not to speak of any other sort of evidence.

In the hearing of evidence, especially in the extraction of it in the shape of testimony, much labour must be expended, and little power is exercised. In the making of presumptions, especially if, as here, without grounds, no labour is expended, and much power is exercised.

Accordingly, on this occasion as on so many others, the door is shut against evidence, and presumptions made without grounds are substituted to it.

In a large proportion of the whole number of instances in which the instrument of afflictive imprisonment is applied in this character, these presumptions are, to the knowledge of all mankind, every one of them false: but in this as in those instances, in the consciousness of such falsity no impediment is found to their being made.

Of evil in this shape and to this purpose, the application cannot have a just ground, unless from the defendant to the plaintiff not only a debt be due, but a debt exceeding in value the aggregate of all debts, if any, due from the plaintiff to the defendant. Of all points concerning which, in a case of the sort in question, the judge, if justice were his object, would be solicitous to obtain some information, this is one: but concerning this point, English judges, in so far as it has been in their power, have taken care to keep all such information out of their reach.

To the accomplishment of the object proposed—viz. the discharge of the debt, supposing a debt due—is this infliction necessary? Another point this, in relation to which the judge refuses to inform himself. Altogether unnecessary it is, as often as the solvency of the alleged debtor is out of doubt.

Forcing a man to pay money that he does not owe—forcing a man to render in any shape a service that he does not owe—is not justice.

Forcing a man to pay for another, money which not he himself but that other owes, is another result equally incompatible with justice. In this case, as in the other, it is forcing a man to pay money that he does not owe.

By the vicarious suffering thus inflicted, no benefit is produced to the whole community of which these several parties are members. He who trusts his money in the hands of another, does it in contemplation of some benefit—of benefit in some shape or other;—and if it be in no other shape than that of the pleasure of beneficence, it makes to this purpose no difference.

To the relation of creditor, if contracted with the party's consent and knowledge, benefit in some shape or other is always expected, and generally is essentially attached: — to the relation of friend to the debtor — friend able and willing to afford relief to his suffering, by taking up more or less of his burthens — no such benefit is, unless by mere accident, attached.

Upon the face of it, to the purpose in question, the infliction in question — does it carry any sufficient promise of being effectual? Not it indeed.

At the charge of the debtor himself, effectual it cannot be, in so far as property to the amount in question — property fails of being in his possession, or at his command.

At the charge of any other person, in the character of friend, prompted by sympathy to relieve the debtor from this affliction — that it should be effectual, is not for the common good of all persons concerned — is not, as hath been already shown, a desirable result.

At the charge of the debtor himself, when these necessary means are actually at his command, its efficiency, managed as it is, is in a high degree imperfect, in comparison of what it most obviously might and ought to be.

To the many a hell, to the comparatively few a prison, is, though not indeed a paradise, yet however a place of comfort — of comfort obtained at the expense of the injured individual by the interested connivance of the judge.

Solitary confinement — to the purpose to which this severe infliction is least well adapted — to the purpose of punishment — has in a most inordinate degree been with the most unthinking levity but too often applied: — solitary confinement continued for two years together, and the victim not yet heart-broken, nor reduced to a state of melancholy madness.

To the wrenching out of the grasp of the depredator the property of his creditor, nothing that has ever been known by the name of torture, supposing it necessary and at the same time actually effectual, or but for the wilful default of the debtor effectual, would be misapplied: for if, having the property at his command, rather than give it up to him to whom it is due, it be his choice to endure the torture, the proof is altogether conclusive, that be the extremity of the torture what it may, he experiences in the idea of the detention — he experiences, from whatsoever source, a countervailing and more than equivalent, howsoever malignant and unenviable, pleasure.

Happily, to the production of the desirable result, no such alarming, no such dangerous instrument is necessary — no such instrument is so effectually conducive as the familiar — indeed too familiar and simple instrument — solitary confinement.

Two years have scarcely satisfied the unfeeling and unthinking severity by which it has been applied to the purpose of punishment: — two weeks would in most, if not in all instances, suffice for the purpose of compulsion thus directed — for the purpose of compelling disclosure and surrender of effects for the benefit of creditors.

Of suffering, in the character of an instrument of compulsion operating by its intensity — as in the case of what is commonly understood by the name of torture — it is a property, by the stimulus applied to the mind, to excite such a degree of resisting force as hath sometimes been found sufficient to prevent the attainment of the object aimed at by it. Of solitary confinement, especially if alone employed as an instrument of compulsion, accompanied, as it ought to be, with spare diet and perpetual darkness, it is the property to break the spirit, as the phrase is — to infuse weakness into the mental frame, the desired and salutary weakness, — to deprive it of the power of applying what in the present case is by the supposition unjust resistance.

SECTION II.

ITS INAPTITUDE, APPLIED AS IT IS AS AN INSTRUMENT OF PUNISHMENT.

In the character of an instrument of punishment, the infliction in question, — is it well-grounded? — is it necessary? — is it, or does it promise to be, effectual?

Compulsion out of the question, if to any purpose suffering purposely applied and directed to an end be of use, it is to one or other of these three: viz. prevention by example, prevention, viz. of delinquency in the shape in question, on the part of persons other than the delinquent in question; — prevention of delinquency on the part of the person in question, by depriving him of the power of transgression, or by depriving him of the will, the disposition or inclination, i. e. reformation.

In the case in question, delinquency in any shape, has it taken place? Because, if not, all punishment is out of the question — all consideration of the subject of punishment is out of place.

Fraud or *temerity*, — in one or other of these shapes, delinquency, if on the occasion in question it really has had place, must have operated.

SECTION III.

ITS NEEDLESSNESS DEMONSTRATED BY EXPERIENCE.

Unjustifiable in this case in the character of an instrument of punishment — inadequate and unjustifiable in the character of an instrument of compulsion, it is unjustifiable in every imaginable point of view.

To what possible ends or objects can it have been directed?

Not to the benefit of trade, — *i. e.* for the augmentation of the security of traders.

It is in this application of it — if to this purpose application had been made of it, that the colour for it, the colour put upon it, would have been most plausible. But it is precisely in this case in which there would have been the best pretence for it, — in which the pretence for employing it would have been most plausible, that it is not employed — that the insolvent is exempted from it. On giving up all his property, a person deemed a trader is under the name of a bankrupt exempted from imprisonment.*

SECTION IV.

END, OR FINAL CAUSE OF THE INSTITUTION— JUDGE AND CO.'S SINISTER INTEREST.

Benefit of trade — security of property in case of trade—are not, then, the real objects, or among the real objects, to the attainment of which the infliction as applied in this case has been directed.

What, then, has been the real object? In this, as in every other quarter of judge-made law, the advancement of the sinister interest of the makers: — the interest of the sceptre, the interest of the purse, and the interest of the pillow; — the increase of power to the judges,—the putting of money into the pocket of Judge and Co. — and the saving of trouble to the judges.

If within the same walls within which the blameless debtor lies stretched upon a bed of wretchedness, or without a bed lies stretched on the floor — the fraudulent debtor lead a life of ease and plenty — it is because it is the interest of judges, that he who comes thither with other men's money in his pocket should lead that life. Whether it operate in the shape of fees received by his own hand; — whether it operate in the shape of patronage — that is, in other words, fees received by the hands of a nominee — the force and effect of sinister interest is still the same; — with only this difference, that, received by the hands of a nominee, the value of a mass of fees is sometimes, though not always, less when received by the patron through the hands of a nominee, than when received immediately into his own.

Under the name of rent, or under some other name, the comforts enjoyed in a jail by a dishonest debtor are bought with the money of the injured creditor — bought of the jailor: and it is generally by some judge that the jailor is stationed in this his profitable post.

The difference between the rate of mortality in the aggregate body of imprisoned debtors, and the rate of mortality among persons at liberty, would give the number of deaths of which, though not for the purposes of punishment, yet for other purposes, the judges with just reason may and ought to be considered as the authors: — viz. in the joint ratio of the facility with which, if such were their wish, the abuse might be done away, and of the advantage which in every shape they derive from the maintenance of it.

How slight, in comparison, would be the responsibility of an English Chief-Justice, if on the score of untimely death produced by imprisonment for debt, he had no more to answer for than Su-raja Dowla had for the mortality in the black hole!

People of England! when will you open your eyes? — how long will ye be the dupes of sophistry, hypocrisy, and masquerade?

The nature of things will not change itself for the accommodation of English judges. Without evidence, there never has been, never will be, never can be, any such thing as justice. Resolved never to hear evidence — they are resolved never to do justice.

Believe, Honourable Gentlemen — believe, noble and learned Lords — the subject swarms with difficulties: difficulties indeed but too mighty. But the seat and source of them,— where is it? In the nature of the case? Not there indeed: but in the nature of the men from whose hands, if from any, the remedy would have to come. In finding out what is most fitting to be done, in that there is little difficulty. The difficulty is in prevailing upon men, whose interest it is that it should not be done, to cause it to be done, or so much as endure to see it done.

"The House will pause" — "I am not prepared to say" — "Your Lordships will pause:" such are the set phrases in which it would be postponed. Prepared to say? When will you be prepared to sacrifice your interest?

Hear evidence — distinguish between right and wrong — distinguish between degrees of guilt — distinguish between guilt and innocence. Give yourselves at least the possibility of doing so: — No, not you indeed: — it is too much trouble. These are the duties that sit so heavy on you: these are the shapes, the very idea of labour in which is, even in prospect, so intolerable.

Distinguish between guilt and innocence? No: we are not used to it — we cannot bear it — the fatigue would be intolerable.

SECTION V.

MEANS EMPLOYED—MENDACITY AND USURPATION.

Flagitious as was and as has been the end, the means have been like unto it. Depredation the end: mendacity and lying, of the very worst sort, the means.

* The above remarks were written before the passing of the Insolvent Debtors' act. The whole system has at a still later period been materially altered by the 1 & 2 Vict. c. 110. — *Ed.*

By the original constitution, if to a state of society where all power was arbitrary and unsettled, a term with any such signification as at present stands attached to the word Constitution can be employed: — by the original constitution, for a penal cause — *i. e.* for an act that was deemed an offence against the king — a man might be arrested and put into confinement in the first instance: for a non-penal cause, a man could not be so dealt with. For the determination of causes of a penal nature, there was one sort of judicatory, the King's Bench: for determining causes of a non-penal nature, there was a different judicatory, the Court of Common Pleas.

Money extorted by power from distress under the name of fees, constituted then a part of the income of a Judge — a Westminster-Hall Judge. With the share allotted to them out of the spoil, the judges of the King's Bench were not content: a contrivance was hit upon for giving increase to it. Quoth the Chief-Justice to the Serjeant-at-law, who had for his client a creditor, or pretended creditor — "If you will charge a crime upon your debtor, I will take him up as for that crime, and I will not let him go till he has paid your client his demand, or given security for it; — you and the serjeant on the other side pleading *pro* and *con* in the meantime." Such, if not in tenor, was in purport, in substance, and effect, the arrangement that was made.

Here, then, was double injustice — here was a most complicated system of injustice and immorality in other shapes. The debtor was illegally deprived of his liberty: — the judges of the proper judicatory were cheated of their fees. Such being the effects produced, the means were suitable: — a conspiracy between the judge and the lawyers that practised under him — a conspiracy, and the means employed for giving effect to that conspiracy, a vile and notorious lie.

Thus commenced the practice: commenced in the King's Bench, how it opened the court, many words will not be necessary to show. Vice is a fruitful stock — lies beget lies. The lie of which the birthplace was the stronger court, the King's Bench, was an aggression; the lie taken up in and by the Common Pleas was in self-defence: and, not to be left altogether in the lurch with such examples, up stood the Exchequer at last, and put in for its share. Truth was a weapon of which neither of them understood the management: on all sides of Westminster Hall, falsehood had been the instrument by which everything had been done.

They have forged a bond upon you, have they? Don't stand to contest the genuineness of the bond, — that will be a waste of trouble and uncertainty. I will tell you what is your shortest and surest course: — forge a release. Such, says the common story, was the advice given by one attorney to another. But if reference had been safe, there would have been no need of story. On all the benches, if not precisely in this shape, in a shape much more dishonest, falsehood is daily practised.

SECTION VI.

AFFIDAVIT PREVIOUS TO ARREST, ITS UNFITNESS.

To the misery produced by imprisonment for debt on mesne process, in the earlier part of the last century, in the shape of the angel of beneficence, the demon of chicane suggested and carried a wretched palliative — viz. the sort of affidavit by which the necessary warrant for arrestation has ever since been preceded.

In addition to the general assurance of the existence of a debt rising to a certain amount, if the averment of its being over and above all debts due *per contra*, as also of the arrest being, in the persuasion of the creditor necessary to the eventual securing of effectual justiciability or personal forthcomingness on the part of the alleged debtor, had been required, the number of the sort of arrests in question, and with it the profit of Judge and Co. would have undergone no inconsiderable diminution. Accordingly, obvious as those amendments were, effectual care was taken that neither of them should be made.

Loss by the unjust imprisonments thus prevented — profit upon the affidavits thus rendered necessary, — which was the greatest? Loss was probably the answer: for on this, as on all other occasions in which great good to the many cannot be produced but at the expense of evil in less amount or quantity to the domineering few, great was the reluctance experienced in the admission even of this wretched palliative.

"Oh! what a blow did that act give to business! Before that act was passed, the richest merchant in London might be taken off, charged — aye, by any man whatever, by a man to whom he had never owed a farthing in his life." Never shall I forget the tone or the countenance with which, some fifty years ago, that lamentation was uttered to me by an experienced practitioner, by whom it was expected that it would have called forth my sympathy, instead of being met with the secret emotion, which is not less distinctly recollected.

SECTION VII.

CONSEQUENCE OF THE EXCLUSION THUS PUT UPON EVIDENCE.

UNDER the influence of such principles — I mean always, in the first place, the principle which shuts out the light of evidence — which keeps innocence for ever confounded with guilt, and each shade of guilt with every other — it has been impossible to do otherwise than very badly, and not easy to do worse than has been done.

Insolvency and bankruptcy form, in the nature of things, but one case. Who and where is the man who, having it in his power, ought not be made to pay his just debts?—who and where is the man who, being blameless, ought to be punished for not doing what he cannot do?

Insolvency and bankruptcy form, in the nature of things, but one case. It is by the demon of chicane — it is by the sinister interest of the possessors of power, that it has been split into the undistinguished parts, for the designation of which these denominations have been employed.

To the same evil spirits in conjunction may be referred the several corresponding and harmonizing distinctions: — the distinction between non-trader and trader — the distinction between insolvent and bankrupt — between insolvency the condition of the one, and bankruptcy the condition of the other.

Never was technical jargon and sham learning employed to a viler purpose: — never was fouler corruption covered by whitened sepulchres.

SECTION VIII.

ADVOCATES FOR THE ABOLITION OF IMPRISONMENT FOR DEBT — THEIR ERRORS.

So completely is the idea of right confounded with the idea of judges' will in the mind of an English lawyer — so completely is the difference between right and wrong understood by him to be dependent upon that will, that when a practice, howsoever established, happens by whatsoever cause to have been brought under his displeasure, — no notion can he form to himself of any other mode of combating it, than by insisting that it is illegal: — in other words, that it is not established.

Humanity is a virtue which in England, for at least several generations past, has in no class of men been altogether wanting — not even among lawyers.

Among lawyers, accordingly, and in more instances than one, there have been found those, who under the impulse of this motive have raised their voices against this abuse. They have argued against it; — they have complained of it; — they have filled volumes with their complaints. They have argued against it, — but how? By showing the mischievousness, the impolicy of it? Something more or less to this effect: — but so long as the legality of it remained unquestioned, they felt what they could not but feel, how unimpressive would be all arguments drawn from such contemned and neglected sources. Yes, it was illegal. Imprisonment for debt illegal? Then what else is there that is legal? If in this case, practice of justice — practice persisted in century after century, does not make law, in what other instance does it make law? If by its mischievousness the practice of English judges be rendered illegal, in what quarter of the whole field of law will any legal practice be to be found?

Illegal? No: the great grievance is — not that it is illegal, but that it is legal: — not that at the hands of the authors of the mischief a remedy may be hoped for, but that it is hopeless.

Strenuous and persevering has been the contest in this quarter of the field of legislation. Parties have formed themselves upon the ground: — the debtor has had his champion, the creditors have had theirs, — each has chosen his watchword, each has chosen his virtue. Humanity, in her soft colours, decks the breastplate of the debtor's champion: Justice, in her grave and sombre tints, that of the champion of the injured creditors. In the eye of the man of humanity, all virtue is on the debtor's side — on the creditor's, nothing but vice. The man of humanity has neither eyes, nor ears, nor feeling, for anything but the oppression exercised by obdurate creditors, and the miseries endured by naked and famished debtors: — the man of justice has none but for the frauds and prodigality of dishonest debtors, and the depredations committed upon the property of their injured creditors.

All along, and on both sides, in the pictures drawn of vice and misery, there has been but too much truth. In the theories formed for the purpose of accounting for these disastrous phenomena, the same error has prevailed on both sides. In shutting their eyes against the only cause of these disastrous phenomena — in the successful exertion made on both sides to avoid seeing the sole authors, the sole creators, the sole preservers of all this vice and all this misery — both sides have constantly been agreed.

If misery have been produced, it is because on this ground the production of it is the object to which the exercise of power has been directed. If vice have been produced, it is because, whilst the matter of punishment has not been employed in the prevention of it, the matter of reward has, by the hand or under the eye of power, been employed or suffered to be employed in the production of it.

If the blameless debtor from whom, he having nothing, no human power could extract anything, has been consigned to useless suffering, it is because the judge got money by consigning him to it.

If the blameless debtor, in whose instance all punishment is undue, be consigned to a course of suffering more severe, because more protracted, than any which the worst of criminals would have been consigned to under the name of punishment,—it is because it would be requisite to learn, whether he were blameless or blameable, that trouble which the judges have one and all been resolved not to take.

Shall the man be let out of jail?—shall he be kept in? On this ground is the everlasting contest between the man of humanity and the man of justice. "Ah! let him out! let him out!" cries the noble sentimentalist, who gets nothing by his being kept in. "Nay, but he shall be kept in," says the noble and learned disciplinarian—the value of whose patronage would be diminished in proportion as the population of the jail were thinned.

Seeing him where he is, "Let him out!" says the man of sentiment; for thus far does the force of his optics penetrate. Yes: true enough, if there he be, and have nothing wherewith to pay, nor have done anything for which it is fit he should be punished, the sooner he is let out the better. But do you know whether he have wherewith to pay?—do you know whether he have done that for which he ought to suffer?—and above all and before all, do you know, how and why, he came there?—by whose power, and to, not to say for, whose benefit? These are of the number of those questions which would be *invidious*, and which are therefore never asked. For in an assembly so polite as the first assembly in the united kingdom, and therefore in the universe, unless it be for a party purpose—a question to which, to a noble person especially, if to boot he be a learned one, it would be impossible to find an answer, and unpleasant to look for one—is of the number of those questions that ought never to be asked. Justice in low places—politeness is the first of virtues in a House of Lords.

Conceive a question of this sort bolted out from one of a coroneted head, by some eccentric tongue,—and by none but a most eccentric tongue would any such question be put; up would start some duke, and lest such impertinence should find approving hearers, move that the people whose liberties are at stake, shall under the name of strangers be driven out.

Of such universal indistinctness of vision, or rather of such blindness—the result of browbeating effrontery on the part of lawyers, and awe-struck ignorance and timidity on the part of the well-meaning among the non-lawyers—the result has been that inconsistency which pervades the whole mass of the wretched piece of legislative patchwork which has bankruptcy for its subject.

The inconsistency, though with so little fruit, has found even lawyers more than one to take notice of it.

By *Severus*, every bankrupt is considered as a criminal: and out comes a law to squeeze and punish him. By *Clemens*, every bankrupt is considered as the blameless child of misfortune: and out comes a law for his relief. In the eyes of *Severus*, the interest of the creditor is everything; he is at all times as spotless as he is injured: what the wicked debtor may suffer is not worth a thought. In the eyes of *Clemens*, every creditor is an extortioner: stone is the material of which his heart is made; if it break, where is the damage?

SECTION IX.

SCOTCH LAW—CESSIO BONORUM, ITS INADEQUACY.

UNDER Scottish law, after suffering a month's imprisonment, every insolvent, on giving up his property for the benefit of his creditors, is set free.

This is an arrangement beyond comparison less bad than that of the English law, whether that part of it be considered which concerns insolvency at large, or that part which concerns bankruptcy: and in the way of experiment made, and precedent set, and pretence taken away, great is the use of it; great at any rate the use that might be made of it.

But the necessary month!—there lies the absurdity; there lies the mischief—there the indication of the sinister interest in which both the absurdity and the mischief took their rise. A month in a jail?—and to what purpose? Not to the purpose of compelling the cession: for that purpose, provision is made by the imprisonment of indefinite length, which till the object be accomplished, would without it take place of course. Not any such purpose as punishment: for, like the perpetual imprisonment under English law, this month's imprisonment under Scottish law falls like the dew and rain and occasionally the lightning from heaven, upon the just and the unjust—and among the unjust, upon the more and less unjust alike.*

Neither to the creditor nor to the debtor any possible use being to be found for it, remain the myrmidons of the law, whose use and interest, and whose alone, it evidently was, that caused

* By 6 & 7 W. IV. c. 56, a cessio may be pursued by any person in prison, or who has been imprisoned and liberated, or against whom a writ of imprisonment has been issued, for a civil debt. By the same act, the process which was liable to all the expense and delay of the Court of Session, is made competent before the Sheriff's local court. In Scotland there is no arrest in *mesne* process, unless circumstances be proved from which the debtor's intention to leave the country must be inferred.—*Ed.*

it to be established. Fees upon putting a man in, fees upon letting him out; — profit to this and that man during his stay — profits, none of which would have been reaped, had the man, without being sent to prison, been admitted to deliver up his all, to and in the presence of the judge.

For this cause it is that he is put into a jail, where he will do — what? Anything but labour without impediment in that vocation which is the source of his subsistence: — and in particular imbibe the sort of instruction which, as everybody knows, is the natural growth of that sort of school: — learn, if he be honest, how to become dishonest, — and if he be dishonest, how to become worse.

Use of it as an example, as an experiment, as a precedent, as a lesson, to wit to all who will suffer their eyes to remain open to it: — though not to any whose interest, and therefore whose determination, is to keep them shut against it.

It would show to England, if the case of bankruptcy were not sufficient to show, that for imprisonment in case of debt, there is no need, nor therefore any use. On the north of the Tweed, is security for property of less value than on the south side of the Tweed? Is property, in point of fact, in so far as depends on the law of debtor and creditor, less secure?

SECTION X.

AGENDA — COURSE PROPER TO BE TAKEN ON THE OCCASION OF INSOLVENCY.

A few points of subordinate account excepted, so obvious is the course which in this case is pointed out by common sense, that the imputation of trifling seems to impend over the hand that should set about delineating it.

So wide from this most obvious course, so tortuous and complicated, and in a word so palpably weak and foolish, in any other character than that of a system of oppression and depredation, is the system set on foot and all along carried on by and for the benefit of Judge and Co., that unless their sinister interest be admitted to have been the only end to which it was really directed, it will appear to have had for its authors, not men, but some inferior race of beings. But of the determination to adhere in all points to the technical system — to consider the abuses of which it is composed as first principles, the propriety of which, lest it should be found to admit of doubt, is not so much as to be taken for the subject of consideration; — of the determination to consider every path of wisdom, or rather of common honesty and common sense, as closed and sealed up for ever, — the consequence is, that in their generation, let men on other points be ever so wise, some track or other of folly is the only track in which it is left to them to tread.

On the part of the commander of an invading or defending army, suppose a fixed determination never from any person, on any occasion, to receive any sort of intelligence: — on the part of such a military commander, the system of tactics would be an exact counterpart of the actual system of judicial procedure: — the aptitude of such commander for military command would be the exact counterpart of the aptitude for judicature manifested on this occasion by English judges.

For satisfaction to the creditor under existing law, what is the provision made? Nothing can be more inadequate — nothing can be more complicated. And when to the creditor it is made, matters are so ordered that it is frequently at the expense of some person or persons from whom it is not due — some friend or friends of the debtor — that it is made, and not at the expense of the only person from whom it is due.

But in Judge and Co. may be seen the great firm to which satisfaction in every instance, by the power of that same great confraternity, is in the first place always made.

In the case of insolvency, punishment ought to be applied to him, and him alone, on whose part there has been blame. Various, and by no means more difficult to distinguish in this than in other cases, are the shapes and degrees in which blame on the part of an insolvent, where there is any, may be seen exhibiting itself.

To all these distinctions, under the guidance of Judge and Co., existing Law inexorably shuts her eyes. Why? Because, as so often observed, to make these distinctions it would be necessary for the judge to hear evidence, — to hear evidence from the best source, in the best shape, and at the properest time; — against all which he sits resolved.

Of this wilful deafness, what is the consequence? Everything that is most contrary to common honesty and common sense.

Woe to the blameless child of misfortune! Thrown into prison for debt, he will lead a life of uninterrupted misery, from which, bating accidents, no relief is found but in death.

Welcome to the swindler! — to the man chosen by the judge, who, instead of restoring to his creditors the property of which he has defrauded them, carries it with him to the house of entertainment which is kept open to money so acquired! His guilt is the deeper, the greater the quantity of other people's money which he has contrived to bring with him into that place; — but the greater the quantity of that money, the more comfortable will his condition and situation be rendered in that place.

The reward thus heaped together in the lap

of the guilty debtor — the punishment thus heaped upon the head of the blameless debtor — is not all. The measure of punishment would in the eyes of these legislators have been incomplete, if the injured creditor had not come in for a share of it. While the debtor, instead of being compelled to give up what he has in his power, if anything, for the satisfaction of his creditor, is either rioting or starving in jail — (who knows or who cares which?) — the injured creditor is fined 4d. per day for keeping him there; and he must submit to this additional loss, or forego whatsoever chance there may be of recovering any part of his original loss.

If we consider what ought to be the practice, we shall find, that in the case of debt, the first point on each occasion to be ascertained is — what on the part of the alleged debtor is the real cause, of the resistance made by him to the demand, and thence of the suit. Is it any real difference of opinion as to the question of right, which has any share in the production of that resistance? or does it arise from no other cause than a present unwillingness to part with the money, or a present inability to provide it?

The next point to be considered is — Solvency on the part of the defendant debtor, — is it out of doubt? If yes, then any vexation in the shape of confinement, whether in a prison, a spunging-house, or in the custody, real or fictitious, of sureties under the name of bail, is unnecessary.

For ascertaining these points, a few minutes — a question or two put by the parties to each other in the presence of the judge — would suffice.

Whether solvent or insolvent, the next point to be provided for is, as far as possible, the satisfaction of the creditor. But satisfaction at whose expense? At the expense of the debtor himself, and not of any other person, those excepted, such as his wife and children, whose subsistence is dependent upon his.

Next to satisfaction, in the event of insolvency — *i. e.* deficiency in respect of the quantum of such satisfaction — comes punishment: — But in what case? — in a case where, on the part of the insolvent, there has been no blame? To a question of this sort, so far from finding it possible to answer yes, common sense cannot for shame answer simply and without apology in the negative.

And note, that as on other occasions, so on this occasion, every infliction, in respect of whatsoever evil is produced by it, which might be avoided and is not avoided, may be, and ought to be, placed to the account of punishment.

APPENDIX C.

FALSE THEORY OF EVIDENCE — (GILBERT'S.)

"The Theory of Evidence" is the subject which, in his work entitled "The Law of Evidence," Lord Chief-Baron Gilbert undertook to make his pupils understand. The theory? Yes, "the true theory." And in pursuit of so laudable a design, the course taken by him, — what was it? To establish in the first place, to serve as a groundwork for this whole theory, a division which was to be all-comprehensive — a division in one or other of the two branches of which the whole subject-matter of it was to be found comprised.

Of real evidence, so called with reference to its source, and in contradistinction to personal evidence, he says nothing: — to his conception, things considered in the character of sources of evidence, capable of furnishing it, of presenting it to the senses of the judge, through or even without the intervention of persons and the evidence of persons, appear not ever to have presented themselves.

Makeshift evidence in its various modifications, preappointed evidence in its various modifications, in point of natural and usual trustworthiness — the first-mentioned below, the other above the ordinary standard, — as little, to a mind like Gilbert's, could any such objects, any such distinctions, have presented themselves.

Of the distinction between genuineness and verity — between the genuineness of a written statement and the verity of the several facts or supposed facts stated in it, — as little was the faculty of forming to himself anything like a clear conception within his reach.

That on this part of the field of law there should be any work to do for the legislator, calling by the nature of it for the hand of the legislator, was a conception which either never presented itself to his mind, or, if so be that it ever presented itself to his mind, could not but have been rejected with abhorrence.

That on any such subject as that of evidence — that in any part of the vast and important demesne of evidence, anything in the way of general rules should be the work of the only hand which they will venture to speak of in direct terms as competent to make law, — that it should be the work of any hand but that of a judge, that is, of a functionary to whom adequate means of information, legal power, legitimate interest, and thence proper inclination, — everything whatsoever that is necessary to the proper execution of this work, as of every work, is wanting, — of a sort of functionary with whom no arrangement good or bad can originate, who on no part of the field can take so much as the first step unless called upon by this or that individual in the character of a suitor, and who to the end of time would remain motionless as a puppet, in whom the very faculty of motion depends altogether upon external agency — motionless as the puppet-king in the showman's box, but for some unhappy or dishonest person, who, led by necessity, in the character of plaintiff repairs to the shop, and obtains the necessary parchment, the purchase of which gives to the cause, and to the authority of the judge who is to try it, that birth and life which is given to the puppet-king by the showman's touch of the animating wire, — is an idea which either never arose in his mind, or was instantly rejected by him.

To put aside the hand of the legislature— of that body by which the people are represented — to put aside its authority, to discountenance its interference, to misconstrue and construe away its laws — to present their own bubbles and crudities as so many advantageous substitutes, — has been the constant course of those creatures of the crown, of whose *caste* he was so worthy a representative. *They* call for the assistance of the legislator's hand! No: — they know better things: they make quicker work. By half-a-dozen threads spun out of their own bowels, as — " Christianity is part and parcel of the law of England,"—ten words exactly told,—they will make you a whole system of penal laws applicable at pleasure to the end of time, to the purposes of every Judge to whom an Attorney-general has made his bow.

Out of words in number one, two, or four— *policy, sound policy*, or *policy of the law*—they will make you a whole system of political economy or anything else, in despite of Adam Smith, on whose unlearned speculations men in their high situations disdain to bestow a glance.

In the book entitled " The Law of *Nisi Prius*," Judge Buller, the favourite pupil of Lord Mansfield, touched, of course, on the subject of evidence; and in the compass of nine rules, with the cases given under each for illustration, undertook to compress the whole law of evidence. Written in the spirit of the Lord Chief-Baron, they constituted a body of instruction altogether worthy of the source from which they had been derived. But not to overload with rubbish a sketch which, in its first design, was to have been throughout highly compressed, a view of these rules is among the matters which must here be laid aside.

" The design of the law," says Gilbert, " is to cause a rigid demonstration in matters of right; and there can be no demonstration of a fact without the best evidence that the nature of the thing is capable of;—less evidence doth create but opinion and surmise, and does not leave a man the entire satisfaction that arises from demonstration." p. 3.

" Records . . . . . are the memorials of the legislature, and of the king's courts of justice . . . . . they are the proper diagrams for the demonstration of right." p. 5.

" If the question be, whether certain land be the land of J. S. or J. N., and a record be produced whereby the land appears to be transferred from J. S. to J. N., — this is called knowledge by demonstration." p. 2.

" . . . . . Report from others . . . . is one step further from demonstration, which is founded upon the view of our own senses; and yet there is that faith and credit to be given to the honesty and integrity of credible and disinterested witnesses attesting any fact under the solemnities and obligation of religion, and the dangers and penalties of perjury, that the mind equally acquiesces therein as on a knowledge by demonstration." p. 3.

Report from others *is one step further* from demonstration ! — as if a record, proof from which is according to him demonstration itself, were anything but a report from others! Of this miraculous receptacle, according to his conception of it, one property (it thus appears) then is, — the being at a distance from itself.

Two questions which he confounds at the very outset, and is never tired of confounding, are the question of authenticity and the question of verity — the question concerning the authenticity of a script, and the question concerning the verity of the assertion contained in it.

As to the question of verity, the constant falsity of a large — and what makes the mischief, not always distinguishable—proportion of the assertions contained in a record (the instrument so styled in the Westminster-Hall Courts,) is confessed and delineated even by Blackstone, and is such as ought to be, if it be not already, proverbial.

As to authenticity, neither can even this property be with strict truth ascribed to it.

Take the judgment itself which is there pronounced: — It presents itself in the character of a written discourse, having for its authors the judges of a certain judicatory and as being expressive of an act of the intellectual faculty, followed by a corresponding act of the volitional faculty, concerning the allowance or disallowance of the claim or demand preferred by the plaintiff in the cause:—having these men for its authors, and expressive of that which, on the occasion in question, was the state of their minds, a state into which they had been respectively brought by the reception given to the allegations and proofs adduced on behalf of the parties on both sides, or at least on one side.

Such, as far as concerns the question of authenticity, is the account given of the matter by and on the face of the record. How stands it in point of fact? That unless by mere accident, the judges do not any of them know anything about the judgment which is thus uttered and put off as theirs. By whose hand or under whose order it is penned, even this, unless by mere accident, is unknown to them. When the record which ought to be made up, and for the making up of which some person or other in the character of suitor and client is made to pay, is really made up, which is not always the case, it is by some attorney's clerk,* under directions from his master: but even this is an event which does not always take place.†

A decree — for this is the name which in an equity court is given to the sort of instrument, which in a common-law court is called a judgment—(and these are the sorts of distinctions the momentary oblivion of which would to the eye of a learned censor present itself as a mark of unpardonable ignorance) — an equity decree is really the expression of a will actually formed and declared by the judge whose name it bears — the mechanical contrivance upon the strength of which an article so expensive as human reason, especially if it be to be furnished by a judicial mind, is dispensed with, not having yet been completely adopted in and applied to the business of a court of equity.

A decree is therefore *authentic*, and thus far, at any rate, the matter of it is true. For this, or for some other equally good reason, it is not, by the judges of the common-law courts, recognised in the character of a record: — it is no such "diagram"—it contains no such "demonstration of right."

According to Gilbert himself, it is not *a record*, or any part of the record: nor should the difference naturally have been unknown to him, he being Chief Judge of that amphibious judicatory, the Court of Exchequer, which is both a common-law court and an equity court — a court of record, and a court not of record — and which in this its inferior capacity, ties up its own hands, stopping and overruling the proceedings carried on under its eye in its superior character of a court of record, viz. a common-law court.

After dispatching the testimonies of the highest rank, the testimonies that are of record, — the first sort of testimonies, says he, that are not of record, are the proceedings of the Court of Chancery. "The reason why the proceedings in Chancery, and the rolls of the court (in which are contained the decree) are not records, is this — because they are not the precedents of justice: for the proceedings in Chancery are founded only in the circumstances of each private case, and *they cannot be rules to any other.*" This from the Lord Chief-Baron himself, chief judge of a judicatory exercising the powers of the Court of Chancery! Had the hand from which it issued been an unlearned one, even though it had been a noble one, how petrifying would have been the taunts of ignorance which it would have drawn down upon itself from learned lips!

The decrees by which, in the court of which he was the Chief, sitting on the equity side of that court, he was overruling the judgments, the demonstrations of right pronounced on the common-law side of that same court, these overruling decrees not being of record, while the overruled judgments were of record, — what, according to the rules of evidence as laid down by himself, must have been the consequence? Records being put by him in the first place, as having "the first place in the discourses of probability," (p. 5,) and matters not of record being with reference to records "matters of inferior nature," (p. 5,) — and the two halves of his mind being in flat contradiction to each other, — the preference must, by the whole of it, have been given to the common-law half. By the common-law half, the right had been *demonstrated* to be in the plaintiff at common-law. By the equity half, it had been *decreed* to be in the plaintiff in equity —the same unhappy person to whose hard lot it had fallen to be defendant at common law, and now, together with his adversary or adversaries, to be hustled between the two sides of the court, — between the law half and the equity half of these the reverend deniers and vendors of law and equity; — for, the representation given by the equity half not being among the precedents of justice, his whole mind, not altogether without reason, refused to believe that representation to be true: — but of the two conflicting halves, the equity half being the stronger, while the opposite side was the more trustworthy, it was to the representation made by the stronger side that the effect was given by the whole, the weaker being left to comfort itself with the reflection, that though equity and power were on the other side, truth and demonstration, as well as law, were on its own side.

"To understand the true theory of evi-

* Impey's Common Pleas, p. 318.

† Compton's B. R. and C. B. by Sellon.

dence:" — such is the purpose for which, Gilbert states, it is necessary that the arrangement which he proceeds to give should be "considered."

Testimony being all along employed as a word exactly synonymous to evidence — circumstantial evidence completely out of his mind, until, not by that name, but under the name of *presumptions*, at the end of his 246 pages, he comes to consider it.

Testimony he divides into "*written*" and "unwritten," — written into "public and private,"—public into "records and matters of inferior nature."

"Speaking of written and unwritten, in the first place," says he, "we are to consider which of these two sorts of evidence is to be preferred in the scale of probability, when they stand in opposition to each other. —Cicero," says he, "gives a handsome turn in favour of the unwritten evidence," p. 4: whereupon comes the handsome turn: "But the balance of probability," continues he, "is certainly on the other side," p. 5: "therefore," continues he again, "we shall begin with the written evidence; that has the first place in the discourses of probability."

Under the head of public records, come the following sorts of evidence, ranged according to the intimation above given, in the order corresponding to their respective altitudes in the scale of probative force: —

In the first place, though without any separate title in large letters, come those records which, according to him, are the precedents of the demonstration of justice (p. 6,) and instruments of justice; *i. e.* the above-mentioned compounds or reservoirs of truths and lies undistinguishably shaken together, penned by nobody knows who, and kept under the orders, how seldom soever, if ever, actually subjected to the eyes of the judges of Westminster Hall. Then comes a score of other heads in the following order: —

1. Statutes, p. 9; — 2. Copies of all other records under seal, and not under seal, p. 11;—3. Copies sworn, and office-copies, p. 17;—4. Records, recoveries, &c. p. 21;—5. Verdicts, evidence, p. 31;—6. Writs, p. 34;—7. Acts of parliament, p. 36;—8. Public matters not of record, chancery proceedings, p. 41;—9. Bills in chancery, p. 42;—10. Answers, p. 43;—11. Affidavits, p. 45;—12. Comparison of hands, p. 47;—13. Voluntary affidavits, p. 49;—14. Depositions, p. 52;—15. Decree, sentence in the spiritual court, p. 60; — 16. Evidence, p. 61;—17. Of the proceedings in the spiritual court, p. 63; — 18. Wills, p. 64.

19. The above being his list of sorts of public evidence that are records, next comes the head entitled "Of the public matters that are not records," p. 67.

20. This dispatched, next comes in great letters, title, Deeds, p. 70, which, says he, is only private evidence between party and party.

Under this same head of private evidence, after title, Deeds, comes once more title, Wills, p. 91; then Deeds cancelled, p. 96; Bills of exchange, notes of acceptance, p. 99.

With this sub-title ends title, *Written evidence.* After all these comes, title, Witnesses p. 205; *i. e.* as he expresses it, "the under written (it should be *unwritten*) evidence, or the proofs from the mouths of witnesses."

And now comes the only case, viz. that in which the testimony of the witness is delivered, in the shape denominated on the present occasion, by this teacher of the theory of evidence, unwritten—and on other occasions, by him and all other lawyers, *parol* evidence—in which it occurs to him that a witness is capable of standing exposed to the action of interest in such manner as to indicate the propriety of a head entitled "Witnesses interested," p. 107.

In any such form as that of a bill, an answer, an affidavit, or a deposition—what had not entered into his conception was, that testimony should ever be exposed to the action of sinister interest. In all these several forms, testimony "*is a record;*" that is to say, "*not a record:*" — and a record being the diagram in and by which right is demonstrated, whatever assertion is happy enough to obtain admittance into any one of those receptacles of truth, becomes truth demonstrated.

Such being the arrangement, and such the nature and order of the matters comprised in it, observe now the reasoning on which it is grounded: — "Contracts reduced to writing" (says he, page 5) "are the most sedate and deliberate acts of the mind," and so forth; — and "therefore" it is that with him "written evidence" has the first place "*in the discourses of* probability:" meaning, as it should seem, in discourses holden on the subject of the *order* of probability: — and therefore it is, that though "depositions," as he himself observes (p. 3,) fall short, viz. in probative force, of examinations *vivâ voce*, yet in the scale of probative force he assigns to them a place higher than that assigned by him to unwritten evidence — *alias* parol evidence — *alias* evidence extracted by examination *vivâ voce;* as if depositions themselves were extracted by anything else but by examinations *vivâ voce:* and therefore it is, that putting affidavits which are not extracted by examination *vivâ voce*, before depositions which are, for a reason which, even according to his own account of it, applies only to contracts, amongst so many other things which are not contracts, he ranks affidavits before depositions.

In the same strain of anility, garrulity, narrow-mindedness, absurdity, perpetual misrepresentation, and indefatigable self-contradiction, runs the whole of this work, from which men are to understand the true theory of evidence.

Although as a whole, the whole of it taken together can scarcely be taken for the subject of serious study, without danger of insanity, it may however be labour not altogether thrown away, to dip into here and there a page — and any page may serve — for two purposes, and in two points of view: —

One is, that it may be seen to what a degree of debasement, even so late as the middle of the eighteenth century, it was possible for the human understanding to be brought down by the study of English law: — another is, that it may be seen by what sort of an understanding it is, that down to that late period, not to descend lower, a man was not disqualified from filling, even with the universal applause and admiration of the learned brotherhood, the highest situations.

Such is the work, which notwithstanding its never having "received the last corrections of its author," (as if susceptibility of correction were among the properties of such a work,) is nevertheless, in the eyes of the author of a so much better work on the same subject,* so excellent, that so far as relates to this part of the law of evidence (viz. "the section on records," of which a sample has been seen above,) "which may be considered as coeval with the law itself, it must form the basis of every subsequent work on the subject."

Whether the expositor (meaning the Lord Chief-Baron) be not well suited to the subject, as well as whether the subject be not well suited to the expositor, the reader may now find himself in a condition in some measure to judge.

* Peake, Preface.

RATIONALE

OF

JUDICIAL EVIDENCE,

SPECIALLY APPLIED TO

ENGLISH PRACTICE.

FROM THE MANUSCRIPTS

OF

JEREMY BENTHAM,

BENCHER OF LINCOLN'S INN.

(FIRST PRINTED IN 1827.)

CONTENTS.

(IN VOL. VI.)

PREFACE, ... page 201
PROSPECTIVE VIEW, ... 203

BOOK I.

THEORETIC GROUNDS.

CHAPTER I.

On Evidence in General, ... 206

CHAPTER II.

Of Evidence, considered with reference to a legal purpose; and of the Duties of the Legislator in relation to Evidence, . 210

CHAPTER III.

Of Facts, the Subject-matter of Evidence, 214

CHAPTER IV.

Of the several Species or Modifications of Evidence, ... 218

CHAPTER V.

Of the Probative Force of Evidence.

§ 1. Ordinary degree of probative force, what, ... 220
2. Probative force, by what circumstances increased, ... 221
3. Probative force, by what circumstances diminished, ... ib.

CHAPTER VI.

Degrees of Persuasion and Probative Force, how measured.

§ 1. Importance of a correct form for expressing degrees of persuasion and probative force, ... 223
2. Application of the principle to different cases in judicature, ... 227
3. Incapacity of ordinary language for expressing degrees of persuasion and probative force, ... 229
4. Roman school—its attempts to express degrees of probative force, . . 230
5. English school—its attempts to express degrees of probative force, . . 231
6. An infinite scale inapplicable, though the only true one, ... 232

CHAPTER VII.

Of the Foundation or Cause of Belief in Testimony.

§ 1. That the cause of belief in testimony is experience, ... 235
2. Objections against the principle, that the cause of belief in testimony is experience, answered, ... 238

CHAPTER VIII.

Modes of Incorrectness in Testimony, . 244

CHAPTER IX.

General View of the Psychological Causes of Correctness and Completeness, with their contraries, Incorrectness and Incompleteness, in Testimony, . . 247

CHAPTER X.

Of the Intellectual Causes of Correctness and Completeness in Testimony, with their opposites, ... page 250

CHAPTER XI.

Of the Moral Causes of Correctness and Completeness in Testimony, with their opposites.

§ 1. The moral causes of correctness and completeness in testimony, with their opposites, are motives, . . 256
2. Any motive may operate as a cause either of veracity or of mendacity, 259
3. Of the four sanctions, considered as causes of trustworthiness or untrustworthiness in testimony, . . 260
4. Operation of the physical sanction, for and against correctness and completeness in testimony, . . . 262
5. Operation of the moral or popular sanction, for and against correctness and completeness in testimony, . 264
6. Operation of the legal sanction, for and against correctness and completeness in testimony, ... 268
7. Operation of the religious sanction, for and against correctness and completeness in testimony, ... 270

CHAPTER XII.

Ground of Persuasion in the case of the Judge—Can Decision on his own knowledge, without Evidence from external sources, be well-grounded? . . 276

BOOK II.

OF THE SECURITIES FOR THE TRUSTWORTHINESS OF TESTIMONY.

CHAPTER I.

Object of the present Book, ... 278

CHAPTER II.

Dangers to be guarded against in regard to Testimony, by the Arrangements suggested in this book, ... 279

CHAPTER III.

Internal and External Securities for the Trustworthiness of Testimony, enumerated, ... 282

CHAPTER IV.

On the Internal Securities for Trustworthiness in Testimony, ... 286

CHAPTER V.

Of Punishment, considered as a Security for the Trustworthiness of Testimony.

§ 1. Species of falsehood—Necessity of substituting the word *mendacity* for *perjury*, ... 291
2. Rules for the application of punishment to testimonial falsehood . 295
3. Defects of Roman law, in regard to the punishment of testimonial falsehood, 302
4. Defects of English law, in regard to the punishment of testimonial falsehood, 303

CHAPTER VI.

Of the ceremony of an Oath, considered as a Security for the Trustworthiness of Testimony.

§ 1. An oath, what? . . . . page 308
2. Inefficacy of an oath, as a security for the trustworthiness of testimony, 309
3. Mischievousness of oaths, . . . 315
4. How to adapt the ceremony, if employed, to its purposes, . . 318
5. Oaths, how applied as a security for the trustworthiness of testimony, under past and present systems of law, . 321
6. Should an oath, if employed in other cases, be employed or not, on the examination of a defendant *in penali?* 325

CHAPTER VII.

Of Shame, considered as a Security for the Trustworthiness of Testimony, . . 326

CHAPTER VIII.

Of Writing, considered as a Security for the Trustworthiness of Testimony, . 327

CHAPTER IX.

Of Interrogation, considered as a Security for the Trustworthiness of Testimony.

§ 1. Uses of interrogation, as applied to the extraction of testimony, . . . 332
2. Exceptions to the application of interrogation to the extraction of testimony, 333
3. On whom ought interrogation to be performable? 334
4. By whom ought interrogation to be performable? 335
5. Affections of the several proposed interrogators and respondents towards each other, how far presumable, 346
6. Distinction between amicable interrogation and interrogation *ex adverso,* 347

CHAPTER X.

Of Publicity and Privacy, as applied to Judicature in general, and to the collection of Evidence in particular.

§ 1. Preliminary explanation. Topics to be considered, ... 351
2. Uses of publicity, as applied to the collection of the evidence, and to the other proceedings of a court of justice, 355
3. Of the exceptions to the principle of universal publicity, . . . 359
4. Precautions to be observed in the application of the principle of privacy, 369
5. Cases particularly unmeet for privacy, *ib.*
6. Errors of Roman and English law in respect of publicity and privacy, . 372

BOOK III.

OF THE EXTRACTION OF TESTIMONIAL EVIDENCE.

CHAPTER I.

Of the Oral Mode of Interrogation, . 383

CHAPTER II.

Notes, whether consultable? . . . 386

CHAPTER III.

Of Suggestive Interrogation.

§ 1. Reasons against the absolute prohibition of suggestive interrogation, . 392
2. Conditions of allowance, . . 397

CHAPTER IV.

Of Discreditive Interrogation, . page 400

CHAPTER V.

Of the demeanour of the adverse Interrogator to the Witness, considered in respect of Vexation, ... 406

CHAPTER VI.

Of the Notation and Recordation of Testimony.

§ 1. Uses of notation and recordation, as applied to orally-delivered testimony, 408
2. In what cases should notation and recordation be employed? . . 410
3. In what manner, and by what hands, should notation be performed? . 412
4. Of notation and recordation, under English law, ... 414
5. Of the authentication of minutes, . 415

CHAPTER VII.

That the Evidence should be collected by the same person by whom the Decision is to be pronounced, ... 419

CHAPTER VIII.

Five Modes of Interrogation compared, 423

CHAPTER IX.

Epistolary Mode of Interrogation, in what cases applicable.

§ 1. Reasons for employing the epistolary mode of interrogation in certain cases, 429
2. The cases particularized, . . 431
3. Should testimony extracted by epistolary interrogation be deemed of itself sufficient to ground a decision? . 433
4. Epistolary interrogation should not shut the door upon subsequent examination *vivâ voce,* 434
5. Incongruities of English law in regard to the application of epistolary interrogation, ... 436

CHAPTER X.

Epistolary Mode of Interrogation, how to apply it to the best advantage.

§ 1. Rules to be observed, what? . . 437
2. First Rule—That the deponent speak always in the first person, . . *ib.*
3. Disregard shown to the first rule in English law, ... 439
4. Second Rule—Paragraphs short and numbered, ... 441
5. Disregard shown to the second rule in English law, ... 443

CHAPTER XI.

Helps to Recollection, how far compatible with Obstructions to Invention? . 446

CHAPTER XII.

Of Re-examination, Repetition, or Recolement.

§ 1. Re-examination, with faculty of amendment, how and in what cases proper, 451
2. Faculty of amendment, in what cases refused in English Equity practice, 455

CHAPTER XIII.

Of Spontaneous or Uninterrogated Testimony.

§ 1. In what cases ought uninterrogated testimony to be received? . . . 458
2. How to lessen the imperfections of uninterrogated testimony, . . 460

3. Abusive applications made of uninterrogated testimony in English law, p. 462

CHAPTER XIV.

General View of the Incongruities of English Law in respect of the Extraction of Evidence, ... 465

CHAPTER XV.

Mode of Extraction in English Common-Law Procedure, its Incongruities.

§ 1. Case, penal—offence, a felony—procedure, by indictment, ... 471
2. Case, penal—offence, a misdemeanour—procedure, by indictment, . 474
3. Case, penal—offence, a contempt—procedure, by attachment, . . 476
4. Case, penal—procedure, by information, ... 477
5. Case, non-penal—procedure, by jury-trial, ... 479
6. Case, non-penal—procedure, without jury-trial—cause originating in a motion, ... 480

CHAPTER XVI.

Mode of Extraction in English Equity Procedure, its Incongruities, . 482

CHAPTER XVII.

Mode of Extraction in English Ecclesiastical and Admiralty Courts, its Incongruities, ... 492

CHAPTER XVIII.

Incongruities of Roman Law in respect of the Extraction of Evidence, . . 499

CHAPTER XIX.

Of Confrontation, under the Roman Law, 501

CHAPTER XX.

Recapitulation, ... 504

BOOK IV.

OF PREAPPOINTED EVIDENCE.

CHAPTER I.

Of Preappointed Evidence in General.

§ 1. Preappointed evidence, what? Topics for discussion enumerated, . . 508
2. Objects or ends of preappointed evidence—cases to which it is principally applicable, ... ib.
3. Advantages and inconveniences incident to preappointed evidence, . 510
4. Means employed—formalities, . 512

CHAPTER II.

Of Instruments of Contract in general.

§ 1. Uses of preappointed evidence as applied to contracts, ... 513
2. Formalities in use in the case of contracts, ... 515

CHAPTER III.

Of the Enforcement of Formalities in the case of Contracts.

§ 1. Absolute nullity, in general an improper means of enforcement, . . 517
2. Means of ensuring the notoriety of the formalities, and of the consequences of their non-observance, . . 521
3. Note of suspicion, a proper substitute to nullity, ... 523

CHAPTER IV.

Formalities, what proper, and in what cases.

§ 1. In what contracts ought scription to be required? . . . . page 525
2. Use of attesting witnesses—a notary should be one, ... ib.
3. Use of a notary for securing the propriety of the contract, . . 526
4. Honorary notaries proposed, . . 529

CHAPTER V.

Of Wills, as distinguished from other Contracts.

§ 1. Utility of wills, deathbed wills included, 530
2. By requisition of formalities, if peremptory, more mischief is produced than prevented, ... 532
3. Use of autography in wills—recommendations in relation to it, . 535
4. On the attestation of wills, . . 537
5. Distinction between regular wills and wills of necessity, ... 541
6. Aberrations of English law in regard to the authentication of wills. Examination of the Statute of Frauds, in so far as relates to wills, ... 542

CHAPTER VI.

Of preappointed Evidence, considered as applied to Laws, ... 551

CHAPTER VII.

Of Public Offices at large, considered as Repositories and Sources of Preappointed Evidence.

§ 1. Official evidence, what? Topics for discussion, ... 553
2. Uses derivable from official evidence, 554
3. Sources of trustworthiness and untrustworthiness in the case of official evidence, ... 556
4. Rules for estimating and securing trustworthiness in the case of official evidence, ... 559

CHAPTER VIII.

Of Official Evidence, as furnished by Judicial Offices.

§ 1. Uses of the official evidence furnished by judicial offices, . . . 561
2. Neglect of English judges and legislators in regard to this kind of preappointed evidence, . . . 564

CHAPTER IX.

Of Preappointed Evidence, considered as applied to legally-operative Facts at large.

§ 1. Use of registration, as applied to legally-operative facts, ... 565
2. Facts calling for registration, what? ib.
3. Registration, by whom performable? 567
4. How to secure the verity of the evidence thus provided? . . 569

CHAPTER X.

Of the Registration of Genealogical Facts; viz. Deaths, Births, and Marriages.

§ 1. Uses of registration as applied to genealogical facts, ... 570
2. Aberrations of English law in regard to the registration of genealogical facts, 573

CHAPTER XI.

Of Offices for conservation of Transcripts of Contracts.

§ 1. Uses of transcriptitious registration as applied to contracts, . . *page* 575
2. Mode of adapting the system of transcriptitious registration to its uses, 576
3. Limits to the application of the practice of transcriptitious registration, 580
4. Importance of reducing within compass the matter to be transcribed—aberations of English practice in this respect, ... 581

CHAPTER XII.

Of the Principle of Preappointed Evidence, as exemplified in the case of Real *Evidence (Evidence from Things,)* 582

RATIONALE

OF

JUDICIAL EVIDENCE.

PREFACE.

The papers, from which the work now submitted to the public has been extracted, were written by Mr. Bentham at various times, from the year 1802 to 1812. They comprise a very minute exposition of his views on all the branches of the great subject of Judicial Evidence, intermixed with criticisms on the Law of Evidence as it is established in this country, and with incidental remarks on the state of that branch of law in most of the continental systems of jurisprudence.

Mr. Bentham's speculations on Judicial Evidence have already been given to the world, in a more condensed form, by M. Dumont, of Geneva, in the "Traité des Preuves Judiciaires," published in 1823: one of the most interesting among the important works founded on Mr. Bentham's manuscripts, with which that "first of translators and *rédacteurs*," as he has justly been termed, has enriched the library of the continental jurist. The strictures, however, on English law, which compose more than one-half of the present work, were judiciously omitted by M. Dumont, as not sufficiently interesting to a continental reader to compensate for the very considerable space which they would have occupied. To an English reader — to him at least who loves his country sufficiently well to desire that what is defective in her institutions should be amended, and, in order to its being amended, should be known — these criticisms will not be the least interesting portion of the work. As is usual in the critical and controversial part of Mr. Bentham's writings, the manner is forcible and perspicuous. The occasional obscurity, of which his style is accused, but which in reality is almost confined to the more intricate of the theoretical discussions, is the less to be regretted, as the nature of the subject is of itself sufficient to render the work a sealed letter to those who read merely for amusement. They who really desire to possess useful knowledge do not grudge the trouble necessary to acquire it.

The task of the Editor has chiefly consisted in collating the manuscripts. Mr. Bentham had gone over the whole of the field several times, at intervals of some length from one another, with little reference on each occasion to what he had written on the subject at the former times. Hence, it was often found that the same topic had been treated two and even three times; and it became necessary for the Editor to determine, not only which of the manuscripts should supply the basis of the chapter, but likewise how great a portion of each of those which were laid aside might usefully be incorporated with that which was retained. The more recent of the manuscripts has in most cases been adopted as the groundwork, being generally that in which the subjects were treated most comprehensively and systematically; while the earlier ones often contained thoughts and illustrations of considerable value, with passages, and sometimes whole pages, written with great spirit and pungency. Where these could conveniently be substituted for the corresponding passages in the manuscript chosen as the basis of the work, the substitution has been made. Where this was thought inexpedient, either on account of the merit of the passages which would thus have been superseded, or because their omission would have broken the thread of the discussion, the Editor (not thinking himself justified in suppressing anything which appeared to him to be valuable in the original) has *added* the passage which was first written, instead of *substituting* it for that which was composed more recently. From this cause it may occasionally be found in perusing the work, that the same ideas have been introduced more than once, in different dresses. But the Editor hopes that this will never prove to be the case, except where either the merit of both passages, or the manner in which one of them was interwoven with the matter preceding and following it, constituted a sufficient motive for retaining both.

The plan of the work having been altered and enlarged at different times, and having ultimately extended to a much wider range of subjects than were included in the original design, it has not unfrequently happened that the same subject has been discussed incidentally in one book, which was afterwards treated directly in another. In some of these cases the incidental discussion has been omitted, as being no longer necessary; but in others, it contained important matter, which was not to be found in the direct and more methodical one, and which, from the plan on which the latter was composed, it was not found possible to introduce in it. In such cases, both discussions have usually been retained.

The work, as has been already observed, not having been written consecutively, but part at one time, and part at another, and having always been regarded by the author as an unfinished work, it has sometimes (though but rarely) occurred, that while one topic was treated several times over, another, of perhaps equal importance, was not treated at all. Such deficiencies it was the wish of Mr. Bentham that the Editor should endeavour to supply. In compliance with this wish, some cases of the exclusion of evidence in English law, which were not noticed by Mr. Bentham, have been stated and commented upon in the last chapter of the book on Makeshift Evidence, and in two chapters of the sixth part of the book on Exclusion.* He has likewise subjoined to some of the chapters in the latter book, a vindication of the doctrines which they contain, against the strictures of an able writer in the Edinburgh Review. A few miscellaneous notes are scattered here and there, but sparingly: nor could anything, except the distinctly expressed wish of the Author, have induced the Editor to think that any additions of his could enhance the value of a work on such a subject, and from such a hand.

For the distribution of the work in Chapters and Sections, the Editor alone is responsible. The division into Books is all that belongs to the Author.

The original manuscripts contained, under the title of Causes of the Exclusion of Evidence, a treatise on the principal defects of the English system of Technical Procedure. This extensive subject may appear not to be so intimately connected with the more limited design of a work which professes to treat of Judicial Evidence only, as to entitle a dissertation upon it to a place in these pages. On examination, however, the parenthetical treatise was thought to be not only so instructive, but so full of point and vivacity, that its publication could not but be acceptable to the readers of the present work: and the additional bulk, in a work which already extended beyond four volumes, was not deemed a preponderant objection, especially as the dissertation, from the liveliness and poignancy with which it exposes established absurdities, gives in some degree a relief to the comparative abstruseness of some other parts of the work. It stands as the eighth in order of the ten books into which the work is divided.

A few of the vices in the detail of English law, which are complained of both in this book and in other parts of the work, have been either wholly or partially remedied by Mr. Peel's recent law reforms; and some others may be expected to be removed, if the recommendations of the late Chancery Commission be carried into execution. The changes, however, which will thus be effected in a system of procedure founded altogether upon wrong principles, will not be sufficient to render that system materially better: in some cases, perhaps, they will even tend to render it worse; since the *malâ fide* suitor has always several modes of distressing his adversary by needless delay or expense, and these petty reforms take away at most one or two, but leave it open to him to have recourse to others, which, though perhaps more troublesome to himself, may be even more burdensome to his *bonâ fide* adversary than the former. Thus, for instance: in one of the earlier chapters of Book VIII. the reader will find an exposure of one of those contrivances for making delay which were formerly within the power of the dishonest suitor; I mean that of groundless writs of error. Mr. Peel has partially (and *but* partially) taken away this resource, and the consequence, as we are informed, has been, not that improper delay has not been obtained, but that it has been obtained by way of demurrer, or by joining issue and proceeding to trial; either of which expedients (though perhaps somewhat less efficacious to the party seeking delay) are equally, if not more, oppressive in the shape of expense to the party against whom they are employed, than the proceedings in error.

The truth is, that, bad as the English system of jurisprudence is, its parts harmonize tolerably well together; and if one part, however bad, be taken away, while another part is left standing, the arrangement which is substituted for it may, for the time, do more harm by its imperfect adaptation to the remainder of the old system, than the removal of the abuse can do good. The objection so often urged by lawyers as an argument against reforms, "That in so complicated and intricate a system of jurisprudence as ours, no one can foretell what the consequences of the slightest innovation may be," is por-

* The Editor has not thought it necessary to consult, on the state of the existing law, any other authorities than the compilations of Phillips, Starkie, and others. These works were sufficiently authoritative for his purpose; and if the state of the law be such, that even those experienced lawyers can have misunderstood it, this simple fact proves more against the law than any remarks which the Editor can have grounded on the misconception.

fectly correct; although the inference to be drawn from it is, not (as they would have it to be understood) that the system ought not to be reformed, but that it ought to be reformed thoroughly, and on a comprehensive plan; not piecemeal, but at once. There are numerous cases in which a gradual change is preferable to a sudden one; because its immediate consequences can be more distinctly foreseen. But in this case, the consequences even of a sudden change can be much more easily foreseen than those of a gradual one. Whatever difficulties men might at first experience (though the difficulties which they would experience have been infinitely exaggerated) in adapting their conduct to a system of procedure entirely founded on rational, and therefore on new, principles, none are more ready than lawyers themselves to admit that still greater difficulty would be felt in adapting it to a system partly rational and partly technical.

For such a thorough reform, or rather reconstruction of our laws, the public mind is not yet entirely prepared. But it is rapidly advancing to such a state of preparation. It is now no longer considered as a mark of disaffection towards the state, and hostility to social order and to law in general, to express an opinion that the existing law is defective, and requires a radical reform. Thus much Mr. Peel's attempts have already done for the best interests of his country; and they will in time do much more. A new spirit is rising in the profession itself. Of this the recent work of Mr. Humphreys, obtaining, as it has done, so great circulation and celebrity, is one of the most gratifying indications. The reform which he contemplates in one of the most difficult, as well as important branches of the law, is no timid and trifling attempt to compromise with the evil, but goes to the root at once.* And the rapidity with which this spirit is spreading among the young and rising lawyers, notwithstanding the degree in which their pecuniary interest must be affected by the removal of the abuses, is one of the most cheering signs of the times, and goes far to show, that the tenacity with which the profession has usually clung to the worst parts of existing systems, was owing, not wholly to those sinister interests which Mr. Bentham has so instructively expounded, but in part at least, to the extreme difficulty which a mind conversant only with one set of securities feels in conceiving that society can possibly be held together by any other.

It has appeared to the Editor superfluous to add one word in recommendation of the work. The vast importance of the subject, which is obvious to all men, and the consideration that it has now for the first time been treated philosophically, and by such a master, contain in themselves so many incitements of curiosity to every liberal mind, to every mind which regards knowledge on important subjects as an object of desire, that volumes might be written without adding to their force.

* It may not be impertinent here to remark, that the suggestions of Mr. Humphreys, admirable as they are, have received most valuable improvements from Mr. Bentham's pen. —See an article in the *Westminster Review*, No. XII. (reprinted in this collection.)

[At an interval of more than ten years from the first publication of this work, the original Editor feels that an apology is due from him for the air of confident dogmatism perceptible in some of his notes and additions, and for which he can only urge the palliation of their having been written in very early youth—a time of life at which such faults are more venial than at any other, because they generally arise, not so much from the writer's own self-conceit, as from confidence in the authority of his teachers. It is due, however, to himself to state, that the tone of some of the passages in question would have been felt by him, even then, to be unbecoming, as proceeding from himself individually: he wrote them in the character of an anonymous Editor of Mr. Bentham's work, who, in the trifling contributions which the author desired at his hands, considered (so far as mere manner was concerned) rather what would be accordant with the spirit of the work itself, and in Mr. Bentham admissible, than what would be decorous from a person of his years and his limited knowledge and experience. His name was subsequently affixed, contrary to his own strongly expressed wish, at the positive desire of the venerable author, who certainly had a right to require it.]

December 1837.

⁂ The notes of the Editor of the original Edition are distinguished from other annotations by the word "*Editor*" being printed at full length.

PROSPECTIVE VIEW.

Before entering on the perusal of the following work, it may afford some satisfaction to the reader to understand, from a general intimation, the nature and extent of the information which he may expect from it.

The results may be comprised in three propositions: the one, a theorem to be proved; the other two, problems to be solved.

The theorem is this: that, merely with a view to rectitude of decision, to the avoidance of the mischiefs attached to undue decision, no species of evidence whatsoever, willing or unwilling, ought to be excluded: for that although in certain cases it may be right that this or that lot of evidence, though tendered, should not be admitted, yet in these cases the reason for the exclusion rests on other grounds; viz. avoidance of vexation, expense, and delay. The proof of this theorem constitutes the first of the three main results.

To give instructions pointing out the means by which what can be done may be done towards securing the truth of evidence: this is one of the two main problems, the solution of which is here attempted. The solution of it is the second of the three main results.,

To give instructions serving to assist the the mind of the judge in forming its estimate of the probability of truth, in the instance of the evidence presented to it; in a word, in judging of the weight of evidence: this is the other of the two main problems which are here attempted to be solved. The solution of it constitutes the third of the three main results.

Of these propositions, the first, which is the only one of the three by which an opinion is announced, can scarce have failed to present to the mind of the professional lawyer the idea of novelty, and not of simple novelty only, but of paradox. Of my own country I speak in the first place; and the observation may, without much danger of error, be extended to every other of the most highly enlightened nations. Many and extensive are the masses of evidence against which an inexorable door is shut by obligatory rules. But, of the masses of evidence thus excluded, the composition is more or less different as between nation and nation.

As to the third problem,—to give instructions for judging of the truth of evidence,—so far as the proposition contained in the leading theorem is contradicted by authoritative practice, the solution of this problem is rendered unnecessary. An exclusion put upon a lot of evidence saves all discussion respecting the degree of weight to be allowed to it. Shut the street door in a man's face, you save the trouble of considering the degree of attention that shall be shown to him in the house.

Objections, the effect of which (if allowed in that character) is to exclude the testimony of a witness altogether, are in the language of English law styled objections to his *competency*.

Translated, then, into the language of English law, the following is the import of the first of the three propositions:—In the character of objections to competency, no objections ought to be allowed.* Willing or unwilling, witnesses of all descriptions ought to be heard: the willing not to be excluded on any such grounds as those of imbecility, interest, or infamy; the unwilling not to be excused on any such ground as that of their unwillingness, either established or presumed; not even in any such cases as those of family-peace-disturbing, trust-betraying, self-convicting or accusing, self-disgracing, or in any other way self-prejudicing evidence.

Of the matter contained in any English law-book bearing the word Evidence on its title-page, a principal part consists of references to decisions by which objections to evidence have been either allowed or disallowed in the character of objections to competency. In the character of objections to competency, so far as the proof here given of the first of the three above-mentioned propositions were deemed satisfactory, they would be disallowed, all of them, in the lump.

But even in this case, the experience and reflection which dictated the allowance given to those objections in judicial practice, would not be altogether lost. Disallowed in the character of objections to competency, there is not one of them (those only excepted, in which the exclusion turns on the ground of unwillingness) that would not be to be allowed in the character of an objection to credit—to credibility. And it is in this character that they will afford so much matter to be employed in the solution of the latter of our two problems: they will serve in the framing of the rules or instructions for estimating the weight of evidence.

In stating the dispositions of the English jurisprudence on the subject of evidence, there will be occasion to lay down and establish the following propositions:—

1. That the system, taken in the aggregate, is repugnant to the ends of justice: and that this is true of almost every rule that has ever been laid down on the subject of evidence.

2. That it is inconsistent even with itself; and in particular, that there is not a rule in it which is not violated by a multitude of exceptions or counter-rules, which are observed in cases in which the reason of the rule so violated applies with as much force as in the cases where it is observed.

3. That this inconsistency has place, not only as between rule and rule, but as between period and period: between the system observed in former periods, and the system observed in later periods.

4. That, consequently, the objections drawn from the topics of innovation, subversion, &c.

* Understand, so far as rectitude of decision is the only object. If on any other ground any exemption be established, it will be on that of delay, vexation, or expense; viz. on the supposition, that the certain mischief flowing from one or more of these sources will be more than equivalent to the contingent mischief apprehendible from the danger of wrong decision, in consequence of the exclusion of the evidence.

do not bear, in the present case, against the introduction of a rational and consistent system: inasmuch as reasonable dispositions might be substituted, in many if not most cases, by the mere adoption of the exceptions, to the exclusion of the general rule.

5. That the fittest hand for introducing improvement into this branch of legislation, would be that of the legislature.

6. But that it might be introduced even by the judicial authority, without that inconvenience which would attend the making changes by this authority in the texture of the substantive branch of the law. The exclusive rules relative to evidence belong to the adjective branch of the law: the effect of them is to frustrate and disappoint the expectations raised by the substantive branch. The maintenance of them has this effect perpetually: the abolition of them, even though by the judicial power, would have no such effect, but the contrary.*

If the discovery of truth be the end of the rules of evidence, and if sagacity consist in the adaptation of means to ends, it appeared to me that, in the line of judicature, the sagacity displayed by the sages of law was as much below the level of that displayed by an illiterate peasant or mechanic in the bosom of his family, as, in the line of physical science, the sagacity displayed by the peasant is below the sagacity displayed in the same line by a Newton. No peasant so stupid as to use a hundredth part of the exertion to put it out of his own power, for his own benefit and that of his family, to come at truth and to do justice within the circle of his family, as what have been employed by those sages to put it out of their power to discover truth and do justice for the benefit of their fellow-subjects within the circle of the state.

Such were the reflections that presented themselves to an uninformed, but happily a new and uncorrupted understanding, on the opening of the grand fountain of legal instruction on the subject of evidence, the work of the Lord Chief-Baron Gilbert.

At the distance of half a century, the first conceptions of youth have been submitted to and confirmed by the cautious scrutiny of riper years. The result of that scrutiny is now submitted to the public eye.

It appeared to me, that no private family, composed of half a dozen members, could subsist a twelvemonth under the governance of such rules: and that, were the principles from which they flow to receive their full effect, the utmost extravagance of Jacobinism would not be more surely fatal to the existence of society than the sort of dealing, which in these seats of elaborate wisdom calls itself by the name of justice. That the incomprehensibility of the law—a circumstance which, if the law were wise and rational, would be the greatest of all abuses—is the very remedy which in its present state preserves society from utter dissolution; and that, if rogues did but know all the pains that the law has taken for their benefit, honest men would have nothing left they could call their own.

Such was the prospect that presented itself to me on my entrance upon this branch of moral science. I had come warm to it from the study of physical science. I had there seen the human mind advancing with uninterrupted and continually accelerated progress towards the pinnacle of perfection: facts wanting, but, by the unmolested and even publicly assisted industry of individuals, the deficiency continually lessened, the demand continually supplied: the faculty, the organ, of invention sound, and by wholesome exercise increasing in vigour every day: errors still abundant enough, but continually and easily corrected, being the result not so much of prejudice as of ignorance: every eye open to instruction, every ear eager to imbibe it. When I turned to the field of law, the contrast was equally impressive and afflicting.

Plowden, one of the heroes of jurisprudence, of the growth of the sixteenth century, was a deserter from one of those professions which are built on physical science: he flourished towards the latter part of the reign of Elizabeth. From the report of a cause relative to a mine, he took occasion to unfold to the eyes of his brethren of the long robe the wonders of mineralogy: a *terra incognita*, as strange to them as America had been to their immediate progenitors. "The theory of mineralogy," said he, "is to the last degree a simple one. In sulphur and mercury, the Adam and Eve of the mineral creation, the whole tribe of metals behold their common parents. Are they in good health? the two perfect metals, gold and silver, are the fruits of their embrace. Do they labour under any infirmity? the effects of it are seen in the imperfect metals, their imperfect progeny."

It rests with the reader to judge, whether the principles of mineralogy as delivered by Plowden, are more absurd in comparison of the principles of the same science as delivered by Lavoisier, than the principles of the law of evidence as delivered by Gilbert, and practised by the infallible and ever-changing

* The terms, *adjective* and *substantive*, applied to law, are intended to mark an important distinction, first pointed out to notice by this author; viz. the distinction between the commands which refer directly to the ultimate ends of the legislator, and the commands which refer to objects which are only the means to those ends. The former are, as it were, the laws themselves; the latter are the prescriptions for carrying the former into execution. They are, in short, the rules of procedure. The former, Mr. Bentham calls the substantive law; the latter, the adjective.—*Editor.*

line of succeeding sages, will be found when compared, I will not say to the truest principles, but to the rules unconsciously conformed to in the humblest cottages.

The peasant wants only to be *taught*, the lawyer to be *untaught:* an operation painful enough, even to ordinary pride; but to pride exalted and hardened by power, altogether unendurable.

Supposing all this to be true — supposing the law of evidence to be in so bad a state, all the world over, as it has here been represented, so incompetent on every occasion to the discovery of truth, so incompetent therefore, on every occasion, to the purposes of justice, — how could things have gone on as they have done? how could society have been kept together? Such are the observations that would be apt enough to present themselves on this occasion to an acute and discerning mind.

The answer is — that, all the world over, what has been done by the law towards the preservation of society, has, on this ground, as on so many other grounds, been done, not so much by what the law is in itself, as by the opinion that has been entertained of it. But as the conception, such as it is, that non-lawyers have had it in their power to obtain, and have been accustomed to entertain of it, has been derived from the only source from which it could have been derived, viz. the account given of it by lawyers; and as, according to all such accounts, the law has at all times, and through all its changes, been the perfection of reason; such, therefore, it has in general been taken to be, by the submissive and incurious multitude. By their own experience, its imperfections must all the while have continually been exhibited to their view; but experience is not sufficient always to open the eyes that have been closed by prejudice. What their experience could exhibit to them, was the *effect:* what their experience could not exhibit to them, was the *cause.* The effect, the sufferings themselves, that resulted to individuals from the imperfections of the law, were but too indubitable: but the cause to which they were imputed, was the invincible and irremediable nature of things, not the factitious and therefore remediable imperfections of the law. The law itself is perfect: this they heard from all quarters from whence they heard anything about the matter: this they heard at all times, and on all occasions, from the only men who so much as pretended to know anything about the matter.

The law is an Utopia — a country that receives no visits, but from those who find their account in making the most favourable report of it.

All this while the violations of justice have been continual. But had they been ever so much more frequent, they would scarcely have contributed more effectually than they have hitherto done, to lay open the real state of the case, the true cause of the mischief, to the public eye. To individuals, that is, to the suffering party in each case, and his immediate connexions, the suffering produced by those violations was more or less acute: but even to the individual who suffered, his own suffering, considering the source it was seen to flow from, scarce presented itself in the character of a grievance. To the public at large, it could never have presented itself in any such character: because, to the public at large, it has always been impossible to know anything about the matter. To lawyers, the suffering has all along been known, and fully known: but to lawyers, how, in the nature of men and things, has it been ever possible that it should have presented itself in the character of a grievance? What sensation is ever produced in the breast of an angler, by an impaled and writhing worm? in the breast of a butcher, by a bleeding lamb? in the breast of an hospital surgeon, by a fractured limb? in the breast of an undertaker, by the death of a father or mother of an orphan family? If a fly were to be put on the hook, in a month when a worm is the proper bait — if the lamb were to be cut up into uncustomary joints — if, in the tying up of the stump after amputation, a three-tailed instead of a five-tailed bandage were to be employed — if, in the decorations of the coffin, the armorial bearings of the deceased were to be turned topsy-turvy — if the testimony of a duke or an alderman, exposed to the temptation of a sinister interest to the value of the tenth part of a farthing, were to be admitted, and an oppressed widow or orphan family gain their rights in consequence — if the rules established in the several professions, established with reason or against reason, were to undergo violation: — these are the incidents by which, in the several classes of professional men, a sensation would be produced; meaning always a sensation of the unpleasant kind.

In English legislation, the causes — meaning the ultimate and original causes — of the imperfections the removal of which is endeavoured at in the present work, are no other than those from which the whole swarm of imperfections with which the whole body of the law is still infested, derive either their existence or their continuance.

Inclination, power, knowledge — these three preliminary requisites concurring, the work, whatever it be — the work, how useful soever, how arduous soever, is accomplished. Any one of them failing, it remains unaccomplished; the accomplishment of it is impossible. And in so far as any one of them fails, in so far must the accomplishment, should it have proceeded to a certain length, remain imperfect.

For a work which is at once so arduous and laborious, adequate inclination cannot be looked for with any rational prospect of success, unless it have been committed to some workman, and he a competent one, under the character of a duty.

A duty, be it what it may, will never be fulfilled, any farther than it is the interest of each person concerned in the work, to do that which is his duty.

Apply these well known and undisputed and indisputable principles to the work in question — the removal of the imperfections in question, as well as all other imperfections of the law.

Of the three altogether indispensable requisites, power — power in quantity and quality altogether adequate, cannot be denied to be in existence. It is the only one of the three that is.

As to inclination, and, in the first place, as to duty: what is every man's business is no man's business; what is every man's duty in name, is no man's duty in effect. Among the sharers of legislative power — that power being supreme, and the sharers in it collectively irresponsible — legislation, *i. e.* the proposition of laws, is to each one a right, to no one a duty.

Taking the whole body of the laws together, or with an exception made of this or that particular branch of it, — were the imperfections ever so much more numerous and pernicious than they are, there is not that individual to whom any one can say with justice — "The fault is in you; you have been neglectful of your duty."

It not being to any effectual purpose the duty, still less is it the interest, of any one alive. With or without knowledge, there exists not, nor in the present state of things can exist, that man whose interest it can be said to be.

Were it the interest of every individual in the whole community, that interest would in each instance be worse than unavailing, if in any instance it were found to exist undirected by the requisite stock of appropriate knowledge.

One class of men there is, by whom the stock of knowledge, appropriate to this purpose, is completely monopolised and engrossed. There is not one of them whose interest acts towards the accomplishment of this most arduous of all possible works: there is not one in whom the force of interest does not act in direct opposition to it. Of all those who have any concern of any kind with the established system, there is not one who would be a gainer by its being better than it is; there are few, very few, who would not be gainers by its being worse than it is

Yet, as often as a proposition, of the smallest or of the greatest moment, but more especially of the greatest, is presented to the legislature, a question put at the outset is, Has it the approbation of the gentlemen of the long robe? If silence, or an answer in the negative, is the result, down drops the proposition dead-born, and a mixture of contempt and indignation, instead of respect and good-will, is the return made to the proposer.

What is more, how ample soever the stock of knowledge may be that is to be found among the exclusive possessors of the appropriate knowledge necessary to the work, in quality it would yet be found far indeed from being adequate. The stock in hand is adapted to its intended purpose, but is not suitable to this other purpose.

In regard to such arrangements as may in the course of the following work be brought to view in the character of remedies to the abuses of which the existing system is composed, two general observations may be found applicable — two observations respecting the reception they may naturally expect to meet with from the two different classes of persons of which the public is composed.

To a non-lawyer, in proportion as an arrangement of this sort appears conducive and necessary to the ends of justice, it will be apt to appear needless. So perfect the system, can it have failed to make provision — the best provision which the nature of things admits of, for the attainment of those ends? The best possible provision — which is as much as to say, either the proposed arrangement, if it be a good one, or one still better.

To a lawyer, in the same proportion, it will accordingly appear odious and formidable. Conscious that no such arrangement is established — conscious that not so much as the semblance of an equivalent, much less any preferable substitute, is established — conscious, if his own horn-book be not completely strange to him, that these abuses are the stuff of which it is made, that to the mischief with which these abuses are pregnant, it contains nothing that is, or can be, or was ever intended to be, a remedy, — the light in which it will be his business to represent the remedy, represent it with the best possible effect to the non-lawyer, and therefore, if possible, to himself, will be that of a wild, fanciful, visionary arrangement, — too alien from practice, and therefore too bad or too good — no matter which, either character will serve — to be a practicable one.

On the present occasion, his task, however, will not be altogether an easy one: for in the arrangements which will be proposed in the character of remedies, there is nothing, or next to nothing, that is not in practice, everywhere and every day, before his eyes. Extension, it will be seen, is all they stand in need of.

BOOK I.—THEORETIC GROUNDS.

CHAPTER I.

ON EVIDENCE IN GENERAL.

EVIDENCE is a word of relation: it is of the number of those which in their signification involve, each of them, a necessary reference to the import expressed by some other; which other must be brought to view at the same time with it, or the import cannot be understood.

By the term evidence, considered according to the most extended application that is ever given to it, may be, and seems in general to be, understood, any matter of fact, the effect, tendency, or design of which, when presented to the mind, is to produce a persuasion concerning the existence of some other matter of fact—a persuasion either affirmative or disaffirmative of its existence.*

Of the two facts thus connected with each other, the latter may, for the purpose of expressing the place it bears in its relation to the other, be distinguished by the appellation of the *principal* fact, or matter of fact: the other, by that of the *evidentiary* fact, or matter of fact.†

Taking the word in this sense, questions of evidence are continually presenting themselves to every human being, every day, and almost every waking hour. of his life.

Domestic management turns upon evidence. Whether the leg of mutton now on the spit be roasted enough, is a question of evidence; a question of which the cook is judge. The meat is done enough; the meat is not done enough: these opposite facts, the one positive, the other negative, are the principal facts—the facts sought: evidentiary facts, the present state of the fire, the time that has elapsed since the putting down of the meat, the state of the fire at different points during that length of time, the appearance of the meat, together with other points perhaps out of number, the development of which might occupy pages upon pages, but which the cook decides upon in the cook's way, as if by instinct; deciding upon evidence, as Monsieur Jourdan talked prose, without having ever heard of any such word, perhaps, in the whole course of her life.

The impression, or something like an impression, I see in the grass—the marks of twisting, bending, breakage, I think I see in the leaves and branches of the shrubs—the smell that seems to present itself to my nostrils—do they afford sufficient evidence that the deer, that the enemy, I am in chase of, have passed this way? Not polished only, but even the most savage men—not human kind only, but even the brute creation, have their *rules*—I will not say, as Montesquieu would have said, their *laws*—of Evidence.‡

If all *practice*, much more must those comparatively narrow branches of it, which are comprehended under any such names as those of *art* and *science*, be grounded upon evidence.

Questions in natural philosophy, questions in natural history, questions in technology in all its branches, questions in medicine, are all questions of evidence. When we use the words *observation*, *experience*, and *experiment*, what we mean is, facts observed, or supposed to be observed, by ourselves or others, either as they arise spontaneously, or after the bodies in question have been put, for the purpose, into a certain situation.

Questions even in mathematics are questions of evidence. The facts, the evidentiary facts, are feigned; but the question concerning the inference to be drawn in each instance, from the feigned existence of the evidentiary facts, to the existence of the facts sought—the question whether, in the way of analogy, the supposed evidentiary facts afford a sufficient ground for being *persuaded* of the corresponding existence of the principal facts—is not the less a question of evidence. The matter of fact, which, presented to the mind in one point of view, is called by this one name, is it the *same* matter of fact which, when presented in another point of view, is called by this other name? Do two and two make four? and for example, the two apples on the right-hand side of the table, added to the two apples on the left-hand side of the same table, are they the same apples, and the same number of apples,

* In the word evidence, together with its conjugates, *to evidence*, *evidencing*, *evidenced*, and *evidentiary*, the English language possesses an instrument of discourse peculiar to itself; at least as compared with the Latin and French languages. In those languages the stock of words applicable to this purpose is confined to the Latin verb *probare* and its conjugates: a cluster of words with which the English language is provided, in addition to those which, as just observed, are peculiar to itself.

† When the persuasion, if any, which is thus produced, is complete, and at its highest point, the principal fact may, in a more expressive way, be termed the fact proved: the evidentiary, the probative fact. But of this pair of appellatives, the range occupying but a point in the scale, the use will, comparatively speaking, not be frequent.

‡ Esprit de Lois, L. I. ch. I.

that constitute all the apples now lying before me upon the table? In this question of identity — in this question of nomenclature disguised under scientific forms, we see a question of evidence.*

The first question in natural religion is no more than a question of evidence. From the several facts that have come under my senses relative to the several beings that have come under my senses, have I or have I not sufficient ground to be persuaded of the existence of a being distinct from all those beings — a being whose agency is the cause of the existence of all these, but whose separate existence has never at any time, by any perceptible impressions, presented itself, as that of other beings has done, to the cognizance of the senses?

Evidence is, in every case, a means to an end — a particular branch or article of knowledge, considered in respect of its subserviency towards a course of action in which a man is called upon to engage, in the pursuit of some particular object or end in view.

In the case of a branch of science — physical science — cultivated by a private individual, that object may be the producing some physical effect, whether of a customary or of a new complexion; or perhaps nothing more than the general advancement of the science — the making an addition to the mass of knowledge, applicable in common to the production of useful effects, customarily produced, or newly discovered, as it may happen.

On this ground, a great part of the business of science in general may be resolved into a research after evidence. The usefulness of it, with reference to the interests of mankind in general, will be in proportion to that of the department of science to which it belongs, and to the place it occupies in that department.

When the conduct to which the evidence in question is subservient — the conduct for the guidance of which the facts in question, and the knowledge obtainable in relation to them, are searched after — when the conduct thus at stake is the conduct of government as such — of men occupied, on the occasion in question, in the exercise of the powers of government, — the importance of the evidence, and of the conduct pursued in relation to it, take a proportionate rise.

In the map of science, the department of judicial evidence remains to this hour a perfect blank. Power has hitherto kept it in a state of wilderness: reason has never visited it.

In the few broken hints which, in the form of principles, may be picked up here and there in the books of practice, little more relevant and useful information is to be found, than would be obtainable by natural philosophy from the logicians of the schools.

The present work is the result of an attempt to fill up this blank, and to fill it up with some approach towards completeness. Not the minutest corner has been left unexplored: the dark spots have not been turned aside from, but looked out for.

Among the subjects here treated of are several concerning which not any the slightest hint is to be found in any of the books of practice.

Should this endeavour be found successful, it may be regarded as a circumstance not disadvantageous to the science, that the survey of the subject happened to be postponed to so mature a period in the history of the human understanding. So much the less rubbish to clear away: so much the less prejudice to contend with.

Should it happen to this work to have readers, by far the greater part of the number will be composed of those for whose use it was not intended — those to whom, were it not for the predilection produced by professional interest in favour of the best customer, Injustice, and her handmaid Falsehood, — justice and injustice, truth and falsehood, would be objects of indifference.

The class of men for whose use it is really designed, is a class composed as yet of those, among whom a personal or other private interest, hostile to that of the public, will prevent it, if not from finding readers, from finding other than unwilling and hostile readers — readers whose object in reading the work will be, to consider by what means, with the fairest prospect of success, the work and the workman may be endeavoured to be crushed.

The species of reader for whose use it was really designed, and whose thanks will not be wanting to the author's ashes, is the legislator; the species of legislator who as yet remains to be formed — the legislator who neither is under the dominion of an interest hostile to that of the public, nor is in league with those who are.

* The difference, in respect of evidence, between questions of mathematics and questions of purely experimental science — of chemistry, for example—is merely this: that the evidence applicable to the former, is that description of evidence which is founded upon general reasoning; while the evidence applicable to the latter, is evidence of that description which is derived immediately from matters of fact, presenting themselves to our senses. To point out the peculiar properties of these two kinds of evidence, and to distinguish them from one another, belongs rather to a treatise on logic than to a work like the present; which, considering evidence almost exclusively in regard to its connexion with judicature, excludes all general speculations which have no immediate bearing upon that subject.—*Editor.*

CHAPTER II.

OF EVIDENCE CONSIDERED WITH REFERENCE TO A LEGAL PURPOSE; AND OF THE DUTIES OF THE LEGISLATOR IN RELATION TO EVIDENCE.

So much for evidence in general; evidence taken in the largest sense of the word, condered under every modification, — of the subject to which it may come to be applied — of the nature of the fact sought, — the fact, to the proof of which it may come to be applied. Hereafter, the only sense in which the word is used, is that in which the application of it is confined to juridical, or say legal, evidence.

Under this limitation, then, evidence is a general name given to any fact, in contemplation of its being presented to the cognizance of a judge, in the view of its producing in his mind a persuasion concerning the existence of some other fact — of some fact by which, supposing the existence of it established, a *decision* to a certain effect would be called for at his hands.

To give execution and effect throughout to the main, or substantive, branch of the body of the law, is, or ought to be, the main positive end or object of the other branch, viz. the adjective, or that which regulates the system of judicial procedure.*

Of the system of procedure, one principal part is that which regards the presentation, or say exhibition, of the *evidence* — the delivery, and receipt or extraction, of the *evidence*.

Preparatory and necessarily antecedent to every operation, or series of operations, by which execution and effect are given to an article of substantive law, is judgment, decree, decision.

Whatever be the decision by which a cause or suit at law is, as to all except execution, terminated, this decision has for its subject-matter two constantly concomitant points or questions: the point or question of *law*, and the point or question of *fact*.

So far as regards the question of fact, the decision, in so far as it is just, depends upon and is governed by the evidence.

Judicature, like all the other operations of government, consists in rendering a service to some person or persons: to the plaintiff, if the decision be in his favour; to the defendant, if in his.

The service rendered by the judge to the plaintiff, by a decision in favour of the plaintiff's side of the cause, consists, according to the nature of the demand, either in putting him in possession of some right, or assemblage of rights; or in administering to him satisfaction in respect of some wrong or wrongs, whether in the shape of compensation to himself, or of punishment to the wrongdoer.

The service rendered by the judge to the defendant, by a decision in favour of the defendant's side of the cause, consists in exonerating him of the obligation sought to be imposed upon him by the plaintiff's demand.

The state of the facts, as well as the state of the law, being such as to confer on the plaintiff a title to such or such a right, or to satisfaction on the score of such or such a wrong, — if evidence, and that of a sufficient degree of *probative force* to satisfy the judge, of the existence of the necessary matter of fact, be wanting, — the law, in that instance, fails of receiving its due execution and effect; and, according to the nature of the case, injustice in the shape of non-collation † of rights where due, non-administration of compensation where due, or non-administration of punishment where due, is the consequence.

If either the state of the facts, or the state of the law, fails of being such as to confer on the plaintiff a title to the service demanded by him as above, injustice to the prejudice of the defendant's side would be the consequence, were the judge to impose upon him the burthensome obligation to which it is the object of the plaintiff to subject him. And so far as his title to an exemption from such obligation is constituted by a matter of fact, so far it depends upon evidence: and if, such matter of fact having on the occasion in question been in existence, the evidence necessary to satisfy the judge of its existence be wanting, so far injustice, as above, is the consequence of such want of evidence.

Hence arises one natural and proper object of the legislator's care; viz. to see that the necessary evidence be *forthcoming*.‡

---

* See *antea*, p. 17, note.

† By collation of rights, Mr. Bentham means that species of service which the judge renders to any person by putting him in possession of a certain right. Non-collation of rights has place when that service is not rendered — when the person in question is not put in possession of the right.

So, collative facts are those facts which have been appointed by the legislator to give commencement to a right: thus, under English law, in the case of the right to a landed estate, collative facts are, a conveyance executed in a particular form, a devise, and the like: in the case of the rights of a husband over a wife, and *vice versâ*, the collative fact is the ceremony of marriage; and so on. Collative facts are also sometimes called by Mr. Bentham *investitive* facts.

In like manner, *ablative*, or *divestitive* facts, are those which take away rights: as in the case of property, gift or sale to another party: in the case of several of the rights of a father over his child, the child's coming of age, &c. &c. — *Editor*.

‡ There are many other judicial purposes for which it is necessary that things and persons should be forthcoming, besides that of being presented to the judge in the character of sources

But if the effect of such evidence as comes to be presented to the judge be to produce in his mind a material and decisive deception, viz. the persuasion of the existence of some matter of fact which was not in existence — the consequence of such persuasion being an unjust decision to the prejudice either of the plaintiff's side, or of the defendant's side, as above — the effect of such fallacious evidence may be the same as that which might have been produced, as above, by the failure, the want, the deficiency of evidence.

Hence arises another natural and proper object of the legislator's care; viz. guarding the judge against the deception liable to be produced by fallacious evidence.

Subordinate to this object, are the following two: — 1. To give instructions to the judge, which may serve to guide him in judging of the probative force of evidence; 2. To take securities that the evidence itself shall possess as great a degree of probative force, in other words, shall be as *trustworthy* as possible.

The properties which constitute trustworthiness in a mass of evidence, are two: correctness and completeness.

The property that presents itself in the first place as desirable on the part of an aggregate mass of evidence is — that, as far as it goes, it be correct; that the statement given in relation to the matter of fact in question, be as conformable as possible, at least in respect of all material circumstances, to the facts themselves. In proportion as it fails of possessing the perfection of this property, in the same proportion will the mass of evidence fail of attaining the maximum of trustworthiness — in the same proportion will be the danger of deception and consequent misdecision on the part of the judge.

First desirable property in an aggregate mass of testimony, *correctness*.

Another property, the desirableness and essentiality of which is no less obvious on the part of an aggregate mass of testimony, is that of being *complete:* that the statements of which it consists comprehend, as far as possible, and without omission, the aggregate mass of all such facts, material to the justice of the decision about to be pronounced, as on the occasion in question really had place.

Let the aggregate mass of evidence be deficient in respect of completeness, its correctness, instead of a cause of trustworthiness, may be a cause of the opposite quality: instead of a security against deception and consequent misdecision, it may be a necessarily efficient cause of these undesirable results.*

Applied to evidence, the term *incompleteness* designates different objects, according as it is applied to a single lot or article of evidence, such as the testimony of a single individual, or to a body of evidence considered in the aggregate. In the latter case, the body may be rendered incomplete, either by incompleteness on the part of any one or more of the articles of which it is composed, or by the entire absence of any one or more of the articles which might and ought to have entered into the composition of it.

Neither incompleteness nor incorrectness have any tendency to produce deception any farther than as *partiality* is the accompaniment or the result: but unless in the rare and just imaginable case, where the incompleteness and incorrectness operate on both sides, and in such manner as to produce on each side a diminution of probative force exactly equal — partiality, intended or unin-

of evidence. The subject of Forthcomingness, therefore, belongs to the general subject of Procedure. And as the arrangements necessary to secure the forthcomingness of persons and things to serve as sources of evidence, do not differ from those which are necessary to secure their forthcomingness for any other judicial purpose, they do not properly form part of the subject of the present work. — *Editor.*

* Suppose two witnesses, both veracious and correct; the testimony of each, of a nature to belong to the head not of direct, but of circumstantial evidence: the facts which Primus is enabled to prove, none but what are of a nature to afford inductions, which, if admitted, and standing alone, will be decisive in favour of the plaintiff's side: the facts which Secundus is enabled to prove, none but what are of a nature to afford inductions decisive in like manner in favour of the defendant's side. Suppose now the testimony of Primus received, while that of Secundus is not received, or *vice versâ*, the consequence is obvious.

Suppose again but one witness, veracious and correct as before, having two facts to state, of the nature of circumstantial evidence, as before, but one of them of a nature to afford, supposing it to stand alone, inductions decisive in favour of the plaintiff's side: the other of a nature to afford, in like manner, inductions alike decisive in favour of the defendant's side. By situation and personal character, moral and intellectual, the witness, being subjected to examination, is disposed to state with perfect correctness whatsoever facts the questions propounded to him appear to call for, but no others. Examined by the judge, the questions put to him are such, whether by design or inadvertence, as to draw from him those facts alone which are favourable to the plaintiff's side, or those facts alone which are favourable to the defendant's side: in either case, the consequence is as obvious as before.

Instead of being put by the judge, suppose that the questions propounded to him are selected and put by the plaintiff only, or by the defendant only: the alternative brought to view in the case of the judge — the alternative of design or inadvertence, has, in this case, no longer any place: that such facts alone as are favourable to the plaintiff's side will be fished for by the plaintiff's questions, is too natural a state of things not to be reckoned upon as certain: and so, *vice versâ*, in the defendant's case.

tended, to the prejudice of one or other side, will always be the result.

To the qualities of correctness and completeness, impartiality could not with propriety have been either substituted or added: not substituted, because the intimation conveyed by it would be an intimation rather of the state of the deponent's mind than of the quality of his evidence; not added, because the intimation conveyed by it would be that of an imperfection distinct from both: whereas, supposing the evidence neither incorrect nor incomplete, neither can the evidence itself be other in its tendency than impartial, nor is the state of the deponent's mind material to the purpose.

Again: the operations necessary to the presentation of the evidence to the senses and cognizance of the judge, are in every instance unavoidably attended with a certain degree of inconvenience, in one or more of three shapes; viz. delay, vexation, and expense. If in any instance it should happen, as in many instances it may and does happen, that the relative magnitude and weight of this inconvenience is such as to render it preponderant over the mischief of whatever chance there may be that injustice, as above, may be produced for want of the evidence; on that supposition, it is better that the evidence in question be not presented, than that it should be presented.

And here we see a third natural and proper object of the legislator's care, viz. guarding against the production of inconvenience in the shape of delay, vexation, or expense; — to wit, in so far as such inconvenience is either superfluous, or, in comparison with the mischief attached to the injustice resulting from the exclusion of the evidence, preponderant.

Vexation and expense being incident to the presentation of evidence, legal powers adapted to that purpose will be requisite: in every case, powers of the compulsive kind, operating by means of punishment; and, in some cases, powers of the alluring or attractive kind, operating by means of the matter of reward.

To arm the judge with powers of this description, applicable to the nature of this case, will thus constitute a specific object of the legislator's care, referable to the general head above brought to view; viz. securing the forthcomingness of evidence. But this being among the operations that fall under the head of procedure, belongs not to the present work.

A condition necessarily previous to any determinate operation directed to the causing of this or that article or source of evidence to be presented to the cognizance of the judge, is the knowledge, or at least the conjectural conception, of its existence. Of evidence, the existence of which is not known at the outset of the suit, the existence may sometimes be discovered in the course of it. Either immediately, or with the intervention of any number of links, one article of evidence may lead to the discovery and to the successful investigation of another.

To arm the judge, and, through the medium of the judge, the parties on either side, with the powers necessary to the investigation of evidence, constitutes accordingly another natural and proper specific object of the legislator's care, subordinate to the same general object—securing the forthcomingness of evidence. But this likewise must be referred to the subject of procedure, not coming within the design of the present work.

In contemplation, and for the eventual support, of a right or rights already created and conferred, or considered as about to be created and conferred, the providence of individuals, and in some instances of government itself, is in use to create or appoint a correspondent and appropriate species of evidence, which, in consideration of such its destination, may be distinguished by the general denomination of *preappointed* evidence.

To favour the institution of this useful species of evidence, constitutes another specific object of the legislator's care, subordinate to the same general head — securing the forthcomingness of evidence.

Under each of these several heads (those only excepted which belong more properly to the subject of Procedure) a view will be presented — in the first place, of what seems *proper* to be done in the way of legislation; in the next place, of what *has* been done in the way of legislation; including the work of which so little has been done — the work of the genuine legislator, and the work of which so much has been done — the work of the pseudo-legislator, the judge, — the judge making, as he goes, under pretence of declaring, that part of the rule of action which has the form of law.

Speculation, to whatever extent pursued, is of no value, except in so far as it has a practical purpose. In the present work, the extent to which the speculative discussions contained in it are pursued, is considerable: but the view with which they were written is altogether practical. The object was to find an answer to this question, — What ought to be the part taken by the legislator in relation to evidence?

The subject of Evidence being but a branch of the subject of Procedure, both have their foundation in one common set of principles. These principles are—the ends, the direct and collateral ends, of justice, the proper and legitimate ends of procedure: on the one hand, rectitude of decision; which may be said to have place when rights are conferred, and obligations imposed, by the judge, on those persons, and those only, on whom the legislator intended that they should be conferred and imposed: on the other hand, the avoidance of unnecessary delay, vexation, and expense. The first may be called the direct end; the three latter, the collateral ends of justice.

These ends are the ends, and the only ends, aimed at in the arrangements proposed in the course of this work. In the form of reasons for the several arrangements, their subserviency to those ends is all along brought to view. Subserviency to these ends is in like manner the standard to which the merit or demerit of the corresponding arrangements of actually established law are all along referred.

But, when tried by this standard, the arrangements of the existing systems of law being found in every part enormously, and to all appearance purposely, defective, the inquiry would, it seemed, have been imperfect, and, comparatively speaking, uninstructive, if the cause of such their aberration had not at the same time been pointed out. This cause appeared to lie in the opportunity which the authors of these arrangements had of directing them, as under the impulse of sinister interest it appears they did direct them, to the prosecution of certain false ends, and in particular their own professional and personal emolument and advantage.

To the pursuit of the legitimate ends, as far as they have been pursued, the system which may be distinguished by the name of the natural system of procedure has owed its birth; to the pursuit of the spurious and sinister ends, the technical system of procedure. Of the natural system, in every family the domestic, and in most states various courses of procedure comprehended under some such name as the summary, may afford exemplifications.

For the purpose of ascertaining what arrangements under each head promised to be most conducive to the attaiment of the ends of justice, it seemed necessary to trace up to their sources or causes the several mischiefs opposite to these ends; the evils, in the avoidance of which the attainment of those ends consisted. When on this occasion a circumstance presented itself in the character of an immediate cause of any of those evils, that immediate cause was seen to originate in a higher cause — that higher in one still higher — and so on; in some instances as high as through four or five degrees or removes. These causes presently distributed themselves into two divisions: *natural*, the original and irremediable work of nature; *factitious*, the work of human agency or omission, of human artifice or imbecility. In the factitious causes might be seen the result partly of folly, partly of improbity — of that improbity on the part of the authors of those arrangements, which consists in the pursuit of the sinister ends above mentioned.

The principal divisions of the subject being thus pointed out, it may be useful to exhibit a summary view of the topics that might be expected to be handled in a work on Evidence, but of which some belong more properly to a work on Procedure at large: others are included under the foregoing head.

1. *Examination* of deponents, — mode of conducting the examination so as to avoid producing deception on one hand, or preponderant vexation, expense, and delay on the other. See Book II. *Securities*, and Book III. *Extraction*.

2. Of the *number* of witnesses to be required.—Requiring two witnesses is excluding every witness that does not come accompanied with another. The propriety of this exclusion stands upon different ground in the two cases of *ordinary* or *casual*, and *pre-appointed*, evidence. See Book IX. *Exclusion*, and Book IV. *Pre-appointed*.

3. Of *conclusive* evidence.—Making any evidence conclusive, is *excluding* all evidence on the other side. See Book IX. *Exclusion*.

4. *Authentication* of evidence; including as well orally delivered, as ready-written, evidence. — See the Book so entitled (Book VII.)

5. *De-authentication*, or detection of unauthenticity: by this is done, in regard to authenticity, what by examination and counter-evidence is done in regard to truth. See Le Clerc's *Ars Critica*, and Book VII. as above.

6. Of *appropriate* evidence.—Under this head might come all discussions on the appositeness of evidence in relation to the terms of the instrument of *demand* or the instrument of *defence*. But the foundation of this inquiry is not in the nature of things, but merely in the technical forms of English common law. It has no place in Roman, nor even in English equity law. It belongs more properly to Procedure at large than to Evidence.

7. Of the *onus probandi:* on whom it lies. — Another title, the importance of which arises chiefly out of the imperfections of English common law; and in particular of that feature of it which forbids to draw the relation from the mouths of the parties; that is, from those who are likely to have been best acquainted with the facts. In general, the proof of all facts necessary to constitute the ground of a demand, lies upon the plaintiff, by whom the demand is made; and so upon the defendant, in the case of the defence. Any exceptions should turn upon

proportions, as between delay, expense, and vexation, on each side, arising out of the particular nature of each species of demand or defence; that is, of the matters of fact of which the ground of each is composed. This topic, too, seems to belong rather to Procedure than to Evidence.

8. Of the means of causing evidence to be *forthcoming;—i. e.* of causing persons and things, in the character of sources of evidence, to be forthcoming, and to yield the evidence of which they have the capacity to become sources.—This topic belongs clearly to the subject of Procedure.

9. Of *indicative* evidence.—Indicative evidence is a name that may be given to any evidence, in respect of its being so, not in relation to the principal fact in question, but in relation to the existence of this or that person or thing, in the character of a source, from whence evidence, which is such with relation to the fact in question, may be derived. When evidence of the fact in question is *investigated*, it is through the medium of indicative evidence. This belongs to Procedure.

10. Of *spontaneously-delivered* evidence.—Spontaneously delivered, is a name which may be given to evidence when delivered without interrogation. See Book II. *Securities*, and Book III. *Extraction*.

11. Of evidence *sine lite*.—An example of this is, where, to enable a man to receive money from an officer employed in the payment of public money, evidence showing his title must be produced. Here, as elsewhere, the object is to guard against deception in the most effectual way possible, without preponderant or unnecessary vexation, expense, and delay.*

12. Of *scientific* evidence—a name that may be given to information delivered by persons whose capacity of furnishing it is founded on skill and experience in some particular line of art and science. Persons of this description, though in English law confounded with witnesses, and, not without advantage, treated as such, are in fact a sort of assistants to the judge, and as such treated by Roman law.

In the case of Le Brun, a domestic servant, erroneously convicted of the murder of his mistress, Madame Mazel, at Paris, by a sentence of the Lieutenant-criminel, dated 18th January 1690,† mention is made of five sorts of professional persons, to whom the denomination of *experts* is applied, and of whose evidence the substance is reported. Locksmiths, to explain the nature of a master-key, known to have been in his possession, and its relation to other keys belonging to the same locks. Cutlers, to say whether there was any relation between a knife found upon the person of the defendant, and another knife which appeared to have been made use of in his committing the murder, but had been found in another place. Peruke-makers, to say whether a few hairs, that had been found in the clenched hand of the deceased, might have been the defendant's, and plucked from his head. Washerwomen, to make a comparison between the shirts and neckcloths of the defendant, and a bloody shirt and neckcloth that appeared to have belonged to the murderer, and to have been stained with blood in the course of the struggle. Rope-makers, to say whether there was any resemblance between some cords that had been found in the possession of the defendant, and a strange cord which, it was thought, might have been made use of, or provided for the purpose of the murder. All these *experts* are mentioned as having been nominated by the Lieutenant-criminel, the judge.

13. Of time and place—their influence on the subject of evidence.—The principles brought to view in an already published work,‡ will be applied to this ground, wherever necessary, in the present publication.

14. English technical writers reviewed, with a view to the method observed, and the rules laid down by them on the subject of evidence.—Comments of this description are incidentally introduced, wherever they appear to be called for by the occasion.

CHAPTER III.

OF FACTS—THE SUBJECT-MATTER OF EVIDENCE.

THE term *evidence*, as has already been remarked, is a relative term. Like other relative terms, it has no complete signification of itself. To complete the signification of it, to enable it to present to the mind a fixed and complete idea, the object to which it bears a necessary reference must be brought upon the stage. I have to produce evidence. Evidence of what? Evidence of a certain *fact* or *facts*. Facts, then, matters of fact, are the subject-matter, the necessary subject-matter of evidence: facts in general, of evidence in general. Before we come to speak of evidence in detail, it will be necessary to

* On this subject a few pages had been written by Mr. Bentham, but he had never completed the inquiry, and the manuscript in the hands of the Editor was so incomplete that he has thought it best to suppress it.

† Causes Célèbres, vol. iii. p. 309.

‡ Essai sur l'Influence des Temps et des Lieux en Matière de Législation,—published in vol. iii. of "Traités de Législation," edited by M. Dumont.—[See *Essay on the Influence of Time and Place*, &c. in Vol. I. of the present collection.]

say something of facts in general, considered as the subject-matter of evidence.

Of facts? Yes: but in what point of view considered? Not in every point of view, but in the particular point of view in which the contemplation of them is pertinent to the design and object of this treatise: not in a physical, not in a medical, not in a mathematical point of view; not in a barren, and purely speculative, logical point of view; not in any point of view, but a legal.

The facts then, or matters of fact, the species of facts, the individual facts, here under consideration, are those facts, and those only, concerning the existence or non-existence of which, at a certain point of time and place, a persuasion may come to be formed by a judge, for the purpose of grounding a decision thereupon.

Thus, then, the circle, within which the class of facts in question is comprised, presents itself as a comparatively narrow one.

In the next view that requires to be given of it, the extent of it will appear boundless. Nor indeed does it admit of any other limits than those which are set to it by the nature of the end or purpose, with a view to which the world of facts is brought thus upon the stage.

Facts, then, considered as the subject-matters of legal decision, and for that purpose of evidence, may be distinguished in the first place into *principal* and *evidentiary*.

What is meant by the words *principal fact*, and *evidentiary fact*, has been seen in a former chapter.* The question now is, what facts are to be considered principal facts, and evidentiary facts, with reference to a legal purpose.

By *principal* facts, I mean those facts, which, on the occasion of each individual suit, are the *facts sought*, for the purpose of their constituting the immediate basis or ground of the decision: insomuch that, when a mass of facts of this description, having been sought, is deemed to have been found, the decision follows of course, whether any other facts be considered as found or not.

By evidentiary facts, I mean such facts as are not competent to form the ground of a decision of themselves, nor otherwise than in as far as they serve to produce in the breast of the judge a persuasion concerning the existence of such and such other facts, of the description just given, viz. principal facts.

Here then it is that the circle expands itself, and seems to break all bounds. Under the term *principal facts*, when the mass comes to be analyzed and divided, facts of a particular description, and that a limited one, will be seen to be comprised. But under the description of *evidentiary facts*, all facts whatsoever — at least all facts that are capable of coming under human cognizance — will be seen to be included. For there is no sort of fact imaginable, to which it may not happen to serve as evidence with relation to some principal fact. It is only by the consideration of the purpose for which the mention of them is introduced, that the view we are called upon to take of them is circumscribed.†

The mass of *principal* facts, so termed with relation to judicial investigation and evidence, comes now to be dissected and spread out. The task would have been a long and laborious one, had it not already been performed for other purposes.

In a work which is already before the public,‡ the mass of facts coming directly under the cognizance of law has been thus divided: —

In the penal branch, the facts that become the subject-matter of regulation to the legislator, and thence of decision and inquiry to the judge, are —

To be proved by evidence adduced on the part of the plaintiff —	1. Facts of an inculpative, or say criminative tendency. 2. Facts of an aggravative tendency.
To be disproved by evidence on the part of the plaintiff, — or proved by evidence on the part of the defendant —	1. Facts of an exculpative, or say justificative tendency. 2. Facts of an exemptive tendency; viz. with reference to the punishment or other burthensome obligation. 3. Facts of an extenuative tendency.‖

To every distinguishable species of offence, to every modification of delinquency, belongs its separate train of principal facts, as characterized by the above distinctions.

In the non-penal branch of substantive law and procedure —

* *Suprà*, Chap. I.

† In a succeeding chapter, a distinction will come to be exhibited between what is called *direct*, and what is called *circumstantial* evidence. Direct evidence is testimony, or other evidence, applying immediately to some *principal* fact as above distinguished: circumstantial evidence is evidence applying immediately not to any such principal fact, but to some evidentary fact — to some other fact which is evidentiary with relation to such principal fact.

‡ Dumont, — Traités de Législation Civile et Penale — Paris, 1802. [See Vol. I. of the present collection.]

‖ Facts of these respective tendencies, as thus applied, are also termed *circumstances*— circumstances of inculpation, exculpation, &c.; for any fact may be a circumstance with reference to any other fact. *Circum stantia:* objects by which a given object is considered as encompassed — which are considered as *standing round* it.

To be proved by evidence adduced on the part of the plaintiff —	*Collative*, or say *investitive* facts; viz. with relation to the right which he claims to have *conferred* on him, with which he claims to be *invested*, by the decision of the judge.*
To be disproved by evidence on the part of the plaintiff, — or proved by evidence on the part of the defendant —	*Ablative*, or say *divestitive* facts; viz. with relation to the right which the plaintiff claims to have *conferred* on him: the right which can not be conferred on the plaintiff, but by imposing on the defendant the obligation correspondent to it.†

To trace the connexion between the several principal facts (whether individual facts be meant, or species of facts,) and the several evidentiary facts respectively related to them in that character, would be, practically speaking, if not strictly and literally, an endless task: at any rate, it will not be attempted here. Volumes, equal in bulk and number to those of an encyclopedia, might be written on this one subject. That the connexion between such and such classes of principal facts, and their correspondent evidentiary facts, is a subject on which it is impossible that any light should be thrown by rules or observations, is more than I would take upon me to assert. But in this case the field of inquiry is so vast, that it appears questionable whether any light which the subject could be capable of receiving from investigation or discussion, would be capable of compensating for the obscurity that would be thrown upon it by the mere quantity of the words, the accumulation of which would be necessary for the purpose. The task would at any rate be a separate one — a task perfectly dstinguishable from that of the present treatise.

Hitherto the operation of judging of the degree of connexion — of the closeness of the connexion between a principal fact and an alleged evidentiary fact, has been an operation of the instinctive class: an operation which has never been attempted to be subjected to rule, or at least to any other rules than what have been completely arbitrary and irrational. To take the business out of the hands of instinct, to subject it to rules, is a task which, if it lies within the reach of human faculties, must at any rate be reserved, I think, for the improved powers of some maturer age.

* Events, or other facts, constitutive of title.

† Events, or other facts, destructive of title.

Facts at large, whether considered as principal or as evidentiary, may be divided into classes, according to several different modes of division.

If, on the occasion of judicial procedure in general, and the evidence elicited for the purpose of it, no practical benefit were derivable from the considering facts in this point of view, and under these distinctions, the mention of them would not have found its place in this work. But the conception entertained respecting the nature of the facts, in relation to which evidence will come to be elicited, and the nature of the evidence so applied, and of the application made of it, would, without close attention to these distinctions, be inadequate, and in practice delusive.

Applying, as they will be seen to do, to every part of the field of thought and action, including that of art and science, the instruction, if any, which may be found derivable from them, will not be the less useful in practice.

Applying, as they will be seen to do, to judicial procedure, sometimes directly, sometimes through the medium of the correspondent substantive branch of law, — the utility of the mention here made of them will not be diminished by any application which may be capable of being made of it to any other portion of the field of art and science.

I. *Distinction the first.* — Facts physical, facts psychological.

The source of the division here is, the sort of beings in which the fact is considered as having its seat.

A physical fact is a fact considered to have its seat in some inanimate being: or, if in an animate being, by virtue, not of the qualities by which it is constituted animate, but of those which it has in common with the class of inanimate beings.

A psychological fact is a fact considered to have its seat it some animate being; and that by virtue of the qualities by which it is constituted animate.

Thus motion, considered simply as such, when predicated of any being, is a physical fact: true, it is an attribute of animate beings, but not in virtue of those qualities which constitute them animate, since it is equally an attribute of inanimate ones.

But if, to the word motion, we add the word voluntary, we then introduce, over and above the physical fact of the motion, another fact; viz. an exertion of the *will*, considered as preceding and causing the motion. This last fact is a psychological fact; since it is not capable of having its seat in any other than animate beings: nor in them, by virtue of any other qualities than those by which they are constituted animate.

Of these two simple facts — one a physical, the other a psychological fact — is composed the complex fact, ***voluntary motion;*** a fact of a mixed character, partly physical, and partly psychological.

The classification and arrangement of physical facts must be left to natural philosophers. The classification and arrangement of psychological facts must, in like manner, be left to metaphysicians. It may not be improper, however, to give in this place a short indication of some of the principal classes of psychological facts:—

1. Sensations: feelings having their seat in some one or more of the five senses — sight, hearing, smell, taste, and touch.

Sensations, again, may be subdivided into those which are pleasurable, those which are painful, and those which, not being attended with any considerable degree of pleasure or pain, may be called indifferent.

2. Recollections: the recollections or remembrances of past sensations.

3. Judgments: that sort of psychological fact which has place when we are said to assent to or dissent from a proposition.

4. Desires; which, when to a certain degree strong, are termed passions.

5. Volitions, or acts of the will &c.

II. *Distinction the second.* — Events, and states of things. Source of the division in this case, the distinction between a state of motion and a state of rest.

By a fact, is meant the existence of a portion of matter, inanimate or animate, either in a state of motion or in a state of rest.

Take any two objects whatever; consider them at any two successive points of time: they have, during these two portions of time, been either at rest with relation to each other, or one of them has, with relation to the other, been in motion — has in the course of that length of time changed its place.

The truth is, that, as far as we are able to judge, all portions of matter, great and small together, are at all times in motion: for in this case is the orb on which we exist, and, as far as we can judge, all others which come under the cognizance of our senses. When, therefore, in speaking of any portion of matter, rest is attributed to it, the rest ascribed to it cannot be understood in any other sense than a relative one.

Whether they or one of them be in motion, or whether both of them be at rest, any two portions of matter may be considered and spoken of in relation to one another; and in this case, the most obvious and simple relation is the relation of distance.

Thus it is, then, that, considered in the most simple state in which it can be a subject or object of consideration, a fact may be either a state of things or a motion; and under one or other of these descriptions it cannot but come.

By an event, is meant some motion, considered as having actually come about in the course of nature. Thus, whatever be the occasion, the ordinary subjects of consideration and discourse come under the general denomination of states of things, or events, or both.

The fall of a tree is an event; the existence of the tree is a state of things: both are alike facts.

An act, or action, is a name given to an event in so far as it comes to be considered as having had the human will for the immediate cause of it.

A fact, then, or a matter of fact, is either the existence of two or more things, considered, in relation to one another, as being in a state of rest during successive portions of time, — or an event: in the idea of which event, is uniformly included that of motion on the part of some portion of matter, *i. e.* a change in its relative position to, and distance from, some other portion of matter.

An act or action — a human act, a human action — is either external or purely internal. In the instance of an external act, there must of necessity be something of complication; for to the external action of the body or some part of it, must have been added an antecedent act of the will — an internal act, but for which, it would have been on the footing of those motions which are exhibited by the unanimated, and even by the unorganized ingredients in the composition of such parts of the world as are perceptible to us.

An internal act may, on the other hand, be of the simplest kind, unattended by any motion on the part of any portion of matter exterior to the individual whose act it is.

It being understood, that it is to the mind that it is ascribed and attributed, the term motion may still be employed in the designation of it, although, in what happens in the mind upon the occasion in question, no change of place can be observed; for, in speaking of what passes in the mind, we must be content, for the most part, to employ the same language as that which we employ in speaking of what passes in and about the body, or we could not in any way make it the subject of discourse.

III. *Distinction the third.*—Facts positive and negative.

In this may be seen a distinction, which belongs not, as in the former case, to the nature of the facts themselves, but to that of the discourse which we are under the necessity of employing in speaking of them,

In the existence of this or that state of things, designated by a certain denomination, we have a positive, or say, an affirmative fact: in the non-existence of it, a negative fact.

But the non-existence of a negative fact is equivalent to the existence of the correspondent and opposite positive fact: and unless this sort of relation be well noted and remembered, great is the confusion that may be the consequence.

The only really existing facts are positive facts. A negative fact is the non-existence of a positive one, and nothing more: though, in many instances, according to the mode of expression commonly employed in speaking of it, the real nature of it is disguised. Thus, by *health*, is meant nothing more than the absence, the non-existence, of disease; by *minority*, the individual's non-arrival at a certain age; by *darkness*, the absence of light; and so on.

For satisfying himself whether, in the case of a certain fact, it is the existence or the non-existence, the presence or the absence of it, that is in question, the course a man may take is to figure to himself the corresponding image: he will then perceive whether, by the expression in question, it is the presence or the absence of that same image that is indicated and brought to view.

CHAPTER IV.

OF THE SEVERAL SPECIES OR MODIFICATIONS OF EVIDENCE.

Of evidence, as of any other sort of thing, the number of *possible* species has no other limits than what are set by the number of points of difference observable by the human mind, in the several individual objects, for the conjunct designation of which, the generic term in question is employed.

Of the species or modifications of evidence actually distinguished in the course of this inquiry, and, for the purpose of it, designated, each of them, by its appropriate name, it may be of use to give a simultaneous intimation at this early stage.

In the present work, our concern is chiefly with judicial evidence. With regard to evidence in general, as contradistinguished from judicial evidence in particular, only one distinction shall be brought to view in this place. Such others as may hereafter become needful, will be noticed as the occasion shall arise.

The evidence by which, in any mind, persuasion is capable of being produced, is derived from one or other or both of two sources: from the operations of the perceptive or intellectual faculties of the individual himself, and from the supposed operations of the like faculties on the part of other individuals at large.

For distinction's sake, to evidence of the first description, the term evidence *ab intrà* may be applied: to evidence of the other description, evidence *ab extrà*.

The modifications of which evidence *ab intrà* is susceptible, are — perception, attention, judgment, memory: imagination, a faculty little less busy than any of the others, and but too frequently operating in the character of a cause of persuasion, being excluded, as not appearing capable of being with strict propriety ranked among the modifications of evidence.

Evidence *ab extrà* has place, in so far as the persuasion has its source or efficient cause in the agency of some person or persons other than he whose persuasion is in question.

The sort of agency from which such persuasion is derived, is either *discourse* or *deportment*.*

So much for evidence in general. We have now to notice the several species into which we shall have occasion in the sequel to consider judicial evidence as divided.

Of evidence, as of every other sort of thing, the aggregate mass, considered as a whole, may, in idea, at one division, be divided into two or any greater number of parts, in any number of different directions, by divisions taken from so many sources of division: just as a field may be divided into two parts any number of times, each time by a line drawn from any point in any one of its boundaries to a different point in any other of its boundaries. So many different points to or from which the division is made, so many different sources of the several divisions thus made.

In the determination of the species of judicial evidence of which there will be occasion to make mention, in the course and for the purpose of the present work, the following are the sources of the principal divisions, of the first order, that have been made: —

1. Source of division, — nature of the source of the evidence. The species which are the result of the division made in this direction, and from this source, are — personal evidence, and real evidence. *Personal* evidence, that which is afforded by some human being — by a being belonging to the class of persons: *real* evidence, that which is afforded by a being belonging, not to the class of persons, but to the class of things.

2. Source of division, in the case of personal evidence, — state of the will, in respect of action or inaction, on the occasion on which it issues from that its source. Species resulting from the mode of division deduced from this source, — voluntary personal evidence, and involuntary personal evidence.

Voluntary personal evidence may be termed, all such evidence as is furnished by any person by means of language or discourse;

---

* Discourse comes mostly under that sort of evidence which there will be occasion to distinguish by the appellation of *direct:* deportment, serving or contributing to produce persuasion, but not operating in the way of discourse, belongs exclusively to the class of circumstantial evidence. See Book V. *Circumstantial.*

or by signs of any other kind, designed by him to perform the function, and produce the effect, of discourse. *Testimonial* is the term by which evidence of this description will henceforward be designated.

To the head of *involuntary* personal evidence may be referred all such personal evidence as, being the result, sign, and expression of some emotion, is exhibited not only not in consequence of any act of the will directed to that end, but frequently in spite of the will and every exertion that can be made of it. To this head belong, for example, all involuntary modifications of which the deportment, and all involuntary changes of which the countenance, is susceptible.

3. Being in both cases personal and voluntary, and thus testimonial, the lot of evidence in question may either have been brought into existence on the occasion of the cause in which it is exhibited, or otherwise than on the occasion of the cause. Source of division, in this case, — relation of the evidence in question, at the time of its coming into existence, to the cause, on the occasion and for the purpose of which it is produced. Species of evidence deduced from this division, — depositional testimonial evidence, and documentary evidence.

4. The signs by which, at its coming into existence, the article of evidence in question, being depositional testimonial evidence, stands expressed, — may be either of the evanescent kind (such as sounds, and those visible signs which through necessity are sometimes employed instead of these audible ones,) or permanent, such as written or printed words or figures. Source of division, — nature of the signs employed for the delivery (viz. the original delivery) of the testimony. Species of evidence deduced from this division, — oral or orally-delivered depositional testimony, and scriptitious or scriptitiously-delivered depositional testimony.

5. In the case of testimonial evidence, the subject of the testimony is either the very fact, the existence or non-existence of which is the principal matter of fact in question; or some fact which, though distinct from it, is considered as being *evidentiary* of it. Source of the division in this case, — identity or diversity of the matter of fact asserted by the deponent in the instances in question, with the principal fact in question in the cause. Species which are the result of the division made in this direction and from this source, — *direct* evidence, and *circumstantial* evidence.

All evidence which comes under the description of real evidence, is circumstantial evidence.

6. Of the lot of testimonial evidence in question, the trustworthiness or legitimately probative force will depend upon the number and efficiency of the several securities for correctness and completeness that have been or can be brought to bear upon it. If, in the instance in question, the list of these securities be complete, the article of evidence may be said to be in an ordinary degree trustworthy, and may be termed ordinary evidence: if any one or more of these securities be wanting, it will be in an inferior degree trustworthy; and, however different from one another in all other respects, the several species of evidence that agree with one another in this particular, may be comprehended, any or all of them, under the appellation of *makeshift* evidence.

7. Whatever written evidence is adduced on the occasion and for the purpose of the cause in question, was, at the time of its being brought into existence, created either *with* the design of its being employed on the occasion and for the purpose of a cause or suit, or *without* any such design. In the last case, it may be termed casually-written evidence. To this head belong private letters and memorandums. If created with the design of being employed in a cause or suit; it either was intended to be employed on the occasion and for the purpose of some *determinate* and *individual* cause or suit, or else to be eventually employed on the occasion and for the purpose of *some* suit or cause of this or that particular species, but *not* individually determined. Source of the division in this case, — determinateness or indeterminateness of the suit or cause, for the purpose of which, the article of evidence in question, being of the written kind, was brought into existence. Species which are the result of the division made in this direction and from this source, — unpreappointed written evidence, and preappointed evidence.

Thus, the affidavit of a witness, delivered in the usual way, on the occasion of a cause of any kind in which that sort of evidence is admitted, is unpreappointed evidence; since it is created with a view to be employed on the occasion and for the purpose of this particular cause. But a deed of conveyance of an estate is preappointed evidence; for it is created for the purpose of being eventually employed in *some* suit or suits, should any such happen to arise, but it is *not* created with a view to any *determinate* suit; since, at the time when it is created, it is as yet uncertain whether any suit of the particular kind in question will ever arise or not.

8. The evidence being testimonial; source of the division, — identity or diversity as between the *narrating* or *deposing* witness and the alleged and supposed *percipient* witness. Species of evidence deduced from this source, — original evidence, and unoriginal evidence.

The evidence may be termed *original*, when the deposing witness — the witness by whom, for the information of the judge, a statement is made concerning the matter of fact in question, — was the very person to whose senses the matter of fact in question did, at the time and place in question, in so far as such his deposition is true, present itself.

The evidence may be termed *unoriginal*, in so far as the narrating witness in question speaks of some *other* person, and not of himself, as the person to whose perceptive faculty the supposed matter of fact in question did, at the time and place in question, present itself.

CHAPTER V.

OF THE PROBATIVE FORCE OF EVIDENCE.

§ 1. *Ordinary degree of probative force,— what.*

Of the several objects that come within the present design, the first being the *prevention of deception*, I proceed to take a concise view of what may be proper to be done for the production of a result so essential to justice.

Deception is a relative term: judgment, regarded as false, is so regarded with relation to some other judgment taken as a standard; which standard, by the unalterable constitution of the human mind, and of the language by which its perceptions are undertaken to be expressed, can never be other than the judgment of the individual by whom the term *deception* is employed.

A mass of evidence being produced on the plaintiff's side of the cause; and on the defendant's, no matter whether a mass of counter-evidence or none (say, to simplify the matter, none;) the judge, grounding on this evidence his decision, so far as the question of fact is concerned, decides in favour of the plaintiff's side.

Taking note of this decision, and of the evidence on which it was grounded, the judgment or opinion delivered by me on the subject is, that, in this instance, *deception*, with the misdecision that has followed upon it of course, has had place.

Developed, my opinion, as expressed above, will be found to amount to this: of the body of evidence collected by the judge, the *probative force* is not, in my opinion, great enough to warrant the conclusion he has drawn from it; to wit, a conclusion, expressing his belief of the existence of the matter of fact undertaken on the plaintiff's side to be proved, viz. by the delivery of this body of evidence.

In this opinion of mine, thus declared, it is assumed and implied, as a notorious matter of fact — that the quality by which testimony or other evidence delivered by an individual in relation to a matter of fact, produces, on the part of another individual, a belief of the existence of that matter of fact, is susceptible of degrees in point of *quantity:* that in my own mind the quantity of this quality was not sufficient to produce that effect which it produced on the mind of the judge: and this being the case, it is impossible for me not to regard the judge as having, in respect of such his opinion, been deceived.*

The quantity of probative force incident to a body of evidence, is manifestly, as above explained, susceptible of degrees: and what is equally manifest is, that, to warrant a decision conformable to the tendency of the evidence, it is not necessary that the probative force of it should in every instance be at the highest degree.

To form, for the purpose of discourse, a nominal standard of comparison; let us take a mass or lot of evidence, of such a description, as, in the judgment of the ordinary run of mankind, is found sufficient (if not contradicted or otherwise counter-evidenced,) to produce a belief of the existence of the matter of fact which it asserts: and this mass of evidence, let it be the deposition of an individual taken by lot, and unknown to the judge; the witness who thus *deposes* asserting, that, in the situation of *percipient* witness, the matter of fact presented itself, under the circumstances stated by him, to the cognizance of his senses.

Let us call the probative force possessed by an article of evidence of this description, the *ordinary* degree of probative force.

What is manifest to every man is, that, by evidence of this description, belief is frequently, indeed most commonly, produced; and that, in the greatest number of cases, of the belief so produced, right judgment, and not deception, is the consequence.

Unfortunately, what is equally notorious, is, that, of belief thus produced, deception is but too frequently the consequence.

In another case, in which the quantity of probative force has been, to a certain degree, greater than it was in the one first mentioned, deception has not been so frequently the consequence.

Here, then, we have an assumed nominal standard of comparison for the probative force of evidence. A lot that comes up to this standard, but does not rise above it, is what is meant by an ordinary mass or lot of evidence:

* On an occasion of this sort, the ultimate standard of rectitude can no more be exterior to the mind in which the opinion declared is formed, in the case of the most diffident, than in the case of the most confident, of mankind. Instead of taking my own view of the matter for the ground of the opinion so declared by me, suppose me to take that of Hypercrito, the judge of appeal, superordinate to the judge first spoken of: the opinion of Hypercrito is the standard of rectitude, so far as assumed by me for that purpose: but, in pronouncing that the opinion, whatever it may have been, pronounced by Hypercrito, is right, my judgment has not assumed any standard of rectitude exterior to itself.

a mass or lot that is considered as rising above it, may be termed a mass or lot of superordinary or superior evidence: any mass or lot that is considered as falling short of it, may, in like manner, be termed a mass or lot of infra-ordinary or inferior evidence.

The greater the quantity of probative force in the mass of evidence produced on one side, deduction made of that which is produced on the other side, the more certain in the eyes of a bystander will be its effect on the mind of the judge, and the greater in the mind of the judge will be the ease and satisfaction with which the judgment of belief pronounced on the strength of it will be accompanied.

As it is the business of the legislator so to order matters, that, on each occasion, the obtainable quantity of probative force shall be as great as possible; so it is the business of the judge to be aware of all the several circumstances by which that quantity is capable either of being augmented or diminished.

§ 2. *Probative force, by what circumstances increased.*

A quantity of probative force being thus marked out for a standard, let us proceed to observe by what circumstances that quantity is capable of receiving increase and decrease.

1. One source of increase is derived from the *quality* of the supposed *percipient* or observing witness, thus standing forth in the character of a *narrating* or *deposing* witness. In the case of that witness, the probative force of whose testimony was assumed above as the standard quantity, the deponent was taken from the middle rank or level, in respect of the qualities, moral and intellectual, the union of which is necessary to trustworthiness. But, suppose that this or that visible situation or station in life (whether constituted by opulence, rank, power, or official function, or any combination of these circumstances) is by general experience found to render a man less apt, on the sort of occasion in question, to deliver a statement in any respect incorrect or incomplete, than a man of a different condition, inferior or even superior, it is not at present necessary to determine which,—here, viz. in the *quality* or *condition in life* of the person (the narrating or deposing witness,) we see one source from which the probative force of an article or mass of evidence may receive increase.

To this head belongs, and on this ground stands, whatever superior degree of credence has in practice been, or may with propriety be, given to *official* evidence in general, or to the testimony of persons invested with judicial offices in particular.*

2. Another, and a much more distinct and unquestionable source of increase, is that which is derived from the *number* of the witnesses. Here the mode of the increase being of the utmost possible simplicity, the degree of it is susceptible of mensuration, with that exactness which is the exclusive property of mathematical operations. To the testimony of what number of ordinary witnesses, the testimony of what lesser number of superordinary witnesses shall, in respect of probative force, be equivalent, it may not be easy, or indeed possible, to determine. But take the witnesses from either, or from any other level (it being the same for all of them,) the increase which the aggregate probative force of the whole mass will receive from the increase of the number will be always determinable with mathematical exactness.

Suppose that—instead of operating all on one and the same side, viz. in proof of the fact in question—the respective testimonies of a number of witnesses, all of the same level, are divided, some operating in proof of the fact, others in disproof of it: in this case, the mode of measuring the probative force will be nearly as simple, and altogether as certain, as in the former. In the former, it was the *sum* of the testimonies that was taken; in this, the *difference*.

3. Number of the witnesses, and a more than ordinary degree of presumable trustworthiness on the part of those witnesses respectively, are not the only sources of increase to the probative force of a mass of evidence. Another quarter from whence it is capable of receiving increase, and to an indefinite amount, is evidence of that sort which may be termed *real evidence*—evidence of which some object or objects belonging to the class of *things* is the source.†

§ 3. *Probative force, by what circumstances diminished.*

Circumstances, the tendency of which is to diminish the probative force of testimony, may be distinguished, in the first place, into such as regard the *source* of the testimony—such as regard the *shape* in which it is delivered—and such as regard the remoteness

---

* Unless it be a superior presumption of non-exposure to the seductive influence of sinister interest.

Persons to whose testimony, in consideration of the offices occupied by them respectively, a superordinary quantity of probative force is attributed, being placed in those offices by appointment, and that appointment previous to the point of time at which it happens to them to deliver such their testimony,—testimony of this description will be among the species of evidence to be spoken of under the head of *preappointed* evidence.—See Book IV. *Preappointed.* Chap. VII. *Official Evidence.*

† Of this, particular mention will principally be made, under the head of Circumstantial Evidence. As to written Evidence, it is nothing but personal, delivered through the medium of real evidence.

of the testimony, as delivered, from the supposed seat of perception.

I. Circumstances regarding the source of the evidence:—

The trustworthiness of a person, considered at once in the character of a supposed *percipient*, and, as such, in that of an actually *deposing* witness—in other words, the probability of *correctness* and *completeness* in his testimony, and thence its probative force—is liable to be diminished by an imperfection in the *intellectual*, or by an imperfection in the *moral* or *volitional* part of his frame. Imperfections in the intellectual part may be comprised under the head of *imbecility*, or intellectual weakness: and these apply to him in both the above characters; viz. that of a supposed *percipient*, and that of a *narrating* or *deposing* witness.

Of the circumstances tending, as above, to diminish the probative force of a man's testimony, those which regard the volitional or moral part of his frame operate by their tendency to produce, on the part of his testimony in the character of a narrating witness, a disposition to incorrectness or incompleteness.

Of these, such as tend to operate in that direction upon his will in the character of motives, are referable to the head of *interest*. viz. *sinister interest:** such as tend to dispose him to yield to the force of interest acting in that *sinister direction*, are referable to the head of *improbity*.

When, the deposition of the witness being considered as either incorrect, or as to material circumstances, incomplete, he is considered as being, at the time of his delivering it, conscious of such its incorrectness or incompleteness—such incorrectness or incompleteness is said to be the result of, or accompanied by, *mendacity;* which, according as the ceremony of an oath happens to have been applied or not, is or is not converted into *perjury*. Where, though produced by the action of sinister interest, he is considered as not being conscious of it, the imperfection is said to have *bias* for its cause.

II. Circumstances regarding the *shape* of the evidence:—

By the *shape* of the evidence or testimony, I understand the *form* or *mode* in which it is delivered on the part of the witness, received or extracted on the part of the judge.

On looking over the practice of nations and judicatories (not to speak of families) in this view, a variety of operations may be observed as having been employed in the character of *securities* or *tests*, applied to the testimony so delivered on the one part, so received or extracted on the other; *securities*, for the purpose of increasing the probability of correctness and completeness on the part of the testimony, before or during the delivery of it; *tests*, as assisting the judge in forming his judgment concerning the correctness and completeness of it, during and after the delivery of it.

Of these securities or tests, the assortment employed on each occasion constitutes the *shape*, the *form*, the *mode*, in which on that occasion the testimony is delivered, received, extracted.

In the list of them, some little difference is liable to be made by a corresponding difference in the nature of the case. This noted, any case being given, the union of the several securities, as above, applicable with advantage to that case, will constitute the *shape most proper* to be given to the evidence in that case: and, so far as *shape* is concerned, the non-application of any one of them, yet more of any greater number, or the whole number, of them, will have the effect of denominating the evidence an *inferior* sort of evidence—a sort of evidence, the probative force of which has, by the operation of that deficiency, suffered a *decrease*.

So far as the nature of the case (meaning in each instance the individual case) is such as to render the application of the several securities practicable,—so far the degree of probative force given to it depends upon the will, and is at the option of the legislator—or, under unwritten law, of the judge, in his disguised, but not the less real, character of legislator.

The person who is the source of the evidence in question, being forthcoming, or in some other way accessible and justiciable, it depends upon the legislator, and upon the judge as legislator, whether to receive or call for his testimony under the securities afforded by oath and examination together (as before a jury,) or without either (as in case of common-law pleadings,) or under oath without examination (as in case of affidavit evidence,) or under examination without oath; and the examination performed either in the oral mode, as in jury-trial, or in the epistolary mode, as in the case of a *bill in equity*.

III. Remoteness of the testimony, as delivered, from the supposed seat of perception:

In the case of the above-supposed standard lot of evidence, the testimony or statement of the fact was delivered to the ear or the eye of the judge in an immediate way, from the mouth or the pen of the deponent by whom, in the character of a percipient witness, the fact was supposed to have been observed. But, between the mouth of the percipient witness and the ear of the judge,

* Interest should to this purpose be understood in its largest and most comprehensive sense; viz. as including not only self-regarding interest, but the interest constituted by sympathy or antipathy, as towards any other persons, taken individually or in classes.

any number of mouths may have intervened; of which that one, by which the statement was conveyed, without the intervention of any other, to the ear of the judge, is the mouth of the deposing witness. For every one of these intervening mouths, the evidence, it is manifest, cannot but lose a proportionate share of its probative force. In like manner, between the pen of a percipient witness and the eye of the judge, may intervene any intermediate number of pens: like loss of force for every intervening pen as for every intervening mouth; though not in equal degree from the intervention of pens as from the intervention of mouths.

As mouths may succeed mouths, and pens pens, so may mouths and pens succeed one another in every variety of alternation. To these varieties correspond so many specific modifications of the genus of transmitted or transmissive evidence — modifications, some of which, being noticed in practice, require distinctive names.

A circumstance that contributes in a principal degree to the diminution of the probative force that takes place in the case of transmitted evidence, is, that the factitious securities applicable to the testimony of the deposing witness, do not reach nor apply to the station of the percipient witness.

It often happens, that the very fact in question has not fallen within the reach of human perception or observation. In this case, the judge is left to infer the existence or non-existence of it, from the ascertained or supposed ascertained existence or non-existence of some other fact or facts, so connected with the existence or non-existence of the principal fact as to be considered *evidentiary* with relation to it; *i. e.* as serving to prove to us the existence of it — to persuade, to satisfy us of the existence of it, with an indefinitely variable degree of force. Evidentiary facts, thus connected with the principal fact, constitute what, in the language of jurisprudence, is called *circumstantial* evidence.

In this denomination may be seen an appellation familiar, in the language of England, to lawyers, and even to non-lawyers, but not so in the language of any of the nations trained up under Roman law.

The species of evidence designated by this appellative, agrees in one respect with the above-mentioned modifications of *unoriginal* evidence, viz. in respect of remoteness from the source. In every instance, the image presented by it is the image — not of the fact itself which is in question, — but of some other fact, the tendency of which is to produce, or contribute to produce, a belief of the existence of such principal fact.

With few or no exceptions, all *real* evidence will be found to come under the head of *circumstantial:* but there is a species of evidence, which, though not properly testimonial, may yet, inasmuch as it has a person for its source, be called *personal.**

To this head may be referred *deportment,* and in some cases even *discourse.*†

CHAPTER VI.

DEGREES OF PERSUASION AND PROBATIVE FORCE, HOW MEASURED.

§ 1. *Importance of a correct form for expressing degrees of persuasion and probative force.*

PERSUASION admits of, and exists in, different degrees of strength, different degrees of intensity; for strength, force, and intensity, are here synonymous.

Of these differences, the practice of wagering affords at the same time a proof of the existence, and a mode of expression or measurement for the quantities or degrees: in which latter character it will claim, farther on, a more particular notice.

Another matter of fact not less notorious is, that by these theoretical differences and supposed degrees of difference, in whatever mode and with whatever degree of accuracy expressed and measured, human conduct is on a variety of occasions governed: instance once more the practice of wagering, and the various applications of the principles of insurance grounded on it.

Not only the persuasion of an ordinary man on an ordinary occasion, but the persuasion of a judge on a judicial occasion, is capable of existing in different degrees of strength.

Whenever a fact comes in dispute, the belief of which on the part of the judge is necessary to produce and warrant such a de-

* Any sort of circumstantial evidence, which, though it have for its source a person, serves not to convey any indication of his mind, may with more propriety be ranked under the head of real than of personal evidence: as, for instance, the appearance produced on the body of a man already dead, or still alive, by a wound, and considered as affording circumstantial evidence, indicative of the instrument or hand by which the wound was inflicted.

† A person being accused of a crime of any sort, suppose him, for argument's sake, guilty. On an occasion judicial or extrajudicial, he has joined with others in discourse, bearing in some way or other relation to the fact, the principal fact, in question. So far as what he says is regarded as true, it is of the nature of direct evidence, and comes under the denomination of confessorial evidence: so far as it is regarded as false, evasive, or in any other way tending to deception, it is of the nature of circumstantial evidence; falsehood, evasion, deception, or the endeavour to deceive, being so many evidences, presumptive evidences, of guilt, *i. e.* of the commission of the criminal act in question, whatever it be. — See Book V. *Circumstantial.*

cision as shall give effect to a right, the *first* object aimed at by the legislator ought to be, as already stated, so to order matters, that evidence of the highest possible degree of probative force in proof of that fact, shall be forthcoming: the *next* object, that the judge may always form the same estimate of the probative force of the evidence, as the legislator would do if it were possible for him to take an estimate of it.

But every element of judicature is subject to variation in quantity and degree.

In the case of circumstantial evidence, the probative force of the evidentiary fact, considered as indicative of the existence of the principal fact (which is as much as to say the strength of the persuasion produced by it,) is susceptible of every variety of degree in the bosom of the judge.

In the case of immediate testimonial evidence (setting aside the consideration of any supposed improbability of the fact stated, and any supposed imperfection in the disposition and character of the witness,) the strength of persuasion on the part of the judge will be as the strength of the persuasion expressed on the part of the witness: which is, in other words, to say, — the probative force of the testimony delivered by the witness will be exactly as, or rather will be the same thing with, the strength of the persuasion expressed by him in the delivery of it.

The strength of the persuasion expressed by the witness will, if clear of wilful falsehood, be (in so far as the means of discourse at his command admit of correctness) exactly the same in degree with the strength of the persuasion actually felt and entertained by him at the time.

But the strength of the persuasion so entertained by him is subject to be diminished in any degree by each of two causes: viz. 1. By weakness on the part of his percipient faculty, *i. e.* want of clearness and distinctness on the part of the conception formed of the fact at the time; 2. By weakness on the part of his retentive faculty — want of strength and distinctness on the part of the impression made on the memory by the first-formed conception.

Of incorrectness in one quarter, error and consequent misdecision in another is thus a natural result.

If, on comparing together the testimonies delivered by a number of witnesses — say by *three* witnesses — it appears to the judge that they joined, all of them, in regarding the existence of the fact as more probable than the non-existence of it; whereas, in truth, the force of the persuasion, when thus compounded together, lay not on that side: here an instance of misdecision will have taken place on the part of the judge; and no worse could have happened, had these testimonies been none of them forthcoming, or had they all, after joining in a tale of wilful falsehood, obtained credence for it as if it had been true.

In what has been already said, reason will probably be seen for regarding a correct mode of expressing degrees of persuasion and probative force as an object of no inconsiderable importance; and the further we go into the examination of the subject, the clearer will be the light in which the importance of it will present itself.

Unfortunately, the language current among the body of the people is, in this particular, most deplorably defective: — I know — I believe; — the fact happened so and so — I believe it happened so and so: and there the gradation ends.

Among men of law, to whichsoever of the two great schools of law belonging, nothing better is to be found.

The language of mathematicians will be seen to afford two different modes or principles.

One is perfectly correct: it is the mode of expression used in speaking of the doctrine of chances. But unfortunately it will be found not applicable to the present purpose.

Another, as applied to the present purpose, will be found incorrect. It is that which, assuming the greatest possible quantity to be a finite quantity, proceeds to divide it into parts; as a circle, which, how small soever, constitutes a whole, has, according to the usage of mathematicians, been divided into 360 degrees. Happily, incorrect as it is, its incorrectness will not be found attended with any practical inconvenience; since, on each occasion, whatever degree of correctness can on that occasion be of any use, can always be attained.

In truth, between infinite and finite, there is no medium; between the one mode and the other, there is accordingly no alternative. Of that mode which considers the greatest possible degree of probative force as being (what it really is) an infinite quantity, it will be seen that it is altogether inapplicable to the purpose of judicial decision: there remains, therefore, as the only mode applicable, that which considers it as a finite quantity, having the number of its parts limited and determinate.

Suppose a number of witnesses deposing to the principal fact in question, in the way of direct evidence — there being no need of any such inference as has a necessary place in the case of circumstantial evidence; and suppose, moreover, that no doubt has place in the mind of the judge respecting the character and disposition of any of those witnesses; whatsoever be the aggregate force of persuasion entertained by all those witnesses put together, such, of course, will be the strength of persuasion on the part of the judge.

Conceive the possible degrees of persuasion, positive and negative together, to be thus expressed:—

The degrees of positive persuasion—persuasion affirming the existence of the fact in question—constitute one part of the scale; which call the positive part.

The degrees of negative persuasion—persuasion disaffirming or denying the existence of the same fact—constitute the other part of the scale; which call the negative part.

Each part is divided into the same number of degrees: suppose ten, for ordinary use. Should the occasion present a demand for any ulterior degree of accuracy, any degree that can be required may be produced at pleasure, here, as in other ordinary applications of arithmetic, by multiplying this ordinary number of degrees in both parts by any number, so it be the same in both cases: the number *ten* will be found the most convenient multiplier. In this case, instead of 10, the number of degrees on each scale will be 100, or 1000, and so on.

At the bottom of each part of the scale stands 0; by which is denoted the non-existence of any degree of persuasion on either side—the state which the mind is in, in the case in which the affirmative and the negative, the existence and the non-existence of the fact in question, present themselves to it, as being exactly as probable the one as the other.

Such is the simplicity of this mode of expression, that no material image representative of a scale seems necessary to the employment of it.

The scale being understood to be composed of ten degrees—in the language applied by the French natural philosophers to thermometers, a *decigrade* scale—a man says, My persuasion is at 10 or 9, &c. affirmative, or at 10 or 9, &c. negative: as, in speaking of temperature as indicated by a thermometer on the principle of Fahrenheit, a man says, the mercury stood at 10 above, or at 10 below, 0.

If ulterior accuracy be regarded as worth pursuing, to the *decigrade* substitute (giving notice) a *centigrade* scale: and if that be not yet sufficient, a *milligrade.*

Three persous make their appearance in the character of witnesses in relation to the existence of the same fact: an option is given to them of three declarations, of which, one or other, in the instance of each witness, it is evident cannot but be true; viz. 1. I believe the fact exists;—2. I believe the fact does not exist;—3. I am unable to form any belief concerning the fact, whether it does exist or does not. Being asked, each of them, what number of degrees in the scale comes nearest to expressing the strength of his persuasion, it being, as already declared by each, on the affirmative side; they answer by indicating, each of them, the same number—number 1.

In these three instances, the force of persuasion is at the least amount at which it can stand on either side.

Take now, in relation to the same fact, two other witnesses; and in the instance of each of them, let the force of persuasion be at its maximum, represented as above by the number 10.

Of these two witnesses, the persuasion may be on the same side as that of the three witnesses; or it may be on the opposite side.

Suppose it on the opposite side, viz. the negative. Out of 30 degrees of persuasion which the three witnesses might have had, they have but 3; while of the 20, the utmost number which the two were capable of having between them, they have the whole.

Observe now the variation which the decision of the judge must experience, according as he has or has not the means of hearing and noting down the differences which are in every instance liable to have place in regard to the quantum of persuasion on the part of witnesses.

If, as hitherto, these differences are unascertainable (the indications afforded by character and by probability being by the supposition out of the question,) the judge can do no otherwise than decide according to the number of the witnesses—according to the difference between the numbers on each side: his decision will be—*the fact does exist.*

If, being ascertainable, these differences are ascertained, as above,—the force of persuasion on the part of the witnesses on both sides taken together, being now his guide, and beyond dispute his proper guide, his decision will be—*the fact does not exist.*

Thus much as to the station of witness: let us come now to the station of judge.

Casual modifications apart, the persuasion of the judge has for its efficient cause, the persuasion of the witness: persuasion on the part of the public at large has for its efficient cause, the persuasion of the judge.

But among three, and even as far as nineteen witnesses, in relation to the same point, the aggregate force of persuasion, it may easily happen, shall be less than among two witnesses.

In like manner among three, and even as far as nineteen judges, in relation to the same point, the aggregate force of persuasion may be less than of two other judges.

For want of an adequate mode of expression, the real force of testimony in a cause has hitherto been exposed to perpetual misrepresentations.

For want of an adequate mode of expression, the real force of judicial opinion and authority in a cause has in like manner been hitherto exposed to similar misrepresentations.*

Of a scale of this sort, supposing the use of it allowed, five things, it should seem, might be predicated, viz. —

1. That when employed, it would be employed without confusion, difficulty, vexation, or other inconvenience in any shape.

2. That, at first more especially, it would not however be in frequent use.

3. That by degrees, as the human understanding improved, the use of it would become more and more frequent.

4. But that at no time would the number of occasions calling for it (*i. e.* the number of the occasions on which, for the purpose of giving a correct expression to the degree of persuasion felt by him, the individual felt the need of such an instrument) be very considerable.

5. That the greater the importance of the cause, the more likely would the instrument be to be called into use.

Being altogether optional, all possibility of vexation is by that circumstance excluded from the use of it.

Everything of difficulty and confusion stands equally excluded: a man will not call for the scale unless he knows perfectly well how to use it—and it seems not easy for a man not to know. If he makes no use of the scale, the effect of his testimony or his suffrage is as if he had placed the index at No. 10, the highest degree in the scale: if it be his desire to make use of the scale, he places the index at No. 9, or any lower number, as he pleases.

The use of it, says the third observation, would be gradually more and more frequent.

Increased correctness, in effect, is the natural result of increase of attention: in proportion as the attention of man fixes itself closer and closer to any subject, advancement in science, as well as increased correctness in art and practice, gradually creep on. It is by increased closeness of attention that discoveries are made, and advances effected, in every path of art and science.

Old measures of every kind receive additional correctness; new ones are added to the number: the electrometer, calorimeter, the photometer, the eudiometer, not to mention so many others, are all of them so many productions of this age. Has not justice its use, as well as gas? †

* In the history of English judicature, an instance is upon record, in which a jury, finding a difficulty in settling the degree of their respective persuasions, sought for their consciences a relief, which, by men of hardened consciences, was imputed to them as a crime. The verdict, the result of the aggregate of their persuasions, was left to the decision of cross and pile. The verdict was set aside, and those who pronounced it (if I mistake not) were punished.

The state of their minds is sufficiently declared by this their act. In one thing they were agreed, viz. in finding themselves under an incapacity of forming a persuasion, an opinion, either on one side or the other. They accordingly referred the matter to a more competent judge, viz. as some would say, to Chance — as others would say, to Providence. They would not profess themselves able to form an opinion, when in truth they were not.

An expression of sincerity so decided and so novel was not to be endured by a set of men among whom the expedient of employing torture to force men to declare as their own, opinions opposite to their own, has been established in the character of a practice indispensably necessary to justice.

To a class of men by whom, in their own instance, sincerity has been cast off as a habit incompatible with profession and with office, every symptom of sincerity in others would of course be matter of ill-will and jealousy.

[There are several cases in which the circumstance of a jury deciding by lot has come under discussion. In Prior *v.* Powers, Mich. T. 16 Ch. II. "Orlaby prayed a new trial, because the jurors in Bedfordshire being divided six and six, they agreed by lot, putting two sixpences into a hat, that which the bailiff took, that way the verdict should go, which was for the plaintiff, and twopence damages: But the court denied it, because it appeared only by pumping a juryman, who confessed all; but being against himself, it was not much regarded. Also the court cannot grant new trial without punishing the jury, which cannot be by this confession against themselves." (1 *Keble*, 811.) In Hale *v.* Cove, Mich. T. 12 Geo. I. the jury having sat up all night, agreed in the morning to put two papers into a hat, and so draw lots, and their finding "happened," says the reporter, "to be according to the evidence and the opinion of the judge." The verdict was set aside. (1 *Strange* 642.) In Philips *v.* Fowler, Easter T. 8 Geo. II. the fact of the jury having determined by lot being undisputed, the same decision was given. (*Barnes* 441.) In Owen *v.* Warburton, 2d July 1804, an affidavit was produced from the foreman of the jury, to the effect that one of the jury having determined to hold out, though in a minority, was finally prevailed on to abide by the decision of lot, and that two pencils of unequal length were accordingly put into the hand of a juror, the jury consenting that their verdict should be that represented by the pencil first drawn, the long one representing one verdict, the short another. It was solemnly decided that such an affidavit could not be received. (1 *Bos. & Pul.* 326.) This precedent was followed in the Scotch case of Stewart *v.* Fraser, 10th March 1830. (5 *Mur.* 166.)—*Editor of this Edition.*]

† In the present instance, the seat and station of improvement, if the idea have any title to that name, is in language; but language, though itself the instrument of all other improvement, and standing to the full as much in need of improvement as any other instrument, is in a more particular degree averse to improvement: at least in those points of it which, not belonging, or not appearing to belong, to the demesne of any particular art or science, are conceived to belong in common to the great body of the people. Chemistry, for example, having for its subjects a multitude of things with which none are conver-

§ 2. *Application of the principle to different cases in Judicature.*

Strength of persuasion belongs to that class of *facts* which has already been distinguished by the name of *psychological* facts.* Among the properties of the facts of this description, is that of not being indicated by direct testimony, other than that of the one individual in question: under that exception, not being indicated by other than circumstantial evidence.

Of a persuasion on the one side or the other, the declaration has on various occasions been rendered matter of obligation in legal practice. But as to the force or degree of persuasion, no distinction having ever been called for on any occasion, so accordingly not on this.

The fact of the existence of a persuasion on the affirmative side, or on the negative, has been considered as being, when untrue, susceptible of being disproved; and so thoroughly susceptible, that, in case of falsity, such falsity has been deemed, and in practice constituted, a ground for punishment. In every instance of the *crimen falsi* — in every instance in which falsehood, howsoever expressed, whether by discourse or by deportment, enters into the composition of the offence — such is the case; for a false assertion is the false declaration of a persuasion in relation to some fact or facts.

On pain of eventual punishment, a man is thus continually called upon to declare persuasion, and punished in the event of his being deemed to have placed it on the wrong side of 0. But even supposing the scale of persuasion in use, it would scarcely for a long time, if ever, be deemed consistent with justice to punish him on the ground of his being deemed to have placed his persuasion at a wrong point on the right side.

In case of adverse interest striving to produce deception, there appears therefore but little if any hope, that any considerable beneficial effect could be produced by an instrument of expression, the use of which is, in the respect in question, to put the means of correct expression in men's hands.

But, happily, instances are by no means wanting in which interest is neuter; insomuch that, whatsoever be the real force of a man's persuasion, it would be on the score of interest not disagreeable, and on the score of love of justice, and other social affections, positively agreeable, to make declaration of that in preference to every other.

In the intercourse of life, and for self-regarding purposes, nothing (as hath been already intimated) is more common than for men to give expression to the force of their persuasion, and upon a principle closely analogous, to the utmost nicety. *Wagering* in all its forms, whether in the way of sport or in the way of business, under the guidance of forecasting prudence, has already been mentioned in this view.

Under the influence of a principle of action comparatively so faint, in the greater number of minds, as the love of justice, or any other modification of the social principle, equal correctness cannot reasonably be expected, since attention equally close cannot reasonably be expected. But, that everything that could be wished cannot be obtained, is no reason why that which can be obtained, should, if useful, be neglected; and by the help of a scale of persuasion, as here brought to view, it is easy to see how high a degree of correctness might be attained in this particular, in comparison of everything that has been as yet exemplified.

Apply it first to the case of a witness.

At present, when a witness has delivered his evidence, if stated in a simple manner, without any expression of doubt, it is under-

sant but those who have devoted themselves to the science, amendments of every kind, to that part of the language, are daily suffered, and received without murmur or repugnance. Not so in the case of morals: this is considered as common land, and every improvement is resisted as an encroachment: always excepted those productions of lawyer-craft which have been forced into the language of the law, beyond all power of resistance, by the combined force of coercive power and imposture.

In chemistry, the prodigious advances which the present generation has witnessed could not have been made, but for correspondent advances in the arts of method and expression — in the structure and composition of the correspondent part of the language.

This is not, by a good many, the first instance in which numbers have been employed for the designation of psychological quantities.

Among the first, if not the first of all, is that in which this mode of expression was employed by De Piles, for expressing the degrees in which, in his judgment, the several perfections desirable in a picture stand exhibited in the works of some of the most celebrated painters. These perfections being numerous, say a dozen; and the same number of degrees assigned to each, say twenty; here were twelve scales, with twenty degrees in each scale, ranged side by side, and all together constituting a sort of table.

Of the original idea thus exhibited, copies after copies have at different times made their appearance in newspapers and other periodical publications. Amongst others, I remember seeing a tabular sketch, exhibiting some of the most eminent characters amongst the judges and other lawyers of the day, with the degrees in which they were supposed to possess the several qualities which are considered as desirable in that line.

An indication given by a single judge, expressive of the degree of force with which his own persuasion applied itself to the existence of a particular fact that had presented itself to him for his decision, would be somewhat less invidious, and more useful, and would present a somewhat better title to confidence.

* See Chap. III. *Facts.*

stood of course as being at its maximum. But if any doubt or diffidence — anything tending, as supposed, to call upon the judge to make any defalcation from that maximum, is manifested, the subject is thereby thrown into a sort of confusion, in the midst of which, the language in use not affording a clue, the judge acts according to the humour or interest of the moment; and as the interest of the moment never fails to urge dispatch, chance, at the best, shares the decision of the cause with justice.

In the use of the instrument by which the point in the scale of persuasion is fixed, there need not be any greater difficulty than in the use of the dial-plate of a clock or watch, or the instruments respectively employed for reckoning at a game at billiards or a game at cribbage.

If the importance of the cause appear such as to pay for this small portion of vexation and delay, the persuasive scale is presented to the witness, with liberty and discretion to place the index either at the highest point, if that be considered as the ordinary one, or at any inferior point by which, according to his own conception, the force of his persuasion may be more accurately designated.

Apply it now to the station of judge.

In this commanding station, men are without difficulty considered as exempt from, or proof against, the action of all sinister interest — proof, at any rate, against all temptation to any such mal-practice as that of misrepresenting their own opinions.

No objection, therefore, except to the novelty and utility of it, would, in the instance of judge, stand opposed to the taking a man's own account for the inward strength of his own persuasion, and reducing the outward effect of it to a conformity with the real state of it so declared.

If the effect of such a liberty were to augment his power, the objections would be insuperable; but a man may, without much danger, be trusted with the faculty of reducing it.

In this case, be it observed, the grant of this faculty need not be confined to the question of fact: the import, or state, of the law (the import of it if in the form of statute law, the state of it if in the form of judge-made law) constitutes a no less proper subject of *persuasion* — in a word, a no less proper subject of *opinion* — than the question of fact.

Under this general head, a variety of particular cases will exemplify the utility of this instrument of accurate judicature.

Case 1. Judges divers, and the number equally divided. — In this case, the supposition acted upon is, that on the part of every one of them, the force of persuasion was at the same pitch — on the part of each of them, at its *maximum*. The instrument employed, it would turn out, perhaps, that in each of them the force of persuasion was different; on one side or other an aggregate force of persuasion clearly preponderant.*

Case 2. Appeal. — The decision become the subject of an appeal to an ulterior judicatory.

Not unfrequent are the occasions on which the real aggregate force of persuasion on the part of the original judicatory may, on just grounds, be taken into consideration by the ulterior judicatory. Suppose, for example, a question of fact, and evidence thereupon delivered *vivâ voce*. In some cases, the testimony of the witness cannot be received in the oral form on any terms by the ulterior judicatory: at any rate, by the repetition, the colour of the evidence, especially so much as is afforded by *deportment*,† is liable to be changed. To be informed of the impression made on the original judicatory by the same testimony, and in its freshest state, might on such an occasion be of considerable use.

Case 3. Pardon. — In a penal case, the judgment being a judgment of conviction, a question proposed is, whether the power of the sovereign shall be applied to the remission of it.

Among the most justifiable causes for the exercise of this power, is a doubt whether the defendant, who has been deemed guilty as above, was really so.

Sometimes the cause of such doubt is to be found in some article of information subsequently brought to light, and, in the character of evidence, sufficiently established for this purpose. But at other times, the doubt has for its cause a doubt on the part of the judicatory: on the part of some judge or judges, the persuasion entertained of the delinquency of the defendant not being at so high a pitch as, to warrant an operation to such a degree afflictive, it is conceived it ought to be. Pardon or no pardon turning in this case upon the degree of persuasion on the part of each member of the judicatory,

* In a case considered as being of importance, in English practice, shades of difference in the form of persuasion on the part of this or that judge, have not unfrequently been endeavoured to be expressed in ordinary language: matter of vague dissertation, and sometimes of secret history.

Among the many and transcendent merits of Lord Chief-Baron Comyn's matchless Digest of the Law, is the attempt to express some of those shades. *Dub.* for *dubious; semb.* for *semble, it appears*, — are among these imperfect, but still useful, approximations.

Applied to the constitution of a jury, under which torture is applied to the purpose of forcing any number of the members, from one to eleven, to deliver persuasions opposite to their real ones, a nicety of the sort above proposed will be apt, in the eyes of an admirer of everything that *is*, to appear preposterous in the extreme.

† See Book V. *Circumstantial.*

the importance of accuracy in the expression given to those several degrees is sufficiently manifest.

Even although the principle of judging from the aggregate of persuasion, instead of the number of persons persuaded, should not be adopted for judicial decision, it might for pardon.

Case 4. The same question moved elsewhere, in another judicatory and in another cause.

So far as concerns the question of fact,—unless where, being considered as having received a decision in the antecedent judicatory, that decision is considered as conclusive,—the opinion of the members of any such antecedent judicatory is not usually taken for an object of regard.

But in so far as any question of law is concerned, great anxiety is commonly testified to learn with the utmost correctness the degree of persuasion entertained in such antecedent judicatory, supposing it not subordinate with relation to the judicatory now in question.

Case 5. Punishment or satisfaction to be administered *pro modo probationum*.

A topic this, which, though it be in the Roman school, and in particular in the French form of that school, that it has received a name, is in practice not altogether disregarded in the English school. Various are the instances in which a degree of probative force, which would not be considered as sufficient to warrant conviction for the purpose of punishment, is considered, and not without reason, as sufficient to warrant a decision by which satisfaction in some shape or other is awarded. The only expression that can be given by a judge to the conception entertained by him of the degree of probative force appertaining to the evidence, being a declaration of the degree of strength of the persuasion of which it has been productive, it seems sufficiently obvious how material it is to this purpose, that a mode of expression the most correct that the nature of the case admits of, should on this occasion be capable of being employed.

Case 6. Scientific evidence.—Scientific is the denomination that, for distinction's sake, may be given to the judicial declaration of a species of functionary, in whose function the character of judge is in some sort combined with that of witness. It comes to be exercised as often as—for the guidance of the opinion of the regular judge in relation to some matter of fact, a just conception of which is considered as requiring some particular *skill*, such as falls not to the lot of all members of the community, nor in particular, unless by accident, to the lot of the regular judge,—the opinion of a person considered as being in an adequate degree possessed of the species of skill in question, is called in.

In the Roman school, this species of functionary is named by the judge, and treated on the footing of a sort of judicial officer acting under the judge.

In the English school, he is named by the party to whom it occurs to expect that an opinion extracted from that source will be serviceable to his side of the cause; and is treated on the footing of any other witness.

On whatever footing his opinion, in other words his persuasion, in relation to the matter of fact in question, is called in, it cannot be matter of doubt how beneficial it cannot but be to the interests of justice, that the means should be in his hands for giving to the expression of the degree of force of his persuasion whatsoever degree of accuracy he thinks fit.

§ 3. *Incapacity of ordinary language for expressing degrees of persuasion and probative force.*

Such, as above brought to view, are the advantages deducible from an adequate mode of expressing degrees of persuasion and probative force, supposing it to be found. If the current language were adequate to this purpose, there would be no need to look out for any other. That to this hour it remains as far from being so as it is possible for it to be, is perceived upon a general view at the first hint. But, by a particular observation or two, the nature of this penury may be rendered more distinctly perceptible.

In a word, the only adequate mode of expressing degrees of persuasion is by *numbers*. But hitherto, neither in ordinary language, nor in the scientific language of jurisprudence, have numbers been employed. The result, in point of imperfection and inadequacy, will be conspicuous.

Persuasion, the only term equally proper in all *cases*—that is, in all *degrees*—is accordingly the term that has all along been employed here.

Opinion, though in some cases capable of taking its place, is not synonymous with it; since opinion is scarcely considered as being, like persuasion, susceptible of degrees.

In addition to this term, which, comparatively speaking, is not in very frequent use, come two others, both of them in perpetual use, viz. *knowledge* and *belief*.

In ordinary discourse, applied to ordinary topics, the word *belief* seems to be applied to designate *any* degree of persuasion; and accordingly it cannot be employed to designate any one, to the exclusion of any other.

Among religionists, applied to the topic of religion, it is employed to designate the very highest degree, and to the exclusion of every other; since it is not any inferior degree that will satisfy them.

Among lawyers, on the contrary—to wit,

among English lawyers, it has been employed to designate any inferior degree of persuasion, to the exclusion of the highest.

For giving expression to the highest, what they have declared themselves to expect, is, that a witness shall either employ the forms of naked assertion — such a thing is so and so — or introduce the word knowledge. *Belief*, in certain cases, they have admitted of, recognising it as designative of an inferior degree of persuasion; but in other cases, in the character of an expression of the degree of persuasion, nothing will satisfy them but *knowledge* — a degree of persuasion above belief.

If your persuasion falls short of amounting to belief, the priest, so far as depends upon himself, consigns you to everlasting punishment in a life to come:* if it fails of mounting above belief, the man of law, the judge, consigns you, and in a manner more visibly efficient, to punishment in the present life.†

Knowledge, with its logical conjugates, comprising the verb *to know*, not only expresses the highest degree of persuasion possible, but in some circumstances expresses that highest degree of persuasion as existing in two different minds at a time. If I say — *I know that London lies to the north of Paris*, I speak of my own persuasion only; but if I say — *You* know that London lies to the north of Paris. I speak of my own persuasion as well as yours — of yours alone expressly, but of my own by implication, and that a necessary one; for were my persuasion on the subject short of the highest point, the expression would be a contradiction in terms.

In this instance, as in so many others, the *indirect* mode of assertion has the effect of expressing a stronger degree of persuasion than can be expressed by the *direct*.‡

In the language of English as well as other lawyers, a case is spoken of as *proved* — as fully proved. In regard to the state and degree of *persuasion*, and of the nature of the cause by which, on the part of the judge, it has been produced, what is understood by this expression? Answer: That, the evidence being either direct — or, if circumstantial, of that sort which is commonly received either as an equivalent or as a necessarily receivable substitute to direct — the strength of persuasion expressed by it on the part of the witness is such as (it standing unopposed either by any objection, or at least by any preponderant objection, to the trust-worthiness of the witness, or by any counter-evidence, or at any rate by counter-evidence of preponderant force) will naturally, on the part of the judge, be productive of such a degree of persuasion, in affirmation of the existence of the fact in question, as shall be sufficient to authorize and require a decision on that side.

In speaking of evidence as having been delivered in relation to the fact in question, — suppose an occasion to arise for avoiding to pronounce decidedly concerning the direction or strength of the persuasion of which it may have been productive: in this case, instead of speaking of the fact as having been proved, the usage is to speak of it as having been attested, affirmed, or denied, in or by deposition or evidence.

§ 4. *Roman school — its attempts to express degrees of probative force.*

The Romanists, in expressing their sense of the importance of giving correctness to the description tendered of the degrees of persuasion entertained in each case, betray, and in a manner confess, their incapacity of finding a solution for the problem thus proposed.

1. Full — 2. More than half-full — 3. Half-full — 4. Less than half-full: — Such, if Heineccius is to be believed, are the degrees of probative force that have been distinguished, and have received denominations, in his school of fraud and nonsense.‖

But of these distinctions the application is confined to the aggregate mass of evidence taken together — the mass produced on one side of the cause. They are not applied either to the force of persuasion on the part of the judge, or so much as to the probative force of the evidence of any one witness when considered by itself.

That they should have had any application to the probative force of the evidence of any witness taken singly, would indeed, according to the notion of that school, have been somewhat difficult: seeing that, according to what, by him, is given as the better opinion, the probative force of the evidence of any one witness, be he who he may, is equal to 0:

* English Liturgy, Athanasian Creed, &c.

† Harrison's Chancery, I. 222. Rules and Orders of the Court of Chancery, p. 99, edit. 1739. — See *infrà*, section 5..

‡ Thus, in the English language, the command intimated by that future which is expressed by the word *shall*, is more imperative, indicative of a stronger exertion of will, than the command expressed by the word to which alone the denomination of *imperative mood* has been commonly affixed by grammarians: the command expressed by *you shall pay me*, is more strongly imperative than the command expressed by the words *pay me*. By the imperative, so called, nothing more is expressed than the bias given to the will of him who speaks. By the future above mentioned, not only the existence of the will is denoted, but the futurity of the event which is the object of it, is predicted as certain; an intimation being moreover given of the event as being about to have for its cause the will that has been thus expressed. Such is the power of my will, that the event of which it seeks to be productive cannot fail of taking place.

‖ Elem. Jur. Civ. (ad Pandect.) pars iv. § 18.

insomuch that, of the party by whom any such article of evidence has been produced, and no more, the condition ought not to be better than if he had produced none at all.*

In the French form of the Roman school, another scale, of a somewhat different construction, was in use, according to M. Jousse,† in the particular case in which the cause was of that sort which, if decided against the defendant, subjected him to capital punishment, and, by way of preparation for that punishment, to torture.

1. Highest degree of probative force, the degree sufficient to warrant conviction.

2. Next highest, or second degree of probative force, the degree expressed by the words "*urgent and indubitable.*" The practical effect of this degree of probative force was sufficient to subject him to torture, with power to the judges to subject him to any punishment short of capital, if the torture, the object of which was to prevail upon him to confess whatever he was accused of, failed of producing that desirable effect.

3. Third degree of probative force, the degree expressed by the words *less than* "*most violent.*" Practical effect, subjecting him to torture, but without any such power to the judges: the torture having, when the probative force was at this degree, and not above a "purgative" quality, and that of so particular a sort, as to "*purge the proofs*" (what is meant is probably *to purge away the proofs*) whatever they may be, that have operated to his prejudice in such manner as to subject him to the torture.

§ 5. *English school—its attempts to express degrees of probative force.*

1. Positive proof—2. Violent presumption—3. Probable presumption—4. Light or rash presumption: such are the degrees of probative force that have been distinguished and denominated in the English school.

Such are the explanations that have been given as instructive by Lord Chief-justice Coke,‡ and accepted and passed off as such by Mr. Justice Blackstone.‖

At the head of this scale, under the appellation of positive proof, is designated direct evidence, however trustworthy the source: below it, circumstantial, however great its force: and to make the distinction so much the clearer, "violent presumption," we are told, "is many times equal to full proof;"—"probable presumption hath also its due weight;"—"light or rash presumptions have no weight or validity at all."

The degree of probative force indicated by the light or rash presumption of the English school, is thus exactly equal to that expressed by the half-full proof of the Roman school; each of them being equal to 0.

But the Roman school has risen to a pitch of accuracy by which the English has been left at a distance; the Romanists having a degree of force which is less than equal to 0, and which, though incapable of producing in the breast of the judge any degree of persuasion whatsoever, is still probative force.

The scale thus exhibited is a scale of probative force abstractedly considered—considered without distinction made as to the quantity and composition of the evidence to which the probative force is considered to belong.

It has accordingly no connexion with, or reference to, that other scale above mentioned, which is a scale of persuasion merely, and of which the degrees are two, and but two, expressed by the words *knowledge* and *belief*.

No such suspicion appears to have found its way into either of these learned bosoms, as that of a connexion between any such objects as *persuasion* on the part of a *witness*, *probative force* on the part of his testimony, and *persuasion* on the part of the *judge*—all susceptible of variation on one and the same scale.

The observation of the connexion between these clearly distinguishable, though so closely connected, objects, was, as far as it goes, an observation in psychology—an observation made of the invariably observable phenomena of human nature; and it is among the characteristics of technical law learning, as of Aristotle's system of dialectics, in which his system of physics was comprised, to look down with indignant disdain on the invariably observable phenomena of human nature.

In both instances, the notion entertained of science seems to have been that it was confined to words; that it consisted in a perpetual substitution of words to words; and that—in addition to words—ideas, clear and distinct ideas, were no better than an incumbrance

1. Unqualified assertion;—2. Assertion qualified by the words "to his remembrance," or, "as he believeth:"—such are the forms of speech devised by the Earl of Clarendon when chancellor of England, for expressing two degrees of persuasion, which it seemed necessary to him to distinguish.§

---

* See Book IX. *Exclusion.* Part VI. *Disguised.* Chap. I. *Exclusion for want of multiplicity.*

The following is the passage from Heineccius, referred to p. 230, n. ‖:—Juris interpretes probationem in plenam et minus plenam, et hanc iterum in semiplenâ majorem, semiplenam, et semiplenâ minorem, dispescunt. Quamvis verius sit, ex juris Romani principiis, unius testimonium plane non admittendum esse, licet præclaro curiæ honore præfulgeat, adeoque non meliorem esse debere conditionem ejus qui semiplene, quam qui nihil, probavit."

† Ordonn. Crim. p. 375. ‡ Coke Litt. 6.

‖ Bl. Com. III. 371, chap. 23.

§ Rules and Orders of Chancery, as published by the Lord Chancellor Clarendon, and the

This second or inferior degree of persuasion is the degree which he permitted to be expressed in the case of a defendant interrogated by an instrument called a *bill in equity*, as to a matter charged as his [the defendant's] own act, in any other case than "if it be laid to be done within seven years before;" not saying before what, but probably enough meant to designate the day on which the matter of the written instrument met his eye.

But if it be laid to be done within seven years before, then it is that the proposed respondent must (on pain, it should seem, of being punished, if he persists, for *contempt*, as having put in an insufficient answer) take care not to suffer to stand as part of his answer either of those forbidden forms of speech; "unless the court, upon exception taken, shall find special cause to dispense with so positive an answer."

The circumstance by which, on this occasion, the attention of this learned person appears to have been engrossed, is the distance in point of time: among the circumstances that appear to have escaped it, are, the importance of the fact (regard being had to the situation and character of the deponent,) the differences of which that importance is susceptible, and the influence of these differences upon the memory. Another consideration, alike overlooked, seems to have been the influence of time of life upon memory, and the difference in this respect between immaturity, maturity, and caducity.

But the faculty of having recourse to the wisdom and justice of the court "*upon exception taken*," presented a solution for every difficulty, a remedy for every inconvenience; a faculty which, to the merit of being to the suitor a source of relief, added the much superior, though so little published, merit, of being, to the judge, his friends, and dependents, a source of fees.

On the present occasion, however, the mode of constructing the scale, and giving denomination to the degrees of which it is composed, constitute the proper subjects of consideration: not the application or applications made of them.

"You shall swear that what is contained in this your answer, so far as concerns your own acts and deeds, is true, and that what relates to the acts and deeds of any other person or persons, you believe to be true. So help you God." (Before commissioners,)—such is the form of the oath at present exacted of a defendant in an equity court, or, at any rate, on the equity side of the court of Exchequer.* Of two things, one: either there is something in the air of the court of Exchequer that strengthens a man's memory, and relieves it from the need of having recourse to that indulgence which has just been seen to be allowed in the court of Chancery: or the indulgence of the court has been silently withdrawn in practice, while the continuators of Mr. Harrison's book continue to represent as still in force the regulation by which it was granted.

Master of the Rolls Sir Harbottle Grimstone, without date, but at a period immediately preceding the 27th February, 19 Car. II. 1667, p. 99, edition of 1739; and quoted as subsisting in Mr. Parker's edition of Harrison's Practice of the Court of Chancery, 8th edit. 1796.

* Fowler's Exchequer, I. 421, anno 1793.

§ 6. *An infinite scale inapplicable, though the only true one.*

In respect of persuasion and probative force—persuasion, in the first place on the part of a witness, in the next place on the part of the judge—probative force on the part of the evidence, of whatsoever nature it be, direct evidence or circumstantial evidence, evidence of persons or evidence of things;—an infinite scale (it has been already intimated) is the only sort of scale by which the truth of the case can be expressed. For what can that mass of evidence be, to the probative force of which no addition is made by the addition of a mass of evidence, exactly of the same composition in every respect, and twice as great?

Unfortunately, a scale to such a degree correct would not, physically speaking, be capable of being applied to the particular purpose here in view.

The use, and only use, of the sort of scale in question, would be to enable the witness to give to his testimony, or the judge to his opinion, a less degree of effect in practice than what it is productive of without the employment of any such scale.

At present, the effect given to any such testimony in practice is as great—never less than as great—as the utmost effect of which the highest possible degree of persuasion in that single breast could be productive. On the side of augmentation, then, nothing remains to be done. The persuasion is considered as being, in every instance, at the highest degree; or at any rate, in practice, the same effect is given to it as if it were.

At the same time, many are the instances in which it may be rendered manifest beyond a doubt, that the degree of persuasion, to which in practice all the effect is given that could be given to the highest, really falls greatly below the highest degree of which the force of persuasion is susceptible.

1. In the case of the *witness*, this deficiency can scarcely be rendered manifest by any considerations of a nature to operate alike on all minds to whom they are presented: where it exists, it is matter not of demonstration, but of sensation only; viz. on the part of the witness in question, by whom alone the force

of the persuasion, of which the seat is in his own mind, can be perceived.

Even the witness, the individual himself whose persuasion is in question, — though his perception may have informed him, that, of two cases, his persuasion has been stronger in the second than in the first; still it is only by calling in the aid of numbers that it will be possible for him to declare, or so much as to settle with himself in his own mind, *how much*: of numbers, as, for instance, by saying, — in the first case it seems to me that the probability of the fact is as 2 to 1, in the second case as 4 to 1; insomuch that, were it matter of necessity to me to lay a wager on the subject, such and no more are the odds that I would lay or take in the two respective cases.

2. In the case of the judge, on the other hand, the deficiency may be rendered manifest to third persons.

On the subject of a question of fact, deposed to by a number of witnesses — the fact having nothing of improbability in its nature, nor the witnesses anything to distinguish them in point of trustworthiness, nor their testimonies respectively anything to distinguish them in respect of the degree of persuasion manifested — the degree of persuasion on the part of the judge will of course be as the number of the witneses.

This being the case, — by every witness added on the same side, an additional degree of force will be added to the persuasion of the judge: and if this be true with regard to a second and a third witness, it cannot be otherwise than true with regard to a hundredth or a thousandth.

Long before the number of witnesses has reached to the height of a hundred, the mind of the judge (it may be said) will have obtained all the satisfaction it could desire: long before this, the multitude will have appeared to him so abundantly sufficient, that he will have refused to give admission to any more.

This may, and naturally will be, the case. But should he even have refused admission to all the witnesses after the second, it will be impossible for him to deny but that, after a thousand have been heard, an addition will still be made, by any other such witness, to the aggregate probative force of the whole mass of evidence thus composed. Had he been the only witness, the testimony of this thousandth and first would of itself have been sufficient to determine the opinion of the judge. Such being the probative force of this testimony, if taken by itself, can there be any colour of reason for saying of it, that it will be destroyed by the addition of a quantity of the same force, a thousand times as great?

If such be the case while the witnesses are supposed to be all of them on the same side, still more manifestly will it be so, if, so many speaking in affirmation of the fact, so many others in negation of it, the number of them be supposed to be on each side the same. In this way, let there be two thousand of them, the probative force of the two thousand and first will be no less perceptible and efficient than if he had been the only one.

Moreover, by this same example it seems manifested, that it is not possible that the probative force of testimony, nor, therefore, that the force of persuasion on the part of the judge (to which may be added, on the part of any witness taken by himself) should, on the side of augmentation, have any certain limit. It can never be so great but that it would be capable of being rendered still greater.

In these circumstances, to allow to any person, either in the station of witness or in that of judge, the faculty of adding at pleasure to the declared force of his persuasion, would be to allow of an operation at the same time endless, useless, and ridiculous. Whatever latitude would in this respect be allowed to any one such person, would be to be allowed to every other. But the tendency of persuasion in one mind being to propagate like persuasion in other minds, and every such act of propagation being an exercise of power, the natural tendency of such an allowance would be a sort of auction, on the one part between witness and witness, on the other part between judge and judge; and in both cases, an auction that would have no end. It being of the number of those cases in which insincerity and abuse would be altogether incapable of detection, it would also be of the number of those cases in which insincerity is universal, or little short of it.

But suppose again (impossible as the supposition is,) that the highest possible degree of persuasion could, by means of such a scale, be reached and expressed, still in practice it would be useless; since no greater effect could be given to the maximum, the expression of which is the supposed result and fruit of the scale, than at present is given to the ordinary assertion, expressed in ordinary language, and without the use of any such scale. Of this simple assertion the effect is to act with the whole probative force of the testimony of the witness — with the whole force of the suffrage of the judge; and from the highest degree of persuasion, — were it possible, by the help of any such scale, to reach it and express it, — no greater effect could ensue.

From the allowance of a scale of the opposite description, limited on the side of increase (limited in effect by its being raised up, as under the present practice, to its maximum, in every case in which no scale is employed,) beneficial effects might be produced in some cases, no evil could be produced in any case.

Of the good effect, the nature has already been brought to view: the decision rendered conformable to justice, in cases in which, without the benefit of this instrument, it could not be conformable.

Abuse there could be none — insincerity there could be none: whether in the station of witness or in that of judge, a more irrefragable proof of sincerity could not be given, than by having recourse to such allowance.

By representing the force of his persuasion as lower than it is, what advantage could a man gain by the use of such a scale, more than he could gain without it?

Yes (it may be said,) a man may in this way diminish the declared force of his persuasion, and thence the probative force of his testimony, contrary to truth, and yet without risk. Placing it on the wrong *side*, the falsehood of the declaration might be proved from other sources, and he punished for it as in case of perjury: but placing it on the right side, though at the wrong end, viz. at the very bottom — at 1, when it ought to have been at the very top, viz. at 10 — he may thus, without risk, strike off nine-tenths of the force of his testimony; which defalcation, if there be many testimonies on both sides, may turn the scale.

Answer: True; in this case, he will save himself from punishment: but neither will he produce the mischief aimed at. Whatever force of counter-evidence would, in case of his placing his declared persuasion on the wrong side, have been sufficient to convict him to the purpose of punishment, the same counter-evidence will, now that he has placed it at the wrong end of the scale, though on the right side, be, notwithstanding his endeavours, sufficient to prevent the abatement thus made in the degree of persuasion declared, from producing the corresponding diminution of probative force. He will not have it in his power to cut off a part of the force of his testimony from the side of truth, except in circumstances which would have allowed him with safety to throw it entire into the scale of falsehood.

NOTE BY THE EDITOR.

M. Dumont, in a note to the *Traité des Preuves Judiciaires*, has brought forward several objections against the scale which Mr. Bentham has suggested for the measurement of degrees of persuasion and probative force. It is fair that the reader should have the means of judging for himself, what degree of validity these objections possess. I quote from a recently published and very well executed translation of M. Dumont's work. [See "A Treatise on Judicial Evidence, extracted from the MSS. of Jeremy Bentham, by M. Dumont, translated into English, 1825." 8vo. p. 45.

"I do not dispute the correctness of the author's principles; and I cannot deny that, where different witnesses have different degrees of belief, it would be extremely desirable to obtain a precise knowledge of these degrees, and to make it the basis of the judicial decision. But I cannot believe that this sort of perfection is attainable in practice. I even think, that it belongs only to intelligences, superior to ourselves, or at least to the great mass of mankind. Looking into myself, and supposing that I am examined in a court of justice on various facts, if I cannot answer 'Yes' or 'No' with all the certainty which my mind can allow, if there be degrees and shades, I feel myself incapable of distinguishing between two and three, between four and five, and even between more distant degrees. I make the experiment at this very moment; I try to recollect who told me a certain fact: I hesitate — I collect all the circumstances — I think it was A rather than B: but should I place my belief at No. 4, or at No. 7? I cannot tell.

"A witness who says, 'I am doubtful,' says nothing at all, in so far as the judge is concerned. It serves no purpose, I think, to inquire after the degrees of doubt. But these different states of belief, which, in my opinion, it is difficult to express in numbers, display themselves to the eyes of the judge by other signs. The readiness of the witness, the distinctness and certainty of his answers, the agreement of all the circumstances of his story with each other, — it is this which shows the confidence of the witness in himself. Hesitation, a painful searching for the details, successive connexions of his own testimony, — it is this which announces a witness who is not at the *maximum* of certainty. It belongs to the judge to appreciate these differences, rather than to the witness himself, who would be greatly embarrassed if he had to fix the numerical amount of his own belief.

"Were this scale adopted, I should be apprehensive that the authority of the testimony would often be inversely as the wisdom of the witnesses. Reserved men — men who knew what doubt is — would, in many cases, place themselves at inferior degrees, rather than at the highest; while those of a positive and presumptuous disposition, above all, passionate men, would almost believe they were doing themselves an injury, if they did not take their station immediately at the highest point. The wisest thus leaning to a diminution, and the least wise to an augmentation of their respective influence on the judge, the scale might produce an effect contrary to what the author expects from it.

"The comparison with wagers and insurances does not seem to me to be applicable. Testimony turns on past events: wagers turn on future events: as a witness, I know, I believe, or I doubt; as a wagerer, I know nothing, but I conjecture, I calculate probabilities — my rashness can injure nobody but myself: and if a wagerer feels that he has gone too far, he often diminishes the chances of loss by betting on the other side.

"It appears to me, that in judicial matters the true security depends on the degree in which the judges are acquainted with the nature of evidence, the appreciation of testimony, and the different degrees of proving power. These principles put a balance into their hands, in which witnesses can be weighed much more accurately than if they were allowed to assign their own value; and even if the scale of the degrees of belief were adopted, it would still be necessary to leave judges the power of appreciating the intelligence and morality of the witnesses, in order to estimate the confidence due to the numerical point of belief at which they have placed their testimony.

"These are the difficulties which have presented themselves to me, in meditating on this new method."

On these observations of M. Dumont it may, in the first place, be remarked, that if applicable at all, they are applicable only to the use of the scale by the witness, not to the use of it by the judge; which latter use, however, is perhaps the more important of the two. In the next place, even as regards the witness, I doubt whether any great weight should be attached to the objections. For, first, what almost all of them seem to imply is, that because we cannot in all cases attain the degree of exactness which is desirable, therefore we ought to neglect the means of attaining that degree of exactness which is in our power. The witness who does not know the degree of his persuasion — the witness to whom the scale would be useless — will not call for it: the judge will at all events have the same means of appreciating *his* testimony, as he has now, and will not be the more likely to be deceived by a witness who does not use the scale, because it has happened to him to have received the testimony of one who does.

Secondly, the most formidable in appearance of all M. Dumont's objections — I mean that which is contained in his third paragraph — seems to me, if it prove anything, to prove much more than M. Dumont intended. The wise (says he) will place their degree of persuasion lower than they ought, the foolish higher than they ought: the effect, therefore of the scale, is to give greater power to the foolish than they otherwise would have, and less power to the wise. But if this be true, what does it prove? That different degrees of persuasion should not be suffered to be indicated at all; that no one should be suffered to say he doubts. It is not the scale which does the mischief, if mischief there be. There are but two sorts of witnesses — the wise and the foolish: grant to them the privilege of expressing doubt, or any degree of persuasion short of the highest; and the foolish, says M. Dumont, will make no use of the privilege, the wise will make a bad use. But if so, would it not be better to withhold the privilege altogether? Is it the scale which makes all the difference?

The truth seems to me to be, that the scale will neither add to the power of the foolish witness, nor unduly diminish that of the wise one. It will not add to the power of the foolish witness; because he cannot place his persuasion higher than the highest point in the scale; and this is no more than he could do without it. It will not unduly diminish the power of the wise witness; because the wise witness will know tolerably well what degree of persuasion he has grounds for, and will therefore know tolerably well whereabouts to place himself in the scale. That he would be likely to place himself too low, seems to me a mere assumption. The wiser a man becomes, the more certainly will he doubt, where evidence is insufficient, and scepticism justifiable; but as his wisdom increases, so also will his confidence increase, in all those cases in which there is sufficient evidence to warrant a positive conclusion.

CHAPTER VII.

OF THE FOUNDATION OR CAUSE OF BELIEF IN TESTIMONY.

§ 1. *That the cause of belief in testimony is experience.*

THAT there exists in man a propensity to believe in testimony is matter of fact — matter of universal experience; and this as well as on every other occasion, and in any private station, as on a judicial occasion, and in the station of judge.

The existence of the propensity being thus out of dispute, then comes the question that belongs to the present purpose — is it right to give way to this propensity? and if right in general, are there no limitations, no exceptions to the cases in which this propensity must be admitted?

To the first question the answer is — Yes; it is right to give way to this propensity: the propriety of doing so is established by experience. By experience, the existence of the propensity is ascertained; by experience, the propriety of acting in compliance with it is established.

Established already by experience — by universal experience — it may be still further established by direct experiment, should any one be found willing to be at the charge of it. Continue your belief in testimony, as you have been used to believe in it, — the business of your life will go on as it has been used to do: withhold your belief from testimony, and with the same regularity as that with which you have been in use to bestow it, — you will not be long without smarting for your forbearance. The prosperity with which the business of your life is carried on, depends on the knowledge you have of the states of men and things; viz. of such men and such things as your situation in life gives you occasion to be acquainted with: and of that knowledge, it is but a minute and altogether insufficient portion that you can obtain from your own experience, from your own perceptions alone; the rest of that of which you have need must come to you, if it comes to you at all, from testimony.

And what is it that, by thus rendering it a man's *interest*, renders it *proper* for him to bestow a general belief on testimony? It is the general conformity of testimony to the real state of things — of the real state of things to testimony: of the facts reported upon to the reports made concerning them.

And by what is it that this conformity is made known? Answer again — By experience. It is because testimony *is* conformable to the truth of things, that, if you were to go on treating it as if it was not conformable, you would not fail of suffering from it.

And by what is it that this conformity is produced? The question is not incapable of receiving an answer; and therefore, being a practically important one, it is neither an improper nor an unreasonable one: a little further on, an answer will be endeavoured to be given.

Forasmuch as, in man, whether on a judicial occasion or on a non-judicial occasion, in a judicial station or not in a judicial station, there exists a general propensity to believe in evidence; and forasmuch as, in general, the giving way to that propensity is right, being found to be attended with consequences advantageous upon the whole; so when, — on a judicial occasion and in a judicial station, a man having received evidence has grounded his belief on it, pronounced a decision in conformity to such belief, and in the exercise of judicial power acted in conformity to such decision, — there exists on the part of men at large, failing special and predominant reasons to the contrary, a propensity to regard such belief as rightly bestowed; and to yield to this propensity also is right, and in general productive of beneficial consequences, as is also established by experience.

Ask what is the ground — the foundation — or more simply and distinctly, the efficient cause of the persuasion produced by evidence — produced by testimony? An answer that may be given without impropriety is — *experience:* experience, and nothing but experience.

Experience? — of what? Of the conformity of the facts which form the subjects of the several assertions of which testimony consists, with the assertions so made concerning these respective facts.

In the course of the ordinary and constant intercourse between man and man in private life, propositions* affirming or disaffirming the existence of this or that fact are continually uttered in a vast variety of forms. For the most part, as occasions of obtaining perceptions of and in relation to the facts in question present themselves, the perceptions thus obtained are found conformable to the description given by those assertions. Testimony being thus for the most part found true in past instances, hence the propensity to expect to find it true in any given future instance: hence, in a word, the disposition to belief.

On the other hand, in some instances, instead of such conformity, disconformity is the result presented by the surer guide, perception: hence the disposition to disbelief.

The number of the instances in which, to a degree sufficient for practice, this conformity is found to have place, is greatly superior to the number of the instances in which it is found to fail. Hence the cases of belief constitute the general rule — the ordinary state of a man's mind; the cases of disbelief constitute so many cases of exception; and to produce disbelief requires some particular assignable consideration, operating in the character of a special cause.

The disposition or propensity to belief may, in this sense, be said to be stronger than the disposition, the propensity, to disbelief. Were the proposition reversed, the business of society could not be carried on — society itself could not have had existence; for the facts which fall under the perception of any given individual are in number but as a drop of water in the bucket, compared with those concerning the existence of which it is impossible for him to obtain any persuasion otherwise than from the reports, the assertions, made by other men.

But why, it may be asked, does experience produce a propensity to believe in the truth of human assertions? — why does experience of the truth of testimony in time past, give rise to an expectation that it will be true in time to come?

Next in point of utility to the knowing o

* The word *testimony* is on this occasion avoided: the reason is, lest by that word the proposition should in any instance be considered as meant to be confined to the cases in which the assertion is supposed to be made on a judicial occasion.

a thing, is the knowing that it is impossible to be known. By the former acquisition, power, in various useful shapes, is acquired; by the latter, pain, in the shape of useless labour and frequently-recurring disappointment, is saved. The instances in which the former acquisition is attainable, are impressed upon the eye of curiosity by every object on which it alights. The other, as unacceptable as it is useful, is turned aside from, in many instances in which, upon a calm and attentive examination, it might be secured.

The relation of causality—the relation between cause and effect, is a soil in which the greatest understandings have toiled with great labour and no fruit: words, and nothing but words, having been the seed; words, and nothing but words, have been the produce.

Words being the names of things,—and, for some time, to judge from the structure of language, there having been no words but what were the names of real entities, of really existing things—as often as we take note of a distinct word, we are apt to assign to it, as an accompaniment of course, the existence of a distinct thing, a distinctly existing real entity, of which it is the accompaniment and the name; and this whether there be any such distinctly existing entity or not.*

Ask what is the foundation or cause of belief?—of persuasion? I answer, without difficulty, *experience*. Ask what is the foundation, the cause, of the belief in the truth of human testimony?—of the persuasion entertained by one man of the truth of the statements contained in the testimony of another, in any given instance? I answer again, the experience of the truth of testimony in former instances. Discard the substantive word *cause*, and give me, instead of it, the import of it in disguise—disguised under the adverbial covering of the word *why*;† and ask me why I find myself disposed, in most cases, to believe in the truth of the statements made in my hearing by my fellow-men? I answer,—because, in the greater part of the instances in which such statements have been made, the truth of them has been made known to me by experience. In the experience I have had of the truth of the like statements in past instances, I view the cause of the propensity I find in myself to believe the truth of the statement in question in the present instance—to pronounce, in my own mind, the sort of judgment indicated by the words *I believe*.

Press me further, and ask me *why* it is that, on recollection of the truth of such statements in former instances, as certified to me by experience, I believe?—ask me why it is that such experience produces belief; what is that ulterior and deeper or higher cause, that causes experience to be the cause of belief?—you ask me for that which is not mine, nor anybody's, to give; you require of me what is impossible.

It may probably enough have appeared to you that what you have been doing, in putting to me that question, amounts to no more than the calling upon me for a proposition, to be delivered to you on my part. But the truth is, that, in calling upon me to that effect, you have yourself, though in an obscure and inexplicit way—you have yourself, whether you are aware of it or no, been delivering to me a proposition—and a proposition which, if my conception of the matter be correct, is not conformable to the truth of things. The proposition I mean is, that—over and above, and distinct from, those objects which you have in view, in speaking of the words *experience* and *belief*, of which the first represents the cause, and the other the effect,—there exists a distinct object, in the character of an ulterior and higher cause, which is the cause of the causative power exercised by that first-mentioned cause: such is the proposition which is comprehended and assumed in and by your interrogative proposition beginning with the word *why*; but, to my judgment of the matter, this indirectly-advanced proposition presents itself as erroneous. For, upon looking for such supposed distinct object, as the archetype of, and thing represented by, the word cause, as now, on the occasion of this second question, employed by you, it does not appear to me that any such object exists in nature. If ever it should happen to you to have discovered any such archetype, do me the favour to point it out to me, that I may look at it and examine it. Till you have done so, it will not be in my power to avoid considering as erroneous the proposition which you have been delivering to me in disguise.

What I have been able to see in the matter is as follows, viz.—

1. Certain facts, viz. of the physical kind

* In the instances of the everlastingly occurring appellations *cause* and *power*, David Hume has pointed out the illusion flowing from this source: but that he has pointed out the constitution of human language as the source from whence the illusion flows, is not, to my conception, alike clear.

† Of the single word,—the *adverb*, as it is called,—the verb *why*, the import, when developed, is found to be an entire proposition, and even a complex one. *My will is, that you name to me that thing which is the cause of that other thing.* So great was the error of the ingenious author of Hermes, when, in his analytical view of the grammatical forms called *parts of speech*, he attributed to the object represented by the adverb, the same simplicity as to the object represented by the noun substantive. Here, by the single adverb, we find represented, amongst others, the several objects respectively represented by no fewer than six nouns substantive.

(for such alone, to simplify the case, let us take) — the facts presented to me by experience.

2. Another fact, viz. of the psychological kind, the sort of internal feeling produced in my mind, and designated by the word *belief.* Both these are really existing objects: my feeling — my belief, — an object possessing at any rate whatever reality can be possessed by an object of the psychological kind, — and those physical objects, by which it seems to me that it has been produced, or at any rate in consequence of which it has made its appearance on my mind. The aggregate of all those physical facts is what, on this occasion, I look upon as the *cause:* the feeling produced in my mind — the belief — is what I look upon as the *effect.*

What higher, what deeper, what intermediate — in a word, what other cause, would you have? What can it be? — what should it be? If, which is possible, your request were to be complied with, what would you be the better for it? Would you be any the wiser for it, the richer? or even the more contented? Alas! no: no sooner had you got this higher cause, than you would be returning again to the charge, and asking for one still higher; and so on again, without end. For, by the same reason (if there were one) by which you were justified in calling upon me for this first arbitrarily assumed and phantastically created cause, you will be justified in calling upon me, and, indeed, bound to call upon me, for another; and so another and another, without end.

By pressing me still further — between the set of physical objects, the aggregate of which is spoken of as constituting the *cause,* and the psychological object *(my belief)* spoken of under the name of the *effect,* — you may, if you insist upon it, oblige me to interpolate a number — almost any number, of intermediate causes. But among these intermediate causes, be they multiplied *ad infinitum,* you will never find that recondite, that higher seated or deeper seated cause, which you are in quest of. From the material physical objects in question, came the appearances, evanescent or permanent, issuing from those material objects: from those appearances, presenting themselves through the medium of sense to the minds of the several percipient witnesses in question, came the feelings of the nature of belief, in the minds of those several witnesses: in the minds again of those witnesses, by the agency of this or that motive, were produced the exertions by which the discourses assertive of the existence of those several objects were conveyed to me: by those assertions, thus conveyed to my mind, was produced, on each occasion, in the interior of my mind, a correspondent feeling of *belief:* by the recollection, more or less distinct and particular, or rather by an extremely rapid and consequently indistinct and general recollection of the aggregate of those feelings, or rather of an extremely minute part of them (for in one extremely minute part is contained all that is possible, and yet quite as much as is sufficient) was produced the belief which my mind entertains at present, affirmative of the existence of the facts contained in the particular statement delivered to me by the particular individual whose testimony is now in question.

Such is the chain, the links of which may be multiplied almost to infinity. Between every two links you may call upon me, if you please, for the cause by which the latter of them is connected with the former; but, in each instance, the answer, for the reason already given, must be still the same — there is no such latent, recondite cause. In your imagination, the picture of it? — yes, if you say there is: in external nature, the original of it, nowhere.

§ 2. *Objections against the principle, that the cause of belief in testimony is experience, answered.*

It is with rules of morality, and propositions in psychology, as with laws: when the indication of reasons, and these reasons grounded on experience, is regarded as unnecessary, any one man is as competent to the task of making them as any other; and, to the number and variety of them, all with equal pretension to the character of goodness, there is no end. To make good laws, requires nothing but power; to make good rules of morality, or good propositions in psychology, requires nothing but a combination of arrogance with weakness.

Thus it is, that as America — British-born America — swarms with books full of laws, Scotland swarms with books full of rules of morality, and propositions of psychology, mixed up together, and undistinguished, the propositions from the rules.

In morals, as in legislation, the *principle of utility* is that which holds up to view, as the only sources and tests of right and wrong, human suffering and enjoyment — pain and pleasure. It is by experience, and by that alone, that the tendency of human conduct, in all its modifications, to give birth to pain and pleasure, is brought to view: it is by reference to experience, and to that standard alone, that the tendency of any such modifications to produce more pleasure than pain, and consequently to be *right* — or more pain than pleasure, and consequently to be *wrong* — is made known and demonstrated. In this view of the matter, morality, as well as policy, is always matter of account. On each occasion, the task to be performed consists in collecting together the several items on both sides, and, in the instance of each item an estimate being formed of its value, regard being paid to the several elements of value,* to determine on which side — on that of pleasure or pain, of profit or loss, the difference is to be found; in a word, to strike the balance.

But to make up an account of this sort requires thought and talent: to apply the principle of common sense, or moral sense, or any other purely verbal principle, requires nothing but pen, ink, and paper. Hence it is, that as from the application made of these verbal principles—these pretences for governing and directing without reason, there can never be any fruit, so neither to the number of them need there ever be any end.

What the logic of the Aristotelian school was to physical science—that science to which for near 2000 years it officiated as a substitute — such are the sciences of morals and legislation as taught by the application of these verbal principles, to the same sciences as taught by applications made of the principle of utility: by reference, unceasing reference, to experience — experience of pain and pleasure.

In the school for Latin and Greek at Westminster, instruction in the art of making nonsense verses under that name, precedes the art of making such verses as pretend to sense. The Aristotelian logic, had it styled itself with equal candour, in its character of a substitute to experimental physics, might have styled itself *nonsense physics:* and, in like manner, and with equal justice, the ethics which consist in the application of the principle of moral sense, that is, in the repetition of the words moral sense, *nonsense ethics:* and the psychology, which points to an innate propensity as the efficient cause of persuasion, independently of, and in opposition to, experience of human correctness and incorrectness — *nonsense psychology.*

A curious spectacle enough would be, but rather more curious than instructive, to see a partisan of moral sense in dispute with a partisan of common sense, or two partisans of either of these verbal principles in dispute with one another. Let the common sense of one of them command what the moral sense of another leaves indifferent, or forbids; or let the common sense of one of them forbid what the moral sense of another leaves indifferent, or commands; or let the like conflict have place between two philosophers of the common sense, or two partisans of the moral sense. When each of them has delivered the response of his oracle according to the interpretation put upon it by itself, all argument should, if consistency were regarded, be at an end; as, at a Lincoln's-Inn exercise, where one of the pleaders has declared himself for the widow, and the other against her, the debate finishes.

In such a case, when a disagreement happens to take place (for when men talk thus at random, it can but happen to them to disagree,) if to either of them it appears in his power, and worth his while, to gain the advantage, he betakes himself for support to the only principle from which any support is to be had — to the principle of utility. But, as often as he betakes himself for support to a quarter so widely distant, so often does he desert, and by implication, by necessary implication, acknowledge the inanity of, his own principle. For if, by pronouncing the words moral sense, a man can learn what is right, what indifferent, and what wrong, in any one case, why not in every other? And if the tendency of an action to produce most pleasure or most pain be the criterion and measure of its claim to be pronounced right, indifferent, or wrong, in any one case, — in what other can it fail of being so?

But the course which hitherto men have followed, in undertaking to philosophize, to learn and to teach the science of legislation, ethics, or psychology, is this: — In the first place, under the joint direction of custom, that is, of prejudice — of interest, under whatever shape — and of unreflecting and unscrutinizing caprice, — a man makes out his list of favourite tenets. These tenets he determines to adhere to and advocate at all events: and, this determination formed, all that remains for him to devise is the form of words which, under the name of a principle, presents itself as best adapted to such his purpose.

The conclusion is, — there are two distinguishable branches of philosophy, which, as they have been taught upon the *ipse dixit* principle, confer on the science a claim above dispute to the title of the philosophy of nonsense.

1. Nonsense ethics. — This is the science taught by him, by whom an alleged propensity, on his own part or on the part of any other person or persons in any number, to approve of any sort of act, is represented as imposing on persons in general an obligation, or bestowing on them a warrant, to approve of it, and to exercise it; and, *vice versâ*, a propensity to disapprove of it, as imposing on persons in general an obligation to abstain from it, or conferring on them a licence to forbear exercising it; and this without regard to the effects of it upon the aggregate welfare of the community in question, in the shape of pain and pleasure.

2. Nonsense *pisteutics.*† — This is the sort of science taught by him, by whom an alleged

* See Dumont's "*Traités de Legislation,*" and Bentham's "*Introduction to the Principles of Morals and Legislation*" in Vol. I. of this Collection.

† From πιστευω, to believe. The reader will excuse this convenient barbarism.

propensity, on his own part or on the part of any other person or persons, to give credit to testimony (or say *assertion* or *report*) concerning any supposed fact or class of facts, is represented as imposing on the will of persons in general an obligation, or affording to their understanding a sufficient reason, to entertain a persuasion of the existence of such fact or class of facts; and this without regard to the probability or improbability of such fact or facts, as indicated by experience.

To an act of judgment, having for its subject the existence of a supposed matter of fact asserted in the way of testimony, substitute a judgment on any other subject without distinction; and nonsense *pisteutics*, receiving a proportional increase in the field of its dominion, becomes nonsense *dogmatics*.

So long and so far as science is taught upon this principle—if, where there is nothing to be learnt, the word *teaching* can be regarded as applicable,—the greater the number of books of which it becomes the subject, so much the further are the readers, (supposing the number of the readers, and their expense in the article of attention, to increase with the number of the books,) from making any advances in true knowledge.*

When, by a consideration of any kind, a man is determined to maintain a proposition of any kind, and finds it not tenable on the ground of reason and experience,—to conceal his distress, he has recourse to some phrase, in and by which the truth of the proposition is, somehow or other, assumed.

Thus, in the moral department of science: having a set of obligations which they were determined to impose upon mankind, or such part of it at any rate as they should succeed in engaging by any means to submit to the yoke,—phrases, in no small variety and abundance, have been invented by various persons, for the purpose of giving force to their respective wills, and thus performing for their accommodation the functions of a law:—law of nations, moral sense, common sense, understanding, rule of right, fitness of things, law of reason, right reason, natural justice, natural equity, good order, truth, will of God, repugnancy to nature.

A similar exhibition of scarcely disguised ipse-dixitism has been made in the field of *pisteutics*, as in that of ethics.

Improbability—the improbability of the fact in question as related by the witness, is a species of counter-evidence, operating against this testimony—a species of counter-evidence, of the nature of *circumstantial* evidence: and so, whatsoever be the number of the witnesses.

Of the two opposite results, which is the most probable? That the fact in question, improbable as it appears, should notwithstanding be true? or that the testimony of the witness in question should, by some circumstance or other, have been rendered incorrect in respect of the report made concerning it?

No: it has been said. There are certain cases in which the improbability of a fact—improbability though in ever so high a degree—ought not to be considered as acting with a disprobative force great enough to outweigh the probative force of a mass of direct testimony, affirming the existence of it. Why? Because the allegation, by which a fact is said to be improbable, can have no other basis than human experience: but the probative force of direct testimony, let the fact asserted by it be what it may, rests upon a foundation anterior to, and more solid than, that of experience; viz. an innate propensity in human nature—a propensity on the part of a man to give credit to what he hears affirmed by others—a propensity which, commencing at the very moment of his birth, renders itself manifest in the very earliest infancy, as soon as any propensity has time to manifest itself—at a period antecedent, if not to all experience, at any rate to all experience of conformity between facts reported, and the testimony by which they are reported.

The debility of this argument is sufficient of itself to betray the occasion on which, and the cause in support of which, it was invented. The occasion was of the number of those in which belief, or the *assertion of belief*, being predetermined by considerations operating not on the understanding but on the will—by good and evil, by reward and punishment, by hope and fear; what remained was to find arguments to justify it—arguments which, the more obscure and irrelevant they were, would be but the more difficult to be refuted. Whether the cause had really any need of such arguments, is an inquiry that belongs not to the present purpose.

Innate ideas, the principle so fully exploded by Locke, constituted the medium of proof employed in his time, for the proof of whatsoever proposition was determined to be

* The propensity on the part of writers to attach to the idea of *practice* the idea of obligation, and that not declaredly in the way of inference, but silently and without notice in the way of substitution,—this propensity, and the confusion spread by it, not only over the whole field of moral science, but over the adjacent territories to a great extent, was noticed, and perhaps for the first time, by Hume, in his Treatise on Human Nature. But such is the force of habit and prepossession, after pointing out the cause of error, he continued himself to be led astray by it. On some occasions the principle of utility was recognized by him as the criterion of right and wrong, and in this sense the efficient cause of obligation. But on other occasions the *ipse dixit* principle, under the name of the moral sense, was, with the most inconsistent oscitancy, seated by his own hands on the same throne.

proved, and could not, as supposed, be proved by any other means.

To innate *ideas*, the doctrine here in question substitutes — if it be not rather an exemplification than a substitution — an innate *propensity*.

But, admitting the propensity, what is the use thus made of it? To prove the truth of the following proposition, — viz. that whatever is said, probable or improbable, is, by being said, if not rendered, at least proved, to be true?

All the extravagances — all the false conceptions that ever have been entertained, may by this argument be proved to be true; for there is not any of them but is the result of this propensity to believe what is said by others — this propensity, so strangely supposed to be antecedent to experience; as if anything subsequent to the moment of birth could be antecedent to experience.

Two propositions are here implied — two propositions, of each of which the absurdity strikes the mind upon the first mention: — 1. That a disposition to believe testimony has an efficient cause other than experience; — 2. That if it had, it would afford an adequate reason for believing in opposition to experience.

But it is in children (it is said) that the reliance on testimony is strongest — strongest in man at that time of life when he has had least experience. Such is the argument, on the strength of which it is concluded that man's reliance on man's testimony has not experience for its ground — experience of the conformity of that testimony to the truth of things; but is produced by an independent innate principle, made on purpose, and acting before experience. Before any experience has taken place, this confidence is at its maximum: as man advances in life, it grows weaker and weaker; and the cause that renders it so, is experience.

A child's reliance on testimony, on the truth of human assertion, antecedent to experience! As if assertions, and experience of the truth of them, were not coeval in his perceptions with the very first instances of the use of language!

Banish the phantom, the offspring of distressed imposture, the innate principle; consult experience, man's faithful and steady guide; and behold on how simple a ground the case stands. In children, at an early age, the reliance on assertion is strongest: why? — Because at that age experience is all, or almost all, on one side. As age advances, that reliance grows weaker and weaker: why? — Because experience is acquired on both sides — experience certifying the existence of falsehood as well as that of truth. The proportion of falsehood to truth commonly itself augments; and, though it should not itself augment, that which cannot fail to augment, and of which the augmentation answer the same purpose, is the habit, the occasion, and the facility of observing it.

But if a ferry-boat (says an argument in the same strain) — if a ferry-boat, that had crossed the river 2000 times without sinking, should, by a single supposed eye-witness, whose character was altogether unknown, be reported to have sunk the two thousand and first time: here is a highly improbable event, improbable in the ratio of 2000 to 1, believed upon the testimony of this unknown, and single witness; — believed, and who will say, not rightly and rationally believed?

An improbability of 2000 to 1? No, nor of 1 to 1. Yes, perhaps, — if a ferry-boat, being a thing unlike everything else in nature — or a ferry-boat, and everything else partaking in respect of submergibility of the nature of a ferry-boat — had been known to cross water 2000 times, and never known once to sink. But the aptitude of things in abundance — the aptitude of the materials of which ferry-boats are composed, to sink in water, when pressed by other bodies lying in them, is a fact composed of an immense mass of facts made known by an immense body of experience. Boats of almost all kinds, it is sufficiently known by experience, are but too apt to sink: which thing being considered, — of all those who have seen or heard of a ferry-boat, is there a single person to whom, though the same boat should be known to have crossed the water in question 10,000 times instead of 2000, the report of its having sunk should present itself as in any degree improbable?

Yes: if a boat, composed solely of cork, and that of the same shape with the ferry-boat in question, except as to the being solid instead of being hollow — if a boat of such description were reported to have sunk, and without anything drawing it down, or pressing upon it, — here, indeed, would be an improbability, and such an improbability, as, to the mind of a man conversant with the phenomena and principles of hydrostatics, would not be rendered probable or credible by the report of a thousand witnesses, though they were all of them self-pretended eye-witnesses.

Experience is the foundation of all our knowledge, and of all our reasoning — the sole guide of our conduct, the sole basis of our security.

Of the argument now under consideration, the object is to persuade us to reject the counsel of experience: to credit, on no better ground than because this or that person or persons have asserted it, a fact, the superior incredibility of which is attested by experience. This is, in other words, to throw off the character of rational beings, and in cold blood to resolve to act the part of madmen.

It is by experience we are taught, that in by far the greater number of instances individually taken, the testimony of mankind — the assertions made by human creatures — are either true, or, if in any respect false, clear of all imputation as well of temerity as of wilfulness. It is by the same experience we are taught, that in a part of the whole number of instances, these assertions are not only false, but tainted with one or other of those two vices; and that, even so far as concerns wilful falsehood, or, in one word, mendacity — though, comparatively speaking, relation being had to the aggregate mass of human assertions, the instances of mendacity are numerically small, — yet so vast is that aggregate, that, absolutely taken, the same number in itself is immense.

It is by experience we are taught, that, as in the case of every other modification of hnman conduct, so in the case of assertion (and all discourse, interrogation not excepted, is in one shape or other *assertion*,) no action is ever performed without a motive: no act of mendacity is therefore without a motive. But a proposition that will be made good as we advance, is, that as there is no modification of interest, no species of motive, by which mendacity is not capable of being produced, so there is no occasion on which there can be any certain ground of assurance that the assertion uttered is not mendacious: no human being, in whose instance there can be any certain ground of assurance that his assertion is altogether untainted by that vice.

The proposition — *all men speak always true*, — is therefore a proposition which itself is not true, but with an innumerable and continually accumulating multitude of exceptions. But in regard to facts of the physical class, there are facts in abundance, which are true without a single exception. Take for instance, that iron is heavier than water. Accordingly, it is not by the testimony of a thousand witnesses, that to a well-informed mind it could be rendered in a preponderant degree probable, that in any one single instance a mass of iron had been found less heavy than an equal bulk of water. Supposing a fact of this kind thus asserted, and supposing what could never be proved, that in the instance of any number of the witnesses the assertion was altogether pure of mendacity, — the conclusion would be either that that which was taken for iron was not iron, but some other substance — wood, for example, with the appearance of iron superinduced upon it; or that that which was taken for water was not water, but some other liquid — mercury for example, with a coat of water lying upon it; or that that which was taken for a solid mass of iron, *i. e.* for iron only, was a hollow mass of iron, *i. e.* a mass of air, or a void space, inclosed in a cover of that metal.

"The improbability of a fact affords no reason — no sufficient reason, for refusing to believe it, if attested by witnesses — by witnesses whose character is not exposed to any special cause of suspicion." Such is the notion which has been endeavoured to be inculcated. But to accede to any such doctrine — to suppose that there can be any imaginable case in which it can be just — is to give up, and to call upon all others to give up, the use of human reason altogether, on every question of evidence; which is as much as to say, on every question of fact.

In the same strain, the only language with which it is possible to reason upon the subject shall be protested against, and denounced as figurative, improper, and unsuited to the subject: in the same strain, and with perfect consistency. The end in view is, by dint of *ipse dixit*, with obscure terrors at the back of it, to engage men to believe, with the utmost force of persuasion, certain supposed facts, which some men have asserted, or have been supposed to assert, in whatsoever degree improbable. But, to this design all consideration of improbability being hostile, — all language in which improbability and its degrees are brought to view, and made the subject of description, will of course be equally so.

When reason is against a man, a man will be against reason. In this he is consistent: as consistent as he is the contrary, when reason, or something that calls itself reason, is employed in proving, that on such or such a subject, reason is a blind guide, and that to be directed by her is unreasonable.

When a man is seen thus occupied, sapping the foundations of human reason, and with them the foundations of human society, and of human security in all its shapes, how shall we account for such preposterous industry? Before him lay a parcel of facts, which, be they what they may to other eyes, to his, at any rate, seemed improbable. Improbable as they were, a determination had been taken that they were to be believed at any rate. Readers were to be persuaded to believe them, and to consider him as believing them likewise; and thus the argument was to be constructed: "There is an innate propensity in every human being to believe whatever is said by any other: to believe probable things; to believe, moreover, improbable things. That the propensity is innate, is evident; for it manifests itself in each human being, at a period antecedent to the commencement of his experience: of his experience (to wit) of the agreement of facts with the reports made by men concerning them. It manifests itself with peculiar strength in children: with the greater degree of strength, the younger they are: with the greatest degree of strength, in those who have least experience. But, forasmuch as this propensity exists on all occasions, therefore man ought to yield to it on all occasions."

Good; when the propensity exists; admitting always, that whatsoever propensity exists in a man, it is good for him to yield to. But in the instance of a man in whom it does not exist, what argument does it afford? Is one man obliged to believe, or is it reasonable for him to believe, a thing, and that an improbable thing, only because another man has a propensity to believe it? Are men obliged to believe—is it reasonable for them to believe—improbable things, because children do?

Being then good as a reason for believing, apply this innate propensity to action. Correspondent to the believing of improbable things, is the doing of foolish ones: what the one is in theory, the other is in practice. Foolish belief, if there be any such thing, what is it? It is neither more nor less than the belief of improbable things. A has a propensity to do foolish things; therefore it is incumbent on, and reasonable for, B to do foolish things: children are apt to do foolish things; therefore, so ought men.

NOTE BY THE AUTHOR.

Dr. Price, to whose honest, but rather unfortunately successful, mathematical labours, England is indebted for the sinking fund system, gives us in one of his essays, a mathematical demonstration of the probability of improbabilities. Imagine a lottery, says he, with a million of blanks to a prize: take No. 1, No. 1,000,001, or any intermediate number; and suppose yourself to hear of its gaining the prize: would you find any difficulty in believing it? No, surely: yet here is an improbability of a million to one; and yet you believe it without difficulty. If this ratio does not import sufficient improbability, instead of millions take billions; or, instead of billions, trillions, and so on.

Well then, since we must stop somewhere, we will stop at a trillion. This being the nominal ratio, what is the consequence? Answer: That the real ratio is that of 1 to 1. One little circumstance of the case had escaped the observation of the mathematical divine. Of the trillion and one, that some one ticket should gain the prize, is matter of necessity: and of them all, every one has exactly as good a chance as every other. Mathematicians, it has been observed (so fond are they of making display of the hard-earned skill acquired by them in the management of their instrument) are apt not to be so scrupulous as might be wished in the examination of the correctness and completeness of the data which they assume, and on which they operate.

A book on ship-building will be filled with letters from the close, and letters from the beginning and middle, of the alphabet; and a ship built upon the plan proved by it to give the maximum of velocity, shall not sail perhaps so quick as one built by a carpenter, whose mathematics had terminated at the rule of three. Why? Because, of the dozen or half dozen influencing circumstances, on the conjunct operation of which the rate of sailing depends, some one had unfortunately escaped the attention of the man of science

Halley, whose deficiency in Christian faith was not much less notorious than his proficiency in astronomy and mathematics, thought he had given a deathblow to revealed religion, when he had published in the Philosophical Transactions a paper with x's and y's, showing the time at which the probative force of all testimony would be reduced to an evanescent quantity. Yes, if testimony had no other shape to exhibit itself in than the oral. But, not to speak of the Shasters and the Koran, —the Bible, against which the attack was levelled, comes to us in the written form: and whatever may be the difference in point of extent, as measured by numbers, between the judgment that will be passed on it ten thousand years hence, and the judgment passed on it at present, it will not be easy to say on what account its title to credence should by that length of time, or any greater length of time, be considered as diminished.

FARTHER NOTE BY THE EDITOR.

When Dr. Price affirms that we continually believe, on the slightest possible evidence, things in the highest degree improbable, he confounds two ideas which are totally distinct from one another, and would be seen to be such, did they not unfortunately happen to be called by the same name: these are, improbability in the ordinary sense, and mathematical improbability. In the latter of these senses there is scarcely any event which is not improbable: in the former, the only improbable events are extraordinary ones.

In the language of common life, an improbable event means an event which is disconformable to the ordinary course of nature.* This kind of improbability constitutes a valid reason for disbelief; because, universal experience having established that the course of nature is uniform, the more widely an alleged event differs from the ordinary course of nature, the smaller is the probability of its being true.

In the language of mathematics, the word improbability has a totally different meaning. In the mathematical sense of the word, every event is improbable, of the happening

---

* See Book V. *Circumstantial.* Chap. XVI. *Improbability and Impossibility.*

of which it might have been said *a priori* that the odds were against it. In this sense, almost all events which ever happen are improbable: not only those events which are disconformable, but even those events which are in the highest degree conformable, to the course, and even to the most ordinary course, of nature. "A corn merchant goes into a granary, and takes up a handful of grains as a sample: there are millions of grains in the granary, which had an equal chance of being taken up. According to Dr. Price, events which happen daily, and in every corner, are extraordinary, and highly improbable. The chances were infinitely great against my placing my foot, when I rise from my chair, on the precise spot where I have placed it; going on, in this manner, from one example to another, nothing can happen that is not infinitely improbable." *Traité des Preuves Judiciaires*, —translation, p. 282.

True it is, in all these cases (as well as in that of the lottery, supposed by Dr. Price) there is what would be called, in the language of the doctrine of chances, an improbability, in the ratio of as many as you please to one: yet it would obviously be absurd to make this a reason for refusing our belief to the alleged event. And why? Because, though it is in one sense an improbable event, it is not an extraordinary event; there is not in the case so much as a shadow of disconformity even to the most ordinary course of nature. Mathematically improbable events happen every moment: experience affords us no reason for refusing our belief to *them*. Extraordinary events happen rarely: and as respects them, consequently, experience *does* afford a valid reason for doubt, or for disbelief. The only question in any such case is, which of two things would be most disconformable to the ordinary course of nature: that the event in question should have happened; or that the witnesses by whom its occurrence is affirmed, should have been deceivers or deceived.

CHAPTER VIII.

MODES OF INCORRECTNESS IN TESTIMONY.

An analytic sketch of the different shapes in which falsehood is wont to show itself, will not be altogether without its use: its particular uses in practice will be pointed out presently.

The modifications of falsehood may be deduced, either from the consideration of the part taken by the *will* in relation to it, or from the consideration of the *facts* which are the subject-matter of the picture thus deviating from the line of truth. Those which result from the former topic will be brought to view in the next chapter. There remain those which respect the nature of the fact in question, or the form of the assertion of which it is the subject.

Cause, homicide. Titius is under examination. Question: What do you know about this business? Answer: 1. Reus struck Defunctus; 2. Reus did not strike Defunctus; 3. I know not whether Reus struck Defunctus or no. Any one of these answers, it is evident, is as susceptible of falsehood as another. In the two first cases, the falsehood consists in false assertion — affirmative in one case, negative in the other; in the third case, it consists in allegation of ignorance.

1. Falsehood, in the way of positive or affirmative assertion; 2. Falsehood, in the way of negative assertion; 3. Falsehood, by alleged ignorance.

Falsehood by allegation of ignorance, it is evident, is altogether as susceptible of mendacity, as falsehood in the way of assertion; and whenever mendacity is an object meet for punishment, it is as much so in this shape as in the other. Unfortunately, it is not so open to disproof as the other. Why? Because, in this case, the fact which is the subject of the false testimony has nothing physical in it — is purely of the psychological kind. Were it exempt from punishment, there would be no witnesses but those who are called *willing* ones. The condition of a delinquent, whatever were the crime, would be subject altogether to the good pleasure of the individuals whose testimony was requisite to ground a decision on that side: to afford him impunity, to grant him a virtual pardon and protection, nothing more would be needful on their part than to say, I know nothing, or I remember nothing, about the matter.

To protect a witness (his testimony being necessary to conviction) to protect him against cross-examination when uttering a falsehood of this sort, is to hold out impunity to the whole catalogue of crimes. On a memorable and never-to-be-forgotten occasion, English judges, all with one voice and hand, scrupled not to aim this mortal stab at penal justice.* Impunity to a crime of the deepest die — a plot for the assassination of the sovereign — has been among the fruits of it in practice.† Since that time, judges have slunk in silence from the precedent.‡ But the decision remaining unreversed, and, but for legislative authority, unreversable, the consequence of the departure is not the restoration of justice, but, on each future occasion, justice or impuinty at the option of the judge.

Question: About what thickness was the stick with which you saw Reus strike his wife Defuncta? Answer: About the thickness of a man's little finger. In truth, it was about the thickness of a man's wrist. Falsehood

* Trial of Warren Hastings.

† Trial of Crossfield. ‡ Trial of Codling.

in this shape may be termed falsehood in *quantity*.

Question: With what food did the jailor Reus feed the prisoner Defunctus? Answer: With sea-biscuit, in an ordinarily eatable state. In truth, the biscuit was rotten and mouldy in great part. Falsehood in this shape may may be termed falsehood in *quality*.

Under what tree was the act committed? said Daniel to each of the Elders, separately. Under a mastic tree, said the one: under a holme tree, said the other. In truth, not being committed at all, it was not committed under any tree. Falsehood in this shape may be termed falsehood in *circumstance*.

The distinction between fact and circumstance, it should here be noted, is extremely apt to be obscure and indeterminate. It supposes the individualization of each fact — the boundary line which divides that from all other facts — to be clear and determinate; whereas, nothing is more apt to be indeterminate. It supposes the distinction between fact and circumstance to be clear and uniform; but nothing is more variable. The term circumstance is but relative: a circumstance is itself a fact, any one of a number of facts considered as *standing round* the principal fact.

The falsehood that respectively accompanied the above-mentioned assertions, — Reus struck Defunctus — Reus did not strike Defunctus — presents itself in a shape different from any of the above three: it went to the act, and did not confine itself to quantity, quality, or circumstance. It may be termed falsehood *in toto*.*

Falsehood in quantity and in quality, is that sort of falsehood which is most apt, and indeed almost exclusively apt, to be produced by bias. Whether produced by bias or by mendacity, it is in general peculiarly difficult to disprove: it is accordingly in this quarter, so far as concerns physical facts, that mendacity finds its surest refuge.

It is, however, liable enough to be disproved where the fact in question is of a nature to afford *real* evidence, and that of the permanent kind: if, for example, the stick, or the unwholesome food, having been impounded and preserved, come to be produced in court. But if the thing, the condition of which was the subject of the falsehood, be not forth coming — whether from its nature (for example wind or running water,) or by accident — this means of detection fails. The size of the stick is not out of the reach of subsequent measurement: the force with which the blow was given, is; except in so far as it may be guessed at from the appearance of the wound or bruise.

* But as circumstance is a name that may be given to a fact of any sort falsehood in circumstance and falsehood *in toto* may in this respect coincide.

The practical use of these distinctions is this: — In the case where the falsehood is only in quantity or quality, the aberration of the evidence from the truth may be accompanied, or not, with that consciousness which gives it the denomination of *wilful* in ordinary language: in the case where the evidence is false *in toto*, the falsehood cannot but have been accompanied with that culpable consciousness — it cannot have been otherwise than *wilful*, unless it have risen from that sort of disorder in the imagination, which may be set down to the account of insanity while it lasts.

Of evidence false *in toto*, the sort of evidence so unhappily frequent in penal causes, and so familiar accordingly in legal language, under the name of *alibi* evidence, may serve as an example. The defendant is accused of having killed a man with a hedge-stake, at a certain place and time: a witness is produced, who says, I am well acquainted with him; he was conversing with me at another place, considerably distant (naming it,) in a small room, exactly at that time. The evidence may be true or false; but what is certain is, that, if it be false, the falsehood cannot be otherwise than wilful, barring the possibility that one man may have been taken for another. A man cannot be at two distant places at the same time; and, with the exception just stated, a man cannot, in the compass of a small room, really conceive himself to have been seeing and holding converse with another man, who, in fact, was never there.

What was the size of the stake, the degree of force with which the blow was given? — did the deceased, on his part, aim a blow at the defendant, or merely endeavour to ward off the defendant's blow? — all these are so many circumstances, in respect of which the mendacious conciousness may or may not be present, although the testimony were more or less unconformable to the exact truth of the case — in a word, were *false*.

Falsehood *in toto*, and falsehood *in circumstance*, will be found, accordingly, to differ, in a number of points of very essential importance in practice.

1. Falsehood *in toto* is, in a decidedly pre-eminent degree, exposed to detection and disproof: in the case of falsehood in circumstance, in quantity, or quality, the facility, and even possibility of detection, will depend upon the degree of aberration from the truth.

2. In the case of falsehood *in toto*, the aberration, as already observed, cannot but be accompanied with mendacious consciousness: falsehood in quantity, quality, or other circumstance, may be produced by *bias*, by the influence of motives on the affections, without being accompanied by any such consciousness.†

† For the explanation of *mendacity* and *bias* see the next chapter. The meaning of the term,

3. Falsehood *in toto* is accordingly that species of falsehood of which a man is in general convicted, when he is convicted of perjury. Perjury, in respect of quantity, quality, or other circumstance, may have been committed a hundred times, without the possibility of a single conviction upon sufficient grounds.

Question to Reus: What was your intention in striking Defunctus? Answer: To disable him, so as to put it out of his power to hurt me. In truth, it was to deprive him of life. Question: By what motive were you instigated to strike Defunctus? Answer: By self-preservation; the desire to save my life. In truth, it was enmity: his own life was in no danger. In both these cases, the subject-matter of the falsehood, it is manifest, was a psychological fact: in the preceding cases, it was a physical fact.

Psychological facts, it is evident, present a more inviting field to mendacity than is commonly presented by physical facts. But this does not hinder the application of punishment, as for mendacity, to falsehood in the one shape, any more than in the other. If it did, — in this case, as in the preceding one, impunity would be secured to many a crime. Not but that, as already observed, psychological facts are much more satisfactorily proved by circumstantial than by direct evidence. In the way of direct evidence, a fact of this class cannot be proved by any person but the one person whose mental faculties are the seat of it.

The field of motives is an open and ample field for the exercise not of mendacity only, but of bias. The tendency of bias is to attribute the greatest share, or rather the whole agency, in the production of the act, to a particular motive; to the exclusion of, or in preference to, whatever others may have concurred in the production of it. Few indeed that are able, scarce any that are willing, to give, on every occasion, a correct account of the state of the psychological force by which their conduct has been produced.

Ask Reus for his own motives, — they are the most laudable, or, in default of laudable, the most justifiable, or at least excusable, of any that can be found. Ask a friend of Reus for the motives of Reus, — the answer is the same. Ask Actor for the motives of Reus, — the same gradation, the order only reversed. Ask Reus for the motive which gave birth to the prosecution on the part of Actor, — the motive of course is the most odious that can be found: desire of gain, if it be a case which opens a door to gain; if not, enmity, though not under that neutral and unimpassioned, but under the name of revenge or malice, or some other such dyslogistic* name. Ask a friend of Reus, or an enemy of Actor, — the answer is the same. Ask an enemy of Reus, or a friend of Actor, — his motive was public spirit, the purest public spirit.

Ask an English lawyer, — his answer will also be, public spirit: or if, under the name of revenge or malice, he concludes enmity to have had its share, he requires, in many cases, no other ground for dismissing the prosecution: such is the simplicity of English lawyers, so profound their ignorance of the causes and effects of human actions, and of the difference between the cases in which the nature of the motive is material and discoverable, and those in which it is irrelevant and inscrutable.

Put the same question to a man to whom the springs of action are known, and the mechanism of the human mind familiar, — he will scorn to pretend to know what is not capable of being known. He will answer, — desire of gain, enmity, public spirit; — these motives (not to speak of casual ones) any one exclusively, any or all conjunctively, and in any one of the whole assemblage of imaginable proportions — the proportions never the same for two days or two hours together, nor understood, or so much as inquired into, by the individual himself.

On this part of the ground of the evidence, a work replete with instruction would be a collection of cases of prosecutions for perjury; the cases ranged under heads expressive of the shape in which the falsehood presented itself, as above. The mischief is obvious and indisputable, if there were any shape in which it could give itself a promise of impunity complete and sure. At first, the prosecutions, it seems natural to suppose, confined themselves to some of the grosser shapes. As human intelligence advances, — in this as in other lines, the field of punishment will naturally approach nearer and nearer to a complete coincidence with the field of crime.

Hitherto I should expect to find falsehood *in toto* a much more frequent subject for a prosecution of this kind, than falsehood either in *quantity* or in *quality*.

When the word falsehood is mentioned, the modifications that will be by far the most apt to present themselves, are those ordinary ones which have been already mentioned; viz. those in which the vehicle used for the conveyance of it, is ordinary language, and in which falsehood, if tinctured with mendacity, and uttered under the sanction of an oath, is understood to come under the denomination of perjury.

But language, verbal discourse, though the most common and convenient vehicle for the

is in general sufficiently well understood to render an anticipated explanation of them in this place unnecessary.

* The word *dyslogistic* is employed by Mr. Bentham in the sense of *vituperative*; as opposed to *eulogistic*.

conveyance of ideas, is not the only one. Accordingly, under the head of circumstantial evidence, it becomes necessary to add *deportment*, as a necessary supplement to language.*

To this head belong the following modifications of falsehood, some of which have been already mentioned:—

1. Graphical forgery.—Forgery in relation to written documents: the species of forgery most commonly understood under that name.

2. Monetary forgery.—Forgery in relation to the current coin.

3. Forgery in relation to evidentiary marks of ownership; *ex. gr.* landmarks: the owner's name upon his linen, or other goods.

4. Forgery in relation to evidentiary marks of authorship: *ex. gr.* the marks of a manufacturer or vender, upon goods made or sold by him.

5. Forgery of *real* evidence at large: in particular, forgery in relation to the traces of delinquency, under its several modifications.

The Romanists, and after them the English lawyers, in some instances, have ranked under the common generical appellation of the *crimen falsi*, forgery (at least in some of the above instances) as well as perjury: falsehood in this *quasi-colloquial* shape, as well as in the shape of ordinary discourse. Of mendacity, except where, by the sanction of an oath, it has been made to receive the denomination of perjury, it has not been common to take notice, either under that or any other name.

* See Book V. *Circumstantial.*

CHAPTER IX.

GENERAL VIEW OF THE PSYCHOLOGICAL CAUSES OF CORRECTNESS AND COMPLETENESS, WITH THEIR CONTRARIES, INCORRECTNESS AND INCOMPLETENESS, IN TESTIMONY.

IN a tolerably sufficient degree for the various purposes of life,—private and public, domestic, commercial, scientific, political, judicial,—is human testimony in general found conformable to the truth of things. At the same time, in instances but too numerous, it fails of being so. The conformity has its causes: the disconformity has its causes likewise. In a work on evidence, all these causes have a claim to notice. Where mischief, as it is but too apt to be, is the result of such disconformity,—*deception*, false judgment, is the name either of the mischief itself, or of the proximate cause of it. And for the prevention of this mischief there is no other course so sure as that which includes the endeavour to avert it, by removing or counteracting the operation of its causes.

The inquiry into the causes of trustworthiness and untrustworthiness in evidence, will probably, without much difficulty, be acknowledged to be an interesting pursuit: interesting not merely as a field of speculation, but with a view to practice.

But when the mode of applying to practice whatever information may be obtainable, comes upon the carpet, opinions will not, at first view at least, be alike uniform.

The practical uses, and the only uses, which present themselves to my view as proper to be made of it, are as follow:—

1. To put the legislator and the judge as fully as possible upon their guard against the causes of untrustworthiness.

2. To show how far and in what instances they are without, and how far within, the reach of remedy.

3. In so far as they are within the reach of remedy, to point out, under the name of the causes of trustworthiness, what are the proper remedies, and in what way they may be employed to the best possible advantage: in such manner as to leave to the causes of untrustworthiness as little influence as possible.

To the above operations, which are but endeavours, the practice of men of law, of judges and legislators, has not been content to confine itself: it has taken a line of conduct presenting the idea of greater efficacy; viz. the excluding from the function of a witness every individual in whose character or situation any mark or symptom of untrustworthiness has presented itself.

The light in which the subject has presented itself to my view, has compelled me to conclude that the idea of exclusion is altogether without foundation in reason and utility: that, though it be employed by lawyers in all nations, no nations, in this respect, are consistent with one another, nor any one consistent with itself: that the practice is not reasonable in any single instance: that it is mischievous in the exact degree in which it is extensive: that, if in any nation it had been consistently pursued, which however is impossible, it would long ago have given a complete impunity to every imaginable crime, and cut up society by the roots: that, in the minds of its authors, it has its seat,—as far as regards their intellects,—not in any comprehensive, but in a wonderfully narrow conception of the springs of action, and the mechanism of the mind:—as far as regards their will,—not in attention and anxiety, as might be supposed, but in indolence, negligence, and indifference.

Nevertheless, as a system of law in which this supposed remedy has not been adopted, and to a greater or less extent employed, is perhaps nowhere to be found—as the body of prejudice to be put down is thus colossal—it cannot but be perceived that he who undertakes to overthrow it, cannot make his ground too sure.

For this purpose, and because the practice of exclusion has no better nor other cause than the observation that, in each instance, the testimony of the witness is exposed to the influence of some *motive*, acting upon him in a sinister direction, and soliciting him to deviate from the path of truth, — it will be necessary to take a complete survey of the whole catalogue of motives, to the action of which the will of man is exposed. It will thence be seen, that for the same reason for which, in the character of a witness, any one class of persons ought to be excluded, so ought every other: and that, in the character of a preservative against mendacity, a consistent system of exclusion would be no wiser a remedy, than an universal deluge, and without an ark, would be against any other vice.

By the same survey by which the unreasonableness of exclusion is thus indicated, the reasonableness of suspicion will all along be brought to view: and if in this way it be seen to fulfil the double purpose of affording wholesome instruction, and guarding against pernicious error, the labour of travelling through it need the less be grudged.

The application of the lights thus collected, to the subject of exclusion, will be the business of a separate book. In the present book, lest the theoretical survey should in any of its points be suspected of being without use in practice, it seemed necessary to show that the practical question, as between exclusion and non-exclusion, is the chief mark which it had in view; and that the solution of that question was the chief of the objects to which it owed its birth.

To begin, then. The conformity or disconformity of the testimony of a witness to the truth of things, to the real state of the facts which constitute the subject-matter of his report, depends upon the state of his mental faculties; viz. partly upon the state of the intellectual, partly upon the state of the moral or volitional, department of his mind.

Incorrectness and incompleteness in testimony have received different names, according as they are supposed to arise from causes the seat of which is in the intellect, or from causes the seat of which is in the will.

By the supposition, the picture is in some respect or other disconformable to the original. Is the witness completely unconscious of the disconformity? the cause of it is to be found in his intellectual faculties merely: his will has no share in the production of it: the falsehood was not on his part a wilful one. Is he conscious of the disconformity? the cause of it is to be found in the state of his volitional faculty.

But for an act of his will, that picture which his understanding had represented to him as false, would not have been exhibited by him as true. The falsehood is therefore, in this respect properly, as in ordinary discourse it is familiarly, spoken of as a wilful one.

In this latter case, and this alone, the falsehood in the language of Roman law is said to be accompanied with *dolus; i. e.* deceit, or at any rate the intention to produce deception — to deceive: with *dolus;* as also with *mala fides* — an inexpressive term, the import of which has been placed out of doubt by use, but of which the connexion with its import, and with its synonyme, as above, would not be very easy to make out.*

Dolus remains peculiar to the Romanists. *mala fides*, not to speak of its negative *bona fides*, has been borrowed from them, and been adopted by English lawyers. Of both of them the use has been extended, from crimes of falsehood, to all other crimes; from delinquency by false testimony, to delinquency in every other mode.

The intellectal faculties concerned in testimony may be comprised under four heads: perception, judgment, memory, expression; under the latter being included, the use of the corporeal faculties in respect of the sensible signs, audible or visible, by means of which the expression is performed.

When, with reference to the matter of fact which is or ought to be the subject of report, these four faculties are all of them in a sound and perfect state, free from infirmity, — correctness and completeness on the part of the testimony, so far as depends upon the state of the intellectual compartment of the deponent's mind, are the result: when in any one of them infirmity or deficiency has place, incorrectness or incompleteness on the part of the testimony is liable to be the consequence: nor, so far as depends upon the state of the intellectual part of the witness's frame, can these defects in his testimony be referable, either of them, to any other cause.

To present a more particular view of the ways in which an infirmity or weakness of which these several faculties are respectively the seats, produces, or contributes to produce, in the testimony of a witness, one or other of these defects, will be the business of the next chapter.

The moral faculties concerned may be comprised under two heads; viz. veracity and attention: adding, or including, their respective opposites or negations, viz. mendacity, and temerity, or negligence: temerity being principally displayed by action, *i. e.* by utterance; negligence, by forbearance, *i. e.* by silence.

Veracity has place, in so far as it is the will, the wish, the desire, the endeavour, of the witness, that his testimony, and the conclusions drawn from it, be conformable to the real state of the case.

* For *mala fides*, say, perhaps, insincerity: for *bona fides*, sincerity.

Mendacity has place, in so far as it is the will, the wish, the desire, the endeavour, of the witness, that his testimony, or the conclusions drawn from it, be in any respect unconformable to the real state of the case.

As the will can scarcely exert itself, at least with any considerable degree of vigour, but the intellectual faculty must, in a more or less considerable degree, be impressed with a consciousness of the exertion so made by the moral faculty; hence falsehood, when in this way wilful, is generally, and in a manner of course, in the mind of the witness, accompanied with self-consciousness — with a consciousness of its own existence. The two expressions, *wilful falsehood* and *self-conscious falsehood*, become thus interconvertible and nearly synonymous.

Verity has place, in so far as — whatsoever be the state of the will, of the volitional or moral faculty of the witness, on the occasion in question, — the report made by him concerning them, in and by his testimony, is conformable to the real state of the case.

Falsehood, or rather *falsity* (the word being used without reference to veracity or mendacity,) has place in so far as — whatsoever on the part of the witness be the state of his will, in relation to the matters of fact in question — his testimony fails of being conformable to the real state of the case.*

Be the *attention* of the witness, ever so closely applied to the subject, or ever so anxiously occupied in giving a correct and complete expression to the facts, the image of which is presented by his *memory*, — falsity on the part of his testimony may in any degree happen to be the result; *ex. gr.* owing to some infirmity in one or other of the four branches above mentioned of the intellectual faculty.

But where, mendacity having no place, falsity has place notwithstanding, it has frequently for its cause a deficiency in respect of that due measure of attention, by which, had it been, as but for his default it might have been, present, the picture given of the fact by his testimony would have been rendered more nearly resembling to the original — to the real state of the case.

The witness has uttered what was untrue; but he was not aware of its being so. Was he in any such situation as called upon him, in regard to justice, before he undertook to give the picture in question, to take measures for assuring himself of the correctness of it, — such measures as, had he taken them, would have saved him from falling into the error, and caused him either to have declared his inability to give any picture of the transaction, or if he gave any picture, to give a true one? If he was, his testimony, though free from the blame of insincerity, is not considered as free from blame altogether. In respect of the judgment, the erroneous judgment, thus formed and expressed by him, — that judgment being, for want of that attention which he might have bestowed and ought to have bestowed upon it, an erroneous one, — blame, viz. the blame of temerity — rashness, is imputed to him, and to such his testimony.†

In case of falsehood, there is yet another state of the mind which requires notice. In English, the word *bias* is employed for the expression of it: it is the state which a man is in, when he is said to have a *bias* upon his mind. The causes of bias cannot be understood any further than as the causes of mendacity are understood. But to understand it, viz. by means of its relation to mendacity, — for the present, nothing further is necesary than to understand, that mendacity has constantly for its cause some one or more *motives* (motives acting upon the will in a sinister direction — in a direction tending, in matters

* A state of things not frequently exemplified, but by no means incapable of being exemplified, is, when a witness, wishing and endeavouring to render his testimony in this or that respect disconformable to the truth of the case, and even believing himself to be so doing, renders it notwithstanding, and in the very same respects, conformable.

In this case, his will is in the same vicious state as in case of mendacity; and yet neither falsity, nor consequently mendacity, is the result.

In the system of ethics or moral philosophy taught in some of the English schools, a distinction is taken between *logical* and *ethical* falsehood. By logical falsehood is meant falsehood in general, whether referable to the case of mendacity, as above described, or not: by ethical falsehood is denoted mendacity, as above described.

But, for the case where, as above, falsehood being intended, truth is notwithstanding the result, the nomenclature of that system furnishes not any appellative; unless ethical falsehood, unaccompanied by logical, be taken for that appellative.

Of him who, meaning and thinking to utter a falsehood, speaks truth notwithstanding, the act may be considered as an attempt, though an abortive attempt, to commit mendacity: and in respect of consequences — mischievous consequences, the relation of the inchoate offence to the consummate offence is the same in the instance of this, as in the instance of any other offence, and with equal propriety is susceptible of having punishment attached to it.

† In the language of the Romanists, *culpa* and *temeritas*. These terms, however, are scarcely so much in use with reference to falsehood, an instrument in the hands of delinquency in general, as with reference to this or that particular species of delinquency. English lawyers have scarce got to the length of this distinction: with reference to delinquency in general, not with any approach to uniformity: with reference to the offence of false testimony, not at all. In a prosecution for perjury, mendacity in judicial testimony delivered upon oath, they know of no medium between self-criminative consciousness and innocence.

of testimony, to produce mendacity,) and that bias is produced by the action of these same causes.

Bias, then, is a tendency to falsehood in testimony, produced by the same causes as those by which mendacity is produced—a tendency, which, even when reduced to act, is not accompanied with that self-criminative consciousness which is of the essence of mendacity, and which distinguishes it from unmendacious falsehood, accompanied or not accompanied by temerity. The mind of Titius is under a bias: his situation exposes him to the action of some motive by which he is urged to depart from the line of truth. He resists the impulse, or yields to it; he adheres to the line of truth, or deviates from it: but, if he deviates, he is not conscious of his doing so; it is not his will, his intention, so to deviate: the falsehood, if there be any in his testimony, is not a wilful one.

When the tendency produced by bias is reduced into act, by the supposition there is no mendacity in the case, though the effect is produced by the action of a cause of the same nature as those by which mendacity is apt to be produced. Is there, or is there not, *temerity?* The answer is not easy: nor happily very material. Men in general are not so indulgent as to be thus nice. If the testimony of Titius is seen to be exposed to any of the causes of mendacity, and falsehood in any respect is understood to have been the result, such falsehood will not ordinarily be understood to be exempt from blame. The best that can easily happen to it, is to be understood as accompanied by temerity: most men would be apt to refer it to mendacity, without staying to think of bias.

Bias, being thus nearly related to mendacity, will require little separate mention to be made of it: having the same causes, it has, when it has any effect, the same effects; and (with the exception of punishment, punishment applied in a direct way by appointment of law) presents a demand for the same remedies.

CHAPTER X.

OF THE INTELLECTUAL CAUSES OF CORRECTNESS AND COMPLETENESS IN TESTIMONY, WITH THEIR OPPOSITES.

When a statement given of a matter of fact is an exact picture of it—agrees with it in all points, it is then correct, and as correct as it can be: when it fails of coinciding with it in any point, in proportion to the degree of such failure it is incorrect. Correctness, properly speaking, is not susceptible of degrees: whatever degrees there are in the scale, are degrees of incorrectness.

A statement which, without any intention on the part of the testifier to depart from the truth, is incorrect in any respect, may, as already observed, be either false *in toto*, or false only in circumstance. When it is false *in toto* — when the picture which it exhibits has not for its original any real fact whatever, or any feature or circumstance of any fact, — it is in that case the mere work of the imagination: of which afterwards. When it is false only in circumstance — when, though it departs from the original in some points, it has an original from whence it was taken, — the cause of the departure lies, in this case, in one or more of the intellectual faculties — perception, judgment, memory, or expression — enumerated above.

In the case of perception, where sight was the sense through the medium of which the cognizance of the fact was obtained, the light in which the object was placed may have been faint; or a part of it only, and not a sufficient part, may on that occasion have presented itself to his eye.

In the case of hearing, in like manner, the sounds which reached his ear may have been faint; or, of those which on that occasion were produced by the sonorous body, parts only, and those broken and interrupted, reached his ear: in the case of words spoken, the voice of the speaker may have been faint, the distance at which he stood considerable, and, from one cause or the other, of the words of which the discourse was composed, some excited, some failed of exciting, a distinct perception. And so on through the less instructive and less constantly active senses — the touch, the smell, the taste.

So intimate is the connexion between the two phenomena, — the perception, the impression made on the organ of sense, — and the act of the judgment performed in consequence, the inference drawn from the impression, the inference made by the judgment in relation to the supposed cause of it; so prodigious is the rapidity with which, in most instances, the consequent judgment succeeds to the antecedent perception;* that, by him who has not by some special motive been led to the making of the analysis, the distinction will be apt to pass unperceived.

Among the topics of disputation, which, having been handed down from past ages, are agitated, or used at least to be agitated, in

* Conceive a song, sung by a female to her harpsichord, with a bar in it composed of demi-semiquavers, or other notes expressive of the quickest time: suppose her to play and sing from the score, playing constantly either three or four parts at once, and singing at the same time a fourth or fifth: not one of these notes, the production of which has not been preceded by an act of vision, a perception of the musical character, and a judgment declarative of its cause and signification, its relation to the rest of the notes in tone and time, &c.

the logical schools at the English universities, one is, the question whether sense is or is not capable of being deceived? To give a just answer to this question, the process conveyed to the mind by the words sense, sensation, requires to be decomposed as above. Deception is an attribute of the judgment only: to have been deceived, is to have passed an erroneous judgment, a judgment more or less disagreeing with the fact. So far, then, as judgment is not concerned in sensation, sensation is not capable of being deceived: so far as judgment is concerned in sensation, sensation is capable of being deceived. An impression either has been received, or it has not: if it has, there is no deception in that case; if it has not, neither is there any deception in that case. The impression is, in case of sight, the sort of sensation produced by the striking of rays of light arranged in a certain order upon the retina; in case of hearing, the sort of feeling produced by the vibration given to the air by the sonorous body, and from the air communicated to the auditory nerve.*

When the judgment has been rendered erroneous by want of attention, and that defect of attention has been produced by want of interest — that is, of motive — this modification of the cause of error in testimony is to be considered under the head of moral, not of intellectual, causes.

Perception may have been rendered faint or indistinct by old age: attention may have been rendered indifferent, judgment hasty, negligent, and erroneous, by want of knowledge, general or particular, absolute or relative — the fruit of relative experience, observation, information, and meditation. Want of relative knowledge may be indicated by condition in life, by immaturity of age, and by insanity. False opinion, a still more powerful cause of incorrectness than simple ignorance, may be indicated in some instances by the like marks.

Where the chemist and the physician see a dangerous poison, the kitchen-maid may see nothing more than an immaterial flaw in one of her pans; the cook may behold an innocent means of recommending herself to the palate through the medium of the eye.

Where the botanist sees a rare, and perhaps new, plant, the husbandman sees a weed; where the mineralogist sees a new ore, pregnant with some new metal, the labourer sees a lump of dirt, not distinguishable from the rest, unless it be by being heavier and more troublesome. The same distinction may be pursued through the whole field of social occupation, and through every walk of science.

Under *insanity* are included *idiocy* and *lunacy:* the former a permanent disorder, and thence indicated by permanent marks; the other an occasional one: the former, therefore, presenting itself with greater certainty to the cognizance of the judge. Lunacy does not so much weaken the judging faculty, as disturb and delude it with false opinions, the product of the imagination; and thus belongs to an ensuing head. In both shapes, insanity may differ from itself in strength, by an infinity of shades — few, if any, distinguishable by any exact criterion, or measurable by any applicable scale.

Another intellectual cause of incorrectness in human testimony, is failure of memory. A failure of this sort may have had for its cause, either some original faintness or indistinctness in the act or acts of perception, as above described, or else the lapse of time — the length of the interval between the point of time at which the fact presented itself to the conception of the witness, and the point of time at which it happens to him to exhibit his statement of it for the information of the judge.

From the weakness of the memory may result two different, and in some respects opposite, effects: non-recollection, and false recollection.

Though the *correctness* of the conception entertained of the fact admits of no gradations upwards, yet this is not the case with regard to the *vivacity* of it — the quality on which its correctness at any subsequent and widely distant point of time so materially depends. Perfect correctness of conception may be stated as a result more usual, more ordinary, perhaps, than any degree of incorrectness: but were it possible to determine the most ordinary degree of vivacity, we should find as many gradations above that mark, perhaps, as below it. The highest point in it might

* When, by the extrusion of the preternaturally opaque humour of the eye, a person born blind has received his sight at an age somewhat advanced, at a time when the judgment, so far as it has had ground to exercise itself upon, has been matured, — all objects have at first appeared to be equally near. The picture painted on the retina cannot in this case have been different from what it would have been in the case of a person of the same age, by whom the art of seeing had been acquired in the usual gradual manner. It has been the judgment, then, and not sensation, that has in this case been in fault. It is only by degrees, by incessant exercise of the judgment, by comparing the sensation produced by an object at a less distance with the sensation produced by the same object at a greater distance, that the judgment has learnt, with that variable degree of accuracy which belongs to the human judgment in such cases, the art of placing objects at their proper distances.

A sensation similar to that produced by rays of light, may be produced by a different cause: for instance, a slight blow when the eyes are shut, or a galvanic stream. But though the judgment pronounces the cause of the sensation to be different in the two cases, the sensation itself is the same.

be described as being immediately below that at which a morbid suspension of the sensitive faculty, or a morbid disturbance of the reasoning faculty—insanity, in a word, transient or permanent—would ensue.

Importance in the fact, as above described, is the quality with which the degree of this vivacity will have been connected. This, like the vivacity which is its effect, will be susceptible of all manner of degrees—above, as well as below, the middle mark. There are some facts (and such are the infinite majority of the whole number of facts observed,) so unimportant as to be capable of escaping out of any man's memory the next minute after that in which the perception of them has taken place: there are others, of which the importance, either absolute or relative, with regard to the individual, is so great, that, unless on the supposition of an almost total decay of the faculty, through old age or disease, it will not be credible that the picture of them should have been effaced out of his memory by any length of time.

As importance may rise to any degree in the scale above the middle, so any degree of faintness that might have been produced by staleness, may have been compensated for by importance.

The importance of the fact may be either intrinsic, or in the way of association merely; viz. in respect of the property it has acquired by the influence of the principle of association, of calling up and presenting to the mind the idea of some other fact, which has an importance of its own. A drop of blood observed in a particular place may serve to indicate a murder: a knife of a particular appearance, found in a particular place, may serve to indicate the person of the murderer. Connected in the mind of a percipient witness with the idea of that atrocious crime, these circumstances will possess the degree of importance due to them: their apparent importance will, in his mind, stand on a level with their real importance. Taken separately, and without any such connexion, their apparent importance would have been as nothing; and no sooner had they found their way into the conception, than they would have made their escape out of the memory. In a butcher's shop, neither the knife nor the blood—neither a few drops of it nor a whole puddle, would have attracted the slightest notice.

Oblivion—forgetfulness—is not the only failing of which the memory is susceptible: erroneous recollection is another. Without any the least false consciousness as to any point whatever—without any intention or desire of departing in any point from the strict line of truth—a supposed recollection may be false, not only in quantity, quality, or other circumstance, but even *in toto*. I can speak from experience. Recollection false even *in toto* is what it has every now and then happened to me to detect myself in. I should expect to find this to be the case more or less with everybody. I speak of recollections devoid of all importance, and the expression of which has never gone forth, nor been intended to go forth, out of my own breast: and in respect of which, all inducements to mendacity, all causes of bias, have consequently been out of the question.

One circumstance, however, has been common (if in this instance too I do not misrecollect) to all these instances of misrecollection and false recollection: the image of the supposed transaction has been faint and dubious. It has been deduced, as it were, in the way of inference, from some real and better recollected facts, which have operated as evidentiary facts with relation to these false ones. It might be regarded as the work of the imagination, were it not for its having a distinct and solid ground to rest upon in the truth of things.

A proof of the difference has been afforded, when, for the purpose of confirming or disconfirming the truth of a dubious recollection of this sort, I have communicated it to some other person, whose opportunities of observation or means of judgment have appeared to render him more or less qualified to help me out. By his recollection or opinion, my own supposed recollection has been influenced. Supposing his persuasion to a certain degree strong, it has determined mine: my supposed recollection has appeared true or false to me, according as it has appeared true or false to him.

On the other hand, when the recollection the internal evidence, is clear and strong to a certain degree, there is no room left for any such external evidence to operate. To every man, recollections must present themselves in multitudes—recollections even of the most ancient facts, against which the evidence of all mankind would not predominate in his breast.

A recollection which is false in circumstance only, may be so, either by being superadded to such parts of the recollection as are true, or substituted to one or more of them. The case of substitution, though the more natural and usual case, is in its description the least simple. It is resolvable into the two opposite modes of falsehood, obliterative and fabricative: a true part of the scene, as it once stood painted, is rubbed out, and a false object painted in the room of it.

A recollection false *in toto*, is as easy to describe and conceive as a recollection false in circumstance. It, however, scarcely admits of being realized. Recollection, if it be recollection, must have had some ground, how narrow soever, in the truth of things, to serve as a foundation for the conception of the false facts. Take away this portion of the true ground, the picture is the work, not in any respect of the recollection, but of the imagination merely. The original picture is completely rubbed out by the hand of oblivion; and fancy has painted a picture of another imaginary fact in the place of it.

There are two causes, by the influence of which memory may be *refreshed*, and by that means rendered, at the time of deposition, more vivid than, by reason of the joint influence of the importance of the fact and the ancientness of it, it would otherwise be.

One is, intermediate statements; by which are supposed, intermediate recollections. The oftener a man has had to give an account of a fact, the less likely he is to have forgotten it, or in any point misremembered it. If in writing, the refreshing touch will naturally have been so much the stronger; inasmuch as the committing of a statement of any kind to writing, calls forth unavoidably a greater degree of attention than the exhibition of it *viva voce* in the way of ordinary conversation.

Another is, fresh incidents — perception of fresh incidents, or receipt of any statement, oral or written, of any fresh incidents — connected in the way of association with the fact in question. The sight of the spot where I have once met a friend, now far distant, recalls a vivid recollection of the friend himself; and not only of himself, but of what passed between us in that place.

Of intermediate recollections which have not been productive of any fresh statement — of mere *intransitive* recollections, which have never, through the medium of either the tongue or the pen of the witness, made their way out of his mind — the effect, though not equal in degree, will of course be of the same kind. By recollection, even of this silent sort, the picture cannot but have received a degree of refreshment — a degree the more considerable, the oftener this mental operation has been repeated. The circumstance is here mentioned, lest the conception given of the subject should be incomplete: but in practice, no application can be made of it.

When the memory of a witness, whose testimony is exhibited in a court of justice, is known to have been refreshed, this circumstance will naturally have a considerable influence on the degree of persuasion produced by his evidence. If the agreement between the two statements be substantially complete, the persuasive force of the evidence may in this way receive considerable increase. If there be any material variance, it will be a sign that, in one or the other of the two statements — the judicial, and the prior non-judicial one — there must have been a tincture of incorrectness, accompanied or not by mendacity, as the case may be. And the stronger the degree of refreshment, the less likely the incorrectness to have been unaccompanied by consciousness.

The last of the causes of incorrectness in evidence, above enumerated, is inaptitude of expression. The picture of the fact, as painted in the memory of the witness at the time of deposition, may be ever so correct; yet if the copy exhibited by the words and other signs employed by him for the expression of it be otherwise than correct, such accordingly will be his evidence. By an infelicity in the expression, the fruit of the most correct perception, and the most retentive memory, may be rendered abortive.*

On comparing the aberration liable to be produced by inaptness of expression, with the aberration producible by non-recollection or false recollection, the following differences appear discernible. —

The aberration by expression seems liable to be more wide than the aberration of the memory. It is capable of giving to the evidence a purport even directly opposite to the true one. The reason is, that a recollection, however false, if it be not false *in toto*, will, in some feature of it, be conformable to the truth: and the improbability of a recollection false *in toto* has already been exhibited. Recollection (as contradistinguished from mere imagination,) having its basis in truth, can scarcely be removed from that basis altogether. Expression, on the other hand, has no necessary tie by which the words are confined to any degree of conformity with the ideas they were intended to represent. The aberration is capable in this case of being so complete, that the fact, as actually expressed, may be

* In the history of French jurisprudence, a case, it is said, may be found, in which inaccuracy of expression cost a man his life. A witness having been examined in the presence of the defendant, and having been asked whether he was the person by whom the act was done, which he had seen done, answered in the negative. "Blessed be God!" exclaims the defendant — "here is a man — *qui ne m'a pas reconnu* — who has not recognised me." What he should have said — what he would have said, had he given a just expression to what he meant, was — "Here is a man *qui a reconnu que ce n'étoit pas moi* — who has recognised, declared, that it was not I." — See Voltaire, "Essai sur les Probabilités en fait de Justice, Politique," tom. ii.

Entire provinces, and even nations, have been taxed by a common opinion with a sort of endemial inaccuracy of expression. Nations the most distinguished for talent and genius, may be referred to as examples: and, in the case of these nations, inaccuracy of testimony has been in an equal degree the subject of remark. Of this inaccuracy, supposing it to be real, the state of the moral faculties appears commonly to have been looked to as the principal, if not the only, cause: but in the production of the effect, there seems little reason to doubt but that the state of the intellectual faculties may have possessed a considerable share.

the exact opposite of the fact as intended to be expressed. In the English language, two negatives, in correct and polished language, are equivalent to an affirmative: in the language of the illiterate classes, they amount frequently to no more than a negative. In the French tongue, negative is added to negative, on many occasions, without reversing the proposition, in the language of all classes.

On the other hand, an aberration arising from this cause does not appear to be altogether so natural, or likely to be so frequent, as an aberration arising from weakness of memory: at least, not to such a degree as to have any considerable effect on the persuasion of the judge. The reason is, that if the aberration be apparent, it will naturally receive correction from the remarks and questions that in each case may be expected from the judge; whereas a defect of recollection is little capable of receiving any such assistance.

In this respect it stands on a different footing, according to the form in which the testimony is presented to the judge — according as it is exhibited in writing, or *vivâ voce*. Exhibited in writing, it is less exposed to be incorrect in point of expression, on account of the assistance it will naturally receive from the hands of the professional assistant of the party whose evidence it is, if a litigant party,* or by whom the evidence was called for:† but in this case it has no chance of receiving correction from the judge. Exhibited *vivâ voce*, it is much more exposed to be incorrect at first utterance, but has the advantage of being open to correction from the judge; viz. either from the judge immediately, or, under his authority, from the professional assistant of one or other of the parties.

Incorrectness from this source, in the course of a *vivâ voce* examination, can, therefore, seldom take place in any very essential circumstance, without some degree of blame on the part of the judge; nor, on that and other accounts, without some degree of blame on the part of the system of procedure.‡

In the case of *vivâ voce* examination, timidity is, perhaps, the most frequent cause of incorrectness in the expression. Of this timidity, the causes of a higher order are principally to be found in inferiority in respect of rank, sex, and age. The degree of it is of course susceptible of an infinity of gradations, according to the idiosyncrasy of the individual. The highest gradations will be found in the case where it has sex for its cause; especially when that cause is combined with that which results from age. It will be influenced in a very considerable degree by the degree of intercourse which a person has had with the world; by the number of persons whom he has been in the habit of living with, — a circumstance of which the influence is perhaps greater in this case than that of *rank*. But though sensibility of this kind, derived from weakness of sex, immaturity of age, inferiority of rank or of social intercourse, bears, with reference to the phenomenon in question, the relation of cause to effect; it would be an abuse of logic to state the effect in those cases as running in any regular proportion with the degree of the cause. In the female sex, it will also be naturally influenced by condition in life, in respect of matrimony. The sort of person likely to be affected in the highest degree from the joint influence of all these causes, is probably an unmarried female, about the age of puberty, and a few years afterwards.

Timidity, upon a closer view, will be found to be, on this occasion, neither more nor less than an extraordinary degree of sensibility to the force of the three tutelary sensations, as applying themselves in this instance: viz. the moral, the political, and the religious; but more especially the moral.‖

This timidity will be influenced in a considerable degree by the publicity of the examination: and the error, which is but too apt to arise from this source, is among the inconveniences which require to be set in the scale against the still preponderating advantages which will be seen to result from that cardinal security for truth.

An intellectual cause of incorrectness in testimony, not yet brought to view, and which could not be enumerated among the causes which apply to correctness and incorrectness, because it is applicable to the latter alone, is the imagination, taking the place of recollection.

In weak and undiscerning minds, the simple idea, the mere conception, of an object, be it substance or event, matter at rest or matter in motion, may come to be but faintly discriminated from, may come even to be confounded with, the belief of its existence. At this moment, I have in my mind three ideas: one of a hill of pure sand, another of a hill of pure gold, a third of a hill composed of gravel, chalk, and flints, with a miscellaneous intermixture of animal and vegetable remains. The idea of the golden hill is as vivid, as well as distinct, in my mind, as that of the sand hill: it is more so than that of the composite hill. But to the idea of the composite hill, as well as of the sand hill, is annexed an act of the judgment, importing belief — the belief which I am hereby expressing, of the existence of hills — an indeterminate number of hills, of that

* As in case of an answer in equity, under the English law.

† As in the case of an affidavit, for or against a motion for an information or attachment.

‡ See Book III. *Extraction*.

‖ See the next Chapter for the explanation of these terms.

sort, — a belief, the expression of which is a proposition to this effect: Sand hills exist in nature; the idea I have of a sand hill has its archetype in nature. To the idea of the golden hill is annexed, likewise, a proposition analogous to the former, but of the opposite cast: No hill of pure gold exists in nature — of the idea I have of a golden hill, there is no archetype in nature. In a weak uncultivated mind, this act of the judgment is sometimes passed on any the slightest evidence—on what, to a stronger and more exercised mind, would seem no evidence. Put into the hands of a child of three years old, under the name, not of a story-book, but of a book of natural history — a book in which the existence of golden hills is assumed, as well as that of sand hills, —the judgment of belief will, in his mind, as readily attach itself upon the existence of the one sort of hill as upon that of the other. Show him at a little distance a hill covered with grass, and tell him that under the grass it is all solid gold, — and let nobody in his hearing ever intimate any suspicion to the contrary,— the belief of the existence of a golden hill may thenceforward present itself to his mind as having been demonstrated to him by the evidence of his senses.

Of the false facts presented to the imagination, and at the same time presented under the guise of real ones at the time, — the only ones the experience of which is common to everybody, are the facts presented in dreams. In infant minds, minds as yet but little exercised in the art of applying attention to the operations of the judgment, the distinction between the state of waking and the state of dreaming, between the waking and the dreaming thoughts, is for some time so faint as to be occasionally evanescent. In my early childhood, at a time when I was just able to go up and down stairs alone, being at the top of the staircase, and having made a false step, it seemed to me that, instead of falling headlong and rolling down the stairs, I felt myself gently wafted, as it were, from top to bottom, and there landed safe, my feet not having come in contact with anything the whole time. At present I have no more difficulty in recognising these sensations to have presented themselves in a dream, than anybody else would have: but I have all along preserved a distinct recollection of a time, and a time of considerable duration, during which the imaginary scene was accompanied in my mind by a belief of its existence. To this recollection is superadded a recollection of my communicating to some person, but I forget whom, the relation of this incident, as an adventure not more extraordinary than true. Had a dream to this same effect been dreamt by Wesley, the recollection of it would probably have remained numbered among his real recollections to the end of his life. In his journal are contained the histories of more than one adventure, in which the deviation from the laws of nature is little, if anything, more considerable. A text, which that incident used not unfrequently to recall to me, might, with the help of a Wesleyan imagination, have been unalterably associated with the conceived event: —"He shall give his angels charge over thee, to keep thee in all thy ways; they shall bear thee up in their hands, lest thou dash thy foot against a stone." Such was the passage in one of the songs of David,* as quoted to his divine descendant by the devil:† and although, among the attributes of that mysterious personage, he numbers that of being *the father of lies*, — for this time, at any rate, his quotation was correct. An angel holding the favourite infant by the hand as it glided down the staircase, might have added neither an unapt, nor an unnatural, embellishment to the scene.

Thus fugitive and precarious, in an unformed mind, is the distinction between the mere conception of an object, and the belief of its existence: thus apt is the judgment, embracing and including the image, to be confounded with the image alone. In this sort of confusion we may behold a principle which not only took possession of, but contributed largely to the generation of a system in, the mind of the sceptical and sagacious Hume. Belief of the existence of an object is, according to him, neither more nor less than a certain degree of vivacity in the idea introduced by the object into the mind. By what kind of *photometer* shall that degree of vivacity upon which belief attaches, be distinguished from those fainter ones to which no such act of the judgment is annexed?

Between the ages of eight and nine, the metamorphoses of which Ovid is the historian, and the prodigies of Jewish history (such was, and such continues to be, the course of instruction at the royal school of Westminster) were presented together to my tender and susceptible mind. On the one hand, the devil in a variety of shapes, — on the other hand, the scenes in Ovid (Baucis and Philemon, I remember, for one) would ever and anon present themselves to my dreaming, as well as my waking, thoughts. Which was the more agreeable class, I well know:—which was the more lively, I could not engage to say. Yet, under this uncertainty in respect of superiority of vivacity, in respect of belief there never was any the smallest doubt. Parental solicitude was too steadily at its post to suffer any the smallest confusion to prevail in those tints by which belief, disbelief, and conception pure from each, are characterized and distinguished.

The reader will approve or disapprove, as

* Psalm xci. 11, 12.
† St. Matthew, iv. 6. St. Luke, iv. 10, 11.

it seems good to him, this exhibition of egotistic evidence, in a case which admits not of any other.

If, in a susceptible and unformed mind, the mere idea of an object is found to operate as sufficient evidence of its existence, — much more frequently will it be sufficient, when the way for its reception in that character has been prepared by popular opinion operating in favour of it, in the character of a mass of remote indeed, but most extensive, and thereby impressive, circumstantial evidence. Hence it is that those terrific spectres, ghosts, witches, devils, and vampires, which, for the last time let it be hoped, have haunted the seat of justice, have not yet ceased to haunt the garret and the cottage.

Under the head of imagination — that is, under the head of incorrectness of testimony considered as flowing from that source — it was necessary to introduce the world of phantoms. The occasions on which false evidence, created by the imagination, has in this way had religion for its source, have been but too frequent. The cases in which false evidence, pure from all mixture of mendacity, has been generated by the imagination, without the benefit of any such supernatural assistance, will hardly be to be found.*

There are two cases in which the result produced is simple incorrectness — pure, or nearly so, from mendacious consciousness, but of which, nevertheless, the causes belong to the moral department. These are, the case of *bias*, — a case that has already been slightly brought to view; and the case of *indolence* — the case where the departure from the direct line of truth has a sort of unconscious indolence for its cause.

To what end the above analysis? To the following ends :—

1. To give a view of the cases in which falsehood is incapable of being prevented.

2. To save the judge from imputing mendacity where there is none — where there is none of that false consciousness which is essential to it.

3. To facilitate the recognition of mendacity where it exists : — a task which will be the easier, the clearer the light in which the characters of simple incorrectness are presented.

4. To give assistance to that one of the parties who has truth and justice on his side — whose interest it is that the truth should be brought to light—by suggesting to him topics for investigation and examination.

So obvious are most of the considerations above presented—so much in the way of every body's observation, that, under the name of instruction, they have scarce any pretension to be of any use. But, what a man has had in his mind, he has not always at hand at the very moment at which it is wanted : what conveys no instruction, may serve for reminiscence.

Minute and trivial as the distinctions may be, the sketch was necessary, to complete the anatomical view which for this purpose it was necessary to give of the human mind. In corporeal anatomy, to trace out the ramifications of the nerves was no amusing operation, but not the less a necessary one. Hunter, the Garrick of lecturers, would sometimes turn it over to his assistant Hewson, but he never would have held himself warranted in omitting it.

CHAPTER XI.

OF THE MORAL CAUSES OF CORRECTNESS AND COMPLETENESS IN TESTIMONY, WITH THEIR OPPOSITES.

§ 1. *The moral causes of correctness and completeness in testimony, with their opposites, are motives.*

Of action (including, in so far as it is the work of the will, inaction, or forbearance) — of action, in whatsoever shape displayed, the efficient causes are *motives;* and it has no others that are perceptible.

Utterance of testimony is action. Whatever verity there is in testimony, is therefore produced by motives: and again, whatsoever mendacity there is in testimony, is also pro-

* The sort of work here in question — the production of false, yet unmendacious evidence — may be styled the extraordinary work of the imagination. The ordinary work consists in exhibiting, for the purpose of amusement, facts, which had indeed no archetypes in nature, but which are known by the individual operator to be in that case, and are not seriously exhibited by him as true, either to a judge acting as such, or to anybody else. This ordinary work of the imagination has consequently nothing to do with evidence, and is altogether clear of those pernicious effects with which its extraordinary work is so apt to be attended. Novel-writers and poets must not be confounded with false witnesses.

Another work, which may also be reckoned among the extraordinary works of imagination, is the exact converse of the one at present under consideration. In the case of false evidence produced by this cause, facts having no existence are averred seriously to exist: in the other case, facts really existing have imagination for their cause. I speak of the class of effects which make so conspicuous a figure in the history of medicine: diseases sometimes removed or suspended, sometimes produced, by the influence of belief upon the mind — mere belief, without any ground in nature. In this belief, religious opinion has in some instances had a share; but instances are much more numerous in which, in the production of the effect, that hyperphysical power has had no share. I need only allude to animal magnetism, which obtained so many partisans at one time in the capital of France; and to the metallic tractors, which had about the same time so much vogue in this country.

duced by motives. Even when the result of mere temerity or negligence, and therefore not referable to the head of mendacity, falsity may be referred to motives: that deficiency of attention, of which the falsity in question is the result, being itself the result either of the love of ease (an article having, as will be seen, an indisputable title to a place in the catalogue of motives,) or at any rate, of the absence of some motive, by which, had it been present, the requisite degree of attention — the degree requisite to the production of correctness and completeness — would have been produced.

A *motive*, is the idea or expectation of good or evil: — of good, as eventually about to result from the mode of action or conduct with reference to which the idea or expectation of it operates as a motive; of evil as eventually about to be produced by the opposite mode of action or conduct.*

Motive, being a conjugate of *motion* — *motive* (though the only word in ordinary use for the purpose of expressing the efficient cause of the mode or line of conduct observed by a man on every given occasion) is in its import too narrow for the purpose: for, be the result *action* or *inaction* — motion (whether of the physical or psychological faculties) or rest, — and, in case of offences for example, be the offence produced an offence of the *positive* or the *negative* cast, — an appellative for the designation of the efficient cause of the effect thus produced, is alike necessary.

To supply the deficiency, either such a signification must be added to the signification of the word *motive*, as involves a sort of contradiction in terms — a motive producing, not motion, but the absence of it, viz. rest; or some other appellative, simple or composite, must be employed instead of it: simple, as *determinative*, — compound, as *principle of conduct*, source of conduct, efficient cause of conduct.

Rest being the result of the absence of motives — action, positive action, being, when motives are present and operating, the more usual and more conspicuous result of such their operation — hence, to designate the efficient cause of action, the word *motive* came *originally*, — and, for want of conceptions sufficiently clear and comprehensive on the part of moralists, has continued — *exclusively* to be employed. Of imperfect conceptions, imperfect expression has, throughout the whole field of conception and language, been the necessary result.

The relation borne by the signification of the word *interest* to the signification of the word *motive*, has on this occasion been rendered a necessary object of attention, and a necessary subject of explanation, not only by the use made of it in common language, but by the use made of it, and the gross and pernicious errors propagated by means of it, to so prodigious an extent, and with such baneful effect, by lawyers.

Correspondent to every species of pain or pleasure, is a species of motive; correspondent to every species of motive, is a modification of *interest*.†

A *motive*, is an *interest* considered as being in a state of action—as being, on the occasion in question, actually exerting its influence on the mind of the individual in question.

An interest, is a motive considered in an abstract point of view; viz. as possessing the faculty of being called into action, but without presenting to view any particular occasion in which it is considered as employing itself in the exercise of such faculty. When the word *motive* is employed, the object designated by it is in general not considered as pointing any further than to the particular *good* which is considered as being in view. Interest—when I say *such is my interest*, or, *it is my interest to do so and so*—points not only to the attainment of that good, but to the general effect of that event upon the sum of my well-being.

* As to *good* and *evil*, neither have the objects respectively signified by those words any value, nor the words themselves any meaning, but by reference to *pain* and *pleasure*.

By the word *good*, where it has any determinate meaning, is meant, either a determinate lot of pleasure; or the absence of a determinate lot of pain; or the chance, or the *efficient cause*, of a determinate lot of pleasure, or of exemption from a determinate lot of pain; or some combination of advantage, in any of these different shapes.

By the word *evil*, in like manner, is meant, either a determinate lot of pain; or the absence or loss of a determinate lot of pleasure; or the chance or *efficient cause* of a determinate lot of pain, or of the absence or loss of a determinate, and not in every event unobtainable, lot of pleasure; or any combination of disadvantage in any of these different shapes.

† The word *interest*, and the word *motive*, are, or at least might and ought to be, exactly co-extensive; the difference being no other than what consists in the difference between the sets of words respectively necessary to make them up into a sentence. A man has an *interest* in doing so and so, when, by the force of some motive, he is urged to do so and so. The interests corresponding to the self-regarding sorts of motives are, it is true, the sorts of interest most commonly in view where the word *interest* is employed. But to give the use of the word the extension which is requisite for the purpose of conveying just conceptions, and of which it is not unsusceptible, it must be extended so as to take in the dissocial motives, and even the purely social motives. *L'interêt de la vengeance* (or *vindictive interest*, as it may be rendered in English) is an expression already familiar enough in the French language: and why should I not be permitted and admitted to take an *interest*, though it be not a self-regarding one, in the prosperity of mankind, my country, my profession, my party, or my friend?

The word *interest* is used in an abstract sense; viz. for the purpose of designating either some particular species of interest, but without designating what; or every species of interest without distinction; or all taken together: this acceptation is wanting to the word *motive*.

The word *sinister* is applied as an epithet indifferently to the word *interest* or to the word *motive*. Employed in the way it usually is, it leads to error; conveying the intimation that there are particular species of interest to which the property thus designated belongs; viz. either constantly or incidentally, but in both cases to the exclusion of others. The truth, however, is, that there exists not any species of interest—any sort of motive, in which this property may not occasionally be found. By a *sinister* interest or motive, is meant an interest or motive that acts in a sinister *direction*, *i. e.* that excites or leads to evil—an interest or motive, by the force of which a man is prompted or excited to engage in some evil line of conduct: but there is not any species of interest—any species of motive, to which it may not happen to act in this, as well as in the contrary, direction.

If this part of the field of language were filled up upon any regular and complete plan, opposite and correspondent to *sinister* as applied to interest, we should have *dexter* as applied to the same subject: forasmuch as interest is no less apt to lead to good than to evil. As every man has a right side as well as a left side, so, in heraldry, every scutcheon has a *dexter* side as well as a *sinister* side: but the language of psychology, though a science rather more useful than heraldry, is not equally well provided.

Of the three classes, to one or other of which all pleasures and pains, consequently all motives, may be referred, viz. the *self-regarding*, the *social*, and the *dissocial* or *anti-social*,—the word *interest* is more frequently applied to designate those of the self-regarding class, than those of either of the two others; and among those of the self-regarding class, most frequently of all to that which stretches over so much larger a portion of the field of action than any other of them, viz. the love of money.

Accordingly, this is the only species of interest which the man of law, at least the English, recognises under that name. *Good*, he knows of none but money: *evil*, he knows of none but the want of money: interest, he knows of none but *pecuniary* interest: *interest*, *motive*, *passion*, he knows of none but the love of money.

Accordingly,—be it as it may in regard to other trangressions—to offences, to crimes, committed by other means, by the aid of other instruments,—*mendacity* is a transgression to which, according to his conception of the matter, no man can be engaged by any other modification of interest than *pecuniary* interest: nor is there, according to him, that particle of this sort of interest, so impalpably small, to the force of which, if exerted in exciting him to mendacity, it lies within the sphere of possibility that he should oppose an effectual resistance.*

Of this error in theory, the practical consequence (it will be seen) is no less than perpetual injustice, with that perpetual insecurity, and that perpetually renewed affliction, which are among the fruits of it.

In the objects designated by the words *pleasure* and *pain*, we see two articles, of which the importance does not seem much exposed to be undervalued, or the nature very liable to be misunderstood.

By reference to pleasure and pain, the word *motive* in all its several acceptations, and the species of objects comprised under that genus in all its several modifications, receive, now at least (and, so far as concerns the subject of *evidence*, now for the first time,) a clear and determinate signification. So many distinguishable sorts of *pleasures* and *pains*, so many distinguishable sorts of motives.

On the one hand, veracity, and, so far as depends on attention, verity—on the other hand, mendacity—being the result of determinate motives or combinations of motives,—what remains, so far as the *will* is concerned in the production of those opposite results, is to observe, on the one hand, in what cases, and in what manner, the efficient causes in question operate in the beneficial and desirable direction indicated by the words veracity and verity—that is, in favour of correctness and completeness; on the other hand, in what cases, and in what manner, the *same* efficient causes (for in both instances they will be found to be at bottom the same) operate in the pernicious and undesirable direction indicated by the word mendacity.

Considered in the character of an efficient cause of veracity and verity in testimony, a motive of any description may be termed a veracity or verity-promoting, or mendacity-restraining, motive.

Considered in the character of an efficient cause of mendacity or bias, and thence of falsehood, a motive of any description may be termed a mendacity-prompting, exciting, or inciting, motive.

On these definitions may be grounded a sort of aphorism or axiom, which, in the character of a help to conception and to memory, may be not altogether without its use. On every occasion, the probability of veracity, and thence, so far as depends upon *will*, of correctness and completeness in testimony, is as the sum of the force of the mendacity-restraining, to the sum of the mendacity-exciting motives.

---

* See Book IX. *Exclusion*.

§ 2. *Any motive may operate as a cause either of veracity or of mendacity.*

Of the causes of mendacity and veracity, the list is the same as that of the causes of human action: no action so good or so bad, that it may not have had any sort of motive for its cause. This is what has been already stated, and, if I mistake not, put beyond doubt, by a general survey of the whole stock of motives elsewhere.*

No action, good or bad, without a motive: an action without a motive, is an effect without a cause. Yet men stand excluded by whole shoals and classes from the faculty of being made to serve in the character of witnesses, for no other reason than their standing exposed to the action of this or that species of motive!

No action, good or bad, or even of the class of those termed indifferent (a class which, strictly speaking, has no existence†) — no action whatsoever without a motive. To actions of atomical and almost invisible importance, correspond motives of atomical and equally invisible force.

To judge whether a motive be capable of giving birth to mendacious testimony exhibited in a court of justice, it will be necessary to observe what sort of result it must be that is expected to ensue from the evidence in question; that is, from the decision which will naturally and properly be grounded on that evidence, taking it for true. Applying this test to the several sorts of motives, we shall find that there is not one of them that is not capable of giving birth to mendacious testimony; that there is not one that would not, in certain cases, be necessarily productive of that effect, supposing the force of it to be unchecked by that of any other motive or motives. As there is no sort of pleasure or pain to which it may not happen to a man to be subjected in consequence of the decision of a court of justice, — it follows of course, that there is no sort of motive by which he may not be urged to do whatever is in his power, towards procuring the decision by which the pleasure in question may be secured to him, or the pain averted. And unless the force of any such motive be counteracted by a stronger motive, it will of course lead him to commit mendacity in that view, if mendacity be the most probable means which occurs to him of effecting his object.

As in the whole catalogue of motives there is none which is not capable of producing mendacity, so in the whole catalogue there is none, the force of which is not liable occasionally to act upon the mind in a direction tending to insure its adherence to the line of truth.

On the same individual occasion, a motive of the same kind operating on different persons at the same time, may prompt one of them to speak true, the other to speak false.

Take the motive of self-preservation — self-preservation from legal punishment. In the character of defendants on a criminal charge, two persons are under examination. One of them is innocent: his interest is manifestly to speak true; every true fact he brings to view, that is pertinent to the object of inquiry, operates in his favour in the character of circumstantial evidence. The other is guilty: the true facts, if brought to view, would operate towards his conviction, in the character of articles of criminative circumstantial evidence: accordingly, under this apprehension, he either suppresses the mention of them, or denies their existence, substituting, or not substituting, in the room of them, false facts of his own invention, adapted to the purpose.

On the same individual occasion, the self-same motive, operating on the same person at the same time, may prompt him, in relation to one fact to speak true, in relation to another to speak false.

The guilty defendant is under examination as before. Various questions are put to him, tending to draw from him the admission or the denial (say the admission) of so many various facts. These facts are all true; all of them in their tendency operating against him in the character of circumstantial evidence. Within the compass of twenty-four hours, suppose he was at four different places specified. Self-preservation is his object—an object he is willing to purchase, and at any price. In regard to three of the four facts, mendacity, he sees clearly, presents not the smallest chance of being of use: these facts, he understands, will be proved against him by other evidence; and mendacity being thus detected, would operate against him in the character of a criminative circumstance: the fourth, he hopes, may not be thus capable of other proof. What in this case will he do? He will admit the three first facts, and in respect to those facts, speak true: he will deny the fourth, and in respect to that, speak false.

Mendacity or veracity will in each instance be the result, according as, in that particular instance, the force of the mendacity-prompting, or say seducing motives, or that of the veracity-insuring, or say tutelary motives, is the strongest.

* "*Introduction to the Principles of Morals and Legislation*," in Vol. I. of the present collection; Chap. X. *Motives*.

† Whatever act affords any the minutest particle of satisfaction, of pleasure, or removes or prevents any the least particle of pain, is, in so far, good. In this case are the great majority of human acts, even in the instance of the most atrocious malefactor that ever lived.

There is no species of motive but what is capable of existing in, and acting with, any degree of force, from the lowest to the highest or — at least, a degree in practical effect equal to the highest.

There is no species of motive, of the effective force of which, in any given instance, any tolerably well-grounded estimate can be formed, without a survey made of the several influencing circumstances in the situation of the witness, on which the effective force of the motive depends; which survey cannot be completely made without a *vivâ voce* examination taken of the witness himself, having for its object the bringing of those circumstances to light.

There is no one species of motive, of the effective force of which any certain prediction can be made, even after a survey taken, and taken in the best manner, of the several influencing circumstances above mentioned.

Although there be some species of motives, of which the force is upon a medium considerably greater than that of others; yet, as they are capable of acting, each of them, according to circumstances, with any degree of force, from the highest to the lowest, it is impossible to form any tolerably well-grounded prediction with respect to the comparative probability of mendacity or veracity, from the mere observation that, on the occasion in question, the witness is subjected to the action of this or that species of motive.

These two axioms cannot be too often repeated.

No species of motive but is capable of operating in the character of a mendacity-exciting cause.

With but slight exception, and with none that is worth noticing for this purpose, no species of motive but is capable of operating with any degree of force.

In the non-observation of these fundamentally important truths, lies the main root of the exclusionary system already spoken of — that system of misrule, the exposure of which in detail is one of the principal objects of this work.

§ 3. *Of the four sanctions, considered as causes of trustworthiness or untrustworthiness in testimony.*

By interests and motives, so far as depends upon the state of the *will*, are (as hath been seen) produced, in so far as it happens to them to be produced, correctness and completeness in testimony. By those same psychological powers, so far as depends upon the will, are, on the other hand, produced, in so far as it happens to them to be produced, the directly opposite qualities, incorrectness and incompleteness.

But, in each pair, the opposite qualities are in such sort opposite, as to be mutually incompatible. Incapable of existing both of them in the same instance; in each instance, which is it that shall have place?

All depends upon the occasion: of the two opposite sets of forces — on one occasion we shall see the one set prevail — on another occasion, the other.

One leading distinction, however, may be remarked at the outset. Of the tutelary forces, the efficient causes of correctness and completeness, the operation (as will be seen) is constant — operating on all occasions: while of the seductive forces — the efficient causes of incorrectness and incompleteness — the operation is but casual, brought about by particular incidents and situations.*

The general prevalence of correctness and completeness over the opposite qualities in testimony, is a matter of fact out of the reach of dispute, and a state of things the existence of which may be regarded as indispensably necessary to the existence of mankind: it is to the general predominance of the tutelary forces over the seductive, that this prevalence of truth over falsehood is to be ascribed.

Be it in the *correct* direction, or in the *sinister* and *seductive* direction, that it acts — it is still by *interest*, operating in some shape or other in the character of a *motive*, that (so far as depends upon the state of the will) the state of the testimony in respect of correctness and completeness is produced. But whether it be the act of giving testimony, or any other sort of act, that constitutes the occasion on which they are considered as operating, — these forces, considered in respect of the direction (viz. the straight direction) most frequently and habitually assumed by them, have in another place† been considered as acting in various groupes; to each of which groupes the name of a *sanction*, in conformity to a usage already found established, has been attached: the principle of combination being, in each instance, the source from whence the pains and pleasures, acting thus in the character of interests and motives, are seen or supposed to flow.

According to this principle of division, there are four distinguishable sanctions: the *physical*, the *legal* or *political*, the *moral* or *popular*, and the *religious;* which three last may, in consideration of the seat of the pains and pleasures immediately belonging to them, be comprised together under the collective appellation of *psychological.*

To the *physical* sanction may be referred all pains and pleasures which are capable of

* By a tutelary motive, is meant any motive which on the occasion in question prompts the person in question to do right. By a seductive motive, any motive which prompts him to do wrong. — See *Introduction to the Principles of Morals and Legislation*, Chap. X. *Motives*, Vol. I. p. 46.

† *Ibid.* Chap. III. p. 14.

being produced, and habitually are produced, by the operation of causes purely natural; without the intervention of any of the powers, from which the pains and pleasures belonging to any of those other sanctions derive, or are supposed to derive, their existence.*

To the *legal*, or say the *political*† sanction may be referred all such pains or pleasures as are capable of being expected at the hand of law and government: pains which, expected from that quarter, and considered as expressly designed to influence action, assume the name of *punishment:* pleasures which, expected from that quarter, and considered as designed to influence action, assume the name of *reward.*

As there is scarce a pain or pleasure, whether of the physical class or the psychological, which may not immediately or remotely be produced by the hand of political power, and thus assume the shape of punishment or reward; hence it may be understood, that the circumstance by which the pains and pleasures capable of emanating from the legal or political sanction, are distinguished from those of the physical, is, not so much the nature of the sensations themselves, as the *quarter* whence they are looked for—the *source* from which they are expected to flow.

To the *moral*, or say the *popular*‡ sanction, may be referred all such pains and pleasures as are capable of being expected at the hands of the community at large—that is, of such individual members of it, within the sphere of whose action it may happen to the condition of the individual in question, in his supposed character of *witness*, to be comprised: such individuals acting, on the occasions in question, in pursuance of whatsoever liberty of indifference is left to them by the law; and accordingly, at pleasure, rendering, or forbearing to render, to him, any such services as they are left at liberty to render or to withhold at pleasure; and producing on his part, or forbearing to produce, any such uneasinesses as, in his instance, they are in like manner left at liberty to produce at pleasure.

From the catalogue of the pains referable to this sanction, are obviously excluded all those severer pains which, for their infliction, require the uncontroulable and irresistible hand of law. But, with this exception, the pains as well as pleasures referable to this sanction, and emanating from this source, may be said nearly to coincide with the pains and pleasures referable to the artifical source just mentioned. When *negative* action is taken into the account as well as *positive*—*negative* action, to which much greater liberty is, and in the nature of the case must be, left by law than to *positive*,—it will be seen, that of the pains to which a man can be subjected by law, there is not one to which, in a way more or less immediate, it may not happen to a man to be subjected by the free agency left to individuals; viz. in this sense, that, by means of some service or other which it was left free to them to render or not, he might by this or that individual have been preserved from it.

To the religious sanction are to be referred all such pains and pleasures as are capable of being expected at the hands of an invisible Ruler of the universe.

In so far as the pains and pleasures expected from this supernatural source are regarded as eventually liable to be experienced in the present life, they comprehend and coincide with the aggregate multitude of the pains and pleasures belonging to the other sanctions: in so far as they are regarded as liable to be experienced in a life to come, they are inconceivable and indescribable as the Being from whose hand they are expected to emanate.

* Under this head must also be included (although, the seat of them being in the mind, the sanction belonging to them should in that respect be referred to the psychological class) all such pains and pleasures as consist in, or are attached to, the *expectation* of pains or pleasures purely physical. For, strictly speaking, it is not so much by the physical sensation, as by the prospect of it, that the effect in question, produced on human conduct, is produced.

† *Legal or political.*] Though in general the objects designated by these epithets will be found to coincide, the hand of law being the hand mostly employed by political government in the distribution of good and evil on the score of reward and punishment, more especially on the score of punishment,—they are not, however, absolutely identical; the political sanction comprising in its extent the whole mass of good and evil capable of being distributed and applied by the hand of government. Good and evil, especially good, are capable of being distributed, and in practice are distributed, by the hand of government, and that not only on other scores, but even on the scores of reward and punishment, especially reward—by other hands than that of *law;* at least, by others than that of the judge: and this not only, as they are but too apt to be, improperly, but to a considerable extent even consistently with strict propriety—especially on the score of reward.

‡ *Popular or moral.*] *Popular*, in respect of the persons at whose hands the pains and pleasures, the good and evil in question, are expectable; viz. the members of the community at large, acting in their individual and private capacity, and not any of them, as in the case of the political sanction, in the character of public functionaries: *moral*, in respect of the degree in which the rules of action received in the character of rules of *morality*, rules for the government of moral conduct (abstraction made of the force of law, and the other motives referable to the political sanction,) depend upon this sanction for their observance. Abstraction made of the force of the political sanction, and of that of the religious, it is by the popular sanction, as above described, in conjunction with the physical, that human conduct in all its modifications is determined.

§ 4. *Operation of the physical sanction, for and against correctness and completeness in testimony.*

In the case of the political, popular, and religious sanctions,—among the pains and pleasures respectively belonging to them, there is not one, the expectation of which is not capable of operating in the character of an efficient cause of, or at least a security for, correctness and completeness in testimony; since, in all these several instances, the production of the pain or pleasure in question, in the bosom of the supposed witness, is the result of a *will* different from, and extraneous to, his own—the will of some *other* being or beings; and in each case, among the several pains and pleasures, the production of which is in the power of the being in question, it depends upon his will to apply, in the case in question, whichsoever of those forces he pleases.

In the case of the pains and pleasures of the physical sanction, in so far as applying to the purpose here in question,—no such extraneous will, nor indeed any will at all, taking any part in their production,—the only pain or pleasure that has place is one that grows of itself out of the nature of the case. This, it will be seen, is a pain only; and this pain, the pain of labour (mental labour) or exertion: and the *motive* corresponding to this pain, is the *love of ease.*

To relate incidents as they have really happened,* is the work of the memory: to relate them otherwise than as they have really happened, is the work of the invention. But, generally speaking, comparing the work of the memory with that of the invention, the latter will be found by much the harder work. The ideas presented by the memory present themselves in the first instance, and as it were of their own accord: the ideas presented by the invention, by the imagination, do not present themseves without labour and exertion. In the first instance come the true facts presented by the memory, which facts must be put aside: they are constantly presenting themselves, and as constantly must the door be shut against them. The false facts, for which the imagination is drawn upon, are not to be got at without effort: not only so, but if, in the search made after them, any at all present themselves, different ones will present themselves for the same place: to the labour of investigation is thus added the labour of selection.

Hence an axiom of mental pathology, applicable to the present case—an axiom expressive of a matter of fact, which may be stated as the primary and fundamental cause of veracity in man. The work of the memory is in general easier than that of the invention. But to consult the memory alone in the statement given, is veracity: mendacity is the quality displayed, so far as the invention is employed.

The love of ease—in other words, the desire of avoiding the pain of mental exertion—is therefore a motive, the action of which tends, on every occasion, with more or less force and effect, to confine the discourse of a man within the pale of truth.

But the pain which in this case acts on the side of veracity,—which acts as a sort of punishment attaching upon the first tendency and leaning towards the path of mendacity—which acts, therefore, as a sort of restrictive force, confining the discourse within the path of truth,—is a punishment which arises immediately and spontaneously out of the offence; which arises of itself, without need of the interposition of the will of any other being, divine or human, to apply it, as in the case of the other three sanctions. The sanction to which this pain, this motive, belongs, is therefore that which has been termed the physical. It is the same sanction by which a man stands prohibited from striking his hand against the edge of a knife, or holding it in the flame of the candle.

Such would be the case, even if the chance in favour of correctness rested on no other basis than the influence of the physical sanction, as above described, taken by itself. But when the influence of the moral sanction is brought upon the carpet, the disproportion receives an ulterior increase.

The act of reporting as true that which is not true,—such a transgression of the line of truth, even when not attended with a consciousness of the departure, is a mode of conduct against which the moral sanction points its censure with a certain degree of force: much more, when the departure is regarded as attended with that vicious consciousness. The labour of invention, consequently, is increased: since the story must be framed, not only so as to answer a present purpose, by deceiving the person to whom it is addressed, but, if possible, so as not to draw down upon the inventor the pain of public disesteem, by being subsequently discovered to be false.

The axiom above brought to view is not a mere barren speculation, but of very high importance with reference to practice. Applied to English law, it will serve to justify the admission of a class of evidence which of late years has been admitted, but which in former times had been excluded: I mean the testimony of non-adults of a tender age. Is the child sufficiently instructed in regard to

* I mean, as to the narrator they have really appeared to happen. With this explanation, the expression, *as they have really happened*, may be used, instead of the more correct expression, to save words.

the nature and consequences of an oath? Upon the ground of this question has the decision, with regard to the admission or rejection of the child's testimony, been customarily placed. In another place, I shall have occasion to show the fallaciousness of such ground. In return to the suddenly put and unforeseeable question that will be respectively grounded upon each preceding answer,—is it, under these circumstances, most likely that the memory, or the invention, shall on each occasion be the fund to which, for the matter of each respective answer, he will have recourse? Of the two, this would seem to be the more reasonable question.

In the matter of fact of which the above axiom is the expression, we already find a cause adequate to account for the predominance of veracity over mendacity—a cause, of the due consideration of which, the natural tendency will be to confirm or increase our confidence in human testimony, independently of whatever security for veracity may be afforded by the influence of the three other sanctions.

Children — (says a proverb one sometimes hears) children and fools tell truth. There is something offensive in the proverb: there is a sort of immoral turn in it — a sort of intimation, as mischievous as it is false, of a natural connexion between veracity and folly. On the first mention of it, one conceives it to have had for its author a species of knave, who, as such, is a species of fool; for, though all folly is not knavery, yet there is no knavery that is not folly. When the covering of immorality and folly is stripped off from it, its foundation, however, appears to be laid in nature. It had been observed as a matter of fact, that veracity in man was more frequent than mendacity— truth than falsehood; that this frequency was particularly great among such classes of persons as, by the complexion of their understandings, were less sensible to the action of a distant interest —such as that sort of interest commonly must be, by which, on occasions of importance, such as those which come before a court of justice, a man can be influenced to step aside from the path of truth. By the first impulse — by the impulse of the universal principle above delineated — by a sort of instinctive impulse, the line in which a man's discourse is urged is invariably the line of veracity—of truth: it is only by reflection — reflection on the distant advantage supposed to be obtainable by falsehood, that a man's footsteps can be turned aside out of that line.

Whatsoever be its direction — in the absence of all rival powers, the love of ease, minute as is the greatest force which on these trivial occasions can be applied by it, is in every instance omnipotent — the power that worketh all in all.*

But, — that, in every instance, to the insuring of verity in contradiction to falsity, the force of this commanding principle applies itself; — to this proposition, before it can be brought to an exact coincidence with the line of truth, some limitation, and that not an inconsiderable one, will require to be applied.

To prevent the testimony from being false *in toto*, will indeed require less exertion than the opposite course: but to render it, and in every circumstance, a correct and *complete* picture of the fact, will at the same time frequently require more exertion than, without some degree of uneasiness, could be bestowed. In proportion as the balance inclines to this side, — here then, supposing the result to depend on the physical sanction alone, here would be a mixture of truth and falsehood.†

The result is, that, under the physical sanction (supposing its force the only force in action,) so far as depends upon *will*, falsehood *in toto* would never have place; false-

* The extreme minuteness of the quantity of labour, the desire of avoiding which composes, in this case, the motive or determinative force, ought not to be considered as constituting any objection against a theory which consists in nothing more than the simple enunciation of a few indisputable facts. It is by forces thus impalpably minute, that the whole system of psychological conduct is regulated and determined. In a material balance, constructed as some have been known to be constructed, one five-hundredth part of a grain has been known to be sufficient to determine the descent on either side: and were it not for *friction* and the *vis inertiæ*, a five-millionth part would be equally efficacious.

† Operating by itself, the efficiency of the physical sanction is not altogether so sure in regard to the production of *completeness* in tesmony, as in regard to the production of *correctness*. Production of completeness requires *attention*; viz. attention directed to that purpose: to attention, as well as to invention, when raised to a certain pitch, exertion, labour of mind, is necessary — labour over and above what is necessary to the giving expression to imperfect fragments. Here, then, is a force which, to be overcome, requires an exciting force over and above what is sufficient to produce correctness. This exciting force cannot be any other than that of some special *interest*. If, then, no such interest is acting upon the mind, completeness, unless by accident, will not have place: the testimony, how correct soever, as far as it goes, will not, to the purpose in question — will not, to the purpose of preventing deception — be complete.

The possibility of incompleteness will, it is evident, be greater and greater, in proportion to the complexity of the matter of fact which constitutes the subject of the testimony: and if the probability of incorrectness, in respect of such parts as are reported, receives increase also from the same cause, still the ratio of increase will not, in regard to incorrectness, be so great as in regard to incompleteness.

hood in circumstance would be frequent: truth would, in every case, constitute the ground; but that ground would be frequently receiving a tincture of falsehood: and the more complex and extensive the ground, the deeper and more extensive would the tincture be naturally apt to be.

Thus far, no interest is supposed to have place, other than that weak, though, in default of all opposing interest, adequately-operating interest — the interest created by the aversion to labour. But let the case be open to any other interest — to any other motive — acting in a sinister direction; there is not any *species* of interest so weak, the force of which is not capable of existing in a degree sufficient to overcome the correctly-acting force of the physical sanction, and in such sort that falsehood, even *in toto*, shall be the result. All these motives, however, act more frequently on the side of truth than on that of falsehood.

The more particularly the nature of human intercourse comes to be considered, the more thoroughly we shall be satisfied that it is not by the general and standing interests alone, but by the particular and fleeting interests of each moment also, that the property of truth is secured to the general tenor of human discourse. In particular, it is only by making known, and that truly, something that he thinks, that a man can obtain what he wants. For a number of years, reckoning from the commencement of the power of locomotion, we are all necessarily subject to the perpetual exertion of the power of command. But the power of command can obtain its gratification on no other terms than by the most correct adherence to the line of truth. By every act of command, a desire is made known; and, in proportion as the desire fails of being truly stated, it is certainly frustrated.

§ 5. *Operation of the moral or popular sanction, for and against correctness and completeness in testimony.*

Happiness, in almost all its points, is, in every individual, brutes scarcely excepted — the most brutish savages not excepted, more or less dependent upon knowledge; the word *knowledge* not being on this occasion confined in its application to the knowledge of those recondite facts which belong to the domain of *science*. But in all cases, except that of a life carried on from beginning to end in a state of perfect solitude, knowledge depends in the largest proportion upon testimony: and except in those cases of comparatively rare occurrence, in which falsehood itself serves to lead to truth,* it is only in so far as it is expressive of truth, that testimony is productive of knowledge.

All the confidence we can ever have, or hope to have, in mankind, either under the law or without the law, — all the reliance we can place on the expectation we entertain of any of the innumerable and daily services, obligatory or free, which we stand in need of for the sustentation and comfort of our existence, — all depends, by a connexion more or less close and immediate, on the preponderance of men's disposition towards the side of veracity and truth.

The force of the moral or popular sanction coinciding in the main with the force of general interest, — hence it is, that, throughout the whole field of intercourse between man and man, in every state of society (the rudest not excepted,) the moral or popular sanction is, with only here and there a casual exception, found in action constantly on the side of truth.†

Of the degree of force with which the moral or popular sanction acts in support of the law or rule of veracity, a more striking or satisfactory exemplification cannot be given, than the infamy which so universally attaches upon the character of liar, and the violent and frequently insupportable provocation given by any one who, in speaking to, or in the presence of another, applies to him that epithet. ‡

There has not, I suppose, existed anywhere, at any time, a community, — certainly there exists not among the civilized communities with which we have intercourse, one in which the appellation of a liar is not a term of reproach. Among the most egregious and notorious liars that ever existed, I cannot think that there can ever have been a single individual to whom it must not have been a cause of pain as often as it happened to him to hear the appellation applied to himself — to whom it would not have been matter of relief and comfort, had it been possible for him to have disburthened his character from the load of it.

Such is the power of the moral or popular

* See Book V. *Circumstantial*, Chap. V.

† Of the moral or popular sanction, however, except where the force of it is assisted by interrogation — of the moral or popular, as well as of the physical sanction, and from the same causes, it may be observed, that it acts with less efficacy in the production of completeness than of correctness.

‡ Like other imputations, this imputation is not the less galling, but apt rather to be the more galling, to a man, from his being conscious of its being merited, and thence of the probability of its being known to be merited. Accordingly, no two characters are more naturally united, in the same person, than the liar and the bully; the function of the bully being to give protection to the liar.

The man who, on hearing imputed to him a supposed act of mendacity, — instead of endeavouring to show the groundlessness of the aspersion, challenges him from whom it came, — gives up the reputation of veracity, as it were in barter, for the pleasure of revenge, and the reputation of courage.

sanction, when applied to extrajudicial testimony — to that sort of discourse which has place between man and man in the miscellaneous intercourse of life.

But the force with which it acts in behalf of truth is applied with much more energy, as well as with much more constancy, when (the importance of truth being the same in both cases) the testimony is of the judicial kind — delivered on a judicial occasion — or even, when not delivered on a judicial occasion, if delivered in contemplation of its being eventually applied to a judicial purpose.*

In the main, and upon the whole, the force of the moral or popular sanction acts in a direction favourable to general happiness and virtue. In the main, accordingly, the direction taken by this same force is favourable to that particular branch of virtue which consists in veracity.

But, to the proposition by which this predominant tendency is announced, ere its limits can be brought to coincidence with the line of truth, considerable exceptions will require to be made.

One capital exception has for its cause the repugnancy — the inbred and irremovable repugnancy, that exists between the aggregate mass of the precepts by which it prescribes good conduct in general and prohibits vice in general, and that particular precept by which it prescribes veracity, and reprobates the opposite vice.

Avoid vicious conduct—conduct prejudicial to the general interests of the community of which you are a member, yourself included; avoid vicious conduct, or the ill opinion, and consequent ill will and ill offices, of the community, will attach upon you. Avoid vicious conduct in every shape, and in the several shapes of mendacity, and falsehood through culpable inattention, among the rest.

Thus far we have the result of its action on the side of virtue. But now comes its action on the side of vice. Whatsoever vicious conduct it has happened to you to fall into, conceal it at any rate from the public eye: for it is only in proportion as it falls within the compass of the knowledge or suspicion of the public, that the evil consequences held up to view will take place. But, by him by whom vicious conduct is confessed, it is not concealed — by him by whom, after it has taken place, it is denied to have taken place, it is, or may be concealed, in so far as it is in the power of mendacity to conceal it.

No really existing person could with truth and propriety be represented as delivering on one and the same occasion these repugnant precepts. But if the word *precept* be on this occasion employed, and the form of a precept given to the discourse in which it is employed, it is in pursuance of one of those unavoidable metaphors to which language is so frequently compelled to have recourse. What there is of strict reality in the case, consists of two motive forces — two interests, acting at the same time in opposite directions on the human mind: and between these motive forces the opposition in question may be seen actually to have place. By confessing what he has done, the individual in question would expose himself to shame: but by denying what he has done, he also exposes himself to shame.

Acted upon as he is by these two opposite forces, — by which of them will the line of his conduct, in regard to testimony, be determined? By that one of them by which, at the moment in question, the interest of the greatest *value* is presented to his eyes, — certainty and proximity, those two never-to-be-over-looked dimensions, being taken into the account of value.

On this occasion (let it not be forgotten) the question is, — not what is most fit and proper, but what is most likely, to be done. The dilemma, be the occasion what it may, is a distressing one. By one only course may the dilemma be avoided. Avoid vice in other shapes, and the temptation to plunge into mendacity for the hope of escaping from that shame which follows at the heels of vice, will not assail you: such is the advice in which the virtue of veracity joins with the other virtues.

Of the other exceptions to the truth-promoting tendency of the moral sanction, the origin may be seen in the opposition between particular interests, and general. The force of the moral sanction, of the popular sanction, taken in its greatest extent, is composed of the general interests of the community at large. But, in every political community, smaller communities or aggregations of individuals will be found; each aggregation having an interest common to all its members, but opposite to that of the all-comprising aggregate to which they all belong; and to every such partial, though still composite interest — to every such section of the community, corresponds a section of the popular or moral sanction, and of the moral force with which it acts.

A sort of honour is to be found among thieves. So it has often been observed, and truly: but this honour is neither more nor less than a disposition to pursue that interest — to be impelled by that detached portion of the general moral force, by which the members of the predatory community in question are bound together. The whole community has its popular or moral sanction upon an all-comprehensive scale: the several com-

* As in case of pre-appointed evidence. See the book so entitled (Book IV.)

munities of thieves, smugglers, and all other communities having particular interests acting in opposition to the general interest—all those, recognised or not recognised as being included in the more comprehensive class or denomination of malefactors,—have each of them a sort of section of the popular or moral sanction to itself.*

It is the interest of the community at large that truth alone should be uttered; that the language of mendacity and deception should be abstained from on every judicial occasion, and on almost every other occasion: abstained from, although, and for the very reason that, the commission of it threatened to be beneficial to the particular interests that act in opposition to the general interests: — to the common interests, for example, of thieves and smugglers.

It is the interest of the community that truth should be revealed, as often as the disclosure of it *promises* to be conducive to the bringing down of punishment upon the heads of thieves and smugglers. But it is the interest of thieves and smugglers that truth should never be revealed, but always concealed, as often as the disclosure of it *threatens* to be conducive to the bringing down punishment on the heads of thieves or smugglers. Among these malefactors, therefore, the section of the moral sanction, which applies to testimony, prescribes mendacity while it prohibits, and, as far as may be, punishes veracity, as an act of vice and treachery.

In any community composed of thieves or smugglers, is any act of depredation committed by one member to the prejudice of the rest? The force of the moral sanction changes now its direction, though not its nature: the force of this section of the popular sanction now joins itself to that of the whole; — mendacity is recognised as a vice — veracity, as a virtue.

The interest which these communities of malefactors have in mendacity, would not, however, have succeeded in perverting the moral feelings of the great bulk of the community, who have no interest but in the universal prevalence of veracity, had not the sinister interest of thieves and smugglers found to this purpose a powerful auxiliary in the sinister interest of lawyers.

Under every system, every mercenary lawyer — under the fee-gathering system, every lawyer without exception — has an interest, as unquestionably, though not as uniformly, opposite to the general interest, as that which forms the bond of union in communities of thieves or smugglers. Under that system, every lawyer without exception — the whole fraternity together, with the judges at their head — have a particular interest in common with the interests of malefactors and wrongdoers of every description, not excepting thieves and smugglers. It is their interest that lawsuits, — understand those and those alone which are pregnant with fees, — lawsuits, by whatsoever name distinguished—action or prosecution — may abound to the utmost pitch. That prosecutions may abound, it is their interest that crimes of all sorts may abound: that actions may abound, it is their interest that wrongs of all sorts may abound; as well those wrongs of which the hand of the judge is the pretended avenger, as those of which it is the unacknowledged instrument. It is their interest that wrongs of all sorts be sometimes punished, lest plaintiffs be discouraged, and the mass of litigation and profit be diminished at one end: it is their interest that wrongs of all sorts remain sometimes unpunished and triumphant, lest the mass of litigation and profit be diminished at the other end. It is their interest that every modification of vice, by which litigation with its profit can be produced, may abound; and thence. in a more especial degree, that mendacity, the instrument and cloak of every vice, may abound.

Neither to thieves nor to smugglers, nor to wrongdoers in any other shape than that of judges, has any such power been given as that of granting impunity, and, by means of impunity, licence, to the vice of lying: accordingly, neither by thieves, nor by smugglers, nor by wrongdoers of any other denomination, has any such licence been ever granted.

Judges, under favour of the oscitancy or connivance of the legislature, have given to themselves that power: and such is the use they have made of it, that the whole system of judicial procedure is one continued tissue of lies — of allowed, protected, rewarded, encouraged, and even necessitated, lies.

In this instance as in every other, power, in proportion to its magnitude, serves as a shield as well to every vice as to every crime. Contempt is that modification of the punishment of the moral sanction, that is more particularly attached to the character of liar, —

* Instances in which particular classes have joined in making one moral rule for their conduct among themselves—another and a totally different rule for their conduct towards all other persons, are not unfrequent. Such is uniformly found to be the case where particular classes are possessed of so much power as to be in a great degree independent of the good or ill opinion of the community at large. In the moral code of the West-India slaveholders, many acts which would be among the worst of crimes if committed against a white man, are perfectly innocent when the subject of them is a negro. For white and black, substitute Mahomedan and Christian, and the same observation holds good with respect to Turkey. Substitute orthodox and heretic, it at one time held good in all Catholic, not to say in all Christian countries, as well with regard to the other virtues in general, as to that of veracity in particular. — *Editor.*

and power, in proportion to its magnitude — power, though it affords not protection against hatred, affords it effectually against contempt.

Hence it is, that, as well the mercenary advocate, whose trade and occupation consist everywhere in the sale of lies, as, under the fee-gathering branch of the English system of procedure, the fee-fed judge, who deals in the same ware,* remain untouched by that infamy, with which, if the dictates of the popular sanction coincided uniformly with the dictates of general utility, they would be covered; and by which the occasional and unprivileged liar, whose lies are many hundred times less frequent, is overwhelmed. The power constitutes a vantage-ground, by which the head of him who is stationed on it is raised above the flood in which the undistinguished, but less guilty herd, are drowned.†

Thus, by the incessant action of comparative knowledge upon invincible ignorance, has the force of the moral or popular sanction been divided and turned against itself. In correspondence with this schism, the aggregate mass of mendacious testimony has been divided, in the contemplation of the public, into two parcels: — whatsoever portion the judge has found it more for his advantage to punish than to permit or to reward, remains in a state of proscription as before, and is continued under the denomination of vice: whatsoever portion he finds it more for his interest to reward or to permit than to punish, is regarded either with indifference or with approbation, and is ranked under the denomination either of innocence or of virtue.

Mendacity is not only permitted, but in some cases properly permitted, by the moral sanction. That cases exist in which a departure from truth is, and ought to be, either prescribed, or at least allowed, by the moral or popular sanction considered in its true and largest sense, is out of dispute. Being in many instances cases of considerable intricacy and delicacy, it happens fortunately, that, to the purpose of the present inquiry, any very particular description of them is neither necessary nor pertinent.

1. In some cases, departure from truth is prescribed by the moral sanction as a duty. Such are all those in which mischief to another would be the certain or probable effect of verity, while from falsity no evil at all, or at least no equal evil, will, with equal probability, be the result: as, if a madman or assassin, with a naked weapon in his hand, asks whether his intended victim be not there, naming the place where he actually is.

2. To this same head may belong falsehoods of *humanity* or beneficence: as when a physician, to save pain of mind, gives hopes which he does not entertain himself.

3. To this same head may be referred what may be termed falsehoods of *urbanity;* which is but humanity or beneficence applying itself to interests of inferior moment: as where, on being interrogated by Artifex concerning the degree of estimation in which he holds a production of Artifex, — for fear of applying discouragement, Crito gives for answer, a degree higher than that which he really entertains: and so in regard to conduct in life, taste, and so forth.

4. As to cases in which departure from truth is *allowed* without being *prescribed.* A footing on which this matter is commonly placed seems to be, that, where a man has no right to the information sought by him, the information need not be given to him. But granting, that were probity, or the duty of one man to another, the only consideration to be attended to, a liberty thus ample might and would be allowed,—the latitude will be found to receive very considerable limitation, when those considerations are attended to, which concern a man's self-regarding interest, and belong to the head of *prudence.*

So dishonourable and pernicious to a man is the reputation of habitual or frequent falsity — so honourable and so valuable to him that of never having violated truth — that, without the least prejudice to any other individual, by even a single departure from veracity it may happen to a man to do irremediable mischief to himself.

The wound thus given by a man to his own reputation will be the more severe, the more intense and deliberate the averment by which the truth is violated: and thus it is, that after a falsehood of humanity or urbanity, uttered with a faint or ordinary degree of assurance, — if urged and pressed, stronger and stronger asseverations being on the other part called for in proof of the verity of the preceding ones, a man may, for the preservation of his own character, find it necessary to give up the enterprise of humanity or urbanity and declare, after all, the naked truth.

A disquisition of no small length and intricacy might be employed on the subject of the exceptions proper to be made to the general rule of verity: a disquisition, curious and in-

* Not that they deal (either of them) in lies and nothing else: the ware they deal in consists in a mixed assortment of truth and lies, made up in whatever proportions happen best to suit the purpose of the customer: — in what proportion, would, to the manufacturer and dealer, be matter of indifference, were it not that, of the two sorts of ware, lies are that by which his skill is most conspicuously displayed.

† To the advocate, as such, belongs no such power, no such coercive power, as that which constitutes the characteristic attribute of the judge: but it is by the tongue of the advocate that the hand of the judge is moved: the power of the advocate, though in respect of intensity less in *degree,* is in *specie* the same with the power of the judge.

teresting at any rate; but, whether subservient or not upon the whole to the interests of morality and happiness, would depend upon the manner in which it was conducted.

§ 6. *Operation of the legal sanction, for and against correctness and completeness in testimony.*

The force of the moral sanction was found insufficient to secure good conduct in general: it was found necessary to add to it the force of law.

The force of law itself cannot be applied but through the instrumentality of testimony; and testimony is of no use but in so far as it leads to truth. The same deficiency which produced the necessity of adding the force of the legal to that of the moral sanction, for the purpose of securing good conduct in general, produced the necessity of applying the same auxiliary force to the particular purpose of securing that particular modification of good conduct which consists in attaching the good qualities of veracity and verity to whatsoever testimony comes to be delivered on a judicial occasion or for a judicial purpose.

Many and extensive are the portions of the field of law, in relation to which the popular sanction has nowhere as yet fashioned, — nor (till it has received that sort and degree of improvement which it may yet for a good while have everywhere to wait for) will it fashion — its dictates, so as to bring them to an exact coincidence with those of the principle of general utility. In relation to those same portions of that field, the regulations of the legal sanction are naturally and generally found to approach nearer than those of the popular sanction to so desirable a coincidence. The quarter in which this deficiency is most conspicuously observable, is that which regards those transgressions which are properly termed public; viz. such offences, by the mischief of which, though it be seen to hover over the heads of the whole community, no assignable member of that community is seen to be afflicted.*

One of the advantages of the political, as compared with the moral sanction, is the greater constancy with which it can avail itself of interrogation — an operation which in many instances is indispensably necessary to the verity of testimony, more particularly in so far as concerns completeness. In some instances, this security may chance to have been applied in such sort that the force of the moral sanction may have had the benefit of it; some individual or individuals, willing to apply this instrument and so circumstanced as to be able to apply it with effect, being at hand at the moment at which the testimony is delivered. But the application of this instrument is an act of power: and it is only in the hands of the administrator of the force of the legal sanction — it is only in the hands of the judge, that power of this description is sure at all times to be found.

The force of the political sanction, like that of the moral sanction, may be considered to be one of the standing causes of veracity— standing counter-forces, acting in opposition to mendacity. Like that of the moral sanction however, and from the same cause, it is capable of being by accident brought to act on the adverse side,

Punishment, legal punishment, is, in every civilized country, annexed to mendacity in judicature. But wherever the effect or tendency of true testimony would be to subject the deponent to any obligation of the burthensome kind, — whether on the score of punishment, satisfaction to be rendered to a party injured, or right to be conferred on the adverse party,—so much of the occasional force of this sanction is made to act in opposition to its regular and standing force. In every such case, — abstraction made of every other species of motive, — whichever of the two antagonizing forces of the same sanction, its standing force and its occasional force, happened on each occasion to be the greater (certainty and proximity, as well as intensity, of the punishment, being taken into account on both sides,) on that side human conduct would be sure to be found. If, for example, the offence for which a man were under prosecution, was a species of fraudulent obtainment, the punishment of which consisted of transportation for three years, — while the punishment for the perjury, in case of his answering falsely while under examination on that occasion, was transportation for seven years, — and the probability of conviction appeared exactly the same in both cases; abstraction made of all other motives, veracity in this case ought, in every instance, to be regarded as certain: while on the other hand, all things remaining as before, — if, instead of transportation for three years, the punishment for the fraud were transportation for fourteen years, perjury might in every instance be set down for certain in this case, as veracity was in the other.

This is the casual operation of the legal sanction, to the prejudice of truth: but many instances there are, in which it is made to operate in that mischievous direction by design.

If the administrator of the force of the legal sanction had all along and everywhere been faithful to his trust, the application made of that force to judicial testimony would have

* Take for example any of that infinite variety of offences, the mischief of which consists in the defalcation which they make from the public revenue. That these offences are not treated by the moral sanction with so much severity as they deserve, is notorious, and the cause is equally plain

been uniform and proportionable: applying itself to all cases in which it happened to such testimony to be delivered, and in a degree regulated by the quantity of force which the opposing force to be surmounted, and the importance of the case (that is, the magnitude of the mischief liable to take place in the event of falsity on the part of the witness, and consequent deception and misdecision on the part of the judge,) required.

But, under every civilized government that has had existence, the administrator of the legal sanction has, as will be seen, been in this particular unfaithful to his trust. Everywhere, at first by the inexperience, and consequent ignorance and unskilfulness — afterwards by the oscitancy or corrupt connivance of the legislator,—the formation of the law of evidence has, along with that of so many other branches of the law, to so immense an extent been abandoned to the judge. Left without allotted recompence by the indigence, the penuriousness, or the improvidence of the legislator, and at the same time with powers adequate to the practice of extortion without stint, the judge has in every country converted the sword and scales of justice into instruments of fraud and depredation.

Having been suffered to convert all judicial demands into a source of profit to himself, he has applied himself to the multiplication of unjust demands: having been suffered to convert all judicial defences made before himself into a source of profit to himself, he has applied himself to the multiplication of unjust defences: having been suffered to convert all judicial expense into a source of profit to himself, he has applied himself to the multiplication of judicial expenses: having been suffered to convert all judicial instruments, and all judicial operations, into sources of profit to himself, he has applied himself to the augmentation of the magnitude and multitude of judicial instruments, and of the multitude of judicial operations. Beholding in delay an encouragement to unjust demands as well as unjust defences, and at the same time, on the occasion of all demands and defences without distinction, a source of incidents which beget occasions or pretences for additional instruments and additional operations, he has applied himself in like manner, with equal energy and success, to the multiplication of delays.

Beholding in mendacious statements a pretence for the reception and entertainment of unjust demands, of unjust defences, of useless expenses, of needless and useless instruments and operations, and of groundless delays (sources of those needless and useless expenses, instruments, and operations,) he has occupied himself in cherishing with one hand that mendacity, which he has been occupied at the same time in punishing with the other. Attaching punishment to those unprivileged lies, in which individuals at large, in the character of suitors, or in other characters, have been concerned by themselves, he has attached reward to those lies in the utterance of which they have employed, as accomplices or substitutes, his subordinate instruments and partners: and, lest with all these lies there should not be yet enough, — having been suffered to convert his own lies into a source of profit to himself, he has multiplied his own lies, lies signed by his own hand, without limit and without shame.*

In holding up therefore to view the force of the legal sanction in the character of a tutelary force, utterance was given to a general rule, of a nature not to be reduced within the limits of truth till after it had been cut into by extensive and numerous exceptions: for, if it were to be held up in the character of a force uniformly and faithfully exerted on the side of truth, regard would be to be had not to what it is, or ever has been, but to what it ought to be, and is so generally, though so erroneously, supposed to be.

I say, supposed to be; for among the delusions which inbred mendacity has, from first to last, been occupied in propagating with so much industry and success, in none has it been more completely successful than in persuading the people, in contradiction to their own eyes and their own feelings, to mistake impunity for purity, and prostrate themselves before the den of mendacity and of depredation, as if it were the sanctuary of truth and spotless justice.

The effect of this perversion of the legal sanction, in occasioning a correspondent perversion of the moral sanction, has been brought to view in the last section. But this is not the only ravage committed by an abuse of the legal sanction upon the force of the moral, even in that part of the field that belongs to testimony.

To an abuse of the power of the political sanction, the nature of things admits of no other check than the resisting force of the moral or popular. A determination to destroy this only check, and thus render the power of the political sanction, by whatsoever vile hands wielded, completely arbitrary, has been not only indefatigably prosecuted, but openly avowed. Judges have been found so insensible to the voice of censure, or so secure of not incurring it, as to maintain for law, and thus to establish for law, that, — when misconduct in any shape is, in any printed and published or written and communicated paper, charged upon a man in power, themselves not excluded, — the truth of the charge, so far from being a justification, shall be deemed to operate as an aggravation; and so far as

* See the work entitled, "Scotch Reform opposed to English Non-reform." Vol. V. See also Book VIII. of the present work.

depends upon themselves shall operate in aggravation of punishment — of that punishment by which, and by which alone, at the command of shameless despotism, the quality of guilt is impressed upon meritorious innocence.

That the triumph over truth may be the more complete, a definition of the sort of instrument called a libel is said to have been given — a definition which requires but to be consistently acted upon, to level whatsoever difference may exist between the constitutions of Britain and Morocco. A libel is any discourse, by which, it being put into writing and made public (whatsoever is to be understood by public,) the feelings of any individual are hurt, injured, violated, wounded, or whatsoever other word it be, that, to answer the purpose of the moment, is presented by the powers of harmony to the rhetoric of despotism. Not that, by this law, the manufacturers of it would wish to be understood as the less friendly to the interests of truth and liberty: for, so often as twelve men, under the name and character of petty jurymen, can be found to join with one voice (speaking upon their oath) to declare their persuasion that the feelings of a malefactor receive no hurt from his seeing himself held up to view in that character — in other words, that it is matter of indifference to a man, guilty or not guilty, whether he be thought criminal or innocent — in a word, that, whether innocent or guilty, man in general has not any such sense belonging to him as the sense of shame, — so often are they at liberty to save him who has been ruined by prosecution, from being ruined over again by punishment.

Towards destroying altogether the force of the moral sanction, the most extensively operating security for individual good conduct, and the only effectual security against the despotic tendency of power — towards rooting out of the human bosom all regard for truth, and at the same time for liberty and virtue, — it seems not easy to say how, with any encouragement from public blindness, it would be possible for the artifice or audacity of usurped legislation to go further

In such a state of things— under a legislation that connives at such usurpation, and a people that submit to it without remonstrance, — it is a question not altogether exempt from difficulty, whether the force of the moral sanction is or is not with propriety to be numbered among the powers by which human conduct in general, and in particular so far as regards the truth of testimony, is influenced and directed. To-day, yes: and so long as the acquiescence under such law continues to be regarded as short of certainty: to-morrow, perhaps not: to a certainty, not a single moment longer than the design manifested by such doctrines shall continue unaccomplished.

§ 7. *Operation of the religious sanction, for and against correctness and completeness in testimony.*

In the case of this sanction, as of the others, its utility, in the character of an efficient cause of truth in testimony, depends partly upon the *direction* in which, partly upon the degree of *force* with which, it acts.

In respect of its direction, nothing can be more favourable, more steadily and uniformly favourable: provided always, that in the case of *book-religions*, the original and authentic repositories of the rule of action be taken for the standard, not any glosses that in later ages may have been put upon them.

On considering the differences — the very wide differences, observable between the several book-religions in other respects, — an observation that would be apt enough here to present itself is, that in this respect likewise, any proposition that were to be predicated of them in the lump, would possess but a feeble chance of being true.

But in this particular, causes, viz. interests and motives, being in all religions the same, effects, viz. precepts and other actions, will naturally, not to say necessarily, fall into the same coincidence. Taking in a certain sense for the author of the religion, the penman by whom the discourses constitutive of the matter of it were committed to writing, — in the instance of every one of them it may with equal truth be observed, that his interest, in respect of the object he had in view, required that the disposition to veracity should, on the part of his adherents, be as strenuous and as uniform as by any means it could be made.

In the case of a leader of this sacred, as in the case of a leader of any profane, description, the success of his designs would be in no small degree dependent upon the correctness of such information, of such testimony, as, on such an infinite variety of occasions, that design might lead him to require at their hands.

In the Jewish religion, the story of the leprosy of Gehazi — in the Christian, the story of the sudden death of Annanias and Saphira — may serve for illustration.

If there were any decided difference, the steadiness of the religious sanction to the cause of truth would be found more rigorous and entire, not only than that of the legal sanction, of which the unsteadiness has above been brought to view, but even than that of the moral. The moral sanction acknowledges the exceptions that have been seen: it has its falsehoods allowed, if not prescribed, of urbanity — its falsehoods of humanity — and even its falsehoods of duty.

The religious sanction, — if the Jewish (which to a great though undefined extent is at the same time the Christian) be taken for an example, and the text of the sacred writings be taken for the standard of that religion, — acknowledges no such exceptions. When Jephthah, the chief of that religion, having vowed in case of victory to sacrifice to the Lord the first object that presented itself, and having beholden in his own daughter that first object, "did with her according to his vow," it was for no other reason than that he had said upon his oath that he would do so, though unquestionably without having, in so saying, had her in his thoughts. Not only humanity, but duty, even parental duty, were on this occasion held to be considerations of inferior moment, when compared with the duty of adherence to truth, that duty having been reinforced by the ceremony of a vow — of that solemn appeal which is common to oaths and vows.

Though the text of the sacred writings, the text recognised in all ages as the standard of obedience, remains in all ages the same, or nearly the same, the interpretation put upon it varies from age to age: and, in each age, it is by the interpretation put upon it in that age, that the effectual direction taken in that age by the religious sanction — the practical effect produced by it, is determined. The age in which the text of the sacred writings was first committed to writing, was not, in the instance of any of the book-religions, an age in which any such qualities as those of precision, accuracy, and particularity of explanation, belonged in any considerable degree to the public mind. To reduce the precept to a state adapted to practice, it has become more and more the custom to fill up from the precepts of the moral sanction, the reputed deficiencies manifested in these particulars by the religious sanction. In a delineation which at this time of day should come to be given, of what the religious sanction prescribes in relation to truth and falsehood, the exceptions above mentioned as applied by the moral sanction to the general requisition of veracity and verity — the particular allowances as well as counter-prescriptions made by the moral sanction, in favour of the several classes of falsehoods designated as above by the several appellations of falsehoods of duty, falsehoods of humanity, and falsehoods of urbanity, — would probably not be omitted.* But, whether proper or otherwise, it is in the law of the moral sanction only, not in the law of the religious sanction, as delivered in the text of either the Jewish religion or the Christian (not to speak of the Mahometan,) that any of these exceptions are to be found.

Cases, however, in which the force of the religious sanction has operated on the side of perjury, even in Christian countries, are neither impossible, nor without example. Paris, no longer ago than the middle of last century — Paris, so lately, not to say at present, the centre of unbelief — yielded a batch of false miracles, regularly attested, vying in extraordinariness with the less-regularly-attested prodigies of Jewish history. In the testimony by which these false miracles were proved, it is difficult, if not impossible, to say how much there was of mendacity — how much of simple incorrectness, the honest work of the imagination. That mendacity was not wholly without its share, can scarcely admit of doubt. True miracles are not wanting (says a man to himself on this occasion,) true miracles have not at least been wanting, on this our side, the side of sacred truth. But unhappily the true are not quite sufficient; sufficient for other times, but unhappily not for the present incredulous age, in which, somehow or other, the source of miraculous evidence appears to have run itself dry. Profiting by the occasion, let us do what depends upon us towards supplying the deficiency. Truth must indeed be departed from: but the end will sanctify the means. What end can ever approach to it in importance? and falsehood, the instrument we mean thus to sanctify, as Pagan temples have been sanctified by being converted into churches, how often has it not been applied to the most flagitious, the most impious ends!

Of all the religous codes known, the Hindoo is the only one by which, in the very text of it, if correctly reported, a licence is in any instance expressly given to false testimony, delivered on a judicial occasion, or for a judicial purpose: and in this instance, among the cases pitched upon for receiving the benefit of the licence, are some which, viewed through an European medium, will be apt to appear whimsical enough.

* Mr. Bentham might have quoted, in illustration of this remark, the following passage from Paley — a writer of undisputed piety, who, in a system of morals professing to be founded upon the will of God as its principle, makes no difficulty in giving a licence to falsehood, in several of its necessary or allowable shapes: —

"There are falsehoods which are not lies, that is, which are not criminal; as, where the person to whom you speak has no right to know the truth, or, more properly, where little or no inconveniency results from the want of confidence in such cases; as where you tell a falsehood to a madman, for his own advantage; to a robber, to conceal your property; to an assassin, to defeat or divert him from his purpose. The particular consequence is, by the supposition, beneficial: and as to the general consequence, the worst that can happen is, that the madman, the robber, the assassin, will not trust you again; which (beside that the first is incapable of deducing regular conclusions from having been once deceived, and the two last not likely to come a second time in your way,) is sufficiently compensated by the immediate benefit which you propose by the falsehood." — Moral and Political Philosophy, book iii. chapter 15.—*Editor.*

Cases, some extra-judicial, some judicial, and upon the whole in considerable variety and to no inconsiderable extent, are specified, in which falsehood, false witness, false testimony, are expressly declared to be allowable.

1. False testimony of an exculpative tendency, in behalf of a person accused of any offence punishable with death. Three cases, however, are excepted; —viz. 1. Where the offence consists in the murder of a Bramin; or 2. (what comes to the same thing) a cow; or 3. In the drinking of wine, the offender being, in this latter case, of the Bramin caste.*

"Whenever a true evidence would deprive a man of his life, — in that case, if a false testimony would be the preservation of his life, it is allowable to give such false testimony; and for ablution of the guilt of false witness, he shall perform the *Poojeeh Sereshtee;* but to him who has murdered a *Bramin* or slain a cow, or who, being of the *Bramin* tribe, has drunken wine, or has committed any of these particularly flagrant offences, it is not allowed to give false witness in preservation of his life."

In the representation of the other cases, scarce a word could be varied, without danger of misrepresentation: word for word they stand as follows: —

"If a marriage for any person may be obtained by false witness, such falsehood may be told; as upon the day of celebrating the marriage, if on that day the marriage is liable to be incomplete, for want of giving certain articles, at that time, if three or four falsehoods be asserted, it does not signify; or if, on the day of marriage, a man promises to give his daughter many ornaments, and is not able to give them, such falsehoods as these, if told to promote a marriage, are allowable.

"If a man, by the impulse of lust, tells lies to a woman, or if his own life would otherwise be lost, or all the goods of his house spoiled, or if it is for the benefit of a *Bramin*, in such affairs, falsehood is allowable."

To the religious sanction — consideration being had of the undoubted magnitude of its influence on some occasions — on an occasion of this importance and extent, a place cannot be altogether refused. Yet, if, — in preference to theories, however generally received. and rendered plausible by the collateral experience just mentioned — experience in the exact direction of the case here in question, and that no less unquestionable than the other, be admitted as the test, — the more closely it is scrutinized into, the less efficient in the character of a security for the truth of testimony in all ways taken together, or even in the character of a security against wilful and self-conscious mendacity, will it be found.

To judge of the real and proper force of any power, try it, measure it, not when acting in combination with other forces, but when acting alone. If, as applied to forces of the physical class, the propriety of this rule be clear beyond dispute, it will scarcely be less so when applied to any force of the psychological class.

That, when the force of the religious sanction is accompanied and conjoined with the two human forces, the force of the moral and legal sanctions, or even with either of them alone, the force of these powers united is in a high degree efficient — so much so, as to throw into the state of exceptions taken out of a general rule the cases of its failure. — is out of dispute. But take a case — take any case, in which it may be seen to come into the field alone, and without support from either of those indisputably powerful coadjutors, the scene will be found to experience a total change.

If there be a mode of conduct which, being clearly and universally understood to stand prohibited by the force of the sanction in question (viz. the religious,) is nevertheless, generally, and as far as can be seen, universally, or almost universally, practised,— so far as concerns the prevention of *that* mode of conduct at least, the body of force in question, however composed, cannot but be acknowledged to be in a correspondent degree inefficient. If, in the formation of that body of force, the force of all these sanctions were comprised, the degree of inefficiency thus demonstrated would extend to all three: if the force of one of the three, and that one only, — it is to that one that the demonstration of inefficiency will stand confined.

If, the mode or species of conduct in question being mendacity, wilful and self-conscious falsehood, — the utterance of that falsehood be accompanied by a more than ordinary and most ample degree of deliberation, — the demonstration of the inefficiency of the sanction in question will be the more conclusive.

If either the practice of this wilful falsehood, or what to this purpose comes to the same thing, the approbation — approbation avowedly and publicly bestowed upon it — be the practice, not of men taken promiscuously from the herd, but of men carefully and anxiously selected for the occasion, under the persuasion of their being in a more than ordinary, in even the highest, degree, sensible to the influence of this sanction — the proof of the inefficiency of this sanction will be seen to possess from these circumstances a still higher force.

The examples in which this proof of the inefficiency of the religious sanction in respect of the prevention of wilful and deliberate

* Halhed's Code of Gentoo Laws, printed by the East-India Company, anno 1776, p. 129, 4to. chapter iii. section 9.

falsehood stands exhibited, may be comprised under the following heads:—

1. Cases in which—under the influence of a manifestly-operating sinister interest in the shape of wealth, power, dignity, or reputation—such declarations of opinion are made, as, from the nature of the facts asserted, cannot, consistently with the nature of the human mind, be in all points true; but without any particular proof of falsity operating in the case of one such false declarer more than another. To this head may be referred all solemn declarations of opinion on the subject of controverted points respecting facts out of the reach of human knowledge, delivered in the shape of pre-appointed formularies, adopted and authenticated by the signature of the witness in question, or otherwise; the declaration enforced or not by the ceremony of an oath.*

2. Cases where—under the influence of a mendacity-exciting interest, constituted by the fear of present and unavoidable corporeal sufferance terminating in extinction of life—declarations of opinion respecting individual facts, or supposed facts, actually in dispute, are delivered by a numerous company (twelve, for instance,) the members of which are forcibly kept in that state of affliction, until, and to the end, that they may in conjunction declare themselves to be all of one opinion, whether they really be so or no, in circumstances in which, in relation to these same points, immediately before such conjunction, different opinions, in all numbers less than that of the whole company, have been declared. To this head belong the pretendedly unanimous opinions delivered under the name of *verdicts* by companies of occasional judges, assembled together under the collective name of a *jury*, in the judicial practice of English law, under the technical system of procedure.

3. Cases where—under the influence of mendacity-exciting interest, constituted by so weak a force as that of sympathy for the sufferance of a stranger—declarations of opinion are delivered with one voice by an equally numerous company, in circumstances in which it is morally impossible that such declarations should be other than wilfully false in the instance of any one of the members. To this head belong the innumerable instances upon record, in which juries, to shield criminals from the unduly-severe punishments prescribed by a bad law, have solemnly and on their oaths declared, that articles of property, which they knew to be of the value of five, ten, or twenty pounds, were under the value of forty shillings.

4. After the above, it is a sort of anticlimax to bring to notice, in this point of view, the course of practice under the technical system of procedure—under which, in the instance of every individual suit without exception, judges, judicial officers their subordinates, professional lawyers of all descriptions, and suitors, unite in the utterance of an indefinitely extensive congeries of wilful falsehoods: judges, with their subordinates and brethren of the profession, voluntarily, under the influence of the profit derived from these enormities; suitors, under the influence of the rewards and punishments by means of which they are in some instances encouraged, in others compelled, by the judges, to join in the habitual perpetration of the same or the like enormities, according to the nature of the instruments and operations into which the tincture of falsehood is infused.

On this occasion, two descriptions of persons standing in so many different situations, require to be distinguished:—1. The individuals who, clothed or not with any authority, engage in the practice of wilful falsehood—the practice thus undeniably reprobated by the religious sanction—engage in it not of their own motion, but either excited by the reward, or compelled by the punishment, held up to them by their superiors: in this situation stand all the members of the community (except in so far as the people called Quakers form an exception,) as well as a select portion of them in the character of jurors; and 2. Those their superiors, under whose constantly observing eyes, and never-withholden approbation, this irreligious practice is carried on, and, in an immensely extensive mass of instances, cherished and inforced by the united powers of reward and punishment.

In this situation may be seen bishops and judges: bishops, to whom, under the notion of there being endued with a more than ordinary degree of sensibility to the action of the motives belonging to the religious sanction, and of their devoting their time to the endeavour of screwing up to its *maximum* that sensibility in the minds of the rest of the community, such enormous masses of emolument, power, and dignity, are attached;—judges, to whose situations, masses of emolument in some instances still more ample, together with masess of power in every instance much more ample, are, if not under an equally strong persuasion, at least under a like notion, also attached.

5. A still more striking instance of the inefficacy of the religious sanction, when unsupported by the other sanctions, to the pro-

* Every person taking orders in the English church, signs a declaration of his full belief in the whole of the thirty-nine articles of that church. Some of the most pious members of it have not, however, scrupled to declare, that it is not necessary that this declaration should be true: that it is allowable for a person who does not believe in the whole, but only in a part, of the thirty-nine articles, to sign a declaration professing himself to believe in the whole.—*Editor*.

duction of truth, is that of university oaths. Every student who enters the University of Oxford swears to observe certain statutes, framed long ago by archbishop Laud for the government of the university. From the frivolity and uselessness of the observances which these statutes prescribe, public opinion does not enforce an adherence to them. The moral and the legal sanction stand neuter; the religious sanction, however, remains, and that in its most powerful shape — the shape which is given to it by the ceremony of an oath. This, then, is an *experimentum crucis* on the force of the religious sanction. If it be notorious that there is not a single student who does not openly and undisguisedly violate those very statutes, which he has solemnly invoked eternal vengeance upon his head if he does not rigidly observe, — violate them, and that as often as the minutest conceivable inconvenience would be incurred by adherence to his oath, — then, surely, the weakness of the religious sanction, considered as a security for veracity, to say nothing of any other virtue, is demonstrated. But every person who has been at the University of Oxford, can testify that this description is literally true.

The weakness manifested in all these instances by the religious sanction, is among those facts which, how little soever adverted to, are most notorious and undeniable. In all these instances, falsehood is committed by high and low, without concealment, scruple, or reluctance. Why? Because it is by the force of this sanction alone that the practice stands prohibited — a sanction composed of pains and pleasures removed to an indefinite distance in point of time, and none of which have ever been presented by experience to any human being.

In other instances, and to a still greater extent, the practice of falsehood is in a very considerable degree repressed, and, in so far as committed, not committed without great reserve, and the most anxious exertions made to conceal it from every eye. Why? Because it is by the force either of the political sanction, or the moral sanction, or both together, that the practice stands prohibited; — of one or both; but, to the production of those symptoms, the force of either is of itself sufficient.

In the case of an interest, by the action of which violent passion is liable to be produced — desire of great pecuniary gain, for instance, fear of great pecuniary loss, sexual desire, or fear of immediate death or severe bodily affliction, — in the case of a contest between the hopes and fears belonging to the religous sanction on the one hand, and any such powerfully-acting motive or interest on the other, and the occasional triumph of the more immediate over the more remote, and as it will he apt to appear, less certain, interest, — the inference afforded of the weakness of the religious principle, by the event of such a contest, would not be so conclusive. The power of the religious principle is in general strong (it might be said) and in a great degree efficient; but (owing to the frail and variable texture of the human mind) not so strong as not to be liable to be, in here and there an instance, borne down by the violence of these stormy passions.

But among the above examples we see one, in which the power of the religious principle is brought into the field in the utmost force of which it is susceptible, and still, habitually, and as it were of course, gives way to an interest of the very weakest species, viz. sympathy for the suffering of a single individual — an individual who is a perfect stranger to all the members of the judicatory by which the contempt of religious principle is thus manifested — and he a criminal, in whose instance, in the judgment of the supreme and competent authority of the state, the suffering from which by this act of mendacity it rescues him, ought to have been inflicted.

In another of the above examples, that of university oaths, the whole force of the religious sanction, exerted in the strongest and most binding of all its shapes, fails of producing any, even the slightest, effect. Is it that it has some violent, some uncontroulable, passion to contend with, such as it might fail of overcoming, without affording any strong inference against its general efficacy? No: but by fulfilling an obligation, contracted under the sanction of so solemn an engagement, some slight inconvenience, some little trouble, might in some instances be incurred. The minutest possible quantity of trouble being thrown into the scale against the obligations of religion, is found, not in the case of an insulated individual, but of every Oxford student without exception, sufficient to outweigh them.

In the case of that pretended unanimity, which has so wantonly and unnecessarily been rendered compulsory on the occasions of the decisions pronounced by juries, the religious principle, it is true, finds itself encountered by the force of one of those almost irresistible motives above mentioned, viz. desire of self-preservation from death, aggravated by long-protracted torture: at the command of him who has the strongest stomach among you, yield, some or all of you, to the number of from one to eleven out of twelve — yield, and perjure yourselves. Immediately after the oath, by which you have engaged to your God not to join in any verdict but the one which, in your judgment, is true, join notwithstanding in a verdict which, in your judgment, is not true: — do thus, or inevitable death, preceded by insupportable torture, is your doom. Thus saith the law, — that is, — thus, in one knows not what age of barbarity and ignorance, have said those unknown judges, by whose authority this combination of torture with perjury was forced into judicial practice. Here, it must be confessed, the force of the physical sanction, with which that of the religious sanction has to contend, is no light matter: — the choice is between perjury and martyrdom.

But though, in the instance of the individuals themselves, on whom, in the character of occasional judges or jurymen, this obligation of trampling upon religious principle is imposed, the force by which it is subdued is thus mighty and irresistible, — no such force does that principle find to contend with, in the instance of those exalted functionaries, by whose hands the anti-religious obligation is, with such undisturbed serenity and undissembled complacency, habitually imposed. Until the perjury shall have been committed, and to the end that it may be committed, the judge holds himself prepared to torture the jurymen: but by no torture is the judge compelled or excited to manifest the satisfaction so habitually and cordially manifested by him at the thoughts of the practice in which he bears so capital a part — a practice which has torture for its means and perjury for its end.

How unpleasant soever, this comparative estimate was with a view to practice altogether indispensable. To depend, on every the most important occasion of life, upon the force of a principle which, on the occasions here in question, not to speak of other occasions, has been demonstrated by experience to be nearly, if not altogether, without force, would continue to lead, as it has led, to mischievous error and deception, to an indefinite extent. The topic of *oaths*, and the topic of exclusionary rules, grounded on the supposition of a deficiency of sensibility to the force of the religious sanction, will furnish proofs and illustrations.*

The opinion above expressed is not new. Divines of the most undisputed piety have repeatedly given their sanction to it.

The inefficacy of preaching *(l'Inefficacité de la Prédication)* constitutes the title, as well as the subject, of a work, published about the middle of the last century, by the Abbé Coyer, a French divine of the Romish church. To prove, or endeavour to prove, the inefficacy of preaching, is in other words to prove, or endeavour to prove, the weakness of the religious sanction; after and notwithstanding, all the force that could in that church be given to it by the most richly-rewarded eloquence.

The same proposition is (if auditors are to be believed) among the propositions habitually brought to view, as being habitually either maintained or assumed, and too manifest to be denied or doubted of, — brought to view in his sermons by a clergyman of the church of England, distinguished, even among those of the Methodist persuasion, for the union of zeal and eloquence.

The occasions on which, in both these instances, the weakness of the religious sanction stands confessed, or rather maintained and advocated, is that of its application to the purpose of meliorating the moral conduct of mankind; viz. in the dealings between man and man, and the conduct of man in regard to his own happiness, in the trifling business of the present transitory life.

To have endeavoured to disprove its efficacy in all respects, would have been an endeavour as vain as it is unexampled.

Various are the purposes to which its efficacy, in a greater or less degree, seems out of the reach of dispute: —

1. In causing men to try to believe, — to succeed in a considerable degree in their endeavours to believe — and whether they succeed or no, to say they believe, — improbable, and even impossible things: and with the more energy, the greater the improbability; and with most energy of all, those things which, not being facts either true or false, but contradictions in terms, are of all things most palpably and flatly impossible.

2. To cause men to profess to regard, and really to regard, with hatred and contempt, and to treat with unkindness — and, when power and opportunity occur, with oppression — those whose belief is not, or is suspected of not being, directed to the same objects, or not with the same energy, as their own belief.

3. To cause men to regard with fear, and in many instances with fear worked up to the pitch of insanity, and to profess and endea-

* See Book II. *Securities*, Chapter VI., and Book IX. *Exclusion*, Part III. Chapter V.

Cases no doubt there are, and those very numerous, in which the religious sanction appears to exercise a much stronger influence than is here ascribed to it. That which is really the effect of the moral sanction, or of the legal sanction, or of both, is continually ascribed to the influence of the religious sanction. From causes which it would be easy, but foreign to the present purpose, to explain, religious persons are apt to suppose, that an act, if virtuous, is more virtuous — if vicious, more excusable, when the motive which prompted it belonged to the religious class, than when it belonged to any other: and even in some cases, that an act which, if produced by any other motive, would be vicious, becomes virtuous by having a motive of this class for its cause. Thus it becomes the interest of every one, to whom the reputation of virtue is an object of desire, to persuade others, and even himself, that as many as possible of his actions, be they good or bad, emanate from that class of motives.—*Editor.*

vour to regard with love, a being, to whom none of those sentiments can be of any use.*

CHAPTER XII.

GROUND OF PERSUASION IN THE CASE OF THE JUDGE — CAN DECISION ON HIS OWN KNOWLEDGE, WITHOUT EVIDENCE FROM EXTERNAL SOURCES, BE WELL GROUNDED?

A DECISION pronounced by a judge on a question of fact, what efficient cause can it have had, so it be conformable to justice, other than evidence? None whatever, is the answer that naturally presents itself.

To this rule, however, four cases may on further reflection be apt to present themselves in the character of exceptions: four cases, of the first of which it will be seen, that its title to that character will, on examination, be affirmed; while in the three others, it will be disallowed.

Case 1. — The only perceptions on which the decision concerning the fact is grounded, are perceptions obtained by the judge himself, without any report made to him, by any other person, in the character of a percipient witness. In this case, the functions and characters of percipient witness and judge are united in the same person: deposing witness there is none, there not being either need or room for the appearance of any person in that character.†

Case 2. — No person appears on either side in the character of a deposing witness: but the facts on which the decision is grounded are, for the purpose of the decision, established by the admission, express or implied, of the parties on both sides.‡

Case 3. — The facts in question are deemed too *notorious* to stand in need of being established by special evidence.

Case 4. — Facts on one side having been deposed to, and in such manner that, supposing the deposition credited, they would have been established by evidence, — a decision in disaffirmance of those facts is formed, on the mere ground of *improbability*.

Of these four cases, the first mentioned alone, viz. decision on *view*, will be found, as already observed, a real exception to the rule. It is a decision without evidence.

Without evidence? The judge, in this case, has he not the evidence of his own senses? Doubtless: but, in this case, the expression is but figurative: nor does the word *evidence* designate the same idea in this, as in other cases: his senses are detached from his person, erected into so many independent persons, and in that character introduced as witnesses. To keep clear of this confusion, — instead of decision without evidence, say rather decision without *testimony*: not that the confusion will, even in this case, be entirely avoided.

Without evidence? Be it so then. But the ground of the decision, — is it not still firmer than if it were composed of evidence? Yes, certainly — if the only mind, the satisfaction of which were worth providing for, were that of the judge by whom in the first instance the decision were to be pronounced. Supposing his opportunities of observation sufficient, and those opportunities improved — a report, however trustworthy, made of the fact by any other person concerning the supposed perceptions of that other person, will be but a very inadequate succedaneum to any perceptions obtained by himself. Whatever be the superiority which immediate possesses over hearsay testimony, the same will internal perception on the part of the judge possess, in comparison with persuasion grounded on the testimony of another, or any number of others.

If, then, the mind of the judge were the only mind, the satisfaction of which were worth regarding, perception obtained by the judge would be a ground of decision, not merely equal, but far superior, to evidence. But unless absolute despotism, seated in the breast of the judge himself, be the only eligible form of government, the mind of the judge is not the only mind the satisfaction of which is worthy of regard. So far from it, that it is only in the character of an instrument of satisfaction to some other mind or minds, that satisfaction afforded to the mind of the judge himself is of any use. In the

* If this view of the matter be just, two practical consequences seem to follow: —

1. That it is a misapplication, a degradation, a profanation, to endeavour to apply so sublime an instrument to so mean a cause. It is applying pearls to the fattening of swine: the pearls are thrown away, and the swine not fattened.

2. That the instrument, not being applicable by government with advantage to any good purpose of government, the best course that can be taken in relation to it is the course so generally taken in relation to it in the United States, viz. to leave the application and enforcement of it to the sincere and unbought exertions of individuals.

† Under English law, this state of things is exemplified in the case in which the judge has been authorized to convict on "*view*:" to pronounce a man guilty of having committed an offence of this or that description, on the ground that the act of transgression was committed under the observation of the judge himself.

‡ Under English law, on admission express on both sides, as when a case is stated by them in conjunction, for the opinion of the court: on admission presumed, on howsoever slight a foundation, by the judge, from the deportment of the defendant, in the case when he omits to perform this or that operation, the performance of which is exacted of him on pain of his being considered as having admitted the facts necessary to establish the demand on the plaintiff's side: as in the case of judgment for default, *Bill* taken *pro confesso*, &c.

case of unbridled despotism seated in some one superior breast, as in Morocco, it is of the mind of the despot, and of him alone: in the case of any government simply monarchical, or in a greater or less degree popular, in which the affections of the public are, or are professed to be, an object of regard, it is the mind of the public, the satisfaction of which must (if propriety or consistency be regarded) be said to be the ultimate object in view.

Of this theoretical disquisition, what then is the practical use? To ascertain whether under any, and if under any, under what conditions, power should in any case be allowed to the judge for deciding on the ground of his own perceptions, without the support of personal evidence *ab extrà*.

The answer seems to present little difficulty. In the first instance, and for saving delay, vexation, and expense, as well as to prevent mis-decision, or non-decision for want of demand, let the judge's own perception be a sufficient ground for decision — for a decision to be pronounced by himself.

In case of *appeal*, which, in a case of this sort, ought ever to be allowed, — to guard against ultimate misdecision, let it be incumbent on the judge, if so required, to officiate in the character of a deposing witness, and in that character state the facts, subject to counter-interrogation,* exactly in the same manner as any other witness.

Even in the first instance, if the judicatory be, as it ought if possible to be, so constructed as to admit and contain an audience, — in pronouncing his decision, the judge might and ought to deliver, in his character of percipient witness, in the face of that audience, the facts which that decision takes for its ground.

Many, as will be seen, are the cases in which, to help to form the ground for decision, cognizance of this or that matter of fact is, under every system of law, obtained, in the way of immediate perception, by men occupied in the exercise of judicial functions: but, in these cases, perception constituting but a part of the ground of decision, and forming no more than a sort of supplement to testimony, they come not under the head of decision without evidence.

We come now to the cases in which the absence of evidence is but apparent, or regards no more than a part of the aggregate mass of legally operative facts: —

1. First comes the case of admissions, as above explained — express, or implied.

Admissions are but evidence, are but testimony, under another name.

When the admission is express, being the declaration of a party, and the effect of it operating, so far as it goes, in disfavour of him whose declaration it is, it comes under the head of self-disserving evidence.

Evidence of this description is, it will be seen, not only evidence, but the most trustworthy of all evidence: understand always, so far as the application made of it — *i. e.* the decision grounded on it — is confined to the interest of him whose declaration it is, and such other interests (viz. the interests of his representatives) as, being placed at his disposal, are considered as included under his.

When the admission is, as above explained, not express but only implied, the evidence is not direct but circumstantial: evidentiary fact, the negative act, the species of *default* above exemplified; principal fact, or fact evidenced, admission of the fact by which the interest which the admitting party has in the cause, is disserved.

2. Next comes the case where the fact is of the number of those which, being considered as placed by *notoriety* out of the reach of dispute, have therefore no need of being established by *special* evidence, — by evidence adduced for the single purpose of the suit actually in hand.

If to the purpose in question (viz. the purpose of serving, or helping to serve, as a ground for judicial decision) the fact be really notorious, it is notorious to the judge: a persuasion of the existence of it — a persuasion strong enough to give support to decision — is already formed in the bosom of the judge: this being assumed, all special evidence — all evidence the object of which is to endeavour to form such a persuasion, is, by the supposition, so far as *his* persuasion alone is deemed sufficient, superfluous and useless.

But, unfortunately, between facts that to the purpose in question are sufficiently notorious, and those that are not so, no distinct line is to be found: and where, in regard to this or that fact, a general persuasion of its existence is sufficiently prevalent, and to a sufficient extent, yet, in regard to this or that material circumstance, the persuasion is not perhaps sufficiently extensive and distinct. A fact regarded as notorious by one man, may be matter of dispute to another: a fact regarded as notorious by the plaintiff, may be matter of dispute to the defendant, and even to the judge.

From this indeterminateness, the practical inference seems to be as follows: — To save delay, vexation, and expense, it ought always to be in the power of the judge, at the instance of either party, to pronounce, and, in the formation of the ground of decision, assume, any alleged matter of fact as notorious. On the other hand, to guard against misdecision, it ought at the same time to be allowed to the party, — viz. to the party to whose prejudice the fact, if assumed, would operate

* See Book II. *Securities*, Chap. IX. *Interrogation*.

—to deny the notoriety of the fact, and in so doing, call for special proof to be made of it: provided always, that for a false assertion to this effect, as for a false declaration of his persuasion to any other effect, he should stand exposed to suffer—whether by burthen of punishment, or by burthen of satisfaction, or both—as for wilful, *i. e.* self-conscious, falsehood, or falsehood through temerity, as the case may be.

When a fact is really to such a degree notorious, as that a man will not, without the imputation of falsehood, be heard to deny his persuasion of its existence, or to speak of himself as doubting of it,—in such case, if, in addition to a simple call for proof of it, an express declaration of such disbelief or doubt be made requisite to the existence of the obligation of complying with such call, shame,—fear of disrepute, will in general be sufficient to prevent any such call from being made, in a case in which the declaration, if made, would be otherwise than sincere: but if no such declaration be required—if the obligation follow upon the call—such call ought to be expected as a matter of course, in every case in which, by a chance of misdecision in favour of him who makes the call, or by delay, vexation, or expense, created by it to the prejudice of the other side, a sinister advantage may in any shape be reaped from it.

Under the existing systems of technical procedure, spun out everywhere under the impulse of an interest directly opposite to every end of justice,—the object, so far as concerns evidence, has everywhere been, not to lighten, but to aggravate, the load of unnecessary evidence: accordingly, proof made by one party, of facts of which on the other side there is no doubt,—proofs, in a word, substituted to admissions, are among the resources drawn upon for the advantage of the actual and mischievous ends of judicature: and as to this, so to other purposes, to prevent those explanations, by which injustice in all its shapes would be prevented, is among the objects which have been but too effectually accomplished.

It will seldom if ever happen that, for the substantiating either the plaintiff's demand, or the defendant's defence, no other facts than such as are already notorious will require to be believed: it is seldom, therefore, if ever, that evidence, special evidence (admissions as above included,) will altogether be to be dispensed with.

3. Lastly comes the case in which, in disaffirmance of facts affirmed by evidence on one side, a decision is pronounced on the ground of the improbability of these same facts.

Though not pronounced altogether without evidence, a decision thus grounded might seem to be pronounced without evidence adduced on the side in favour of which it is pronounced.

But, upon examination, it will be found that even in this case the decision is not without support from evidence. The evidence belongs indeed to that class which has received the name of circumstantial evidence—a modification of circumstantial evidence, composed of all those facts, all those sufficiently notorious facts, the existence of which is regarded as incompatible with the existence of the facts to which it is thus opposed; or, at any rate, as affording inferences of their non-existence—inferences strong enough to be regarded as *conclusive*, and, in that character, to govern and determine the persuasion of the judge.*

* The subject of improbability will be treated at considerable length in the Book on *Circumstantial Evidence*, (Book V.)

BOOK II.—ON THE SECURITIES FOR THE TRUSTWORTHINESS OF TESTIMONY.

CHAPTER I.

OBJECT OF THE PRESENT BOOK.

In the preceding Book, a survey has been taken,—on the one hand, of the standing causes,—the psychological causes, of trustworthiness in human testimony,—on the other hand, of the occasional causes of untrustworthiness; including the incitements to mendacity, the seducing motives, the sinister interests, by which the tutelary influence of the causes of veracity is liable to be counteracted and overborne.

In the planning of the system of judicial procedure, with a view to the main end of procedure, viz. the rendering of decisions conformable on all occasions to the predictions pronounced by the substantive branch of the law; the object of the legislator will be to strengthen as much as possible, the influence of the causes of trustworthiness; to weaken as much as possible, the influence of the causes of untrustworthiness—the sinister interests of all kinds; that is to say, interests, motives, of all kinds, as often as it may happen to them to be acting in this sinister line.

To exhibit a view as complete as may be, of the several arrangements of procedure, capable of being made to operate in the character of securities for trustworthiness in testimony, and thence as securities against deception from that quarter, and consequent misdecision on the part of the judge, is the business of the present book: to show, in the first place what may be done, and ought to be done, to this end; in the next place, what, in the Roman and English modifications of the technical system, has been done on this subject, in pursuit of whatsoever ends the authors have on such occasions set before them.

A mass of evidence, consisting of human testimony, brought into existence for the occasion and on the occasion, (without any mixture of *real* evidence, pre-appointed written evidence, or other written evidence antecedently brought into existence by other causes,) a mass of evidence of this description is about to be presented to the cognizance, and to serve as a basis for the decision, of the judge. By what means, within the power of the legislator, shall its trustworthiness be raised to a maximum? By what means shall the danger of deception on the part of the judge, and, from that or other causes, of misdecision on the ground of the evidence, be reduced to its minimum? To find an answer to these questions, is the problem the solution of which will be the object of the present book.

The mass which is the subject of our problem, is the whole mass, and every mass, to which it may happen on any occasion to be taken into consideration for the purpose of forming, by means of it, a ground for a judicial decision. It must therefore be considered in respect of every modification, of which, in judicial practice, a mass of this description is susceptible. It may be simple to the utmost degree of simplicity — complex to any degree of complexity. It may consist of the testimony of no more than a single person, and consequently on one side only — the plaintiff's side; it may consist of the testimony of any number of persons, and that either on the plaintiff's side, or on the defendant's as well as the plaintiff's — each side being again to this effect divisible into as many sides as there are parties ranged on it, with different, and actually or possibly conflicting, interests. It may consist of the testimony of an extraneous witness or witnesses only, or of a party or parties only, or of a mixture of testimonies of both descriptions. For all these diversifications, provision must be made in the system of arrangements destined to serve as securities for trustworthiness in testimony.

CHAPTER II.

DANGERS TO BE GUARDED AGAINST, IN REGARD TO TESTIMONY, BY THE ARRANGEMENTS SUGGESTED IN THIS BOOK.

THE proper object of the judge, according to the most general description that can be given of it, is, on every occasion to pronounce such a decision as shall be called for by the law, on the ground of the facts of the case: and, for that purpose, to form, in relation to each material fact, by means of a statement afforded by human testimony or otherwise, a conception exactly conformable to the truth; so far at least as is material to the decision which he is called upon to pronounce: —

In this endeavour he will be liable to be defeated by any of the following results.

1. If in relation to any such material fact the testimony be in any point incorrect, although such incorrectness be unaccompanied with that self-consciousness which mendacity implies.

2. If in relation to any such fact it be incorrect in the way of mendacity, as above.

3. If the collection of the facts thus presented to his conception, be in any respect incomplete.* By such incompleteness, the

* Regarded in a certain point of view, the two imperfections — falsehood (including incorrectness and mendacity,) falsehood and incompleteness — may appear to coincide. Previous to the exhibition of the testimony, an oath, suppose, is exacted from the deponent — an oath promising completeness. Such oath having been taken, if the deposition be in any respect incomplete, it is in so far false.

Answer: Say rather perjurious, than false: — an oath is violated, but the oath thus violated is, in this respect, not an assertory oath, but a promissory one: a promise is broken, but no falsehood uttered.

Reply: But suppose a general assertion made at the conclusion of the deposition. *What I have deposed contains everything material that fell under my observation; at any rate, everything material that I recollect.* Or, instead of an oath in the promissory form (as it most commonly is, when the form in which it is exhibited is oral deposition,) suppose it not promissory but assertory; as it most commonly is when the form is that of a deposition already written.

Here, at any rate, the distinction vanishes: in so far as the deposition is incomplete, just so far it is false.

Rejoinder: Incomplete, and therefore false: — admitted. But the proposition in which the falsehood resides is altogether different in this case from what it is in those. In this case, the false fact is but one, and that one, whatever be the matter in dispute, always the same; viz. the completeness of the narration that has just been exhibited. Whereas, if the narration, so far as it goes, contains false facts, false assertions, of any other kind, every one is distinct from every other — every one of a complexion peculiar to the individual cause.

The difference which exists between falsehood

rendering of the decision duly adapted to the case may be as effectually prevented as by incorrectness or mendacity itself. To warrant a decision (say on the plaintiff's side,) let proof of certain facts, in a certain number (say four,) be necessary. If three of these only be proved (say each of them by two witnesses, the testimony of each witness being correct in the extreme) and not the fourth, the plaintiff will be as effectually debarred of his right, as if there had not been a single particle of truth in the testimony of so much as one of their number.

Incorrectness, mendacity, and incompleteness — such are the imperfections from which it will be the object of the legislator to preserve, on each occasion, the evidence that, in the shape of human testimony, comes to be presented to the judge.

The idea of incorrectness being included in that of mendacity, the mention of the word incorrectness may be apt to appear superfluous.

The distinction will, however, be found to be highly material, and that to more purposes than one: —

1. In the first place, as will be seen, the list of securities is not the same in the two cases. Suppose *bona fides*, for example: — prompting — suggestive indication and interrogation, would in many cases be highly conducive to the correct and complete disclosure of the truth of the case; highly useful against false asseveration, false negation, and, in particular, false omission; and, comparatively speaking, free from danger: suppose *mala fides*, the same sort of assistance may be to be guarded against with the legislator's utmost anxiety and diligence.

2. The other purpose regards punishment. Unaccompanied with temerity, simple incorrectness presents, it is obvious, not the least demand for punishment: accompanied with temerity, it may present a demand for punishment, viz. in some comparatively inferior degree, not rising above that which is insuperably attached to the burthen of rendering pecuniary satisfaction in case of injury: accompanied with *mala fides*, it rises into that serious crime, which, by a very intimate, though, as will be seen, a very unfortunate association, has, in the cases where punishment has been attached to it, been designated by the name of perjury.

So far as the failure is accompanied with *bona fides*, the legislator finds, by the supposition, no *will* acting in opposition to him; he has scarce any difficulty to contend with; the demand for securities is inconsiderable. When, on the contrary, the transgression is accompanied by, and originates in, *mala fides*, it originates in design, in fraud: he finds human *will*, perverse will, acting against him with all its might; and all the securities he can muster, with all the force it is in his power to give to them, prove but too often inadequate to his purpose.

Were it possible for the legislator, viewing each transaction from his distant station, to draw a line in each instance between the two cases, and say to himself, this man is in *mala fides*, but this other in *bona fides*, his task would still be comparatively an easy one. Unfortunately, from the distant station he occupies, no such determinate line can be drawn: of one sort of man, he may say he is most likely to be in *mala fides*, as in the case of an accomplice; of another sort, he is most likely to be in *bona fides*, as in the case of *official* evidence:* but, with sufficient grounds of assurance, he can never ground his arrangements exclusively either on the one supposition or on the other, in any instance. A determination of this kind must either be abandoned altogether, or (under favour of the appropriate information extractible from each individual case) intrusted to the probity and prudence of the judge.

There being no individual whatever, of whom the legislator, in his position, can be warranted in regarding himself as completely sure that his testimony will be altogether pure from *mala fides* — there is no individual soever, for whose case he can avoid providing — to be applied eventually at least, and sooner or later — whatever securities it is in his power to supply, for the purpose of combating those sinister motives, to the action of which human testimony can never cease to be exposed.

To the three imperfections above enumerated, must be added, for practical reasons that will be presently seen, that of *indistinctness* — an imperfection which, though not exactly synonymous either with incorrectness or incompleteness, may, according to circumstances, have the effect of either. In truth, one of the two effects it *must* be attended with, to be capable of giving birth to deception, and thence to misdecision: if it be not productive of this bad effect, the only remaining bad effects of which it is capable of being productive (and of those it is but too apt to be productive,) are reducible to the heads of vexation, expense, and delay.

To the consideration of the dangers to be guarded against by the securities in question, must be added that of the *stations* to be guarded against those dangers: these are, all

consisting in a false assertion of completeness, and falsehood at large, is not the only reason, nor the chief reason, for expressing the two modes of imperfection by different appellations. They constitute two different objections against the trustworthiness of evidence: objections, of which the one may exist without the other.

* See Book IV. *Preappointed*, Chapter VIII. *Official Evidence*.

of them, reducible to two—that of the deponent, and that of the judge.

Under the designation of deponent must here be comprised, not only extraneous witnesses, but each and every party in the cause, where it happens to him, whether at his own instance or that of an adversary, to deliver his testimony in the cause.*

The quarter from which the imperfections above mentioned are most to be apprehended, is evidently that of the witness. But as judges, as well as witnesses, are men, both of them exposed, though not altogether equally exposed, to the seduction of sinister interest, the station of the judge is not, any more than that of the witness, to be wholly overlooked in the precautionary arrangements taken on this ground. As it may be, in a certain sense the interest, and at any rate the endeavour, of the witness, to suppress the truth, in the whole or in part, so may it be that of the judge: as it may be the endeavour of the witness to convey false impressions to the judge, so may it be that of the judge to receive, or to have a pretence for acting as if he had received, such false impressions, in preference to true ones. In a certain sense, the judge will always have an interest in receiving the evidence in an incomplete state; because the farther it is from being complete, the less his trouble. One species of sinister interest there is, the *love of ease*, by which, on every occasion, the judge will be prompted to receive the evidence in an incomplete state. The influence of this cause of seduction will become but too manifest as we advance.†

This interest is, on this occasion, the more dangerous, inasmuch as it is opposed with so little force by the tutelary sanctions, the political and the popular, and its agency is so little apt to betray itself to the eyes of those to whom the application of the castigatory force of these sanctions respectively appertains. The exertions a man makes in this way, to preserve himself from trouble, are often-

---

* Witness (to speak here of deposing witness) is an appellation that with propriety may be, and sometimes at least of necessity must be, applied to the designation of every person whose discourse, when exhibited to a court of justice, is employed in the character of *testimony*, or say *evidence*. If this be true, it must be applied, every now and then, to those who are *parties* in the cause, as well as to persons who, not being parties, are more commonly meant when the word witness is employed.

At any rate, it must surely appear strikingly inconsistent and incongruous—after speaking of a person as one who has been deposing, giving testimony, whose testimony, or deposition, or ex-examination, has been given in—to deny that he has acted in the character of a deponent, an examinee, or a *witness*.

Yet, somehow (such is the perversity and inconsistency of language,) a notion seems generally to have obtained, of a sort of incompatibility (whether natural or factitious, seems not to have been distinguished) between the character of a party and the character of a witness: insomuch that, when Titius or Sempronius is spoken of as being a party in the cause, we conceive of him, as of course, as not having acted, nor being about to act, in the character of a witness: and *è converso*, if he is spoken of in the character of a witness in the cause, we conceive of him, as of course, as not bearing any such relation as that of party to the cause.

This conception, partial and erroneous as it is, is receiving continual support from one of those maxims of technical jurisprudence, which, familiar as they are, are yet, in every imaginable sense, false. *Nemo* (to take it in the language in which it probably originated)—*nemo debet esse testis in propriâ causâ*. That it ought not, in any case, to be considered as founded in utility, reason, and justice, is an opinion which will be receiving continual support in the progress of this work. That, in point of fact, in the practice of men of law, it is not acted upon with anything like consistency,—that the extent in which it is departed from, is little, if at all, less than that in which it is observed,—will also appear as we advance. No man, not even a judge, was ever absurd enough to pay the smallest regard to it in the bosom of his own family. Yet, somehow or other (such is the force of prejudice, especially when produced and supported by power,) it has had the effect of causing the characters of party and witness to be generally considered as incompatible and mutually exclusive.

It will be seen, as we advance, that among the numerous instances in which a party is admitted, and even compelled, to act in the character of a witness, there is not one in which his reception in that character can in that instance be justified but by reasons which apply with equal force to justify it in every other instance,—in the instances in which he is not compelled, or not admitted. By the caprice or sinister policy of men of power, a man may be excluded from being heard in the character of a *deposing* witness; but at any rate, he cannot be prevented from having existed in the character of a *percipient* witness. He may be excluded from speaking in a court of justice; but he cannot be prevented from having seen, or heard, or felt, whatever may be to be seen, or heard, or felt, in other places.

Meantime, numerous (as it will be seen) are the cases, in which arrangements that apply with propriety to the case of a witness who is at the same time a party, do not apply with propriety to the case of a witness who is not a party to the cause; and *vice versâ*. On this account, in speaking of a witness, it is absolutely necessary to adopt some mode of distinction, to denote whether he does or does not stand in the relation of a party to the cause. To this purpose may be employed, on the one hand, the adjunct *extraneous*, the phrase extraneous (or say non-litigant) witness; on the other hand, the phrases *self-regarding witness*, litigant witness, deposing or testifying party. Of the extraneous or non-litigant witness, the *testimony*, the *deposition*, the *evidence*, may accordingly be termed *extraneous* testimony, deposition, evidence: of the litigant witness, the deposing or testifying party, *self-regarding* testimony, deposition, evidence.

† See Book IX. *Exclusion*.

times scarce perceptible even to himself. Against corruption on the part of a judge, all mankind are up in arms — all mankind are constantly upon the watch; ready to impute it upon strong grounds, upon slight grounds, and sometimes without any grounds. To precipitation, to inattention, on the part of the judge, — his suitors, his auditors, his superiors—in short, mankind in general, are comparatively inattentive.

The transgression of the deponent is as nothing, any farther than as it is productive either incidentally of vexation, expense, and delay, or ultimately of misdecision, the transgression of the judge. But of the judge's possible sphere of transgression, that of the deponent forms no more than a part. On the part of the judge, misdecision may indeed have been produced by some transgression (occasioned either by his inattention, or by his ill-directed attention) on the part of the evidence. But it is equally possible for the judge to transgress, to misdecide, without any regard to the evidence.*

Correspondent to the nature of the several imperfections, is that of the respective remedies. To incorrectness and mendacity, — detection, and thence, if possible, correction, by the substitution of correct evidence in the place of it. To incompleteness, — detection of the incompleteness, and thence acquisition of evidence concerning the facts not brought forward by the evidence in its original incomplete state.

A remedy of a higher nature than the above — a remedy never to be lost sight of in such remedial measures, such securities for trustworthiness, as come to be employed, — is *prevention* in the first instance—prevention of incorrectness and mendacity, especially the latter; prevention also of incompleteness.

But the two objects — detection on the one hand, prevention on the other — these two objects, distinct as they are in a theoretical view, will, in a practical point of view, be found to coincide. Why? Because the one of them cannot be pursued but through the other; the means by which the prevention of the malpractice is aimed at, being no other than those, by the use of which, supposing the malpractice hazarded, detection, it is wished and expected, may ensue. The witness is incompassed with the fear of detection, and of the unpleasant consequences in its train—a misadventure which he sees ready to befal him, in the event of his swerving from the path of truth. The prospect of this miscarriage is before his eyes; and, by the fear which it inspires, the wish and expectation is, that his footsteps will all along be confined to that desirable path, the only one that leads, directly at least, to justice.

By the detection and correction of the above several imperfections on the part of the evidence, the danger of the correspondent failures on the part of the judge—viz. deception and non-information, and in either case misdecision, is obviated, as far as that danger has its source in the tenor of the evidence.

To the above imperfections and dangers, the remedies immediately applicable are as above. These, however, being altogether obvious — too completely so to be the objects of remark, are not the remedies, are not the securities, we are in quest of. If they are worth mentioning here, it is only in the way of memento, not of instruction, and for the purpose of keeping the line of investigation and arrangement unbroken and complete. The remedies that require research, and are of a nature to pay for it by their importance, are those remedies of a higher order that will meet us a little farther on, under the appellation of *securities* for trustworthiness in testimony.

Among these, so far are they from being obvious, we shall find some, and those among the most efficient, which, with a comparatively narrow exception, have hitherto remained hidden from the eyes of the most enlightened nation on the globe.

CHAPTER III.

INTERNAL AND EXTERNAL SECURITIES FOR THE TRUSTWORTHINESS OF TESTIMONY ENUMERATED.

Correctness and completeness may be called the primary qualities desirable in testimony. There are others, which may be called secondary qualities, and which are desirable for the sake of the primary.

To facilitate the conception and comprehension of the several secondary qualities that promise to operate, on the part of an aggregate mass of testimony, in the character of securities for its trustworthiness — that is to say, for its correctness and completeness, — it may be of use that the reader should, in the first place, be in possession of a naked list of them. From the inspection of that list, some general conception may be formed of them in the first instance: by a separate consideration of each article, that conception will be cleared and fixed as we advance.

To avoid the harsh effect which would result from the finding or making an abstract appellation correspondent to each quality, it may be necessary to discard the correspond-

* In general, whatever security serves to guard the station of deponent by operating as a check to transgression in his sphere, will apply, with more or less efficiency, to the station of judge, by operating as a check to transgression in that superior sphere. But there are some — publicity, for example — that apply, either exclusively, or with a more particular energy, to the station of judge.

ing list of substantives, and confine ourselves to adjectives.

In relation, then, to an aggregate mass of evidence, and to each the several testimonies of which it may happen to be composed, there will be, or there may be (let us say) reason to desire that it may be as follows:—

1. *Particular;* as particular as possible: as special as possible, down to individuality: and besides that, circumstantial; of which distinction in its place.

2. *Recollected;* sufficiently recollected: the deponent, before the delivery of his testimony is concluded, having possessed and employed whatever portion of time may have been necessary to his bestowing upon it the primary qualities of correctness and completeness.

3. *Unpremeditated;* that is, not sufficiently recollected for any such purpose as that of mendacious invention. This and the preceding quality are evidently opposite to each other, and to a certain degree incompatible. To determine how to reconcile them in so far as they may be reconcilable, and which to sacrifice in so far as they may be irreconcilable, will be amongst the nicest and most difficult problems that can be presented by the subject to the skill of the legislator.

4. Assisted by suggestions *ab extrà*— viz. in so far as such suggestions may be necessary to the assistance of recollection — true unfeigned recollection.

5. Unassisted by mendacity-serving suggestions *ab extrà;* unassisted by any such suggestions, true or false, as, in case of a disposition to mendacity, may enable the deponent to give to his mendacious statements an air of truth, so as to enable him to produce the deception he aims at producing in the mind of the judge. Another pair of opposite qualities — further demand for reconciliation as far as practicable, and, beyond that point, for sacrifices on one or both sides.

6. *Interrogated:* called forth by interrogation: by examination — questions — interrogatories, — and, for the sake of correctness and completeness, these questions put on all sides — put by every individual in whose person a mass of appropriate information, qualifying him for putting *apt* questions (*i. e.* questions calculated to contribute to the trustworthiness of the testimony, either in the article of correctness or in the article of completeness) is united with a degree of interest, and thence with a degree of zeal, sufficient to produce the exertion necessary to the purpose.

7. *Distinct* as to the expression. Of indistinct expression the consequence may be, either to cause the testimony, though correct, to produce the effect that would have been produced by testimony of a different purport, and failing in respect of correctness or completeness; or, by appearing to express something, when on a clear examination it would be found to express nothing, to preserve a witness whose discourse has been no more than equivalent to silence, from affording those indications which silence, when manifest, affords in the character of circumstantial evidence to the prejudice of the sincerity and probity of him by whom such reserve is persevered in.

8. Expressed by *permanent* signs; such, for example, as those of which written discourse is composed. If, destitute of the support of those permanent signs, it be limited to such evanescent signs as those of which oral discourse is composed, it will be liable to produce deception, as in case of indistinctness; unrecollected, when occasion comes for recollecting it, it will be tantamount to silence, except as to the affording of those instructive indications which silence is so frequently calculated to afford in the character of circumstantial evidence: misrecollected, it will, though originally correct, be converted into some modification or other of incorrect, erroneous, and perhaps deceptitious, evidence.

If substantives correspondent to these several adjectival expressions — abstract terms corresponding to those several concrete terms — were already in use, or capable of being put into use, they would be equivalent to those which follow; of which, some are already in use — others have been constructed for the purpose:—

1. Particularity.
2. Recollectedness; viz. to the purpose of correct and complete information.
3. Unpremeditatedness; viz. to the purpose of mendacious invention.
4. Suggestedness; viz. in so far as necessary to the purpose of correctness and completeness.
5. Unsuggestedness; viz. when not necessary to these purposes; more especially when conducive to the purpose of mendacious incorrectness, or its equivalent, intentional suppression, productive of intentional incompleteness.
6. Interrogatedness; if a conjugate of so harsh a form may, for the purpose of the moment, be endured.
7. Distinctness; viz. in point of expression.
8. Permanence; viz. in respect of the nature of the signs to which it is committed.

Such is the list of qualities that have presented themselves in the character of securities, *internal* securities, for trustworthiness, for correctness and completeness, in the aggregate mass of testimony. It remains to bring to view those arrangements which present themselves in the character of *external* securities, with reference to the same purpose: arrangements tending to secure, on the part of a mass of testimony, those desirable qualities which have been enumerated under the name of internal securities. These seem all of them referable to one or other of the following heads, viz. —

1. Punishment: (including, in case of special injury to individuals, the burthen of satisfaction in so far as it tends to operate in the character of punishment:) arrangements calculated to attach punishment, in the character of an eventual consequence, to incorrectness or incompleteness of testimony, when accompanied with blame, whether in the shape of mendacity or temerity. In case of manifest mendacity or intentional silence, on the part of defendant or plaintiff, when called upon to depose, — loss of cause, that is, loss of the advantages, or subjection to the inflictions, at stake upon the cause, may be considered as a sort of virtual punishment, growing naturally out of the offence.

2. Oath: arrangements attaching the sort of ceremony so called to the act of deposition, for the purpose of causing punishment from a supernatural source to attach upon the act, in case of mendacity; a species of misbehaviour which, on the occasion of the association so formed, receives the appellation of *perjury*.

3. Infamy: arrangements followed, or designed to be followed, by the effect of attaching to false testimony, through punishment or otherwise, the sort of ideal burthen characterized by a variety of denominations, such as infamy, ignominy, shame, disgrace, dishonour, disrepute: in other words, causing the punishment of the moral or popular sanction to attach upon the offence.

4. Interrogation: arrangements conferring on the different classes of persons already spoken of, those powers, the application of which to the deponent produces on his part an obligation more or less coercive and efficient in respect to the furnishing such ulterior information as the questions put in virtue of such powers, call for at his hands. To this head belongs, in the language peculiar to the English law, cross-examination, and its opposite, examination-in-chief.

5. Reception in the *vivâ voce*, or ready-written form, or both, according to circumstances: arrangements leaving it in the power of the judge, under such restrictions (if any) as may be needful, to receive the testimony in the one form, or in the other, or in the one after the other, according to the exigencies of each individual case: in the *vivâ voce* form, to save the superior expense, delay, and vexation, incident in general to the ready-written form, and to avoid giving facility to mendacious invention: in the ready-written form, when ulterior time for recollection and methodization seems requisite to the purpose of correctness and completeness, and when the expected advantage in these respects is such as promises to overbalance the delay, vexation, and expense.

6. Notation: or say recordation, registration, scription, note-taking, minute-taking, minuting down the evidence: the operation by which testimony, when delivered in the *vivâ voce* form, is made to receive the above-mentioned quality of *permanence;* and in that respect is, or may be, put upon a footing with ready-written testimony.

7. Publicity: arrangements tending to increase the number of the persons to whose cognizance the testimony, on the occasion of its issuing from the lips or the pen of the deponent, may convey itself. The virtue of this security applies itself partly to the station of the deponent, partly to the station of the judge: to that of the deponent, by leaving or throwing open the door, in case of incorrectness or incompleteness, to correction and completion by opposite or supplemental evidence: to both stations, by giving (by the same means) increased probability to eventual punishment, viz. legal punishment, and by introducing and strengthening the force of that punishment of the moral sanction, which for its application neither requires, nor is accompanied by, the forms and ceremonies of procedure.

To this head belong the arrangements indicated by the words *open doors*, courts of sufficient amplitude, liberty of publication, publication by authority, whether of the minuted *vivâ voce* testimony, or of the ready-written depositions.

To this head also belongs the opposite of publicity, *privacy* or *secresy*, in so far as any case may arise presenting a sufficient demand for arrangements directed to that end. In some cases, secresy may be subservient to correctness and completeness; viz. by withholding from a mendaciously-disposed deponent, mendacity-serving information: in other cases, whatever use it is susceptible of will be confined to the prevention of vexation — of that vexation, which, it will be seen, is liable to spring in various shapes out of the communications liable to be made by the unrestained divulgation of judicial evidence.

8. Counter-evidence: arrangements for giving admission to such evidence from whence opposition may come to be presented to the testimony in question: evidence tending to the correction of it, and thence convicting it of incorrectness, or to the filling up of the deficiencies intentionally or unintentionally left in it, and thence convicting it of incompleteness.

9. Investigation: arrangements designed or tending to promote the discovery of one article of evidence through the medium of another: the discovery of a lot of testimonial evidence, for example, of a sort fit to be lodged in the budget of ultimately employable evidence; whether the article, by means of which it is

discovered, be, or be not, itself fit to be so disposed of—fit to be attended to in that character: the finding out, for example, a person who was an eye-witness of the transaction, by the examination of a person who was not himself an eye-witness of it, but heard the other speak of himself as having been so.

Arrangements competent to the process of investigation, as here described, are in every case necessary, to preserve the aggregate mass of evidence from being untrustworthy and deceptitious on the score of incompleteness.*

The list of arrangements presenting themselves as capable of being employed in the character of securities against deception and misdecision, being thus numerous and multifarious — to enable the mind to obtain a clear and comprehensive view of them, in respect of their mutual relations—to observe in what respects they severally agree, in what others they disagree, and how it is that these different means co-operate in their several spheres, and become conducive to the common end — it may not be amiss to divide them into groups: —

1. In the first group come the topics of punishment, oaths, and shame—all considered as capable of being applied for the prevention of false testimony; each of them indicative of a mass or source of evil, by the fear of which it is designed that a person exposed to the temptation of delivering false testimony shall be deterred from the act. So far as these three articles are concerned, the object of the legislator is, so to manage, as that a person exposed to the temptation of falling into that species of delinquency by which false testimony, and with it the danger of deception, is produced, may never be without an adequate motive (at least a motive bidding as fair as possible to prove adequate) for strengthening him against the temptation, in such manner as to prevent his yielding to it. The course taken by these three securities for restraining the person in question from falling into the obnoxious practice, is by operating upon his will; and that in such manner as to overcome, in a direct way, whatever inclination he might otherwise have to do those things, which in this case ought not to be done.

2. In the next group come the securities which, without applying directly to the will of the deponent, aim at doing whatsoever may without preponderant inconvenience be possible to be done, towards depriving him of the power (supposing on his part the existence of the inclination,) to give into the obnoxious practice. To this head belong the taking away the faculty of premeditation (premeditation considered as a source of falsehood,) so far as can be done without prejudice to recollection — to recollection considered as a source of truth; and the depriving him of the faculty of receiving, from without, mendacity-serving information (information considered as a source of falsehood) without prejudice to the faculty of receiving, also from without, veracity-serving information—information considered as a source of truth; that is, information for the assistance of the faculty of recollection, the only way in which information from without can in any way be contributory to that useful purpose.

3. To the third group belong those securities which operate by lending the powers of the law to the procurement of all such evidence as the case happens to afford, thereby preventing such incorrectness and incompleteness in the aggregate mass of evidence (incompleteness amounting, in some cases, to the total absence of all evidence) as might be the result of such evidence, when delivered, as happened to present itself without the assistance afforded by those powers: — 1. General powers for compelling answers to interrogatories; 2. Powers for insuring the production of evidence operating as counter-evidence to what would otherwise have been delivered; 3. Powers for investigation of evidence — *i. e.* for obtaining the testimony of one man, by means of indications given of it by the testimony of another.

4. By itself (there being nothing either to contrast or match with it) comes *publicity:* an instrument of multifarious application and use: an instrument, the destination of which seems to be (like that of the grindstone and the hone) to give power and efficiency to all those other instruments; augmenting the tutelary force of punishment and shame, and extending and promoting the application of it to all the characters of the forensic drama — to parties, extraneous witnesses, and judges — care being taken not to push the application of it in such manner as, by affording mendacity-serving information to the ill-disposed, to contravene the ends of justice in one way, more than it promotes them in another; nor by preponderant vexation to outweigh the advantage produced in respect of those direct ends, by inconvenience produced in respect of the collateral ends of justice.

5. By itself, again (there being nothing either to contrast or match with it,) comes the use of *writing;* the application of that handmaid of all the other arts and sciences to the particular use of judicial practice, and of

* This last article in the list of securities, which, as the reader will have seen, is a security, not for the correctness of any one article of evidence, but for the completeness of the whole mass, belongs to the head of Forthcomingness, which was reserved by the Author to form part of a work on Procedure.—*Editor.*—[See *Principles of Judicial Procedure*, (in Vol. II. of this collection) Chap. X. *Judicial Communication*, and Chap. XXII. *Prehension.*]

that branch of it in particular which concerns testimony: a security to which publicity itself is indebted for the greatest part of its existence, and all those other securities (including testimony itself) for their permanence.

For the exhibition of these arrangements, no novelty will be produced — no force of invention will be employed. I do but copy: the pattern, approved by the experience and applause of ages, is furnished by established practice: what features of novelty may be found, will be confined to the exhibition of the use and reason of each arrangement, and to the claim made to the tribunal of common sense and common honesty for the steady and constant use and employment of those instruments of truth and justice, the existence of which is indisputed and indisputable.

Yes, so it is: it is from the established order of things, and from that alone, that the above list of securities for testimonial trustworthiness is deduced: but, if the virtue of them were turned to the account to which it might and ought to be turned, the changes that would be made in the established order of things would not be inconsiderable.

In the estimation of the propriety and utility of these several securities, — the main end, rectitude of decision, with the more particular ends on this occasion subordinate to it,— viz. prevention of incorrectness, mendacity, incompleteness, and consequent deception, as above—will not be the only objects to be kept in view. The collateral end — the avoidance of collateral inconvenience, in its triple shape of vexation, expense, and delay, ought never to be out of sight.

The uses pointed out as resulting from the several proposed securities — the uses employed in the capacity of *reasons* to justify the recommendation given of them — will be drawn partly from one of these sources, partly from the other.

At the tail of the group of expedients, in and by which it is altogether proper, and more or less customary, for the legislator to take an active part in the service of truth and justice, seems to be a proper place for putting him upon his guard against the expedient, of which in the same view so abundant, and in every instance so unhappy, a use has been made; viz. the exclusion of proffered testimony — not on the ground of its irrelevancy, of its uselessness in that character, of its worse than uselessness in respect of the expense, vexation, and delay with which the delivery and receipt of it would be attended, — but on account of the danger of its becoming productive of deception, and thence of misdecision, on the part of the judge; a vain, but unhappily too prevalent terror, of the vanity of which proof will require to be given in its place.

CHAPTER IV.

ON THE INTERNAL SECURITIES FOR TRUSTWORTHINESS IN TESTIMONY.

1. First internal security, *particularity* of the statement.

In this respect, we may conceive the statement as resting altogether in generals, or as descending lower and lower in the region of particulars, till at last everything is in such a degree particular as to become individualized: persons, things, portions of space, and portions of time.

The more particular it is, — the more instructive, the more satisfactory, the more trustworthy. Why? The reason is very simple. The more completely it thus descends into particulars, the more matters of fact it contains and exhibits, in respect of each of which, supposing it to vary from the truth, its variation is liable to be disproved, and the witness convicted of mendacity, or error at least, by other evidence. Every step it takes in the region of particulars, whether downwards in the *Porphyrian* scale, or sideways all round in the field of *circumstances*, affords an additional security. The degree of particularity proper to be insisted on in each case cannot be indicated by any description applicable to all cases. But, in jurisprudential practice, examples are not wanting of a degree of generality so vague, that, to a judgment unblinded by prejudice, it will be manifest at first glance, that scarce any the slightest degree of trustworthiness can reasonably be attached to it. Yet, in these very instances, the testimony has not only been received, but treated as conclusive.*

Hence one cause of the comparative untrustworthiness of purely spontaneous testimony. Why? Because, by the supposition, there being no room for interrogation, the degree of particularity rests altogether at the deponent's choice. In the function and right of putting questions, is included the right of commanding the deponent to descend to any degree of particularization, of which, with or without any deceptious design on his part, he may have stopped short.

Give to any person — for example, to the judge — this scrutinizing power, — the testimony, supposing it to abide this test, possesses a degree of trustworthiness which otherwise could not have belonged to it.

Under the head of particularity, two qualities may be included: — speciality, or rather individuality — and circumstantiality: qualities, which, how intimately soever connected, will be found distinct in their nature, and in some respects in their application to the purpose now in hand.

---

* *Ex. gr.* Wager of Law.

For the purpose of forming a ground for decision, so long as the fact is in other respects exposed to doubt, a relation is never particular enough, unless the fact be individualized, that is, fixed and circumscribed in respect of time and place.

Titius has killed a man: a relation to this effect is as yet no evidence; though repeated by a hundred deponents, each declaring himself an eye-witness, this would not as yet be ground sufficient for a decision pronouncing Titius convicted of homicide. Titius has killed an Englishman or a Frenchman, an old man or a young man, a tall man or a short man: by no such specification would the deficiency in the former relation be sufficiently supplied. Titius has killed Sempronius: this is nearer the mark, but neither is this sufficient. At what *time* was the act committed? In what year, month, day, hour? — in what *place?* — in what province, township, road, field, garden, house, room in the house? It is not till all these points have been fixed, that the fact has been individualized: and till the fact has been thus individualized, the evidence is scarce as yet brought to the level of direct evidence; it hangs still in the air, in the character of circumstantial evidence.

"*Quis? quid? ubi? quibus auxiliis? cur? quomodo? quando?*" says a verse, useful for memory, and to be found in the institutional books of ethics.

By the *ubi* and the *quando*, place and time are designated; and by the answers to those questions, if sufficiently particular for the purpose, the fact is *individualized.*

As to the other questions, so far as they go, — by the answers to them, the fact, besides being individualized, is circumstantialized, circumstantiated.

So many circumstances, so many criteria by which, supposing the testimony false in any point, the falsity of it may be indicated and detected. Hence, the more circumstantiated the testimony, the greater the security it affords against deception and consequent misdecision on the part of the judge.

Between speciality and circumstantiality there is this difference: Circumstances which contribute to the giving speciality, down to individuality, to the statement, will all of them be found relevant to the purpose or object to which the testimony is directed — to the substantiating the demand, or the defence — to the showing that the individual fact in question belongs to the species of fact to which the law has intended to annex such and such consequences. They belong, accordingly, to the list of those circumstances, which, in so far as they happen to be present to his recollection, it is proper that he should bring to view in the first instance.

To the head of circumstantiality, considered as distinct from speciality and individuality, belong all those circumstances which, without being relevant to the purpose in question, may yet serve as tests or criteria of the correctness of the deposition — of the veracity and attention of the deponent.

Being, with respect to the purpose in question, irrelevant, they will not come with propriety from the deponent in the first instance. But if (as by interrogation) it be required of him to give to his statement the additional extent in question, an extent that shall embrace the circumstance or circumstances indicated to him for that purpose, — in that view it is, that, the question being relevant, the answer will be so too, and both question and answer proper and instructive.

Take, for example, the case of Susanna and the two Elders. To the head of speciality, down to individuality, belonged the several circumstances which these false accusers thought it advisable to bring to view of their own accord, for the purpose of producing in the mind of the judge a persuasion of the delinquency of the intended victim of their malice.

But, by way of test of their veracity, the ingenuity of her advocate suggested, and called upon each of them to speak to, a topic in itself irrelevant. Affirming that it was under a tree that the fact was committed, and that in the supposed scene of the transaction trees of different sorts were included, — of what sort was that tree? The witnesses being examined out of the hearing of each other, each out of the way of receiving mendacity-serving information from the other, — one pitched upon a tree of one sort, the other upon a tree of a different sort; and, by this mutual contradiction, the falsity of their statement was detected.

Whether under a tree, or not under a tree, — and if under a tree, under what sort of tree, — were circumstances, the irrelevance of which, with relation to the guilt of the supposed transaction, was altogether manifest; but, from the contradiction thus produced, these irrelevant circumstances acquired a sort of accidental relevancy; and the purpose for which they were brought to view was accomplished.

2 and 3. *Recollectedness* and *unpremeditatedness.*

These qualities are, as logicians say, *simul naturâ:* and *primâ facie* directly opposite, and mutually exclusive of one another.

Recollectedness to every good purpose, unpremeditatedness to every bad purpose: recollectedness to the purpose of a man's searching into the storehouse of his memory, and spreading out before the judge the articles it contains: unpremeditatedness to the purpose of a man's setting his judgment and invention to work upon these same articles, in the view of suppressing, disguising, or altering, any of the facts his memory has furnished him with, or delivering false facts in lieu of them, or along with them. Even in this closer view, the two qualities still present themselves as mutually exclusive and incompatible. For, if recollection be necessary, time must be allowed for it: and unless it be by the allowance of suggestion (of which presently,) it is only by the allowance of time that any assistance, tending to put the testimony in question in possession of this quality, can be afforded by the legislator. But if time be allowed for this honest and desirable purpose, what shall hinder its being employed for the opposite dishonest and undesirable one?

Notwithstanding these unfavourable appearances, a still closer view will show it not to be altogether out of the reach of the ingenuity of the legislator to afford the necessary assistance to the desirable result, and at the same time to throw no inconsiderable obstruction in the way of the undesirable one.

No man but must have felt — no man but feels every day of his life, the necessity of recollection for his own use, — the necessity of recollection, and thence of time to be applied to that purpose: for his own use, and therefore when the existence of any desire to deceive is impossible.

As to the quantity of time that may by possibility be necessary to this purpose, — necessary to a man in the character of a deponent, — there is scarce any assignable limit to it. Does Titius owe anything, and what, to Sempronius? To enable the deponent to find an answer, and that with truth and full assurance, perhaps not a second of time may be necessary — perhaps a number of weeks, or months, not to say years. Titius and Sempronius are both merchants, dealing to all parts of the world: the accounts between them are long and complicated: — or, Titius is an executor, his testator a man possessed of large property in a variety of shapes, burthened with a variety of debts; among assets and among debts, a number of articles depending upon so many diversified contingencies.

Nor is the demand for recollection terminated in every instance by the moment which completes the delivery of the testimony: — forgetfulness or mis-recollection is but too frequent, when it is for a man's own use that he makes his search, and when, as before observed, the existence of any desire to deceive is impossible. But if the testimony brought out in the first instance has been in any material respect incorrect or incomplete, there remains a demand for ulterior recollection on the part of the same deponent: recollection, if possible, of new facts, for the correction or completion of the mass delivered in the first instance.

It is for this contingency that we shall see provision made by design, though with a hand not always equal, and sometimes rather scanty under the names of *repetition* and *recolement*, by the Roman law: as also (though without a name, because without design, and consequently in some instances with great redundance, in other instances not at all,) by English law.

4 and 5. *Suggestedness* and *unsuggestedness:* the quality of having been assisted by suggestions to every good purpose, and the quality of not having received any such suggestions to any bad purpose.

Between this pair of antagonizing qualities and the former, there is manifestly a very intimate connexion. And here again recurs the mystery, by what contrivance the good purpose can be promoted without the bad — the bad obstructed without the good.

The same experience — the same constant and universal experience, which evinces to every man the need he may have of whatever information can be derived from his own memory, evinces to him also the need he may have of whatever assistance can be derived to his memory from the memory of others: and that, too, where the existence of any desire to deceive, or to be deceived, is alike impossible.

On this ground, as on the former, first appearances are apt to be fallacious; shutting out a hope which a closer scrutiny will show not to be an unreasonable one. To suggestions from without, what possible obstruction can ever be thrown, it may be asked, by any obstacle which it lies within the power of the legislator to apply?

When a man delivers false testimony, what there is of falsification in it may be either of his own invention, or of the invention of some one else — either home-made or imported.

Made at home or abroad, the inventor of it must have had a stock, a ground, composed of true facts, to work upon.

To the true man, knowledge of facts — of any other facts than what are presented to him by his own memory, is of no use. Why? Because all true facts are consistent with each other: his facts being true, they cannot receive contradiction from any other facts that are so likewise.

To the mendacious deponent, on the contrary, knowledge of other connected facts is indispensable: his stock of this sort of information cannot be too extensive for his security against detection; it can never, indeed, be sufficiently extensive: because every true fact that has any discoverable bearing upon the case, presents a rock upon which, if unseen, his false facts, one or more of them, are liable to split.

So they be but relevant, true and false information may be alike subservient to the purpose of the mendacious deponent: or rather, on the single condition of being relevant, truth cannot but be of use to him; whereas, the use he can make of suggested falsehood will depend, not only upon its being well adapted to his mendacious purpose, but also upon its being better adapted than any which his own invention could, on that same occasion, have supplied him with.

Upon this view, the importance of the quality of unsuggestedness appears already in its true light: at the same time, the difficulty of promoting it by any arrangements within the power of the legislator, presents itself as yet in a false, and, happily, an exaggerated light. What are the problems that seem to present themselves to him for a solution? Required, on the present occasion, to exclude a man from all intercourse with his fellow men, — on the former occasion, to deliver him from all access to his own thoughts, from all communication with himself.

Thus much indeed is true, that in every instance there exists a point of time, down to which recollectedness and suggestedness are qualities of which no man's testimony can be deprived, unpremeditatedness and unsuggestedness, qualities which no ingenuity on the part of the legislator can endow it with. Equally true it is, that from and after that point of time, no inconsiderable degree of security is actually produced (not to speak of what may be produced) by arrangements lying within the power of the legislator and the judge. What will also be seen is, that from the commencement of this period there is no such absolute incompatibility as hitherto there has appeared to be, between the antagonizing qualities compared with one another — between recollectedness and unpremeditatedness — between suggestedness and unsuggestedness: no such incompatibility but that a sufficient portion of time to a good purpose — time applicable to the purpose of recollection, and opportunity sufficient for receiving information assistant to that same purpose, may be allowed to a deponent; while the time and information capable of being employed in the fabrication, or receipt and adoption, of false and mendacious testimony, may in no inconsiderable degree be kept out of his reach. But the designation of this critical point of time, as well as the delineation of the requisite system of arrangements commencing at that same date, will be more clearly apprehended, when, under the head of external securities, we come to speak of interrogation.

6. *Interrogatedness.* — A mass of testimony, extracted from a man by the process of interrogation, will almost always be more or less different, in substance as well as in form, from the testimony of the same man on the same occasion, if spontaneously delivered, without the assistance or controul of any such operation. To the external security created by that process, corresponds, therefore, an internal security, afforded by the texture which, under the influence of that operation, the testimony itself has been made to assume. Nor is the case materially different, where, a mass of testimony having been delivered in the first instance without the aid of interrogation, the extractive force of that process is afterwards employed in adding to the original a supplemental mass.

It is by interrogation, and not without interrogation, that testimony too general for use is brought down to individuality, and clothed with instructive circumstances: it is by interrogation, and not without interrogation, that indistinct testimony is rendered distinct — cleared from the clouds in which it has involved itself, or been involved.

It is by interrogation, aptly and honestly applied, though not exclusively by interrogation, that testimony is assisted by information, subservient to it in respect of correctness and completeness. It is by the skilful application of this instrument, that a mass of testimony, while left in possession of that degree of recollectedness which is necessary to correctness and completeness, is deprived of the quality of premeditatedness in a state of things in which the time demanded on pretence of recollection might be but too apt to be employed to the purpose of fraud.

7. *Distinctness.*—Distinctness, like health, is a negative quality in the garb of a positive one. Health, in the natural body, is the absence of disease: distinctness, in a body of evidence, is the absence of a most pernicious disease called indistinctness — a disease for which, as will be seen under the natural system of procedure in its original simplicity, there is no place — a disease which owes its birth in most cases to the implanting hand of the regular-bred practitioner. Even when not planted by art, the seeds of it are attached, as it were, to the nature of written evidence: in *vivâ voce* evidence, if for a moment it makes its appearance, interrogation, if admitted, drives it out the next.

An article of testimony, so long as it is indistinct, may be neither general nor particular, and neither true nor false. Until subjected to that process, by which it may be ascertained whether the confusion in it be the result of honest weakness or of dishonest artifice, no indications, no decision, can be justly grounded on it. It is worse than false evidence — it is worse than no evidence: for from falsehood, when seen to be such, as well as from silence, indications highly instructive may be, and are, every day deduced: but from indistinct testimony, till it be understood to be tantamount to silence, nothing can be deduced.

8. *Permanence.* So great, as must be ob-

vious to everybody, is the importance of this quality, that, till the means, the only means of producing it, came into use, justice must everywhere have stood, or rather floated, upon a basis comparatively unstable.

Purport depends upon tenor — effect and substance, upon words: and if the words are forgotten, or doubtful, or in dispute, on what sort of foundation is it that the decision has to ground itself? Everything may come to depend on the question whether this word or that word — whether this word has or has not—been employed: and when the decision on this question rests on the memory of one man, opposed by the memory, or pretended memory, of another, justice is thus left to be the sport of fortune.

For the effects of all kinds produced by it at the first moment after its utterance, a mass of testimony depends upon itself; but at every moment after the first (one may almost say without exaggeration) it depends upon its having, or not having, received the quality of permanence; — in a word, on its having, or not having, been clothed in the form of written discourse. Divest it of this security, it becomes each moment more and more liable to be changed or lost; having been correct— to become incorrect, having been complete — to become incomplete: for, the instrument whereby the effect is produced upon the mind of the judge, and of all other persons taking upon themselves at any subsequent period to contemplate it in the point of view in which it is contemplated by the judge, is — not the testimony itself, but that picture of it only which is present to the conception of him by whom it is so contemplated. So that, by the want of this one security, whatever care has, with whatever success, been taken to endow the testimony with those other qualities, may be lost.

Nor is it merely by its existence that this quality is productive of the desirable effects in respect of correctness and completeness: even upon the mind of the deponent, at the very instant of giving utterance to his testimony, the assurance that nothing of it will be misrepresented or lost, will, by the force it gives to the truth-ensuring motives (whatever they may be,) to the action of which he is exposed, operate with no inconsiderable force as a security for the attention requisite on his part to invest it with those primarily essential qualities.

Such is its importance in the case of a *bonâ fide* deponent: for even in the case of a *bonâ fide* deponent (especially if, being without interest of any kind, he be completely indifferent to the issue of the cause) a certain degree of attention on his part will be necessary to his bestowing upon his testimony whatever degree of correctness and completeness it happens to be in his power to bestow upon it.

But to the supposition of *bona fides* and complete indifference, substitute that of mendacity, or even bias. In what case now lies the chance for correctness and completeness? It is not merely that there may be a deficiency in the force of the motives necessary to secure the measure of attention necessary to these qualities; but the motives by which the bias, or determination of mendacity, has been produced, act in a manner without check. The punishment or the shame a man may be exposed to by the falsehood of his testimony, — every security of this sort depends upon the words of it, upon the recollection which somebody has, or pretends to have, of them; and the words of it are liable at all times to be mis-recollected, or forgotten.

Before writing came into use, — in order to give the best hold that could be given upon the memory, — laws, moral sayings, and whatever other discourses were judged most worthy of remembrance, were clothed in rhyme or measure. But even among Italian improvisatores, where is the man who, along with correctness and completeness, could give measure and rhyme to testimony?

Strictly speaking, it is only in respect of its influence on the mass of testimony in question — on the correctness and completeness of it, that the consideration of the quality of *permanence* belongs to the present head. But the correctness and completeness — the trustworthiness, of testimony itself, is no otherwise of importance than in the character of a security against misdecision on the part of the judge. Suppose, then, the testimony vanished, or the purport of it a subject of doubt and dispute, — and, from any cause whatsoever, a disposition to misdecision, wilful or temerarious, on the part of the judge, — in what condition is the only check that can be opposed to it?

Independently of desert, — power and authority never fail to invest with a prodigious body of factitious credit the assertions, direct or implied, of every man who speaks from so commanding a station as the seat of judicature. Be the reclamations of the losing party ever so well founded, what degree of credence can they hope to find, when this security is wanting against the testimony — the implied testimony, of the judge?

In this state of things, when, either from the mendacity of a deponent, or from the unrighteousness of the judge, a suitor has received an injury, on what basis stands his chance for redress?

Nor are the benefits that depend upon the permanence of testimony confined to the station of the suitor. If in this imperfect quality the unrighteous judge finds a necessary check, the righteous judge finds in the same quality a most desirable protection. On the testimony, as really delivered, he pronounces a decision aptly deduced from that testimony. But, from the clamour of rash or mendacious tongues, the testimony, or the extra-judicial accounts thus given of it, being misrepresented and mutilated, he finds himself covered with the obloquy and disrepute due only to wilful misdecision and injustice.

Take away this security, and mark the contrast, the deplorable contrast, which is liable to be exhibited by the fates of the unrighteous and the righteous judge. The former reaps insecurity, the fruit of his unrighteousness: the latter, the righteous judge, suffers under the affliction which ought to have fallen upon the unrighteous one.

When justice was left to totter upon this fluctuating basis in the case of original judicature, what must have been its condition in the case of judicature upon appeal?

1. On the occasion of this fresh inquiry, if the evidence be collected *de novo*, every day, by helping to rub out the impression left upon the memory of the deponent, will lessen the probability of correctness and completeness in the testimony.

Every day, while it thus lessens the assurance for trustworthiness on the part of the testimony of the deponent, will lessen in the same proportion the security for probity, and on that ground the security against wilful misdecision, on the part of the judge.

If no part of the original mass of testimony but what is thus delivered *de novo*, be admitted, every day adds to the chance of deperition, by death, absentation, or latency, designed or casual, on the part of the deponents of whose testimony it was composed.

The expense and vexation attached to this second exhibition, is, moreover, so much added to the account of collateral inconvenience.

2. If the same witnesses be not thus heard over again, there remains no other alternative but that of hearing an account of the supposed substance of their testimony from some person who has been, or pretends to have been, present at the time of its being delivered.

But, in this way, all the above-mentioned probabilities of incorrectness and incompleteness receive an indefinite increase: the whole mass of direct evidence is transformed and degraded into hearsay evidence.

Of the importance of publicity, a view will come to be taken in its place: but in how great a degree that external security will, for its possible extent and magnitude, be dependent on the permanence of the signs to which the testimony is committed, is obvious to every eye.

When the testimony was destitute of the quality of permanence, how precarious at best must have been the chance for justice, is but too apparent. But a circumstance not altogether so evident, nor yet unworthy of regard, is, in how great a degree this chance, such as it was, must have depended upon promptitude: understanding by promptitude, the shortness of the interval between the time of receiving the testimony, and the time of pronouncing the decision grounded on it.

Give permanence to the evidence, — delay no longer adds, to its own appropriate and certain mischiefs, the danger of being productive of misdecision and ultimate injustice. A body of evidence hastily delivered, must be followed in every instance by a decision hastily pronounced: lest the traces left upon the memory of the judge be obliterated or distorted, the decision must be pronounced at a period before the time necessary for due reflection has been completed, and before the tumult that may have been raised in his passions has had time to subside.

Many are the instances in which it happens that a mass of evidence, delivered or extracted on the occasion or for the purpose of one suit, may be applied with advantage to the just decision, or (what is much better) to the prevention, of another. But in how great a degree its use in this respect depends upon the permanence or impermanence of its form, is obvious at first sight. Give it but permanence — commit it but to writing, — the same mass of evidence may be applied to the decision or prevention of any number of suits, and this without any considerable addition to vexation or expense; whereas, without this instrument of economy, the quantity of each inconvenience would be to be multiplied by the number of such suits.

CHAPTER V.

OF PUNISHMENT, CONSIDERED AS A SECURITY FOR THE TRUSTWORTHINESS OF TESTIMONY.

§ 1. *Species of falsehood — Necessity of substituting the word Mendacity for Perjury.*

AT the head of the fictitious securities for the trustworthiness of testimony, punishment — punishment by appointment of law — must stand without dispute: it is indispensable for the purpose of securing the preponderance of the tutelary over the seductive motives. After this security, a number of others will be brought to view: but a property common to almost all of them, is, the assuming the existence of this primary security: they will be found to consist principally of so many expedients, having for their object the application of this indispensable security to the best advantage.

Falsehood, as already intimated, may be either free from blame, or accompanied with blame. When free from blame, it is rendered so by circumstances (such as invincible ignorance), the effect of which is to preclude the possibility of employing punishment to any advantage.

When accompanied with blame, it is, in the mind of the individual, either accompanied or not with the consciousness of its own existence. If accompanied with that criminal consciousness, it then comes under the denomination of *mendacity*.

If not accompanied with the consciousness which renders it thus criminal, and yet accompanied with blame,— it is because, though a man had no complete persuasion — possibly not so much as that faint commencement of persuasion called *suspicion* — that what he was saying was false, yet had he bestowed on the subject that attention which on legal or moral grounds was due, the falsity of such his testimony would have been perceived by him, or at least suspected: in which case, if, without making known such his suspicion, he had delivered such statement notwithstanding, it would thereby have been accompanied and tainted by mendacity. Falsehood thus accompanied with blame, but with an inferior degree of blame, may be termed falsehood through or with *temerity*. And thus we fall in with a known and most useful distinction of Roman law.*

In a former Book, occasion presnted itself for observing how close the connexion — how frequently undistinguishable the boundary, between the functions of sense and that of the judgment — between perception (with its consequent recollection) and inference.† In another Book, manifold occasion, in like manner, will present itself, for observing the same sort of connexion between direct and circumstantial evidence. Where a man speaks from simple perception, without the necessity of having recourse to inference, the testimony he gives is purely direct evidence: in so far as what he says is grounded on inference, though it be on inference drawn from his own perceptions — grounded on inference, and seen by others to be so, — his testimony, with whatever propriety it may be ranked under the head of direct evidence, cannot but be seen to involve in it a proportionable mass of circumstantial evidence.

On the other hand, intimate as this connexion is between perception and inference in some cases, in others it may be remote, to every imaginable degree of remoteness: and instances may be found in abundance in which it will be universally recognised, that from the erroneousness of the inference, howsoever ascertained, no such imputation as that of mendacity (in other words, of a thorough

* With *mendacity*, a work on the law of evidence has no direct concern, any further than as the falsehood thus characterized is delivered on a judicial occasion or for a judicial purpose.

When thus delivered, it is apt to be accompanied with circumstances, from whence it has derived so many appropriate names. A brief mention of them can scarcely be dispensed with here.

1. Where, for impressing on the mind of the individual in question the desire and endeavour to steer clear of falsehood by adhering to the line of truth, the sort of ceremony known by the name of an oath (of which further on) has been employed, — mendacity in this case has received the name of *perjury*.

2. When the mendacious assertion has had for its subject-matter an article of written evidence, being employed in the endeavour to obtain credence for a spurious script fabricated, or a genuine one altered for the purpose of deception, — it has received the name of forgery; though, in strictness of speech, the appellation of the forgerer belongs only to the man who, for the purpose in question, fabricates or alters the script; and who, for the application of it to its intended criminal purpose, frequently trusts to some other individual, by whose mendacious representations endeavours are to be used for causing it to pass for true. In this case, if the criminal labour be divided between two persons, and the appellation of forgerer be applied to both, the one may be distinguished by the name of the *operative* forgerer— the other by that of the *uttering*, *exhibiting*, or *circulating* forgerer. In this shape, even when employed on a judicial occasion, the false conception may be conveyed, the mendacity uttered, by *deportment* as well as by language.

3. Mendacity considered as having deception for its object (and it seems difficult to conceive it without ascribing to it a reference to that object) has received the general name of *fraud*. When, for the conveyance of the false conception, language is employed, — mendacity is the term more likely to be used; when deportment, — fraud.

4. When the mendacity, the fraud, has for its subject-matter the person of any determinate individual, — consisting in the endeavour to cause one person to be taken for another, it has in English obtained the name of *personation*. Or if the substantive *personation* be not as yet in common use, at any rate its conjugate, the verb to *personate*, is in familiar, as well as in legal, use. Mendacity in this form is, under English law, subjected to capital punishment, and thus put upon a level with what is regarded as the most criminal modification of *forgery*, and above the level of perjury, to whatsoever purpose applied.

5. When the deceit has for its object the obtaining the possession of some material object, in relation to which the person guilty of the deceit is conscious of his having no legal title, — it constitutes a particular species of offence against property, and may be termed *fraudulent obtainment*.

To the designation of this species of offence, under the Roman law, the single-worded appellation *stellionatus* is applied in some cases. In English law it is no otherwise designated than by the circumlocutory expression, "obtaining by false pretences;" except in some particular cases, in which it is familiarly called *swindling*.

In none of the above cases will the names respectively designative of the several modifications of delinquency be employed, unless the falsehood is understood to be accompanied by that blameworthy consciousness which stamps upon it the character of *mendacity*: to the case of falsehood through temerity, they will not be understood to reach.

† Book I. Chapter VIII.

consciousness, on the part of the witness, of the non-existence of the fact, the existence of which is represented by his testimony as having been inferred by him) can justly attach.

After this explanation, and subject to the limitations brought to view by it, the following propositions will be found to be true, with a degree of correctness sufficient to enable them to be employed to good account in practice:—

1. In a case which is clearly that of mendacity, the testimony consists of pretended recollections of pretended perceptions which never did take place.

2. Of falsehood through temerity, one case is that where,—from a recollection of certain facts (call them evidentiary facts) actually made known to the witness by perception, by the evidence of his senses,—he avers the existence of other facts, (call them principal facts)—grounding his persuasion of the existence of these principal facts, on inferences of his own, drawn from these evidentiary facts; which principal facts, and consequently the inference on which his persuasion of their existence was grounded, prove to be untrue.

3. Another case of falsehood through temerity is that, where the persuasion entertained or professed to be entertained by the witness is grounded, or purports or professes to be grounded, on the relation of some other person or persons; which relation turns out not to be true.*

Observe, that,—though inference, the work of the judgment, is the proper field for temerity,—the sort of operation in which the representation of falsehood is most apt to have been the result of mere temerity (*i. e.* of insufficient attention,) and to have stood altogether clear of mendacity,—yet neither is this case less susceptible of mendacity than the first. From the fact of my having seen Titius aim a blow at Sempronius, of whose death he stands accused, I may have deposed to the fact of Sempronius's having received the blow (representing the matter as if, in my judgment, consideration being had of their relative positions, it was impossible that the hand of Titius, moving in the direction in which I saw it move, should have failed of lighting upon Sempronius:) whereas in fact I was in my own judgment persuaded that the blow did not take effect; no such inference being really drawn by me, as must have been, had it really been my persuasion that the blow took place.

Again, from the fact of my having heard Sempronius say that he was so struck by Titius, I may have alleged the existence of a persuasion on my part of his having been so struck: whereas in truth it may have been, either that Sempronius never told me any such thing; or that, though he told me so, I did not believe him, but on the contrary in my own mind was fully persuaded that what he so said to me was false: as if, for the purpose of giving a colour of truth to a knowingly and wilfully false deposition on my part, I had myself suggested to him the telling me a false story, invented by myself for that very purpose.

In a word, two sorts of occurrences there are, of which by personal experience no man living but must have been abundantly conscious: one is, the having believed, on the ground of an inference from other facts, the existence of a fact, which, without any imputation upon his attentiveness, or even his sagacity, turned out not to be true: the other is, the having believed, also on the ground of inference, a fact which turned out not to be true, and to which, had he applied his attention with the utmost degree of closeness with which on some occasions it has been applied, he would not have given credence. Supposing him to have deposed according to such his belief, the first is a case of falsehood in the way of simple incorrectness, without temerity; the other is a case of falsehood accompanied with temerity.†

* This case might have been comprised under the second head; inasmuch as persuasion grounded on the testimony of another person, is necessarily matter of inference. But the two cases, that of inference from a man's own perceptions, and that of inference from exterior human testimony, are, in respect of the opening for error, so widely different, that the latter could not but be referred to a separate head.

† It is only in consideration of the *purpose*, the mischievous purpose, to which the falsehood is applied—the mischievous *effect* of which it is or tends to be productive, that punishment can properly be employed to check it. In respect of quality as well as quantity, the demand for punishment will of course vary with the nature of the mischief, and consequently with the *occasion* on which it is produced, or liable to be produced. To the modifications of falsehood already brought to view, will therefore come here to be added a view of those which result from the particular occasion on which it is uttered: the general description of the occasion being that of a suit at law, either actually instituted, or in contemplation to be instituted.

Distinction I.—Falsehood *in penali* (*i. e.* on the occasion of a penal suit)—falsehood in *non-penali.*

II. Distinctions of falsehood *in penali.*

Distinction 1—Falsehood inculpative (including *criminative*,) and falsehood exculpative.

Distinction 2—Inculpative, distinguished into inculpative at large, and self-inculpative: the latter conceivable, but altogether improbable and rare; yet not so rare as to be altogether without example. For, in human nature, where is the conceivable inconsistency and extravagance, of which examples are not to be found?

Distinction 3—Exculpative falsehood, distinguished in like manner into exculpative false-

In the sketch about to be given of the arrangements made by existing institutions in relation to judicial falsehood and its three modifications as above distinguished, there is one circumstance, which if it were not noticed at the outset, would be apt to encounter and embarrass us at every turn.

This is the non-employment of any such word as *mendacity* on these occasions, and the practice of substituting to it, where anything at all is substituted to it, the word *perjury*.

One operation there is, and that an indispensable one, by which mendacity is converted into perjury: and that is, the previous connexion established between the act of giving testimony, and the ceremony of an oath.

What is evident enough as soon as noticed is, that between this ceremony (how great soever may be its use) and the mischief of the act, the act of mendacious testimony, which it is employed to prevent, there is not the smallest natural connexion. The mischief exists, exists in all its force, independently of the oath; and it is with the view of helping to prevent that mischief, that the ceremony is employed.

To the applying of legal punishment (and that in a lot as well assorted to the species of delinquency in question as the lots of punishment are that are applied to the respective species of delinquency in other cases,) the previous performance of this ceremony, how beneficial soever it may be, is by no means necessary. To the punishing of Testis for a false and mendacious deposition of his, the consequence of which has been loss of life to Insons, it is (setting aside institution and custom) no more necessary that Testis should have taken an oath not to put his testimony purposely in a false shape, than, for punishing him in the case of his producing the same disastrous effect by his own hand, it was necessary to have made him take an oath promissing to abstain from employing that other member in the commission of the same crime.

Yet so it is, that, with a very few exceptions, in the practice of nations, judicial mendacity — mendacity on a judicial occasion or for a judicial purpose, is scarce ever punished, but in the case where, by means of this collateral and casual additament, it has been previously converted into perjury.

The consequences of this state of things have been, in no small degree, and in no small variety of ways, prejudicial to the interests of truth and justice.

1. All the mischief, all the guilt, all the demand for punishment really attached to mendacity, having thus been transferred in idea to the case in which, by positive institution, it may happen to have been converted into perjury, — the demand for punishment and for infamy (the punishment of the popular sanction) having thus been transferred from the right ground to a wrong one, — the consequence has been, that, where there has been no perjury (that is, where there has been no oath) there has been — in the conception of the bulk of mankind, and even of their rulers — comparatively speaking, no harm done, — no harm, at least, of such sort and degree as to create any demand for punishment.

First inconvenience from the misnomer, — *punishment for mendacity*, and, in that respect, security for veracity *not co-extensive with the demand.*

The mischief would not have been so great, if, on every occasion on which mendacity of this description were capable of being committed, care were taken to convert it into perjury. But there exists as yet perhaps no country, in which such care has actually been taken. To take it, would have required, in every country, on the part of the sovereign and his assistants, a commanding view of the ends of justice, and of the means most suitable to their accomplishment.

2. Of the thus resting, in this case, the demand for punishment upon a wrong *ground*, another evil consequence has been, the applying to it a wrong *measure*. The ceremony necessary to the commission of perjury being in all cases the same ceremony, the profanation of it by the utterance of the falsehood

---

hood at large, and self-exculpative: both but too natural; both unhappily but too frequent.

Distinction 4 — Distinction of falsehood, as well exculpative as inculpative, according to the division of the offences, with reference to which it may respectively be productive of those effects. Distinction of offences, in the first place, into private, self-regarding, semi-public, and public offences; and so on through the orders and genera of those several classes. For those ulterior divisions, reference may fortunately be made to another work.[a]

III. — Distinctions of falsehood *in non-penali.*

Distinction 1 — *Collative*, or say investitive, (with reference to the right in question,) and *ablative*, or say divestitive.

Distinction 2 — Onerative, or say *impositive*, (with reference to the obligation in question,) and exonerative.[b]

Distinction 3 — Falsehood collative (or say investitive,) ablative (or say divestitive,) onerative (or say impositive,) and exonerative, *at large*; — falsehood self-investitive, or self-exonerative, as before.

Falsehood self-divestitive and self-onerative, possible, but not natural or frequent.

[a] Dumont's "Traités de Legislation." See also Bentham's "*Introduction to Morals and Legislation*," Vol. I. of this collection.

[b] A right can never be conferred on one party, but a correspondent obligation is imposed upon another. A right being a thing beneficial in its own nature, and indeed incapable of being otherwise, no mischief can result from its being conferred on one party, otherwise than in virtue of the correspondent and inseparably concomitant obligation imposed by the same operation on some other party.

which it had been employed to prevent, has been regarded in every instance as one and the same sort of offence; whereas the real mischievousness of it, the real demand for punishment on all scores taken together, varies in effect from almost the top to almost the bottom of the scale.

Second inconvenience, —*quantum of punishment not proportioned to the demand.*

3. A third bad consequence is, that in several instances, where the legislator has not forgotten to make such provision for the punishment of mendacity as was to be made for it by that collateral and imperfect operation, his provision has been rendered ineffectual by an unlooked-for circumstance. To the punishment of a man in the character of a witness as for perjury, it is necessary that he should have performed his part in the ceremony of an oath. But the ceremony being understood to be a religious ceremony, sects of religionists have started up, who, actuated by religious motives, have refused to bear their parts in this ceremony. What was to be done? To render these sectaries punishable without the ceremony, as they would have been in consequence of the ceremony, would have been to depart from custom, the ordinary substitute to reason: to attempt to force them into the ceremony, would have been persecution, and, in that respect, against custom, and against reason too. What, then, was the result? To sit still and do nothing; to deprive the public of the benefit of their testimony; to put them, and those in their company, out of the protection of the law; to leave open in so far the door of impunity to all injustice and all crimes.

Third inconvenience, — *exclusion of the testimony of all who are unwilling to go through the ceremony of an oath.*

Besides the mischief to the public, from this same source results no small degree of embarrassment to the writer, who, by the view of that mischief, is excited to apply his industry to the correction of it. Speak of it as flowing from the perjury,—the impression you convey is erroneous and deceptious: you must therefore either discard the word altogether, or give warning of the error every time the word comes to be employed. This appellation, therefore, this improper and deceitful appellation, must at any rate be discarded: another appellation, mendacity, the only appellation by which it is possible to avoid deception and confusion, must be employed in the room of it. At the same time, the appellation thus unavoidably discarded, is the one, and the only one, which the public is at all in the habit of seeing employed: it is the one which they will be upon the look-out for at every turn; and not finding it, every thing they meet with on the subject will be apt to seem defective and irrelevant.

Moreover, the appellation which they find instead, is one which they are altogether out of the habit of seeing employed to this purpose: they will misconceive, they will undervalue, the force of it; they will wonder, and fancy they see error and injustice, when they see the guilt and punishment of perjury ascribed to a species of misbehaviour, which to their eyes may present itself as no more than a naughty schoolboy's trick, a venial peccadillo: while, on the other hand, when, to express the misconduct of men in power, as well as of men subject to power, they observe no other appellation employed than one, which in their experience has never been employed to characterize any species of misconduct so high in the scale as even the lowest punishable offence, they will be apt to slight, as scarce worth regarding, what with due attention would be found to be a national disgrace, and a mischievous and most crying grievance.

To give warning, then, once for all,— let the following indisputable, howsoever unwelcome truths, never be out of mind with the reader of these pages. By *mendacity*, as often as the word presents itself to his view, let him understand that species of misbehaviour, which, if the legislator had done his duty, would have been to be characterized by the word perjury: and in so far as, by the design or negligence of any special person, the practice of mendacity in law proceedings has, for want of such restraint, been left in possession of the profit aimed at by it, — the guilt of such person wants nothing of subornation of perjury, but the punishment and the name.

§ 2. *Rules for the application of punishment to testimonial falsehood.*

Rule 1. Punishment, employed as a check to falsehood, should attach throughout upon *temerity*, as well as upon *mendacity:* diminishing only in degree, in proportion to the diminution of the demand, produced by the difference between the two cases.

Reason 1. Wherever, in the case of mendacity, mischief is among the consequences of falsehood, so is it in that of temerity. In degree, indeed, it is throughout inferior in this latter case:* but such inferiority is a reason, not for withholding punishment altogether, but only for reducing it in degree.

The distinction between criminative consciousness, temerity, and delinquency clear of both those aggravating accompaniments, is a distinction that runs through the whole system of offences. In every instance, the mischievous consequences of the delinquency, and in particular the mischief of the second order — the danger and alarm* — are either constituted or increased by temerity, in how much

* Dumont, "Traités de Legislation," — "*Introduction to Moral and Legislation*," *ut supra.*

less soever a degree than by criminal consciousness. But by falsehood, in one way or other, may be produced, as will presently be shown, mischief in all sorts of shapes — the mischiefs respectively producible by all sorts of offences.

Reason 2. If temerity be not taken as a distinct ground for punishment, distinct from that of *mendacity* (the only species of falsehood convertible into *perjury*,)—in that case, in every instance of falsehood accompanied with temerity, but not with that complete self-consciousness which is necessary to denominate it mendacity, the consequence is, either absolute impunity, or punishment as for mendacity; that is, if converted into perjury, as for perjury; and thence punishment in excess.

It has already been remarked, that one of the most common cases of temerity is that in which incorrect inferences are drawn from real perceptions — in which, from one fact which did happen, the existence of another fact which did not happen, is inferred.

As the closeness of connexion, real and apparent, between fact and fact, is susceptible of variation *ad infinitum*, so is the degree of the temerity imputable to a man, in the case where, the first being true and the others not, he has notwithstanding asserted the existence of the second, inferring the existence of it from that of the first. The more palpably remote the connexion is in the eyes of those to whom it belongs to judge, the less in that case will they be disposed to look upon the pretended error as sincere, to regard the false representation as having had temerity and not mendacity for its accompaniment. But suppose the temerity, the culpable want of attention, to have risen to such a pitch as in its effects on testimony to be undistinguishable from mendacity; the quantity of force necessary to be employed in the two cases in the way of punishment for the prevention of it, may also be undistinguishable: and thus it is, that while for mendacity the lowest lot of punishment may be fixed at a considerable height on the scale, — in the first place it would leave a wide and mischievous door to falsehood, if temerity were left altogether without punishment — and in the next place, the punishment for it ought to be made susceptible of all manner of gradations, from the lowest punishment for perjury, or even above, down to 0.

For fixing the attention of man to whatever happens to be his duty, punishment may be no less necessary than to any other purpose to which it has been employed. Were it not for this, a nurse might with impunity starve her child, a jailor his prisoner; saying, and perhaps with truth, *I never thought about it:* and so with regard to the payment of taxes, and all manner of other active duties.

In particular, in regard to the attention necessary to preserve a man from giving, without actual mendacity, falsehood for truth, — if the want of such attention were generally known to be sufficient to secure a man against punishment, he would take care to clear himself of so inconvenient an incumbrance, as often as the falsehood, which it should have prevented, held out a prospect of answering any profitable purpose. Where is the profitable absurdity so gross, that men have not professed — do not profess (and in many instances doubtless without mendacity) to believe? Is there any imaginable absurdity so enormous and so gross, that, for the sake of money, or rank, or power, or a mixture of all these, the bulk of mankind are not at all times ready (and, doubtless, in a large proportion, without downright mendacity) to profess themselves to believe? And in these cases, how is it that they keep clear of mendacity, when so it is that they do keep clear of it? By fastening their attention with all their might, to whatever arguments can be found in favour of the object of belief, and by suffering it, with all their negligence, to be put aside by the force of interest, from all arguments that act in opposition to that object.

Rule 2. On this occasion, as well as on every other, punishment — the punishment provided by the legislator — ought to be such as shall appear to him to be of itself adequate to the purpose, without any assistance from either the popular or the religious sanction.

Why? Because the punishment appointed by the legislator himself, is such as he thinks fit it should be: it is pointed at such objects, and adjusted, moreover, in such quantity and quality, as to adapt it in every respect to the purposes he has in view. On neither of the two other sanctions, powerful and useful as their assistance will be to him, can he in any of these respects place any such entire dependence.

The instances are but too many, in which falsehood, and even perjury, have, and even by the highest authorities and on the part of official men, been held up to view as meritorious.*

Rule 3. In determining the quantity and quality of the punishment applicable to this offence in each case, regard must be had to the nature of the mischief of which it is productive.

In respect of the mischief producible by it (viz. by means of the deception, and thence of the misdecision, of which it may happen to be productive,) the field of its influence is nearly co-extensive with the whole field over which *wrong* has it in its power to range.

Exercising itself within the non-penal branch of the field of law, and to the prejudice of the plaintiff's side of the cause, it may have the

* See Book I. Chapter XI. § 5.

effect of depriving a man of every kind of right, of satisfaction for every imaginable species of wrong.

Exercised in the same branch to the prejudice of the defendant's side, it may have the effect of imposing on him unduly the obligation corresponding to every kind of right which, at his charge, is capable of being conferred on a plaintiff.

Exercising itself in the penal branch of the field of law, and to the prejudice of the plaintiff's side of the cause, it may give impunity to the delinquent of any and every description, and by that means be productive of alarm and danger, in any shape, and to any amount, to determinate individuals — to a determinate class of persons — to the community at large.

Exercising itself in the same (viz. the penal) branch of the same field, and to the prejudice of the defendant's side of the cause, it may have the effect of subjecting an individual altogether innocent, to any article or mass of punishment which has been, or can be, inflicted under the authority of the law.

The mischiefs, therefore, producible by false testimony considered as an eventual cause of deception, and thence of misdecision, on the part of the judge, are, in this view of them, as numerous and as various as the mischiefs producible by misdecision itself.

Neither in the way of punishment, nor in any other way, is there any mischief which, being producible by the exercise of judicial authority, is not producible by judicial falsehood.

The mischief being thus diversified and extensive, the application of the punishment destined to serve as a security against this mischief ought to be correspondently extensive and diversifiable.

No reason can be given why a wrong,— which is followed by satisfaction, or punishment, or both, if committed by any other means, — should go without satisfaction, or without punishment, if committed in this way by a guilty pen or tongue. By either of these instruments, destitute as they are of physical strength, life may be as effectually destroyed as by the cannon or the sword.

To attempt to fix, either in point of quantity or quality, the mode of punishment best assorted to each modification of delinquency thus commissible, belongs not to a design so limited as the present. Principles destined to both purposes are already before the public in two other works.*

One hint only in respect of quantity: —

The alarm inspired by mischief arising from this species of fraud — from a fraud which, like this, has for its theatre the theatre of justice — seems to be not altogether so great as that which springs from a fraud operating upon a more private theatre. In the case of swindling, for example, a man beholds for himself no other security than in his own (perhaps unexperienced) sagacity and discernment: in the case of testimonial mendacity, no otherwise commissible than in so public a theatre as that of a court of judicature, he beholds for his security, besides the unexperienced sagacity of the jury, the thoroughly exercised sagacity of the advocate and the judge.

One other hint in respect of quality: —

A punishment which, in the practice of English jurisprudence, stands upon the list of those which, on the occasion of testimonial mendacity (when duly erected into perjury,) awaits the option of the judge, is the pillory, —an instrument devised for the purpose of inflicting the punishment of corporal ignominy. But considered as applied to testimonial mendacity, the pillory has nothing belonging to it that can serve in any respect to point the attention of the observer to the nature of the crime.†

If, on this occasion, as on others, a proper object be to give to the punishment that species of analogy, or characteristicalness, which is given to it by exhibiting the offending member in a state of sufferance, real or apparent,—the offending member is in this case not the neck, with both the hands for company, but the one offending hand (viz. the hand that gave motion to the offending pen,) or else the offending tongue.

Rule 4. In both shapes, as well that of temerity as that of mendacity, punishment should embrace every case of false statement uttered by any person in the course or for the purpose of judicial investigation — every false statement, at least, from which, in any shape, advantage or inconvenience can accrue to anybody. Neither on this occasion nor on any other, should a man be suffered *"to take advantage of his own wrong."*

Reason. If, in the course of procedure, (or on any other occasion in which pecuniary interest, or, in short, any other species of interest, is at stake,) a man is allowed to derive advantage in any shape from false assertions, — false assertions may in every such instance be expected from the generality of mankind. In the course of judicial procedure, in particular — if, in the case of any such assertion, nominal as well as virtual, or virtual only, no punishment be either appointed by positive regulation, or commonly applied in practice, the party who sees an advantage to be gained by such falsehood, will look upon it as allowed: and the habit of such falsehood will thus become general, not to say universal, among suitors.

In such case, whatever injustice results

* Dumont, "Traités de Legislation." "*Introduction to Morals and Legislation, ut supra.*"

† This punishment is abolished by 7 W. IV. c. 23. — *Ed.*

from such falsehood, whether in the shape of direct or in the shape of collateral injustice (vexation, expense, or delay,) ought to be set down to the account, not of the party, but of the legislator and the judge.

For any of the differences, the abolition or prevention of which is prescribed by this equalizing rule, no reason ever has been — no sufficient reason ever can be, given. Whatever may be the sanctions, the force of which employs itself, or is employed, in the endeavour to confine men's discourse, for the purposes of justice, within the path of truth — sanctions of law, sanctions of morality, sanctions of religion, — they are not less necessary on one side of a cause than on the other — on the part of one of the dramatis personæ in the theatre of justice, than on another: on the part of the professional agent, for example, than on the part of the client. In one station, the natural force of the improbity-and-mendacity-restricting motives acting with more power than in another, the demand for factitious power, acting in the same direction, may not perhaps be quite so great. But, be the station what it will — if the power of the mendacity-restraining motives be inferior to that of the mendacity-promoting motives, mendacity is the certain consequence.

That the interests of truth and justice neither require nor admit of any such distinction, is too self-evident to require proof, or to admit of it. Turn to practice, the distinction is exemplified to a prodigious extent. To a prodigious extent, spontaneous allegations are, in case of mendacity, exempt from those punishments which attach upon it in the case of allegations *ex interrogato*, which would attach upon the same falsehoods if drawn forth by questions.

The cases in which this licence — the *licentia mentiendi* — is granted, are sufficiently indicative, as well of the quality of the authors, as of the final cause of it. *Concessum est oratoribus*, says a famous orator, *aliquid mentiri in historiis. Concessum est:* By whom? Such is the licence, but who, it may be asked, are the granters? Instead of *oratoribus*, put *litigantibus*, — the proposition is at once more determinate, and more unquestionably true. In this case, that the licence is granted, and who the granters are, are two points equally and simultaneously conspicuous: nor will the third point — why it is granted — be much less so.

When a cause has run out its length, the man of law has nothing to lose by the punishment of mendacity; on the contrary, he is a gainer by it: the mendacity may afford matter for a fresh cause; and it is in a fresh cause, if at all, that the inquiry is performed; how satisfactorily soever the fact of the offence may have been established in the course of the cause which gave birth to it. Applied at this stage, — whatsoever it may contribute in regard to the prevention of mendacity in future contingent causes at large, — it contributes little or nothing to the prevention of it in the individual cause in the course of which the falsehood is uttered. If by punishment, or whatever other means are necessary to the production of the effect, truth were not rendered, to appearance at least, more probable than falsehood in judicial causes, there would be no such causes instituted. Accordingly, at this time of day, punishment is almost universally applied to persons called witnesses, (meaning extraneous witnesses,) as likewise to the litigants themselves, when, with reference to the main point in dispute, they come, either of them, to be examined in the character of witnesses.

This community of interest between the professional lawyer and the public — between the class of persons by whom law, especially jurisprudential law, is made, and those for whose interest it is supposed to be made — is, however, by no means co-extensive with the whole extent of the cause: and where it fails of taking place — *i. e.* to whatsoever point the opposition of interest extends — there, of course, the interest of the governing class governs, and that of the governed is sacrificed to it.

If the truth of the facts on which the commencement of a cause is grounded, were vouched for on the part of the litigant party by whom it is commenced — those which are said to have fallen within his own perception, by a direct deposition on his part — those in respect of which his persuasion is grounded on circumstantial, or on extraneous testimonial evidence, by a declaration of persuasion adapted to the nature of the case, — a most extensive description of causes would thus be nipped in the bud: all causes in which the plaintiff, being completely conscious of a total want of merits, was at the same time assured, either of his inability to produce any sufficient proof (*i. e.* any proof that would be sufficient if it were believed,) or of seeing the force of it overborne by counter-proof: or (to come to the point at once) all those in which the loss of the cause would, in case of mendacity or temerity on his part, subject him, if not to the legal punishment, to the moral shame, of perjury. Here then is a large description of causes, or rather a large proportion of causes of all descriptions, of which the profit would be lost.

Should it be asked, in what way a man thus circumstanced can find his interest in the institution of any such cause, the answer is but too obvious: Every case in which a man, having oppression for his object, beholds, in the person of his intended victim, a person either unable or unwilling to bear the quantity of expense and vexation which in this case has been attached to the faculty of self-defence. In such case, where the inability is total, or the unwillingness immediate, the profit of the profession is confined to the earliest stage, or first stages, of the cause: if either the one or the other bar to the continuance of the cause does not present itself before a later period, the intermediate stages constitute by so much the longer line, with which the current of profit is co-extensive. As to the *malâ fide* plaintiff (bating the casualty of pecuniary support afforded to the intended victim by the casual generosity and ability of his friends,) the relative degrees of opulence being given, the operations of this system of warfare may be reduced to certainty. That, in a siege, how long the power of self-defence may be expected to be protracted, may be known, by means of the proper *data*, if not to a day, at least to a week, is a point that seems to be sufficiently settled by the general opinion of the professors of that branch of the art military. But in the judicial warfare, at what expense a man perfectly honest, and completely innocent and irreproachable, may be either enslaved or ruined by a villain — any villain whatsoever, who happens to be in a certain degree richer than himself, — is a result, the certainty of which, under the system of policy in question, is not at all affected by the uncertainty which, to the prejudice of him who has right on his side, is but too well known to be attached to the operations of the law. The prospect of obtaining redress in any degree is deplorably uncertain: the prospect of obtaining complete redress is, with few exceptions indeed, altogether hopeless: the prospect of oppressing with impunity may be reduced, and every day is reduced, to a complete certainty.

Uttered on a judicial occasion or for a judicial purpose, spontaneous statement will, according to the usage of established language, be understood to require a different appellation, according as it is in the character of a witness or in that of a party that the person is understood to express himself: if in the character of a witness, whether extraneous or self-regarding, *deposition*,—if, in the character of a party merely, and not in that of a witness, *allegation*. From *depositions*, the licence for mendacity has been, in general, taken away— to *allegations*, it has been, in general, extended; and if, in here and there an instance, it has at different times been withdrawn, the proposition by which the existence of it has been affirmed, continues still to constitute the general rule: nor can the reasonableness and experienced utility of the exceptions be maintained by any arguments, which will not with equal force evince the mischievousness and depravity of the general rule.

In the character of a witness, or of a party under examination in the place of a witness, a man must take care what he says; he is expected to confine his discourse within the pale of truth: but no sooner is he freed from the incumbrance, than all restraints of legal obligation are thrown off along with it; the word of command is, *stand at your ease:* the field of mendacity is thrown open to him, and in that field he beholds a play-ground, in which fancy and sinister interest are allowed to gambol without restraint.

Depositions and allegations — depositions on the one side, allegations on the other — differ in name; by positive institution, as above, they differ in effect: but, after making due allowance for the slight distinction in nature which gave rise to the difference in name, there is no reason why the one, more than the other, should be exempt from the law of truth. In both cases, the immediate subject of the assertion is the existence of a fact — a psychological fact: in both cases, it is the existence of the same fact; viz. a persuasion concerning the existence of some other fact. In the case of a deposition, where the evidence is strictly and purely direct, without mixture of circumstantial, — the fact constituting the subject of persuasion is the recollection of certain perceptions entertained by the deponent himself, at a point of time more or less remote. In the case of a deposition which explicitly or implicitly involves a mixture of circumstantial evidence, — the fact constituting the subject of persuasion consists, *pro tanto*, of certain inferences drawn from certain perceptions, so entertained, as above. Where the fact which is the externally apparent subject of the allegation, is a fact the persuasion of which never had the immediate perceptions of the person in question for its ground, — that persuasion has a different ground to rest upon; but, on the part of a veracious speaker, its existence is not less indisputable in this case than in the other: nor is the assertion of its existence less susceptible of mendacity in this case than in the other.

A horse belonging to the defendant has broken into my inclosed field, and damaged my growing corn: deposition or allegation, this at any rate is an assertion on my part — an assertion by which the existence of a persuasion on my part (a persuasion of the past existence of an individual fact belonging to the species of facts designated by these words) is expressed. If this persuasion has for its ground the recollection of a correspondent perception on my part—viz. the sight of the horse when occupied in the act of treading down the corn, and feeding upon it — and if, at the same time, by the terms by which such assertion is conveyed, I declare it to have had such perception for its ground — my assertion is of the nature of a deposition, and is properly susceptible of that name. If I speak of the same fact as a fact which I look upon as proved, or capable of being proved, by my own testimony, — although the fact which presented itself to my senses was not the very fact so described as above, but an evidentiary fact, or assemblage of evidentiary facts (which on account of their supposed necessary connexion with that principal fact, produce on my part a persuasion no less satisfactory of its existence,) — say, for example, my having seen the horse running in a line leading from the field, and in a part of that line commencing immediately without a hedge that bounds the field, the hedge being broken behind, and footsteps tallying with those of the beast discernible on each side of the hedge, — in this case my assertion is not less susceptible than in the former, of presenting itself in the character of a deposition.

If, on the other hand, my persuasion is spoken of by me as not having had any such perception of my own for its ground — neither the perception of the principal fact itself, nor the perception of any physical fact operating on my mind — in relation to it, in the character of an evidentiary fact; but the existence of a set of perceptions of either of the above descriptions on the part of a third person, Titius; — then, and in such case, my assertion cannot, according to the notions and language of jurisprudence, bear with propriety the name of a deposition (except in so far as hearsay evidence is received in depositions:) of the two names in question, it cannot with propriety bear any other than that of an *allegation*: the deposition, if there be any, must be the work of Titius. But whether the assertion, by which the existence of the principal fact in question is pronounced — the fact on which I ground my claim of satisfaction — the fact which, with reference to my title to such satisfaction, I rely on, in the character of an investitive or collative event — whether such my assertion be of the nature of a deposition, or in the nature of a bare allegation, it is equally expressive of a persuasion: and the declaration of the existence of that persuasion is equally susceptible of truth and falsehood — of veracity, mendacity, and temerity; and the fact of such mendacity or temerity, where it exists (though it be an internal psychological fact, the seat of which is in my mind) is, like so many other facts of that same nature, equally susceptible of proof — of proof of a texture strong enough to afford a ground for the burthen of satisfaction, or for the burthen of punishment.

A declaration assertive of such persuasion, and that (in case of its being knowingly false) on pain as for mendacity, may therefore with equal propriety be insisted on in the case of a party, as in the case of an extraneous witness.

There remains, as capable of being included in the allegation, the point of law — the proposition expressive of a man's persuasion in regard to the state and condition of the law, so far as respects the subject-matter of his claim.

The reality of the distinction between mendacity and temerity, and the necessity of preserving it (viz. for the sake of avoiding the mischief of applying excessive punishment on one hand, or giving impunity to delinquency on the other) have been already brought to view. Of the two points — the point of fact and the point of law — the latter is the one in relation to which temerity (in contradistinction to mendacity) is most apt to be the accompaniment of erroneous assertion. In regard to matter of fact, persuasion may be the mere copy of perception, the simple result of recollection: in regard to matter of law, it can never be produced without the aid of judgment and inference.

In a general view, the uncertainty of the law is a quality, unhappily, but too strongly stamped upon it, even in those countries in which the mischief is least flagrant: and upon a view thus general and indiscriminating, it may naturally enough seem a harsh arrangement to fix upon an alleged persuasion (how erroneous and groundless soever) the imputation of mendacity, or even of temerity: at least, if followed up by inflictions of a penal or otherwise burthensome nature, in practice.

Unquestionably, the points in which the aspect of the law may appear uncertain, and that even to the most penetrating eyes, are in every system of established law but too numerous; but this partial uncertainty does not hinder but that, in respect of the subject-matter of this or that individual suit, the state of the law may have been much too clear to admit of any possibility, psychologically speaking, of its having been mistaken. No man who, upon a moment's search directed to that view, will not meet with objects of property in plenty, to which he will be satisfied that, at the existing point of time, be it what it may, he cannot, under the existing state of the law of his country, be it what it will, possess the least shadow of a claim; insomuch, that if, in relation to any such object, he were upon oath to declare, on his own part, the existence of a persuasion pronouncing that object to be included by law in the mass of his property, such declaration could not but in his own mind be accompanied with a consciousness of the guilt of perjury. Well then, let him, for the purpose of the argument, fix upon any one or more of all that infinite variety of objects: let him, if he pleases, include in the list the contents of the firmament and the host of heaven. If the commencement of a suit at law, for the recovery of an object of property, be understood as involving a declaration of a man's persuasion, affirming on his part the existence of a right to that object as given him by the dispensations of existing law; a declaration to that effect, under most, if not all, systems of established law, may, in relation to any such object, or number of such objects, be uttered by any man that pleases, without exposing himself to any sort of punishment, — or to any worse consequences than what would ensue from the disallowance of a claim, of the legality of which, a man of the soundest judgment and most intimate acquaintance with the state of the existing body of the laws, might, with ever so clear a sincerity, declare himself persuaded.

Falsehood — false declaration of opinion, accompanied with mendacity; error, declaration of an opinion really entertained but erroneous, accompanied with temerity; error, declaration of an opinion really entertained but erroneous, unaccompanied with temerity: such, in regard to the subject in question, are the broad lines of difference. Of these different states and aspects of the mind, there is not one that is not frequently, the two first but too frequently, exemplified in practice. Of these several facts, all of them of a psychological nature, there is not any one, of which those to whom it belongs to judge of legal facts, are not as competent judges — as capable of framing a well and sufficiently grounded judgment, as of any other fact belonging to the class of psychological facts. Even of mendacity, of perjury, in these cases, the existence, as already shown, is by no means incapable of being pronounced, and on perfectly sufficient grounds. If even of perjury, much more of temerity: of which — inasmuch as (considered in the character of a species of delinquency) the number of degrees and shades of which it is susceptible is infinite, reckoning from perjury down to absolutely blameless error, — so accordingly may be the corresponding shades and degrees of punishment.

In the case of theft, no man is ever convicted of that crime, unless the judge (in English law, the jury) be as fully satisfied in regard to his persuasion concerning the question of law, as, in case of a conviction of perjury, they are in regard to his persuasion concerning the matter of fact. Let it be ever so clear, that the thing supposed to be stolen has been taken by him; still, if there appear to be any degree of probability, how slight soever, that he regarded it as being his own by law, he is no more convicted of theft than if he had never meddled with it.

Suppose it a case in which the suitor has no professional adviser (for in no country is the case absolutely without example:) it is upon the suitor, and upon him alone that, in the case of the offence in question, whether it be temerity or mendacity, the imputation must attach; together with whatever penal or other burthensome consequences may have been annexed to it. But if, in the case of an individual taken at large, — an individual taken from the most numerous, which are necessarily the least informed, ranks in life, — error thus accompanied, may, without oppression or injustice, be taken as a ground for punishment; much more may it in the case of a man by whom the sort of knowledge in question is professed, and whose title to the remuneration he receives, is grounded on the possession he professes to have of that knowledge. So far as facts are concerned, it may have happened to him to be deceived by his client: though, in regard to any declarations made by him on that subject, even on that occasion recurs the question as between mendacity, temerity, and blameless mispersuasion. But, so far as the question of law is concerned, the blame (if any blame there be) must press upon him, in full and undiminished force: and as to the difference between fact and law, if there be any occasions or purposes for which it is determinable, this is one of them. In the case of the ignorant, the irreproachably ignorant, day-labourer or mechanic, to whom any tolerably adequate acquaintance of the law has been rendered impossible — ignorance (according to a maxim generally maintained and acted upon by those by whom the impossibility of knowledge has been created) is no excuse: shall it in *their* favour alone be an excuse, who profess, and who in so peculiarly abundant a degree are paid for professing, peculiar, and even exclusive science?

The surgeon, or even the farrier, who does injury to his patient, for want of the scientific skill, the possession of which he undertakes for (though it be but by the assumption of that professional name,) is, for compensation to the party injured, taxed by them without scruple; and not without reason, even though it be without the least suspicion of his having intended injury. The man of law, — although on his part the intention, the consciousness of injury, be out of doubt, — shall he alone be exempt from that responsibility which by his own arrangements has been made to attach upon comparative innocence?

The more clearly the question of law, with all declarations of opinion respecting it, is separated from the question of fact, with the corresponding declarations, the easier of course will it be, in the station of the judge, to determine as between mendacity, temerity, and blameless error, and to act accordingly. Turn to established systems, we shall see the two questions lumped together, not to say confounded, by one and the same expression; and punishment, as for perjury, attached to mendacity — to mendacity, and on whose part? — on the part of the suitor, and him only;

not in any case on the part of his professional adviser, the man of law.

So much for the rules themselves, and the reasons on which they are grounded. In the remaining sections of this chapter, the light of exemplification will be thrown upon them, by the instances in which they have failed of receiving due observance from established practice. All-comprehensive in their extent, the practical importance of them will be found proportionable.

§ 3. *Defects of Roman law, in regard to the punishment of testimonial falsehood.*

Under the ancient Roman law (if Heineccius's account of it is to depended upon,) falsehood, mendacious falsehood, — though punished on a variety of extra-judicial occasions, mostly bringing it under the denomination of fraud, — yet, when committed on a judicial occasion, in the shape of mendacious testimony, was in general exempt from all legal punishment. One exception is noted, and but one: viz. when, being in the shape of criminative perjury, it had the effect of murder: in this case, it was, with a consistency not yet attained by English law, punished as murder: murder thus committed by the tongue, was punished as it would have been if committed with any other instrument.

In other cases, *calumny* appears to have been treated on the footing of a punishable offence; and punished as such, sometimes with pecuniary punishment, at other times with the complex and heterogeneous punishment expressed by the name of *infamy*.* By calumny, appears to have been meant false testimony, when given on the criminative side. Committed on the exculpative side in penal cases, and on either side in cases not penal, mendacity would hardly be understood to come under the name of calumny: in those cases, therefore, it should seem, no punishment would attach to it.

As to perjury; in the ordinary course of judicial testimony, and on the part of an extraneous witness, it could not be committed: —why? because, in that case, the act of deposition was not accompanied by the ceremony of an oath: by that ceremony by which mendacity is converted into perjury. The only cases in which the ceremony of an oath was employed in judicature, were those in which the witness was a self-regarding witness — the testimony was of the self-regarding kind: and then, to complete the absurdity, it was rendered incontrovertible and conclusive.†

Once upon a time, indeed, it is said that a gang of false witnesses were thrown from the Tarpeian rock: to judge from what is said of them, one must suppose that, in some way or other, they had entitled themselves to the name of *perjurers*. Be this as it may, the misadventure seems to belong to the head of casualties at large, rather than to that of legal executions: it is noticed, by a collector of anecdotes, as a thing that *had* taken place; not by a legislator, as a thing that, according to the determination of him, the legislator, was in future to take place.

Till the Roman empire was far gone in its decline, — that justice should have truth rather than falsehood for its foundation, was a point not thought worth providing for: always excepting the narrow cases above described, in which falsehood, being preceded by an oath, as well as accompanied by mendacity, received the name of perjury. By the joint tenants of the Roman empire, Arcadius and Honorius, perjurers, we are told, were threatened with infamy: but if it had been made possible for us to know whether any, and what, false witnesses, were on this occasion included under the name of *perjurers*, or what was meant by *threatening; i. e.* whether the legislator actually made a law to such effect, or only threatened to make one; or what sort of a punishment the *infamy* was that the delinquents in question were threatened with; neither would the law have been Roman law, nor Heineccius the expositor of it.

Perjury itself (whatever was meant by perjury) does not seem to have been treated as a punishable crime, except in the particular case where, the avenging deity being the *genius of the emperor* (whatever was meant by the *genius of the emperor*,) perjury, in this case, was consequently a species of high treason, or rather a sort of compound of high treason and blasphemy, and consequently could not be too severely punished. Not applying in general to testimonial, commonly called assertory oaths, its application must have been confined for the most part to promissory oaths.

Quitting the masters, we must now apply to the scholars: on this, as on other occasions, let us apply to the head scholars in preference: to the French, as being the most enlightened as well as the most numerous nation of continental Europe.

Among these modern Romanists, at any rate, mendacity, in so far as it has happened to have been previously converted into perjury, has been punished under that name.‡

By these scholars too, as by their masters, homicide committed by means of perjury, has been punished as homicide.‖

Looking at the established course of procedure, under the old French law; on the

* Halifax, p. 104.

† Vide infra, Chapter VI. Section 5.

‡ Code Pénal, p. 160 — viz. by imprisonment, with forced labour, on board the galleys.

‖ Ibid.

part of the suitors, as such, falsehood seems to be altogether without a check. No affidavits, as in English judicature, to establish facts for the purpose of introductory or interlocutory decisions. In respect of facts to be established as grounds for the definitive decision, the parties, though interrogated as witnesses, are interrogated upon oath; consequently, in case of proved mendacity, punishable as for perjury. But in respect of assertions made for the purpose of laying a foundation for this or that step, or train of steps, in the track of procedure; ransacking for this purpose a quarto volume of 864 closely-printed pages,* I can see no trace of impending punishment. No oath required or received; every allegation wears the form of a simple affirmation; and cases are mentioned, and that to an undefined extent, in which, though the fact be within the cognizance of the party, the affirmation may be made by proxy, the attorney speaking for his client.†

In an argument of Linguet's, on the contested marriage of the Vicomte de Bombilles, there is a passage which exhibits a faithful enough picture of a cause, as carried on at that time, under the technical system of Romano-Gallic procedure.‡ "En raisonnant, en dénaturant, en falsifiant ainsi les choses, les mots, et les écrits, on réussit à remplir un Plaidoyer ou un Mémoire : . . . mais le public instruit fait justice."

Where a party is exposed to no punishment, in case of mendacity,—is never subjected to the obligation of giving a word of answer to any question put to him by the adverse party, in the presence of the judge, — has, upon the terms of uttering a lie to this or that effect, a right to continue the series of delays and expenses in one court, or to commence a fresh series in another; if, under such a system, a man, conscious of being in the wrong, suffers the day on which a definitive decision can be pronounced to arrive, he may seek the cause of his defeat in his own ignorance or indolence, rather than in any obstacle opposed to his success, by the discernment, and zeal or activity, of the legislator or the judge.

In most established systems of law, the triple distinction, between delinquency accompanied with self-criminative consciousness, delinquency accompanied with temerity, and delinquency clear from both these accompaniments — and therefore free from moral blame, — has obtained more or less notice. On the other hand, in no established system have these important distinctions been clearly conceived and expressed in words, nor therefore applied with any uniformity in practice.

The distinction is in itself applicable, with few or no exceptions, and with equal propriety, to all manner of offences: but it is only in here and there a scattered instance that any such application has been made of it.

To testimonial falsehood it is applicable, with as much propriety as to delinquency in any other shape. But, that in established practice any such application has been made of it, appears by no means probable.

In the Roman law, though self-criminative consciousness has been no otherwise indicated than by the inexpressive and inapposite appelatives of *dolus* and *mala fides*, the distinction is not unfrequently, how far soever from uniformly, brought to view. Accordingly, where *dolus* or *mala fides* is considered as not proved, the absence of it is not always considered as exempting a delinquent completely from all punishment: *culpa*, sometimes styled temerity, is, in certain cases, understood to create likewise a demand for punishment, in effect at least, if not in name; though to an inferior amount.

To the case of testimonial falsehood, indeed, the distinction could scarcely have extended. If testimonial falsehood were converted by the previous ceremony of an oath into perjury, it was matter of doubt whether among the Romans it was considered as generally punishable, under that name at least, even in the most attrocious cases.‖

On this head the modern Romanists have gone far and usefully beyond their guides, the Romans. By the latter, the distinction between *dolus* and *culpa* appears to have scarcely gone beyond the case of misbehaviour relative to contracts,§ with or without the addition of that of homicide.¶ By the former, it seems to have received a pretty general application to the higher ranks of offences.

§ 4. *Defects of English law, in regard to the punishment of testimonial falsehood.*

The first great defect of the English law, in regard to the punishment of judicial falsehood, is the absolute want even of anything like an approach to a graduated scale of punishments.

Mendacity, when punished at all, being punished not as mendacity, but as perjury; the profanation of the ceremony being regarded as constituting the principal part, if not the whole, of the guilt; — that profanation being the same, whatever be the occasion on which, or the purpose for which, the crime is perpetrated, or whatever be its effects when perpetrated, — no distinction is made in the punishment.

Common sense dictates, that, if there be a difference in guilt, and a difference in the demand for punishment, as between him who assaults a man with intent to kill, and him

* Ravaut, "Procédure Civile du Palais," Paris, 1788.
† Ibid. p. 66.
‡ Linguet's Plaidoyers, tom vi. p. 404.

‖ Hein. ad Pan. P. iii. § 31.
§ Ib. i. 473 — ii. 66, 87 — iii. 114.
¶ Ib. vii. 200.

who assaults with only the intent of inflicting a slight bodily pain, there is at least an equal difference in guilt — an equal difference in the demand for punishment, as between the man who gives false testimony for the purpose of taking away the life of an innocent person, and the man who performs the same act for the purpose of subjecting him to a penalty of five shillings.

Among the Romanists, as has been already observed, murder, when thus perpetrated by the tongue, was treated nearly as if the same crime had been committed by means of any other instrument.

In English judicature; as, in the case of a poor delinquent, there was nothing to be got for the king by punishing the offence, — no knife value sixpence, or sword value six shillings, to be forfeited; no murder could in this case be discerned. In latter times, propositions have been started for treating murder as murder, when committed by these means: but the difficulty of saying what forfeitable commodity a man could on any such occasion be said to have been holding in his right hand, threw out the innovation, and there the matter rests.*

But this is not all: in English law no distinction is made between two offences generally so widely different in point of enormity, as falsehood through mendacity, and falsehood through temerity.

In English jurisprudence, the confusion of men's conceptions on this subject is evidenced and perpetuated by the inappositeness of their language. For the *dolus* of the Romanists, they have sometimes *malice*, sometimes *mala fides*: for the *culpa* of the Romanists they have nothing at all. *Malice* accordingly means, in some cases, existence of the self-criminative consciousness: but it means a hundred things besides. The short account of the matter is, that, when men of law talk of *malice*, they do not know what they mean: this, though so short an account, differs little, if anything, from the true one. For discovering what they mean, there is one course to be taken, and but one; and that is, to observe the treatment they give to a delinquent, to whose conduct this feature is ascribed. Malice is either *express* or *implied*. With this distinction at command, if a fancy happens to take you to punish a man as for *malice*, it is impossible for you to be under any difficulty. Whatever you happen to mean by malice, if you can prove it, you prove it: if you cannot prove it, you imply it.

But, though the distinction is neither conceived by them, nor expressed, — though, for want of being clearly understood, it is unexpressed, and, for want of being expressed, it is not understood, — it cannot be said to be altogether unfelt: accordingly, so far as discretion in judicature extends, the distinction, in both its branches, may not unreasonably be expected to be seen applied in practice. In general, a man whose delinquency is altogether pure from temerity, as well as self-criminative consciousness, will not, in every instance, be so hardly dealt with — under or not under the name of punishment, — as a man in whose instance delinquency is accompanied with that cause of blame. A man whose delinquency is characterized by temerity, and nothing worse, will not be punished with so much severity as the delinquent whose conduct shows that a full view of the several circumstances, on which the criminality of the act depends, was all the time before his eyes.

In homicide, for example; although a lawyer, bewildered as well as tied up by precedents, will imply malice, where, in the sense annexed by everbody to the word *malice*, neither he nor anybody else sees any such thing, although, in support of that implication, he will be urgent with a jury to convict as for murder a man who, through temerity, without either self-criminative consciousness or ordinary malice, has committed an act of homicide; yet in another place, another lawyer, or perhaps the same, will betake himself to the fountain of mercy, and substitute, in such a case, to the punishment insisted on by common law, a punishment suggested by common humanity, with the support of common sense.

In regard to the offence of testimonial falsehood, scarce any, even the obscurest, notion of the distinction in question (I mean, so far as temerity is concerned) appears, as yet, to have found its way into English jurisprudence. In a case of temerity, a man must either be punished as in a case of self-criminative consciousness, or go unpunished. Falsehood — falsehood committed in giving testimony — is either perjury, and punishable as such, or remains without punishment, because it remains without a name; † and by *perjury* is understood (how inadequately and improperly soever expressed) falsehood not only preceded by the ceremony of an oath, but accompanied, in the mind of the delinquent, with the self-criminative consciousness so often spoken of.

In the case of Elizabeth Canning, a girl under age, who, in 1754, was convicted of perjury at the Old Bailey, for that, on her disappearance from home for about four weeks, she had sworn to her having been confined during that time, and robbed, in a house of ill fame, by the mistress Mary Wells, and a

* State Trials — Elizabeth Canning's trial.

† Except the case of a Quaker, which applies not to this purpose. [By 5 & 6 W. IV. c. 62, which abolished oaths in certain cases (see Note, Vol. V. p. 188,) Justices are prohibited from taking affidavits on oath, except where they are authorised by act of Parliament; but they may receive declarations, and the making such declaration falsely is a misdemeanour.] — *Ed. of this Collection.*

gipsy woman, then a lodger in the house; on which evidence of her's, Wells and the gipsy had been capitally convicted; — a majority of the jury, as well as a bare majority of the judges, had regarded the narrative as false *in toto*, having for its object the saving herself from the imputation of a voluntary residence in company, by which, if known, her character would have been destroyed. This consequently was, in their eyes, a case of self-criminative consciousness. But, to a part of the jury, it appeared that the story was false in circumstance only; and that the falsity was accompanied with nothing worse than temerity, not self-criminative consciousness. That she had been incorrect in her statements, could not be doubted by any one; since in a variety of circumstances it was not only contradicted by extraneous witnesses, but inconsistent and self-contradictory. Temerity on this account — want of the attention which might have been bestowed, and which, had it been bestowed, would have saved her from the stating of so many particulars, of the falsity of which there could be no doubt — could not but be imputed to her by everybody: since, on the occasion on which they were uttered, the lives of the persons actually convicted on her testimony were at stake. But of her consciousness of the falsity of her own statements (it appears) they were not persuaded: at least as to any of the circumstances essential to the conviction of the persons convicted on her evidence. With this exception, they were satisfied of her having committed *perjury;* and on that account had joined in the verdict convicting her of the crime so denominated. But, in their conception, the perjury was not wilful and corrupt: the wish declared by them, accordingly, had been, that, in the instrument attesting, the words expressive of that imputation should be omitted.

In the words *wilful and corrupt*, we may observe an endeavour to express a circumstance, which, at the time when the locution was first hit upon, the progress of intelligence had not qualified men to express by clear and apposite words. By the word *wilful*, a psychological fact, the seat of which is in the understanding, was referred to the will: *wilful* the assertion could not but be, unless uttered by the perjurer in a state of delirium, or in his sleep. The circumstance meant to be expressed by the word *wilful* was, that the perjurer, at the time of his uttering the assertion in question, was persuaded — was conscious — of its falsity — of its want of conformity to the truth. The word *corrupt* is a term intensely but vaguely dyslogistic: what it does express, though still in a vague manner, is the quantity, — what it endeavours, though unsuccessfully, to express, is the quality, — of the blame.

In this case we may observe an occurrence, the exemplification of which is not unfrequent in English judicature: the probity and unsophisticated good sense of the occasional judges (or jury,) coming forward with a request, which the scientific intelligence of their professional instructors does not enable them to comply with. We are not satisfied of the existence of self-criminative consciousness; we are satisfied of the existence of temerity: what we wish is, to give such a verdict as shall subject the defendant to the punishment adapted to that inferior degree of delinquency, but not to the superior. Such was, in substance, the language of these conscientious jurymen. But the established language and practice of the law was not such as to enable the keepers of the *officina justitiæ* to satisfy so reasonable a demand. They were forced to leave it unsatisfied; they had no such articles in their warehouse. If you want law for wilful and corrupt perjury, there it is for you: as to perjury that is not wilful and corrupt, there is no such thing — no such thing that we know of. Wilful and corrupt perjury is, therefore, what you must convict the defendant of, or else acquit her altogether.

In the practice of English law (with but a single exception) if any punishment be annexed to the practice of mendacity, the sanction of an oath is employed, as a medium of connexion, to attach the punishment to the offence. Mendacity, when the sanction of an oath has been employed as an instrument to bind the conscience of the individual to an adherence to the opposite virtue, is termed perjury. Perjury, accordingly, in these cases, not mendacity, is the denomination given to the offence: insomuch that mendacity, if it fall not within the case of perjury — if it be not punishable as perjury, — is not punishable at all.

The single exception, spoken of above, is constituted by the case of examination taken by the House of Commons, or a committee of the House.

Not that, in that legislative tribunal, truth is of less importance than in a cause about the value of a pot of beer, or a packet of pins. But the helplessness, in this respect, of the most efficient of the three branches of legislature is a great point of constitutional law: and (according to common intendment,) in the constitutional branch beyond every other, it belongs to utility to give way to usage.

Nor yet is mendacity, on these occasions, altogether exempt from punishment. It is called a contempt; and, as such, is punishable with imprisonment; to which, by means of fees exacted by the house for the benefit of the jailor, is added pecuniary punishment. With imprisonment — but mark the consequence. The imprisonment being limited in its duration by that of the tribunal which inflicts it, and the maximum of the latter being seven years, the longer it has sitten, the weaker it has become, in this point, not to mention others. On the one hand, the utility of the law depends on the goodness of the information on which it has been grounded; on the other hand, the most efficient of the three branches of the legislature is less and less adequate to the task of procuring good information, the longer it lives, till at last it finishes its career in downright impotence.

Rabelais, living in a distant province, and wanting to see Paris, forged a quantity of *real* evidence calculated to throw upon him the suspicion of a state crime, and, upon the strength of it, travelled at free cost. On a favourable conjuncture, the trick might not be altogether incapable of being done into English, by a political adventurer, richer in boldness than in the gifts of fortune. Towards the conclusion of a parliament, he commits a contempt, and is committed to the custody of the serjeant at arms. What is the serjeant to do with him? To starve him is forbidden, not only by the law of humanity, but by the law against murder. He lodges and boards him: and, no sooner is the parliament dissolved, than out walks the delinquent, and with him all prospect of fees.

The English procedure, in almost every branch of it, affords but too many examples, in which mendacity, not being stamped with the name of perjury, remains altogether unpunishable, and secures to the offender, in this respect, the fruit of his offence.

I. In the penal branch of procedure, — in the present state of it, — the encouragement given in this way to mendacity bears but a small proportion to that which we shall see dealt out with so profuse a hand in the non-penal branch.

The only instance in the penal branch, in which an encouragement is given in this way to mendacity, and that encouragement productive in a direct way of consequences immediately prejudicial to justice, — is the practice which has obtained in capital cases and cases next to capital, of dissuading a guilty defendant from the confession he declares himself ready to make, and in a manner forcing him to substitute, in pre-appointed language, what is called the plea of not guilty, that is, a false and mendacious averment of his not being guilty, in the room of it. If, in this case, the extraneous evidence exhibited on the other side fails of coming up to the description of that allotment, which, according to the established rules of evidence, is necessary to conviction, — so often as any such failure takes place, so often does a guilty defendant escape, — so often is the escape attended with a failure of justice. If the evidence be sufficient, and conviction takes place accordingly, even then the satisfaction of the judge and of the public fails of being so complete as it would be if the disposition on the part of the defendant to speak truth had not been checked, by those whose duty, at least in the moral view of the word, it was to cultivate it.

Evidence of inferior quality is in this case received alone, to the exclusion of evidence of a superior quality — of a nature which cannot fail of being more satisfactory to every mind to which it ever comes to be presented. The mendacity thus bespoken, and in a manner commanded, from the highest ground, on pretence of a regard to justice or humanity, but in reality for the purpose of gaining an unmerited popularity at the expense of justice, is sometimes fatal, and in no case of any use, to justice.

Compared, however, with the state of things in this respect as it stood till little above a century ago, the abuse thus noted is a prodigious improvement. A century has scarce elapsed since the practice was abolished, according to which, in a capital case, the witnesses for the defendant were examined without oath, and thence (in case of mendacity,) without being exposed to punishment.* The practice thus abolished was, in both points of view, pernicious: favourable in the highest degree to guilt, by leaving the door wide open to mendacious evidence on that side: unfavourable to innocence, by depriving veracious witnesses of whatever share of confidence it is in the power of the sanction of an oath, in these circumstances, to inspire.

The instances in which mendacity is forced upon the *pen* of the other party (the plaintiff or prosecutor,) by those who, to the more especial duty, add the exclusive power, of cherishing and enforcing on all occasions the opposite virtue; — these examples, unhappily but too numerous, of corruption issuing in torrents from above, will be apt on this occasion to present themselves to a discerning mind.† But the mischief, great as it is, belongs not to this place. If, by the contempt of veracity and the fondness for mendacity thus displayed, the morals of the profession, and (through that commanding channel) the morals of the community, are tainted in the most vital part; the interests, however, of justice, receive not in this way any immediate prejudice: for, so far as the law in favour of mendacity is complied with, neither plaintiff nor defendant, neither innocent nor guilty, are in any respect the better for it. If, indeed, in any respect, compliance on the

* Hawk. iv. 446. 1 Ann. c. 9. § 3.

† *Ex. gr.* Cases in which facts that are either false or unascertainable are required to be averred in indictments, on pain of nullity: that the crime was committed at the instigation of the devil, — that the instrument employed in the commission of it was of such or such a determinate value, &c. &c.

part of the plaintiff is deficient, a flaw is thereby produced, through which the defendant, if guilty, makes his escape. But the source from whence the advantage given to the defendant in this case is derived, is not the commission of mendacity on that side, but the omission of it on the other.

2. In non-penal procedure—in both branches of it, the common law and the equity branch, —it will now be seen in what abundance invitation is held out to mendacity on the part of the litigants on both sides, and in what abundancy of produce the fruit thus cultivated may naturally be expected.

In the common-law branch, the regular course, in the shape in which it is pursued at present, can scarcely in the minds of those who planned it, have had any other view. If, at the outset of every cause, the parties, in the presence of each other, and each of them interrogated by the other, were to produce at once the whole budget of their allegations, and their suspicions, as well as their demands, and that under the sanction of an oath: mendacity would not be hazarded by a man, in the station of a party, any more than in that of a witness. But the fundamental allegation, or body of allegations, termed the *declaration*, is made without any such check. This declaration gives commencement to the cause — operates as an introduction to the several steps and instruments that follow it. A man may be completely conscious of the badness of his own cause; he may be conscious that the facts alleged or assumed by himself are not true; he may be conscious that facts, such as, if proved on the part of the defendant, would defeat his (the plaintiff's) claim, did really exist; whether the defendent be supposed to be in a condition, or not in a condition, to bring proof of them. In any of these ways he may be fully conscious of the falsity of his averments, and yet withuot being deterred from making them: these being among the occasions on which falsehood has received a licence to come forward and effect its purposes. As to costs of suit — besides that this species of partial satisfaction is not in English procedure applied, with anything like consistency or uniformity, to the cases that call for it, — the inadequacy of it to the purpose in hand will be hereafter brought to view.

The whole system of what is called *special pleading*, is an edifice erected upon the corrupt foundation just described. The counter-allegations, — such reciprocal ones as the nature of the case admits of — these *pleadings* (as they are called) — instead of being extracted from the parties speaking *viva voce*, and face to face, under the authority and in the presence of the judge, — are kept back to be exhibited in writing, in a protracted succession, at distant intervals; and, be they ever so mendacious, no other punishment attaches upon the mendacity but the inadequate and irregularly applied punishment of costs.

In no respect whatever is direct justice benefited by this practice: collateral injustice, in its triple shape of vexation, expense, and delay, is produced by it in abundance.

The commencement as well as final cause of it — the origin of it in both senses — is distinctly before our view. We know of a time in which the abuse had no existence. Like libelling and forgery, it has grown out of the art of writing. But forgery conducts men to the gallows, special pleading to the bench.

In summary procedure it is unknown: as happily and completely so, as in the domestic procedure—which, in forensic practice, serves as a model for summary procedure,— and from which the regular mode may be considered as being for the most part a causeless deviation.

On a variety of occasions it is excluded: the general issue is allowed to be pleaded: and the party to whom such permission is given, is the defendant, — the party whose interest on each such occasion insures his availing himself of it. The propriety of such exclusion is, in these several instances, unquestioned and unquestionable: but on no one of these occasions can it be justified, but by reasons which with equal cogency prove the propriety of the exclusion — the impropriety of this mode of procedure — in the several instances in which it continues to be employed.

Common law, the old original law of the country — common law, though "the perfection of reason," was here and there a little scanty, and here and there a little harsh. Under the name of *equity*, a new and smoother kind of law has been half imported, half manufactured, to fill it up and smooth it.

In common-law procedure, for the benefit of the lawyer, mendacity on the part of the suitor enjoys (as has been seen) an almost unbounded licence. If falsehood is, by those whose duty should naturally have been to suppress it, connived at and rendered profitable, and in that way encouraged; if such encouragement be a mode of subornation; at that mode, however, it stops: understand, at common law.

Would you see it in a stronger and more efficient mode, you must look to equity. It is there that the apparatus of subornation is complete: it is there that the effect of it is altogether irresistible.

In equity procedure, the altercations between the parties, including the examination of one of them by the other, are carried on in the way of written correspondence. The cause opens by the plaintiff's address to the judge, who never reads it: to which the defendant, to whom it is not addressed, is to return an answer. This epistle is called a bill. The bill is composed partly of allegations, partly of questions. In the allegations are stated, on the one hand, the facts,—such facts, designed to constitute a ground for the plaintiff's claim, as the plaintiff *knows*, or is made to pretend to know; on the other hand, such facts as he does not know, but which, by means of so many confessorial statements to be extracted from the defendant, he, the plaintiff, wishes and endeavours to *learn*. For this purpose the court lends its authority to the plaintiff (in equity, the complainant) with the readiness that may be imagined. It however makes one condition with him, viz. that every interrogatory put by him to the defendant shall have a *charge* to support it. In itself, the rule is sufficiently obscure and vague: but practice has explained and fixed it. If, for example, to make good your title you want a deed, but know not where it is; if you tell the truth, and say you don't know where it is, you will never get it. You must begin with saying you *do* know where it is; you must say that the defendant has it; and so, having complied with the condition, and said on your part what you know is false, you are allowed to call upon the defendant to declare on his part what is true.

In respect of delay, vexation and expense, the consequence of this sort of justice is not to the present purpose. In respect of mendacity, the effect produced on the state of the public morals by that vice is another topic that belongs not to this place. Upon the administration of justice, and the advantage derived to judicature from evidence received in this mode, the effect in point of extent may be tolerably conceived from a fact soon stated. The answer being upon oath, may be true or not true: the bill, not being upon oath, is regarded as altogether unworthy of all credit.* In the character of defendant, what a man says may be true or not true: in the character of plaintiff, what the same man says is not a syllable of it true. Why? Because, in the character of defendant, he is made to take an oath: in the character of plaintiff, he is neither subjected nor admitted to any such ceremony. And why, in the character of plaintiff, is he to enjoy this licence for mendacity? To justify him for subjecting a man to the torment of the most tedious and expensive of all suits,—to justify him for stopping him in the pursuit of less expensive and vexatious remedies,—has the court any better, or other, warrant, than the assertion of a man who, by its rules and maxims, is unworthy of all credit?—whom it first forces to make himself a liar, and then stigmatizes for being so.

Besides the radical absurdity of the rule, in any other character than that of a contrivance to corrupt and oppress suitors for the benefit of lawyers; the uncertainty with which it is pregnant is without end. What breadth of charge shall be sufficient for the support of the interrogatories that a man may see occasion to exhibit? To furnish an answer to this question, adapted to all the modifications of which the case is susceptible, is of itself a topic, the discussion of which might be made to fill any number of volumes. Meantime, on every occasion, the prudence of the draughtsman fails not to satisfy him, which is the safe side. From the omission of any portion of matter, which, in the eye of the judge *ad hoc*,† may chance to present itself as necessary to enter into the composition of the charging part, to enable it to support the interrogatories grounded on it, inconvenience to his client, in the shape of vexation and delay, as well as increased expense, may ensue: from the insertion of any quantity beyond that which, on a just view of the matter, might appear strictly necessary, no inconvenience in any degree approaching to equality can ensue: to the expense an addition, but that comparatively a very small one: to the account of delay and vexation, none. These things being duly considered, the conclusion is but natural. To give the reins to invention, and augment *ad libitum* the quantity of this species of poetry, will, so long as the above rule remains unrepealed, continue for ever the most natural and pleasant, as for ever it will continue to be the safest course.

CHAPTER VI.

OF THE CEREMONY OF AN OATH, CONSIDERED AS A SECURITY FOR THE TRUSTWORTHINESS OF TESTIMONY.

§ 1. *An oath, what?*

On a former occasion, mention was made of the three great sanctions — the political, the popular, and the religious, — as so many powers usually, and in a certain sense naturally, employed, in the character of securities for trustworthiness in testimony. But their efficacy in that character will depend, in no small degree, on the mode in which application is made of them to that use. Although not expressly invoked, nor so much as regarded, by the factitious arrangements of judicial procedure; they might, notwithstanding, be by no means devoid of efficacy. But, in point of fact and general usage, a particu-

* In here and there a scanty instance, the current of mendacity has indeed received a check: the facts stated in the plaintiff's bill being required to be verified by affidavit. But the same considerations, by which the attention of the legislator is proved in these odd corners in the field of equity jurisdiction, demonstrate his negligence — his self-conscious negligence — in every other quarter of that vast expanse.

† In the Court of Chancery, the master; in the Court of Exchequer, the barons, the judges themselves.

lar instrument has been employed for the special purpose of pointing their force to this special use. This instrument is the solemnity, or say ceremony, called an oath.

Contemplated in themselves, and abstraction made of the application of this instrument, they might be considered, in a certain sense, as so many natural securities for testimonial trustworthiness: contemplated as applied to this special purpose by the intervention and assistance of this factitious instrument, their united force, so augmented and applied, may be considered as a sort of factitious or artificial security for trustworthiness, superadded to those natural securities.

But, in perhaps every civilized nation upon earth (unless the Chinese nation, the most numerous of all civilized nations, be an exception,) the ceremony distinguished by the name of an oath, or what in other languages is equivalent to that word, has been designed or understood to involve in it an address (or at least a reference) to a supreme being or beings — to invisible, supernatural, and omnipotent, or at least superior, agents: and the object of this address or reference has been to engage those superior powers, or to represent them as engaged, to inflict on the witness punishment, in some shape or other, at some time or other, in the event of his departing knowingly from the truth on the occasion of such his testimony.

Unfortunately in some respects, this same ceremony, with the address or reference included by it, has (besides the above use) been employed as an instrument to bind men to the fulfilment of miscellaneous promises of all sorts: promises having no connexion with testimony.

It has been applied promiscuously, and without any discrimination or distinction so much as in name, to purposes of the most heterogeneous nature: to the securing of veracity and correctness on the part of the swearer, on judicial occasions, and thence to the prevention of deception and consequent misdecision on the part of the judge; and, besides that, to the securing the performance of other acts of all sorts.

At present, our view of the ceremony is confined to the case in which the purpose for which it is employed is that of securing the truth of testimony.

§ 2. *Inefficacy of an oath, as a security for the trustworthiness of testimony.*

Consistently with the opinion so generally entertained by unreflecting prejudice, a place upon the list of securities for the trustworthiness of testimony, and thence against deception, and consequent misdecision and injustice, could not be refused to the ceremony of an oath. But, whether principle or experience be regarded, it will be found in the hands of justice an altogether useless instrument; in the hands of injustice, a deplorably serviceable one.

1. The supposition of its efficiency is absurd in principle. It ascribes to man a power over his maker: it places the Almighty in the station of a sheriff's officer; it places him under the command of every justice of the peace. It supposes him to stand engaged, no matter how, but absolutely engaged to inflict — on every individual, by whom the ceremony, after having been performed, has been profaned, — a punishment (no matter what) which, but for the ceremony and the profanation, he would not have inflicted.

It supposes him thus prepared to inflict, at command, and at all times, a punishment, which, being at all times the same, at no time bears any proportion to the offence.

Take two offenders: the one a parricide, by whose false testimony his innocent father has been consigned to capital punishment; the other, by whose false testimony a neighbouring householder has been wrongfully convicted of the offence of laying rubbish on the highway. Take the offence in both cases on the mere footing of false testimony, one sees how unequal is the guilt, — and how widely different the punishment, which, consistently with the principle of religion, cannot but be expected at the hands of divine justice. Take it on the footing of perjury, the guilt is precisely the same in both cases: for in both cases the ceremony is the same; and in both cases it is alike violated and profaned.

In a certain sense, and with reference to a certain relative point of time, the consent of the beneficent power over which authority was supposed to be exercised by a subordinate power could hardly have been looked upon as wanting. It must have been considered as having been given, in general terms, at some anterior period: but, — being thus given, by an engagement, express or virtual, contracted by the superior being, — so long as the engagement thus entered upon was adhered to, the conduct of the superior being would not be less under the command of the inferior, than if the relation had from the beginning been reversed; and whatever promise the superior being might, by means of the oath, be called upon by the inferior being to enforce, — to such promise, so long as the engagement was adhered to, it would not be in the power of the superior being to refuse his sanction.*

* In *specie* it was the same sort of authority as that which was supposed to be exercised by magical incantations: exercised only over a different sort of supernatural person, and to different and even strongly contrasted purposes. The authority exercised by a testimonial oath, was exercised over a divinity spoken of in the character of a beneficent divinity, and for purposes spoken of in the character of beneficial purposes: the authority exercised by a magical incantation, was

Will it be said, Nay: for, after and notwithstanding this ceremony, God will govern himself by his own good pleasure, as he would have done without it: though the act which the oath-taker engaged himself thus to perform be unperformed, if that act be a criminal one, God will not punish him for the omission of it: commission, not omission, is what God punishes in crimes? Be it so: God will not punish the violation of an oath, when the act engaged for by it is the commission of a crime: God would not have punished Jephthah, had he omitted to put to death his unoffending daughter, notwithstanding his eventual promise so to do. Be it so: but, this being supposed, here is an end of the efficacy, the separate and independent efficacy, of an oath.

To the purpose in question, the authority given by the oath to the inferior being over the superior, must have been understood to be absolute, or it must have amounted to nothing. Were there any exceptions or limitations? If so, the imagination is set to work to look out for the terms and grounds of such exceptions and limitations: to inquire, for example, into the species and degree of *mischief* that in each instance might be expected to result from the violation of testimonial truth. But if *this*, then, be the ground of the supernatural punishment attached to the violation of the oath,—then the mere violation of the oath itself, independently of the mischief resulting from the falsehood, is not that ground; that is,—the effect produced by the oath, considered in and by itself, amounts to nothing.

In vain would it be to say, No; when God punishes for perjury, though he punishes for the profanation, that does not hinder but that he may punish for the false testimony in proportion to the mischievousness of the effects produced by it. Whatever reason there is for supposing him to punish for the false testimony, there is the same reason for supposing him to punish for that crime, whether the profanation be or be not coupled with it. Whatever punishment is inflicted by him on the score of the false testimony, is not inflicted by him on the score of the profanation: whatever is inflicted by him on the score of the profanation, is not inflicted by him on the score of the false testimony.

Either the ceremony causes punishment to be inflicted by the Deity, in cases where otherwise it would not have been inflicted; or it does not. In the former case, the same sort of authority is exercised by man over the Deity, as that which, in English law, is exercised over the judge by the legislator, or over the sheriff by the judge. In the latter case, the ceremony is a mere form, without any useful effect whatever.*

exercised over a maleficent divinity, and for pernicious purposes.

* "The alternative to which Providence is by consequence reduced, of either giving up that country to everlasting superstition, or of working some miracle in order to accomplish its conversion." Such are the words in which (in the Edinburgh Review for April 1808[a]) a reverend divine is represented as describing one of the consequences which, in his view of the matter, will ensue, should the arm of government be employed in restraining, by coercive measures, the exertions directed to the extension of the benefits of christianity to the natives of Hindostan. "The idea of reducing Providence to an alternative!!" exclaims the reviewer in a double note of admiration: "and by a motion at the India-House, carried by ballot!"—"Providence reduced to an alternative!!!!!"—another exclamation by notes of admiration five deep. Then—for the declared purpose of representing the idea as the *ne plus ultra* of irrationality—this and that and the other idea, represented as irrational, is said to be pure reason when compared to it.

The ground on which the line of conduct thus protested against, as tending to reduce Providence to an alternative, is censured, is that of its being too great a power for human imbecility to exercise, or so much as to attempt to exercise, over divine omnipotence. But the power, the supposed exercise of which drew from the reverend divine the apprehension and the censure expressed in the above passage—this power, if indeed it reduced the Supreme Being to an alternative, left him, at any rate, in possession of an alternative: and an alternative which does not present itself to human conception as pregnant with any considerable degree of distress.

But the notion which represents the common ceremony of an oath as entailing, and without recovery, guilt—with its inseparable appurtenance, future punishment—on the violators of it,—and this independently of, and over and above, whatever may be attached to the occasion,—leaves to divine omnipotence no alternative. Bailiff to and under the human magistrate, the divine functionary has given bond for the execution—the constant and punctual and sure execution—of whatsoever writ shall be sent from the court below to the court above: for, when the idea is so self-contradictory, language is at a loss how to phrase it.

The human power, which, reducing divine omnipotence indeed to an alternative, leaves it at any rate in possession of an alternative, is not proposed to be exercised by any other hand than one, and that the hand of the supreme authority in the state: the power which leaves omnipotence no alternative, is a power which any and every individual in the state, who is rash enough and foolish enough, may exercise at any time, and any number of times, at pleasure: on so simple a condition as that of getting a justice of peace to join in the performance of the instantaneous ceremony.

God made man after his own image, says the text: man has returned him the compliment, says I forget what commentator. "Every man his own broker" is the title of one book; "Every man his own lawyer" of another: difficult as it is for any (not to speak of every) man to be his

[a] Page 180.

2. To justice it is not of any the smallest use. The only character in which it is in the nature of it to render — in which it has ever been supposed to render — service to justice, is that of a security against a man's doing what (on the occasion in question) he has engaged not to do: viz. assert what he knows or believes to be false. But that in this character it is altogether without efficacy, is matter of daily and uncontroverted and uncontrovertible experience. On the part of the most exalted characters, it is seen every day yielding to the force of the weakest of all human motives.

Comparison being had with the motives of the two other classes — viz. the self-regarding, and the dissocial — the weakest upon the whole, in the great mass of mankind, are those which, belonging to the social class, may be referred to the head of sympathy: of which that sort of sympathy towards an individual, commonly characterized by the term *humanity*, is one.

But, of all descriptions of men (hangmen perhaps excepted, butchers certainly not excepted,) the lawyer, and, among the lawyers of all nations, the English lawyer, is he on whom, — judging from situation, from habitual exposure to the action of opposite interest, or from historical experience, — the principle of humanity may with reason be regarded as acting with the smallest degree of force. For, under the existing mode of remuneration (viz. by fees,) there is no other class of men whose prosperity rises and falls in so exact a proportion with those miseries of mankind which it is in their power to increase or decrease: nor any set of men, who have had it so effectually in their power, and so determinedly and inexorably in their will, to preserve those miseries from decrease. Unfortunately, this hostility (though undeniable) not being perceptible without such an insight into the system of procedure made by them, as scarce any but themselves find adequate inducements for obtaining, can never be rendered so easily perceptible, as, for the preservation of the rest of the community, it were so desirable that it should be.

Weak as, in the breast of an English lawyer, this weakest of all human motives cannot but be — and more especially in the breast of an English lawyer whose acknowledged experience has raised him to the situation of judge, — in that situation it is found habitually strong enough to overpower whatever regard, if any, is lodged in the same bosom, for the ceremony of an oath.

Many and notorious are the occasions on which, in violation of their oaths, a set of jurymen, — for the purpose of screening a criminal from a degree of punishment to which the legislature has declared its intention of devoting him, — ascribe to a mass of stolen property a value inferior in any proportion to that which, to the knowledge of everybody, is the real one; and this under the eyes and direction of a never-opposing, frequently applauding, or even advising judge: so that here we have in perpetual activity as many schools of perjury as there are courts of justice, having cognizance of these the most frequently committed sorts of crimes; schools in which the judge is master, the jurymen scholars, and the by-standers applauders and encouragers.

Not that there exists, perhaps, any other nation, in which a due regard to veracity on the occasion of testimony is more general. But, of this regard (be it more or less extensive,) the *cause* must be looked for in the influence of those other *really* operative securities, to which, in compliance with usage, this delusive one has been so undeservedly associated. What is not only possible, but probable, is, that, in the production of this regard, the religious principle, the fear of God, has no inconsiderable influence. What is certain, as being rendered so by the above experience (not to mention so many others as might be adduced,) is, that in the application thus supposed to be made of it, the religious principle has no influence.

Under the ceremony of an oath are included, it is to be observed, two very different ties, — the moral, and the religious. The one is capable of being made more or less binding upon all men; the other upon such only as are of a particular way of thinking. The same formulary, which undertakes to draw down upon a man the resentment of the Deity in case of contravention, does actually, in the same event, draw down upon him (as experience proves) the resentment and contempt of mankind. The religious tie is that which stands forth, which makes all the show, which offers itself to view; but it is the moral tie that does by far the greatest part of the business. The influence of the former is partial — that of the latter is universal: nothing, therefore, could be a mark of greater weakness and

own broker, much more his own lawyer, no man finds any difficulty in being his own God-maker: and when a man has made his God, we see the sort of work he puts him to. The God of the good sort of man is himself a good sort of man: but the God of the vulgar, great and small, is what the God of Samuel Johnson was — a devil, with the name of God written in great letters on his forehead.

O that, in making his God, man would but content himself in making him for his own use! But no: it is not for his own use, it is not for his own benefit at least, that man makes his God; but for the destruction of others, of all others who presume to differ from him; and who, for this offence, are, on any the slightest pretence, doomed to unutterable torture without end in another world, together with such as can be inflicted by the present and ready-prepared engines of the civil magistrate in this.

imprudence than to cultivate the former only, and neglect the latter. As to the religious tie,—not only are there many on whom it has no hold at all—but in those on whom it has a hold as well as the moral, that of the moral is beyond comparison the strongest. Can anybody doubt, that among the English clergy (for example) believers are more abundant than unbelievers? Yet, on some occasions, oaths go with them for nothing.

What gives an oath the degree of efficacy it possesses, is, that in most points, and with most men, a declaration upon oath includes a declaration upon honour: the laws of honour enjoining as to those points the observance of an oath. The deference shown is paid in appearance to the religious ceremony: but in reality it is paid, even by the most pious religionists, much more to the moral engagement than to the religious.

It is, in truth, to the property which the ceremony of an oath possesses, of weakening the power of the only really efficacious securities, that what influence it has is confined. In the character of a security for veracity, take it by itself, it is powerless, and may plainly be seen to be so.

Applied to judicial testimony, if there be an appearance of its exercising a salutary influence, it is because this supposed power acts in conjunction with two real and efficient ones: the power of the political sanction, and the power of the moral or popular sanction. When, to preserve a man from mendacity,—in addition to the fear of supernatural punishment for the profanation of the ceremony, a man has the fear of fine, imprisonment, pillory, and so forth, on the one hand; the fear of infamy, the contempt and hatred of all that know him, on the other; it is no wonder that it should appear powerful. Strip it of these its accompaniments—deprive it of these its supports—its impotence appears immediately.

But of a case in which it is thus deprived of its supports,—and in which impotence, complete impotence, is the consequence—the notorious consequence of such deprivation,—the bare word *custom-house oaths* is sufficient to present to view the complete exemplification.*

So long as two forces, pointing towards the same object, are followed to a certain degree by the effect they aim at, without its being apparent in what proportion they have repectively contributed to the common end; the credit of the result may be given to whichever of the two is most in favour. Watch them, and catch them acting separately, or in opposition: then is the time to see how far the credit given has been due. In certain cases, the tie of an oath is seen to have a powerful effect upon mankind. Where?—in what cases? Where the force of public opinion acts under its command: where it employs itself in insuring the veracity of parties or witnesses in courts of justice (especially in civil causes: or in criminal ones, where falsehood has not the plea of compassion or self-preservation to extenuate it.) In other cases, oaths are cobwebs, or at best, hairs. In what? In all in which the force of public opinion runs counter, or does but withhold its aid: in the case of jurymen's oaths, in a variety of instances: in the case of a variety of other offices: in the case of university oaths: in the case of custom-house oaths: in the case of *subscriptions*,—which, considering the solemnity of the act, and the awfulness of the subject, may be placed on the same line with oaths.

If you wish to have powder of post taken for an efficacious medicine, try it with opium and antimony: if you wish to have it taken for what it is, try it by itself.

That in England, in the governing part of the public mind, there has always prevailed a sort of tacit sense of the inefficacy and inutility of this ceremony in the character of a security for testimonial veracity, is evidenced, not by any explicit verbal declarations indeed, but by tokens still more trustworthy—by long-continued practice.

On the occasion of the inquiries carried on by the House of Commons—whether by the whole House in the form of a committee, or by detached committees—no oath is administered (at least in general practice) to any persons examined in the character of witnesses. The ceremony is suffered to remain unperformed. Why? Because, none of the really efficient securities* being wanting, the want of this inefficient one is thought not worth supplying.

This branch of the legislature, not possessing, like the other, ordinary judicial powers, possesses not (it may be said) the power of exacting the performance of this ceremony. Be it so: but this, instead of a refutation of the proposition above advanced, is a confirmation of it. Is legislation of less importance than judicature? So far from it, the importance of an act of legislation is to that of an act of judicature, as the whole number of subjects in the empire is to 2. Is information concerning matters of fact less necessary to constitute a just ground for an act of legislation than for an act of judicature? Nor that neither.

Had the performance of this ceremony been really necessary, or been really thought necessary, to the forming of sufficient grounds for legislation, would the most efficient of the three branches of the supreme power have

* By 1 & 2 W. IV. c. 4, declarations were substituted to oaths in this department.—*Ed. of this Collection.*

* Subjection to interrogation *ex adverso*, backed by fear of punishment and of loss of reputation, to enforce compliance.

acquiesced thus long under the non-possession of it?

Conceive the courts of justice throughout the country, all of them abundantly provided with the power of administering oaths, all of them destitute of the power of applying punishment, — in what degree of vigour would have been the power of these courts? For what length of time, in that case, would society have held together?

If, in the character of a security for testimonial veracity, this ceremony were seriously looked upon as possessing any considerable value,— the occasions to which the ordinary judicial securities failed of applying, at the same time that the value at stake is equal to any pecuniary value that is ever at stake in judicature,—these are the occasions on which this supernatural security would (at least supposing any tolerable degree of providence or consistency on the part of the ruling powers) have been resorted to with particular care. I speak of the cases where money is to be received by individuals at any of the public offices instituted for that purpose—the Bank of England, the Navy and Army pay-offices, and so forth. For one pound paid by the appointment of a court of justice, fifty or a hundred pounds perhaps are paid in and by these non-judicial offices. In these pay-offices, there being no adverse party to contest the claim, all those ordinary securities, to the application of which the diligence of an adverse party is necessary (cross-examination, faculty of counter-evidence, and so forth,) are of course inapplicable. For the protection of so prodigious a mass of property, under the deficiency of ordinary securities, what does legislative providence? Does it call in, with peculiar anxiety and exclusive or superior confidence, this extraordinary security?—does it employ oath without punishment? On the contrary, it employs punishment without oath.*

Another proof of the inefficiency and inutility of the ceremony of an oath, in the character of a security for the truth of testimony. Of the modes of delivering evidence — of delivering what is equivalent to testimony,— that which is susceptible of having the ceremony attached to it, is but one. Of the modifications of mendacity (or, what is equivalent to it, the endeavour to gain credence for false facts,) that which is chargeable with the profanation of this ceremony, — that which is, in consequence, susceptible of the appellation of perjury, — *mendacious deposition*, — is but one. The others (as we have seen) are, forgery commonly so called (forgery in respect of written evidence;) forgery in respect of *real* evidence; fraudulent obtainment; and personation.† For the prevention of these modifications of *malâ fide* falsehood, *punishment*, simple punishment, has all along been trusted to: without any assistance from the ceremony of an oath, and apparently without any suspicion of deficiency on the score of the want of such assistance.

True it is, that in those several cases it may happen to the species of fraud which is not perjury, to be supported by deposition delivered to a court of justice; in which case, the punishment appointed for those several offences will receive, from the ceremony of an oath, whatever support it is in the power of that ceremony to give. But this is but a contingency; and that, comparatively speaking, but seldom exemplified: the case in which the punishment annexed to these offences respectively derives no support from the oath, is by far the most common case.

To the persuasion thus indicated on the part of the governing class, add the like persuasion as indicated on the part of all persons without distinction, in the character of suitors and their law advisers.

Supposing a man wrongfully deprived of the possession of any moveable thing belonging to him; and supposing him to demand restitution of it by the only species of action by which specific restitution is so much as professed to be given; in that case, if the defendant,—performing the ceremony of an oath in conjunction with twelve other men speaking only to his character, and not so much as professing to know anything about the matter — will take upon him to say, in general terms, that the plaintiff's demand is not a just one, — the plaintiff therefore loses the cause: neither can any question be put to the defendant for the purpose of bringing down from generals to particulars such his self-regarding and self-serving testimony; nor are any witnesses in support of the plaintiff's demand permitted to be examined. The man who proffered this curious kind of evidence, was said to *wage his law*.

By what exertion of fraud or imbecility, any species of demand (or *action*, as it is called) was thus paralyzed, or why one species more than another, are questions which, at this time of day, must be left to the industry of antiquarians. In point of fact, so

* In some of the above cases, the title to the money rests solely upon the authenticity of a script, an order, or other voucher, produced in the character of an article of written evidence. In these cases, he who, instead of an authentic, produces a counterfeit script, subjects himself to the punishment (generally capital) appointed in case of forgery.[a] In others of these cases, the mere identity of the person is the efficient causes of title. In these cases, he who, not being the person entitled under a certain name to receive a certain sum of money, represents himself as being that person, and receives the money accordingly, subjects himself to the punishment (generally capital) appointed for this offence, under the name of *personation*.

[a] Capital punishment has now been abolished in such cases, by 7 W. IV. and 1 Vict. c. 84. — *Ed. of this Collection*.

† See the last Chapter, § 1.

it is, that to a man who claims the thing itself, this species of defence is still liable to be opposed; while, to the man who, instead of the thing itself, claims money in the name of satisfaction, this same sort of defence is not capable of being opposed. What has been the consequence? That the action of *detinue* — the only action at common law by which a man can claim the thing itself — has for ages been abandoned altogether: the action called *assumpsit* — the action by which a man, instead of the thing, demands money under the name of damages, — is the action employed in lieu of it. Men—all men—have all this while, under the guidance of their law advisers, chosen to give up everything moveable they had been accustomed to call their own, rather than trust to this supernatural security, to the exclusion of the other natural ones.

As to judges (I speak of English judges, and more particularly of the highest stages in that office,) the contempt universally entertained by them for this ceremony stands evidenced by every day's practice.

No jury is ever impannelled, but their entrance into their ephemeral office is prefaced by what is called their oath. Each man bearing his part in this ceremony, promises that the verdict in which he joins shall be according to the evidence, *i. e.* according to his own conception of the probative force of the evidence. What is the consequence? That, so far as in relation to this probative force (*i. e.* as to that one of the two sides of the cause, to which the greatest quantity of probative force applies) there is any ultimate difference of opinion, some proportion out of the twelve, any number from one to eleven inclusive, has committed perjury. Lest the consummation of this perjury should be delayed for an inconvenient length of time, a species of torture has, by the care of those judges by whom the foundation of this species of judicature was laid, been provided for the purpose: a species of torture, composed of hunger, cold, and darkness. Hence judicature by jury is a sort of game of *brag*, in which the stake is won by the boldest and the most obstinate: they or he remain unperjured — all the others perjured. Of all the men of law that ever sat upon the official bench, by what one could this carefully-manufactured and perpetually-exemplified perjury have been unknown? — by what one of them was it ever spoken of as matter of regret?

On the contrary, Englishmen of all classes — — non-lawyers and lawyers—have been at all times vying with one another in their admiration, their blind and indiscriminating admiration, of an institution into the basis of which a necessary course of perjury had been wrought: and, at the same time (as if to crown the inconsistency) the oath, the sacred oath, has ever been sounded in men's ears; as if in *that* consisted the principal, if not sole, security, for whatever regard for justice is looked for at their hands.

Nor yet is it to the *inevitable* perjury, the perjury without which the business could not go on, — nor yet is it to the complacency with which this really accidental accompaniment is regarded, — that the proofs of the contempt entertained for the ceremony by all classes, judges and jurymen as well as suitors, lawyers as well as non-lawyers, is confined. Business would not the less go on, although effects to which jurymen are called upon to set a value (the true value) upon their oaths, were accordingly to be appreciated, appreciated without exception, at their true value: although a purse of money, with money of the real value of three pounds, were appreciated at three pounds, instead of being appreciated at nine and thirty shillings. Yet what sessions ever passes over at the Old Bailey, without giving birth to instances, more than one, in which effects, known by all mankind to be worth three pounds, or ever so much more, are valued at less than forty shillings?* Valued, thus under-valued, and for what purpose? For what but to set their power above that of the law; and, in the very teeth of the legislature, consign to a less degree of punishment, some criminal, for whom a greater degree of punishment has been appointed by parliament? When a judge is really displeased with a verdict, his practice and his duty is to send them back to their box, or their room, with a recommendation to reconsider it. What instance was ever known of a judge sending back a jury with a recommendation to exonerate their consciences of a load of perjury thus incurred? On the contrary, — whether by judges, by lawyers of other classes, or by non-lawyers, — in how many instances has such perjury been ever spoken of with any other note of observation, than what has been expressive of approbation and applause? Mercy — humanity — such are the eulogistic names bestowed, regularly bestowed, upon the profanation of this ceremony: as often as the object of the profanation has been to usurp a power lodged by the constitution in other hands, and put the most marked contempt that can be put by a subordinate authority upon superior law.

Blessed effect of this ceremony and its vaunted sanctity! Judges designating by the self-same name the practice they punish, and the practice they encourage! Punishing at one time — promoting, enforcing, at another — the same thing, or at least what they bid men look upon as the same thing: for, to cause two things to be looked upon as the same thing, what shorter or more effectual course can a man take, than to call them by the same name?

In the well-known epigram of Prior, the

* By 7 & 8 G. IV. c. 29, § 12, the amount is raised to £5. — *Ed. of this Collection.*

story of the fat man in the crowd, complaining, in terms of impatience, of the inconvenience of which in his own person he was in so great a degree the cause, presents, as it flows from the pen of the poet, no other sentiments than those sentiments of ridicule and pleasantry which it was intended to excite.

Sentiments of a somewhat different complexion may perhaps be excited, in the instance of the mischief now upon the carpet — that of perjury — when, in the persons of the most constant complainers of it, and indefatigable declaimers against it, we find the chief and unceasing encouragers, and, as far as encouragement goes, authors: encouragers in every mode and form in which encouragement can be administered, — example, precept, commendation, reward, punishment: punishment attached, not, as might have been supposed, to the incurring of the guilt, but to the abstaining or omitting to incur it; — the punishment here spoken of being not that which is administered in ceremony, half a dozen times perhaps in the year, with the professed view of curbing it, but that which is administered without ceremony every day in the year, not merely in the design, but with the indisputable effect, not merely of promoting, but of securing, the perpetration of it.*

* "*Oaths*" the seed, "*perjury*" the "*harvest.*" Such is the husbandry which by Blackstone[a] is spoken of as actually pursued; and of which, by the mention made of it in these terms, his disapprobation is pointedly enough declared. O yes! bad indeed was such husbandry *in that case.* And why in that case? Because, in that case, the husbandman was a competitor in trade: the judge, or the practitioner, in a rival set of judicatories; which — though (under the auspices of the fee-gathering system) united by a common interest with his own — had also for a source of rivalry and discord, its separate interest. Never can he bring himself to speak without a sarcasm, of the business of those decayed and petty traders (once, in the good old times, at the head of the trade,) whom the vast firm to which he belongs have now, for such a length of time, kept like toads under a harrow. Viewing in every rival an usurper, he grudges them even their wretched remnant in the trade of wickedness.

On this occasion, could he but have looked at home, — had the range of his optics been somewhat more extensive, and somewhat more under command, — he would have thought a second time, before he had hazarded an imputation so easily retorted, and with such increase of force.

In the nursery of a spiritual court is no such *forcing frame* as a *jury-box* — no such horticulturist as a lord chief-justice. In the spiritual nursery, perjury is but a sort of weed — an accidental product: the system, if *purposely*, is at least not *avowedly*, directed to the production of it: when it does spring up, the cause of its growth is not in the cultivator only, but in the soil likewise. But in the profane nursery, the cultivator is actively and conspicuously employed in *forcing* it: nor is that soil to be seen anywhere in which it can fail to grow.

[a] II. 344; and see IV. 361.

§ 3. *Mischievousness of Oaths.*

Inefficacious as is the ceremony of an oath to all good purposes, it is by no means inefficacious to bad ones.

Shift the scene, — give to another set of lawyers the benefit, — and perjury now becomes *pious.* Employ it (as above) in the jury-box, to debilitate the understanding, as well as taint the morals, of the people, and thus render them passive tools and unresisting victims in the hands of this domineering and now uppermost set; and the choicest epithet, how incongruous soever, is not too good for it.

Pious is, of all others, the epithet chosen by Blackstone[b] for perjury, when (under the direction of common-law judges) employed by jurymen to rescue criminals from a punishment to which they have been devoted by the legislature. "*Pious perjury:*" as who should say — loyal treason, humane assassination, honest peculation, chaste adultery. *Humane* perjury — yes, in this case, beyond dispute: *moral* perjury — even that might pass: but, of all imaginable eulogistic epithets (eulogy being the strain to be pursued at any rate) why pitch upon that of *pious* to affix to perjury? — why thus volunteer a flat contradiction in terms? Why, but to reconcile to the practice those pious persons, who, looking down upon morality, look up only to piety, as that in comparison of which all other objects are unworthy of regard. With these — whatsoever of humanity, or utility in any other shape, might appear predicable of the practice — the impiety of it might be apt to be considered as an objection to it, and that objection an insuperable one. What is to be done? Give them to understand, that (in this instance at least,) perjurious as the practice is, here may still be piety in it, — the objection is removed, and "everything is as it should be." When every other argument fails, then is the time to try what can be done by a bold paradox: the bolder it appears, the more difficult it is for the disciple to be persuaded, or to suffer himself so much as to entertain the suspicion, that, without some sufficient reason at bottom, so great a master would have given utterance to it.

In the eye of the man of law (not to speak at present of the priest,) whether an act be right or wrong, is a question that depends never on the act itself, but always on the quality of the persons by whom it is practised.

Practised by a "bishop," that bishop being a papist, "subornation of perjury" was a bad thing: no *piety* in it: sheer "wickedness," and nothing else.[c] On this occasion, a system of contrivance is reported, by which, — when a clerk (meaning here by a clerk, perhaps a clergyman only, perhaps any man who could read) — when a clerk had in a capital crime been defendant, — if in that character he had been convicted by a lay jury, he used to be saved from punishment: the contrivance consisting in making him pass through the formality of a sort of *new trial*, in which the bishop sat as judge; the jury being, as Judge and Reporter Hobart represents it, "compounded of clerks and laymen;" or as Blackstone, referring to Hobart, finds it more convenient to misrepresent it, "composed of twelve clerks."

On every such occasion (to take the account of the matter from Blackstone) might be seen "a vast complication of perjury and subornation of perjury, in this solemn farce" (so he calls it) "of

[b] IV. 239. [c] Blackstone, IV. 360.

1. Under the name of the *mendacity-licence* will be hereafter treated of, at full length, one of the principal among the devices by which, under the fee-gathering system, judges — the authors of unwritten law in both its branches, the main or substantive branch, and the adjective branch, or system of procedure — have, with so disastrous a success, pursued the ends — the real ends — under the fee-gathering system the only ends — of judicature. It is by the licence granted to mendacity on both sides of the cause, that judges have given encouragement and birth to their best customers, the *malâ fide* suitors. It is by means of the vain and pernicious ceremony of an oath, that they have been enabled to grant and vend the mendacity-licence. The punishment due to testimonial mendacity has been artfully attached, not to testimonial mendacity, but to perjury: not to testimonial mendacity in all cases without distinction, but to testimonial mendacity in such cases, and such cases alone, in which mendacity has by their authority been converted into perjury: which conversion cannot be effected without the previous ceremony of an oath; of which ceremony they have, at pleasure, caused, or forborne to cause, the performance: and, when the religious ceremony has been withheld, they have not only exempted the offence from punishment, but, by exempting it from punishment, they have exempted it from infamy also.

2. The ceremony having acquired a technical denomination, that of an *oath* — a substantive which is understood to have for its *quasi-conjugate* the verb *to swear* — religionists of different descriptions (in particular those called *Quakers*) have, by a principle of religion, been prevented from taking a part in it. The consequence has been a licence, *inter alia*, to commit, to the prejudice as well of Quakers as of all other persons, every imaginable crime, of which, in whatsoever number, Quakers, and they alone, shall have been percipient witnesses.

From the class of wrongs called *civil*, the licence has, by an act of the legislature, in case of a Quaker witness, been withdrawn; viz. by substituting to the words *oath*, and *swear*, the words *affirmation*, and *solemnly affirm*: but to the encouragement of the class of wrongs called *criminal* (to which class belong those which are of the deepest die) the licence continues to operate with unabated force and efficacy.*

3. The last which shall be here mentioned of the wounds inflicted upon justice by this disastrous ceremony, is one, of which, on the present occasion, a short hint is all that can be afforded.

Of the mischief done to justice by the door

---

a mock trial; the witnesses, the compurgators" (twelve of them) "and the jury, being all of them partakers in the guilt: the delinquent party also, though convicted before on the clearest evidence, and conscious of his own offence, yet was permitted, and *almost compelled*, to swear himself not guilty: nor" (adds he) "was the good bishop himself," (*good* being the epithet applied to this papist to make the sarcasm the more caustic;) "the good bishop himself, under whose countenance this scene of wickedness was daily transacted, by any means exempt from a share in it."

Against this "perjury and subornation of perjury," lest our indignation should not be strong enough, the learned commentator sets out with informing us, that "in the beginning of the (then) last century it was remarked on with much indignation by a learned judge," viz. Judge Hobart, whose reports constitute the authority to which he refers.[a]

On this occasion, the learned judge, it must be acknowledged — without any apparent scruple, reserve, or affected delicacy, such as, in this age of refinement, a non-lawyer, an unlicensed person at least, might be expected to observe — speaks out, and calls things by their names. "The perjuries, indeed," quoth he, "were sundry: one in the witnesses and compurgators; another in the jury, compounded of clerks and laymen; and of the third, the judge himself was not clear, all turning the solemn trial of truth by oath, into a ceremonious and formal lie."

As to the ceremony of riding off on the backs of twelve compurgators; in civil cases, to a great extent, under the learned judge's own sort of law, it then was, and still is, law at this day.[b] It might be brought into exercise any day, and would be every day, but for a more modern quirk, by which the original quirk is evaded.

As to the "ceremonious and formal lie," it is no other than that which, under his own sort of law, is pronounced, as often as, among the Rev. Dr. Paley's "twelve men taken by lot out of a promiscuous multitude,"[c] any difference of opinion has place: and this in virtue of the torture applied with the knowledge and under the authority of the judge, but without the need of any work and labour done by the reverend artificer, in the subornative line, for the purpose of giving existence to the lie: not to speak of the cases in which — the perjury (when committed) being of the *pious* sort recommended under that name by Blackstone — the learned judge, ambitious of taking his share in the praise of piety, makes special application of that "countenance" which, had the judicatory been of the spiritual law, instead of the common-law class, would have made the scene of perjury and subornation a scene of wickedness, and himself, in the bitter sense of the word *good*, a "good judge."

As to the "*complication*" with which the mode employed on this occasion by these ecclesiastical judges, for the giving impunity to criminals, appears so justly chargeable, it must be imputed to a comparative deficiency in respect of those associated endowments of genius and courage, which with such brilliant success have been displayed by their lay brethren of the trade: by so simple an invention as that of a flaw in the indictment, all this "*complication*" might have been saved.

* By 9 Geo. IV. c. 32, the evidence of Quakers is taken in affirmation in criminal cases. — *Ed. of this Collection.*

[a] Hob. 289, 291.

[b] Wager of Law.

[c] Paley, II. 263.

so inconsistently shut against evidence from the most satisfactory source, viz. confessional evidence, if presented in the best shape, — while, to evidence from the same source, on condition of its being presented in some less trustworthy shape, the same door is left wide open, — mention will be made in the sequel.* To an exclusion thus prejudicial to justice, it seems as if the ceremony of an oath, with the prejudices that cluster round it, had been in some degree necessary. That sacred regard for the ceremony of an oath, — that awful sense which, if it ever was alive, is seen to be so effectually dead, in judges and jurymen — has been supposed to be essentially and tremblingly alive in robbers, murderers, and incendiaries. If (what is not endurable) a man of any of these descriptions were, on his trial, to be subjected to examination, as well as his accomplice, on whose testimony he is about to be convicted, the oath so regularly tendered to the one must not be tendered to the other, for it would be a snare laid to his conscience: and thus it is, that, not being to be interrogated upon oath, he is not to be interrogated at all.

Note, that to one who is really innocent, neither oath nor question can be a snare. It is only on the supposition of his *being* the robber, the murderer, or the incendiary, which he is supposed to be, that his conscience can be afflicted with the qualms supposed to be infused into it by that ceremony, which is trampled upon even to ostentation by jurymen and judges.

In compelling a man, in the character of an extraneous witness, to declare what he knows touching a transaction in which he has no pecuniary, or other reputedly considerable, interest, — and, on the occasion of such a declaration to such an effect, to join in the ceremony of an oath,—the man of law, the English lawyer for example, finds not the smallest difficulty. In compelling a man, in the character of a party — in the character of a defendant — always with the same ceremony, to make a declaration, in consequence of which (if true) he may find himself divested of the possession of an estate to any magnitude, the property of which, till the question had thus been put to him, he had conceived no apprehension of not carrying with him into his grave — the man of law, and again the English lawyer, finds as little difficulty.

But now comes another case: the defendant is under prosecution for a crime, for which, if convicted, he will be punished with death. Now then, shall a man thus circumstanced be put to his oath? Forbid it, religion! forbid it, humanity! What! subject him to a temptation, under which it is not possible he should not sink! force him, and at such a time, to commit perjury! His body is to be sent to the worms: and, before it has time to reach them, is his soul to be consigned into the hands of the devil — of the devil, at whose instigation the crime, if committed, was committed, — his soul to be consigned over to the devil, to be plunged immediately into hell!

Whence comes all this tenderness, this delicacy, this difficulty? It arises principally, if not entirely, out of the oath. Take the man out of the court of justice — out of that place, where everything that passes, passes in the face of day; where, — either by threats, promises, or other undue influence — by threats of severity, by promises of mercy or positive reward — the idea of seducing his testimony from the line of truth is hopeless and without example; — take him into a forest, or a dungeon — into a recess of any kind, into which no third eye can penetrate; in this case, whatever he may have been made to say, though to his own indubitable condemnation, is unexceptionable evidence. Why? Because, in that case, there is no oath, no perjury: if his body goes to the worms, and his soul to the place of endless torment, it is for whatever he has done; it is not for what he has thus said — it is not for the perjury.

But the mischief, and the difficulty, the inconsistency, end not here. Not only when life may be saved by perjury, may not the temptation be too great? May it not also be too great, when liberty, reputation, property, the great bulk of a large property, may at this price be saved? and so down to a fine of five shillings? Would not this, too, be laying a snare for men's consciences? Was not this the cruelty practised by the wicked judges of the star-chamber? Could it be proved that a judge of the star-chamber ever folded a piece of paper in three folds — would not the wretch who should presume, at this time of day, to fold a piece of paper in three folds, deserve to be held in execration by all posterity?

Thus it is, that, in the case of a defendant, you must not have the security, the supposed security, that an oath would give: and because you must not have the sham, the hollow security that this ceremony could give, you must not in this same case have the real, the substantial security that punishment would give — punishment applied to mendacity in this, as in any other case.†

* See Book IX. *Exclusion.*

† What, then, it may be asked — by threatening a man with inferior punishment in case of mendacity, would you expect to see him, by veracity, subject himself to superior punishment? By threatening him eventually with punishment short of death, would you expect to see him subject himself for a certainty to the very punishment of death? No, surely: nor in that case is it necessary to subject a man, in case of mendacity, to any separate, independent punishment. Un-

It was simply in the character of a security for veracity, and in respect of its inefficiency and inaptitude in that character, that the ceremony of an oath fell to be considered here. Its efficiency, its unhappy efficiency, in a very different character, that of an instrument of tyranny and improbity, by serving to bind men to the performance of engagements fraught with the most pernicious consequences to themselves and others, belongs not directly to the present purpose. The purposes to which it has thus been applied, belong not the less to the list of the objections to the use of it: but, not being directly applicable to the purpose in hand, to mention them *pro memoriâ* may, in this place, be sufficient.

Suppose but an atom of punishment attached to the profanation on its own account merely — on its own account merely, and, if that be the case, inseparably attached to it; so far as that supposition extends, so far the institution of an oath is mischievous, and purely mischievous. It gives to man, weak, frail, sinful, wicked man — it gives to man *pro tanto* (so he be but clothed in temporal authority) the command, the absolute command, over a proportionable part of God's power — applicable to the worst, as easily as to the best of purposes. It makes man the master, God his servant: and not his servant only, but his slave — his slave bound to a degree of unerring obedience such as no human master ever received, or could have received, from any slave.

Attach to the ceremony, and thence to the profanation of it, but the smallest particle of punishment, and that particle inseparable; then has every man a sure recipe for binding himself, and any such other man as the influence of a moment can put into his power for this purpose, — for binding them, with a force proportioned to the quantum of this particle, to the commission of all imaginable crimes: then has man, by grant from God himself, a power over God, applicable at any time to the purpose of converting God himself into an accomplice of all those crimes.

Let this be the supposition built upon, then would Jephthah, by the amount of this inseparable particle, — then would Jephthah, had he spared his daughter, have been punished by God's power — punished, not for the taking of the rash vow, but for the breaking of it.

Then would the assassin of Henry IV. (punished, or not punished for making the attempt) have been punished, and by divine vengeance, had he refrained from making it.

Assassination, — assassination through motives of piety, is the natural, — in case of consistency the necessary, and as history testifies, the too frequent, — fruit of the popular persuasion relative to the nature and effect of oaths.

It was in the earliest stages of society — in those stages at which the powers of the human understanding were at the weakest — that this, together with so many other articles in the list of supernatural securities, or substitutes for testimonial veracity, took their rise. Ordeals, in all their forms: trials by battle: trials without evidence (understand human evidence:) trials by supernatural, to the exclusion of human, evidence: trials by evidence secured against mendacity by supernatural means — by the ceremony of an oath.

As the powers of the human understanding gain strength, invigorated by nourishment and exercise, — the natural securities rise in value, the supernatural, understood to be what they are, drop, one after another, off the stage. First went ordeal: then went duel: after that, went, under the name of the wager of law, the ceremony of an oath in its pure state, unpropped by that support which this inefficient security receives at present from those efficient ones which are still clogged with it: by and bye, its rottenness standing confessed, it will perish off the human stage: and this last of the train of supernatural powers, *ultima cœlicolûm*, will be gathered, with Astrea, into its native skies.

The lights, which at that time of day were sought for in vain from supernatural interference, are now collected and applied, by a watchful attention to the probative force of circumstantial evidence, and a skilful application of the scrutinizing force of cross-examination.

§ 4. *How to adapt the ceremony, if employed, to its purposes.*

Objectionable as the ceremony of an oath, considered in the light of a security for the trustworthiness of testimony, has appeared to us to be; still, if it is to be applied to that purpose, it cannot be a matter of indifference to know in what way the little efficiency which it possesses may be made as great as possible.

An oath acts in three ways: it carries with it the operation of three different sanctions: of the religious sanction, from its nature and

detected, it cannot be punished in any case; detected, it will in general subject him to the proper punishment: to the very punishment from which, by that fresh crime, the natural consequence of every former crime, he struggled to escape from it.

Not that, even in this case, punishment as for mendacity would be necessarily without its use: for a man who is innocent has everything to lose by mendacity, nothing to gain by it: and it may happen that, though the former crime which he has committed may not be susceptible of sufficient proof, yet among the lies which he has uttered, in his endeavours to escape from the imputation of such his former crime, there may be this or that one so ill-contrived as to be susceptible of the clearest refutation.

essence; of the legal sanction, whenever punishment has been attached to the profanation of the ceremony, as such; of the moral or popular sanction, because that which points the force of the legal sanction upon any object, generally points at the same time the force of the moral sanction, and brings to bear the punishment issuing from that source, also.

Suitable to the nature of the three different sanctions concerned, will be the arrangements calculated to raise to its maximum the salutary agency of the ceremony, as applied to the purpose in hand. The practical utility of introducing into practice this or that particular arrangement on the occasion in question, will depend so much upon the state of public opinion in each respective country — upon the prejudices, and humours, and caprices, of the people and their rulers,—that the hints which follow on the subject cannot be adapted to any other purpose than that of illustration. For that purpose, a concise (and as it were) *short-hand* mention of them will be sufficient, without attempting to enter into details, distinctions, modifications, or justifications.

I. Arrangements for adapting the ceremony of the oath for the purpose of pointing the force of the *religious* sanction: —

1. Form of words, appropriate and impressive.*

2. Different form of words, rising one above another in solemnity and impressiveness; partly according to the importance of the occasion, as measured by the mischievousness of the offence, according to the modifications above exhibited; partly according to the apprehension of falsehood, excited by the individual circumstances of the case in the bosom of the judge.†

3. On occasions of superior importance, attitudes and gestures directed to the same end — lifting up the hands and eyes to heaven,‡ &c.

4. Appropriate graphical exhibitions, constituting in this view a regular part of the furniture of every court of justice. Copy, in painting or engraving, of the death of Ananias and Sapphira (capitally punished on the spot by divine justice, for mendacious testimony of the *self-investitive* or *self-exonerative* kind,) a subject treated by Raphael in one of his cartoons. Over the picture or print, explanations and applications, in characters legible to all spectators.

5. Other appropriate exhortations and observations taken from scripture.

6. The oath administered, not by a lay-officer of the court, but by a minister of the established religion.‖ On extraordinary oc-

* To show how much in this case may depend on form, when in substance the ceremony is the same, I have heard at different times many more instances than I can recollect of the importance attached to particular forms among sea-faring men and other individuals belonging to the unlettered classes — forms not established, but cast by chance in each man's particular imagination. Say, you wish your tongue may rot off — say, you wish your eyes may drop out of your head this moment, — if you ever saw any such thing. By an adjuration in some such form, or varying from it by some whimsical embroidery which I have now forgotten, and which, if remembered, it might perhaps not be decent to repeat, has a man been made to bring out some truth, which, till then, he had masked by a profusion of false protestations, uttered without scruple; and which could not have been extracted from him by all the force that could have been brought to bear upon him in a court of justice.

Unfortunately, illustration is the only purpose that can be answered by this observation. The comparative impressiveness of each such formulary depending upon the inscrutable texture of individual idiosyncrasy, it can never be applied to any judicial purpose; unless possibly at the suggestion of a party, apprized by habitual intercourse, of his adversary's state of mind in this respect: in which case, however, it would always be to be *added* (since it could never on sufficient assurance be *substituted*) to the regular oath.

† With a view to solemnity and impressiveness, the choice of a formulary is matter of no small difficulty. It is exposed to this dilemma; employ the same form on all occasions, the most trifling as well as the most important, — applied to the most important, it fails of being so impressive as it might be; or else, when applied to the least important, it sounds bombast and ridiculous. Employ divers forms, rising one above another in impressiveness, — then comes another danger: on the occasions on which any form short of the most impressive is employed, the witness, knowing that there is another which is regarded as more efficacious, may conceive lightly of that which, on the occasion in question, is tendered to him, and regard it as wanting in some particular which is necessary to endow it with a completely binding force.

The only effectual remedy would be, not to employ the ceremony at all, or, if at all, only on the most important occasions.

The following might be two of the gradations: —

The evidence I {am about to give, shall be / have been giving, is} the truth, the whole truth, and nothing but the truth.

If, in any part of the testimony I {have been giving, / am about to give,} I knowingly utter anything that is false, or in any respect conceal, disguise, or misrepresent the truth, I acknowledge myself to be deserving of the wrath of Almighty God, and of the contempt and abhorrence of all mankind.

‡ Scotch covenanter's oath.

‖ On the ground of English law, — if the faculties possessed by ecclesiastical functionaries were not, by a sort of mutual (though tacit) understanding, set down among the sorts of talents better kept under the napkin than drawn out for use, — the application might be made of this principle in a variety of obvious instances: —

1. In a bench of justices of the peace, sitting in general sessions, it seldom happens but that one or more clergymen are spontaneously present. In this case, the principle might be applied,

casions (the witness professing a religion other than the established) — power to the judge to call in the assistance of a minister of the witness's own religion, for the purpose. On occasions of extraordinary importance, prayer by the minister, short but appropriate.

II. Arrangements for adapting the ceremony, on extraordinary occasions, to the purpose of pointing the force of the *political* sanction: —

1. In front of the station of the witness, as he stands up to deliver his evidence, — a table, in characters large enough to be read from every part of the court, stating the punishment for perjury, according to its various gradations. While the witness is pronouncing the oath, an officer of the court, with a wand, points to the particular modification of punishment attached to the particular modification of perjury, which on the occasion in question, would, in case of mendacity, be incurred.*

2. On extraordinary occasions (for example, when the temptation or the proneness to mendacity is apprehended to be particularly great, and, at the same time, the cause important,) a curtain draws up, and discovers a graphical exhibition, representing a convict suffering the characteristic punishment for perjury, whatsoever it be. The officer, with his wand, directs the attention of the witness to it, as above.

III. Arrangements for adapting the ceremony to the purpose of pointing the force of the *moral* sanction: —

1. In the wording of the oath, express and distinct reference made to the punishment from this source, as well as from the religious. In the event of mendacity, the witness recognises himself as about to incur, and as meriting to incur, the contempt, or (according to the nature of the case) the abhorrence of all good men.†

2. In case of suspicion of falsehood (whether arising from extraneous contradiction, from self-contradiction, from inconsistency, or improbability,) but without ground sufficient for prosecution; the publication of this particular part of the evidence in the newspapers, authorized, encouraged, or ordered, by the judge: warning given of this arrangement to the witness at the time. Concerning the publicity to be given to judicial examination in general, see a subsequent chapter of this Book.‡

3. To this head may likewise be referred the several arrangements exhibited under the

---

* The institution of binding a man to his good behaviour, by obliging him (in the language of English law) to enter into a recognisance, bears, in one respect, an analogy to this arrangement. Considered on the mere footing of a contract, an engagement, an agreement, — so far as the cognizor himself is concerned, and without adverting to the persons joining with him in the obligation in the character of sureties, the operation is useless and nugatory: to what end employ the compulsive force of law, to engage a man to consent to submit to an eventual obligation, which it would be just as easy to impose upon him without such forced consent, as with it? The only real use of the instrument is to fix the penal sum which, on the deprecated event in question, a man will have to pay; and to notify to him the amount of it.

† A very few words, indeed, well chosen and well placed, will be sufficient. There is no sort of incompatibility between the one object and the other. Among men not under the influence of religion, an oath bearing reference to religion and nothing else, is in danger of losing the whole, or a great part, of that respect, which might be secured to it by a prudent attention to their opinions. All men *ought* to be under the influence of religion — therefore, whether they are or no, we ought to deal with them as if they were — is a most deplorably self-deceiving, though unhappily but too frequent, logic. But deplorable would be a man's own error — deplorable the misfortunes of his subjects — if, on any practical occasion, any such assumption, any conceit thus hatched, should be taken up by him in the capacity of a legislator, and acted upon as a ground for any of his measures.

‡ Chap. X.

---

without the smallest additional trouble or expense.

2. At the assizes, it scarcely ever happens but that one or more of the neighbouring clergy are present, drawn by curiosity or business.

3. At the Old Bailey, in the intervals of meals, might not the Lord Mayor's chaplain be as suitably and profitably employed in this line of serious service, as in saying grace before and after meat at the Mansion-house? As a simple spectator, the Ordinary of Newgate is often present.

4. In Westminster Hall, of the five chiefs, three are commonly members of the House of Lords, and in that character give title (if not occupation) each of them to a certain number of chaplains. Might not these, with or without the assistance of other such labourers in the sacred vineyard, suffice amongst them for the discharge of a function so well assorted to their other functions? At whatever price the labour was estimated, the chief judge of the chief court of equity has in his hands assets singularly well adapted to the purpose of affording it its reward.

5. In the House of Commons, the Speaker has a chaplain, whose duty consists in offering up prayers and thanksgivings, which, happily for his congregation, they are not obliged to join in. Might not his time be employed to rather more advantage, in giving solemnity to the oaths administered to witnesses before committees?

6. In the ecclesiastical establishment, for the greater advancement of piety and religion, are contained (as everybody knows) in no inconsiderable number, dignities and other benefices, composed of reward altogether pure from service. Would the reward be less profitably bestowed, if service, in this or some other shape, were attached to it.

Among our Saxon ancestors, in the county courts (at that time competent, as they should never have ceased to be, to all sorts of causes,) the minister of justice never sat without the minister of religion at his elbow.

two former heads. Whatever discourses and exhibitions are addressed in this way to the witness, make their way at the same time to the public at large, and through that channel (circuitous as it is) are reverberated upon him with augmented force.

Preach to the eye, if you would preach with efficacy. By that organ, through the medium of the imagination, the judgment of the bulk of mankind may be led and moulded almost at pleasure. As puppets in the hand of the showman, so would men be in the hand of the legislator, who, to the science proper to his function, should add a well-informed attention to stage effect. Unhappily, among the abundantly diversified shapes in which severity has displayed itself in penal exhibitions, scarce the faintest trace of ingenuity is anywhere to be found. No marks of any progress made in the study of human nature—no sign of any skill, or so much as thought, displayed in the adaptation of means to ends. Ends are scarce so much as looked at. Blind antipathy is the spur—blind practice the only guide. To do (though it be to fail) as others have done before him, is each man's only aim, is each man's highest praise.

Next (if not superior) in importance, to the study of augmenting the efficacy of the ceremony by these corroborative circumstances and accompaniments, is the attention not to spend its force upon the air — not to consume it upon inadequate objects — nor to debilitate it and bring it into contempt, by employing it upon occasions in which its utter inefficacy is demonstrated by experience: not to persevere in employing it in the character of a security for veracity, in cases where mendacity is the constant and notorious result.

The following are such further rules, as may with advantage be observed in the wording and administering of the oath: —

Rule 1. Let the words of the oath be pronounced by the witness himself: not simply heard, and tacitly assented to, as they issue from the mouth of a third person — such as the person by whom the oath is said to be administered.

Reasons: 1. A ceremony — a discourse — will naturally appear to a man to be the more unequivocally and indisputably his own, the more active the part is which he takes in it. Whatever issues out of a man's own mouth, will naturally appear to him to be more completely his own, than what he silently hears while spoken by another. Silence, says the proverb, gives consent: True; but not so clear and unequivocal a consent as is given by direct speech. Where the inclination is reluctant, nothing more inventive than the imagination — nothing more flimsy than the subterfuges which it will make or catch at. I did not hear — I did not attend — I did not comprehend: no excuses too weak for a man to pass upon himself, howsoever it be with others. What you yourself pronounced, you cannot but have heard: what you yourself pronounced, you cannot but have attended to: what you yourself pronounced, you cannot but have comprehended; it being that sort of proposition, which a man cannot fail of comprehending, so he have but given it that measure of attention, without which he could not have pronounced it. Such are the bars which the voice of conscience, or of any monitor from without, has to oppose to the propensity to evasion in the case of audible enunciation, but not in the case of silent auditorship.

2. Any denunciation of infamy, though it be but eventual and hypothetical, is reflected upon a man in a more forcible manner, when the mouth from which it is known to have issued is his own. "Thy own mouth condemneth thee, not I."* "Out of thy own mouth will I judge thee."†

Rule 2. In the words which the witness pronounces, the verbs and pronouns should be in the first person, *I swear*, *I declare*, and so forth.

Reason: This feature in the oath is necessary to give complete fulfilment to the intention expressed in the rule last preceding; to raise to its maximum the force of the inflicted infamy; to raise to its maximum the force of the impression made by the oath upon the mind of him who takes it.

This form, though not only the most apposite, but the most natural, is not however so necessary as to render the opposite form without example. The form, in which the judgment eventually passed upon the conduct of the witness, and pronounced by the witness, is expressed, may be that of a judgment passed upon it, not by himself, but by others, viz. the authors of the disposition of law, by which the oath is instituted.

Rule 3. The form should be as concise as is consistent with the preceding rules.

Reasons: 1. In proportion as a discourse is drawn into length, especially if without material addition to the ideas conveyed by it, the impression made by it is weakened.

2. Where witnesses are numerous (especially where the time allowed for the examination is limited and scanty,) the time consumed in this way may be a material object, in respect of vexation, expense and delay; and at any rate, in respect of the time consumed on the part of the judge.

§ 5. *Oaths, how applied as a security for the trustworthiness of testimony, under past and present systems of law.*

Under the original Roman law, the ceremony of an oath (as already mentioned‡) does

* Job xv. 6. † Luke xix. 22.

‡ See last Chapter, § 3.

not appear to have been employed in general on the occasion, nor consequently for the purpose of adding to the securities for the truth of testimony. Not extending in general to what are commonly called assertory declarations, it must have been for the most part confined to those occasions on which it has been distinguished by the appellation of a promissory oath.

At one period or other, on here and there an occasion, the ceremony does indeed appear to have been employed for this purpose. But if the intention was really sincere, so shallow was the conception, so clumsy the manipulation, that the interests of truth seem upon the whole rather to have suffered by it, than to have been served.

An oath, in so far as a breach of the engagement is exposed to detection, operates, it is true, as a check to mendacity. But, if the breach of it is entirely covered from detection, it operates, — in here and there a mind of more than common delicacy, as a check to mendacity, — but on minds of vulgar mould, rather as an encouragement. By presenting a colour of efficiency to a check which in reality amounts to nothing, it furnishes a certificate of veracity to any liar who thinks fit to apply it to that use. It gives him credit for virtue which he does not possess; secures to him all the profit of mendacity without any of the risk; and enables him to combine the benefits of mendacity with the reputation of the opposite virtue. When, by the tie of so awful a sanction, a man is bound to the observance of the laws of truth,— can you, without a violation of the law of charity, refuse to take him at his word? Such, on these occasions, is the joint cry of the hypocrite and the dupe.

In case of falsity, the testimony given by a man is the more thoroughly exposed to detection, — in the first place, the more particular and circumstantial it is at the first delivery,— in the next place, the more completely it is subjected to the test of cross-examination. Remove this test, you already grant to mendacity a sort of half-licence. But if, instead of calling upon a man for particulars, you admit of a declaration in general terms, — nothing is more easy, more natural, or more common, than, by the generality of those terms, to render the licence complete.

Such, at any rate, is the effect. More than one cause (speaking of psychological causes) may, any of them, have been adequate to the production of it. In some instances, fraud: the futility of the remedy being understood by the hand that administered it. In other instances, honest imbecility: the prescriber being himself a believer in the efficacy of his own quack medicine.

In what, if in any, cases, the general declaration has been *substituted* to particular statement, such as would naturally be extracted by examination,—in what cases, if in any, *superadded*,— does not appear clearly, on the face of such reports as are before me. What seems probable is, that the reporter himself had no clear conception of the difference: what seems equally probable is, that the judges, whose practice he has in view, had not themselves any clear conception of the difference. Sometimes the one course may have been pursued, sometimes the other, according to the occasion, and the object (public or private, good or bad) that happened to have been principally in view. Substitution would be suggested by indolence or favour—addition, by despair and lassitude. In the latter case, the judge stands in the predicament of the miser Harpagon, in Molière: after searching till he was tired, and finding nothing on the supposed thief — " Rends moi," says he, "sans te fouiller, ce que tu m'as volé."

Among the Romanists, the following present themselves as the principal instances in which this sort of mock security appears to have been employed: —

1. The *juramentum expurgatorium*. The sort of case here is a criminal one. The process of examination must have been already undergone; for to employ it, was the constant practice in these cases. The evidence thus extracted was found insufficient: it was so, even with the addition of the extraneous evidence. Had an oath been administered before the examination? then to what use repeat it afterwards? Had no oath been administered at that stage? then why discard it at a time at which (if at any) it might have been useful, reserving it for a time at which all chance of its being useful was at an end?

2. The *juramentum suppletorium*. The case is here a non-penal one. The plaintiff, for example, demands a debt. The extraneous evidence he produces is deemed insufficient. To supply the deficiency, he is admitted as witness in his own behalf: but on what terms? Not on the terms of submitting to examination, like an extraneous witness,— but on the terms of repeating, in general words, what in general words he had said before. Of so untrustworthy a sort is the testimony, that, so long as any other is to be had, it is not to be received at all: this same untrustworthy evidence, when it is received, is to be received free from those essential checks, which, in the case of the most trustworthy witnesses are deemed indispensable.

3. The *oath of calumny:* placed by Bishop Halifax at the head of those arrangements the object of which was to restrain what he calls temerity (he should have said *mala fides*) on

the part of litigants. I believe my cause is a good one,— says the suitor, plaintiff or defendant. To a suitor by whom these words have been pronounced, what judge can be so uncharitable as to impute any but the purest wishes and the purest motives? By these words, as surely as by a talisman, everything that savours of temerity is to be restrained. What grounds have you for looking upon your cause to be a good one? A question of that sort would have been too dangerous: a customer who could not answer it, might every now and then be driven from the shop, the *officina justitiæ*, as Blackstone so truly calls it.

On the *vivâ voce* examination of a witness, the form observed in English procedure, on the occasion of a trial before a jury, is as follows: — An officer of the court, having put into the hand of the witness a book containing the Christian scriptures (viz. that part which is purely Christian, the New Testament — or, in case of a Jew, that part of the Christian scriptures which is recognized in common by Jews and Christians — the Old Testament) — addresses himself to the witness, and says to him as follows: — The evidence you shall give on the issue joined between our sovereign lord the king and the defendant — or, the prisoner at the bar — or, the parties—shall be the truth, the whole truth, and nothing but the truth — so help you God. The witness thereupon, either of his own accord or at the suggestion of the officer, puts his lips to the book: and then, and not till then, the oath is considered as having been taken.

As to the description of the testimonial duty, it seems happily enough imagined: — comprehensiveness, conciseness, and emphaticalness, are qualities, the praise of which seems to be justly merited by it. Of the three members of the clause — "the truth," "the whole truth," "and nothing but the truth" — the sense might perhaps be conveyed by the two last, without the first. But so useful is the first for filling the period, and strengthening the impression made upon the mind through the medium of the ear, that, supposing it omitted, the force of the phrase can scarcely but appear to have sustained a considerable loss. Instead of being considered as an additament purely superfluous, the general expression *the truth* may be considered as containing in itself the whole of the sense: in which case, the two other members may be considered as added by way of exposition; lest, for want of sufficient particularity, either of the ideas (in particular that of integrality) should fail of presenting itself to notice.

In other respects, if the above rules be considered as affording a proper test, the above exhibited formulary seems ill qualified to abide it. So far as enunciation goes, the witness is purely passive: he is a hearer only, not a speaker, though in a concern so much his own. Not speaking at all, the rule which requires him to speak in the first person is unobserved of course. The kissing of the book is an exhibition altogether vague and inapposite. If it be understood to convey an expression of respect, there is nothing to direct it to any object beyond the book: if it contain an expression of respect for the book, and the objects from which it derives its title to respect, it bears not any express assurance of the veracity of the statement about to be delivered.

Considered as an instrument for calling in the force of the religious sanction for the purpose of binding the witness to the observance of his duty, the phrase *So help you God* seems but very feeble and inadequate. It contains an allusion to God's favour, but scarce the faintest allusion to God's wrath. It brings good alone to view, not evil — reward, not punishment. It holds up to the witness the prospect of a sort of special grace, an extraordinary and unknown reward, to be hoped for by him in the one event; but is silent as to reprobation and punishment, in the other, The worst that is represented as about to befal him in any event — in the event of his defiling himself with the crime of perjury,— is the failure of this special grace: a sort of acquisition, the idea of which not having been ever stamped upon his mind, the apprehension of missing it is not of the number of those by which sensible and serious alarms are wont to be excited. What salutary terror can be expected to be excited in the mind by the faint and altogether oblique intimation of a possible loss, of which neither the value, nor so much as the nature, has in any perceptible degree been ever present to a man's mind? If a working man (and of such is the bulk of the species) has a burthen to raise, and wants help to lift it, whom has he been used to look to? — not God, but his next neighbour.

In the Danish law, no great value appears to be set upon the judge's time. In causes of a certain degree of importance, each witness, before or after he takes the oath, is to hear what is called an "exposition" of it, extending to the length of three quarto pages; an expense of time the more wanton, inasmuch as this dissertation is to be kept constantly exposed to view, in every court of justice.*

According to the Danish code, a witness swears with his fingers—the thumb and the two next being held up together, one for each person of the Trinity.†

Of this sort of theology, observe the moral consequence. If murder or incendiarism (for example) be committed in presence of Arians or Socinians in any number, and of no others (not to speak of Jews,) either the crime is to

* Code Dan. l. 1. cap. xiii. § 8. p. 58.

† Expositio Juramenti, p. 545.

go unpunished, or the witness is to be duly plagued in form of law, till he submit to swear against his conscience.

In case of perjury, besides forfeiture of all forfeitable property, the witness is to lose two fingers,— two of the three offending fingers, it seems natural to suppose, — and thus far analogy seems to have been consulted. Pity an equal regard had not been shown to economy, not to speak of humanity and common sense. The convict, if not already a pauper, was to be converted into one by the forfeiture; and, by the same sentence, his means of livelihood were to be cut of.

As to the punishment of the religious sanction, if any particulars are desired concerning it, reference may be made to the Hindoo code, and to the Danish code.

In respect of quality, the Hindoo code does not afford us much information: in respect of quantity, it is precise to admiration. The misfortune is, every quantity is relative: and what the correlative is, is not explained.

If the subject be a cow (whether the cause be penal or non-penal is not specified,) the guilt of perjury is equal to that of the murder of exactly ten persons: if a horse, guilt equal to one hundred murders: if a man, one thousand murders: if a piece of gold, the number of murdered persons on the other side of the equation is rather difficult to reckon; it is equal to all the men that ever were born, *plus* all that ever will be.

" If the affair be concerning land," the ratio of this lot of guilt to the preceding one seems rather difficult to measure: it is that of the murder of all the creatures of all sorts living in the world; but at what period is not specified.

Another difficulty turns upon the distinction between an animal having hair upon its tail, and an animal having none: in the former case (kine and horses excepted as above,) the number of murders, to the guilt of which that of the perjury is equal, is exactly five: when the tail has no hair upon it, the degree of guilt is left to be discovered by the faint light of human reason.

For exculpative perjury (at least for self-exculpative,) when the punishment is capital, there is an express licence — a few cases of particular atrocity excepted, such as the cases of murdering a cow, or drinking wine :* and, for the encouragement of marriage, three or four falsehoods may be told, to promote so laudable an end. At the same time, so much better a thing is gallantry without marriage, than marriage itself, that in the former case the quantity of " falsehood" pronounced " allowable" is unlimited.†

In the Danish code, the punishment of the religious sanction says nothing of proportions, and seems to have but one and the same lot for all offences, whatever be the unhappy occasion, — men, land, horses, gold, animals without hair upon their tails, or cows. In respect of quality, it furnishes considerable information. Besides being excluded for ever from the company of the inhabitants of heaven, with the three persons of the Trinity at their head — a privilege the loss of which might, by want of the experienced enjoyment, have been rendered the more tolerable, — besides this, together with a variety of other negative punishments of the same complexion, — the perjurer's body and soul are to stand devoted to Satan and his crew (who, for the occasion, are loaded with sad epithets,) and with them in the depth of Erebus, are to be surrounded and tossed about in everlasting and unextinguishable fire, always consuming, never liberated. Another punishment, which in case of perjury the witness is to be understood to wish for, is one that is to be borne, not by himself immediately, but by his cattle. They are not to be roasted, like their master, in Erebus, but to pine away upon earth, and be emaciated, till they have lost their value. Such, it is explained, is to be his wish: but as to the cattle, whether the wish is to be accomplished, is not stated.

By the Swedish law, if the letter of it is to be depended upon,— be the cause what it may — in a cause of property, be the value in dispute what it may, — every man is at liberty to perjure himself for forty dollars: a sum considerably less than the ten pounds, which, in English equity law, is deemed so very a trifle as not to be worth restoring to a man who is unjustly deprived of it. One would think that all the absurdity in human nature had crowded itself into the department of science in which the demand for intelligence is the most urgent.

In the same code, the oath, though little more than a tenth of the length of the Danish explication, is still too long for ordinary occasions. It occupies a dozen quarto lines.‡ No written exposition here, as, on extraordinary occasions, in the Danish code: but, whatever be the occasion, the witness is condemned to hear, and the judge to pronounce, on the subject of it, an extempore admonition, which may be of any length. Much scope for eloquence is not indeed afforded to the sermon, where the text is no more than forty dollars. The pain of being *intestabilis* (whatever be meant by *intestabilis*) will not make any very efficient addition to the dollars: if the privilege from which a man is debarred be the making of a will, the terror will not be very great where he has nothing to leave, or is satisfied with the will that the law has made for him: if it be that of serving again as a witness, it is so much trouble saved, the

* Halhed's Code of Gentoo Law, pp. 129, 130.
† Ibid. p. 130. See above, p. 262.

‡ Page 364.

only inconvenience being to a possible somebody else, whom he does not care about: unless the case be his own, and then the exclusion may cost him his life.

§ 6. *Should an oath, if employed in other cases, be employed or not on the examination of a defendant* in penali?

When a defendant, in a cause of a penal nature, is examined — in other words, where the testimony extracted or received is of the self-regarding kind, and, in the event of conviction, self-disserving, and self-convicting, — shall an oath be administered to him or not? If not, then the security thus afforded for veracity is left unemployed: and in what cases? In those in which the discovery of the truth is of most importance. If the ceremony be extended to these cases, then comes a hardship, which to some eyes may be apt to appear so tremendous as to be intolerable. In case of perjury, the suffering, being supernatural, may be infinite; while, in case of delinquency, such is the frailty of human nature, more particularly in so guilty a bosom, that the temptation to incur this infinite punishment may be irresistible.

Another difficulty. Suppose it desirable, that, under such circumstances, a defendant should take the oath: what if he refuse? Acquiesce in the refusal, the security is lost, —lost to the most important class of causes. Refuse to acquiesce in the refusal, what resource is there for compelling it? To endeavour to compel it, is but in other words to employ torture. But admitting torture to be a warrantable expedient in any case, is this a case in which to employ it?

Not to pursue, as it were in a parenthesis, an inquiry of such intricacy, a solution for the difficulty presents itself, and such a one as seems equally simple and unexceptionable. Tender the oath: if he accepts it, swear him; if he declines it, do not attempt to force him, but warn him of the inference. From a refusal to take the oath (particular religious persuasions excepted) the inference — an inference which, at the suggestion of common sense, every man will draw immediately, — is exactly the same as that which would be drawn from non-responsion under the oath, or from non-responsion on an occasion of an extrajudicial nature, and which accordingly admits not of an oath.

This course seems to be equally advantageous, whether guilt be supposed, or innocence. In case of innocence, all objection vanishes: being innocent, a man embraces with alacrity this as well as every other means of impressing the court with the persuasion of his innocence. In case of guilt, if he declines taking the oath, a species of circumstantial evidence operating in proof of the guilt — a sort of evidence tantamount to non-responsion, is thus obtained. If, notwithstanding his guilt, and thence his consciousness of guilt, he takes the oath — takes it in the view of avoiding to bring to bear against himself that species of circumstantial criminative evidence, — a result more or less probable is, that, to the symptoms of perturbation produced in his deportment by the apprehension of the legal punishment which he has incurred, may be added those of an ulterior degree of perturbation, produced by the contemplation of the guilt of perjury.

Will it again be said — still you ought not thus to lay snares for consciences; it is cruel, for any temporal advantage, thus to subject a sinful soul to so serious an addition to its guilt? If this reasoning were conclusive, you should abstain from the use of this security altogether: in cases non-penal, as well as penal — in the case of extraneous, as well as in that of self-regarding, testimony; wherever you saw a man determined, as you thought, to commit perjury, this security for veracity ought, in that instance, to be laid aside: the more hardened and determined in mendacity a man were, the more safe.

The mischievous consequences that would ensue from the notion that the profanation of the ceremony were accompanied with any guilt, moral or religious, over and above whatever may be attached to the mendacity by which the profanation is effected, have been already stated: together with the radical incongruity and inconsistency attached to the notion of a frail and weak being, such as a man, disposing, at his pleasure, of the power of a Being all-powerful and all-wise. If the conclusion be just, the above objection, respecting the peril of future supernatural punishment, falls to the ground.

At any rate, the objection can never come with any tolerable consistency or grace from the lips of any one by whom the application made of this ceremony to the function of a juryman, on the occasion of an English trial, is approved. An oath, forced into the mouth of twelve such judges, to oblige them to declare their real opinion; and torture applied to force some number of them, in case of diversity of opinion, to declare (each of them) that to be his opinion which is not! — a mode of judicature so contrived that it could not go on, unless the judges, in unknown numbers, were continually forced by torture into perjury!

True it is, that the incongruity of one such practice does not give congruity to another: but if, for fashion's sake, a certain quantity of perjury must at all events be preserved, better preserve a sort which is of some use, than a sort which is as useless, as in every other point of view it is incongruous.*

* For the principal alterations in the law regarding oaths, which have taken place since the above chapter was first published, *vide supra*, pp. 312 & 316, and Vol. V. p. 188.

CHAPTER VII.

OF SHAME, CONSIDERED AS A SECURITY FOR THE TRUSTWORTHINESS OF TESTIMONY.

Shame may be considered as operating in the character of a security for trustworthiness in testimony, in so far as, on the occasion of a man's delivering testimony, the contempt or ill-will of any person or persons is understood to attach, or apprehended as being about to attach, upon a deviation, on his part, from the line of truth.

Shame, it is but too evident, in the character of a principle of action, cannot upon all occasions be relied upon as a sufficient security, without the aid of legal punishment. Some men are below shame; some men are above it. Power will, in some situations, place a man above shame. In England, however, power is hardly sufficient to place a man above shame, without a pedestal of false science. In England, a king, were he ever so much inclined, could scarce dare to deliver a notorious falsehood from the throne. In the same country, however, no judge (I except always the judges for the time being) ever yet feared to deliver from the bench notorious falsehoods, under the name of fictions (and the whole system of common law procedure is made up of fiction) — or to suborn jurymen to deliver falsehoods not less notorious, and aggravated into perjury.

Happily, however, for mankind, shame, in this its character of a security for trustworthiness, is not altogether without its influence on uncorrupted minds, — I mean on minds which, howsoever it may be in respect of corruption from other sources, have not the misfortune to be exposed to that corruption which is poured down in such torrents from the heights of English judicature.

In the Danish courts of justice denominated *Reconciliation Offices*, oath is out of the question, punishment is out of the question; truth has no other support than the sentiment of shame. Yet, strange to tell — strange at any rate to an English ear — more causes in that country are determined in these courts, from which the professional lawyer is excluded, than in all the courts put together in which the system of technical procedure, with its apparatus of oaths and punishments, bears sway.

Even in England, cases in which the only punishment that bears upon the case is that which consists in shame, are neither unknown to lawyers, nor unheeded by the legislature. Awards, for the correctness and completeness of the testimony on which they are grounded, having nothing else to trust to: and by an act of the legislature,* the power of the regular tribunals is applied to the giving force to these decisions — decisions pronounced by judges, learned or unlearned, constituted by the joint choice of the parties.†

The force of the moral sanction, as applied to this purpose, is a most commodious and valuable supplement to that of the political. It condemns upon less evidence: it inflicts a punishment *pro more probationum*, reduced in intensity in proportion to the faintness of the evidence: it admits of a middle course between condemnation and acquittal — an expedient which in general cannot be, or at least is not usually, resorted to by the punishment of the political sanction, as applied by judicial procedure: upon the appearance of fresh lights, it is able, without difficulty, to divest itself of any such undecided character, and either fill up the measure of its punishment, or strike it off altogether, according to the complexion of the case.

Much of that which appears to be done by fear of punishment alone, is really done by fear of shame — a fear which, howsoever backed and strengthened by fear of punishment, would not of itself have been by any means without effect.

In the course of this work, we shall have but too frequent occasion to observe the debility that has been introduced into the constitution of the political sanction by the rashness that has given birth to the established rules of evidence. In these cases, the force of the moral sanction — the force of public opinion — steps in, and supplies to a certain degree (however incompletely) the place of that force which, by the unskilfulness of the commanders, has thus been rendered unserviceable. It prevents nominal and apparent impunity from being altogether equivalent to real; and helps to moderate, when it does not do away entirely, the triumph of successful guilt.

When accused for the purpose of punishment, a delinquent, in escaping from punishment, does not always escape from shame. Judges, when by their quibbles — statesmen, when by their intrigues with judges — they save a man from merited punishment, do not always save him from shame. Judge and Co., in selling exemption from punishment,‡ and thus far impunity, do not — cannot (where evidence is heard, and not excluded by other quibbles) sell exemption from shame.

* 9 and 10 W. III. c. 15, anno 1698.

† If, previously to any regular application to a technically proceeding tribunal, a plaintiff were obliged to address his demands in the first instance to a tribunal proceeding in the mode indicated by natural justice, these arbitration courts would in that respect coincide in their nature with the Danish Reconciliation Offices. But these occasional arbitration courts not having existence but by the joint act of both parties, such coincidence is impossible.

‡ *Vide infrà*, Book VIII. *Technical Procedure*, Chap. XIV. *Nullification*.

To the efficiency of this security, unhappily the limits are but too apparent. Shame, to constitute on this occasion an adequate succedaneum to legal punishment, supposes on the part of the deponent a certain degree of moral sensibility—a certain degree of probity. But, be that degree what it may, the cases in which the demand for coercive judicature is the most urgent, are those in which no such degree of probity is to be found.

On this as on every other occasion, the influence of shame depends, in no small degree, upon mutual presence—upon the interchange of the language of the eye, between those on whose part the contempt and ill-will is apprehended, and him in whose breast the apprehension of those sources of incalculable affliction is excited.

On this account, the influence of shame is attached, in no small degree, to that mode of collection in which the testimony is delivered *vivâ voce* — delivered by the deponent in the presence, if not of the adversary, at any rate of a judge, or (what is most usual) an assembly of judges, with his or their ministerial officers and subordinates.

Accordingly, in the procedure of the Danish Reconciliation Courts, this mode of delivery is an essential feature. On the part of the party, or (what comes to the same thing) a non-professional substitute by whose acts and words he is bound — personal appearance, — not sham personal appearance, as at the English regular courts, but real personal appearance — attendance (by what words shall the idea be conveyed to the mind of an English lawyer?)—is an indispensable requisite.

The natural securities for trustworthiness in testimony have been adverted to in the preceding Book:* and of these, that for the designation of which the word *shame* is here employed, was one. In the present Book, this same principle of action has been comprised in the list of factitious instituted securities. Why? Because to this security, standing by itself, no inconsiderable part of the business of factitious judicature hath, as we have seen, been entrusted: because, in the instance of the Danish Reconciliation Courts, the admission of this security, to the exclusion of factitious punishment, required and called forth a positive act of the Danish legislature: and because the choice of that mode of testification, on which the efficacy of this principle of action in so great a degree depends, is another positive institution, in the establishment of which the will of the sovereign must take an active part.

When punishment, factitious punishment, to be attached to the species of delinquency in question by an express act of will to be exercised by the legislator, was the principle of action in question, — rules were found necessary to be brought to view, for the purpose of guiding the application of it: rules, the demand for which, on this occasion as on others, had been created by non-observance. The legislator, on this as on so many other occasions, acting under the guidance of hands engaged by interest to mislead him, has on this as on so many other occasions, acted in continual opposition to the dictates of utility and justice.

The public, whose finger, on this as on so many occasions, the power of shame is in the habit of following, with a degree of obsequiousness such as it knows better than to bestow upon the "finger of the law;"— the public, in its application of the principle of shame to the subject in question (in so far as the force of that principle is at its disposal,) is already in the habit of following those same rules, which, for the direction of the force of legal punishment, it became necessary, as above, to bring to view.

1. Applied to falsehood in the shape of testimony, punishment (says one of these rules) should attach upon temerity, as well as upon mendacity. And so, under the dispensation of the tribunal of public opinion, does the punishment of shame: making the proper distinction between the degrees of delinquency in the two cases.

2. Applied to falsehood in the shape of testimony, punishment (says another of these rules) should apply to every occasion without exception, in which it is uttered in that shape. And so, with this unerring and unsleeping steadiness, under the uncorrupted dispensation of the tribunal of public opinion, does the punishment of shame: making (in proportion to the instruction it has imbibed from the principle of utility) a distinction, in respect of the severity of its punishment, corresponding to the shades of depravity dependent on the occasion on which it may happen to falsehood to be uttered in this shape.

As to the remaining rules brought to view under that head, they will be seen to bear no application to the present purpose.

CHAPTER VIII.

OF WRITING, CONSIDERED AS A SECURITY FOR THE TRUSTWORTHINESS OF TESTIMONY.

THE art of writing, besides its other infinitely diversified applications, has been productive of such important effects, good and bad, in relation to evidence, and thence (as well as in many other ways) to judicature,—that a few words, for the purpose of giving a general and comprehensive view of its application in both directions — in the way of conducive-

* Book I. Chap. XI. *Moral causes of correctness and completeness.*

ness, and in the way of opposition, to the ends of justice, — may not be misemployed.

Of this inquiry the practical object is almost too obvious to need mentioning: to prepare the mind of the legislator, on the one hand, for pushing to its maximum the use — on the other, for reducing to its minimum the abuse — of so powerful an instrument in the hand of justice or injustice.

In this, as in so many other instances, the union between the use and the abuse is unhappily but too close: the chemistry by which they may be separated, and the abuse precipitated, is not of easy practice.

In the character of an external security for the correctness and completeness of testimony, the uses of writing are as obvious as they are various: —

1. Of *distinctness* it is oftentimes a necessary instrument. Where the mass of testimony is small, — the string of facts requiring to be brought to view short, — the employment of this security may be unnecessary. But, let the mass be swollen to a certain bulk, — the deponent who is able to give it the distinctness requisite for producing a clear conception of the whole in the mind of the judge, without using a pen of his own, or borrowing that of another, will not often be to be found.*

2. In the same case, the use of it to the purpose of *recollection* — complete as well as correct recollection — may be equally indispensable. Accordingly — where writing is in common use, and testimony (as under English law) is delivered *vivâ voce*, and the transaction of which a man has been a percipient witness, has, in respect of its importance, appeared to him to be of a nature to create a probable demand for future testimony — it is no uncommon incident for a man to have given ease and certainty to his memory, by committing to writing a statement of the perceptions entertained by him at the time; and by English practice, such memoranda are allowed to be consulted by him while he is in the act of delivering his evidence. At any rate, if interrogation be employed for the extraction of the testimony, and the string of questions be long, and presented to the witness, all of them, or a considerable number, at a time, the having the questions in writing, for the purpose of giving occasional refreshment to the memory under the burthen thus laid upon it, may be altogether indispensable. For, in this case, it is not sufficient for a man to recollect the perceptions presented to him at the time by the mass of facts in question; he must, besides this, have continually present to his mind the conception of the several questions put to him — of the several facts to which he has thus been called upon to depose.

3. It is to the art of writing that testimony is altogether indebted for the quality of *permanence*, and thence for the security which that quality affords for the correctness, as well as completeness, of whatever testimony has been delivered: understand, for its correctness and completeness (when it has swelled to a certain bulk) on any day, not to say hour or minute, subsequent to that on which it has been delivered.

4. One case there is, and that of no small extent, in which testimony is indebted to writing for its very *existence*. This is where, for any cause, the appearance of the witness (the percipient witness) at the judgment-seat — the place where the judicial testimony would have been to be delivered — either is physically, or is deemed to be prudentially, impracticable.†

In every such case, were if not for the use of writing, either the testimony would be altogether lost, or if delivered at all, it would not be delivered without being degraded from the rank of immediate to that of hearsay evidence: suffering thereby, in point of trustworthiness, that defalcation, the nature and value of which will be brought to view in its place.‡

Such is the importance of good judicature to general civilization — such the importance of writing to good judicature—that, — independently of the application of this master art to the several other departments of government, — the absence of it as applied to *judica-*

* On this occasion, a distinction necessary to be kept in view is the distinction between the effect of the *vivâ voce* mode on the quality, the distinctness, of the *testimony* itself, — and the effect of the same mode on the *conception* capable of being formed and retained, in relation to that same testimony, by the judge. On the part of the testimony itself, *vivâ voce* delivery (coupled, as it must be, with *vivâ voce* interrogation) may often be a necessary bar to the indefinite accumulation of irrelevant matter, and consequent increase of indistinctness: on the part of the conception formed of it by those by whom a judgment on it is to be formed, all chance of adequate distinctness would soon vanish, if the assistance of the art of writing were not called in, to give permanence to the words to which it has been consigned.

† As on other occasions, so on the occasion of any operations which may come to be performed in relation to evidence, impracticability may be distinguished into *physical* and *prudential*.

By a case of *physical* impracticability, I ununderstand that case in which the effect in question cannot be produced, or the act in question performed, on any terms.

By a case of *prudential* impracticability, I understand that case in which the effect, whether physically producible or no — the act, whether physically performable or no — cannot (it is supposed) be produced or performed, without the production of a preponderant quantity (probability being in both cases taken into the account) of inconvenience, in the shape of delay, vexation, and expense.

‡ Book VI. *Makeshift*, Chapters III. & IV.

ture would of itself (it is probable) have been sufficient to stop the progress of civilization at a stage greatly below any that we see at present anywhere in Europe.

Causes of a certain degree of simplicity, — and happily the great majority of causes are within this desirable degree,—may, supposing probity on the part of the judicatory, be tolerably well decided without writing: because decision may follow upon evidence before the memory of it in the breast of the judge is become incorrect or incomplete. In a cause involved in a certain degree of complication, the use of writing is in a manner necessary to good judicature. But civilization must have stopped far short of its present advanced stage, if complicated causes had not been susceptible of just decision as well as simple ones.

If, under natural procedure (as in the small debt courts) causes are in general sufficiently well decided without the committing of the evidence to writing, it is because the description of the case is there so extremely simple: and even in these cases, security against misdecision is sacrificed in some degree to the avoidance of vexation and expense.

But though, in respect of their number, the causes simple enough to have been suffered to be decided in the way of natural procedure constitute the most important class; yet, individually taken, causes in the highest degree complicated, possess, in general (so far as property is concerned) a proportionable degree of importance: witness bankruptcy causes, and causes relative to testaments, in each of which property to the amount of millions may be at stake upon a single cause.

If such be the importance of writing, even on the supposition of undeviating probity on the part of the judicatory, its importance is in a much higher degree exemplified in the character of a security against improbity: and, in particular, in the character of an instrument of extensive and lasting publication.

As it is only by writing that the grounds of decision can be made known, beyond the narrow circle composed of the few by-standers; hence, without writing, there can be no tolerably adequate responsibility on the part of the judge. But for writing, a single judge would decide on every occasion as he pleased: an oligarchical bench of judges, as they could agree; a democratical bench (as indeed it is too apt to be the case, notwithstanding the benefit of writing,) — a bench, howsoever composed, if the number be such that the idea of individual responsibility is destroyed, — would decide according to the caprice or passion of the moment.

Of the deplorable state in which, for want of the application of writing to this purpose, the business of judicature may be left in a democratically-constituted tribunal (a tribunal composed of a numerous assemblage of judges, no matter of what rank,) the character of Election Judicature in the House of Commons antecedently to the Grenville Act, will afford an impressive example. Under favour of the confusion, — the absolute want of all permanent memorials of the grounds which the several suffrages had to rest upon, — and the consequent mischief, the equally complete want of all individual responsibility, — no man's vote was ever grounded on any other considerations than those of personal convenience.*

By adding to the *natural* and unavoidable degree of complexity attached to the cause, a suitable dose of *factitious*, a party in the wrong (especially if favoured by the co-operation of a colluding judge) may give to his bad title an equal chance with the best one.

By lumping charges together, and (after a lumping mass of proof) pronouncing a lumping judgment on the whole mass, — a precedent has been set,† under which a delinquent's chance of impunity is not in the inverse, but in the direct ratio of the number of his crimes. Such judicature having been found practicable, notwithstanding the check applied by the art of writing, what would it have been without that check?

In the cases of Peru, Mexico, and Tlascala, may be seen a specimen of what degree of civilization it is possible for society to reach without the application of writing to the fixation of the grounds of decision in judicature: higher than in those instances it could hardly have risen without that help.

In its original constitution, jury-trial, being unaided by writing, would in England have been sufficient to confine civilization within bounds as narrow as those which circumscribed it in Peru, Mexico, and Tlascala. If, under jury-trial, writing has latterly been applied to the fixation of the grounds of decision, it is unhappily in but an accidental and imperfect way. Hence it has happened, that, in cases to a certain degree complicated, this mode of judicature is seen to be inapplicable; being in some cases recognised as such by established

* The great Douglas cause, and the trial of Mr. Hastings, will by many be regarded as exemplifications of a similar result produced by an opposite cause. Why? Because, where writing is concerned, too much may have the effect of too little. By supersaturation, as well as by inanition, the powers of the mind, as well as those of the body, may be destroyed.

If, of the want, or (what may in an extraordinary case be equivalent) of the superabundance, of permanent grounds of judicial decision, the effect has been so disastrous in modern England, notwithstanding its acknowledged pre-eminence in judicial purity,—how much more frequently, not to say constantly, must it have been so, in ages of far inferior morality, under the tumultuary constitution of Athenian or Roman judicature!

† See the Trial of Warren Hastings.

usage, equivalent in force to law—in others, though not by law, in necessary practice.

Writing being of use, and frequently in a great degree even matter of necessity, in all stages of the suit; so is it in the hands of all classes of persons concerned in it.

In the hands of the parties, it serves to give permanence to evidence — to constitute the matter of the instruments exhibited in the character of sources of evidence.

In the hands of the judge, and his official subordinates, it serves to preserve the memory of operations —to *register*, to record, to consign to permanent characters, in proportion as they are performed, the fact of their having been so.

But the delivery of an instrument to this or that effect, is itself a capital article in the catalogue of those operations. Hence registration of instruments, as well as of operations, falls naturally within the province of the judge.

The indication which has been given of the uses of writing, as applied to the subject of evidence, has a sort of claim to be accompanied with a correspondent sketch of its uses, as applied to the business of registration.

Subjects for judicial registration, with their uses: —

1. Representation of operations successively performed, and instruments successively presented, for the purpose of grounding such subsequent operations and instruments, as may come to be called for, or warranted, by such preceding ones.

2. Representation of operations performed, and orders given, or other instruments made, by or under the authority of the judge, on the occasion of the operations and instruments emanating from the parties as above.

3. Grounds and reasons of such operations and instruments, as aforesaid, on the part of the judge.

N.B. To be of use, these grounds and reasons will not consist of argumentation uttered on each occasion by the judge himself, but of the indications given of so many matters of fact brought to light in the course of the cause — indications given in the concisest possible form, under heads prescribed by the legislator for that purpose.

4. At the special instance of either party, this or that proposition, or even word, that may have dropt from the lips of the judge. In the particular suit upon the carpet, be the importance of the subject-matter in dispute ever so trifling, the language used by the judge may be to any degree important. By language (not to speak of deportment, which is not so easily rendered the subject of registration,) disposition is manifested: and, in a judge, the effects of disposition extend to whatever suits are liable to come under his cognizance. Not a blemish of which the judicial character is susceptible, but language may have served for the manifestation of it.

In each house of parliament, whatever word is spoken by any member, is liable to be taken down at the instance of any other. This check, instead of being an infringement, is the most efficient security for that just liberty of speech, without which such assemblies would be worse than useless. The beneficial efficacy is in reality the greater, in proportion as it is less manifested: it is composed of the improprieties that but for this check might have been uttered, but are not uttered.

In the practice of the courts of justice (the regular courts) this institution is not without example. Witness the bill of exceptions. But in that instance the application of it is confined within narrow limits: whereas there, as in parliament, the demand for it has no limits.

Uses of the above registrations: —

1. To the several parties, on the occasion of the suit in hand, the use of them, in a direct way, is already evident.

2. So, in a less direct way, in respect of the check they apply to abuse in every shape on the part of the judge,—corruption, undue sympathy, antipathy, precipitation through impatience, delay through indifference and negligence.

3. With a view to appeal on the occasion of the suit in hand,— the service capable of being rendered by such registration to both parties (and especially to him who is in the right,) by the complete and correct indication of all grounds of appeal, justly or unjustly alleged, seems alike evident.

4. In respect of future contingent suits, considered as capable of being produced, prevented, or governed, by the result of, or previous proceedings in, the cause in hand,— suits considered as liable to arise between the same parties, or their legal representatives, — the utility is alike manifest.

5. In respect of future contingent suits, considered as liable to be produced by like causes, or to give birth to like incidents and occurrences,—causes as between other parties having no connexion with those in question; the use of such registration in the character of a stock of precedents seems alike indisputable.

The service thus capable of being rendered, will be rendered partly to individuals at large, in the character of eventual suitors in such eventual causes, in respect of their respective interests; partly to the judge, in respect of security, facility, and tranquillity, in the execution of his official duty.

6. To the legislator, the guardian of the people, and through him to the people at large, the service rendered by the aggregate

mass of the facts thus registered, will be seen to be more and more important, the more closely it is considered.

By the abstracts made of the body of information thus collected (abstracts prepared under a system of appropriate heads, and periodically presented and made public,) he will see throughout in what respects the existing arrangements fulfil — in what respects (if in any) they fail of fulfilling — his intentions: how far they are conducive — in what respects (if in any) they fail of being perfectly conducive, — to the several ends of justice.

With the sketch of what is here stated as capable of being done, confront the loose sketches that will hereafter come to be given of what is actually established: the difference between use and abuse will present itself in colours not very obscure.

If the services thus rendered to the interests of truth and justice by the art of writing are thus great, neither are the ways in which it is liable to be made to operate, and to a great extent is continually made to operate, to the injury of those interests, by any means inconsiderable.

1. If, on certain occasions, and in certain ways, it is capable of being employed as an instrument of distinctness for giving that indispensable quality to a mass of evidence, — on other occasions, and in other ways, it is but too apt to be employed in such a manner as to give to the evidence a degree of indistinctness, from which, but for the abuse made of this important art, it would have been free.

The reason (meaning the cause) of this abuse is extremely simple. To the quantity of irrelevant matter, to which (under the spur of sinister interest) the pen of a writer is, on this, as on so many other occasions, capable of giving birth, there are no determinate limits: nor yet to the degree of disorder, and consequent indistinctness, with which the whole mass, made up of irrelevant and relevant matter jumbled together, may be infected: and the same mischief which thus, to an infinite degree, is liable to be produced by *mala fides* on the part of the suitor or his professional assistant, may (though in a less degree) be produced by mere weakness of mind on either part: whereas, in the case of *vivâ voce* testimony extracted by, or substituted to, interrogation, — no sooner does an irrelevant proposition make its appearance, than the current of the testimony in that devious direction is stopped, and the stream forced back into its proper channel.

2. When writing is employed in the extraction, and thence in the delivery, of the testimony, — time applicable, and but too often applied, to the purpose of mendacious invention, is a natural, and practically (though not strictly and physically) inseparable, result, as will be seen more particularly in its place.*

3. In the same case, a result no less closely connected with the use of writing than the former, is the opportunity afforded by it for receiving mendacity-serving information from all sorts of sources—a danger from which *vivâ voce* deposition, though by no means exempt, is more easily guarded.

On the other hand,—where writing is employed for the delivery and extraction of evidence, the superior facility which it affords for planning the means of deception is accompanied, and in a considerable degree counteracted and compensated on the part of the adverse party and the judge, by a correspondent quantity of time (and thence a correspondent means) applicable to the purpose of scrutinizing the supposed mendacious testimony, and so divesting it of its deceptitious influence.

Hitherto we have considered the art in no other light than that of its capacity of being made subservient to the purposes of that species of injustice which is opposite to the *direct* end of justice: subservient to deception, and thence to misdecision.

But the grand abuse, and that in comparison of which what has hitherto been brought to view shrinks almost into insignificance, is the perverted application that has been made of it to the purposes of that branch of injustice which stands opposed to the *collateral* ends of justice — of that branch of injustice which consists of factitious delay, vexation, and expense, heaped together for the sake of the profit extractible and extracted from the expense.

In a word, it is in the art of writing thus perverted, that we may view the main instrument of the technical system, and of all the abominations of which it is composed—an instrument by which this baneful system, wheresoever established, has all along operated, and without which it could scarcely have come anywhere into existence.

It is on pretence of something that has been written, or that might, could, or should have been written, that whatever portion of the means of sustenance has, on the occasion, or on the pretence of administering justice, been wrung from the unfortunate suitor, has been demanded and received. Statements that ought not to have been made, have, to an enormous extent, been made: statements that required to be made, have been swelled out beyond all bounds — stuffed out with words and lines and pages of surplusage, oftentimes without truth, sometimes even without meaning, and always without use. This excrementitious matter has been made up into all the forms that the conjunct industry of the demon

* See Book III. *Extraction.*

of mendacity, seconded by the genius of nonsense, could contrive to give to it. Having, by the accumulated labours of successive generations, been wrought up to the highest possible pitch of voluminousness, indistinctness, and unintelligibility; in this state it has been locked up and concealed from general view as effectually as possible. In England it has been locked up in two several languages, both of them completely unintelligible to the vast majority of the people: office upon office, profession upon profession, have been established for the manufacturing, warehousing, and vending of this intellectual poison. In the capacity of suitors, the whole body of the people (able or unable to bear the charge) are compelled to pay, on one occasion or another, for everything that was done, or suffered or pretended to be done, in relation to it — for writing it, for copying it, for abridging it, for looking at it, for employing others to look at it, for employing others to understand it, or to pretend to understand it; interpreting and expounding imaginary laws, laws that no man ever made.

Thus much for this branch of the abuse: thus much for a bird's-eye, or rather an aerostatic, view of it. To consider it heap by heap, is a task that belongs not to this place — a labour that will continue to press upon us through every part of this toilsome and thankless course.

The uses and the abuses of writing in judicial procedure have now been briefly enumerated: the various arrangements which have for their object to bring the use to its maximum, and the abuse to its minimum, will be severally brought to view in the proper place.

CHAPTER IX.

OF INTERROGATION, CONSIDERED AS A SECURITY FOR THE TRUSTWORTHINESS OF TESTIMONY.

§ 1. *Uses of interrogation, as applied to the extraction of testimony.*

In the character of a security for the correctness and completeness of testimony, so obvious is the utility and importance of the faculty and practice of interrogation, that the mention of it in this view might well be deemed superfluous, were it not for the cases, to so prodigious an extent, in which, under English law, it is barred out by judicial practice.

1. The case in which its utility is most conspicuous, is that of *mala fides* on the part of the deponent; and this, being a state of things which in each individual instance may (for aught the legislator can know) have place, is a state of things for which, on every occasion, in the arrangements taken by him, provision ought to be made.

Completeness is the primary quality, with reference to which the demand for it is most obvious: fear of punishment and fear of shame having here less influence than as applied to secure correctness. In case of incompleteness, neither punishment nor shame apply, any further than as it is established that the omitted part came under the perception of the deponent, preserved a place in his remembrance, and presented to him, along with itself, the idea of its importance.

Importance being assumed, incompleteness may indeed become equivalent to, and a modification of incorrectness: but in general it is by interrogation, and by interrogation only, that it is rendered so.

Do you remember nothing more? did nothing further pass, relative to this or that person or thing (naming them?) By interrogations thus pointed, such a security for completeness is afforded, as can never be afforded by any general engagement which can be included in the terms of an oath or other formulary: be the engagement what it may, in the course of the deposition the memory of it may have evaporated: and suppose it borne in mind — yet, without the aid of interrogation, the violation of it by suppression of the truth loses its best chance of detection.

2. *Particularity*, if it be not included under the notion of completeness, is no less indispensable to the purposes of testimony. But suppose a deposition delivered, and, in so essential a point, a deficiency remaining in it; by what means, if at all, shall the defect be supplied? Interrogation, it is evident, is the sole resource.

By particularity only can that repugnancy to known truths be established, by which mendacity is demonstrated.

Under what tree was the act committed? was the question put by the prophet Daniel to each of the two calumnious elders. Under a holme tree, answered the one: under a mastic tree, answered the other. But for the proof of mendacity, the question would have been irrelevant and superfluous; for, supposing the forbidden act committed, what mattered under what tree, or whether under any tree? But, for the detection of mendacity, no question that can contribute anything, can be irrelevant; and the more particular, the better its chance of being productive of so desirable an effect.

By interrogation, and not without, is the improbity of a deponent driven out of all its holds. An answer being given, is it true? It is useful in the character of direct evidence. Is it false? It stands exposed to contradiction, both from within and from without: and, being detected, it operates as an evidence of character and disposition, and thence in the way of circumstantial evidence. Is silence, pure silence, the result? Even this is evidence, circumstantial evidence. The deponent, — is he an extraneous witness? According to the nature of the question, it may afford as impressive a presumption of falsehood, antecedent or subsequent, as could have been afforded by detected falsehood. Is he a party to the cause? Besides the particular mendacity, it may afford a presumption of his own consciousness of the badness of his cause.

The testimony, is it indistinct, nugatory, unintelligible? Such indistinctness, if persevered in, and not the result of mental infirmity, is equivalent to silence.

In no case, be the sincerity of the deponent ever so unquestionable — in no case, either to completeness or correctness, can the faculty of interrogation be a matter of indifference, not even in ordinary conversation between bosom friends.

What father could be satisfied with the narrative of a long lost child, — what lover with that of his mistress,—without a possibility of perfecting his satisfaction by questions?

In no state can a deponent's mind be, in respect to interest, but that interrogation may be necessary to the purpose as well of correctness as of completeness.

In every possible result, does he behold an event of the most consummate indifference? A fact really important may be left out of his narrative, either because not recollected at the time, or because, though recollected, its materiality, with regard to the cause, had not presented itself to his view.

Is he even desirous and eager to bring forward every circumstance that can serve the party by whom his testimony has been invoked? Still a circumstance may have been forgotten, or its materiality have escaped notice.

Supposing even a party in the cause — say a plaintiff — adducing his own testimony, deposing in support of his own demand (under English law, a state of things rarely exemplified in form, but in substance frequently:) a poor person, say, prosecuting in the hope of recovering goods lost by stealth. With all the interest and all the will that can be imagined, intellectual power may be insufficient to bring to light, in a complete body, the material circumstances, without the aid of some superior intelligence in the character of an interrogator, in the person of an advocate or a judge.

In a word, — but for interrogation, every person interested, in whatever way interested, in the manifestation of truth, is completely dependent on the deponent: and on the state not only of the moral but of the intellectual part of the deponent's mind.

§ 2. *Exceptions to the application of interrogation to the extraction of testimony.*

Were security against deception and consequent misdecision the only object that had a claim to notice, the use of the security afforded by interrogation ought never to be foregone.

But, in this case as in all others, the mischief of that injustice which is opposite to the *direct* ends of justice, may find more than a counterpoise in mischief which is opposite to the *collateral* ends of justice, — inconvenience in the shapes of delay, vexation, and expense, jointly or even separately considered.

Take for examples the following cases, in which for avoidance of preponderant collateral injustice, it may happen that the security afforded by interrogation ought to be foregone; that is, in which it will generally or frequently happen, that the mischief resulting from the application of the security, will be greater in value (probability taken into the account) than any mischief that can take place for want of it.

1. Cases where the *delay* necessary to interrogation may be productive of irreparable damage: where, for example, the use of the evidence is to ground an application for stopping, 1. expatriation of the defendant, for avoidance of justiciability;* 2. exportation of property in his hands, for the like purpose; 3. deportation for the purpose of slavery; 4. deportation (the person a female) for the purpose of wrongful marriage or defilement; or, 5. wrongful destruction or deterioration of another's property, by operations clandestine or forcible. To form a ground for arrestation, seizure, sequestration, and so forth, on any of these accounts, testimony is requisite. If time admit of the subjecting this testimony to the scrutiny of judicial interrogation, so much the better; but if not, better that it be received and acted upon without the interrogation, than that any such irreparable mischief should be done.†

* A case for the writ called *ne exeat regno*, in English equity practice.

† In English law, in all the cases in which a man is laid provisionally under restraint *pendente lite*, the testimony on which the restriction is grounded is in the uninterrogated form, that of an affidavit.

For a debt above a certain value, a man is liable to be held to bail (that is, arrested, consigned to prison, and confined there for an indefinite time) unless he finds persons who engage for the eventual consignment of his person to the same fate. The testimony requisite to ground the warrant for this purpose, is the mass of sworn but uninterrogated deposition called an affidavit. What the affidavit must, though only in general terms, assert, is the justice of the claim: but what it need not assert, nor ever does assert, is the necessity of this legal infliction to secure the payment of the debt.

In some cases, a man, against whom another has a claim, may be stopped from going out of the kingdom; and, on this occasion likewise, to ground an application for this purpose, an affidavit is necessary. But, in this case, notice must be given, such as will in general enable the man

2. Cases where the benefit of the security afforded by interrogation may be outweighed by the expense unavoidably attached to the application of it: as, if the seat of the judicatory in which the decision is to be pronounced, be in London or Paris, and the evidence of the deponent in the East Indies.

To determine the preponderance, as between the mischief on the score of direct injustice, and the mischief on the score of collateral inconvenience in this shape, will be matter of detail for the legislator, and under him for the judge.

Interrogation in the epistolary mode, or by judges for the occasion, on the spot, affords, for the giving the evidence the benefit of this security, two other resources: either of which, where practicable, will be preferable to the receipt of the testimony in an uninterrogated state.

As to the case of *vexation*, independent of expense; examples of it will be seen to more advantage in another place; when the cases, where it is proper to put on that ground an absolute exclusion upon evidence, come to be considered.

Where, for the avoidance of collateral inconvenience in the shape of delay, vexation, and expense, the application of this security is dispensed with, the following rules are expressive of the *conditions* which seem proper to be annexed to the dispensation:—1. The exemption ought not to be absolute and definitive. The inconvenience being removed, either *in toto*, or to such a degree as to be no longer preponderant, interrogation ought to take place; either of course, or at the instance, of a party interested, or of the judge. 2. In a case where the deponent (he who has been deposing in the uninterrogated form) is liable as above to interrogation,—if his deposition was either delivered in the ready-written form, or, being delivered in the oral form, was committed thereupon to writing, for which purpose appropriate paper is employed; notice of the eventual interrogation ought to be inserted (as for example it is when ready printed) on the margin.

For, to the purpose of preventing *incorrectness* and *incompleteness* (preventing, in a word, the testimony from being rendered *deceptitious*) it is material that the deponent should be pre-apprized of the scrutiny which it may continually have to undergo: and, for making sure of his being thus pre-apprized, no other expedient can be more effectual than this simple and unexpensive one.

§ 3. *On whom ought interrogation to be performable?*

On whom? Answer: On every individual from whom, in the character of a deponent, testimony is received: saving the case of preponderant collateral inconvenience, as above.

If, at his own instance, at the instance of a co-party on the same side, or at the instance of his adversary, the testimony of a party (plaintiff or defendant) be received, it should of course, and for reasons not less cogent than in the case of an extraneous witness, be subjected to this scrutiny: and it will be shown elsewhere,* that, in no instance, in any of the above cases, should the testimony of a party stand excluded, or the measures proper and necessary for the extraction of it, if called for by an adverse party, be omitted: any more than in the case of an extraneous witness.

Official evidence presents a case in which the demand for interrogation on the score of security against mendacity, and thence against deception and misdecision, will, generally speaking, be at its *minimum:* while on the other hand, the inconvenience, in respect of vexation, may be at its *maximum*, comparison being made with individuals whose residence is at no greater distance: inconvenience, of which part will be to be placed to the account of the individual (the officer,) part to that of the public service.

But unless, by being placed in the office in question, a man is purified from all the infirmities (intellectual as well as moral) incident to human nature; in the instance of no such office can the exemption from this security be with propriety regarded as unconditional and definitive.

---

to get off. So in case of irreparable destruction meditated, time, such as in general will be sufficient, is in like manner allowed him to effect it.

In neither of these cases is the person, on whose uninterrogated deposition the act of power is grounded, liable to be ever subjected to interrogation in any case.

As to the stoppage of effects; for any such purpose the law affords no power on any terms.

In Scottish procedure, on the petition of an alleged creditor, any person may, by warrant from a justice of the peace, be arrested on the ground of his being *in meditatione fugæ*, and committed, until he finds security for "giving suit and presence in any action." But, before the warrant is granted, the petitioner appears before the justice, and is examined upon oath, producing a written account of the particulars of the alleged debt. In how high a degree this mode of procedure is preferable to the above English modes, will appear clear enough to any eye that is not averse to seeing it.[a] The fault, as is well observed by Mr. MacMillan, consists in the committing the alleged debtor to prison at once, without giving him an opportunity of being heard by the judge, and in his presence being confronted with the adversary: but this injustice is common to English, as well as Scottish law.[b]

[a] MacMillan's Form of Writings, Edinburgh, 1790, third edit. p. 389.

[b] The law of England on these points has been materially altered by 1 & 2 Vict. c. 110.

* Book IX. *Exclusion.* Part V. *Double Account.*

Applied to official testimony, the objection bears with considerably greater force on oral interrogation than on scriptitious: the oral being the only mode of the two, to which the vexation and expense incident to attendance (at the judicatory,) with journeys to and fro, and demurrage, is liable to be attached.

If the above observations be just, the practice of English law under the technical system must, in cases in great abundance and to a great extent, be radically vicious,—favourable to incorrectness, to incompleteness, to mendacity, to consequent deception and misdecision: — *affidavit* evidence (i. e. *uninterrogated* testimony) being received, and to the exclusion of interrogated testimony from the same individual, — on the *main* question, in a class of causes in great abundance and to a great extent, — and in causes of all classes, on those *incidental* questions by the determination of which the fate of the cause is liable to be, and frequently is, determined:— *official* evidence received without the security afforded by interrogation, as well as without the security afforded by the eventual subjection to that punishment, which, by the penal consequences attached to a violation of the ceremony of an oath, is hung over the head of mendacity at large: — and these securities against mendacity removed with particular care, in the instance of that class of official evidence (I speak of the sort of judicial evidence called a *record*,) each article of which is by no other circumstance so remarkably and incontestably distinguished from every other species of official evidence, as by its being replete with pernicious falsehoods: some with facility enough, others with more or less difficulty, capable of being distinguished from the small proportion of useful truths that are to be found in it.

§ 4. *By whom ought interrogation to be performable?*

To whom ought the power of interrogation to be imparted? Answer: To every person by whom it promises to be exercised with good effect: subject always to the controul of the judge, but for which, any power of command might, on this as well as on any other occasion, run into the wildest despotism.

And by whom is it likely to be exercised with good effect? Answer: By every person in whom suitable *will* and *power* are likely to be found conjoined. *Will*, the product of adequate *interest*, in the most extensive sense of the word, — *power*, consisting, in the present case, of appropriate information, accompanied with adequate ability of the intellectual kind.

Of the extent thus proposed to be given to the power of interrogation, the propriety stands expressed in the following aphorisms, which seem to claim a title to the appellation of axioms: —

1. For every interrogator, in whose person adequate interest and natural power unite, an additional security is afforded for correctness and completeness, and thence against mendacity and temerity on the one part and deception and misdecision on the other.

2. Against the admission of any proposed interrogator, no objection consistent with the ends of justice can be raised, on any other ground than that of mendacity-serving suggestion, or that of preponderant collateral inconvenience in the shape of delay, vexation, and expense: placing to the account of useless delay and vexation every proposed interrogation, that, in the judgment of the competent judge, is either *irrelevant* or *superfluous*.

The individuals in whose persons these requisites may be expected are,—1. The judge (including, in English jury-trial procedure, the jurymen, as well as the directing judge or judges;) 2. The plaintiff or plaintiffs; 3. The defendant or defendants; 4. The advocate or advocates of the plaintiff or plaintiffs; 5. The advocate or advocates of the defendant or defendants; 6. In some cases even extraneous witnesses.

There is a species of procedure in which there is no party on the plaintiff's side: in causes tried under this species of procedure, the function of the plaintiff is really exercised by the judge.

There is another species of procedure, in which there is no party on the defendant's side: in causes thus tried, the function of the defendant is exercised by the judge.

In causes of the above several descriptions, the number of possible interrogators suffers a correspondent reduction.*

---

* The following are cases, in which, if there be interrogation at all, there is but one person by whom it can be applied.

The occasion may be non-litigious or litigious: and, being litigious, the inquiry may be to be performed *ex parte* (on one side only,) or *reciprocally* (on more sides than one.)

1. Occasion non-litigious: an individual to deliver testimony; a judge, or a person acting on this occasion and *quoad hoc* in the character of a judge, to receive it: and either to act or not to act in consequence.

Examples: 1. Where a man makes application for money at a public office, as in England at the Exchequer, the Bank, and so forth. 2. Where a man, in the view of gaining general credence for certain facts, and of perpetuating the remembrance of them, comes forward of his own accord, and makes a solemn statement of them in the presence of a judge; as in England in the case of a voluntary affidavit sworn before a justice of the peace. 3. Inquiries carried on by a person or persons in the character of judges, for the purpose of bringing to light a particular class of facts, without any particular view to individual persons in the character of actors: as by a committee of either house of parliament, or by a commission of inquiry organized by the whole legislature.

When the list of characters capable of bearing a part on the theatre of justice is complete, there are, of proposed deponents, four descriptions; a plaintiff; a defendant; a witness (viz. an extraneous witness) called on the plaintiff's side; a witness called on the defendant's side.

Proposed interrogators, to each proposed deponent, seven. When the proposed deponent is the *plaintiff;* 1. the judge (including, in the case of jury trial, the several jurymen;) 2. this same plaintiff's own advocate; 3. any defendant or his advocate; 4. any co-plaintiff or his advocate; 5. any witness called by this same plaintiff; 6. any witness called by any defendant; 7. any witness called by a co-plaintiff.

From hence, *mutatis mutandis*, may be determined the correspondent proposable interrogators in the respective cases of the three other descriptions of proposed deponents. Proposed deponents, 4: to each one of them, proposed interrogators, 7: by multiplication, total number of cases for consideration, 28.*

If the principle above laid down be correct (viz., that, except as excepted, every interest ought to have its representative in the person of an interrogator,) a consequence which follows is—that, of the above eight and twenty cases of interrogation, in so many as under any system of procedure are peremptorily excluded from having place, so many cases of incongruity stand exemplified.

English common-law procedure exhibits a multitude of different modes of receiving and collecting testimony: Roman and Rome-bred procedure (including English equity, English ecclesiastical court, and English admiralty

In all these several cases, if the propriety of interrogation be supposed, the necessity of its being performed by the person standing *quoad hoc* in the station of judge, follows of course; there being no person else to perform it. In the third case, the interrogation is matter, not of propriety only, but necessity: in the two others, whether it be or be not matter of propriety belongs not to the present purpose.

II. The occasion litigious: but the examination, as yet at least, *unilateral:* on one side only. In this class of cases, the nature of the case affords but one person in a condition to be subjected to the operation; and but one person in a condition to perform it, viz. the judge. This case admits of the following modifications.

1. One person only as yet appearing to be interrogated, and he, as yet at least, not fixed in the character of a party, but examined (at least for the present) in the character of an extraneous witness: the deponent appearing at the judgment-seat, either spontaneously, or by order of the judge.

Example.—A dead body with marks of violence found by two persons in company. One of them gives information to an officer established for that purpose under the name of a coroner: the coroner by his warrant procures the attendance of the other. Both of them, together with such other persons as the nature of the case indicates as likely to be able to furnish information, are examined with a view of finding out the cause of the death. What may happen in this case is, that one of them shall, in the course of the inquiry, be fixed in the character of defendant; the other, in the character of plaintiff. Such, accordingly, was the result in the case of Captain Donnellan, executed for the murder of Sir Theodosius Boughton by poison.

2. One person only as yet appearing, and he in the character of a plaintiff, exhibiting in that character a criminal charge or non-criminal demand against a person not as yet appearing or having appeared. Examples in English law: 1. In regular procedure, application to a justice of the peace, by a person complaining of an assault, for a warrant to compel the appearance of the assailant. 2. In summary procedure, information given of an alleged offence to a justice of the peace, to ground a summons or warrant for compelling the appearance of the alleged delinquent.

3. One person only as yet appearing, and he in the character of a defendant: the function of plaintiff being (either throughout or in the first instance) united to that of judge. Example: in Roman law the species of procedure called *inquisitorial*, in contradistinction to *accusatorial*, which presents a distinct person in the character of plaintiff.

In these several cases likewise, if the propriety of interrogation be supposed, the necessity of its being performed by the judge follows of course, there being no other person to perform it.

* I. A plaintiff deposing, may be interrogated by or in behalf of the characters following: viz.

1. The judge.
2. His own advocate.
3. A co-plaintiff or his advocate.
4. A defendant or his advocate.
5. A witness called by himself.
6. A witness called by a co-plaintiff.
7. A witness called by a defendant.

II. A defendant deposing, may be interrogated by or in behalf of the characters following: viz.

1. The judge.
2. His own advocate.
3. A co-defendant or his advocate.
4. A plaintiff or his advocate.
5. A witness called by himself.
6. A witness called by a co-defendant.
7. A witness called by a plaintiff.

III. A witness (viz. an extraneous witness) called by the plaintiff, may be interrogated by or in behalf of the characters following: viz.

1. The judge.
2. The said plaintiff or his advocate.
3. Another plaintiff or his advocate.
4. A defendant or his advocate.
5. Another witness called by the plaintiff by whom he was called.
6. A witness called by another plaintiff.
7. A witness called by a defendant.

IV. A witness called by the defendant, may be interrogated by or in behalf of the characters following: viz.

1. The judge.
2. The said defendant or his advocate.
3. Another defendant or his advocate.
4. A plaintiff or his advocate.
5. Another witness called by the plaintiff by whom he was called.
6. A witness called by another plaintiff.
7. A witness called by a defendant.

court procedure) another multitude: in many, or most of them, the list of proposed deponents and interrogators is more or less different, and the difference not governed by any consistent regard (if by any regard at all) to the grounds of exception above brought to view. Of these established modes of practice, that all are wrong, will, if the above principle be correct, be found more than probable; that all are right, will be found absolutely impossible.

All the parties, and on both sides of the cause, have been placed upon the above list of persons, on whom, in the character of witnesses (each of them as well at his own instance and at the instance of a party on the same side of the cause, as at the instance of any party on the opposite side of the cause,) the process of interrogation may with propriety be performed. Under the established forms of procedure, under the general rule (so far as, in the midst of such diversity and inconsistency, anything under the name of a general rule can with propriety be spoken of,) both these classes of proposed deponents stand excluded: excluded, if proposed at their own instance or that of a party on the same side, on the score of *interest;* if proposed at the instance of the opposite side, excluded (principally in the case of a defendant) on the ground of *vexation.*

But on the ground of interest, so futile is the pretence, that, in cases where to any amount the impulse of sinister interest is more forcible, the exclusionary rule is itself excluded: and on the ground of vexation, when the vexation is not less galling, and (by reason of the inferiority of the species of evidence) attended with a much greater probability of deception and misdecision, the exclusion on this ground has no place: and moreover, at his own instance, the same party, who is not admitted in the guise of a party, is admitted with the sinister interest acting in full strength in his bosom, under a variety of disguises.*

In so great a multitude of proposed cases for interrogation, two clusters shall be here selected for special explanation: the case of the advocate under all its diversifications, and the case of the extraneous witness under all its diversifications. The other cases are sufficiently simple to require no special notice.

In case the second of the twenty-eight, it is assumed, that a plaintiff ought to be capable of being interrogated by his own advocate. To an English lawyer on one side of the great hall, the necessity of the admission will be apt to appear so palpable, that every word employed in proof of it would be so much thrown away. But on the other side of the same hall, the door of the evidence-collecting judicatory is inexorably shut against the interrogating advocate, as well as against every other interrogator but the underling, who to this purpose stands in the place of judge.

In the cases of interrogation here proposed, are included two assumptions: the propriety of admitting as the representative and assistant of a party, a person who is not a party; and the propriety of his being a professional advocate: the professional advocate being of course understood to be included under the appellation of advocate.

Of the occasional admission of a person in the character of an assistant to the party (supposing it a case in which admission may with propriety be given to the party himself,) the necessity stands demonstrated by the following causes of infirmity and relative incapacity, under which a party is liable to labour: 1. Infirmity from immaturity of age, or superannuation; 2. Bodily indisposition; 3. Mental imbecility; 4. Inexperience; 5. Natural timidity; 6. Female bashfulness; 7. Lowness of station, in either sex.

True it is that there sits a judge, whose duty (it may be said) is, on this occasion as on others, to act as an advocate — not indeed on either side, but on both.

But on the part of an advocate, to enable him to fulfil his duty in an adequate manner, two endowments are necessary: appropriate information in all its plenitude, and the zeal that is necessary to turn it to full account. On the part of a judge, neither requisite (in a measure sufficient for all causes, or even for the general run of causes,) can on any sufficient ground be expected: much less both.

In the particular case here supposed, the party is by the supposition, present: but he may be absent, and that unavoidably.

Of a substitute to the party, the necessity is co-extensive with the cases where the attendance of the party is either in the *physical* or the *prudential* sense impracticable.

On the occasion here in question, as on other judicial occasions, the necessity of giving admission to a professional advocate is indicated by the following considerations:—

1. An adequately qualified non-professional and gratuitous assistant or substitute would not always be to be had.

2. In so far as appropriate learning is necessary (and all the art, as well as all the power, of the profession has been employed for ages in rendering that necessity as universal and cogent as possible,) a non-professional assistant or substitute would very seldom be adequately qualified.

True it is that (so far as matter of fact only is in question) neither in point of appropriate information nor in point of zeal, can the professional advocate be naturally expected to be so much as upon a par with the friendly and unpaid substitute or assistant. Though

* See Book IX. *Exclusion.*

in practice Judge and Co. have taken too good care of themselves and one another not to exclude all such odious interlopers; yet the exclusion is the result of positive and abusive institution, not of the nature of the case.

Besides those which, as above, are the result of artifice, — two other advantages are, on the occasion in question, naturally enough attendant on the intervention of the professional, in contradistinction to the non-professional, advocate: advantages which may be reckoned as such, even with reference to the cause of justice.

But for this resource, a wrongdoer may, to the prejudice of the party wronged, possess on this occasion two advantages of a very oppressive nature: the advantage of the strong over the weak in mind; and the advantage of the high over the low in station. In a cause of a doubtful or intricate nature, nothing but such a union of talent and zealous probity, as would be too great to expect with reason on the part of an ordinary judge, more especially of a juryman, can prevent these advantages (even in a separate state, much more when united) from operating in a degree highly dangerous to justice. But, unless in case of a species of corruption, which is not of the number of those over which fashion throws its veil, the advocate is the same to all,—to low as well as high.

Unfortunately, however, in this supposition is included the being in a condition to purchase such high-priced assistance: and the great majority of those who have need for justice, are far from being in that condition.

But though the advocate (whatsoever may be the ascendant attached to his rank in the profession,) being the same to all, will not be more apt to make an abusive application of it, to the advantage of the high and opulent (as such,) in their warfare with the low and indigent; this sort of impartiality will not hinder him, it may be said, from employing it in another manner, more directly and certainly prejudicial to the cause of justice.

Under the name of *brow-beating* (a mode of oppression of which witnesses in the station of respondents are the more immediate objects,) a practice is designated, which has been the subject of a complaint too general to be likely to be altogether groundless. Oppression in this form has a particular propensity to alight upon those witnesses who have been called on that side of the cause (whichever it be) that has the right on its side; because the more clearly a side is in the right, the less need has it for any such assistance as it is in the nature of any such dishonest arts to administer to it.

But, of the assistance of a professional advocate to the cause of justice, where such assistance is to be had, the utility is grounded in the nature of things: whereas the abuse thus characterized by the name of *brow-beating*, is not, as will be seen, altogether without remedy.* Brow-beating is that sort of offence which never can be committed by any advocate who has not the judge for his accomplice.

In respect of appropriate information (with relation to the purpose in question,) under the technical system the advocate is but too apt to be deplorably deficient: the advocate seeing nothing of the facts but through the medium of another professional man, rich in opportunity, and prompted by interest in a variety of shapes, to misrepresent or intercept them. But the sinister advantage which the technical system has contrived to give itself in this respect, depends upon the fundamental arrangement by which it excludes the parties, on all possible occasions, from the converse and presence of the judge. On the occasion here in question, the presence of the party in question is supposed.

In the particular case here in question, that of a party (the plaintiff) in the cause, proposed to be interrogated by his own advocate, an objection, obvious enough in theory, grounds itself on the danger of prompting or suggestive questions, — in a word of mendacity-serving information. But on a closer examination this danger will be seen to lose much of its magnitude: † meantime it may not be amiss briefly to observe, that in the shape of actual mischief it does not appear to have been felt in English practice.

Compared with this second case, case ninth (in which, the deponent's own advocate being still the proposed interrogator, the party proposed to be interrogated by him, instead of being as in the former case the plaintiff, is the defendant,) presents some slight difference: — in a criminal case, especially in a case where the punishment is raised to the highest pitch of severity, the incitement to afford mendacity-serving information in the shape of a question is in itself much greater; at the same time that the topic of humanity presents an excuse, beyond any that applies in the other case. But, that even in this case, the objection is not weighty enough to be preponderant, will be seen in the place referred to as above.

Be this as it may: whether for this or for any other reason, or (what is on all occasions at least equally probable) without any consideration on the ground of reason, in English criminal law, — though the plaintiff, under the name of prosecutor, is allowed to be interrogated by his own advocate, — that allowance is not extended to the defendant. But an observation to be made at the same time is, — neither is he allowed to be inter-

---

* Book III. *Extraction.* Chap. V. *Browbeating.*

† Book III. *Extraction.* Chap. III. *Suggestive Interrogation.*

rogated by anybody else: he tells his own story if he pleases; but, however deficient it may be, either in point of correctness or completeness, effectual and anxious care is taken that (in this way at least) the deficiency shall not from any quarter be supplied.

In twelve, out of the eight and twenty cases, it is assumed that a witness ought to be considered as capable of being admitted to act in the character of an interrogator, *i. e.* to put questions, as well to a party as to a witness, on either side of the cause.

To an English lawyer, on either side of the great hall, the idea will be apt to appear too strange and visionary to have ever been exemplified in practice. It was, however, in common practice, at any rate in the French modification of the Roman system of procedure, in criminal causes of the most highly penal class. *Confrontation* was the name of a meeting which the judge was in most instances bound to bring about between the prisoner and the several witnesses on the other side — the witnesses by whom he was charged: and, on the occasion of such meeting, each was allowed to put questions to the other: the judge present, and (except a clerk for minuting down what passed) no one else.

If so it be that cases may happen, in which, in the most higly penal class of criminal cases, questions put by an interrogator of this description may be conducive to the ends of justice,—so may it in all other classes of criminal cases: and if in criminal cases, so also in non-criminal. Whatever may be the demand for the use of it, the propriety of that demand will not be varied, either by the distinction between most highly penal and least highly penal cases, or by that between criminal on the one part, and non-criminal on the other.

Cases are not wanting in which, on the score of the direct ends of justice (in other words, in respect of the merits of the cause,) interrogation, if performed by the sort of interrogator here in question, promises to be more efficient than if originating from any other source.

A contradiction, real or apparent, takes place (suppose) between the testimony delivered by an extraneous witness, and that delivered by a defendant in the character of a witness, a plaintiff in the character of a witness, or another extraneous witness, called, whether on the same side, or (what is more apt to be the case) on the side opposite to that on which the first was called. By reciprocal interrogation, in which (on one side or on both) an extraneous witness takes a part, truth will acquire a better chance for being brought to light than it could have without this assistance: the seeming contradiction may be cleared up, or the incorrect testimony shown to be so.

True it is, that the same end might be arrived at, without admitting any extraneous witness to perform the function of an interrogator; viz. by the instrumentality of the party, or his advocate.

But in the case in question, it is only by means of the witness that the party can be apprized of the facts, or supposed facts, on which the questions are to be grounded. By interposing, between two individuals to whom (if to anybody) the facts of the case are known, another individual to whom they are unknown (besides the useless consumption of time), no help to truth can be gained, and much help may be lost.

Both were present (suppose) at the same transaction: how prompt and lively in such a case is the interchange of questions and replies on both sides! How instantaneously the points of agreement and disagreement are brought to view! How instructive is the *deportment* exhibited on both sides on the occasion of such a conference! Of the advantage possessed by the oral mode of extraction in comparison with the epistolary, much (as will be seen*) depends on the promptitude of the responses — on the exclusion thereby put upon mendacity-serving reflection and invention. Interpose between the two individuals (both privy to the transaction) another who is a stranger,— both the advantages in question (viz. the promptitude of succession as between question and answer, and the *real* evidence furnished by deportment) are in great measure lost.

Other cases there are, in which the regard due to the interest of the witness himself (the proposed interrogator) calls for the admitting him to the exercise of that function.

1. The witness happens to have a collateral interest in the matter of dispute. In the testimony delivered by another deponent (plaintiff, defendant, or extraneous witness on either side,) incorrectness has taken place to the prejudice of such collateral interest. The testimony (suppose) will be, or is liable to be, divulgated and recorded. — It seems unreasonable, that, from a dispute having place between two parties, a third should suffer an irremediable prejudice. Here we see the case of a *special* interest: and an interest susceptible of almost as many diversifications as any which can be at stake in the principal cause.

2. His reputation for veracity is, by the proposed interrogator, seen to be put in jeopardy by the incorrect statement delivered by another witness as above. Why for this, any more than any other injury, should a man stand precluded from the means of self-defence?

Attacked in his person, the law would not

* Book III. *Extraction.* Chap. VIII. *Modes of Interrogation compared.*

refuse him permission to defend himself on the spot: the protection which it grants to his person, why should it refuse to his reputation? Here we see the case of a sort of *general* interest, the interest of reputation: or (to employ the denomination more in use in the language of evidence) of *character*.

Causes (says an objection) would at this rate grow out of one another, and thence litigation without end.

Nay (says the answer) it is not the demand for litigation, it is not injury, that would in this way be increased: it is only the means of redress for injury, that would in this way be afforded: redress rendered incomparably more easy and effectual than at present.

It is not by the fear of an excess, but by the fear of a deficiency, of litigation, that, under the fee-gathering system, this undilatory, unexpensive, and comparatively unvexatious, mode of redress, has been shut out. To open the door to such explanations would be to rip open the belly of the hen with the golden eggs.*

All three cases being accidental, and comparatively extraordinary; no doubt but that the admission of a witness to the faculty of interrogation must be committed to the discretion of the judge: grantable either of his own motion, at the instance of the party, or at that of the witness himself, according to the nature of the case, as above.

In the case of the party, liberty of interrogation is a matter of right: since a case cannot be figured in which it ought not to be allowed. Of the several distinguishable descriptions of witnesses, if to any one it were matter of right, so would it be to all: the consequence might be the most intolerable confusion. A *malâ fide* plaintiff or defendant, by calling in adherents and confederates of his own in unlimited numbers, might swell the amount of delay, vexation, and expense, to any height.

One case, that of a party (say the plaintiff,) made subjectable, on the occasion of delivering his testimony, to interrogation by a person whom he is about to call in the character of an extraneous witness, affords a particular objection on the ground of the danger of mendacity-serving information. By the supposition, the witness — the extraneous witness — has no interest, no avowable and rightful interest, in the cause. If then he be to be admitted to interrogate, it can only be in the character of an advocate; an agent of the party whom it is proposed he should interrogate. But, between the character of an agent and the character of a witness, there is a sort of incompatibility: on the part of an agent, partiality ought to be supposed; on the part of a witness, impartiality is a quality that ought to be cultivated and guarded with all imaginable care. To admit interrogation from such a quarter, is to incur a needless danger of bias or of mendacity on the part of the extraneous witness, and thus of mendacity-serving information from him to the plaintiff-deponent.

Answer: 1. From a man's being disposed to afford that assistance, the affording of which is consistent with the laws of probity (viz. affording information in a direct way by his own testimony, and in a less direct way by questions tending to extract information from another person,) it follows not that he will be effectually disposed, or so much as at all disposed, to afford mendacity-serving information.

2. Between the character of a witness for one of the parties, and the character of an agent for the same party, there neither ought to be any such incompatibility, nor is in general in established practice; at any rate not in English practice. A man known to be an agent of the party, is admitted to depose at his instance, and in that respect on his behalf, without difficulty.

3. If the danger on this score were serious enough to be conclusive, excluding the witness from acting in this case in the character of an interrogator would not suffice to obviate it: for so long as any other person alike partial to the interest of the plaintiff (say the plaintiff-deponent's own advocate, say a fellow-plaintiff or his advocate) were permitted to interrogate, the same sinister end might be compassed, as well by the witness's commu-

* In case of supposed perjury, for the purpose of eventual forthcomingness and justiciability, power has, by a special law, been given to the judge to commit the supposed perjurer on the spot, and to order prosecution at the expense of a public fund.

So far so good: but why not to try him, and convict or acquit him on the spot? It may be, that, besides the evidence which gave birth to the suspicion in the bosom of the judge, the case affords other evidence which is not on the spot: in that case, the necessity of adjournment is manifest. But a state of things that may equally be, and probably most frequently is, exemplified, is, that the case does not afford, nor by the supposed perjurer would be so much as pretended to afford, any other evidence. In that state of things, the impropriety of adjournment is equally manifest.

After a lapse of months, hours are, in the postponed trial, employed in greater number than the minutes that would have been sufficient on the impromptuary one. Meantime, recollection fades, evidence perishes; and the question whether a trial shall so much as take place, rests on the arbitrary decision of a secret tribunal; which cannot know more of the transaction, and may, to any amount, know less, than the one by which, to so much advantage, conviction and punishment might have been made to attach instantaneously upon the offence.

The ends of justice take their chance: but fees, the objects of judicature, are made sure: objects, which in the other case would not, or at least need not, have existence.

nicating the proposed question to these allowed confederates, as by his propounding it himself.

Thus stands the matter on the footing of *sinister* interest; interest prompting the individual in question to promote the departure of the deponent from the line of truth. But in the case of an extraneous witness (considered with a view to his appearance in the character of an interrogator) there exists a naturally-operating *tutelary* interest, tending to engage him to employ the information he is master of in framing questions, the tendency of which will be to confine the testimony of the deponent within the pale of truth. The deponent has been delivering his testimony—the extraneous witness has had communication of it, or heard or read the minutes taken of it: a passage that he has remarked in it strikes him as deficient (no matter from what cause) in correctness or completeness —in those respects, one or both, it disagrees with the testimony which he himself has delivered. Independently of all personal interest (honest or dishonest) in the cause; what desire can be more natural, what more general, than, by questions, or any such other means as are allowed, to interpose in the view of supplying the deficiency? Let the permission of satisfying this desire be allowed, a sort of contest springs up, a sort of combat takes place, between the deponent and the interposing witness: a clashing of counter-assertions and counter-interrogatories, — a collision from which truth and justice have nothing to fear, everything to hope.

Instead of this immediate collision between the deponent and the proposed interrogating witness, substitute an examination performed by the party interested or his advocate, without other assistance than that of the proposed interrogating witness: who does not see that this operation will be, comparatively speaking, languid and ineffective? When two persons, each a percipient witness of the transaction of which they both speak, stand up in contradiction to each other, the guard of artifice is beat down: mendacious invention, unable to find apt matter at such instantaneous warning, is confounded, and driven into self-contradiction, or self-condemning silence.*

For the deponent, instead of the plaintiff (as above,) put the defendant; making at the same time, in the description of the interrogator, the correspondent changes: you will find the arrangement subjecting him to be interrogated by the three other sort of persons proposed in that quality, recommended by the same reasons.

Such and so various are the descriptions of persons by whom it may be of advantage to the interests of truth and justice that the process of interrogation should be performed. Performed, and to what purpose? To the purpose so often mentioned, viz. that of making what provision can be made for the completeness, as well as correctness, of the aggregate mass of evidence.

And in what view and intention were these several classes of persons looked out for? — In the view of collecting the requisite stock of appropriate skill and appropriate information: whatever skill (derived from experience) might reasonably be looked for as requisite and sufficient for the purpose, applied to whatever information the particular circumstances of the individual case might happen to afford.

But without the requisite share of zeal to put those means into action, and give them a suitable character, all the skill and all the information imaginable would still be of no use. It was for this purpose that all the distinguishable interests, which, in each individual case, the nature of the case might happen to afford, were carefully looked out for; for, supposing any one such interest left out, and the case so circumstanced as to afford a fact which no other but that interest would prompt an interrogator possessing the requisite share of skill and information to call for, — the necessary consequence is that *pro tanto* the mass of evidence remains incorrect or incomplete: and howsoever it may fare with other persons having other interests, misdecision and injustice to the prejudice of the possessor of that interest will be the probable consequence.†

* The same reasons will serve to show that a plaintiff, on the occasion of his delivering his testimony, should be subjectible to interrogation, even by or in behalf of a fellow-plaintiff. If the interest of the fellow-plaintiff coincide with that of the plaintiff who is about to depose, there is at any rate the chance of additional skill, added to that of additional appropriate information: if the interest of the fellow-plaintiff is different in any respect from that of the plaintiff who is about to depose, the situation of the fellow-plaintiff coincides in that respect with that of a defendant. On the score of danger of mendacity-serving information, the same objection as above may be brought, and the same answer may be given to it.

† Whatever be the number of persons whose interest in any shape is at stake in the cause, each having a separate interest, and demanding to be allowed to do whatever may be lawful and necessary for the support of such his interest (be his demand positive or defensive,) there is as much reason for acceding to one such demand as to another. *Audi alteram partem* — hear the other side — is the phrase by which this universally applicable and universally undisputed conception appears commonly to have been expressed: such, at least, is the interpretation which that maxim requires to be put upon it, ere it can be admitted to have embraced on this ground, to their full extent, the exigencies of justice. By *altera pars*, understand every separate interest: for each part, each interest, is *altera* with reference to to every other. Under *audi* comprehend the giving allowance to every lawful act, the performance of which is necessary to the support of each such interest. To adduce or exhibit

Thus much then is, I flatter myself, pretty clearly understood; viz. that when all the interests at stake in a cause are comprehended, and the faculty of interrogation allowed to the possessors of those several interests without exception, over and above the faculty of adducing such testimony as they themselves may happen to have it in their power to adduce; the best provision is made that can be made for correctness and completeness (so far as information and zeal at least are concerned:) and that, on the other hand, while there be any one such interest to which that faculty is denied, the provision made is imperfect, and pregnant with deception, misdecision, and injustice.

But what (I think I hear an English lawyer crying out and saying) — what is all this but a round-about way of observing, that in every cause *cross-examination* ought to be allowed?

In answer, what may be admitted is, that, towards conveying the conception above meant to be conveyed, this word (to which no equivalent seems to be afforded by any other language than the English) does more than can be done by any other single word in actual use.

What on the other hand requires to be observed, is, that, had this word and no other been employed, the conception conveyed by it would, as well in point of correctness as in point of completeness, have been in no slight degree discordant with the truth of things, for, —

In the first place, the salutary effect in ques-

sources of evidence, is one such act: to take a part in the extraction of the evidence from the several sources adduced, by whomsoever adduced, is another: to present to the judge observations on the evidence so extracted, is again another. In any given cause, if the allowance of any one of these operations be necessary to justice, so is that of every other: if in any one cause the allowance of them all is necessary to justice, so is it in every other. If, among three operations such as these, to all of which it may happen to be necessary to justice that they should be respectively performed, there be any one which is less certain of being necessary than the two others, it is the one last mentioned, viz. that of presenting observations. The testimony of Titius, in the character of an extraneous witness, may of itself be so correct and complete, as to supersede all demand for skill and labour to be employed in the extraction of any supplemental testimony from the same source: its application to the demand may at the same time be so plain and obvious, as to render it plainly impossible for it to receive any additional persuasive force from any observations that could be grounded on it. Scrutinized or unscrutinized, evidence may speak, and speak sufficiently for itself: but in a question of fact, observations without evidence would be a discourse without a subject.

Such, and no less extensive, is the import which it seems necessary to give to this most familiar of all judicial adages, ere it can be rendered commensurate to the ends of justice: I say familiar, for, between the being familiar to the ear of every man, and the presenting a clear conception, and that the same conception, to the mind of every man, there is (in most questions of the field of morals, and more especially of the field of jurisprudence) a most wide and lamentable difference.

Very different is the import affixed by the professional lawyer to the word *audience*. According to his conception of the matter (at least as far as conception is to be understood to be well interpreted by practice,) there is indeed a *one thing needful* to justice, but it is not any one of these three.

Let every party, let every person, who claims to have an interest in the cause, be heard by counsel: which again, being interpreted, is — let matters be so ordered, that every man, on pain of seeing his interest perish, shall be admitted (that is, shall be compelled) to employ a lawyer; that is, to employ a multitude of lawyers, of as many different sorts as possible, to make their observations on the cause. If these observations have any evidence for their ground, so much the better, and the more evidence the better; because, the more evidence, the more ample the ground and room for observations: if labour be applied to the extraction of the evidence from those sources, so much the better, and the more labour the better; because the more abundant the labour, the more abundant the source of reward. Provided they are accompanied by the observations (understand always from the professional quarter above designated,) any or all of them may have their use: but without all these documents, or any of them, the observations (provided always it be from that quarter that they come) are of themselves capable of answering every purpose that is worth providing for: without the observations, neither any one of them nor all of them put together, have any claim to notice.

But, above all errors, take care at any rate not to fall into so gross a one as that which for *pars* on this occasion would understand *party*, — each of the several parties in the cause. Unless it be here and there in the station of witnesses, these, of all others, are the persons who, from the beginning to the end of the cause, are neither to be seen nor *heard in it:* not to bear a part in the extraction of the evidence, still less for the purpose of presenting observations grounded on it.

Such are the commands of scientifically instructed justice. Let no man, on any occasion on which it is possible to prevent his being heard, be heard in any way by himself: let every man be compelled to be heard on all manner of occasions, and in all manner of ways, by counsel: this is the one thing needful: so counsel be but heard what he has to say when he is heard is of minor consequence; and so this one thing needful be but performed, whether there be evidence or no evidence, and whether the evidence (if there be any) be correct or incorrect, complete or incomplete, is not worth a thought on the part of the judge: understand of a judge professionally bred and instructed, the only sort of judge who is entitled to the name.

Such is the interpretation put upon the maxim *audi alteram partem* by the professional lawyer; by those from whose lips interpretation has the force of law. Will proof be asked for? The answer is, *Circumspice.*

tion will be seen to be obtained in a variety of cases in which no such operation as that denoted in English practice by the word *cross-examination* is performed.

In the second place, cases will be seen in which an operation called by the name of cross-examination is performed, and the salutary effect in question is either not promoted at all, or promoted in a mode and degree very imperfect in comparison with that which is generally understood as attached to the performance of the operation so denominated.

There is another and a perfectly sufficient reason, for not being contented with saying that cross-examination should be allowed. This work, if it be of any use to any one nation, may be of no less use to any other: if it be of any use to-day, its use will not be obliterated by cycles of years succeeding each other in any number. If to the substance of the practice denoted in the English language by the word cross-examination, there be attached (as it appears to me there is attached) a virtue in a peculiar degree salutary to justice; it would be too much to say or to suppose that an acquaintance with the language of this small part of the globe is indispensable to it; that it is only by understanding English that a man can understand what is necessary to justice.

Thus extensive, and in themselves occasionally almost unbounded, are the demands presented by the direct ends of justice,—the latitude demanded in respect of the number of persons to be admitted to the faculty of interrogation, to make it absolutely sure, that of the persons (whatsoever may be their number) having each a separate interest in the cause, no one shall be exposed in any degree to suffer for want of it.

But on this, as on every other occasion, the operations prescribed by the direct and ultimate ends, find their necessary limit in the regard due to the collateral end, of justice. On this as on every other occasion, care must be taken — taken by the legislator, and discretionary power in corresponding amplitude allowed by him to the judge,— that, for the avoidance of a possible mischief in the shape of a misdecision, a certain and immediate mischief be not admitted to a preponderant amount in the shape of delay, vexation, and expense. But for this, the number of persons standing together on the defendant's side of the cause, and possessing each a distinguishable interest, might, by the nature of the cause, be every now and then swelled to such a pitch, that, by conjunct operation (with or without concert and conspiracy,) the value of the service demanded (how considerable soever,) might eventually, or even to a certainty, be overborne by the weight of the delay, vexation, and expense thus attached to the prosecution of it; and thus, sooner or later (over and above all the collateral inconvenience,) direct and certain injustice to the prejudice of the plaintiff's side would be the necessary result.

On the part of the judge exists the requisite allotment of skill: this, provisionally at least, must all along be supposed. At the command of the judge lies the whole stock of information which, in each individual case, the nature of the case affords: for this may all be supposed, — understand always, in so far as the information possessed by one man can, to this purpose, be deemed with propriety to be in possession of another.

In the exercise of judicature in every country, among the occupations of the judge — among the obligations which the judge is expected to fulfil, is that, of applying that skill and that information to the discovery of the truth through the medium of evidence. If, then, interrogation be indeed, as it was not denied to be, an apt instrument for that purpose, why, it may be asked, look out for any other hands to lodge it in? What is there in his station to hinder him from employing it? and employing it to the utmost advantage to which it is capable of being employed?

What should hinder him? Two deficiencies: —deficiency in respect of two out of three endowments (not to speak here of probity,)* the union of which is necessary to the discharge of this function to the best advantage: appropriate information, and zeal.

1. Appropriate information: for the faculty of obtaining possession is not itself possession: to have a chance, and but a chance, of possessing a thing some days hence, is not the same thing as the actual possession of it at this very instant: information at second hand is not the same thing as information at first hand. These considerations have already been mentioned among the reasons for allowing the judge to admit a witness to the exercise of this function, as well as a party or his advocate.

2. In the article of zeal, the inferiority of the judge as compared with the party, is not less obvious or undeniable. Equality in this respect is an endowment which seems hardly to be wished for, were it even attainable: as being incompatible with that characteristic

* If, on the part of the judge, improbity (which in this case will be a determination or inclination to decide in favour of one side or other, in opposition to the dictates of justice) be supposed; the chance in favour of justice is, in this case, reduced perhaps even lower, than if, the judge being excluded, the right of interrogation were allowed exclusively to the party on one side. For the judge, by the supposition, in point of affection, is, in this case, what the party would be in the other: and for giving effect to his sinister views, the judge possesses powers of which the party is destitute; powers adequate to the accomplishment of the sinister ends.

calmness and impartiality, for the want of which no other endowments can atone.*

In this general point of view, the deficiency natural to the station of the judge is, indeed, sufficiently obvious: although in Roman practice the recognition of it has not had any such effect as to have produced (except in a comparatively narrow case) the communication of any share of it to any other of the stations in the cause; that of a party or that of an extraneous witness.

But what is not quite so obvious, nor is yet altogether unworthy of remark, is the different degrees of zeal which, in causes or inquiries differently circumstanced, will naturally be apt to infuse itself into the station of the judge.

1. In one class of causes, and that more numerous than all the others put together, his zeal may be set down as being naturally at its *minimum*. This is the class of causes between man and man; the class composed of non-criminal causes.

Not but that, even here, the indifference so natural, and frequently so observable, in the situation of the judge, may be referable, in no inconsiderable degree, to a collateral and not altogether inseparable cause: viz. the natural state of procedure under the technical system; which, in these cases, never fails to afford, on some terms or other, to each of the persons an advocate, or advocates: one sure way of realizing which state of things, is the refusal to listen to the party unless he employs an advocate.

In this state of things, by one sort of interest, to the action of which the judge, like every other man, is continually exposed (viz. the interest corresponding to the love of ease,) he is continually urged to get through the business with as little trouble to himself as possible. Here then we have a sinister interest, which (supposing it to stand alone, or without being encountered by any interest, acting in a tutelary direction, of sufficient force to overcome it) will be sufficient to render the faculty of interrogation, as far as he is concerned, altogether nugatory.

In the view that will come presently to be taken of the existing modifications of technical procedure, we shall see this sinister interest acting with very little opposition from any tutelary one: but of this in its place.

In the employment of this instrument to the best advantage, the advocate, in so far as he is admitted to wield it, has an obvious, and in a considerable degree efficacious, interest: his bread, in many cases, depending on his professional reputation; and the reputation of the advocate having a natural and intimate connexion with the success of the client.

In this interest, the judge, it is evident, has not the smallest share. His reputation is, indeed, in a certain degree, dependant on the apparent justice and propriety of his decisions; and on their actual, in so far as their apparent depends upon their actual, justice. But the apparent justice of a decision grounded on a body of evidence depends upon that evidence: depends upon the evidence, not as it might have been, but as it is. In this state of things,— so long as the evidence, as collected by him, does not *appear* to be either incorrect or incomplete, — in what degree it really *is* so, is to the interest of his reputation a matter of indifference. Moreover, so far as appearances are concerned, everything depends upon publicity: insomuch that, supposing perfect secresy, it is with this part of the business as with every other, — let it be done as well as possible, or as ill as possible, his reputation is exactly in the same state.

2. The case in which the zeal of the judge on this occasion may be expected to be found at its *maximum*, is that of the species of procedure already described under the name of inquisitorial procedure: a case which comprehends the whole of the criminal branch, — in so far as the business of receiving, collecting, and investigating the evidence against the defendant, rests (especially if it rests exclusively) in the hands of the judge,—without any co-operation, (or at least without the necessity of any co-operation) on the part of any other person in the character of prosecutor (the name, in this branch, given to those who act on the plaintiff's side of the cause.)

In this case, that in the article of zeal there should be any considerable deficiency on the part of the judge, will not, on a general view, be found natural to the case.

To repress his activity, the same *vis inertiæ* the love of ease, is operating, in this as in the other case: but in this case it is natural to it to find counter-forces (and these adequate to the surmounting of it) such as do not apply to that former case.

Here is an end to be accomplished; an end which (setting aside particular and casual interests and affections) men in general have an interest in seeing accomplished, and an

* Another remark: to extort the truth from the bosom of an unwilling, an unscrupulous, and strong-minded witness, is among the most of difficult tasks: and a pre-eminent degree of fitness for it is one of the brightest and rarest accomplishments that the war of tongues affords to natural talent improved by practice. The judge (as such) never having been, by any motive force equal to that under the action of which the advocate is continually operating, excited to those exertions which are necessary to the exercise of that function with a superior degree of efficiency and success, cannot reasonably be expected to be on a par, in this respect, with an advocate whose stock of experience has been equally abundant.

interest which, in some degree or other, is pretty generally felt by the judge himself, along with the rest: and his is precisely that particular situation from which the general interest will naturally be viewed in one of its strongest lights. To accomplish this end, is a task committed, and universally known to have been committed, to his charge — a task not forced upon him, but voluntarily accepted by him, along with the other functions attached to his office; his reputation for professional skill, as well as industry, is attached to the due execution of this power, and, in the case of real delinquency, to the successful execution of it.

Under these circumstances, — to produce a considerable, and in general an adequate, degree of zeal and exertion on his part — neither to excite it in the first instance, nor, *à fortiori*, to keep it up, is any such interest as pecuniary interest, in the shape of a mass of fees depending in any way upon success, necessary. Of the hunter who toils the whole day to catch a stag or a fox, whom he lets go as soon as caught, the zeal is neither awakened nor kept up by any such prospect as that of fees.

In so wide a field, general principles of action are liable, in certain cases, to be overborne by particular ones. But upon the whole, that in this case the situation itself is literally adequate to the production of the quantum of zeal requisite for the effectual discharge of the function, directly and principally attached to it (viz. the receiving, collecting, and investigating evidence, and, by means of the instrument of interrogation, giving correctness and completeness to it,) at least in so far as the operation of the evidence tends to bring about the conviction of the real delinquent, seems pretty generally testified by experience.

In this view may be cited — 1. Under the Roman system, the conduct of the business, from beginning to end, in the case of those crimes of high degree, which, affording no individual prompted by peculiar interest to take upon himself the vexation and expense attached to the station of private prosecutor, are left to be prosecuted for, as well as decided upon, by the judge. 2. Under the English system, the preparatory inquiry conducted by a justice of the peace, in the case of a crime of the rank of felony. 3. Under the same English system, the inquiries conducted by tribunals organized on special occasions, for special purposes — whether by the authority of either house of parliament, under the name of a committee — or under the authority of the whole legislature, under the name of a commission of inquiry.

Excess rather than defect of zeal has in these cases been the more frequent topic of complaint. In the case of that tribunal (the inquisition) to which the denomination of this species of procedure has become attached, — as if it were the only tribunal in which the two functions of prosecutor and judge had ever been united, — the complaint has risen long ago to a height become proverbial.

It is from the abuse made of the faculty of interrogation, on the occasion of its being applied to the disastrous purpose there in view, that criminals of all sorts, co-operating in this way without the need of concert — criminals of all sorts, with their accomplices after the fact, and abettors of all sorts — have taken occasion to labour, and with but too much success, in deluding the public mind, and setting it against the application of the same instrument to the most necessary purposes — laboured, and with as much reason, and even appearance of reason, as if their endeavour had been to stamp the like infamy upon the power of judicature itself, or upon the use of the interrogative mood as applied to any of the other common purposes of social intercourse.

Though interrogation by the parties is of itself, in general, a more effectual security than interrogation by the judge, the former, nevertheless, does not supersede the latter.

Though, in respect of special information applying exclusively to the facts appertaining to the individual cause in hand, the parties will (one or other, or both of them) be better qualified for the task than the judge, — yet, in many instances, the superiority of general information, discernment, and promptitude, naturally resulting from the superiority of experience, will enable him to bring to light facts, for want of which the testimony would have been incomplete, or mendacity, if employed by the witness, would have escaped detection. In no case, it is evident, can such assistance be deemed superfluous; but there are various circumstances by which the demand for it may be increased: if there be any deficiency in point of intelligence or exertion on the part of the advocate on either side; if on either side there be no advocate, — and the party (by mental weakness, the result of sex, age, bodily indisposition, want of education, natural dulness, and so forth) be in any particular degree disqualified from conducting his own cause with due advantage.

As to zeal: though in this point the jndge cannot reasonably be expected to be upon a par with the party interested; yet, with the advantage of professional education and experience, a much inferior degree of exertion will frequently enable him to render much more effectual service; — so that, upon the whole, in the character of an interrogator, the judge, though but an inadequate substitute, may, with reference to the party, be deemed an indispensable assistant.

§ 5. *Affections of the several proposed interrogators and respondents towards each other, how far presumable.*

Such or such a person in the character of an interrogator,—shall it be permitted to him to interrogate such or such another person in the character of a proposed respondent? To settle the answers to these several questions is one practical use of the double list of proposed respondents and interrogators.

But, in judicial practice, rules have been grounded on the supposed affections of this or that person in the character of a respondent, to this or that other person in the character of an interrogator, or *vice versâ:* rules prohibiting or allowing such or such a mode of interrogation in the several instances.

Here, then, we have another practical use of the list: inquiring into the nature and solidity of the grounds for ascribing to such or such a situation such or such a state of the affections; and thence into the propriety of the prohibitions and permissions respectively administered by these rules.

In most instances we shall find ground for a presumption ascribing to a party in one of these situations, with relation to a party in such or such another of these situation, such or such a state of the affections. But in each of these instances it will be manifest, that, from one cause or another, such presumption is liable to fail: from which inconclusiveness and uncertainty, follows, in every instance, the impropriety, whether of prohibition or of permission, if established by any such peremptory and unbending rule.

1. Proposed respondent, an extraneous witness called by the plaintiff; proposed interrogator, the plaintiff or his advocate.

The superior probability is, that the affections of the proposed respondent are either neutral, or favourable as towards the side from which the interrogation proeeeds. For, supposing the party to have his choice of witnesses, he will pitch upon such as he expects to find favourable to him, or at least neutral: he will avoid calling such as he expects to find adverse.*

But this probability, such as it is, is manifestly much exposed to failure. It is not of course, and always, that a party has any such choice of witnesses: those cases which afford no such choice are the most apt to be productive of legal dispute. Of whatever number of distinct facts it may be necessary to the plaintiff to prove, if there be a single one which cannot be proved by any other evidence than the testimony of a witness rendered adverse to himself by any repugnancy of interest or cause of antipathy, or (what comes to the same thing) rendered amicable towards the defendant by any tie of interest or sympathy; he must either give up his right altogether, or, instead of finding the road to information smoothed by the neutrality or sympathy of the proposed respondent, find it obstructed by his ill-will and reluctance.

2. Proposed respondent, an extraneous witness called by the defendant; proposed interrogator, the defendant or his advocate.

Under these different names, to the purpose here in question, this second case is in substance the same as the first.

3. Proposed respondent, a plaintiff; proposed interrogator, a co-plaintiff or his advocate.

Here the presumption is, that the affections of the proposed respondent are not merely neutral, but highly favourable to the proposed interrogator, and *vice versâ;* because here, in respect of the cause itself, is a declared community of interest.

In this third case, the presumption, it is evident, is much stronger than in either of the two former.

* Independently, too, of all other causes of favourable partiality, there is something in the relation between party and witness that has a tendency to conciliate the affections and wishes of a witness to the side of that party by whom his testimony is called in.

1. Confidence, as being a mark of esteem, has, by the force of sympathy, a tendency to produce good-will on the part of the individual towards whom it manifests itself.

2. In proportion to the importance of the cause to the party, and of the evidence to the cause, the witness is placed by the party in a situation of superiority with relation to himself — himself in a situation of dependence with reference to the witness. A species of power, with the pleasures attendant on that possession, is thus conferred upon the witness, and conferred upon him by the party. Hence, another source of good will, produced by the power of sympathy.

3. In proportion to this double importance is that of the part which the witness is, by the choice thus made of him by the party, enabled and called upon to act. A species of distinction, a situation of honour, is thus conferred upon the witness, and conferred upon him by the party, as before. Hence another cause of good-will, produced by the power of sympathy, acting in the shape of gratitude.

4. Where witnesses are called in on the same side in numbers, a sort of party is formed, animated by the spirit of party, and a sort of social and more extended sympathy is thus generated, and adds its force to that of the personal sympathy of which the individual is the object. This effect will of course be the more conspicuous where the cause itself has anything in it of a public or semi-public nature — where, instead of an insulated individual, an entire class (more or less extensive) has a direct and common interest in the event. But even when there is no common interest, it does not follow that the effect will not be produced. In an election riot, a passer-by, seeing an affray, resolves to have a share in it: before he began, it may have been a matter of indifference to him with which side he should take part, but he will not shout Blue or Yellow the less lustily afterwards.

But here also it is liable to failure. 1. Under the apparent bond of union, an original opposition of interests may be concealed.* 2. The declared interest which the proposed respondent has in common with the proposed interrogator, may be outweighed by some undeclared and secret opposite interest: or, between the proposed interrogator and a party or parties on the other side of the cause, collusion may have place.†

4. Proposed respondent, a defendant; proposed interrogator, a co-defendant or his advocate.

Presumption here the same as in case 3: causes of failure also the same. But in this fourth case the presumption is weaker; the existence of a cause of failure being more probable. For, without his own consent, no man can be made a plaintiff—any man a defendant. Into the station of defendant it rests with any individual in the character of plaintiff to force any number of individuals actuated by mutually opposite interests.

5. Proposed respondent, a witness called by the defendant; proposed interrogator, the plaintiff or his advocate.

Here the presumption is, that the affections of the proposed respondent are adverse to the proposed interrogator. But, under the first case, it may already have been seen in how high a degree, in the present case also, that rule is exposed to failure.

6. Proposed respondent, a witness called by the plaintiff; proposed interrogator, the defendant or his advocate.

What belongs to this sixth case may be seen in what has been said of the last preceding one.

7. Proposed respondent, a defendant; proposed interrogator, the judge.

Here the presumption — the first presumption at least — is, that, as towards the defendant, the affections of the judge are neutral.

But where the case has been a criminal one, and more particularly of the most highly penal class, under the secret modes of inquiry which have been generally in use in the Roman school,—the judge, in many instances, uniting to that neutral the partial function of plaintiff, — a suspicion that has trod fast upon the heels of that presumption is, that an occasional wish has place on the part of the judge (whether in prosecution of his own inclinations or those of some other member or members of the government) to find pretences for misdecision to the prejudice of the defendant's side.

After the above exemplifications, the extension of the inquiry to the several other diversifications of which the relation as between proposed respondent and proposed interrogator is susceptible, will, it is imagined, be found to present but little difficulty.

§ 6. *Distinction between amicable interrogation and interrogation* ex adverso.

Not for completeness only, but for correctness likewise, suggestion *ab extrà*, such as it is of the nature of interrogation to afford, and occasionally perhaps almost any suggestion that it is in the power of interrogation to afford, may be necessary; and this, whatever may be the state of the interests or affections of the respondent, as towards the person by whom, or in whose behalf, he is interrogated.

It may be necessary where the affections of the respondent are indifferent, or even partially favourable, as towards the interrogator; for, on any ordinary occasion on which you seek for information (if the subject be of a certain latitude,) apply to your most intimate friend — let him be fluent in speech as well as communicative in disposition—how seldom will it happen that a single question (how comprehensively soever framed) will be sufficient to draw from him all the information you wish to receive!

Interrogation from an interrogator, between whom and the respondent the affections are in either of these states, may, to distinguish this case from the opposite one, be termed amicable interrogation.

But the case in which the demand for this security is by far the stronger and more conspicuous, is that where between the two interlocutors there exists a contrariety of interests or affections.

Interrogation in this case may be termed *adverse* interrogation: interrogation *ex adverso*, or *ex opposito*.

In a former section, different descriptions of persons, in considerable and almost indeterminate variety, have been brought to view, as being upon occasion capable of rendering service to justice by contributing to the extraction of the light of evidence; in particular, the parties on both sides (with their representatives,) the judge, and extraneous witnesses.

In the language of English law, there are two descriptions of persons, and but two, from the consideration of whose relation to the cause the operation of interrogation or examination receives a particular denomination. When the deponent (being an extraneous witness) is interrogated at the instance of the party by whom his testimony was called for, he is said to be examined *in chief* — his examination is styled the examination in chief:

---

* Example *in civili:* Two persons, each in the character of creditor, join in making a demand upon a testamentary executor or other manager of an insufficient fund: it is the interest of each that the other should fail in the proof of his debt.

† Example *in criminali:* Two persons join in the prosecution of a supposed criminal: one of them, for money, or through compassion, is secretly determined to endeavour to bring about the acquittal of the defendant.

when, immediately after such his examination in chief, he is interrogated on the part of a party whose station is on the opposite side of the cause, he is said to be *cross-examined* — the examination is termed his cross-examination.

Attached in general to the circumstance of his being examined by that side of the cause by and from which his testimony was called for, is the notion of his affections being favourable to that side of the cause, and thence of a willingness on his part to give a correspondent shape and complexion to his responses. Attached in like manner to the circumstance of his being examined on that side of the cause which is opposite to that by and from which his testimony was called for, is the notion of his affections being unfavourable to that side of the cause, and of a corresponding adverse shape and complexion given to his responses.

And, from this supposition, practical rules of no slight importance have been deduced.

Were this notion uniformly correct, then, and in that case, examination *ex adverso* would be synonymous with cross-examination. But we have already seen how far this notion is from any such uniform correctness.

To the supposition of an agreement or disagreement of interests, that of a correspondent relation of affections naturally attaches itself. Concerning this relation (of whichsoever of the two opposite kinds it be,) the natural supposition is, that it is mutual, and even (in default of reasons to the contrary) equal. Neither this equality, nor even that mutuality, is, however, as is sufficiently known to everybody, constantly verified in practice. When either the term amicable interrogation, or the term adverse interrogation (or rather interrogation *ex adverso*) is employed, then the above-noted irregularities ought not to be overlooked.

Where the exertions of one of two parties (the interrogator) are employed in the endeavour to bring to light a fact, or other object, which the exertions of the other party are all the time employed in the endeavour to keep back, — on the part of that one of them on whom the force is thus endeavoured to be put, the existence of an emotion of the angry kind, to a degree more or less intense, can scarcely be supposed to be altogether absent: more especially if, with reference to the respondent, the obvious consequences of the disclosure be of a nature decidedly and eminently penal; such as the loss of property, liberty, reputation, or life.

At the same time, on the part of the interrogator, on that same afflicting occasion, the supposition of an emotion of the angry kind (looking towards the unhappy respondent) is far indeed from being a necessary one; as in the case where, on that same occasion, the melancholy function is in the hands of a humane and upright judge.

To warrant the employment of this necessary term, it therefore is not necessary that the emotion or the natural ground should exist on the part of both interlocutors: it is sufficient if it exists on either part. Be it reciprocal, or but unilateral, — in either case there will be the same reluctance on the part of the respondent — the same sort of unwillingness as to the yielding the information which it is the endeavour of the interrogator to extract: the same psychological difficulties and obstacles will therefore be exerting their force in the endeavour to prevent the testimony from possessing that degree of completeness and correctness with which, for the purposes of justice, it is so necessary that it be endowed.

Nor is this sort of dialogue between interlocutor and interlocutor, the only relation by which the sort of opposition above described, and the consequent danger of incompleteness and incorrectness, is liable to subsist.

The interrogator being a party (say the defendant,)—let the respondent be an extraneous witness, called by an opposite party (the plaintiff,) and already interrogated by or in behalf of that party; and, in point of affections, let the witness be, with reference to each party, altogether unopposite — equally indifferent, to both, or equally a friend to both. The string of questions put to the witness being completed, will his evidence be altogether correct, as well as complete? Correct, seldom; complete, still more seldom. Why? Because, in quality as well as quantity, the facts delivered by the respondent will naturally have been influenced, more or less, by the nature and object of the questions, and hence by the object which the interrogator had in view: and the object which the interrogator had in view probably embraced the keeping back a part (more or less considerable) of the facts considered as likely to operate to his prejudice; and almost to a certainty did not embrace the bringing forward any such facts.

In this case, then, the interrogation, — though not adverse with relation to any interest, or affection, or emotion, of the person interrogated, — may, with not the less propriety, be termed interrogation *ex adverso* — *ex adverso* with relation, not to the respondent himself, but with relation to an antecedent interrogator.

In the case just put, the affections of the respondent were, with reference to the party by or in whose behalf he is under interrogation, supposed to be in a state of indifference. But a case not less natural, and indeed considerably more natural, is a state of favourable partiality. In this case, the obstacles tending to prevent the completeness and correctness of the testimony, the obstacles which the interrogator has to contend with, act (it is evident) with additional force.

On the other hand, while it is certain that the interests and affections of the preceding interrogator will be opposite with relation to the interests and affections of the succeeding interrogator, a case which, though comparatively unfrequent, is notwithstanding sometimes verified, is, that the affections of the witness shall be partial, in favour not of the party by whom he was called, but of the party adverse to the party by whom he was called.

This being the case, the force tending to produce incorrectness and incompleteness on the part of the testimony, — the force against which the second interrogator has to contend, — this force, considered in respect of its dependence upon the state of the affections of the three several individuals bearing a part in the business, admits of three cases or gradations:—Case 1. The respondent favourable to the second interrogator: Case 2. The respondent indifferent: Case 3. The respondent adverse to the second interrogator.

When the respondent is a mere witness (an extraneous witness,) himself without interest or affection in the cause,— on the part of the judge, the process of interrogation is scarcely susceptible of either of the pair of adjuncts, amicable or adverse. The witness has no desire to keep back anything: the judge has, or at least ought to have, a desire to get out everything — every fact and circumstance (in favour of whichsoever side it may chance to operate) that promises to be material to the cause. To prevent the judge from getting whatever evidence the source affords, there is nothing on his part but want of skill, want of appropriate information to direct his interrogatories, and deficiency of zeal, as above.

When the respondent is a party, the judge, in the character of an interrogator, cannot fulfil his obvious and acknowledged duty, — cannot do in every instance what depends upon his exertions towards giving completeness and correctness to the aggregate mass of testimony, —without occasionally presenting to the party (according to the nature and tendency of the fact sought — according to the side in favour of which it operates) two opposite aspects; the one amicable, the other adverse: amicable, in so far as the fact sought for promises to operate in favour of the respondent's side; adverse, in so far as it promises to operate against that side, or (what comes to the same thing) in favour of any opposite side.

Of the questions put by the judge to an extraneous and indifferent witness, not one (it has just been observed) can be termed either amicable or adverse in relation to such respondent witness. But, of the same questions, not one (so it be material to the purpose) can fail of being at once amicable and adverse with reference to the parties: amicable, with relation to the one; adverse, in the same degree, with relation to the other.

In a criminal case—at least if it be of that class of criminal cases which presents no individual in the character of a party injured, — there being but one individual whose interest is at stake (viz. the defendant,) — in the language naturally employed on this occasion, that one individual is the sole object in view: and he, and he alone, is the party with relation to whom the adjuncts *amicable* and *adverse* are employed.

Considered, then, with relation to this individual, it will be always true to say, in speaking of the whole string of interrogations put to him by the judge, that the aspect manifested by the judge, in respect of them, to the defendant, ought to be at once *amicable* and *adverse*. and on this occasion, each of these adjuncts may be employed with propriety, so the other be at the same time employed with it; neither can, without the most flagrant impropriety, be employed alone.

That, in respect of his interrogatories, the aspect of the judge ought to be *adverse* to the defendant (who, in a case where the arrangements of procedure bring him into court in a state of confinement, is called, in the language of English law, the prisoner,) if nothing be said of what it ought to be on the other side, — is a proposition too monstrous, too revolting, to have ever been advanced. How often soever it may have been pursued in practice, in discourse no such monstrous maxim has ever been professed.

That, in the same respect, the aspect of the same public functionary ought to be *amicable* to the prisoner, in the sense just mentioned as attached in this case to the term *amicable* (the same silence being observed as to the opposite aspect, with which it is necessary it should be accompanied, if it be reconcilable to the ends of justice,) is a proposition equally monstrous, though in an opposite way; and equally repugnant to the ends of justice; but, unhappily (such has been the weakness of the public mind,) not equally revolting: and it is under favour of this weakness that currency has been given to one of those sophisms, under which, by the artifices of hypocrisy, the grossest selfishness and the most sordid corruption have succeeded in imposing themselves upon mankind under the names of humanity and virtue.

I speak of the current maxim, that the judge ought to be of counsel with the prisoner—meaning the defendant, in a prosecution which subjects the defendant to provisional imprisonment for safe custody. This proposition, being in one sense indubitably true and consonant to justice, but liable to be taken, and most commonly taken and applied, in a sense in which it is false and hostile to justice, bears no inconsiderable part among the causes that concur in keeping up the stock of crimes in its present state of abundance.

In every cause, these are at least two sides — that of the plaintiff, and that of the defendant. In every cause it is the indisputable duty of the judge to do what depends upon him towards bringing to light all the material facts which the cause is capable of furnishing; whatever facts make in favour of the one side — whatever facts make in favour of the other. To apply his endeavours to bring to light such of the facts as promise to operate in favour of that side of the cause on which he is engaged, is at any rate the function (not to enter into the question of duty) of the counsel, the advocate, on that side — in favour of the defendant's, the prisoner's side, when engaged on that side. In this sense it is the equally indisputable duty of the judge to be of counsel with the defendant. His duty? Yes: but on what condition? On condition of being of counsel in the same sense, and to the same purpose, on the opposite side — on the side of the prosecutor, or other plaintiff. On every occasion, and to whatever purpose — on which side soever the truth promises to operate, it is his duty to use his endeavours to bring it out. Giving this double direction to his endeavours, he serves both sides of the cause.

Now, of the man who serves both of the opposite sides of a cause, it cannot be denied but that he serves each of them. Take which side you will, it cannot be denied but that he serves that side — it cannot be denied but that he acts as counsel on that side.

Here, then, lies the mischief. Beneficial and justifiable in one sense, — the proposition is employed in another sense, in which it is pernicious and unjustifiable. It is only on condition of his occupying himself with equal industry in favour of the opposite side, that it is the duty of the judge — that it is otherwise than a crime in the judge — to occupy himself in the way in question, or in any other way, in favour of the other. Set aside this indispensable condition, it is a crime on the part of the judge to occupy himself in favour of either side. In point of propriety, next after impartial activity comes impartial negligence.

Fairly translated, stripped of its disguise, what is the argument of this sophism? It is the duty of the judge to be impartial; — therefore it is his duty to be partial.

Question of duty once more set aside, — it is the function, at any rate it is the constant occupation, of the counsel for either side — of the counsel for the defendant, of the counsel for the prisoner — to use every endeavour that the law does not forbid, towards procuring success for that side — towards procuring an acquittal for the defendant his client; whether he be innocent or guilty, whether by truth or falsehood (so the falsehood be unpunishable,) are questions which make no difference — questions not worth thinking about — questions that in practice are not thought of, nor, according to current axioms, have any need or title to be thought of.

A man has committed a theft; another man, who, without a licence, knowing what he has done, has assisted him in making his escape, is punished as an accomplice. But the law (that is, the judges, by whom in this behalf the law has been made,) have contrived to grant to their connexions acting in the character of advocates, a licence for this purpose. What the non-advocate is hanged for, the advocate is paid for, and admired.

Among the expedients that have been contrived for selling impunity to such criminals as have wherewithal to purchase it, is the invention which will be hereafter spoken of under the appellation of a decision on grounds foreign to the merits.* To discover all grounds of this sort that can be discovered, and, as often as any such ground can be discovered, to call for a decision productive of an acquittal to the delinquent defendant, is among the functions of the counsel when enlisted in the criminal's service. Justifying, and even commending, on the part of the judge, discoveries of the same kind, is one of the most favourite of the services on which the maxim here in question is wont to be employed. It is the duty of the judge to do that which, if he were not a judge, or a man of law in some other shape, he would be punished (and not without reason,) in the character of an accomplice, for doing.

Of a rational and honest aphorism on this subject, what would be the purport and effect? That the judge ought to be counsel for all parties, and that in all sorts of causes. Not in criminal causes alone, and such criminal causes alone in which the defendant is in the condition of a prisoner, — and in those causes on the side of the defendant alone; but alike for all parties, and in all sorts of causes. Where is the cause in which any the slightest departure from the rule of impartiality is, in the eye of justice and reason, anything less than criminal on the part of the judge? Not that a mere negative impartiality is sufficient; a positive, an active impartiality, must be added to it: to be equally active in his endeavours to search out the truth on both sides, — that is the true impartiality, the only true and proper sort of impartiality, befitting the station of the judge.

Thus much is true, indeed, — that, next to the positive and negative impartiality conjoined, comes negative impartiality alone:

* Book VIII. *Technical Procedure;* Chap. XIV. *Nullification.*

next to his taking equal pains to search out the truth on both sides, is his not giving himself any concern to search it out on either side.

The psychological cause of this adage — is it worth looking for? In the currency given to it, humanity, or rather childish weakness, may possibly, in here and there an instance, have had a share; — hypocrisy, selfishness covering itself in the mask of virtue, is in every instance a more probable cause. It is among the artifices employed by lawyercraft to reconcile the public mind to the sale of indulgences, elsewhere spoken of. Decision in favour of the defendant on a ground foreign to the merits — decision grounded on a quirk or quibble — is among the instruments by which this species of traffic has ever been carried on.

In the individual instance in which the quibble is not only applied to this purpose, but discovered, by the judge, no immediate profit, perhaps, results to anybody: either there is no counsel, or if there be, the counsel, without the quibble, and for the mere chance of his finding out that or some other quibble, has received his fee.

But the practice itself is, in its own nature, shocking to common sense and common honesty: the public mind, had it not been duped and gulled, could never have contemplated it without the indignation and scorn it merited. A sophism, therefore, was to be invented for that purpose—a lying spirit was to be sent forth to deceive the people; and this was the imp that offered itself.

The traffic would not have been borne in any case, if the credit of the commodity had not been kept up in all cases: and nothing could contribute more powerfully to keep up the credit of the sophism, than the distributing it through the pure (and to appearance unpaid) hands of the judge. The policy is no secret to any species of impostor: like the husbandman, he knows when to scatter as well as how to gather in: the quack, that he may sell the more of his pills at one time, distributes them gratis at another.

Without strict search, assertion is not to be ventured: but, from principle, I should not expect to find that the adage had ever been employed to any other than a bad purpose. How should it? Good wine needs no bush: putting a pertinent question, bringing to light the innocence of the innocent, needs no apologies, no adages.

Nothing can be more artful than the sophism — nothing more guarded, more impregnable. Who shall contest the truth of it? Fallacious in the highest degree, no one can say that it is false. It is like one of the two sides of a correct account. So far as it goes, it is all pure justice: stop there and sink the other side, it is the quintessence of injustice. But so sure as the account thus drawn up by lawyercraft is produced, so sure is one of the sides sunk.

The English judge — would he dare to put to a guilty defendant so much as a single question that might throw light upon his guilt? Not he indeed. The sophism nursed up so carefully by his predecessors for the benefit of the common cause — the sophism here in question, is not of the number of those which a judge can bring forward or put aside as caprice may dictate: firm as a rock, his power would be shaken by it, were he to venture to attack it.

The policy has still deeper root: it is for this cause that cruel punishments are to be multiplied; and in particular that the punishment of death (a punishment not good in any case) is, as opportunity serves, to be extended to all cases. The more barbarous the punishment, the less disposed is the public mind to scrutinize into the pretences by which here and there a victim is preserved from it.

For this cause amongst so many others, the punishment of death has ever been, and (so long as lawyercraft reigns) will ever continue to be, a favourite policy with the English lawyer.

A connexion, says Cicero, may be traced between all the virtues: a connexion still more obvious may be traced between the several branches of injustice. Injustice to the defendant's side, injustice by excess of punishment, — and injustice to the prosecutor's side, injustice operating by quibbles, — are consanguineous vices — vices that act in partnership, and play into one another's hands.

CHAPTER X.

OF PUBLICITY AND PRIVACY, AS APPLIED TO JUDICATURE IN GENERAL, AND TO THE COLLECTION OF THE EVIDENCE IN PARTICULAR.

§ 1. *Preliminary explanations — Topics to be considered.*

Considered as applied to judicial procedure, and in particular as applied in the character of securities for the correctness and completeness of evidence, — of the mass of evidence which a judicial decision, pronounced on the question of fact, takes for its ground; publicity, privacy, and secrecy, are qualities which cannot, if considered at all, be considered otherwise than in conjunction.

Publicity and privacy are opposite and antagonizing, but mutually connected, qualities, differing from one another only in degree. Secrecy might be considered as exactly synonymous to privacy, were it not that, upon the face of it, it seems to exclude gradation, and to be synonymous to no other than the greatest possible degree of privacy.

For the correctness and completeness of the mass of evidence, publicity is a security in some respects: privacy—its opposite, in some other respects.

Publicity and privacy have for their measure the number of the persons to whom knowledge of the matters of fact in question is considered as communicated, or capable of being communicated.

The degree of actual publicity will be great or high, in the direct ratio of the number of persons to whose minds the knowledge of the matter or matters of fact in question has been communicated: the degree of privacy, in the inverse ratio of that same quantity.

The highest conceivable degree of publicity is that according to which the matter of fact in question would be present at all times to the minds of all the inhabitants of the globe. This highest *conceivable* degree of publicity being in no individual instance ever exemplified or capable of being exemplified, is consequently greater or higher than the highest *possible* degree of publicity.

The highest conceivable degree of privacy, is that in which the number of the persons to whose minds the knowledge of the matter in question is capable of being present (so it be present to any one such mind,) is the smallest number conceivable. This number is, of course, unity. But that in this or that instance there should be one person, and no more than one person, to whose mind the knowledge of the matter of fact in question has, on the occasion in question, been communicated, is a case the exemplication of which is neither impossible, nor so much as difficult.

Some matter of fact, for example, applicable in the character of circumstantial evidence, to the question of fact on which a decision is to be pronounced, — suppose that by some accident it has happened to it to have presented itself to the senses of *the* judge or *a* judge by whom the decision is to be pronounced; and suppose matters so ordered, that, until the time when the decision is to be pronounced, this matter of fact has not been communicated to any other mind.

Thus it is, that of publicity, the highest degree conceivable and the highest degree possible do not coincide: the highest degree possible falling short of the highest degree conceivable. But of privacy, the highest degree conceivable and the highest possible do coincide. The case in which they both have place, is that in which there is but one mind to which the knowledge of the matter in question is present, and that one mind the mind of the judge.

The highest conceivable degree of privacy, and the lowest conceivable degree of publicity, coincide: the two expressions are synonymous.

In the examination bestowed upon these opposite and antagonizing qualities, it is that of publicity that must take the lead. In publicity will be seen a quality, of which, for the most part, the highest conceivable degree can do no harm; and of which a very high degree, and such a one as cannot without some attention and exertion be secured, will be subservient and conducive at least, if not indispensable, to the purposes and ends of justice.

This being the case, establishment of publicity (and without any limits to the degree of it but what are set by the consideration of the collateral inconveniences of delay, vexation, and expense) will stand recommended by the general rule, as being, in most cases, conducive to the direct ends of justice: whereupon the cases in which privacy (viz. in a mode as well as degree adapted to the nature of this or that particular case) is conducive to those ends, will, with reference to that general rule, wear the character of *exceptions*.

On the present occasion, correctness and completeness of the mass of evidence are the points and objects to be provided for and secured: qualities, in relation to which, the most effectual and eligible mode of securing on each occasion the existence of them, is the problem to the solution of which it is the object and endeavour of the contents of this part of the work to contribute.

But, as the mass of evidence itself, so the correctness and completeness of that mass, is not itself an ultimate end, but a means only with reference to an ulterior end. This ulterior end is rectitude of decision; viz. on the subject of the matter in question; which, in so far as evidence is concerned, is the existence or non-existence of some matter of fact.

For what reason, it may be asked, on the present occasion, bring this distinction in view?

The answer is: For giving, on the sort of theatre in question, to rectitude of decision its best chance, it will not be altogether sufficient, either that the chief instrument of security, *publicity*,—or that *publicity* and *privacy* together (each in its proper place) — be applied to the mass of evidence and to that alone (or to this or that portion of it, as the case may require:) it may be necessary that these same safeguards should respectively be applied to this or that *other* article; for example, to the declared grounds and reasons of the decision, considered as delivered, or capable of being delivered, and rendered more or less public, by the deciding judge.

And forasmuch as (considered with relation to the correctness and completeness of the mass of evidence) the degree of consideration necessary to be bestowed on the subservient qualities of publicity and privacy will be in no slight degree ample, it may be advisable to give to the inquiry that degree of extension (beyond the proper subject of the present book, as announced by its title) which will be necessary to enable it to comprehend such other of the instruments and operations of procedure, as these same qualities of publicity and privacy may, according to the nature of each case, be found applicable to, with advantage.

In relation to publicity and privacy, the following are the topics that present themselves for consideration:—

I. The operations and instruments (judicial operations and judicial instruments) capable of being the subject-matter of publicity or privacy—of divulgation or concealment.

These seem reducible to the following heads, viz.

1. The mass of evidence in question, of whatsoever materials composed, viz. real or personal which again is either testimonial or documentary.

2. The interrogatories whereby, of what is testimonial, such part as is not spontaneously exhibited, is elicited and extracted.

3. The arguments delivered by the parties or their representatives, in the character of observations upon the evidence.

4. The interrogatories (if any) that come to have been administered by the judge.

5. The recapitulation (if any;) *i. e.* the summing up of the mass of evidence, performed (with or without observations of his own) by the judge.

6. The decision pronounced by the judge on the question of fact; with or without reasons.

II. The different characters in which it may be of use that, by the means and instruments of publicity employed, different members of the community should receive communication of these several matters.

These characters will be found to be those of—1. Eventual witnesses—(percipient witnesses)—furnishing ulterior and supplemental testimony, in relation to the matters of fact which are the subjects of the inquiry.

2. Witnesses who—in the character of percipient witnesses of the testimony exhibited by the principal witnesses—may eventually, in the character of deposing witnesses, be of use, by deposing in confirmation or disaffirmance of the correctness and completeness of the *minutes* taken of the testimony delivered by the principal witnesses.

3. Judges, who, in quality of administrators of the force of the popular or moral sanction, take eventual cognizance of the whole proceeding, for the purpose of passing a judgment of approbation or disapprobation on the conduct of the several actors in the judicial drama, (viz. parties, agents, representatives of parties, witnesses, judge or judges, subordinate judicial officers acting under the direction of the judge or judges.)

4. Executioners, viz. of the judgment pronounced, by themselves and colleagues, on the conduct of the several actors, as above: executioners; viz. by the bestowal of their good or ill opinion, their good or ill will, and hence upon occasion (as the substantial fruits and results of such good or bad opinion and will) their good or ill offices.

III. The mode in which, by the members of the public (as above) in their several characters (as above,) communication of the matters of fact (viz. the evidence in question) is capable of being received.

This mode of reception will be determined by, and will be correspondent to, the form in which the evidence is delivered; viz. according as, in virtue of such form, it comes under the denomination of *oral* (otherwise called *vivâ voce*) testimony, or *scriptitious* evidentiary matter, already consigned to writing at the time of its being delivered.

If it be oral,—to the reception of it by any person at the time of its delivery, and in the character of orally-delivered testimony, it is necessary that, at the very time, he be present at the delivery of it. If it be scriptitious,—all that is either necessary or possible is, that the writing, or the contents of it, be present to his mind in time enough for the performance of the function (whatever it be) which it is desirable he should perform in relation to it. If it be an article of real evidence, of the evanescent kind, it stands in this respect upon the footing of orally-delivered testimony: if of the permanent kind, it stands, in this respect, upon the footing of scriptitious evidence.

IV. The means, or instruments, capable of being applied to the purpose of giving publicity to the evidentiary matter in question; together with the several degrees of publicity capable of being given to it by those means.

Of the degree of publicity in each instance, an exact measure is afforded by the number of the persons to whose minds, on the occasion in question, in time for the purpose in question, the evidentiary matter in question is present.

In the case of testimony orally delivered and not consigned to writing, the greatest possible number of such cognizant persons, if the judicial theatre be a closed room (as is always the case in England, and, with few or no exceptions, in modern Europe,) will be determined and limited by the magnitude and structure of the room.

In the case of evidence consigned to writing, the number of such persons will be determined, in the first place, by the number of exemptions made; in the next place, by the number of persons to the mind of whom it happens to each such exemption to be present, as above.

In both cases, the means or instruments of publicity may be distinguished into natural and factitious. Natural, are those which take place of themselves, without any act done by any person (at least by any person in authority) with the intention and for the purpose of producing or contributing to the production of this effect. Factitious, are such as, for this very purpose, are brought into existence or put in action by the hand of power.

Considered in itself, a room allotted to the reception of the evidence in question (the orally delivered evidence) is an instrument rather of privacy than of publicity; since, if performed in the open air and in a plain, the number of persons capable of taking cognizance of it would bear no fixed limits; it would, in no individual instance, have any other limits than those which were set to it by the strength of the voice on the one part, and the strength and soundness of the auditory faculty on the other.

Considered on the other hand in respect of its capacity of being so constructed as to be in any degree an instrument of privacy, — the room in question, the place of audience, may (in so far as, in the magnitude and form given to it, the affording room and accommodation to auditors in a number not less than this or that number is taken for an end) be considered, in this negative sense, as an instrument of publicity.

If — in the view of securing what (for the purposes in question, as above, and in the character in question, as above) is looked upon as a requisite or desirable number for the *minimum* number of the audience — means are taken by public authority for securing attendance on the part of persons of such or such a description, in such or such a number,—whether the means thus taken be of the nature of reward or punishment, or both in one (as is the case where attendance is made matter of duty to an official person, who receives a recompense for the performance of the duties of his office,) such means are an example of the sort of means above described under the appellation of factitious means.

If, while in the act of *vivâ voce* utterance, or afterwards, the purport or tenor of the evidence be committed to writing, the same means and instruments of divulgation become applicable to it, which have place in the case of that sort of evidence which is scriptitious in its origin.

But in the case of *vivâ voce* evidence, there is a demand, not only for those means and instruments which are necessary and sufficient to any given degree of divulgation in the case of evidence which is in its origin scriptitious, but also for such antecedently employed means and instruments as are necessary to the purpose of bringing about this perpetuation. Minuting or note-taking, copying, printing, publishing,— these are so many successive operations, which, according to the degree of divulgation or publicity given or proposed to be given to the matter, become necessary in the character of means of publicity: and so many as there are of these operations performed, so many are the instruments or sets of instruments, personal and real, that come to be employed about it.

These means and instruments (like those others that were brought to view in the case of orally-delivered evidence, considered as being thus delivered without being consigned to writing,) may be distinguished from each other by the epithets of *natural* or *factitious*, according as the hand of authority is or is not employed in the giving existence or aid to them.

The place of evidence itself being, on the occasion in question, naturally, and usually and properly, in the hands and at the command of the judge; and the several operations conducive to divulgation being (like any other operations) capable of being interdicted, not only on each particular occasion by the judge, but on every or all occasions by the legislator; — hence, in so far as forbearance is in any instance given to the exercise of such prohibitive power, a sort of negative means of publicity comes to be, by the hand of authority, employed. Admission given, extra-accommodation given, to note-takers — permission of publication or republication at length, in the way of extract or abridgment, given to the editors of newspapers, and other periodical papers, — in this way (on the occasion in question, as on other occasions,) whatsoever mischief is by the hands of authority forborne or omitted to be done, is naturally and frequently placed to the account of merit, and taken for the subject of approbation and praise.

Instruments of privacy. — In this character, two sorts of apartments, both of them fit appendages to the main theatre of justice, may be brought to view, viz. —

1. The witnesses' chamber or conservatory.
2. The judge's private chamber, or little theatre of justice.

Of the nature and destination of these two apartments, explanation will come to be given under another head.

As, when publicity is the object, the magnitude of the theatre is among the instruments employed for the attainment of it; so, when privacy is the object, the smallness, if not necessarily of the apartment itself, at any rate of the company for which it is destined, qualifies it for operating in the character of an instrument of privacy.

§ 2. *Uses of publicity, as applied to the collection of the evidence, and to the other proceedings of a court of justice.*

The advantages of publicity are neither inconsiderable nor unobvious. In the character of a security, it operates in the first place upon the deponent; and, in a way not less important, though less immediately relevant to the present purpose, upon the judge.

1. In many cases, say rather in most (in all except those in which a witness bent upon mendacity can make sure of being apprized with perfect certainty of every person to whom it can by any possibility have happened to be able to give contradiction to any of his proposed statements,) the publicity of the examination or deposition operates as a check upon mendacity and incorrectness. However sure he may think himself of not being contradicted by the deposition of any percipient witnesses, — yet, if the circumstances of the case have but afforded a single such witness, the prudence or imprudence, the probity or improbity, of that one original witness, may have given birth to derivative and extra-judicial testimonies in any number. "Environed, as he sees himself, by a thousand eyes, contradiction, should he hazard a false tale, will seem ready to rise up in opposition to it from a thousand mouths. Many a known face, and every unknown countenance, presents to him a possible source of detection, from whence the truth he is struggling to suppress, may, through some unsuspected channel, burst forth to his confusion."*

2. In case of registration and recordation of the evidence, publicity serves as a security for the correctness in every respect (completeness included) of the work of the registrator.

In case of material incorrectness, whether by design or inadvertence, — so many auditors present, so many individuals, any or each of whom may eventually be capable of indicating, in the character of a witness, the existence of the error, and the tenor (or at least the purport) of the alteration requisite for the correction of it.

3. Nor is this principle either less efficient or less indispensable, in the character of a security against misdecision considered as liable to be produced by misconduct in any shape on the part of the judge. Upon his moral faculties it acts as a check, restraining him from active partiality and improbity in every shape: upon his intellectual faculties it acts as a spur, urging him to that habit of unremitting exertion, without which his attention can never be kept up to the pitch of his duty. Without any addition to the mass of delay, vexation, and expense, it keeps the judge himself, while trying, under trial: — under the auspices of publicity, the original cause in the court of law, and the appeal to the court of public opinion, are going on at the same time. So many by-standers as an unrighteous judge (or rather a judge who would otherwise have been unrighteous) beholds attending in his court, so many witnesses he sees of his unrighteousness; — so many ready executioners — so many industrious proclaimers, of his sentence.

On the other hand,—suppose the proceedings to be completely secret, and the court, on the occasion, to consist of no more than a single judge, — that judge will be at once indolent and arbitrary: how corrupt soever his inclination may be, it will find no check, at any rate no tolerably efficient check, to oppose it. Without publicity, all other checks are insufficient: in comparison with publicity, all other checks are of small account. Recordation, appeal, whatever other institutions might present themselves in the character of checks, would be found to operate rather as cloaks than checks — as cloaks in reality, as checks only in appearance.†

4. Publicity is farther useful as a security for the reputation of the judge (if blameless) against the imputation of having misconceived, or, as if on pretence of misconception, falsified, the evidence. Withhold this safeguard, the reputation of the judge remains a perpetual prey to calumny, without the possibility of defence: apply this safeguard, adding it as an accompaniment and corroborative to the security afforded (as above) by registration, — all such calumny being rendered hopeless, it will in scarce any instance be attempted — it will not in any instance be attempted with success.

5. Another advantage (collateral indeed to the present object, yet too extensively important to be passed over without notice) is, that, by publicity, the temple of justice adds to its other functions that of a school — a school of the highest order, where the most important branches of morality are enforced by the most impressive means — a theatre, in which the sports of the imagination give place to the more interesting exhibitions of real life. Sent thither by the self-regarding motive of curiosity, men imbibe, without intending it, and without being aware of it, a disposition

* Bentham's *Plan of a Judicial Establishment in France*, Vol. IV. p. 317.

† The constitution of the judicial establishment, including the question as between unity and multiplicity in regard to the number of the judges sitting and acting at the same time, belongs not to the present work. Meantime, as well with regard to division as with regard to subordination of judicial powers, let it be noted that it operates no otherwise as a guard to probity, than in as far as the chance of disagreement and altercation presents a faint chance of occasional publicity.

to be influenced, more or less, by the social and tutelary motive, the love of justice. Without effort on their own parts, without effort and without merit on the part of their respective governments, they learn the chief part of what little they are permitted to learn (for the obligation of physical impossibility is still more irresistible than that of legal prohibition) of the state of the laws on which their fate depends.

Uses of leaving it free to all persons without restriction, to take notes of the evidence:

1. To give effect, in the way of permanence, to the general principle of publicity—to the general liberty of attendance, proposed to be allowed as above. From no person's attendance in the character of auditor and spectator, can any utility be derived, either to himself or to any other individual, or to the public at large, but in proportion as his conceptions of what passes continue correct: and by no other means can he make so sure of their correctness as by committing them (or at least having it in his power to commit them) to writing, with his own hand, at the very time.

But for this general liberty, there would be no effectual, no sufficient check at least, against even wilful misrepresentation on the part of an unrighteous judge. Against written testimony from such a quarter, what representation could be expected to prevail, on the part of individuals precluded by the supposition from committing to writing what they were hearing—precluded from giving to their testimony that permanence on which its trustworthiness would so effectually depend?

2. To afford a source of casual solution or correction to any casual ambiguity, obscurity, or undesigned error, in the representation given of the evidence by the judge or other official scribe: —*

Rule: Allow to persons in general the liberty of publishing, and that in print, minutes taken by anybody of the depositions of witnesses, as above.

Reason: Without the liberty of publishing, and in this effectual manner, the liberty of penning such minutes would be of little use. It is only in so far as they are made public, that they can minister to any of the above-mentioned uses (except that which consists in the information they afford to the judge.) By a limited circulation, room is left for misrepresentation, wilful as well as undesigned: by an unlimited circulation, both are silenced: by the facility given to an unlimited circulation, both are prevented.

Look over the list of advantages by which the demand for publicity is produced in respect of the *evidence;* you will find them applying (the greater part of them, and with a force quite sufficient) to the extension of the demand to all *observations* of which the evidence is the subject, whether on the part of the judge, or of the parties or their advocates. Security to suitors (to the suitors in each individual cause) — and through them to men in general, in the character of persons liable to become suitors — against negligence and partiality on the part of the judge; security to the judge against the unmerited imputation of any such breach of duty; instruction to the people at large, in the character of occasional spectators and auditors at the theatre of justice, and occasional readers of the dramatical performances exhibited at that theatre.

The evidence itself is so and so: from this evidence, the decision which the judge proposes to ground on it, and the conclusion necessary to warrant that decision, are so and so. This conclusion, is it a just and proper deduction from the evidence? In some instances the conclusion may follow so plainly and inevitably from the evidence, that any words which should be expended in displaying the propriety of it would be thrown away; while, in other cases, the conclusion (though clear enough to him who with full time before him shall take upon himself to bestow upon the subject an impartial and attentive consideration) may yet present itself to the hearers under such a veil of obscurity as may well require explanations on the part of the judge, to satisfy them that he has not availed himself of the obscurity to any such sinister purpose as that of pronouncing a decision not warranted by the truth of the case.

If, previously to the decision for the purpose of which the inquiry is performed, debate should arise, with arguments on both sides; — in such a case, under the auspices of publicity, a result altogether natural (whether obligatory or no) is, that the judge should state, in the presence of the by-standers (his inspectors,) the considerations — the reasons — by the force of which the decision so pronounced by him has been made to assume its actual shape, in preference to any other that may have been contended for. In such a situation, that to any judge the

* The security thus afforded against misrepresentation (wilful or not wilful) on the part of the judge, may be apt to present itself as belonging in strictness to the subject of procedure at large, or to that of the organization of the judicial establishment, and not to that branch of the subject of procedure which is the subject of the present work — the branch, particularly, relative to the topic of *evidence.* But as the quality of trustworthiness in a lot of evidence is no otherwise valuable than as a *means* to an *end*, and rectitude of decision is that end, — when the reasons of a rule directed to a subordinate object come to be assigned, the reasons which indicate on the part of the *same* rule a still higher and more important utility, viz. its immediate subservience to the ultimate end, can scarcely be out of place.

good opinion of such his judges should be altogether a matter of indifference, is not to be imagined. In such a state of things, that which the judge is to the parties or their advocates, the by-standers are to the judge: that which arguments are in their mouths, reasons are in his.

Publicity therefore draws with it, on the part of the judge,—as a consequence if not altogether necessary (since in conception at least it is not inseparable,) at any rate natural, and in experience customary, and at any rate altogether desirable — the habit of giving reasons from the bench.

The same considerations which prescribe the giving an obligatory force to the one arrangement, apply in like manner to the other, subject only in both instances to the exception dictated by a regard to preponderant inconvenience in the shape of delay, vexation, and expense. Whenever the reason of the arrangement made by the judge is apparent upon the face of it, entering into a detailed explanation of it would be so much time and labour lost to everybody.

So difficult to settle is the proportion between the advantage in respect of security against misdecision on the one hand, and the disadvantage in respect of delay and vexation on the other, that the practice of giving reasons from the bench can scarcely be made the subject of any determinate rule acting with the force of legal obligation on the judge. Of courts of justice it may be said, that they shall be open, unless in such and such cases; while, in the description of these cases, a considerable degree of particularity may be employed, designative of the species of cause, or of the stage at which the cause (be it what it may) is arrived in the track of procedure. But of the judge it cannot be determined with any degree of precision, in what cases he shall, and in what cases he shall not, be bound to deliver reasons.

This, however, is but one out of the multitude of instances in which, though an obligation of the legal kind is inapplicable, an obligation of the moral kind will be neither inapplicable nor inefficacious. Specifying reasons is an operation, to the performance of which, under the auspices of publicity, the nature of his situation will (as already observed) naturally dispose him to have recourse. Consigned to the text of the law, an intimation to the same effect, in terms however general, can scarce fail of producing upon the minds of the persons concerned, the effect on this occasion to be desired: in the minds of the public, a more constant disposition to expect this sort of satisfaction from the mouth of the judge — in the mind of the judge, a more constant disposition to afford it.

In legislation, in judicature, in every line of human action in which the agent is or ought to be accountable to the public or any part of it, — giving reasons is, in relation to rectitude of conduct, a test, a standard, a security, a source of interpretation. Good *laws* are such laws for which good reasons can be given: good *decisions* are such decisions for which good reasons can be given. On the part of a legislator whose wish it is that his laws be good, who thinks they are good, and who knows why he thinks so, a natural object of anxiety will be, the communicating the like persuasion to those whom he wishes to see conforming themselves to those rules. On the part of a judge whose wish it is that his decisions be good, who thinks them so, and knows why he thinks them so (it is only in proportion as he knows why he thinks them good that they are likely so to be,) an equally natural object of anxiety will be the communicating the like persuasion to all to whose cognizance it may happen to them to present themselves; and more especially to those from whom a more immediate conformity to them is expected.

In neither case, therefore, does a man exempt himself from a function so strongly recommended as well by probity as by prudence; unless it be where — power standing in the place of reason — the deficiency of psychological power being supplied by political, of internal by external, — he exempts himself, because it is in his power to exempt himself, from that sort of qualification which, feeling himself unable to perform well, he feels it at the same time in his power to decline performing.

Oughton, in his Treatise on the Practice of the Ecclesiastical Courts, maintains without reserve, that the practice of examining witnesses in public is a bad practice.

In support of this censure he adduces two reasons: —

1. **The witnesses, in this case, have the faculty of entering into a confederacy, and of fashioning their stories in such manner as to preserve them from inconsistency.**

True; this faculty they possess where the examination is performed in public: but this same faculty,—is it less open to them where it is performed in secret?

The danger peculiar to the system of publicity, is confined to the short space of time during which, if the requisite and not impracticable precaution be not taken, a mendacious witness about to depose may profit by hearing the deposition, as it issues, of a preceding witness, deposing in evidence to the same fact.

This danger, as it is frequently worth obviating, so neither is it incapable of being obviated: and this (as will be seen) it may be, without depriving the process of the benefit of publicity.

The observation of Oughton is confined to

the case of mutual concert. But the advantage derivable by a mendacious witness from the knowledge of the purport of the anterior deposition of another witness, does not require any such complicity on the part of such other witness: it is equally derivable from the testimony of an adverse, as from that of a friendly, witness

2. Fear of the resentment of one or other of the parties might operate upon the witness, so as to produce in his testimony a departure from the truth. It might occasion him to keep locked up in his breast some fact, which, if disclosed, might operate to the prejudice of the party by whom his testimony was called for, or of the opposite party.

To this objection the following observations seem applicable: —

1. In a cause between individual and individual, whatever interest one party has in the witness's speaking false, the opposing party has a correspondent interest in causing him to speak true.

2. The disposition of the witness, even if left to himself, might be, on this or that point, to speak false: at the same time that, for confining him within the pale of truth, there is no other chance than that power of contradiction and refutation, which depends upon a mass of information which the party in question, and he only, is in possession of.

3. The secrecy in question is but temporary. Upon this, as upon the other system, when the cause comes to be heard, the depositions are divulged. Whatever is contained in the deposition, of a nature displeasing to either party — the invoker or the adversary — is then disclosed.

True it is, that this applies only to actual deposition: it does not apply to silence. By the apprehension of the displeasure of one of the parties, it may happen that by the witness something should be suppressed, which, had it not been for such presence, might have come out. But this inconvenience is too slight to be put for one moment in comparison with the transcendent benefits of publicity: it can never afford ground for anything more than an occasional exception.

By the admirers of the technical system as it exists in England, the bar has been spoken of as constituting the best, if not the only necessary, public — as a most excellent and efficient check upon the bench.

Thus far may be admitted, — that, in the character in question (viz. that of uncommissioned inspecting judges,) so far as either practical experience or technical science are concerned, no other persons, in equal number, can come up to them; that they are scarce ever altogether wanting; and that upon the whole, the number of them bears (as it were to be wished it should do) a proportion to the importance of the cause.

Thus stands the matter under the technical system. But were any one to say, that under the natural system this check would be wanting, and that therefore, under the natural system, there would be no sufficient security for good judicature, — in such a case, its title to the character of an indispensable security would require a more particular scrutiny.

1. So long as the technical system were the object to be pursued, — to the conduct of a set of judges acting under that system, no other adequate inspectors could be found than a set of persons alike impregnated with technical science. Remove those features and arrangements, which, being peculiar to the technical system, are repugnant to common sense as well as common honesty, — and unlearned inspectors might be nearly as competent to that function, as those learned ones are at present.

2. Of the incongruities, absolute or relative, into which the judge is liable to fall, it is with reference to those only which are such in relation to the technical system as it actually stands at present, that the eyes of those technical inspectors can afford any security. So far, indeed, as the technical system has for its ends in view the ends of justice, so far the inspection exercised by these watchmen might serve, and does serve, to confine the course of judicature within the proper track of justice. But in proportion as these only legitimate ends have been neglected or contravened, in so far that same system of inspection, instead of being subservient, is adverse, to the ends of justice. Wherever misdecision has for its source either the sinister interests that gave birth, or the prejudices that have given support, to the technical system, — far from operating as a check to misdecision, the presence of these technical inspectors will operate as a security in favour of it. In how many instances does the technical system not only authorize, but prescribe, and that professedly and avowedly, decisions contrary to the merits, on grounds foreign to the merits? What, in these cases, will be the effect of a system of inspection administered by such inspectors? Not to diminish the frequency of such injustice, but to give it security and increase.

The faculty of appeal may be apt to present itself as an effectual succedaneum to publicity in judicature. In many countries — under the Rome-sprung system in general — under Anglican law in some instances, it is the actual, and in some, the only one.

The utility of appeal in general — its efficacy in regard to the particular points here in question — will depend in no small degree upon the arrangements made in relation to that branch of procedure; a detail which belongs not to this work.

But, that the faculty of appeal, however conducted, cannot operate in any such way as to supersede the demand for publicity in the collection of testimony, may even in this place be made sufficiently evident by various considerations.

1. Appeal, howsoever conducted, is clogged by an unavoidable mass of delay, vexation, and expense. Publicity is in no case productive of considerable delay; and, so far as concerns open doors — in a word, as to everything but the official registration of the evidence, when that operation is thought fit to be prescribed (concerning which, see further on,)—is altogether unattended with expense.

2. In the case of appeal, as generally established, the evidence, as registered, is the very basis on which the appeal, so far as concerns the question of fact, is made to stand. But of the instruments to which the tenor or purport of the testimony is professed to be consigned, the correctness is taken for granted, and not suffered to be disputed. Appeal, therefore, in this point of view, howsoever it may be an auxiliary, is no succedaneum to publicity. Is publicity necessary to secure the correctness of the registration for the purpose of the immediate decision? — then so is it for the purpose of the appeal. Appeal, instead of rendering it unnecessary, increases the demand for it.

3. If grounded on the same evidence, it affords no sort of security against incorrectness or incompleteness, whether from mendacity, bias, or blameless misconception or omission, on the part of the evidence: in all points, the correctness of the evidence is taken for granted.

4. Punishment or disapprobation, experienced or apprehended from the judge above, in virtue of the appeal, operates, even without publicity, as a check and remedy more or less effective, against misconduct (whether through mental weakness, improbity, or negligence) in the judge below. But the judge above,—where is the check upon misconduct on his part in any shape? What possible check so effectual as publicity?— and if the court above is at the highest stage, what other possible check is afforded by the nature of things?

5. Publicity, a principle of the most simple texture, is so much the less liable to be out of order; — nor is it in the power of mismanagement to do much towards the destruction of its efficacy. Of the principle of appeal, the utility depends altogether upon the details — upon the propriety of the arrangements taken in relation to it: among which, this of publicity is one of the most natural.

"Appeals without publicity, are an aggravation, rather than a remedy: they serve but to lengthen the succession, the dull and useless compound, of despotism, procrastination, precipitation, caprice, and negligence."

§ 3. *Of the exceptions to the principle of universal publicity.*

The uses and advantages of publicity have already been brought to view: so far as those uses are concerned, the most complete and unbounded degree of publicity cannot be too great.

But in other ways, in particular cases, publicity, if carried to this or that degree, may on this or that score be productive of inconvenience, and the mass of that inconvenience preponderant over the mass of the advantages. To the application of the principle of publicity — of universal and absolute publicity, these cases will present so many exceptions.

Let us observe what these cases are — observe, in regard to each, what the circumstance is, by which the demand for the degree of privacy in question is presented, — appreciating, in each instance, as near as may be, the proportion as between inconvenience and advantage.

1. Publicity is necessary to good judicature. True: but it is not necessary that every man should be present at every cause, and at every hearing of every cause. No — nor so much as that every man should be so present, to whom, for whatever reason, it might happen to be desirous of being present.

A man, a number of men, wish to be present at the hearing of a certain cause; and in what view? To disturb the proceedings — to expel or intimidate the parties, the witnesses (or, what is worse and more natural, this or that party, this or that witness,) or the judge. Because judicature ought to be public, does it follow that this ought to be suffered?

2. Publicity is necessary to good judicature. True: but even to him to whose cognizance it is fit that a cause, and such or such a hearing in the cause, should come, it is not absolutely necessary that he should be actually present at the hearing, and that during the whole of the time. Nor, again, is it necessary that any one person should be present, over and above those whose presence is necessary and sufficient to ensure the rendering, upon occasion, to the public, at a subsequent time, a correct and complete account of whatever passed at that time.

3. What is more: — suppose a cause absolutely devoid of interest to all persons but the parties to the cause, and those parties agreeing in their desire that the doors shall be open to no other person, or no other than such and such persons as they can mutually agree upon: in this case, where can be the harm of the degree of privacy thus required? As to unlimited publicity, the existence of the inconvenience that would result from it is sufficiently established by the suffrage of

those who by the supposition are the only competent judges.

If the guarding the parties against injustice in the individual cause before the court, were the only reason pleading in favour of unrestrained publicity, — this reason would cease in every case in which unrestrained publicity being the general rule, all the parties interested joined in an application for privacy; or in which, privacy being the general rule, no application were made by either of them for publicity. For by common consent they might put an end to the proceedings altogether; and where no proceedings existed, there would be none to make public.

But neither by any such joint application, nor by any such joint acquiescence, would more than a part (and that scarcely a principal part) of the demand for publicity, unrestrained publicity, be removed. 1. In the character of so many schools of morality, the courts of judicature would, by every such exception, lose more or less of their practice and their influence. 2. What is much more natural, the habit and sense of responsibility would be proportionably weakened on the part of the judge. 3. If privacy were the general rule, both the above inconveniences would receive a great increase: and in other respects this arrangement, as compared with the opposite one (publicity, subject to exception if on special application,) would be highly unfavourable to the ends of justice. The main use of publicity being to serve as a check upon the judge, no particular application could be made for it without manifesting a suspicion to his disadvantage. Much, therefore, as a party might conceive himself to stand in need of this security, he would have no means of obtaining it without exposing himself to the displeasure of the judge.

4. The supposition is, that all parties who have any interest in this question (at any rate any special interest) join in the consent given to the privacy. But this supposition is very apt to prove erroneous: nor will it perhaps be easy to pitch upon any individual case in which there can be any very perfect assurance of its being verified. More interests, it will frequently happen, are involved in a cause, than those of the individuals who appear in the character of parties to the cause.

At any rate, this case has been exemplified as often as evidence, delivered in a cause between two parties, has come to be relevant in a cause having any other party or parties. True it is, that, by compromising the suit in question, or compromising their difference before the commencement of any suit, they equally had it in their power to withhold from all third persons the benefit of all such evidence as would otherwise have been called into existence by that suit: but true it also is, that on the occasion of the delivery of the evidence, each party, whether he prejudiced his own interest or no, might prejudice the interest of such third persons, not being parties to the suit.

In consenting to the privacy, either party, or even each of them, may, in one way or other, have done prejudice to his interest: in this case, the public, and perhaps individual third persons, will have participated in the inconvenience resulting from such imprudence.

The cases which present themselves as creating a demand for a certain degree of restriction to be put upon the principle of absolute publicity, each for an appropriate mode and degree, — these cases, as expressed by the several grounds of the demand, may be thus enumerated: —

Object 1. To preserve the peace and good order of the proceedings; — to protect the judge, the parties, and all other persons present, against annoyance.

Object 2. To prevent the receipt of mendacity-serving information.

Object 3. To prevent the receipt of information subservient to the evasion of justiciability in respect of person or property.

Object 4. To preserve the tranquillity and reputation of individuals and families from unnecessary vexation by disclosure of facts prejudicial to their honour, or liable to be productive of uneasiness or disagreements among themselves.

Object 5. To preserve individuals and families from unnecessary vexation, producible by the unnecessary disclosure of their pecuniary circumstances.

Object 6. To preserve public decency from violation.

Object 7. To preserve the secrets of state from disclosure.

Object 8. So far as concerns the taking of active measures for publication, — the avoidance of the expense necessary to the purchase of that security, where the inconvenience of the expense is preponderant (as in all but here and there a particular case it will be) over the advantage referable to the direct ends of justice. This case will be considered in another book.*

Object 9. (A false object.) To prevent the receipt of information tending to produce undue additions to the aggregate mass of evidence.

Purpose 1. Securing the persons of the judge and the other dramatis personæ against violence and annoyance.

The importance of this object, the necessity of making due provision for it, is too obvious to be susceptible either of contestation or proof. Being thus incontestable, the

* Book III. *Extraction*; Chapter VI. *Notation and Recordation.*

necessity is the more apt to be converted into a plea for abusive application for undue extension.

Suppose the judge destitute of all controuling power, the place of audience being alike open to all comers,—the whole quantity of room might be engrossed at any time by a host of conspirators, coming together for the express purpose of intimidating the judge, and causing injustice to be done.

What seems necessary to this purpose is, therefore, that, of the whole number of seats or stations contained in the judicatory, a certain number should, upon a declaration made by him of the presumed necessity, be at any time at his command, to be filled by persons nominated by himself, and armed in such manner as he thinks fit; all other persons being precluded from bringing arms of any kind.

But to enable a man to contribute his physical force to the preservation of the peace in a room or apartment of this kind, it is not necessary that the place occupied by him should be among those which are most effectually adapted to the purpose of enabling a man to comprehend distinctly the conversations that have place there. The stations allotted to these eventual guards to the person of the judge, should therefore be such as to leave free to promiscuous visitants such as are best adapted to the purposes of sight and hearing.

On such occasion, to warrant the assumption of this power, it should be necessary for the judge to declare his opinion of the needfulness of such a precaution; the declaration to this purpose being notified by a placard signed by the judge, and hung out in a conspicuous situation on the outside of the court.

But for this precaution, a natural result would be his taking to himself, as his own property, such part of the judicatory as were allotted to him in trust for that purpose, and in some way or other disposing of it to his own profit.

Doors open to persons of all classes without distinction: but any one whose presence would, by disease, or filth, or turbulence, be a nuisance to the rest, individually, and on that account, excludible.

Nor is pay, exacted for places of superior convenience, inconsistent with the spirit of the principle—not in the theatre of justice, any more than in any other theatre. The more elevated the spectator's condition in life, the better his qualification to act in the character of guardian to the probity of the judge. But a man bred up in the delicacy of the drawing-room, will not willingly frequent any place in which he is liable to be elbowed and oppressed by men whose labours, how much soever more profitable to the community than his indolence, have just been employed in the foundry or in the slaughter-house. For purposes of this sort, rate of payment is perhaps the only practicable principle of selection; at any rate, the least invidious possible.

Purpose 2. Prevention of mendacity-serving information.

Wheresoever, on the part of a deposing witness (party or not party to the cause,) there exists a propensity to mendacity,—the probability of preventing his giving way to that disposition, or (in the event of his giving way to it) of preventing his dishonest endeavours from being productive of their intended effect,—depends in no small degree upon the measures taken for preventing him from obtaining, in time to avail himself of it, information concerning the testimony delivered or about to be delivered by this or that other person in relation to the same matter. The co-witness,—is he on the same side with the supposed mendaciously-disposed witness?—the purpose for which he needs to be apprized of such testimony, is the giving to it what confirmation may be in his power, and the avoiding to contradict it. The co-witness, is he on the opposite side?—the use then is, that he may be enabled either to overpower it, or to avoid being overpowered by it, according to the probable degree of its probative force. By the nature of the case, or the mass of accordant evidence, does it appear too strong to be overborne?—in this case, for fear of being overborne and discredited by it, he avoids, as much as may be, touching on the main points; as, in the opposite case, he touches upon those same points with care and preference.

To a propensity, at the same time so unavoidably prevalent, and so pernicious to truth and justice, every obstacle ought of course to be opposed, that can be opposed.

When (as in the Roman school) the mode of examination is private in the highest degree, or in a degree near to the highest,—this purpose is in a great measure effected of course, with or without thinking of it. The testimony delivered by a witness not being known, but either to the judge himself, or to some other person or persons on whom it is supposed that (whether *equal* or no) at least *sufficient* dependence may be placed, his testimony, or such part of it as the judge thinks fit, is committed to writing,—and thereupon (until the time comes for hearing arguments, and pronouncing a decision grounded on it) remains wrapt up in darkness.

There remains, in the character of a means of divulgation, the discourse—the extra-judicial discourse—of the examinee himself. Against this source of mendacity-serving information, if the process of examination is not finished at the first meeting, there exists no remedy—unless his case be that of a person in whose instance immediate commitment to safe custody is for this or other purposes regarded as warrantable.

On the other hand, if the case be such as is understood to warrant such commitment, accompanied with the seclusion of the person, for the time requisite for this purpose, from promiscuous intercourse (personal as well as epistolary;) in that case, this source of mendacity-serving information is sealed up of course.

Even when the mode of examination is public, and no such power of commitment has place, still, so long as the examination is begun and concluded at the same meeting, the nature of the case does not refuse a remedy. The persons about to be examined being predetermined and foreknown at the time appointed for the examination, they repair to one and the same room (a room allotted to the purpose;) in which, under the custody of an officer appointed to prevent conversation, they remain together, each person not being suffered to quit the room till called for to undergo his examination: which performed, he is permitted to go at large, but not permitted to return to the room and company from which he came.

In cases where a second examination of a witness is expected to be necessary, with a view to confrontation or subsequent sifting, he is reconducted out of court, to prevent his hearing the information communicated by any other witness, and kept in the place of safe custody in which he was before, till again called.*

To give to the system of precautions demanded for this purpose, the utmost degree of efficiency of which the nature of things allows them to be susceptible — to determine on this occasion what shall be the fittest decision, between the antagonizing claims of the direct ends of justice on the one hand, and the collateral ends of justice on the other — belongs not so much to this subject as to that of procedure at large.

The reason why it was necessary that mention should be in this place made of it, is, that whenever such seclusion has place, a correspondent degree of relative privacy necessarily has place. During the time he is thus kept in the witness's waiting-room, each such *paulò-post-future* examinee remains precluded from the faculty of rendering himself a member of the assemblage of persons of whom the audience is composed.†

Purpose 3. Prevention of disclosures subservient to non-justiciability, through non-forthcomingness.

* This is precisely the practice adopted in Scotland. — *Ed.*

† The misfortune is, that, besides the expense of whatever architectural arrangements may be necessary to give full effect to the principle of separation thus applied, a considerable measure of delay will be found unavoidably attached to the employing of this security. After the plaintiff (for example) has told his story out of the hearing of the defendant, the defendant has to tell his, and to tell it out of the hearing of the plaintiff. Thus far, all is smooth and easy. But for the purpose of sufficient security, the defendant must have the faculty of putting questions to the plaintiff, in order to draw from him, in explanation, completion, and perhaps refutation, of allegations or depositions, such parts of his case as he might otherwise have suppressed. Moreover, to obtain any explanation of the testimony which the plaintiff has been delivering, it is necessary that the defendant should be correctly apprized of the purport, or rather the very tenor, of the testimony. But, at the time when it was delivered, he was, for the other purpose, studiously excluded. This being the case, of two things one: either, after having delivered his testimony out of the hearing of the defendant, the plaintiff must, for the purpose of the scrutiny, deliver it over again in the hearing of the defendant; or, minutes having been taken of his deposition on the first occasion, those minutes must on the second occasion be read, to serve as a ground for the questions which the defendant is to have the liberty to put to him: — and so, *vice versâ*, for the purpose of the cross-examination to be performed by the plaintiff on the defendant. But to this arrangement, it is evident, no inconsiderable quantity of delay will be attached; and since, if this order of proceeding be invariably observed in all suits, this collateral inconvenience will be produced in many instances in which it will be of no use, — here comes an option to be made between the certain inconvenience produced in the shape of delay, and the contingent profit produced in the shape of security against mendacity, and consequent deception and misdecision.

It will be proper in this case, for a basis for the cross-examination, to refer to the minutes of the plaintiff's original deposition, in preference to the causing him to be re-examined for the same purpose.

Reasons: — 1. Because it may happen, that (either with or without blame on the part of the plaintiff) such rehearing might differ more or less, in reality or in appearance, in circumstances material or in circumstances immaterial, from the standard prototype: and in that case the difference might draw on discussions and delay. Such departure might be produced, not only by a variation in the allegations, depositions, or answers, but by a variation in the purport or order of the questions in such second examination, as compared with those of the first.

2. In the original hearing, more or less matter of conversation may have been extracted or received, which, being palpably irrelevant, may, and with propriety have been left out of the minutes. In the case of a rehearing, this irrelevant matter, more or less of it, might be liable to reappear. Upon the whole, reading the minutes will therefore in general consume less time, be productive of less delay, than a rehearing of the plaintiff.

Upon his cross-examination, it may happen to the plaintiff, with or without blame, to wish to vary more or less from his original testimony. From this advantage, where it operates in favour of truth, he will not be precluded by the substitution of the reading of the minutes to a rehearing; since, in his answer to the cross-questions, nothing will hinder him from bringing forward such new matter as he may think fit.

The fulfilment, in each case, of the direct ends of justice (in other words, *rectitude of decision,*) depends, in so far as concerns the question of fact, upon the complete forthcomingness of all things and persons whose presence is necessary thereto in the character of sources of evidence. The *efficiency* of the decision depends upon the complete forthcomingness of all things and persons which, for the purpose of justiciability, it is necessary should be at the disposal of the judicatory.

There exists not that sort of cause in which, to this or that party on one or other side of the cause (but more especially on the defendant's side,) it may not happen to have an interest in preventing the forthcomingness either of persons or things, to one or other, or both, of the judicial purposes just mentioned.

There exists not that species of cause in which it is not the interest of each party that every witness whose testimony would, if delivered, operate to his disadvantage, should be prevented from delivering it. Nor is this interest necessarily, and in all cases (though naturally and in most cases it will be,) a sinister one. For, in the instance of any given witness, suppose his testimony about to be false, and at the same time likely to gain credence. Though on account of the impossibility of establishing, to any legal purpose, the existence of both these facts, it could never be right for the law itself to lend its assistance to any such evasion, nor so much as to leave the attempt dispunishable; yet in a moral point of view, supposing the expectation of the eventual union of the two disastrous incidents sincere, and to a certain degree intense, it would not be easy (it should seem) to find in it a just ground of censure.

As little exists there that species of cause, in or on occasion of which it may not happen to this or that party on either side (more particularly on the defendant's side) to be, by decision of the judge (direct or incidental,) subjected to some obligation, which, for the fulfilment of it, requires the forthcomingness of this or that person, or this or that thing or aggregate mass of things, to the purpose of his or its being at the disposal of the judicatory; — some obligation, the fulfilment of which, as being attended with evil in some shape or other to the party on whom it should be imposed, it will be his interest (and thence naturally his inclination) to escape from.

It is evident, that all information calculated to assist either of the parties in removing out of the way, either sources of evidence, or anything else which for purposes of justiciability ought to be forthcoming, should (if practicable without preponderant disadvantage) be withheld. The demand for privacy on this account is chiefly confined to investigatorial procedure: when the case is ripe for being brought to trial, it will in general be practicable to take other securities against the frustration of the ends of justice in this way. Discretionary power ought therefore to be vested in the judge, to give temporary privacy to the preliminary examinations taken in the course of investigatorial procedure. Their subsequent publication would in general be a sufficient security against the excercise of this power for any but proper purposes, or on any but proper occasions.

Purpose 4. Preservation of pecuniary reputation.

The demand for the application of the principle of secrecy to this purpose, is of great extent and variety.

In almost every court of justice, in almost every day's practice, cases present themselves in which, without a correct acquaintance with the pecuniary faculties of one or both parties, nothing that deserves the name of justice can be done.

On the other hand, neither are cases much less frequent, in which a public disclosure of those circumstances would, on whichever side it fell, be productive of inconvenience, preponderating in some cases over every advantage derivable from such knowledge.

1. For the purpose of punishment, a necessary point of knowledge is the pecuniary ability of the one party, the delinquent.

2. For the purpose of satisfaction, the finances of two parties (the delinquent and the party injured) are included in the demand for knowledge.

3. Let the suit be one in which costs are incurred. Not to speak of any such enormous and undiscriminating and oppressive load of factitious costs as that which, under judge-made law, has, by the power and to the profit of judges and their confederates, been created and preserved,* there are few causes individually taken, and no sort of cause specifically taken, in which costs, necessary and unavoidable costs, have not place. Of these, at the conclusion of the cause or causes, some disposition cannot but be made. Nor can that disposition be conformable to utility and justice, unless, for the prodigious disproportion which may happen to have place between the pecuniary circumstances of one party and the pecuniary circumstances of another party, some eventual provision be made, and thereupon some account be rendered liable to be taken.

4. Knowledge of the circumstances of the debtor is necessary to the judge, to enable him to do justice as between him and his creditors — whether on a criminal, or on a non-criminal score.

5. In case of danger to ultimate solvency, knowledge of the time or times, mode or modes, to which, without ultimate, or at

* See "*Scotch Reform,*" Letter I. in Vol. V.

least without preponderant, prejudice to the creditor, the payment may be adjusted,— may be necessary to the judge to enable him to preserve the defendant debtor from unnecessary ruin.

6. In addition to the knowledge of the aggregate amount of his debts, knowledge of the circumstances of the creditors to whom they are respectively due may be necessary to the judge, to enable him to preserve from unequal and unreasonable loss, third persons, not parties to the suit by which the demand for the inquiry has been produced.

To an English lawyer, considerations such as the above will scarce appear worthy of a thought. In his hands, the knots in question (like so many others) are cut, as with a sword, by a magnanimous contempt for all such niceties. It is by such magnanimity that the coffers of English judges are gorged with the accumulated pittances of the distressed — the promiscuous spoils of creditors and debtors.

It is only by the examination of the party— the *vivâ voce* examination, that his pecuniary circumstances can in general be established with any approach to accuracy. But (especially if performed in time) this operation would, in nine cases out of ten, or nineteen out of twenty, dry up the source of profitable misery. Hence it is that the presence of the creditors is accordingly not less intolerable to the eye of the insolvent debtor, than that of creditor and debtor is to the English judge. In cases to a vast extent, the ear of the judge is inexorably shut to all evidence respecting the pecuniary circumstances of parties. On what occasion is any such disposition manifested, as that of adjusting time and mode of payment to ability? On what occasion is any regard paid to the interests of co-creditors, who, unsuspicious of the danger, are not parties to the suit? What steam-engine is there, that, beating upon a mass of iron, would pay less regard than is paid by an English judge, with his *capias* or his *fieri facias*, to all such trifles?

On these points, is his ear open to anything in the shape of evidence? It is open to inference — open to the very worst that can be found, to the exclusion of this best, evidence: open to what, in the character of a witness, a third person (perhaps a stranger) shall suppose in relation to the party's circumstances: open to what the party himself shall think fit to say of them, delivering his testimony without the possibility of being questioned — delivering it in the shape of affidavit evidence.

Purpose 5. Fifth purpose of privacy. Prevention of needless violation to the reputation of individuals and the peace of families.

On the occasion of those disputes which are liable to have place between individuals, instances are frequent, in which, either no such blame as deserves punishment has place on any side, or none but such, for the repression of which, the quantity of suffering (in the shape of expense, and other shapes) unavoidably attached to the process of litigation, is of itself sufficient: much more if any part of that vast load of factitious vexation be added to it, which is so much in use to be added to it.

At the same time, in many a cause of this kind, such is the quantity of suffering produced on the part of this or that party, or perhaps all the parties, by the mere exposure of such incidents as have happened to have place in the course of the dispute (in particular, of the conduct maintained by them in the course of the dispute,) that, in comparison with the suffering thus unintentionally produced, any suffering, that by any express, act of the judge, would on the occasion in question be intentionally produced, would be to any degree inferior in its amount.*

* This is more particularly true in the case of disputes in which the disputants are nearly related to one another — more especially between husband and wife, parent and child.

Under the anti-revolutionary constitution of France, when the institution of *lettres de cachet* was attacked on the ground of abuse, their subservience to the purpose of secrecy was brought to view in the way of justification or extenuation, and placed to the account of use. The persons thus consigned to imprisonment were persons of distinction, members of high families, who, had they not been taken care of by a sort of extraordinary justice, would, under the dispensations of ordinary justice, have experienced a severer fate. Good in so far as it served to palliate the mischief of the institution, the plea was bad in so far as it served to reconcile men to the continuance of it.

Before the accession of Louis XVI. the power of confining any number of persons for any length of time, for any cause or for none, was committed to single hands: and blank *lettres de cachet* were, it is said, an object of sale.

At the accession of that weak but well-intentioned monarch, the evil was rendered more tolerable, and thence, had anything endured, more durable. A court consisting of judges was established for the management of this business;— a set of men who, setting out (as may naturally be supposed) with dispositions prone to philanthropy, would as naturally in the cavern of mystery have gradually worn them out, and put on the character of theologo-inquisitorial despotism in their stead. Habits of general publicity, with a withdrawing room for the purpose of occasional secrecy, would, as above, have been the true and only remedy. But in that country (as under the Roman system, wheresoever in use) the whole system was too radically bad to admit of this or any other remedy.

The judge who, sitting singly, takes all examinations in his closet, might have been required, under the requisite limitations and exceptions, to take them in open court. Few things would have been more easy, but nothing more radical, than such a change.

In so far as (without prejudice to the interest of the community in general, in respect of the direct ends of justice and of that sense of security which depends upon the persuasion entertained of their being faithfully pursued) any such suffering can be prevented from taking place, the general happiness of the community will (it is evident) receive proportionable increase.

Vexation, whether to individuals or to the public, is brought to view under the head of Exclusion,* as a ground on which the door may sometimes with propriety be shut against evidence. But if in any case, without preponderant inconvenience, the door of justice may be shut against the evidence itself, with much less inconvenience may it in that same case be shut against this or that individual, or against the public at large, in quality of co-auditors of the evidence.

By means of this temperament, the direct ends of justice may be fulfilled, in many instances in which otherwise it might have been necessary to make a complete sacrifice of them to the collateral ends. The light of evidence, instead of being extinguished altogether, may be set to shine under a bushel — under a bushel, and nevertheless, though in so confined a situation, fulfil its office.

Of these considerations, if just, the following is the use which (it should seem) might be made in practice: —

In cases in which punishment, for the benefit of the public, and for the sake of example, is out of the question, the subject of the contest being some matter of private right; — supposing it sufficiently established that either party was desirous of substituting the private to the public mode, and the other not averse to it, it might, generally speaking, be of use, that (unless for special cause to be assigned by himself) the judge should, on the petition of either party, substitute to the ordinary or public, the private mode.†

By a regulation to this effect, no small part of the vexation incident to litigation might be saved: a species of vexation teeming with a degree of suffering frequently exceeding in its amount that which is produced by the expense, even under the vast increase which such part of the expense as is necessary and unavoidable receives from the amount of such part as is factitious and useless.

Against an arrangement to this effect, three objections may be apt to present themselves:

1. One is, that, by intimidation, this or that one of the litigants may be (as it were) compelled to join in the application; or at any rate to forbear opposing it.

2. Another is, that, in a case in which it would have been for his advantage that the proceeding should have been public, he may by false or fallacious representations, have been deceived into the giving his consent to its being carried on in the private mode.

3. A third is, that, in many instances in which the private mode is substituted (as above) to the public mode, the use of the theatre of justice in the character of a school of moral instruction will be done away.

To the first and second objections it may be answered, that against the mischief thus apprehended, two remedies present themselves: —

One consists in the probity of the judge. If in his opinion the case is of the number of those in which publicity would have been more subservient to the purposes of justice than privacy; in this case, though the possibility of letting in the public at large in the character of spectators is gone by, yet, by himself, or by some person under his direction, minutes having been taken of what passed, — it will rest with him to take order for the publication of those minutes, laying the burthen of the expense on whichever shoulders seem best adapted for it.

If, in the course taken by any party for the obtaining the consent of any other to the substitution of the private to the public mode, any sign of intimidation or fraud should be observed, it may rest with him to inflict moreover on the offending party whatever censure may appear suitable to the case; viz. by expression of disapprobation, or by addition made to the expense of divulgation (as by adding to the number of copies to be printed at the offender's expense,) &c.

The punishment will then be analogous to the offence; and that in such a way as to give it its best chance of being efficacious. Good repute was the possession, to the value of which his sensibility stands indicated and proved, by the sinister course which he took for the preservation of it: reputation is accordingly the possession upon which the punishment attaches, in such a way as to make a defalcation from it.

The other remedy is one that may be left in the hands of the party himself. This remedy consists in the liberty of printing and publishing the minutes at his own expense.

---

* Book IX. *Exclusion;* Part II. *Proper.*

† The proper mode of limitation seems not unobvious: particular individuals on both sides to stand excluded, with or without consent, by authority of the judge. Under the same authority, persons admissible on each side, to be settled (either individually, or only as to number) by blank tickets of admission delivered to the respective parties.

The principal and only constant use of publicity is reducible to the setting as a watch over the conduct of the judge, such persons as, in case of misconduct on his part, may naturally be expected not to be backward in proclaiming it. The inspecting eyes of a few persons thus selected, would be more steadily effectual than those of a promiscuous multitude.

For the purpose of doing all that in this case seems proper or necessary to be done for the repression of such inconvenience as is liable to be produced by such publication, in cases in which the suffering produced by it will be excessive, — the judge might be allowed to mark upon the minutes his disapprobation of any such publication: which note of censure, the party who persists notwithstanding in the design of publication, shall be under the obligation of including in it.

Here, then, should publication be made notwithstanding, the effect of it will be to prefer as it were an appeal to the bar of the public, from the decision pronounced as to this point by the judge. In this way, between the judge and the litigant in question, a sort of silent litigation will take place, in the course of which the judge will act (as it is desirable he should) with all that advantage which it is in the nature of his commanding situation to put into the hands of him who occupies it.

To the third objection, two answers present themselves: —

One is, that, to whatever services the theatre of justice is capable of being made to render to society in the character of a school of moral instruction, no determinate number of causes is necessary. When all are defalcated which the purpose here in question requires to be defalcated, there seems no determinate ground for any such apprehension as that the remainder will not be sufficient for this collateral purpose.

The other is, that forasmuch as, in every such case, it would be in the power of the parties (agreeing in the manner in question) to deprive the public of the use of the theatre of justice in the character in question, either by not commencing the suit, or by compromising it (in which case the public would also be deprived of the use of it in that its principal character,) — any such inferior loss as (to preserve individuals from unnecessary vexation) the public may be subjected to in respect of this collateral and inferior use, seems the less to be regretted.

In causes in which the peace and honour of families is concerned, so long as there is any hope of reconciliation, there cannot be any sufficient objection to secrecy.

Publicity in these cases (understand always if administered in the first instance) can have no better effect than that of pouring poison into whatever wounds have already been sustained.*

Should the pacific endeavours of the judge have proved ineffectual—should reconciliation prove hopeless, hostility and suspicion still alive, and seeking every advantage,—then is

* In the account given of the species of tribunals established in the Danish dominions under a name corresponding to that of Reconciliation Offices, secrecy is spoken of as a universally extensive and inviolable law.

Reasons may be conceived, which, under an institution circumstanced as that was, might operate in justification of that universality, at the same time without lessening its incompetence in the character of a general principle in judicature.

1. From the cognizance of that institution, the class of causes in which generally the demand for the principle of publicity is at its highest pitch (viz. penal causes) are exempted.

2. It is obvious, as already observed, how intimate the connexion is between secrecy of procedure and hope of reconciliation.

3. The powers of that extraordinary tribunal do not extend to the pronouncing a definitive decision, unless by consent of parties. Supposing, therefore, that, in the ordinary courts, the course of proceeding has more or less of the light of publicity to illuminate it,—this light it rests with the party to take the full benefit of, if he please. The decision of the Reconciliation Court is pronounced: is he satisfied with it? publicity is of no use to him; is he dissatisfied? the ordinary courts are open to him: do they afford publicity? he has the benefit of it; do they refuse it? the secrecy of the procedure in the Reconciliation Courts is at any rate no new imperfection in the system of judicature.

4. At the commencement of the institution in question, it was natural that the persons to whom the management of it was intrusted should be persons at once possessing and deserving the highest share of public confidence: stimulated, and at the same time confined within the pale of probity, by that enthusiasm, without which no considerable reforms can ever be so much as attempted. The demand for publicity in its most essential character, that of a check to improbity, might, therefore, in these individual instances, be not altogether without reason, considered as superseded and rendered unnecessary. But a confidence of this sort, how well soever placed in those individual instances, might be very much misplaced, if, by being rendered perpetual, it were extended to an indefinite line of successors; of whom nothing could be known, except that to their case no such securities for zeal and probity, as above described, would have any application.

5. Of this extraordinary system of tribunals, the object — the principal, if not only, object — was the rescuing the people from the depredation which, in that country as well as in every other, has, under the auspices of the technical system, been the real object of the established course of procedure. The sensations excited in the breasts of the men of law of all descriptions (official and professional) attached to the regular tribunals, would of course be such as those with which a flock of half-starved wolves might be supposed to be tormented, when a flock of sheep has just been rescued by the shepherd from their fangs.

In this state of things, any little errors into which the newly-established magistrates might chance to fall — any weaknesses which it might happen to them to betray — would of course be fastened upon with avidity, commented upon with malignity, painted in aggravated colours, and circulated with unwearied assiduity in all circles from which defeat or obstruction to the new system could be hoped. Against such hostility, secrecy, if not a necessary or eligible, was at any rate a very natural, and at least excusable, defence.

the time for either of the parties (though even then at his peril) to demand his pound of flesh, his right of tormenting his adversary, by dragging into daylight all those shades in his character, which (for the tranquillity or reputation of one or both parties, their families, and other connexions) had better have remained in darkness. I say at his peril; for if, upon the continuance and completion (that is, in part, if necessary, the repetition) of the investigation in public, it should appear that this sort of appeal had for its cause the malignant satisfaction of inflicting on the adversary this species of vexation, and that no real apprehension of partiality or misconduct in any other shape bore any part of it,—there seems no reason why malicious vexation in this shape should go unpunished, any more than in any other. The character in which the vexation operates is that of an offence against reputation—an offence of which the hand of the judge, as in case of conviction on a false accusation, has been made the unwilling instrument.

Let but the right of appeal be reserved—in that case,—though in the court below publicity were ultimately and peremptorily refused by the judge, the only serious part, of the mischief against which publicity is particularly calculated to operate as a security, would be avoided. At the court of appeal, it is here assumed that, sooner or later, even in causes in which the demand for secrecy is the strongest, it is in the power of the appellant (alway at his peril) to force publicity.

But such (it may be still observed) is sometimes the force of malice, that, notwithstanding any punishment that can be thus denounced, one of the parties, for the pleasure of injuring the reputation of the other—of perpetrating the mischief, whatever it be, to which the family or any part of it is exposed,—will persevere to the last in the demand of publicity. Possibly: since men are every now and then to be found, who, for the pleasure of depriving an adversary of life, are content to risk their own. Against defamation, when practised in any of the ordinary ways—by word of mouth, by writing, or in print—the punishments appointed for that offence are not always effectual. True: but that is no more than may be said of every other sort of offence, and every other sort of punishment: and after all, the worst mischief arising from publicity is always a limited one; whereas the mischief attached to inviolable secrecy in judicature is altogether boundless. Whatever may be the punishment annexed to defamation when committed in any of the ordinary ways, and whatever in these cases may be its degree of efficacy, a much superior degree of efficacy may be expected from it where it has for its object defamation committed or attempted to be committed in this extraordinary way. In the former case, the passion finds nothing to oppose it: in the latter case, it finds itself opposed by whatever can be done, either in the way of advice or examination, by the authority of the judge. Finding security (security purely pecuniary, constituted by the apprehension of the loss of a fixed sum of money) is the remedy in common use against known or apprehended malice: and among the instances in which it is employed, how small is the proportion of those in which it fails of answering its intended purpose!

Purpose 6. Regard to decency.

Among the cases in which the demand for secrecy is created by a regard to the peace and honour of individuals and families, those in which the injury has its root in the sexual appetite, claim the like attention by this additional title.

If on this score it be proper that exclusion from the right of attendance should be pronounced upon any description of persons by the authority of the legislator and the judge, the classes it would fall upon would naturally be the female sex in general, and, in both sexes, minors below a certain age; more especially in the case of any of those irregularities of the sexual appetite, in which the error regards the species or the sex.

On a subject of this sort, reason stands so little chance of being regarded, that reasoning would be but ill bestowed. The topic being thus brought to view, discussion and decision may be abandoned to those in whose eyes all the others might comparatively appear of small importance.

Minors being under power, it will rest with parents and guardians to keep them out of such scenes, or of any other such scenes by which their morals may be put in jeopardy. Answer *per contrà:* It is easier for the judge to guard the entrance into court, than for a parent or guardian to guard all the roads that lead to it.

How shall age be tried for this purpose? An attempt to try age by view produced the insurrection under Wat Tyler and Jack Straw. A discretionary power of exclusion on this ground to be exercised on view (view of the countenance without ulterior scrutiny,) shall it be lodged in the hands of the judge?

In England, the resort of persons of the female sex to scenes so little suited to female delicacy, has been a frequent subject of animadversion. Exclusion in this case (supposing it worth while) could no otherwise be effected than by the authority of the judge. The subject, however, can scarcely present itself as of light importance to the sort of reformers who of late years have busied themselves so much about print-shops, and who, when they have excluded loose characters from this or that house or garden, conceive themselves to have extinguished looseness; like those politicians who, when without increasing capital they have increased the number of places capable of being traded with, conceive themselves to have increased trade.

Suppose courts of justice as well as print-shops sufficiently fenced, what is to be done with bathing places? amongst others, with the sea coast and the shores of rivers?*

Purpose 7. Preservation of state secrets from disclosure.

To give the question a body, and that the discussion may be somewhat more useful than a mutual beating of the air in the dark, let us frame a feigned case out of a real one. On the occasion of the peace that ensued in 1806 between France and Austria after the battle of Austerlitz, and the change that took place soon afterwards in the British administration, parliament received from the departing ministry a communication of the negotiations that had preceded the rupture terminated by that peace. The communication thus made, was charged with imprudence: the military weakness of your late unfortunate allies, the weakness of their councils, the intellectual weakness of the persons by whom those councils were conducted, the designs entertained in your favour by other powers who were in a way to become your allies; — all these (it was said) you have betrayed: such is the imprudence; and what is the probable consequence? That on future contingent occasions, powers who otherwise might have become your allies, will shrink from your alliance, deterred by the apprehension of the like imprudence.

Such was the imputation: as to the justice or injustice of it, it is altogether foreign to the present purpose. To adapt the case to the present purpose:—suppose that the conduct of the British administration, antecedently to that disaster, had been made the subject of a charge of corruption; and suppose that, for the pronouncing a judicial decision upon that charge, it would have been necessary that the communication spontaneously made as above should have been produced in the character of evidence; and, for the argument's sake, suppose it sufficiently established, that, from the unrestricted publicity of that evidence, the inconveniences above spoken of would have ensued; and that the weight of those circumstances would have been preponderant over any advantage that could have been produced by the punishment of the persons participating in that crime.

Here, then, would have been two great evils, one of which, under the system of inflexible publicity, must necessarily have been submitted to: on the one hand, impunity and consequent encouragement to a public crime of the most dangerous description; on the other hand, offence given to foreign powers, and the country eventually deprived of assistance which might be necessary to its preservation.

By a considerate relaxation of a system, which, inestimably beneficial as it has been in its general tendency, was introduced without consideration, and has been pursued in the same manner, both these evils might in the supposed case in question be avoided.

To give a detailed plan for this ideal purpose would occupy more space than could be spared. But, as to leading principles, precedents not inadequate to the purpose might be found without straying out of the field of English practice. The privacy of secret committees, though as yet confined to preparatory inquiry, might on an emergency of this sort be extended to definitive judicature: the mode in which, in equity procedure, the examining judges are appointed by the parties — appointed out of a body of men to a certain degree select, — and (to come nearer the mark) the mode in which two of the fifteen judges are chosen in the House of Commons for the trial of election causes, — would afford a more promising security for impartiality than could be afforded by any committee chosen (though it were in the way of ballot) in either House.

---

* When a person of the female sex has received an insult of a nature offensive to decency (especially if to youth and virginity refined habits of life be added,) it is no small aggravation of the injury to be obliged, on pain of seeing the author triumph in impunity, to come forward, as in England, and give a description of it, in the face of a mixed and formidable company of starers, many of them adversaries. Females have been seen to faint under such trials. The endeavour on the part of lovers and male relations to supply in this respect the deficiencies of law, is among the causes that give birth to duels. When death ensues, then comes the judge, who, in the case of this species of misery, taught by his books to regard the difference between consent and non-consent as of no importance, urges the jury to consign the defender of a sister or a daughter's honour, to the fate allotted to midnight assassins and incendiaries.

When the injury is greater, as in case of rape, the trial of the injured is less severe. By the horror of the crime, and the idea of the punishment, lighter thoughts are to a certain degree subdued in the bosoms of the audience: while the like sentiments, acting as a stimulus on the mind of the injured sufferer, support her spirits under the conflict.

When life — the life of the defendant — is at stake, any additional danger that might be looked upon as attendant upon a mode of examination comparatively secret, might appear to some too high a price to pay for the preservation of female delicacy. Place that catastrophe out of the question, the proportion between inconvenience and inconvenience will show itself in a point of view materially different: the suffering of the injured, greater — the danger to the supposed injurer, of less magnitude.

§ 4. *Precautions to be observed in the application of the principle of privacy.*

Whatever be the restriction applied to the principle of absolute publicity, care must be taken that the mischief resulting from the restriction be not preponderant over the advantage; that the advantage, consisting in the avoidance of vexation (the inconvenience opposite to the collateral ends of justice,) be not outweighed by any considerable abatement of the security necessary with reference to the direct ends, or rather to all the ends, of justice.

The following are a few precautions, by the observance of which, whatever advantage depending on the relaxation of the principle of publicity be pursued, the more important security afforded by the general observance of that principle may (it should seem) be maintained, either altogether undiminished, or without any diminution worth regarding: —

.. In no case should the concealment be foreknown to be perpetual and indefinite. For to admit of any such case, would be to confer on the judge under whose direction the evidence were to be collected, and the inquiry in other respects carried on, a power completely arbitrary; since, in relation to the business in question, let his conduct be ever so flagitious and indefensible, by the supposition he is, by means of the concealment in question, completely protected from every unpleasant consequence; protected not only against punishment — legal punishment, but against shame.

At all events, in the hands of every party interested must be lodged (to be exercised on some terms or other,) in the first place, the power of establishing each act, each word, by proper memorials; in the next place, the power of eventually bringing those memorials to light. If, in the case of a secret scrutiny, the examination be performed *vivâ voce*, questions and answers both should be minuted *ipsissimis verbis*, and the authenticity of the minutes established in the strictest and most satisfactory mode.

2. In no case let the privacy extend beyond the purpose: let no degree of privacy be produced (if one may so say) in waste. For every restriction put upon publicity, in tendency at least (whether in actual effect or not) infringes upon the habit, and weakens the sense of responsibility on the part of the judge.

3. Care in particular should be taken not to have two different sets of tribunals; one of them reserved for secret causes. The tribunals reserved for secret causes will be so many seats of despotism; more especially if composed of judges who never judge but in secret. Under a judge trained up (as it were) from infancy to act under the controul of the public eye, secrecy in this or that particular cause will be comparatively exempt from danger: the sense of responsibility, the habit of salutary self-restraint, formed under the discipline of the public school, will not be suddenly thrown off in the closet.

4. Instead of secret courts, of which there should not anywhere be a single one, let there be to every court a private chamber or withdrawing room: behind the bench, a door opening into a small apartment, into which the judge, calling to him the persons requisite, may withdraw one minute, and return the next, the audience in the court remaining undisplaced.*

In this way, just so much of the inquiry is kept secret as the purpose requires to be kept secret, and no more. In one and the same cause, the interrogation of one deponent may be performed in secret, that of another in public: even of the same deponent, one part of the examination may be performed in the one mode, another in the other mode.

§ 5. *Cases particularly unmeet for privacy.*

In cases of a non-criminal nature, between individual and individual, — so long as the faculty of attendance for himself and a sufficient number of his nominees is secured to each person having a distinct interest in the cause, the privacy can be attended with no other inconvenience except the loss of the casual security afforded for the correctness and completeness of the evidence, by the chance of ulterior witnesses, as above explained (a chance which will only apply to here and there a particular case,) and the infringement made in the habit of responsibility on the part of the judge.

In the case of offences of a criminal nature, — and in particular those in the punishment of which the members of the government† or the public at large‡ have an interest, — privacy is far from being equally exempt from danger.

The interest which the public at large have in the conformity of the procedure to the several ends of justice, added to the general

* In this way, no such affront would be put upon the public as is habitually, and (though naturally enough) not necessarily, put upon it, in the two houses of the British parliament, by the operation of *clearing* the house.

† *E. g.* endeavours to overturn the government; endeavours to excite resistance to the government; endeavours to injure the reputation of the governing body, or this or that particular member of it; actions against any member of th governing body for abuse of the powers or functions attached to his station; election causes; suits relative to the right of occupying this or that public station.

‡ Predatory offences,—theft, highway robbery, housebreaking; rape; incendiarism; homicide, in some cases.

reasons that plead in favour of publicity (as above,) seem sufficient to establish the rule of unrestrained publicity in the character of the general rule. What remains to be considered is, whether, among the above-mentioned reasons in favour of privacy, there be any which in a case of this class can constitute a sufficient ground for the establishment of an exception to that general rule.

1. The judge without the concurrence of either party — the judge alone, could not present so much as a colourable reason for any mode or degree of privacy.

2. Nor yet the judge and the prosecutor together. In other words, it would not be eligible that the judge, at the instance of the prosecutor alone, should, for any cause, withdraw the procedure from the cognizance of the public at large.

Whatsoever be the form of government — monarchical, aristocratical, democratical, or mixed — the sort of dependence or connexion which can scarcely fail of subsisting as between the judge and the members of the administration, is such, that, to a person in the situation of defendant in any cause in which any member of that body (as such) has any personal interest, the eventual protection of the public eye is a security too important to be foregone: the vexation — the greatest vexation — that could befal the public functionary for want of that privacy which, in a case between individual and individual, might without preponderant danger be allowed, would be confined to the individual: but, in case of misdecision to the prejudice of the defendant, and undue punishment in consequence (besides that to the individual the affliction of the punishment in this case would be so much greater than that of the vexation on the other,) the alarm which a bare suspicion of such unjust punishment is calculated to excite, would, in respect of its extent, be an additional and more serious evil: and although there were no other cause, the simple fact of a desire on the part of the prosecutor, and a consent on the part of the judge, to withdraw the procedure from the cognizance of the public eye, would of itself be a ground of alarm, neither unnatural nor unreasonable.

The minutes being in this case taken, and taken *ipsissimis verbis*, — if, when the proof had been closed, the minutes were to be read in the presence of the defendant and of the open committee of the public — if, in answer to appropriate questions, the defendant were then, in the presence of the public, to recognise the correctness of the statement, — the security thus afforded to him against misrepresentation, would (it might be supposed) be sufficient for the purpose.

If, however, throughout the whole of his examination, the defendant were to be altogether destitute of assistance and support (as in Roman procedure is actually the case,) no such security would be sufficient. Having no one to bear witness for him, intimidations of all kinds may, on the part of the judge, or on the part of the judge and prosecutor, be applied to him, and (if unsuccessful) disavowed. On the occasion of the public hearing (as above,) it may happen to him to come ready-instructed—and by such irresistible authority—what to say, and what not to say.

Corrupt indeed must be the state of justice, where such abuses are not at the worst extremely rare; but (be the abuse itself ever so rare) what in the midst of such darkness cannot reasonably be expected to be rare, is the apprehension of it.

What if, no such abuse being really practised, the defendant, temerariously, or through *mala fides*, should set up a false complaint of it? If indeed he is prudent, and at the same time not without hope of what is called mercy (absolute or comparative,) he certainly will not pursue a course at once so injurious and so offensive. But, that hope of mercy should be altogether wanting, cannot, in a case of this class, be an unfrequent occurrence: nor yet, where revenge can promise itself an immediate gratification, is any such imprudence out of nature.

Under every government, cases will occur, in which (not to speak of pretences) there may be just grounds for wishing that the evidence may be, more or less of it, kept secret. Suppose, for example, the occasion of the supposed offence to be a transaction, the disclosure of which would betray the military projects or the military weakness of the state; or a transaction, exposing to obloquy the conduct of some foreign state. Be the mischief of publicity preponderant or not, few indeed will be the political states (none, perhaps, but the English and the Anglo-American) in which the members of the administration, whose conduct might by the disclosure be exposed to censure, would have self-denial sufficient to forbear availing themselves of the plea for withdrawing it from the scrutiny of the public eye.

In a case of this kind, a sort of middle course might be observed. In the class of professional lawyers, there can never be wanting, in every country, men of reputation, adequate to be trusted with such secrets, if bound to secrecy by an oath, or other the most solemn engagement in use. Out of a list formed for this purpose, but formed at a period anterior to that in which the individual cause could have come into contemplation, let the defendant, in such case, have the liberty of choice. The professional assistant thus chosen, without being near enough to prompt the defendant in his answers, might be present to the purpose of witnessing any impropriety of conduct (supposing it to take place) on the part of the judge, and by that means to serve as a security against its taking place, and to attest its not having taken place.

What if the defendant should be too poor to pay, on the occasion, the price of professional assistance? He must, on this as on other occasions, obtain it through charity, or remain destitute of it. But in a case of this sort, which is always a case of extensive expectation and interest, charity for this purpose can scarcely fail of being at hand, either on the part of sellers, or on the part of purchasers.

3. Nor yet would it be conducive to the ends of justice, that in a case of this description it should rest with the judge to withdraw the procedure from the cognizance of the public at large, at the instance of a defendant; to withdraw it, at any rate but so that, the prosecutor (if there be one) be present on each examination, with at least one professional assistant, by way of witness, at his choice. Without this check (supposing, on the part of the judge, any undue partiality in favour of the defendant's side) matters might easily be so arranged as that the acquittal of the defendant, though guilty, might be the result; and this without being productive of any of that disrepute which would naturally attach upon the conduct of the judge who should give impunity to a malefactor whose guilt was written in legible characters upon the face of the evidence.

The objection to the privacy extends not, however, beyond the case in which, in consideration of the interest which the public at large has in the suppression of the offence, the judge stands interdicted from remitting the punishment attached to it. For wherever the power of remission obtains, the worst that can happen from the privacy is the exercise of that same power — the exercise of it in an indirect way, instead of a direct one.

4. Nor yet, in the class of cases in question, would it be eligible that the mode of privacy in question should take place, although it were even at the joint solicitation of both parties (or say all parties,) as well as with the consent of the judge.

The reason is, that here (as before) there is a party interested (viz. the public at large) whose interest might, by means of the privacy in question, and a sort of conspiracy, more or less explicit, between the other persons concerned (the judge included) be made a sacrifice. Here (as before) if the case be of the number of those in which, by the concurrence of those several parties (or, much more, if by any two or one of them) the punishment incurred or supposed to be incurred by the defendant may avowedly be remitted, the objection against privacy extends not to this case.

So publication in the scriptural mode were kept open, privacy, as against publicity in the *vivâ voce* mode (it might seem,) might be maintained without inconvenience; at any rate, if ultimate decision and execution were not admitted till the public had had time sufficient for taking cognizance of the communication made to it.

Several causes, however, concur in preventing the latter of these securities from being an equivalent to both together.

In the first place, it is not the whole of the evidence that is capable of being expressed by writing. Deportment (an article constituting a considerable branch of circumstantial evidence, and itself distinguishable into a considerable number of varieties) is an article not communicable but in a very imperfect manner, to any that are not at once auditors and spectators.

In the next place, the discourse published under the name of the depositions delivered *vivâ voce* on the occasion in question, — is it really, in tenor or in purport, the very evidence — neither more nor less than what on that time or occasion, was actually delivered? For the completeness, as well as correctness, of the evidence, the presence of an unrestricted assemblage of bystanders affords a security which on some occasions may be absolutely necessary to the prevention of misconduct on the part of the judge (misconduct, the fruit of which may be the violation of all the ends of justice) — a security, of which, in some cases, privacy, as against publicity in the *vivâ voce* mode, may be absolutely destructive.

In the third place (the evidence being, or not being, represented as it was actually delivered) — that which was delivered under the degree of privacy in question, — is it exactly the same as would have been delivered had the conduct of the judge been carried on under the controul of the public eye, in a state of unrestricted publicity?

The advantages of publicity, — whether considered in themselves, or in comparison with the advantages of secrecy (*i. e.* with the disadvantages of publicity) in the several cases in which the demand for secrecy presents itself, — will be apt to appear different, according to the state of the constitutional branch of law in the country in question—according as the degree of influence possessed by the body of the people is more or less considerable. Under the republican institutions of British America (for example) it is evident that the value set upon publicity should be at the highest pitch: nor, in this respect, should one expect to see British Europe in any considerable degree behind.

Not that in respect of the real value of publicity in this character of a security for good judicature, there is any very distinct and assignable difference. But in monarchies, the difficulty (if there be any) will naturally be to prevail on the government to give to the application of the principle of *publicity*, the extent which abstract utility would require. Under a mixed constitution like the British, or a republican constitution like the Anglo-American, the difficulty would be to prevail on the people to view with complacency any such extent given to the principle of *privacy* as the dictates of abstract utility might be thought to require.

The class of causes in which, under a constitution more or less popular, it is more particularly material that the principle of publicity should be maintained, are such as may be termed constitutional causes—causes in which the government of the country may naturally be expected to take a more particular interest, and in which (if in any) the sinister influence of government (that is of the other members of government) might be apprehended as likely to act with effect in the character of a sinister influence upon the probity of the judge. Such, for example, are—

1. *In penali*, Prosecutions for endeavours to subvert the government.

2. Prosecutions for endeavours to excite resistance to the power of government on this or that particular occasion.

3. Prosecutions for endeavours to injure the reputation of the public functionaries of the higher orders.

4. Actions by individuals against the public functionaries, especially of the higher orders, for abuse of power or influence.

5. In non-penali, Election causes: suits in which the right to the possession of this or that public office is the subject-matter in dispute.

Of all these sorts of causes (which, however, are given but as examples,) there is not any one that comes within any of the classes marked out for secrecy. Thus far, therefore, the advocate of a popular constitution need find no objection to the application of the principle of publicity.

Even under the most absolute monarchy, in a constitutional cause (as above described) it will not often happen to the sovereign to wish to see injustice done; it can never happen to him to be content to be regarded as harbouring such a wish.

In all cases, therefore, except such in which he is seriously anxious that injustice should be done, he might at least suffer the *evidence* to be collected in public, without prejudice to his wishes.

But the arguments? — the arguments of advocates in favour of the prisoner, — might it not happen to them to be delivered in too popular a tone, especially where a question of law came to be discussed? In pursuit of professional celebrity and the praise of eloquence, might it not be a natural endeavour on the part of the advocate to raise the spirit of the people, and point their passions against the existing order of things? Supposing this inconvenience a preponderant one, the bar of secrecy might be applied to these effusions of rhetoric, leaving the evidence to be collected in public notwithstanding.

English jurisprudence, supposing it on this ground to rest upon any rational principle, goes much farther in this track. In penal causes of the rank of felonies (high treason only excepted, and that by statute,) it imposes absolute silence upon the defendant's advocate, so far as the question of fact is on the carpet. So jealous were the founders of the system, of the power of professional rhetoric over the affections of their favourite class of judges — so jealous (always supposing them to have consulted reason on the subject, which very likely they never did)— that by putting a gag into the mouths of the advocates, they determined to give the same sort of security to their judges that Ulysses, when amongst the Syrens, gave to his companions — by putting wax into their ears.

If there were no other option than between publicity in all cases and secrecy in all cases, there can be no doubt in favour of which side it ought to declare itself. It is only in here and there a particular case, that secrecy is of any use — that publicity is liable to be productive of any inconvenience. The inconvenience, where it does happen, confines itself to a few individuals, and that in a few sorts of causes: the evil attached to secret judicature strikes against the whole body of the community — deprives the public of an indispensable security for good judicature — runs counter to all the ends of justice.

§ 6. *Errors of Roman and English law in respect to publicity and privacy.*

Such (as far as it can be represented by rough outline) is the course which, as between publicity and privacy, seems, at the present advanced state of society, to be naturally suggested by a solicitous and attentive regard to the ends of justice.

Such, or not very different from it, would have been the course pursued in the civilized states of Europe, and in England in particular, if, being devised and put together at any such advanced stage in the career of civilization, they had had for their authors men who had proposed to themselves the ends of justice as the main object by which their labours were to be guided, and towards which they were to be directed.

At the time when the system of procedure had arrived at such a stage as to have taken a form and character of which it could not, without an extensive and sudden change of lights and views and interests, be divested;

unhappily, both the two elements of aptitude, the two requisites to the pursuit of the right path as above sketched out (viz. probity and wisdom,) were, on the part of those in whose hands the power was lodged, everywhere wanting.

In every country, the fashioning of the main body of the laws, and with it, of its necessary appendage the system of procedure, was in the hands of men who, from the blindness which had place as well below them as above them, derived the faculty of taking for the main object of their exertions and arrangements their own personal, separate, and sinister interest:—the interest of the public, of the community in general, and thence the ends of justice, being either in no degree at all, or at best in a very subordinate and inferior degree, the objects of their regard.

For the pursuit of those sinister ends, everywhere the stock of wisdom existing on the part of this class of men was abundantly sufficient: while, for the pursuing of the several ends of justice on every occasion by the most direct and proper course, even had the suggestions of probity been listened to, the stock of wisdom could not but (as we go farther and farther back in the track of history. cutting off thereby more and more of the now-accumulated stock of experience) have been proportionably deficient.

Two opposite systems, the English and the Roman—both of them harsh, unreflecting and unbending—both of them running to extremes, blindly pursuing a general principle to the neglect or contempt of all requisite exceptions—divided between them, in England itself, the field of power; while, upon the continent of Europe, the principle of privacy, pushed to the pitch of absolute secrecy, covered the whole expanse.

In the Roman procedure, as exemplified on the continent, the whole business of examination is performed *in secreto judicis:* in a place which, whether actually the private closet of the judge or not, is at any rate equally inaccessible to the public at large. Screened by this means almost entirely from the force of the moral sanction, from the tutelary inspection of the public eye,—improbity and (what is still more common) indolence and indifference, may accomplish their ends with comparatively little risk. The court above (for, under the Roman law, the check of appeal, being the only one, is almost uniformly applied)—the court above, were they to discover any marks of improbity apparent to their eyes, would naturally prevent it from taking effect. But under the system of privacy, it is only from the information given them by the inferior judges themselves, that the superior judges obtain what information they acquire concerning what is done by those inferior judges. In case of mere indolence, impropriety of conduct may rise to such a degree as to be continually giving birth to wrong decision, and frustrating the purposes of justice, without betraying itself by any such indications as would necessarily find their way to the eye of the court above. And in case of improbity, or prepossession,—if the seducing motive or prejudice were either imbibed by the inferior judges from the superior, or shared with them in any other way, a check which at best (as we have seen) is but inadequate, would by that means be reduced to nothing.

Happily for England, that one of the two rival principles to which good fortune rather than wisdom had given the ascendant, was the principle of publicity. At first, the small body of men who in each district, under the name of freeholders, lorded it over a larger body of slaves and other humble dependents, then, by degrees, a sort of select committee of that body,—gained or preserved, together with the right of access and the duty of attendance, a sort of influence which (by the favour of fortune) operated as a check upon the king's completely dependent creatures, who in this department of goverment operated as instruments of his will under the name of judges.

But of the attendance of every such tribe of assessors—whether the promiscuous body of freeholders, or the committee of twelve under the name of jurors—publicity (and that in a degree unrestrained by any bounds but such as in this or that place came to be applied by casual and local and accidental circumstances) became a natural, and, as good fortune would have it, at length an inseparable, concomitant.

In English judicature, therefore, the principle of publicity predominates over the principle of secrecy; and it is to this predominance, added to two or three other very simple principles, and not the less salutary for being simple,* that, taken in the aggregate, the system of procedure is indebted for its being perhaps the least bad extant, instead of being among the worst.

In English judicature, the genius of publicity predominates over its antagonist. In some parts of the system it is established: and in those parts, loud and universal and incessant are the praises of it. In other parts it is discarded: in those parts the principle of secrecy is watched over with a degree of attention and anxiety much beyond what is manifested for the maintenance of publicity. Publicity is adored—secrecy cultivated: in despite of adages, in despite of consistency, God and Mammon are served in the same breath.

In common law, all is light: in equity law,

* Such as cross-examination and the use of juries, however inconsistently, scantily, redundantly, and inappropriately applied.

all is darkness. The light is admirable: the darkness no less admirable. Think not that the darkness, where darkness reigns, has any rational cause, or anything approaching to a rational cause. The circumstances presenting a demand for secrecy have above been brought to view: scarce any of them have any application to any of the sorts of causes of which equity takes cognizance. At any rate, if a selection were made of the sorts of causes least apt to present a demand for secrecy, those of which equity takes cognizance might stand first upon the list. "I think; therefore I exist," was the argument of Des Cartes: I exist; therefore I have no need to think or be thought about, is the argument of jurisprudence.

What are, and what are not, equity causes, I cannot (happily it is not here necessary) undertake to say: those by whom this exquisite sort of law is administered, do not themselves so much as profess to know. Two things, however, a man may venture to say, with some assurance: that there is not any sort of fact whatever inquired after in this extraordinary, this less trustworthy, this secret mode, that may not at any time be sent to be inquired after in the ordinary, the more trustworthy, the public mode, by virtue of what is called *directing an issue:* that, — in this division of cases, to which the capacity of being inquired after in the secret mode is confined, — the sorts of transactions in which the peace and honour of families are most liable to be wounded, those in which the laws of decency are most liable to be violated, and those in which pecuniary credit is most liable to be injured, are not comprised.

The reason for this secrecy (for there is a reason for it) is altogether curious: it is, lest the evidence delivered on each side should be opposed by counter-evidence delivered on the other.

And why not suffer the testimony to undergo this correction and completion? Why not? (for this reason has likewise its reason, its superior reason.) Why not? For fear of perjury.* Such is the reason for not suffering evidence to be opposed by counter-evidence. Had it been the express object of these sages to encourage perjury, few means better adapted to that purpose could have been devised.

* Gilbert's Forum Romanum [History and Practice of the Court of Chancery 1758,] p. 109— "But if the supplemental bill be moved for after publication" [viz. of the depositions taken in consequence of the original bill,] "the court never gives them leave to examine anything that was in issue in the former cause, by reason of the manifest danger of subornation of perjury, where they have a sight of the examination of the witnesses."

P. 117—"One of the judges of the court himself anciently examined, and therefore he might form the interrogations out of the articles as he pleased: but the adverse party was to exhibit interrogations for the judge to examine upon; because the matter upon which the defendant might cross-examine to invalidate, might not be within the articles: but no copies of the interrogatories were to be given to the adverse party." [*N. B.* The above in the Roman Law.]

P. 120—"Afterwards," [after expiration of rule to show cause why publication should not pass,] "there could be no examination of witnesses, unless by the special direction of the judge, upon good cause shown, and an affidavit of the party, that he, or those employed by him, had not, nor would see the depositions of the witnesses, which were published, by reason of the manifest danger of perjury and subornation of witnesses, in case examinations should be allowed after publication. But after publication there might be *editio instrumentorum*, till the conclusion of the cause, because there was no danger of perjury, upon the proof of such notorious instruments." — [Perjury and subornation they therefore regard as more probable than the honest need of counter-evidence or counter-interrogation. If this were right, this should be a bar to all *new* trials.]

P. 127—"The fair examination by commissioners is not to adjourn without necessity; because that would be to harass the defendant by obliging him to travel from place to place to cross-examine...... And this affair must be performed as far as possible *uno actu*, that there be as little opportunity as possible to divulge the depositions, that neither side may better the proof."

P. 131—"If due notice be given, one side proceeds and examines his witnesses; the other, if he does not examine, shall not have a new commission, unless affidavit be made of some reasonable cause of his non-attendance, and that neither the party who did not examine, nor any for him, or by his direction or knowledge, has seen, heard, or been informed of the depositions taken, or any part of them, nor willingly will see, &c. till he has examined, or till publication: this is, that the defendant may not have an opportunity of knowing what has been proved for the plaintiff, and so be able to contest it."

P. 137—"If it shall appear to the court, by affidavit or certificate of the plaintiff's, that the defendant's commissioners attended during the whole time of the execution of the commission, and never exhibited any interrogatories, — in this case, the court will never grant the defendant another commission, and he must take it for his pains; since he lay upon the watch and catch, only to see what the plaintiff proved, and then, at another commission, to exhibit interrogatories adapted to such matters and questions as might tend to overthrow all that he had done: and he shall never be admitted to have this unfair advantage over his adversary; for if he is admitted, after having knowledge of all that his adversary has proved, to exhibit interrogatories, he may easily conceive what interrogatories to exhibit, and how to hit the bird in the eye."

P. 138—"And care must be taken (if a new commission is granted) that neither party add to or alter their interrogatories: they must examine upon the old interrogatories, which were exhibited at the former commission, and are not to add any new ones without special leave from the court; and they are to be settled by a master, and are never done but in extraordinary cases."

The notion that seems to be implied, and in a manner assumed, in this arrangement, and the reasoning by which it is supported, is curious enough. It is, that there exists a sort of natural fund of evidence, upon which it is in every man's power to draw for any quantity for which he happens to have a demand: or else, that every man possesses a sort of manufactory of evidence, in which it depends upon himself to manufacture at any time whatsoever quantity of the article he has occasion for, for his own use.

This unlimited fund of evidence—of what sort is it supposed to be?—true and relevant evidence, or false evidence? If true and relevant, what advantage did the legislator propose to justice from the suppression of it? If false evidence, what is there in this arrangement that can tend to discourage the manufacture? The party who, in consequence of what he has heard of the evidence (true or false) that has been produced by his adversary, sets about the production of false evidence, has therefore as well the will as the power to manufacture false evidence—whatever false evidence suits his purpose. What a supposition! and where is it that anything can be found to countenance it?

Will it be denied that true evidence is rather more frequent, and more easy to obtain, than false evidence? But if so, the evidence suppressed by the arrangement in question is more likely to be true than false.

Is it, that evidence is more likely to be false than true? and being false, to be deceptitious? If this theory were correct, the practical inference would be, that the best course to take would be never to receive any evidence at all.

In the criminal branch, the open inquiry is regularly preceded by a secret one.* To what use the secrecy here? Oh, it had once a use, though the use is gone:—no matter, it is not the less admirable.

P. 141—"And since the very life and vitals of almost every cause, and of every man's property, lies in keeping close, and secreting his evidence, till after the depositions are published, because after that there is an end of examining."

P. 144—"Neither the examinations nor depositions, which are taken by commission, can be published in any case whatsoever, till publication is duly passed by rule in the office, or by motion or petition; for it may be done either way."

P. 146—"And in this case the plaintiff or defendant (as the case falls out) must make oath, and so must his clerk in court, or solicitor, 'that they have neither seen, heard, read, or been informed of any of the contents of the depositions taken in that cause; nor will they hear, see, read, or be informed of the same, till publication is duly passed in the cause.' And upon such affidavit it is usual for the court to enlarge publication, and give the party an opportunity to examine his witnesses."

* Grand jury.

The use of the secrecy having for centuries been lost (lost without being missed by anybody,) the secrecy itself continues. What is the consequence? In the seat of secrecy, what could not but be the consequence,—despotism: in another place, caprice, in this or that odd corner of the field of judicature, taking upon itself to controul that despotism—caprice, acting without rule, and tolerated (though not always without grumbling) because despotism jostled and counteracted by caprice, is better than despotism pure and simple. Would informations in any case be endurable, if, in that same case, grand juries were not a source of impunity, an obstruction in the way of justice?

The original purpose of this secrecy was, to avoid divulging to the defendant the evidence that might come to be produced against him in the definitive inquiry (called the trial) before the petty jury. Not divulge it to him? why not? Lest, by absconding, he should elude the hands of justice. Observe, that at this period he has already heard the evidence against him, defended himself against it as well as he has been able, and is already in the hands of justice.

Another case of secrecy at common law is that of the examination of a married woman, on the occasion of her joining with her husband in the alienation of a landed estate held by them in her right. This in itself has nothing to do with judicature. But some centuries ago, the judges of one of the great courts of Westminster-Hall (the Common Pleas) having contrived to introduce themselves into a share of that sort of business, which on the continent of Europe is performed by notaries who are not attorneys, and in Britain by attorneys,—the ceremony thus described has been introduced accordingly into the list of the ceremonies performed by a judge. Whatsoever may have been the origin of it, the effect is innoxious (at least if the expense and vexation of personal attendance be laid out of the question,) and what was probably the object is laudable: the property originating with the wife, the object was to ascertain that her consent to the parting with it was free, not extorted by ill usage.

The veil of secrecy is thrown over examinations and other inquiries, as carried on in the common-law courts, as well as in the equity courts, by the sort of subordinate judge called in most instances the Master—in the other instances, designated by some other name which is regarded as synonymous.†

The matters of fact inquired into by this sort of subordinate judge, are in general such as are regarded but as accidental with relation to the principal matters on which the

† On the equity side of the court of Exchequer, the Deputy Remembrancer; in the Common Pleas, the Prothonotary.

cause hinges, and which form the subject of the ultimate decision pronounced by the principal judge or judges.

The business of the examiner so denominated — of the subordinate, who, sitting in the office called the examiner's office, collects the personal evidence — is confined altogether to that narrow function. By him the evidence is collected, but it belongs not to him to pronounce any decision grounded on it. Were he not to commit the testimony to writing, his operations would have neither object nor effect.

Not so the Master. To pronounce decisions is the principal function of his office: another function, subservient to the former, is the making inquiry into the matters of fact on which these decisions are to be grounded. Of the testimony relative to these matters of fact, that he should commit to writing minutes of some sort or other (possibly and eventually for his justification, but at all times for the assistance of his own recollection) may naturally, or rather must necessarily, be presumed. In the present instance, however, everything of this sort is left to chance. For any general proposition expressive of the state of the law or the practice on this head, no sufficient warrant is to be found in any printed book of law. How should there? Operations which are left throughout to be the sport of chance, how should they in any way form the subject of a rule?

A cause, on the occasion of which the testimony, after having been extracted and collected in the sunshine of publicity, is carefully committed to writing by judges of the highest rank, may be to any degree destitute of importance. A decision adjudging to the plaintiff, in the name of damages, the sum of one shilling (a fraction of the value of one day's labour of an ordinary labourer) is in every day's experience: a decision adjudging to him no more than the forty-eighth part of that sum, is not without example.

A cause, on the occasion of which the testimony (after having been extracted and collected, in the darkness of a small sitting room, by judges of too low a rank to be spoken of under that respected name) is either committed or not committed to writing, — and (if in any form) in a form more or less adequate or inadequate to the purpose, as indolence, caprice, or any other motive may have prescribed, — may be important to any the highest degree of importance — at least of pecuniary importance.

In the case of the inquiry carried on as above in the examiner's office, secrecy (as hath already been mentioned) is an object expressly avowed, and anxiously provided for. With a degree of strictness not much less anxious than that which is observed on the occasion of those spontaneous and confessional declarations which in some countries religion is considered as prescribing, the door is avowedly shut against the public at large — against every person besides the two necessary actors in the forensic drama—the examiner and the examinee.

In the case of the inquiry carried on before a Master, no traces of any such anxiety are to be found anywhere in print; no authoritative political bar, visible in that form, has been opposed to the entrance of miscellaneous visitors. Bars of the physical class (such, for example, as brick walls) are, however, not less efficacious; and of these there is no want. The walls which bound a space in which not more than twenty persons can find standing room, are at least as peremptory a bar to the admission of three score, as any act that was ever printed in the statute book, or any proclamation that was ever inserted in the Gazette.

An experiment I should not choose to make, is the attempt to gain admission into a master's office, not being attorney, or advocate, or witness about to be examined in the cause. Courts of justice — English courts of justice (as any English lawyer will be ready to assure you) are always open: but an argument I should not choose to pay for, is an argument on the question, whether in this sense a master's office is or is not a court of justice.

In ecclesiastical court procedure, again, as in equity procedure, all is darkness. Why?— because in those courts of narrow jurisdiction the demand for secrecy is particularly urgent? Not for any such cause, most surely: that cause would be a rational one. It is because this smaller branch, as well as the larger, was imported ready-grown from the Roman world. In both instances, who were the importers? Men who, whatever was the cause, loved darkness better than light.

Within the jurisdiction of these courts are included causes relative to adultery: and in these causes is not the peace and honour of families concerned? Yes, surely, if in any. Here, then, at least (it may be added) is not the veil of secrecy well applied? applied fortunately at least, if not wisely? Yes, verily, if it were applied to any effect. But is it? To the delivery of the evidence, the public is not admitted, because it would be against custom and against principle. But the evidence, when delivered, is made public—as public as the press can make it. While concealed, it is not because concealment is favourable to decency: when made public, it is not because publicity is favourable to justice. When concealed, it is not because judges have regard to family peace, to female honour, or to decency; but because judges, or those who act under judges, have a regard for trade. The secrets of the Arches are opened by the same key — the same patent key — by which the courts in Westminster and Guildhall are closed.

There are moral obstacles, and there are physical ones — there are prohibitions, and there are stone walls: the walls are of rather the firmer texture. In the highest criminal court, the King's Bench, when the doors are not shut, the proceedings are said to be public: and when in a popular mood, magnificent are the eulogiums pronounced on the publicity by learned judges. When the doors are not shut, the proceedings are said to be public: but within these doors, in what numbers it is possible for men to come, or (being come) to hear, is not worth thinking of. When the doors are not shut, the proceedings are said to be public: and so are they when the doors are shut, so long as it is in the power of money to open them. Would you know what becomes of the money? Ask the door-keeper, or the Lord Chief Justice: the door-keeper, who either keeps the money or pays it over; the judge, who either gives the place or sells it.

So much for that branch of publicity which consists in the admission of spectators into the theatre of justice. Next, as to that which consists in the printed publication of the whole of the proceedings, including at any rate the evidence; — publication of the *trial*, as we say in English. In that part of the cause which is called the trial, is contained (with scarce an accidental exception) as much of it as is capable of exciting, on the part of a non-professional reader, the least particle of interest: all the rest of the proceedings being of a nature common to all causes of that class, and not contributing to add to the conception of the characteristic features of the individual cause. In this document are exhibited; — 1. The cause of action, as set forth in the declaration or indictment, according as the cause belongs to the non-penal or penal class; 2. The evidence, as contained in the questions put to the witnesses, whether by advocates, judge, or jurymen, and the answers given in consequence; 3. The arguments of the advocates on both sides; 4. The substance of the evidence as recapitulated by the judge, with any such observations as he thinks fit to make on it, for the instruction of the jury.

In England, the faculty of printing and publishing the trial, as thus explained, is, in the instance of all causes at the hearing of which the public is permitted to be present, open to any person who may find himself disposed to exercise it. It is exercised as often as (in the instance of a party concerned) the care of his reputation, or (in the instance of a bookseller or reporter) the prospect of profit, presents an adequate inducement — an incident that frequently does happen, and may happen in any case, for any assurance that any person interested in the concealment of improbity or negligence or imbecility could ever give himself to the contrary. In this way, not only the parties to the cause are upon their trial before the bar of the public, but all the other actors in the drama: witnesses, advocates, jurymen, and judges.

The fixation of the evidence in this way, by signs of an unevanescent and imperishable nature, affords (it is evident) to the correctness of the expression a much more permanent security than could be afforded by the mere publicity of the transaction — by the faculty afforded to the public at large of catching by the ear such a transient impression as that organ is capable of receiving. Expense apart, the thing to be desired would be, that such complete publication should take place in every case. In the bulk of cases, the magnitude of the expense operates as a bar: but, by a happy coincidence, the more important the cause, the better the chance it possesses of obtaining this matchless security for propriety of conduct on the part of all persons in any way concerned in it.

In this country, an account, more or less particular, of the proceedings of the principal courts of justice, has, for many years past, formed a constant ingredient in the composition of a newspaper. The degree of interest likely to be taken by the public, is in this case the natural measure of the space allowed to the history of each cause. Wherever, according to the calculation made by commercial speculation, the degree of interest promises to spread to a certain extent, the history of each cause forms a separate publication.

The causes which serve to hold up to the view of the public the conduct of the public functionaries, are among those by which the most extensive interest will naturally be excited.

Thus intimate is the connexion between intelligence, curiosity, opulence, morality, liberty, and justice.

Another advantage of this publicity, and one that applies more directly to the present head, is the chance it affords to justice, of receiving from hands individually unknown, ulterior evidence; for the supply of any deficiency, or confutation of any falsehood, which inadvertency or mendacity may have left or introduced. In this way, though it furnishes not altogether the same inducement — (the motive grounded on the religious sanction,) it may be capable of answering in other respects (and if with less efficacy, on the other hand with less danger) the purpose of the French *Monitoire*.

Such might be the use made of it: and by this means, in penal causes of the two highest classes, a powerful barrier might be erected against the influx of that most copious of all causes of mendacity and consequent impunity, alibi evidence. But as matters stand at present, the rule which forbids *new trial** in this the most important class of causes, prevents the application of the principle to this use

* In English criminal law, two opposite, but alike baneful, principles, — one of thoughtless cruelty, the other of equally thoughtless laxity, — are constantly at work together: the one infusing its poison into legislation, the other into judicature — the one inimical to all enlightened policy, the other to all substantial justice.

By the one, — at the suggestion of some individual member of the legislature, engrossed by the view of some narrow object, without so much as a thought about any that are on one side of it, — penal laws are heaped upon penal laws, in a progression the ultimate tendency of which is to extend to all cases a mode of punishment too radically incongruous to be fit to be employed in any. Between delinquency and punishment, between temptation and check, between impelling causes and restraining causes, between delinquency and delinquency, between mischief and mischief, — on these and the like occasions, not the faintest idea of proportion seems ever to have made its way into those seats of public sapience. In this state of things, if a mark which is never aimed at should not unfrequently be missed, the wonder will not be great.

The other principle is employed, in the hands of the judge, to frustrate the laws altogether, by preventing them from being executed: it is the principle which will be so often spoken of in this work, under the name of the principle of nullification; and its instruments are quirks, or (as they are generally called) decisions on grounds foreign to the merits.

Each, as if by consent, with blind and wayward industry, tampers in his own way with the cords that bind society together: the legislator in straining them, the judge in fretting and enfeebling them: and the farther the advance made in the system of indiscriminating tension, the stronger the passion, and the more plausible the pretence, for equally indiscriminating and still more extensive relaxation. The two functionaries, playing a seemingly adverse part, each in pursuit of his own narrow and sinister interest, play in fact (with or without thinking of it) into each other's hands. The one obtains the praise of wisdom, by the sacrifice of all enlarged and consistent policy — the other the praise of humanity and science, and at no greater expense than the sacrifice of the interests of truth and justice and public security.

Partly to this desire of ill-earned popularity, partly to the habit of blind adherence to blindly established rules, may be ascribed the maxim which declares, that when the proceedings of one trial have not been sufficient to warrant the conviction of a prisoner, there shall never be another. If neither truth nor justice were of any value, there would be no objection to this rule: but, supposing either to be worth caring for, the mischievousness, as well as absurdity of it, will be equally incontestible.

Completeness of the mass of evidence is a point no less essential than correctness. It is accordingly an object at which, by cross-examination and a variety of other means, English procedure never ceases to aim; except in so far as its endeavours are stopped and diverted by some blind and sinister prejudice. In cases not penal (except as excepted — for in English jurisprudence no general proposition is true till after an indeterminable list of exceptions has been taken out of it) — in cases not penal, to whichsoever side the result of one trial has been favourable, the door is open to another. In criminal cases, no: this must not be. If a guilty man has in this way been let loose, there is no harm done: so he might have been by a thousand other causes, none of them having, or so much as professing to have, any regard or relation to the merits. If a man not guilty has been convicted, — no, not then neither: he is to be saved or not, as he can find favour: the credit of saving him is to be taken out of the hands of open and discerning justice, and made a perquisite of, for the benefit of secret yet ostentatious mercy. As if every praise bestowed on mercy were not purloined from justice; as if the very distinction between justice and mercy had anything but blindness and weakness for its source; as if such mercy were anything better than tyranny, with hypocrisy for a covering to it.

The ways in which justice may be, and every day is, knocked on the head by the instrumentality of this rule, are infinite. Papers for the moment put out of the way — witnesses locked up, kept in a state of drunkenness, sent away on fools' errands, or misinformed as to the appointed day or hour — and so forth.

Two sorts of occasions alone shall here be brought to view in any detail; partly on account of the frequency of their occurrence, partly on account of the facility, as well as the imperative propriety, of obviating them. One is the case of *character* evidence — an article to be hereinafter spoken of in the character of a species of circumstantial evidence. The inconclusiveness of it in some cases, the importance of it in others, will be fully brought to view. The circumstance which calls for the mention of it for the present purpose, is the encouragement afforded to mendacious evidence of this description by the adherence to the above blind rule. A good character is given to a guilty defendant by accomplices, whose character, being inscrutable, must be taken for good. The defendant is a thief; and the receivers, who are his customers, come with a panegyric on his honesty. What risk is encountered by such evidence? what door is left open for the detection of it — especially at the only period when detection would come in time? To both questions, the answer is in the negative. To the purpose of the conviction of the guilty principal, — after the verdict by which he stands acquitted, the clearest proof of the worthlessness of the eulogist, the accomplice, would come too late. As to punishment for this species of mendacious testimony, it is, at any rate, without example. To convict a man of mendacity, for an opinion (however false) delivered in general terms, — to warrant on the part of the judge a persuasion adequate to that purpose, — is not in itself an easy task.

The other case is that of *alibi* evidence (as above.) Here, the evidence being in its nature so much the more conclusive, the mischievousness of the factitious bar opposed to the proof of its falsity (where it happens to be false) is the more serious and the more palpable. Conviction, as for the mendacity, would here indeed, in the nature of the case, be as easy and comparatively certain (understand always in case of prosecu-

—prevents the deriving of any advantage to justice from this source. To point out a remedy for that mischief, and (what is of much more difficulty) to inquire whether the remedy, which is obvious enough, would be worth the purchase,—belongs to another Book.*

Such as our exigencies are, such is our nomenclature. For alibi evidence—a branch of perjury springing out of English procedure—English jurisprudence, and that alone, affords a familiar name. At the expense of delay, which, in the system of Roman procedure, has no bounds, that system frees itself from this source of undue acquittal and impunity. Were a guilty defendant to attempt to prove the impossibility of his crime by his distance from the spot—the prosecutor, convinced of the falsity of this evidence by the true evidence which it contradicts, would not fail either to demand or to obtain the time requisite for the confutation of it.

In France, even under the *ancien régime*, a custom prevailed which could not but have operated in a very considerable degree as a succedaneum to the constant publicity and frequent publication of the English trials. I mean that of printing *mémoires* in every stage of a cause, and even before the commencement of it: *mémoires* by or on behalf of the parties, for the purpose of explaining to the body of the public the grounds of their several pretensions. If at the time of the publication of a *mémoire* of this sort, a decision had already been given by a court of the first instance, the evidence would of course be exhibited and commented upon: and by this means, supposing *mémoires* published on both sides (as would naturally be the case,) the effect, and in some respects more than the effect, of an English trial, would be produced. Supposing even the publication of the *mémoire* antecedent to the commencement of the cause, the attention of the public would at any rate be drawn to it, and a guard be thus set upon the probity of the judge.

A circumstance that rendered the demand for this guard more particularly urgent, was the practice of *solicitation*—a practice not only tolerated, but in a manner necessitated; by which was meant that of paying a visit to the judge, out of court and in secret, to endeavour to obtain his favour, and beg his vote and interest in favour of the solicitant or his friend. Money, or anything to be bought for money, was not to be offered: but neither sex was excluded, either by law or custom; and the advantage afforded by beauty on such occasions was too palpable to be neglected, and too notorious to be denied. The other circumstances contributed to enhance the mischief: the tumultuous multitude of the judges, a circumstance by which the idea of individual responsibility was in a manner obliterated; the common interest possessed by the judges of a superior court as members of a political body; and the constitution of the state, which exempted them from any such prosecutions as that which, under the name of impeachment, English judges are exposed to undergo, at the instance of one of the three branches of the sovereign body, with the members of the others for their judges.

In England, if a man who had a cause depending before a judge should have the option forced upon him, either to spit in the judge's face, or to wait upon him to solicit him in the *ci-devant* French style, he would probably choose the first mode of helping his cause as the least dangerous of the two. I can speak only from conjecture: for, as both compliments are equally unexampled, it is impossible to speak from experience.

In England, publications of the cases of litigant parties are altogether unusual; and, if distributed for any such purpose as that of influencing the decision of the jury, would be liable to be treated on the footing of an offence against justice. The censure thus passed upon the practice in England is grounded on reasons which pass no condemnation

---

tion,) as in the other it is difficult and precarious. But, for the vexation and expense of prosecuting for this excretitious crime, who is there that shall find adequate motives? Neither public spirit, nor even vengeance, are in general found equal to such a task. A prosecution of this sort is, if not altogether without example, extremely rare; while, unhappily, nothing is more common than the offence.

Meantime, although punishment as for the perjury were actually to take place, the conviction of the criminal in whose favour it was uttered, and by whom or in whose behalf it was suborned, would be never the nearer. Had the crime been a non-penal one, and the matter in dispute some petty right of property, yes: but upon a criminal, the laws are to go unexecuted, rather than that, to the two superfluous inquiries that have been seen, a necessary one should require to be superadded.

In regard to remedies,—two, equally obvious, present themselves; each alike applicable to both these species of circumstantial evidence.

One is,—in case of the acquittal of a prisoner on the ground of such evidence, the rendering the acquittal provisional:—reversible on subsequent proof of falsehood on the part of the evidence. The other is, the requiring (according to a practice already established in some cases) timely notice to be given of the nature of the evidence so intended to be produced, and of the persons of whose testimony it is to consist. As to the combination of these two securities, or the option to be made between them, these are among the topics which belong not to *evidence*, but to *procedure*.

* Book V. *Circumstantial;* Chap. XVI. *Improbability and Impossibility;* Section 11, *Alibi Evidence.*

on the practice just described as prevailing formerly in France:—

1. In the first place, in England there is no such demand and use for it as that which has already been exhibited as resulting from it in France. No solicitations: judges acting singly, whose conduct, without the need of any such occasional lights, is transparent on every occasion and on every point.

2. In England, the ground for the prohibition put upon these *ex parte* publications, is the danger of their exercising an undue influence on the minds of the jury. This reason, whatsoever may be the force of it, had no application to the judicial establishment as constituted in France. On professional and cultivated minds, engaged by the necessity of office to procure the whole mass of evidence and argument, the premature exhibition of a part would rather be turned aside from as useless, than apprehended by anybody as dangerous. It was to the eye of the public at large, and not to the eye of any person whose office called on him to act in the character of a judge, that these statements were addressed. In what way could the probity of the judge be endangered by receiving at one time a part of those documents, the whole of which would come before him of course? Even in England, the reason on which the prohibition relies for its support has more of surface than of substance in it. The representations given by publications of this sort will of course be partial ones; the colour given to them will be apt to be inflammatory; the judgment of a jury will be apt to be deceived, and their affections engaged on the wrong side. Partial? Yes: but can anything in these printed arguments be more partial than the *vivâ voce* oratory of the advocates on that same side will be sure to be? The dead letter cannot avoid allowing full time for reflection: the *vivâ voce* declamation allows of none. The written argument may contain allegations without proofs:—true; but is not the spoken argument just as apt to do the same? When, of the previous statement given by the leading advocate, any part remains unsupported by evidence, the judge of course points out the failure: whatever effect this indication has on the jury, in the way of guarding them against that source of delusion in spoken arguments, would it have less efficacy in the case of written ones?

ADDITIONAL NOTES TO BOOKS I. & II.

CHIEFLY WITH REFERENCE TO ALTERATIONS MADE IN THE LAW SINCE THE DATE OF THE FIRST EDITION, — *viz.* 1827.

1.

P. 244, col. 2, *Note* *.

The doctrine laid down on this occasion by the judges was, that it was not proper for the counsel for the Crown to press an unwilling witness called by themselves, as such a course would end in destroying the credit of their own witness. In Crossfield's case, where the same doctrine was laid down by the Lord Chief-Justice Eyre, the witness who was thus protected swore the very reverse of what he had sworn at his prior examination. This doctrine is now in abeyance, and the usual course which is pursued, is to allow the examination in chief in such cases to assume the style of a cross-examination. It seems to have been first allowed at the trial of Codling and others in 1803, for feloniously destroying a brig on the high seas. The mistress of one of the prisoners was called by the counsel for the Crown, and cross-examined by him.

2.

P. 273, col. 2, line 5—"*forty shillings.*"

The act 7 & 8 Geo. IV. cap. 29, which abolished the distinction between grand and petty larceny, makes the value of the property stolen immaterial in the case of simple larceny: but stealing in a dwelling-house, property to the value of £5 or more, is by the 12th section made punishable with death. The death-punishment has, however, been abolished by 3 & 4 Wil. IV. cap. 44.

3.

P. 286, col. 2, end of 3d paragraph.

The wager of law, one of the instances here alluded to was abolished by the last Law Amendment Act, 3 & 4 Wil. IV. cap. 42, § 13.

4.

P. 292, col. 2 of Note, line 9—"*personation.*"

To personate another, for the purpose of fraud, is a misdemeanor at common law. 2 East, P. C. cap. 20, § 6, p. 1010. The personation of proprietors of shares in the public funds and stocks, was made a capital offence by various statutes; and lastly, by 11 Geo. IV. and 1 Wil. IV. cap. 66, § 6, in cases where any transfer or receipt of money actually took place. The 2 & 3 Wil. IV. cap. 123, takes away the punishment of death, and substitutes transportation for life. A former act appears to have been overlooked, viz. 2 & 3 Wil. IV. cap. 59, which was passed for the purpose of transferring the management of certain annuities from the Exchequer to the Commissioners of the National Debt. By the 19th section, the personation of any nominee is made a capital felony. The 7 Wil. IV. and 1 Vict. cap. 84, abolishes the punishment of death for this offence, and substitutes transportation, or imprisonment for not less than two years; whereas the 2 & 3 Wil. IV. cap. 123, takes away all discretion from the Court in the numerous cases to which it refers.

5.

P. 294, col. 2, line 22—"*perjury.*"

By the English law, all judicial mendacity, though upon oath, is not perjury; for a necessary ingredient in the crime of perjury is, that the matter sworn to, shall be *material to the issue* in question, on each individual occasion, as well as wilfully false. 5 Bac. Abr. *Perjury.* 1 Hawk. P. C. cap. 69, § 8. Thus it frequently happens, that witnesses wilfully perjure themselves *in foro conscientiæ*, though not in point of law, because the false testimony may not be material to the issue, upon the record. By the late legislative alterations which substitute declarations for oaths (see some of these noticed above, Vol. V. p. 288,) the punishment of perjury has been awarded against false declaration.

6.

P. 295, col. 1, line 37—"*crimes.*"

By the 3 & 4 Wil. IV. cap. 49, Quakers and Moravians are allowed to make an affirmation in all cases, criminal as well as civil, in which the law requires an oath: a false affirmation being punishable as for perjury. The same relief is granted to the sect called Separatists, by the 3 & 4 Wil. IV. cap. 82. By 1 & 2 Vict. cap. 77, the same privilege is conceded to those who declare themselves to have been Quakers or Moravians, though they have ceased to belong to either of such denominations of Christians, if they continue to entertain conscientious objections to taking oaths. In the session 1838–9, a bill was brought in to allow all persons professing conscientious objections to oaths, to give evidence on solemn affirmation, under sanction of the pains of perjury in case of falsehood. It was thrown out by the House of Commons, where it was introduced.

7.

P. 301, col. 2, par. 1.

The remarks in the text apply only to the class of barristers, who are exempted from responsibility on the fiction that their employment is merely honorary. For the same alleged reason, physicians are exempted from responsibility. Special pleaders, however, and attorneys, like surgeons, are responsible for the want of care, knowledge, or skill, in the same manner as other mandatories.

8.

P. 304, col. 1, line 22—"*means.*"

By the ancient common law, this *was* considered as murder, Mirror, cap. 1, § 9, Bract. lib. 3, cap. 4; 3 Inst. 91. In 1756, three persons were indicted for murder, for having taken away the life of an innocent person, who had been convicted and executed upon their false testimony. The prisoners were convicted; but the judgment was respited, in order that the point of law might be more fully considered upon a motion in arrest of judgment. The point, however, was not argued by the then Attorney-General, from prudential reasons altogether unconnected with the law of the case. There seems to be good ground for believing that the opinions of the judges were in favour of the indictment. Fost. 132, 1 Leach. 44. 4 Black. Com. 196, note (*g.*) 1 East. P. C. cap. 5, § 94, p. 333, note (*a.*) 1 Russ. p. 427.

9.

P. 333, col. 2, line 30—"*defilement.*"

The 9 Geo. IV. cap. 31, declares that the carrying off of any woman (having an interest in any real or personal estate,) with intent to marry or defile her, is *felony.* If the woman has no property, it would still be an offence at common law; and the offenders may therefore in either case be taken into custody at once. The same observation would of course apply to the third case supposed by the author, if such a case should occur in this country.

10.

P. 338, col. 2, line 14—"*intercept them.*"

In criminal cases, the counsel for the prisoner may now, by the 3d section of 6 & 7 W. IV. cap. 114, have the depositions which the witnesses may have made before the committing magistrate. The counsel for the prosecution always had access to them.

11.

P. 340, par. 1 of Note *.

The special law here referred to, is the 3d section of the 23 Geo. II. cap. 11, which says, that judges of assize may direct any witness to be prosecuted for perjury at the public expense. It appears doubtful whether any such clause were necessary. The judges are in the daily habit of ordering prosecutions to be instituted against witnesses for other misdemeanors, and also for felonies; in particular, for receiving stolen goods.

12.

P. 345, col. 1, line 54—"*rank of felony.*"

Although this is the usual and most proper course of proceeding, it is by no means obligatory, as a prosecutor may, and sometimes, but very rarely, does, go before the Grand Jury at once.

13.

P. 351, col. 2, line 27—"*English lawyer.*"

Happily, since this passage was written, the punishment of death has been abolished to a very considerable extent, and is now limited to the most heinous crimes, and offences accompanied with personal violence. The last statutes on this subject are the 7 Wil. IV. and 1 Vict. cap. 84 to 89 inclusive, and cap. 91.

14.

P. 358, col. 2, end of par. 4—"*the only one.*"

Under the English law, there is no appeal in criminal cases (properly so called.) For what is called a writ of error, lies only upon some matter of *law* apparent on the face of the record.

15.

P. 368, col. 1, line 8—"*bathing places?*"

In Rex *v.* Crunden, 2 Campb. 89, it was laid down, that if a man undresses himself on the beach, and bathes in the sea, near inhabited houses, from which he might be distinctly seen, he is guilty of a misdemeanor.

16.

P. 372, col. 2, end of par. 2—"*their ears.*"

The prisoner's counsel is now allowed to address the jury on the facts of the case, by the 6 & 7 Wil. IV. cap. 114.

17.

P. 377, col. 1, end of par. 2—"*or sells it.*"

The public are not admitted into the Central Criminal Court, except on the payment of money. No such tax is now imposed in the courts at Guildhall.

BOOK III.

OF THE EXTRACTION OF TESTIMONIAL EVIDENCE.

CHAPTER I.

OF THE ORAL MODE OF INTERROGATION.

Such being the means which the nature of things furnishes for securing the correctness and completeness of testimony; what remains to be considered is, how to employ them to the best advantage.

Punishment, shame, oath, publicity, privacy: of these securities, sufficient has been said under their respective heads.

In the process of interrogation, we see an instrument, the application of which is susceptible of much greater diversification. It will constitute, though not the sole object, yet the principal object, throughout the course of the present book.

So far as testimony delivers itself of its own accord (as in the case of affidavit evidence,) *interrogation*, *extraction*, are out of the question.

Where testimony is extracted, it is by interrogation that it is extracted. Where interrogation is employed, it is administered in one or other of two simple modes, the *oral* and the *epistolary*. But, out of these two, other modes of a complex nature are capable of being made up. Of this number, what is called *examination upon interrogatories* — extraction of oral responses by ready-written interrogatories — is one. This demands special notice, in consideration of the so unhappily abundant use made of it in practice.

That the fullest possible scope should be given to examination *ex adverso* — that every person who can by possibility have an interest in rendering the testimony correct and complete, should have the power of employing interrogation to that end — has been shown in the last book.

Four rules still remain to be explained, on which the utility and efficiency of the oral mode of extracting and delivering testimony appear chiefly to rest: viz. 1. Answers impromptuary; 2. Questions put singly; 3. Questions arising out of the answers; 4. The process carried on in the presence of the judge.

I. First point, — promptitude of the response.

On the promptitude of an answer depends its unpremeditatedness; and thence the degree of security afforded against the exercise of the faculty of *invention*, considered as applicable to the purpose of mendacious evidence.

The security it thus affords, depends upon a matter of universal experience, expressible by this axiom — memory is prompter than invention: (understand, of such statements as, though false, shall not be capable of being shown to be so.*)

This restriction must be carefully preserved in mind. Without it, the proposition will frequently be untrue. When memory has length of time, or the obscurity of original perception, to contend with, and neither punishment nor shame is the apprehended consequence of incorrectness or incompleteness, invention may be the more prompt of the two. Hence the comparative inaccuracy of the ordinary narratives to which common conversation gives birth.

Of the oral form of interrogation, promptitude of response is the natural, but not the absolutely necessary, accompaniment.

So, of the epistolary mode, tardiness of response is the natural accompaniment; but, as anybody may see, not even here the necessary one.

As to the degree of promptitude, it must, in each individual instance, be left to the judge. In regard to the demand for recollection, the scale of variation has no determinate limits. Here, as in ordinary conversation, the time proper to be allowed will be indicated by the nature of the case.

One answer, that, with little modification, can be returned, in any case in which a particular answer cannot be returned, is — at the instant I cannot recollect; by the help of a little time for reflection, perhaps I may.

But, in general — when, in obedience to a summons from justice, a man stands forth to deliver testimony, — his time for recollection has begun, if not from the moment of the transaction, at any rate from the moment of his receiving the summons, or being applied to in a less formal manner to know what he will have to say. So far as this is the case, there will be little need of any time for reflection at the time of his examination.

Protracted beyond the natural and proper time, delay becomes silence; and, under cer-

* *Vide supra*, p. 262 — Book I. Chapter XI. *Moral Causes of Trustworthiness:* § 4. *Physical Sanction.*

tain circumstances, silence becomes, to the disadvantage of the proposed deponent (if an extraneous witness,) a presumption of a propensity to mendacity, or deceptitious *reticence;* (if a party) of the like propensity, and, what is more directly material, of a consciousness of his not having right, and thence of his actually not having right, on his side.

II. Second point, — questions put one by one, not in strings.

Of the oral mode of interrogation, neither is this feature a physically necessary accompaniment — an accompaniment essentially inseparable.*

On the part of an interrogator, what is possible, not only in this judicial but in ordinary conversation, is, — to deliver question after question — to let fly (as it were) a volley of questions, without waiting for the answers. But of such a proceeding the possibility is not more manifest, than the absurdity and inutility to every beneficial purpose.

String together a multitude of questions, immediate confusion will demonstrate the inconvenience of the practice. With equal clearness, two questions, not included one in the other, can no more be answered at once, than, with equal clearness, two objects can be seen at once. While one of the questions is receiving an answer, the attention must be divided and strained, to keep the other from escaping out of the memory.

Where the questions are presented in the ready-written form, this source of confusion has no place. Ink does not lose its hold on the paper, as facts do on the memory. While the first question is receiving its answer, any number of others may, for any length of time, be waiting for theirs.

Confusion is not the only evil of which this stringing together of questions would be productive. Force the interrogator to produce at once all the questions he would wish in any event to produce; force him to produce any more than he would wish to produce; force him, in a word, to produce any more than a single one, than the least number that can be produced at a time; — you may force him, in many instances, to furnish a mendaciously-disposed deponent with information subservient to such his sinister purpose. By the nature and quantity of the information a man calls for at other hands, no bad measure may, in many cases, be formed of the nature and quantity of the information of which he is already in possession.

* The necessity which the judge is under of summing up the evidence to the jury, affords him a strong motive for compelling singleness of interrogation, and singleness in the answers: it is also the interest generally of the party in whose favour the evidence preponderates, to extract it as clearly as possible. Under the combined influence of these motives, the English examinations are free from the vice here adverted to. — *Ed.*

III. Third point, — questions arising out of the answers.

This is as much as to say — of the answer made to each preceding question, communication received by the interrogator, with liberty to ground on such preceding answer each succeeding question.† *N. B.* This hinders not but that the first question, or one of the first questions put, may be of a nature to draw out the main substance of the testimony in the form of a single answer, viz. in the form of one continued and complete narrative. As for instance — What do you know in relation to this affair?

Of the oral mode of interrogation, knowledge of the answers, with the faculty of grounding ulterior questions upon them, is an accompaniment no less natural than the obligation of presenting the questions one by one.

But, though a natural, and a too obviously useful one to be separated in practice, the faculty is not (any more than the obligation) an inseparable accompaniment.

The first question having been delivered; before the answer were delivered, the interrogator might be sent out of court, and not let in again to put his second question, till after the answer to his first were finished. Absurd as the arrangement may seem in the oral mode of interrogation, it is not the less a possible one, and in effect in the epistolary mode it is realized. When a chain of written interrogatories is upon the anvil, it is frequently by the nature of the case rendered much more certainly impossible for the interrogator, in framing his second interrogatory, to know what the answer to the first will be, than on the occasion of an examination performed in the oral mode it could be rendered by the mere physical operation of putting the interrogator out of court — unless his senses

† This feature, though naturally connected with the one last mentioned, is not so connected with it as to be undistinguishable from it. An arrangement easily conceivable is this: — In the first place comes a string of questions calling for answers; in the next place, a string of answers in return to those questions; in the third place, a second string of questions, arising out of the answers delivered in return to the first. Here — though the questions have come, not singly, but in a string, or rather in a lump, — it is not the less open to the interrogator to ground questions upon preceding answers — ulterior questions upon the answers extracted by preceding ones.

Suppose a bill in equity with its string of interrogatories, — answer thereto consisting of a string of responses, — amendments to the bill, including a fresh string of interrogatories grounded on those responses; — suppose these several instruments spoken extempore, and at the same meeting, by the several interlocutors. In this imaginary dialogue we should have a set of questions not put singly, and yet some of them arising (viz. the second set) out of the answers.

of seeing as well as hearing were destroyed, antecedently to his being let in again.*

In such a state of darkness—after any one question has been delivered—to know what, for the purpose of giving completeness as well as correctness to the testimony, the next question ought to be, will frequently be, no less impossible than, in a game of chess or draughts, to know what your next move ought to be, without knowing what your antagonist's last preceding move has been.

Even in a conversation with a confidential friend, where both interlocutors are alike desirous, the one of receiving the whole and exact truth of the case, the other of communicating it:—consider with yourself whether, the subject being a matter of importance to your personal interest or your affections, it would be a satisfaction to you to know beforehand, that, after an answer given to your first question or string of questions, it would be impossible to you to put another.

This done,—setting aside your veracious and willing respondent, call up in his place any person who, on the ground of improbity, and that disposition to mendacity which is so natural an accompaniment of it, has happened to attract your notice: then think with yourself what would be your chance for extracting from him a truth which a powerful interest urged him to conceal, if, attached to the known necessity of making a full answer to your first question or string of questions, he possessed the assurance that, however false his answers might be, no ulterior questions could ever be grounded on his lies.

True it may be, that there are occasions on which, from the extreme simplicity of the case, the answer or answers to a first question or string of questions may by a person of ordinary sagacity be foreseen with sufficient correctness and completeness; and upon the first answer so imagined, a second question framed, suitable to the purpose of succeeding to it. But the cases are perhaps not less numerous, in which such forecast would to any man, or (what to this purpose comes to much the same thing) to the ordinary run of men, be plainly impossible. But even were such forecast sure for the first question—for a question of the first degree, who would venture to assure it, for a second, for a third degree, and so on? for the utmost number of links of which it can happen to be requisite that a chain of questions and answers thus connected shall be composed?

A case which may serve to place in a clearer light the general impossibility of this kind of forecast in a degree adequate to all purposes, is one that has already been brought to view: viz. the case where, for the purpose of setting indubitable facts in opposition to the testimony of a mendacious witness, questions are put to him, calling for statements on his part relative to circumstances in all other respects irrelevant—relevant and instructive by accident only, and with reference to this single purpose.—What had you for supper? To the merits of the cause, the contents of the supper were in themselves altogether irrelevant and indifferent. But if, in speaking of a supper given on an important or recent occasion, six persons, all supposed to be present, give a different bill of fare; the contrariety affords evidence pretty satisfactory (though but of the circumstantial kind) that at least some of them were not there.

But to reach beforehand, either by provision or so much as by imagination, all the false facts to which in the agony of the conflict it may happen to a mendacious witness to give utterance—to pre-comprehend all these facts,—and on them, when so pre-comprehended, to ground a set of questions adequate to the purpose of bringing their falsity to light in the manner that has just been mentioned, is a task, the general impracticability of which appears too clear to need any further elucidation.

IV. Fourth point,—responsion performed in the presence of the judge.

From the *oral* mode, this feature, like the preceding one, is separable in idea, and in possibility: in the *epistolary* mode, it has no place in fact; in the *mixt* mode (oral interrogation according to written interrogatories,) it has place, but (as will be seen, and from the causes that may already be suspected) to very little good purpose.

Not to repeat what has been said of the faculty of interrogation on the part of the

* It is even conceivable, that, in the course of a *vivâ voce* conversation,—a question or string of questions being put by the interrogator, and an answer or correspondent string of answers given in a breath by the deponent,—the lips of the interrogator may thereupon be closed, as those of a frog are for a certain part of the year, and then the examination may end.

It is conceivable this arrangement, and accordingly it stands exemplified: for of human, and especially juridical absurdity, no conceivable modification can be mentioned that does not stand a good chance of being somewhere or other exemplified in practice.

Cause, a criminal one; mode of procedure, by indictment; inquiry, the principal one—that in which the decision is pronounced by a jury: offence, a crime of the rank of felony. Officer of the court to the defendant, called here the prisoner: Prisoner, hold up your hand (hand held up)—How say you? Guilty, or not guilty? Prisoner: "Guilty," or "Not guilty." In either case, here the interrogation ends. Whichever be the response, not another question can ensue.[a]

[a] If a prisoner refuse to plead, the Court may order the proper officer to enter a plea of "Not guilty," under the authority of the 7 & 8 Geo. IV. cap. 28, § 2. See R. v. Bitton, 6 C. & P. 92. —*Ed.*

judge,—a faculty naturally indeed as well as properly, but not necessarily, connected with that of his presence,—the use of this presence is, in case of *mala fides*, to afford to him, by observance of deportment, circumstantial evidence of the emotion of fear: and thence (as above observed) of a disposition to mendacity, if the respondent be an extraneous witness; of the like disposition, or (what is more material) of a consciousness of not having right on his side, if he be a party, whether defendant or plaintiff.

In using the word *presence*, a reference more or less explicit is or ought to be made, as well to the occasion or purpose, as to the particular sense or senses upon which the object, in virtue of its presence, acts. At the same instant of time, two men being in every sense present to each other, the self-same object is present to one, not present to another. Objects removed to an infinite distance with relation to all the other senses, are still present to the sight.

In a Grecian court of judicature, a point was made (we are told) that the parties should not be visible—should not, in this sense, be present—to the judges. The story has much the air of fable: perhaps (as in relations of all sorts of transactions, judicial more than any other, is so apt to be the case) an individual instance was magnified into a general rule. Supposing the existence, what was the reason of this rule? By a female bosom, too deep an impression had been made (it seems) upon judicial eyes. If we believe the story, a constant and most instructive source of evidence was thus cut off, for the momentary chance of preventing a rare and casual and possible abuse. A shawl, or whatever equivalent to a shawl was then in fashion, would have been as simple and a rather less expensive remedy.

A material point is, that the testimony be delivered in the presence of *a* judge; of an official person, who, in case of mendacity—mendacity detected on the spot—shall be armed with authority competent to the following it up with punishment: with punishment, seizing the delinquency in the very act—not crawling after her at a snail's pace (as under the technical system,) to afford time for squeezing the injured and the injurer with undiscriminating pressure, while the judge, by the hands of his workmen, is wire-drawing them through the offices.

Another material point is, that the presence in which the testimony is delivered be the presence of *the* judge—of the judge by whom the decision, to be grounded on that evidence, comes afterwards to be framed. Change the judge,—the circumstantial evidence, the important evidence above spoken of, almost entirely perishes.*

* *Vide infra*, Chap. VII.

CHAPTER II.

NOTES, WHETHER CONSULTABLE?

In any, and (if in any) in what cases, shall the liberty of recurring to ready-written notes or memoranda in his possession, be allowed to a proposed respondent, pending the process of interrogation (viz. in the oral mode?)

Suppose him deprived of this faculty, cases exist in great variety and to a great extent, in which correctness and completeness would, on the part of his testimony, be physically impossible.

Suppose him left in possession of this faculty,—the advantage occasionally derivable, in case of *mala fides*, from the promptitude, and thence from the unpremeditatedness, of the answers, is in a considerable degree lost.†

To the extent of the class of cases above alluded to,—certainty of incorrectness and incompleteness being the result of the *exclusion*, and not more than a chance of these causes of deception and misdecision being the result in case of admission; by this statement, upon the face of it, the proper practical course seems to be already indicated.

The demand for this help to memory depending not so much on the species of the case, as on the individual circumstances of the individual case; drawing the line between the cases in which the faculty shall be allowed, and those in which it shall be disallowed, cannot, with safety and propriety, be the work of the legislature. If drawn at all, it must be left to the discretion of the judge.

1. On the part of the mass of facts required to be deposed to, suppose a certain degree of complication,—the union of completeness and correctness will, in the instance of every man (prodigies excepted,) be manifestly impossible: take, for instance, a mass of pecuniary accounts.

2. To memories of all sorts, some classes of circumstances will be more difficult to retain than others. The most difficulty retained of all is a mere date, *i. e.* an individual portion of time: except in the case where some other circumstance has intervened, whereby to distinguish that portion from like contiguous portions—some circumstance, whereby, in virtue of some connexion or other which it has with the deponent's interest (the word interest being taken in its largest sense,) his attention has been drawn to it with a peculiar degree of force.

3. But (not to speak of figures) for one purpose or another, a history of any kind or length may come to be required for evidence.

† The practical rule of the English courts is, that if no sinister motive for making a note can be detected, the note adds much to the probative force of the witness's testimony, he being allowed to use it only to refresh his memory.—*Ed.*

In the capacity of a public functionary, the conduct of a man through a great part of his life, may, by being rendered the subject of legal inquiry, be rendered the subject of evidence.

4. To a memory below the average or ordinary degree of retentive force (whatever be that average degree,) helps may be necessary, such as to a memory above that standard would be superfluous. But between memory and memory who shall draw the line? And not only memory is in question, but appropriate firmness of mind; regard being had to the presence of the judge — not to speak of an unknown circle of bystanders.

Whatever danger of mendacity and consequent deception and misdecision may be attached to the admission of this help to recollection or instrument of mendacious invention, may be more or less reduced by conditions annexed to the faculty of utterance. It is not till after the reduction practicable in this way has been effected, that the propriety of admission or exclusion can be fairly estimated.

1. Whenever a deponent, being under examination, asks leave to look at notes, he should, in the first place, at the instance of the adverse party, be examined, and that on both sides, before he has looked at his notes.*

Why? Because, if he be honest, be his answers at that time what they may, neither he nor the side on which he deposes has any thing to fear. Suppose him to say — I am absolutely unable to recollect anything about the matter without my notes: even an answer to that effect may be highly instructive; for, on recurrence to the nature of the transaction, as delineated in his notes, it will be a point to be judged of, whether it be probable that his oblivion of it should be thus entire.

Being honest, whatever he says, he need not have anything to fear. Of the matter of fact which, under these circumstances, he advances, more or less may be erroneous, and proved to be so: inconsistent with facts proved to be true by evidence from other sources — inconsistent with his own statements, as delivered in his notes. Still, if he be honest, it is not the mere falsity of his *vivâ voce* statements, that under these circumstances will mark him out as having knowingly and wilfully deviated from the line of truth: at the same time that, in case of dishonesty, it may very well happen that the nature and circumstances of the deviation shall betray it.

2. Before such recurrence on his part, and after his examination performed as above on both sides, his papers should (at the instance of the judge, or at the instance of an adverse party, by order of the judge) be handed up to the judge, with liberty to the judge thereupon to continue his examination, by further interrogatories grounded on the paper and its contents.

3. Like liberty to the judge to hand the paper down, for the like purpose, to the party or advocate on the adverse side.

4. Should it so happen that the paper, in addition to the relevant matter, contains other matter, in the disclosure of which no one of the parties has any interest, and by the disclosure of which the deponent, or any third person, would, without any legal transgression on his part, suffer a prejudice to any amount — would be exposed, for instance, to contempt or ridicule, or to vexation in any other shape; here would be an opportunity for the judge so to order matters, that, in the communication made (as above) to hostile hands, this collateral inconvenience be avoided.†

5. Power, again, to the judge, of his own accord, or at the instance of the party concerned, to *impound* the script,‡ that, like any other article of written evidence, it may be subjected to scrutiny, with whatever degree of time and attention may be requisite. Power again to the judge, either to cause the script itself to be redelivered to the deponent, or to retain it, delivering or not delivering a copy in its stead.

6. Power to the judge, of his own accord, or at the instance of either side, to appoint another day for the re-examination of the deponent on the ground of the paper of notes; after time taken for the examination and consideration of it, as aforesaid.

It is almost superfluous to observe, that, on this as on all other occasions, the demand

* The English practice is, when a witness is seen referring to any written paper, to ask first what it is; and if from the answer it appear that it consists of notes made by the witness himself, and that he uses it to refresh his memory, the counsel who is adverse to the evidence is entitled to look at it, and afterwards to use it as an assistance in cross-examining the witness upon his previous testimony. — *Ed.*

† If the proposed rule in question have received that effectual degree of promulgation which every rule of law might and ought to receive; the script being, by the supposition, in the deponent's own possession, the faculty of performing such obliteration for himself will accordingly have been all along in his power. But, in this as well as other cases, negligence is a case too common not to require provision to be made against it by legislative vigilance: add to which, that it may happen, that not the deponent himself, but some third person, shall be the person exposed to suffer by the disclosure.

‡ In the English system, the judge has the power to impound, but it applies only to written papers which are evidence of themselves, independently of any oral testimony. Notes made by an eye-witness or an ear-witness to refresh his memory are not of this kind: they are not evidence which is read to the jury; they are mere grounds of belief for the witness himself, and have no force or technical use, except as aids to his memory. — *Ed.*

for all this delay, vexation, and expense, will be preponderant or otherwise, according to the importance of the cause itself, and the importance of the evidence in question to the cause.

On this occasion, an intimation given of a few particulars to which it may happen to be found proper subjects for inquiry, may be not altogether without its use.

1. The person by whom the notes were penned: whether the proposed respondent himself, or any other person.*

2. The time at which the transaction, or supposed transaction, is supposed to have happened: whether at such a distance from the time of interrogation, as to have produced a sufficient demand for recurrence to such helps.

3. The time at which the script was penned: whether at, or how long after, the time of the transaction of which it contains a statement. Not that it will always be material at what distance of time. Whenever an apprehension of relative failure of memory presents itself, then is the time for obviating it.

4. The cause (final cause) of its being penned.

5. If by the respondent himself,—whether it be the original memorandum, or a transcript made of it by himself? if a transcript, for what reason made?

N. B. A very natural and not censurable cause is, the original's having been mixed with other memoranda (as in an ordinary memorandum-book,) material to the writer, and not material to the cause. But what may notwithstanding be with reason insisted upon, if for special cause, is, that the original, in whatever state, be produced.

6. If not by the hand of the witness,—by what other hand?

7. Whoever were the penman (whether the witness himself, or any other person)—whether it were worded by the writer himself, or written from dictation, by any, and what, other person?

8. If it be not in the witness's own hand, from what cause came it to be in another hand than his own? whether from a physical cause, such (for example) as his inability to write,—or from what other?

9. In the hand of what person soever it be alleged by the witness to be, a case may happen in which it may be material (though at the expense of a distinct inquiry) to authenticate or deauthenticate it by ulterior evidence.

Objection: Allow the proposed respondent to recur to notes not in his own handwriting, you allow a suborned witness to deliver a mendacious story, framed for him by his suborner.

Answer: But, for the exclusion of such helps, on the ground of the possibility of such a case, in this instance, no reason can be given but what (if admitted) would put an exclusion upon them in any case. May it be that a third person has happened to invent a false tale for the witness? So may it that the witness has invented one for himself. May it be that the witness has received from a third person a false story penned for him by the inventor? So may it that he has transcribed with his own hand a false story, written originally by the inventor in his (the inventor's) hand.

Refuse such recurrence absolutely, veracious testimony may stand excluded, while mendacious is admitted and gains credence. A liar with a good memory may remember a mendacious statement, better than an honest man, with a bad memory, will, without the help in question, remember his own real perceptions and observations.

With, or even without, the above-proposed inquiries and conditions,—in no case can the admission of this subsidiary species of evidence be so much in danger of being productive of deception, as in the case of other species of evidence admitted in English practice.

1. Wherever the process of interrogation is conducted in the epistolary mode, the liberty of recurrence to notes is necessarily unbounded. If, in all cases, such liberty were upon the whole prejudicial to justice, this of itself would be a sufficient reason for interdicting altogether all interrogation in the epistolary mode.

True it is, that, in English practice, the epistolary mode is not applied to extraneous witnesses: true it likewise is, that in the application of it to extraneous witnesses, there would be a danger of deception, over and above what has place in its application to a party. But of this in another place.†

2. After the death of the writer or supposed writer, memoranda in writing are, in cases to a great extent, received without scruple, in the character of evidence. By death, the writer is withdrawn out of the reach of interrogation, with the security of which it is pregnant: but in the present case, there he is, and in the act of undergoing it.

3. At the instance of a party on the other side, a memorandum or letter of any person, being a party, is received as evidence. He is alive, and perhaps in court: but,—for the purpose of giving completeness and correctness to this frequently incorrect and almost always incomplete fragment of evidence,—neither at the instance of his own side, nor at that of the opposite side of a cause, is a question admitted to be put to him; unless when, under the mask of an extraneous witness, the

* If the notes are not penned by the respondent himself, he is not in the English courts entitled to use them to refresh his memory.—*Ed.*

† *Post*, Chap. IX.

interest which he has in his real character of a party be disguised.

4. In whatever cases evidence is admitted in the shape of affidavit evidence, the faculty of recurring to notes is, by the very shape of the evidence, possessed and exercised without stint.

This, the most deceptitious of all shapes, is the only shape in which, by English judges, when left to themselves, testimony is ever received.

If, in whatever hand, and under whatever circumstances penned, a proposed respondent were to deliver a paper of notes (whether penned by himself or no) declared to be his testimony, he refusing to answer a single question,—a paper of notes under these circumstances would, in point of trustworthiness, be at least upon a par with the best affidavit evidence.

On this, as on many other heads, should any example be needed to show how completely it is in the power of prejudice to render a man blind to transactions daily passing before his own eyes; how completely it is in the power of indifference—indifference, to say no worse, to the ends of justice,—to render a man unconscious of the obvious nature and character and tendency of his own act; this topic will afford sufficient examples drawn from English practice.

Cases on this subject, all reported in Term Reports, III. 749, 754:—

1. Principal case, Doe *v.* Perkins, B. R. 11th June 1790.

2. Case thereupon cited by Buller, J.—Tanner *v.* Taylor, Hereford Spring Assizes, 1756; a manuscript case thus bolted out after a sleep of 34 years.

3. Case cited by Kenyon, Ch. J., from the MS. of the late Lord Ashburton, then Mr. Dunning: Anonymous, 3d December 1753, at Lincoln's Inn Hall, before the Lord Chancellor (Lord Hardwicke), a cause in equity: a manuscript case bolted out after a sleep of 37 years.*

Doe *v.* Perkins, B. R. 11th June 1790. III. Term Reports, 749. A variety of reflections are suggested by the statement given in relation to this case.

1. That the evidence, the production of which had been omitted (viz. the original book, with the entries made in it at the instant,) would have been better evidence, more trustworthy, than the extracted copies made of those same entries from that same book, by the same person who himself made some of the entries and saw the others made. And this for the reason given by the counsel, viz. that it might happen in a variety of instances, that something would appear upon the original paper itself which would do away the effect of the evidence, but which might be suppressed in a copy, and still more easily in an extract.

2. That, therefore, the court acted in a justifiable manner in doing what they did—viz. in ordering a new trial; the effect of which order was to disallow the evidence in question, by setting aside the verdict, of the ground of which it formed either the whole or a necessary part.

3. That, if they had acted in a manner directly opposite, *i. e.* had they refused the new trial, they would have acted in a manner equally justifiable.

4. That, though in either case they would have acted justifiably (viz. taking for the standard of reference the established course of practice;) yet, in neither did they act, nor was it in their power to act on the occasion, without enormous trespasses committed in a variety of ways against the ends of justice: the established course of practice being itself, in a variety of ways, repugnant to the ends of justice, pregnant with injustice in a variety of shapes.

5. That, had the same points come before a justice of peace, acting in the mode of procedure called summary, none of those injustices would necessarily or probably have taken place: but that the whole procedure might have been, and in all probability would have been, in a state of perfect conformity to all the ends of justice.

Supposing the extracts in question to have

* Note on the Anonymous Equity Case, No. 3, before Lord Chancellor Hardwicke:—

"Should the Court connive at such proceedings as these, depositions would be no better than affidavits." 1. In the first place, not true. In the case of affidavit evidence, the deponent is completely exempt from interrogation; from interrogation on all sides: from the judge, as well as the adverse party. In this case, the deponent had actually been subjected to interrogation; to a species of cross-examination—to what goes by that name in equity practice; to cross-examination from written interrogatories drawn up by the advocate of the party adverse, and administered by judges *ad hoc*, a commissioner appointed by the party adverse, in conjunction with another appointed by the party invoking: in a word, to the most efficient mode of scrutiny which the practice of his Lordship's Court allows of.

2. In the next place; supposing it true that the deposition taken in the mode in question was no better than an affidavit, what would be the result? That it was upon a par with the only sort of evidence which a court of common-law judges, sitting without a jury, ever vouchsafes to hear: the only sort of evidence which his Lordship, sitting in that same place, ever suffered himself to hear, when the cause, instead of commencing by an instrument called a Bill, commenced by an instrument called a Petition: the sort of evidence which, in preference to depositions (by deponents examined *vivâ voce* by the examining clerk, or by commissioners named on both sides,) and even to the exclusion of such depositions, he was at least as much in the habit of hearing, as of hearing depositions. Connive at such proceedings!

been at once complete and correct copies of the original entries (that is, of so much of the contents of the whole book as applied to the facts in question,) the propriety of the verdict is out of dispute. But there appears strong reason for concluding them to have been trustworthy in both those points, and scarce any reason for suspecting them to have been untrustworthy in either.

"On his cross-examination, Aldridge" declared (*confessed*, says the report) "that he had no memory of his own of those specific facts." This declaration seems a pretty convincing proof of his veracity and trustworthiness: for, had it been an object with him to gain credence for the facts stated in and by the entries, those facts being false, what should have hindered him from deposing to the truth of them at once? why qualify his testimony by a "confession" so likely to destroy the supposed intended effect of it? Yet it is this very declaration that constitutes the whole of the ground on which the whole of his testimony taken together was pronounced unfit to constitute the ground, or any part of the ground, of the verdict.

A multitude of lights which might have been thrown on the case, appear, somehow or other, to have failed of being thrown on it.

Between the day on which this testimony was delivered, and the day on which the entries were supposed to have been made, what length of interval was there? On this head, utter silence. Suppose twenty years:—it might be natural enough that the facts constituting the subject-matter of the several entries (answers given by the several tenants to the question, At what time of the year did your holding expire?) should have left in his memory little or no trace. Instead of twenty years, put half as many months, such utter oblivion would seem scarcely probable: and in this case, and this only, a suspicion might have presented itself. The entries made by you were not true: you knew they were not: were you now to swear them to be true, by the testimony of those tenants or some of them, you might (so you apprehend) be convicted of perjury. It is to avoid the danger, hoping at the same time to have the benefit, of a false oath, that you now confine your declaration to the fact of having made those entries; that being a fact which is true.

Question 1. When you made those respective entries, did you at the time look upon them as true, or as being in any instance or in any respect not true?—Answer in one way: I have no recollection of my being conscious of their being false in any respect: I cannot, therefore, but be persuaded of their being true: for, had it been my intention to make an entry known by me to be false, it must have been in pursuance of some plan of fraud, a matter too remarkable (not to speak of the wickedness of it) to have been so soon forgotten by me.—Answer in the other way: Though it was by me that the entries were made, I cannot but acknowledge that at the very time of making them I was conscious of their not being true.

Question 2. The memoranda, of which the paper you now produce is composed, are not original memoranda made by you at the time, but copies made, in the way of extracts, from the memoranda really made at the time; which memoranda were entered in a book. This transcript which you now produce, does it contain all the entries in that book that bear any relation to the matter in question? if not, then, of the whole number of relevant entries that are in that book, how many, and to what effect, are those which you omitted to include in this your transcript? and for what cause did you omit them respectively? Most probable Answer: In this transcript is contained everything whatsoever that bears any relation to the matter in dispute: the other entries were nothing more than entries of payments made by the tenants at different times, payments which have no relation to the matter in dispute.

Question 3. Here, instead of the book in which the original entries were made, you bring a paper containing memoranda which you say are transcripts made from such of the entries as bear relation to the matter in dispute. How comes it that you have not brought the book itself? How came you to put yourself to all that trouble?—Probable Answer: In the book, these memoranda were a little dispersed: being ranged (as in other books of account) according to their dates, they were intermixed with entries relative to other matters. To have searched for them here, would have consumed I know not how much of the time of the court. As the effect of the whole statement was at any rate to depend on the credit that might be thought due to my testimony, it did not occur to me that my bringing that book would be either necessary or of use.

By the part taken in the business by the judge that tried the cause (Lord Loughborough,) it is clear that by that learned Chief Justice of the Common Pleas, afterwards Lord Chancellor, the production of the original book was deemed not necessary. Is it to be wondered at, if a conclusion to the same effect should have determined the conduct of the unlearned witness?

All these questions, so obvious, so natural, and not one of them put: neither by the counsel employed to impugn the evidence, by the counsel employed to support the evidence, nor by the learned judge, whose support in other ways it received. Was it that unlearned reason and law-learning are mutually exclusive of each other? Was it that, in the opinion of learned gentlemen, it was time to go to dinner? Was it that causes calling for judicature were many, and that (as in the nature of things must commonly be the case in current practice) there was not time for doing justice to any one? Was it that the parties were known to be rich and sturdy, and that, by a sort of professional instinct so natural to learned gentlemen, it was felt that the less the expenditure of untimely reason, the more ample room there might be for supplemental law?

In fact, no fewer than five learned gentlemen, all of them then or since of distinguished eminence, were listed, though in vain, in the support of this evidence: and, before this argument, the cause had been rich in intervening incidents.

The more thoroughly the history of the cause is understood, the less the wonder will be, if the unlearned witness and the learned judge joined in one common error. They were wrong; for the Court of King's Bench, with Lord Kenyon at the head of it, pronounced them so. They were in an error: but how came they to have fallen into it? The want of having made acquaintance with a law never promulgated — a law never made, but which by learned imagination was capable of being made, in the way of jurisprudential abstraction (that is, of imagination,) out of two decisions, with either of which it was not possible for them to have been acquainted; and which, after having been buried as soon as born, were dug up for the occasion out of the *limbus infantum* in which they slept: the one by Mr. Justice Buller, after a sleep of thirty-four years; the other by Lord Kenyon, after a sleep of thirty-seven years.

For thus it is, that, on pretence of being declared, laws upon laws, laws fighting with laws, are made throughout the manufactory of common, that is, of judge-made, law. That B may receive warning (warning which it is neither designed nor expected should ever reach him), A must first have been consigned to distress or ruin. Gulfs by the side of gulfs cover in its whole expanse the field of jurisprudential law: nor can any of them take its chance of being closed, till the property or liberty of some involuntary Curtius has been thrown into it.

Had the matter come before a court of conscience, or a justice of the peace (and nothing hinders but that a case, the same in principle, may have come ere now before either of those seats of unsophisticated common sense;) had it come (say for exemplification sake) before a justice of the peace, how would he have dealt with it? If the above-proposed rules, obvious as they are, are indeed conformable to the ends of justice, he would have proceeded (for what should have hindered him?) according to the spirit of those rules. By questions such as those above brought to view, he would have scrutinized into the *bona fides* of the witness; and (if satisfied as to that), into the correctness and completeness of the evidence, when all had been extracted that could be extracted from that source. Previously to his decision, he would have insisted or not insisted upon the production of the book, according to circumstances.

He would have insisted upon the production of it, had any doubts remained on his mind of the correctness or completeness of the alleged transcripts; had the like doubts remained upon the mind of the adverse party; at any rate, if only a few minutes, or only a few hours, or even (if fraud were suspected, or the magnitude of the stake appeared to warrant the delay, vexation, and expense) a few *days*, were understood to be necessary, in respect of time, to the production of it: nor would he even have grudged days, or weeks, or months, with whatever burthen in respect of expense the burthen in other shapes might be understood to be aggravated, if the party applying for the scrutiny were content to take, and did actually take, the burthen, absolutely or provisionally, upon himself.

He would not have insisted on it, if — the answers given to all such questions as the above proving completely satisfactory, he had been assured that the book was at the other end of the country, and that not less than a week's or a fortnight's journey on the part of the witness (it being under his lock and key) would be necessary to its being forthcoming, — if the call made for it on the other side appeared to originate in *mala fides*, the demander refusing to come into any reasonable measures for indemnification present or eventual, — and to have no other object than that of subjecting the opposite party to vexation and expense.

He would have had recourse to any one of a variety of expedients, rather than, by unconditional order, or unconditional refusal, subject in any shape either the one party or the other to preponderant and unnecessary inconvenience. He would determine in favour of the transcripts in the first instance, subjecting the decision to eventual reversal within a limited time, means of inspection being secured to the adverse party within that time. He would determine against the transcript in the first instance, subjecting the decision to eventual reversal within a limited time, on the production of the book before himself, or the examination of it in other trustworthy hands, agreed upon by both parties, or too notoriously trustworthy to be with any colour of reason objected to by either; the book being in either case found to be correctly and completely represented by the transcripts.

It would be an almost endless task to exhibit on this occasion an exhaustive view of all the expedients, the *mezzi termini*, to which, under the possible diversifications of which the convenience of the parties in a case of this sort may be susceptible, recourse might have been had. To assist conception, the above may be sufficient for a sample. In the choice of expedients having the legitimate ends of justice for their object, common sense and common honesty would not in practice—when they act by themselves they do not—find any insuperable difficulty. It is only common law, or its faithful ally in the war against justice, English equity, that, by a noble disdain of the convenience and interest of all parties, contrives for its own sinister purposes — contrives by unbending rules — to involve in one common violation all the ends of justice.

The question here on the carpet is of the number of those which respect the admission and exclusion of evidence. At the trial, whether it be in the metropolis at *Nisi Prius*, or in the country at the assizes, it is always in an abstract point of view that they are considered. In all cases alike, there is a something which is abstracted and set aside: and what is that something? — the interest of all individuals concerned, in the character of suitors; their interest, in respect of the important points of delay, vexation, and expense. In theory, accordingly, the decision may be wrong or right: in theory, and in this abstract point of view, it is actually right, as often as it puts an exclusion upon evidence of inferior trustworthiness, where superior might have been had from the same source. In theory, therefore, it is sometimes (though, on the whole ground of exclusion taken together, perhaps not once in fifty times) right: but in practice, — if in delay, vexation, and expense — all factitious, all manufactured for the sake of the profit to be extracted out of the expense — there be anything of injustice, it is always richly fruitful in injustice. Take the assizes, the circuit business, as the fairest sample of the whole field of common-law regular judicature; embracing the whole territorial expanse, with the exception of the metropolis. The only article of evidence produced, and that an article which (supposing it received and credited) is decisive of the cause, turns out to be of such a sort as to indicate as obtainable from the same source another article: and that other, an article of such a complexion, that, with the help of a micrometer, if viewed with a microscope, it might be seen to stand in the scale of trustworthiness an infinitesimal part of a degree above that one which, being in court, is actually offered. What follows? Considered in the abstract point of view above mentioned, there is nothing to be said against the rejection of the inferior evidence. But in a practical point of view,—in respect of everything that is worth considering — in respect of the interest, the feelings, the property, the well-being, perhaps the being, of the suitors, — observe the consequence. At the end of six or twelve months, or twice as much — at the expense of fifty guineas, or a hundred, or several hundreds — at an expense which not one individual out of fifty would be able to defray, though he were to leave himself as bare as when first brought into the world, the ideal imperfection may or may not receive its corrective; but in the meantime, some one out of a hundred accidents has happened: the better evidence is lost; the party that should have profited by it is dead, heart-broken, or ruined; his life, or his money, or his courage, are extinguished.

Could a respite of half a dozen hours have been allowed, perhaps the theoretically-superior evidence might have been made forthcoming, and the requisite satisfaction given to the delicacy of learned consciences. To an unlearned magistrate, to a dozen of ignorant shopkeepers sitting in a court of conscience, it would as soon have occurred to hang a man without a hearing, as to refuse him any such respite. But neither six hours, nor half the number, can ever be allowed to any such purpose. Necessity, the offspring of professional convenience, opposes an insuperable bar to all such weaknesses. Under the auspices of the learned magistrate, in whose eyes the cosmography of circuit-judicature is a miracle of wisdom and justice; in whose computation four days out of the three hundred and sixty-five are in every place sufficient, and in some places too many by half, for justice; in whose estimate, the time which is sufficient for the collection of fees must needs be sufficient for judicature;—under such auspices, the wheel of judicature can no more be stopped to save a man's fortune, than a mill-wheel to save his body from being crushed.

CHAPTER III.

OF SUGGESTIVE INTERROGATION.

§ 1. *Reasons against the absolute prohibition of Suggestive Interrogation.*

By a *suggestive* interrogation, is meant an interrogation by which the fact or supposed fact which the interrogator expects and wishes to find asserted in and by the answer, is made known to the proposed respondent. Is not your name so and so? You live at such a place, do not you? You live as a servant with the defendant?

The term is from the Roman school of law; but, without suggesting the idea of Roman or any other law, to the mind of every person to whom the English language is familiar, it suggests readily enough the import above ascribed to it.

Leading is the word employed instead of it by English lawyers. To a non-lawyer, the import meant to be conveyed is not suggested so readily and distinctly (if at all) by this word, as by the word suggestive. It affords, however, the convenience of being applied in cases in which the word suggestive is not applicable. You must not lead your own witness, says one rule one hears among English lawyers: you may lead your adversary's witness, says another rule one hears in the same school.

Concerning the propriety of these rules, and of the distinction on which they turn, inquiry will presently be made.

That the response ought in every instance to be the expression of the actual recollection of the proposed respondent, and not the allegation of another person, adopted by the respondent, and falsely delivered as his own, is sufficiently manifest. That whatsoever measures may be necessary for the prevention of this effect should constantly be taken, is in like manner manifest. But they belong not to this head.*

The purposes for which an interrogation of the suggestive kind may be not only not prejudicial, but conducive, to the ends of justice, seem reducible to two heads, viz. dispatch, and assistance. In the first case, the interrogation is suggestive in form only; in the other, in substance and effect.

Take, in any individual case, any individual interrogation, — and suppose it subservient to the purpose of dispatch, and of dispatch only, not yielding in any shape any assistance to the proposed respondent; the innocence and the utility of it are by the supposition established: the innocence, by its not being subservient to incorrectness or incompleteness on the part of the testimony, nor thence to deception and misdecision; the utility, by its being subservient to dispatch, thence operating in diminution of delay and vexation.

In this case, the substance of the matter of fact which the interrogator expects and wishes to find asserted in and by the answer, is made known to the proposed respondent; and therefore the interrogation is *suggestive.* But the fact made known to him for this purpose being no other than what was known to him already, the suggestion is, by the supposition, of a sort from which no assistance to any plan of mendacity can be derived.

From the purposely short exemplification given above — a specimen by which, as yet, little dispatch is gained, little circumlocution saved — a conception may, without much difficulty, be formed, of much greater savings.

* The subject they belong to is rather *procedure* than evidence. Among the arrangements requisite, those that belong to architecture constitute the basis of the est.

You live at such a place? no saving as yet: *Where do you live?* would be still shorter. *You live as servant with the defendant?* some saving already. Under a rigorous prohibition of suggestion, the interrogation might have been drawn into some such form as this: — Have you any acquaintance with either of the parties to this cause? Yes. — With which of them? The defendant. — *Of what nature is your acquaintance with him, and whence derived? I live with him as his servant.*

In the way of supposition, — and even in practice, where, on the part of the party really concerned in interest, the requisite degree of confidence is not wanting, — the use of suggestion to the purpose of dispatch will assume a greater latitude; if the proposed respondent be a person to whom no disposition to make any such deceptitious use of any fact made known to him can be ascribed; or if the fact, though as yet unknown to the proposed respondent, be of such a nature that, though he were even disposed to make any such improper use of it, it would not be in his power.

The appearance of suggestion affords naturally a sort of suspicion of *mala fides:* information, therefore, which he knows how to obtain without that appearance, a man will not naturally choose to purchase at that price: to incur a suspicion of that sort, and without use, will be a mark of unskilfulness. Hence, in this way, a young advocate of little experience, who, as such, stands exposed to the imputation of unskilfulness, will not naturally hazard the taking liberties, such as an advocate whose eminence has placed him above the imputation, will take without scruple.†

The second ground for admitting suggestive interrogation, is assistance to recollection.

From what has been said under the head of *recurrence to notes,* it must have been abundantly manifest that cases exist in which, to the correctness and completeness of testimony, helps to recollection cannot but be necessary.‡

† The saving thus made in point of time is among the many causes which concur in rendering it more pleasant to the judge to have to do with advocates of old established eminence, in preference to juniors.

‡ In the case of any such help to recollection, it may exist in the shape of a written document, and that document in the possession of the proposed respondent: in that case, the help is afforded by recurrence to notes.

But a case that may also exist, is, that it shall be in the possession, not of the proposed respondent, but of the interrogator. Here, then, if not in the particular shape of suggestive interrogation, at any rate suggestion, is justifiable. *Look upon that paper* — the contents of it are a long account (suppose) of receipts and payments: — *do you know anything of the contents? are any and what of them true?* By

In the ordinary intercourse of life,—in cases where the interest, the manifest and recognised interest, of all the parties, requires that the truth, the whole truth, and nothing but the truth, be brought to light,—where from falsehood (supposing it to come out instead of truth) every interest would be prejudiced, none promoted;—no one but must have frequently experienced how useful and necessary suggestions from without are to the correctness as well as completeness of the statement which requires to be delivered.

By such suggestion, a result which, it is true, may happen is, that (honest recollection not being the object) assistance may be given to mendacious invention, and the production of deception may be the consequence. But from this possibility, no just conclusion against the propriety of admitting the suggestion can be deduced.

In favour of the admission, provided certain conditions be observed, several considerations appear to plead.

1. If the bringing to view the fact or circumstance in question be necessary to the giving effect to the right of the cause, on which side soever it lie—in other words, to the prevention of misdecision; at the same time that, without the assistance in question, recollection of the fact or circumstance cannot take place;—exclude the suggestion, misdecision is the certain consequence.

On the other hand, admit the suggestion, and,—though it should happen that, of the request made for the admission of it, a plan of mendacious invention was the final cause,—still deception and misdecision are far, very far, from being the *necessary* result.

2. The probability of the failure of true evidence through want of recollection, is greater than the probability of mendacious evidence in consequence of assistance afforded by suggestive questions.

On the one hand, honest failure of recollection (a weakness that requires assistance from another quarter, to enable a man to declare and make known the fact as it really happened) is an incident extremely common, and therefore proportionably probable. It is what may happen to every man; and is happening to every man continually, in every man's experience.

Failure of recollection is most apt to happen in the case of a timid witness, who is least likely to be a mendacious, and in particular a successfully mendacious, witness. By the perilousness and novelty of his situation, it frequently happens that the exercise of a man's mental faculties, and in particular his memory, is greatly disturbed and weakened. From the facts that constitute the subject-matter of his deposition,—from the traces left by the past perceptions in question in his memory,—his attention is irresistibly called off to the variety of sensible objects with which he is encompassed, and which are so many sources of terror to his mind.

So far as the effect of the suggestion (whether exhibited in the form of a question or in any other) is merely to bring back to the recollection of the witness a true matter of fact, which was really there before,—the effect of it is not prejudicial to truth and justice, but advantageous, and frequently altogether necessary.

The case, therefore, in which the effect of such suggestion is beneficial to the interests of truth and justice, is in experience frequent, and in prospect probable.

On the other hand, the case in which the effect of it is prejudicial to the interests of truth and justice, viz. by promoting mendacity—mendacity successful, that is, productive of deception on the part of the judge,—presents itself (at least in the state of things most frequently exemplified in English practice, in which the interrogation is performed in an open judicatory, on a day foreknown to both parties, and by professional advocates on both sides) as likely to be extremely rare.

1. The mischievousness of suggested information is confined to those cases in which the proposed respondent is pre-disposed to make use of it to a mendacious purpose.

2. Supposing the existence of a disposition to mendacity to be productive of any such pernicious effect, the fact thus conveyed to the knowledge of the proposed respondent, must be a fact the knowledge of which could not have been conveyed to him at any earlier period than the commencement of this his examination. For, at any antecedent point of time, the intimation of it might have been conveyed to him without exciting any suspicion: whereas, conveyed in the way in question, it cannot but be productive of a degree of suspicion such as leaves little danger of its being productive of the effect aimed at by it.

3. In the shape of notes or memoranda supposed to have been taken by the proposed respondent for his own use, the information might, at any antecedent point of time, have been furnished to him,—and that in the permanent form of a written document, much more surely subservient to the proposed sinister purpose, than any such verbal information as is supposed, can be.

4. Even within this narrow space of time, it cannot be conveyed to the proposed respondent (however prone to mendacity), other-

By the same causes by which recurrence to notes may be necessitated, suggestion from without may be necessitated.

In the case of recurrence to notes, was seen the necessity of referring the allowance or disallowance to the discretion of the judge: in this case (as will be seen presently) the same necessity prescribes the same arrangement.

wise than in the case of a correspondent disposition to the correspondent species of subornation, on the part of the interrogating advocate.

5. In the station of advocate, misbehaviour in this shape is not at all conformable to the natural state of things: the profit would be improbable, and would accrue to the party: the loss, in the shape of loss of reputation, would be probable, and would fall on the supposed delinquent, the advocate, himself.

6. Suppose the two requisites to the species of improbity in question conjoined; viz. on the part of a proposed respondent, a disposition to apply the information to the purpose of a mendacious statement, and on the part of the advocate, a correspondent disposition to furnish it; and suppose the mendacious statement delivered accordingly: still no harm takes place, unless, mendacious as the statement is, it obtains credence, and deception and misdecision are the consequences.

But the probability of any such deception on the part of the judge, in consequence of the mendacity of the witness, and thence of mendacity itself from this source, is, again, much reduced by the remedial virtue of *vivâ voce* interrogation *ex adverso.*

Where the answer to the suggestive question would be decisive, and the truth of it not liable to undergo ulterior scrutiny from a quarter interested in the detection of the falsity of it (if false;) here, indeed, the prospect of success in a confederacy of this kind would be highly favourable, and the probability of the attempt proportionable.

Such, accordingly, would be the case, in the instance of the sort of examination carried on in the Roman mode of procedure in causes in general, and in English procedure in the courts of equity. An advocate of the party frames the question in writing; the officer standing in the place of the judge propounds those questions to the witness *vivâ voce;* the witness gives his answer accordingly; no advocate present on the side opposite to that in favour of which the witness (in the case of a mendacious witness) violates the obligation of veracity; no advocate to ground a fresh string of questions upon the mendacious answer, for the purpose of bringing the falsity of it to view.

But, under the tutelary influence of cross-examination, the chance of success to a conspiracy of this kind cannot but be rendered highly precarious. The assistance which it is in the power of the supposed confederate, in the station of examiner, to give to the examinee, is but momentary. What he does, is to suggest the supposed matter of fact, the existence of which is to be asserted by the response. But, the suggestion once given, the power of support is gone. The next moment, the mendacious witness sees himself delivered into the hands of the adversary; from whose merciless lips will issue an unknown string of questions, all conspiring to bring to light the truth he has endeavoured to disguise; to expose to view the falsehood he has had the imprudence to advance.

7. As in case of false responsion, — where an attempt has been made that fails of producing deception, the natural effect is to put the judge upon his guard: the natural tendency is thus to prevent deception, and to give birth to a decision in favour of the other side.

Of a question of this nature, the distinctive character is too manifest to be in any danger of escaping the observation of the advocate on the other side, or even of the judge. The degree of suspicion and discredit which it will throw on that side of the cause in favour of which the attempt is made, may be set down as (comparatively speaking) a constant and certain effect; while the undue benefit derivable from it, is but an accidental and precarious one.

In a dubious case, or in a case in which success (bad or good) admits of degrees, undue prejudice to the side on which it is employed, is perhaps upon the whole a more probable result than undue advantage. If, by the advocate on one side, any such attempt be made with his eyes open to the tendency and consequent impropriety of it, it must be in confidence of its meeting with no common degree of incapacity on the part of the advocate on the other side, as well as no common degree of incapacity, or carelessness, or worse, on the part of the judge.

Where it is the known destiny of the evidence to be minuted down and published, the probability of any transgression of this sort seems very small indeed: nor, it is supposed, would the exemplifications of it (if any) be found otherwise than very unfrequent in the printed trials, at least of modern times.

The difficulty of drawing any clear line of demarcation, between the cases to which the prohibition of such suggestions shall, and those to which it shall not, be understood to extend, constitutes another objection to the utility of the prohibition. Look at the histories of these proceedings; documents which English judicature furnishes in such instructive abundance: instances in which the questions, put by an advocate to the witness called in on his own side, wear this suggestive form, present themselves, and present themselves unaccompanied with any objection on the other side, at every page.

In fact, when is it that any objection to the use of them appears to be made? On those occasions on which the use of them presents to view any probable prejudice to the other side. These are but few: and of these few, the cases in which the real cause of the objection is not the adverseness, but the serviceableness, of the suggestion to the extraction of truth, would (I am inclined to think) be found to compose the major part. The witness (an honest witness) is bewildered: a hint to refresh his recollection would set him in the right path. It is for this reason that the party who has truth on his side, endeavours to supply him with that assistance: it is for this same reason that the party who has truth adverse to him, is upon the watch to deprive him of that assistance.

The impossibility of marking out beforehand the cases to which the liberty of suggestive interrogation shall extend, will appear sufficiently manifest to any one who considers the tenor of the two rules of English law mentioned above: rules which, taken together, are by much too absurd to experience (even under the technical system) an undeviating obedience; rules which (like most, if not all, other rules of that system) experience double honour, sometimes in the breach, and sometimes in the observance.

Not lead your own witness?—Why not? Because your own witness is partial to your side; and to such a degree partial as to be ready on all occasions to adopt, and deliver as his own testimony,—to adopt, knowing it to be a lie,—any lie that, from your brief or otherwise, you may be disposed to put into his mouth. Thus measured, thus rational, are the professors of this pretended science, in the conclusions they draw in the way of circumstantial evidence. Principal fact, partiality, even to the length of perjury, on the part of the witness called on any side,—partiality on the part of every witness in favour of any suitor by whom he is called upon to depose. Evidentiary fact proving the partiality, the need I conceive myself to be under of calling upon him for his evidence: the accident of his having been present at the transaction, on the proof of which my chance of justice happens to depend.

What if he happens to have been called on both sides?—a case every now and then exemplified in practice. According to this argument, he must in that case be partial on both sides: determined, in case any such question should be put to him, to perjure himself; and so sure of succeeding in his perjury, and of making each side gain the cause, that he must not be heard on either side.

Lead my adversary's witness? Why may I on all occasions lead my adversary's witness? on no occasion lead my own? Because, your adversary's witness (the witness on whose testimony your adversary's claim happens to stand) being on that account sure to be partial to your adversary, and against you, you may offer to put into his mouth as many untruths as you please, he will not open it to one of them.

Not to speak of any such outrageous force as to plunge a man into the acceptance of an invitation to commit perjury,—in what proportion of the whole number of causes, may a bias more or less strong in favour of the inviting party (the testimony not having been called for on both sides) be expected? There are three cases—partiality for the invoker's side, partiality for the adversary's side, partiality for neither side. Antecedently to particular reasons pleading in favour of the several cases, the aggregate list of witness should be equally divided between the three. That the list of cases in which the partiality is on the invoker's side* will naturally be the most numerous, is indeed evident enough at the first glance: that it can never be so numerous as to swallow up both the others, might, one should have thought, have been at least equally evident.

Observe that, should it so happen that my adversary's witness, the witness technically so denominated, the witness whose testimony my adversary is so unfortunate as to be obliged to call for or lose his chance of justice—that this witness of my adversary's in name, should, in affection, be my witness;—in this case, in the regular course of things, the check opposed to mendacity by interrogation *ex adverso* has no application. For, it being on behalf of my adversary that this witness has been examined in chief, the examination to which he is subjected on my behalf is the cross-examination: the supposed adverse examination, which, being itself the check upon the examination in chief, is the last of the two parts of which the whole examination is comprised: the last of all, and which, being itself but a check, has no other to be a check upon it.

In this case, therefore, the security of the cause against mendacity by the assistance of suggestive questions, rests on the honour and regard to character on the part of the advocate and of the judge, not on the preventive power of the prohibitive rule.†

* See Book II. *Securities*; Chap. IX. *Interrogation*; § 5. *Affections of the interrogators and respondents towards each other, how far presumable?* p. 346.

† Of the two corresponding rules, thus equally pregnant with theoretical absurdity, the use made in practice may be expected to be considerably different.

When, in the person of his adversary's witness, an advocate finds himself in possession of a deponent whose affections are (as, from his relation to the parties or the cause, they frequently will be) manifestly and strongly on his (the advocate's) side; shame will naturally and almost instinctively restrain him from plying the witness with suggestive questions. Of the two rules—the *prohibition* absurd in itself, the *permission* absurd by its inconsistency and undiscriminating generality,—the *permissive* one (it seems probable) is scarce ever in practice productive of any detri-

But, forasmuch as it rests on this basis entirely in this case, and to a certain degree in all cases, why should it not rest entirely on this same basis in all cases? that is to say, in the sense of the court respecting the propriety or impropriety of suffering the intimation in question to be conveyed to the witness under examination, regard being had to the interests of truth and justice. Every now and then it happens, that a candid witness, conscious of a defect in his memory, speaks out and says (supposing it for instance the name of a person or a place)—"I cannot this moment recollect the name, but if any person will mention to me that name amongst others, such mention will bring it back to my memory, and I shall be able to distinguish it from the rest." In virtue of the prohibitive rule here contended against, such assistance is, I believe, generally refused. What I contend for is—

1. In the first place, that, when thus requested on the part of the witness, it should not be refused, but rather granted of course, reserving to the discretion of the judge the power of refusing it.

2. In the next place, that,—when, upon the hesitation or declaration of non-recollection on the part of the witness, the advocate conceives it to be a case in which he may honestly make known a disposition to afford to the recollection of the witness that assistance which it appears to stand in need of,—it should be allowable and customary for him to submit such his desire to the judge. To do so *vivâ voce*, and therefore openly, might not be in every instance practicable, consistently with the reserves necessary to prevent the communication from being actually made by means of the application by which the liberty of making it is prayed. For maintaining this necessary reserve, one expedient is the handing up to the judge in writing (which might also be done through the hands and with the privity of the advocate on the other side) the suggestion proposed to be made: the other is, to cause the witness to withdraw while the question on this subject is under debate.

In this way, it should seem, might frequently be obtained much light, which otherwise would be lost. And where the information thus afforded *ab extrà* happened to be at once apposite and true, it would often happen that the truth of it, and the truth of the ulterior testimony drawn forth by this means, would manifest itself by tokens sufficient to put the matter out of doubt. Often will it happen that one fact, thus replaced in a memory from which it had escaped, shall draw out from thence other facts, in a stream, the copiousness and rapidity of which shall leave no doubt of its flowing from the right source: from memory, the seat of truth; not from invention, the source of falsehood.

No objection (it should seem) can consistently be made to the committing it to the judge's discretion to afford assistance of this sort, in whatsoever case it promises to be subservient to the interests of truth and justice. On this occasion, as on all others, the judge must be supposed fit for his office: all such precautionary arrangements must be supposed to have been made as appear necessary, and without preponderant inconvenience promise to be conducive, to that effect. Such is the presumption on which all reasonings must be built.

§ 2. *Conditions of Allowance.*

That, during the process of interrogation, information under the notion of a help to recollection ought not to be communicable by an interrogator to a proposed respondent, without permission openly applied for and granted by the judge; and that, in the event of such permission, it ought to be communicable; has been already intimated.

What remains is, to bring to view the cases in which, with propriety, permission to that effect may be, on the condition above mentioned, granted by the judge.

1. If, on being applied for, it appear to you that the information in question would be more likely to assist the framing a mendacious state-

ment to the interests of truth and justice. It is so flagrantly absurd, that, in a case where the application of it would be productive of the mischief with which it is pregnant, no man has the effrontery to put it in practice.

The corresponding and opposite rule will, naturally speaking, be far from being alike innocent in practice. In this case, no shame being attached to the enforcement of the rule, the enforcement of it will experience little difficulty. Instances in which, by the influence of this rule, testimony may be sure to be rendered incomplete, and decision thus placed on the wrong side, will indeed be not unfrequently presenting themselves. But a spectacle of this sort is too frequent to make any sensation, or (if it were to make any) too favourable to the general interest and propensity of the men of law, to make any other than an agreeable one. It is an article belonging to the list of exclusionary rules: a set of rules of which almost the whole of the jurisprudential law of evidence is composed: rules which are at once the engines of his power, and the foundation of his claim to the reputation of superior wisdom, and recondite science: rules which, being worshipped one moment, trampled upon the next—adhered to in favour of A, broken in favour of B,—throw open the shop of justice and injustice, leaving no right secure, nor any iniquity without hope.

[Mr. Phillipps (Law of Evidence, 6th Edit. i. 256) says, "If a witness should appear to be in the interest of the opposite party, or unwilling to give evidence, the court will in its discretion allow the examination-in-chief to assume something of the form of a cross-examination." It appears therefore that this rule of judge-made law has to a great degree been set aside by other judge-made law, subsequently enacted.—*Editor.*]

ment (and that in such manner as to render it detection-proof, and so promote deception), than to improve the testimony either in point of correctness or completeness, — refuse to permit the yielding it: in the opposite case, allow it.

A rule to this effect would be extremely general. But it seems scarcely possible to narrow the power thus given, without diminishing the utility of it.

2. There is one case in which the permission ought evidently to be granted: where, from the multitude and variety of the facts to be spoken to by the proposed respondent, it cannot reasonably be expected that the whole mass of them should have been borne in memory, in such sort as that it shall be in his power, without such assistance, to deliver his testimony in relation to it in a state of correctness and completeness.

Instances might be mentioned in which the necessity of refreshment would be obvious, even in the case of a witness of the most practised memory. An account (for example) containing a hundred items on one side, and as many on the other: disbursements or receipts, all having taken place by or with the privity of the deponent. Some of these, perhaps, it may happen to him to recollect of himself: but is there one man out of a hundred, or a thousand, that (especially if called upon on the sudden) would be able to recollect the whole? At the same time, present to him a list of them, there may be none of them to which he may not be able to speak with decision and with truth.

Accordingly, the presenting to a deponent in this way a ready-drawn account, is matter of general practice; yet what can be more clearly leading, more clearly suggestive?

But here the line between the cases in which on this ground the permission ought to be given, and those in which it ought not to be given, cannot (it is evident) be drawn by any general form of words. The necessity, and thence propriety, of the permission, will depend partly upon the length of the account, partly upon the simplicity or complexity of it, partly upon the mental powers of the proposed respondent.

3. Setting aside the case in which, without any application from the proposed respondent himself, it may be proper that, in the shape of a written document, assistance to his recollection should be administered of course; a rule that upon the face of it seems a reasonable one is this:

Unless the proposed respondent, perceiving (as he says) the need of information from without, in regard to this or that one of the points concerning which he is interrogated, makes application for such information accordingly, (which application will of course be openly made;) let it not be furnished to him. If such application be made by him, it will then rest with the judge to allow it or not, according as (regard being had to rule the first) to his discretion shall seem meet.

4. But if, for want of his being apprised of some matter of fact (which, having or not having been matter of dispute, is sufficiently established,) the proposed respondent has, on the occasion and in the course of his testimony, fallen into some erroneous statement, or assumption, or supposition, by which in any particular, without blame on his part, his testimony has been rendered more or less incomplete or incorrect; in such case it should be allowable to the judge, whether at his own motion, or (if he thinks fit) at the motion of any party, or the advocate of any party (the party by whom the testimony of the proposed respondent was called for not excepted,) to correct the mistake: communicating to the proposed respondent whatever information shall be necessary to that purpose.

5. So, in case of need of suggestive information, manifested by the proposed witness, otherwise than by direct confession or unintentional and blameless error (as above;) for instance, by deportment, in the way of hesitation or otherwise, it may be allowable to the judge, of his own motion, or at the instance of a party (as above,) to tender to the proposed respondent such assistance as shall be requisite: and upon his request to administer it accordingly.

6. Such assistance, if administered, should be administered in such manner as to afford no more information than what, on the supposition of veracity on the part of the proposed respondent, may be absolutely necessary; leaving to be done by his memory whatever can be done by it.

Example. If the name of a person form a material part of the testimony: and the witness, hesitating about the name, declares that if he were to hear it he should recognise it; — give him, along with other names taken at random, the name or names stated as true, by the suggestion of either or both the parties; to the intent that the proposed respondent may make his choice: in which case, let it be the care of the judge so to present to notice the whole list of names, that the names, so chosen respectively by the parties shall not be distinguishable by him from the rest.*

7. Excepting cases in which (as in that above exemplified) the length and intricacy of the string of facts to be spoken to, puts the necessity of suggestive information out of doubt; a precaution that may be of use (at least where

* The device commonly known (more particularly among sea-faring men) under the name of a *round robin*, exemplifies the principle; how different soever the purpose has been, to which, in this instance, it has been most apt to be applied.

the circumstances of the case are of a nature to mark out the testimony for suspicion) is the going through with the examination of the witnesses on both sides, without the suggestive information; and then, and not till then, administering the information, if the demand for it be deemed to continue.*

Under the system of procedure above supposed — under a system of publicity such as the English, — a relation of amity, operating to the prejudice of truth and justice, is, as between the proposed respondent and the interrogator, the source, and only source, of whatever mischief is apprehended from the suggestion.

Under a system of darkness, such as that of the Roman school, the opposite relation (a relation of hostility) constitutes an additional relation from which, in case of suggestion, mischief has (and not without reason) been apprehended; the nature of the suit being penal, the interrogator the judge, the interrogation oral, and no other person present, except a scribe, acting in a state of dependence under the judge.

Accordingly, among the rules of that system are to be found rules prohibiting the use of suggestive questions, and to that end requiring that the interrogator's proposition shall have for its subject the name of a *species*, and not of an *individual*. "Did you see a person, any person, there at that time?" A *person* — not *Titius* or *Titia*: no, nor so much as a *man* or a *woman*, if anything turn upon the sex.

In the cases which gave occasion to those rules, the mischief was but too real. But the cause of it was not the suggestiveness of the interrogation, but the darkness in which the power exercised on the occasion was involved; involved and screened from the controuling and salutary influence of the public eye.

In the security afforded by such darkness to judicial misconduct, to the prejudice of either side at pleasure, — it is no more than should be expected, that in this or that instance, the judge will be disposed to bestow impunity on a delinquent, — in this or that other instance, to let fall on the head of innocence the punishment due to guilt.

In the latter case, different expedients will, according to the circumstances of the case, offer themselves to his choice. By dint of terror he may so confound the intellectual faculties of the defendant as to extract from him a sort of assent to any or every question that appears to call for it: by a sort of compact (more or less explicit,) he may engage the defendant to confess a less severely punishable offence of which he is innocent, in hopes of saving himself from the punishment attached to a more severely punishable offence, of which he is also innocent: or, to save all this trouble, he may at once extract from his terror, or his ignorance, a signature, by which he is made to recognise, as a true expression of his mind, a discourse of the confessional cast, the contents of which had never been really presented to his mind.

All this while (as above observed) the cause of the mischief lies merely in the secrecy.

Establish the secrecy, the injustice may be perpetrated, and securely, without the improper mode of interrogation. Substitute due and appropriate publicity to the secrecy, the injustice cannot, with any assurance of safety, be perpetrated by means of that improper practice. Supposing this or that interrogatory to be, in the way in question, improper; by the entering of the interrogatory on the minutes, and the publication of the minutes, the interrogator with his injustice will be exposed to shame. By putting the suggestive question, the judge would but expose himself; unless, by causing the insertion of it to be omitted, he were to falsify the minutes: and, supposing this fraud to be in his power, and practised, the other is of no use.

Remove what there is dangerous in the secrecy, and, at the same time, place all relation of undue amity out of the case, — suggestion, be it ever so pointed and particular, not only is capable of being practised without danger, but, without any inconvenience, is in ordinary use. The invitation given to a man to prejudice himself may be ever so pointed; he may be trusted to for not accepting it.

In English equity practice, interrogatories put on behalf of a plaintiff to a defendant, are rendered suggestive without reserve. So, in English common law practice, in the case of the interrogatories put by the advocate on one side to the witness, who (with or without reason) is, from the side on which he has been called in the cause, presumed to be friendly towards the other.

In the Roman school, in cases not penal, interrogatories propounded by the judge to the defendant, have been drawn up for the purpose by the law-assistant of the plaintiff; and in this case, the darkness being in a considerable degree lightened, and the motives for judicial oppression having little application in comparison with what they have in penal cases, (especially in those in which government is a party, in affection as well as name,) little more inconvenience is produced from the source in question, than in the case of English equity practice, as above.

* This precaution is the exact counterpart of that which will be found to be suggested in Chapter XI. under the head of *time for recollection*. Examination in the first instance *vivâ voce*, to preclude the opportunity of mendacious invention: then (if any special demand for recollection-time be presented by the nature of the case) interrogation *ex scripto*, to be answered in the same mode.

CHAPTER IV.

OF DISCREDITIVE INTERROGATION.

But for a fallacy, no less pernicious in practice than gross and palpable in theory, neither the demand for this chapter, nor consequently the chapter itself, would have had existence.

There stands a witness, whose testimony appears to my apprehension stained with mendacity; and that mendacity of a nature to operate to my prejudice. By the questions I put to him, shall it be permitted to me to endeavour to bring to light his mendacity, or the reasons which I have for suspecting him of a disposition to launch into that crime?

Yes, if he be my adversary's witness: but no (says a rule of English law,) if he be my own witness.

It is the interest of English judges that chances may never be wanting in favour of any the worst cause: that no cause, how bad soever, may be given up as desperate. Among the vast variety of devices which they have set on foot for this purpose, one is, — to grant to every witness a mendacity-license, subject only to this condition, that, of two parties in a cause, it must be employed against that one by whom the witness has been called upon for his testimony.

In this witness, I behold a person to whom it happened to be a witness — a percipient witness — and perhaps the only percipient witness, of a fact, on which my right, and my hope of success in the cause, is founded. This being the case, I could do no less than call upon him to appear in the character of a deposing witness, and give his statement in relation to the case.

In a loose way of speaking, this person, to whom it may equally happen to be my friend, a person altogether unknown and indifferent to me, or my enemy, may be termed *my* witness.

On so flimsy a ground as that of a verbal inaccuracy — a loose way of employing a possessive pronoun, — have been raised in judicial practice, three or four most deceptitious rules of very diversified tendency, each of them susceptible of very extensive application, and, in fact, but too frequently applied.

1. You may lead your adversary's witness.

2. You must not lead your own witness.

Of these two rules, the impropriety was shown in the preceding chapter.

3. You must not discredit your own witness; viz. in the way and by means of counter-interrogation: by means of facts extracted out of his own lips in the shape of *confessorial* testimony.*

4. You must not discredit your own witness; viz. in the way and by means of coun-

---

* Trial of R. T. Crossfield for high treason, at the Old Bailey, 11th and 12th May 1796; his crime, a conspiracy to assassinate his late Majesty [Geo. III.] by shooting a poisoned arrow out of an air-gun. By men, whose purposes it answered to speak of the affair as a good joke, it was called the *popgun plot.* A paper was produced to one of the witnesses called by the crown (Peregrine Palmer), who, on his own showing, had been of the party with the prisoner, when a tube, for the purpose of an air-gun, had been looked out for. Question put to him, whether he had ever seen it before? After a page or two of shuffling and pretended non-recollection,—question by the counsel for the crown,—" I ask you once more upon your oath, have you never said when you was upon your oath that you had seen a paper similar to that?" Question by counsel for the prisoner,—" Does your Lordship think this is the proper way of examining a witness in chief?" Lord Chief-Justice Eyre: — " The whole course of this species of examination is not regular. This is a witness for the crown: if he disgraces himself, which it is the tendency of this examination to make him do, they lose the benefit of his testimony. The idea of extracting truth from a witness for the crown who disgraces himself is, in my apprehension, and always has been, a thing perfectly impracticable; for the moment he has gone to the length of discrediting his testimony by the manner in which he shuffles with your examination, there is an end of all credit to him. You recollect upon a very solemn occasion, the judges were all of opinion that that kind of examination on the part of a prosecution was improper, for that it always ended in destroying the credit of your own witness."

Thus far the learned judge. The decision evidently alluded to by him will appear from the following document:—

Extract from p. 43 of a printed paper, entitled " Report from the Committee of the House of Commons, appointed to inspect the Lords' Journals in relation to their proceeding on the Trial of Warren Hastings, Esq. Ordered to be printed 30th April 1794."

" Appendix, No. 2. Questions referred by the lords to the judges, in the impeachment of Warren Hastings, Esq.; and the answers of the judges. Extracted from the Lord's Journals and Minutes.

" Question 1. Whether, when a witness produced and examined in a criminal proceeding by a prosecutor, disclaims all knowledge of any matter so interrogated, it be competent for such prosecutor to pursue such examination, by proposing a question, containing the particulars of an answer supposed to have been made by such witness before a committee of the House of Commons, or in any other place; and by demanding of him whether the particulars so suggested were not the answer he had so made? Feb. 29th, 1788:" p. 418.

" Answer. The Lord Chief Baron of the Court of Exchequer delivered the unanimous opinion of the judges, upon the question of law put to them on Friday the 29th of February last, as follows: — ' That when a witness produced and examined in a criminal proceeding by a prosecutor disclaims all knowledge of any matter so interrogated, it is not competent for such prosecutor to pursue such examination, by proposing a question containing the particulars of an

ter evidence: by means of facts established by evidence other than as above.

5. Of kin to the above, is a rule confined to equity-court practice. When, in the epistolary mode, in the character of plaintiff, you have interrogated a man in the character of defendant, and in this way extracted from him a mass of ready-written evidence, called his *answer*; — if you abstain from employing it, or any part of it, in the character of evidence against him, he shall not read it, or any part of it, in the character of evidence for himself: but if there be any part of it, of which you make use as above, it rests with him to make the like use of the whole, or any part, of the remainder.

In support of the three last of these five rules (the two others having already been disposed of,) two arguments, such as they are, — two arguments, in some measure distinct, may be collected from the books. Without confining myself to exact words, the authority of which (for such throughout is the texture of unwritten law) can never be depended upon, my endeavour shall be to display them to the utmost advantage possible.

1. By calling for his testimony, you have admitted him to be a person of credit, acknowledged his trustworthiness: to seek to discredit him would be an inconsistency; and the success of your endeavours would be fatal to your cause: for, if his testimony be not to be believed, and you have none but his, then is your side of the cause without evidence.

2. Were this to be permitted to you, the permission would be attended with consequences fatal to truth and justice. You would call in an untrustworthy person: if you found his testimony in your favour, you would then keep back the means you have in your hands of demonstrating his untrustworthiness: if, on the other hand, his testimony proved disadvantageous to you, then, and then only, would you employ the means you have in your hands to the purpose of discrediting it. Choose, then, which you will have him to be—trustworthy, or untrustworthy: both he cannot be. If untrustworthy, you shall not call him; it is not fit he should be heard: if trustworthy, then whatsoever he says is by your own admission entitled to credence; you are *estopped* from saying otherwise.

Such are the arguments. They rest upon two grounds.

One is a false axiom of psychology—a proposition enunciative of a complete ignorance of, or inattention to, the universal and universally-known constitution of human nature.

The other is an equally complete inattention to the tutelary and veracity-promoting influence of the securities employed (as above) for insuring the veracity, the correctness, and completeness of testimony—those very securities, of which counter-interrogation (of the benefit of which it is the endeavour of these arguments to deprive the cause) is among the most efficient and impressive.

The false axiom is this:—All men belong to one or other of two classes—the trustworthy, and the untrustworthy. The trustworthy never say anything but what is true: by them you never can be deceived. The untrustworthy never say anything but what is false: so sure as you believe them, so sure are you deceived.

To place the absurdity of this theory in its true light, would be to anticipate the contents of a future book.* But, by an eye not wilfully closed by sinister interest, the true character of it can hardly fail to be seen stamped in sufficiently strong marks upon the face of it. No man is so habitually mendacious as not to speak true a hundred times, for once that he speaks false: no man speaks falsehood for its own sake — no man departs from simple verity without a motive; and that of sufficient force to more than countervail those motives which we have seen acting upon him in the character of securities for his veracity.

But suppose, in this particular, the disposition of a man ever so depraved. In the present case, that man is the most depraved, in whose bosom the force of the standing tutelary and veracity-promoting motives has least influence; who is most apt to be overborne by the force of any interest or interests whatever, acting on him in a sinister or mendacity-promoting direction. But, if not exposed to the action of any sinister interest, a man of the most depraved disposition will not be more apt to speak false, against so strong a current as that of the motives which tend

answer supposed to have been made by such witness before a committee of the House of Commons, or in any other place; and by demanding of him whether the particulars so suggested were not the answer he had so made.' April 10th, 1788." p. 592.

The above is the first in a list of twelve questions, with their respective answers. To each of the eleven others is subjoined this memorandum, — "*and gave his reasons.*" If, from this statement, any man should suppose, that, among so many millions of men as are bound by these decisions, there is so much as a single individual breathing by whom the possibility of obtaining cognizance of these reasons is possessed, he would be much mistaken. The reasons were kept purposely from the knowledge of the very party to whom the decisions were professing to do justice; — viz. the managers of the House of Commons. "Against their reiterated requests, remonstrances, and protestations, the opinions of the judges were always taken secretly." Pp. 13, 20.

The scene was changed from London to Morocco. Happy would it have been for the interests of justice, if the same darkness which covers the reasons, had involved the decisions likewise.

* Book IX. *Exclusion*.

to keep his testimony within the pale of truth, than the most upright one.

But suppose him as much under the governance of sinister interest as it is possible for a man to be. He has then taken his side: being (such for the argument sake he shall be supposed) an extraneous witness, he has taken his side: his wishes, and consequently the leaning of his testimony, are constantly (say) against the plaintiff's side, in favour of the defendant's.

Be the occasion what it may — take what man's testimony you will, you will scarce ever find the whole of it false: some parts of it at any rate will be kept within the pale of truth, were it only to give credit, or escape the danger of giving discredit, to the rest.

Of this dishonest witness the testimony will thus be resolvable into three parts: one part, which, in pursuance of his plan, he has rendered favourable to the defendant's side: another part, which, it not having appeared to him to be in his power to render it favourable to the defendant's side, is neutral, or at least has appeared so in his eyes: a third part, which (as far as it goes) is favourable to the plaintiff's side, unfavourable to the defendant's; the dishonest witness, in spite of his wishes and endeavours, not having deemed it advisable to render it otherwise

Exhibit in the strongest possible colours the untrustworthiness of your witness — his partiality to your adversary's side, and his improbity of character; you discredit so much of his testimony as makes in favour of your adversary, but in the very same proportion you increase the trustworthiness of all that portion which makes in favour of yourself.

A man's testimony cannot be believed where it makes for his wishes — therefore it cannot be believed where it makes against his wishes: in other words, a man will be as ready to tell lies to thwart his own purposes, as to forward them. Was ever proposition more directly in the teeth of the plainest common sense?

Such is the proposition assumed and built upon in the intimation, that "the credit" of your own witness (meaning a witness called upon by you through necessity, though in wishes adverse to you) "is destroyed," in regard to facts extracted from him in *opposition* to his own wishes, if his credit be destroyed in regard to facts stated by him in *furtherance* of his own wishes.

Of this same witness, whose credit is thus said to be destroyed, in relation to all facts disclosed by him in opposition to his own wishes, now that, by his having been summoned by you, a pretence is given for calling him *your own witness*: of this same adverse witness, whose credit as to all such facts is thus said to be destroyed by the name thus given to him, — the credit would, as to all such facts, have been in full vigour, had it so happened that he had been summoned by your adversary, and the self-same answers had been extracted by you, by virtue of the self-same questions. Had the examination which brought out the facts been called a cross-examination, they would have been true; but as the examination they are brought out by is not called a cross-examination, they are false.

The reason, if it were good for anything, would be a reason, not against the adverse examination of a man's own witness, but against the adverse examination of any witness.

Disbelieve all he says in favour of his adversary when examined by his adversary in the first instance, you must disbelieve all he says when examined by his adversary in the second instance. This you must admit; unless you maintain that the same man is credible or incredible, honest or dishonest, according as it happens to be this or that man who first stands up to question him.

A man's moral disposition being as yet unknown (which, in truth, will on these occasions be in most instances the case,) his situation is such as (suppose this out of doubt) exposes him to the action of a naturally strong sinister interest: apprised of such his situation, confidence in him you have none. But, unfortunately for you, so it has happened, that in his presence, and no other, the transaction of which it is necessary to you to make proof took place. In his testimony, therefore (viz. in so far as, notwithstanding his manifest situation and his presumed wishes, it may not happen to him to render it incorrect or incomplete to your prejudice,) you behold your only chance.

Among the means which the nature of things affords you for extracting the truth from this or any other unwilling bosom, is interrogation: counter-interrogation it may in one sense be called, in respect of its contrariety to the current of his wishes. *No* (says one of the rules;) *this shall not be permitted to you.* Why? says justice: because (adds the rule) this witness, this enemy of yours, is *your* witness. And so, because the nature of things has made you unfortunate enough to stand in need of this testimony — a testimony which, to your prejudice, has so strong a tendency to become false, — the fee-fed judge, with his technical and arbitrary rules, is to step in, and deprive you of the use of an instrument, without which you have no chance of preserving the testimony from being false, and decisive to your prejudice.

In favour of your claim to apply his testimony to this touchstone, your argument is this — (and where is the inconsistency of it?)

The leaning of this man's wishes, as is manifest from his situation, is strongly in disfavour of my cause. The truth of the case, which to him is perfectly known — the truth (if he would but speak it, the whole of it, and nothing else) would be decisive in my favour. As yet, what I have been able to extract from him in my favour is not sufficient; and, insufficient as it is, it has been counteracted by false statements that have accompanied it—statements operating in favour of the other side. But this man, honest or dishonest, would naturally not be willing to find himself (whether in danger, or not in danger, of legal punishment) set down in the account of all persons to whose cognizance this cause may happen to present itself, in the character of a false witness. By the apprehension of standing convicted of falsehood by the inconsistency of his testimony, on this occasion, with this or that known matter of fact (whether known by his own testimony delivered on a former occasion, or from any other source,) let me see whether I may not be able to make him confess a part of the truth, which as yet he has not confessed, and retract or explain away, before it be too late, a part of the falsehood which he has hazarded.

Thus much for the endeavour to discredit him by *interrogation* — by counter-interrogation: remains what concerns the endeavour to discredit him by *counter-evidence.*

On some other occasion, the testimony delivered by him has been found to be false: or he has been known to be guilty of one of those crimes which, without indicating any particular disposition to improbity in this particular shape (the shape of mendacious testimony,) indicate, however, a general depravity of disposition, in such sort, that in case of temptation to fall into this crime, resistance to the temptation cannot, in the instance of a person so disposed, be with reason depended upon as being in a preponderant degree probable.

Proofs of such former mendacity, or such improbity in another shape, are in your power: and the current of his testimony having upon the whole run against you, yet not in such sort as to deprive you of all hope (*his* not being in the present instance the only testimony you have adduced,) you apply for liberty to produce them. On what ground should it be refused to you? His testimony being incorrect and incomplete, and being so to your prejudice, what reason is there by which you should be prevented from bringing to light this truth, any more than any other pertinent and instructive truth? In the grammatical expression, *your witness*, howsoever applicable to him, what is there that should prevent your having permission to paint his disposition, any more than the disposition of any other person, in its real colours?

Not to discredit him? Why not, as well as anybody else? To discredit him is to render probable, either by direct proof, or by circumstantial (of which nature is character-evidence operating in diminution of his general trustworthiness,) that the testimony he has been giving, is giving, or (as supposed) is about to give, is, or will be, deficient in respect of correctness or completeness. This counter-evidence, upon which the exclusion is thus put, — is it to be supposed false, or to be supposed true? Suppose it false, there is the same reason, and no other, for the exclusion of this, as for the exclusion of any other false evidence. As there is no knowing whether evidence be or be not false, without hearing it — to know whether the supposition of falsity be just, the evidence must be heard. On the other hand, suppose it true, to what end would you exclude it? What has truth to gain by the exclusion of true evidence?

The testimony which the witness gives, is (by the supposition) incomplete or incorrect. What has truth to gain by its being taken for complete and correct, when in reality it is otherwise?

The tendency of this your counter-evidence is to place the value of your witness's testimony in its true light. No, say the lawyers; we will not have it placed in its true light: the situation, the moral situation, in which the witness is placed — the sinister interests to the action of which he is exposed — shall not be presented to view.

Oh, but what you contend for is an inconsistency: you want the same man to be regarded as credible and incredible—as speaking true, and speaking false.

Not the smallest inconsistency: what we want to have thought true of this man, is no more than what is true of every man, — at least, of every man of whom it could not be said that he has never, from his birth to the moment in question, said anything that was not true.

Part of his testimony (viz. that part which operates to your prejudice,) you regard as being false; and of the testimony which you have to produce from other sources, the tendency, and (in your expectation) the effect, will be, to cause the judge to regard it as likely to be false. Why? Because, from his situation or other sources, you have shown a great probability that the current of his wishes runs in a direction opposite to your side of the cause; and, by the evidence which you apply for liberty to adduce, a disposition on his part is proved, such as indicates in his instance a greater probability than in the instance of another (an ordinary) man would be indicated, of his testimony being turned aside out of the path of truth by the current of his wishes.

Supposing this then to be his disposition, as I believe or suspect it to be, what will be the effect of it upon his testimony? To divide it into two parts: that which comes out *with* the current, and that which comes out *against* the current, of his wishes. But if, with respect to one of those two parts of his testimony, he is less credible than an average man — than a man endued with an ordinary degree of this branch of probity, — with respect to the other, he is not at all less credible.

If there be a difference, he is more credible. The stronger the sinister current of his wishes, the less likely, in comparison with an ordinary man, he is to deliver out any matter of fact, the consequences of which are sure to militate against those wishes.

In a criminal cause, in which, in the character of defendant, a man is subjected to examination,* are you not the more fully persuaded of the truth of any fact he discloses, the more forcibly it tends to his conviction, and the severer the punishment to which it thereby tends to subject him? No doubt you are: because, the more forcible those tendencies, the more improbable that a man should disclose, should confess, the fact, if he were not fully conscious of the truth of it. To both men it has happened to be placed in a situation in which one part of their testimony comes out in opposition to the current of their inclinations. In both instances, the opposite character of the two branches of their respective testimonies is alike conspicuous: that which comes out with the current is the worst — that which comes out against the current is the best — of all evidence.

But, such as it is (says the last argument,) you have had the benefit of his testimony. Had it turned out favourable to you, these proofs which you say you have of his mendacity, (whether experienced, or rendered probable and presumable by experienced improbity in some other shape,) would not have been produced by you, but suppressed: therefore (continues the argument) now that his testimony has turned out unfavourable to you, they shall not be produced by you; they shall be suppressed: it is I (says the judge) that will not suffer them to be produced; it is I that will cause them to be suppressed.

The witness proves dishonest, following his wishes instead of his duty, and, on pretence of non-recollection, refuses to produce the information which he possesses: instead of disclosing truth for your advantage, he utters falsehood to your prejudice. Before you were driven by your distress to take your chance, slender as you thought it, for his assistance, his character afforded you but too much reason to apprehend the improbity that ensued. You have been injured by falsehood, and you are not suffered to call in truth for your defence. The mischief has been done to you, and you are not suffered to apply the remedy. You are not to account for the turn his evidence has taken to your prejudice: you are not to show his character in its true light. Why? Because, if, contrary to your expectations, he had proved honest, you would not, in this case, have given your reasons for apprehending he would prove otherwise. You shall not give the evidence, now that it is necessary; because, had it not been necessary, you would not have given it. Such is the argument, when cleared of its false gloss. Not to speak of the supposition involved in it; as if general bad character were a sort of thing which one of two parties, by putting into his own pocket, conceals from the other, and keeps in his pocket or pulls out at pleasure.

Of your forbearance, no such thing as *suppression of evidence* is the result. There stands the evidence: no measure, no active step, was, by the supposition, taken by you, for any such purpose as that of suppressing it. There stands the evidence; and if it can be produced by him to whom (if to anybody,) and to whom alone, the production of it can be of any use, let it be produced: no hand of his is arrested by your forbearance.

Oh, but in this way you had an advantage, and an unfair one, and you ought not to be suffered to make use of it. This counter-evidence of yours was known to yourself, it was not known to your adversary: he could not make use of it; therefore neither shall you.

Oh, hypocrites! what an objection in your lips! On what other occasion did it ever occur to you to say, that, because the evidence that lies without my knowledge is out of the knowledge of my adversary, it shall not be in my power to make use of it? Not to speak of lawyer-craft, — in point of common sense, what a reason is this for shutting out the light of evidence!

To this deficiency (such as it is) it is most completely congenial to the system of reason to afford the remedy, — as completely as it is to yours to refuse it. In the system of common sense, common honesty, and (everywhere but with common lawyers) common practice, there are no secrets. Do you suspect me of being apprized of evidence of which you are not apprized? Ask me, and I stand bound to you. From what party, under your system,

* In English practice, a prisoner or defendant cannot be examined upon his *trial*: he may make any statement he pleases. It may have happened, that previous to his trial he has given answers to any number of questions put to him by a police-officer or a private individual. Although this in reality is an examination of the prisoner, yet his answers are received in evidence against him at the trial, provided no threat has been made, or promise held out to the pursuer to induce him to answer, by the person or persons who carried on the examination. The practice in Scotland is, for the statements made by the prisoner in presence of the magistrate at the preliminary examination, to be recorded in an attested writ along with the circumstances under which the declaration is taken, the whole being read as evidence at the trial.—*Ed.*

is any such information ever permitted to be so much as asked for.

Here is so much truth, say you, but it shall not be brought to light. Why not? Because there is a somebody who does not know of it. Such is your argument — such the reason by which you stand determined to shut the door against material evidence, — against that evidence, without which there will be no justice!

At the very first mention, there is a hollowness in the argument, by which it must, I think, have betrayed itself to every eye not shut against reason by professional interest or prejudice. But there was a fallaciousness in it that seemed to call for exposure; and that fallaciousness consisted in the muddiness of the ideas which it was the tendency of it to excite — in the confusion which it was its tendency to spread over the whole field of evidence. Unhappily, so thick was the confusion, that to dispel it required no inconsiderable mass of words. Such is the jargon of which the great force of unwritten law is composed. So monstrous is it in its mass, — to unpractised minds, so oppressive the weight of it, — that in mere despair they are content to sink under it, rather than be at the pains of wrestling with it.

By the rule, "you must not discredit your own witness," you are, among other things, prevented from asking him whether he made a different statement on a former occasion. In this manner, to injustice operating by mendacity and aggravated by treachery, the sophism involved in the use of the words *your own witness*, secures a certain triumph.

Called upon by an agent of yours, or offering himself to you spontaneously, — a man who, by ill-will towards you (the party wronged,) or by sympathy towards, or secret community of interest with. the wrong-doer, has been engaged to practise the fraud in question, states himself as having been a witness (a percipient witness) of the transaction in question; painting it in such encouraging but false colours, as promise to you, the plaintiff, a certainty of success. Relying on this assurance, the party wronged either institutes against the wrong-doer an action, which without this encouragement he would not have instituted; or if, on the strength of other evidence less promising, he was at any rate determined to bring his action, deprives himself of the benefit of the honest evidence which he might have; placing his whole confidence on a testimony, the offer of which had no other object than, by deception, to make him lose his cause. On the trial, or other judicial hearing, the witness speaks the truth, which being by the supposition not sufficient to warrant a decision in favour of the plaintiff, loss of the object at stake upon the cause, together with the costs on both sides, follows as a necessary consequence.

Out of court, on the extra-judicial occasion, what the witness said was replete with falsehood, — falsehood studied, and expressly contrived for this base purpose. But of this plan of falsehood, under English rules of evidence, the success is sure — detection is impossible. Out of his own mouth you stand debarred from so much as the chance of exposing his treachery; debarred by that part of the rule which relates to interrogation. From exposing it by your own testimony you stand doubly debarred: first, by that branch of the rule which regards counter-evidence; next, by the rule which, unless under the cover of some disguise, excludes the receiving the testimony of a party.

Without the slightest provocation on your part, you have been abused, insulted, wounded, by a malignant enemy. You propose to yourself to seek redress at law. In the hearing of a known friend of yours, in pursuance of a plan concocted with the wrong-doer, and founded upon this rule (for, with how much care soever the knowledge of the law is kept in general from the body of the people, bad laws are frequently no secret to the wicked, whose study it is to profit by them,) a confederate of his, who, having been an eye-witness of the transaction, has full knowledge of the nature and circumstances of the injury, relates, as if in the course of casual conversation, everything as it really took place; expressing such sentiments on the occasion as are calculated to impress the assurance of his fulfilling, if called upon, the duty of an honest witness. You call upon him accordingly, and rest your cause upon his evidence. When the cause comes on, instead of stating the transaction according to his former statement, — a statement exactly agreeing with the truth of the case, — he suppresses some circumstances, adds others, makes you the aggressor, and, instead of redress, you are loaded with expense and infamy. Would you ask him whether, on that former occasion, his statement did not wear a different complexion? Your mouth is stopped by this rule.

Such being the absurdity of this cluster of rules, and so sure the mischief of them — a question that naturally presents itself is — what may be the proportional amount of that mischief?

The question has little more than curiosity in it: for, the existence of mischief being established, and that pure from all advantage, be the amount greater or less, the practical inference is the same.

To a first glance, such would be the effect of the rule, that, in one case out of every two, it would exclude a party from the benefit of interrogation: and thus lay justice at the mercy of every mendacious witness.

Blows take place in consequence of a quarrel you have with a man at the house of one of you, and on the occasion of which you prosecute. In point of probability, the house may as well be his as yours. If it be yours, in the natural course of things the evidence which it affords is friendly to your side of the cause: if it be his house, in a course of things altogether as natural, the evidence it affords is hostile to you. Friendly or hostile, if, prosecuting, you have need of it, and, having need of it, call for it, it is (in the practical phrase) *your* evidence, and (as such) not to be discredited by you; that is (be it ever so mendacious) is not to be shown by you in its proper colours.

To a first glance, the quantity of injustice and mischief thus produced should be enormous: in practice, great as it is, it is found to be not to such a degree enormous as would naturally be supposed. The circumstances by which the amount of it is reduced are various: too various, and requiring too much room to be enumerated here.

CHAPTER V.

OF THE DEMEANOUR OF THE ADVERSE INTERROGATOR TO THE WITNESS, CONSIDERED IN RESPECT OF VEXATION.

This subject presents itself as of the number of those which scarce afford any hold for any determinate rules. A few observations, however, in the way of warning, may not be altogether without their use.

What liberty ought, on this occasion, to be allowed to the adverse interrogator? 1. In the first place, the liberty of doing and saying anything which promises to promote the discovery of material truth, and which at the same time is not productive of vexation to the witness; 2. In the second place, every liberty, the effect of which (although it should be productive of such vexation) promises to be attended with more of advantage in respect of its subserviency and necessity to the discovery of the material truth, than of mischief in respect to any such vexation of which it may be productive.

What liberty ought, on the other hand, to be refused? 1. In the first place, every liberty, the exercise of which, being or not being productive of vexation, has no tendency to promote the discovery of truth; 2. In the next place, every liberty, by the exercise of which (however it may possess that useful tendency) too great a price is paid in the shape of vexation, for the advantage purchased in the shape of furtherance of justice.

Rule 1 Every expression of reproach, as if for established mendacity: every such manifestation, however expressed—by language, gesture, countenance, tone of voice (especially at the outset of the examination,) ought to be abstained from by the examining advocate.

If the tendency of such style of address were to promote the extraction of material truth, at the same time that the action of it could not be supplied to equal effect by any other plan of examination,—the vexation thus produced (how sharp soever) not being of any considerable duration, the liberty might be allowed, with preponderant advantage for the furtherance of justice.

But, on a close investigation, no advantage, but rather a disadvantage, even in respect of furtherance of justice, seems to be the natural result of an assumption of this kind. The instrument by which mendacity is detected, or deterred from the attempt, is the representation of facts inconsistent with the false assertions advanced or meditated: facts established on other grounds, viz. improbability of the opposite facts, indubitable testimony from other quarters, or other assertions advanced by the witness himself on other occasions or on the occasion in hand. The effect of any such contradictive and damnatory manifestations will be in itself sufficiently impressive, and needs not the assistance of any such force as it may be in the power of the advocate, in the way of rhetorical or dramatical artifice, to apply. Their operation will be proportioned to, and dependent upon, the cogency of the argument derived from the contradiction afforded to the statement of the witness by those other adverse testimonies.

Even in the *course* of the examination, and after having received whatever warrant it is capable of receiving from whatever symptoms of mendacity may have transpired,—it seems to be neither necessary, nor (in comparison with such unobjectionable resources as have just been mentioned) preferably conducive, to the purposes of truth and justice.

At the *outset* of the adverse examination, and therefore before this style of demeanour can have received any warrant (at least in the eyes of either the judge, the by-standers, or any person besides the advocate himself who is displaying it,) it seems adverse to the interests of truth and justice; and that in more ways than one.

Of the legitimate mode of attack — the attack by the force of adverse facts — the impressiveness depends upon the force of such adverse facts, and is stronger and stronger in proportion as the mendacity is more enormous, and (if undetected) pernicious: the magnitude of the force rises, with the legitimate demand for it, occasioned by the improbity of the individual to whose mental feelings it is applied.

Of the opposite mode of attack, the impressiveness proportions itself, not to the improbity of the witness, but to his sensibility, his natural timidity — a weakness much more naturally allied to probity than to its opposite. By reproachful and terrifying demeanour on the part of a person invested with, and acting under, an authority thus formidable, it seems full as natural that an honest witness should be confounded, and thus deprived of recollection and due utterance, and even (through confusion of mind) betrayed into self-contradiction and involuntary falsehood, as that a dishonest witness should be detected and exposed. The quiet mode above described is not in any degree susceptible of this sort of abuse: the outrageous mode seems more likely to terminate in the abuse than in the use.

In another way,—far from being conducive to the detection or prevention of mendacity,—it has a tendency to serve the side of injustice, by exciting in the mind of the judge (especially in the case of a non-professional and unpractised judge, the juryman,) prepossesions injurious to an honest witness, and prejudicial to the interests of truth.* The contagiousness of persuasion, real or pretended, is no secret to the observing mind.

In the sort of treatment thus given to a witness, two distinguishable injuries may commonly be seen united: the imputation of guilt cast upon the witness, in the way of assumption, frequently without any ground at all, and always without the justification afforded by antecedently apparent grounds; this unwarranted imputation, coupled with the assumption of a sort of magisterial authority over the witness by the advocate. Howsoever it may be in respect of the imputation, the assumption of the authority cannot but be acknowledged to be without ground. For any authority over the witness there is no better pretence on the part of the advocate than there would be on the part of the party: on the part of the agent than on the part of the principal, in whose place he stands, in whose behalf he acts. That the witness is all the while under the pressure of an obligation, moral as well as legal, is not to be disputed: that the party, to the prejudice of whose cause the testimony tends, possesses a right corresponding to that obligation, is as little to be denied: that the advocate, standing in the place or by the side of his client, is entitled to the exercise of that right in its full extent, is equally clear: but as to power, authority, anything of that sort, there is but one sort of person to whom any privilege of that sort can with propriety be ascribed, and that is, the judge.

As to the advocate: whatever restraints in respect of moderation and decorum are binding upon the party, are, in point of justice, equally binding upon this his representative.

Rule 2. Such unwarranted manifestations, if not abstained from by the advocate, ought to be checked, with marks of disapprobation, by the judge.

In the presence of the judge, any misbehaviour, which, being witnessed at the time by the judge, is regarded by him without censure, becomes in effect the act, the misbehaviour, of the judge. On him more particularly should the reproach of it lie; because, for the connivance (which is in effect the authorization) of it, he cannot ever possess any of those excuses, which may ever and anon present themselves on the part of the advocate.

The demand for the honest vigilance and occasional interference of the judge will appear the stronger, when due consideration is had of the strength of the temptation, to which, on this occasion, the probity of the advocate is exposed. Sinister interests in considerable variety concur in instigating him to this improper practice.

1. In the way above mentioned, an advantage is naturally derived to his cause: especially (or rather exclusively) if it be a bad one; labouring therefore, in proportion to its badness, under the need of seeking its support in such undue advantages.

2. His zeal in behalf of the interest of his client, finds in this sort of impassioned demeanour an occasion of displaying itself.

3. The love of power, the appetite for respect and deference (passions inherent in the species, and in a particular degree brought into exercise by the profession,) find in this display of superiority a gratification suited to their nature.

Rule 3. When, on the false supposition of a disposition to mendacity, an honest witness has been treated accordingly by the cross-examining advocate (the judge having suffered the examination to be conducted in that manner, for the sake of truth)—at the close of which examination all doubts respecting the probity of the witness have been dispelled,—it is a moral duty on the part of the judge to do what depends on him towards soothing the irritation sustained by the witness's mind; to wit, by expressing his own satisfaction respecting the probity of the witness, and the sympathy and regret excited by the irritation he has undergone.

* The English practice affords no adequate security against the effects of brow-beating, grimace, and the misleading arts of an adverse counsel. If no witnesses are called for the defendant, the plaintiff's counsel not having the right of reply, can administer no antidote or corrective to them: if, on the other hand, witnesses are called for the defendant, the plantiff's counsel has the last speech and last cross-examination, and the defendant's counsel has no opportunity of applying an antidote or corrective. The judge indeed has the opportunity of checking such improprieties, but he generally confines his correction to the imputations which may be cast on a witness without evidence to support them. It should be added, however, that as juries have improved in taste and civilization, the practices alluded to have become less prevalent. The Grimaldis of the law have become less in request, and are not considered its ornaments.—*Ed.*

That, in any considerable degree, any such sympathy should in any such station really have been felt, is not reasonably to be expected: any more than, on the part of the hunter, for the agonies of the deer whom he has been running down. But the occasions in judicature are not wanting, in which a sense of decorum, and a usage that has been grounded on it, has commonly the effect of giving birth to demonstrations of that kind. In a case of expectation, by which the sympathetic feelings of the by-standers are understood to be excited, when sentence comes to be pronounced upon a criminal, — along with the naturally and properly predominant expressions of sympathy for the suffering interests of the public, expressions of sympathy for the sufferings of the guilty individual are as naturally and properly intermixed. It is one of the common-places of judicial oratory — of judicial acting, upon the forensic theatre. The addition presents itself as one that would neither be unuseful nor undue, if, to these expressions of sympathy for the individual justly wounded by the hand of law, correspondent demonstrations were as regularly added, having for their object the healing the wounds unjustly inflicted by the hand of the lawyer.*

The subject is manifestly of the number of those which admit not of regulation, in any coercive shape. But the more completely unsusceptible it is of regulation, the more urgent the demand it presents for *instruction;* which, where regulation is inapplicable, is the sole, nor by any means inefficacious (though to English law almost unknown) resource. The more inapplicable the force of the political sanction is, the greater the need for calling in that of the moral, and applying it to the best advantage. That the strongest checks to misconduct cannot be applied, is surely no reason why the benefit of even the mildest and gentlest should be refused.

* Under the spur of the provocation, I remember now and then to have observed the witness turn upon the advocate in the way of retaliation. On an occasion of this sort, I have also now and then observed the judge to interpose, for the purpose of applying a check to the petulance of the witness. For one occasion in which, under the spur of the injury, the injured witness has presented himself to my conception as overstepping the limits of a just defence, — ten, twenty, or twice twenty, have occurred, in which the witness has been suffering, without resistance and without remedy, as well as without just cause, under the torture inflicted on him by the oppression and insolence of an adverse advocate. Scarce ever, I think, had I the satisfaction of observing the Judge interpose to afford his protection to the witness, either at the commencement of the persecution, for the purpose of staying or alleviating the injury, or at the conclusion, for the purpose of affording satisfaction for it—such inadequate satisfaction as the nature of the case admits of.

The remedy most applicable (and from being so simple it is not the less efficacious,) is publicity.

Against malpractice more directly and obviously adverse to the ends of justice, a remedy applied by the legislature at a very early period of the history of the judicial system, is to be found in the instrument called a bill of exceptions. Whatever, in the judge's charge to a jury, is regarded as being improper, is, at the instance of the party or his advocate, committed to writing, and the judge, on being called upon, is bound to recognise it; whereupon, in case of appeal, the very words are referred to the cognizance of a superior judicatory.

If, without the formality of an appeal to a legal judicatory, provision were in like manner, in the case here in question, made, for laying the history of the transaction duly authenticated before the moral judicatory of the public, — the abuse would find, in an expedient thus simple, a check too efficient to be consented to by those whose power of inflicting injury on pretence of justice would be thus put under restraint.

In the case of those trials of which, in respect of their importance, it is foreknown or expected that what passes in them, being taken down word for word by short-hand writers, will be printed for general sale; this abuse is exemplified (if at all) in a very inferior degree

A set of monitory rules (and it would not need to be a voluminous one,) hung up in the form of a table, in characters large enough to be legible to all eyes at once, — a set of rules, prescribing what is proper to be prescribed, forbidding what is proper to be forbidden, respecting the deportment of the several classes of the dramatis personæ on the forensic theatre, — (to be prescribed or forbidden, with or without penalties, according as penalties were applicable or inapplicable) — would, surely, not be an unsuitable article of furniture in a court of justice.

If, in such a table of rules, the practice of brow-beating were noticed (though it were but in the gentlest terms) as a practice to be avoided, it is scarcely possible to doubt that it would be eradicated altogether.

CHAPTER VI.

OF THE NOTATION AND RECORDATION OF TESTIMONY.

§ 1. *Uses of notation and recordation, as applied to orally-delivered testimony.*

Of the use and importance of permanence in testimony — of the necessity of writing, as being the sole instrument or efficient cause of permanence — of the nature of minuted testimony, as contradistinguished from ready-written testimony — of the use there may be for each in preference or in addition to the other, and of the advantage possessed by minuted testimony, in the essential points of dispatch, and security against mendacity-serving information and reflection, — enough has been said already.

The operation whereby *vivâ voce* testimony is converted into minuted testimony, is or may be called notation, minute-taking, recordation of testimony, registration of testimony: is, or may be called; for, somehow or other, though the name of the work thus produced is of frequent occurrence, the like frequency cannot be predicated of the name of the operation by which the work is produced.

Permanence in the testimony is of use, — notation, therefore, considered as an efficient cause of permanence, is of use, — in two very distinguishable ways, and on as many distinguishable occasions; — viz. to the judge, and against the judge.*

To the judge, notation is of use, to enable him, — at all times down to the moment which gives birth to the last word of his decree, — to refresh his memory, and render his view of the testimony on which that decree is to be grounded as correct and complete as the purpose of each moment can require.

Against the judge, for the protection of suitors — for the protection of the interests of truth and justice against any errors (voluntary or involuntary) on the part of the judge, — recordation, and thence notation, are of use, for the purpose of giving correctness and completeness to the opinions and decisions of such persons (if any) by whom, in the character of superordinate judges, the question may come to be re-judged, and his conduct in relation to it judged.

To the class of superordinate judges may be referred, on this occasion, in the first place, official judges — judges to whose lot it may fall to take cognizance of the cause itself in the way of appeal, for the purpose of reviewing, and either confirming or abrogating or altering, the decision so given in the first instance: in the next place, the public at large; who, without any authority to abrogate or modify the decision, will, when thus informed, be not the less competent to sit in judgment on the conduct maintained by the judge in respect of it; rewarding or punishing him, according to their conception of his good or ill deserts, — rewarding him with their esteem, punishing him with their disesteem and displeasure.

Let us recapitulate. Use of notation to the judge, — presenting him at all times with a correct and complete view of the ground on which his decision is to be built. Use of recordation as against the judge, in case of appeal, — presenting to the judge of appeal a view of the same ground, as correct and complete as may be: — as may be; for, unhappily (as will be seen) the view taken by the judge of appeal can never be altogether so correct or complete as that which may have been taken by the judge in the first instance. Use of recordation, with or without appeal, — presenting to the public, in their capacity of judges of the conduct of the judge, a view, as correct and complete as may be, of the same ground.

Between notation and recordation (recordation as applied to evidence) a shade of difference may already have been observed. Recordation implies preservation: notation, not. To the judge, considered by himself, notation expresses all that is of use: against the judge, not notation only, but preservation, recordation, is necessary. No sooner is the decision pronounced, than the notes taken by the judge, or by any one for his use, might be destroyed — destroyed, not only without inconvenience to him, but oftentimes to his no small easement and convenience. But, for the use of a judge of appeal, and of the public in their character of judges of judges, it is necessary that the notes taken be not only taken, but preserved.

Reference being had to the occasion, the use of notation and recordation to the judge admits of diversifications which require to be distinguished.

For divers purposes, the testimony of the same deponent may, at different times, require to be repeatedly brought to view: before the judge below, for confrontation with itself, or for confrontation with other testimony delivered by other deponents — (with itself, for elucidation, for proving or disproving the consistency, and thence the trustworthiness, of the deponent:) before the judge of appeal, for the purpose of the appeal. If, on the appeal, the deponent be re-examined *vivâ voce*, as in the first instance; the minutes taken at the first trial will serve to confront, or (in case of deperition, or for dispatch on points to which the dispute does not extend) to stand in lieu of re-delivered *vivâ voce* evidence: and, in the like case, testimony delivered in one suit may be employed with

* Understand here by the *judge*, the functionary by whom, for the purpose of decision, the testimony is to be collected, and by whom, on the ground of the testimony when collected, the decision is to be pronounced. These two functions may (for the purpose of the argument at least, let us hope) be considered as being discharged by one and the same person. The world is not so unfortunate but that this union is actually realized in numerous instances. The unnatural and disastrous arrangement by which they have in so many instances been separated, has not been quite so universal, as to have rent in twain, throughout, the veil of the temple of justice.

advantage or of necessity in another; sometimes in any number of other causes, on to the end of time.

From this comprehensive enumeration of possible occasions, may be deduced the following list of particular and subordinate uses of the connected operations of notation and recordation:—

1. On the occasion of a different examination or inquiry,—confrontation with the testimony of the same deponent: for example, to prevent backsliding.*

2. Ditto with ditto of other deponents.

3. In the case of the death or non-forthcomingness of the same deponent,—to serve instead of his re-examination *vivâ voce.*

4. To serve instead of, or in addition to, *vivâ voce* re-examination, in case of appeal.

5. To serve, on the occasion of future disputes between the same or other parties, for the prevention, or (if that cannot be) for the decision, of other suits.

§ 2. *In what cases should notation and recordation be employed?*

Such being the uses of recordation, in what cases shall it be employed?

Were security against misdecision the sole object,—in all cases without distinction: for where is the case in which it may not be productive of such security, in virtue of some one article, in virtue of several articles at once, in the above list of uses?

But, on this occasion as on all others, regard for any one or more will require to be tempered by due regard to the other ends of justice. By security against misdecision, the direct ends of justice are provided for; but, in this case as in all others, the advantages obtainable in this shape are not to be obtained but at the expense of collateral inconvenience, in the shape of delay, vexation, and pecuniary expense.

If, to the taking cognizance of a demand of a quantity of corn to the value of no more than 5s., writing which cannot be had for less than 10s. is, in any court, rendered necessary, it is obvious that for a quantity of corn to that value no man has any security; nor, consequently, for the whole quantity of corn in the whole country, or any part of it, does there exist any adequate security, as far as depends upon that court.

If each parcel, how minute soever, be not secure to a man, neither is the whole: if each grain of corn in his granary be not secure to him, neither is the whole granary: if each might be taken from him without redress, so might every one.

It is in this point of view that causes (suits) will come to be distinguished into two classes: causes recordation-worthy—causes not recordation-worthy. The problem will be, in the instance of each cause, and occasionally in the instance of this or that examination that may come to have place in the course of any given cause, to which of these two classes it shall be referred.

Every cause is recordation-worthy, abstraction made of the delay, vexation, and expense: every cause is recordation-worthy, unless, in so far as some special reason can be shown to the contrary—in so far as a sufficient reason can be shown for regarding the inconvenience in the shape of delay, vexation, and expense, as being preponderant over the advantage of security against misdecision (regard being had to the several eventual causes contained in the above list.)

But though no sort of cause, nor any individual cause, can with propriety be placed on the list of non-recordation-worthy causes without special reason, it follows not that that list must be less numerous than the opposite one. On the contrary, it will probably be found by far the more numerous, whether the natural system, or the technical system, in any of its existing modifications, be considered:—the actual proportion under the system by which *malâ fide* suits in such multitudes are bred, and *bonâ fide* suits smothered, or the proportion that would take place in a system under which the encouragement and discouragement were to change places.

The reason is, that, on the one hand, under every system of procedure (actual and possible,)—the quantity of evidence delivered, and the mode of delivering it, being given,—the delay, vexation, and expense attached to the recordation of it (I speak of the mere manual operation of committing it to writing) must be the same. On the other hand; out of the whole number of suits of all sorts that receive their commencement, it is happily to a very small proportion only that any considerable demand for notation and recordation, as a security against misdecision, will apply. In by far the greater number, the necessity of a claim in form of law is produced, not by any ability (real or so much as supposed) on the part of the defendant, to oppose a sufficient defence to it,—but either by reluctance, or absolute inability, to comply with it. And even among the cases which do afford matter for a *bonâ fide* defence, it will only be in a comparatively small number that the evidence will furnish matter of any such difficulty, or for any such difference of

* In cases of felony and misdemeanour, Justices of the Peace are required, by the 7 Geo. IV. c. 64, to take down in writing the examination of the witnesses, and to send such examination to the court where the trial is to take place. At the trial, the testimony of a witness may thus be confronted with his original deposition; but it is necessary in the first instance, to prove that the deposition in question was duly taken before the justice.—*Ed.*

opinion, as to attach any considerable importance to the operation whereby a perpetual existence is given to the words of which the tenor of it is composed.

A line, therefore, must be drawn, somewhere and somehow: but where and how? At first view, the difficulty will be apt to present itself as insuperable: on each side injustice, inevitable injustice; on neither, anything better than a choice of injustice; and that choice a task not for reason but for fortune. Draw the line where you will, — on one side will be an expanse, within which, for want of so efficient a check, the machinations of *mali fide* suitors, whether plaintiffs or defendants, will take sanctuary, and find themselves in force.

On a closer view, means may perhaps be found, by which the separation may be made with somewhat less disadvantage. The line being drawn, and (for experiment and argument) say, in the first instance, through any point at pleasure, —all above the line will be the group of recordation-worthy causes; below it will be the place for non-recordation-worthy causes. In both instances, for causes recordation-worthy and non-recordation-worthy: but in what sense? how taken? Not individually, but only *in specie.* In the door left open for admitting into the recorded class individuals belonging *primâ facie* to the non-recordation-worthy class — in this temperament lies the resource against ultimate and preponderant injustice.

Let the suit (for example) be of a pecuniary nature, and the line drawn on the ground of value: in all causes above £50 value, the evidence to be recorded of course; in all causes where the demand rises not to that value, no such recordation of course. But, on this occasion as on every other, the *pretium affectionis* is an object to be attended to, and one that will be attended to by every legislator to whom the feelings of individuals (the matter of which the prosperity of the state is composed) is an object of regard. And even when, considered by itself, the subject-matter of the dispute is not susceptible of any such value; as where it consists of a mere sum of money, payable in a number of articles (pieces of money,) in their individual character referred absolutely to the debtor's choice; still, a value, beyond the current value of the sum, may be attached, to victory, by the circumstances of the dispute. This considered, let it (for argument's sake) depend on either party to take the suit out of the lower, the non-recordation-worthy, and place it in the higher, the recordation-worthy, class.

Good: but, by this arrangement, is there the value of a single atom subtracted from the account of delay, vexation, and expense?

No, certainly: to annihilate that mass of inconvenience is not possible: but what is possible, is to place it upon the shoulders of him by whom an extraordinary value is set, or professed to be set, upon the advantage to be purchased at the expense of it. There, then, let it be placed—at any rate in the first instance.

When the nature of the cause comes to be understood (understood in all its circumstances,) it is with the judge that it must rest to say on whose shoulders the burthen shall, in the last instance, lie.

Good again: but, the party who has need of the security,— what is to be done if he be unable to defray the expense?

In this extraordinary case, must be suffered to take place, — with that concern and regret which, on every such occasion, a lover of mankind, and of justice for the sake of mankind, can never fail to experience—that which, by the conductors of the technical system, is, without any such emotion, suffered, or rather made, to take place in all ordinary cases: — the indigent man must be left to bear the penalty of his indigence.

Not that he will always be condemned to bear it without hope. The security to be purchased at this price, is a security as against the judge. It is because (on some score or other, intellectual or moral) the disposition of the judge is an object of suspicion, that the party is thus anxious to purchase it. But it can seldom indeed happen to the judge to be the object of suspicion, scarce ever to be the object of well-grounded suspicion, to an individual, without being so on the same account (or at any rate at the same time) to a portion, more or less considerable, of the public. But the expense, which to the individual would be an insuperable bar, will to this committee of the public be but as a straw: and it is only by gross prejudice (inherited perhaps from other and far different times,) or by a spirit of aristocratical oppression, that the principle can be discountenanced which points out the voluntary contributions of the opulent as a desirable fund for occasionally bringing within the reach of injured indigence that necessary of life in which all other necessaries are included.*

That a line, the direction of which should be inflexibly determined by the consideration of the species of the cause, without regard to the individual circumstances of the parties, would, on this occasion as on so many others, be pregnant with injustice,—is a proposition which an example or two will suffice to place in a clear light. Titius inflicts on Sempronius that sort of personal injury, which in respect of physical pain or uneasiness amounting almost to nothing, is frequently on a moral account but the more intolerable. Is Sem-

---

* See "*Defence of Usury,*" Vol. III., and "*Protest against Law Taxes,*" Vol. II.

pronius in point of age a school-boy, or in point of condition of life a day-labourer? — the offence amounts to nothing: the evidence cannot be worth the committing to paper, though it were not to occupy ten lines. Is Sempronius, as well as Titius, a person occupying a certain station in the state? scarce any business can be more serious: volumes upon volumes might not be ill-bestowed upon it. Suppose, by a stretch of imagination, a chancellor and a primate thus engaged; the whole country might ring with it, and continue ringing with it for years.

The question, whether the evidence in a suit is or is not recordation-worthy, depending in so great a degree upon the circumstances of the individual suit,—all that can be done is to give, in the way of sample, an indication of such as are most apt, and of such as are least apt, to afford, by their importance in any shape, an adequate counterpoise to the delay, vexation, and expense.

Examples of suits most apt to be recordation-worthy, are—

1. Among penal causes, all such in which punishment other than pecuniary, or pecuniary punishment to the value of such a number of days' labour (according to an average of the wages paid for a day's ordinary labour in husbandry,) is assigned.

2. Among causes not penal, all causes by which any right is claimed, having for its subject-matter any article belonging to the class of immoveables; all causes relative to last wills; and all causes in which condition in life (for example, in respect of marriage and parentage) is concerned.

To the class of causes least apt, to the extent in question, to be recordation-worthy, may be referred (for example) causes relative to debts contracted on any of the ordinary grounds, and causes relative to simple personal injuries. And of the individual causes belonging to these classes are composed no fewer perhaps than nineteen-twentieths of the whole aggregate of causes.

§ 3. *In what manner, and by what hands, should notation be performed?*

Considered in respect of the accuracy or fidelity of the result, the process of notation is susceptible of two very distinguishable degrees. What is committed to writing may either be the *tenor*, the very words of which the testimony was composed, or no more than the supposed *purport* of it: notation *ipsissimis verbis*, notation in *substance*.

The distinction is a very material one. Application, utility, inconvenience,—in all these respects the two modes or species of notation differ from each other.

Notation *ipsissimis verbis*,—being the more accurate of the two, and that upon a scale extendible *ad infinitum*, by reason of the infinite degrees of aberration of which the looser mode of notation is susceptible,—is the only one of the two that is completely adapted to all purposes: it is consequently the standard of reference, from which, without special reason (that is, without preponderant inconvenience in the shape of delay, vexation, and expense,) no departure ought ever to be made.* It is the only one of the two that is capable of serving completely as *against* the judge.

If, however, the judge be the only person for whose use the minutes above taken are intended,—notation in substance (especially if performed by the judge himself, or under his immediate direction,) may answer the purpose as well as, or even better than, notation *ipsissimis verbis:* better, because, the degree of amplitude being capable of being exactly adjusted to his own exigencies, every part of the matter that in his view of it is irrelevant, or immaterial, and thence superfluous, will of course be left out, and his memory will be exonerated of so much incumbrance.

In the case of recordation *ipsissimis verbis;* the subject-matter and result of the operation being the very words, and all the words, of the testimony,—much room for direction or discussion respecting the mode of recordation (it will naturally be supposed) can scarce be left.

In respect of the testimony itself, true: but what does require to be mentioned, is, that, without the interrogations, the view given of the testimony by the only part of the matter that in strictness of speech comes under the denomination of the testimony, (viz. by the responses) would be in effect and substance incomplete. *To* the judge, and for his own use, the responses alone will be sufficient, and much more than sufficient; but as *against* the judge (the judge below,) and for the use of the judge above (if there be one,) and at any rate of the public, cognizance of the interrogatories is indispensable.

Let the judge have misbehaved himself—and let his misbehaviour have been ever so gross and dishonest,—what remedy does the nature of the case admit of, unless the very words, in the utterance of which the misbehaviour consists, are ascertained and registered?

To this subject applies therefore, of course, what has been said in a former place,† con-

* The minutes of what has passed at a trial, or (to use the common abbreviation) *the trial*, as committed to writing by a skilful scribe using the art of short-hand, affords an example, so happily familiar to every English eye, of this most perfect, or rather only perfect, mode or species of notation.

† Book II. *Securities*; Chap. VI. *Oath;* § 4. *Mode of application: supra*, p. 318.

cerning the impropriety of the grammatical change from the first person to the third. As the respondent, so let the interrogator, whatever be his station—party, fellow-witness, advocate, judge—speak for himself: let not the scribe take upon himself to speak for any of them: as from his other works of all sorts, so let every man be judged from his own words. *Verba " suos teneant auctores."**

In the case where the only person for whose use the discourse is destined is the judge—the only case in which the security afforded by recordation in substance is an operation completely adequate,—in this case, the proper mode, and the proper hand, are pointed out by obvious and pretty conclusive considerations:—

1. In this case, the object, and sole object, consulted, is and ought to be the convenience of the judge: and to no other person can it be so well known what suits with that convenience, as to himself.

2. By his own conception of the quantity and quality of the words necessary and sufficient to keep the substance of the testimony in his mind, during the time and for the purpose for which his attention is to be fixed upon it, should the quantity and quality committed to writing be regulated.

3. In him alone rests the power of regulating the pace of the discourse in the mouths of the several interlocutors, in such manner that the time thus employed may be sufficient, and not more than sufficient, to admit of his committing to paper the quantity of writing he finds necessary and sufficient for his purpose.

4. What to the conception of another man would present itself as a correct and complete representation of the substance of the discourse, would seldom present itself in exactly the same character to the conception of the judge.

5. At the pace to which, on pain of no inconsiderable waste of time, the course of the pen must on this occasion be kept up, the handwriting of a third person would seldom, to the eye of the judge, be equally legible with his own; or so much as legible at all, without difficulty and waste of time. Writing on such occasions for his own use, every man naturally has recourse to little modes of abbreviation, more particularly adapted to his own individual practice and habits.

As to the possibility of the judge's uniting in his own person the commanding function of that office, with the sabaltern and almost mechanical operation of the scribe, one proof of it is afforded by English practice. In trials of all sorts in which a jury bears a part, it is a customary feature: on the occasion of giving a *charge* (as it is called,)—that is, a speech of direction to the jury,—it is, in the state of most men's memories, a necessary one: in all instances in which a *new trial* is liable to be moved for (a fresh inquiry liable to be applied for,) it is an indispensable one.

To a document possessing in so pre-eminent a degree the character of trustworthiness, the sort of regard one would naturally expect to find generally bestowed, at least by the authors themselves, whose works these may in some measure be said to be, is of the most confidential and reverential kind. But he by whom any such persuasion should have been entertained, would not apply it long to practice before he would find the necessity of making great abatements. For the single purpose of constituting an eventual ground for a motion for a new trial, yes: and, in point of time, for and during the space of time allowed for such motion; viz. the four first days of the *term* following the trial, the renovation of which is thus prayed. But no sooner is this short *terminus fatalis* expired, than whatever little share of trustworthiness this document may have possessed, is deemed to have expired likewise; it is completely converted into waste paper.

In the course of a prosecution (for perjury, for example), a point which it is become necessary to prove is the testimony that was given by somebody (suppose the defendant in the prosecution for perjury) on the occasion of a former trial. To what source (would any one suppose) is reference made for the tenor or purport of such testimony? To the judge's notes?—the judge by whom the cause was tried? Not so indeed: on the contrary, to any the most suspected source, rather than this, of all conceivable sources the most trustworthy and unsuspectible. To a note, taken or said to have been taken at the time, by the professional agent of either of the parties,†—nay, to a mere recollection, or supposed recollection, on the part of that or any other individual, without so much as a written word to fix it,—there would be no objection: but as to any such document as the minutes made by the judge who tried the cause,—of a reference made to any such source, of the admission of any such evidence, no instance is anywhere to be found.

A mass of evidence which has had for its

* Such, accordingly, is the practice in the British House of Commons. If the language used by any Member is pointed at as calling for censure, a preliminary motion always is, that the words be taken down by the clerk: and so likewise in the House o. Lords.

† So likewise, " minutes taken by the solicitor for a prosecution, on the examination of a person before a magistrate" (the examination performed without a jury, previously to the trial by a jury) " may be read in evidence at the trial, though not signed either by the prisoner or the magistrate."—*Leach's Crown Cases*, 3d edit. p. 727. *The King against Thomas.*

scribe one knows not what clerk, employed for that purpose in the examiner's office, is (not only in that cause, but on the occasion of other causes tried by other courts) admitted without scruple. A mass of testimony, from the same witness and to the same effect, collected by one of the twelve judges, in the sunshine of publicity, is a species of evidence too extraordinary to have been so much as thought of.

So much for the case in which the only person, for whose use recordation is designed, is the judge. So far as concerns the other cases that have been mentioned, the question, *by what hands?* will receive a different answer.

For this purpose, while the faculty of taking minutes should be allowed to any person who pleases, an official scribe, a short-hand writer, ought to be employed:* power being given to either party to employ whatsoever expedients shall be found necessary for securing the completeness as well as correctness of the notes thus taken; and for that purpose, as often as the importance of the matter appears to him to warrant the additional vexation, power to call for the momentary stoppage requisite to be applied to the delivery of evidence.

In the early ages of modern jurisprudence, writing was rare, short-hand writing unexampled. Should the ends of justice take place anywhere of the ends of judicature, this talent would be regarded as an indispensable qualification in a judicial scribe.

§ 4. *Of notation and recordation under English law.*

Whatever objection there might be in point of reason to the indiscriminate recordation of the evidence in all causes, none could come with any degree of consistency from the lips of an English lawyer. In causes of a certain class, this security has been inexorably exacted. What are these causes? Precisely the class of causes which, individually taken, are of the least importance,—suits for penalties to the lowest amount (as low as a few shillings,) brought before single justices of peace, out of sessions. And by whom was the obligation imposed? Not by the legislature, but by the Court of King's Bench: by this section of the twelve great judges, legislating in their own way, in the way of *ex post facto* law. Parliament, by whom the jurisdiction was given in this large class of cases to these subordinate magistrates, imposed not, in any instance, any such duty: the judges of the Court of King's Bench took upon them to impose it in every instance. How? By quashing convictions, on pretence of the non-fulfilment of a duty that had never been imposed. The prosecutor was punished—that is, the public was punished—because a justice had not complied with a regulation of the Court of King's Bench, which that court had no right to make, and had never made.

By the act of contempt thus committed against the legislature, two favourite points were gained by the men of law: 1. They made business for themselves, by bringing into their own court causes of which it was the manifest intention of the legislature not to give them the cognizance; 2. They threw discouragement and discredit upon a rival mode of procedure, which, by its conformity to the ends of justice, was and is a perpetual satire upon their own.

Had the usurpation remained altogether unchecked, society would have been dissolved. The legislature has interfered: but how? Instead of punishing the usurpers, it has stolen back by degrees the authority thus filched from it. For a considerable time past, as often as a new offence has been created by act of parliament (a case that takes place many times over in every session,) and cognizance given of it to these subordinate judges, a form of conviction has been prescribed by the act; and in this form, nothing being said of the evidence, the obligation of setting forth the evidence is virtually dispensed with.

The task thus set to unlearned magistrates was a curious one: satisfaction was, on every occasion, to be given to a set of men who had neither the will nor the power to declare what it was would satisfy them—whose interest it was, never to be satisfied—and whose ideas a man might be sure never to meet, by following the dictates of common sense.

The pretence was, the affording to the defendant a security against misdecision to his prejudice—against the being convicted on insufficient grounds. That this formed any part of the real inducement, let him believe whose faith is strong enough. In the character of a security, the information required was not worth a straw; it was not the *minutes*, the tenor of the evidence, but whatever account (true or false) the subordinate judge might think fit to give of it. To secure the correctness of this account, no measures either were or could be taken by those who thus took upon them to require it; as they well knew. Correct or incorrect, it remained equally exposed to be tried, and either condemned or acquitted—(condemnation or acquittal would serve equally well)—by rules made hot and hot, at the moment they were wanted: by rules which, to have been known, required to have been communicated; and to have been communicated, required to have been made.

* The Central Criminal Court is the only court in this country in which an official short-hand writer is employed. To his notes the judges occasionally refer with great advantage, in order to ascertain the exact words made use of by a particular witness.—*Ed.*

So much for summary procedure: a few words will serve for regular.

In the common-law branch, so far as the evidence is concerned, no recordation takes place—nothing, at least, that goes by that name.

A sort of instrument there is, indeed, called the record; but in this instrument, composed chiefly of lies and nonsense, no notice is taken of the evidence.*

Minutes, indeed, are customarily taken by the professional, the directing, judge: they are called the judge's notes. But it has been already observed, that of these minutes (a sort of document unknown to the system in its original constitution) little notice is taken, in comparison with what might be expected. When taken (which they are not necessarily nor always,) they are not authenticated by any other signature. They do not profess to contain the tenor of the evidence. What they contain is, what, in the view of the judge who penned them, constituted the general substance of the evidence. The purpose for which they were originally taken, was no other than the private purpose of the judge. It being customary for him to give, for the instruction of the jury, a recapitulatory view of the evidence they had been hearing,—the memoranda he took were subservient to that and no other purpose.

When, about the middle of the seventeenth century, the practice of granting a *new trial* by a fresh jury, without punishing the former jury, came into use,—the notes of the presiding judge constituted a ready document, the only existing one, and the best that could have existed for that purpose.

Then, however, as to this day, no such document as this was known to the genius of jurisprudence; the supply of it was matter of private accommodation from judge A to judge B. Regularly, there were no grounds to go upon: if judge A had taken no notes, there was no remedy. So long as the lies and nonsense were regularly entered,—whether the truth and sense of the case were regularly entered or no, was a matter of no consequence.

In the minds of the original framers of the system, the demand for recordation (it may be thought) was superseded by the unlimited confidence reposed in the judges taken from the body of the people. Vain thought! In an English jury, corruption of the grossest kind was regarded, and not altogether without reason, as every day's practice; but, in the age of primeval barbarism,—error, innocent error, on the part of those unlearned judges, was not possible. All twelve together, in a mass, they were consigned to utter ruin. The prosecution having this for its object was called an *attaint*; and, in those days, prosecutions in the way of attaint seem scarcely to have been less common than motions for new trials now.

A judgment by which twelve judges were to be consigned in the lump to indigence, perpetual imprisonment, and infamy, should have had (one would have thought) some fixed ground made for it. No such thing. What they were punished for was, for deciding otherwise than according to the evidence; but what the evidence had been, was a matter scarce worth thinking about: the functions of the recording scribe extended not to any such minutiæ. Of men capable of writing down what they had been hearing, the state of society afforded no abundance.

When the liberty, entire property, and reputation, of twelve men, were at stake upon the correctness of the conception formed of the evidence,—committing it to writing as it was delivered, was an operation, the benefit of which, in the eyes of a learned judge, was not worth the trouble. When a small number of shillings, the price of a few days' labour, limited the value of the stake, then it was that the judgment of an unlearned judge, on whom no such duty had been imposed, was to be overthrown, for want of his having performed it.

Under the equity branch of regular procedure, the evidence is committed to writing, every tittle of it, and carefully authenticated with undiscriminating particularity. That which is extracted from the pen of the defendant, comes into the world in the form of ready-written evidence. That which is extracted from an extraneous witness, comes authenticated by the signature of the obscure clerk, who to this important purpose is suffered to exercise the function and power of a judge.

Such is the course in all equity causes, be their importance ever so great, or ever so little: always understood, that, in the eye of English equity, a sum that does not exceed £10 (more than a twelvemonth's subsistence for an average individual) is of no importance; and that the factitious part of the expense of an English equity cause is sufficient to give high importance to a cause which otherwise would have none.

§ 5. *Of the authentication of minutes.*

A written discourse is exhibited, purporting to be the minutes of what passed on the occasion of an examination. Good: but is it really what it purports to be? If given for no more than the substance of what passed, may it be taken for the exact substance? Is it in a sufficient degree a correct and complete

* The forms of pleading against which this observation is directed, have been much altered since the recent Law Amendment Act, 2 W. IV. c. 39. It must however be confessed, that the pleadings require still farther purgation.—*Ed.*

representation of the tenor? If given for the tenor,—the words it consists of, are they exactly the same words, and are they the whole of the same words, that on the occasion in question were pronounced?

If the identity required regards the substance only—if, in regard to the person for whose use the notes or minutes are desired, there be but one such person, and he the judge (the judge by whom, after the evidence has been collected by him, the decision grounded on that evidence is to be pronounced)—and if, as is natural, the person by whom the minutes are so taken for the use of the judge be no other than the judge himself,—the business of authentication neither presents, nor is even susceptible of, difficulty. Arrangements for securing the authenticity of the written discourse purporting to contain notes or minutes of the testimony in question, with the interrogatories which called it forth, are superseded by the consideration of the person by whom they have been penned; as, in the case of the testimony itself, the operation of taking minutes of it is superseded by the mode of expression employed when it is delivered in the first instance in the form of ready-written evidence.

When the identity required regards the words themselves—when (as in that case will naturally be the case) the hand by which the minutes are taken is a hand other than that of the judge—when, as in the same case will also be natural, it is as against the judge that the document in question is intended to serve,—it is in this case, and in this alone, that difficulties respecting the securing the authenticity of the minutes are liable to present themselves.

There are two opposite dangers with which the nature of the case is pregnant: 1. In some way or other, it may happen to the minutes to be really wanting, materially wanting, in point of authenticity; 2. Not being in any respect wanting in point of authenticity, it may happen to them to be charged (and here, by the supposition, falsely charged) with being so. And again, the falsity of the charge may either be not accompanied, or accompanied, with mendacity.

This last-mentioned case is far from being an imaginary one. Suppose, on the ground of testimony thus recorded, a malefactor to be condemned to death: if the want of sufficient proof be recognised as a sufficient ground for invalidating the judgment, and in this or that individual case any such deficiency be recognised to have taken place, the malefactor, how well convinced soever of the groundlessness of the charge, cannot reasonably be suspected of any backwardness to avail himself of it.*

Moreover, besides the imputation of failure in point of authenticity or genuineness, it may happen to the sort of instrument here in question (as to an instrument of contract, or any other legally-important instrument) to be charged with want of freedom or fairness. In regard to the testimony, it may be alleged, that—though, in the very terms in question, delivered by the deponent—it would not have been delivered by him, had it not been for some undue inducements (whether of a coercive or an alluring nature) in the shape of undue punishment or undue reward, held out to him, at the very time of the delivery of his testimony, by the judge. I say by the judge: for if by any other person, or if by the judge himself at any prior point of time, the mischief will not be within the reach of the remedial arrangements applicable to the present case.

The dangers thus being brought to view, the next thing to be brought to view is the remedy by which all difficulty in regard to the obviating of these dangers is removed. This is no other than publicity—the grand panacea in the system of procedure.

But (as hath already been seen) cases are not altogether wanting in which the propriety of waiving the benefit of this security may be indicated by particular and preponderant considerations. Accordingly, for these cases at least, such arrangements will require to be provided, as, when employed, may upon occasion shut the door against all such imputed deficiencies as may be liable to be urged by the eagerness or insincerity of any party to whose side of the cause the tendency of the evidence in question may happen to be adverse.

Before the breaking-up of the court, let it be incumbent on the judge,—either at the instance of the deponent, or (if he be an extraneous witness) at the instance of either party,—to afford him the faculty of examining into the correctness of the minutes taken of his deposition; and, having so done, to call upon him, in token of his assent, to annex his signature to a short sentence or phrase expressive of such assent—or, if in any particular he objects to them as incorrect, to state in what respect—suggesting, if he thinks fit, the words (if any) that would have the effect of rendering them correct, in tenor or in purport.

To afford him the faculty of ascertaining the correctness or incorrectness of the minutes, let some such course as the following be pursued:—

1. Let the passage in question be read aloud

* In England, at least, if this or any other such token of probity and sincerity on the part of a malefactor were to betray itself, it would have to encounter the most determined opposition, not only from the advice of counsel, accessaries after the fact, in the character of advocates and attorneys, but from the hypocritical and trust-breaking humanity of judges.

(either by the judge, or, under his authority by some officer of the court) to the deponent; and with such slowness and such pauses as shall be sufficient to enable him on each occasion to fix upon any word or phrase, and object to it as incorrect.

2. If, for the purpose of enabling himself to obtain a clearer conception of the contents,—being able to read, he signifies a desire to have the paper in his own hands, that he may peruse it more at leisure,—let such liberty be allowed: such precautions being taken, as (in case of his being a person under suspicion of criminal delinquency) may be necessary to prevent his employing such liberty to a bad purpose; for example, vexatious delay,—or the discovery of the contents of any part of the minute to which the testimony of any other co-deponent is consigned,—or tearing or otherwise defacing or destroying the paper of minutes, or any part of its contents.

If, on any such occasion, objecting or not objecting to any part of the minutes as incorrect (viz. in the character of an incorrect expression of the discourse of which it purports to be the minute, viz. the discourse delivered by him at the time,) he gives it to be understood, that, in the character of testimony, the discourse so delivered by him was in any particular incorrect; and prays accordingly that he may be admitted to correct it, viz. by the suggestion of such additions, omissions, or substitutions, as are thereupon uttered by him for that purpose;—in such case, let such his application be complied with: and let the tenor (or at least the substance) of what passes upon that occasion, be entered forthwith upon the paper of minutes, in the same manner as any other part of the evidence.

If he declines writing his signature, on the declared ground of his inability, let it be written for him by some one else; as (for example) by the person by whom the other parts of the minute are penned; and, to the signature so written for him, let him annex his mark: but, if he refuses, or wilfully forbears, as well to make his mark as to write his signature, let mention be made of such refusal or forbearance upon the minutes.

On any such occasion, let it be in the power of the judge to call upon all or any of the persons present to attest by their signatures the correctness of the minute so made: and to such order let them be bound to pay obedience, as to any other order issued by the judge in execution of his office. Provided always that, instead of an affirmance (as above,) every such person shall be at liberty to enter a denial; subject, in case of falsity, to such penalty as is annexed to the offence of judicial falsehood in other cases.*

In Rome-bred law, in general, provision is made for obtaining such evidence, as is deemed sufficient, of the authenticity of the minutes. The deponent is called upon to authenticate them by his signature: if, whether through inability or unwillingness, he fails of so doing, mention of such failure is, in general terms, entered upon the minutes.

By this arrangement, the appearance of authenticity and correctness (authenticity applies to the whole, correctness to any and every part taken by itself) is sure enough to be obtained: but as to the reality, how ineffectually it is provided for is but too manifest. To sign or not to sign—such indeed is the option given him: if he does not sign, mention is made of such failure, or (as in the language of French law it is called) his refusal: but as to any grounds which he may have had, or not had, for such refusal, no light is ever afforded by these minutes. They may have been spurious in the whole, or incorrect in every part; yet, upon the face of them, everything in them may appear as completely regular in this case as in any other.

Along with the deponent, there is, indeed, besides the judge, another person—his official secretary. But, should these two persons (through mendacity, temerity, or even blameless misconception,) agree in a statement in any respect false or erroneous, or the inferior be overawed by the superior into acquiescence; it seems impossible to conceive what remedy the nature of the case can afford. In the case of a person of the clearest character, what weight can the testimony of one non-official person have, capable of overpowering that of two official ones? And if that be the helplessness even of a person clear of all suspicion, what must be the condition of a man whose character stands loaded with the imputation of a first-rate crime?†

* The course pursued in taking examinations before a justice of the peace, is as follows:—While the witnesses are giving their evidence, a clerk writes it down in a book. If after all the evidence has been heard, the justice dismisses the case, there is an end of the matter; but if the justice determines to send the case for trial, then the evidence of each witness is read over to him; he is asked if it is correct, and whether he wishes to add anything to it. The deposition is altered or not, according to the answer of the witness. After this it is copied out, on separate sheets of paper, by the clerk, from the book in which it was originally entered: it is again read over to the witness, and he then signs his name or puts his mark to it. If he declines to do so, a memorandum is made to that effect. When all the depositions relating to the case in question have thus been copied out and signed by the witnesses, the justice puts his signature at the end. These depositions so authenticated, are returned to the court in which the case is to be ultimately tried.—*Ed.*

† In one of the Anglican modifications of the Rome-bred mode, there is one person less than

How ill soever a man may be disposed to think of the English judges, no man can think worse of them than in this respect they appear to have been thought of by parliament and by one another.

On other occasions, to authenticate an instrument of any sort (a judicial writ, for example) by which the authority of any of the great courts of Westminster Hall is exercised, the signature of any of the judges is regarded as sufficient evidence of his participation in the act: not to speak of the case in which the signature of the chief of the four judges is regarded as sufficient evidence of the participation of all the rest.

It now and then happens, that in the course of a trial before a jury, presided over by one of the twelve judges, some instruction or direction is given by the judge in relation to some point of law — for example, as to the admission or rejection of this or that article of evidence — an instruction by which it has always been customary to the jury to be governed in the pronouncing of their verdict. On the occasion of such direction, at a very early period of juridical history, provision was made by parliament for giving to the party prejudiced by it the faculty of appeal to another court. The instrument by which an appeal on this ground is expressed, is called a bill of exceptions. For this purpose it is necessary, that, if not in tenor, at least in substance, the direction given by the presiding judge should be established. It is curious enough to observe the formalities prescribed on this insulated occasion, on which, for any useful purpose, extraordinary formalities would seem to be particularly unnecessary; and the extraordinary distrust with which all persons concerned (judges among the rest) appear, nor altogether without reason, to have been regarded.

The statute by which this remedy is provided, is a statute of Edward I. To save critical discussion, let us take the account given by Judge Buller. "By Westminster 2," says he, "13 E. I. c. 31, it is enacted, that, if one impleaded before any of the justices allege an exception, [an expression vague and insignificant enough, but practice has found a sense for it,] praying that the justices will allow it, and if they will not, if he write the exception and require the justices to put their seals to it, the justices shall so do, and if one will not, another shall. And if the king, on complaint made of the justices, cause the record to come before him, and the exception be not in the roll [the apprehension being that the justices, to avoid having their proceedings canvassed, would suppress it,] on showing it written with the seal of the justice, he shall be commanded at a day to confess or deny his seal; and if he cannot deny his seal [effrontery, not improbity, being the quality in respect of which it was thought it might happen to him to be deficient,] they [who?] shall proceed to judge, and allow or disallow, the exception."* Thus far Buller. They? who? Not certainly the judges thus appealed from, but the person appealed to, viz. the king, that is, the judges of the court of King's Bench, with the king sitting, or rather not sitting, in the midst of them.

It was on the ground of this statute, that, nothing less having been deemed sufficient to prove that the seal of the judge had not been forged, the first Earl Camden (then Lord Chief-Justice Pratt, chief-justice of the court of Common Pleas,) having set his seal to a bill of exceptions, and "*not being able to deny it*," appeared personally and confessed it in the court of King's Bench, then presided over by the first Lord Mansfield.† Reflection upon reflection here presents itself. What use of a *seal*, which a judge (if so disposed) might deny to be his? Why not that best of all instruments of authentication, the name written by the person whose name it is; the instrument that, without any such useless locomotion, served even then in so many other cases of superior importance? In the case of an illiterate non-lawyer, yes: but as to lawyers, as to judges (even at this early period) was there ever one instance of a person aggregated to this fraternity at all times distinguished by the epithet of *learned*, and at the same time unable to write his name?

The real danger was, not that, after having given his attestation to the instrument expressive of his own words, a judge should deny his own hand-writing, or (what came to the same thing) the seal which was so absurdly substituted in the room of it; but that the attestation thus required of the judges should not be given by them, or any one of them. That "one will not," is the case put, with primitive simplicity, by the statute: but if any one find courage to refuse, — to adopt such refusal requires on the part of any other

even in the Romano-Gallic; from which the practice of the other nations by which the Roman mode has been adopted, may in this particular, be presumed not to be materially different. I speak of the case where the operation is performed under the authority of the Court of Chancery, in what is called the examiner's office. But, on this occasion, any misbehaviour to the effect in question on the part of the obscure person by whom the examination is performed, would be exposed to so much danger, — in the first place of censure, and perhaps loss of his office, on extrajudicial complaint to his immediate superior — but more especially in case of a public prosecution, to which he might be subjected in more forms than one, — that, of any complaint of this sort, no traces have presented themselves in the books.

* Buller's *Nisi Prius*, p. 315.

† Burrow, p. 1694, anno 1765.

much less courage: and so on, the probability of a refusal going on in an increasing ratio, till the whole number, viz. four, or five (which at one time was the number,) be exhausted.

"If the judges refuse to sign the bill," continues Judge Buller, referring in the margin to the Institutes of Lord Coke,* "the party grieved by the denial may have a writ upon the statute, commanding the same to be done, *juxta formam statuti*; it recites the form of an exception taken and over-ruled, and it follows, *vobis præcipimus quod si ita est, tunc sigilla vestra apponatis*; and if it be returned [viz. by the judges in question] *quod non ita est* [an incident natural enough, or it would not have been provided for,] an action will lie for a false return [an action, suppose, against a judge or judges of the King's Bench; but before whom? Themselves? or their subordinates of the Common Pleas?] and, thereupon, the surmise will be tried, and if found to be so, damages will be given; and upon such a recovery, a peremptory writ commanding the same." And if the same cause which produced the first mal-practice, should continue its influence, and produce a second, what was to come then? An *alias* peremptory writ, and then a *pluries*; and thus, in the form of a legal repetend, pluries upon pluries without end.

That, to a set of lawyers, to whose power this remedy was intended as a check, it might happen not to be very forward in lending their hand to the application of it, was a surmise, neither improbable in itself, nor altogether unsanctioned by experience.

If there was one sort of case, in which, as compared with another, this sort of remedy was particularly needful and important, it would be a penal case, as compared with a non-penal one: and in particular, among penal cases, a capital, in contradistinction to a non-capital, one. "In Sir H. Vane's case," continues Buller, "who was indicted for high-treason," [it was along with the regicides concerned in the murder of Charles I.] the court refused to sign a bill of exceptions." Refused? why? "Because," continues Buller, "they said criminal cases were not within the statute, but only actions between party and party." There the statute is, and throughout the whole of it there is no such absurdity as that of refusing the remedy (such as it is) to the most important class of cases. A man impleaded in a criminal case, is he not "impleaded?" But when a statute was found troublesome, in what instance was it ever an effectual bar to the wishes of an English judge?

Actio personalis moritur cum personâ, says a maxim of English jurisprudence, the design of which (if it had had any) would have been to encourage murders, especially slow and secret ones. Well or ill-grounded, the bill of exceptions being denied, the regicides died: and with them died the "action for a false return," the "*surmise*" that should have been "*tried*," the "*damages*" that should have been "given," and the "*peremptory writ*" by which "*the same*" should have been "commanded;" commanded with as much effect as by the non-peremptory one.

The above example may suffice to show that the sorts of cases which, under the system of modern manners, may seem the most unlikely to occur, require not the less to be provided for: and the more effectual the provision made for them, the greater the assurance of their non-occurrence:—and that, on this as on every other occasion that can be named, the provision made by the technical system, constantly adequate to what have been, is wretchedly inadequate to what ought to have been, its purposes.

On another occasion, a bill of exceptions had been tendered by a man who was indicted for a trespass. A trespass, though not so great a crime, is in English jurisprudence as much a crime as murder: indictment is the mode of prosecution employed in the one case as in the other. No such exceptions had at this time been discovered in the statute, as the judges in Vane's case found it convenient to dream of: but the trespasser was not a regicide. It was after this decision, and in the teeth of the warning given by it, that the dispatchers of regicides dreamt their dream.

* 2 Inst. p. 426.

CHAPTER VII.

THAT THE EVIDENCE SHOULD BE COLLECTED BY THE SAME PERSON BY WHOM THE DECISION IS TO BE PRONOUNCED.

ONE person to receive, and help to extract, the testimony—another person to decide upon it. Any such division of labour,—ought it to be made? No, surely: unless in cases (if any such there be) where the union which it cuts asunder is either physically, or (in respect of delay, vexation, or expense) prudentially, impracticable.

To what one of all the ends of justice can it ever be subservient? What one of them all is there that is not counteracted by it?

On which side, and in what way, can it in any conceivable case tend to prevent misdecision on the ground of the evidence?—misdecision to the prejudice of the plaintiff's, or to the prejudice of the defendant's, side?

Death, incurable infirmity of mind or body, a motion from the office or from the spot,—in each of these we see an event that may at any time intervene to render the function of decision physically impracticable to him by whom, in the function of receipt and extraction, a progress of any length, from commencement down to termination, has been made. Has any such irremediable impediment taken place? Either ultimate non-decision, with the consequent injustice to the plaintiff's side, must be the result, or a decision (if pronounced) must be the work of another judge.

Infirmity of mind or body, to appearance not incurable, but (as in respect of future duration, all such indisposition is) of uncertain promise, — time of vacation (if any) to be allowed to the judge, for the pursuit of his personal health, business, or amusements:— in what cases shall these temporary causes of cessation be allowed to have the effect of transferring the business from the hands of one to those of another judge? Topics these of particular detail, the solution of which, depending in no inconsiderable degree upon circumstances of a local and temporary nature, will hardly be looked for here.

The subject of inquiry here is, — where no natural impediments stand in the way of the finishing of the cause by the same hands in which it took its commencement, the deciding upon the evidence by the same person by whom it was collected, — shall the two functions be consigned to two different persons?

From the severance, no advantage can be seen to result in any shape: no advantage (understand) with reference to the ends of justice; how abundant soever (of which presently) the advantage with reference to the actual ends of judicature.

Disadvantages may, on the other hand, be seen in abundance.

1. Loss of the benefit of that most instructive species of circumstantial evidence, which is afforded by deportment: concerning which, see the book on Circumstantial Evidence.*

It is not in every suit, that, from deportment, any instructive indication can be derived. True: in every individual suit, not: but in every imaginable species of suit, yes.

2. Danger of incorrectness and incompleteness on the part of the written minutes, in the character of representations of the testimony orally delivered. In this respect, the infirmity of the evidence is of the nature of that which is essential to *hearsay evidence*.†

Hence, danger of deception and consequent misdecision: hence, in other words, disadvantage with reference to the direct ends of justice.

3. By this division, writing, minutation and recordation (as will be seen farther on,) is necessitated: necessitated, as well in such causes as are not recordation-worthy, as in those that are so.‡

Hence, inconvenience in the shape of delay, vexation, and expense: disadvantage with reference to the collateral ends of justice.

To the reasons which thus plead against the severance, no just reasons in favour of it can be opposed.

In vain would it be said, To a head which is competent to collect the evidence, it may happen not to be competent to the framing of the decision which is to be grounded on it.

1. It is with a view to whatsoever decision may be proper to be grounded on the evidence, that the collection of the evidence ought to be performed: without such view, it will not be appositely performed. Decision is the end; collection of the evidence on which that decision is to be grounded, is the means: the head that is not adequate to the end, is not adequate to the means.

2. In the process of collection, the whole body of the evidence will necessarily have passed under the review of the judge (for such he is) by whom it has been collected. In the course of this process, it can scarcely happen (supposing, as is the most common case, the whole of it thus collected at once, and by the same judicatory) but that an opinion in relation to it, *i. e.* in relation to its probative force in regard to the fact in question, must have been formed. But, the opinion formed, the decision follows of course; and it requires but a minute or two, and a word or a line or two, to pronounce it. The decision pronounced; if all parties are satisfied with it, there ends the cause: if on either side a party is dissatisfied with it, then, and then only, is appeal of any use. The ulterior judicatory is thus charged with the suit, in those instances alone (but in all such instances) in which, in the judgment of those to whom it properly belongs to judge, it can be of use.

At whose instance should any such transference be made?

1. At the instance of the collecting judge? This is what has been called *remitter*. For declining to pronounce a decision, what can be the pretence? Knows he not how? Is his judgment unable to satisfy itself? Let him at any rate try whether he cannot satisfy the parties. Better decide by cross and pile, than not decide: if the parties are satisfied with the decision, everything is as it should be: if either be dissatisfied, the worst that can happen is, the doing for that good reason, what, in the other case, it is proposed to do without reason.

2. At the instance of a superior judge? This is what is called *evocation:* but still evocation without reason. Whether in any and what cases evocation can be grounded on sufficient reason, is a question that belongs not to this place. Is it to put an end to delay?—at any rate, the delay, the ill-grounded delay, ought to have been proved, and (if this be the only ground) an option given for

* *Vide infra*, Book V. *Circumstantial.*

† Book VI. *Makeshift*; Chap. IV. *Hearsay Evidence.*

‡ *Vide supra*, Chap. VI. § 2, p. 410.

the removal of it by decision pronounced within the time.

3. At the instance of a party? This is what is called *appeal*. But, before a party prefers an appeal, let him stay till a ground is made for it: before he complains of the decision, let him stay till he knows what it is. And what must the malcontent party say in this case? Stop, pronounce not your decision, for fear lest, when I hear it, it should not be agreeable to me.

When, however, judicature cannot be performed in the best mode, it follows not that it ought not to be performed in any inferior mode: judicature must be badly performed indeed, if denial of justice be preferable to it.

1. A case that will sometimes happen, is, that the whole of the evidence is to be sought for at the hands of one or more proposed respondents (whether parties or extraneous witnesses,) of whom no one, to the purpose of forthcomingness in order to testification, is subject, in point of *fact*, to the power of the judicatory by which the decision is to be framed.

In the case of *expatriation*, this bar may have been opposed by the insuperable nature of things: in the case of *exprovinciation*, by the shortsightedness or negligence of the legislative branch of government.

2. Another case that may happen, is,—part of the necessary evidence *is* thus forthcoming; another part, not.

3. In either of the above cases, it may happen, that the securing the requisite forthcomingness is an operation which, though not *physically*, is *prudentially*, impracticable: not practicable without preponderant inconvenience in the shape of delay, vexation, and expense.

4. Another case that sometimes happens, is this: A mass of evidence, which, at any distance of time, was collected for the purpose of another cause,—whether on the occasion of the same or a different demand,—between the same parties, between parties altogether different, or between parties in one or more instances the same, in others different,—may contain in it matter applicable to the suit in hand: of the witnesses in question, the forthcomingness being at present either physically or prudentially impracticable.

Whether it be more conducive to the ends of justice, that evidence in this inferior shape be, or that it be not, admitted, will depend upon the class of the cause, and the side on which the admission is applied for: whether the cause be of the non-penal or of the penal class: whether the side on which the admission is called for be the plaintiff's or the defendant's side. But for such details this is no fit place.

When the judicatory by which the decision grounded on the evidence is framed, is different in any respect from the judicatory by which the evidence was collected, the difference may be complete, or partial: complete, if the deciding judicatory does not contain any one member who was a member of the collecting judicatory; partial, if it does contain one or more.

If the separation be thus complete, the mischief of it stands exactly upon the footing above represented. If the deciding judicatory contains in it one or more persons who were members of the collecting judicature (say, for example, *one*,) the mischief stands upon a footing somewhat different:—1. The benefit of *deportment* evidence is not so completely lost. There sits the collecting judge, by whom some account, such as he pleases, may be given of it to the rest. 2. The danger of incorrectness and incompleteness on the part of the minutes is not quite so great. There sits the collecting judge, who, in answer to any doubts or inquiries that may be started on that head, may give any such elucidations—make any such confessions—as it is agreeable to him to make.

The mischiefs of severance are thus in some indeterminate and ever-varying degree diminished, but far indeed from being removed.

In this case, we see a judicatory composed of a number of members, one of whom is perfectly, the others but imperfectly, competent to the purpose of the decision, in the formation of which they bear each of them an equal part.

Supposing them all equally instructed,—all, except one, are (if what has been endeavoured to be shown elsewhere* be just) much worse than useless: still more, if all above one are comparatively uninstructed. Do the rest suffer themselves to be governed by that one? A decision which in fact had but one author, enjoys (in the event of its being erroneous) so many other apparent co-authors, to compose a screen for the error, and save it from the merited censure.—Do the rest disagree with that one? Here, then, is a number of judges comparatively ill instructed, opposing themselves, and with success, to the only one who is, comparatively, well instructed.

In the French and other continental editions of the procedure of the Roman school, the mischief of the severance has commonly this palliative. In the several English editions of that procedure, viz. those used in the equity courts, the ecclesiastical courts, and the admiralty courts, it has no such palliative. In the Scotch editions, it is for the most part, though not completely, without the palliative. In the principal and highest judicatory by which the decision on the evidence is framed and pronounced, it may

* Scotch Reform, Vol. V. Letter I.

happen, and now and then (but rarely) has happened, that some one among the fifteen judges, in the character of Lord Ordinary on oaths and witnesses, had in charge, and (if so) singly in charge, the collection of it.

In this instance, as in every other, the cause of whatever is amiss in judicial procedure may, by every eye that can endure the light, be seen in the opposition between the ends of judicature and the ends of justice. Love of power, ease, profit,—all these persuasive considerations concurred in pleading for the severance.

1. It is by *decision*—an act of the *will*—that power is exercised. Previous inquiry—receiving and collecting evidence—hearing arguments on both sides—and supporting the decision by reasons,—all these acts of the *understanding* are not additions to the power, but clogs upon the exercise of it.

To decide, is an operation that does not necessarily require more time than it is agreeable to the decider to bestow upon it. The performance of those other operations—of those exercises of the understanding,—and in such manner as not to expose a man to disrepute,—requires, for the purpose of each decision, an expense of time any number of times greater than what is necessary for the formation and utterance of the decision itself.

If the extent and quantity of the power in question be measured by the number of decisions pronounced within a given space of time (say a year,)—a hundred, a thousand, any number of times the power may be exercised within the year by the judge who is unshackled, that can be exercised by one who is shackled, with those clogs. And, where the importance of the case is given, this is the fair and proper measure.

2. Witnesses are persons of all castes: and as the great majority of the people are of a low and ignorant caste, they constitute in proportion *bad company* with relation to the judge. In the advocates on both sides, by whom the comments on the evidence when collected—no matter by whom or how—are delivered, the judge beholds so many brethren, and these brethren learned ones; men of the same caste, superior to all other men, inferior only to himself; in every respect the very pleasantest of company.

Ease, accommodation, convenience (whatever word be the most convenient and agreeable,) are thus, along with power, promoted and augmented by the severance.

3. Where, on the evidence collected by one man or set of men, a decision is to be pronounced by another, writing is an operation not merely of use but of necessity. In the early ages of jurisprudence, writing was an art, the exercise of which was too rare not to be well remunerated: the *art* even by itself; much more when found in conjunction with the still rarer science of jurisprudence. The greater the expenditure in the article of art and science, the greater the receipt necessary in the article of profit—pecuniary profit—to balance the account.

Profit thus added its influence to those of power and ease.

Whatever part of the business could be turned over to subordinates, those subordinates would take care to be paid for: and the fee paid to the subordinate would be in addition to the fee paid to the principal. Hence, so much patronage *in præsenti*: and patronage *in præsenti* becomes, in some shape or other, profit *in futurum*, if it suits the inclinations and situation of the patron to apply it to that use.

Besides being so much more favourable to his interest, this arrangement was much more directly and certainly in the power of the judge, than the only one that would have been well adapted to the interests of the suitors and the ends of justice. Subordinates could be employed by his own authority: co-ordinates could not be obtained but by the authority of his superiors. The quantity and quality of the business turned over to the subordinate, might be adapted to the convenience of the superior: the quantity and quality of the business done by a co-ordinate would not be thus obsequious.

For illustration, look to the English Court of Chancery.

In the beginning, when causes were comparatively few, the Chancellor,—this new sort of judge, to whom a commission had been given to judge *secundum æquum et bonum*, (it being but too manifest how widely the rules pursued by the established judges differed from this character,)—this new-made judge proceeded (as any man would naturally proceed in his place)—proceeded as the inferior judges called justices of the peace proceed at this day. He heard the evidence, and then he decided upon it. The evidence on which he was about to decide, he heard with his own ears.

It could not be long before business of this judicial kind would crowd upon him in a much greater quantity than his other business, of which he had no inconsiderable quantity, would allow him time for. What was to be done? Of a co-ordinate, a rival in office, a sharer in the dignity, power, and emoluments attached to it, it was not natural that he should be desirous; nor, had he even been desirous, could he have been sure of obtaining of the king any such coadjutor; at any rate, without such solicitations as it suited not to him to make. From the first, he had of necessity (were it only for the mere mechanical, the writing, part of his business) a number of clerks under his orders; the number of these clerks soon rose to twelve. In process of time, these clerks, not being yet enough, contrived to have other clerks under them: the original sort of clerk became distinguished by the name of *Masters*. As the writings accumulated, — many of which, if not all, were for some reason or other to be preserved, and for the purpose of occasional consultation, to be put and kept in some sort of order, — this charge, a charge of no small trust, was committed to one of those clerks, who thus became distinguished from and above the rest. In those days, paper had not been invented, or at least was not in common use: parchment was the only substance to which the characters, which written discourse is composed of, was applied: the art of bookbinding was little in use: economy suggested, as the most convenient mode of adding sheet to sheet, and in such successive quantities as came to be required by successive incidents, the tacking them together in such manner that the whole length might be wound up together in the form of spiral rolls. The clerk, in whose keeping these rolls were, was thus distinguished by the name of the clerk of the rolls. When clerks became masters, the clerk of the rolls became Master of the Rolls.

Of the business committed to the Chancellor, such business as was least pleasant to him to do himself, he turned over, of course, to these his clerks. In some instances, entire causes, — decision, as well as collection of evidence. But in general it came to be felt that decision was a more pleasant operation than inquiry: decision has more of power in it — inquiry more labour: inquiry takes up more time, and creates a greater demand for patience. The business of collecting the evidence thus fell into the hands of the twelve master clerks: but more particularly of the head one amongst them, the clerk of the rolls.

The evidence thus collected, was collected by the clerks: but the Chancellor, by whom a decision was to be grounded on it, — how was the purport of it to be presented to his knowledge? The surest channel was the *tenor*: but that required it to be committed to writing. So much the better: on the account of the suitors, in respect of security against misdecision, for obvious reasons: on the account of this great officer, and these his subordinates, for other reasons not less obvious. Writing is labour: — but the labourer is worthy of his hire: and the labourer acted under the orders of one, in whose hands were vested the easiest and surest means of exacting from his employer, the suitor, whatever it should be thought prudent to demand, on the score of hire.

On interlocutory points, the power of decision, provisional decision, subject of course to appeal to the principal judge (the only judge recognised in that character,) came thus, little by little, to be exercised by all these clerks. Even on definitive points, the like power, though always subject to appeal, came by degrees to be exercised by the chief clerk, or the Master of the Rolls.

Of the whole business of procedure, the part that afforded most trouble, and by assignment had been made to afford additional profit, was that which consists in the collection of the oral part of the evidence: This portion of the business had overflowed (we have seen how, and at how early a period,) from the hands of the Chancellor, into the hands of his head clerk or official servant: the same causes continuing to operate, made it necessarily overflow into still lower and lower channels. The clerk, now become master, of the rolls, turned it over to his "*servants*." Servants, not so much as distinguished by the name of clerks, were deemed good enough for this laborious part of the business: what sort of servants (pages, footmen, grooms, or stable-boys) is not said.

These servants kicked it down to servants or deputies of their own.

From page, or foot-boy, or whatever else happened to be his original occupation, the servant rose into a clerk, — the examining-clerk, — the examiner. The examiner has long been rich enough to be above his business: he keeps a deputy, and the deputy acts by his clerks, all for the good of the public, not forgetting the master of the rolls. All these offices have their value: to all of them the nomination is in the master of the rolls: whatever may be the rational cause, the historical cause is at any rate sufficiently apparent.

The king's turnspit used to be a Member of Parliament:* the clerk of the deputy of a servant of a clerk of the keeper of one of the king's seals, is still a Judge.

CHAPTER VIII.

FIVE MODES OF INTERROGATION COMPARED.

PUTTING together the three considerations — of the form of the intercourse, the quality of the interrogator, and the publicity or unpublicity of the process, — we have five modes of interrogation, all of them in use; viz.

1. Interrogation in the oral mode, *per partes, publicè, coram judice;* the mode pursued under natural procedure and jury trial.

2. Interrogation oral, *per judicem, sine partibus, secretò;* as under Roman procedure in general.

3. Interrogation oral, *per judicem, sine partibus, publicè;* as in English procedure, on the occasion of the preliminary examinations taken by justices of the peace.

* Burke's Speech on his Economy Bill.

4. Interrogation oral, *per judices à partibus electos; i. e.* by commissioners named, one or more on each side; as under the English edition of the Roman school, viz. in the equity courts, in some cases.

5. Interrogation in the epistolary mode.

Compared with each other, what are the advantages and disadvantages attached to these several modes?

The appositeness and importance of the question are sufficiently manifest: but the solution of it belongs not altogether to the head of evidence. Yet in this place the view of the subject would be apt to appear imperfect, if these several modes of obtaining, or professing to aim at obtaining, the same result, were to be left altogether unconfronted and uncompared.

Follows a parallel of the oral mode of collection, and the epistolary, compared with one another: the oral being viewed in the first instance without any reference to any of those distinctions above noticed; and both together being considered with reference to the secondary qualities above noticed as desirable in a mass of evidence, in the character of efficient causes of the primary qualities of correctness and completeness.

1. In respect of *particularity* and *interrogatedness*, the two modes of collection are exactly upon a par. In either way, the process of interrogation is alike capable of being employed; in either way, by means of that operation, the quality of particularity is capable of being, in an equal degree of perfection, given to the mass of evidence.

Take days, or weeks, or months, or years enough, — you may, in the way of written correspondence, render the testimony of the deponent as particular, perhaps, as you would have rendered it in the course of a few minutes by *vivâ voce* examination in the presence of the judge.

2. So in respect of *permanence:* provided that, in the case of orally-delivered testimony, the operation of writing be employed (as it always may be) to give fixity to the discourse as it issues from the deponent's lips.

3. In respect of the faculty of obstructing mendacious *invention* (viz. by the promptitude with which interrogations and responses succeed one another without prejudice to the faculty of receiving, upon occasion, from without, such interrogations as may be subservient to honest recollection;) the advantage is all on the side of the oral mode.

In the epistolary mode, it is not only impossible to oppose to a design of mendacious invention those obstacles which, in virtue of the promptitude of response required, and the symptoms of evil consciousness so apt to be betrayed by deportment, stand opposed to it of course in the oral mode; — but in the very form of the epistolary mode there is a circumstance which, in spite of the exertions of an adverse, or even favourably partial, interrogator, gives aid to invention on the part of a *malâ fide* and mendacious respondent. In the epistolary mode, the questions not coming out singly, nor consequently arising out of the answers, but the whole string of them being displayed at once; hence by the nature of the questien it may every now and then happen, that, to a mendaciously-disposed respondent, information, though in an oblique and unintended way, shall be communicated; information, the effect of which may be to aid him in the accomplishment of such his dishonest purpose.*

The advantage is thus on the side of the mendacious respondent. On the other hand, the correspondent and opposite disadvantage presses upon his interrogator. For the purposes of justice, the respondent, when mendacious, cannot know too little; his interrogator cannot know too much. Here we see what, for the purposes of justice, for the correctness and completeness of the evidence, is, on the part of the mode of interrogation employed, desirable. Now let us observe what, in the case of the epistolary mode, contrasted with

* On this occasion, a cautious reserve would be the resource, and the only resource, of a man of truth and honour. Confined by circumstances to this disadvantageous mode (a case that, as will soon be seen, is but too frequently exemplified,) his care will be, that, by the declarations he is obliged to make, by the string of interrogations he is obliged to bring forward at the same time, as little as possible shall be afforded of that information, which, in the hands of a *malâ fide* adversary or mendacious witness, might prove auxiliary (or, in the language of an English lawyer, ancillary) to that sinister purpose.

A reserve thus dictated by prudence and allowed by truth, would be the sole resource of a man of sincerity and honour. Mendacity—a resource more familiar to their hands, more congenial to their tastes, more gainful to their pockets, has been the resource of English lawyers. Under the licence granted from the bench, the practitioner at the bar, in his endeavours to extract truth from the pen of the adversary, puts into the pen of his own client whatever lies present themselves as best adapted to this purpose. Under the ancient regime (I know not how it is under the modern) a French judge, with the view, real or pretended, of extracting the truth out of the bosom of a criminal under examination, would tell him (for example) that an accomplice has confessed, when perhaps no accomplice has been heard. Such advocates are worthy to practise under such judges. Not that the difference is more than apparent: for the lie of the bar is the lie of the bench by which it is permitted. Not that in this instance the part taken from above, in the manufacture of lucrative mendacity, is simply permissive. In the station of plaintiff in equity, a man is not simply permitted to stuff his narrative with lies: he is forced to it. On no other condition will the judge so much as profess to do him justice.

the oral, virtually has place. In the oral mode, whatsoever be the question addressed to the proposed respondent, whatever questions are intended to come after it remain concealed from him: in the epistolary mode, they are all disclosed to him at once. To the interrogator in the oral mode, on the occasion of each question, all the answers that have been made in compliance with preceding questions are revealed: in the epistolary mode, all the answers that will be given to such antecedent questions, are unrevealed, and undiscoverable.

Physically speaking, what indeed is not altogether impossible, is, that, for the collection of evidence in the epistolary mode, the correspondence shall be so conducted that no more than one interrogation shall be transmitted at a time: just as games at chess have been known to be carried on, each move being announced by a letter written for the purpose.

In this way, the unwilling assistance liable to be lent by an interrogator to a mendacious respondent, would indeed be kept back: and thus far, in the instance of the epistolary mode, its subserviency to the direct ends of justice would be upon a par with that of the oral.

Accordingly, in the only case in which, in English practice, the epistolary mode of interrogation has place (viz. the string of interrogations addressed to a defendant — to a defendant alone, not to a plaintiff or an extraneous witness—in a court of equity,) the correspondent point of policy is naturally and frequently observed by the professional scribe: in the first edition of the instrument, a part more or less considerable of the string of interrogations proposed to be eventually emitted (together with the correspondent averments that have so unnecessarily been made requisite,) is kept back — purposely kept back — till it be seen what answers are given to the first flight; kept back, and reserved for a second edition, which, under the name of *the amended bill*, commonly succeeds the first.

But, besides that in respect of promptitude of response, and the obstruction in that way given to a plan of mendacious responsion, the epistolary mode would even thus remain inferior to the oral, — it is easy to see at how vast an expense of inconvenience, in the shape of delay, vexation, and expense, this diminution of disadvantage, in respect of danger of deception and consequent misdecision, is purchased.*

4. *Recollectedness*. This quality (to any degree beyond that which common conversation admits of, but which, even for the judicial purpose in question, will in ordinary cases be sufficient) is, by the supposition, out of the question: the very arrangements above brought to view as necessary to the perfection of the *vivâ voce* mode, have for their object the exclusion of it.

It is in this article that we see one of the advantages peculiar to the written mode: it is on this account that, as often as extraordinary cases (cases not comprehended in the description of the ordinary cases above spoken of) present themselves, it may become necessary to have recourse, in due time, to the written mode. But of this hereafter.

5. Remains the quality of *distinctness*, in regard to which the advantage is in some respects on the side of the epistolary, in others on the side of the oral, mode.

Where the epistolary mode is the mode employed, a respondent who (being in *malâ fide*) takes for his object the withholding and misrepresenting of the truth so far as it can be endeavoured at with safety, takes of course for his principal means the expedient of indistinctness — as not exposing him in the first instance to those perils to which

* Exercise for a student: a student, not in the art of depredation under the mask of law, but in the art of legislation; in that art which seeks to show by what means the objects professed to be aimed at by those who have the power, may in reality be attained: in the art of legislation, should any man ever arise, to whom an art so unprofitable and thankless should present itself as having any claim to notice. Exercise for a student: — Take up a bundle of printed trials: look out a suitable one — such a one more particularly in which the truth has been wrung, by this engine, out of the bosom of an unwilling witness. Follow out the genealogy of questions and answers; take note of the number of degrees; pitch upon a case in which, by the answer to question the first, a second question is suggested — a question which, had the answer come in another shape, might not have been put: out of the answer to question the second, in like manner, a third question; and so on, as long as the string is found to run. Take out your watch; repeat to yourself aloud each question with its answer, and note the length of time they occupy. Add up the several lengths of time, and divide by the number of consecutive questions or degrees. Apply the same process to the ready-written mode, taking for each degree three months, or whatever other length of time (greater or less) may appear necessary to found a fairer average. You will probably find the number of minutes occupied in the one case somewhere between the number of months and the number of years consumed in the other. Not that in the ready-written mode, an example of a genealogical tree or string of this sort would probably be found of equal or nearly equal length to that of the longest afforded by the *vivâ voce* mode: not that any such real parallel would be to be found. But why? Only because it is not in the nature of a mode which gives full scope to mendacity-serving premeditation, suggestion, and consultation, to afford any such instances of detected mendacity, or extorted truth, as those which, in such abundance, are furnished by the mode which affords to *mala fides* no such helps.

he would be exposed by disprovable mendacity or pertinacious silence. Either of these courses would be evidently the result of a vicious state of the will; *indistinctness*, and to any degree, is not altogether incapable of being the result of an infirm state of the understanding: he therefore heaps together words upon words, throwing the whole matter into the completest state of disorder possible, for the chance of propagating a correspondent state of confusion in the conception of the adversary whom he has to deal with, and thus finally saving from observation and detection as large a proportion as possible of his misrepresentation and reticence, over and above the certain advantage of the delay thus fabricated. In a word, *evasion* is the safest resource of all whose purpose is to conceal the truth, and *indistinctness* is the quality which his discourse receives from the attempt.

Where the collection is performed in the epistolary mode, there are no bounds to the quantity of nebulous matter thus capable of being raised.

The matter of writing, accessible in an unlimited quantity, is to the dishonest party or the mendaciously-disposed witness, what the forest is to the fox — what the ocean is to the fish. Complain of indistinctness in the first effusion, he increases it in the second: complain of the remedy, he adds to the disease; and so on without end. Will alone is necessary. Stupidity and acuteness are both but too fully competent—both almost equally competent, to the task. A man goes through with it, even without assistance — without that assistance which appropriate learning is so competent and so ready to afford. He goes through with it, even without such assistance; though, with the assistance, he will go through with it (whether with better effect and success, or no) with more fluency, more copiousness, and less shame. The labyrinth increases, and increases without end. Could you find your way through it, distinguish the parts of it, and find names for them, you would be able to point out the *mala fides* lurking in it, and the indications by which it is betrayed. But the difficulty is to find your way through it: for, as to parts, form, or figure, it has none: a chaos, like a point, has no parts.

Turn now to *vivâ voce* examination, and observe how all such clouds — all such labyrinths, vanish before it. The power of interrogation, considered as an instrument of distinctness, has been already mentioned: it resides almost exclusively in the *vivâ voce* mode. After the apposite interrogation, indistinctness in the answers becomes tantamount to irrelevance. Irrelevance is, in that situation, seen to be equivalent to silence. Silence, in the same circumstances, is seen to be equivalent to confession: on the part of a plaintiff or defendant under examination, to confession of want of merits; on the part of an extraneous witness, to mendacity, or that wilful suppression which is equivalent to it; and betrays what it strives to cover up from view.

On the other hand, in the oral mode, *browbeating*, a species of mal-practice to which on the part of the interrogator that mode stands exposed, and from which the epistolary mode is altogether secure, is but too apt to operate as a cause of indistinctness; and in the instance, not of the *malâ fide*, but of the *bonâ fide*, respondent. Clothed in authority derived from the authority, and in symbolic robes analogous to the robes, of the judge, — the hireling advocate, observing in an honest witness a deponent whose testimony promises to be adverse, assumes terrific tones and deportment, and, pretending to find dishonesty on the part of the witness, strives to give his testimony the appearance of it: suppressing thus one part of what he would have had to say, and rendering what he does say, — in part, through indistinctness, unconceived, or misconceived — in part, through apparent confusion and hesitation, unbelieved.

I say the *bonâ fide* witness: for, in the case of a witness who by an adverse interrogator is really looked upon as dishonest, this is not the proper course, nor is it taken with him. For bringing to light the falsehood of a witness really believed to be mendacious, the more suitable, or rather the only suitable, course, is to forbear to express the suspicion he has inspired. Supposing his tale clear of suspicion, he runs on his course with fluency, till he is entangled in some irretrievable contradiction, at variance either with other parts of his own story, or with facts notorious in themselves, or established by proofs from other sources.

This cause of indistinctness is no inefficient one: but it inheres not, as in the case of epistolary interrogation, in the very essence of the mode. It originates in abuse: and that abuse, howsoever interwoven and intrenched in the general mass of abuse, has been shown in a former chapter not to be in its own nature unsusceptible of correction.

Compare now with each other the four modifications of the oral mode.

On the occasion of the comparative view given of the two modes, the oral and the epistolary, it was from the first-mentioned of the three modifications of the oral mode — interrogation *per partes, publicè, coram judice* — that the conception of those qualities was taken: because it is in that case that the advantages resulting from these qualities are capable of being made to exist in the greatest perfection. If either of the two other modes be substituted, — in that case, in the degree at least in which these qualities should be expected to be found existing, a considerable abatement will require to be made.

Answers *instanter*—questions propounded singly—questions arising out of the answers—and the operation performed under the eye, as well as authority of the judge,—these were mentioned as so many *sub-securities* for correctness and completeness, securities exclusively attached to the oral mode.* To all the several modifications of the oral mode here in question, these several peculiar securities apply, but in all of them with different force: in all of them the faculty of making use of those securities exists, but in no one of the three last can any *zeal* equal to what may be looked for with confidence in the instance of the first, be expected to animate the exercise of it.

When, for instance, the judge is split into two parts—the collecting part and the deciding part,—the collecting part is always of inferior mould to the deciding: the judge, to whom both originally belonged, reserving to himself (as above noticed) the more palatable function, and turning over the labouring oar to the rib detached by himself from his own substance. By the superior, the deciding judge, all the attention which the public eye has to bestow is engrossed: for his subordinate, the collecting judge, whose bench is in a dark closet, no part of it is reserved. The public not thinking about *him*, *he* thinks as little about the public: the public not thinking anything about him, his official superior thinks about him as little: the underling does accordingly as he pleases. By bringing Truth out of her well, he has no more to get, in any shape, than by leaving her there; by attempting to draw her out, he would lose labour: he lets her lie where she is. If he is paid by salary—paid thus for his whole time—he makes *short* work, the shortest that he can with safety: if, being paid by fees, he is paid in proportion to the time, he makes *long* work—as long as he can contrive to make it.

1. When it is by the judge *ad hoc*, by this subordinate functionary, that the testimony is collected, the mode employed is in effect neither oral altogether, nor epistolary altogether, but something between both: another reason why the sub-securities promised by the oral are not employed in equal force nor in equal degree by this degenerate mode. The promptitude with which the answers are made to follow upon the questions in the dark closet, may or may not be equal to that with which they come out in the open judicatory. The questions may be, and probably (forasmuch as they ought to be) generally are, administered singly; but it is only in a very uncertain and intermitting stream that the questions can be made to issue out of the answers. To constitute the necessary fund of information and direction to this essentially careless judge, a string of interrogatories is always drawn up and prepared by the professional agents of the parties. But within the path marked out by this string, the operations of the judge are confined: so that if from the respondent on any occasion an answer happens to come out which has not been foreseen by the party (that is, not by the party, but by his professional draughtsman, who himself never has any personal communication with the party,) and which, not having been foreseen by the party or the draughtsman, cannot have had a correspondent interrogatory deduced from it by the draughtsman; the benefit deducible in that shape from the oral mode, is, by this contrivance for making business and breeding lawyers' profit, lost.

Thus it is, that, in the factitious gloom of this dark closet, mendacity finds naturally a safe hiding-place. In daylight, there is a known and efficient process for dragging it out: but the operation is not compatible with a string of pre-determined interrogatories. That they may not be capable of being provided against by the mendacious respondent, these interrogatories must always be, in the obvious sense, *irrelevant:* relevant to the general purpose of proving mendacity, by self-contradiction or opposition to known truths; irrelevant, with relation to the particular fact in question. Defendant Susanna committed adultery with a man in that garden, said the two mendacious Elders. Under what tree? said defendant's counsel, Daniel. Being examined apart,—Under a mastic tree, answered the one: Under a holme tree, answered the other. Under what tree it was committed, or whether under any, supposing it was committed, was nothing to the purpose: nor, had a string of interrogatories been to be drawn up by Susanna's counsel, was it much to be expected that by the draughtsman the circumstance of the tree should have been thought of, nor consequently that anything should have been said about it in the interrogatories. Had even the first answer been foreseen, and an apposite interrogatory grounded on it, the foresight would hardly have extended so far as the second; if the second, still less likely so far as a third; and so on.

Paid, whether by salary or by fees, a judge, not nominated and employed by either party, would certainly not—and even though nominated and employed by a party, probably not—hold himself warranted in going out of his string to act the part of Daniel, as above mentioned.

2. Let a judge, or a couple of judges, be named for the business on each side—named of course in that case, and paid by the parties. Paid by salary they cannot be: if paid by

* *Supra*, Chap. I.

fees, paid by the piece they cannot easily be, because it is not easy to foresee what quantity of time will be necessary. Paid by the day, time enough will be taken for the business: but as to the employment given to the time, *that* will depend upon their own convenience. Being considered as judges, and not as agents for the parties, none of that zeal which is so fluently displayed by avowed agents will be displayed: but in the construction put by them on those rules of impartial justice, for which the regard will on both sides be equal and inexorable, it will be convenient for them to run into disagreements; and, being in station as well as in number equal,—equals all, and without a superior,—the length of the disagreement will naturally, and without any kind of contest, adjust itself, with more or less correctness, to the estimated depth of the plaintiff's or defendant's purse.

With a tribunal thus composed, publicity is not absolutely incompatible: publicity, that is, so far as consists in the liberty to strangers of being present if they please. But,—in the case of a judicatory so composed, and especially of a set of judges thus by a tacit engagement pledged to one another that on each day as little shall be done as possible; that the affluence of strangers should be considerable, even in a case of the first importance and of the most attractive complexion, is very far from probable.

Collection by judges named on both sides by the parties, is a sort of middle course between the natural mode of collection, and the pure Roman mode, as performed in his dark closet by an underling of the deciding judge. Taking for its ground the pure Roman mode, it may be considered as a sort of amendment of that mode,—a palliation of the disorder of which it is composed.

Uniting to the character of the judge that of the advocate; attention to the interests of their respective employers, though subordinate to the study of collecting plunder on both sides by made business, will not on the part of these nominees of the parties be so completely deficient, as on the part of the nominee of the deciding judge.

The effect, therefore, of the amendment, is to render the procedure somewhat more subservient to the direct ends of justice, though at the expense of the collateral ends of justice. On the part of the aggregate mass of evidence, the chance of correctness and completeness is somewhat increased; but the mass of collateral inconvenience, in the shape of delay, vexation, and expense, is still more certainly increased.

The advantageousness of it increases therefore in the joint ratio of the importance of the cause and the opulence of the parties. But as the individuals who are altogether unable to support the increase of expense are more numerous than those who are capable of supporting it, the mischief seems upon the whole to be preponderant over the advantage.

3. Collection, when performed by the judge alone, but in public, is, though in appearance widely, in effect not very considerably, different (at least in the instances in which it is in use) from interrogation also in public by the parties or their agents, under the eye as well as authority of the judge.

Of this mode, a well-known exemplification may be seen in the preliminary examinations taken under the English system in the most frequently exemplified species of criminal offences, by single justices of the peace.

In appearance, the function of the judge goes not in these cases beyond that of the evidence-collecting-judge, as above described: but in effect that of the deciding judge is united to it. On the decision of the magistrate it depends, on these occasions, whether the proposed respondent shall or shall not be committed to prison;—shall or shall not be subjected to eventual forthcomingness and ulterior justiciability by being held to bail.

Moreover, to the functions, character, and name of judge, the magistrate unites in effect, though not in name, the functions of advocate for one of the parties concerned; viz. the public: and acting at the same time (in the metropolis at least) under the discipline of the public eye, the care which he takes naturally of the interests of the public will in general not be very decidedly inferior (so far as it is conducive to the ends of justice that it should be equal) to the care which is taken by the advocate of the interests of his client.

They are, it is true, in the habit of betraying the interests of their client the public, and counteracting the direct ends of justice, by the warning which it is customary for them to give to the defendant, not to say anything that shall be capable of operating to his prejudice; thereby authorizing and encouraging him to keep his testimony incomplete, depriving justice of the best and safest species of evidence it can have.

But, of the acts of immorality committed in this shape, the cause is to be found in the example set by, and even coercion apprehended from, their learned superiors, and the vulgar errors and prejudices that have in that example found their source. Nor, on this occasion, is the force of example so uniformly prevalent, as not to be occasionally surmounted by the united powers of common honesty and common sense. But of this more at large, in the Book which has for its subject the system of exclusionary rules, by the force of which, to so prodigious an extent, the light of truth has been shut out from the theatre of law, and the door opened to triumphant wickedness and injustice.

CHAPTER IX.

EPISTOLARY MODE OF INTERROGATION, IN WHAT CASES APPLICABLE.

§ 1. *Reasons for employing the epistolary mode of interrogation in certain cases.*

THAT the oral mode may be applied without the epistolary, and this (unless in particular cases) without any prejudice to correctness or completeness, is manifest enough.

The epistolary mode,—shall it in any case, and what cases, be employed without the oral, in such sort, as that, for the formation of a decision, testimony thus extracted shall of itself be capable of being taken for a sufficient ground?

One objection presents itself *in limine*. This mode of receiving evidence, being in so high a degree and in so many points inferior to the *vivâ voce* mode, ought not to be employed instead of it, but for special reasons.

These reasons will be found reducible to two heads:—1. Impracticability; 2. Preponderant collateral inconvenience: meaning by collateral inconvenience, here as elsewhere, the aggregate of delay, vexation, and expense.

Impracticability—absolute physical impracticability, will of course be admitted as a reason, without further discussion, supposing the existence of a case in which it takes place: but this is a supposition that will seldom, if at all, be verified. A case that at first sight might be apt to present itself as belonging to this head, would, on examination, be probably found to amount to no more than a high and manifestly preponderant mass of collateral inconvenience. The matter in dispute is the value of a day's labour; and, to give the cause the benefit of *vivâ voce* examination instead of written examination, it would be necessary to fetch a man from the antipodes. This, in common parlance, might well pass for a case of *impracticability;* whereas, in strictness, supposing the full power of government seriously employed in the overcoming of the difficulty, the objection amounts to no more than the indication of a manifestly preponderant mass of delay, vexation, and expense.

One case, however, of utter impracticability, may at any rate be found; and it is this: —The residence of the defendant is in a foreign country—a country which, by the nature of its system of procedure, is disabled from affording the necessary power; or by possibility is, on the particular occasion in question, induced to refuse it. Powers for causing the defendant to be examined *vivâ voce* by the judge of the court within the jurisdiction of which he has his residence, do not exist, or are suspended. In this case, the *vivâ voce* mode being precluded, the receipt or extraction of his testimony must, if at all, be performed in the way of written correspondence. The former may be impracticable, and at the same time the latter practicable without difficulty.* Though, with relation to the court *in quâ*, the defendant be not only absent, but absent with a full determination of never being present,—means of effective jurisdiction may be possessed by it in abundance:' an estate in land, a valuable office exercised by deputy, debts due to him and capable of being sequestered, may serve for examples. A paper containing the interrogatories is dispatched to the defendant, at his foreign residence. The plaintiff has at that same place a correspondent, to whom it goes in the first instance, by the common conveyance (say the letter post;) and the correspondent, having himself delivered it to the defendant in person, or left it at his house, writes to this effect to the court; the plaintiff deposing to the authenticity of the letter, and to his persuasion of the truth of its contents, and being in other respects responsible for the truth of it. Silence on the part of the defendant so *served* (as the phrase is) with notice, would in this case form as reasonable a ground for decision in favour of the plaintiff (at least for a provisional one,) as if the place of delivery had been within the jurisdiction of the Court.

Prudential impracticability is another word for preponderant inconvenience.

The case of sickness excepted, and (in very particular cases) the inconvenience that might result from disturbing public functionaries of different classes in the exercise of their respective functions,—the only remaining cause of inconvenience consists in mutual distance of abode. Supposing all persons whose simultaneous presence is requisite at the seat of judicature,—supposing parties and witnesses, all of them,—to have, for the time in question, their abodes within a short distance of the seat of judicature; then, and in that case, no inconvenience results from the proposed ordinary mode of testification, viz. deposition *vivâ voce*. Suppose the abode of any one of them distant by a certain space from that of the rest, then comes the inconvenience. If,—the abodes of the plaintiff and the defendant being at any given distance from one another, and the defendant's abode being within the *convenient* distance of the seat of judicature, —the plaintiff, having occasion to examine the defendant, is willing (for the benefit of performing the examination in the best and most trustworthy mode) to bear the trouble and expense of conveying himself for that purpose,—the defendant can have no reasonable cause of objection; and so far all inconvenience and all difficulty are removed. But if he is not willing so to do, or if parties and witnesses are dispersed, according to any one of a great variety of changes that might be rung upon the possible modes of dispersion,—then comes the inconvenience; and then the option between the inconvenience produced, according to the nature of the cause, by the less trustworthy mode of examination and deposition, on the one hand; and the inconvenience consisting of the delay, expense, and other vexation, resulting from the requisite modes of *exprovinciation* or *expatriation* necessary to complete the judicial meeting, on the other. All these several points would require to be settled by apposite provisions of law, grounded on the consideration of the importance of the respective classes of causes, modified by the local and other idiosyncratic circumstances of each political state. But the adjustment of these points belongs neither to the present book nor to the present work, but to the subject of procedure.*

Of this less trustworthy mode of examination and deposition, the only use (it is to be observed) is, to save the personal inconvenience, which, in case of dispersion of abode (as above explained,) is liable to attach upon the more trustworthy mode. In proportion as the mass of the examination is more complicated, the inconvenience attaching (as above) upon the less trustworthy mode increases: and as the precise degree of complication may not always be to be determined beforehand, it may sometimes happen that, in the instance of a cause commenced (and that with propriety) in the way of written correspondence, it may at last be necessary to have recourse to examination or deposition *vivâ voce*. If the complication appear to have for its cause the misconduct of any one of the correspondents (viz. either in the way of criminal consciousness or temerity;) in such case, the obligation of being subjected after all to *deplacement*, for the purpose of *vivâ voce* examination or deposition at a tribunal convenient to some other party or witness, and inconvenient to himself, will operate in the character of a punishment, and the apprehension of it in the character of a preventive.

In the way of legislative provision, the adjustment of these details, in subordination to a sort of compound end, compounded of the direct and collateral ends of judicial procedure, will be matter of considerable nicety: — it will require considerable detail in any country, and considerable variation according to the different circumstances of different countries. In the existing systems, this part of the business of judicature presents, in comparison, little difficulty: why? because the ends of justice are little regarded; the course of procedure having been originally chalked out in some barbarous age, and governed by principles extraneous to the ends of justice. Untied in no case, the knot is cut, sometimes in one way, sometimes in another. In one place, or in one sort of cause, examination and deposition by written correspondence is unknown, and the *vivâ voce* mode is exclusively practised, at whatever inconvenience; in another place, or in another sort of cause, the converse takes place: very frequently, where distance and dispersion are considerable, the party in the right is left altogether without redress, the main ends of justice being sacrificed altogether, without necessity and yet without regret, to the collateral ends.

Nowhere has the established system of procedure been grounded on any distinct and comprehensive view of the mutually conflicting and difficultly-reconcilable ends of justice: everywhere have the foundations of it been laid at a period antecedent to the establishment of transmarine colonies and other distant dependencies: everywhere at a period prior to the institution, or at least to the present improved state, of the public establishments for the facilitation of written correspondence.

No case so complicated, but that provision must be made for it. By neglect, the mischief of unavoidable complication will not be lessened, much less removed, but aggravated. Happily, the cases of greatest complication, though generically they make the greatest figure, are individually much the least frequently exemplified. †

* Viz. under some such title as that of *forthcomingness*, *i. e.* the means of providing for the forthcomingness of individuals, in the respective characters of parties and witnesses — extraneous witnesses. [See *Principles of Procedure*, Chap. XVIII. § 4. "Procedure *inter distantes*," Vol. II. p. 99.]

† The mode of receipt and extraction by written correspondence would hardly have suggested itself to a person whose views were bounded by the line that circumscribes the range of the Roman mode of procedure: it would hardly have suggested itself to a mind unacquainted with English practice.

Under the Roman system, such as it is, the even, and in general not altogether scanty, distribution of judicial tribunals (such as they are,) secures, on condition of their consent and co-operation, the faculty of performing the examination of any individual by the mouth of the judge, without the necessity of the party's moving himself to any such distance from his abode as would be productive of very material inconvenience. In general, it will be rather a rare case if there be a dwelling situated at such a distance from the nearest court, that a man might not convey himself thither, undergo his examination, and return home, within the compass of the same day.

Britain is the country in which, if not to the exclusion of every other, at least more readily than in most others, the idea of performing the business of examination in this recently-invented (though less trustworthy) mode, would naturally present itself, and accordingly has actually been exemplified. In Britain, the three metropolises of the three compound kingdoms are, each of them in its kingdom, to many purposes, the only seats of judicature. Of local jurisdictions, but more particularly in England, a deficiency presents itself to a degree in any other country altogether without an example: the superior me-

§ 2. *The cases particularized.*

The proposed deponent being in circumstances in which preliminary interrogation *vivâ voce* (understand *coram judice*) is physically or prudentially impracticable, — shall deposition *ex scripto*, accompanied by interrogation in the same form, be admitted in the first instance?

Case I. Proposed respondent, the defendant.

Place the proposed deponent in the station of a party; and in the first instance in that of defendant.*

The option may here without danger be given to the plaintiff. Suppose the plaintiff in *bona fides*, the advantage of a personal discussion with the defendant, in the presence of the judge, is too palpable to be foregone. But, by the supposition, this advantage is not obtainable: the residence of the defendant is under the dominion of a foreign government, and where no such conference is to be had. In such case, the option of the plaintiff lies between justice on those comparatively disadvantageous terms, or no justice at all. Between this extraordinary mode, and the ordinary mode by confrontation *coram judice*, the difference is altogether to the advantage of the defendant.

In this case, two obvious duties present themselves to the judge; at least, on the supposition that the residence of the plaintiff is within the geographical limits of his jurisdiction.

The plaintiff making his appearance in court, the judge receives his spontaneous testimony, interposing such questions as appear requisite for the correction and completion of it.

If, on this occasion, the assistance of a professional advocate† be admitted, in this case the testimony may as well be previously digested in the form of a ready-written deposition, annexed to the instrument of demand, of which it presents the grounds. But in this case, as in the other, the personal appearance of the plaintiff, and his personal interrogation by the judge, are securities not to be dispensed with.

2. If the judge, on hearing the case thus stated on one side, thinks fit to subject the proposed defendant to the obligation of standing in that character, and putting in an answer in consequence, — then comes the drawing up the tenor of the instrument of interrogation. If there be no advocate, this will be work for the judge, and may be performed on the spot: if there be an advocate, it will be work for the advocate. But at any rate, carrying with it the authority of the judge, it must have the *fiat* of the judge; and for the same reason, his should be the person in which it speaks.

Another option that in this case may be left to the discretion of the plaintiff, is, — where the case happens to afford extraneous testimony on his side, — whether to collect it or no: and, when collected, whether to communicate it or no to the defendant, in such manner as that it may reach his cognizance before his answer to the instrument of interrogation has passed out of his hands. If any part of such extraneous testimony runs coun-

tropolitan tribunals having, by circumstances foreign to the present purpose, been enabled nearly to swallow up the authority of the inferior provincial ones.

* Of this nature is the mode of procedure, as far as it goes, in the English equity court. The first instrument that makes its appearance is called a bill. In this bill (in the first part of it, called the charging part) the plaintiff, without oath, delivers his testimony; to which, it being without oath, no credence is given by the judge. The second part, called the interrogative part, is the instrument he is allowed to employ for the extraction of the defendant's testimony: which, being delivered upon oath, is considered as having, with certain limitations, the force of testimony. Such is the mode of procedure, even if the plaintiff and defendant live in the same house; or if, being attorneys practising in that same court, they meet one another in court every day in the presence of the judge: — but such, it is evident, and with somewhat better reason, might be the practice, if, one or both residing out of the jurisdiction of the court, the relative situation of the parties were at the antipodes.

No man was ever absurd enough to imagine that interrogation, with three months time to prepare (with the assistance of professional accomplices) a lying or evasive answer, — that this mode of collection by itself was of a nature to afford a better security for the extraction of the truth, and the whole truth, from the bosom of a deponent urged by interest to keep it back, than examination *vivâ voce*, with subsequent allowance of time for recollection in case of need (and not otherwise.)

But, by interrogation *vivâ voce*, that is, by the extraction of the truth, and the whole truth, with the least quantity posssible of delay, vexation and expense, no other end would have been answered than the ends of justice. The only ends that have ever really been arrived at in the development of this or any other branch of technical judicature, the extorting money from suitors on pretence of administering justice, would have been relinquished by it.

† Few cases present themselves as more proper than this, for imposing on the party the obligation of recurring to the assistance of a professional advocate.

An indispensable exception is, indigence on the part of the plaintiff — indigence, and consequent inability to engage the assistance of an advocate: but if there be a professional advocate employed by government for managing the causes of indigent plaintiffs (an arrangement which seems to require a correspondent officer for the assistance of indigent defendants,) this function will fall with more propriety to their shares respectively, than to that of the judge. Paper (on this as on all other occasions,) appropriate promulgation paper, as of course. — *See the next Book.* [See Vol. IV. p. 384, *et seq.*]

ter to the testimony contained in his instrument of response, it may perhaps be necessary that he should receive communication of it, and have an opportunity of replying to it, and making observations on it, before a decision is pronounced to his prejudice. But as to the seeing any extraneous evidence, before his own is delivered in the first instance, — this (as already explained) is a sort of information, which to a mendaciously-disposed witness may be eminently subservient, but which to a veracious witness can scarcely be of use.

Another point to be left to the discretion of the judge, may be, whether, on the ground of the plaintiff's testimony thus scrutinized, (supported or unsupported by extraneous evidence,) provisional arrangements shall or shall not be taken for securing the forthcomingness of the subject-matter in dispute, and preserving it against irreparable damage: the whole, on condition of the plaintiff's giving adequate security for eventual *restitutio ad integrum*.

Case II. Proposed respondent, the plaintiff.

Let us now suppose the respondent to be the plaintiff in the cause: he having obtained the judge's *fiat* for the interrogation of the defendant, as above.

In this state of things, the plaintiff stands upon ground very different from that of the defendant. Against the defendant, the disadvantageous mode of proceeding, the interrogation *ex scripto*, has been embraced by the plaintiff — embraced by him under the pressure of necessity, the defendant being out of the way of being reached by any other mode. But the plaintiff himself (by the supposition) the person of the plaintiff himself, is within the reach of the judge — of the very judge by whose authority, at the instance of him the plaintiff, and on the ground of his *vivâ voce* deposition, the instrument of interrogation was just addressed to the defendant. Without sufficient assurance of his eventual forthcomingness for the purpose of justiciability (*vivâ voce* interrogability included,) the *fiat* of the judge will not have been given. Two modes of interrogation accordingly present themselves for the option of the defendant: 1. Interrogation *ex scripto*, interrogation in the same mode in which he himself has been interrogated; 2. Interrogation *vivâ voce*, by the mouth of an agent, non-professional or professional, appointed by him for that purpose.

That he should embrace the makeshift mode, when the ordinary and more advantageous mode is open to him, will be seen not to be in the natural and ordinary course of things: the rather, when it is considered, that, even after the *vivâ voce* interrogation, the scriptural mode (if in the judgment of his proxy the delay given by it should appear necessary to the purpose of allowing the plaintiff respondent any such time as may be necessary for recollection), will still be open to him.

Case III. Proposed respondent, an extraneous witness.

In the case of an extraneous witness, the propriety of admitting this mode of interrogation stands upon very different grounds.

Suppose, indeed, *bona fides*, and absolute impartiality — this mode will (in this as in other cases) be not merely equal, but preferable, to the *vivâ voce* mode: but (except in the case of official evidence*) to ground arrangements upon any such presumption would be sufficient to lay all rights whatsoever at the mercy of dishonest plaintiffs or defendants supported by mendacious witnesses. A security which is good only against *bona fides*, is good only in the case in which it is least wanted, — which affords the least demand for it.

Witnesses being at every man's choice, so it be their choice to appear in that character, — and witnesses who, in the case of mendacity, have by the supposition nothing to fear from the power of the judge; a man who should propose to himself a plan of conquest to be carried into effect by the power of the law, would have the whole world to range in, in quest of false witnesses. The only caution necessary in this case would be, not to set a witness to speak in the character of a percipient witness to a transaction, the scene of which lay in a place at which it were notoriously impossible he should have been present at that moment of time.

A merchant in London, with the assistance of two or three correspondents in Paris, ready to depose *ex scripto* in the character of extraneous witnesses, might prove false debts to any amount upon any number of persons in London. A person in Paris, with the assistance of two or three persons in London, might prove false debts to any amount upon any number of persons in Paris.

Perilous as this state of things would be to the interests of truth and justice, — is not a state of things still more perilous (it may be asked) actually exemplified in England, and in every day's practice? On the occasion of the sort of suit called a petition in a matter of bankruptcy, are not debts to any amount proved by a still less trustworthy species of evidence, by ready-written affidavits — by depositions *ex scripto*, altogether exempt from the check of adverse interrogation?

Yes: and had the matter rested upon the wisdom and probity of the unprofessional framers of this branch of jurisprudential law, the mischief would long ago have been felt in its full force; and, on this as on so many other occasions, society, if preserved (as of course it would have been) from perdition,

* See Book IV. *Preappointed*; Chap. VII.

would have been indebted for its preservation to the interposition of the legislature. But, against a danger which (unless for the purpose of giving extension and increase to it) has never been thought of, a barrier has all along been opposed by an arrangement which, in this point of view, seems to have been as little thought of. An affidavit to be made use of in a court in which the Lord Chancellor presides, must have been sworn to, either at an office in the district of the metropolis, or (if out of that district) before some person having a standing commission from the Chancellor for administering oaths on occasions of that description. The only sort of person to whom commissions of this sort are usually granted, is an attorney, whose residence is in some part or other of that part of the united kingdom called England. And thus, and thus only, it happens, that testimony, delivered in so eminently untrustworthy a shape, can seldom issue but from a person ultimately amenable (viz. by a prosecution as for perjury) to English judicature.

But where it happens that, after having on an occasion of this sort sworn to an affidavit, a person disposed by character to lend himself to a scheme of depredation finds soon afterwards occasion to quit the country, — or meets with an employer who makes it worth his while, after rendering a service of this sort, to quit the country on purpose, — the accidental barrier above mentioned yields, it is evident, no opposition to the scheme: and the mischief above mentioned as attached to the proposed arrangement, hangs in full force over the existing state of things.

By these observations, it will probably have been made sufficiently apparent, what certain and extensive ruin might be the consequence, if it were made obligatory upon the judge to regulate his decision by testimony thus circumstanced. On the other hand, — when the symptoms of untrustworthiness attached to evidence of this description are once pointed out, and placed in full daylight, there seems not any sufficient reason why, on the mere score of security against deception, a peremptory exclusion should be put, in this case, any more than in any other, upon any information that can bear the name of evidence.

Frequent as mendacity is, it is not yet quite so frequent, let us hope, as truth: and if this proposition be not the reverse of true, how unfavourable to the interests of truth and justice a peremptory exclusion put upon this sort of evidence would be, seems sufficiently manifest.

Instances will not unfrequently present themselves (especially among persons in the mercantile line) in which a person altogether and for ever out of the reach and power of the court may, in the character of an extraneous witness, possess in equal degree the confidence of both parties. An instance still more frequent will be, that, after a witness thus circumstanced has delivered his testimony, the party to whose disadvantage it operates will not only in his own mind give credit to it, — but, when with judicial solemnity called upon to say whether he does or does not, will by general probity of character, or at least by the sentiment of shame, be deterred from answering in the negative.

On this footing stands the danger to the interests of truth, in the case where the side on which the proposed species of evidence is proposed to be adduced, is the plaintiff's side. Placed on the opposite side, the danger, in other respects the same, will be apt to present itself, at least to a first glance, as not rising to equal magnitude. In the character of plaintiff, — give to a person disposed to depredation a full assurance of success, — the number of such predatory enterprises that will of course be engaged in, is plainly infinite. But the number of defendants, it may be added, is limited by the number of plaintiffs: which being the case, the number of defences, of *malâ fide* defences, constructed upon the ground of the species of fraud in question, can never exceed, nor so much as equal, the number of *bonâ fide* demands.

On a more attentive consideration, the *primâ facie* inequality, though perhaps it will not vanish altogether, will, however, lose much of its magnitude. Various and many are the cases in which the station of defendant and that of plaintiff will present themselves as being equally capable of being occupied in the prosecution of a plan of dishonest enterprise looking to mendacity for its support. At one time, the power of the judge will present itself to the adventurer as an instrument *sine quâ non* for putting him in possession of the object of his concupiscence: and then it is, that the side he possesses himself of is the plaintiff's side. At another time, either force or fraud in some other shape will present itself as the more eligible resource: — in this case he will put himself in possession of the object without any help from the judicial power, trusting to his plan of testimonial mendacity for the continuance of the advantage: and then it is, that having so done, he will stand at his ease, ready to act in the station of defendant, should the time arrive.

§ 3. *Should testimony extracted by epistolary interrogation be deemed of itself sufficient to ground a decision?*

In this case, the party against whom it is most natural that the testimony should operate, stands deprived of the use of counter-interrogation applied in its most searching and efficacious mode.

That testimony extracted in this inferior mode should be admitted, even when there is no possibility of its being encountered by testimony extracted in the superior and more searching mode from the same source, is what has already been observed.

If admitted, in circumstances where, physically or prudentially speaking, the encountering it with testimony extracted from the same source in the more searching mode is not practicable,—shall it be regarded as sufficient to ground a decision on that side, when and although unsupported by testimony extracted in that best mode from any other source?

The proper answer will, in both instances, depend upon the importance of the suit: and of importance the most prominent criterion (though, without ulterior distinction, by no means a determinate one) is the distinction indicated by the words *penal* and *civil*, in the sense in which *civil* is used as synonymous to *non-penal*.

There are some cases in which the possibility of a decision grounded on such evidence, if to the prejudice of the defendant's side, might be productive of such a degree of alarm as it might be found eligible to obviate. Such are—

1. Criminal causes in general, of that class which, the offence not striking against any one individual more than another, would naturally have government itself for its prosecutor, by the instrumentality of some public officer appointed for that purpose. Offences against the authority of the government—offences against justice (and not affecting individuals)—offences against the revenue—may serve as examples.

2. Even in the case of those offences which, though striking in the first instance only against a determinate individual, are (in consideration of the magnitude of the mischief with which they are pregnant) marked out as objects for punishment, in addition to the burthen of satisfaction—the mischief of misdecision, in case of injustice, to the defendant's side, may still appear too formidable to justify the leaving men exposed to suffer punishment on the ground of such untrustworthy evidence.

Even in any the most trifling class of cases, supposing the decision of the judge bound by the evidence (or, though not so bound, supposing him not sufficiently upon his guard,) the mischief that might be done by the testimony of expatriated and unjusticiable witnesses might be boundless.

But (as will be shown in its proper place*) it is contrary to justice, that, by a mass of evidence of any description or to any amount, decision should in any case be forced; and, as to the judge's being upon his guard against weak evidence, it is no more than what he ought to be in every case: and evidence of a complexion beyond comparison weaker than this ever can be, is under every system received without scruple and without inconvenience.†

Of the heap of blind and mischievous exclusionary rules, which in every system of procedure are set in array against justice, one mishief is,—that testimony to such a degree deserving of confidence, that the party against whom it would operate would, through consciousness of its trustworthiness, be ashamed to declare any distrust, is nevertheless, on his application (or even without his application,) by the wayward zeal of the judge, set aside. Such would be the consequence, if the impracticability of subjecting the testimony of the witness to the test of counter-interrogation in the oral mode, were established in the character of a peremptory bar to the reception of it.

§ 4. *Epistolary interrogation should not shut the door upon subsequent examination* vivâ voce.

A person deposing (whether spontaneously or *ex interrogato*) in the way of written correspondence—ought he to remain liable, at the discretion of the judge, to be examined *vivâ voce?*

He ought.—Reason: That, while deposing under this less close scrutiny, his testimony may be the more effectually confined within the pale of truth, by the prospect of being subjected, upon occasion, to the still closer scrutiny.

This prospect may be expected to have upon the mind an effect not much inferior to the thing itself. The inconveniences, the consideration of which gave birth, in the character of a final cause, to the substitution of the less efficient security for truth to the more efficient, are in so far avoided; at the same time that the advantage looked for from the more efficient security, may frequently, in a considerable degree, be obtained.‡

* Book IX. *Exclusion;* Part VI. *Disguised;* Chap. IV. *Conclusive.*

† See Book V. *Circumstantial;* and Book VI. *Makeshift.*

‡ In the British government, in the instance of some of the taxes imposed of late years upon income, this exemplification of the maxim *fortiter in re, suaviter in modo,* has been employed, and apparently with very good effect. A deposition, expressive of the particulars of a man's income, was received from him, according to a prescribed form, in the way of written correspondence, power being at the same time given for examining him on the subject, if thought necessary, *vivâ voce,* in the first instance, upon oath. Under this power the usage has been to perform the examination in the first instance without the administration of the oath; it being

The employing in the first instance the less trustworthy and efficient, but at the same time less dilatory, vexatious, and expensive, mode of scrutiny, is a sort of experiment, the object of which is to save the quantity of inconvenience which, in the shape of delay, vexation, and expense, would, under the circumstances of the case (circumstanced as the persons concerned are, with relation to each other, in respect of local distance,) be inseparable from the employment of the more trustworthy mode. Does the experiment fail? then, unless the more trustworthy mode be employed in *dernier resort*, misdecision, failure of justice, or positive injustice, must be the consequence.

The mischief of the failure of justice, or positive injustice, being given, — the comparative eligibility, as between one mode and another, depends upon the magnitude of the collateral inconvenience. But if, on the occasion of the investigation, an act of mendacity, an act of perjury, comes to have been committed, — here comes a fresh offence, the impunity of which (were the offence to prove successful) would be to be added to the original injustice. A mass of collateral inconvenience, which would not have been worth producing for the sake of rectifying the original injustice, may now be worth incurring, when, in addition to the redressing of the original injustice, comes the benefit to be reaped from the punishment of the incidental crime. Were even the mode of examination by written correspondence out of the question,—to fetch a man from a place at the distance of a month's journey, to decide a dispute relative to the value of a week's labour, would hardly be worth the while. But the account of profit and loss wears a very different face, when, to the rendering of justice in the original dispute, comes to be added the benefit of stripping of its nefarious profit so mischievous a crime as perjury.

The door ought not to be shut against the employment (when needful) of both modes, alternately and repeatedly, in any order.

Reason, as above: As a necessary security against incorrectness or incompleteness, and thence against misdecision, in certain cases.

To the demand which, in some cases, will present itself for the repeated examination of the same person, and even in a certain sense to the same facts, there are no uniform and certain limits.

The demand which, after *vivâ voce* examination, may present itself for ready-written deposition, has already been brought to view. But there is no sort of writing — no sort of written testimony, to which it may not happen to require explanation, and that (as already observed) ultimately by word of mouth: which is as much as to say, by *vivâ voce* examination: and in this case (as well as so many others which frequently occur,) to the sort of alternation and repetition here in question there are evidently no certain limits.

1. The testimony of Primus has been received. Comes Secundus, and gives a testimony which seems difficultly, if at all, reconcilable with that of Primus: for explanation, it seems necessary that Primus be re-examined. By confrontation, the doubt might have been cleared up; the two conflicting testimonies reconciled, or the truth of one of them, and the falsity of the other, established. But, by the supposition, such confrontation, — that is, the appearance of both in the presence of each other and of the judge, — is either physically or prudentially (as yet at least) impracticable.

2. Primus and Secundus have or have not been confronted as above. But, since that time, Tertius, another witness, with or without an article of written evidence or an article of real evidence in his possession, has been discovered. Hence demand for explanation — further demand for examination at the hands of Primus, and perhaps of Secundus.

To the chain of these contingencies there is evidently no determinate assignable end.

Observation. In respect of the possible length of delay, vexation, and expense, the prospect just given may be apt at first sight to appear formidable. But, whatever it be, it is produced by the nature of things; and, whatever it be, it requires to be provided for. It is produced by the nature of things, and not by any particular system of procedure; much less by the natural system, in contradistinction to the technical, — the technical, by which such an enormous load of factitious and unnatural complication has everywhere been produced.

To whomsoever else the view may present itself as formidable, — to the eye of an English lawyer there is nothing in it, which, with anything like consistency, he can find any pretence for being startled at. Twice, three times, four times over, under his system, we shall see the testimony of the same individual received to the same facts; and this not on account of any particular demand that there is for it, any demand presented by the particular nature of the case, but because (with-

understood at the same time, that, should it appear necessary, the oath may be administered at any time. Under these circumstances, the apprehension of the oath (there seems reason to believe) may in general have exercised an influence not materially inferior in effect to the oath itself. For, in case of previous mendacity or evasion, no sooner would the oath have been administered, than, upon a repetition of the examination with the assistance of that sanction, the delinquent would be reduced to the alternative of risking the future consequences of perjury, or exposing himself to immediate shame.

out regard to the demand) such has been the practice in this or that sort of suits, of which the plaintiff sometimes has not the choice. In one individual instance out of ten, this reiteration may perhaps have its use (viz. as a security against misdecision:) it is accordingly employed in the other nine, in which it is useless, and where delay, vexation, and expense, are the fruit, and the only fruit, of it.

§ 5. *Incongruities of English law in regard to the application of epistolary interrogation.*

As to the form of testimony, we have seen that which, wherever practicable, viz. as well prudentially as physically, is the most eligible; viz. the *vivâ voce* form, subject to cross-examination, and fixed by writing as it issues. We have seen at the same time, that, in this form, cases are not wanting in which, either in the physical or the prudential sense, it is not practicable: the impracticability being, in either case, either temporary or definitive, as the case may be. In the case where, in either sense, the obtainment of the best species of testimony is impracticable,—and in such case, whether the bar be but temporary or perpetual,—it is necessary to recur to another, which of course ought to be the next best mode. Lastly, we have seen what is this next best mode; viz. examination in writing, or delivery in writing subject to examination in writing, in the way of written correspondence.

Another thing that either has been observed already, or (if not) will naturally be assented to as soon as mentioned, is, that in the just-mentioned scale of eligibility no variation can be produced by any variation in the relative quality of the examinee—by any relation it can have happened to him to bear to the cause; whether, for example, that of an extraneous witness, or that of a party (whether plaintiff or defendant) in the suit. Setting aside the associations produced by habit—the prejudices which never fail to grow out of existing institutions,—what could appear more capricious or absurd than to say, In the case where the deponent is a party, the examination (if any) shall be performed in the way of written correspondence; and this although he be close at hand, ready to be examined *vivâ voce*;—in the case where the examinee is an extraneous witness, he shall never be examined in the way of written correspondence. If provision has been made by law for the examining him in the *vivâ voce* way, so be it; if not, he never shall be examined at all!

This absurdity—this inconsistency—this source of palpable injustice, is on the list of those absurdities, inconsistencies, and sources of injustice, which never cease to be contemplated with such imperturbable complacency by English judges.

In common-law procedure, in cases not penal, no party (on which side soever of the cause he stands) can depose or be examined in either mode. In equity procedure, the plaintiff cannot, in either mode: the defendant may be, and indeed cannot but be, in one mode; but it cannot be any other than the ready-written mode. To perform such examination is the function of the bill, as it is called—the instrument with which the suit commences.

You have agreed with Fundarius for a piece of land, which he was to sell or let to you; but it was with an agent of his, and not the principal, that the business was all along transacted: except from the report made to him by his agent, the principal knows nothing of the matter. What says equity to this?—English equity? The principal, who knows nothing about the matter,—him it forces you to examine in the first instance; the agent, who knows everything,—him, in the first instance, it does not suffer you to examine.

Not that, in the case of an extraneous witness, deposition in the ready-written form is uniformly prohibited. On the contrary, it is in most abundant use. In use—but upon what terms? Upon these terms, viz. that the test and security of cross-examination be not applied to it. So this check to incompleteness, incorrectness, temerity, and mendacity, be but out of the way, judges (English judges) are never tired of hearing it: among pecuniary causes, those of the highest importance are every day decided upon this unscrutinized evidence and no other.

Let it not be thought that, in the reception given to this species of evidence, prudential impracticability—inconvenience to any amount in the shape of delay, vexation, and expense—has had any the smallest influence. The witness may be actually in court under their eye; if it be a case for affidavit work, they are better taught than to hear him open his lips upon the subject, much more so than to put a question to him, or suffer a question to be put to him by anybody else. Practice forbids it—forbids it in those regions where reason is a pigmy, practice a Colossus. Be the man who he may, be he where he may, the examining him cannot (it is evident,) unless by factitious institution, be clogged by any greater mass of expense, vexation, and delay, in the case of his being an extraneous witness, than in the case of his being a party to the cause.

The inferior, the less trustworthy, mode, is admitted; but on condition that nothing be done by which its untrustworthiness may be mitigated:—admitted, and that to the exclusion of the mode universally acknowledged to be the most trustworthy; and in cases where the excess of expense, vexation, and delay, is on the side of the least trustworthy mode.*

For illustration's sake, apply to *vivâ voce* deposition this exemption from adverse scrutiny, and observe the consequences. In the sunshine of a trial by jury, or in the darkness of an examiner's office, suppose an extraneous witness produced to tell his story, and telling it accordingly—no man living being allowed to put a single question to him—neither the examining clerk at the office, the invoking party, the adverse party, nor the judge at the trial;—the absurdity being without a precedent, or nearly so, in English law, the imagination of an English lawyer starts at it.—Instead of being delivered *vivâ voce,* let a testimony from the same person and to the same effect be delivered ready-written, *i. e.* in the form of an affidavit; the case is now reversed. The imagination of the sage is now no less grievously shocked by the idea of putting any such questions, than before it was by the idea of not putting them. By precedent, reason is turned into absurdity, absurdity into reason—vice into virtue, virtue into vice.

CHAPTER X.

EPISTOLARY MODE OF INTERROGATION, HOW TO APPLY IT TO THE BEST ADVANTAGE.

§ 1. *Rules to be observed, what?*

As between the oral, or say colloquial, mode of interrogation, and the epistolary,—the epistolary, being unsusceptible of some of the securities with which (under the name of *sub-securities*) the oral mode has been seen to be provided,† is not the most eligible. But (as hath been seen) there are cases in which the oral alone is not sufficient; others, in which it is not capable of being applied.

The epistolary mode being therefore a mode of extraction not to be dispensed with,—remains the problem, how to apply it to the best advantage.

To apply it to the best advantage, is to apply the best remedies which the nature of the case admits of, to the disorders to which both modes are exposed, but the epistolary in a manner peculiar to itself.

The remedies are these—

1. Let not the deponent speak otherwise than in the first person,—*I did* or *saw* so and so; exactly as when interrogated in the colloquial mode: not in the third person,—*defendant* did or saw so and so; as, under the technical system, has become the general practice. *Deposition never but in the first person.*

2. Let both discourses, that of the interrogator, and that of the proposed respondent, stand divided into parts, *uncompounded,* short, and numbered: the interrogatories, that the responses may be thus short and manageable; and the responses, even in cases where, the statement or narrative drawn forth by a single interrogatory being long and complex, the interrogatory admits not of any correspondent comminution. *In the instruments on all sides, the paragraphs short and numbered.*

§ 2. *First rule—That the deponent speak always in the first person.*

The first of these rules is so obvious, that it would have been unnecessary to make mention of it, but for the frequency of the contrary practice—a practice, the absurdity of which is too flagrant to be covered by anything but *custom;* that veil, by which no absurdity, nor any improbity, is too flagrant to be masked.

To no honest purpose was a man ever made or suffered to speak in the third person, in the way of testification. On his examination before a jury, conceive a witness speaking in the third person, in a manner in which, when a pen is put into his hand, he is forced to speak by lawyers—speaking of himself as if he were *one beside himself,*—what a burst of scorn and laughter among those same lawyers! He would be treated as if he were one beside himself in another sense.

Thus simple is this arrangement: it is purely negative. On this important occasion, adhere to those modes of speech which in common conversation no man ever thinks of swerving from. Abstain from those artificial forms which probably had deceit and depredation for their object, and certainly have never had any other than mischief for their effect.

Read as you would speak, is the fundamental precept in the art of reading: it is the precept of good taste. Write as you would speak, at any rate in the same person as you would speak in,—is a law in the enactment of which good taste concurs with probity.

Prevention of incorrectness and incompleteness, especially when incurred through temerity or suggested by mendacity, is the main advantage: prevention of indistinctness and

* What is scarce worth observing (unless it be for illustration) is, that in cases where examination in the *vivâ voce* mode is impracticable, if there were any reason why examination in the ready-written mode should be admitted in the one case and not in the other, it is rather in the case of an extraneous witness that this less coercive mode should be allowed of,—in the case of a party whose testimony is desired on the other side, that it should not be allowed of. Why? Because, in the case of a party (the defendant,) you are sure of an interest—an interest acting in a sinister direction, and of a strength running in proportion to the whole relative value of the matter in dispute: whereas, in the case of an extraneous witness, it is but by accident that there is any such sinister force to cope with; and though there be, it is not likely to be equal in strength to that, the influence of which the veracity of the defendant stands exposed to.

† *Vide supra,* Chap. I. *Oral Interrogation.*

redundance are ulterior advantages attached to it—advantages of subordinate rank, yet surely not to be despised.

1. Prevention of incorrectness and incompleteness. When a man speaks in his own person, he considers what he says to be his own discourse, and himself to be in the highest degree responsible for it. To a man expressing himself in this form, the idea of responsibility is in the highest degree impressive. When he is made to speak in the third person, — to speak of himself as he would of another person, the idea of responsibility is apt to be in a considerable degree fainter. He scarce knows in what character to consider himself — whether in that of the author, or only of the subject of the discourse. Does he find himself tempted to swerve from the line of truth? Self-deceit conceals from him his own image in the character of the author, bids him consider himself as the subject, and look for the author in the person of the professional scribe by whom he is thus spoken of, and who, in fact, is the author of the words.

2. Prevention of indistinctness—prevention of ambiguity and obscurity, and thence unintelligibility (temporary at least,) in the language; whence ultimately delay, vexation, and expense, perplexity, and frequently incorrectness, on the part of those who have to study the deposition and reply to it. When the author of the discourse is spoken of, not in that his distinctive character, but in that character which is common to him with every other person — to know, on each occasion, which is meant, is matter of perpetually-recurring, although it should be but momentary difficulty.*

3. Prevention of circumlocution and unnecessary voluminousness; whence again delay, as above, with the *etceteras* in its train. One *he* not being of himself distinguishable from other *hes*, an addition such as *this deponent* is a sort of badge which it becomes necessary to pin upon him, as often as he makes his re-appearance upon the stage.

On all legal occasions on which spontaneous deposition in this form is employed (and in established practice there are few instances in which it is employed in any other form,) the transfiguration is of course the work of the man of law. Whatever may have been the object — in point of tendency and effect it may be reckoned as one of the most efficient of the numerous arrangements by which the distinctive points of individual character have been worn down, and the important boundary-line which separates sincerity from insincerity, — veracity from mendacity, rendered more and more obscure. A court of justice is thus converted into a sort of masquerade, to gain admission into which, instead of a domino, the suitor or other witness is obliged to swaddle himself up, not in a fool's coat, but in a sort of knave's coat; or (to use an appellative not many years ago applied in vulgar language to a particular sort of surtout) a *wrap-rascal*—an habiliment manufactured for him, and sold to him at masquerade price by his lawyer.

Nothing can be more commodious than this dress to the wearer, where he happens to be in the wrong, and conscious of being (what it is the tendency of this dress to render him) a knave. At any rate, be the wearer honest or dishonest, nothing can be more convenient than it is for the tailor who has the making of it. Between the one and the other, responsibility, no small portion of it, evaporates, and is lost. The lawyer scrawls through thick and thin, and fears nothing: let the mendacity be ever so great, and though it have been brought under the predicament of perjury, not on him will attach the punishment, or so much as any part of the shame. The suitor, or the partial witness, bribed by his wishes to regard as right that which he feels to be so favourable to his purpose — the respondent, be he a party, be he a hired or partial witness, — signs with convenient obsequiousness whatever is pronounced to be right by one who knows so much better what is right than he does. Though here and there a point may present itself which does not coincide exactly with the rigid line of truth, it may (for aught he sees, or chooses to see, to the contrary) be among those points of form, which in law are so numerous, so sacred, and so inviolable. By lawyers of all classes on an infinity of occasions, and by suitors in all causes, under the compulsion of men of law, I see uttered (says he) in abundance, propositions upon propositions, which are known by everybody to be false. So much falsehood in law, and so much of it by which I am prejudiced — shall all opportunity of compensation be neglected? Shall there be none by which I am to be served? And, after all, if there be falsehood, whose falsehood is it? Not mine: it is not I that speak — I am the person spoken of: it was not I (says he) that penned it—not I, but one who knows so much better than I — the professional guardian of my conscience.

True it is, that a mental apology of this sort will not save a man from the pillory — it will not engage him to set his hand to falsehood, when he understands clearly that there exists sufficient proof of it, and that prosecution will be the consequence. But when he understands as clearly that proof sufficient for conviction is

* The perpetual confusion of persons attached to the practice of writing in the third person on the occasion of epistolary correspondence for the trivial purposes of common life (I say *writing*, for absurdity has not got the length of *speaking* in this mode), is a well-known source of ridiculous embarrassment, distressing enough in English, and still more in French, and most (if not all) other European languages. It seems to have been among the inventions of cold pride, to keep inferiors and intruders at a distance.

wanting, or that (though it exists) prosecution is not to be feared—in a case like this (and how abundant are such cases!) if downright open-eyed mendacity be not the result, how natural and frequent will be a relaxation of that vigilance which is so necessary to weed out from the ready-prepared and scientifically-planted ground every germ of serviceable incorrectness? Thus slippery, on an occasion of this sort, is the position even of the most cultivated mind: how much more so that of a mind taken at random from the ignorant, and undiscerning, and precipitate, and, on such occasions, blindly obsequious multitude?

It is not without an exertion of intelligence, as well as probity, that a simple man can bring himself to contradict a misrepresentation thus put into his mouth: before he attempts it, he has to surmount the awe which self-conscious ignorance cannot but feel at the thought of opposing itself to reputed science. Thus stands the case, while he is hearing or poring over a dark and unaccustomed formulary, to which indeed he is to set his hand (for so the forms require,) but in which he is spoken of as if he were somebody else, by an unknown somebody. But the pronoun *I*—the interesting pronoun *I*, with which so many lively ideas, so many acute sensations, are associated,—the pronoun *I* acts as a spur to attention, and preserves the innocent from dropping into the abyss of falsehood, while slumbering and nodding over the lullaby of his nurse.

As to the man of law, besides that he has nothing to lose by the falsehood, he has much gain by it: he has everything that is to be hoped from the exultation and gratitude of his client, and the reputation of success, and of the ability and science that insured it.

Viewed in the light of incongruity, nothing can be more grossly absurd than this practice. The deponent is the person spoken of: but who is the speaker? Nobody. Instead of the plain truth, you have an absurd and useless (besides being, as shown already, a mischievous) fiction: the man is split into two persons, the one speaking of the other: or, he remaining unsplit, an ideal person is fabricated to speak of the real one. Evidence of prime quality—immediate evidence—is thus converted into evidence of a bad and slippery texture—hearsay evidence: the supposed or percipient witness is the so-styled deponent, but the deposing witness is nobody knows who.

In point of history (not to speak of motives, and other such causes) whence comes this sophistication? Evidently from the man of law. To the production of this effect, even the relative situation of lawyer and client seems of itself sufficient, with or without the aid of sinister policy and reflection on the part of the directing mind. To *vivâ voce* discourse, whether in the way of responsive or spontaneous statement, no man so simple as not to be competent: the talent of writing was a possession so rare (I speak of the times when law was in her cradle) the talent of writing was the object of little less than a monopoly—the talent of writing for law purposes was the object of a complete monopoly—in the hands of the man of law. In this way, the simple and unlearned suitor or witness was altogether unable to give any sort of account of his own thoughts: whatever account (if any) was to be given of them, came necessarily, and (as far as individual words were concerned) really and truly, from a third person; and that third person was the man of law. The unlearned man being incapable of giving in this learned way any account of his own thoughts, his learned guardian took upon himself to give a learned and proper account, to his friends and brethren upon the bench, of the poor client's thoughts. Hence comes the division of functions, or at least of characters and situations: the persons spoken of, the client; the spokesman, the man of law.

Even when the art of writing came to be more generally diffused, this assistance was not without pretence, nor even without use. Left to himself, a deponent—an average deponent—will run wild: the testimony he delivers will be whatsoever it is most pleasant to himself to deliver, so as not to be unsafe: relevancy, if at all an object, will be at best but a secondary one. It will be continually wandering from the mark: his lawyer—a professional lawyer—stands engaged, by a sort of professional responsibility, to keep him to it.

In the oral mode, every excursion of this sort is stopped at the first step. Being productive of so much unprofitable delay—producing vexation to all present, and no increase of profit to the man of law,—the advocate on the same side, no less than the judge, and the advocate on the opposite side, is upon the watch to stop it. The closet, in which the epistolary response is penned, affords no such bars.

Thus natural, and even thus useful, it was and is, that, in the framing a mass of testimony to be delivered in the ready-written mode, a deponent, not being a lawyer, should have a lawyer at his elbow.

But that the discourse so delivered, and with this assistance, should, in form any more than in substance, be the discourse of any person other than of him whose discourse it is said to be, neither was, nor is, nor can ever be, of any use: on the contrary, in the shape of an encouragement to incorrectness and incompleteness, as well in the way of mendacity as of temerity, we have seen of what mischief it is productive.

§ 3. *Disregard shown to the first rule, in English law.*

Comparatively speaking, the ground on which interrogation *ex scripto* has found its exemplification under any branch of the technical system, is extremely narrow.

Under the Roman system, no such arrangement is to be found. Under that system, either interrogation has no place — or, if employed, it is performed *coram judice*, and in the *vivâ voce* mode, and *by* the judge only, as well as in his presence.

It is only under the English system that any example of it can be found; viz. that which is afforded by a bill in equity. In this case, the respondent is always a party; and that on one side only of the cause, the defendant's side: the interrogator likewise is never other than a party, and he on the opposite, the plaintiff's, side of the cause. The defendant, who is punished if he does not answer (punished in the first instance as for contempt of court, and ultimately by loss of the cause,) is not permitted to answer by himself. To entitle himself to the privilege of delivering in an answer, he is forced to take in a partner for the manufacturing of it: in fact, two partners—one of the attorney class, whose name does not appear in the firm — another of the advocate class, whose name does and must appear in it. The iniquity of thus forcing upon a man this burthensome assistance, and the shallowness of the pretences on which this part of the system of extortion has been attempted to be justified, belong not to this place.

What does belong to this place is, that, — if the different orders of leeches thus fastened upon a man were ever so necessary, and ever so much more numerous than they are, — the propriety of the respondent's being suffered and made to speak in his own person (in other words, the propriety of suffering and obliging the proper person to speak in his own person, and not suffering a wrong person, known or unknown, to speak of and for him,) would not be the less, but rather the more, incontestable. Neither reason, nor so much as pretence, can apply to anything more than the stopping him from saying something that ought not to have been said: neither reason nor pretence can assign to the man of law any other function than that of obliteration: whatever is said, whatever is suffered to be said, it is from the non-lawyer surely, not from the lawyer, that it is intended it should come. But, if the testimony delivered by the defendant in the character of deponent is really to be his, and not the lawyer's — the produce of the client's recollecting, not of the lawyer's inventing, — it is surely in the person of the real deponent, not in the person of another man who knows nothing about the matter, that whatever is delivered ought to be expressed.

The part which the suitor has thus been forced to call in a lawyer to take, in the delivery of his (the suitor's) testimony, accounts in a satisfactory manner, in the character of an *historical* cause, for the absurdity which gives to what is (or at least ought to be) immediate evidence, the form of hearsay evidence. But in the character of a *rational* cause, a cause demonstrative of the propriety of the effect (that is, of its conformity to the ends of justice,) it is as incompetent as, under the technical system, the historical cause of the existing arrangement is almost in every instance sure to be.

That the absurdity here reprobated is the work, not of the non-lawyer — of the party or witness, — but of the man of law—that it is amongst the frauds of the technical system, is evident enough. When, on a judicial occasion, a man expresses himself in writing, nowhere is he suffered to express himself in his own words.

Under the Roman system, though a respondent answers *vivâ voce*, and though a discourse pretended to be his is committed to writing and employed in evidence, the discourse thus given for his is never his: in purport, perhaps, sometimes; in tenor, never. The judge, scribe, and deponent, being shut up, without any other person present in the closet of the judge, — the judge puts a question — the deponent speaks in answer; the scribe sets down as the substance of the answer what the judge pleases — the deponent signing it, or entry made of his refusal to sign it.

Under the English system, it is only in the equity courts that interrogation is permitted, and, in these, one of the parties only (viz. the defendant) is allowed to be interrogated; and, being interrogated, it is in this scriptural mode only that he is interrogated — it is in the scriptural mode alone that he is admitted to deliver his responses. To deliver his responses? No: not his (singly, at least,) but responses delivered in partnership — in partnership with an attorney for a non-apparent partner, and an advocate for an apparent as well as real one. The party signs, and the advocate signs: the party or the attorney has the initiative, but the advocate has a negative upon every syllable.

A negative, how and why? Why, because, without the signature of an advocate, the answer will not be received. If he does not give in an answer, he is punished — punished as for a contempt of the judge in the first instance, and ultimately by the loss of his cause. If he were to give in an answer, it would not be received — not received, until, being tinkered by the advocate, it ceases *pro tanto* to be the answer of the client. Well then and properly may he be spoken of, since it is not he that is permitted to speak. The judge, with a sword called the sword of justice in his hand, forces him into the shark's mouth.

To power, pretence is never wanting: and where power is irresistible, no pretence so shallow but it may serve. Left to himself, the non-lawyer, forsooth, might stray into the path of irrelevancy—he might write surplusage. What is certain is, that the man of law writes surplusage. A certain quantity of that commodity is sanctioned by professional custom: the man of law finds himself under a happy impossibility of omitting it. A certain and constant inconvenience is thus produced, on pretence of preventing a possible inconvenience of the same kind. Nor yet without an attorney, is a man, here any more than elsewhere, admitted to defend himself. What is there in the attorney, that should hinder him from being responsible, and of himself sufficiently responsible, for the non-insertion of unaccustomed surplusage? But the attorney has not been the brother in trade, and companion of the judge: the advocate has.

If such tinkering be necessary, or in any degree serviceable, to the interests of truth and justice, why not give *vivâ voce* testimony the benefit of it? Why not, in a trial at common law, station an advocate between the jury and the witness, to receive his testimony and improve it—to make it what it ought to be, and keep back what it is?

One plain proof there is that this ostensible ground is not the real one. Take it all together—take the whole stock furnished by all the courts—the quantity of uninterrogated evidence delivered in this mode, exceeds by far the quantity of interrogated. Even in the courts of equity themselves, the number of affidavits is not inferior to the number of answers: for, though interrogated written evidence is not admitted but on one side (the defendant's side,) uninterrogated evidence is delivered, affidavits are delivered, in indefinite numbers, on both sides. No advocate's name is ever signed to an affidavit. Why is it not? Is there anything in the want of interrogation to render surplusage impossible?

This improvement remains yet to be made: for in this line there has never been any backwardness to make improvements; nor, under the technical system, ever can be.

In Anglican procedure, in the courts called Common-law courts, where the trial is by jury, the testimony is in general delivered in the form of a deposition *vivâ voce* and *ex interrogato: interrogato autem non solum judicis, sed etiam, et præcipue partium.* No official perpetually-remaining minute being in this case taken by any special scribe (for, as to the judge's notes, the treatment given to them is the same which was given to the Sybil's leaves;) it is not known in what person it is, whether the first or the third, that in these recondite documents the defendant is made to speak; in the first or the third, according to the inspiration received by the modern Sybil in each particular instance.

But in a number of instances much greater (I speak of individual instances,) in almost all instances in which the information thus collected is treated as if it were worth preserving, the testimony is delivered in the ready-written form: and in all those instances, the only person in which the deponent is suffered to speak is the third.

Take up an English trial (I speak of trial at common-law:) if the subject be interesting, the very evidence is amusing: it is in the form of ordinary conversation; it is in the dramatic form; it is the drama of real life.

Take up the history of an old French law-suit, the evidence is absolutely unreadable: it is the same dull formulary in every case. Of the witness you see nothing—you see nothing but the lawyer: what you see plainly is, that nothing could have really passed exactly as it is there represented to have passed: what you cannot hope to see, is, how anything really passed. Accordingly, in the *Causes Celébres*, you know nothing of the evidence: all that you see—all that you could bear to see, is the account (faithful or unfaithful) given of it by the advocates, together with the observations which they ground on it.

In a suit in equity, the evidence is collected and worded exactly as under the old French law. The evidence, of course, is equally uninstructive, uninteresting, unreadable. Accordingly, you scarce ever meet with a publication containing at large the evidence taken in a court of equity.

In the English Romano-ecclesiastical courts the evidence is on the same footing. Here, indeed, histories of causes—publications answering to trials at common law—are at least sufficiently abundant. Why? Because the subject is adultery: and on this subject at least, the adage holds good: *Historia quoque modo scripta delectat.*

§ 4. *Second rule—Paragraphs short and numbered.*

The other rule which has been already mentioned as essential to the proper application of the epistolary mode of interrogation, is, that both discourses, that of the interrogator and that of the respondent, be divided into numbered paragraphs: or, more particularly, thus:—

1. Questions uncompounded, short, and numbered.

2. Answers numbered in correspondence with the questions.

3. Replies, if necessary (as in the case of *exceptions* for supposed insufficiency) numbered in correspondence with the answers, and thence with the questions.

4. Ulterior answers, if called for, numbered in correspondence with the exceptions, and

thence with the original answers and the questions.

All these several arrangements, though in themselves distinct and distinguishable, require to be considered at the same time.

Of the answers (articles 2 and 4) original and ulterior, consists the evidence. It is for the sake of securing distinctness to this part of the conversation, that the principle of distinctness, the division and numeration, are required to be given to the questions, and to the exceptions or other observations.

Of these arrangements the object is to give the maximum of simplicity, and thence of facility, to the task of the interrogator: that the point of view under which the testimony is presented to him may be as clear and as distinct as possible: that in this mode the process of interrogation may be as clear as possible from that entanglement, to which (as we have seen) it is scarce in any degree exposed in the *vivâ voce* mode.

Of the above divisions and distinctions, what is the object and practical use? That, with as much certainty and as little trouble as possible, the interrogator may discern whether, of the questions contained in the instrument of interrogation, there be any, and if any, what, to which either no response has been given in return, or such a one as in any (and what) respect is insufficient.

Of the importance of the quality of distinctness — of the proneness of *bona fides* to be let fall by mental imbecility into the opposite evil quality, without intending it — of the natural eagerness with which *mala fides* avail itself of the opportunity of promoting its purpose undetected — of the readiness with which the inconvenience finds its remedy under the *vivâ voce* mode — and of the unhappy facility afforded by the scriptural mode to *mala fides* for swelling out the inconvenience, — enough has already been said. On the present occasion, what remains is, to show by what means the weakness incident to *bona fides* may receive the most effectual support, and the artifices of *mala fides* be most effectually obviated and counteracted.

Divide et impera, is a maxim of no less use when applied to the operations of intellectual power, than to those of physical and political power. The fable of the old man and his sons and the bundle of sticks, should on this occasion never be forgotten: nor yet (how widely different soever the fields of the two images) the emblem of the cuttle-fish — the fish which, to blind and confound its pursuers, deluges with a flood of ink the medium in which it moves. The special pleader and the equity draughtsman might interplead at the Herald's Office for the privilege of taking for an armorial bearing this original manufacturer of troubled waters.

Division, however, is but of little use without nomenclature: without nomenclature, indeed (at least when intellectual objects are in question,) it can hardly be said to be performed. For to what use is division without distinction? And how can distinction be preserved without a name? Divided one moment, the parts of an idea unite again or are dissipated the next: it is by nomenclature, and by nomenclature only, that the division is either rendered permanent for the benefit of the operating mind, or communicable to any other.

In natural history, in botany, the objects themselves — the individual objects, are distinct enough, and, without the aid of names, distinguishable, while present to the material eye: but it is by nomenclature, and nomenclature only, that the attribute of distinctness can be preserved to them any longer, — that any one species (one might almost add individual) can be so much as spoken of. Accordingly, an observation that has every now and then been brought forward by those who have felt themselves disposed to depreciate that amusing study, is, that it consists of little more than a system of nomenclature. True: but what a fund of ingenuity, added to what a fund of knowledge, does it not require, in any branch of science, to bestow upon it a good system of nomenclature? It is because the subject of legislation is as yet in so barbarous a state, that its nomenclature is so too.

Among the logicians, an instrument of universal empire in the regions of intelligence was supposed to have been discovered by the invention of the syllogism. Yet, in truth, what is the exploit achieved by it? The dividing an argument into three parts or members, distinguished from each other by so many names, — names, in the invention of which (of two of them at least) not quite so much felicity has been displayed, as in those for which we are indebted to the genius of Lavoisier and Linnæus.

Characteristic names are names [illegible] [illegible] species, and for ever. Numbers are names, and names adequate to the purpose, for the individual; which, when they have performed their transitory office, may slide into oblivion without damage to mankind: or even for the individual, however permanent, when, for the purpose of human intercourse, no species requires to be moulded on it. Numeration, therefore, is the sort of nomenclature most advantageously applicable to the different parts of which the ready-written testimony of a witness is composed: including the questions, if it is by questions that the testimony is called forth.

When the questions are thus distinguished one from another, so may the answers be; — otherwise, not. Suppose twenty questions duly distinct and numbered: so many questions, so many statements, or groups of statements, in form of answers. Each question having a name (viz. a number) which it may be called by, each answer has a name which it may be called by. The examinee, viewing each question separately, sees whether he has given a sufficient answer to it: so many questions to which he has thus given a sufficient answer, so much of his task is gone through: seeing this, as far as he has thus proceeded, he fears not to see his answers excepted to for insufficiency. The examiner, on his part, when the examination of the examinee comes to be transmitted to him, performs the same review with great facility. With each question he confronts the answer given to that question. To judge whether question 1 has received an answer, and that answer sufficient, he has no more of the examination to look for than the answer to question 1; and so in regard to question 2, and every other article in the list of questions.

Leave the questions unnumbered, what is the consequence? On the occasion of each question, the examiner has the whole of the examination to look over and study, for the purpose of judging whether, upon the whole, an answer sufficient with reference to that one question be to be found in it. The labour is thus twenty times as great as on the plan proposed; and the inlet to incorrectness, mendacity, incompleteness, delay, vexation, and expense, as above, twenty times as wide.

The more complex the interchange of communication is between examiner and examinee (as above,) the more involved will the mode of distinction by numbers be, as above.* But the more involved it is, the more necessary: for, without it, the more complex the above interchange, the thicker the confusion.

A numerical nomenclature of this sort is the only check that can be applied to the studied confusion that will naturally be manufactured by *malâ fide* suitors, and, occasionally at least, by the law-agents of *bonâ fide* as well as *malâ fide* suitors. When the whole examination is one unbroken chaos, and of the length that it is so apt to be, a *malâ fide* examinee makes or endeavours to make his escape, under favour of the confusion, and leaves questions unanswered, or insufficiently answered: an insufficiently attentive or *malâ fide* examiner, or his insufficiently attentive or *malâ fide* agent, overlooks, or pretends to overlook, answers; imputes or pretends to impute insufficiency to answers really sufficient; and takes exceptions accordingly. But as, in the proposed rule, the subject of attention is in each case drawn to a point, censure may the more readily attach upon insufficiency on the one hand, and groundless exception on the other; and so, by the fear of censure and of shame, abuse will be the more frequently prevented.

In case of obscurity, for want of employing the prescribed means of distinctness, the culpable party should be liable to the burthen of satisfaction: — Reason 1. To prevent misdecision. 2. To prevent, or make satisfaction for, expense, vexation, and delay.

Were it not for a provision of this sort, the consequence might be, that, by confusion, produced through carelessness, or even by design, considerable inconvenience in the above shapes might frequently be produced. A *malâ fide* suitor, or an extraneous witness under the guidance of a *malâ fide* suitor, might, by studied and persevering confusion, delay justice, and heap upon the head of the injured party expense and vexation without end.

Under the existing technical systems of procedure, the costs, mostly factitious, are so high, that, when properly applied, they operate in this way with still greater force than could have been wished. But, if the factitious part were removed, the burthen of bearing the remainder might frequently not be sufficient to restrain a *malâ fide* suitor from purposely producing those delays and vexations that might so easily be produced by those means. In certain cases, therefore, a suitor transgressing in this way ought to be subjected to an ulterior burthen in the shape of punishment. Otherwise he might be without a motive operating so as to restrain him from producing, to the injury of himself and others, the delay and vexation producible from this source. Where there is no assignable individual by whom any injury can be said to have been sustained, as in the case of a prosecution for an offence purely public, there is no party to whom satisfaction can be rendered, unless in so far as the nature of the offence may be to subject the public to a pecuniary loss. In such case (the case not admitting of satisfaction) if no burthen could be imposed under the name of punishment, the party under temptation might be frequently without a motive tending to restrain him from the offence.

It will generally be proper to subject a man, in such a case, to *vivâ voce* examination. Reason: Because, as already observed, *vivâ voce* examination is a sovereign remedy, and in some cases may be the only effectual remedy, against all such confusion as (by design, or through imbecility) is likely to take place in ready-written statements framed by designing or illiterate persons.

§ 5. *Disregard shown to the second rule in English law.*

In English law, it is to the practice of the courts called courts of equity, that we must

* Response 1, 2, or 3, to interrogatory 1, 2, or 3. Again, exception 1, 2, or 3 (exception, in English equity practice, means re-interrogation,) exception 1, 2, or 3, to response 1, 2, or 3, to interrogatory 1, 2, or 3.

look for the only exemplification of the scriptural mode of interrogation, as above described.

In those courts, the business of interrogation is conducted upon two completely different plans.

1. In the initial instrument called the bill, — to a string of allegations not upon oath, nor expected to be true, succeeds a string of questions. The whole string constitutes one unbroken undivided chaos: not being broken down into paragraphs, it has, like a mathematical point, or an English statute, no parts: it has nothing to which numbers can be applied.

In spite of the cloud-compelling power of the draughtsman, a sort of natural principle of division will show itself. The force of the common interrogative proposition, "my will is, that you declare so and so," being combined with different particles, as *when*, *where*, *who*, *what*, *how long*, and so forth, — as often as one of these particles is changed for another, a fresh and distinguishable question is brought to view. In spite of all the powers of darkness, this circumstance is sufficient to diffuse over the interrogative part a glimmering of light, such as cannot ever be discernible in the assertive part.

In reply to this instrument called the bill, comes from the defendant's side of the cause an instrument called the answer.

The questions being squeezed together in one undivided mass, so of course are the responses of which the answer is composed.

The sort of person to whom, in the character of respondent, this mode of interrogation is applied, is the defendant, and the defendant only: not the plaintiff, he not being subject to interrogation in any mode: not any extraneous witnesses, they not being interrogated but in a different mode, which will come next to be described. The interrogator is the plaintiff, or rather the plaintiff's advocate. For, lest the utterance of the falsehoods without which the judge would not give any effect to the bill, should experience any impediment from the probity of the unlearned client, he is neither called upon, nor permitted, to authenticate it by his signature.

2. When an extraneous witness is the sort of person whose testimony is to be collected, he is interrogated indeed, but upon a plan altogether different. It is in the Roman mode that the respondent is now interrogated.

This mode is a sort of mixed mode, partaking in some respects of the nature of the scriptural, in others of that of the *vivâ voce*, mode. It has (as will be seen) the disadvantages of both, without the advantages of either.

A string of interrogatories is drawn by the party at whose instance the testimony of the respondent is called for: by the party — that is, not by the party (for by the party they are not signed,) but by the party's advocate, by whom, if made use of, they must be signed: for it is only on condition of seeing a learned brother fee'd, that this indispensable part of a judge's duty will be executed by the judge: by the judge, that is, not by the judge by whom the decision grounded on this evidence is to be pronounced, but by another judge *ad hoc*, who has nothing to do with it.

The string of interrogatories thus drawn by an advocate, and an advocate who would take it as an affront if it was proposed to him to have any personal communication with his ultimate client — with the suitor — the only person who, of his own knowledge, is capable of affording him any information, — the string of interrogatories, thus framed, is put into the hands of the judge: understand the judge *ad hoc* — a sort of person of two different and almost opposite descriptions,* but which agree in this, that in neither case is he to bear any part in the decision of the cause, — that is, in applying to its only use the testimony he has collected.

Thus far the interrogation is performed *ex scripto:* interrogatories are committed to writing. But, though the interrogatories are committed to writing, it is in the *vivâ voce* form that the responses are delivered: delivered in the *vivâ voce* form, though thereupon the purport of them, or something which is to pass for the purport of them, is noted down, and drawn up in the usual official style. Interrogatories have been committed to writing: but it is not in writing that these or any other questions are communicated to the respondent. The only person to whom these written interrogatories are communicated, is the judge: to him they serve for *instructions:* and on him, besides serving simply in the way of information, they exercise thus far a sort of binding force, that, in so far as any of the questions contained in the instrument remains without an answer, the task given to him is not done.

Though to him communicated all together, — by him to the respondent they will of course be communicated separately: so that the mendacity-serving instruction, which in some cases might be deduced from a simultaneous view of the whole assemblage by a mendacious respondent, will not in this place be to be had.

Nor, by the tenor of the interrogatories thus put into his hands for his instruction, is the judge ever understood to be so strictly bound, but that he is at liberty to propound

* In London, and within twenty miles, the judge *ad hoc* is a clerk in an office called the Examiner's Office: beyond that distance, two persons called Commissioners, nominated one by each party: or, in some instances, two on each side. See above, Chap. VII.

to the respondent any such other questions as may have been suggested by the respondent's answers: which power the judge will of course employ, in a manner depending partly on his own individual turn of mind, partly on the relation which the interest arising out of his position bears to the interests of truth and justice: if nominated by the parties, each commissioner using his industry with more or less zeal for the benefit of that one of the parties by whom he has been employed; if otherwise selected, getting through the business as soon as it is in his power to get through it, observing that to each question there be some sort of answer—whether true or not, being no concern of his. Be this as it may, the mass of interrogatories is constantly broken down into articles, and those articles numbered: and it is to an article thus distinguished and denominated, that the answer entered upon the minutes bears reference by name: and it is always under the head of the interrogatory by which it has been extracted, that the response is entered; "to the first interrogatory this deponent saith," and so forth.

The defendant comes sometimes to be interrogated upon the plan above described as calculated for the station of the extraneous witness. For interrogated, say re-interrogated: for, in his own station, and in the mode calculated for that station, he must always have been interrogated in the first instance.

In the case of the defendant interrogated in that character—interrogated in and by the plaintiff's bill,—if the answer fail of being satisfactory, if in any part it be deemed incomplete or indistinct, an instrument is grounded on it on the part of the plaintiff, under the name of *exceptions*. In this paper (as in the paper of interrogatories framed, as above, for the interrogator of the extraneous witness, by the judge,) the mass is broken down into articles, and those articles are numbered.

For the purpose of grounding ulterior interrogations on the responses of which the defendant's *answer* is composed—or when the answer, though complete and distinct, presents itself as being in any respect incorrect, —in the hope of exposing such its incorrectness, the plaintiff frequently, indeed most commonly, is advised to make amendments in his bill. These amendments, according to the number of the words respectively contained in them, are either inserted in the way of interlineation in the authentic exemplar of the bill, or subjoined in a separate mass. But, though subjoined in a separate mass, this supplemental mass, like the original mass, is one mass; the unity of the second not being, any more than that of the first, violated by any such operation as that of breaking it down into articles.

In the choice thus made of the two modes of interrogation—in the application made of them respectively to the respective stations—in the refusal of the principle of distinctness to the one case, in the allowance of it to the other,—there is nothing more than natural.

The more indistinct, as well as voluminous, the bill with its interrogatories, the more difficult will it be for the learned gentleman by whom the answer with its responses must be drawn, to make sure of having given to each interrogatory its complete and distinct response,—and thereby to take away, if by miracle he were so inclined, all occasion for exceptions. Thus it is that (here as elsewhere, under this as well as every other part of the system) by and out of business, more business is made. The more unintelligible the bill is, the more certain is the demand for work for the same learned hand, in the shape of *exceptions*.

The shoemaker when he makes a shoe, the tailor when he makes a coat, does not make a hole in his work for the sake of having it to mend. But, besides that flaws are not always so conspicuous in ideal as in physical work, no shoemaker finds a judge disposed to support him in the making of bad shoes: every advocate finds a judge determined to support him in making, in the way here described (not to mention so many other ways,) bad bills, and consequently bad answers.

To the instrument composed of interrogatories, this principle of distinctness is not refused. The reason—(I speak here of the historical and physical cause, not certainly of the justification)—the reason is no less simple in this case than in the opposite one. By putting or leaving in a state of confusion a mass of interrogatories, technically so called —of interrogatories that are to serve for instruction to the examining judge, nothing is to be got. By the learned drawer of the interrogatories, nothing; by the examining judge, by whom those instructions are to be made use of, perhaps as little: but, be that as it may, it is no concern of the draughtsman—no sort of relation subsisting between him and the obscure clerk, or the unknown country attorneys, to whom this indispensable part of the business of a judge (of every judge in whose eyes justice appears preferable to injustice) is turned over, as a matter of no importance, to the judge by whom the decision is to be pronounced.

On this head, as on others, the state of the practice (however in the first instance it may depend upon the subordinate lawyer, upon the office-clerk, the advocate, or the attorney) depends ultimately upon the superintending and ruling lawyer—the lawyer who, on pretence of expounding, legislates—the judge.

Originally, to all appearance, the judge to

whom it belonged to decide upon the testimony, was the person, the same person, by whom the questions (if any) that were propounded to the deponent, were formed, and the answers to them received. But, in causes between party and party, such as those here in question,—the judge of himself knowing nothing, and caring not much more,—an arrangement always useful, sometimes necessary, was, that, in respect of the points to which the testimony of the deponent was to be obtained, information should be furnished by him whose purposes were to be served by it.

No man who is not paid for being perplexed, and in proportion as he is perplexed, likes perplexity. Every judge who does not make a preponderant profit by judging ill, derives a profit from judging well: that is, from being thought to judge well; for which the really judging well is the simplest and surest recipe. Even under the technical system, every judge, when he has no particular interest to the contrary, finds it his interest to judge well: for it is upon whatever reputation may be to be got by judging well, that he depends more or less for the patience with which the deluded public submits to the load of factitious delay, vexation, and expense, out of which, under that system, his profit, and even honour, is extracted.

Having, in case of confusion, certain perplexity to suffer from it in the first instance, together with a chance of disrepute in case of misdecision—nothing could in this state of things be more natural, than that so obvious a principle of distinctness should be laid hold of by the judge. When you lay before me a statement of the points which I am to examine, do not throw them altogether into a confused mass, but break them down into articles, distinguishing the articles by numbers. By this means, I shall see my way all along as I go; I shall see the progress I have made, and, as fast as an article is answered to, I shall mark it off as answered, and go on to the next.

But in the world of law, as in other world's, when motion has once got into any track, *vis inertiæ* keeps it in the same track: and thus —when, for the accommodation of the ruling judge, this principle of facility had taken root —afterwards, when this principal part of a judge's duty came to be turned over to an underling, the benefit of the accommodation fell, along with the duty, to the underling's share.

The principle of distinctness, the division, thus refused to the parts of a defendant's answer, but applied to interrogatories, is also applied to exceptions: to the instrument composed of a list of the points in respect of which the defendant's answer is charged on the part of the plaintiff with being defective. Why to these exceptions, as well as to these interrogatories? For a like reason. The paper of exceptions being given in; if, by advice of his professional advisers, the defendant preferred the not giving in a further answer, the propriety of those exceptions was matter of argument before the judge. In this case, therefore, as in the other, some sort and degree of distinctness—something better than utter chaos, was matter of personal accommodation to the judge. The exceptions, therefore (as in the former case the interrogatories,) were to be, and were numbered. In the first exception, my lord, it is stated that, to the question to this effect, no sufficient answer has been given: if any such answer be to be found, the learned gentlemen on the other side will produce it.

The demand on the part of the judge for the principle of distinctness ceasing, the accommodation ceased along with it. If, instead of arguing the exceptions, the defendant, always under the orders of his professional advisers, submitted to make further answer,—in such further answer no mention was made of any particular exceptions. It was for the sake of the judge, that the principle of distinctness was employed: his profit was not diminished, his ease was served by it. The judge being here out of the question, the use of the principle ceased. With reference to the professional lawyer, the defendant's advocate, it was useless: what was there for him to gain by breaking this second answer into numbered parts corresponding to the exceptions which gave birth to it? The first was not thus classified: to what use should the second be? In this case, as in the former, distinctness would, with reference to the only interests which had any claim to be considered, be worse than useless. From the second answer, if kept in a state of as convenient confusion as the first, may come a demand for a second set of exceptions: to which second set of exceptions a third answer would come to be made.

CHAPTER XI.

HELPS TO RECOLLECTION, HOW FAR COMPATIBLE WITH OBSTRUCTIONS TO INVENTION?

Correctness and completeness are, both of them, qualities, the union of which is necessary in every aggregate mass of evidence. Of a deficiency in respect of either, deception and consequent misdecision may be the result.

If, on the part of the witness, the testimony be the product of the imagination, instead of the memory,—incorrectness is, in so far, the quality given to it.

If, for want of such helps to which on the particular occasion it may happen to be necessary, recollection fail to bring to view any such real facts as with these helps might and would have been brought to view, — incompleteness in the mass of the evidence is the result.

But, by the same suggestions by which, in case of veracity, memory alone would be assisted and fertilized, it may also happen, and is but too apt to happen, that *invention* (which, where testimony is in question, is synonymous with mendacity) shall also be set to work, and rendered productive. To administer assistance to recollection, to veracity — to administer, not assistance, but obstruction, to invention, to mendacity, — in these we see two opposite, and, to a first view, irreconcilable, pursuits. How then to reconcile them? or, at any rate, to do what is possible to be done towards it? In this question may be seen a problem, the solution of which is no less conspicuous for its difficulty than for its importance.

The first point to be considered is, the natural opposition between the two ends. In the instance of any arrangement by which recollection is assisted, how natural, if not necessary and unavoidable, it is, that mendacious invention should receive assistance likewise? In the instance of any arrangement by which mendacious invention is obstructed, how natural, if not necessary, it is, that recollection should be subjected to interruption likewise?

From the observation of these several relations, results the following practical inference: —

To put a negative upon the use of an arrangement designed for the assistance of honest recollection, it is not sufficient to say, "Nay — for so it may happen, that mendacious invention shall moreover be served by it." So again —

To put a negative upon the use of an arrangement designed for the obstruction of mendacious invention, it is not sufficient to say, "Nay—for so it may happen, that honest recollection shall moreover be obstructed by it."

In each case, the question will be, on what side is the preponderant probability in regard to deception: be the measure a measure of assistance or a measure of obstruction, is it by the adoption or the rejection of it that deception is most in danger of being produced? For (except with relation to that effect), whether recollection be or be not obstructed, whether invention be or be not employed, is, with relation to the individual cause in hand, a matter of indifference. I say, with relation to the individual cause in hand: for, to the general interests of morality, whether mendacious invention be or be not practised, can never be a matter of indifference.

The next point to be considered is, how far the nature of things admits of the throwing obstacles in the way of mendacious invention. For, wherever things are so circumstanced that the offering of any effectual obstruction to mendacious invention is either of itself impossible, or not possible by any means that will not, in an equal or superior degree, have the effect of depriving recollection of the helps necessary to the completeness and correctness of the testimony, — then one of the two pursuits, viz. obstruction of invention, ought clearly to be abandoned.

Antecedently to the delivery of the interrogatories to the proposed deponent — or at least (when the proposed deponent is made a defendant in the cause, and the cause is such as to warrant his commitment to provisional safe custody) — antecedently to the moment of his arrestation, — all the powers of government are insufficient to keep from him whatsoever time for mendacious invention he may have thought proper to employ. In the case of the *malâ fide* suitor, whether plaintiff or defendant, from the moment of his delinquency, or rather from the moment of his beginning to form the plan of delinquency—in the case of the *malâ fide* and mendacious witness, from the moment in which he has reason to expect that his testimony will be called for — his thoughts will with more or less assiduity be employed in the task of mendacious invention.

On this occasion, among the tasks given to his imagination will be the representing to him such adverse questions, as, when the time comes for the delivery of his testimony (willing or unwilling,) may be expected to be propounded to him on the part of his adversary or adversaries: and it is only in so far as his imagination has failed of executing the task to perfection, that it will be possible for him to be taken unprepared — that it will be possible for his answer to have been unpremeditated.

The only interval, therefore, in which obstruction to mendacious invention, acting independently of all assistance by suggestion from without, can find room to place itself, is (on the occasion of the examination of the supposed delinquent) the interval between each interrogatory and the response returned to it. Of the obstruction capable of being thus applied, the influence will, however, be seen to be far from inconsiderable.

Howsoever the general tendency and scope of the system of interrogation may be anticipated, — it will seldom happen, especially if the function of interrogation be lodged in able hands, that the separate particular import of each interrogatory taken separately can be exactly divined. So far, then, as in any instance the purport of this or that interrogatory fails of having been foreseen, and a response provided for it — a response which though mendacious shall not be discovered to be so,—the length of time which invention has for the performance of its task, has for its limit the length of the interval above described.

In the case where the process of interrogation is performed in the epistolary mode, the length of this interval may, to the purpose in question, be considered as being without limit. Under the *oral* (or say *colloquial*) mode, its limits are extremely narrow: and hence, to any such purposes as that in question, the prodigious advantage of the colloquial over the epistolary mode.*

When the form is that of oral conversation, the time allowed for recollection is naturally and usually extremely short: to speak at hazard, seldom so long as a minute.

Nor yet is it necessary that the faculty of veracious and honest recollection should in any degree receive obstruction from the promptitude thus exacted in the first instance. A veracious deponent, on those occasions, has nothing to fear—sees no cause for fear: whatever facts his recollection presents to him, he utters without hesitation: all true facts being consistent with each other, he fears but little the being contradicted, at least with effect, by others—he fears not at all the being contradicted by himself. If, for the purpose of searching in the store-room of his memory, a certain interval of time be unavoidably employed by him,—having nothing but real facts to search for, having no other receptacle than memory to search into for them, he fears not the result: it is in the honest and unhazardous task of recollection that he employs himself, not in the dishonest and perilous task of invention. In the course of his exertions to hunt out the truth, should it happen to him to have taken up and brought to view error in its place, and thereupon to have discovered his mistake,—still the contradiction, which he perceives himself thus to have given to himself, will not be productive of confusion: no sinister views being harboured by him, no sinister views are disappointed by what has happened; there being nothing dishonest to conceal, nothing dishonest has been betrayed by it. A misrecollection on his part has indeed been brought to light: but in this, what cause is there for shame or apprehension? The failure is neither more nor less than that sort of failure, of which every man of the purest probity has, in his own instance, the continually repeated consciousness—which is continually happening to a man in cases where his dearest interest, his most decided wishes, call upon him, were it possible, to avoid it.

Between recollection previous, and recollection subsequent (both having respect to the time, and consequently to the process, of interrogation,) the distinction has already been brought to view.†

---

* Between the use of writing, and the existence of an interval of time applicable alike to the purpose of veracious recollection and mendacious invention, the connexion is customary, and altogether natural, but not strictly necessary.

What is altogether natural, exclusively usual, and in general reasonable, is, that, as between written and unwritten, in whichsoever of the two forms the interrogations are presented, in the same should the depositions in answer be presented. But in the nature of things there is nothing to hinder this more obvious arrangement from being deviated from in either of two ways:—

1. The interrogations may have been presented to the deponent in the ready-written form; and, immediately upon his receiving them, answers from him, to be delivered *vivâ voce*, may be insisted upon, just as if the interrogations had also been delivered *vivâ voce*.

2. The interrogations themselves may have been delivered to the deponent in the *vivâ voce* form: and notwithstanding their having been so delivered, answers from him to be delivered in the ready-written form may be insisted upon,—to be delivered upon the spot, just as, in return to questions put *vivâ voce*, answers, if delivered *vivâ voce*, would naturally be delivered on the spot.

An example may be found in the following extract from the *Mémoires de Bezenval*, tom. iii. p. 125. 8vo. Paris, 1805:—

"Le jour de l'Ascension de l'année 1785, toute la cour remplissant le cabinet du roi, le cardinal de Rohan, en rochet, et en camail, attendait sa majesté qui alloit passer pour la messe, où sa charge de grand aumônier l'appeloit. Le roi le fit demander dans son cabinet interieur, où il fut un peu étonné de trouver la reine en tiers. Le roi lui demanda ce que c'étoit qu'un collier qu'il devoit avoir procuré à la reine? 'Ah, sire,' s'écria le cardinal, '*je vois trop tard que j'ai été trompé!*'—'*Mais*,' lui dit la reine, '*si vous avez cru si légèrement, vous n'auriez pas dû vous méprendre à mon écriture, que sûrement vous connoissez.*' Sans lui répondre, le cardinal, s'adressant au roi, protesta de son innocence. 'M. le cardinal,' reprit le roi, 'il est très-simple que vous soyez un peu troublé de cette explication; remettez-vous; et pour vous en donner le moyen, et que la presence de la reine ni la mienne ne nuisent pas au calme qui vous est nécessaire, passez dans la pièce à côté; vous y serez seul, vous y trouverez du papier, une plume et de l'encre; écrivez-y votre déposition, que vous me remettrez ensuite; prenez tout le temps qui vous sera nécessaire.' Le cardinal obéit, resta à peu près un demi-quart d'heure, rentra, et remit un papier au roi."

In this latter case it is, however, manifest that the degree of unpremeditatedness cannot be so great, the security against mendacious invention so perfect, as in the former, in which the answers are delivered in the *vivâ voce* form: since writing in a form that shall be readily and generally legible, necessarily takes up a considerably greater length of time than a discourse of the same tenor delivered *vivâ voce;* and, under the cloak of the real necessity, it would be easy for mendacious fraud to possess itself of a considerably greater length of time, without exposing itself to censure, or any decidedly prejudicial inference.

† Book II. *Securities;* Chap. IV. *Internal Securities.*

If adequate time for subsequent recollection be but allowed, supposing the nature of the case to call for it (understand always of the individual case in hand,) the time allowed for previous recollection can scarcely be too short. Why? Because, in case of mendacity, the shortness of the interval applicable to the purpose of invention is a capital security, and, in the first instance at least, the only one.

But what (it may be said)—what if the answer be (and a more natural answer there cannot be, whether on the part of a *bonâ fide* or on the part of a *malâ fide* witness,) I do not as yet remember:—unless time be given me for recollection, I cannot speak to the purpose? Certainly: nothing more natural, nor more frequent: but, in case of mendacity, in case of an actual recollection at the time, and this answer given—an answer by which the act of recollection is denied,—the purpose of the question is in some degree fulfilled: the evidence, presumptive at least, of mendacity, is obtained, or a way opened for the obtainment of it, just as in the case of a decided answer denying the fact spoken of.

You say you have forgotten what happened? How can that be, the transaction being of a nature so unlikely to be forgotten? For there are incidents, incidents in abundance, such as (supposing a man to have been a percipient witness of them, and the intervening length of time not extending beyond a certain length, according to the nature of the case) it is morally impossible that a man should fail of recollecting: such, at any rate, that, if oblivion in relation to them be possible, mendacity will always be much more probable. Nor is the comparative estimate any other than what a man, to whose lot it falls to weigh evidence against evidence, finds himself continually called upon to make.

You say you have forgotten what happened. How can that be, on this occasion,—you having, on other occasions not very remote, given an account of it to other persons? How can that be, considering the account that has been given of it by others, whose opportunities of observation were not better than your own? How can that be, considering what you yourself have already been stating relative to that same transaction, since you have been called upon to speak to it?

It is with non-recollection, the alleged non-recollection of the moment, as with evasion, indistinct responsion, and silence. If none of these courses of action were capable of affording any indication, mendacity would be impregnable—interrogation a vain resource.

Observe, that, though the interval of time allowed for recollection subsequently to the putting of the question be thus short, perhaps not a minute, perhaps not half a minute,—the time previously applicable to the purpose of recollection is not thus short. Was the fact, upon the face of it, of a nature to be likely to become the subject of deposition in a court of justice? a fact exhibiting itself as evidentiary of a crime, of an atrocious injury to person, to property, to reputation? The time applicable, and which naturally would be applied, to the purpose of recollection, dates from the very moment at which the fact presented itself to the deponent's cognizance. Was the fact, upon the face of it, ever so indifferent,—the time applicable to the purpose of recollection would take its commencement, at any rate, from the moment at which information was given to him (with or without the forms of law) that his deposition in relation to that fact would be called for to a judicial purpose.

Mendacious invention, then, having been either prevented, or encompassed with dangers, by the *vivâ voce* questions followed immediately by the *vivâ voce* answers,—should any time be needed by honest recollection, either for searching out what could not be searched out at so short a warning, or for rectifying any misrecollections fallen into through the shortness of the warning; then comes the occasion for the judge, under the guardianship of his probity (consideration being had of the nature of the case, and the colour and complexion of the language, countenance, and deportment of the witness,) to exercise his discretion (of his own motion, or at the instance of the witness himself or either of the parties) in the allowance or refusal of a further length of time to be employed in the forming of ready-written interrogatories on the one part, followed by ready-written answers on the other: the minutes of the *vivâ voce* deposition, with the minutes of the interrogatories by which they were extracted, serving as a standard of reference and comparison: the interrogator, at any rate, being furnished with the document; the deponent furnished or not furnished with that source of instruction, according to the complexion of his preceding testimony, at the discretion of the judge.

Meantime, *vivâ voce* interrogation is (as hath already been seen) the only remedy, from the application of which, mendacious invention (the mischief to which the interval necessary for interrogation and deposition in the way of ready-written correspondence affords such opportunities) can receive adequate check. For obtaining in full perfection the testimony of a *bonâ fide* deponent, the mode that allows full time for recollection is not only a sufficient, but by far the best adapted, mode. But, for protecting justice against the artifices of determined mendacity, the mode that allows the least possible time to the premeditation necessary to that criminal purpose, is the only mode adequately adapted to the purpose.

When, in order to allow the necessary time for recollection, and perhaps for research and methodization, depositions in the form of ready-written answers have been allowed to succeed on the one part to ready-written interrogations on the other,—the faculty of examining the deponent *de novo*, in the way of *vivâ voce* interrogation, must still be reserved to the discretion of the judge. As the minutes taken of the *vivâ voce* examination served as a standard of reference and comparison to the examination in the way of ready-written correspondence, so will the deposition obtained in this latter form serve as a standard of reference and comparison for the second *vivâ voce* interrogation of the same deponent.

So much for *invention*. Next, as to mendacity-serving *suggestion*.

For depriving a man of the faculty of receiving suggestions from without — suggestions to all purposes, and consequently to the purpose of assistance to mendacious invention — the nature of things offers but one expedient: and that is, close confinement.

But, of close confinement, misdecision to the prejudice of the individual so confined, if in the character of defendant, is, unless obviated by due conditions, a contingent result; vexation, and that in an intense degree, a certain accompaniment.

For the purpose of receiving advice, as well as collecting evidence, unlimited communication with the world without doors will in general be necessary: therefore, co-existently with justice, close confinement can never be continued to the time of the trial or other definitive hearing.

But (setting aside those factitious suspensions of judicial procedure, so conducive to the ends of judicature, so adverse to the ends of justice,) — in the instance of a defendant whose case was deemed to warrant eventual confinement for the purpose of forthcomingness — between the moment of arrestation and the moment of the commencement of the process of his interrogation, no other interval would (unless by accident) be necessary, than what was employed in the journey to the seat of the judicatory. In the event of any such accident, or supposing the process of interrogation too long to be completed at one sitting, the judge might be, and ought to be, furnished with power for subjecting the defendant to close confinement, in such manner as to exclude him completely from the faculty of receiving, from without, any communications, but what were seen and allowed of by the judge.

The testimony of the individual being thus collected, under circumstances by which mendacious invention stands precluded from all assistance from without, and has undergone all the obstructions which the nature of things allows to be opposed to it,—then is the time for the doors of the place of confinement to be thrown open to all communication from without: and not only must this communication be allowed of, for the purpose of just defence in case of innocence, but moreover the allowance of it is attended with less advantage to delinquency than might at first view be supposed. The statements made under these circumstances by the delinquent (for let delinquency be supposed for the purpose of the argument) being consigned to writing, it will rarely happen, that, for the purpose of mendacious invention, any subsequent information can be of use.

On receipt of the information, the delinquent, pretending that in this or that point his statement had by misrecollection been rendered erroneous, or by non-recollection incomplete, demands another hearing for the purpose of amending the pretended defect. With a demand to this effect, compliance can scarcely ever, consistently with justice, be refused. But, in the original testimony, the judge possesses a standard of comparison, with which every subsequent testimony from the same source will have to be confronted and compared: and, supposing a variance and inconsistency, it will rest with the judge to satisfy himself which of the two presents the image of truth in the strongest characters, and whether it be to honest recollection, or to mendacity-serving suggestion from without, that the change is to be ascribed.

Thus much for the case of a *defendant*, considered in the character of a source of testimonial evidence. The case of an extraneous witness stands, in relation to these points, on grounds in a considerable degree different. Suppose him (whether on the particular occasion in question an accomplice or not) an habitual confederate or intimate of the defendant, and, as such, ready to deliver whatsoever testimony (true or false) promises to be of use to him. By the close confinement of the defendant, the witness stands as effectually precluded (so far as the defendant alone is concerned) from the faculty of receiving, as from that of communicating, mendacity-serving suggestions. But, supposing mendaciously-disposed witnesses of this description more than one, — to their case, be they ever so numerous, the effect of the obstruction does not extend.

Here, then, suppose the collateral ends of justice not attended to, or suppose the case such, that the mischief, consisting of the vexation necessary to be inflicted on the extraneous witness in question, is outweighed by the benefit attached to the additional security obtained for the fulfilment of the direct and positive end of justice; here the same reason which has been seen urging the application of the security afforded by close confinement to the case of the defendant, will be seen applying, and with equal force, to the case of the extraneous witness.

The extraneous witness being, by the supposition, not a partaker in the supposed course of delinquency — being by the supposition not guilty, — should not (it may be said) be treated as if he were guilty. True: on the score of punishment, unquestionably he ought not. But on this score, neither ought the defendant himself, in this incipient stage of the cause. If it be fit that the defendant should be thus treated, it is because probability appears of his being found guilty: if it be fit that the extraneous witness be thus treated, it is because a probability appears that his being thus treated is necessary to the removing of the obstacles that might otherwise be opposed, by mendacious testimony, to the conviction of the guilty defendant.*

What is manifest is, that the price thus considered as capable of being paid for an additional security against the liberation of a guilty defendant by mendacious testimony, is not a small one. Whether there be any, and (if any) what, cases, in which a practice of this kind ought to be considered as likely to be upon the whole an advantageous one, are questions that belong not to this place.

Whatsoever be the species of delinquency, of the vexation in question the magnitude will be the same. The proportion between the two mischiefs, between the two benefits, or between the benefit on one hand and the price paid for it in the shape of mischief (viz. vexation) on the other hand, will depend in every case upon the magnitude, that is, upon the mischievousness of the offence.

Against undue suggestions from bystanders while the witness is under examination, or waiting for it, such remedies as the nature of the case admits of, are on the one hand not very difficult to discover, nor on the other very efficient. They are of a purely physical nature, and consist of the temporary exclusion of the individual from whom any such undue suggestion may be apprehended.

Objects capable of being brought to view by such suggestion may be referred to the class of *means* or that of *motives:* means of mendacity, — information true or false: motives to mendacity, — by addresses made to the hopes of the witness, or to his fears.

The use of such exclusion, for the purpose of guarding the mind of the witness from the action of seductive motives, or (to use the common language) from undue influence, may be exemplified by the case of a non-adult witness, — a parent, or other person under whose direction he has been accustomed to act, being in the number of the bystanders. Of undue partiality on the part of the superior, mendacity on the part of the inferior will naturally enough in these circumstances be the apprehended consequence. To the mischief apprehended from this source, the temporary removal of the superior will in this case be an obvious, and in general an unobjectionable, remedy.

Other relations of dependency will naturally present themselves as affording a ground for the more extended application of the same remedy.

The wife being about to depose, the husband may in like manner be required to withdraw: the apprentice, — the master of such apprentice. The principle thus stated, the discussion of the particular applications of which it may be susceptible, will scarcely afford payment in the shape of utility for the place it would fill up. A discretionary power in the hands of the judge presents itself as preferable, in every such instance, to an unbending rule.

* Cases every now and then occur, in which a prosecutor, or an extraneous witness, even where he is not suspected of being implicated in the offence of which the defendant is accused, is sent to prison by the justice to ensure his forthcomingness at the trial, or to prevent his being tampered with; — for instance, when the prisoner happens to be a man of rank and fortune, and the prosecutor or witness a child in a state of poverty. The necessity, however, for this extreme measure of precaution, would not have place were the system proposed by the author, in the instance of a defendant, adopted in that of an extraneous witness, inasmuch as the judicatory in which the evidence was elicited would at once decide upon the case, unless, as he observes (p. 450) by accident, or supposing the evidence too long to be elicited at one hearing, it became necessary to adjourn the case. — *Ed.*

CHAPTER XII.

OF RE-EXAMINATION, REPETITION, OR RECOLEMENT.

§ 1. *Re-examination, with faculty of amendment, how and in what cases proper.*

UNDER the head of repetition, in French *recolement*, we have to speak of an operation, the nature and the use of which will be apt to appear strange to an English eye. In England, no such thing was ever heard of: whence can come the demand for it anywhere else? Are witnesses a different set of people, testimony a different sort of thing, elsewhere, from what they are in England?

Repetition, however, is no less familiar on the north side of the Tweed, than it is strange on the south side. It is a term borrowed by Scotch from Roman law. Recolement is exactly the same thing in French law. French recolement, though in point of signification in an irregular sort of way, is a conjugate of Roman and English *recollection.* A deponent or his testimony is in Scotch said to be *repeated*, in French *recoled (recolé* or *recollé)*, when, after having been interrogated at one time, he is at another time brought again to the judgment-seat, for the purpose of its being put to him whether to abide by his antecedently-delivered testimony, or amend it.

Not that, under any system of law, opportunities of this sort can be altogether wanting. Under English law, if in some sorts of causes they are altogether wanting, in other sorts of causes (and those grounded on the same facts) they present themselves in abundance. But, in English law, they present themselves without design — without any thought on the part of the legislator or the judge. Under Roman law, the faculty in question is the subject of anxious care and inflexible regulation: care, that is to say, as applied to a certain sort of causes, and as complete neglect in all the others. Problem for an academical prize: — Which of the two sets of jurists, the Roman and the English, has on this occasion shown itself blindest to the ends of justice?

In one quarter or another, three distinguishable objects appear to have been aimed at in the institution of this process: — 1. Providing for the correctness and completeness of the testimony taken by itself, all seductive influence out of the question; 2. Preserving the purity of it from being violated by seductive influence, whether terrific or alluring, on the part of the judge; 3. Guarding against incorrectness and incompleteness, from this or any other cause, such minutes as may happen to have been taken of it.

Of these three objects, the first is the only one that appears to have met with any considerable regard under the original and generally prevalent system of Roman procedure.

In regard to the two other objects, the only system in which any indications can be found of their being looked to on this occasion, is the ecclesiastical branch of Anglo-Roman law. The deponent, after having been examined in the first instance by one sort of judge at one time and place, is, for the purpose of a sort of repetition (though in very general terms) brought before another sort of judge, a judge of superior dignity, at another time and place. The object of this change is made no secret of. It is to give the deponent, in case of misbehaviour to his prejudice on the part of the judge below, protection and redress at the tribunal of his superior.

No such advantage could have been looked to by the framers of the French ordinance. In France, at any rate, if the judge before whom the re-examination were taken were a different person from him by whom the original examination had been taken, he would have been a judge from the same bench — a judge of co-ordinate rank, not superordinate. But, if any such change took place, it could only be by accident: for in the ordinance it is assumed, or at least presumed, that, on the occasion of the several successive operations, the learned operator is the same.*

To the prosecution of these two collateral objects, a change in the person of the judge is an arrangement, the necessity of which seems obvious and indisputable. On the part of one and the same judge, seduction, if effected on the first occasion, would be persevered in on the second: if, by the tenor of the minutes, the testimony actually delivered had been misrepresented at the one time, the misrepresentation would hardly be corrected at any other.

On any such second occasion, the power of the check would of course be rendered more impressive by superordinate power on the part of the judge: but (though superiority were out of the question) the check afforded by the intervention of another person, though it were only in the character of a witness, much more if in character of a co-ordinate magistrate, could not but be in a very considerable degree impressive.

An objection is, — the information gained by the first judge, including the whole body of circumstantial evidence afforded by the *deportment* of the respondent, would be lost to the second judge. The objection is good in itself; but, by the legislators in question, not receivable. For under their system, be the number of judges by whom the evidence is decided on ever so great (and, were it not for the expense, the notion there is, or at least was, that there could never be too many,) no more than one of them is ever to set eyes on the evidence, or any species or part of it.

Henceforward, then, in speaking of this security, let us consider it in its application to the first object only; viz. the making better provision for the correctness and completeness of the testimony, by affording opportunity for the delivery of amendments on the ground of their having presented themselves since the time when the original mass to which they are applied was delivered.

On the principle of utility, the course which presented itself as proper to be taken in relation to this point, has been already brought to view: in the first instance — (to prevent, in case of *mala fides*, mendacity-serving recollection, and at any rate to save unnecessary delay, vexation, and expense) — interrogation on all sides *vivâ voce*, if practicable: then (if by the judge deemed necessary for the assistance of recollection, and not otherwise,)

* Predicated of the recolements only: implied probably of the confrontations. In regard to the recolement, in the first draught the identity was pointedly insisted upon: "que le même soit commis pour faire le recolement." (Art. 4.) In conclusion the point was taken off — "que le recolement se fasse par devant lui," — probably in contemplation of casual impediments. — *Procès Verbal des Conferences*, p. 175, edit. Louvain, 1700.

interrogation on all sides *ex scripto:* then again, interrogation *vivâ voce ad explicandum,* if deemed by him necessary for explanation of the scriptural testimony so obtained in the second instance, and its reconciliation with the original or first extracted mass of *vivâ voce* testimony, according to the minutes taken of it: the third again, if deemed by the judge necessary for the clearing up any doubts or differences remaining, according to his conception, upon the face of the two first,—and not otherwise: in each succeeding instance, the opportunity afforded, in case of special and adequate reason, but in no instance, of course.

By what description of persons, on each such occasion, it seemed proper that the process of interrogation should be performed, has also been brought to view: a system of all-comprehensive interrogation having on that occasion been proposed, as alike adapted to all sorts of causes: to all parties having a distinct and opposite interest, the faculty to be considered as belonging *de jure:* as likewise to the judge: and to extraneous witnesses, not without special allowance from the Judge, for special cause, in a case of difficulty.

If, with or without such supplemental and extraordinary (though regular and established) examinations, a suggestion should be presented from any of those quarters, urging on special ground the propriety of receiving from any such deponent an alleged amendment to his already delivered testimony,—better the door should (at any time before judgment, or even before execution) be opened, though out of time, than that incorrect or incomplete evidence should prevail, and misdecision and ultimate injustice be the consequence.

On these conditions, and these conditions only, does any operation analogous to the repetition or recolement of Roman law present itself as conducive to the ends of justice.

On the contrary, if no such special demand for re-interrogation should present itself, to what end have recourse to any such process? the delay, vexation, and expense attached to it, would be so much inconvenience in waste.

In any sort of cause, so to order matters as that the performance of the operation shall be matter of necessity, is entailing upon the public a certain and constant inconvenience, for the sake of a casual advantage.

And if one such re-examination must come of course, why not another? and so on, another and another without end?

In the three forms or stages of examination above proposed (*vivâ voce* once for all, or primary; ready-written; and *vivâ voce* explanatory,)—the application for each succeeding examination has been supposed to originate with one or other of the parties: the demand being presented, in the case of the second examination (the object of which is to afford the necessary time and opportunities for recollection, and opportunities of investigation and arrangement) by the nature of the case, in the instance of the third examination, by some casual inconsistency, real or apparent, between the two preceding ones.

In the present instance, the object to be provided for is that of a casual recollection, or alleged recollection, on the part of the deponent himself—operating in correction or completion of the deposition antecedently delivered. Supposing such alleged recollection sincere and real, no doubt surely can be entertained of the propriety of its being received—no reason suggested why deception, and consequent misdecision, should be admitted, for want of lights attainable from this quarter and in this mode, any more than for want of lights attainable from any other quarter or in any other mode.

In fact, it is from this quarter and in this mode alone, that it was the object of the Roman institution of recolement to throw lights upon the cause: for it is only in the case where the application proceeds from the quondam deponent himself, that any addition is on this occasion made to his evidence. Do you persist in your former evidence? If his answer be in the affirmative, no fresh interrogatory is put to him. If indeed his answer be, Yes, but my wish is, that an addition be made to such or such an effect, or that an alteration be made to such or such an effect,—then indeed, if in what he says on that occasion there be anything which in the conception of the judge requires elucidation, nothing can be more natural, or frequently more necessary, than that question should succeed question, until such a set of answers as shall have appeared productive of the requisite degree of distinctness, have been obtained. This being the case, a recolement exhibits, as it may happen, the characters of an additional examination, or those of a pure and simple confirmation of the testimony delivered on a preceding one, according to circumstances.

The fixation of an interview on purpose, at a more or less distant period of time, for the purpose of affording an opportunity for alterations in testimony, whether the deponent applies for it or no, and whether the judge thinks it of any use or no, forms a strange contrast with the blind confidence reposed in the Roman judge in so many other respects, especially in that of the total absence of publicity. The power of the judge being left without controul in so many other points, the coercion imposed upon him in this respect may be numbered among the inconsistencies of this system, as well as among the incongruities.

The capital feature, the radically pernicious and corruptive feature, of close secrecy, being established, partly upon avoidable grounds, partly upon unavoidable ones—partly for the obstruction it afforded to mendacious invention, partly for the facility it afforded to corrupt judges for doing as they pleased; the pretence it afforded for a regular addition to the mass of official and professional profit in the shape of fees, had probably at least as large a share as any other circumstance, in the composition of the mass of psychological and final causes.* For, that the expenses of criminal procedure were considerable, and that, by the particular operation here in question, a considerable addition was made to the aggregate mass, are facts sufficiently established.

Moreover, if in any one sort of cause, why not in every sort of cause? Is there any one sort of cause in which it may not as well happen to a man to forget a fact at one time, to recollect it at another time, as in any other? The principal circumstances on which the demand for recollection-time is apt to depend, are, 1. Impressiveness of the transaction (i. e. its relative importance in the eyes of the percipient witness;) 2. Complexity; and 3. Remoteness or staleness. The degree of these respective qualities being given, the natural result should be, that the transaction should be more correctly and completely present to the mind at any antecedent point of time, than at any subsequent one. True: and so it will be in general: on the other hand, in virtue of the principle of association, so it will now and then happen, — so in every man's experience it does happen, — that a circumstance which at one time will not present itself, notwithstanding the sincerest and most anxious search that can be made for it, shall, by means of some train of ideas with which it has happened to it to have associated itself, be brought up, as it were, by accident, at some subsequent point of time.

At any rate, — on whatever it may be that the demand for opportunity of amendment may happen to depend,—what it never does depend upon is the nature of the cause, as characterized by any such terms as criminal and civil, criminal and non-criminal. If, therefore, it be fit that the opportunity be afforded in all criminal cases, so is it in all other cases.

No (says somebody;) it is not that in criminal causes the probability of a demand for recollection is greater than in non-criminal ones; but that, should the mischief of misdecision take place for want of recollection, for want of that amendment which the recollection would have given to the aggregate mass of evidence, this mischief is much greater in the one case than in the other, and consequently creates a greater demand for this as well as all other securities that present a chance for the prevention of it.

True: but, in the first place, all that can be admitted in regard to the superior importance of criminal causes, as compared with non-criminal ones, resolves itself into this, viz. that, upon an average of all sorts of each description, the importance of a criminal suit will be greater than that of a non-criminal one. But, this being admitted, it will not be the less true that there will be many and many a non-criminal cause superior in importance to many and many a criminal one.

In the next place, whatever be the superior importance of an average criminal cause, it will never follow, either that, in a criminal cause, recollection-time, with the delay, vexation, and expense attached to it, should be given where it is not wanted; or that, in a non-criminal cause, it should be refused where it is wanted.

It certainly is not in every instance, in every individual instance, that the need of this opportunity presents itself. In English law it is not granted, *eo intuitu*, in any instance.

If this be true, it might surely have been sufficient so to have left the door open to it, as to have rendered it obtainable on special order of the judge, either of his own motion, or at the application of the deponent himself, or of some other person having an interest in the correctness and completeness of his testimony.†

* See the Ordinance, its commentators, and the *Causes Célèbres*—*passim*.

† In a criminal cause, the ground of the question will be apt to admit of very considerable variation, according to the deponent's station in the cause; the station of a defendant, or that of an extraneous witness: a defendant, exposed to punishment (and that perhaps capital,) or a witness, exposed to no such danger, nor anything at all approaching to it.

It is from a defendant that, in case of his being guilty, *mala fides* is next to certain. From an extraneous witness, in so far as the tendency of his testimony is to criminate the defendant, the absence of *mala fides* may be presumed to be not much less certain; criminative perjury, in capital cases at least, being happily among the rarest of all crimes.

In this station, at any rate, the penalties for blameable falsehood, especially on the criminative side, being everywhere so heavy,—falsehood on that side is not to be presumed as a matter of course.

The distinction is material. It is on the side of the extraneous witness only, that the probability, comparatively speaking, of honest recollection (viz. oblivion or non-recollection at one time, and deposition accordingly, followed by true and corrective recollection) is considerable.

On the part of a defendant who is guilty (as, under the worst system of criminal procedure that ever was established, a vast majority of the whole number of persons prosecuted always have been)—on the part of a guilty defendant, an application for liberty to amend his deposition will commonly have this origin:—Revolving in his mind the testimony he has been delivering, this or that fact or circumstance will present itself to him as being disproved and rendered untenable

§ 2. *Faculty of amendment, in what cases refused in English Equity practice.*

If the practice of English equity courts be tried by the standard which we have now laid down, it will be found inconsistent in a most extraordinary degree.

In equity, a deposition is sometimes called a deposition, sometimes not. I shall begin with the depositions which are not called depositions, and then go on to those which are.

I. Depositions called *answers*, containing the testimony of a party on one side, viz. the defendant.

In some instances, the equity courts have allowed a defendant to amend his answer: and in all those instances they have done well.

In other instances they have refused this liberty: and in all these instances they have done ill.

In the sort of thing called an answer, two instruments of very different kinds are confounded: 1. Claims, or demands; viz. on the part of a defendant (for a plaintiff in equity never makes answers,) counter-claims, counter-demands; and 2. Responses, in the way of testimony, extracted by the interrogatories.

On this occasion, as on many others, to refuse to a man, at any time, the faculty of preferring any such claims as he conceives himself able to make good in law, is manifest iniquity. A claim may indeed be ill-timed; and, on that ground, the reception of it may with propriety be refused at that time. But that is not the ground of refusal here; for, in a variety of instances, amendments to answers have been permitted.

Rational cause, none: probable historical, psychological, final cause, desire of making business. Let it not be thought that the counter-claim, be it what it may, would never be entertained. No claim can be framed so unreasonable as not to be received; but there must be another suit for it. File your bill, defendant; change yourself into a plaintiff, and treat the court with a fresh suit: that you may do, and welcome.

To refuse to a man whose testimony has been incorrect or incomplete, the liberty of making it correct and complete, is iniquity equally gross, and something worse: it is producing the effect of false testimony, without incurring the punishment.

Oh, but, instead of adding truth to falsehood, he may add falsehood to truth.

Answer 1. The objection, if good in any instance, would be good in all instances. Yet still your cases are open to applications for this liberty.

Answer 2. What if that which he now wishes to add be false, — are you under any obligation to believe it? The second deposition, will it prove inconsistent with the first? Inconsistency is one of the means of detecting falsehood.

Answer 3. On an indictment in the King's Bench for an assault, the same deponent, the prosecutor, tells his story three or four times over: three or four times, on the occasion of so many stated inquiries, besides any number of casual times on the occasion of the first of those three or four inquiries.

But when, in order to make the amendment, a part of the answer is obliterated, the inconsistency does not appear. It is only in one of two modes of amendment that this can happen: nor in that can it happen, but by your fault. First you make the inconvenience, and then you plead it.

The amendment which the defendant wishes to make, — the tendency of it may be to his advantage, or it may be to his adversary's advantage. In the latter case, the iniquity is doubled: you will not suffer the defendant to speak truth — you will not suffer the plaintiff to have justice.

"An answer," it is said, "shall not be amended, after an indictment for perjury, preferred or threatened, in order to avoid the indictment."* "Upon a motion to amend a schedule to the defendant's answer, an indictment for perjury having been preferred, or at least threatened, the Lord Chancellor refused to interfere, although he took it to be clear that the defendant did not intend to perjure himself, as he had no interest in so doing. The question would be proper before the Grand Jury, who, if they thought the defendant did not intend to perjure himself, would throw out the indictment: on the other hand, if there were ground for the indictment, it would be wrong for him to interpose."

"The reporter" (says a note) "has been informed, a similar application had been rejected a few days before, in the case of Vaux *v.* Lord Waltham, where, however, the Lord Chancellor seemed inclined to grant the motion, if the affidavit had *clearly* shown it to be a mistake."

The amendment not made, the Grand Jury would have found the bill or thrown it out: and the amendment made, what should have

by counter-evidence, either *ab intra* or *ab extra:* by its inconsistency with some fact, true or false, of his own advancing, or with some fact sufficiently established by evidence from some other source. In these circumstances, opportunity of amendment being then presented to him, he will be apt enough to embrace it: why? Because some scheme has occurred to him, by means of which he hopes to get rid of the inconsistency, and make up his statement to such a consistence, as that, though in many points it be false, it may in the material points afford him a chance of being believed.

* Bro. Ch. Rep. I. 419.

hindered them from doing exactly the same thing? If those to whose prejudice the refusal operated had not been thus injured, in what way, unless by positive and needless institution, would the authority of the Grand Jury have been obstructed?

Observe the wavering: a natural effect, where reason is unknown, and precedents, as usual, opposite. Observe too the process: testimony actually received, to know whether testimony, and from the self-same person to the self-same point, shall be allowed to be received: folios upon folios written and received, to know whether a word or two of the words contained in them shall be received.

On this footing stands the business of repetition, or of making amendments to answers, in the practice of English equity. By what combination of power and industry could it have been placed on any footing more favourable to the maintenance of profitable uncertainty,—less favourable to the extraction of truth and the maintenance of justice? "Shall the amendment be permitted?" is a point always subjected to contestation. But, if it be received, it is received in the mode in which falsehood receives as little discouragement as it can receive: — no room for ulterior interrogation — no room for *vivâ voce* scrutiny.

Besides whatever number of unreported cases that may remain lost to the world, *carent quia vate sacro*, the books afford I know not how many reported ones: in some of these the liberty was granted, in some refused: and, upon the whole, the man of law may read for his encouragement, and the suitor, if he has eyes for looking into such books, to his dismay, that "there are no certain rules for amending answers." *

Take a case in which the object of the defendant in his amendment was to speak, not in the simple character of a deponent, recollecting himself, correcting himself, and delivering confessorial testimony, but in the mixed character of a deponent and a party defendant, delivering self-serving testimony, asserting a fact for the purpose of grounding on it a fresh counterclaim. At a time subsequent to that of the putting in the answer, the fact wished in this way to be brought to view had taken place. The fact is true: is the defendant to be suffered to allege it? The claims founded on it are just: is he to be suffered to take the benefit of them? Not he, indeed. And why is he not? because he would have his due a year or two sooner: because the man of law, in all his hundred shapes, would thus be defrauded of his prey.

" To order the cause to stand over, till a new bill, in which the fact can be put to issue,

---

*1. Answer not to be mended after issue joined.	Chettle *v.* Chettle.	9 Car. I.	Foth. 10.
2. Liberty given to defendant to amend her answer, she being surprised therein.	Chute *v.* Lady Dacres.	Mich. 15 Car. II.	1 Ca. in Chan. 29. Freem. Rep. 173. S.C.
3. Defendant, having by answer consented that an award made by her father might be confirmed, prayed she might amend her answer, she having made oath that she never read the award, and that her answer was prepared by her father, who had wronged her in the award. Motion denied per Cur.	Harcourt *v.* Sherrard.	East 1702	2 Vern. 434.
4. There are no certain rules about amendments of answers, for those amendments are in the discretion of the court.	Woodgate *v.* Fuller.	East 1740	Barnard Rep. 50.
5. An answer may be amended even after a prosecution for perjury commenced against the defendant for what he has sworn in his answer, where it plainly appears to be a mere mistake. Ib.	Ib.	Ib	Ib.
6. Where an answer not allowed to be amended, barely upon the affidavit of the defendant.	Ib.	Ib.	Ib.
7. Liberty given to amend an answer so as to explain an admission therein of assets.	Dagly *v.* Crump.	July 1719	1 Dick. Rep. 35; sed vide Roberts *v.* Roberts. 2 Dick. Rep. 573.
8. Answer allowed to be amended by adding facts.	Bedford *v.* Wharton.	May 1742	1 Dick. Rep. 84.
9. Liberty given to defendant to amend his answer by striking out the admission of the plaintiff's pedigree after publication.	Kingscote *v.* Banisly.	June 1773	2 Dick. Rep. 485.

be brought to a hearing with the original suit,"—this is what, in the eyes of the then learned, and since by such learning ennobled, treatise-writer, "seems to be the proper way." Suitor, would you grudge your hundred pounds, or your two hundred pounds (supposing you to have it)? Can you be so unreasonable, when you are informed that, in the eyes of the same supremely learned person, a bill for this purpose seems to be in the nature of a plea *puis darrein continuance* at common law?—so that equity, it seems, consists in catching with avidity at every pretence for the manufacture of delay, vexation, and expense, that can be found in the storehouse of the special pleader. The fact is ready to be seen, but the man of law is not yet ready to see it: the parties must first have been under a fresh course of vexation and pillage for a few months or years. All this while, observe that, by the plea *puis darrein continuance*, the party receives the benefit of a fresh fact without the misery of a fresh suit: and the proposal here is, that the party shall not have the benefit of any fresh fact without a fresh suit: such is the logic, such the morality, of this learning: such is the improvement made upon common law by equity.

Think of what any one suit in equity is; think of what an additional suit must be; and think of the judge who would force men into it for such a cause!

Objection. — Was it not your own plan, that the making or not making amendments to testimony should be committed to the discretion of the judge?—Yes: on the supposition that the testimony is collected in the mode acknowledged to be the only good one, viz. by interrogation *vivâ voce*. Why? Because this mode, though so much more trustworthy than every other with reference to the direct ends of justice, involves a sacrifice in the way of delay, vexation, and expense. But, in the case where under the technical system the faculty of amendment is so often refused,—in the case of the answer in equity, amendments might succeed one another in any number without addition to the expense. The amendment not being to be subjected in any case to interrogation, the transmission of the few lines, or few words, that in such a case would be necessary, would not be attended with any expense worth regarding—(factitious expense excepted, to which of course there are no bounds.) The receiving it quietly without argument, would not be attended with any expense. What creates the expense, is the dispute whether it shall be received, after it has been received already for the purpose of the dispute.

On the proposed plan, everything turns upon the proportion between the advantage in respect of the direct ends of justice, and the inconvenience in respect of delay, vexation, and expense: to take measure of this proportion is what the judge is called upon to do in every case, and the only thing he has to do in any case. On the existing plan, not a thought is ever bestowed on the delay, vexation, and expense, unless it be in the manner that has been seen, for the purpose of giving increase to them.

II. Depositions called depositions: containing the testimony of extraneous witnesses.

This case is less complex than the preceding: claims confounded with testimony are here out of the question: claims are the claims of parties only: witnesses, as such, have no claim.

Six cases relative to the amendment of depositions are afforded by the books:* in the earliest and latest the faculty was refused; in the four others it was allowed.

In the 4th (Greills and Gansel) the language of the Lord Chancellor (Lord King) is so consonant to the ends of justice, so dissonant to the general tenor of the language of law and equity, that I cannot refuse myself the satisfaction of contemplating it in the very words:—"When it appears to the Court that either the examiner is mistaken in taking the deposition, or the witness in making it, I think it for the advancement of truth and justice, that the mistake should

* 1. No amendment of a deposition after publication.	Chamberlain *v.* Pope.	39 & 40 Eliz.	Foth. 77.
2. A witness after examination supplies his deposition to inform the conscience of the court.	Wynn *v.* ———	5 Car. I.	Foth. 77.
3. Upon affidavit of a witness that the examiner had mistaken him, his deposition amended, on examination in court.	Penderill *v.* Penderill.	5 Geo. I.	Kely, Rep. 25.
4. Petition to amend a deposition after publication granted, the witness, according to order, having attended in court, and been there examined.			
5. Depositions of a witness amended.	Rowley *v.* Ridley.	Nov. 1786.	2 Dick. Rep. 677.
6. Motion to amend depositions after publication refused.	Ingram *v.* Mitchell.	Mar. 1800.	5 Ves. jun. 297.

be amended, and the sooner this is done the better, in regard the witness may be dead, or in remote parts, before the hearing: it will be hard and unjust to pin a witness down to what is a mistake, by denying to rectify it: as to what has been objected of the inconvenience of amending the deposition after publication, it was impossible to know it until publication: whereupon let the deposition be amended, as desired, and the witness swear it over again."

This was the language of a man of sense and honesty—a spring in an Arabian desert: but it was not of a nature to run long. Anno 1800, the digested index affords this note: "Motion to amend depositions after publication refused." Ingram *v.* Mitchell, March 1800, 5 Ves. jun. 297.

Compare what Lord King says about amending depositions, with all that is said and done, as above, about amending answers: see whether there be anything in the situation of a defendant, that should render the interests of truth and justice less worthy of the regard of a Lord Chancellor than in the situation of an extraneous witness; or anything in the testimony of the one that should render the rectification of a mistake in it less conducive than in that of the other, to the advancement of truth and justice.

Compare the language of sense and honesty in the mouth of Lord King, on the subject of amending depositions, with the language of everybody else on the subject of amending answers: but of all things forget not to compare it with the use above proposed to be made of the plea of *puis darrein continuance*.

A not the least curious circumstance in this business is the utter want of reference between the cases relative to depositions and the cases relative to answers. Between two objects, in themselves so nearly approaching to coincidence, the difference of denomination seems to have raised up a barrier impenetrable to every learned mind. No allusion in arguments—no reference in books of practice, or abridgments, or indexes. The light of reason had shone upon the expanse, the whole expanse of the subject, in both its branches, from the mind of Lord King: but it was not that light that was suited to the sensibility of learned eyes. The light shone in darkness; but the darkness comprehended it not.

CHAPTER XIII.

OF SPONTANEOUS OR UNINTERROGATED TESTIMONY.

§ 1. *In what cases ought uninterrogated testimony to be received?*

In the description given of the mode of bringing facts, or supposed facts, under the cognizance of the judge, a supposition all along, though tacitly, made, has been, that, for the eliciting of the facts, a correspondent question or series of questions has been employed. To the best, or rather only proper mode of conducting the business, such introductory interrogations are, as has been seen, necessary. For what reason they are necessary, has also been fully shown. But, in whatever degree this mode is preferable *in general* to the opposite mode, it is by no means the only one in use. Hence comes the necessity of another distinction on the subject of evidence:—1. Evidence brought out in answer to questions, or, more shortly, evidence by examination; 2. Evidence *spontaneous*, issuing from the source of its own accord.

Of this sort is that species of testimony, the expression of which (so much of it as is exhibited by one and the same deponent, *uno flatu*, in one and the same instrument) forms the tenor of what, in the spurious latinity of English law, has obtained the name of an *affidavit*. Say, then—1. Evidence by examination; 2. Evidence by affidavit.

When I spoke of the opposite form as preferable to this, I subjoined (what was necessary to be subjoined) a mark of limitation, expressed by the words *in general*. Cases there certainly are, in which this mode of exhibiting evidence may be preferable to the other. Abused as it will be found to be, it is by no means without its use.

As a mode of coming at the truth of the case, where the extraction of the truth is attended with any considerable difficulty, nothing can be more palpably incompetent than the use of this irregular shape, when confronted in this point of view with the regular shape in which evidence is exhibited in ordinary cases. Yet evidence in this shape is employed in a multitude of instances, and with indisputable advantage. It is so in English practice, it is so in French practice; nor can I conceive how the use of it can well be avoided in the practice of any other political state.

Cases, therefore, being to be found in which it is employed with advantage, what are those cases? By what marks are they to be recognised?

The regular mode of extracting evidence being (with reference to the main end of procedure, viz. rectitude of decision) the only tolerably competent mode in most cases, and not inferior to this irregular mode in any case,—if in any case it can be proper to resort to this extraordinary mode in preference—to depart from that which is in general the only eligible mode—it must be in respect of some special advantage to be derived from such departure. This special advantage, if the list of the several subordinate ends of procedure (viz. avoidance of delay, of vexation, and of expense) is rightly made up, must be referable to one or more of those ends. Thus far, then, we are arrived, viz. that it is only for the sake of some saving to be made in the articles of delay, vexation, and expense — one or more of them — that the sort of evidence called spontaneous, evidence by affidavit, ought to be received.

What cases come within this limitation? They are comprisable under the following description: viz. cases where the extraction of the truth is not attended with any considerable difficulty. How, then, to search out these cases?

To quadrate with the mass of facts requisite to be brought to view, the evidence exhibited in each instance must in the first place be correct—conformable to the facts as far as it goes; in the next place, complete — corresponding in its extent to that of the whole mass.

But how to make sure of its covering the whole mass? To make sure of it in each instance, a complete description of the whole mass requisite must be capable of being given in each instance. This is actually done in all cases where the nature and extent of the facts sought is described and settled by pre-appointed forms. A form of this sort, has it been pre-appointed by the legislator? He has framed then to himself a conception of the exact purport and description of the mass of facts, the existence of which he wishes, for the purpose in question, to see ascertained: he has given expression to it in and by that form. Being according to that form, it cannot, in the legislator's own view of the matter, fail of being complete.

In the drawing up of a form of this sort, two cautions present themselves as highly material to be observed: viz. 1. That the description of the mass of facts to be averred shall, if possible, be of such a description, that the averment of it (if false) cannot be made without subjecting the deponent to the imputation, at least, of perjury; 2. In the next place, that, in case of perjury, the facts pitched upon in this way for attestation shall be such (if possible) as that, of the perjury, if committed, the nature of the case shall afford a probability of a mass of contrary proof sufficient for conviction.

An example sufficient for the illustration of the above rules may be found in the case of an affidavit made requisite (suppose) to entitle a man to receive a periodical payment due upon an annuity granted for the term of another man's life.

1. Suppose the form of the deposition to be in these words: — Juratus (the deponent) maketh oath and saith, that the said Vivant Denom (the person in question) was living at the city of Paris on the first day of this instant January. Affidavits of life, of a tenor not more precise than this, have, I am inclined to think, been received. But can perjury be *assigned* (as the term is) upon an affidavit thus worded? I should much doubt it. Vivant Denom was no longer living at that day. Juratus, on being prosecuted as for perjury, produces a man who deposes, and that truly, that he, the deponent, had, previously to the taking of the affidavit, in the presence of Juratus, mentioned Vivant Denom as a person then alive: the deposition may easily enough have been true: it may have been equally true, whether the deponent at the time of the above conversation believed Denom to be then alive, or believed, or was even certain, by the evidence of his own senses, to the contrary. Yet, after a deposition to this effect, would Juratus be convicted of perjury?

Instead of being worded as above, let the form run thus: — Juratus maketh oath and saith, that the said Vivant Denom was living at the city of Paris on the first day of this instant January, inasmuch as he (this deponent) did, on the day aforesaid, of the month aforesaid, at the place aforesaid, see the said Vivant Denom, he the said Vivant Denom being then alive. In this case, supposing it established by sufficient evidence, either that Denom was then dead (say, to put the matter out of doubt, several days before,) or that Juratus was in no part of France near that time, — so far at least as depends upon the wording of the form, no doubt could exist to prevent a conviction as for perjury.

Among the variety of steps that come to be taken in the course of any system of procedure, facts in abundance may be found simple enough in their nature to give occasion to affidavits, printed forms for which might be framed by the appointment even of a legislator. But, over and above the cases of this description, others might, from time to time, present themselves, in which, at the instance of the party calling for the evidence, a form might be prepared, in conformity to the above rules, under the eye and with the allowance of the judge. It would be his care to provide that the indulgence prayed for, on the ground of a saving in point of delay, vexation, and expense, should not be purchased by too great a sacrifice (if by any sacrifice at all,) in respect of rectitude of decision, the main end of judicature.

But, how commodious and eligible soever it may be that evidence should (to save the trouble of personal attendance in the course or on the occasion of a suit, or, where there is no suit, to prevent a suit) be received in this form in the first instance, it by no means follows that the evidence thus given should not, so long as the deponent were living and forthcoming, be on any subsequent occasion subjected to scrutiny in the ordinary mode. The expectation of such a scrutiny would, at the time of making the affidavit, be a very powerful check to incorrectness as well as mendacity — a very powerful security for the correctness as well as veracity of the testimony contained in it.

At present, under the English law, no such check, no such security, exists—at least in any sort of regularity. In the case of a non-litigant witness, the having made an affidavit in regard to any fact, would not indeed exempt him from being called upon to give his evidence *vivâ voce*, in the ordinary way, in any cause in which he might have been called upon for this purpose had there been no such affidavit made. But as, according to the general rule, no defendant can be examined *vivâ voce* in a cause of either kind, penal or non-penal, nor any plaintiff in a non-penal one, the consequence is, that, upon the whole, it can seldom happen that a person who has given his testimony in this unscrutinized shape, can look upon himself as liable to be called upon to speak to the same points under the check of the regular *vivâ voce* scrutiny.

At present, the only security there is for the truth of testimony taken in this way, is the prospect of a prosecution as for perjury. Several causes concur in rendering this remedy a very inadequate succedaneum to the proposed eventual *vivâ voce* examination.

1. Where the side of the prosecution could produce but one witness, the prospect of producing by such evidence the degree of persuasion requisite for conviction, would at best appear extremely precarious, commonly hopeless: in this case, the common phrase is, *it is but oath against oath*: and though it is in words only that the equality is constant, in real amount accidental and even rare, yet the simplicity of the argument gives it weight which cannot but be expected to be in general prevailing.

2. In the next place, how fully soever the falsehood of a statement in an affidavit may be put out of doubt, there cannot be, any more than there ought to be, any expectation, that, in a case where that falsehood is regarded as standing clear from mendacity, a prosecution for perjury (supposing it instituted) would be followed by conviction.

3. In the third place, this remedy (a vexatious one to the party already vexed, as well as severely penal to the author of the vexation) cannot be administered but by a suit on purpose.

4. In the fourth place, the satisfaction to the party injured is not either immediate or certain, but remote and even precarious.

On the other hand,—suppose the expectation of an eventual *vivâ voce* examination and cross-examination to hang over a man's head,—an expectation to this effect would afford a degree of security for correctness as well as veracity, much beyond what hitherto men have been accustomed to experience, or so much as conceive.

The expectation of this scrutiny will in no inconsiderable degree answer the purpose of the actual application of it—as in the case of the declaration of property, required for the purpose of the income tax, alluded to in a former place.

Upon the whole, the admission of affidavit evidence appears to stand on similar ground to that of unsanctioned and thence unscrutinized official evidence. In both instances, evidence, in a shape evidently inferior, is received in lieu of evidence in that shape which, on account of its manifest superiority, is become the ordinary shape. In both instances, the presumption is, that, in respect to the security for veracity and correctness, and thence for rectitude of decision, the evidence which in other cases would be manifestly inferior, is not so, practically speaking (at least, in such a degree as to forbid the employment of it,) in the particular circumstances of these two cases. In both instances, the reason for departing from the superior and regular mode, consists in the saving made in point of delay, vexation, and expense, or at any rate of vexation. In both instances, therefore, the substitution ought to be no more than provisional; the superior and regular mode being liable to be recurred to after it, on either of two suppositions: if the saving in point of delay, vexation, and expense, together, is looked upon as not worth regarding; or if on any particular account the danger of deception (whether by mendacity or simple incorrectness,) and thence of undue decision, threatens to rise to such a pitch as to constitute a mass of disadvantage more than equivalent to the saving in point of delay, vexation, and expense.

§ 2. *How to lessen the imperfections of uninterrogated testimony.*

How eminently ill-adapted to every useful purpose testimony is when deprived of the security afforded by interrogation, has already been observed. The more imperfect it is in the essential part of its nature, the more diligent should the legislator be in doing what depends upon him towards lessening its imperfections, to the end that, where the exhibition of the testimony in question in any less imperfect form is either physically or prudentially impracticable, it may in this unavoidably imperfect shape make its appearance under the least possible disadvantage.

In the case where two masses of testimony in this form are opposed to one another,—each, it has already been observed, by the opposition it cannot but receive in case of falsity, serves as a sort of security for the trustworthiness (as far as respects correctness) of the other: acting in this respect as a sort of succedaneum, though a very inadequate one, to the process of interrogation.

To apply it in this character to most advantage, all that can be done for it in respect of securities, is to make what provision can be made for it under the head of *distinctness*.

The arrangements which presented themselves as favourable to the production of this quality, have already been brought to view, when considered as applicable to a discourse of the same nature considered as subjected to the process of interrogation.* The application of them to a mass of uninterrogated evidence will be an operation little more than mechanical. *Mutatis mutandis*, they apply of course; and to discover what the *mutanda* are, the slightest glance will serve. The requisite changes being made, the description of the arrangements will stand as follows:—

1. The statements should be divided into articles, distinct and numbered. Though the reasons which render such distinctness desirable are the same in this case as in that of the questions and answers in the case of deposition taken on examination, unfortunately the facility of securing it is far from being so. Questions naturally clothe themselves in the form of distinct and short and simple propositions: if, instead of being simple, a question happens to be of a complex nature, it is easily seen to be so, and in what respect it is so: and it being seen that it is complex, and in what respect, it is commonly seen in what way it requires to be decomposed, in order to its being resolved into simple ones. Where the framer of the question really wishes for a clear answer, his wish will dispose him to make the question as simple and distinct as possible: even where it happens not to be his wish to obtain a clear answer (as in the case of a party wishing to involve the cause in confusion by written examinations for the sake of delay, or his law-agent for the sake of the profit to be extracted from it,) the very form of the interrogation, by betraying the complexity, serves in a considerable degree to betray the *mala fides* that gave birth to it.

In the case of an examination, whether *vivâ voce* or in writing, the most uninformed interrogator knows therefore where to stop, and does stop accordingly, before the proposition has extended to any unmeasurable degree of complexity. In the case of spontaneous deposition—a species of discourse, which, not being broken into by questions, presents itself in the form of one continuous narrative—the above principle of distinction and division has no place. What, then, in this case, is to be done? Suppose a professional agent employed, the difficulty will not be insurmountable, nor very considerable: the statement being required to be broken down into numbered articles, the number of words allowed to be put into each article may be limited. But, in many cases, it is only because the importance of the suit will not pay for the expense of the superior mode of examination and deposition, that the inferior mode is here proposed to be admitted of: and if this costly assistance must necessarily be called in, the cost of it is necessarily (because the labour as well as skill is necessarily) much augmented by the substitution of this inferior mode. To inscribe a logical proposition within a circle of given extent, is a sort of geometry to which the suitor, even though not altogether a stranger to the art of writing, will in general be incompetent. Supposing him indeed to have written what he has to write, what he has thus written will at any rate be divisible (though not always by himself) into grammatical sentences.†

The laws of punctuation are not so universally agreed upon, nor so thoroughly settled, as that the boundary line between every two sentences shall in every case be beyond dispute or doubt: but in each instance—so it be settled (which it may always be) so long as there is somebody whose duty it is to settle it—the mode in which it is settled, and the degree of simplicity resulting from such mode, will comparatively be a matter of indifference. Supposing the statement, in its way to the party interested, to pass through the hands of the judge, or a scribe acting under the direction of the judge,—such judge or scribe would always be able to divide it for this purpose into numbered articles, with scarce any more time and trouble than would be requisite for the simple reading of it.

The above, however, in case of legal intercourse by written correspondence, is far from being the only or the greatest difficulty. In the production of an imperfectly instructed mind, the great difficulty is, not to know where one sentence ends and another begins, but to obviate the confusion resulting from incomplete, inexplicit, indistinct, ambiguous, incoherent, and inconsistent statements. In the case of *vivâ voce* examination, all these defects are prevented, or all material aberration corrected, by the steady line traced out by the questions put, and the immediate *veto* opposed to aberrations by the judge. In the case of examination and deposition by written correspondence, this present guide is wanting: and, unless a professional assistant be called in, many will be the instances in which a correspondence thus carried on will be too rambling and irrelevant to answer the intended purpose.

* *Vide supra*, p. 383, *et seq.*; and p. 437, *et seq.*

† Under the discipline of the stamp duties, the number of words allowed to be put into a page is limited, in many (if not most) instances, in Britain, France, and probably other countries.

In the English translation of the Christian scriptures, the matter is broken down into verses, and it is not always that the grammatical sentence is concluded in the verse.

The danger of such confusion, and the difficulty of avoiding or remedying it, will depend, in a great degree, on the greater or less degree of complexity in the case: and, though now and then a case may run out into a prodigious degree of complexity, happily, in by far the greater number of cases, the degree of complexity will not be such as to oppose any very troublesome bar to distinctness of statement or narration.

2. The deponent should speak in the first person, and not in the third.

Reasons, again, the same as in the case of written deposition *ex interrogato;* and in an equal degree.

3. It is rarely that a spontaneous deponent can, from his own knowledge, bear testimony to all the facts which he may have occasion to allege. It will be proper therefore to require, for the expression of his persuasion, different terms, corresponding to so many differences in the source from whence that persuasion is derived.

Reason: — For the sake of comprehending them all alike under the obligation to abstain from mendacity and temerity. A persuasion grounded on the relation of others, or on inferences drawn by a man from the relations of others, or from his own perceptions (present or past,) cannot, in point of intensity, stand altogether upon a level with a persuasion grounded either on his own present perceptions, or even his past perceptions, if presented to him by a clear and lively recollection. To these latter the term *knowledge* is regarded as applicable: to the former, not: no term expressive of any more intense persuasion than what is expressed by the term *belief*.

In the use of *vivâ voce* examination, a description of the intensity of persuasion, if not drawn forth with sufficient precision by one question, may be drawn forth with greater precision by another or another. In the case of ready-written testimony, the deponent, having time sufficient before him to choose his words, may be expected and called upon to choose them accordingly.*

§ 3. *Abusive applications made of uninterrogated testimony in English law.*

Of the narrow description of cases in which the use made of this comparatively untrustworthy species of testimony may be reconcilable to the ends of justice, a view has just been given: the occasion is now come for observing the use that actually has been made of it in judicial practice.

Neglecting for once the order of precedence as between the Roman and the English mode, the exemplifications afforded of this miserable species of evidence, may, for the sake of illustration, be ranged in a climax, the steps of the ladder rising one above another in the scale of absurdity.

1. Reciprocal affidavit evidence, affidavits and counter-affidavits, in the English mode: averments on one side upon oath, liable to be encountered by averments on the other side, also upon oath.

2. Reciprocal allegations without oath: averments on one side without oath liable to be encountered by averments on the other side, also without oath. Allegations relative to the main points in issue: allegations called pleadings, and in use as well in English as in Roman law.

3. *Ex parte* affidavit evidence: averments upon oath, but on one side only (and without any faculty of encountering them allowed on the other side,) rendered decisive: a practice in use in many instances under the English system, but in such manner as to command not a definitive decision relative to the main points of the cause, but a decision, actual or virtual, relative to some incidental point — a decision giving effect to some incidental application.

4. *Ex parte* deposition without oath, but not without particularization: deposition rendered conclusive in such manner as to command the decision on the main points of the cause: exemplified in English practice in the case of a *return* to a *mandamus*.

5. *Ex parte* deposition upon oath, but without particularization: deposition commanding the decision on the main points of the cause: exemplified in Roman practice, in the averments called respectively Oaths purgatory, suppletory, &c., and in the English *wager of law*.†

To prove the incongruity of these several exemplifications of uninterrogated evidence, argument will not here be necessary: they are condemned when classed. Enumeration and elucidation are the tasks to which the present chapter is confined.

On the historical cause of such of them as are applicable to the purpose of giving *commencement* to a *malâ fide* cause — a cause which, under the immediate obligation of more trustworthy evidence, would not have been commenced, — or *continuance* to *any* cause, — of the psychological or final cause of these arrangements, the cause which gave birth to them in the minds of the inventors, nothing need here be said, in addition to what has been said under another head. The more writing, the more business: the more business, the more profit — the more delay, vexation, and expense, at the charge of those whose interests are not regarded; but the more profit to those whose interests alone were ever the real objects of regard.

Of such of them as establish, for the ground of the ultimate decision, such bad evidence

* See Book I. Chap. VI.

† Wager of law is now abolished. — *Ed.*

in concurrence with, or to the exclusion of, better evidence,—the psychological cause is not equally obvious: imbecility seems to claim a share equal at least to that of improbity in the composition of it.

A species of evidence the most completely divested of all intrinsic securities for truth—a species of evidence standing in the very lowest point of the scale of trustworthiness—a species of evidence not fit, as we have seen, to be trusted to in any contested case, nor so much as in an uncontested one without being supported by the eventual faculty of scrutinizing the same testimony in a better mode: such is the mode to which an exclusive preference has been given by English judges: such is the sort of information, the only sort, which, for their own use, they will allow themselves to receive: such is the only sort of evidence on which they will ground any of their decisions, final or incidental, of which, without the clog of a jury, they assume to themselves the cognizance.

When performed by the judge alone, without the benefit of that zeal and appropriate information on both sides, which cannot be expected from any other quarter than that of the parties,—so sensible is the judge of the comparative imperfection even of the mode by examination, when performed in this way, that—as often as the importance of the cause or the intricacy of the question presents to his mind a warrant for the expense, vexation, and delay—he dismisses the question from his own tribunal, and sends it to be tried at another, before a very different and less experienced judicature; for the benefit of adding examination by the parties to the examination by the judge. Affidavit work has not the benefit of any sort of examination—not so much as of that loose and incurious sort of examination that may be expected from a judge's deputy, to whom the function of deciding upon it does not belong: affidavit evidence is altogether exempt from scrutiny; and this is the only sort of evidence which an English common-law judge will ever suffer to come before him—the only sort of evidence on which he will suffer any decision of his to be grounded!

Here follow, for illustration, some of the principal applications of it.

In criminali, where the mode of prosecution is by information, the cause is tried upon this improper evidence, to know whether it shall be tried upon proper evidence.

In criminali,—whether the mode of prosecution be by information or by indictment,—after a trial on proper evidence, or rather by evidence in a proper shape, before a jury, the cause is tried over again upon this bad evidence.

If, making no defence before the jury, the defendant suffers judgment to go by default,—in case of indictment the cause is tried for the first time—in case of information for the second time—upon this bad evidence.*

When the prosecution is by attachment (be it really a criminal suit, be it a non-criminal suit in the form of a criminal one) the cause is tried upon no other evidence.

In non-criminali, in all the courts, but more especially in the common law courts, an extensive and numerous class of causes hereinafter distinguished by the name of *motion causes*, are never tried on any other evidence.

When brought before the Chancellor in the form of a petition, questions relative to the estates of bankrupts (questions, the value of which may rise to any amount) are tried on no other evidence.†

In every regular court, whether of the common law or equity class, where, in the course of a cause brought on in any of the established modes (whether indictment, information, action, or bill,) any incidental application comes to be made, grounded, as in almost every case it must be, upon some specially alleged matter of fact,—the fact is tried upon no other evidence.—*N. B.* Before the principal inquiry comes on (if destined to come on at all,) the fate of the cause is liable, perpetually liable, to be disposed of by this or that incidental one.

---

* In the King's Bench, in case of an indictment, for example, for an assault, if the defendant, having witnesses whose partiality is in his favour, thinks them capable of standing cross-examination, he pleads not guilty, and stands trial: if not, he suffers judgment of guilty to go by default; and, in mitigation of punishment, antecedently to his receiving judgment (say *sentence*,) he produces their testimony in the shape of affidavit evidence.

So much in course is the observance of this policy (it would be superfluous to say by whose advice,) that when it is not employed, the omission is publicly made a merit of. "My lord, gentlemen of the jury, we produce our witness (you see) to stand cross-examination:" it depended upon us to have preserved him from it.

This is but one out of a swarm of abuses that cling to the trial of a misdemeanour, as performed before a learned judge in the King's Bench or at the Assizes, in contradistinction to the trial for the same offence, performed before a company of unlearned men at the Sessions.

† Unless (what does not happen in one cause out of twenty) the Chancellor thinks fit to direct an issue; *i. e.* a suit to be carried on in a common-law court, for the purpose of trying the question (it being a question of fact) before a jury, and consequently by evidence presented in a proper shape, as above. But, in this case, so far from being a loser, the partnership is a gainer by the admission of the proper evidence: the trial of the issue being a suit within a suit: the suit with the evidence in a good shape being not substituted, but added to the suit with the same evidence in a bad shape. The same observation applies for the most part to issues sent to be tried out of the equity courts.

Why so exclusive a predilection for the worst evidence? — why this inviolable determination never to decide but upon the worst grounds? The reason (meaning by reason not surely the justificative cause, of which sort of reason there is none — but the historical and psychological cause) — the reason in this sense is not difficult to perceive, to any one who is not determined not to see it.

1. Affidavit work brings grist to the official and professional mill: *vivâ voce* examination brings none.

2. Having extracts read from ready-written and manufactured testimony, when occasionally referred to in argument by a brother of the long robe, is comparatively an easy process: watching and assisting the extraction of testimony, in its genuine colours, and in all its plenitude, from willing and unwilling witnesses, is a task comparatively laborious.

Two interests, two all-mighty interests, and both sinister ones, have therefore concurred in determining the arbiters of man's fate never to judge but upon bad grounds: the interest of their purses, and the interert of their ease.

When evidence was to be received by them, by them who had all possible modes at their choice, — what mode of all modes did they choose? The mode the most repugnant to all the ends of justice — the mode the most lucrative and most easy to themselves, their dependents, and their friends.

Nor is it in their power to plead in self-defence, that this bad mode of extraction is employed by them to save the delay, vexation, and expense, which might be the consequence of requiring the testimony to be delivered *vivâ voce*.

He whose testimony is desired, — let him be all the time within view of the great hall, and all the time known to be so; let him be the whole time in court, as the several attorneys of the court, for example, always are supposed to be, and sometimes are; — would any judge of the court suffer the man to be examined *vivâ voce*, instead of receiving the testimony in the shape of affidavit evidence? — Not he indeed.

One of their rules is — You must give the best evidence the nature of the thing admits of. Behold in this example one specimen of the regard paid to the engagement taken by that rule!

Cases there are, and happily to a large extent, in which the choice in question — the choice of the form to be given to evidence, was not open to them. In these instances, and in these alone, they did consent to receive it — consent, as it were per force, to receive it in some less improper shape. But in every instance (one excepted, of which presently, in which choice was absolutely chained,) they took effectual care not to be sufferers from the exchange.

A rule, not (like the other) proclaimed, but observed, and with a degree of fidelity with which no rule ever proclaimed is ever observed, is, never to suffer the light of evidence to find its way directly to the eye of the judge: never but through some impure medium, by which one part is absorbed, another part distorted into false colours: written affidavits, through the pen of one sort of lawyer — an attorney; written answers through the pens of two sorts of lawyers (a barrister being forced upon the party by modern regulation, to make up for the assumed untrustworthiness of the attorney:) even *vivâ voce* testimony delivered in that pure state to the jury, must first have been misrepresented, curtailed, and added to, by the venal eloquence of a lawyer hired for the purpose, whose falsehoods and sophistry it is part of the duty of the judge (if he happens to be in the humour), to persuade them, if possible, to blot out of their minds.

What if any unlearned judge — what if any court of conscience — what if any justice of peace — were to take it upon them to try a cause upon affidavit evidence? Even in the way of supposition, the idea is scarce endurable. Absurdity thus palpable, iniquity thus flagrant, never yet found its way into the practice, scarcely into the imagination, of any unlearned judge. To try causes without any evidence but such as is unfit to be received in any cause, is among the uncommunicable (in this instance the happily uncommunicable) privileges of learned judges.

Decisions of unlearned judges, decisions of justice of the peace, are quashed without mercy — quashed for no reason, quashed on no pretence, except that, what no law had ever ordered them to do, they had omitted to do, viz. to set forth the evidence.* Set forth the evidence? — to what end? Unless they had omitted the ceremony of an oath, and usurped the privilege of granting the mendacity-licence so regularly granted by their learned superiors, was there any danger of their grounding their decisions on any evidence so bad as the only evidence which those their superiors ever suffer themselves to hear? No: nor so much as a possibility of it.

When a course of guilt rendered necessary by ill-constructed laws, and become inveterate by habit, is become so familiar to the eye as no longer to be productive of any perceptible sensation; men, though in the theatre of justice accustomed to talk morality, as a poor player in the like character might do upon the stage, — such men will, like the poor player, sometimes forget their part. The men I have in view shall not be named by me;

* By 3 Geo. IV. cap. 23, a general form is given for the record of convictions. It requires the evidence to be set forth. — *Ed.*

they are particular men, and there are more than one of them: I was never set against them by any the least cause of enmity; enmity, had there ever been any, would long since have been extinguished in the grave; they would scarcely, were they alive, regard the observation so much as a token, or even as a cause of displeasure: but I will not, on this occasion, refuse to mankind the benefit of this my testimony. Oftentimes have I observed them, while affidavits have been reading, looking about to their brethren on the bench, or across the court to their quondam brethren at the bar, with sympathetic nods and winks and smiles, noting perjury, and treating it as a good joke. Such, while suitors are men, and while judges are men, must be the consequences of affidavit evidence. These were old men—I was then a young one: youth, where there is any virtue, is the season for it: virtue, at a distance from temptation, may be practised without difficulty. Whatever be the cause, well do I remember that no such jokes, especially when followed by such marks of relish, have ever met my eyes or ears without exciting a mixed sensation of disgust and melancholy.

Are judges insensible to the impropriety of this species of evidence? No: they are not insensible of it. How often have I not heard them speaking with displeasure of the task imposed upon them, or attempted to be imposed upon them, of trying a cause by affidavits! Why then submit to it at all? Because, in certain cases, like so many other unpleasant tasks (unpleasant, at least, in proportion to a man's love of justice,) it stands imposed upon them by the inviolable law of usage.

When the decision is by a judge without a jury, could not the examination be carried on without a jury likewise, at the same time carried on in other respects as if there were a jury to hear it, and decide upon it? Oh no: not for the world. Was ever proposition so extravagant? Littleton, with Coke upon his back, would rise out of his grave to protest against it.

Locke, in his Essay, speaks of a student in the art of dancing, who could not practise unless an old trunk he had been used to see in the rooms, were in the particular place he had been used to see it in. An English judge would not know how to lend an ear to the examination of a witness, unless he saw a dozen tradesmen sitting in the box in which on these occasions he had been used to see them.

So much for affidavit evidence. Bad as it is, this species of evidence must be acknowledged to be a great improvement on the sort of information to which, in all incidental, as well as initiative applications, the effect of evidence was at that time, and still continues to be, given, in the courts established on the Roman model, in most parts of the continent of Europe.

CHAPTER XIV.

GENERAL VIEW OF THE INCONGRUITIES OF ENGLISH LAW IN RESPECT OF THE EXTRACTION OF EVIDENCE.

TAKING the ends of justice, and, in so far as any contrariety or opposition is discernible on the part of any one as compared to any other, taking the aggregate interest of justice, as constituted by the preference due to this more important end,—the above rules, are they conformable to those ends? If yes, every arrangement contrary to any one of them, is, *pro tanto*, contrary to the ends of justice, and (in so far as the ends of justice meet with regard on the part of those on whom the state of the law depends) will not be suffered to continue. So many instances of departure from the above rules, so many instances of incongruity in the established practice.

To any one to whom the general spirit of the established systems (which is as much as to say, the existing modifications of the technical system) is known, it must already be pretty apparent, that whichsoever of them be taken, and subjected to this test of propriety, will be found altogether incapable of abiding it.

Referred to this test, the incongruities of the Anglican modification of that system will be found more numerous and more flagrant than those of any other. Not that it is upon the whole more adverse, perhaps, than every other to the ends of justice; but that the others, or at least its grand rival the Roman system, being in its deviation from the rule of right more uniform, those of the Anglican system will be found more numerous, more diversified, more inconsistent, and, in respect of their inconsistency, upon the whole more revolting to the scrutinizing eye.

As to the possible modes of incongruity, or deviation from the track marked out by the ends of justice,—in this part of the course, as in every other, they are of course innumerable. Imagination being here at fault, it is to observation that we must have recourse for examples. Directed to the field of English procedure, observation will accordingly afford us but too ample a stock. At every line it will become more and more evident, that, taking altogether the arrangements which will be referred to, or brought to view, it is scarce possible that, in the framing of them, any sincere regard should ever have been had to the ends of justice.

The standards of congruity, and thence the tests of incongruity, having already been established, no more remains to be done at present, than, upon a view of the several leading arrangements of Anglican procedure (so far as the present part of the subject is concerned,) to mark out — in the first place, the several incongruities, — in the second place, the several institutions in which they have respectively been exemplified.

The following are the heads under which the principal incongruities belonging to this part of the field of evidence appear reducible :—

1. Receiving testimony in the ready-written, that is, the less trustworthy, form, without any regard to expense, vexation, and delay; and thence, in instances in which the sacrifice of the direct ends of justice is pure and simple, uncompensated by any saving or advantage, having respect to these incidental or collateral ends.

2. Receiving testimony exempt from that security which is afforded by punishment against mendacity and temerarious falsity; and that in cases in which punishment is applicable for that purpose, with no less propriety than in any of the other cases in which punishment is actually thus applied.

3. Receiving testimony exempt from that security which is afforded against mendacity and temerarious falsity by the sanction of an oath; and that in cases in which that sanction is applicable for that purpose with no less propriety than in any other of the cases in which it is actually thus applied.

4. Receiving testimony, whether in the *vivâ voce* or the ready-written form, exempt from that security which is afforded as well against mendacity and temerarious falsity as against undesigned incorrectness and incompleteness, by the faculty of special interrogation, especially by or on behalf of the party adverse to him by whom the testimony has been called in; and this too not on any such score as that of a regard to preponderant inconvenience in the shape of expense, vexation, and delay.

5. Receiving testimony (*vivâ voce* testimony) in secret — *i. e.* without the benefit of publicity, in cases in which no ground of demand for secrecy applies: in cases in which the general advantages attached to publicity do not stand counterweighed by any of the inconveniences which, in the shape of vexation, are apt in particular cases to result from the employment of that security.

6. Receiving testimony (*vivâ voce* testimony) in public, in cases in which either no considerable advantage results from the employment of that security, or such advantage (if any) is outweighed by the inconvenience resulting, as above, from the employment of that security in particular cases.

7. In the case of testimony delivered *vivâ voce*, neglecting to make any express provision, or any provision at all, for recordation: and — where, without any such provision, such means have actually been brought into existence as it were by accident — making no adequate use of them, but suffering evidence of a less trustworthy, and comparatively highly untrustworthy, complexion, to be employed, and even to the exclusion of the most trustworthy sort above mentioned.

8. Providing to causes of one denomination, viz. *criminal* causes, one mode or plan of collection; to causes of another denomination, viz. *civil* causes, another mode or plan of collection altogether different: allowing, at the same time, the same individual case to be inquired after in either or both of those widely different modes.

9. Applying to suits of the same denomination (viz. *criminal* causes,) modes or plans of collection altogether different, according as this or that arbitrarily allotted sub-denomination happens to have been given to them, such as indictment, information, attachment: allowing, at the same time, the same individual case to be inquired after in any one, or in several together, of those modes; amongst which, as compared one with another, the difference is again extremely wide.

10. Applying in like manner to divers suits, all comprehended under the same general denomination of *civil* suits, modes or plans of collection altogether different, according as this or that arbitrarily allotted sub-denomination happens respectively to have been given to them, such as action, bill in equity, petition in bankruptcy, suit in ecclesiastical court: allowing here also the same individual case to be inquired after in any one, or in several together, of those modes; amongst which the difference is again extremely wide.

11. Applying, in the course of the same suit, modes and plans of collection altogether different, according as the fact or question forming the subject of inquiry were the principal, or an incidental one, and the inquiry thereupon considered as definitive, or but preparatory: and this, although in both the importance be exactly the same, the fate of the cause being as effectually determined by a decision on the incidental question, as by a decision on the principal question.

12. Rendering it necessary that one and same fact or question should in all cases be inquired into several times over; and this not in respect of any special demand which in this or that individual instance may present itself for such repetition, but in virtue of a general unbending rule, grounded on the *denomination* under which the species of cause or demand happens to have been aggregated, by an appointment altogether arbitrary, as above.

Should it enter into the conception of any admirer of technical procedure to fancy, or pretend, that, in the allotment of the modes of collection to each case, any regard has really been paid to the different demands presented by different cases for closeness and elaborateness of scrutiny; or, in other words, that any symptoms have been manifested in it of any consideration had of the interests of truth and justice, unless it be in the view of making the more complete sacrifice of them on the altar of professional profit; let him take into mind the following example, and then answer, if he has courage enough for the task.

Læsus, having (as he says) sustained a personal injury from personal violence offered to his person by the hand of Furius, has it in contemplation to call him to account in the way of law. In this, one of the most simple and common of all cases, the following are the options he has, in the first place, of the courses or modes of procedure which he will pursue, and thence of the modes of collection which will be pursued in relation to the testimony by which the fact of the offence is to be established.

I. In the first place, he may proceed by *action* — civil action: and in this case the collection of the evidence is twice performed, each time in a different mode; viz. 1. At the outset of the cause, by the *declaration:* the instrument so called, in which the plaintiff, without the sanction of an oath, and without being subject to examination, is made to assert in general terms the fact of the offence, coupled with the designation of the person of the offender, and the individual person who has been the subject of the offence. 2. At the trial: but on this occasion, so far from being deemed necessary, the testimony of the plaintiff is universally excluded. Extraneous witnesses, such, if any, as the transaction happens to have furnished, are (unless excluded upon some other pretence, out of the legion of pretences which, in the technical system, men of law have started upon this ground) heard and examined *vivâ voce*, in the mode in that behalf already indicated.

II. In the next place, he may proceed by *indictment*, with or without previous application to a justice of the peace. In the case of the indictment, he is twice heard, if he thinks proper, in the character of a witness in his own behalf, in his own cause, with or without extraneous witnesses, as the case may be (the same person who, had he proceeded in the mode of procedure called action, would have been too untrustworthy to be heard;) both times deposing *vivâ voce*, and subject to interrogation on the part of the judge — 1. At the inquiry before the grand jury, without being subject to cross-examination by or in behalf of the defendant; 2. At the definitive trial, before the petit jury, subject to that scrutiny.

As to the defendant, Furius: — at the inquiry before the grand jury, he cannot depose, either for or against himself, being excluded from both faculties by the physical bar of absence: at the inquiry before the petit jury, he stands also excluded from both, but by the legal bar of positive institution. No question can be put to him by the advocate on the other side; no question can be put to him by his own advocate. He has a right, if he thinks fit to exercise it (a right which, if he listens to the advice of his advocate, he will not exercise,) to speak, as the phrase is, in his own defence: but as the oath cannot be tendered to him on his own application, any more than at the instance of the adversary, what he says is not considered as testimony.

3. Previously to the application to the grand jury for the allowance, on their part, necessary to the production of the evidence before the petit jury, Læsus has, if he has thought fit, made application to a justice of the peace: on which occasion, Furius having also, by summons or warrant (*i. e.* without or with bodily force,) been brought before the magistrate in the presence of Læsus, the whole transaction may have been completely brought to light by a mass of testimony collected in a mode not differing by any features worth expatiating upon, from the mode just mentioned as observed on the occasion of the definitive inquiry, the trial before the petit jury.

III. In the third place, he may proceed in the way of *information:* in which case are exhibited the two or the three courses of inquiry and masses of testimony above stated under that head, viz.

1. Affidavit work, on the occasion of the motion made by the advocate of Læsus for the rule upon Furius to show cause why the information proposed to be exhibited against him by Læsus should not be *filed; i.e.* entered among the records, to form a groundwork for the definitive inquiry called the *trial.* On this occasion, Læsus exhibits his own testimony, his own ready-written and uninterrogable testimony, in the shape of an *affidavit*, together with the testimony of any such extraneous witnesses as (the transaction having happened to furnish them) can be persuaded voluntarily to join their affidavits to his.

2. On the occasion of showing cause, as above, comes, on the part of the defendant Furius, his own testimony in his own behalf; which, being in the ready-written form, and secure against the scrutiny of adverse interrogation, is therefore admitted without scruple. Of course, unless subject to any special objections, so are the affidavits of as many extraneous witnesses as he can prevail upon to take part with him: for in this stage the cause affords not, on either side, any compulsive process for the obtainment of evidence: so that, on this stage, upon which the remaining ones are built, there cannot be any other witnesses than partial ones.

3. At the time of the trial, the evidence and the mode in which it is collected stand

on the same footing here, in the case of information, as above in the case of indictment. But, compared with the views of reason and justice entertained or professed to be entertained at an anterior stage, procedure by information affords a contrast not exhibited in the procedure by indictment. The self-same person who, on the preliminary inquiry, discoursing in the way of ready-written and uninterrogable testimony, has been received to depose upon oath, is now, on the trial, subjected to the same disadvantage, and screened by the same privilege, as in the case of the indictment. He can neither be compelled by questions, with or without the sanction of an oath, to bring forward or admit such truths as make against him; nor suffered, under the same sanction of an oath, to bring forward such truths as make for the advantage of his cause. The oath which, in the same case and the same cause, was no hardship, is now become, on a sudden, an intolerable one: the same individual, upon whose credibility the fate of the cause has been depending, now becomes so completely incredible as to be unreceivable.

4. In case of conviction, after the trial, comes (though not necessarily yet frequently, perhaps most frequently) the fresh batch of affidavit work, as above described. The credibility, the trustworthiness, now remains or is revived on all sides: the incredible prosecutor (incredible, had his suit been called an action) is now encountered, and for the second time, by the lately incredible, and now again credible and trustworthy, defendant. They are now again both credible: why? Because it is in the least trustworthy of all modes of testification that they both of them make application to be heard.

IV. It was (suppose) on the occasion of the serving on Furius the process of the court (the court in which the new mode of procedure now to be spoken of is instituted,)—that is, of conveying a summons issued from the court, or ministering in some other way to the power and authority of the court,—that Læsus received from him the injury complained of. It is a case that happens every now and then, and may happen at any time. In this case, another option he has, is, to proceed by way of *attachment*.

1. Affidavit work, the least trustworthy of all modes of collection, now completely supersedes and renders unnecessary every other, that is, every better, mode. Grand jury and petit jury are now found to be mere lumber, and, as such, thrown into the dust-hole. Both fools' baubles being thus put out of the way, the Chief justice, like Cromwell in the House of Commons, wields the rod of power and punishment at his ease: and this he is suffered to do by the worshippers of the idol with twelve heads: always on condition of his acting upon improper evidence—upon evidence too untrustworthy ever to be offered to that idol.

2. When, on the ground of the mass of evidence thus collected, the defendant Furius has been convicted and consigned to punishment (to imprisonment) in consequence of the attachment's having gone against him, as the phrase is; then comes the fresh inquiry above mentioned under that head—the inquiry by interrogatories. This mode, being different from the former, can therefore scarcely avoid being better. Though the questions be premeditated, and (unless by a discretionary latitude assumed by the subaltern judge) incapable of being accommodated, each succeeding one, to the preceding answers, the answers at any rate are unpremeditated: or at least may be, for aught that appears to the contrary, if the judge *ad hoc* (the master) thinks fit to insist on their being delivered on the spot. But, lest the mode of inquiry should be too good, it is now carefully wrapped up in official darkness: and, after everything has been brought to light that was deemed necessary to warrant the punishment imposed, a deep secret covers the rest. The party injured, too—the prosecutor Læsus—from whose suggestions further questions and further lights might have been expected with more reason than from anybody else, had any such further lights been necessary,—finds the door of this secret court shut against him, as against everybody else. As far as zeal is worth looking for on the part of the master, the subaltern of the great judge, against whose authority the contempt has militated, as much may perhaps be not unreasonably looked for, as may in general be sufficient for the purpose. But all the zeal in the world will not stand in the place of information: and, if the case were of a sort to need any, the only person on whose part it can rationally be looked for, is the prosecutor; on whose face, for anything that appears, the door of the closet is shut, as well as against every other but the examiner and examinee, with or without a third person in the character of scribe.

Meantime, should that be true which has pretty much the air of being so, viz. that the supplemental inquiry is an inquiry without an object, unless it be the extracting from the examinee the fees for the exercise thus given to his patience,—any defects observable in the plan of operation will be the less to be regretted.*

* If, after an offender has been convicted, the process of subjecting him to an examination of the inquisitorial kind,—this is the appropriate denomination, I use it not in the character of a vituperative one,—if this process be a useful process in any case, why in this case to the exclusion of all others? Why not in many other cases as well as this, or in preference to this? Why not, for

V. Let Læsus be a clergyman: the misfortune is of the number of those to which a clergyman, no less than any other man, is exposed. In this case he has the option of yet another remedy,—a remedy by suit in the ecclesiastical court. The badness of the mode of extraction employed in courts of that class will be hereafter seen.

Amidst all these remedies, with the corresponding manipulations for the collection of testimony — a question that to a thinking reader can scarce fail to present itself, is — can they all, or any, and which of them, be employed together? To meet this question by an all comprehensive and at the same time determinate set of answers, is what the most experienced lawyer would scarcely take upon him.

When, for an injury of this nature, a man has prosecuted the wrong-doer in the way of indictment and (the indictment still pending) has afterwards sued him in the way of action, — instances have been known where (on application made in the way of motion) the court have compelled the plaintiff to make his election between the two remedies, by staying, or threatening to stay, the action, till he has undertaken not to go on with the indictment.

On inquiry, it would perhaps turn out that the restraint thus put upon multiplied litigation, for the same cause, may have been modified in other ways besides the above. But the changes that might be rung in this way would, if taken in hand by a mathematician, be found in no small degree numerous; and amongst them might perhaps be found as many for which, for want of precedents, a circumspect lawyer would not take upon him to answer, as of those concerning which the oracle would not scruple to pronounce: especially as ecclesiastical law would require to be included in the sphere of his meditations; and, the law (ignorance of which is not excused in any man) being, for the general convenience of the practitioners, divided into divers branches, some of them having little communication with their rivals, the judge who is erudite in the one, confesses himself, with habitual modesty and reciprocally-requited candour, less than a tyro in the other.

For example: though, in the order above exemplified, the restriction is applicable, it follows not that it would be so, were the order, as between remedy and remedy, reversed. By an action for the injury, a man recovers damages — obtains money under the name of damages: it follows not by any means, that an indictment brought afterwards for the same offence could be got rid of on that ground. In case of conviction, in considering the amount of the penalty (if pecuniary) to be inflicted, the court might, and probably enough would, consider the prior burthen so imposed: but, though the penalty should be reduced to a nominal one, the costs would remain without reduction; and, in comparison with that part of the burthen which is not capable of being adjusted to merits and demerits, the part which is capable of such adjustment is commonly very inconsiderable.

Another consideration which the oracle would know better than to bring to view, is, that, for a man to take his chance of getting rid of one such burthen, it would be necessary for him to begin with taking upon himself another. For, in an English court of justice, nothing is done out of the way without *motion*, nor any regard paid to a motion unless supported (and in general with the faculty of being combated) by affidavit work: a sort of contest which is in fact a suit of itself, in everything but the name; being, as hath already been seen, that sort of suit in which matters of any degree of importance may be and are determined.

One point on which a man may venture to pronounce with greater confidence, is, that, in the case of the clergyman (for example,) the three *remedies*, as they are called, each with its proportion of irreducible and previously unascertainable costs, must each of them be brought into action, or a correspondent end of justice (at least according to Blackstone's, which is the technically correct conception of the ends of justice) remain unfulfilled. Reparation of the breach made in the king's peace, reparation of the damage sustained by the party injured, and reparation of the damage done by the sin to the sinner's soul, — these are the objects to be provided for; and, where money is the healing matter, it requires for each a different sum to be levied by a different set of hands.† By a sum of ten pounds, for example, conveyed into the pockets of the individual injured, the injury sustained by that individual (that is to say, to the extent of the sum, and in consequence of its repairing or healing property,) is repaired. But by this ten pounds no sort of repair is applied to the breach that had been made in the king's peace: to make this second repair requires an-

example, to ascertain the state of his finances, for the purpose of observing the weight of the pecuniary burthen he is able to bear in the character of satisfaction or of punishment? Why not, in case of apprehended insolvency, for the purpose of securing what remains for the benefit of creditors, in just proportions? Why not, in the case of criminality in the way of depredation, for the purpose of investigating former depredations, and restoring to the persons injured such fruits as may be to be recovered? Why not—but questions of this nature proceed on the supposition—the perpetually-disproved supposition, that the arrangements of technical procedure have for their objects the ends of justice.

* *Vide infra*, Chap. XVII.

† Bl. Comm. IV. Chap. 15.

other sum, suppose a like sum of ten pounds, by which, if duly conveyed into the pocket of the king—(what in law is said of the king is commonly a fiction, but here it is plain truth)—duly conveyed into the royal pocket by the surveyor of the green wax (there is much learning in that green wax,*) may be presumed to produce that salutary effect.

As little, although put into the pocket of a clergyman, does this same ten pounds contribute to the repair of the damage done by the assault to the sinner's (the assaulter's) soul: the soul remains as sinful and as sick as ever, unless and until a third sum, say also of ten pounds (according to Blackstone, it must be a *round* one,) has found its way into the pockets of the officers of the court, by way of "commutation of penance."† Thus stands the matter according to Blackstone, to whose peering eyes depredation is an object of scorn or adoration, according to the power of the depredator; and by whom every fee that finds its way into the pockets of those by-practitioners is regarded as so much stolen from the superior college.

If Blackstone were to be trusted to, "these three kinds of prosecution may, *all* of them," (he says not, *any* of them,) be pursued for one and the same offence. Interrogated about the stop that might be put to the action, he might probably enough have replied, that to pursue is one thing, to pursue with effect is another. But he who, on any occasion, trusts to Blackstone, leans on a broken reed: and it is among the privileges of an interpreter of English jurisprudence, that his interpretations may always be deceitful, without ever being false.

On the subject of testimony, the following presents itself as a tolerably correct and tolerably complete list of the sources from whence the distinctions struck out by the sinister industry of the man of law have been derived:

1. The relation borne to the cause by the proposed deponent: that of an extraneous witness, with or without interest—(not that his being without interest is a point that, to the purpose of its sinister effect on the mind, ever can be ascertained)—or that of plaintiff, or that of defendant, in the cause.

2. The modification given to the course of procedure, as distinguished by the terms *criminal* and *civil*.

3. The sub-modifications given to that course, as further distinguished by the appellations of indictment, information, appeal, criminal suit in the spiritual or ecclesiastical court, action, mandamus, prohibition, bill in equity, petition, civil suit in the spiritual or ecclesiastical court.

4. The stage to which, according to the sub-modification to which it has been referred, the inquiry by which the evidence in question is called for happens to belong:—on an indictment for felony or breach of the peace, the preparatory examination; the inquiry before the grand jury; the trial (except in case of felony;) the supplemental affidavit work, preparatory to the pronouncing of judgment or sentence:—in an information, the preparatory affidavit work; the trial; the supplemental affidavit work preparatory to the receiving judgment or sentence: and so on.

5. The station of the demand on the occasion of which the testimony is proposed to be received; viz. whether it be the principal demand, which gave beginning to the cause, or some incidental demand, made (whether by the plaintiff or by the defendant) in the course of the cause.

6. The person at whose instance the testimony is proposed to be exhibited; whether the proposed deponent himself, the judge, a plaintiff, a defendant, a co-witness, or an advocate, on the one side or the other: and (in each case except the two first) whether the party on whose side the deponent was first called upon to depose, or any other person calling for his testimony on the same or on the opposite side.

7. The willingness or reluctance, whether on the part of the proposed deponent himself, or on that of either party or any co-witness, in respect of his coming to act in that character: according to which modifications, his testimony, if admitted, is admitted either without compulsion or on compulsion; if excluded, is excluded either on the score of reluctance, or notwithstanding willingness.

8. The condition of the testimony in respect to particularity: whether resting altogether on generals, or descending more or less deep into particulars, through the fixation of limited or individual portions of time and place, and the designation of the things and persons that are the subjects of it, by classes, determinate assemblages, or individuals.

9. The occasion, whether judicial or extrajudicial, on which the testimony in question is proposed to be, or has been, delivered.

10. The nature of the signs by which it has been or is proposed to be expressed, at the moment of its first utterance, or afterwards: *i. e.* whether delivered by evanescent signs, as *vivâ voce*, or by permanent signs, as in the state of a ready-written document; and if by evanescent signs, whether fixed or not fixed, during its utterance, or at any subsequent period of time, as by written notes or minutes.

11. In case of falsehood with mendacity, or falsehood through temerity (though this latter species, materially as it differs from the

* See 23d Report of the House of Commons Committee on Finance, anno 1798.

† IV. Comm. Chap. 19.

other, is scarcely distinguished;) the annexation or non-annexation of punishment to a deviation from the path of truth.

12. In the above cases, the performance or non-performance of the ceremony called swearing, or taking an oath—a ceremony instituted for the purpose of binding witnesses the more effectually to an adherence to the line of truth, on the occasion of their acting in the character of deposing witnesses.

It is of distinctions like these that nineteen parts out of twenty of the chaos of jurisprudential law are composed. It is from effusions like these, that the manufacturer of that chaos of fraud and imbecility derives, from his accomplices and his dupes, the praise of ingenuity and science.

To the eye of common sense and common honesty, looking to the ends of justice, all these distinctions are the baseless fabric of distorted vision. In the estimation of common sense and common honesty, it matters not—

1. What relation the individual whose testimony is in question, bears to the cause—whether that of extraneous witness (interested or not interested,) plaintiff, or defendant.

2. Nor whether the suit be called criminal or civil.

3. Nor, in either case, by what capricious, or accidental, or obsolete, or insidious modifications, the course of procedure in it has been diversified, and by what denominations those modifications have been distinguished.

4. Nor in what stage the inquiry is: and so on, as the reader may easily pursue for himself, through the twelve sources of distinction.

CHAPTER XV.

MODE OF EXTRACTION IN ENGLISH COMMON-LAW PROCEDURE—ITS INCONGRUITIES.

§ 1. *Case, penal: offence, a felony: procedure by indictment.*

WHERE the punishment rises to a certain pitch, the offence is called a felony: below that pitch, it is called a misdemeanour. Without endless details, any more precise account would be impossible.

The mode of collecting the evidence is, in these different cases, distinguished by material differences; but these differences are made to depend, not upon the nature of the case, but upon the nature of the punishment.

In the case of a felony, the evidence is collected (the whole or the principal part of it) three times over: each time by a different tribunal, and according to a different set of arrangements. Once, by an inferior and non-professional sort of judge called a justice of peace, without a jury: in this case, the hearing or hearings are called the *examination*. A second time, by a sort of jury without a judge, called the grand jury. And a third time, by, or rather with, another sort of jury (directed by a judge, inferior or superior, non-professional or professional,) called a petit jury. It is on the last occasion only that the hearing is called the *trial:* a term for which no other language affords anything like an equivalent.

So in the case of a misdemeanour, regarded as amounting to a breach of the peace.

In the case of a misdemeanour not so regarded, the preliminary examination has no place. The cause comes, in the first instance, before the grand jury; unless where the proceeding is by *information*, of which afterwards.

We shall begin with the case of felonies.

I. Inquiry before a justice.

Before this tribunal there are commonly at least two hearings. At the first, comes a person in the character of a prosecutor, to state the fact of the supposed offence, and the person of the supposed offender, for the purpose of thus forming the ground of his application for a *warrant.** A warrant is an order, to be directed to a proper officer by the justice, for the arrestation of the defendant, that he may be brought before him for examination, and, in the meantime, committed to a proper prison, to secure his forthcomingness for that purpose.

At this first hearing, the absence of the defendant is supposed by the nature of the case.† The plaintiff, or (as he is called) the prosecutor, being first put on his oath, states his case in the way of spontaneous deposition. the judge on his part interposes what questions he thinks fit; which questions, it is evident, so far as their operation or tendency is in favour of the defendant, have the effect of adverse interrogation.

This *ex parte* examination is either altogether private, or more or less public in any degree, according to accidental circumstances, and the discretion of the judge. By a provision of statute law, minutes of such examination ought to be taken by this magistrate. Whether they ever are taken, does not appear in print. What does appear is, that there are instances in which this statute is disobeyed;

* In consequence of the efficiency of the new police, applications to the magistrates in the metropolis, for warrants to apprehend individuals charged with felony, are now very rare. When for the first time the magistrates hear of the matter, the person accused is, generally speaking, already in custody.—*Ed.*

† Unless where the delinquent, being caught in the commission of the offence, is by individuals (with or without the assistance of a constable) brought to the magistrate in the first instance, before any warrant granted by him for the purpose, and therefore without any such warrant. In this case, the first *ex parte* inquiry is of course wanting, or (what comes to the same thing) converted into a reciprocal one.

in which ill consequences arise from this disobedience; in which the superior judges are apprized of the disobedience, see the ill consequences of it, and take no notice of it.*

Next comes the reciprocal hearing: when, the defendant being produced in the character of a prisoner, the prosecutor (being, as before, upon oath) tells his story as before. He is confronted with the defendant; the defendant puts what questions to him he thinks fit, which questions have of course the effect of an adverse examination: to the one, as well as to the other, questions such as the occasion demands are put of course by the judge. With or instead of the above-mentioned first witness, may have come on this occasion any number of other witnesses, according to the individual circumstances of the case. The defendant, on this occasion, is not upon oath: he is neither required nor permitted to subject himself to the ceremony. In case of an illegal attack made upon a man's person in the way of physical force, the faculty of self-defence is allowed to him for his protection, by English as well as other laws. In England, for his protection against legal accusation, the faculty of mendacity, with its attendant, non-responsion, is (on this occasion as on others) carefully reserved to him, as a branch of the lawful faculty of self-defence. In putting questions to a defendant thus under examination, it is a sort of fashion to give him warning that he is at liberty to answer them or not as he thinks fit; for, though whatever a supposed delinquent is supposed to have said, out of the presence of a judge, to his own prejudice, is heard with perfect readiness,—yet, whatever evidence of the same nature it might have happened to him thus to furnish against himself in the presence of a judge, is carefully prevented from coming into existence. The criminal (for to a criminal alone can the intimation be of any use) the criminal, if the case admit of his availing himself of this friendly warning, avails himself of it, and is eventually turned loose again into society to afflict it with fresh crimes. The judge obtains the praise of patriotism and humanity and legal science, at no other expense than that of the interests of truth, justice, and public security. A deluded public pays a man with its praise for betraying its own interests. Sometimes it may happen that the public, besides being duped to its own prejudice, is duped for its own advantage. The magistrate, wishing to reconcile, if possible, the merit of serving the public interest, with the praise of having betrayed it, extracts the confessorial testimony where the cause stands in need of it, reserving the warning for the cases in which he perceives the inutility of it. But all this is matter of chance.

The number of these examinations depends of course upon the exigency of the individual case: upon the number of the witnesses, the remoteness of their situation, and the several other possible causes of unavoidable complication and delay.

Of the evidence thus obtained, the aggregate constitutes what, under the Roman procedure, would constitute ground sufficient for a decision in the first instance—for a decision which, supposing no appeal, would be definitive.

In English procedure, the acts of this tribunal serve but as a passport to the two others. In a large proportion of cases of this class (perhaps the greater number,) the truth is as effectually brought to light in one hearing (that hearing being a reciprocal one,) as it could be in fifty: but, because ulterior inquiry is in some few cases necessary, it is employed in all; including those in which it is useless, and worse than useless.

II. Inquiry before the grand jury.

Applied to the class of cases still in question, the operations of this intermediate tribunal may be set down as purely mischievous. They had once an object, but that object has been done away: it might be seen to be so, if bigotry had eyes; but bigotry is blind: the incumbrance keeps its place; lawyers and their dupes never speak of it but with rapture.

The object was to preserve an innocent man from the vexation incidental to prosecution: and innocent he might well be pronounced, if, even upon the face of the evidence produced against him by the adversary, delinquency did not appear probable.

The design was laudable: and to this design, the procedure, whatsoever might be the inconveniences attached to it in other respects, was naturally enough adapted.

1. Evidence was received only on one side —on the side of the prosecutor: on the side of the defendant, not; for to call upon him for his evidence would be to subject him to the very vexation from which it was intended he should be preserved.

2. The evidence was received and collected in secret; that is to say, in so far as secrecy was compatible with the presence and participation of a number of persons (the persons composing the grand jury) from twelve to twenty-three. In the same intention, these jurymen were sworn to secrecy. Why? Because, at this period, the defendant knew nothing of the matter. The bill being found by this jury (*i. e.* the accusation pronounced to have had a sufficient ground in point of evidence to warrant the ulterior inquiry,) thereupon went an order for his arrestation. Had it not been for the oath, a friendly jury-

* Leach's Cases, 3d edit.

man might give intimation, and the defendant make his escape.

In the first place, then, the institution is useless: it has been so about these two hundred and fifty years. The defendant has been already subjected to the vexation from which he was thus to have been preserved. From the middle of the sixteenth century, the examinations above described have taken place.

In the next place, it is mischievous. It is so in no small degree. One of the great boasts, as well as one of the greatest merits, of English procedure, is its publicity. This security, it has been seen, is sacrificed: sacrificed, and so continues to be, after the object for which the sacrifice was made is gone. The consequence is, an unlimited domination to popular prejudice; to party, if not personal interest and affection; to false humanity; to caprice under all its inscrutable modifications. In practice, many a bill which ought to have been found, is thrown out without reason—many a mischievous delinquent turned loose. In the abuse of this useless institution may be seen the sole use and justification of the inquiry by *information;* of which presently in its place.

Under the auspices of publicity, for example—as at the succeeding inquiry before the petit jury, causes in other respects the same, could not be productive of equal mischief. Whatsoever became of the legal sanction, the moral would not lose its hold. Of a guilty man, who is seen and known to be guilty, the proof of his guilt is itself a punishment.

Nor, as applied to the judges themselves, is the tutelary genius of publicity altogether without its influence. In the way of legal punishment, they are indeed exempt from responsibility altogether. In the way of moral reproach,—though, by the want of individual responsibility, the security by publicity against misdecision is, on the part of these ephemeral judges, sadly diminished,—it were too much to look upon it as altogether destroyed.

III. Inquiry before the petit jury, called the *trial.*

The doors are now thrown open: under the auspices of publicity, collection and registration of the evidence are performed, each in its best mode, with no other exceptions than those which will be mentioned as we proceed.

At this stage, the defendant is necessarily present, as being necessarily in custody: on which account it is that he is never designated by any other appellation than that of the prisoner: if he were not present, the trial would not be legal.*

Being present, one question, and but one, is put to him, and that at the outset of the inquiry: "Are you guilty or not guilty?" If his answer were Guilty, and he were to abide by it, the trial would be at an end: Guilty would of course be the decision—the verdict (as it is called) of the jury.†

That this species of confessorial evidence ought not of itself to be regarded as sufficient to warrant conviction—that it ought to be followed up and confirmed by a detailed narrative—is a proposition which will be maintained in another place.‡ That mendacity, and subornation of mendacity, is no more necessary or conducive to the ends of justice on this than on any other occasion, is a proposition, the truth of which may be left to rest upon its own evidence.

Where it happens to a prisoner to answer in the affirmative—in appropriate language, to *plead guilty*—if he insists on it, the general understanding seems to be that he has a right to have such his plea recorded: in which case there is a necessary end of the trial, and the verdict follows of course.

In practice, it is grown into a sort of fashion, when a prisoner has returned this answer, for the judge to endeavour to persuade him to withdraw it, and substitute the opposite plea, the plea of not guilty, in its place. The wicked man, repenting of his wickedness, offers what atonement is in his power: the judge, the chosen minister of righteousness, bids him repent of his repentance, and in place of the truth, substitute a barefaced lie. Such is the morality, such the holiness, of an English judge.‖

* Why not legal? Because, if not present, he stands bereft of two essential faculties, both necessary to his defence—the faculty of cross-examining the witnesses on the other side, and the faculty of producing evidence on his own side. To preserve him from this disadvantage, what is the course taken by the law? In case of his non-appearance, he is outlawed—subjected to an unfathomable mass of punishment, of which the punishment appropriated to the particular sort of offence of which he stands suspected, constitutes but a part.

† If he pleads "not guilty," in a case of felony, he is also told that he may challenge the jury, by objecting to any of the jurymen as they come to be sworn.—*Ed.*

‡ Book V. *Circumstantial;* Chap. VI. *Spontaneous self-inculpative Testimony.*

‖ A rule which in itself has no reason, affords, so long as it is suffered to exist, a reason, and even a use, for this preposterous subornation. Unless the defendant will plead not guilty, the particular facts by which his guilt is evidenced cannot forsooth be brought to view.[a] Why not

[a] When a prisoner pleads guilty, the usual course in England, is for the judge to read the depositions, and examine the witnesses, if he thinks it necessary, in order to determine what degree of punishment should be inflicted. In Scotland, this practice is not adopted; but in that part of the empire it is not customary for the judge to offer any recommendations as to the prisoner's plea.—*Ed.*

It would be some extenuation, though by no means a justification, if it were clear that the supplying the defectiveness of the general proposition by a detailed narrative, were the sole or principal object of this unnecessary, and (were it not that custom is a cloak for every enormity) unseemly, subornation. But, such an apology would be but a surmise, and that (to judge by analogy) not the most probable one. When a general disregard to truth, or (to speak more correctly) a fondness for falsehood, coupled with a general propensity to sacrifice the interests of justice to popular prejudice, to curry favour with the people at the expense of moral duty, pervades the whole system, breaking out on a variety of occasions into so many overt acts; it seems much more consistent with probability to ascribe the effect to this known actual cause, than to any other purely conjectural one.

When the witnesses in support of the charge have been respectively subjected to primary examination performed by the advocate for the prosecutor—or by the judge, in the few instances in which it has happened that no advocate has been employed,—the prisoner, by himself and advocate, exercises, in so far as he thinks fit, the right of cross-examination: the witnesses, of course, all of them upon oath.

When the evidence on that side has been gone through, then comes the time for the prisoner to make what is called his *defence*. For this purpose no advocate is in these cases (cases of felony) allowed to him:* in private, the advocate may, in the way of advice, speak *to* him; but, in the address to the judge and jury, must not speak *for* him: an arrangement, the propriety or impropriety of which belongs not to this place. The defence therefore consists of a discourse, shorter or longer, according to the nature of the case, and the rhetorical powers of the prisoner; in which, whatever suggestions promise to his conception to promote his cause, are brought forward without distinction: testimony and argument, facts (or pretended facts) and inferences from these facts, all produced without distinction, all uttered in the same breath.

On other occasions, and on the opposite side, the sanction of an oath, and the use of cross-examination, are magnified, the former far beyond the extent of its real efficacy, as the most indispensable securities for truth and justice: on this occasion, and as against the defendant on behalf of the public, neither is permitted to be employed.

Out of court, under circumstances favourable to every species of abuse, the faculty of interrogating the defendant has been open to every man without distinction, and without regard to fitness; and the hearsay account of the result of such adverse examinations, in any number, is admitted in evidence without scruple. In court, under the eye of the judge, in circumstances in which the possibility of abuse (unless the judge himself were to be supposed a party to it) is excluded, all exercise of that faculty is forbidden; nor must a single question be put to a defendant in that view.

§ 2. *Case, penal: offence, a misdemeanor: procedure by indictment.*

Let us next pass to the case of misdemeanors attended with breach of the peace.

The nomenclature is not here very expressive or determinate; but it is such as English jurisprudence furnishes. Offences attended with violence to person or property, but not in such sort as to be punished with the punishment of felony,—is a description that seems to come as near the mark as any other that could be given without limitations, exceptions, and dissertations.†

Here too come the same three inquiries as before. The first, however (viz. that before a justice of the peace,) is not so uniformly resorted to as in the case of felonies. Of this inquiry, the principal use and object is prospective—to put a stop to a course of intended or apprehended injuries. It is for this purpose that power is given to the magistrate to oblige the defendant, on pain of imprisonment, to find sureties for abstaining from such transgressions in future.

Here, as above, a but too obvious remark is, that, if justice had been the object in preference to plunder, this one of the three inquiries

be brought to view? What should hinder them? Why not receive his confession in general terms, and at the same time receive the confirmation of it by the relation of all the particulars? That, in point of reason, confessorial evidence conceived in general terms does not by any means supersede the demand for the statement of the facts in detail, will be shown in another place: but, to this purpose, mendacity on the part of the criminal—subornation of mendacity on the part of the judge, is no more necessary, or so much as conducive, than it is to any other useful and commendable purpose. In the nature of things, the plea of guilty would no more prove an obstacle to the continuance of the inquiry, than the plea of not guilty. But so familiar and so delightful is falsehood to the ear and the lips of an English lawyer, that without it he would be perpetually at a stand: it is the oil, with which the wheels must at every turn be greased, or the machine would stand still.

* By 6 & 7 Wil. IV. cap. 114, counsel for the prisoner may now address the jury in cases of felony.—*Ed.*

† *Peace* is a word without meaning, in the mind of an English lawyer. The peace is broken by an unsuccessful attempt to give currency to a forged note or a bad shilling. Adultery, though committed by consent, is never committed any otherwise than by force and arms.

would in general have been the only one. To warrant, in point of natural justice, the imposition of this burthensome obligation upon the defendant, the magistrate cannot but have been satisfied of his delinquency—satisfied of it with that degree of persuasion which warrants him in passing a sentence of conviction to other purposes, in the cases where power to that effect has been conferred upon him by the law. Satisfaction, or punishment, or both (according to the nature of the case,) might as well be administered at the end of this first inquiry, when the state of the evidence is ripe for it, as at the end of ever so many more. But, by any such arrangement, the *regularity* of the procedure would have been destroyed: it would have been cut down, and reduced to summary; every application of which is an injury to the profession, useful only to the public and the suitors.

In this case, the registration of the evidence has not been made obligatory, as in the case where the subject-matter of the inquiry belongs to the class of felonies. Being unperformed where commanded, whether it be performed where uncommanded, may be easily imagined.

As between the two parties to the quarrel, the same want of reciprocity is observable as in those other cases. That one of them who happens to have come forward in the character of plaintiff, narrates and answers upon his oath; the defendant, not.

In virtue of the established principle, here as there, the defendant may refuse to make answer if he pleases: but, forasmuch as from the nature of the case it is in general more for his advantage to be explicit than to be silent, the effect of the privilege is scarce perceptible in practice: and, forasmuch as the praise of humanity and patriotism is not to be reaped in so large a proportion in this case as in that, by the protection of guilt and the obstruction of justice, the practice of cautioning the defendant against the imprudence of speaking truth is not here so fashionable.

This (it must further be observed) is among the cases in which the party grieved has his option, whether he will consider the act of delinquency on the footing of a crime, or of what is called a civil injury. In the first case (to speak strictly rather than correctly,) he obtains punishment without satisfaction; in the other case, satisfaction without punishment. In this latter case, those three stages of inquiry are out of the question, and the inquiry is conducted in the purely non-penal mode, of which in its place.

Among the circumstances which a man has to take into account for the purpose of this option, one is, the absence or presence of a sufficient mass of extraneous evidence. If the mode of procedure be of the non-penal, called the *civil*, kind (in which case it is called an *action*,) the party seeking redress is not trustworthy, and, in the character of a self-serving witness in his own behalf, cannot be heard. If, as above, it be of the penal kind (in which case it is called an *indictment*,) the same individual is trustworthy, and his testimony in his own behalf is accordingly admitted.

The reason given for the distinction is, that, in the case of an action, he has money at stake upon his testimony, whereas, in the case of an indictment, he has nothing at stake but revenge: as if, in the eyes of the bidder, revenge were not worth to a man the money he is content to pay for the prospect of obtaining it. In point of fact, the reason is notoriously untrue:* but, in the reasoning of English jurisprudence, falsehood is a virtue, truth at best a superfluity; nor is the argument weakened by the want of it.

For injuries of the self-same description, there is yet another mode of procedure, which is called an *information;* of which by and by in its place.

In this, again, the mode of inquiry and the rules of evidence undergo many material changes. The first inquiry — that before a justice of the peace — does not usually take place. The second — that before a grand jury — never can take place: an essential object of this form of procedure being to preserve justice against the obstruction apprehended from that secret, and consequently arbitrary, tribunal.

Among the advantages of the natural form of procedure, is that of its fixing the evidence in the earliest stage, and thus saving it from deperition. The first of the three above-mentioned inquiries,—viz. the examination before a magistrate — the inquiry which, if it were the only one, would denominate the procedure summary instead of regular, — possesses this great advantage. In procedure by indictment without such previous examination, and in procedure by action, and (as it should seem,) in procedure by information, this benefit has no place.

English lawyers and their dupes are in raptures at the thoughts of so rich a variety of remedies (the list of which is not yet exhausted,†) all for the same injury. But, as there is not one of them that gives more than a fragment, a scrap, of a remedy, the plain fact is, the greater the number of them, the more inadequate to the object: — understand here the *professed* object — the fulfilment of the ends of justice: for as to the real object, there is no want either of contrivance or success.

The greater the number of these forms of

---

* See Book IX. *Exclusion.*

† Ecclesiastical Court.

procedure, and the greater the variety of the arrangements they present in respect of the rules of evidence, the more impenetrable is the darkness, which has for so long a time been thicker than Egyptian, and without a miracle.

The case of misdemeanor not attended with breach of the peace, calls not for any remarks, over and above those which have been given under the other heads.

In these cases, the preliminary inquiry before a magistrate has no place. The first inquiry is the *ex parte* inquiry before the grand jury. In this, as well as in the last stage, the same observations apply to this class of offences as to the two others.

§ 3. *Case, penal: offence, a contempt: procedure by attachment.*

Causes determined without a jury: the commencement by motion: the inquiry carried on by or before the professional judge or judges.

Now opens a scene of point-blank contradiction. Every rule of evidence, every principle held sacred where the species of cause gives occasion for the pronouncing of the magical word jury, is now completely abandoned. On a system of procedure completely opposite to the former, the inquiry is conducted; always by the same persons, always with the same self-satisfaction and content.

In the species of procedure here in question, the court is one of the superior courts in Westminster Hall. The cause commences by motion — motion for a rule to show cause: an application made to the court by the plaintiff's advocate, praying that an order (a *rule*, the technical word is) may be addressed to the intended defendant, commanding him to show cause why that should not be done (whatsoever it be) which at his charge the plaintiff wishes to see done.

The evidence in this case is composed wholly of affidavit work.

At the time of the motion, and as a necessary ground for it, an affidavit is produced containing the discourse of the plaintiff. That affidavit is commonly corroborated by other affidavits, exhibiting the testimony of extraneous witnesses: the testimony of divers witnesses being sometimes conjoined in a single affidavit.

The plaintiff, in his affidavit, exhibits his own testimony in his own behalf: the sacred and inviolable rule, *nemo debet esse testis in propriâ causâ*, is thus regularly violated.

In vain would it be said — "The cause is not his own, he has no interest in it;" by which, in English law language, is meant no pecuniary interest. In the first place, many are the cases in which he has a direct and manifest interest of the strictly pecuniary kind, and that unlimited in respect of magnitude. In all cases he has the sort and degree of pecuniary interest created by *costs* — the eventual obligation of reimbursing to the adversary his share, in case of miscarriage. Even laying out of the case such eventual obligation, which may or may not be imposed; supposing him not to have any pecuniary interest in the cause, he has at any rate some other interest of stronger quality — stronger than the interest created by the money which in the shape of costs (his own costs) he sacrifices in pursuit of the service which he thus claims.

Vivâ voce deposition, by the general confession, or rather the proclamation, of all English lawyers, is the only completely trustworthy form of testimony: this only fit ground of decision is here abandoned.

Nor let it be said that considerations of convenience — convenience in respect of avoidance of the vexation and expense attached to personal attendance, had any the smallest share in giving birth to this aberration from the line of universally-acknowledged rectitude. The sort of case in which, more frequently than in any other, this mode of procedure is employed, is a case in which this species of vexation is at its minimum, if not equal to 0. Among the cases which find most employment for this species of procedure, is that of a dispute between attorney and attorney, not in a cause of their own, but on the occasion of the cause of their respective clients — a dispute having for its subject, on one part or the other, a supposed deviation from the established rules of procedure. In a case of this sort, both deponents are, in supposition always, in reality commonly, present in court — present at the same time. They are a sort of officers of the court: it is by belonging to the court, that they are what they are styled, attorneys of the court. Though not present as deponents, they are all the while present as attorneys. It is commonly in the hearing of the deponent himself, that the studied and manufactured vehicle of his testimony is read.

Along with *vivâ voce* deposition, vanishes cross-examination: even that inadequate and comparatively inefficient and untrustworthy species of cross-examination, which we shall see not banished by institution, any more than by the nature of things, from examination in the way of written correspondence.

There stands the plaintiff; close by him the defendant: each speaking — that is, hearing himself speak, by borrowed lips, in the character of witnesses. To neither of them is it possible to put a single question to the other: the court would never suffer it.

Of the utility — in some measure the necessity, of the practice of breaking down into numbered articles a mass of literary matter the destination of which (in whatever shape) is to constitute or help to constitute a ground for judicial decision,—mention has been made already in its place. Further on, instances will be brought to view, in which so important a help to comprehension has not been refused to English practice. The present is not of the number. Of an affidavit, though it were of a length to reach from one side of the Hall to the other, the whole contents would not the less remain in one shapeless undivided mass. On the part of the plaintiff, —his chance of success depending upon the goodness of his case as it stands impressed upon the face of his narrative,—his endeavour (that is, the endeavour of his attorney, in so far as, in respect of intelligence as well as probity, he is qualified to do justice to his client,) is naturally to put it into the clearest order, as being best adapted to that purpose. On the part of the defendant, if so it happens that in his own view of the matter he is in the right, the endeavour to speak clearly will be equally strenuous; and in this case the order pursued by the one will naturally be adopted and followed by the other. If, as is most likely to be the case (for the probability of right is for obvious reasons naturally on the plaintiff's side,) he is conscious of being in the wrong,—so surely will it be his study, and that of his professional assistant and licensed accomplice, to keep clear of that order, and of every sort of order; in a word, to render as thick as possible that confusion, in which alone he can behold a probability of escape.

It would be something—nay, a good deal, if this unscrutinized species of testimony were, in any court, on any future occasion, liable, and known to be liable, to be subjected to scrutiny, by being extracted over again in the most trustworthy and only proper mode. But this is altogether without example. The bare idea of any such innovation would be enough to strike horror into a professional and learned mind.

If reason had any the smallest concern in the business,—the less trustworthy the source of the testimony, the more searching and efficient would be the arrangements taken for counteracting and checking the propensity to falsehood on the part of the witness—for guarding against deception the mind of the judge. Throughout the system of English jurisprudence, a directly contrary policy (if a term so clearly expressive of thought be applicable) has been pursued. When a man's testimony is received in his own behalf, it is received in scarce any other form than that of an affidavit—in the form of an elaborate and preconcerted instrument in writing, neither divided into parts, nor liable to be disconcerted by questions. As often as the least trustworthy species of evidence—evidence from the least trustworthy source—is received, it is the inviolable rule to receive it in the least trustworthy shape, and in the least trustworthy modification of that shape.

§ 4. *Case, penal: procedure by information.*

Procedure in the way of information—information in criminal cases, is commenced by motion praying a rule to show cause: a rule, or order, upon the defendant, to show cause why an information, a species of accusation, should not be exhibited against him.

This species of procedure, like the other species of procedure in which a jury is employed, is of the composite kind. It contains two distinct inquiries: the definitive one, in which the rules of evidence are exactly the same as in the case of an indictment, as above mentioned; and a preliminary one, in which, as in procedure by attachment (of which already,) the evidence is exclusively composed of affidavit work, as above.

In this species of procedure, the previous examination—the mode of inquiry which, with little alteration, might, with advantage, supersede both of those which follow it—the mode of inquiry with which, as we have already seen, the procedure commences in the case of felony—is not admitted: a deficiency, the effects of which, in respect of the faculty of investigating and following up a thread of evidence, are but too sensible.

The inquiry by affidavit work is here a succedaneum to the inquiry before the grand jury: like that, it is worse than useless, though rendered so by a different cause.

In the inquiry before the grand jury—an inquiry conducted in secret by a tribunal the decisions of which are altogether arbitrary, the members being neither punishable by law, nor so much as subject to the restraint of shame,—the principal danger consists in the grant of impunity to guilt.

The use of the grand jury inquiry is, in the event of the non-delinquency of the intended defendant, to save him from judicial vexation—the vexation and expense attached to the obligation of defending himself against the charge: and such (supposing the bill thrown out) is, and that very completely, the effect of that inquiry. What is the effect of the previous inquiry in the way of information? It does not merely fail of diminishing the vexation: it does more than double it. An inquiry is carried on, to know whether an inquiry shall be instituted: an inquiry is carried on in a bad mode, to know whether an inquiry shall be carried on in a good mode: a cause is tried upon bad evidence, to know whether the same cause shall be tried upon good evidence.

This is not all. If, in the inquiry called the *trial*, the defendant is convicted, a third inquiry scarce ever fails of taking place: and this, like the first, is carried on by affidavit work. On the day of trial, the evidence is exhibited before the jury, under the direction of a single judge. When the defendant comes to receive judgment, it is in the court of King's Bench, in Westminster Hall, a tribunal composed of four, and those professional, judges. On this occasion, the defendant, on his part, is admitted to state (provided always it be by affidavit) any such facts as may be thought to operate in mitigation of his punishment: the prosecutor is, on his part, at liberty to bring forward, always in the same way, any facts, the tendency of which may be to operate in aggravation of the punishment: and each party will, in general, be admitted to contest, by counter-affidavits, the representations given by the other.

Among the facts which the prosecutor is thus admitted to bring forward, are any facts constitutive of subsequent bad behaviour on the part of the defendant — bad behaviour subsequent to the day of trial, on which the conviction took place; not to speak of the anterior period intervening between that day, and the date of the offence, as charged in the instrument of *information*. Here, then, for the hundredth time, we have the bad mode, the acknowledged bad mode, used promiscuously with the good mode — the (by lawyers) never enough to be admired and eulogized good mode. Nokes offers a personal insult to Stiles. Being prosecuted for this in the way of information, he is tried in the first place in the affidavit mode; and, if found guilty in that mode, tried over again in the *vivâ voce* mode. Being thus found guilty a second time, — after his conviction he offers to the same person (his prosecutor) a second insult, exactly of the same nature with the first. What is the consequence? For this second insult, he is tried but once, and that by affidavit work, and, if upon the result of that inquiry deemed guilty, punished without any reference to a jury; the punishment for this second offence being pronounced at the same time with the punishment for the first, and indistinguishably confounded with it.

When sentence (*judgment* it is called in this case) is to be pronounced, the personal attendance of the defendant is either insisted upon or dispensed with, as the court thinks fit. But when he does appear, it is for the purpose of hearing merely, and not for the purpose of being admitted to be heard. There he is; and, with him, the physical faculty of being examined in the best mode. No — it cannot—legally speaking, it cannot be. Speak he may, if he pleases: always understood, that whatever, when heard in this best mode, he advances in the way of fact, must go for nothing. Go for nothing? Why so? Only because it is offered in this best mode. The acknowledged bad mode — the mode by affidavit, in which ample time for preparation is allowed, and scrutiny by cross-examination not allowed, is the only mode in which his testimony in the character of a witness — a self-regarding, self-serving witness, is admitted to be heard. To the subjecting him to the vexation of personal attendance, there is no reluctance. The only thing resisted, and that most inexorably, is the employing for the extraction of his evidence that acknowledged best mode, against which the only objection ever made, or capable of being made on the ground of reason and utility, consists in the vexation of attendance — that very vexation to which the party is so readily subjected, on condition of its being of no use.

As to the vexation and the expense attached to this so elaborately complicated and inconsistent plan of procedure (the vexation which is the unheeded result, and the expense which, in the shape of profit, has been so manifestly the final cause,)—these are topics, the handling of which in detail must be referred to the subject of procedure. Of the vices of the system, the only ones that belong directly to the present purpose are those the tendency of which is to weaken the security for truth on the part of the witness, and thence for right decision on the part of the judge.

Elsewhere, it is in the character of an engine of oppression, — here, it is in no other than that of a vast manufactory of mendacity and deception, — that our business is to exhibit the technical system of procedure.

The composition of the tribunal is another point which requires to be carefully abstracted from the present investigation. Procedure by information, and procedure by attachment, were at one time the butts of popular and party clamour. Wherefore? For no other reason than as being rivals and succedanea to the indiscriminately-cherished and never-enough-to-be-idolized trial by jury. Information leaves work but for one out of two juries; attachment, none for any.

As to this matter, thus much is (as I presume) by this time tolerably clear; viz. that, of all the modifications of the technical (*alias* regular) mode of procedure, that in which a jury is employed is the only one tolerably well adapted to the pretended purpose of elicitation of the truth. Well adapted: why? — Because the judges are unexperienced, uninformed, numerous, unresponsible, the minority or majority of them regularly forced by torture into perjury? No: but because it is only when ephemeral judges are called in, that the mode of inquiry, acknowledged to be the only good one, is suffered to be employed. Against the professional, the learned, the veteran class of judges, my complaint (in so many instances) is, not that they have taken upon themselves, without the co-operation of their unlearned colleagues, to exercise the function of judicature, — but that, with their eyes open, and with a degree of pertinacity and assurance not to be exceeded, they have made it an inviolable rule, when left to themselves, never to conduct an inquiry but in a mode which they know to be a bad one; uniformly rejecting the very mode the superiority of which they are continually recognising, and that not only in language, but practice.

§ 5. *Case, non-penal: procedure by jury-trial.*

Compared with the procedure in criminal cases (especially those which stand, or are supposed to stand, highest in the scale of mischievousness,) the mode of procedure, in cases non-penal, presents, under the head of evidence, several important differences.

The cause of these differences need not be a secret, to any eye that has courage enough to look it in the face. In criminal cases, the law had the more pressing exigencies of society for its object, and, for the subjects of its operation, a description of persons in whose purses any considerable quantity of plunderable matter was seldom to be found. In the non-penal branch, the demand for justice was less pressing, and the quantity of plunderable matter ample enough to pay for the detention of the parties in the trammels of procedure.

Accordingly, in the construction of the criminal branch of procedure, the interests of justice seem to have taken the lead; views of plunder being comparatively inefficient and subordinate. In the formation of the plan of procedure in non-penal cases — in cases in which the title to rights of property forms the principal object of dispute — plunder, and the means of extracting it from both parties in the greatest possible quantity, would be the main object; justice, the collateral result, having, in the mind and intention of the founders of the law, afforded little more than the occasion and the pretence.

In criminal procedure there has accordingly been no fear, or at least no equal fear, of bringing the parties together, face to face, in the first instance, in the presence of the judges; nor in general has any apprehension manifested itself of seeing the cause pushed to too speedy a conclusion.

It is in the non-penal branch alone that an arrangement thus imperiously prescribed by the most obvious dictates of natural and universal justice, has been so systematically and pertinaciously excluded by men of law: except on the few occasions on which, in spite of their reluctance, the dictates of genuine justice have, under the spur of necessity, been obeyed by legislators.

Reciprocal explanation and interrogation between the parties, under the sanction of an oath, with the fear of present shame as well as future punishment staring in the face that one of the parties who, being in the wrong, is conscious of being so, — would have nipped in the bud all *malâ fide* causes. By a view jointly taken at the outset, of all the evidence afforded by the nature of the cause, together with a survey of all other causes (if any) natural and unavoidable, of delay and complication, which happened to be attached to the individual matter in dispute, — causes of both descriptions, *malâ fide* and *bonâ fide* causes together, would receive of course the speediest termination of which they were respectively susceptible.

To prevent *malâ fide* causes from being themselves prevented — to keep the doors of justice open to the best class of customers, — one fundamental rule accordingly was, that an unlimited licence for mendacity should be granted to all mankind in the character of plaintiffs.

Another was, — from the first to the last, never to admit the parties, much less bring them by compulsion, into the presence of the judge.

To the joint influence of these rules, suitors are indebted for everything which in English common law goes by the name of *pleading*.

The plaintiff has a demand (suppose for a sum of money) on the defendant. Plaintiff and defendant live (suppose) within a stone's throw of one another, and of the seat of justice. In the summary mode of procedure, had that mode been permitted to take place, the grounds of the dispute might be liquidated — evidence, such as the case affords, heard — and a decision pronounced, all within the compass of an hour. The ground being a note of hand, — whether the sum be £2 or £200, makes, in regard to the proof, and the time necessary for the exhibiting of it, not the smallest difference. The plaintiff, in this case, coming forward spontaneously with the statements made in his own way of the facts relied on by him as the grounds of his claim, general allegations and particular statements might naturally enough in this way come mixed; but a few questions from the judge would be sufficient to effect the decomposition, and place each under its proper head.

Under the technical system, — instead of appearing before the judge, and there stating the grounds of his demand, subject to counter-interrogation, and under those securities for veracity which have place in the instance of an extraneous witness, — the plaintiff (or, more properly speaking, his attorney) produces a written paper, called the *declaration*, from which almost all such information as could be of use for acquainting the judge or the defendant with the nature and grounds of the claim, is carefully excluded; an enormous mass of surplusage, garnished with innumerable lies, being substituted in its place. This paper the plaintiff's attorney deposits in an office, whence the defendant's attorney obtains a copy, on payment of a fee. If the defendant pleads the general issue — that is, contents himself with a general denial of the justice of the claim, the cause then goes to trial. If the defendant pleads any special plea — that is, makes any answer, other than such general denial, the matter of this answer is expressed in another instrument called a *plea*, which is also filled with surplusage and lies. To this plea the plaintiff may answer by a third instrument, called a *replication;* to which the defendant may further reply by a *rejoinder;* and so on, without any certain limit.

No security whatever being taken for the veracity of all this testimony (for testimony it is in the eye of reason, though not of technical law) — neither punishment, oath, interrogation, nor any other check, being applied to falsehood in this shape, — the consequence is, that, saving just so far as it is the interest of the party who gives in the testimony that it should be true, not a word of truth does it ever contain.

But of this more fully hereafter.*

At length, when the stock of reciprocal scrawls is exhausted, when the quiver of useless arrows is on both sides emptied, the first and only inquiry, the trial before a petty jury, takes place. On this occasion, the meeting of the parties in the presence of the judge — the first stage in every system of procedure that has really the ends of justice for its ends in view — this harbinger of reconciliation, and condition *sine quâ non* to thorough explanation, though purely accidental, is at least not impossible.

On this occasion, if so it happens that both parties are in a state of *bona fides*, each conceiving himself to be in the right, — in such case, whether both or either of them are or are not present, a scene of mutual frankness and expansion of heart may not unfrequently be observed. A spectator who, not knowing or not adverting to the stage at which these amicable demonstrations present themselves, should be witness only to the effect, would be apt to wonder how it should happen that between parties so well meaning, assisted by agents at once so faithful and so ingenuous, a difference capable of plunging them into litigation should ever have subsisted. In one consideration, and one only, can any cause be found adequate to the production of so remarkable an effect. The cause has, at this stage of it, furnished to the lawyers of all classes whatever pickings are to be had out of it. The stage in which agreement thus takes place, if it takes place at all, is that in which, if the cause did not end in this way, it would alike find its termination in another way. The stage at which all this virtue manifests itself, is that in which the parties have little or nothing to gain by it—their lawyers little or nothing to lose by it.

On this happy occasion, the advocates on both sides appear seldom backward in contributing their parts towards so salutary a result. Why should they? Before things are come to this pass, the learned gentlemen have had their fees.

By termination in the ordinary way—viz. by a verdict in favour of one party or the other—nothing farther would be to be got. By a termination in some extraordinary way, in virtue of an agreement for that purpose, ulterior fees may be to be got in more ways than one; and if the overture be made, as it commonly is, before the evidence is begun to be heard, so much time and trouble is saved.

By agreement, the result may come to be modified, amongst others, in either of the following ways: —

1. By a direct compromise upon the spot.
2. By reference to arbitration: in which case, after a bad mode of inquiry, the cause is subjected to the only good one. To a good mode of inquiry — even to the very best — lawyers have no objection, when it is not substituted for, but given in addition to, their own, the bad one.

§ 6. *Case, non-penal: procedure without jury-trial: cause originating in a motion.*

In the criminal class of suits, we have seen causes that take their commencement in motions: of this description are informations. We have seen others, that, having begun in motions, end there, without passing into any other mode of inquiry: such, unless in the accidental and comparatively rare case of supplemental interrogation, are attachments. Inquiry, in these cases, but one, and that by affidavit work.

The non-penal division furnishes, in like manner, causes (comparatively speaking) of the like simple texture: to this head belong causes arising out of *awards*, and causes arising out of judgments without previous litigation, or judgments (as they are called) by consent.

Incidental applications of all kinds — applications grounded on incidents arising out of a cause already commenced in some one or other of the above regular modes, — are introduced by motion, and carried on by affidavit work.

The class of causes here in question, though in substance and effect original, are in form and appearance incidental. Judgment as for debt, entered up (as the phrase is) on a warrant of attorney to confess judgment, is, in

* Book VIII. *Technical Procedure;* Chap. XVI. *Written Pleadings.*

effect and substance, a mere contract between the creditor and the debtor—the supposed plaintiff and the supposed defendant; the judge, whose decision the enrolment of judgment professes to deliver, never having actually heard anything of the cause: but, according to the course of mendacity established in that behalf, the judges of the court in question are said to have taken cognizance of the pretended cause, and pronounced judgment accordingly; and by this means an inquiry, in reality original, assumes the form of an incidental one.

The like observations may apply to the case of motions grounded on awards, without much other difference than this,—viz. that the jurisdiction in this case, instead of being woven in the loom of jurisprudence by the shuttle of fiction, was fashioned in the proper manufactory, and put into the hands of the judge by the well-meant providence of the legislature.

The award—a decision formed by arbitrators, a sort of judges chosen by the parties—is made a rule of court: it is by that means placed on a footing with the judgment by consent, as described above.*

In this case, does the cause originate with the party who is satisfied with the award? A motion is made for an attachment against the other for non-performance of the award—for not rendering that service, the non-reddition of which has, by the conversion of the award into the equivalent of a judgment, become an offence against the authority of the court.

Does the cause originate with him who is dissatisfied with the award? It comes in the shape of a motion made by him, to set aside the award: the virtual judgment, though pronounced, is one the execution of which would not, it is contended, be consistent with the dictates of justice.

In the case of the judgment by consent, there has been no previous inquiry: the consent, the confession implied in that consent, stands in lieu of inquiry, and supersedes the use of it.

In the case of the award, there has been a previous inquiry; and that inquiry conducted in the best mode—the natural mode: examination *ex interrogatu judicis et partium* (cross-examination included) by *vivâ voce* answers to *vivâ voce* questions.

From the unlearned, the cause is brought before the learned, judge: and in what mode is it now conducted? In the very worst of modes. How so? Because it is a rule with them, an inflexible rule, when assembled four of them together, and without a jury, never to receive evidence in any other mode than the worst in use.

Compared with the general run of causes,—motion causes, causes originating in affidavit work, whether they end there or not, but more especially if they end as well as begin there, have one advantage: they bring the kernel of the cause to view at once, without the husk—the evidence, without the mass of useless and mendacious allegation on both sides, which neither is received, nor is intended to be received, as evidence. In comparison with the main body, they are a sort of summary causes.

* In the minds of the contrivers, these arbitration courts (it seems not impossible) may have originated in the honest wish of diminishing litigation—of extending the benefit of justice to those to whom it might otherwise have been inaccessible, and saving them, at the same time, from the fangs of the men of law. But the projector, whoever he may have been, if not a lawyer, appears in great measure to have been either deceived by the wiles, or overborne by the power of lawyers: what they have gained by the institution is rather more ascertainable than what they have lost; that is, than what has been gained to justice.

1. Parties examinable, and of course examined: but no oath, consequently no punishment; licence for mendacity, as against everything that goes by the name of punishment—as against everything but shame, that punishment to which those only against whom the forms of judicature are least necessary, are sensible.

2. No such tribunal capable of being instituted, but by consent of both parties. Let there be a spark of *mala fides* on either side, no such tribunal will be instituted, unless it be in virtue of an expectation on one part, of profiting by the *bona fides* and consequent veracity on the opposite side, reserving to himself the benefit of mendacity on his own side.

3. Care has been taken, as above, that on both sides an appeal shall be open to the learning and probity of the regular tribunals, sitting by themselves, without the incumbrance of a jury. But, neither on these nor on any other occasions, do these masters of wisdom ever determine a question upon any other than that which, in respect of the mode of collection, is the worst evidence—evidence delivered in that form in virtue of which a *malâ fide* suitor and a *malâ fide* deponent act to most advantage.

4. There is a class of causes, nor that a scanty one, to the cognizance of which, as Blackstone confesses,[a] a tribunal with a jury in it is physically incompetent; and which, if not tried by this sort of voluntarily appointed tribunal, would, as he also intimates, not be tried at all—disputes having for their subject-matter long-winded and intricate accounts between merchant and merchant, for example. In respect of so many of these disputes, therefore, as, having been carried on in the first instance before the irregular tribunals, pass from them to the regular, the institution is so much clear gain to the regular ones: and as the mode of trial is such as holds out every encouragement to mendacity and dishonesty, if the source thus opened of litigation is not productive, it is no fault of the man of law.

[a] Book III. Chap. I. *Arbitration*, Vol. III. p. 16.

Compared with the regular causes, these summary ones afford this instruction to the eye that is not afraid or ashamed to look at it; viz. that, by the implicit, but not less clear and undeniable, confession of those by whom regular and summary procedure are administered with the same imperturbable complacency, so much of the regular as consists in the sham inquiry, is so much sheer abuse.

What, in a word, is the character of this species of procedure? It wants nothing of being coincident with the domestic, the natural, the truly and solely just mode of procedure, but this one circumstance, viz. the conducting the inquiry in the best mode instead of the worst.

If the most learned persons who sit in judgment over the award, did but receive the evidence in the same mode as the unlearned persons who pronounced the award, "everything would be as it should be."

Everything would be as it should be, if those who sit in judgment over inferior judgments would allow themselves the possibility of coming at the truth, instead of giving the monopoly of it to inferior hands.

CHAPTER XVI.

MODE OF EXTRACTION IN ENGLISH EQUITY PROCEDURE — ITS INCONGRUITIES.

Equity is the name that has been given to law (jurisprudential law,) when the inquiry into the matter of fact and other proceedings are carried on according to a particular mode.

The origin and history of Equity, or rather of Equity courts, will be given in a subsequent book.*

It is in the mode of procedure pursued, and in nothing else, that the difference between common law and equity is to be sought. Law—common law—is that sort of jurisprudential law (understand, substantive law,) the arrangements of which are formed and carried into effect according to the system of procedure pursued in the courts originally styled simply courts of law, now occasionally, by way of distinction, courts of common law. Equity is that sort of law (jurisprudential substantive law,) pursued in the courts of more modern institution, which have by degrees acquired the name of courts of equity. That between law and equity there is any natural, intrinsic, original distinction, is a shallow conceit, the offspring of prejudice and ignorance. *Equity* itself is a mere word; the *thing*, of which it is the name, is the mere creation of the imagination. The arrangements of substantive law, to which men with the word equity in their mouths give effect, are, in many instances, different from the arrangements to which men with common law in their mouths give effect: but, — for distinguishing the one set of arrangements from the other, or the cases in which it is proper, from those in which it is not proper, that the courts of equity should interpose, and, by proceeding according to their system, establish such arrangements as they are in use to establish, — there is not in the word *equity* anything from which any the slightest direction can be obtained.

In the courts called courts of equity, the procedure is said to be by bill; that is, the instrument by which the suit is commenced (understand, the first instrument after the mere instrument of summons — the first instrument in and by which either party is considered as speaking) is thus denominated. Not but that, in the lexicography of English jurisprudence, the same denomination is given to a thousand other sorts of things.

In this procedure, both modes of delivering and extracting testimony are employed — the ready-written, and the *vivâ voce* mode: the one of them employed upon the one description of deponents, the other upon another; the one upon parties speaking in the character of witnesses, the other upon extraneous witnesses.

In this mode, as in the common-law mode, — lest *malâ fide* litigants should stand excluded, and lest, between *bonâ fide* litigants, the business should be settled too soon, and at too small an expense of words to the lawyers and money to the suitors, — the door is of course left open to mendacity in the first instance. In the written instrument, the bill, by which the suit commences, the plaintiff, not upon oath, enjoying a complete licence for mendacity, tells whatever story suggests itself to his professional fabricator as best adapted to whatever may be the purpose. In this bill (the length, and by that means the expense, of which, is whatever he is pleased to make it,) he possesses an engine of destruction, by the use of which, the stock of plunderable matter at the command of the defendant being given (not exceeding a certain quantity,) the victim may be consigned to certain ruin. To this purpose, it is not necessary that, from the beginning to the end, the bill should contain a single syllable of truth: and (that the licence given to him in this respect may be the more complete and uncontradicted) besides that he is freed from all apprehension on the score of punishment, he is not, even in this comparatively unimpressive mode, subjected to any such check as that of cross-examination. From the burthen of costs, it is true, he is not altogether exempted. In case of ultimate failure, in most, though not in all cases, he is liable to bear, not only the whole burthen of his own

* Book VIII. *Technical Procedure*; Chap. XIX.

disbursements, but a considerable part (probably in general the greater part) of those incurred by his adversary. But, of this compensation on the one part, this check to oppression on the other, the time is postponed to the conclusion of the suit: a point of time which it depends upon the author of the suit to postpone, always for several months, and commonly for years — a length of time, previous to the expiration of which, the ruin of the defendant, and by that means the attainment of the object of the suit, without either right or shadow of right, may have been reduced to certainty.

Thus it is that, by the essential structure of the system, mendacity, in the character of an instrument of oppression, receives ample licence and encouragement. Truth, at the same time, and on the part of the same person, enjoys no licence: mendacity is not simply permitted — it is in large quantities, on various occasions, and in various shapes, compelled. A plaintiff whose delicacy should shrink from it would be punished with the loss of his cause. Not that, in the natural course of things, his delicacy is likely to be put to the test. The answer to this sort of bill must be the defendant's own, and, besides his oath, he is made responsible for it by his signature. The bill is, on the contrary, the discourse, not of the plaintiff, whose discourse it purports to be, but of his lawyers: neither swearing to it nor signing it, in the ordinary course of things he never so much as looks at it.

The mendacity thus bespoken by authority, forced into the mouth of the suitor by the hand of power, may be distinguished into two masses — the unappropriate, and the appropriate.

By the unappropriate, I mean that which is of the same tenor or purport in every individual instance. This trash (besides that the quantity of it is, in comparison with the other, not very abundant,) being generally known, at least by lawyers, for what it is, produces, in the character of a mass of falsehood, a degree of mischief comparatively inconsiderable: no other than what consists in the exposing to the eye of the world the spectacle of intellectual debility, in conjunction with moral insensibility, occupying the seats of judicature, — the depraved taste which can endure the eternal repetition of so much useless nonsense,—the moral insensibility which, sheltering itself behind the plea of usage, is content in such sort to abuse its power, as to force one party to write falsehood, that both parties may be forced to pay for it.

By the appropriate mass of falsehood, I mean those particular false allegations which the rules of the court compel a plaintiff to employ his law assistant to stuff and stain his bill with, on pain of losing his suit.

In the matter of every bill, as before observed, there are two distinguishable parts: in the one, the plaintiff exhibits his own testimony in his own behalf; by the other, he endeavours to obtain, to extract, the testimony of his adversary the defendant. Aiming at the latter object, he is permitted to clothe, and accordingly does clothe, a correspondent portion of the matter of his bill in the form of questions or interrogations. So far, so good: but if this were all, the quantity of trash manufactured and sold, the quantity of profit extractable from the manufacture and sale of it, would not be sufficient. To supply the deficiency, a rule of practice has been established, and it is this: *every interrogatory must have a charge to support it.* What is here meant by the word *charge?* An assertion, commonly false, whereby the plaintiff, applying to the defendant for information concerning a matter of fact of which he (the plaintiff) frequently is altogether ignorant, declares his knowledge of it. The defendant, for example, is executor of the will of a deceased testator, by which a legacy has been left to the plaintiff. The plaintiff, knowing nothing of the state of the testator's affairs, knows not whether, after payment of debts, there will be any and what pecuniary matter left for the payment of the legacy. Simply to put the question would be exhibiting an interrogatory without a *charge* for the support of it. To steer clear of this irregularity, the draughtsman turns to his common-place book for an inventory of the several shapes in which property is capable of exhibiting itself; and without resorting to his employer (a recourse which would be altogether useless,) speaking always in the person of his principal, he gives a list of all these modifications, and without more ado alleges and asserts that the testator had property in some, or if he thinks fit (for it makes no sort of difference) in every one, or all, of these shapes.

The same rule extends itself over every part of the case. To obtain a true statement, you must begin with giving a false one; and the object of the false statement being to exhaust the whole stock of modifications of which the fact in each case is susceptible, the mass of mendacious matter must be proportionally voluminous. The power of the judge is indefatigably displayed in enforcing the observance of this immoral rule.*

* As everything has its reason (good, bad, or indifferent,) so has this: and at first glance it is rather a plausible one. If, for every question, a charge—a correspondent allegation, were not to be required, interrogation might run riot: there would be no end to questioning: a door would remain open, and that a boundless one, to impertinence. Plausible thus far: but where is the real utility at the bottom of it? What is required, is, that to every question there should be a charge: what is not required in the instance of any charge,

On this occasion an option addresses itself to the prudence of the draughtsman — an option to be made between the present interest of his purse, and the permanent interest of his professional fame. Of any sort of deficiency in the charging part, a natural result is a corresponding deficiency in the answer of the defendant — especially if the fact be of the number of those which are material to the support of the plaintiff's claim, in which case a faithful adviser will be alert in the discovery of the flaw, and in enabling his client to take due advantage of it. The consequence is, that the correspondent interrogatory remains unanswered. This produces the necessity of an amendment to the bill; which accordingly comes back to be new tinkered up by the same hand by which the hole in it had been left. Infirmity is the general lot of human nature; but it is in the practice of the law only that a man may be sure to gain by it. Designed or undesigned, it is upon the head of the unlearned that the transgressions of the man of learning are avenged.

When, in this system of procedure, the individual subjected to examination is not a party but an extraneous witness, we shall see the mass of interrogative matter very properly broken down into distinct questions, and these questions numbered. Under the eyes of the same court, and in the same cause — in this initial stage of the same individual cause — this source of distinctness, this principle of order, is uniformly, and as it were carefully, steered clear of: the interrogative part is one undivided mass, the charging part is another undivided mass, placed before the interrogative. If, the charging part being divided into articles, the interrogative were divided into a correspondent number of articles, a deficiency in either would too readily be observed; the licence to evasion on one part, the demand for amendment on the other, would be too unfrequent: this must not be.

The charging part is accordingly elaborated into one shapeless mass, agreeing in that respect with the sort of composition which in common-law procedure we have been viewing under the name of an affidavit: differing only in respect of the licence for mendacity — a liberty which, in the case of a bill, is conducive (as hath been seen) to the professional and real ends of judicature; in the case of an affidavit, not so.

The charging part is worked up into one such mass, the interrogative into another. Not that the nature of the interrogative suffers its elementary parts to be quite so undistinguishable as in the other case; inasmuch as, if not a complete division, a sort of *joint* is naturally formed, as often as any of the interrogative parts of speech — the *what*, the *when*, the *where*, the *whether* — come to be repeated. The questions, and consequently the propositions to which answers are to be adapted, — these portions of the discussion, though not denominated, though not numbered, are in some sort (though thus insufficiently) distinguished.

When the established sources of delay have been exhausted (delay, a mischief which belongs not to the present work,) comes at length the defendant's answer. The established licence to mendacity, having given birth to the suit — having, if the suit be a *malâ fide* one, thus fulfilled its obviously intended purpose — is now withdrawn: what a man says in the character of a defendant, he is made to deliver upon oath.*

is, that that charge shall be a true one. What follows? That the apprehended impertinence, instead of being checked, is doubled. To constitute a legal ground for each question, pertinent or impertinent, it is prefaced by an allegation, which allegation, as often as it is false (which it is perhaps still oftener than it is true,) cannot possibly be of any use. Thus stands the matter on the ground of utility; particular utility with reference to the particular object in view, viz. the obtaining a just ground for a decision to a particular effect, by the discovery of a particular mass of truth. With a view to the influence of this practice upon general probity, upon the public disposition to veracity, occasion will occur for noticing it in another place.

* He cannot, however, be punished for mendacity, unless upon the evidence of at least two witnesses.

"No decree, it is said, can be made against a man's answer, upon the proof of one witness." (1 Vern. 140. 3 Chanc. Cas. 123. 1 Ventr. 213 in Parker's Harrison I. 224.)

This is as much as to say, that a court of equity cannot or will not form that sort of judgment which is exercised every day by a jury, and to which the meanest jury is acknowledged to be in every sense fully competent; — a judgment concerning the comparative trustworthiness of the opposite testimonies of two deponents. — To what considerations are we to impute this self-created incompetence on the part of these great and learned personages? Is it that, in their own judgments, the mode of inquiry they are content to pursue is completely ill-adapted to the ends of justice? — or is it, that, to their own consciousness, their own minds are so vitiated and enfeebled by false science, as to be unfit for a task for which no unfitness is to be found in a company of unlearned tradesmen?

The effects of this disclaimer are not unworthy of observation.

1. In the character of defendant, the testimony of one man, of every man — so long as he has but the testimony of one extraneous witness to oppose him, be that one witness who he may, — is absolutely conclusive: so that, to whomsoever has but one such opponent, the benefit of triumphant perjury is made sure.

2. And what sort of evidence is it, in comparison with which the most trustworthy evidence goes for nothing? A person who is interested by the amount of the whole interest created by the whole value of the cause: and this in the judgment of those sages with whom it is a maxim

If the bill, the instrument exhibited on the part of the plaintiff, were broken down into numbered articles,—in that case, if the matter contained in the defendant's answer were broken down in like manner, the deficiencies in it (if any such were left) would be too clearly apparent: of an allegation unanswered, it would be seen, that it had been left unanswered, and thence virtually admitted to be true—of a question unanswered, it would be seen that it had been left unanswered, and in so far the obligation of furnishing the requisite evidence left unfulfilled. This again is what must not be: for, besides that on every occasion the influence of light is unfavourable to the health of the professional system, it would not be so easy as at present, when the first answer is called in, to increase the bulk of the second answer by groundless *exceptions* (*exception* is the technical appellative,) imputing deficiencies to the first. If *charge* article 2, or *interrogatory* article 2, had, in the corresponding article of the answer, received a fair and full reply, a degree of salutary shame might be felt by a draughtsman, who, in drawing up a paper of exceptions, should be disposed to accuse the answer of insufficiency in relation to these respective articles. But, when the charging part of the bill has been digested into one sort of confusion, the interrogative part into another, and the matter of the answer into a third, the industry and ingenuity of the drawer of the list of exceptions stands happily exempt from all restraint. Full or scanty, explicit or evasive, the answer is (for anything that can be seen clearly to the contrary) alike open to exception. Bill and answer together compose so thick a wood, that a *bonâ fide* traveller may lose his way in it, and a *malâ fide* traveller may, without fear of exposure, make as if he had lost his way in it: whatever be the means, the professional purpose is equally well fulfilled.

When the thread of examination has thus at length been spun on to its end—when papers of exceptions have been followed by fresh answers, these answers by new editions of the bill with amendments, these amendments again by fresh answers, these answers by fresh exceptions, these exceptions again by fresh answers, and so on to an end (if haply the suit be destined to have an end,)—the entire state of the case, so far as depends upon what the parties themselves know of it, is frequently but half exhibited. To complete the picture, what is called a cross bill is necessary. In the cross bill, as may be imagined from the name, the parties now change places: the defendant takes upon himself the character of plaintiff, and the obligation of answering questions is exchanged for the less irksome task of putting them.

In this cross cause, as it is called, veracity is now required from him upon whom in the original cause mendacity had been forced: and the same judge, by whose well practised hand mendacity had been planted in the heart of the suitor, calls for (can it be said expects?) sincerity as the fruit of it.

In other respects, no fresh observations seem necessary on the occasion of this supplemental half of a mercilessly-protracted, yet still imperfect, course of litigation: without any variation worth noticing, whatever has been predicated of the original cause may with equal propriety be predicated of the cross cause.

All this while no other progress has been made in the cause or causes (*singular* or *plural*, which you please) than the extraction of the self-regarding testimony on both sides. There remains to be collected (not to speak of evidence of the real or written kind) the testimony of extraneous witnesses—of whatever witnesses of this description the individual nature of the case has happened to present.

A moment's pause.—In speaking of the testimony of the self-regarding kind—the testimony of the parties themselves, as having been extracted in the course of this process, (meaning the whole of it extracted,) I went too far. What each party has said to his own prejudice is now indeed looked upon as proved; credit is understood to be due to it: but whatever, in the character of plaintiff, either party may have said to his own advantage, is (as already observed) understood to be so much falsehood, and in that character goes for nothing. If, then, of what facts a party happens to have known to his own advantage, any part be, in the instance of either of them, capable of being employed to the advantage of him by whose discourse it is brought to view, it can only be in so far as it is in the character of defendant, that the ingenuity of the draughtsman has contrived to make him come out with it. Even then, great doubts and difficulties seem to have encompassed the question, how far he, of whom it is certain that he has spoken truth in one case, ought to be regarded as capable of speaking truth in the other case: and, for clearing up these doubts and difficulties, recourse has been had, on this as on every other part of the field of evidence—not to the discernment of the judge, judging from the particular circumstances of the individual case—but to unbending rules, binding the judge in each individual case to disregard the circumstances of the case before his eyes, in order to govern himself exclusively by the circumstances of some other case, of which the circumstances have never presented themselves,

---

that an interest, though to a less value than the smallest coin in currency, is sufficient to render a witness inadmissible.

nor can ever be made to present themselves, to his view.

Lest the road of mendacity should not yet be smooth enough, and that the professional hand, which the suitor is forced to hire, may have as much to do as possible, — the change of persons (that species of falsehood, of which, besides the falsity, the mischief in other respects has already been brought to view) is imposed upon the defendant in each cause — upon him who, on pain of punishment as for perjury, is commanded to speak true — as well as upon the plaintiff, that is, upon him from whom (so long as he continues to speak in that character) truth is neither expected, nor so much as tolerated. In the case of the answer, as in the case of the bill, — the discourse ascribed to the party, having the professional assistant for its penman — who again speaks in his own person, if in any determinate person, at any rate not in the person of the party, — the party is thereupon required to swear it, and to sign it. In a language not his own — a language in which, from beginning to end, whatsoever of truth there be, is, if not falsified, at least disguised and travestied — in a language not his own, by a person he knows not who (for between the party and the draughtsman there is never any sort of contact, the attorney being the medium of communication,) he reads or does not read, hears read or does not hear read, hears read correctly or incorrectly, intelligibly or not intelligibly, what he swears and signs. Under these circumstances, if the burthen of legal responsibility is too conspicuous and too formidable not to have made some impression — not to have produced the effect of a check, as to such of the facts to which in the nature of the case it may have appeared applicable, — in the burthen of moral responsibility, if so it happens that he has any feeling of it at all, he is but too apt to feel, not so much a yoke itself, as the shadow of a yoke.

We come now, however, to the mode in use, in this species of procedure, for obtaining the testimony of extraneous witnesses: and now the mode employed is as different as if they were animals of another species, or inhabitants of another world.

Interested allegation, and thence spontaneous exhibition, being now out of the question, — what evidence is to be received from this source falls to be *extracted:* and the extraction is performed in the mode already brought to view under the name of the Roman (or say Romanigenous) mode: understand always a bad modification of that bad mode.

Of the Roman procedure on this head, considered on the footing on which it stands in general, the defective points in this respect have been already brought to view: — cross-examination by the adverse party, none; to the gap left by that deficiency, no adequate supplement; on each side, sole interrogator the judge — on whose part, not so much as in point of appropriate information, much less in point of zeal, can any degree of aptitude approaching to that of the party be reasonably expected.

On the continent of Europe, the operator on this occasion is at any rate a person bearing the official name, the power, the dignity, of a judge — beholding as such the eyes of the public pointed at his proceeding, curious to spy whatever may be to be spied through the crevices of his closet door; nor does this door, against whomsoever else it may be shut, refuse admittance to his official assistant and subordinate — his secretary — by whatsoever name denominated.

In the English mode (understand always the mode which claims to itself the exclusive praise of having equity for its guide,) no secretary — not so much as a judge — no person who bears the name, the dignity, or on any other occasion whatsoever exercises the function, of a judge. On this important occasion — the only sort of occasion which, were the legislator to perform his part, could ever occur to call into exercise the faculties of a judge, — his function is exercised by nobody knows what deputy, clerk, or clerk's-deputy — an unknown and nameless underling, who neither in reputation nor in any other respect has anything to gain by good desert — anything to lose (corruption or other such palpable criminality excepted) by ill desert; and who, on each occasion, has but one interest in the business, which is to get through it in as speedy, and consequently in as imperfect, a way as possible.

The person who on this occasion fills the place that, if filled by anybody, ought to be filled by a judge, — this person being considered as an automaton, is not considered as possessed of the smallest particle of discretionary power; but reciting, as a parrot might recite, such questions as on each side have been put into his hands, receives such answers as the witness thinks fit to give to them: to subtract a word, to add a word, to change a word, all these operations are alike superior to his province. One opening indeed there is to further information, and that not chargeable (it must be confessed) with any deficiency in point of amplitude: the misfortune is, that it lies all of it on one side. Do you know anything further that may be of advantage to the plaintiff? says the concluding article in the paper of interrogatories delivered on the part of the plaintiff. Do you know anything that may be of advantage to the defendant? says a corresponding article in the paper delivered on the part of the defendant. Having no one before him that either knows a syllable, or cares a straw, about the matter—seeing no one before him, of whom it is possible for him to stand in any kind of awe,—the witness remembers on each side as much or as little as he pleases. Fear of consequences may prevent him from telling any falsehood for which he sees reason to apprehend detection and punishment from other sources; but for the utterance of any truth which in his view may appear pregnant with anything unfavourable to the side which his inclinations have espoused, there is nothing in the whole system put together that can afford him the slightest motive.

In the situation of the clerk who on this occasion acts the part of a sort of shadow of a judge, what can be supposed to be his inclinations or endeavours from the opening of the business to the conclusion of it? To get it out of his hands, and put an end to his labour—his obscure and thankless and in every shape unprofitable labour, as soon as possible;—to get some sort of answer to each and every interrogatory,—if such be understood to be his duty, *i. e.* the task, for a failure in which he might be in danger of being punished: to get an answer; but whether true or false, complete or incomplete, distinct or indistinct, intelligible or unintelligible, why should he care?

On this footing is this principal part of the judicial function exercised in that court (the Court of Chancery) by which by far the greatest part of the business called equity business is performed; that is to say, when the examination is performed in the district of the metropolis, being that district in which the greater part of this sort of business is performed. This accordingly is what may be termed the *ordinary* mode.

In the same court, what may be termed the extraordinary mode, the mode less in use, and at any rate employed only as a makeshift, may be pronounced somewhat less imperfect. Where the scene of the examination lies elsewhere than within the district of the metropolis,—on the occasion of each cause, a commission is granted to four persons, commonly attorneys, two of them recommended on each side. The court of justice is a room in some public house: and there it is, that, under the obligation—the anxiously enforced obligation of secrecy, the witnesses are brought together. Compared with the open mode by examination and cross-examination in a public court of justice, with or without a jury, this mode will be seen to be imperfect; though what particular quarter may be the seat of the imperfection may not be quite so easy to pronounce. These commissioners,—to what known class are their function and their station to be referred? Are they judges, mere judges, and nothing more? Then comes the deficiency in respect of appropriate information, and adequate interest and stimulus to exertion, as before. Are they mere agents of the parties by whom they are respectively nominated and paid? In this way of viewing the matter, we behold a judicature without a judge. The official experience, the habitual sense of dignity, the consequent solicitude in respect of reputation,—these endowments, so naturally attached to the station of the permanent judge, are not reasonably to be looked for on the part of these ephemeral judges. On the other hand, more or less of partiality towards the interests of the parties to whom they are respectively indebted for their appointment, and on that account a proportionable degree of zeal and acuteness in the conduct of the examination (which by this means wears in a certain degree the complexion of the reciprocal process of examination and cross-examination,) may not unreasonably be expected. But their zeal, if any such emotion be felt, has not, unless by accident, been excited or sharpened by any personal intercourse with the immediate agents of the parties, much less with the parties themselves: and, as to information with regard to facts, if they possess any beyond what the interrogatories themselves in their naked and unexplained state afford, it is again a matter of accident; and, if the supposition be realized, the information and function of the agents, the attorneys, of the parties, is communicated to these amphibious functionaries.

The only source of information they are sure to possess, consists of the above-mentioned sets of interrogatories, exhibited one on each, or perhaps only on one, side. These interrogatories must, by the rules of the court, have received the signature of an advocate, having been drawn up either by the advocate himself from a paper of instructions given to him by his client the attorney, or by the attorney himself. Drawn by whomsoever they may, they are necessarily presented *uno flatu* to the commissioners, to whom, in their character of judges or agents of the parties, they are to serve in the character of instructions. Comparing the situation of these deputies with that of the parties, it is obvious how indifferently qualified they will be for the putting of such questions as neither have been nor can have been comprised in the paper of interrogatories,—fresh questions arising in unlimited number and variety out of the unforeseeable answers to immediately preceding questions. Thus, in the respect in question, stands this modification of the regular mode, when compared with the summary mode, in which the mutual presence of the parties forms the essential and characteristic feature. Compared indeed with the mode observed in trial by jury, in which the presence of advocates, coupled with the absence or at least the inaction of the parties, is an inseparable circumstance,—the disparity in this respect may not be so great. If, when transmitted to the commissioners, the paper of interrogatories be accompanied by a paper of instructions as full as that which, under the name of a *brief*, has on the occasion of a trial by jury been put into the hands of the advocate,—it follows that (excepting the occasional faculty of *vivâ voce* communication with the attorney at the time of the trial) between the situation and means of information on the part of the advocate so called, and those of the commissioner thus qualified for exercising the function of an advocate, there is no very striking difference.

What might seem extraordinary enough (if in the practice of English jurisdiction any exemplification of inconsistency or of established contempt for the known ends of justice could appear extraordinary) is, that the comparative incongruity of this equity mode of receiving and extracting extraneous testimony is by no description of persons so explicitly and habitually recognised as by the very persons under whose authority it is so regularly pursued. In ordinary cases indeed, in by far the greater number of causes, this wretchedly adapted mode of investigation is suffered to take its course. Yet sometimes it does happen, that the least defective of the existing modes of extraction — the jury-trial mode, by examination and cross-examination, is looked upon as worth being employed; and in this case, trial by jury is the resource. The Chancellor knowing, and, by expression stronger than any words, confessing and proclaiming, that the only mode which he is in the constant habit of employing for the discovery of truth is a bad one, sends the cause (that is to say, this part of it) to another tribunal, the habits of which are less aberrant from the ends of justice. The practice is so familiar as to have acquired an appropriate technical name: it is called *directing an issue*.

The whole character and complexion of English judicature would be belied, if on this occasion as well as so many others, the professional fondness for mendacity were not indulged with its gratification. The operation belonging to the head of Procedure, the details of it belong not to this place. How the parties are forced, or one of them, to say a wager has been laid between them, though it is no such thing — a wager, as to whether the fact in question happened or no; how one of them is made to bring an action for the money pretended to be at stake on the pretended wager, saying that it has been won by him, for that the fact happened as he said — which the other on his part denies; how the connexion is made out between the sham demand and the real object of inquiry; how the court, in consideration of its self-created incapacity of conducting the inquiry in any tolerably good mode, finds itself under the manufactured necessity of sending the cause to another court, which has not precluded itself from the use of a less imperfect mode; how and in what proportion the delay, vexation, and expense, of a suit at law is by this ingenious husbandry grafted upon the stock of a suit in equity; — these are subjects, the exhibition of which will find a more apposite place under the head of Procedure.

The storehouse of inconsistency is not yet exhausted. The cognizance of a court of equity, how ill-defined soever its limits may be in other respects, is at any rate confined to questions of property. Among the largest masses of property apt to come thus in question — among those which give rise to the greatest number of causes cognizable by a tribunal thus denominated — may be reckoned the estates of bankrupts. Claims to the amount of a million or more have come thus to be disposed of on the occasion of the bankruptcy of a single house.* In cases of this sort, though there is nothing to hinder the claim from being preferred by the sort of suit above described under the name of a bill, it is much more common for it to be preferred by a different sort of suit, called a *petition*.† In this case, again, the mode of inquiry is altogether different. To avoid the only natural, and (when practicable without preponderant collateral inconvenience) the only just and rational mode, the same scrupulous and unvarying care is taken in this case as in all others. But neither is the mode pursued in all other cases by the same tribunal, less completely relinquished. The mode now pursued is exactly the mode already described as the worst of all modes — as the one exclusively pursued by the common-law courts on the occasion of every inquiry in which no jury bears a part: — I mean the affidavit mode.

Here, as at common law, the substitution of a less searching to a more searching mode

---

* Gibson and Johnson.

† Petition is the name given to the instrument by which, in cases of bankruptcy, claims are preferred to the Lord Chancellor sitting in a judicial capacity superordinate to that of the commissioners of bankruptcy, before whom the business is transacted in the first instance. To this species of judicature, in scientific strictness the term *equity* is said not to extend itself: it is as Lord High Chancellor that this great magistrate sits, and not as judge of a court of equity. Accordingly, in this branch of judicature, the other high court of equity, the Court of Exchequer, when sitting in its equitable capacity, does not participate. — [The judicature in bankruptcy has experienced considerable alteration by the establishment of a Bankruptcy Court, in terms of Lord Brougham's Act, 1 & 2 Wil. IV. cap. 56. See the author's remarks on the measure, in the pamphlet called "Lord Brougham Displayed," Vol. V. p. 549. — *Ed.*]

of scrutiny, is sufficient to give admissibility and credit to the most decidedly inadmissible and incredible species of testimony. On this occasion as on that, the too-hastily adopted dictate of inconsiderate caution, *nemo debet esse testis in propriâ causâ*, is adopted, with no other change than that of a single word — the change of *nemo* into *omnis*. Call yourself plaintiff, your testimony goes for nothing: — call yourself petitioner, it is as good as anybody's.*

Compared with procedure by bill, procedure in this way by petition may be, not altogether without propriety (as in practice it sometimes is,) styled *summary:* for the pace of an ox, how slow soever when compared with that of a greyhound, is swift when compared with that of a tortoise. But it would have been profanation, as well as confusion, to have degraded the only mode of inquiry dictated by nature, and honestly subservient to the ends of truth and justice, by confounding it with any modification of that factitious mode, which has so evidently had an end of a widely different description for its result, not to speak of its final cause.

The Roman mode of collecting evidence furnishes a source of complication and misdecision from which the English mode is happily exempt. In the English mode there is no medium between existence and non-existence: a proposed witness is either heard or not heard; his testimony is either delivered or not delivered: delivered, it exists, and it has its effect, if not with reference to all persons in general, at any rate with reference to all those who are parties in the cause.

In the Roman mode, the same testimony is susceptible of as many modes of imperfect existence, as the cause has parties: existing as to Titius, it may be non-existing as to Sempronius, and so on, in relation to as many points as there may happen to be found in the juridical compass.

A mass of ready-written evidence is constructed, constructed in private, in the secret workshop of the patent manufacturer, the judge. Thus constructed, it becomes an instrument that may be let out to anybody, refused to anybody: it may be applied to use at the instance of one person, refused to be applied to use at the instance of another.

Two plaintiffs: one of them has delivered assertions concerning the existence of certain matters of fact — assertions capable in their own nature of being employed in the character of evidence. This testimony (so, for argument's sake, let it be called,) shall it be employed, or not? admitted, or not admitted? read (to employ the word in common use,) or not read? It may be read at the instance of that one of the plaintiffs whose testimony it is not — not read at the instance of the other. Being read, no matter at whose instance, it may be allowed to operate in favour of (or, as the phrase is, *for*) the one, not allowed to operate in favour of the other: operate to the prejudice of (or, as the phrase is, against) the one, not operate to the prejudice of the other.

Add now a defendant (or, for dispatch, say two defendants,) to match with the two plaintiffs. The testimony of the plaintiff in question may be read at the instance of one of the two defendants, not read at the instance of the other: it may be admitted to operate in favour of the one, not operate in favour of the other: operate against the one, not operate against the other.

Discard now the two plaintiffs: and let the testimony in question be that of one of the two defendants. The deposition may be allowed to be read at the instance of the deponent, not allowed to be read at the instance of the non-deponent:† or (what will be apt to appear more natural, because less dangerous) read at the instance of the non-deponent, not read at the instance of the deponent. Being read, it may be suffered or not suffered to operate for the deponent, suffered or not suffered to operate against him: and again, suffered or not suffered to operate for the non-deponent, suffered or not suffered to operate to his prejudice.

To reduce to its minimum the burthen of this disastrous arithmetic, two has been taken as the smallest multiplier: two, the number of the sides of a cause, increases the multiplier to four; those other points, *at whose instance, for whom, against whom,* swell it to twelve. But the number of parties in a case may, on either, or each side, be half-a-dozen — it may be half a score — an entire dozen, or an entire score — a hundred, any number of hundreds: a number amounting to divers hundreds may not improbably have been exemplified in practice. Take a parcel of creditors on one side, a parcel of legatees on the

* Some years ago, in the House of Lords (no matter on what occasion) an advocate (such being the exigency of his case) was inveighing against the monstrous absurdity, the notorious injustice, the immoral tendency, of allowing a party to appear as a witness in his own cause. The answer was a simple, but at least, in the character of an *argumentum ad hominem*, a pretty decisive one: — "In a court in which you are every day sitting, it is every day's practice."

† Exemplified at common law, *in criminali*.[a]

[a] The deposition of a prisoner may also be read at the instance of a prosecutor, though the contents of the deposition will not be evidence against a co-prisoner, but only against the prisoner who made the deposition. 1 Phil. Ev. 108. In Scotland, where the prisoner's declaration is almost invariably evidence against him (see above, p. 404, note) the same distinction is adopted. — *Ed.*

other, it will be evident that on neither side has the number any certain limits. Thus it is that the number of changes that are capable of being rung, in answer to the question, *read, or not read?* is plainly infinite. The number of folio volumes capable of being filled with discussions on the subject of these changes, is alike infinite.

The courts which have given admission to the distinctions pregnant with these changes and these discussions — the courts which have sowed the seeds of all this science — are the courts, which by the courtesy of England, have been complimented with the title of courts of equity.

Of all these possible distinctions, the number of those which have actually presented themselves to notice, and called forth decisions, and those decisions ripened into rules, is as yet extremely small: but, as yet, equity is but in her cradle.

Will reason be referred to, as the power by which the number of these distinctions either has been, or is capable of being, limited? Reason rejects them in the lump. If that power by which the existing ones have been fixed (supposing any to have been fixed) be reason, no other number but may equally be fixed by the virtue of the same cause.

That the testimony of one defendant, whether it be in the shape of an answer or in the shape of a deposition, cannot be read for or against another defendant without *special order*, seems tolerably well fixed. Unfortunately, in the words *special order*, a mystery is inclosed. The application by which the special order is called forth, — is it acceded to, as the phrase is, *of course* — that is, without being subject to contestation? In some of the instances where evidence is not admitted but upon special order, the affirmative is the case in every day's practice Special order, in that case, means nothing but a pretence for that for which, to a hand clothed with adequate power, any pretence serves; viz. extracting fees. In this case, if the order be understood to be preceded by reflection, the money extracted on the occasion is extracted on false pretences; for wherever the application (whether called *motion* or *petition*) is acceded to of course, the circumstances of the case are never so much as presented to the conception of the judge. Excepting always the part that consists in the eating of the fees, a wooden judge would be as competent to the business as the living one.

In the particular case in question, do the words *special order* imply faculty of contestation on the part of the adversary, and consequently the exercise of the faculties of hearing and reflection on the part of the judge? If yes, the special order may in each instance be governed and modified by the special circumstances of the case: and then, at the door thrown open by these special circumstances, in comes the goddess of Equity, with her infinity, her incomprehensibility, and all her other attributes, and with a pile composed of an infinite number of volumes for her throne.

From anything that has been said it must not be concluded that the ears of the principal judges in the equity courts are inexorably shut against all *vivâ voce* evidence. They are still open to receive it, in certain cases; and these cases are those in which it is of no use.

Proof of the authenticity of a deed is on one supposition, and one supposition only, of any use; viz. that it may have been fabricated or falsified in the way of forgery. Is forgery suspected? In this case, indeed, the proof of the authenticity of the deed is of real use; provided always that cross-examination and counter-evidence be allowed. On every other supposition, and setting aside this condition, it is a vain formulary — an operation without use.

In how many instances out of ten thousand is any suspicion, real or pretended, of forgery, manifested? If in ten, the proportion seems a large one.

In every other case — at least every other contested case — the probability seems to be, that, on one account or another, *vivâ voce* examination will be of use.

The result is, that this most efficient mode of scrutiny is, among the votaries of equity, reserved, as it were, with care, for the only class of cases in which it is of no use.

Of the myriads of instances in which it has been employed, perhaps not a single one is to be found in which it ever was of use. In the chancellor's court of equity, does a suspicion of this kind present itself? Whatever contestation may arise, it is not the chancellor that will hear it: no; he will send it to be tried before a jury — he will direct an issue.

The collection of this part of the evidence in a mode thus comparatively undilatory, unexpensive, unvexatious — does it then belong to the list of grievances? No, surely: no otherwise than in as far as it stands parcel of the processes of that immense manufactory of expense, vexation, and delay, of which the existence is one continued and prodigious grievance. The fault belongs not to the head of absolute faults, but to the head of inconsistencies — not in the giving this best mode of scrutiny to these cases, but in the refusal put upon it in all other cases.*

* In one other case I find an instance of an examination *viv voce* in court, viz. that before the principal equity judge. It is where two or more affidavits, charged with being contradictory, have been exhibited by the same person. — Wyat's Practical Register, p. 10.

What seems evident enough is, that had the two supposed contradictory depositions been the depositions of different persons, the demand for

If, following the track of his predecessors, it were possible (which it is not) for an English judge to do wrong, the narrow set of instances in which they have done right would only serve to render their conduct the more inexcusable. The result of it is, that they have known what is right—that they have had power to do what is right—but that they have not thought fit to exercise it.

In the accounts which are given by practical writers, of the mode of collecting the evidence, as practised under the authority of a court of equity, the word *cross-examination* every now and then presents itself. But, between the operation here spoken of, and the operation spoken of under the same name on the occasion of the inquiry called a trial, as carried on in a court of law, there is a very material difference. In the common-law operation thus denominated, the examination is performed by the advocate of the party, *i. e.* of the party opposite to him by whom the witness has been examined in the first instance: and, the answers given on that occasion being already known, the questions put in the way of cross-examination have the faculty of grounding themselves on any of those answers; as well as each successive cross-question (if so it may be called,) on the answers given to the several cross-questions that have preceded it. Under the cross-examination of the Romanists,* no such faculty is possessed. The exhibition of that set of interrogatories which is furnished to the examiner by the party by whom alone, or by whom in the first place, the testimony of the examinee was called for, is called simply the examination, and answers to the examination in chief of the common lawyers. The exhibition of that set of interrogatories which is furnished to the examiner by that one of the parties by whom the testimony of the examinee was either not called for at all, or not called for till after it had been called for by the other, is what the Romanists mean when they speak of the cross-examination.

That this cross-examination of the Romanists does not afford any security equal to that which is afforded by the cross-examination of the Anglicans, will appear evident enough. To the lawyer by whom the set of interrogatories furnished by the party opposite to the invoking party are drawn up, it is not possible in every instance to foresee the interrogatories that will be exhibited on the other side: it is still farther from being possible to him to foresee each answer that will be drawn forth by each such question: it is. therefore, on a double account impossible for him to ground on every such answer, such question as in case of incorrectness or incompleteness (from whatever cause, mendacity, temerity, or negligence) might be conducive and necessary to the full and correct disclosure of the facts on which the merits of the cause depend.

To form the best conception that can be formed of the course pursued in this part of English judicature, a Frenchman can do no better than to think of the course pursued in his own country in legislative oratory. From pulpit No. 1, orator No. 1 having read a previously-written declamation, from pulpit No. 2, orator No. 2 reads another prepared declamation, in which (though the thesis is the same) no notice is or can be taken of a single syllable of what has been said in the declamation that preceded.

In the ecclesiastical courts, the examination being conducted in the same manner, the insufficiency of this spurious sort of cross and adverse examination, in comparison with the natural and genuine (the Anglican mode,) is of course felt in equal force.

What is curious enough is, that, in the case of the ecclesiastical courts, not only the effects of it are felt by the parties—felt to the prejudice of that one of them who has right on his side, but recognised and confessed by the institutionalists themselves.†

Speaking of the ecclesiastical courts,—"Imperfect and wretched" (said his Majesty's attorney-general, addressing himself to the House of Lords,‡) "imperfect and wretched" is the "manner, in which cross-examination is managed upon paper, and in these courts." Hearing this in their judicial capacities,—to

such explanation would have been at least as great: so also in case of the like contradiction between two extraneous witnesses, both deposing in whispers to an examining clerk: so also between one such witness, and defendant, in and by his answer: so, in a word, in case of any other contradiction whatsoever.

But in the particular case in question, by some strange accident, in a fit of insanity or inebriety, a chancellor happened to be in a humour to find out the truth—to find out the truth by the force of his own faculties, without sending it to be found out by a jury, in the course and by means of a suit instituted on purpose.

One other instance is upon record, of a person examined in court upon a different ground: but the case is too extraordinary to be worth insisting on.—2. Chancery Cases, 68. 69, 70, in Fowler's Exchequer (Edit. 1795,) ii. 99. After hearing the depositions of other witnesses, one of a set of persons employed as commissioners to take depositions had himself deposed. A ground of suspicion, which in common-law practice is continually presented, and almost as continually disregarded, was here considered as fatal: and in this, at that time, and almost still, unprecedented mode, the witness was re-examined. Profit to the lawyers, one motion and two hearings: what, if anything, the party in the right got by this sort of judicial frolic, does not appear.

* Browne, i. 478; ii. 421.

† Oughton.

‡ Duchess of Kingston's Trial for Bigamy, anno 1776, Hargrave's State Trials, vol. xi. p. 239.

how many of their lordships, in their legislative capacities, in the course of the fifty years that have elapsed, has it ever occurred that it might be matter of duty to endeavour to substitute in those courts a suitable mode of doing the business, to an unsuitable one? Not to a single one. What was said, was said in the presence of at least three law lords: Earl Bathurst, lord chancellor; Lord Mansfield, lord chief-justice of the King's Bench; and Lord Camden, lord chief-justice of the Common Pleas. The same gentleman to whom, in the station of attorney-general and member of the House of Commons, the form of extracting evidence in these courts had with so much reason presented itself as wretched and imperfect, became afterwards lord high chancellor, and a member of the House of Lords: nor in the one station any more than in the other, does it appear ever to have occurred to him that the difference between the bad mode of administering justice and the good one was worth trying to do away. Whether what is established answers its purpose well or ill, is not worth inquiring about, so long as it is established.

Wretched and imperfect, however, as is the manner in which cross-examination is managed upon paper and in those courts, it cannot in any respect have been worse, or materially different, from the only one which is in use, was then, is now, and perhaps ever shall be in use, in those other courts of tenfold greater business and importance, in which this successful votary of the law was then practising at the head of the faculty of advocates, and afterwards for so many years presiding in the character of sole judge.

For profiting by the wretchednesses and imperfections of the law, the reward is rich and ample: for endeavouring to remove them, there is none. To carry on the existing bad course of procedure, according to the existing system of inconsistent and ever-fluctuating rules, is at once a matter of obligation, and a source of honour and veneration. To endeavour to make it less bad, is neither matter of obligation to anybody, nor source of anything but jealousy, hatred, and contempt.

CHAPTER XVII.

MODE OF EXTRACTION IN ENGLISH ECCLESIASTICAL AND ADMIRALTY COURTS — ITS INCONGRUITIES.

In the courts, called in English Ecclesiastical courts, as in the ecclesiastical courts of most other countries in Europe, the old Roman system forms (as everybody knows) the ground-work of the procedure. Hence (as hath so often been observed) a regular, but a pretty uniform and consistent, deviation from the natural mode, the only mode that could have been suggested by a real regard to the ends of justice. Hence at the same time a degree of uniformity, as between the procedure in penal and the procedure in non-penal cases: such a degree as indicated the convenience of bringing to view both branches under one head; especially on considering within what comparatively narrow, though still too ample, limits, the jurisdiction of these courts is, under the domineering controul of the original Anglican courts, confined.

With the exception of a slight regard to general utility, seconded by here and there a ray of the light of human reason let in in very modern times,* the state of existing jurisdictions is in England, as elsewhere, but more particularly in England, the result of the universal scramble, between violence and fraud on the part of each casual occupant of a branch of judicial power, and the like violence and fraud on the part of every other.

For putting in, each for his share (the greatest of course that could be obtained) of the common stock of plunderable matter, each set of learned depredators formed, in a different word or combination of words, a pretence. To the original gang, the original and primeval words law and justice were sufficient. These words having by hard wear been worn down into a certain degree of disrepute came another troop bearing another standard — the word Equity. All this while, in another quarter the attack was carried on by a third set, who were continually pronouncing the words Church, Soul's health, Good of Souls.

That the chance for the attainment of truth will depend upon the mode employed in the extraction of it, and not upon the pronouncing this or that one out of the above, or any other, collection of words, will be evident enough to any man who is not determined not to see it. Yet in this third, as in the two former instances, the change of the word, thus affording a pretence for the exercise of

* Compared with the pure Anglicans (the common and equity lay-lawyers,) the ecclesiastical and other Romanist lawyers (the civilians as they are called) exhibit a perceptible distinction. Acting under the yoke of a predominating power, the latter refer every now and then to the principle of utility, as an oracle from which they look for popularity and for defence against the hand, the weight of which is constantly felt pressing on their shoulders. For such and such a reason (meaning in respect of such or such an article of perceptible convenience or inconvenience,) such or such a feature of Romanistic is preferable to the correspondent feature in Anglican practice. — Such was the language of Oughton, twenty years before Blackstone made his appearance: such was the language of Oughton, at a time when no lay-lawyer, no common lawyer or equity lawyer, had ever deigned to make any the loosest reference of the consecrated established arrangements of procedure to the ends of justice.

judicial power, was accompanied by a change more or less considerable in the mode of inquiry pursued or allowed of, under the notion of coming at the truth.

Of penal procedure, three modes of primary distinction, with so many appropriate names: accusation, denunciation (or say presentment) and inquisition. Accusation, where an individual appears in the character of plaintiff or prosecutor: denunciation, where that function is undertaken by an official person or a set of official persons, a churchwarden or the churchwardens of a parish: inquisition (otherwise styled procedure *ex mero officio*,) where the function of prosecutor is exercised, for a time at least, by the judge.

The accusatorial mode is the mode that seems the properest to be taken for a standard; that of denunciation being only an inconsiderable modification of it, and the inquisitorial (how much soever in use in other countries) a sort of irregular and as it were incomplete mode, in which (as in an enthymeme when compared to a complete syllogism of three terms) one of the members naturally looked for is in appearance wanting, being consolidated with another.

1. First lot of evidence or deposition:— articles spontaneously exhibited by the accuser.

In these articles is included the statement given of the supposed offence by the accuser, he not being upon oath. Except that, from its division into articles (probably numbered articles,) it may be expected to be more particular,—the place it occupies in the cause seems to correspond to that of the indictment or information in the penal branch of the indigenous system of procedure, to the declaration in the civil or non-penal branch, and to the bill in equity.*

As to the imperfection attached to the evidence exhibited in this mode, it consists, here as elsewhere, in its being exhibited without the check of interrogation, and without the sanction of an oath. It is the same imperfection which (as if by an original contract) lawyers of all nations and all times have agreed in planting in the system, as the necessary means for rendering it well adapted to their own professional ends, and proportionably ill adapted and hostile to the ends of justice.

In other respects, we see already how much superior this sort of instrument is to those instruments of indigenous law, to which, in respect of its station in the cause, it corresponds. Digested into articles, and these articles numbered, a source of perspicuity is seen, the utility of which has already been pretty fully brought to view.

None of the technical nonsense—none of the gratuitous, and frequently injurious and insulting, falsehoods, of which those instruments of indigenous law are in so large a proportion composed. Of misplaced rhetoric, placed there for the benefit of the scribe, probably a pretty ample stock. But simple depredation is one sort of abuse—depredation stained by mendacity, and bedaubed with nonsense, is a more aggravated species of abuse.

2. Examination of the defendant, in answer to the above articles.

This examination,—being conducted, in the usual secrecy of the Roman mode, by the judge alone, or his representative, without the presence of the adverse (the accusing) party, or the advocate of either,—is therefore performed in the same way as the examination is performed (as above) by and before the master in the King's Bench: with this difference, that the ecclesiastical examination has an object, viz. the finding out whether the defendant be guilty or no; whereas, in the case of the lay-examination, being performed after he has been deemed guilty, no object is discernible.

In the countenance of the initiative articles, there is one feature very particular, and which affords a curious enough specimen of ecclesiastical justice. Over and above the statement made, in a manner more or less detailed, of the supposed facts and circumstances of the supposed offence,—a distinct fact is stated, viz. that a general report or rumour of it prevails in the neighbourhood: which is as much as to say that it is affirmed extrajudicially, by hearsay witnesses in unknown numbers, and whose statements respectively were removed by an unknown number of degrees, from the original source of evidence.

By the articles, the defendant is called upon to answer,—or at least, in consequence of them, he is obliged (and on pain of excommunication as for contumacy) to answer—as to what? As to the truth of criminative facts contained in the accusation? No: but only as to the existence of such a report, true or false.

Why not as to the only material point, the fact of the offence? For this very good reason,—that in an express statute it is declared, that, by the sort of court in question, no such obligation shall be enforced. Driven from this hold, from this mode of coming at material truth, they betake themselves thus to a lawyer's shift:—Well then, we must not ask you what it was you did, but what is it that people say of you? To common sense and common honesty, nothing could be more idle than this question. Why are you in any event to be punished for what people say of you, unless what they say of you is true? In such a case, if punishment is due anywhere, the authors of the defamation, not the per-

* Oughton, ii. 218, 225.

sons labouring under it, are the persons to whom it is due.

Not so, in the opinion of these ecclesiastics. In their opinion, or at least by their laws, it is on the party defamed that the punishment ought and is to be made to fall — at least if costs imposed under the name of punishment be a punishment. Though not guilty of the fact; — if to your knowledge there be such a report to your prejudice, being (or, if you are a true man, although not being) upon your oath, you can do no less than confess the existence of it: in this case it is expressly declared, that you are to be subjected to costs.* Confess or not, if it be proved that there has been such a report, guilty or not guilty, you are equally to be condemned to costs. *Si fama confessata vel probata fuerit, pars rea condemnabitur in expensis.*

What is again curious is, that, — though without a rumour the defendant could not have been obliged to make answer to questions concerning the truth of the charge, — yet, the existence of a rumour being established, as above, whether by his own confession, or by extraneous testimony, the protection meant by the legislature to be given him against these relevant questions is now taken off by these ecclesiastical judges; and (according to Oughton at least) he is obliged to make answer to all such questions, just as if no such law had been enacted. Obliged? How? By a mode which (it must be confessed) is not only a proper, but the only proper mode: by his being adjudged guilty — to wit, on the ground of his silence, considered in the character of circumstantial evidence.

Here then, we see, ecclesiastical ingenuity has afforded a pretty effectual contrivance for getting rid of the manacles imposed upon these holy hands. Spread a lying report, and then with the fruits of your own lie nullify the act of the legislature.†

If, either by the confession of the defendant or by extraneous witnesses, the existence of the rumour be proved, — a final remedy to which (always according to Oughton) it is competent to the spiritual practitioner to have recourse, is to propose to him (on pain of the ultimate punishment, excommunication) to declare upon oath, and in terms of convenient generality, without the inconvenience of adverse or particular examination, that he is not guilty of the offence charged. Giving a man this invitation to commit perjury, is, in the technical language of Romanigenous, canonical, and spiritual pharmacy, called giving him a purge *(purgatio, purgationis indictio:)* perjury being, it seems, no less conducive than the evacuation of the purse, to the health of souls.

The administration of this cathartic stands prohibited in explicit terms in the Westminster Dispensary.‡ Oughton, though he recommends a reference to the statute, does not on that account think it necessary to represent this branch of practice as being the less in force.‖

To the eye of reason, standing upon experience, the pertinacity of a man refusing to answer questions (when they are permitted to be put) in relation to his supposed delinquency, is a more satisfactory proof of his being guilty, than any that can be afforded by any extraneous testimony. It is after having given this proof of his guiltiness, that the spiritual judge is allowed by the practice of the court to urge the defendant, on pain of conviction and the severe punishment of excommunication, to this protestation of his innocence.

Without any such rumour, confessed or proved, — in the administration of this cathartic, the spiritual judge is equally warranted by circumstantial evidence; provided that it merit the appellation of "vehement,"

---

* Oughton, i. 221, 226.

† The contrivance, — would it hold water? — Apply in the regular way to the Court of King's Bench, and then you will know. In the year 1738, Oughton speaks of it as the then existing practice: in 1767, twenty-nine years after, Burn drops all mention of it. The contrivance is a trick; but on this ground, not to speak of others, tricks are established practice. If, — a man having been excommunicated for an offence of this description, — the spiritual court, for the purpose of causing pecuniary satisfaction to be made to the parties injured, offer, on that condition, to take off the punishment, their proceedings will be annulled.[a] But if, instead of making any such offer, they begin with imposing penance, and then, on the same condition, and for the same purpose, offer to take off the penance, so far so good. By a statute still in force,[b] in the case of this very offence, it is ordained, that, if the offender will redeem it (the penance) of his own good will, by giving money to the prelate, or to the party grieved, it shall be required before the prelate, and the king's prohibition shall not lie. The trick, then, is on the part of the lay judges; who, — when the spiritual judge, to save to the delinquent the expense, vexation, and delay of the previous and useless penance, proceeded to make his bargain by the ordinary means of the excommunication without the penance, — took advantage of this regard for public justice on his part, to nullify his proceedings, and leave the injury without redress.

Tenable or untenable, the mode of procedure on this ground, as it stands in Oughton, will serve equally well for illustration. If, in the character of a description of what can lawfully be done by these spiritual judges, it be incorrect, — in the character of a description of what in that way they have done, or would do, or would have done if they could, it is not the less instructive.

[a] Gibson, 9, in Burn, iii. 185.

[b] 9 Edw. II. c. 3. [Repealed by 9 Geo. IV. c. 31. — *Ed.*]

‡ Stat. 13. C. II. c. 12, § 4.

‖ Oughton, i. 223.

which is as much as to say, provided it be of that degree of strength which, under the indigenous practice, is held of itself sufficient for conviction in the most highly penal cases: another reason for suspecting that, if administered at all, this dose is scarce ever swallowed without carrying down with it at least a *quantum sufficit* of perjury.

One good thing is, that it does not appear there is any obligation upon the judge to make application of this drastic remedy: what I should expect to find, if there were any means of knowing, is, that within the memory of man it has scarce ever been applied.

Instead of being put to his oath, as in the Anglican mode, — at the very instant of his delivering his testimony in the Romanigenous mode, an examinee is made to swear on one day before one person, that he will deliver his testimony another day before another:* on which other day it appears not that any fresh oath is taken. In the promissory oath, does it expressly stand as part of the promise that the testimony when so given shall be true?† If not, the testimony can hardly be said to be delivered upon oath, according to the import annexed to that phrase by common use. The professed object of the oath so tendered is to secure submission in this behalf to the authority of the judge: and this object is attained by the mere act of submitting to examination: howsoever the matter of deposition may stand in respect of truth and falsehood.

In the practice of the ecclesiastical courts, (if the conception entertained by a modern institutionalist be correct) much inconvenience has arisen from the practice of taking the examining judges at the recommendation of the parties; as we have seen to be the practice in the case of *country* causes in the lay equity courts. Each one of these ephemeral judges espouses (it is said) too warmly the cause of the party to whom he is indebted for his appointment: the temper they bring into the business is that of the agent or the advocate, rather than that of the judge.

Since Oughton's time, it has been the practice for the judge himself — the principal and permanent judge — to take upon himself the nomination of these occasional judges: not referring the recommendation to the parties, but choosing some person — some official person for example, some co-practitioner in the same branch of ecclesiastical law, to whom the interests of both are supposed to be alike indifferent. The situation of the person who officiates in that character, is by this means analogous to that of the examiner's clerk, by whom, in the lay equity courts, the business is conducted in *town* causes.

This is spoken of as if it were a prodigious and clear improvement.

It may be too much to affirm, with absolute persuasion, that the change is for the worse: but whether on the whole it be advantageous, is at any rate extremely questionable.

Leave the nomination to the parties, you leave a danger of partiality, and *ex parte* zeal. But the danger is alike on both sides; and excess on either side finds its check and counterpoise in a similar excess on the other.

Give the nomination to the permanent judge; he being in the habit of choosing the judge or judges *ad hoc* among his fellow-practitioners, the danger to which the arrangement is exposed, is that of carelessness and negligence. But to this inconvenience there is no check whatever. From the secrecy so carefully preserved, it derives every facility and encouragement which it would be possible for it to receive.

The only indispensable advantage resulting from the change, is that which is reaped by the judge, and consists in the patronage he has contrived to create for himself by means of it. It affords him the means of throwing business into the hands of some personal friend and dependent.

This circumstance is of the class of those considerations which politicians in their mutual altercations are never backward to bring to view, but of which not the smallest hint is ever to be found in any book which has a lawyer of any class for its author.

For the conducting of the business in the best manner, two opposite endowments (it has been seen) are wanting; such as cannot with reason be expected to be found habitually united in one person or set of persons: — the zeal and appropriate information peculiar to the situation of party; and the moderation and skill derived from exercise — endowments which are naturally looked for on the part of the judge.

Of two systems, one of which affords the first of these qualifications without the second, the other the second without the first, nothing better can be said, than that they are both deficient. But, if the question be, which of the two, upon the ground of general principles, presents itself as most deficient and ineligible, — the answer seems to be, that which threatens the interests of truth and justice with irremediable negligence.

In the lay equity courts, both these defective and opposite courses have from the beginning of things been pursued with equal and equally imperturbable composure. A circle of ten miles' radius is drawn round some central point in the metropolis of England — suppose the cathedral of St Paul's. In all places an inch without that circle, the danger of deficiency of zeal predominates, and the examinations are taken by persons nominated by

* Oughton, i. 217, 218.

† *Ibid.* i. 217, Tit. 141, § 1, 2.

the parties. In all places an inch within that same circle, the danger of excess of zeal predominates, and the business affords a little mine of patronage for the benefit of some great dignitary in the law.

The only indisputable disadvantage attendant on that arrangement which gives the nomination to the parties, consists in the expense. Four functionaries, or at least two, require on this plan to be paid; instead of one. A single person, were it made his duty to do all the business of this kind that comes within the compass of a certain district, might, in consideration of the constancy of his employment, afford to do it upon cheaper terms than those others to whom it affords but a casual resource. These ephemeral judges have moreover a manifest interest in prolonging their existence, for the sake of prolonging their pay. A permanent judge would not be exposed to any sinister interest of this kind; to whatsoever other sinister interests he might stand exposed.*

In the institution of the examiner's office, the geographical limits set to the jurisdiction of it were evidently suggested by considerations of utility and convenience. Within the space in question, less vexation and expense would be produced by sending the witnesses to a fixed tribunal, than by providing occasional tribunals all over the country, within an equally short distance of their several abodes: without that space, the economy of the arrangement would no longer hold. Not that the difference between ten miles exactly and ten miles and a foot, would be worth taking into account; but that all lines of demarcation must be drawn somewhere.

Making amendments of this nature in the equity or any other branch of the technical system, would be like laying new boards on a floor eat up by the dry-rot. But, inasmuch as, at the time when the radius of ten miles was marked out, the means of local communication were much less expeditious, and travelling much less frequent, than at the present day,—if (all circumstances taken into account) the examination at the examiner's office were preferable upon the whole to examination by commissioners, a twenty-miles radius might seem better adapted than one of no more than ten miles, to the present state of things.

But every observation thus pointing to immediate practice stands exposed to this general objection, viz. that it supposes, on the part of those dignitaries on whom the state of the laws depends, the existence of some one person at least, to whom their degree of aptitude with reference to the ends of justice is not a matter of complete and incurable indifference.

In the Anglican ecclesiastical courts, the practice in respect of the mode of collecting the evidence of extraneous witnesses differs not materially from that of the equity courts. The leading features — examination *per judicem solum*, and that conducted under the seal of inviolable secrecy — are in both cases the same.

What differences there are, consist chiefly in an arrangement or two peculiar to the Romanistic courts; which, in so far as they are to be considered as having any of the ends of justice for their object, may be considered as so many sacrifices made to the direct ends, at the expense of the collateral ends.

After the deposition given by the examinee has been taken down by the examiner, it is read over to him article by article; whereupon liberty is given to him to make what amendment he thinks fit.†

The authenticity of the deposition being thus established,—for further confirmation of it, he is on another occasion brought into the presence of the judge; on which occasion the opportunity of making alterations is again afforded him.‡

Other ceremonies there are, which in the ecclesiastical courts appear to be added to those which have place in the lay equity courts. What they do towards making the bill of costs, is evident enough; but, as what they do towards increasing the security against falsehood seems to amount to nothing, they present no title to admission in this place.‖

The mode of collecting evidence in the admiralty courts differs not materially from that which is in use (as above described) in the ecclesiastical courts.§

A pamphlet was written a few years ago under the title of "War in Disguise,"—a pamphlet of considerable celebrity (proceeding from a name, which, though not announced, was not disguised,) having for its object the making it appear that, in the dispute between the British government and that of the American United States on a point of international law, the American government was in the wrong; and, moreover, that, for eluding the authority of those British judicatories to whose cognizance the point in question appertains, perjury was an instrument habitually and regularly employed by the subjects of those states.

That, in the charge thus made, there was a considerable degree of truth, there seems but

* On a system radically bad, observations pointing out, as here, this or that particular defect, together with this or that partial remedy, answer no other purpose than that of illustration. When, instead of being carved out into fair slices by a geographical knife alone, jurisdiction is divided or rather torn into shapeless scraps by metaphysical instruments, the establishment may be oppressively expensive, and at the same time inadequate and insufficient.

† Browne, ii. 421. Admiralty Practice.
‡ See Ch. XII. *Repetition.*
‖ See Browne, and Oughton.
§ Browne, Compend. View, ii. 413.

too much reason for believing; the misfortune is, that, if so it be that it is the truth, it is far, very far, from being the whole truth.

In speaking of what in his language was "war in disguise," it seemed to the gentleman that, in bringing to view the cause of the war, he had completely stripped it of all disguise. Unfortunately, — if, to the cause brought to view by him in the character of the immediate cause (or at least an immediate cause,) that character does appertain with too much justice, — a still higher cause, the cause of that cause, remains still in disguise; in a disguise which the gentleman was not quite so willing, as he was able, to divest it of.

In the case of perjury, as of any other crime, — if the station of the suborners be not too high to leave them within the reach of punishment, — in looking for the perjurers, it is customary not to stop there, but to look out also for the suborners. Unfortunately, in this as in so many instances, the station of the suborners is too high to leave them within the reach of justice. Of justice? of penal infliction? Aye, or so much as of shame.

These suborners are those (need it be mentioned?) by whom, with full and complete consciousness of such its character, a system of procedure thus fruitful in perjuries, having been found created, is preserved — preserved with full and complete consciousness of such its character; and, if not for the sake of the profit, yet surely not without pretty effectual knowledge of the profit, which, in so many shapes — money, power, and ease — in such abundance flows from it.

By what is the perjury supported? By the generally experienced efficacy of it in the courts to which it is presented. And what is the cause of this efficacy? What but a mode for collection of the evidence — a mode by which, whether obtainable or not obtainable in the universally-acknowledged best shape, an exclusion is put upon it in that best shape, while the door is kept open to evidence in the worst shapes from the same source: a mode than which, were the object (as perhaps it was) to encourage, to propagate perjury, none more promising, none more effectual, could have been devised.

For so many hundreds of years past, in more courts than one, and, in each court, in so long and illustrious a line of judges, by whom evidence in these perjury-begetting shapes has exclusively been received, — has there been one to whom the efficacy of this mode for the generation of perjury, its inefficacy for the support of justice, has been a secret, or could have been a matter of doubt? Has there been any one of them to whom trial by *vivâ voce* evidence with questions arising out of answers, and with cross-examination by parties, has been unknown? Have there been many of them to whom, when changes agreeable to them have been to be made, the road to Parliament has been unknown?

Now then, on the score of perjury, how stands the account between the United States and the United Kingdom? In the United States, the system of procedure known on both sides to be thus rich in perjury, has been abolished — long abolished. In the United Kingdom, having been sometimes attacked, it has been, and continues to be, strenuously defended and kept up. In these as in other cases, in regard to this abomination, the government of the United States has done what was in the power of government to do towards the extirpation of it: in the United Kingdom, government has done, and continues to do, what is in the power of government for the preservation of it.

In the United States, the transgressors are, not the rulers — (they have done whatever was in their power to purge themselves of the transgression) — but individuals. In the United Kingdom, the main transgressors — those to whom belongs the wo denounced against those from whom evil comes — are the rulers. As to individuals, members of those states, — if so it be that, in defending themselves against force which in their eyes is injurious, they abstain not from defiling their lips with perjury, — whence is it that they do so? It is from the facility and encouragement which, in the United Kingdom, as above, they receive from its rulers.

In the opinion of the late Dr. Browne, professor of civil (*i. e.* Roman) law in the university of Dublin, and representative in three parliaments for the same, the practice of the ecclesiastical courts (to which may be added that of the admiralty courts) has the advantage (he wishes us of course to understand in respect of conduciveness to the ends of justice) over the practice of the equity courts.*

Two main reasons are assigned by him:—

1. In the ecclesiastical courts, in the course of one and the same suit, each party has it in his power to obtain the testimony (the testimony upon oath) of the opposite party (this supposes only one of a side:) whereas in the equity courts, for the defendant to obtain in this way the testimony of the plaintiff, requires an additional suit, viz. a cross bill.*

If, in the one ecclesiastical or admiralty suit, the quantity of vexation, expense, and delay is (upon the average of the number of cases in each respective court presenting an equal demand for vexation, expense, and delay) less than in the equity courts, — in so far, the practice of the ecclesiastical and admiralty courts has the advantage over the practice of those its rivals, in respect of conduciveness to the ends of justice. How, in these re-

* Browne, i. 472.

spects, the account stands between them, it is impossible for an individual to pretend to say: it is in the power of the rulers of the people to know, should it ever occur to them that these matters belong to the list of "secrets worth knowing."

In the ecclesiastical courts, "I scarcely ever knew," says he,* "even the most complicated last two years. How few equity suits," adds he, "are so soon over." But the suits which come before the equity courts, are they not upon an average of a nature considerably more complicated than those which come before the ecclesiastical courts?

2. The other alleged advantage is, that, in the ecclesiastical and admiralty courts, "the personal answer of the party is demanded to the assertions and charges of his adversary, without putting them into the form of interrogation."† This he calls "superfluous tautology:"† repeating the same story twice, first in the shape of assertion, "and then in the form of interrogation."‡ And this "superfluous tautology" (he informs us) has been "corrected," as he calls it, in the ecclesiastical courts, and not in the courts of equity; which he observes is very remarkable.‖

That there is tautology enough, and to spare, might perhaps, in the instance of which of these courts he pleased, be conceded to him without much danger: but how it should have happened to him to conceive that there is tautology in putting questions after having stated supposed facts, remains to be explained. True it is, that, what a man knows, or chooses to profess to know, he may express in the form of an assertion: but suppose a point, concerning which he really knows not anything, nor conceives nor professes himself to know anything, but wishes for information, and to obtain such information addresses himself to the adverse party, who he supposes may have it in his power to afford it. Where in this case is the tautology? So far as a man is really ignorant, to obtain information, there is but one way, which is to ask for it: to obtain answers, there is but one way, which is to put questions: to obtain information in relation to such and such particular points, there is but one way, which is to name those points.

That in a bill in equity there is commonly no want of superfluity, may safely enough be conceded: but so far as regards the parallel drawn by the learned professor, wherein does it consist? Not in the interrogative part, but in the assertive part — not in the endeavours used to obtain the information which a man does not possess, and has occasion for, but in the false pretensions in which, by weak or wicked judges it has been made necessary to a plaintiff to say that he possesses it, when the sole cause and reason of his asking for it is, that he does not possess it.

The courts of equity have split each suit into two suits; making a separate suit necessary to enable the defendant of the first suit to obtain the confessorial testimony of his adversary, in return for that which has been already furnished to him. The source of vexation, expense, and delay, thus opened, is an improvement made by English equity upon the original Roman practice retained in the ecclesiastical and admiralty courts, as well as in the whole system of procedure pursued in several other nations of Europe, in so far as they have taken the Roman system (as for the most part they have done) for the foundation of their own. But, from another source of vexation, expense, and delay, from which the ecclesiastical and admiralty courts (according to the information of the same learned professor) have made copious draughts, the equity courts have made no such draughts. To the sort of inquiry, on the occasion of which no licence is given to mendacity (viz. that on which each party, at the requisition of the other, deposes upon oath, and which consists of the effect of the equity bill reciprocalized, and in that way doubled,) the ecclesiasticalists have contrived to prefix the sort of inquiry by which the requisite licence is given to mendacity—by which the requisite profit is furnished to the men of law — by which no information consequently is furnished to anybody, nor (excepting the vexation, expense, and delay, to the parties) anything else but the profit to the men of law. In a word, before it suffers any information that can be depended upon to be obtained on either side, it makes it necessary that the men of law should occupy themselves in giving sham information on both sides: it mounts the common-law abuse of special pleading upon the more useful part of equity practice.

That, after everything that has thus been done by the ecclesiasticalists to augment the profitable mass of vexation, expense, and delay, still more has been done in the same line of industry by the dispensers of equity, is maintained by the learned professor, and may perhaps be true enough. If so it be, then it follows that there are grievances still worse than the system which he stood engaged to explain, was accustomed to draw upon for honour and for profit, and became thus disposed to eulogise. To compare one branch of the system with another, when a tempting opportunity offers in this or that particular to display the superiority of his own over a rival branch, — this is what a professor of any one of them, and each of them, may do without much difficulty. But to compare his own branch with the ends of justice — the professor who has courage to make any

* Browne, i. 488.
† *Ibid.* ii. 348.
‡ *Ibid.* ii. 348.
‖ *Ibid.* ii. 347.

such comparison, is still to seek, and ever will be.

As to the supposed improvement in which the learned professor prides himself, it consists, we may see, so far as it takes place, in neither more nor less than cutting down examinations, and reducing them to affidavit work. Whether it be in the nature of this difference to add to the chance in favour of a full discovery of the truth, is a question that has already been considered.

CHAPTER XVIII.

INCONGRUITIES OF ROMAN LAW IN RESPECT OF THE EXTRACTION OF EVIDENCE.

FOR the extraction and receipt of testimony, the Roman system admits of but one of the two modes — the *vivâ voce* mode: the mode by written correspondence has no place in it.

Except in one case, and that a narrow one, viz. the case of *confrontation*, as between a prisoner defendant and the witnesses on the other side (of which presently,) the practice of cross-examination is unknown to it. Cross-examination, a term of English jurisprudence — a term for which (like the terms witness, testimony, right, obligation, and other terms of natural jurisprudence) one should have expected to have found an equivalent in every language — has actually out of Britain no single-worded equivalent in any European language.

Hence the door is left wide open to mendacity, falsehood, and partiality, whether from unblameable incorrectness, from temerity, or from mendacity: against mendacity, in very gross cases, some faint and inadequate prospect, perhaps, of punishment at some future contingent period; but for prevention, cross-examination being unknown, nothing can be done immediately, and upon the spot.

In the perusal of the *Causes Célèbres*, an observation that presented itself almost in every cause, was the extraordinary frequency of the cases of repugnant testimony, in comparison with anything which is presented by the ordinary run of causes on the occasion of the trials conducted in the English mode — a repugnancy which, for want of cross-examination, remains uncleared up; and that in cases where, from the nature of the fact, it appears evident, that by a few questions put in the way of cross-examination, or (in Romano-Gallic language) by confrontation, if confrontation were extended to these causes, the contradiction would be naturally, and in all probability satisfactorily, cleared up.

In looking for the cause of this repugnancy, and of the superior frequency of it in the Romano-Gallic practice in comparison with the English, a more candid and consolatory mode of accounting for it presents itself than would be presented by any supposed difference on the ground of morality between the two nations. False testimony is so much more frequent in France than in England — why? Because the witness, though examined *vivâ voce* and extemporaneously in France as in England, had in France no apprehension of seeing questions put to him in that same way, and on that same occasion, by the experienced sagacity of the legal assistant on the other side.

Whatever be the nature and rank of the cause — higher penal, lower penal, or non-penal, — the person, the only person by whom testimony could be either received or extracted, was the judge. But, unless by mere accident, it is not in the nature of things that the judge should of himself know anything about the facts on either side. In the way of extraction — that is, of interrogation, examination, putting questions, — whatever can be done from that commanding station cannot have any other ground to proceed upon, any other lights for guidance, than such facts or supposed facts as are furnished by one of the parties. The judge is, or ought to be, — the judge is supposed to be (and let him be supposed to be) impartial; but, in the instance of each witness whom he examines, the instructions, the only instructions he acts or can act from, are partial instructions, furnished by one alone of the contending parties, viz. that one by whom the testimony of the witness is invoked.

When each witness is examined by the parties — examined by both parties — examined primarily by the party by whom his testimony was called for (if called for by both,* by the plaintiff,) cross-examined by the adverse party; he is examined by two persons, who, taken together, have every interest which the matter at stake in the cause can give them, to draw from him the whole truth: each having every interest which the value of the matter in dispute to himself can give him, in drawing forth so much of the truth as makes in favour of his side. So far as the extraction of the truth is concerned, justice, under this system, has nothing to fear but such casual deficiency as may happen to take place in respect of the intellectual sufficiency of the parties and their agents in relation to this task.

Deficiency of zeal, the result of deficiency of interest, is not to be apprehended on either side. Excess of zeal, the result of excessive sensibility to the sinister action of interest, may naturally be apprehended on both sides; but its operation on each side is checked and compensated by its operation on the other.

* It is very evidently possible, but from various causes not a frequent case, that the testimony of one and the same witness shall have been invoked on both sides.

When the business, the proper business, of both parties, is taken out of the hands of both parties, and lodged in the hands of the judge, — so far as depends upon the state of the affections, of motives and interests, the business is as badly arranged as possible. General deficiency of zeal, variegated by occasional excess of zeal, and that on one side only — general carelessness, variegated by occasional partiality, both of them almost without controul,—such is the natural result of so incongruous a state of things. Are the parties, both of them, unknown — the interests of them alike indifferent — to the judge? His interest is to get rid of them and their dispute as quickly as possible. The points he cannot help examining the witnesses to, he examines them to: the points he can help examining them to, he suffers to pass without notice. Attentive only to his own ease, inattentive alike to the interests of both parties, the merit of impartiality cannot be denied to be his due. On the other hand, does it happen to him, from amity, enmity, or self-regarding interest, to have any leaning on either side? All facts operating on that favoured side find him eager to draw them forth; all facts operating in favour of the opposite side find him as determined as the care of his reputation suffers him to be, not to think of them. Under the eye of a scrutinizing public, such studied blindness would not at all times be equally safe. But, in the Roman system, whatever is done in this way is done under the veil of secrecy: besides the judge and the person under examination, no one is present but the judge's subordinate, the recording scribe. If the object were to push carelessness and corruption to their *maximum* — to render, in one or other way, misdecision as frequent as possible, — no means could be better adapted to that end.

Under this system, the arrangements recommended (as above) as subservient to the purpose of cross-examination, are indeed admitted; the testimony delivered in the shape of answers to questions; each answer extemporaneous, following immediately upon the question which called for it, and in so far unpremeditated; the questions put separately — not *uno flatu*, in a simultaneous string; each question having the whole string of preceding answers, and in particular the last preceding answer, for a ground to work upon, for a light to work by. True: but of these subordinate arrangements, useful as they are, what is the chief use? Answer — to give effect to cross-examination: but, in the system which thus employs them, cross-examination has no place.

The notes of the evidence are taken down, not by the judge himself, but by a scribe who attends him for that purpose. Of what passes, or of what does not pass, more or less is set down, as the superior and his subordinate can agree. To the account there given of what has passed, or is supposed to have passed, the person examined is indeed made to annex his signature; but the words, even of the answers, are not so much as supposed to be given — much less, of the questions. Of the answers, no more than the substance, or supposed substance; of the questions, not so much as the substance, except such part as is, as it were, seen through the answers—such part without which the answers would not be intelligible. Negligence, violence, subornation effected or attempted by threats or promises, with or without the intention of fulfilling them — misbehaviour in every imaginable shape, may on the part of the judge have been committed, yet not the slightest trace of it need, or is at all likely, to appear upon the face of any of these minutes.

Had it been really an object to guard individuals against a species of injustice, which in capital cases would amount to legal murder aggravated by torture, — arrangements so obvious as those which in this view might be imagined, would hardly have been so universally omitted.

Without being stationed so near the prisoner as to be capable of prompting him without the observance of the judge, — a friend and nominee of the prisoner might be in the same apartment, effectually present to the purpose of hearing everything that passed.

If, for fear of prompting by signs, it were not thought fit that this assistant should be present during any part of the examination, he might at any rate be present at the final reading of the minutes. In case of their being in every respect correct, and acknowledged to be so, he might be present at the time when the prisoner, being finally interrogated concerning their correctness, confessed them to be correct, either by positive assent, or (what would be equivalent) by silence: — present to the purpose of hearing and testifying his assent, observing and testifying his silence. In case of the prisoner's objecting to any part of the minutes as incorrect or incomplete, he might be present to the purpose of hearing, seeing, and attesting the discussion produced in consequence; he might be present to the purpose of doing, what in most cases he would naturally have to do, and think fit to do — viz. to confirm by his subscription the statement drawn up on that occasion by the official scribe, or (in the extraordinary but still possible case of an irreconcilable disagreement) entering upon the minutes his dissent, together with whatever observations he might think fit to add to it.

This assistant would naturally have been a professional assistant, of the attorney or advocate class, as most competent to the business: it might have been a non-professional friend. The prisoner (for no possible case ought ever to pass unprovided for) is too poor to purchase assistance—he is too friendless to obtain it gratis. What is to be done? Shall it rest with the judge to provide him with an assistant? An assistant so named would afford but slender security against any possible mal-practice on the part of the functionary by whom he had been named.

But wherever the Roman system of jurisprudence has been prevalent, other functionaries have never been wanting, whose function, while it has made the exercise of such charity a duty, has secured to them the requisite portion of public confidence. The confessor, for example, by whom the prisoner, if capitally convicted, would have been attended and supported in his last moments, — he, or some one of his cloth, would be the person to guard him (as above) from such oppression as might involve him in any such suffering without its having been his due.

Thus hostile is the Roman system of procedure to every end of justice — thus subservient to the sinister interests by which it has been created and preserved.

By the several governments of the American states — by those republican legislators, though bred in the sink of English corruption, this abomination has for these many years been extirpated.

Even by Napoleon, the most absolute of all despots that the world ever saw, it has been extirpated.

In this, as in its other shapes, republicans abhor corruption — despots have no need of it.

In England alone is it an object of worship; rulers protesting, and people sottish enough to believe, that the very life of the government depends upon it, and that without it everything would fall to pieces.

CHAPTER XIX.

OF CONFRONTATION UNDER THE ROMAN LAW.

CONFRONTATION, considered as belonging to the nomenclature of judicial procedure, is a term peculiar to Roman law. *Ex vi termini*, it denotes the bringing of one person into the presence of another: by institution, it denotes the bringing into the presence of a defendant, a person who, whether in the character of a co-defendant or that of an extraneous witness, has delivered testimony tending to the crimination of such defendant.

Under the head of *confrontation* may be found whatever advances (scanty indeed they will be seen to be) have been made in Roman procedure towards the introduction of that universal and equal system of interrogation above delineated and proposed: consequently whatever part has been covered by Roman law, of the ground covered by the operation called *cross-examination* in English law.

The operation has two professed objects: one is, the establishing the identity of the defendant, viz. that the person thus produced to the deponent is the person of whom he has been speaking; the other is, that an opportunity may be afforded to the defendant, in addition to whatever testimony may have been delivered to his disadvantage, to obtain the extraction of such other part (if any) of the facts within the knowledge of the deponent, as may operate in his favour. At the instance of the defendant, interrogatories suggested by him are accordingly permitted by the legislator (but subject to the discretion of the judge) to be propounded; thereby enabling the operation, as far as it goes, to contribute towards the trustworthiness and probative force of the testimony, as well in respect of correctness as completeness.*

This security has already been spoken of as being in its application confined far within the amplitude demanded for it by the exigencies of justice: the more closely it is examined, the more thoroughly will this conception of it be confirmed. It is narrowed and curtailed in a variety of directions: the quality of the cause; the description of the interrogators and respondents; the plenitude of the right.

1. *Quality of the cause.* It is confined absolutely to criminal causes; and, in general practice, to such criminal cases as may subject the defendant to corporally-afflictive punishment — *peine afflictive*.

The defendant having already been interrogated by the judge in the darkness of his closet; the witnesses in support of the prosecution cited by the judge, where there is no prosecutor, or by the prosecutor (public or private) where there is one, having been examined in the same manner a first time, having under the name of *repetition* or *recolement*† been examined in the same manner a second time (the defendant not present at their examination either time;) a third examination takes place, as secret as before, except that the defendant, and the witnesses, one by one, are now, for the first time, introduced into each other's presence.

Considering confrontation in the character

* Another purpose mentioned, and much dwelt upon,[a] is that of the allowance given to a defendant to exhibit against a witness (an extraneous witness) objections tending to weaken the credit, or bar the admission, of his testimony. Of this I take no further notice; partly because, to that particular purpose, presence is not particularly necessary; partly because the subject will receive ample consideration in another place.[b]

† Chap. XII. *Repetition*.

[a] Ordonnance de 1670, tit. xv.

[b] *Infra*, Book IX. *Exclusion*.

of an instrument for the correction and completion of a lot of testimony, — an observation almost too obvious to be repeated is, that the demand for the use of it (that is, for one all-comprehensive system of interrogation, and for this operation as being among the branches of that system) has no respect whatsoever to the general nature, — to the penality or non-penality, — of the suit. The more highly penal the cause, the greater is the mischief of injustice, supposing it to take place; but as to the probability of its taking place for want of the sort of security in question, it stands exactly upon a par in both cases.

In the cases in which it is not afforded, as well as in the cases in which it is afforded, the importance of it has been not altogether a secret to the technicalists by whom it has been refused. To obtain the benefit of it, a defendant that has been proceeded against in the non-criminal (called the *civil*) mode, has begged to be treated as a criminal. Prayers to this effect have not been rejected; but the adverse party is permitted to oppose the grant of the prayer, on the ground that the importance of the cause is not considerable enough to warrant the expense. It seems, upon the whole, that where the defendant is able and willing to pay the expense of being treated as a criminal, the grace has not been refused.

On the first-mentioned ground, that of establishing the identity of the defendant, the appropriation thus made of the operation to criminal cases is in a double way incongruous.

Cases occur, and without number, in which the witness, though against the defendant a very material witness, has never been in his presence. Goods, for example, stolen in the absence of the owner, are found in the possession of the thief: the owner knows his own goods; but what knows he of the thief?

Cases occur also in abundance, in which, though the cause has nothing criminal in it, the point in dispute (and a point not to be settled without a judicial interview) may be, whether the person of whom the witness has spoken under a name the same as that of the plaintiff or that of the defendant, was in truth the person thus in question, or another. He saw a person, called by a name the same as that of the defendant, execute a deed: but was it really the defendant, or another person, who, perhaps for the occasion only, was called by that same name? — He saw a person called by a name the same as that of the plaintiff, living with an older person of that same name, in the character of his son: the like question again in this case.

So far as the use and application of the principle of confrontation is concerned, in non-criminal and slightly criminal causes, English law (it is true) is no less lame than Roman law. In a cause of another description, on a trial by jury, in the character of an extraneous witness, the attendance of any man may be enforced: in the character of a party, plaintiff or defendant, no man's attendance can be enforced: *mala fides* in every shape finds a veil in absence. Happily, to the purpose here in question, the demand for confrontation does not frequently present itself.

2. *Description of the interrogators and respondents.* Subject to the restrictions that will be mentioned, the faculty of interrogation is allowed to the defendant, against the deponents, of whatever description, that have been testifying on the side adverse to him, whether in the situation of extraneous witnesses or co-defendants: for the caprice which in England prevents one defendant from being examined touching the conduct of another, extends not beyond English ground.

But the judge, it seems, on this third examination, is not allowed to interpose — is expressly interdicted from interposing, any question on his part; — that is to say, any question, which, by the particularity of the responses called for by it, can contribute to the elicitation of fresh lights. He may call upon, and is to call upon, each deponent, to declare over again — to declare, according to the tenor of the ordinance, in general terms, whether the testimony delivered by him on each former occasion was true: but, as to any question that in case of mistatement can help to rectify it, interposition for the purpose is forbidden in express words. On the two former occasions, the judge frames as well as puts all the questions; on this third occasion, he is not suffered to frame one: put questions he may — but such only as are framed by the defendants or witnesses, and by them desired to be put. But of this presently.

The defendant — the individual defendant whose confrontation is performing, — this defendant having put his questions to the co-defendant who is confronted with him, or to the extraneous witness who is confronted with him, — are they respectively at liberty to put questions back to him on their parts? On this head nothing said in the ordinance: on this point as on so many others, the natural result is that the judge does as he pleases — each judge differently, if he thinks fit.

What is clear is, that, when witnesses called for the defendant come to be examined, they are not subject to any interrogation *ex adverso* — to anything that in the language of English common law goes by the name of cross-examination, either on the part of a prosecutor, or on the part of a co-defendant: not on the part of a prosecutor; because, the examination being performed by the judge alone, and in his own cupboard, no prosecutor, no advocate, is let in: not on the part of a co-defendant; because at this time, if we may believe the commentators, the tide is turned, and mercv is the order of the day.

A circumstance that may help to reconcile justice to the sacrifice is, that by this time the defendant may have lain in prison any number of years, by which time any witness that he could have called may have died, or been otherwise disposed of: for it is a rule, that, till the proof on the side of the prosecution has been completed (and the time of its completion depends upon the pleasure of the judge,) no witness at the instance of the defendant can be heard.

3. *Plenitude of the right.* Cut down as we have seen it to be in the confused application left to it by the preceding restrictions, a security thus essential to justice is put into the hands of fortune — *si besoin est,** if need be: and in each case, whether such need exist, is left, without controul, without a word either of obligation or instruction, to the good pleasure of the judge — of the very person on whose conduct it is designed (or at least ought to have been designed) to operate as a check.†

Nor yet is the defendant permitted (at least by the tenor of the ordinance) to put any one question of himself: his right is confined to the petitioning the judge to put it for him. The judge, as we have seen, is forbidden to

* Ordonn. de 1670, Tit. xv. Art i. and ix.

† The subject remains indeed, as usual, involved in thick confusion; the result of which is, as usual, that the judge might, in most cases at least, proceed as he found most agreeable to himself.

In the Ordonnance, in this first article (tit. xv.) after leave has been given to the judge to make the order as to the *recolement* absolute and peremptory, leave is then added for making the order as to the confrontation conditional and discretionary, as above. Si l'accusation mérite d'être instruite, *le juge* ordonnera que les témois .... seront récolés en leurs depositions, et, si besoin est, confrontés à l'accusé....

In art. xi. a supposition is started, that at a point of time not specified, *recolement* and *confrontation* taken together have not been performed; and in that case, leave is given to the judges (*les juges* in the plural — before, it was *le juge* in the singular) to order these operations, so mentioned in conjunction, to be then performed.

In the article immediately preceding (art. viii.) it had been provided, that if an order has been made (it does not say by whom) that the witnesses be recoled and confronted, the deposition of those who have not been confronted shall not be received as proof, except in case of their respective deaths during the (defendant's) contumacy. By this article, confrontation is thus rendered indispensable, viz. in case of an order for that purpose; but as to the making of such order, it is not rendered indispensable: and the article immediately following assumes that recolement and confrontation, one or both, have somehow or other failed of being performed.

As to *le juge* in art. i., and *les juges* in art. ix., the expressions may naturally enough be imagined to be synonymous. No such thing. For the performance of all these several operations, — examinations, recolements, confrontations, — a single judge is in every case sufficient: more than one are scarce ever employed. For pronouncing the bare order for these respective purposes (a matter, of course, that requires much less reflection) a multitude of judges, I pretend not to say how many, was in many cases indispensable. Accordingly, when, as in art. i., the ordonnance itself speaks of but one judge, — according to Jousse, the commentator, three or seven are necessary: three, if in a court appealable from; seven, if in a court appealed to: referring, as to the three, to another title of the same Ordonnance (tit. xxv. art. x.) the provision of which, in this behalf, appears to be such as he represents it.

Another reference he makes[a] is to an arrêt of the Tournelle, by which it is adjudged and thence ordained, that no punishment either of an afflictive or infamous nature shall be pronounced, unless when recolement and confrontation have been both performed: — *adjudged* (I say) *and thence ordained;* for in France it was in this way the custom among judges to make laws avowedly in the prospective way, like legislators, instead of confining themselves to the making them in an unavowed and *ex post facto* way, as in England. But of this Tournelle court, the jurisdiction was limited by that of the Parliament of Paris: so that, in other parts of France, a judge (or the judges) did not find their liberty incommoded by this rule.

As mal-practice is but a casualty, especially among judges, there seems but little doubt that, in practice, conviction seldom took place without previous confrontation. A circumstance that will hardly be thought to weaken the probability on that side is, that, by the application of these subsidiary securities, the expense of the procedure, and with it of course the profit, never failed to receive a considerable augmentation.

As to the original legislator, the penner of the ordinance, — an expression he has let drop may afford at one view a proof of the value set by him on this security, and a sample of a technically-learned mind. In the case of non-forthcomingness on the part of the defendant, — recolement, the opportunity given to him and the other deponents to amend their respective answers, — recolement, a possible re-examination, — is declared to be *equivalent* to itself and confrontation put together: recolement *vaudra* confrontation, not, recolement *tiendra lieu* de confrontation. The logic of this jurisprudence, and the arithmetic, are worthy of each other: if both be correct, 0 must be the exact value of this security; a security which among English lawyers is regarded as so indispensable as to be without equivalent and without price.

Not but that in English law, the treatment given in this same case to a defendant is much worse — the contravention of the ends of justice much more flagrant. Absence, which though a circumstantial evidence with reference to guilt, is evidently a most untrustworthy and precarious one, receives among English judges the effect of a conclusive one. The Roman judge, complete evidence not being to be had, grounds his decision on what, of any that he is acquainted with, is the next best evidence: the English lawyer, shocked at the idea of convicting a man on imperfect evidence, convicts him without any evidence. But of this more fully in its place.

[a] P. 281; Art. i. Note 1.

put a question that has not been proposed by the defendant;* — the defendant is not allowed to put a question that has not been sanctioned by the judge.

That to the judge should be reserved a power to prohibit or exempt a respondent from making answer to this or that question (the question being noted down and recorded) is no more than necessary: otherwise the door would lie wide open to irrelevant and passionate matter without end. But the difference is considerable between making the right to put the question depend in the first instance on an express sanction given to it by the judge, and the allowing it to be put of course, subject only to stoppage for special reason.

On this as on so many other occasions, the real mischief, the root of all the evil, consists in the want of *publicity*. Under that regimen of darkness, a question, though ever so pertinent and important, may be stopped: an answer that would have saved the life of an innocent person may thus be suppressed, and no trace of the iniquity appear anywhere. Under the safeguard of publicity — adequate and appropriate publicity — no danger on the score of misdecision, capable of outweighing the inconvenience in the shape of delay and vexation on the other side, can present any adequate objection to so necessary a check.

The German edition of Romanistic procedure is, on this head, more explicit than the Gallican; and, by being so, more flagitiously and palpably tyrannical and iniquitous—more resolutely and openly bent upon the scarcely dissembled object of enabling the judge to sacrifice the innocent as often as he pleases to the sinister interests and passions of men in power; among which his own are not much in danger of being forgotten.

In English law, in the case of an extraneous witness, cross-examination is in principle regarded as the indefeasible right of each party; in all sorts of causes, penal as well as non-penal, the examination of a witness is never regarded as complete without it. Confrontation, in German as well as Gallic law, is a distinct operation, to be performed or not, according to circumstances; and at any rate not to be performed but at a different hearing, after the examination of the witness has been performed twice over, both times without the application of a check so obviously necessary to truth and justice.

In Germano-Austrian law, whether the imperfect modification of cross-examination called confrontation shall be performed or no, is in every case left in express terms to the arbitrary will and pleasure of the judge.† On the one hand, in no case is the use of it made obligatory upon the judge: on the other hand, partly by implication, partly in express terms, cases are specified in which it ought not to be employed. In one sort of cases, it is in express terms declared to be superfluous: and what, would an Englishman suppose, is that case? Where the defendant has already been "convicted by two *classical* witnesses."‡ And who is a *classical* witness? Any man against whom no particular cause of objection can be produced.|| Two witnesses, not the less false by being classical ones, charge an innocent man with a crime supposed to be committed by him at Vienna: two hundred unbribed witnesses agree in deposing that at the same day, hour, and minute, he was seen by them at Prague. Under these circumstances, is the defendant allowed to cross-examine these two classical perjurers? Not he indeed: the operation would be "superfluous"—too evidently "*superfluous*" to be admissible. The authors of the German Theresian code, and their Latin interpreter Banniza, are altogether clear about it.

After this specimen, to hunt out minor absurdities and atrocities, of which there are a most abundant breed, is an operation that may be spared.

In Romano-German as in Romano-Gallic law, where confrontation ends, there ends adverse interrogation — there ends cross-examination even in that faint shadow of it. In the minor penal branch, and in the whole of the non-penal branch, it is not only not made necessary, but not so much as suffered to be employed. Not that it is forbidden; but that, under any other name than that of *confrontation*, no such thing was ever heard of; and, without the idea of a criminal prosecution to hitch it upon, the idea of confrontation has never been able to find a place in any Roman-law-bred mind.

* Jousse, p. 286; Tit. xv. Art. i. Note 7.

† Brannisa, ii. 219. § 460, referring to Code Therese, Art. xxxv. § 2.

‡ Brannisa, ii. p. 223, § 468. Code Therèse, Art. xxxii. § 15.

|| *Ibid.* ii. 193, § 400, 412, 415.

CHAPTER XX.

RECAPITULATION.

From the view that has above been taken of the practice of English and Roman law in relation to the collection of evidence, the following propositions seem deducible: —

1. That there is but one perfectly good and fit mode of collecting testimony.

2. That this is no other than what common sense suggests: and, as far as power and opportunity admit, and the importance of the occasion appears to demand, is naturally and commonly practised in the bosom of every private family.

3. That, to give precision and permanence to the information thus collected, so as to

adapt it to the use of all times and all places, nothing more or less is necessary than the committing the testimony to writing in proportion as it issues from the lips of the person deposing or examined.

4. That, so far as writing is concerned, there is but one cause that can in any case warrant any departure from this most perfect mode; and that is, the expense, vexation, and delay inseparably attached to that invaluable mode of fixation and perpetuation.

5. That the mode of collecting evidence by means of its delivery *vivâ voce*, and subsequent though immediate consignment to writing, is essentially preferable to the mode which operates by the delivery of the testimony in writing in the first instance.

6. That there are but two justificative causes that can warrant the use of the inferior mode, in contradistinction to the superior mode; viz. physical impracticability, and prudential impracticability — prudential impracticability, in respect of preponderant inconvenience in the shape of expense, vexation, and delay.

7. That, on the part of the superior mode, physical impracticability may for an indefinite length of time be constituted by local distance, for ever by *expatriation*, as contradistinguished from *exprovinciation*;—prudential impracticability, for a time, or for ever, by preponderant expense, vexation, and delay, the result of local distance.

8. That English lawyers, recognising the incontrovertible superiority, not to say the exclusive fitness (where practicable,) of the above-described superior mode, — yet, so far from employing it exclusively on every occasion in which the employment of it is not impracticable, depart from it in all manner of ways, employing inferior and bad modes before it, after it, and instead of it: in cases, too, in none of which can any warrant for such deperture be found under the head of impracticability, either physical or prudential, as above explained.

9. That, on these occasions, so far is the prudential impracticability (viz. in respect of expense, vexation, and delay) from being the cause of the departure from the most trustworthy mode, that, when the less trustworthy modes are attended with a superior share of that triple inconvenience, it is then that they are employed — employed to the exclusion of that superior mode which, besides its superiority of trustworthiness, has the advantage of being comparatively free from that collateral inconvenience.

10. That, taking together the entire system of procedure of which the collection of evidence forms a part, — the inferiority of the technical mode, in the English form more especially, in comparison with the natural mode herein-above recommended, is, in respect of expense, vexation, and delay, too flagrant and notorious not to be recognised by everybody — men of law themselves not excepted: but that, as often as this disadvantage is brought to view, if the system be defended notwithstanding, it is always on this ground, viz. that the mass of inconvenience attached to it in this form is (if not wholly and absolutely unavoidable) at any rate compensated for, absolutely compensated, by a preponderant mass of advantage in respect of superior security against ultimate injustice, whether by misdecision or by failure of justice: against ultimate injustice, from whatever causes derivable — whether from improprieties in respect of the mode of collecting the evidence, or from any other causes: and that, accordingly, it is its supposed superiority in respect of the mode of collecting the evidence, that consitutes either the source or at least one of the sources of that compensation, that ample compensation which it is supposed to afford on the score of superiorly good ultimate justice, for whatever inferiority may be observable in it in respect of the provision made by it against collateral inconveniences, viz. against delay, vexation, and expense.

11. That so far is this supposed compensation from being in any degree real, that in truth its deficiency in respect of security against delay, vexation, and expense, remains altogether unaccompanied by any compensation in any other shape: and that, in respect of security against misdecision and failure of justice (so far at least as the system employed for the collection of evidence is concerned,) its defects are such as to constitute an enormous addition and heavy aggravation to the load of imperfection attached to it in all those other shapes.

12. That it is not in human nature, that, in the forming a system, in which, in the pretended pursuit of the same ends, so many discordant and inconsistent courses are employed (discordant as well with one another, as, all of them, with the modes actually and from the beginning employed in pursuit of the same ends in the daily intercourse of private life,) the ends professed and pretended to have been pursued, viz. the real and genuine ends of justice, should have been the ends and objects really, steadily, and exclusively (not to say ever, and in any degree) pursued.

13. That, under the circumstances under which the existing system took its rise, — as it is not natural that in the adjustment of the detail the faculties of observation and invention should have been, so neither in fact do they appear to have been, steadily and anxiously occupied in any other endeavour than that of adding to the load of inconvenience and mischief in all imaginable shapes, in so far as profit and advantage in all shapes

to be reaped by the authors and contrivers of the system, could be made to spring out of it.

14. That, in like manner, in regard to the real ends of justice, — as it was not natural that in the construction of that system they should have been taken (at least any otherwise than incidentally and occasionally, and in subordination to those sinister ends) for the objects aimed at, — so neither does it appear that in fact they have, if at all, been pursued in any other character: insomuch that the attainment of them, in so far as in fact they have taken place, is to be regarded no otherwise than in general as the accidental result, and at best no otherwise than as the occasional object, of the exertions actually made on this ground.

15. That, for ages together, the object of the contrivers and conductors of the existing system (in so far as anything that can be called an object appears to have been kept by them with anything like constancy and consistency before their eyes) will appear to have been neither more nor less than the employing the powers and privileges attached to their respective offices, and professions in the character of an instrument of depredation—licensed and unpunishable depredation: the ends of justice, as before, being, if ever, only occasionally, an object, and then a subordinate one, though constantly and invariably a pretence.

16. That, as to the existing race of lawyers, taken at any given point of time, — pupils and successors of these learned depredators, — regarding, or pretending to regard, as perfect in its kind (if not in every minute point of detail, at least in respect of its leading features) the work of such their predecessors; — not only their endeavours and wishes, but their very pretensions and professions, are confined to the keeping it, as near as may be, to its present state of assumed and pretended excellence.

17. That, of the modifications of the plan in use for the collection of evidence, the impropriety is fully and unequivocally recognised by those under whose direction it is pursued: but that from this recognition no symptoms are anywhere observable of so much as a wish, much less an endeavour, to substitute, in the room of those which they regard as comparatively unconducive, those which are regarded by everybody (themselves in particular not excepted) as in a superior degree conducive, to the ends of justice.

The best possible mode of extracting testimony — the mode which a considerate master of a family would employ when sitting in judgment on the conduct of a servant or a child — in a word, the mode by oral interrogation and counter-interrogation, — is a production of English growth. If, on a microscopical observation, the germ of it be found discoverable in the Roman process of confrontation, the same scrutiny will show how confined was the use made of it in that its primeval state, and with how much propriety the appellation of a discovery may be applied to the vast edifice that in England has been built, or might be built, upon a foundation so narrow.

If the application made of this discovery has been found neither all-comprehensive, nor comparatively very extensive, the wonder need not be great. To England the glory of it, or at any rate (so far as it extends) the advantage of it, belongs without dispute: but whether, in the establishment of the practice, wisdom or fortune had the greatest share, may not be easy to decide. Had wisdom planned it, wisdom would have carried it as far as it would go, would not have suffered it to be arrested in its progress; but the same system which employs it in one instance, neglects it in another, to which not only with equal propriety, but with equally obvious propriety, it would have been applicable.

A circumstance which contributes in no inconsiderable degree to weaken the claims of wisdom, is, that the value which appears to have been implicitly set upon this feature in the system, has never been explicitly set upon the right ground. All mouths are open in praise of the trial by jury; and this is the mode of extraction employed on a trial by jury. But its connexion with the species of procedure in which the intervention of a court so constituted is employed, is altogether accidental: the same mode of extraction might be employed, and is employed, with equal facility and equal propriety, in a court composed of a number of permanent and professional judges, or in a court consisting of a single judge. It had been observed that somehow or other the ends of justice were more effectually accomplished in that sort of court of which the tribunal called a jury was one feature, and the use of this mode of extracting evidence another, than in other courts of a different appearance in respect of both these features: but to which of them the effect was principally to be ascribed, is a question that seems never to have presented itself. As water was considered till of late years as a simple substance, so was the trial by jury considered as a simple institution: the sagacity by which confused perceptions are rendered clear, and composite objects are resolved into their constituent elements, had never exercised itself (for when has it ever exercised itself?) upon the field of jurisprudence. The feature which consists in the composition of the court, being the feature which on many accounts would strike with peculiar force the eyes of the herd of politicians, — this feature, while it has given denomination to the complex system, seems to have engrossed all the praise of it. Trial by jury! ever blessed and sacred trial by jury! juries for ever! is the cry: not trial by oral and cross-examined evidence.*

It is, however, to this comparatively neglected feature, that that most popular of all judicial institutions would be found to be indebted for the least questionable and most extensively efficient, if not the most important, of its real merits. Against the advantages attending the mode of extraction practised, no objection can be urged, no inconvenience opposed; while the advantages purchased by the peculiar composition of the tribunal are not purchased but by great sacrifices in other shapes: the popularity, the unsuspectedness, is not purchased, but at the expense of appropriate experience; the superiority in probity, by the sacrifice of superiority of wisdom, and of the security which individual responsibility alone can afford either for probity or for wisdom. I speak of the really useful features, in which whatever there is of excellence in the institution is enshrined: not to speak of the errors and abuses that have been worked up with it by the hand of undistinguishing barbarity; the ethnico-theological and apostolic number; the mendacious unanimity, proclaimed by perjury, after having been produced by torture: not to mention a variety of other ingredients, good, bad, and indifferent, which might be modified for the better or the worse, without destroying or very materially changing the general effect.

With these advantages in point of practical efficiency and indisputable innocence, no political institution of real worth was ever kept more completely hidden from general observation. Among those who in its native country are so cordial in their admiration of this mode of trial, there are not twenty perhaps who at this moment are aware that, in contradistinction to Roman jurisprudence, the mode of extracting the evidence on this occasion is as peculiar to English procedure as the constitution of the court. The peculiarity of the practice called in England cross-examination — the complete absence of it in every system of procedure grounded on the Roman, with the single exception of the partial and narrow use made of it in the case of confrontation, — is a fact unnoticed till now in any printed book, but which will be as conclusively as concisely ascertained at any time, by the impossibility of finding a word to render it by, in any other language.

* While coupled with trial by jury, lawyers could join and even lead the popular cry, because trial by jury is trial with lawyers: by itself they could not recommend it without sacrifice of their professional interest: recommendation of this principle purely and simply, would involve a recommendation of the natural system (viz. personal attendance of the parties, with mutual cross-examination,) to the exclusion of all technical ones.

BOOK IV.

OF PREAPPOINTED EVIDENCE.

CHAPTER I.

OF PREAPPOINTED EVIDENCE IN GENERAL.

§ 1. *Preappointed evidence, what?* — *Topics for discussion enumerated.*

We come now to the subject of preappointed evidence: a subject new in denomination, and thence, taken in the aggregate, even in idea: for, without names to fix them, ideas, like clouds, change and vanish as speedily as they are produced.

In every case in which the creation or preservation of an article of evidence has been, either to public or private minds, an object of solicitude, and thence a final cause of arrangement taken in consequence (viz. in the view of its serving to give effect to a right, or enforce an obligation, on some future contingent occasion,) — the evidence so created and preserved comes under the notion of *preappointed* evidence.

The sort of facts which such evidence is employed to prove, are mostly facts constitutive or evidentiary of *right*. Facts constitutive or evidentiary of *wrong*, will not readily find persons able, and at the same time willing, to make mention or join in making mention of them in writing, or any other way in which the memory of them will be preserved.

The rights of which the evidence is in this way endeavoured to be preserved, are mostly either rights to *property* in some shape or other, or rights to *condition in life*.

Preappointed evidence may be distinguished into *original* and *transcriptitious*.

Examples of articles of *original* preappointed evidence are —

1. Registers of deaths, births, marriages: these have been more particularly the objects of public care.

2. Instruments expressive of the different sorts of *contract*, in the most extensive sense of the word; including not only those expressive of obligatory agreements, but those expressive of conveyance, whether by deed at large, or by the sort of deed called a *will* or *testament* — a particular sort of unilateral conveyance, which is not to take place till after the death of the conveyer, and in the meantime is destructible or alterable at his pleasure: as also all other sorts of contract by which a contract of the sort first mentioned is, in the whole or in part, either destroyed or altered.

Examples of the *transcriptitious* species of preappointed evidence are afforded by the register offices established in and for Middlesex and part of Yorkshire, and the offices for enrolment belonging to some of the judicatories in Westminster Hall.

In the course of this book, the following are the topics proposed for consideration: —

1. Ends or objects that are or ought to be aimed at (viz. on the part of the legislator,) in relation to preappointed evidence.

2. Field of preappointed evidence; *i. e.* subjects of proof by preappointed evidence, considered in an aggregate view, and under subordinate divisions.

3. Advantages proper to be aimed at, and inconveniences to be avoided, in relation to preappointed evidence.

4. Description of persons to whom, and occasions on which, the institution of the same mass of preappointed evidence may be advantageous.

5. Means by which, in relation to the different subjects of proof (as above,) the general object in view may most effectually and conveniently be attained.

§ 2. *Objects or ends of preappointed evidence: Cases to which it is principally applicable.*

Not judicature only, but all human action, depends upon evidence for its conduciveness to its end: evidence, knowledge of the most proper means, being itself among the means necessary to the attainment of that end.

Be the *occasion* what it may (it being one that calls for action,) — to possess a stock of evidence suitable to the occasion, is to possess correct and complete knowledge of all such matters of fact, the knowledge of which is necessary to right conduct — to a course of action suitable to that same occasion, whatsoever be the nature of it.

But, be the occasion (the sort of occasion and the individual occasion) what it may, the demand for such suitable evidence will be the same. So far as, without any special care taken in any part of the field on the part of the legislator, it be sure to spring up of itself, so far there is no need of preappointed evidence, or at least of anything to be done on his part towards securing either the existence or the aptitude of such preappointed evidence. If anywhere there be an actual deficiency, or a risk of a deficiency, it is then and there matter for his consideration, whether, by any exertions of his — by any provision made for that purpose, the filling up of such deficiency be at the same time practicable and eligible.

But, on a judicial occasion, as on every other, evidence in almost every instance is liable to prove deceptitious.

Hence two problems looking throughout for solution at the hands of the legislator's guide: — 1. How to secure the existence of true evidence; 2. How to guard the judge against deception, considered as liable to be produced by *false*, or in any other way *fallacious*, evidence.

Evidence being a standing object of research in every line of human action, and in particular in every department of government; it follows that, in proportion to the wisdom of the government, the endeavours on the part of the government to provide itself, in every part of the line, with an apposite stock of evidence, will be comprehensive and unremitted. So far at least as desire and endeavour are concerned, the sphere of operation, in respect of the securing the requisite provision of preappointed evidence, has no other limits than those of the entire field of evidence. Setting aside particular limitation, the general rule of practice would accordingly be, to lay in beforehand a stock of evidence applicable to all purposes, and producible on all occasions: in a word, to leave nothing to chance, to trust no operation to so slippery a ground as that of casual evidence — to cover the whole field of political action, as it were, with magazines of preappointed evidence.

Two considerations, and two only, serve to limit the exertions of government in this line, — *impracticability*, and *expense*.

1. In one class of cases, the nature of things (it will be seen) renders the success of such exertions hopeless. This is the case of delinquency in general. When you have said, whosoever does so and so shall be punished, — for the proof of the fact by which such punishment has been incurred, casual evidence is evidently the sole resource. The nature of man forbids us to expect that the child that has done amiss should, as soon as it has done amiss, come in of its own accord, and present its back to the chastising rod.

2. Expense is another consideration, which on this as on every other ground, sets limits to the operations of every prudent government. By expense, on this as on other occasions, I do not mean mere pecuniary expense, but evil, inconvenience, vexation, labour, in whatever other shape it presents itself. *Gold itself may be bought too dear*, is a consideration which, on this ground as on every other, is never out of the eye of a well ordered government.

Such are the two topics from which will be drawn whatever limitations present themselves as applying to the demand for preappointed evidence.

Looking over the field of evidence at large for objects admitting and requiring preappointed evidence, we shall find them reducible to three classes, viz.

1. *Laws*; viz. laws in the common acceptation of the word: rules of action which derive their tenor or their purport, as well as their binding force, from the legislator alone, without the concurrence of any individual hands.

2. *Contracts*; viz. the word being taken in the largest sense, in which it comprises not only agreements, legally obligatory agreements, but *conveyances*, or instruments expressive of transference of legal rights, and among conveyances, *testaments*.

These are in fact so many *laws*, obligatory rules of action, in the enactment of which the legislator and the individual concur; the individual furnishing the act of volition, and the expression given to it—the legislator furnishing the binding force, and (in quality of necessary conditions and concomitants to binding force) *limits*, and interpretation.

3. *Facts*; *i. e.* legally operative, legally important facts: facts to which the body of the laws, whether general or private contractual (as above,) have given the quality of producing or destroying *rights* or *obligations*: events or other facts *collative* (or say *investitive*,) *ablative* (or *divestitive*:) say, in either case, facts *dispositive*: these in the non-penal (called the civil) branch of law; add to which, in the penal branch, on the one hand, acts, events, and other facts, *inculpative* and *aggravative*; on the other hand, facts *exculpative*, *extenuative*, and (with a view to punishment independently of the consideration of delinquency or innocence) *exemptive*.*

Laws, whether of the purely public or of the private (or contractual) class, as above, have no other object, effect, or use, than in as far as they give birth or termination to rights or obligations: to *rights* purposely, as being the only beneficial products of law — to *obligations* necessarily, inasmuch as no right can be conferred or created without the creation and imposition of a train of correspondent obligations. But, throughout a large portion of the field of law, it is only through the medium of facts to which, in this view, the law has imparted those prolific and distinctive powers, that the law has it in its power to give birth or termination to rights and obligations.†

* Note, that the formation of an obligatory rule of action, whether *law* or legalized *contract*, is itself a matter of fact requiring to be established by evidence, as well as the existence of any of those legally operative facts which derive their operation from laws or legalized contracts.

† If, for three pounds, the price agreed on, payable the first day of next year, a tailor makes for a customer a coat of a certain description,

Of a very extensive and diversified mass of facts, the existence is habitually declared, and the remembrance preserved, by portions of written discourse committed to paper on the occasion of the acts performed in the exercise of the functions attached to the several established public offices, in books kept under the direction of the governing functionaries belonging to those several offices.

Of the several facts thus recorded, there is not one to which, in some way or other, it may not happen to have a legal operation, in manner above mentioned. So many offices, so many sources of evidence which without impropriety may be termed preappointed evidence.

The object to which the labour thus employed is principally, if not exclusively, directed, is very different from that of affording evidence on the occasion of a suit at law. But, be the object to which they are directed what it may, this is not the less among the objects to which these documents are capable of being, and in practice actually are, occasionally, if not habitually, applied.

§ 3. *Advantages and inconveniences incident to preappointed evidence.*

Considered in a general point of view, and without reference to one more than another of the several modifications of preappointed evidence as already indicated,— the advantages deducible from it may be distinguished into those which are *direct*, and those which are *collateral* or *indirect*.

The direct, considering these modifications in the same general point of view, consist in neither more nor less than the effectuation of the objects already indicated under the character of ends in view—contributing on each occasion to give effect in practice to whatever rights and obligations the law has undertaken to constitute and establish. For, be the law as to its other parts what it may, the effect of it depends upon that part of it which concerns the subject of evidence.

---

and delivers it to him; here may be seen a *conveyance*, coupled with an agreement obligatory. The whole contract, if such were the usage and it were worth while, might stand (as it would stand, if, instead of a coat, the subject-matter were a house) expressed in and by an instrument of contract, an article of concurrent preappointed evidence, framed by one of the two contracting parties, and recognised by both of them. What *is* the usage is, that a memorandum of the contract should be entered in one or more of the tailor's account-books, forming an article of *ex parte* preappointed evidence, admitted directly and constantly in French law, not unless indirectly and precariously in English.

Here is a contractual law, framed by the contracting parties, the tailor and his customer, one or both of them—the tenor or purport furnished by the individual contracting parties, the binding force by the legislator; which binding force is *really* furnished, and seen to be furnished, by the legislator, if there be in the general body of statute law an article of a general cast, to the effect of giving a binding force to such contracts; imagined and feigned to be furnished by the legislator, if it be by jurisprudential law (so improperly termed unwritten) that eventual obligations of the nature here in question are imposed.

But,—without a set of facts, correspondent legally important facts, to which the laws in this case, general and contractual together, were intended to apply, and which, when they take place, apply on their part to the law,—no such conveyance could have taken place, no such obligation have been produced, no such obligation discharged.

1. Delivery of the coat:—here we have one legally operative, important, or material fact,—possessing, in virtue of, and conjunction with, the law above mentioned, the effect of a *collative* event, conferring on one party a title to the coat,—all rights in relation to the coat, including the right to make every lawful use that can be made of a coat.

2. Delivery of the coat once more. In this fact or event may be seen operating also, in conjunction with the law, as above mentioned, a fact legally operative in another way, viz. in the character of an *impositive* event, imposing upon the same party the obligation of delivering to the tailor, at the time specified, a sum of money.

3. Payment of the money by the same party to the tailor at the day. In this fact we see,—besides the act of conveyance, conferring on the tailor the title to the metal or paper of which the money is composed,—another legally operative event—an event operating in the character of an *exonerative* event, exonerating the customer from the obligation imposed as above.

4. Writing, and (by the tailor in sign of recognition) signature, of a stamped instrument of receipt, declarative of the delivery of the coat on one part, and the money on the other: in the declaration of which legally operative facts, the mutual declaration and acknowledgment of their legal consequences (as above) is considered as implied. In this instrument we see an article of preappointed evidence—preappointed written contractual evidence.

The coat, thus purchased and received, is carried off afterwards by a thief. In the act of carrying off (physical fact or series of facts,) coupled with the consciousness of want of right (a psychological fact,) may be seen two inculpative facts, the concurrence of which was necessary to compose the crime. It was carried off by the thief in the night time, he having for that purpose broken into the house by night: here may be seen an aggravative fact or circumstance. But the thief was of a very tender age: here we see an extenuative fact or circumstance. Since the commission of the crime, he has moreover lost his senses, having become a perfect maniac: here we see an exemptive fact or circumstance, leaving guilt in every respect as it stood at first, and applying itself solely to the demand for punishment; but applying to it so effectually as to point it out as being unnecessary and useless.

Here we see so many legally operative facts, in so many different ways, operating in a case of a penal nature: always supposing the existence of a law, or assemblage of laws, conferring on the several species of facts in question those several characters and effects.

Rules of action, expressions of will, whether of the nature of laws or legalized contracts, are capable of receiving, from the operation of apposite and preappointed evidence, advantages of a special nature, such as have no application to legally operative facts taken at large.

As between laws and contracts,—of those which apply to *contracts*, the catalogue, it will be seen, is the most ample.

Non-notoriety— viz. with relation to the persons whose rights and obligations are respectively affected by them — non-notoriety (including *oblivion*, which is but non-notoriety at times subsequent to that in question;) *uncertainty* in respect of their *import; spuriousness*, whether *in toto* (the result of forgery in the way of *fabrication*,) or partial (the result of forgery in the way of *alteration*;*) *incapacity*, or unfair procurement in respect of their source (*i. e.* the condition and situation of the individual of whose will they contain the expression;) *injury to third persons* considered as producible by secrecy or privacy on the part of the contract, — *i. e.* by its non-notoriety with reference to such third persons as are concerned in point of interest to have knowledge of its existence: — such are the mischiefs to which contracts are exposed. Such accordingly are the mischiefs, in the prevention of which, the direct advantages deducible from the institution of preappointed evidence are to be looked for, in so far as contracts are concerned.

But, under the head of *preappointed contractual evidence* (preappointed evidence as applied to the case of contracts), these several mischiefs, in conjunction with their respective remedies (the application of which, as far as practicable — to wit, by the instrumentality of the formalities of which the essence of preappointed evidence is composed— constitutes the advantages derivable from the institution of the sort of evidence so denominated,) will be brought to view in detail.

The descriptions of persons to whose use or convenience the institution of preappointed evidence may on one occasion or another be found subservient, may be thus distinguished and designated: —

1. *Individuals*, considered in the character of persons invested or in a way to be invested with the rights, bound or in a way to be bound by the obligations, to the effectuation of which the article of evidence in question is calculated to be subservient: *eventual* parties in the suits which the institution is calculated to prevent; *actual* parties in those suits, if, notwithstanding the means of prevention thus employed, they take place; *privies*, *i. e.* persons respectively connected in point of interest, in some shape or other, with, and eventual representatives of, such parties; persons liable eventually to become parties in future suits, on the occasion of which it may happen to the same article of preappointed evidence to be found applicable; and the like.

2. *The judge*, considered as such, and in respect to the decision which he will have to pronounce on the occasion of such suits as above, when instituted.

It is in so far as persons of these descriptions, and standing in these situations, are concerned, that the uses derivable from the institution of the preappointed evidence in question may be termed *direct*.

3. *The legislator*. The manner in which preappointed evidence may be rendered conducive to the due exercise of the functions of the functionary thus denominated, will present itself in a particularly conspicuous point of view, in the case where the facts, the remembrance of which is in this way preserved, are produced by, or composed of, the transactions of the several public offices; and, still more particularly, of the transactions of judicial offices.

The uses thus capable of being made by the legislator of preappointed evidence, are those which have, as above, been brought to view under the denomination of the *collateral* or *indirect* uses; and consist in the furnishing him with data, with experience, by the consideration of which he may be enabled to render his operations in every department of the field of government, and more especially in the judicial, more and more conducive to what are or ought to be their respective ends.

Under the name of the *statistics* of the several departments (and in particular the department here more particularly concerned —viz. the judicial), may the branch of political science to which belongs the knowledge of facts of this description, tendency, and use, be with propriety designated.

Of the inconveniences incident to the institution of preappointed evidence, some will be found inseparably attached, in a degree more or less considerable, to the principle of the institution; others will depend more or less upon the particular mode or expedient by which the principle is pursued — the particular purposes endeavoured to be accomplished.

Delay, vexation, and expense — the inconveniences which (in a quantity varying from next to nothing, to a magnitude beyond endurance) follow in the train of every step

* The subject to which this distinction between total and partial spuriousness has its application, is rather the collection of signs of which the instrument is composed, than the practical effect: since, by the alteration or insertion of a single word in a genuine instrument, an effect as completely and extensively injurious is capable of being produced, as by the making of one which shall be altogether spurious.

taken by or under the authority of law—may be stated as the only disadvantages inherent in the institution under all its forms, in whatever mode the purposes of it are endeavoured to be accomplished, though in degrees dependent more or less upon the nature of the mode.

These may be ranked together under the head of general inconveniences: the particular inconveniences will stand in a clearer point of view, after the several modes or particular institutions, to which they seem respectively attached, shall have been considered.

§ 4. *Means employed—formalities.*

The operations and instruments employed in the design (real or pretended) of securing, in relation to contracts and other expressions of will, the advantages derivable, as above, from the institution of preappointed evidence, seem to be comprehended under the general and generally-employed appellation of *formalities.*

The particular operations employed under this name seem comprisable under the following denominations, viz.

1. *Scription* (original scription:) viz.—expressing the meaning of the party or parties by a determinate assemblage of words, and those words made to receive permanence—permanence for any length of time that may be required: to wit, by means of the visible characters now for so many ages in general use for that purpose among civilized nations. For the importance of this operation, as applied to evidence, see above, under the head of Securities.*

2. Authentication† (*i. e.* declaration of the authenticity of the script in question) *ab intrà.* Under this head may be included whatever acts are done by a party of whose will the script purports to be the expression—done in the view of causing it to be known, that the will or conception of which it purports to be the expression is really his.‡

3. Authentication (*i. e.* declaration of the authenticity of the script) *ab extrà.* Under this head may be included whatever acts are, immediately upon the performance of some act of authentication *ab intrà*, done by some other person or persons, in the view of causing it to be known—not only that the will or conception of which the script in question purports to be the expression, is the will of the person of whose will it purports to be the expression—but also that such act of authentication has really been performed.*

4. Examination into the *competence* of the party or parties as to the entering into the contract: the examination considered as performable by the individuals by whom the act of authentication *ab intrà* is itself authenticated, as above. This is mentioned rather as a formality that might be used in some cases with advantage, than as one which actually has been introduced into practice.

5. Multiplicate scription, or transcription,—penning many scripts of exactly the same tenor—an operation which, as well in the way of writing with a pen as in the way of printing, has, by the exertions of modern ingenuity, been rendered practicable, as well at the same time as at different times. Whence the distinction, transcription simultaneous or subsequential.

6. Registration. This, considered as distinct from scription, means nothing more than conservation of the script or transcript, the original or the copy, in the custody and under the care of some determinate person or persons, in some appropriate repository allotted to that purpose.

7. Notification, competent and effectual; viz. communication of the script in question, including sufficient information of its tenor, as well as of its existence, to all persons concerned in point of interest so to be informed.

Such are the formalities applicable, and with little exception commonly employed, in relation to legalized contracts. Such, for the most part, are the formalities not in the nature of the subject incapable of being employed in relation to laws.

Laws, however, the direct work of a set of functionaries, all whose operations are habitually exposed to public view, are in general so circumstanced, that the operations above mentioned either have no application, or, if they have, take place and produce their intended effect as it were of course. But, in respect of three of these operations,—viz. scription, transcription, and notification,—practice will be seen to exhibit deficiencies too considerable to be brought fully to view in a work on evidence, and at the same time too important to be passed over altogether without notice.†

As to *facts,*—the class of facts already brought to view under the denomination of *legally operative* facts: of the seven distinguishable operations above spoken of, under

* Book II. Chap. VIII.

† *Authentication*, viz. *extrajudicial*: such being the occasion on which the operation is here considered as being performed. *Judicial authentication* forms the subject of another Book.

‡ Modes of authentication *ab intrà*:—1. Holography; 2. Signature (onomastic or symbolic;) 3. Oral recognition; 4. Recognition by deportment. See Chap. II.

* Were it not for this, the signature of an attesting witness might be applied to the instrument at any posterior point of time.

Modes of authentication *ab extrà*, in point of possibility the same as in case of authentication *ab intrà*: in point of practice, signature; usually onomastic; only in case of necessity symbolic.

† *Vide infrà*, Chap. VI.

the name of *formalities*, as applicable, and with advantage, to contracts, four only—viz. scription, transcription, registration, and notification—are applicable to the purpose of preserving the memory of facts thus taken at large.*

Among legally applicable facts, a distinction has already been made, distinguishing those which have come under review of official persons, occupants of the several established offices, private as well as public; inasmuch as they consist of acts done by or under the direction of those persons, or of facts which, on the occasion of such acts, were taken by them into contemplation. Scription, transcription, and registration, are operations which, in relation to facts of this description, have by the very supposition been to a certain extent performed. But, in relation to every such office, whatsoever other more direct purposes have been provided for by the extent which has happened to have been given to the mass so registered, it may still be matter of consideration, whether (to adapt it to the purpose of preappointed evidence) an ulterior extent, and in a suitable shape, might not in this or that instance be given to the mass, in such manner as to add to the services at present derived from it.

The facts and other transactions that are or ought to be preserved in remembrance under the direction of persons invested with judicial offices,—these judicial facts, together with the advantage which in various shapes might by the legislator be derived from the contemplation of them, are among the objects to which the above observation will be seen applying itself with a peculiar degree of force.†

Such being the operations capable of being applied with more or less advantage to the purpose of communicating, by means of preappointed evidence, the existence of the objects respectively in question,—by what *means* shall the performance of those several operations, in so far as they respectively promise to be subservient to that purpose, be endeavoured to be secured?

In each respective case, shall the performance of these several formalities be endeavoured to be rendered obligatory, according to present usage, by what is called *pain of nullity*, or by punishment in any other (and what) shape? Or, after indication given of such formalities as, in the case in question, promise, in the character of evidence, to be of use, and the doubts that will naturally be produced by the non-employment of them, shall observance be, in any and in what cases, left to the option of the parties interested?

To these questions, answers will be endeavoured to be provided, in so far as they have application to any of the several divisions that have here been made of the subjects of preappointed evidence. The subject of contracts is the only one to which they will be found to apply in such manner as to operate with practical importance.

CHAPTER II.

OF INSTRUMENTS OF CONTRACT IN GENERAL.

§ 1. *Uses of preappointed evidence as applied to contracts.*

Of the advantages or uses derivable from a due application of the principle of preappointed evidence to the case of contracts, a sort of anticipated and general view has been given already.‡ It remains now to bring them to view one by one.

These uses seem comprehendible under the following heads—the description of the use being in each instance taken, as above, from the description of the mischief, in the prevention of which it consists:—

1. Prevention of *non-notoriety* and *oblivion;* viz. with respect to the *existence* of the contract. A contract can no otherwise be of use, than in as far as the existence of it is known. Were it not for the art of writing, the existence of a contract might, after having been known one day, cease to be known the next.

2. Prevention of *uncertainty* in respect of the *import* of it. Writing is little less necessary to this purpose than to the former. Without a determinate set of words allotted to the expression of it, the import can never be other than indeterminate: and it is only by writing that the words can be rendered determinate, and secured as well against total oblivion as against changes.

3. Prevention of *spurious contracts*, and of *spuriousness in contracts*. When the whole contract is spurious, it is the product of forgery in the way of fabrication; when spurious in this or that part, through any other cause than unintentional error on the part of the scribe, it is the product of forgery in the way of alteration: and by obliteration, the import may be rendered spurious, even where there are no spurious words.

4. Prevention of *unfairly obtained*, or in other respects *unfair*, or say *vitious*, contracts. Of the different cases in which the epithets *unfair* or *unfairly obtained*, may be applied to a contract, mention will be made presently.

* Authentication, whether *ab intrà* or *ab extrà*, and examination into competence, are operations which have no application but on the supposition of the existence of a person occupied in the production of expressions of will, of the number of those from which facts of the class here in question derive their effect and essence.

† *Vide infrà*, Chap. VIII.

‡ Chap. I. § 3.

5. Prevention of injury to third persons; viz. such injury as might be the result of non-notoriety of the contract with reference to such third persons: for instance, a contract whereby the property of a debtor is disposed of in favour of a non-creditor, to the prejudice of creditors; or of one creditor, to the prejudice of co-creditors. This use may perhaps be considered as belonging to the class of direct uses: a contract of this description being referable to the head of *unfair* contracts, — unfair, viz. with reference to third persons thus exposed by it to injury.

6. Production of revenue to government.

In this, the last upon the list of purposes, we see an advantage altogether void of all natural connexion with the five preceding ones, and with the general object and use of evidence. But, when the connexion is once formed, it contributes a material assistance to those other original and direct purposes; inasmuch as the advantage derived from the institution in this point of view is carried to account, and serves to be set in the scale against whatever articles are chargeable upon it on the side of disadvantage.*

As to *unfairness:* various are the ways in which it may happen to a contract to have been unfairly obtained, or to be in other respects unfair or vitious: the mode of the vitiousness being determined or indicated, either by the efficient cause of the contract, or by its effects or tendency.

The following are the cases in which its unfairness or vitiousness results from the nature of its efficient cause: —

1. *Undue coercion* — whether physical, by bodily force applied, or *psychological*, by fear of undue suffering (present or future) impressed.

2. *Erroneous supposition of obligation;* viz. legal, or perhaps, in some cases, even though purely moral. This is in fact a case of undue coercion, though no person, other than the party himself, be instrumental in the application of it.

3. Fraud — *positive* fraud — on the part of another party to the contract (or of some other person acting, with or without his commission or privity, in his behalf,) operating by false representations, assertive of the eventual existence of some benefit, by which, supposing it to accrue, the contract would in so far have been rendered a fair one.

4. Fraud — *negative* or *passive* fraud — operating by *silence*, or say *reticence*, a negative act, — by non-disclosure of this or that circumstance of disadvantage, in respect of which disclosure was due.†

5. Erroneous supposition in regard to *value;* viz. an over-value being, in the mind of the party in question, ascribed to the thing acquired to him by the contract, or an under value to the thing parted with. Though there are many cases in which the rescission of a contract in this respect unfair might not be eligible, there are none in which the prevention of it would not be useful; viz. on the supposition that, supposing the real value known, the contract would not have been entered into.

6. *Insanity;* including *non-age*, *caducity*, and *intoxication*, in so far as productive of the same effects. It is only in so far as these circumstances are respectively productive of unfairness in one or other of the modes above mentioned, that the contract ought to be considered as rendered unfair by them.

7. *Injuriousness to third persons*, the public at large included; injuriousness, certain, or more or less probable; provided the amount of such injury, all circumstances considered, be preponderant over the amount of the aggregate benefit to the parties.

8. *Subornation;* the prospect of a benefit considered as derivable from the contract being employed by one party as an instrument of subornation, for the purpose of engaging another in the commission of some injurious act. In this case, the injurious tendency is considered as being in contemplation: in the last preceding case, it may be in contemplation or not.

It is natural to all contracts to be beneficial to all parties to them. A contract neither ought to be, nor commonly is, intended by the legislator to be legalized, but on one or other of two suppositions, — viz. that, at the time of its being entered into, it is (at least in its apparent tendency and promise) beneficial to all parties, and not injurious to any; or in a greater degree beneficial to one party, at least, than it is injurious to all others put together.

In the cases above brought to view, as cases of unfairness or vitiousness, the supposition is, that, if beneficial to one or more individuals, it is not to him or them beneficial in a degree equal to that in which it is hurtful to some other individual, or other individuals, or the public at large, put together.

In cases 1, 3, 4, and 8, blame on the part of some individual or other, naturally but not necessarily a party to the contract, is ascribed: and it is in the wrongful conduct of such individual that the unfairness of the

* This last might perhaps without impropriety be struck out of the list of uses; since a tax on contracts, in whatever manner laid on, is either a law-tax — that is, a tax upon justice, which is perhaps the worst of all taxes, — or a tax upon the transfer of property, which is one of the worst, or both together. — *Editor.*

† As when, for a horse known to be unsound, and no questions asked, the price of a sound one is received.

contract has its source. In the other four cases, no such blame forms any necessary part of the case.

§ 2. *Formalities in use in the case of contracts.*

We have seen the evil qualities, which, in the instance of contracts taken in the aggregate, are liable to have place—*non-notoriety, uncertainty, spuriousness, unfairness:* we have seen the different shapes in which it may happen to unfairness to present itself.

We have seen the expedients which, under the name of *formalities*, are in use, for the apparent purpose of affording to the parties a protection to a certain extent against these evils; viz. scription, authentication *ab intrà*, authentication *ab extrà*, multiplicate scription or transcription, registration, and notification.

Against *non-notoriety* and *uncertainty*, scription, of itself, and without any expense of thought bestowed upon the adaptation of it to those ends, affords, in a considerable (though far from a complete) degree, a remedy. Spuriousness, in the character of an evil,—authentication *ab intrà*, and *ab extrà*, in the character of remedies,—in these may be seen the objects on which the greatest expense of thought appears to have been bestowed.

Of authentication *ab intrà*, practice presents five distinguishable modes: 1. *Autography* or *holography;** 2. *Onomastic* signature; 3. *Symbolic* signature; 4. *Sigillation; 5. Recognition,*—viz. oral, or by deportment.

1. In comparison with the three next mentioned to it, *autography* or *holography* (whichever be the word employed) presents, as against spuriousness, by far the best security. Men (say the English law books) are distinguished by their handwriting, as by their faces. Whosoever be the penman, his handwriting presents (as long as the paper or other substance, and the colour or other marks imprinted on it, last) a sort of *real* evidence, a species of circumstantial evidence, of his identity; and, so far, of the genuineness of the script. Spuriousness *in toto* is the only modification of spuriousness to which the security afforded by any of the three other modes of authenticity applies: against spuriousness *pro parte*, this alone presents a remedy; except that, in case of falsification by simple erasure, holography taken by itself has but little application, inasmuch as, in case of cancellation or abrasion, hands are not distinguishable.

But in some cases this most effectual mode of authentication is physically, in others deemed prudentially, impracticable: *physically*, as where, in case of a single contracting party (as in case of a *last will*,) the party is by want of skill, or by debility, rendered unable to write; and moreover, wherever there are contracting parties more than one—unless the task were divided, each for example writing those clauses and those alone, in and by which himself were bound: *prudentially*, viz. the vexation (the trouble of writing) being more than the party in question chose to submit to.

2. In the *onomastic* mode of signature may be seen the succedaneum so naturally resorted to, where—ability, sufficient at least to the writing of the words that enter into the composition of the man's name, not being wanting—holography has, in any of the ways just mentioned, been rendered impracticable.

3. In the *symbolic* mode of signature may be seen the succedaneum resorted to, where even the degree of ability necessary to the use of the onomastic mode is deficient.

But in this mode, whatever security is afforded by the two other modes (viz. against spuriousness *pro parte* as well as *in toto* by the holographic, against spuriousness *in toto* by the onomastic) is manifestly wanting: a cross (the usual mark) a cross made by one man not being distinguishable from a cross made by another, the *real* part of evidence has no place. Recognition, viz. by deportment, is the only way in which this mode of authentication can be said to operate.

4. *Sigillation*, a succedaneum to (or rather mode of) onomastic signature, was the mode in use in those times of barbarism, when, even among persons of rank, skill adequate to so much as onomastic signature was rare: and so much less attainable for any forbidden purpose was the art of the engraver than the art of the ordinary scribe, that the mode thus substituted was, in the character of a security against spuriousness *in toto*, but little inferior to the mode to which it was substituted.

At present, and since the art of writing has become comparatively common, sigillation, in the character of a source of real evidence, has gone completely out of use. The coat of arms—that substitute for a name, invented for the use of those who could neither read nor write—might in this way be not altogether without its use. But even this is not employed, except by accident.

Sigillation, at one time an efficient and almost the sole security against fraud, has for this long time past degenerated into an idle

* In the language of French law, a will written from beginning to end by the testator's own hand is distinguished by the appellation of *testament holographe.*—[A similar phraseology is employed in Scotland, where a deed written and signed by the granter is termed "holograph." Deeds of this kind are "privileged," and as such are valid without attestation; but if not attested, they do not prove their own dates, against the claim of any one whose interest it is to hold them as executed of a different date from that which they bear.—*Ed.*]

and mischievous ceremony; * answering no other purpose than that of recognition, for which the oral mode might and does serve equally well without it.

5. Recognition, — viz. oral, or by deportment.

When the modes (or any of the modes) of authentication already enumerated have been employed, little good, it should seem, could be done by superadding this operation. They all of them suppose and include in themselves an act of recognition.

That, in the instance of an instrument purporting to contain an expression of my will, it should be put out of doubt that my will has been completely and determinately formed, is a result unquestionably to be desired: but when an operation performed by permanent signs has been already performed, and applied to that use, how an operation not performed by other than evanescent signs is capable of affording any additional security, does not seem easily perceptible. In the case of onomastic signature, the act of writing the name serves not only the purpose of recognition by deportment, but that of real evidence — permanent circumstantial evidence; and as to symbolic signature, though, as above, it is scarcely capable of serving the purpose of real evidence, yet either it answers, and of itself, the purpose of *recognition* (viz. recognition by deportment,) or it means nothing, and answers not any purpose.†

Recognition, if performed by oral discourse, or by two out of the four modes of authentication which have been enumerated (symbolic signature and sigillation,) requires the presence of at least one other person in the character of a *percipient* witness, to see or hear it, so that eventually, on a judicial inquiry, in the character of a *deposing* witness, he may narrate it.

Authentication *ab extrà*, — viz. by attesting witnesses, is therefore the only mode in which the authenticity of an instrument of contract can be proved by direct evidence. Without such additional proof, the fact of the authenticity will have no other basis to rest on than what, as above, is constituted by the *circumstantial*, the *real* evidence.

But, since *significant* onomastic seals have ceased to be in use, it is only in the case of those who are able to write that this *real* proof of authenticity can have place: and even while significant seals were in use, forgery by fabrication of that species of evidence, though but few were capable of so much as attempting it, might with less danger of detection be executed by any of those few, than any imitation by one person of the handwriting of another.

A person in whose presence a party, while performing in relation to any such instrument an act of recognition (oral or by deportment, as above), is seen or heard to do so, acts thereby, whether so required or not, in relation to such act of recognition, in the character of a percipient witness: and, so long as he is in existence, in a state of sanity, and forthcoming, so long there exists a person by means of whose testimony the intrinsic authentication of the instrument in question is capable of being proved by direct evidence.

By the simple perception thus obtained, an additional security is unquestionably afforded: but, if the process of authentication be moreover performed by such percipient witness, the security receives thereby a manifest increase.

1. Although the signature be but symbolic, — yet, if sufficient measures be employed (as they always might be and ought to be) for securing a mode of intercourse with such attesting witness, for the purpose of his even-

* In English practice, seriously mischievous. Under the fee-gathering system, judges, ever upon the watch for occasions of committing safe injustice, have extracted out of the absence of this useless ceremony, a pretence for applying the principle of nullification. Some instruments must have a seal — others will serve without it: more complication, more uncertainty; more disappointment and distress on the one part, more arbitary power and predatory opulence on the other.

† It would be in the instance of a *last will*, if in the instance of any species of contract (and that only in one particular case, viz. that of *holography*,) that the requisition of an act of recognition, as distinct from *scription*, whether in the way of *holography*, or in the way of *onomastic* signature, would be of use. For, of a last will, as contradistinguished from a contract of every other description, it is a distinctive character, that the dispositions made by it are designed by law to remain to the last moment subject to the power of him by whom they were made. But of an instrument written in form of a will, and written by the testator himself, it may be said, that it appears not as yet whether what has been so written had received his ultimate determination; since, having written it to serve as a subject of consideration, it may have happened to him to have kept it by him in that view for any length of time. Some other act (it may be said) — some other act distinct from the mere act of writing it, is necessary to demonstrate that his mind is fixed.

This reasoning, however, does not seem conclusive. If, at the time of his writing, he says, I give such a thing to such a person, it is a sign, and seems a sufficiently sure one, that at that time (*i. e.* down to the moment which gave a finish to the last word) such was his determinate intention. That intention, true it is, may have changed. But so may it, and with equal probability, although in the presence of witnesses he had performed an express act of recognition, by pronouncing a form of words: and whensoever the change may have taken place, there is no more difficulty in his expressing it in the body of the instrument, without any such formal act of recognition, than after it.

tual forthcomingness in the character of a deposing witness, it will thereby secure to the parties and their representatives the benefit of his direct evidence (the accidents of expatriation and exprovinciation and insanity apart) during his lifetime.

2. If the signature be onomastic,—in that case, to the benefit of his direct testimony is added that of the circumstantial real evidence afforded by his handwriting; and that neither defeasible by death, nor by any of the accidents just mentioned.*

CHAPTER III.

OF THE ENFORCEMENT OF FORMALITIES IN THE CASE OF CONTRACTS.

§ 1. *Absolute nullity in general an improper means of enforcement.*

THE benefit derivable from preappointed evidence depends upon the observance of the *formalities*, of which its essential character, as contradistinguished from casual evidence, is composed: which formalities are all comprisable under two heads,—viz. *writing*, and *authentication*. In proportion to the magnitude of that benefit, considered in its application to the several classes of legally operative *facts* to which that application extends, it is therefore desirable that, in so far as is practicable (prudentially as well as physically practicable,) these formalities should on each individual occasion be employed.

By what *means*, then, shall the employment of them be secured? In other words, by what means shall the non-employment of them be prevented?

Consider the non-employment of them in the light of an offence—an offence for which the public, in the persons of the parties, any of them, or any other person, is exposed to receive injury,—punishment would, in this as in other cases, afford the natural and obvious remedy.

But delinquency is here altogether out of the question: the evil of punishment is an evil, the application of which would, in this case, be altogether without use. In the case of a contract, be it of what kind it may, there is always some one person at least, whose interest and whose wish it is that it may be followed by the effect it professes to aim at: its not being followed by that effect is, in his eyes, an evil: such he cannot but understand will be the result, if the memory of it should perish, or the import of it be in such or such a way misconceived. But, to the prevention of that undesirable result, the formalities in question (viz. writing in apt terms and sufficient authentication) are, if not in every case absolutely necessary, at any rate in every case highly and obviously and indubitably conducive. *Will*, therefore (to give birth to which is the function and sole use of punishment,) cannot here, in the nature of the case, be ever wanting. Of the conditions requisite to the production of the desirable result, the only one liable to be deficient is *power*, and in particular that branch of *power* which consists of *knowledge*.

On these occasions, for securing the observance of these formalities, the principle of *nullity*, *pain of nullity*, as in the language of French lawyers it is styled,† is the moving power that by legislators, under the guidance of professional lawyers, has been commonly, not to say universally, employed: pain of nullity, applied in the character of an inducement, a motive, to the will: to the will, a faculty which requires no such factitious moving power; a moving power abundantly sufficient, so far as mere *will* is concerned, operating by the very nature of the case.

* What one should scarce have imagined *à priori*—what would scarcely have been worth mentioning had it not been for the experienced blindness of judges and legislators,—in the case of attestation and registration, a task altogether necessary to perform is that of subjecting to a close scrutiny, and distinguishing from every other fact, the fact which is the true and proper subject of the testimony thus given—the fact which, upon the strength of such testimony, may with reason be taken for proved.

1. In the case of a deed, it is the mere fact of recognition, and nothing more. Venditor acknowledged the instrument in question to be his act and deed—to contain the expression of his volition in that behalf, that expression emitted at a certain time. Thus much—if the attesting (and, in acknowledgment of attestation, subscribing) witnesses, do by such attestation say true—is proved by the attestation: this, but not any other fact whatever. The deed is full of recitals; and not one of these recitals, perhaps, but is false. Of the truth of any one of these recitals, what proof, what ground of persuasion, is given by the subscription? Not the smallest.

So, again, in the case of a will. A man leaves so much money to one friend, so much to another, and so on. The will is attested and subscribed in the most regular manner, by the fullest complement of the most unexceptionable witnesses. What is it that the subscription proves? That he declared the writing in question to be the expression of his last will and testament: thus much, and nothing more. Does it prove him to have left behind him all those sums, or so much as a single farthing of them? No such thing. At his death he was, perhaps, insolvent. Ample bequests, supported by scanty assets, is no very uncommon case. It is no more than what is liable to happen to all wills, whether the testators are aware of it or no, from change of circumstances: but men have sometimes been seen, who appear to have made a sort of sport to themselves out of the anticipated prospect of the disappointment of their expectant relatives.

† The same expression is employed in Scotland. There are several old statutes still in force, enjoining certain solemnities to be used in the execution of all deeds not "*in re mercatoria*," under "pain of nullity."—*Ed.*

Considered in the character of a means directed to an end, and that end the giving effect to genuine and fair contracts, and those such as it has been the declared intention of the legislator to adopt and give effect to by his coercive power, nothing can be more unconducive and inconsistent, not to say treacherous, than the expedient of nullity, employed as hitherto it has been employed. The mischief, the prevention of which is professed to be in view,—the mischief, one great branch of it at least, is the *frustration* to which, for want of the securities in question (or some of them,) fair and genuine contracts are exposed: the destruction of all benefit expected from such contracts, the substitution of the pangs of disappointment to the exultation of success. To prevent this mischief, is one at least of the professed ends in view: and what, in the case in question, are the means employed? The giving birth to the mischief in cases in which it would not otherwise have had place.

Should any one be disposed to justify this, it is only in one or other of two characters that he can think of justifying it.

Is it in the character of a *penalty*, designed to prevent the evil in question, viz. frustration of fair and genuine contracts?—But the penalty involves (as already observed) the production of this part at least of the very evil which it professes to prevent.

Is it in the character of a *conclusion*, an *inference*, drawn from the circumstances of the case; the non-observance of the formalities in question being considered as circumstantial evidence (and that conclusive) of the existence of one or other of the two vices incident to supposed contracts, viz. spuriousness or unfairness?

But, to take the case of *spuriousness*, and to consider the non-observance of these formalities as circumstantial evidence of this vice, and this evidence conclusive—conclusive not only without any support from direct evidence, but against and in despite of any how large soever a body of direct evidence;—no inference can be more unwarranted, more directly in the teeth of a most extensive and notorious body of experience. Of contracts in any way spurious, experience affords, in comparison, but few examples; while of genuine contracts, which are neither committed to writing nor authenticated, but which are nevertheless fair, and fairly fulfilled, on all sides, the number is beyond comparison greater (taking together those of small and great importance) than the number of those which, being committed to writing, are at the same time duly authenticated in form of law.

Not that nullity is in its own nature incapable of being rationally and beneficially employed; for, though it cannot in any case fail of being mis-seated and inconsistent when considered in the character of a penalty, there are cases in which—there are conditions on which—it may be just and reasonable, and thence beneficial, in the character of an inference. But everywhere, under the dominion of the technical, the fee-gathering, system of judicature, these conditions, so necessary to general utility and justice, remain, as naturally they could not but remain, unfulfilled.

The conditions thus spoken of are as follows, viz.—

1. That knowledge of the formalities in question, and of the necessity of the observance of them to the validity of the contract, should be present to the mind of every individual to whom it can happen to be desirous of entering (he at the same time having power and right to enter) into such contract;

2. That observance of these formalities be in his power; and

3. That observance be not too burthensome; *i.e.* the burthen so great as that, taking all the instances of observance together, the aggregate of the burthen attached to them shall outweigh the aggregate of whatever benefit in any shape results from the observance.

Of these three several conditions, let the two first be fulfilled, the nullity of the contract is, in case of the non-observance of the formalities, a rational result, in the character of an inference. The character of them is such, that, unless it be in the way of preponderant delay, vexation, and expense, an honest man, in the character of a contracting party, cannot be hurt by them; he cannot but be benefited by them: while, to the contriver of a spurious contract, observance will be, at any rate, difficult, and, without detection and frustration, it is hoped, impracticable.

Of these same two conditions, let either fail to have place,—*nullity*, *i.e.* spuriousness or unfairness, as an inference, will be manifestly groundless. With what colour of reason can you expect a man to pay observance to formalities, to perform a variety of acts more or less burthensome, when neither the inducement for performing them, nor so much as the idea of them, was present to his mind? What inference to the prejudice either of the genuineness of the alleged contract, or of the fairness of it, can in such a case be grounded on non-observance?

So, again, in regard to *power*. With what colour of reason can you call upon a man to do what he has not power to do? With what colour of justice can you ground any inference whatsoever on his not doing it?

But, let both of these conditions be fulfilled, the spuriousness or unfairness of the contract may not unreasonably be inferred from non-observance of the formalities. A rational man will not enter into a contract of the terms of which he stands assured that, of whichever of them are regarded by him as beneficial to himself, the benefit will not take place: an honest man will not enter into a contract, of the terms of which he stands assured that, of whichever of them are beneficial to whatever other persons are concerned in point of interest, the benefit will not take place. Therefore the alleged contract is either no contract at all, or it is an unfair one: the *will* alleged to have been expressed never was expressed, or it is such a will as (the consequences of giving effect to it being preponderantly or purely mischievous) ought not to be suffered to take effect.

As to the remaining condition,—viz. that the burthen of observance of such formalities as are prescribed be not too great,—on the part of the legislator, the non-fulfilment of this condition amounts in effect to neither more nor less than the disallowance of every contract, in the instance of which the observance of the formalities in question comes to be regarded as too burthensome. To prescribe this condition is neither more nor less than to give a warning to the legislator, that, in the observing of his formalities, he pitch not upon such by the adoption of which any such contract as he meant to allow should in effect be disallowed.

Unhappily for legislators as well as subjects, the prostrate negligence with which all these important duties, and in particular the indispensable one of promulgation, have been universally violated by the possessors of sovereign power, is hitherto the only matter of fact that is notorious in the case.

As with other parts of the law by which the fate of every man is disposed of, so it is with this. They tell him he ought to know it; they say of him that he does know it; they give him no means of knowing it; they see he does not know it; they do nothing to make him know it; they do every thing to keep him from knowing it; they have brought it into a state in which it is impossible for him to know it; they say it is; they insist that it is; they say his ignorance of it is no excuse; and, in all imaginable ways, they punish him for not knowing it.

By no military commander was it ever supposed, so much as for a moment, that, by keeping his orders in his pocket, or mumbling them to himself, or laying them up with a houseful of other orders upon a shelf, where any man that chose to pay for them might have them, he could hope either to gain an advantage over, or so much as defend himself against, the enemy.

By no master of a family, by no old woman, mistress, or housekeeper of a family, was it ever so much as supposed, that, by any such mode of promulgation (if promulgation it could be called,) the daily and hourly business of any the most inconsiderable private family could ever be carried on.

Conceits to any such effect—chimeras, supposable for illustration's sake, like any other chimeras, but never yet realized in practice—would, if they came to be realized, be regarded as marks, not of unskilfulness, but idiocy.

Every law requiring a man, under a penalty, to do that which is not in his power,—every such law, come it from whence it will, is an act of tyranny. Pure suffering—suffering without benefit—pure evil—is the fruit of it.

Every law unpromulgated is, moreover, an act of tyranny. For as well might it be out of a man's power to do an act, as out of his knowledge that he is called upon to do it. To every human act, motives, as well as means, are necessary: as well might a man be without the means as without a motive. In this case, therefore, no less than in the other, pure suffering—suffering without benefit—pure evil—is the result of such a law.

Every law insufficiently promulgated, is an act of tyranny as towards all those in whose conception and remembrance, by reason of such insufficiency, it fails to have implanted itself.

Nebuchadnezzar dreamed a dream: he told it to his wise men, and said to them, tell me what it was, and what it signified. Those whose interpretation did not satisfy him were put to death. A specimen this, sufficiently strong, one should have thought, of oriental tyranny. But the men thus called upon to interpret mystery, were select men—men selected for their wisdom. The Nebuchadnezzars of modern times impose a still more difficult task—and upon whom? Upon all mankind without distinction: and, in this case as in that, not the meaning of the dream, but the very dream itself, is the mystery they are called upon to divine.

Legislation—genuine legislation—has her trumpet: instead of a trumpet, the law of jurisprudence employs a sword—a sword, or a rod: such, and such alone, are the instruments of promulgation that ever are or can be employed by what is called common law.

Punishment instead of instruction—punishment without instruction, without warning;—such is the form in which the law of jurisprudence gives all its lessons.

When a man has a dog to teach, he falls upon him and beats him: the animal takes note in his own mind of the circumstances in which he has been beaten, and the intimation thus received becomes, in the mind of the dog, a rule of common law.

Such is the law—such the unpunishable,

and even inevitable, yet not the less grievous and deplorable, tyranny, to which, through the whole extent of the law of jurisprudence, the legislator abandons the community entrusted to his charge. Men are treated like dogs—they are beaten without respite, and without mercy; and out of one man's beating, another man is left to derive instruction as he can.

The injustice which, in every case of an unobservable or unpromulgated law, stains the conduct of the legislator, is, in the instance of the particular sort of law with which we are at present concerned, aggravated by a sort of treachery—by the breach of an engagement, which, though not declared in express words by the legislator, is not the less clearly understood and acted upon by the subject.

Unless things be so ordered that every one shall know what formalities are required,—every law, or rule of law, imposing, on pain of nullity, the necessity of complying with any such formality, is a breach of faith on the part of the ruling power. The mischief produced by it is of the same sort as that produced by breach of faith on the part of any individual: and, supposing the amount of the loss the same in both cases, the mischief is the same in magnitude. The difference is, that, in ordinary cases of breach of faith, the man of power is prepared to administer satisfaction for the injury; whereas in this case it is the man of power himself who is the prime author of the injury: the individual who, by the invitation of the man of law, comes in and reaps the profit, is but the accomplice.

By a general rule, the power of the law is declared to hold itself at all times in readiness to lend a binding force to the engagements and proprietary dispositions made by individuals. This rule or maxim, taken in the form of generality and simplicity in which (as above) it stands expressed, may, without much violence to fact, without much danger of incorrectness, be said to be known to every adult individual of sound mind: for there can scarcely be any such individual, to whom the knowledge of a rule of law to that effect has not been repeatedly presented by his own particular observation or experience. This law, however, neither is actually enforced, nor consistently with general utility could be enforced, till after having been narrowed in its extent by a variety of exceptions and limitations. Of the particular rules establishing these several exceptions—of the several particular laws annulling *pro tanto*, and repealing (as it were) to a certain extent, the force of the general law,—some will be reasonable, *i.e.* conformable to the principle of utility; others, under the hitherto imperfect state of the science, under the hitherto imperfect application of that sovereign principle, will be unreasonable. But of those of which the abstract reasonableness is most indisputable, the practicable reasonableness and actual utility will depend, if not altogether, at least in a great measure, on the fact of their being actually known—actually present to the mind of him on whose lot they take upon them to decide. For, as hath already been observed, the general rule, though (such hitherto has been the negligence or incapacity of legislators) perhaps in no code of laws consigned to any express form of words, is actually and at all times present to the mind of everybody: I mean so far as it is in the nature of things that a proposition floating as it were in the air, without any determinate assemblage of words to anchor it to, should maintain its hold upon the public mind. Here, then, is a general promise, understood by everybody to be made to everybody by the law. If in any case there exists, in virtue of a particular exceptive law, a known exception to that general law—a disposition made by the law in conformity to that exception, neither does involve, nor, by anybody to whom the existence of the exceptive law is known, is supposed to involve, a breach of promise. But to any one to whom the existence of the general rule is known, and the existence of the exceptive law unknown, every decision contrary to the general rule and founded upon the exceptive law, *does* involve a breach of the implied promise made by the general rule: just as much as a similar decision would do, if the exceptive law had no existence.

The non-promulgation of the rule of action, by which the individuals composing the community are all of them commanded to regulate their conduct, is the grand device of the fee-fed legislating lawyer, for the increase of lawyers' profit by increase of transgressions.

Over and over again I have had occasion to state it as a standing and natural and universal object with the legislator, acting under the guidance of the fee-fed lawyer, or rather with the fee-fed lawyer under whose guidance the legislator is in the habit of acting without thought,—so to order matters, that, for want of knowledge of the considerations which call for compliance, transgressions of all sorts may, on the part of the several members of the community, be as numerous as possible: to the end that, by the hands of fee-fed advocates and attorneys, satisfaction or punishment for transgressions real or pretended, may, in as many instances as possible, at the expense of those who have wherewithal to defray the expense, be demanded at the hands of fee-fed judges.

In the pursuit of this general and all-embracing object, is implied the pursuit of as many specific or less general objects as are comprised in it.

1. That,—as to any really existent rule of action and measure of obedience,—there should, to the greatest extent possible, be no such thing; but, under the notion of a transgression against a rule of what is called *common law* (a mere nonentity,) men should in as many instances as possible, under the name of punishment, or satisfaction, or compensation, or damages, be plagued as if a portion of law to that effect had been enacted and made notorious.

2. That, in so far as portions of real law were really enacted, they should be kept as effectually concealed as possible from those whose lot was made to depend on the observance of them, and who, in manner above mentioned, and to the ends above mentioned, were to be plagued for non-observance.

3. That, in regard to contracts legalized, or professed to be legalized, the following should be the measures taken for rendering transgressions of the real or supposed rule of law as numerous as possible:—

That, in respect of *quantity* and *quality* of matter, the language should be as effectually adapted as possible to prevent the formation of correct conceptions, and to give rise to incorrect ones:

That if, upon the footing of the instrument of contract taken by itself, the conceptions formed in relation to it were clear and correct, such conceptions should be rendered ultimately erroneous, by concealed rules of law, real or pretended, requiring a different interpretation to be put by the judge upon the words from which such clear and correct conceptions shall have been deduced:

That, by sometimes confirming and allowing and giving effect to, sometimes disallowing and frustrating, an engagement endeavoured to be taken or a disposition endeavoured to be made by a contract to such and such an effect—(or, what comes to the same thing, sometimes assigning to it the meaning supposed to be meant by the parties to be assigned to it—sometimes assigning to it some other meaning—any other meaning at pleasure—not so much as pretended to be assigned to it by the parties, or any one of them;) the judges should establish themselves in the *habit*, and thence, to the greatest possible extent, in the *power*, of determining the matter in dispute in favour of the plaintiff's or the defendant's side of the cause at pleasure:

And that, the existence of a rule to this or that effect being throughout supposed, and punishment or vexation, under the name of *nullity*, being predetermined in case of the non-observance of it,—and the supposed rule being (as above) either not so much as made, or if made, kept in a state of concealment,—such operations, and such alone, should be directed and employed under the notion of giving *notice* of the rule (*i. e.* causing it to be made present to the minds of those who were to be punished or otherwise vexed for non-observance of it,) as would in as many instances as possible fail of being productive of the effect so professed to be aimed at.

§ 2. *Means of ensuring the notoriety of the formalities, and of the consequences of their non-observance.*

Such being the conditions proper to be observed by the legislator—the conditions necessary to the reasonableness and utility of whatever formalities he prescribes,—and the fulfilment of those conditions being in each instance within the power of the legislator,—it remains to be shown by what means the observance of those conditions may most advantageously be accomplished.*

Were any other than improbity—general improbity (the necessary result of sinister interest,) the ruling principle that presided over that part of the rule of action which concerns contracts—had common honesty, under the direction of common sense, been the ruling principle,—the arrangements which now wait to be brought to view could never have waited to this time.

When, on the part of the governing members of the community, upon whose will the fate of the rest depends, there exists any real desire that the knowledge of, and with it the possibility of bestowing observance upon, those rules for the non-observance of which the community are in such a variety of ways tormented, should have place,—they never are, nor ever can be, at a loss for effectual means.

As often as the statesman to whose office it belongs to devise taxes, has devised and obtained the imposition of a new tax, knowledge of this obligation is never wanting to those on whose knowledge of it the fulfilment of it depends. Why? Because, of him by whom taxes are thus devised, it is the real desire that the payment of the taxes, and consequently the knowledge of their enactment, should be as universal as possible.

Under the presidence of the lawyer, on whom the state of that part of the law which concerns contracts (not to speak of other parts) depends, knowledge of all obligations established by that branch of the law has all along been, and will continue to be, as scanty and deficient as it can be made to be. Why? Because, of this lawyer, as of all others, it

* In the case of a last will, the means adapted to this purpose will in some respects be seen to differ from the means adapted to every other species of contract. Those which will here be brought to view in the first place, must therefore be understood as not meant to apply in every particular to *last wills*. Those which are peculiar to this particular species of contract, will be brought afterwards to view under a separate head.

ever has been, and (so long as the fee-gathering system continues) will continue to be, the interest, that, in relation to this part of the field as well as every other, the state of the law shall, as long as possible, continue to be as adverse as possible to every end of justice.

1. Let each species of contract which on pain of invalidity is required to be committed to writing, be, on the same pain, required to be written on a particular species of paper, which, in consideration of its destined use, may be termed (by a general appellative) contract paper, or contract promulgation paper.

2. For each distinct species of contract, let a distinct species of paper be provided, denominated according to the species of contract for which it is intended to serve; as for instance, marriage-contract paper, agreement paper, farm-lease paper, house-lease paper, lodging-lease paper, house-purchase paper, money-loan-bond paper,* and so forth.

3. Let a complete printed list be made by authority, of the several species of contracts for which such promulgation paper is required to be employed: and let this list, accompanied by a notice of the obligation of employing for every such species of contract the species of promulgation paper appropriated to it, be hung up in some conspicuous part (such as the inside of a window looking to the public street) of every government office throughout the country: for example, in England, every post-office, excise-office, and house where stamped paper is sold: to which might be added, some conspicuous part of every place of divine worship, as in the case of the table exhibiting the prohibited degrees of marriage.

In the form of a border to the sheet of paper, or at the back of it, or in both places, and (according to the quantity of matter) either at length, or in the way of reference to a separate printed sheet or number of sheets, — let an indication be given of so much of the law, as concerns the species of contract, to the expression of which the paper is adapted.†

Such matter of law as seems applicable to every species of contract, seems comprisable under the following heads, viz. —

1. Modes of authentication allowed, and either prescribed or recommended, for the prevention of spuriousness, whether total or partial.

2. Indication of the different circumstances by any of which the contract in question would be rendered unfair: coinciding with, or including, those by which any contract whatever would be rendered unfair, as above. A circumstance by which, in the instance of each particular species of contract, the entering into it is rendered unfair, is, the contracting parties being, any one of them, incapacitated by law from entering into a contract of that description.

3. Obligations and rights incidental and adjectitious to the species of contract in question: obligations and rights which the law has thought fit to annex to those which are in their nature inseparable from the species of contract designated by that name; distinguishing between those which take place of themselves, without the happening of any fresh incident over and above that of the entrance into the contract, and those which are made to take place respectively upon the happening of such and such incidents: and in both instances specifying those obligations (if any) from which the law permits not one contracting party to be released by another.

4. Circumstances by which the obligations and rights, as well principal and essential as adjectitious, established by the species of contract in question, are respectively made to cease.

5. Where the contract is in its nature to such a degree simple as not to admit of any diversifications other than such as are capable of being expressed by the filling up of a few blanks, let a form for the contract be given *in terminis*, leaving only blanks, such blanks as are requisite for the expression of the *individualizing* circumstances‡ peculiar to the individual contract in each instance.

6. When the contract is *not* in its nature to such a degree simple, let an expository or interpretative view be given of such terms as are most apt to be employed in the expression of a contract of the description in question.

7. Let an intimation be given that the contract, as expressed on the face of the written instrument, cannot, either in the way of addition, subtraction, or substitution, receive any amendment by oral discourse: but that any such amendment may at any time be made by the same party or parties (provided their respective rights in that behalf have not been extinguished by any intervening incident,) viz. either in a different instrument, or, so the process of authentication be reiterated, in the same.

What a blessing to the subject, if, upon his entrance into each condition in life, the law would thus condescend to render it possible for him to be acquainted with the benefits and burthens she has annexed to it! If, on receiving their mutual vows at the altar, the bride and bridegroom were to be presented by the priest with the code of laws indicative of the rights they had been respectively ac-

* So also guardian-appointment paper, apprentice-binding paper, partnership-contract paper, fire-insurance paper, ship-insurance paper.

† See *Essay on the Promulgation of Laws*, Vol. I. p. 158.

‡ Such as names of the parties and other persons, as well as individual things spoken of; designation of times and places, where money is in question, designation of the sum or sums.

quiring, the duties, actual and contingent, they had been taking upon them! If, upon the entrance of a guardian upon his guardianship, the protector, and the infant committed to his protection, were at the same time, by the hand of some proper magistrate, put into possession of the list of their reciprocal rights and duties! If, on the binding of the apprentice, the three parties to the contract—the master, the apprentice, and the father, or the person occupying his place—were to find, each of them, at the back of his copy of the instrument of indenture, the authentic indication of the powers, rights, and duties, attached to the character he had just been putting on!

Always understand, that, the object being to prevent and not produce surprise, though the formal delivery of the code might follow upon the signature expressive of the entrance into the engagement, the reading of the code to or by the parties interested should precede it.

Extend the same observation to the case of partnership—the law of insurance—especially maritime insurance. How light would be the task of putting together the provisions of the law as they stand at present (with or without improvements) relative to any or all these subjects, in comparison with the labour bestowed upon this single work! Ordinary talents—I had almost said talents not superior to those of the worst informed compiler of the law-compilations with which the science is provided—ordinary talents at any rate, would, if invested with the powers of the sceptre, do more towards the rendering the substance of the law fixed and known, than could be done by the most perfect talents unfurnished with these powers.

Happily, neither models for imitation nor marks for avoidance, each in perfection, would be wanting to the hand to whom this beneficent office should be committed. The digest made by Lord Chief Baron Comyns may be mentioned in the first of these characters—an act of parliament constructed according to the present form, in the latter. In the former, not a syllable of surplusage: in the latter, the major part of the text composed of surplusage; and the greater the profusion of surplusage, the greater the quantity of surface exposed to flaws and defects.

§ 3. *Note of suspicion, a proper substitute to nullity.*

By the above expedients, or others (according to the circumstances of the country in question) selected in the same view, one of the three conditions above mentioned, viz. communication of the necessary information, may effectually be provided for.

This being supposed, whether the non-observance of this or that formality shall be made *obligatory*, in such sort that from the non-observance of it the invalidity, the *nullity*, of the contract, ought to be inferred, will in every case depend upon this question—viz. whether, in the instance of the party or parties in question, observance was in their *power*.

Before he can come to a just determination on this question, it will be necessary for the legislator, in the instance of each species of contract, to consider the nature of the species of contract, the nature of the formalities proposed to be rendered in this way obligatory, and the condition of the place (the portion of territory) in question, at the time in question, with a view to the facilities the place affords at that time for the observance of those formalities.

Formalities which it will not in general be in the power of the parties to observe, a tolerably provident legislator will not choose. But what may happen is, that formalities which *in general* are capable, may in this or that particular instance be by accident rendered incapable, of being observed.*

On the supposition that the formalities prescribed are such as no accident can prevent the parties from having it in their power to comply with, and in time,—viz. within the length of time after which either the entrance into the contract would be impracticable, or the benefits that might have resulted from it no longer attainable;—on that supposition, and that alone, nullity may be established in the character of an article of circumstantial evidence, and that *conclusive*, of spuriousness or unfairness.

On the supposition that these same formalities are such as will in general be capable of being observed, but of which the observance may by this or that rare accident, in this or that particular case, be rendered impracticable;—on that supposition, non-observance may still be established in the character of an article of circumstantial evidence of spuriousness or unfairness, but not conclusive:—*probabilizing* either spuriousness or unfairness, but not *probative* with respect to either vice.

In each case, it ought to be stated, as what will naturally be expected of any one by whom the genuineness and fairness of the contract is contended for, that he shall make it appear, by the irresistible power or influence of what

* Suppose (for instance) that, to the validity of a contract of the description in question, the presence of a professional assistant (such as a notary,) in the character of an attesting witness, be rendered necessary. It may be, that one of the parties is in a precarious state of health, or on the point of embarking for a long voyage on board a ship which cannot be detained. Three notaries, and no more, are so situated as to be within reach within the time: and of these, one is too sick to act, another is absent on a long journey, and the third, under the governance of some sinister interest, withholds his assistance. Meantime one of the parties dies, or, as above, expatriates.

circumstance the observance of the formality or formalities was prevented. But, considering that, by length of time or accident, the memory of the circumstances that accompanied the transaction may have been obliterated (especially when the contracting parties are any of them dead, or otherwise not forthcoming,) such explanation ought not to be insisted on as a condition universally and peremptorily indispensable.

But in no case ought the circumstantial evidence of spuriousness or unfairness to be deemed conclusive, in such sort as to be considered as a ground of nullity, unless, — by him who, on the ground of spuriousness or unfairness, demands the nullity of it to be pronounced, — a persuasion, or at the least a suspicion, of its spuriousness or unfairness be asserted; the veracity of such declaration being provided for by the ordinary securities: — except when injury to third persons is the cause of unfairness and ground of nullity.

By the declaration thus proposed to be required, many a fair and genuine contract, and in particular many a fair will, would be preserved, which now, under the encouragement given by lawyers to the species of improbity in question, is defeated. Many a man, who, now that the advantage tendered to him by the improbity of lawyers is to be had as it were gratuitously, embraces it without scruple, would never have sacrificed his reputation for veracity and sincerity for the purchase of it.

Of the application thus made of the principle of nullification to contracts, the sole object, when that object is an honest one, is to preserve men from being injured by unfair or spurious contracts. Whether the formalities have or have not been observed, — if the fairness as well as the genuineness of the contract in question is out of doubt, even with him whose interest, were it either unfair or spurious, would be injured by it, — the only reason that could have called for the defeating of it has no application: the reasons which called for the effectuation of it remain in full force.

By the mere circumstance of indicating the want of the prescribed securities in the character of a ground of suspicion — of an article of circumstantial evidence having the effect of rendering spuriousness or unfairness more or less probable, — such an inducement for observance will be afforded, as will, — in the ordinary course of things, and (in a word) whenever the observance of the formalities in question is not physically or prudentially impracticable, — be sufficient (adequate motive, as above, always supposed) to secure their observance: especially if, the assistance of a professional adviser being called in, nonobservance is on his part rendered matter of delinquency.

An expectation to this effect seems to have received the confirmation not only of general reason, but of particular experience. In no instance has the non-observance of the formalities framed by Dr. Burn, and annexed to his work on the office of a justice of the peace, been prescribed on pain of nullity. Yet, how general the recurrence to these forms has been, experience testifies.*

By placing the non-observance of the formalities in question in the light of an article of circumstantial evidence, probabilizing, and not proving, spuriousness or unfairness,—the prescription of these formalities seems to be placed on its only rational and honest ground: no such spectacle is presented as that of the legislator, in the character of an arbitrary and perfidious despot, violating in detail, and as it were by stealth, the engagements he has entered into publicly and in the gross; or, what is worse,—where the engagements thus taken have been taken by the legislator himself, as in the case of statute law,—the judge presuming thus to break the faith plighted by the legislator, and the legislator regarding with an eye of connivance, perfidy thus aggravated by anti-constitutional insubordination and usurpation.

When, availing himself of the non-observance of any of these arbitrarily instituted

* English legislation has of late years exhibited a practice which accords exactly with the principle recommended in the text; viz. on the occasion of *formalities*, the substitution of instruction, to regulation on pain of nullity. By a fresh statute, fresh offences being created, cognizance of these offences is given to justices of the peace, one or more, judging in the way of natural procedure. For the expression of the judgment, in case of conviction, a formulary is provided; the use of it is authorized, but not on pain of nullity necessitated.

The practice thus recently observed by supreme authority, forms a pleasing and instructive contrast with the practice begun in barbarous ages, and still pursued by an authority which ought to be, though in effect it can scarce be said as yet to be, subordinate. The course taken in this behalf applies alike to contracts, and to operations or instruments of procedure.

A contract is produced: the judge pronounces it *null and void.* Why null and void? Because in the tenor of it, or in the mode of entering into it, the parties have failed to conform themselves to such rule, never yet *made known*—no, nor so much as *made.* First comes the arbitrarily-imputed and inevitable transgression: then, from the undivulgated description of the case in which transgression was thus calumniously imputed, and the party dealt with as if he had transgressed, distil off and catch up who can the imaginary rule.

As of a conqueror, so, under jurisprudential law, ruin thus marks the footsteps of the judge.

Regulation improperly substituted to *instruction*—*will* addressing itself to *will*, where *understanding* should have addressed itself to *understanding*—is, in government, one of the marks of primeval barbarism.

formalities, a man derives to himself a benefit by invalidating a contract entered into by himself—a deficiency in moral honesty on his part is generally and justly regarded as unquestionable. Even where the contract thus invalidated by him, is a contract to which he is not a party, no objection being to be made to it but that his interest is without any injury disserved by it, as in the case of a last will,—probity on his part is at any rate regarded as somewhat lax. By the legislator who sets up, though in the legitimate form of statute law, such grounds of nullity,—much more by the judge, who, without authority from the legislator, institutes them in the way of *ex post facto* law,—premiums are offered for improbity: the taint of corruption is diffused into the mass of the public morals.

CHAPTER IV.

FORMALITIES, WHAT PROPER, AND IN WHAT CASES?

§ 1. *In what contracts ought scription to be required?*

In the instance of what contracts shall scription be made requisite?

In the adjustment of the answer, divers circumstances will require to be considered:

I. The importance of the contract;—viz. taking for the measure of the importance, generally speaking, the amount of the damage (estimated in money) that might result from the non-fulfilment of it.

Some sorts, however, there are, to which this measure could not apply. Such are those by which domestic condition in life is made to begin or cease: such are, for example,—

1. The marriage-contract;

2. Contract by which an apprentice is bound to a master or mistress;

3. Contract by which a guardian is appointed to a minor.

II. The natural complexity of the contract, as estimated by the variety of the obligations and rights of which it is productive,—whether absolutely and in the first instance, or eventually on the happening of such and such events.

The above may serve as examples of contracts to which a considerable degree of complication naturally attaches.

III. The state of the place in question, in respect of the proportional number of the inhabitants skilled in the art of writing, and the facility of obtaining the materials necessary for writing: in particular, the promulgation paper, if any such paper, appointed by authority for the species of contract in question, exists.

Suppose a number of persons out upon a long journey by land or water, and either none of them able to write, or none of them provided with materials for writing. It would be an unnecessary and improper hardship to say, that, amongst a number of persons so circumstanced, let the journey last for ever so great a length of time, no binding contract of any kind should take place.*

§ 2. *Use of attesting witnesses.—A notary should be one.*

Three distinguishable advantages seem to result from the practice of having recourse to the assistance of attesting witnesses:—

---

* A regulation applicable to many useful purposes is this,—viz. that on every instrument of contract, the name, together with a sufficient description, of the writer,—the very individual by whose hand the characters are traced—be expressed.

1. In the case of an autograph last will, the scribe is by the supposition the party, the testator, himself.

2. In the case of an unilateral deed, the scribe *may* be the party himself; but (except in a few cases of the utmost simplicity, as well as frequency of occurrence, such as bills of exchange, promissory-notes, drafts on bankers, and receipts) is not commonly so in English practice.

3. In the case of a bilateral or multilateral deed,—viz. to which there are parties more than one,—the instrument cannot be written, the whole of it, by the party (and him only) of whose will it is the expression.

4. In this case the scribe will naturally be a non-party: in English practice most commonly either the notary (an attorney) by whom the instrument is prepared, or a clerk of his (free or articled,) or (in the metropolis in particular, and perhaps some other large towns) a professional writer, either in a state of independence, or as clerk or journeyman to a stationer.

In the notary and the stationer may be seen two responsible and almost official persons, both having a fixed place of settlement. To them respectively, in the description given of himself by any subordinate scribe, reference ought to be made.

But, as between the notary and the stationer, it is the notary who is the principal—his being the scientific part of the business, that of the stationer only the mechanical. What the stationer does, except in the rare case of his being employed directly by a party, it is by commission from the notary (the attorney) that he does it.

By the designation in question, two distinct services will be rendered:—1. In the case of a genuine and fair contract, a source of intelligence will be afforded, giving additional facility to the operation of judicial authentication, and as it might be ordered (if it were worth while) to the end of any length of time. 2. Against unfair and spurious contracts, especially against contracts spurious *in toto*, it would afford additional security. If, in the instance of the scribe, name and reference be omitted, the penalty (whatever it be) will be incurred, and at any rate suspicion of spuriousness or unfairness: if falsely stated, danger of punishment and miscarriage: if truly stated, here then will be a clue, by which, for the purpose of interrogation and justiciability in other respects, forthcomingness will be secured.

One is, the additional security thus afforded for the fairness of the contract.

But for this security, persons whose mental frame is weak, whether rendered so by age or bodily infirmity, would remain exposed in no inconsiderable degree to the danger of being brought to enter into contracts to any degree disadvantageous, by physical force or intimidation.

2. So, again, for the genuineness of the instrument of contract—at any rate as against fabrication *in toto*. But the chief use of it in this respect is confined to the case where the instrument is not in the handwriting of him who is bound by the obligation constituted by it: the security afforded by that circumstance being of itself so very considerable.

The uses of authentication *ab extrà* (viz. by attesting witnesses) being to support the contract,—while the witnesses are alive and producible, by direct testimony—when they are dead, or otherwise unproducible, by the circumstantial evidence of their handwriting: in these uses may be seen the objects by which the choice of witnesses ought to be guided.

If it be required that witnesses more than one be employed in the character of attesting (*i. e.* percipient and signing) witnesses,—one of them at least ought to be that sort of person, who, as long as he lives, is likely to be forthcoming, and whose handwriting is likely to be extensively known. And, be he who he may, care should be taken on the face of the instrument to give a description of him, so formed, that, so long as he is in being, there may be no difficulty in finding him out—that, when deceased, his decease may be notorious, or easily ascertainable,—and that, for both purposes, the individual may be easily and certainly distinguishable from every other.

These circumstances either concur of themselves, or might easily be made to concur, in the person of a notary: which, in England (where, except in the limited case of the notary-public, no persons but attorneys act in the character of notaries,) is as much to say, in the person of an attorney.*

For reasons already given, it were too much for the law to say, that, by non-attestation by a notary, a contract shall be invalidated; since, in some contracts more especially, cases may happen, in which the assistance of any person in the character of a notary may not be to be had in time, or not without preponderant inconvenience in the shape of delay, vexation, and expense.†

But, what the legislator may very well do, is (at any rate in the case of all contracts that have any intricacy in their nature) to recommend that the assistance of a notary be called in;—directing, moreover, that the absence of such assistance be regarded as a ground of suspicion by the judge.

And what in this same view the legislator may do without difficulty, is, to ordain, and that under a penalty, that wherever a notary is employed in any way in the preparation of an instrument of contract, he shall write his name and description, according to a pre-appointed form, in some appointed part of it.

By an arrangement thus simple, various and important advantages would be derived:—

1. Here would be an attesting witness, always producible during his lifetime in the character of a deposing witness; his decease always easily ascertainable; his handwriting generally cognizable; his identity easily and certainly determinable.

2. Here would be a person of a responsible condition in life, answerable for any circumstance of improbity apparent on the face of the contract itself, or otherwise known to, or discoverable by him.

3. So likewise for any improbity in his own conduct in relation to the business.

4. So likewise for any injury that might befal either parties or third persons, by reason of unskilfulness or negligence on his part.

§ 3. *Use of a notary for securing the propriety of the contract.*

Be the contract what it may, four things are desirable in respect to it:—

1. That no such contract be entered into by any individual by whom in the judgment of the legislator it is not fit that such contract should be entered into, and whom the law has accordingly declared *incapable* of entering into it.

2. That it be not entered into by any person to whose interests it is to be presumed injurious;—fraud or undue coercion having been employed to engage him to enter into it.

3. That,—lest, to his disappointment, it should prove injurious to his interest,—before he enters into it, he should be sufficiently

* It is in the character and by the description of notaries, that attorneys should on these occasions be spoken of. It is not in the character of attorneys, assistants in litigation, that their assistance is on these occasions required: on the contrary, to save the parties from the misfortune of being eventually obliged to have recourse to a man in the character of an attorney, is the very use and purpose of calling in his assistance in the character of a notary.

† By way of an example of a sort of contract to which such professional intervention could not without great inconvenience be required, I will give the common bill of exchange, inland as well as foreign, in use among commercial hands. The delay and vexation of which an obligatory regulation to any such effect could not but be productive (not to speak of expense,) constitutes an objection so obvious and so peremptory, that the barest hint of it may suffice.

apprized, not only of the rights which he will acquire by it, but of the several obligations, certain or contingent, to which he will, or eventually may, be subjected by it.

4. That the contract be not of the number of those which are contrary to law,—*i. e.* in the opinion of the legislator productive of preponderant mischief to third persons, and, in contemplation of such mischief, the fulfilment of, and consequently the entrance into, a contract to any such effect, prohibited.

Wheresoever the assistance of a notary is called in, it depends upon the legislator to render it subservient to all these desirable purposes.

The operations by which it may be rendered so, may be comprised under three heads, viz.—

1. Reception and attestation of declarations (uninterrogated declarations) made by the party or parties, according to preappointed forms prescribed and provided by the law,—viz. in such cases in which such spontaneous declarations are of themselves, and without the assistance of interrogation, regarded as sufficient.

2. Interrogation of the party or parties, when deemed necessary for the more correct and complete extraction of the facts marked out for the subjects of declaration.

3. Notification of the state and disposition of the law;—viz. of the law by which the several rights and obligations, resulting or liable to result from the contract in question, have been determined.

1, & 2. As between requisition and receipt of uninterrogated *declarations* on the one hand, and *interrogation* on the other,—which shall be the species of security employed, will depend upon the nature of the contract, and other circumstances in the case. Either, or both, may be prescribed absolutely; or, declaration, as to certain points being required of course, power, discretionary power, of interrogation, may be given to the notary, without imposing on him the obligation of exercising it.

Interrogation requiring on the part of the proposed interrogator (here, the notary) the union of intelligence and skill with probity, to render it productive of its intended effect, and being never wholly unattended with vexation,—whatsoever can be done without it (*i. e.* by means of declarations alone) ought therefore to be done: and accordingly, whatsoever security can be afforded by declarations alone, ought to be carried to the utmost length that can be given to it. But, as in all other cases, so in this,—wheresoever *mala fides*, self-conscious improbity, has place, the utmost security that can be afforded by naked declarations, exempt from the scrutiny of interrogation, will frequently prove insufficient.

Where, for instance, either fraud or undue coercion have been employed by any party, to engage any other to enter into the proposed contract;—so various are the facts which, for detection of the projected iniquity, will require to be brought to light—so incapable of being comprehended by any of those general expressions, to the use of which preappointed forms are necessarily confined, that the necessity of providing powers of interrogation for supplying the deficiency seems to be out of doubt.

But fraud and undue coercion are extraordinary incidents—not having place, perhaps in one out of many hundred instances. Here, then, we see an instance in which, for the prevention of the possible mischief, power for applying the remedy (viz. interrogation) is sufficient, without the obligation of applying it.*

3. For the notification of the state of the law, provision has already been proposed to be made by the proposed requisition of *promulgation* paper.

But it is one thing to possess a faculty or possible means of doing a thing, and another to have actually exercised it. The state of the law relative to the species of contract in question being (either at large, or in the way of abridgment and reference) presented by the promulgation paper,—*i. e.* by the species of contract paper applying to the species of contract in question,—there it is for each party to read, if he be at the same time able and willing to go through the task: but an illiterate man will not be able, and an idle or careless man may not be willing, so much as to engage in it.

Shall the notary himself be bound to read over to his client the contents of the margin of the contract paper? or shall it be sufficient for him to receive from the client, among the list of declarations (properly sanctioned declarations,) a declaration of having read it, or heard it read over by an individual (naming him,) as the case may be?

The option proper to be made between the two courses will depend partly upon the importance of the contract, partly upon the quantity of matter to be read. The time of the notary must not be occupied in reading

* Take for instance the case of marriage. Prior marriage undissolved,—relationship too near,—age absolutely immature,—age immature for want of consent of guardians:—of all these four causes of incapacity to the contract, the non-existence may perhaps be sufficiently established by appositely worded and sufficiently sanctioned declarations. But in the case of three others—viz. undue coercion, fraud, and insanity—the insufficiency of declarations is obvious. Of any of these causes of incapacitation, should any suspicion in this or that individual instance arise, it is only by particular interrogatories adapted to the circumstances of the individual case, that such suspicion will be capable of being confirmed or done away.

that, or anything else, without his receiving, at the expense of the client, an adequate remuneration for it.

In English practice, it is pretty much in course for the client, in the presence of the notary, to read over, or hear read over, the instrument of contract, before he signs it. To what end receive this information of the contents of it? That he may be assured that no other obligation will on the occasion in question be imposed upon him, than what he is willing to take upon himself.

But, under English jurisprudence, as instruments of contract are penned on the one hand, and as the rule of action in relation to them stands, or rather wavers, on the other, —the obligations which, by reading the instrument of contract, the party is apprized of, are never any more than a part (it is impossible to say what part, frequently the least considerable part) of the obligations which, on his joining in the contract, are imposed upon him.

The proposed contents of the proposed printed margin of the proposed promulgation contract paper, will therefore consist of that sort of matter which there will be no less reason for the party's reading or having read, than for the reading or hearing the contents of the manuscript in the body of it.

Of the contents of an instrument of contract, as prepared by an English lawyer, by far the greater part is regularly composed of a quantity of excrementitious matter, having for its object and effect, partly the exaction of a correspondently superfluous quantity of the matter of remuneration in the shape of fees—partly the production of uncertainty, with the litigation which is the expected fruit of it—partly the impressing the non-lawyer with the persuasion of his inability to give expression, in a case of this sort, to his own will, without calling in the assistance and submitting himself to the guidance of an adviser, whose interest is thus opposite to his own. If this surplusage—this noxious matter—were left out, a vacancy would be left, such as might in general fall little, if at all, short of being sufficient to contain as large a portion of the text of the law (supposing the law to have a text) as would be sufficient to furnish the parties with the information requisite for their guidance.

Not unfrequently, among the rights and obligations which the parties suppose themselves to have established by their contract, are many, and those to any amount in respect of importance, which, by the disposition of the law in that behalf (law distilled by writers from decisions pronounced by judges,) have been changed or omitted. So far as this plan of treachery has been carried into effect, the text of the contract, instead of affording the information, the true information, which it pretends to afford, produces the deception which is intended.

If the reading or hearing the proposed instrument of contract be deferred till the time appointed for authentication, time sufficient for reflection will, in many instances, not have been allowed: and, in case of any change of intention produced by the information thus conveyed, time, which must be paid for, will have been unnecessarily consumed.

An operation which ought therefore to be considered as part of the duty of the notary, is, the putting into the hands of the client a blank instrument of promulgation paper, according to the nature of the proposed contract: and the acceptance of such blank instrument will serve as a proof of the act of engaging the assistance of the notary, and will fix the point of time from which the service is to be computed.

Then will be the time and the occasion for the notary to point out to his client the *declarations* which it is incumbent on him to make, and the *interrogations*, if any, to which it is, or may be, incumbent on him to make answer.

Here, then, will be no surprise, no hurry, no dearly-paid time unnecessarily consumed.

For illustration, the following may be mentioned as so many instances of contracts which, while by their importance they will compensate for the time and labour necessary to produce the most effectual notification, so by the nature of them they will, previously to final agreement, admit, without inconvenience, of an interval of reflection sufficient to the purpose:—

1. Instruments expressive of the rights and obligations established by the marriage-contract.

2. Instruments expressive of the contract constitutive of the correspondent relations of master and apprentice.

3. Instruments serving for the appointment of an individual to act as *guardian* to a given minor, who is thereby constituted his or her *ward.*

4. Instruments expressive of the contract constitutive of the relation of master and servant—hired servant.

N.B. Instruments with marginal laws of different tenor will here be requisite, according to the different lines of service: domestic service, under its various modifications; service in husbandry, in navigation, mining, &c. &c.

5. Instruments expressive of the contract constitutive of the relation between landlord and tenant.

Here also instruments with marginal laws of different tenor will be required, corresponding to the different modifications of which the subject-matter and the quantity of interest in it are susceptible; according as it consists of land without buildings, buildings without land, buildings used for habitation, buildings used not for habitation, but for other purposes; the whole of a dwelling-house, or only an apartment in the house, and so forth.

The object to be aimed at in the distribution is this,—viz. that no person shall, either in the shape of expense or in the shape of labour of mind, be charged with any portion of the matter of law, other than what, for the guidance either of his conduct or his expectations, he is concerned in point of interest to be acquainted with: for example, that, though both come under the general denomination of tenants, the occupiers of a weekly lodging in a house situated in a town, shall not be obliged either to buy, read, or hear read, a string of regulations which apply to the occupier of an agricultural establishment.

The cases themselves are not to such a degree distinct as to render it possible in every case to exonerate each individual from every particle of legislative matter that does not apply to his case. The only use of the principle, nor is it an inconsiderable one, is, that the separation, so far as the nature of the law and the circumstances of the individual case admit of it, shall be made.*

§ 4. *Honorary notaries proposed.*

Some persons there will always be, who, to purposes such as the above, having occasion for the assistance of a notary, will be unable to pay the price for it. Some persons:—and, in England for example, in this predicament stand the labouring classes in general; in a word, the great majority of the people.

To almost any person in such parts of the country as have no considerable town in their

* The principle of distribution here proposed, in which regulation and notification are virtually included, is but an application of the more comprehensive principle,—viz. that all judicature should have previous regulation for its basis, and that regulation effectually notified: in other words, that regulation and notification should everywhere precede judicature: that no man should, on the score of punishment, or on any other score, be made to suffer for not having conformed to a regulation or rule of law, real or imaginary, of the existence of which, supposing it to exist, no means of informing himself had ever been presented to his notice.

If the keeping of the rule of action (so far as it exists in what is called a *written* state, that is, so far as it has any real existence) in one immense and unorganic mass, undistributed, and consequently unnotified, is a contravention of the above principle,—a beyond comparison more flagrant and mischievous contravention, is the practice of disposing of men's fate by the exercise of judicial power, grounding itself on no other basis than that of a rule of action purely imaginary, composed of the fictitious matter of that fictitious entity styled by lawyers *unwritten* law: throughout the whole course of which (there being in truth no real law on the subject—the legislator, the only real and acknowledged legislator, having never applied his mind to the subject, nor expressed any will in relation to it,)—the judge, to reconcile men to the acts of power he is exercising at their expense, feigns on each occasion a general proposition of law, to such an effect, as, if it had been really delivered by the legislator in and for the expression of his will, would, in his view of the matter, have formed a sufficient warrant for the act of power so exercised.

Before that general and habitual course of submission, which is necessary to the establishment of legislative authority, had taken root, this arbitrary mode of judicature, preposterous and oppressive as it is, was unavoidable. But no sooner is the habit of uninterrupted legislation established, as well as the power recognised, and regularly submitted to, than the existence of a mass of fictitious law, under the name of unwritten law, becomes an absolute nuisance, a reproach to the legislator by whom so vast a portion of his authority is suffered to be exercised in a manner in which it is impossible that it should be exercised well, and to the nation by which so afflictive a remnant of primeval barbarism is submitted to without remonstrance.

In relation to any part of the field of law thus usurped (usurped by the judicial power upon the legislative,) propose that the legislator—the legitimate and acknowledged legislator, should form a will of his own, should give expression to that will, and now for the first time render it possible for his will in that behalf to be known and acted upon:—propose this to a lawyer, he will laugh you to scorn, assuring you in the same breath, that what you propose is both needless and impracticable: needless, because the common law is already known to everybody—impracticable, because it is incapable of being written down by anybody; for that, if ten thousand lawyers, without communication with each other, were at the same time set down to give an account of the common or unwritten law, no two of them would give the same.

To what end inculcate thus anxiously the notion of its being impracticable? Because, convinced of its being practicable, their fear is to see it carried into practice.

For the truth is, it is as far from being impracticable as from being needless. Take the code belonging to any one of the various sets of persons: set the thousand lawyers each to give his view of the law as it stands at present: converted into the form of real law, sanctioned (as all real law is) by the legitimate legislator, the worst framed and least warranted account that could be given of it, would, in comparison with the present mass of conjectural law on the same subject, be a blessing. A standard of conformity and obedience, a really existing standard, would then be visible and accessible: and whatever imperfections, whether in point of substance or in point of expression, were discernible in it, would present themselves to the eye, and from the amending hand be ready to receive a remedy.

Yes: converted by the touch of the sceptre into really existing and authoritative laws, the worst penned abridgment that ever was compiled would be a blessing, in comparison of the unauthoritative chaos out of which it is compiled.

near vicinity, it may on various occasions happen to have need to enter into a contract, especially to make a disposition of his property by his last will, and for this purpose to have recourse to the assistance of a notary, at a time when no such assistance is within reach.

But a neighbourhood, many a neighbourhood, which does not afford a professional notary (*i. e.* in England, an attorney,) or does not afford a notary who at the moment of exigence is within reach, may afford a person or persons whose education and habits of life would enable him (at least in respect of such contracts as are not embarrassed with any considerable degree of complication) to discharge the functions of a notary, if furnished with proper instructions by the legislator, in a manner no less effectual than if engaged by profession in that line of service.

Britain is fortunate enough to possess more descriptions of men than one, of whom, on an occasion of either of the above descriptions, service of this nature, if placed on a suitable footing, might, on the ground of experience, be expected: justices of the peace, for example, and ministers of religion;* to whom to some purpose might perhaps be added schoolmasters.

To accept of a pecuniary recompense would in the two first instances be to enter upon a profession which would not be generally regarded as being with propriety capable of being added to their own: and, where it is by the indigence of the client that the need of recourse to the assistance of the patron is produced, the acceptance of such recompense would be repugnant to the end in view. In the adjunct *honorary*, the exclusion of such recompense would be implied.

In the case of the indigent client, the fee, whatsoever it might be, that might be deemed suitable to the service, if rendered by the professional notary, would, by the honorary notary, not be received.

In the case of the client driven to request the assistance of the honorary notary, by the inability of obtaining within the necessary time the assistance of the professional notary, —the considerations of delicacy which would prevent the honorary notary from receiving the fee to his own use, would not prevent him from receiving it to the use of some charity, such as the poor of the parish, or to the use of some professional notary of his own choice.

Of a general and habitual readiness to render such service upon such terms, there seems not in either instance any room for doubt.

In the case of judicature, by far the greatest part of the business of this nature that the country affords is done by unfee'd judges.

* In Scotland, a parochial clergyman may act as a notary in executing a will.—*Ed.*

Applied to this branch of legal service, there seems no reason to apprehend that the same principle should be less efficacious than it is seen to be in its application to the other.

The abode of the patron will of course be the spot to which, as in the case of the judicial business above alluded to, whoever has need of the service will repair for the purpose of requesting it. Under these circumstances, the service rendered, the obligation conferred, will be considerable; the labour of rendering it will not be great.

As to the readiness and frequency with which service of this nature will be rendered, several circumstances may be mentioned, on the joint influence of which it will depend.

1. Upon the simplicity and clearness of the instructions given by the legislator, as proposed, on the margin of the proposed authoritative contract paper.

2. Upon the comparative lightness of the burthen attached in the shape of responsibility to assistance thus bestowed. In the case of the man of charity, whose service is bestowed without anything that is generally understood under the name of recompense, the responsibility cannot be in every point as strict as in the case of him who serves for recompense. The principle, alike recommended by justice and policy, has nothing new in it. It has received its application in the instance of the office of justice of the peace. As to schoolmasters, those of the lower order have every now and then been known to be employed, among the lower classes of clients, in the character of notaries, principally for the purpose of making wills.

With sarcastic exultation, professional lawyers have been heard to speak of men of this description as belonging to the number of their friends — more useful to them by the lawsuits thrown by these usurpers into the hands of the regular practitioners, than hurtful by the notarial business taken out of the same learned hands.

The exultation may perhaps have not been ill-grounded: but it may be accused as carrying ingratitude in its company, if due remembrance be not had of the governing members of the partnership, from whose providence the rule of action has received that well elaborated form by which it has been rendered incapable of being learnt by those whose province it is to teach others.

CHAPTER V.

OF WILLS, AS DISTINGUISHED FROM OTHER CONTRACTS.

§ 1. *Utility of wills, deathbed wills included.*

The demand, in point of use and reason, for the power of giving validity to a last will, differs in several points from the power of giving validity to a contract of any other description, whether obligatory promise or conveyance: and, from the difference as to these points, follows a corresponding difference in respect of the formalities proper to be required, and the means proper to be employed in the view of enforcing observance.

1. A disposition of a man's property, destined to take effect not till after death, and in the meantime, as it ought in general to be, revocable, and subject to indefinite alteration, is a species of conveyance, which, to answer its purpose, must be susceptible of, and, if there be power, will frequently in fact be subjected to, indefinitely frequent changes.

It is liable to change, as it were, at both ends. On the one hand, by death, by increase or decrease of need, by increase of age, by change in condition of life, the claims of those whom a testator would naturally choose for the objects of his bounty, are liable to continual change. On the other hand, the subject-matter, the property to be disposed of, is, in shape or quality as well as quantity, alike exposed to change.

2. A last will requires to be made, in circumstances in which neither the necessity nor the expediency of entering into a contract of any other kind, to any considerable amount in point of pecuniary importance, will in general be apt to have place: viz. on a deathbed, at a time when professional assistance may not be within reach; or in some place in which, or on some occasion on which, neither professional assistance nor promulgation paper (supposing any such implement to be required to be employed) would be obtainable.

By the laws of some countries,* a will made on a deathbed is disallowed.

By such a disallowance, spurious and unfair wills may perhaps be in a degree more or less prevented; but the value of the power in question is to every purpose in a very considerable degree diminished.

Without the power of making dispositions of property to take effect after death, the provision made by the legislator for the comfort of the heads of families, and for the welfare of the members, would be in an eminent degree deficient.

1. This power is of use to a man in the character of an article of property. In this way, value is created, as it were, out of nothing; the value of the property of the country increased in a vast proportion, not to say doubled.

2. In the hands of the aged, it serves as a compensation for the various disgusts which that time of life is so liable to inspire; and as a security against that neglect and contempt to which, on that account, as well as on account of the weaknesses incident to it, they would otherwise stand exposed.

3. In the hands of a person rendered helpless by disease, and dependent for his life on the services of others, this power is a security for life—an instrument of self-preservation.

4. It is useful in the character of an instrument of government, having for its object the welfare of individuals other than the proprietor himself. At an early age, it is necessary to the very being of man that he should be subject to the government—and for a long while after, conducive to his well-being that he be subject to the influence of his superiors in age. If the power of bequest were withholden, the force of this instrument would be in a great degree weakened.

5. As between equals in age, without need of government or docility on either side, the prospect of posthumous bounty forms a bond of reciprocal attachment, and a security for reciprocal good behaviour, kindness, and self-denial, in the minor but continually-repeated concerns of life. It enables one man to obtain the convenient or necessary services of another, for whom, out of his income, and in his life-time, he could not spare a sufficient reward.

6. In the case of those who have no near relations, endeared to them by the ties of nature or long habit,—and in the case of those whose natural relations have, in their eyes, rendered themselves unworthy of their favour,—it contributes to substitute frugality to that dissipation, which would be the natural course of him who should behold whatever were left unexpended by himself entailed on a successor or set of successors who were either odious or at best indifferent in his eyes; and thus (in so far as it checks dissipation from that source) it promotes that slow but constant and general accumulation of the matter of wealth, in the shape of capital, upon which the welfare and comfort of the individual, and the increase of the general mass of comfort by the multiplication of the species, depends.

If a deathbed will—a will made during a last illness—be utterly disallowed, a man is divested of the power of rewarding services on which his life depends, or of punishing neglects (whether wilful or for want of attention) by which death, preceded by suffering to an indefinite amount, may be produced. On a person rendered helpless, and perhaps speechless, by a dangerous disease—in a case in which an apparently trivial service, neglected or even ill performed, may be fatal,—homicide, murder (viz. so committed,) is scarcely an object of legal punishment. If, therefore, there be a single moment of sanity

* At any rate, by the law of Scotland. [By the law of Scotland, a will, technically speaking, *may* be made on deathbed. An alienation of the heritable or real property, however (which cannot be disposed of by will,) is reducible at the instance of the heir-at-law, if made on deathbed. See above, p. 66.—*Ed.*]

during which this power is withheld, and known to be so, a man's life will lie altogether at the mercy of the attendants of a sick-bed, — that is, of dispositions of all shades, from the best to the worst, too many of whom may not be proof against the temptation thus thrown into their hands. Exposed to injury from enemies, a man would feel himself divested of the power of purchasing assistance from neutrals, or animating in the same way the exertions of the well-disposed. In conversation with the devoted victim, so long as no third persons capable of serving as witnesses were at hand, the fatal purpose might even be avowed: and the cup of inhumanity might thus have insult to embitter it.

These things being considered, the propriety of allowing or disallowing deathbed wills, will, in each country, depend in no inconsiderable degree on the state of morality among the people. But, even in the most virtuous state of society, the legislator should never repose on popular virtue any confidence which can be withholden without preponderant inconvenience; he should never hold out, to all, a temptation, under the force of which it may happen to the virtue of any one to sink. Be the quantity of virtue among the people ever so great, necessity alone should engage him to do anything that can tend to lessen it.

§ 2. *By requisition of formalities, if peremptory, more mischief is produced than prevented.*

In speaking of contracts in general; formalities, calculated to throw difficulty in the way of spurious and unfair ones, being proposed to be by authority instituted, and the observance of them recommended, — pointed suspicion, not nullification, was spoken of as being in general the proper and sufficient instrument for securing observance: *nullification, disallowance*, not being reconcilable to general utility on the part of the legislator, nor to good faith on that of the judge, on any other condition than that of a full assurance of its being in a man's power to comply with the formalities, as well as of his being actually apprized of the existence of the obligation by which he is called upon for compliance.

Of contracts of all sorts, taken in the aggregate, so vast and diversified is the field, that, without some determinate species brought forward for illustration, and as an example by means of which a determinate shape might be given to the ideas belonging to such general propositions as should be advanced concerning it, and the truth of those the more readily brought to the test, our conceptions on the subject might be apt to be bewildered. On this consideration it was, that the species of contract called a *last will* was fixed upon, to officiate, as it were, on this occasion, in the character of a representative of the rest.

On the occasion of this, as of other contracts, the legislator, if he be at once honest and enlightened, neither corrupted nor misled, will naturally direct his endeavours to two main objects: to facilitate the formation, and secure the effect, of genuine and fair ones; to prevent the formation, and at any rate the success, of such as are unfair or spurious.

If pain of nullity be imposed, and that arbitrarily and inexorably, without regard to the necessary conditions, viz. power of observance, and knowledge of the necessity for observance, as above specified, — the first of the above objects, viz. the giving existence and effect to fair ones, is, so far as the application of the proposed remedy extends, sacrificed, certainly as well as completely. But, by the certain sacrifice thus made of the one object, no more than a chance of compassing the other is purchased; for, where the formalities, whatever they may be, are to all appearance, or even in reality, observed, still it may and does happen to the pretended instrument exhibited in the character of a last will, to be discovered to be either unfair or spurious.

Force and fraud, the causes of unfair wills (viz. of such as are so to the prejudice of the testator and his natural successors) — force and fraud are no less capable of being employed in the prevention of fair wills.

A set of persons — engaged in a mal-practice of this sort by sinister interest, whether as standing next in succession, or as being or supposing themselves to be favoured by a will already made — beset a man's deathbed, refuse their assistance to the making of a will, shutting the door at the same time against assistance from every other quarter. Here we see a fair and genuine will (*i. e.* one which, had it been suffered to have been made, would have been so) prevented by force.

Suppose three attesting witnesses necessary: two on the spot, ready and willing to officiate in that character, but all others kept off, as above, avowedly, and even by force. Under the inexorable system of nullity, the wickedness would be triumphant: no relief could be obtainable.

In league with the persons interested (as above) against the allowance of a fresh will, a notary falsely declares to the testator that such and such formalities are not necessary, or that, being necessary, they have been observed, when in fact his care has been that they shall not have been observed. Wickedness again triumphant: no relief.

Of the two objects, — the one pursued at the expense of the other — the one openly sacrificed to the other, — suppose the importance equal: how would the profit or loss resulting from the expedient be to be taken account of? It is only upon one supposition that there would be a net profit,—viz. if the number of unfair or spurious wills thus prevented from taking effect or coming into existence, was greater than the number of fair and genuine wills prevented from taking effect or coming into existence. Not (be it observed) the total number of unfair or spurious ones prevented from taking effect or coming into existence by *any* means, but only the number prevented from taking effect or coming into existence by *this* means.

Suppose, then, a country, in which two species of property are to this purpose distinguished: one, to the disposal of which by last will, certain formalities have been made necessary; the other, to the disposal of which in that same way, no such formalities are made necessary.

To any person unapprized of the state of the English law in this respect, the supposition will be apt to appear an extravagant one. A little further on, it will be seen to be realized.*

If, in this state of things, an account were taken of the wills of both sorts, call them *formal* and *informal*, contested within a given period, say ten years — distinguishing, in each case, such as were allowed from such as were disallowed, — by such an account, conclusions in no small degree instructive might be afforded.†.

Suppose that the number of *formal* wills, to which spuriousness or unfairness is in this authentic and deliberate way imputed, and which, on one or other ground, are accordingly contested, is found to be just as great as the number of *informal* wills contested on the same grounds: this will surely amount to a satisfactory proof, that, by the formalities, no effect at all, in respect of the prevention of spurious and unfair wills, has been produced; and that, consequently, the sacrifice made of so many fair and genuine wills as, having been made, have been prevented from making their appearance, has been a sacrifice purely gratuitous: none of that good which the requisition of the formalities had for its object or professed object, — nothing, in a word, but so much pure evil (as above)— having been produced.‡

Whatever be the number of spurious or unfair wills defeated,— prevented, either from taking effect, or from coming into existence — in the case of the species of property subject to formalities, — the mass of good thus produced under the system of formalities sanctioned by nullification, is not all of it to be placed to the account of that system; since a part of that same good, if not the whole, might equally have been produced by the same formalities, if barely recommended: suspicion of unfairness or spuriousness, not nullification, being indicated as the consequence of non-observance.

Under English law, an account of the sort

* Reference is made in this and in subsequent pages, to the state of the law of England with regard to wills at the time when the work was published. The distinction between real and personal property, with regard to testamentary attestation, has been, since that time, abolished by 7 Wil. IV. & 1 Vict. c. 26 (3d July 1837.) By that act, all wills must be in writing, and "signed at the foot or end thereof by the testator, or by some other person in his presence, and by his direction; and such signature shall be made or acknowledged by the testator, in the presence of two or more witnesses present at the same time, and such witnesses shall attest and shall subscribe the will in the presence of the testator, but no form of attestation shall be necessary." The act does not extend to the wills of soldiers, nor to those of sailors and marines in the navy, which are regulated by 11 Geo. IV. & 1 Wil. IV. c. 20.—*Ed.*

† Two items, it is true, would still remain out of the reach of observation; viz. 1. The number of unfair or spurious wills prevented by the formalities from coming into execution; 2. The number of fair and genuine wills prevented by the same means from taking effect: for, by means of the formalities, fair and genuine wills actually made, may, in any number, have been prevented from making their appearance: since, when a will is seen and understood to be unprovided with the formalities, the observance of which has been rendered necessary to its validity, it is given up of course, and never can make its appearance in the character of a subject of contestation.

‡ Nor is this the whole of the evil: for, in the account of fair and genuine wills prevented from taking effect, must be included the number prevented from coming into existence. In other words, to the number of wills of this description prevented from taking effect by want of knowledge of the necessity of the formalities, must be added the number prevented from coming into existence by want of power to comply with those formalities. The number of those which, not having been prevented from coming into existence, have been prevented from taking effect, are those that have been thus frustrated for want of *knowledge:* the number of those that have been prevented by the same formalities from coming into existence, has been the number of those that have been thus frustrated for want of *power* to comply with the formalities. A man who, knowing that writing is necessary to a will, is neither in a condition to write one himself, nor can, at the exigence, obtain the assistance of any other person who is able to write, will not attempt to make a will. A man who, knowing that three witnessess are necessary to attestation, cannot obtain the assistance of three persons in that character, and three competent ones, will not attempt to make a will. In the house in which I am writing this, some years ago, an only daughter, an heiress, being minded to add by her will to a scanty provision that had been made for her mother by the marriage settlement, a lawyer was sent, and a will drawn accordingly. Just as the pen was put for signature into the hand of the testatrix, she expired; and, with her, the intended provision.

hereinabove indicated, might, without difficulty, if the force of authority were applied to the subject, be obtained — if not for a past period, at any rate for a period to come. But even for a past period, say ten or twenty years, there need be little doubt. The official books, notwithstanding the defectiveness and inappositeness of the plan on which official books are kept, would afford considerable information; inquiry among individual practisers would complete it: work for a committee of either house of parliament.

In a cause of great celebrity, the number of formal wills contested, and even disallowed, was, by one of the most enlightened of English judges, asserted to be greater than the number of informal ones in the same case. "The legislature," says Lord Mansfield (speaking of the clauses relative to wills, in the statute called the Statute of Frauds and Perjuries,) "the legislature meant only to guard against fraud by a solemn attestation: which *they thought* would soon be universally known, and might very easily be complied with. In theory, this attestation might seem a strong guard: it may be some guard in practice; but I am persuaded many more fair wills have been overturned for want of the form, than fraudulent have been prevented by introducing it. I have had a good deal of experience at the Court of Delegates, and hardly recollect a case of a forged or fraudulent will, where it has not been solemnly attested. I have heard eminent civilians who are dead, and some now living, make the same observation."*

Hitherto we have supposed that the two evils — frustration of a genuine will, and successful imposition of a spurious one — are of equal magnitude: and even upon this supposition it has appeared, that to incur the first of the two evils for a chance of preventing the second (by peremptory requisition of formalities,) is a bad calculation; the number of fair wills disallowed in consequence, having, in the opinion of a competent judge, practically exceeded the number of spurious or unfair ones prevented. But, even in this way of stating the case, we have not availed ourselves of all the arguments within our reach.

Might it not with considerable show of reason be contended, that (value at stake, and all other circumstances, as nearly as possible the same) securing of fair wills from frustration is a more important object than preventing unfair or spurious ones from taking effect? — that, of two mischievous results, frustration of an intended fair will is more mischievous than effectuation of an unfair or spurious one?

1. Take first the case of a father of a family.

The legislator being unacquainted with the exigencies of individual families, the disposition he makes of the property after death is but a random guess, a makeshift: against its being the best adapted that can be made, there are many chances to one. Unreasonable wills may, it is true, be made, and every now and then are made. But the case of an unreasonable will is an extraordinary case, similar to that of prodigality: and, as it supposes reflection, the absence of which rather than the presence is indicated by prodigality, probably still more rare.

On the part of parent, as well as child, *inofficiosity*, as the Romanists call it, is indeed always liable to have place. But on the part of the parent it seems least so. In descent, love has been observed to be stronger than in ascent. In the superior, sympathy has the pleasure of power to strengthen it: in the inferior, it has the painful sense of restraint to weaken it.

Prodigality is more naturally the weakness of youth than of mature age. Against prodigality on the part of a child, the disposition made of the property of the parent, after his death, by the law, provides no remedy: by the forecast and sympathy of the parent, a remedy will naturally be provided.

* Lord Camden, whose ruling passion was enmity to Lord Mansfield, and who with unprecedented acrimony disputed everything that in the above-quoted argument presented itself as disputable, — even Lord Camden does not dispute the matter of fact exhibited by that instructive experience. "The design of the statute," he says, "was to prevent wills that ought not to be made, and it always operates silently by intestacy. I have no doubt," continues he, ("for this assertion," says he, "cannot be proved,) but that a thousand estates have been saved by this excellent provision. It is called a guard in theory only, whereas almost every delirious paralytic that is suffered to die intestate is preserved by this law, and gives testimony of its utility." So far the noble and learned lawyer. Delirious paralytics, a thousand in number, preserved from imposition by this law! So far as it goes, a happy result indeed, if it be true. Happy, I mean, for the delirious paralytics whose property has happened to be in the shape of what is called *real* property — in that particular sort of shape for the designation of which the lawyers who have invented it have never yet employed or invented any distinctive name. But what becomes of so many other delirious paralytics in much greater abundance, whose property is in any other shape than this indescribable one; whose property is in the shape of moveables, or of that sort of property which, being as immoveable as it is possible for property to be, is spoken of and treated by lawyers as if it were moveable? In a word — of three delirious paralytics, worth £10,000 a-piece, the first in freehold houses, the second in leasehold houses, and the third in stock in trade, — what is there about the two last that should exclude them from the protection, whatever it may be, that is afforded by what his Lordship calls "this famous law, every line whereof, according to Lord Nottingham's opinion, was worth a subsidy?" — *Camden*, p. 25.

When a fair will is prevented, the worst that happens (it may be said) is that the estate falls into the natural course of succession, viz. that which in the eye of the law is the best: whereas, by an unfair will, it may be made to take a course as foreign to the natural course as it would by theft. But, under different systems of established law, courses of succession differing widely from each other are to be found: and among them all it would not be easy to find one to which the epithet of a natural one could with propriety be applied: and even the best natural one, supposing it adopted, would, as already observed, frequently be but ill adapted to the exigencies of the individual case.

A will, leaving everything away from children to strangers, or more distant relatives, is always possible. But, even taking fair and unfair, genuine and spurious, together, such a case is very rare: much more so if fair and genuine ones are left out of the account.

What applies, as above, to the cases of parent and child, applies, though of course with less and less force, to their respective more remote representatives — grand-parent and grand-child, uncle or aunt and nephew or niece, and so forth.

In every case of a *first* will, the operation, if it has any, is to the disadvantage, if not of all natural relatives taken in the aggregate, at any rate of some, as compared with others. But when once a will has been made, the operation of any subsequent will may as naturally be to the advantage of natural relatives, as to their disadvantage.

2. Take next the case of a man without a family — a man who has no blood relations near enough to produce from that source the sentiment of sympathy. Wills (whether fair or unfair, genuine or spurious) made to the prejudice of blood relations, are supposed to belong mostly to this class.

To this case applies the distinction between the mischief of the first order, and the mischief of the second order:* in comparison with which last, where it has place, the mischief of the first order is generally very inconsiderable.

As often as an intended fair will is, by non-observance of formalities, prevented from taking effect, the existence of the mischief is almost always known — the knowledge of it spread over a circle more or less extensive. The more extensive the circle, the wider the alarm, the apprehension, produced of similar mischances in the breasts of other persons, in the character of intended testators.

On the other hand, when an unfair or spurious will takes effect, the instances are rare indeed, in which, the existence of the mischief being known, or at least suspected, any alarm can have been spread by it. If suspected, contestation is the natural consequence. And if wills of this description — wills, the object of suspicion and contestation, are rare, — wills which, being so suspected and contested, have been confirmed by the judge, and, notwithstanding such confirmation, are generally believed to be either unfair or spurious, cannot but be much more rare.

The conclusion is, that, of the two mischiefs — effectuation of unfair or spurious wills on the one hand, and frustration of fair ones (which being fair cannot but be genuine) on the other — magnitude and certainty both taken into the account, the latter is considerably the greatest. But it is this latter, which, under the system of nullification, the legislator produces to a certainty, and as it were without a thought about the consequences, for the purpose (real or pretended) of promoting, not the certainty, but a chance only of the other. For, without evidence of some sort or other, an unfair or spurious one will no more obtain credence than a fair one; and, on the supposition that the evidence is false, there is surely some probability, if not a preponderant one, that it will not be believed.

§ 3. *Use of autography in wills. Recommendations in relation to it.*

So efficient, in the case of last wills, is the security afforded by autography, against fraud in almost every shape — against spuriousness *pro parte*, as well as spuriousness *in toto* — against unfairness as well as spuriousness — that, in point of trustworthiness, even without any attestation, a will thus authenticated seems to stand at least upon a par with a supposed last will, written in a hand other than that of the testator, although authenticated by his onomastic signature.

1. The more words a mass of writing contains, the more precarious will be the success, and thence the greater the labour, of an attempt to fabricate it. Where the only mode employed for authentication *ab intrà* is that which consists of onomastic signature, the quantity of writing to be fabricated is confined to the two or three words (in England most commonly no more than two) of which a man's name is composed: in the case of autography, the number has no limits.

2. An autograph instrument is less exposed to the danger and suspicion of having been the result of undue coercion, whether by physical force or fear, than a will, in the instance of which the operation of authentication has consisted of nothing more than the writing of two or three words. Signature, though it be of the onomastic kind, is the work of a minute: the terror or uneasiness

* For the explanation of these terms, see Dumont — "*Traités de Legislation*," and Bentham — "*Introduction to Morals and Legislation*," Vol I. of this collection.

of the minute suffices for the accomplishment of it. The greater the number of the words, the greater the difficulty of keeping the mind of the patient in the state of coercion requisite to the production of the effect.

3. It is even in some degree less exposed to the danger and suspicion of having been the result of fraud in either of its shapes, viz. positive falsehood, and undue reticence; or even erroneous supposition of inducement, unaccompanied by fraud. Why? Because, the greater the number of words written, the longer the operation lasts, and thence the longer the mind of the writer is necessarily applied to the subject.

4. So likewise to the danger and suspicion of unsoundness of mind. If the testater calls in the assistance of a scribe, more especially if of a professional scribe, whatever words he employs in conveying the expression of his meaning to the scribe, the words written will be those of the scribe: expressions which, in case of want of sanity, might have betrayed the defect, will of course be rejected. For the scribe to reject them, it is not necessary that any persuasion, or so much as a suspicion, of the insanity, should have entered into his mind: they will be rejected as being, in comparison with those which to *his* mind present themselves in the same view, inapposite. The inappositeness — the effect — will present itself much more promptly than the *insanity*, the cause: and the effect will have been perceived in many a case, where the cause has never presented itself at all.

5. When the requisite soundness of mind is wanting, — the longer the instrument, the longer the course during every part of which the mind will be exposed to the danger of taking its flight into the regions of absurdity or nonsense.

6. When the test and proof of genuineness and fairness is thus afforded, amendment in every shape may be allowed to take a freer course than without this security can with equal safety be permitted.

7. Of this contract it has already been mentioned as an effectual and peculiar feature, the being susceptible of requiring frequent and indefinitely numerous changes; and these, in point of importance, to any amount considerable or inconsiderable.

In this way, many a change will present itself, which a man will readily and gladly make, when he can do it by a few lines or a few strokes of his own hand, and without witnesses, but which he would not make, if upon each occasion it were necessary to have to perform the ceremony of calling in witnesses. To employ always the same witnesses, he would excite speculation, and expose himself to the imputation of fickleness or capriciousness: different sets of witnesses, to whom it would be agreeable thus to open himself, it might not always be easy for him to find; and the more there were of them, the greater the danger of their comparing notes, and thence of the imputation of fickleness or capriciousness, as before.

On an occasion of this sort, it is not enough that the testator and the intended objects of his bounty be guarded against receiving injustice: another object to be attended to, is the guarding the circle of which he is the centre from being exposed to suspicion of having been guilty of injustice.

For both these purposes taken together, the following present themselves as being of the number of the recommendations which it might be of use for the legislator to address to testators in general; and in particular to such as, for the expression of such their wills, make use of none but their own hands:—

Let *numbers* be written in words, rather than figures: or (to unite distinctness with security against falsification and misconception) in both ways; as is the practice in draughts made on bankers. To forge an entire name with any prospect of success, requires a degree of skill much beyond what is common: but there is scarce any tolerably good writer by whom one figure could not be converted into another, without leaving a possibility of guessing by what hand the alteration was made. In some instances (such as the conversion of an 0 into a 9) the alteration may even be made without inducing a suspicion that any alteration has been made by the original writer (the testator,) or any one else.

The following recommendations relate exclusively to amendments, considered as incident to last wills: viz. in the case of autography, as above:—

Amendments may be made either in the *informal* or in the *formal* mode: viz. on the face of that part of the paper on which the will was written in its original state (as in the writing of an ordinary letter or memorandum;) or on a separate part of the paper, or on a separate sheet: in either of which last two cases, it is said to be made by *codicil*.

Recommendations concerning the informal mode:—

1. Of amendment or alteration there are three modes: subtraction, addition, and substitution. Substitution is subtraction and addition both in one.

2. Whatever amendment you make in any line, write in continuation of that line (in a margin left for that purpose) your name,— viz. either at length, or by the initial letters of the several words of which your name is composed: if the alteration be an important one, better your name at length. For, supposing any other person disposed to falsify your will,— so far as subtraction is sufficient, it is what may be performed by any person

(viz. by cancelling or obliteration, by drawing lines across, or scratching the word out,) without its being possible for any one to perceive that it was not by yourself that the alteration was made.

3. For subtraction (unless it be an object with you that the prior disposition should not appear,)—cancelling in such manner as to leave the original word still visible, seems preferable to obliteration: for obliteration will be apt to excite doubts and suspicions, which the leaving of the original word still visible will obviate.

4. So, for substitution,—cancelling (as above) the original word, and then, with a mark to indicate the proper place for insertion, writing the added word above, is preferable to alteration of this or that letter in the original word: because, if done by another hand than your own, the difference between one hand and another is more perceptible in an unaltered than in an altered word.

5. If (whether by cancelling, or obliteration, or interlineation) you subtract, or substitute, or add, one more word than in the same line, especially if it be in distinct parts of the same line,—it may be of use to insert the initials of your name, not only in the margin of that line, but over every word so cancelled or obliterated: otherwise, under favour of the acknowledgment which you have given that one such alteration has been made by you, another person may, without possibility of discovery, make more alterations, at least in the way of cancelling or obliteration.

6. It will be an additional security, if, at the end of your altered will, after any alterations which it has undergone, you were (after writing the day of the month and year of the date) to sum up the number of the alterations made up to that date: for which purpose, the lines of which your will is composed would require to be numbered,—for example, by a numerical figure subjoined to every fifth line in the margin: as thus,—

Lines containing Alterations.	Number of Alterations in the several Lines.
Line 6	1
7	1
10	2
13	3
4	7

7. If the alterations be to a certain degree numerous, you will find it advisable, for avoidance of perplexity or uncertainty, to write your will afresh. But, in many instances, as where a sum or a person is concerned, an alteration of any the greatest degree of importance may be effected, by subtraction, addition, or substitution of a single word.

Unless where the alteration consists of new matter, intelligible without reference to the old, the informal mode will frequently be clearer than the formal; *i. e.* the change in disposition will be more clearly made by alteration of a few words in the original text, than by an additional paragraph or number of paragraphs forming a codicil: for in this case, the effect of the codicil at length will only be to give directions for the doing that which, by alterations made in the informal way, is done at once.*

§ 4. *On the attestation of wills.*

The advantages attached to autography have just been brought to view. But in some cases autography is not practicable; in others, a man will naturally be disinclined to practise it.

1. The cases in which it is not practicable, are those in which either the necessary *skill* or *strength* are wanting.

2. Where professional assistance is called in, autography will not in general be in use. The words employed by the man of science will naturally be his own. It is by his hand that they will be committed to writing. To the testator, the labour of writing being thus performed by another hand, labour of copying employed by his own hand will be apt to appear superfluous. If a transcript is wished for, the labour of making it will naturally devolve upon the professional man's clerk; the profit constituting a natural perquisite to the master.

If, among the dispositions to be made, there be any of a complicated nature, as is apt to be the case where landed property is among the subjects to be disposed of,—then, especially if the scene lies in England, comes in a mass of technical jargon, to the non-lawyer an object of terror and disgust or both, from which his pen will be repelled by a sort of instinctive repugnance.

When thus the assistance of a foreign hand is called in, that of the testator himself not being applied to any purpose other than that of authentication, onomastic, or, according to the state of his powers, only symbolic,—then comes naturally the demand for authentication *ab extrà:* and, along with it, the questions, by what and how many hands shall it be performed.

* Apply this to *statutes* as well as to wills. By a simple *erratum*, a clear expression might have been given to many an amendment, to which an always obscure and sometimes ambiguous expression has been given by a *statute at large*. The obscure and ambiguous has however been preferred to the clear. Why? Because, from the obscure and ambiguous form, more emolument in the shape of fees is extracted, than could with equal ease be extracted from the clear and familiar form, by those on whom the choice of forms has depended.[a]

[a] See "*Nomography, or the art of inditing Laws*," Vol. III. p. 231.

One will naturally be that of the assistant, professional or non-professional, who has officiated in the character of scribe: and then comes in the other question, — Shall any, and, if any, how many, other persons, be called in to officiate as attesting witnesses?

1. In contradistinction to a single witness, the chief use of two attesting witnesses is constituted by the increased security it affords against spuriousness; viz. spuriousness *in toto*, the result of forgery in the way of *fabrication*.*

Whatsoever may be the obstacles to success in the case of a single attesting witness,—add another attesting witness (*i. e.* a requisition recommending the calling in of another attesting witness,) these obstacles will be not merely doubled, but more than doubled.

To form the more distinct conception of the use of *two* attesting witnesses, in the character of a security against forgery in the way of fabrication,—let it be considered what the expedients are, which under different circumstances would be apt to present themselves to the consideration of a man who had it in contemplation to commit a fraud of this nature.

For the reason already mentioned, a will purporting to be an autograph will scarcely be chosen by the fabricator for the subject of the fabrication: it will be the less likely, the greater the number of the words that appear necessary to answer the fraudulent purpose.

But, if a supposed autograph be rejected as impracticable, then comes the necessity of an apparent authentication *ab extrà*, to be performed by one or more attesting witnesses.

The author of the fraud must either write the supposed spurious will himself, or procure some other person to write it. Of another person the assistance could scarcely be made effectual to this purpose, without his being let into the secret; *i. e.* engaged to become an accomplice in the fraud. Such accomplice the author will not naturally engage, nor attempt to engage, if he can help it: the accomplice must have his reward, which carries off more or less of the profit: paid *in presenti*, it requires confidence on one side; made payable *in futuro*, eventually (for example) in case of success, it requires confidence on the other side: putting himself in the power of another, who by the supposition cannot but be dishonest, he thus incurs an additional risk of failure, besides exposing himself to the risk of punishment and infamy: and to the danger of infamy he cannot but expose himself by the very proposal, and before he is sure of consent.

The accomplice, unless his timely death be assured, must moreover be such a person, as, upon receipt of such instructions as the author of the fraud has it in his power to give, must be able to stand the scrutiny of counter-interrogation.

In this state of things, suppose the law to have rendered the attestation of one attesting witness necessary, but at the same time sufficient.

First, then, let the supposed testator be a person of whom it is known that he is unable to write his name. Here the task of the forgerer is comparatively an easy one. With his own hand he writes the spurious will—with his own hand he subjoins his own name in the character of that of an attesting witness; then adding, in the character of a symbolic signature performed by the testator, a mark; for which (a cross, the usual mark, having nothing in it that is characteristic of the hand) the forgerer's hand may serve as well as any other.

Next, let the supposed testator be a person whose capacity of writing is out of doubt. Here, then, the signature must be of the onomastic kind. Accordingly, upon a paper on which he has previously succeeded in writing what to him appears a sufficiently good imitation, the author writes in his own hand the spurious will, together with a declaration of attestation signed by his own name in his own natural hand.

How much more difficult the task of the forgerer would be rendered, by requiring two witnesses instead of one, has been seen.

---

* In the case of spuriousness *pro parte*, the danger is narrowed by the impracticability of the fraud to all persons other than the one or few who, in the interval between connexion and exhibition, in the individual case in question, can have had access to the will, with length of time and other facilities adequate to the purpose.

For this same reason, a codicil may be admitted without fresh attestation. By the attestation provided for the will itself, a security is provided against forgery *in toto*,—such security as the nature of the case seems to admit of,—a security that presents itself as superior, upon the whole, to any that has been as yet exemplified. But forgery *in toto* is the species of forgery most to be apprehended. Forgery in the way of alteration presupposes a genuine will, and access to that will on the part of the actor or actors in the fraud. But in this case the possibility of the attempt is limited to a very few persons, and a very few occasions.

Were it not for these considerations, an obvious objection to the indulgence would be,—On what principle, with what consistency, refuse to a testamentary disposition under one name, that of a codicil, a safeguard you look upon as necessary to it under the name of a will? But, by the above considerations, when duly attended to, the objection seems to be obviated. Under the circumstances in question, the safeguard given to the preceding will extends itself in a great measure to the subsequent codicil: the genuineness of the paper, as being a paper actually made use of by the testator for the purpose of his will, is established in this case, with as little room for doubt as in any other that can be mentioned.

Even if the difficulty of finding persons at the same time able and willing to engage in a scheme of iniquity of this description were the only difficulty,—by doubling the number of the persons whose engaging in it were necessary to success, the difficulty would be increased cent. per cent.*

But to this difficulty, with its attendant dangers, are added the several other dangers that have just above been brought to view. By calling for two attesting witnesses in contradistinction to one, the difficulty, the improbability of success, is therefore much more than doubled. *How much* more, depends, in each individual instance, upon the individual circumstances of the case; and cannot, in any one individual case, be brought within the reach of calculation.

More than two attesting witnesses, it appears unnecessary either to require or to recommend; since it does not seem that the absence of a greater number of attestations constitutes in itself a valid ground for suspicion either of spuriousness or unfairness. There is no need, however, to limit the number of attesting witnesses: every additional attestation adds an additional security. Still less should attestation, as in English law, exclude recourse to non-attesting witnesses.

The exclusion put upon non-attesting witnesses on no better nor other ground than that of the existence of attesting ones, claims, by the word *exclusion*, to be posted off to that title. But, as the case in which the door of the judgment-seat is thus shut against the light of evidence bears no reference to anything in the character or situation of the witness, or to any peculiar effect resulting from the evidence, it seems difficult, under the general head of exclusion, to find any particular head under which to place it.

Never surely was iniquity more completely destitute of all support on the ground of reason. What passed, or is said to have passed, was seen by the two or the three persons whose names stand upon the face of the instrument in the character of attesting witnesses; therefore it was not seen by anybody else: such is the least absurd plea that could be urged in favour of the exclusion; supposing any man to have courage to hazard anything in that view. But what does it amount to?

To a last will, being a will disposing of an estate called real, three witness at the least being required,—three witnesses at the least, but three witnesses also at the most, are in common usage called in and made to sign their names. Besides these three, were thirty more present, no lawyer would (without some very particular reason, produced by some very particular state of things) think of desiring any more of the persons present to add their superfluous names to the three necessary ones.†

But, supposing it really to happen, that, in the number of persons present, in addition to these three attestors, thirty non-attesting but equally percipient witnesses were included; neither any one of the thirty, nor all of them put together, could, under the rule, be able to obtain credence for what they saw.

Of good, not a particle can on any supposition be the result of this lawyer-made rule. Of the mischievousness of its tendency, the enormity is such as to baffle calculation.

1. The attesting witnesses being all gained by corruption, and disappearing,—the thirty, if admitted, might, any one of them, defeat the wicked purpose. No: they shall not; nor all of them put together. Why not? Lest the wicked purpose should be defeated, and iniquity, the offspring of lawyer-craft, lose its triumph.

2. The attesting witnesses being all of them dead, remains as the sole obtainable proof (unless the other direct testimony which the case happens to have afforded be called in) the circumstantial evidence composed of the similitude of hands. The hand suggests doubt: shall the doubt be cleared up? Oh no: for to involve everything in doubt, is among the objects of the men of law.

3. Of the three attesting witnesses, one or more exist; and, at one time or other, their testimony may perhaps be obtained; but at any rate not without ruinous delay, as well as a most oppressive load of vexation and expense. Shall mischief in this shape be avoided? Oh no: to accumulate it in this shape, is another of the objects to which the desires and exertions of the law are invariably directed.

Whatever be the number of attesting witnesses required or recommended for a contract in general, for which authentication by witnesses is recommended,—the number of such witnesses required or recommended for last wills in particular should be the same. Why? For this reason: that it may be in a man's power to make a will, without its being known to the attesting witnesses that he has done so.

The persecution and coercion to which, at the approach of death, a man is apt to be exposed at the hands of those in whose power accident or sinister design has placed him in so critical a conjuncture, has been already brought to view. In some instances, their interest will prompt them to engage him to make a will; in other cases, to prevent his making one. If the number of witnesses

* In fact, it would even then be increased more than cent. per cent. The greater the number of persons in whose power the supposed accomplice must put himself, by joining with them in the commission of the offence, the greater will evidently be his danger, and therefore the greater the difficulty of engaging him in the conspiracy.

† *Vide supra*, p. 533, note *.

required in the case of a will were different from the number required in the case of every other sort of contract; and if, by simultaneous presence, or view of the attesting signature, it were manifest to each or to any one of the witnesses that the instrument he was executing was a will; the choice of the persons permitted to approach him for that or any other purpose, being in the power of those in whose power, in these moments of absolute subjection, his person happened to be; in such case, his purpose being thus rendered incapable of being concealed, the iniquity would thus be in possession of the information necessary to its purpose.

But, on the other hand, if, the same number serving for both purposes, a pretence could be found by the dying man himself, or by any faithful friend or friends to whom it might happen to be placed in company with his unfaithful ones,—an additional chance would thus be given him for escape from such iniquitous restraint.

That it would be no better than a chance, is but too apparent; because the spirit of rapacity, which by the supposition is on the alert, understanding him to be desirous of executing an instrument of contract, would naturally be suspicious of its being a will; and, on that supposition, would endeavour to prevent it.

But what might also happen is, that, at that same conjuncture, an instrument or instruments of contract of some other nature might require to be executed by the sick person: contracts which, being in the view of the supposed intended oppressor beneficial or necessary to the interest of the sick person, in respect of the property on which the eye of concupiscence had fastened itself, it might, n the view of the intending oppressor, be for his advantage upon the whole to suffer the execution of the instrument, notwithstanding the risk attending it. And, in a case like this, no chance, however small, that can contribute to preserve the helpless against the machinations of power at that time despotic, ought to be neglected.

The witnesses (supposing two at least,)—should it be required that, at the time of the attestation, they be present to each other, as well as to the party of whose act of authentication their signature is understood to declare their perception,—or should that circumstance be passed by without notice?

By their being *present* to each other, understand in the character of attesting and subscribing witnesses; the act of attestation and subscription being performed at the same time by both, and each of them being apprized of the part borne in the transaction by the other.

Of a requisition to this effect, the advantageous tendency is indubitable: but neither is it altogether free from tendencies of an opposite nature.

1. The advantage consists in the additional difficulty it opposes to forgery in the way of fabrication. If the person to whose profit the counterfeit disposition of property is designed to operate, be not capable himself of penning the instrument, and at the same time annexing his signature in the character of an attesting witness,—then (unless the penner of the instrument, making his own signature in the character of an attesting witness, is able to counterfeit with sufficient skill the handwriting of another person, representing that other person as acting in the character or another attesting witness,) the fabrication cannot be effected or attempted unless two persons, acting at the same time in that criminal and dangerous character, have been engaged.

The first falsely attesting and subscribing witness being procured at one time—the second (it may happen,) with his signature, was procured at another: the instrument (to comply with the supposed requisition of the law) bearing on the face of it a statement, declaring (though falsely) that, at the time of the attestation, both the individuals, whose names, written by themselves, appear together in the character of names of attesting and subscribing witnesses, wrote their respective names at the same time. But, by the supposition, this asserted simultaneity is false: the first was never seen, perhaps, by the second. Here, then, is a story, which, though false, they will each of them, in case of counter-interrogation, have to support as true. In these circumstances, though neither should quarrel with the penner or with each other, the difficulty they will labour under in their endeavours to give credibility to the false story under the scrutiny of cross-examination, will apply to their imposture such a check as would not have applied to it had the requisition of simultaneity been omitted.

2. The disadvantage consists in the difficulty thrown in the way of making a fair and genuine will, in the case in which the interest of the person or persons in whose power the dying testator is placed by the weakness incident to his condition, has engaged them to use their endeavours to prevent it. Suppose him to succeed in engaging the assistance of one faithful friend—that friend, taking advantage of a momentary opportunity, subscribes his name, before there can be a certainty of his engaging another. Some time after, accident, or the industry of the first faithful friend, sends in another to repeat the office and complete the attestation: no other opportunity, no other assistance, presents itself. Under these circumstances, had simultaneity been rendered necessary on pain of nullity, nullity must have been the result.

The two objects being thus in a state of conflict, — to which shall the legislator give the preference?

Answer: To guard against the prevention of fair wills, is the preponderant object.

How important, in the character of a security for life against wickedness or carelessness, the continuance of the right and faculty of making a last will to the latest moment is, has been already brought to view. By the requisition of the formality in question (if on pain of nullity,) the exercise of this important right is rendered more dependent than it would be in the contrary case, on the will of those in whose power the sick man happens to be placed. Being better pleased with the disposition which (whether by the general rule of law, or by a will already made and still in existence) they consider as having been made of his effects, — it is, in this state of things, more easy to them, than in the opposite state of things it would be, to prevent, for this time, his making any different disposition of his effects; and (to make sure of his not doing so at any other time) to prevent his continuing any longer in life.

Against that species of iniquity which consists in giving a man's property a disposition which it was not his wish to make of it, the obstacles that not only may be, but in practice actually are, opposed, are forcible and abundant: punishment, in most countries capital, and everywhere very severe. To the opposite species of iniquity, though in respect of mischief differing by so slight a shade, no such punishment, scarcely anything in the name of punishment, has anywhere been opposed.

To be engaged in a scheme of forgery, is what few persons are competent to, even if disposed: to engage others in the like scheme, and with success, still fewer. On the other hand, to keep out of a sick room those who have no right to enter it, is no more than almost any man is competent to, who, being in the room, is in possession of it.

Such is the difficulty, such the dilemma, where, for securing observance of the formalities regarded as conducive to the prevention of mal-practice in this field, pain of nullity is employed. Obstruct in the way in question (viz. by requiring simultaneity of presence on the part of the attesting and subscribing witnesses) the procuring of unfair, or fabrication of spurious wills, — you obstruct in a still greater degree the making of fair and genuine ones.

To the inflexible pain of nullity, substitute the natural and ever proportionate pain of suspicion, and the difficulty vanishes — the dilemma has no place.

§ 5. *Distinction between regular wills and wills of necessity.*

Taking into consideration, on the one hand, the danger of spuriousness or unfairness for want of *formalities* (whatsoever may be the operations thought fit to be prescribed or recommended in that view,) — on the other hand, the possible, and not altogether improbable case, of the existence of the need, coupled with the desire of making a will, at a time when the observance of these formalities in the whole or in part is impracticable, — a distinction seems to be called for, such as may be expressed by the terms *regular will*, and *will of necessity*.

By the term a *regular will*, may be designated a will, in the expression of which, whatever formalities have by the legislator been prescribed or recommended, have been (that is, upon the face of the will appear to have been) observed; and which, therefore, on the face of it, and setting aside all extraneous indications, is pure from all suspicion.

By a *will of necessity*, may be designated any will, in the expression of which these formalities have all or any of them failed of having been observed: from which deficiency a ground of suspicion will naturally be attached to it; and a warning will be given to the judge to inquire and consider, whether the observance of those formalities which (forasmuch as regularly they *ought* to have been) naturally in case of a fair and genuine will *would* have been observed, was prevented by any necessity.

The supposed will (for example) is not committed to writing, but orally delivered; or, being committed to writing, is written not on *will paper* but ordinary paper: and, in either case, in a handwriting not purporting or appearing to be that of the testator; or without signature of the testator; or without the signature of any attesting witness; or with the signature of no more than one attesting witness.

It being supposed that the law by which the observance of these several formalities has been recommended, has been sufficiently notified, in the manner already explained,* — then comes the question, how — supposing the will to be a fair and genuine one — how can it have happened that the formality or formalities not observed, failed of having been observed?

Examples of states of things in and by which the observance of formalities may, without prejudice to the genuineness or fairness of the will, have been prevented: —

I. Omission to be accounted for, — the will not committed to writing, but addressed to some person or persons, separately or in presence of each other, by word of mouth:

1. Scene, a private ship at sea. The testator a passenger, or one of the crew. The master, — able of course to write, but the

* Chap. III. § 2.

testator and he not upon terms of amity, — is engaged by interest to oppose the making of the will now in question. This interest may arise out of the disposition made by the law in case of intestacy; or out of a will already made, and now proposed to be revoked or altered.

2. Scene, an uninhabited or thinly inhabited country, such as the wilds of America; or a country inhabited by a people alien in language and manners to the testator; for example, a place such as Asiatic Turkey, or Arabia: the testator an European traveller, without any European servant, master, or other companion, able, and at the same time willing, to render the service of penmanship.

3. Scene, a prison, or other place of confinement, domestic or foreign, lawful or unlawful; a mad-house, or other secluded spot, into which the testator has been conveyed by fraud or force, for the purpose of preventing his making a will, which he was supposed to have it in contemplation to make.

II. Omission to be accounted for, — non-use of will paper:—The will made in a place (such as a foreign country) where no will paper was to be had.

III. Omission to be accounted for, — non-employment of a notary:—No notary at hand, or none obtainable within the time: — the testator not able to purchase the assistance of such a person: — the only persons of that description within reach, in a state of enmity with the testator, or on some other account (such as connexion with a party meant to be disserved by the will) regarded as incompetent: — Or, the dispositions in the will too simple to present a demand for professional assistance.

IV. Omissions to be accounted for,—body of the will not in the handwriting of the testator; onomastic authentication not in the handwriting of the testator:—The testator a person rendered (by want of skill, or by infirmity) unable to write.*

Of the formalities brought to view, the observance will, in the case of a *regular* will, be at any rate, at the hands of the legislator, the subject of *recommendation*. In what instances (if in any) the several recommendations should, by pain of nullity, be converted into *requisitions* — indispensable requisitions —will depend, partly on the state of society in the country in question (for example, in respect of obtaining at a short warning the requisite assistances;) partly on the provision made for notification (viz. of the requisition thus proposed to be made obligatory.)

Supposing, in the case of a regular will, the recommendations thus converted into requisitions, — then will come for consideration the question, whether to extend the requisition to the cases above indicated as capable of presenting a demand for the allowance of a *will of necessity*. If here, too, it be thought fit that the recommendations be rendered peremptory, on that supposition the distinction is of no use. If — in the case of the *regular* will the recommendations being rendered peremptory — in the case of the *will of necessity* they be left on the footing of recommendations, — the use of the distinction is apparent. But even supposing them in both instances left upon the footing of recommendations, the distinction will not be without its use: for if, in circumstances which present no demand for the allowance of the will of necessity, the formalities remain any of them unobserved, such non-observance will, in the character of an article of circumstantial evidence tending to probabilize spuriousness or unfairness, operate with much stronger force than in the contrary case.

§ 6. *Aberrations of English law in regard to the authentication of wills — Examination of the Statute of Frauds, in so far as relates to wills.*

If the above principles are right, the course pursued in relation to this subject by the English law must be allowed to be improper and inconsistent in a very extraordinary degree.

In the case of deeds *inter vivos* — a case in which the nature of the transaction admits not only of the employing writing, but of the calling in the assistance of attesting witnesses, — writing is indeed rendered obligatory, but the assistance of attesting witnesses is not rendered obligatory.

On the other hand, in the case of wills — a case in which it must not unfrequently happen, not only that the means of giving to the disposition in question the written form, but also the probability of obtaining the assistance of attesting witnesses, may be wanting, — in one case, and that a case which is looked upon as the case of principal importance, not only a written form for the testamentary discourse, but the assistance of attesting witnesses, and that to the number of three, is inexorably required—required on pain of nullity.

In the case of last wills, a set of formalities are prescribed, and of course on pain of nullity, by a statute commonly and not inappositely termed the Statute of Frauds (29 C. II. c. 3.)†

So far as this species of contract is con-

* If no symbolic attestation be visible on the face of the will, and this (in case of inability to write) be among the formalities required; in this case the omission cannot be accounted for without calling in the supposition of ignorance with regard to the recommendation of the formalities.

† By the act 7 W. IV. & 1 Vict. c. 26, noticed above, p. 533, the 29 C. II. c. 3, so far as it has reference to wills, is repealed. — *Ed.*

cerned, three points in relation to this statute are beyond dispute: the mischievousness of it—the uselessness of it—and the corruption in which it was begotten, and has been preserved.

The mischievousness of it is legible in glaring colours, in the multitude of fair and genuine wills of which it has been destructive, and the enormous mass of litigation and lawyers' profit of which it has been the fruitful parent.

The uselessness of it has been displayed by a course of experiment that has been going on for nearly a century and a half. All this time, one half the property of the kingdom, by much the larger half,* has been left without any such security; and no inconvenience for the want of it has ever been so much as suspected.

The corruption is manifested (if it be possible for corruption when enveloped in long robes to be made manifest) by the enormity of the profit to lawyers, coupled with the enormity of the misery to non-lawyers, of which it has been the efficient cause.

Is it in the nature of it to defeat more fair and genuine wills, than it prevents or exposes unfair or spurious ones? Then why apply it to property in any shape?

Is it in the nature of it to prevent or expose more unfair or spurious wills, than it defeats fair and genuine ones? Then why refuse the benefit of it to property in the shape to which it is not applied?†

From the non-observance of the formalities in question, prescribed as by it they stand prescribed, can any rational conclusion be formed in relation to the fairness or unfairness, the genuineness or spuriousness, of a last will? then is the same last will fair and unfair, genuine and spurious.

Let the testator leave property to the value of £20,000—whereof £10,000 in one of the two shapes, £10,000 in the other. The same last will, authenticated by one and the same act or acts of authentication, is fair and genuine with respect to the one sum, unfair or spurious with regard to the other.

Oh! but immoveables, being a species of property of more importance, require better protection than moveables: a sophism from the crude conceptions of feudal times, carefully preserved, like so many others from the same stock, by the cunning hand of lawyercraft. Ten thousand pounds' worth of land, how much more is it worth than ten thousand pounds' worth of money?

But even that sophism, shallow as it is, has no place here. For the self-same piece of land, the £10,000 worth of land, according as the lawyer has scribbled one sort of jargon or another on the occasion of it, shall be subject to the formalities, or stand exempt from them: and *vice versâ*, money, the £10,000 worth of money, by the effect of another jargon, may have been subjected to the same rules as land.

The difference between what is called real and what is called personal property, turns frequently upon a word, or a phrase. Let the words be, I give to A. my house in D. for ninety-nine years, if he shall so long live:—these words, in the testator's own writing,

* See the estimates which by different writers have of late years, on the occasion of the property taxes, been made, of the value of the masses of property in different shapes: taking into account this circumstance, viz. the large proportion of immoveable property, which, in the sum of what is called *real* property, stands exempted (viz. by marriage and other *settlements*) from the operation of *last wills*.

† To a man whose reason is in his own keeping, it is scarce necessary to observe, that the demand for formalities cannot be varied by the consideration of the shape in which the property happens to be invested: whether, for example, it consists principally of immoveable property, lands, leases, and so forth; or principally of moveable property, such as stock in trade; or of property called incorporeal, such as an annuity, which is neither immoveable nor moveable, but something between both. Still less, whether, having an immoveable mass for its subject-matter, the interest he has in it, being the same in substance, be expressed in the language of the law by one form of words or another. And, moreover, that, if power be given to a man to dispose in this way of a portion of his property without the regular formalities, that portion should be, not a fixed and absolute one, but a relative one, proportioned as near as may be to the circumstances of the parties.

Under the provision made on this subject by the law of England, everything, however, turns upon these irrelevant points. For the share belonging to one of ten children in a quarter of an acre of unproductive ground, nothing less will serve than writing, with three witnesses: for the rents receivable for the space of ninety-nine years for a street of a hundred houses, a will without any witness, so it be in the hand of the testator, or even a will said to be delivered *vivâ voce*, so there be a certain number of witnesses to it, and so forth, will in this case serve. So likewise if the property be in a moveable shape—floating for example, or capable of being floated; rolling, or capable of being rolled—no matter to the amount of how many millions. Address yourself to a lawyer, and ask him for the reason of these distinctions,—he begins telling you a tale of other times, the only sort of reason he ever heard of, or ever wished to hear of. If there ever was or might have been a time to which the provision might have been well suited, no matter how ill suited to the time in which we live: if there ever was a sort of people to whom it might have been beneficial, no matter how inconvenient to ourselves.

Ask him what proportion of a dying man's property should be exempted from formalities? Proportion is theory, a sort of a thing he never desires to hear of: but what is better, he can tell you the proper sum to a farthing:—exactly thirty pounds.

are sufficient—no witness is necessary. Let the words be, I give to A. my house in B. for his life:—witnesses no fewer than three are necessary. In the same page, with his own hand, let a man give to A. one of his houses in the one way, and to B. the next house in the other way,—then is this will of his half genuine, half spurious: it is his will for the one purpose, it is not his will for the other.

Where is the absurdity which the lawyer will not utter?—where is the mischief to which, so long as it can be done with profit and with safety, he will not continue to lend his hand?—where is the absurdity, which, so it come from the mouth of the lawyer, the non-lawyer will not worship?—where is the oppression under which, so long as he sees the hand of the lawyer having a part in the production of it, he will not submit with patience?

Whichever of the two systems of policy above spoken of—the strict or the lax system—be the most reasonable one, it makes no difference with regard to the wisdom of this law. Mischievous by the whole extent of it, or else too scanty by a space greater than the whole extent of it: such is the alternative.

Who the authors were—what their views and intentions, are points that make no sort of difference. A consideration somewhat more material, is the poisonous influence of it upon the public morals. By what it neglects to do, it leaves the door open to wills in multitudes, which, though unprovided with the prescribed formalities, everybody sees to be fair and genuine; and which, as such (the formalities not extending to them) are permitted to take effect. By what it does, it shuts the door against other wills, the fairness of which is equally indisputable; but which, notwithstanding that acknowledged fairness (the formalities not being observed) it crushes without mercy. But, so many wills, not fraudulent or spurious upon the face of them, as it invalidates, so many acts of palpable and notorious injustice does it invite and encourage men to commit. In the author of this law, supposing him a lawyer (and who but a lawyer could be the author of such a law?) an eye unstained by professional prejudices may behold as clearly as in the author of any sort of other corrupt or corruptive law, the legislator of whom the poet speaks, when he says, *leges fixit pretio atque refixit.* In his capacity of legislator, he invites men to possess themselves of property which they are conscious was not intended for them by the lawful owner: he invites them to enrich themselves by notorious injustice, that he or his brethren may come in for their portion of the spoil.

Had the inconsistency been avoided—had the requisition of the formalities been extended to property in every shape,—the real temptation to injustice would have been as great, but the contempt shown for the known laws of justice would not have been so open and scandalous. The legislator might then have been understood to say,—Wherever these necessary formalities are not observed, my opinion is that the will is either fraudulent or spurious. The party interested (whatever might have been his real opinion) might with some degree of plausibility at least, have been allowed to say,—Such being the opinion of the legislator, a person of consummate wisdom and untempted probity, can anybody, consistently with reason and candour, profess to disbelieve me when I declare that his opinion is also mine? With this plea in his mouth, sincere or insincere, a man at any rate could not be publicly convicted of insincerity and injustice. But when, to justify the law in point of prudence and common sense, the same will, made by the self-same person under the self-same circumstances, must be pronounced fair and fraudulent, genuine and spurious—genuine as to property in one shape, spurious as to property in another shape—when the same thing must be pronounced, at the same time and place, to be and not to be,—all pretence of honesty must be at end. What everybody must see, is, that by no man, either in or out of his senses, was any such opinion ever really entertained.

No man ever was or ever will be besotted enough to say, either that a will of land to a given amount is in itself more apt to be unfair than a will of goods to the same amount,—or that, in the case of the will of land, the preventive efficacy of a given set of formalities as against unfairness, will be greater than in the case of a will of goods to the same amount.

Whence, then, came the distinction? Evidently from the narrow views and selfish prejudices of two different sets of lawyers. The common lawyers had possession of the cognizance of wills, so far as concerned lands; meaning always (for such is the absurd and for ever inexplicable and inconceivable distinction) where the quantity and quality of interest denominated the estate a *real* estate. The civilians—a tolerated remnant of a foreign breed of lawyers, the ecclesiastical Romanists,—had possession of the cognizance of the same instrument, so far as concerned every other species of property. In the adjustment of the business under the new invented rule of evidence, each, preserving his own share in the division of power, was to retain the privilege of gratifying his own prejudices. The same fact which was to become false in Westminster Hall, was to continue true in Doctors' Commons. The same will, the same sentence, written by the self-same hand, attested by the self-same pair of witnesses, was to be spurious or genuine, according as a man with fur upon his gown, or a man in a gown without fur, were to sit in judgment on it. So monstrous were the absurdities which the penners of the Statute of Frauds, having been fed with in their respective schools, scrupled not to cram down the throats of their fellow-subjects by the power of the sceptre.

Where, amidst all these lawyers, guides blind and mercenary, was the legislator? — where was the man who, regardless of professional prejudices, possessed probity and intelligence to look to the security of property and the tranquillity of the people? Alas! nowhere. Neither in those days, nor down to the present, has any such character ever appeared. The true shepherd of the people is a comforter not yet born. Look to his place,—you find in it none but hirelings.

Under the English, as under other systems, on the subject of wills and other contracts, as on so large a portion besides of the field of law, the rule of action, such as it is, has had for its authors, not legislators, but judges. In the making of it, the interest the promotion of which has been all along aimed at — to which it has all along been made subservient, has been, not the interest of the community at large, but the private interest of those by whom it has been made: and in the pursuit of this private interest there is no degree of vexation and misery, which, on this part of the field as on every other, they have not been ready and satisfied to produce.

If it were possible that a state of things so manifest and undeniable could be matter of doubt to any one who has courage to look it in the face, this one example should suffice for the removal of the doubt.

Right and wrong, wisdom and folly, felicity and misery, must all be the same thing, ere the conduct of the English legislator, under the guidance of English judges, on this part of the field of law, can find so much as an excuse.

Hold up to the view of the man of law any one of these abuses, — if not so much as the shadow of a pretence can be found for the justification of it, he solemnizes his tone, he knits his brow, and beholds in the air a host of difficulties. But these difficulties, — what are they? None but of his own making: the only difficulties he can find to plead, are the difficulties which he makes.

The course that presented itself as best adapted to the purpose has been brought to view above: were it ever so well adapted, the putting it in practice would not be altogether exempt from difficulties. But a course by which a great part of the abuse would be removed, would not be attended with any the smallest difficulty. Do away at one stroke the distinction between a will of realty and a will of personalty: whatsoever formalities suffice for a will of personalty, let them suffice for a will of realty: repeal *pro tanto* the Statute of Frauds.

The real difficulties lie in removing the film of prejudice from the eyes of non-lawyers—in giving them the courage to look their own interest in the face.

As to the man of law, to cause him to lend a willing hand to the removal of imperfection or abuse in this shape or any other, is matter, not of difficulty, but of moral impossibility. Call upon a body of men, and such a body, to sacrifice each of them his own most important interest to the public interest! — as well might you call upon each and every one of them to jump down his own throat.

Word-of-mouth wills are, in certain cases, allowed by the Statute of Frauds. In the description of these cases, the penman had evidently the case of *necessity* in view. But in the description, or rather the exemplification, which he gives of that case, he is far indeed from covering it with exactness. The case of last sickness, and that too disfigured by obscure and indistinct modifications, is the case he employs for that purpose. But the case of last sickness is far indeed from being well adapted to the purpose. It goes beyond the mark: it falls short of it. There may be sickness — sickness terminating in death, and yet no necessity: no impediment to the fulfilment of the formalities in their utmost latitude. There may be necessity without sickness. A man in health is about to embark in a perilous adventure — no will made, and the means of making a regular will not at hand: to embark in an open boat on a high sea: to attack a robber: to plunge into a torrent to save a person from drowning: to plunge into a deep well to save a person from suffocation.

Among the provisions made by the Statute of Frauds, under the notion of preventing spurious or incorrect last wills, when delivered, or supposed to have been delivered, by word of mouth, one (sect. 20) is in these words: — "After six months passed after the speaking of the pretended" (instead of saying supposed) "testamentary words, no testimony shall be received to prove any will nuncupative" (meaning by word of mouth,) "except the said testimony, or the substance thereof, were committed to writing within six days after the making of the said will."

No person being here specially designated as the person, or as a person, by whom it is required that the recordation or supposed recordation shall have been made, the consequence is, that it may have been made in any manner, and by any person, so that it have been made within the time. But of this latitude another consequence is, that, supposing such recordation to have been made by any one person, and (as is natural enough) by him alone, the validity of the will remains thereby in his power; and he may either, under the influence of ill-will, suppress the testament altogether, or, under the influence of rapacity, sell his testimony or the suppression of his testimony (and all this without exposing himself to punishment as for perjury) to whichsoever of the parties interested will give him the best price.

As to the impropriety of frustrating the known will of the testator, and the honest expectations of any number of persons, for want of compliance with a requisition which nothing is done to make them acquainted with, and which there is an abundantly preponderant probability that they have not been acquainted with in time, — it belongs not to the present purpose.

What does belong to the present purpose is, that, — if, instead of a requisition on pain of nullity, a recommendation were given on pain of suspicion, to call in the assistance of a notary honorary, or even professional,* in the manner above proposed, — the two antagonizing objects — prevention of spurious and unfair wills, prevention of the frustration of such as are genuine and fair — would be much better secured and provided for than under that absurd or treacherous statute.

The matter being thus not only committed to writing, but lodged in safe custody, the door would therefore be effectually shut against the corrupt practice above indicated. Thus far against suppression of genuine wills: and moreover, against unfair wills — against wills rendered unfair, for example, by undue coercion, or by mental infirmity, — there would always be a chance, more or less considerable, of the clearing up doubts, one way or other, or at least of the preservation of otherwise perishable evidence, by such interrogatories as it might happen to the notary to collect answers to, in pursuance of the *instructions* provided by the law.

In the same statute, on the same subject of oral wills, are regulations in abundance, professing to have for their object the frustration of spurious wills of that description, but having for their effect, probably to a greater extent, the frustration of fair and genuine ones, and for their object (as usual) increase of uncertainty, and of litigation, with the sweet attendants for the sake of which it is promoted.

Three witnesses, at the least, required not only to have been present at the writing of the will, but the same three witnesses required to concur in proving it by their oaths: whatever be the distance of time to which it may have been in the power of the dishonest person whose endeavour it is to frustrate a fair and genuine will, to delay the possibility of proving it. Keep on feeing us till one of the witnesses is dead, and the property is yours.*

* See Chap. IV. § 3 & 4.

* If the object of the author of this statute had been to create confusion, he could scarcely have pitched upon any more effectual means than he has done. He foresees nothing: he sees nothing but through a cloud. In § 19, in speaking of a word-of-mouth will, he began with the case where there has been no written will already in existence: and on that occasion he described the conditions on which he will allow it to stand good: the subject-matter being property in any shape but *real*. In § 22 he takes up the opposite case, that of the existence of a written will. In this case, shall a word-of-mouth will be good, or no? That, says he, depends upon the circumstances. Ask him what those circumstances are, — the first and principal one is, that it shall not be a word-of-mouth will, but a will in writing: it must be "in the life of the testator committed to writing, and after the writing thereof read unto the testator, and allowed by him, and proved to be so done by three witnesses at the least." Allowed by him! But how? in what manner? In the same manner as in the case of land, or tenements, &c.? in the shape of real property, as under § 5 & 6? or in any and what different manner? Between the wording of the two clauses of the act — words employed to make provision for the same case — there is not the smallest connexion or analogy. That they should have been the work of the same hand, however unskilful, is morally impossible: they must have been the work of two different, though alike careless and thoughtless, hands. If in the one case it be required (as in § 5) that the will expressed in writing be subscribed by the three witnesses, why not require, in § 22, the same proof of privity in the other case? If the provision requiring the will to be read over to the testator in the case of the non-real estate be a necessary precaution, why not extend the benefit of it to real estates? Why, in the case of the real estate (§ 5,) insist upon three witnesses to *attest* the will, without saying how many of them there shall be to prove it; and at the same time, in the case of the non-real estate, insist upon three witnesses to prove the will (*i. e.* in case of contestation, to depose to the fairness of it) without saying whether there shall be any, and how many, to *attest* it?

A fact which seems to have been a secret to the penner of this clause, but which one may venture to assert without hesitation, is, that all men are mortal. Quære, what is the number of attesting witnesses that a man must procure (and that at a pinch, in circumstances in which a regularly written will cannot be made,) in order to make sure that, at any given distance of time, three of them shall be alive to prove the will in the character of deposing witnesses? To enumerate the things necessary to be known, which our legislator did not know, would be an endless task. One of them is, the difference between an attesting witness and a deposing witness — between writing, at the time when an instrument is authenticated, and speaking, at another time, when that same instrument has become the subject-matter of dispute in a suit at law.

Through such a thicket of confusion, what

In cases of all sorts without distinction, the mischiefs resulting from exclusion of testimony, and in particular from exclusion on the score of interest, will be fully stated hereafter.* In the case of testaments, the mischiefs had been so severely felt, and so

---

shall be the course? Shall fair wills be overturned by wholesale? —or, to prevent such subversion, shall the acts of the legislative power be overturned by the judicial, on the pretence of interpretation? I know not: but, what everybody knows is, that, in the century and a half that has elapsed, the legislator is not to be found to whom it has appeared worth while to pass an act for reconciling on this ground the interests of constitutional obedience with the dictates of common sense and justice.

More caprice, more incongruity, more perplexity, the consequence. Relative to wills of personal estate, this statute found the rules of evidence determined by the ecclesiastical courts, governed by the Roman law. Under that law, a will in the handwriting of the testator is a good will, even without any attesting witnesses. Under the same law, the will, though not written by the testator, yet, if (to use the words of the statute) "read unto the testator and allowed by him," or indeed if allowed by him, whether read to him or no, would then have been, as it still is, good; such allowance being proved by two witnesses. The testimony of two witnesses, therefore, being sufficient to prove the *making* of a will, having property in this shape for its subject-matter, why should not the same quantity of testimony be sufficient to prove the annulling or altering of it? Or if, in the case of property in this shape, *three* are so necessary to render the annulment or alteration of a will a probable event, why should that same number be less necessary, even in the case of property in this same neglected shape, to prove the *making* of a will in the first instance? But this would have put property personal upon the same footing in this respect with property real: it would have rendered the law, if not reasonable, nor favourable to tranquillity nor to probity, yet, in its unreasonableness, consistent and simple, at least: which was not to be endured. It was necessary that, like the law of succession to intestates, the law of testaments should be in a shape which no mortal conception could lay hold of, and which, if laid hold of, no mortal memory would be able to retain.

Nor is this all. Though witnesses are so little liable to die, testators, it seems, are not only liable to die, but apt to allow wills after they are dead. To make provision (as it should seem) for this accident, it is, that before he comes to require that the sort of will in question (the word-of-mouth will) shall be in writing, and allowed by the testator, he takes care to stipulate that the operation of putting it into writing shall be performed "in the life of the testator," for fear of his being put to the trouble of allowing it after he is dead. The confusion would not have been thick enough without the insertion of this surplusage.

By the last of the two provisions contained in § 21, "no nuncupative will shall be at any time received to be proved, unless process have first issued to call on the widow, or next of kindred to the deceased, to the end they may contest the same if they please."

1. The object, probably, which the penner of this clause had in view, was, the making business for Judge and Co. in the ecclesiastical court: and, for this object, the provision made is effectual and secure. What is required is, that the process shall have *issued:* what is not required is, that it shall have been received. If it has not been received, the ostensible purpose has not been answered; but the real purpose, viz. the receipt of the fees, being answered, in this case as in the others, such accordingly is the requisition made. An incident altogether natural and frequent was and is, that the widow or the next of kindred (if there be but one) is, for an indefinite time, and without any imputation upon his or her probity, out of the reach of this process, whatsoever it be. To a man who had *justice* in view, this accident would afford no reason why the required proof, and the will along with it, should perish: but, as on all other occasions so on this, what the learned draughtsman had in view was fees.

"The next of kindred:" it may happen to *him* to be one, or it may happen to *them* to be in any greater number. All are known, or some are not known: whatsoever be to be understood by *process*, and whatsoever be to be understood by *issuing*, process is issued as to some, not issued as to others. In this case, is the will, or is it not, "at any time to be received, to be proved?" Address yourself in a proper manner to Judge and Co., and it is possible that, some day or other, you may know: but it will not the less remain a secret to all who have not paid for it.

The supposed will being in favour of the widow, to the exclusion of the next of kindred; the process, at any rate, being issued, and addressed or not addressed to the widow, is received or not received by her.

The supposed will being in favour of the one next of kindred, to the exclusion of the widow,—the process being at any rate issued, and addressed or not addressed to that one next of kindred, is received or not received by that one next of kindred.

In each of these cases, the words of the act are satisfied. Will the judge be satisfied? Ask him in the proper manner, and it is possible that one day you may know.

A former will has been made, and the persons in whose favour it was made are all of them strangers, none of them either widow or next of kindred: this will subsisting, a subsequent will finds neither widow nor next of kin possessed of any interest to contest it. Process having been duly and regularly issued, if either widow or next of kin have received it, so much the worse for them: but those things of which it was intended that they should be received have been received, viz. the fees.—But (says the learned scribe, or some one for him,) It is no intention of yours, that, after one will has been made, another in the word-of-mouth form, by us called nuncupative, should be made: and to that effect is our very next section.—Answer: if not, so much the worse. What your next section extends to, however, is only the disallowance of a succeeding nuncupative will after a preceding written one: but to a preceding it may happen to have been also nuncupative: and thus it is that the effect takes place, which to you was either an object of desire, or at best a matter of indifference,—that the only persons by whom the pretended notice is received (if by any it be received) are of the number of those to whom it is not of any use.

* Book IX. *Exclusion.*

fully recognised, that about eighty years ago they attracted the notice of the legislature. To do away this ground of exclusion altogether, either in regard to transactions of the sort in question, or in short in regard to any case whatsoever, would have been too great a sacrifice of professional prejudice to public utility — an exertion far beyond the wisdom of the time. Recourse was had to a sort of half measure — an expedient which, though not equal to the cure of the mischief, yet, in the character of a palliative, was not altogether without its use. To do away the nullity altogether, would have been too wide a stretch — too bold a measure: instead of that, they transferred it from the whole will taken together, to each particular bequest. A legacy being given to a subscribing witness, the bequest of this particular legacy was declared void, and, at that price, the attestation and deposition of the legatee, in the character of a witness, were to be held good.

The persons by whom it is most natural that a man's deathbed should be surrounded, are the persons who, in case of his making a will, are, in consequence of his kindness towards them, most likely to find themselves in that sort of situation which will give them an interest in the support of it: near relations — old friends — old servants. But *interest* (it was said) is a sort of taint, the effect of which is to give a legal foulness to a man's evidence. To clear away this foulness, requires a legal purge. There are three purges applicable to this case: receipt of the legacy, refusal to receive it, refusal to pay it: three diaphoretics these, any one of which has virtue enough to carry off the peccant matter.*

Such is the prescription. In point of form, nothing can be fairer. But how stands it in point of effect and substance?

The will is either fair or unfair. Is it a fair one? there is no mischief to prevent: injustice is the fruit of the law, and the only fruit of it. To invalidate the entire will would have been one injustice: to invalidate the legacy, is another injustice. Thus much may indeed be said, — but it is the best that can be said, — the injustice introduced is less than the injustice done away.

If imposition be at work, what is there in the security afforded against it by this arrangement, that can be relied upon for preventing it? The reward for dishonesty, instead of being held up to view upon the face of the will, must be covered up: as, in this like all other cases, it is most natural it should be. Confidence — a certain measure of it — is necessary to all conspiracies. In the case of murder, where the contriving head engages an executing hand, the stroke, if struck, must be struck either before payment, or not till afterwards: in the first case, the assassin trusts the suborner; in the other, the suborner trusts the assassin. Suppose no confidence, an unfair will can no more be set up for hire, than a murder can be committed from the same motive: suppose confidence, an unfair will may be set up as well when the legacy is made void, as when it is made payable.

By the act which this act takes upon itself to amend, three subscribing witnesses are made necessary. Under these circumstances (forgery out of the case,) no unfair will can have been brought into existence, without a conspiracy between that number of subscribing witnesses. But, in case of a set of persons thus linked together by interest and guilt, what difference can it make to them whether a legacy left to a subscribing witness is exigible or not exigible? Such as are the shares agreed upon, such, in so far as the conspirators are true to one another, will be the shares respectively received. If, when the time comes, the executor or other paymaster feels himself disposed to be false to his confederates, the circumstance of their wages being specified in the form of a legacy,

* This act is the 25th Geo. II. c. 6.[a] In the preamble to it may be seen an example of the sort of varnish with which, in English law more especially, the works of legislators, and in particular the works of lawyers in the way of legislation, are so constantly and diligently covered. From lawgivers so wise, what laws ever proceed but wise ones? But, of all marks of wisdom, what (according to the Spanish proverb) more abundant or genuine than doubts? As wisdom increases, doubts accordingly multiply. But, as there is a time for all things, so is there even for the removal of doubts: even of lawyers' doubts. Beards are also marks of wisdom: yet neither is shaving without its use. Too good ever to be altered, neither this law nor any other can ever be too good to be *explained*. A wise and good provision is the provision now in hand; the provision which, for the validity of this and that sort of will, requires "three or four credible witnesses:" but doubts have arisen under it what witnesses are to be deemed *legal* witnesses: the object of the new act is therefore to "avoid" those doubts; or, in other words, to remove them. Such, then, was the pretended function of the act: not alteration, but pure interpretation. What is its real function? Not interpretation, but alteration. Mischief, flagrant mischief, had been experienced: the cause of it was, partly the work of the legislator, the act itself, by which (without any notice to testators) witnesses in such a number were rendered necessary to the validity of a will; partly the work of the judge, by which the testimony of the description of persons most likely to be called in to subscribe, had so rashly been excluded. What, then, does the act? It puts an end to what the judges used to do, and does what it was not in their power to do: it receives the testimony of the so appointed witness, but deprives him of his legacy.

[a] This act is repealed, except as to the colonies, by 7 W. IV. and 1 Vict. c. 26.—*Ed.*

will not prevent his being false to them: if he is disposed to be true to them, the circumstance of their wages not being specified in that form, will not prevent his being true to them. The agreement made, and the executor pitched upon, of what use can it be to him, or to his accomplices, that the wages of their iniquity should be posted up on the face of the will? What security, what advantage can it be in any shape to any of the conspirators? The effect would be — what? Not to give security to the scheme, but to draw suspicion upon it, and endanger the success of it.

Put any case of unfairness — forgery, obtainment by compulsion, obtainment by misrepresentation and fraud; in either case, sanity or insanity: — the argument applies still with equal force.

The utility of the provision is, upon this view of it, greater in appearance than in reality: the mischievousness of it will be found greater in reality than in appearance.

The law of evidence, founded as it has been upon the principles that have been displayed, may be considered as a great school of injustice, in which nothing but injustice is to be learned, and in which every rule and maxim it gives birth to, imbibes the original taint, and comes out a lesson of injustice.

Distribution of the bulk of the property — donation of minor legacies. Such is the distinction, which though nowhere announced in words, nor even capable of being marked out by any precise boundary lines, is not the less perceptible upon the face of the generality of wills. By the former, the bulk of the property is distributed among the nearest relatives: by the latter, tokens of remembrance are given to persons situated without the pale of near relationship — to particular friends, to old and faithful servants. In the eyes of unsuspecting probity and uncorrupted common sense, how natural the association, how amiable the reciprocity, that the persons pitched upon to receive the token of affection should be the persons called upon to accept on their parts the honourable charge — to render on their parts the honourable service.

After making provision for the domestic circle — after taking care of his natural and necessary dependents, and mentioning in his will, not so much for provision as for honour, the most intimate of his friends without the circle, and the most confidential of his servants, — this, says he to them, addressing himself to them in language suited to their respective stations — this, says he, is my will, and be you my witnesses to it. The testator departed, and the will opened, up stands the legislator, and says to the family — *You see the legacies that were intended: do not pay them: you need not, unless you choose.* Do Englishmen in general accept of the offer thus made them by their rulers? I think better of them than to suppose it. The wages of iniquity are held out without ceasing, to corrupt the people; but I believe it is but here and there that in this instance they are accepted.

On this occasion, as on so many others, the iniquity of the law depends in no small degree upon the care taken to conceal the knowledge of it from the body of the people. Suppose the law in this behalf universally known, the effect of it would be simply to oblige testators to provide themselves with persons that are indifferent to their affections, to serve them for attesting witnesses: but in fact it is generally unknown; and thence comes the immoral tendency of the provision, as above held up to view.

Persons who set about the fabrication of false wills — these are the persons who will be sure to make themselves masters, as far as is in their power, of whatever has been done upon the subject by the law. Illiterate they cannot be: persons professionally acquainted with the law they will (some of them, the head manager at least, will) probably be: the suspicion and anxiety inseparably attached to guilt, especially to guilt in this insidious shape, will be almost sure to put them upon this inquiry in the first instance. These, then — the only description of persons against whose dishonesty the expedient is intended as a guard — are the very persons on whom it will not operate. They know, they knew well enough before the act, that a legacy given to any one of them would be enough, if not to destroy, at any rate to endanger, the whole will. By them, care will be taken not to insert any such legacy. The persons, the only persons, by whom any such legacy was ever likely to have been inserted, were real fair testators — testators meaning in the simplicity of their hearts to bestow these manifestations of kindness upon their friends, little suspecting that the same law which openly professes to give effect to a man's will, defeats it by counter-determinations, which it suffers to remain secret ones.

So much for the practical enactments of English law. The nomenclature used by lawyers on the subject of deeds and wills, is, in many instances, remarkably unhappy: the effect of it will naturally be to present erroneous conceptions — at least to all men but themselves.

1. *Deliver* used instead of *declare* or *recognise*. *I deliver this as my act and deed.* To this belongs the conjugate *delivery:* the delivery of a deed. But, in common speech, a thing that is said to be delivered is understood to pass out of the possession of the person by whom it is delivered, into the possession of some other person — the person (if there be any determinate person, which is

what the word seems to imply) to whom it is delivered. And such is the import given to it by lawyers themselves, in other cases: for instance, in the case of an action for goods sold and delivered. But, in the case of a deed, the instrument does not necessarily pass out of the possession of him whose deed it is, and by whom it is said to be delivered: it is only by accident, if it happens on that occasion to be delivered to anybody else; in particular, if at that same time it happens to be delivered to any of the other contracting parties. Of the word *declare*, the import is alike known to every man who is acquainted with the language. It conveys the idea meant to be conveyed: it conveys not to any mind any idea that is not on this occasion intended to be conveyed.

In the case of a will, the term is particularly improper. It is among the characteristic properties of this species of instrument, that no man has a right to have it delivered to him. The most natural and customary, and in most instances the most proper person to have the custody of it, is the testator himself.

True it is that the word *declaration* will not by itself serve to convey the whole of the signification which lawyers have contrived to include in the word *delivery*. This conjugate of the word declare, cannot of itself be made use of in this sense. In the phrase *I declare this to be my act and deed*, the sense is indeed as complete as in the phrase *I deliver this as my act and deed*. But, though the phrase *delivery of a deed or will* has a known meaning, the phrase *declaration of a deed or will* has no such meaning.

2. *Publication*, used as synonymous to *recognition*: publication, instead of *authentication*. In a case where concealment as against the public in general, and, in many instances, secrecy as towards every individual without exception, is a lawful and rational as well as a very common object, — *publication*, a word in general use to denote the opposite of concealment, to put a direct negative on every such idea as that of secrecy and concealment, is particularly incongruous. An object which (as above mentioned) calls for the legislator's care, is the making provision for rendering it practicable to a testator to give a sufficient authentication to his will, at the same time that even the fact of his having made a will remains a secret to all the world. *Secret authentication* is a term I can, on this occasion, make use of without impropriety and without scruple. But *secret publication?* Who could be allowed to speak of secret publication? By whom would any such expression be endured?

The word *authentication*, correct and expressive as it is, I would nevertheless have avoided, could I have found a more familiar one that were equally expressive, to take its place. Why? For this reason, that it is not so familiar as could be wished. By the bulk of the people it would scarce be understood without inquiry and explanation. But a word which, until explained, may chance to convey no idea, is better beyond comparison than a word which, to every one who hears it, presents a false one — produces a degree of misconception such as nothing but long practice in the use of an incongruous language will enable a man effectually to get the better of. For my own part, familiarized as I am with a system of nomenclature which seems to have had confusion and uncertainty for its object, in the present instance I can never get rid of the impression without pain and difficulty. How much more difficult the task to the unlettered peasant, the handicraft, the petty shopkeeper!

This caution will be apt to appear inconceivable to a lawyer. But, to a man to whom it would be matter of regret and even of shame not to be understood, and above all in matters of law, nomenclature is no light matter. On a man who cares not whether the law be understood or no, or who, if he saw to the bottom of his own mind, would acknowledge (as some have done) that it should be either not understood or misunderstood by the generality of his fellow-subjects, matters of this sort sit light and easy.

3. *Execution*, instead of *recognition*. Ambiguity and uncertainty, one would think, were the very ends in view of jurisprudence. She has certainly no dislike to them, nor any the smallest desire to get rid of them. Speaking of a testator, they say he *executes* his will. What then? Is he the executor of his own will? Not he, any more than the executioner of it.* The *executor* is another person. But the *executor* of the will, — of him is it not also said sometimes that he *executes* it?

Connected with the verb *to execute*, is its conjugate the substantive *execution*. Whose act, then, is it, that is expressed by the term *execution?* May it not be the act of the testator? May it not alike be the act of the executor, whose act it can never be in the other sense?

So, again, in the case of a contract. One mode of executing it is to authenticate the instrument by which the obligations are ex-

* The executioner of it, without much impropriety, might be termed the lawyer, and his dupe the legislator; who, satisfied in his own conscience of the fairness of it, puts it to death, because the testator neglected to comply with this or that requisition, the existence of which it had been rendered impossible for him to be apprized of — the knowledge of which had never travelled beyond the breast that hatched it: made, as the requisitions of jurisprudence are so often made, after the man who is punished for the non-observance of them was no longer in existence.

pressed; another way is to fulfil those obligations. What a nomenclature, in which the same word is employed to express the creation of an obligation and the annihilation of it!

CHAPTER VI.

OF PREAPPOINTED EVIDENCE, CONSIDERED AS APPLIED TO LAWS.

PREAPPOINTED evidence having been considered (as above) in its application to legalized contracts — to those private sorts of laws, in the establishment of which the legislator and the individuals empowered by him operate in conjunction, — we come now to speak of the same principle considered in its application to *laws* in the common acceptation of the word; viz. those rules of action, in the establishment of which the legislator operates alone.

Naturally, the consideration of the simple object should have preceded that of the complex. But, by bringing to view the subject of legalized contracts in the first instance, an object of reference and comparison was set up, by which, now that the application of the principle to *laws* is brought upon the carpet, suggestions not uninstructive may be afforded.

Of the four evils, to the prevention of which the application of the principle has been seen to be capable of being directed in the case of legalized contracts, there are two — viz. *spuriousness* and *unfairness* — to the prevention of which, in the case of *laws*, it is in the practice of nations so generally and habitually directed, that the application of it can scarcely be considered as an object of inquiry belonging to the present work.

There remain two other evils; viz. non-notoriety with respect to existence, and uncertainty with respect to import. Happy the lot of mankind — much happier than, in England more especially, it is in a way speedily to be — if, for the defence of the community against these crying mischiefs, the principle of preappointed evidence had received the all-embracing application it is capable of, or even a degree of application equal in extent to that which it has received in the case of contracts.

In the case of a contract, scription, considered in the character of a security against non-notoriety in respect to the existence of the contract and uncertainty as to its import, suggests itself naturally to individual reason; and would, by individual reason, be, in an extensive degree, even without the intervention of legislative authority, adopted.

When the practice of the art of writing had begun to be to a certain degree general, in such sort that any factitious *demand* for service in this line seemed no longer in danger of not being followed by supply, — the legislator was, with few or no exceptions, among the civilized or civilizing nations of Europe, seen to interpose his authority: converting into a legal obligation a precaution to which, till then, had belonged no other origin than individual prudence.

In the instance of individuals, this precaution, in so far as freely adopted, had for its manifest and indisputable final cause, the prevention of those evils. But on the part of the legislator, — at any rate on the part of those by whose counsels the hand of the legislator was on this occasion put in motion and guided, — this precaution had no such final cause.

The class of persons by whose counsels the hand of the legislator was at that time, and in general, throughout the civilized part of the world, continues to be, guided, were and are professional lawyers: men who, whether in their original character of advocates, or in their subsequential and superior character of judges, were and are, under the influence of the fee-gathering principle, knit together into a compact body by the strongest and most indissoluble ties — by one common interest, impelling them in a direction in almost every turn opposite to the interest of the community over which they rule, and which they profess to serve.

Individuals, in the use spontaneously made of writing, had of course (as above mentioned) for their object and final cause, the prevention of the evils above mentioned; viz. *non-notoriety* (including *oblivion*) in regard to the existence of the contract, and *uncertainty* in regard to the import and effect of it.

Lawyers, the persons by whose counsels the hand of the legislator was guided, had not, — in the nature of man they could not have had, — any such object. Their object was, the making of power, influence, and profit for themselves; i.e. *the making of business* — in their case the natural, and naturally the sole, parent of that amiable progeny. So accordingly they ordered matters, that what they had ordained to be written, none but a lawyer could be supposed to be, indeed scarce any could be, competent to write.

Had the prevention of those evils — or of any evils other than the only one to which, in their situation, it was in the nature of man that their sensitive faculty should be sensible, viz. *insufficiency of business* — been in their wishes and endeavours, — the anxiety thus manifested by them to see those same evils prevented, in so far as liable to have place in the case of those expressions of will in the formation of which the individual and the legislator were acting in conjunction, would have applied itself, and with equal force, to all those expressions of the will, in the formation of which the legislator (by himself, or his subordinates and substitutes the judges) acts alone.

But, in regard to the rule of action, by whomsoever framed, the real object has ever been (what, under such circumstances, it never can cease to be) not the prevention of uncertainty, but the increase of it. Hence it is, that, throughout the sphere of their influence, but nowhere with so much zeal and success as under the British constitution (under which their influence has by a concurrence of causes been rendered in a peculiar degree extensive and irresistible,) — it has been a rule of conduct with the legislature to leave the rule of other men's action in a state of as complete uncertainty, or rather inscrutability and non-existence, as possible.

Instead of declaring, himself, what, on each part of the field of his authority, his will is, the course which, under the direction of these his treacherous guides, he has so assiduously pursued, has been to abstain from making known his will, or so much as forming one.

Everywhere (but nowhere among civilized men so completely as in Great Britain,) he has given up his subjects to the tormentors: he has given them up to be tormented without mercy, and in all imaginable ways, for non-compliance with a will which it has been the care of the tormentors should never be declared, nor so much as formed: tormented for non-compliance, where compliance was and is (having been studiously and effectually caused to be so) impossible.

Not but that there has all along been a pretended rule of action—a pretence for vexation and pillage never wanting. But this pretended rule of action, what has it been — what is it? A mere phantom—a figment of the imagination; in the composition of which the legislator himself, whose will it is pretended to be, has never had any the smallest share.

Dragged under the rod (though, where anything is to be got by excluding him, neither compelled nor suffered to come into the presence) of one of these lawyers or companies of lawyers, — a man is in one or other way vexed, and always by them and for their benefit, on pretence of his not having done something which he was never commanded to do, or having done something which he never was commanded not to do. Under the name of punishment, or under some other name, he is thus vexed: and, from such observation as men cannot be prevented from taking of the individual case in which the man is thus vexed, other men are left to frame to themselves, as they can, the conception of a law or rule of law: a rule or law completely imaginary, not framed by the legislator, nor so much as by the immediate author of the vexation, the judge: an imaginary law, such as, had it been real, might have warranted the decision under and by virtue of which he is thus vexed.

Where the rule of action is in the form of common law, there is no such thing, properly speaking, as a law, a general law: there is no such thing as any act of the legislator, any expression of the will of the legislator, in the case. The judge, to warrant his proceeding, is forced to have recourse to fiction — to feign the existence of a law, and, upon the ground of this imaginary law, to proceed as if it were a real one. He takes a survey of the cases that present themselves as bearing the closest analogy to the particular case in hand; he observes the decisions that have been pronounced by judges, by himself, his colleagues, or their predecessors, on the occasion of those cases; he considers with himself what the tenor or purport of a law would have been, supposing a law, a real law, made in terms such as would have warranted the decisions that (as above) he finds to have been pronounced, together with the decision which, in the case in question, he proposes to himself (on the presumption of its conformity to the general complexion of those decisions) to pronounce; and, upon this feigned law, the work of his own imagination, he passes judgment as if it were a real one.

Ask them in what *words* this pretended will stands expressed: — no answer; for answer is impossible.

Ask them at what *time*, in what *place*, it was formed and expressed: — still the same necessary silence.

Ask them by *whom* made or by *whom* expressed: — either silence or stark falsehood. Was it by them, or any of them? God forbid! they know their duty better: their bounden duty, their only right, is, not to *make* law, but *declare* it. Declare what? Declare that to have been made, which to their own perfect knowledge never was made? Give their own fictions, their own interest-begotten falsehoods, for realities?

Nullis lex verbis, à nullo, nullibi, nunquam.
Law, in no words — by no one — never — made.

Such is the phantom, the god of their own making, to which, under the eye of a conniving legislator, they compel obedience, or rather submission, on the part of his subjects; and in the name of which those too-patient subjects suffer themselves to be tormented, as if it were of flesh and blood. This is that idol, so indefatigably bedaubed with praise, in comparison with which all other praise is cold: — the wisdom of ages — the perfection of reason — that of which reason is the life.

Well might they cause it to be ordained, that contracts (those declarations of individual will to which they profess to give binding force) should be in writing, and thence provided with determinate assemblages of words for the expression of them: since, whatever degree of certainty might have been produced by those portions of written law, is obliterated by the patches of this species of unwritten unformed law, with which they are everywhere overlaid. The contract, which forms the apparent and pretended rule of action, is visible: but the practice, or conjectural rule of law, by which it will be found to have been annulled, or misinterpreted, or interpreted away, is not visible; nor can the effect of it be known, till, after the substance of the parties has been consumed in litigation, the existence of this rule is declared, that is to say, the rule is made, by the judge.

Thus it is, that, by requiring contracts to be in writing, they have thrown profit into their own hands. Had certainty been produced, their mass of profit would have been diminished. If, under such strong inducement to the contrary, certainty had been given by one branch of the partnership to the contract as it stood upon the face of its own words, that certainty would by another, the higher banch of that same partnership, be overruled and done away: by dint of nullities, seconded by a set of mutually conflicting and universally flexible rules of interpretation or construction, as they are called, and other unpromulgated, and unenacted, and spurious laws, of the same fantastic fabric: laws, which are neither laws of nullification nor laws of interpretation.

By notification of contracts themselves, nothing effectual is done — no security afforded, any further than as the effect which those contracts will have, is made known. But the effect of those contracts can no further be made known, than in so far as, in effect, and (to that end) in tenor, those rules are made known, by which the effect of the contracts is obliterated or transmuted.

But, by causing the tenor of these rules (that is to say, of any rules that have been or could be framed and settled in relation to the subject) to be consigned to determinate assemblages of words, — and thus, in manner as above proposed, or in any other manner, brought home, on the occasions which call for their being acted under, to the mind of those whose lot in life is made to rest upon them; by any such course, the real object of the whole system would, to so wide an extent, be counteracted and defeated: and hence it is, that as well those as any other arrangements, the effect of which would be to render knowledge possible, where ignorance has been made fatal, will, till they are accomplished (should it be their lot ever to be accomplished,) be reprobated, and pronounced (as everything that is good ever has been, and ever will be, by those to whose sinister interests, and interest-begotten prejudices, its aspect is unfavourable) to be theoretical, and speculative, and visionary, and mischievous, and impracticable.

When, by proper authority (by the authority of the legislator,) a law is abrogated, — the fact of its abrogation is no more exposed to doubt than the fact of its enactment: the same evidence, the same preappointed evidence, that serves for the establishment of the one fact, serves for the establishment of the other.

When, by improper, by usurped authority — by the authority of the sworn servant of the legislator, the judge, overruling and contemning the authority of his master — any such power is exercised, — confusion, confusion ever delightful and profitable to the authors of it, is the consequence.

By some compiler or copyist of statutes, the date of whose labour stands antecedent to the invention of printing, laws anterior to the reign of Henry III. were (at whose, if at any one's, suggestion, or by what authority, is now undiscoverable) omitted. By this man, whoever he was, all those ancient laws were abrogated in the lump — abrogated, to use the language of Scotch law, by desuetude.

But *desuetude* is not a *person*, a legislator by whom laws can be abrogated: abrogated on pretence of desuetude, a law cannot but have been abrogated by the judge.

In Scotland, the expression of the will of the legitimate legislator is thus abrogated — abrogated *ad libitum*, by the judge, the Court of Session: abrogated, in virtue (it should seem) of what in Latin they call their *nobile officium*, — in English, the right, the avowed right, of doing what they please.

If in England this right has been no less constantly, and to a still greater extent, exercised, and by corresponding authority, it has never been avowed; it has as constantly been all the while disavowed and disclaimed.

CHAPTER VII.

OF PUBLIC OFFICES AT LARGE, CONSIDERED AS REPOSITORIES AND SOURCES OF PREAPPOINTED EVIDENCE.*

§ 1. *Official evidence, what — Topics for discussion.*

In respect of the *operation* performed in execution of the functions, powers, and duties, for the execution of which the office was established, or is kept on foot, and the *facts*, or *alleged facts*, on which these operations are grounded, — every office (be its functions, powers, and duties, what they may) may be considered as a repository or source of preappointed evidence; it being among the objects in view in the institution of the office, that, as the facts come into existence or under review, the remembrance of them should be preserved.

Such was the advantage derivable and de-

* See the author's further remarks on this subject in the Introduction to the *Rationale of Evidence*, Chap. XVI. *supra*, p. 72.

rived to justice, in some measure, from official situations; even in those times of intellectual darkness, in which, even among persons constituted in authority, the practice of the art of writing was not in universal use.*

But, by the extension which that master art has acquired, especially after the aid it has received from the operations of the press, whatever use may in this shape be derivable from the several public offices, has received in point of extent a prodigious increase.

In respect of the several legally-operative, or in any other point of view useful and important, facts, in this manner (whether with or without design) more or less effectually secured against oblivion, against concealment, and misrepresentation, — so far as these desirable effects are actually produced, so far all is well: that which is done coincides *pro tanto* with that which ought to be done; and, on this part of the field of legislation, nothing remains to be done by the legislator himself, or heard by him from any other quarter in the way of suggestion or advice.

But, in whatever degree, under the government of each country, it may happen to those several important objects to be actually and habitually accomplished, some considerations may be brought to view, which as yet will not be found altogether undeserving of notice, and which may be ranged under the following heads; viz. —

1. Uses derived or derivable from the masses of pre-appointed evidence, of which the several public offices are, or might conveniently be, rendered the repositories or the sources.

2. By what considerations a just estimate may be formed of the degree of verity or trustworthiness of the evidence thus afforded.

3. By what means the verity of the statements or narrations thus delivered, may most effectually be secured.

4. By what means the quantity of true and instructive evidence obtainable from these repositories or sources, may, upon terms of the greatest, and that preponderant, advantage, be increased: with preponderant advantage, reference being made to the several ends of justice, as well as to the sources derivable from the several departments of government, to which the offices in question respectively belong.

§ 2. *Uses derivable from official evidence.*

Considered in the most general point of view, the evidence furnished by the several public offices, and (in virtue of the evidence so furnished) the institution of those offices themselves, may be seen at first glance to be, in two distinguishable ways, conducive to the ends of justice, and in particular to the support of the rights and obligations established or meant to be established by the law.

1. By means of evidence of that description, a multitude of facts, of which, on different accounts, men are concerned to be informed, and, in particular, facts of the legally operative class, are preserved from oblivion and concealment: — facts of which the remembrance would not otherwise be preserved.

2. The statements or narrations of which the matter of this official body of evidence is composed, present, under certain conditions, in virtue of the situation from which they issue, or into which they have been received, a degree of trustworthiness — a title to credence — beyond what could reasonably be looked for on the part of so many statements or narrations to the same effect, if issuing from so many individuals taken at large.

More evidence, and that better: — such, in five words, are the advantages or uses derived from official situations, considered, in the most general point of view, in the character of *sources* or *repositories* of evidence.

Contemplating now in a nearer point of view the uses derivable from preappointed evidence of this description, we shall find one and the same article or mass of evidence useful in that character to different persons, in as many different ways.

In the carrying on of the various operations included in the aggregate term government, it will frequently happen that the knowledge of the same event or state of things shall be necessary to different functionaries, acting in so many different departments of government. Thus it is that the same article or mass of official evidence is applicable to divers *uses*, correspondent to the different departments to the business of which the knowledge of the fact evidenced by it is subservient.

Take, then, any government office whatsoever: the written evidence of which that

* In the official establishment of the city of London there exists still one officer, the *remembrancer*, whose principal if not sole function originally consisted in the preserving in his memory the *remembrance* of such facts as it might happen to the city, in its corporate capacity, to have a special interest in bringing to view, especially in presenting to the cognizance of the superior authorities.

When the practice of the act of writing, though not unknown, was still comparatively rare, printing not as yet invented, such was the importance attributed to that branch of learned industry, that the bare custody of the fruits of it constituted an office, to which the judicial constituted but an appendage. In proof of this, note the name of *recorder*, by which the principal local and permanent judge is designated in some of the principal towns in England, the metropolis included; and the name of *master* (originally *clerk*) *of the rolls*, the sole appellation of the Equity-Court-judge, whose jurisdiction, though subordinate to, wants little of being co-extensive with, the judicial authority of the Lord High Chancellor, the highest amongst the English judges.

office is the repository, and even the testimonial evidence of which it may eventually be the source, — that is, each or any article, or competent mass of it, — will be found susceptible of a variety of appropriate uses, some direct and constant, others collateral, and, comparatively speaking, indirect.

By the term *direct* uses, may be understood such uses and purposes to which the receipt and conservation of the evidence in question cannot but have been directed: the knowledge of the facts thus evidenced being necessary to the due performance of the operations, for the performance of which the office in question was instituted and established.

What follows concerns the *collateral* uses, to which it may happen to one and the same article of evidence — official evidence — to be applicable.

Suppose, on the occasion of a suit (non-penal or penal) instituted, or in a way to be instituted, between any two or more parties, this or that matter of fact requiring to be proved or disproved, whether in the character of a principal fact, or in that of an evidentiary fact. Evidence of this fact is afforded by the books kept in and for the purposes of the office; or by the testimony of some person to whose knowledge, in virtue of the situation occupied by him in that office, the fact in question happened to present itself. Here we have one sort of *collateral* use derivable from the body of preappointed evidence, of which the particular office in question is the repository or the source.

The sort of collateral use thus capable of being derived from any article of official evidence, may be termed its *judicial* use.

The books of the English office (for example) called the Navy Office or Navy Board, have for their direct object the recordation of such facts to which it may happen to require to be present to the mind of this or that official person employed in giving existence and direction to that part of the national force, in all its several shapes, which has the sea for its field of action. But, in the discharge of this function, it has happened to the persons under whose charge some of the books belonging to that office have been placed, to make entry of the deaths of persons of certain descriptions, who, while living, entered into the composition of that force.

Again; in official situations, as in all other situations, men are liable to misconduct themselves. Suppose in any such office — in a word, in any office whatsoever — an act of transgression committed, or supposed to be committed, by any officer belonging to it: — on the question, whether the act in question has been committed by the official person in question; or on the question, whether such act, if committed, is an act of transgression; recourse is had to the evidence furnished by the books kept, or papers received and preserved, for the purpose of the direct business of the office. Evidence thus applied, having evidently a double use, presents itself under a sort of mixed character. If the transgression, or supposed misconduct, is such as, for the prevention of it in future, and for the rendering due satisfaction for the past, requires not the interference of any public functionary other than the chief of the department to which the office in question belongs,—the use then made of it may be considered as coming under the description of the direct use: and the functionary to whom it is of use, and to the discharge of whose functions it is subservient, is no other than the *administrator* — *i.e.* the chief of the department for the use of which the article in question has been produced, or received and preserved.*

In this same case, suppose the gravity of the transgression, in the eyes of those to whom it belongs to pronounce, to be such as to call for a prosecution — non-penal, for the mere recovery of the money so diverted into an improper channel — or penal, for the punishment of him by whose transgression it was thus diverted: — the evidence, which before was evidence for the use of the administrator only, is now become evidence for the use of the judge.

Suppose that, in consideration of some such instances of transgression already committed (as above supposed,) or in contemplation of any such instances of transgression as being liable to happen for want of proper checks and safeguards, it occurs to the legislator to call for the production of the books of the department in question, in the view of observing upon what principle, and in what mode, the operations of that department are carried on and recorded: — here, in the person of the legislator, we have another functionary—the legislator, to whose use, in such his character, the same article or mass of evidence may happen to be found subservient.

The sort of collateral use thus capable of being derived from any article of official evidence, may be termed the statistic use.†

* Thus, suppose an office belonging to the department of finance. An officer causes or permits the money lying at the disposal of the office to be applied to his own use, or to some other use not comprised in the number of the uses to which it was destined. From the same books, by which, had the application made of the money been proper, evidence of such proper application would have been presented, — evidence of the improper application in question may be deducible.

† Of the official evidence of which the several public offices are the repositories or sources, the statistic use, as above described, is every now and then made, under the British constitution (though not to a degree of extent or constancy nearly sufficient,) by committees of one or other House of Parliament. Of this use, the operations of the House of Commons finance committee, of the

§ 3. *Sources of trustworthiness and untrustworthiness in the case of official evidence.*

In point of trustworthiness, whatever superiority can be possessed by officia. evidence considered as such, presents itself as standing upon one or other of two distinguishable foundations: —

1. Pre-eminent *responsibility:* a degree of responsibility beyond what is to be found in the situation of the majority of the members of the community taken at large. In proportion to the value of the office — of whatsoever elements that value may be composed — emolument, *power,* and *dignity* (the efficient cause of the respect habitually paid to the possessor of the office, as such, by the community at large;) — in proportion to the magnitude of that value, in all those shapes taken together, the man in office has so much more to lose (*i. e.* that he is *capable* of losing) than the man not in office: so much, by the loss of which he is *capable* of being subjected to a species and quantity of punishment, to which an individual at large cannot be subjected.

2. Presumable impartiality: — of the situation in which a man is placed by the possession of the office, the effect (it is supposed) being such as to place him out of the reach of those self-regarding and other interests, to the sinister influence of which, the testimony of an individual taken at large stands exposed.

Of *responsibility,* in the sense above explained, the influence, in the character of an efficient cause of, or security for, trustworthiness in testimony, and in particular in case of official testimony, seems out of dispute.

But, from the efficiency of that influence in the character in question, the same situation affords drawbacks, and those of no mean account, the neglect of which would be productive of much error in practice.

1. Employed in the sense above explained, responsibility — the term responsibility — may be said to be understood in its *beneficial* sense: in the sense in which, so far as it has place, its operation is purely beneficial to the individual in whom the quality of responsibility is considered as inhering. But in this sense responsibility on the part of any person is no otherwise contributory to the trustworthiness of his testimony, than in as far as he is also responsible in what may be termed its *burthensome* sense: a sense extremely different from the other, though so habitually confounded with it under the same appellative. It is only in so far as in case of transgression he is *liable* to lose — actually liable, and eventually subject, to the burthen of loss, or to the bearing of a burthen in some other shape, — that a man's having more, by the loss of which, if lost, he would be a sufferer, affords any reason for regarding his testimony as superior in point of trustworthiness to that of one who has not so much to lose.

years 1797 and 1798, affords the most extensive and efficient exemplification that is to be found in the history of the British or any other nation.

In point of *magnitude* (*i. e.* possible magnitude,) the value of the eventual suffering, of which the responsibility and consequent security is composed, is increased: but, in point of *probability,* it may be diminished.

The existence of responsibility in this its burthensome sense being a *causa sine quâ non* to the efficiency and utility of its influence, in the respect in question, in its beneficial sense, — the *causes* by which a deficiency of it in its burthensome sense is liable to be produced, present a claim to notice.

1. Superior and unamenable power. If, in the case of incorrectness or prejudicial incompleteness on the part of his testimony, the situation of the official person in question be such as to place him out of the reach of punishment in any shape, — the security afforded by his responsibility, in the beneficial sense of the word, amounts to nothing. Instead of being less, he is more apt to transgress in this way, than an individual taken at large. Examples are too prominent to need mentioning.*

In this case, the beneficial influence of eventual punishment is done away, because, even supposing detection performed, and transgression manifest, punishment will not follow.

But, in a situation of the kind in question, whether the application of punishment in case of detection be or be not obstructed, detection itself is apt to be prevented or obstructed.

* Hence, in a constitution such as the British, the danger attendant on placing in any situation of extensive power a person too nearly allied to the crown: the *jus nocendi,* which, by the necessity of onerously responsible co-operators, has been taken away from the monarch himself, is thus conferred upon his relative.

In the reign of Queen Anne, the husband of the monarch was commander-in-chief of the naval force: in the burthensome sense, the domestic superior of the irresponsible monarch could not, practically speaking, be considered as responsible. But to his office a council was attached; in such sort that the power exercised by him was in fact exercised in and by a board — a board, of which the members were not in the onerous sense irresponsible, their responsibility being in this board not destroyed, nor otherwise weakened than in as far as, in every board acting on the ordinary terms, responsibility is weakened.

Other circumstances contributed, moreover, in this instance, to lessen the inconvenience. Being a foreigner, little acquainted with the state of persons and things in England, the Danish prince was in that respect the less disposed to apply to the business with an independent and peremptory will; while the mildness of his temper, as well as of that of his august consort, concurred in promoting the same salutary result.

When the operation is thus exempt from danger, lies are a sort of article, which whosoever, having power, conceives it worth his while to bespeak, may command in any quantity, as well as (subject to the condition of security against detection, as above) of any quality, he can desire. Be the proposition what it will, so that in a competent proportion the matter of reward be attached to the act of signing it, it can never want for signatures. And, in such case, what is really the fact of which the signature affords the proof? Not that the subscriber really believes the supposed fact which by his signature he declares himself to believe; but that in some shape or other he has been paid, or expects to be paid, for writing it.

In this case, — so far as the *responsibility*, in the beneficial sense of the word, is the result of the emolument, power, or dignity attached to the office,— the higher the degree of the responsibility, the more completely is it destructive of the trustworthiness of the office, in regard to the statement or declaration thus made: since the more a man has to gain by falsehood (the force of the tutelary, the mendacity-restraining motives, being the same in both cases,) the more likely he is to commit it.

Take any given mass of absurdity, howsoever palpable: — a man who would not by his signature declare his belief in it for £14 a-year, would with great readiness do so for £14,000, were it only for the sake of the abundance of good which it would be in his power to do with it.

2. If, in the particular instance in question, in case of incorrectness or incompleteness on the part of the statement, the existence of such cause of deception be unknown — unknown to every one but him whose statement it is, — the influence of his situation, on the occasion in question, in the character of a cause of trustworthiness, may be set down as equal to 0.

In this case are all statements concerning any of those self-regarding psychological facts, in regard to which, in case of falsehood, the falsehood finds no physical fact so connected with it as to contradict and disprove it. Take, for example, a declaration of opinion or belief. No absurdity can imagination itself figure to itself greater than many a one in which many a man has declared his belief, and (so far as can be inferred from his actions) even with sincerity and truth. The absurdity of the fact, or rather of the proposition, not being capable of affording any conclusive evidence of the mendacity of the assertion whereby a man declares his belief of it; hence it is, that, so far as the absurdity of the prejudice is a proof of the falsity of the proposition whereby a belief in it is asserted, there is no proposition so absurd, no proposition so palpably false, in which — in office as well as out of office — in the highest, and in the beneficial sense the most responsible offices, as well as in the lowest and least responsible ones — the legislator may not make sure of causing belief to be declared, by any number of persons from whom the extraction of declarations of this sort is regarded by him as conducive to the ends which he has in view.

The words by which the declaration itself is expressed — and, moreover, the fact that it is by the individual in question that such declaration has been made — may be in any degree notorious, known to every member of the community without exception; yet still the *abstruseness of the subject*, howsoever produced, whether by the nature of the subject or by human artifice, may, in case of falsity, afford such a degree of security against detection, and thence against responsibility in the burthensome sense, as shall be sufficient to do away in a great proportion, if not altogether, whatever degree of security for trustworthiness may stand attached to the office on the score of responsibility in the beneficial sense.

Scarce a day passes in which, in the ordinary course of business — that is, of the fee-gathering husbandry — an English judge, of the learned and superior class on which that official title is in a manner exclusively bestowed, does not, by his signature or by his connivance, give utterance and currency to falsehoods in abundance: but, except to those who are either in the habit or the expectation of deriving profit from the same source, either the fact of the falsity is unknown, or, in consequence of the deception that has been practised upon them, men have been taught to look upon such falsehood as being either necessary, or in some unknown way or other conducive, to the attainment of the ends of justice.

3. Aggregation of a number of colleagues in office in such manner as to constitute a *body corporate*, or *board*.

Superiority of power, and non-notoriety of the falsity of the statement made, or (what comes to the same thing) of the part taken by the official person in question in the making of such false statement, have already been mentioned as two circumstances, each of them having its separate operation in the character of a drawback on that degree of superordinary trustworthiness which has the official situation for its source or efficient cause.

By the junction made of the individual in question with others in a board, both these drawbacks are made to centre in the same person. To the power derived from his own situation, each member of the corporate body or board adds the power derived from the situation and connexions of his several colleagues. A board is thus a rampart of defence, behind which each of its members finds a place of security against all attacks of the nature of those of which responsibility in the burthensome sense is the result. Bandied to and fro amongst a number of individuals, on no one of whom it can fasten to the exclusion of the rest, the disrepute (whatever it be) which in the case in question, were it the case of a single individual, would attach itself to the falsity, remains in the present case in a state of suspense, not being able to find any one of them to fix upon. To each of the members which compose it, it is the nature of a *board* to serve as a screen from responsibility in the burthensome sense—a screen from whatever punishment or disrepute is, in the case in question, meant, or pretended to be meant, to be attributed to transgression: to transgression, as in other shapes at large, so in the shape of falsehood—the only shape in which it comes in question here.

By the want of responsibility in the burthensome sense, attached to the essence of a board, inferiority instead of superiority in point of trustworthiness may be attached, not only to such statements in the delivery of which the members of the board speak in the character of percipient witnesses, but to statements which, having been delivered in the like character by officers subject to the authority of the board, receive from the board an attestation of verity, express or virtual, in the way of discourse or in the way of deportment; viz. by being acted upon by the board as if believed to be true.

In any such subordinate situation, falsehood and misrepresentation may be produced by sinister interest, not only in a pecuniary shape, but in the shape of indolence or love of ease: and not only, as above, by a vicious state of the will, but by a weak or vicious state of the intellectual faculties: particularly where the business of the office is of such a nature, that the statements and representations made by such subordinates are such as come under the denomination of *scientific evidence*.

In political administration, a board, in contradistinction to individual management, is an invention which, throughout the sphere of its authority, has for its properties and effects the securing transgression against punishment, the depriving merit of its reward, the extinction of emulation and consequent exertion, the perpetuation of incapacity, indolence, and negligence—in a word, of misconduct in every shape imaginable: and this not so much on the part of the members of the board itself, which by the prominence of its situation engages in some measure the public eye, as on the part of the subordinate functionaries; whose functions, while they have little to attract the eye of the public, have much to repel it, and who are the less looked after by the public, in proportion as they are supposed to be well looked after by their superiors at the board.

The tendency of the sort of institution in question to produce misconduct in any other shape than that of falsehood and misrepresentation, belongs not to the present purpose. But, this chapter having among its objects the showing how to form a just estimate of the trustworthiness of official evidence, and how to render it more trustworthy than it has been found to be in practice, it became a necessary task to inquire by what causes its experienced deficiency in point of trustworthiness is produced: and among these causes, one of the most efficient was found to be, the artificial union thus effected among the highest stationed of the hands by which the business of office is performed; viz. in respect of the deficiency thence resulting in point of *responsibility*, taken in the *burthensome* sense.*

So much for the drawbacks from the superior trustworthiness supposed to be attached to official evidence on the ground of responsibility. Remains to be estimated the amount of the superior trustworthiness supposed to be attached to it on the ground of presumable *impartiality*.

Supposing the impartiality perfect, and the existence of this important though negative quality out of doubt, the trustworthiness of the evidence, in so far as depends upon the state of the moral faculties of him whose statement it exhibits, is beyond dispute.

In the case of official evidence, it is no uncommon case for the testimony, so far as depends upon impartiality, to be in this perfect state. In the case where the purpose to which the evidence is applied is a judicial purpose, be the office what it may, this impartiality may, it should seem, be stated as the natural state of things. In an official book an entry is supposed to have been made of the birth of the plaintiff, or the marriage or death of one under whom he claims. It can only be in consequence of some comparatively rare accident, if the keeper of the official book was, at the time in question, exposed to the influence of any interest by which he could have been so much as excited to suppress an entry

* It would be an error, if, from what is said above, a conclusion were formed that there exists not any case in which government by bodies corporate or boards can be conducive to the legitimate ends of government. Where, in the conduct of the business of the department, neither extraordinary talent nor extraordinary exertion are necessary,—as where money is to be received, kept, and given out, according to directions given by other hands,—at the same time that misapplication of the money, if attempted, would be manifest, or easily detected,—there the force of the objections which apply to it in other cases is either done away altogether, or much diminished: and in so far as division of power is necessary to good government, the institution is indispensable.

to the effect in question—to insert an entry totally false—or, in the description given of the fact in question, to insert a circumstance known by him who inserts it to be false: and so in regard to an entry supposed to have been made in this or that book belonging to this or that judicial office; an entry, for example, of a judicial incidental order supposed to have been made, or final judgment supposed to have been pronounced. Impartiality is, in a case of this sort, the ordinary and probable state of the mind of the official narrating witness. Why? For this, amongst other reasons, viz. that, at the time at which the entry is or ought to be made, the application which eventually comes to be made of the evidence to the judicial purpose in question (whether it bears, when it does take place, any relation or not to his interest) cannot be so much as present to his mind.

But this quality, though a natural accompaniment of official evidence, is not a necessary one: and it would be a mischievous error, if, because in ninety-nine instances out of one hundred, the application of the securities for correctness and completeness is unnecessary, in the hundredth in which it is necessary it should, by any such general conception of superior trustworthiness, be prevented from being made.

In judging of the degree of credit due to the testimony of a witness taken at large, a question that can never cease to be relevant is, Had he any interest in misrepresenting the fact in any respect?—and, in judging of the degree of credit due to the statement of the official testimony expressed in writing or otherwise by one official person, the same question can never cease, in this particular case, to be as pertinent and proper as in the general case.

Among the uses above stated as derivable from official evidence, is the use adapted to that accidental and comparatively unfrequent, but never to be neglected, class of cases, in which, on the occasion of some transgression imputed to this or that official person belonging to the office, the same article of official evidence which in the ordinary state of things is of use only to the *administrator* (*i. e.* to some one or more of the officers belonging to the department in question, or other officers or individuals holding correspondence with it,) becomes evidence to, and to the use of, the judge. But in this class of cases, and it is not a narrow one, nothing can be more obvious or undeniable, than that, so far as depends upon presumable impartiality and nothing more, official evidence—the official evidence in question, so far from being a point of trustworthiness above the level, will stand below the level, of evidence taken at large.

---

§ 4. *Rules for estimating and securing trustworthiness in the case of official evidence.*

Principles being laid down, a few observations, bringing to view (in principle at least) the arrangements that have presented themselves as conducive to the forming, in the case of official evidence, a just estimate of its trustworthiness, may perhaps be not without their use. And the same rules which serve for showing in what degree such evidence of that description as is found in existence is possessed of that desirable quality, will serve for indicating in some measure such arrangements as promise to be conducive to the giving of that same desirable quality to evidence of the like description as it may be destined to come into existence in future.

Rule 1. To form a just estimate of the trustworthiness of an article of official evidence, look out for the several causes of inferiority that are liable to have place in regard to evidence at large;—viz. 1. That which has place in the case of circumstantial evidence; the fact spoken to not the very fact in question, but a fact considered as evidentiary of it;—2. That which has place in the case of unoriginal evidence; where, between the information supposed to have been given by the percipient witness, and the ear or the eye of him to whom it belongs to judge, one or more media of transmission are supposed to have intervened;—3. That which has place in the case of free and uninterrogated statements, where the information in question, as above (whether any such media of transmission have intervened or no,) has been made without being subjected to the influence of interrogation, or eventual punishment, in the character of securities for correctness and completeness;—4. That which, on the part of a witness of any description (viz. extrajudicially percipient and narrating, extrajudicially reporting, or judicially reporting and deposing witness,) has place in the case of diminished trustworthiness; howsoever the diminution be produced—viz. whether by inferiority in point of intellectual aptitude, by exposure to the action of interest acting in a sinister direction, or by improbity of disposition, considered as rendering his effectual resistance to that sinister force by so much the less probable.

The fact in question, the fact spoken to by the official document, or the statement made by the official person,—is it of the number of those facts by which, according as they are credited or not—according to the opinions entertained concerning them—his own reputation, or that of any other person specially connected with him by any tie of self-regarding interest or sympathy, may, either in a favourable or an unfavourable way, be affected? Is it, for example, an act of his own, or any matter of fact or supposed fact, on the belief or disbelief of which his own act was grounded, or on which the propriety or impropriety of his own conduct may be found to depend? If yes, there is an end of that ground of trustworthiness which is composed of *impartiality:* exemption from the action of sinister interest.

Rule 2. For a judicial purpose, in the case where, for the purpose of the official business, the evidence in question, having been already committed to writing, exists in the shape of ready-written evidence,—in that same shape, though unsanctioned and uninterrogated, it may in general be presented to the cognizance of the judge, viz. for avoidance of delay, vexation, and expense, notwithstanding the imperfection and comparative untrustworthiness incident to it in that shape.

Rule 3. But if, on any of the grounds mentioned as above, the trustworthiness of it be regarded as diminished, all such operations ought to be allowed to be performed, as, supposing the information to have issued from any ordinary and non-official source, would be regarded as necessary to place the trustworthiness of it (viz. its correctness and completeness) upon the strongest and surest ground: to wit, by tracing out direct evidence of the fact in question through the medium of the circumstantial, or by tracing out percipient witnesses through the medium of judicially or extra-judicially reporting witnesses, and by applying to the testimony of the respective witnesses the ordinary securities for trustworthiness, viz. interrogation, publicity, denunciation of eventual punishment, &c. as the case may be.

Rule 4. Note, that, without any imputation upon the trustworthiness of the witness (the author or reporter of the narrative or statement exhibited by the article of official evidence,) the application of the process of interrogation may, to the purposes of correctness and completeness taken together, but more particularly completeness, be indispensable. For a mass of testimony, though correct and sincere, may to one purpose be complete, to another incomplete: incomplete, and not capable of being rendered complete by any other means than an interrogatory or series of interrogatories adapted to the individual purpose actually in hand.

A distinction requires here to be noted, between the information sought, and the document in and by which it is supposed to be contained and presented. To either of these objects, where an office of this or that description is the source or repository of the information sought or the document consulted, the term *official evidence* may without impropriety be applied. But a case that may very easily happen is, that—where the matter of the document is more or less false, and would (if trusted to) be deceptitious—true and useful information, information such as to the purpose in question shall be complete, and in every part correct, shall be obtainable and obtained by means of it, viz. by a due and skilful application of the instruments for the extraction of truth—the instruments already mentioned. But, to the ends of justice, the material object is, that the information obtained shall be complete and correct. Whether the document by means of which it was obtained, was or was not possessed of those same qualities, is to this purpose a matter of indifference.

Were this distinction to pass unobserved, official evidence from this source might be in a high degree over-valued or under-valued; and from either error, much practical mischief to justice might be the result. The official documents of which this or that particular office is the repository or the source—*i. e.* the information already contained and presented by them—is very apt to be false: but if the conclusion were to be, Receive not, credit not, any information that comes through that office, and this conclusion were acted upon, here would be a great mass of light extinguished—of light indispensably necessary to the purposes of justice. From the office in question, true and instructive evidence might, by a suitable application of the instruments for the extraction of truth, at any time, and for any of a variety of purposes, be obtained: but if the conclusion were to be, Receive as true whatever information may be presented by any of the documents of which that office is the repository, and this conclusion acted upon, an habitual course of error, deception, and injustice, would here again be the result.

Rule 5. The same rules, which, in the several cases individually taken, serve for *estimating* the trustworthiness of an article or mass of evidence—in the present instance, a mass of *official* evidence—will serve for *securing* the possession of this desirable property to the whole mass of official evidence taken in the aggregate. The instruments of security in question adapted to the purpose, are—1. The arrangements and operations so often mentioned under the name of securities for trustworthiness; 2. The application of these securities to the purpose of investigatorial procedure: tracing out, in relation to each article of information, the percipient witness (if any such there were) through the medium of the reporting witness or witnesses. In each individual case, to employ these instruments in so far as requisite, or permit them to be employed in so far as requisite, is the function of the judge; and it is by performing it that he enables himself to *estimate* the trustworthiness of the evidence, and the verity of the facts probabilized by it. To allow or prescribe, as the case may be, the employment of these same instruments in future, is the function of the legislator: and it is by performing it that he does what depends upon him towards *securing* this desirable result in all future instances.

Of the several purposes, as above distinguished, to which it may happen to official evidence to be found applicable,—the collateral and incidental, the *judicial*, is the only one that, in the observations just delivered, has hitherto been in view. But if, when applied to that purpose, any of them be found applicable with advantage, they will scarcely be found applicable with less advantage to the direct purpose of the several masses of official evidence, of which the several offices are respectively the repositories or the sources. If, in any such office, in the instance of this or that species of document, the matter be regularly replete with falsehood, arrangements and operations have above been pointed out, by means of which that falsehood may, on any occasion, be converted into a source of useful truth.

Here, then, are two other functionaries—the administrator and the legislator, to whom the above suggestions (if useful to the judge) may also be of use: to the *administrator (i. e.* to that branch of the executive authority to whom, under the legislator, the conduct of the business in each several office depends,) that he may take such measures as lie within his competence for the substitution of true documents to false ones: to the legislator, that, in default of his subordinate the administrator, he may apply his own superordinate authority to the same salutary purpose.

CHAPTER VIII.

OF OFFICIAL EVIDENCE, AS FURNISHED BY JUDICIAL OFFICES.

§ 1. *Uses of the official evidence furnished by judicial offices.*

APPLYING to all offices without exception, the matter of the last preceding chapter will be found to apply with no less propriety or advantage to judicial offices in particular. But, in that mass of evidence of which an office of the judicial kind is either the source, or the receptacle and repository, circumstances may be observed, by which, considered as the basis of judicial decision, official evidence will be seen to stand in the scale of importance upon a higher level than official evidence taken at large.

In the character of evidence to the judge, the application of official evidence taken at large is but collateral and incidental. The application of the evidence furnished by a judicial office is direct and constant: and this as well in the instance of that part of the mass of which the office (in this case the *judicial* office) is but the repository, as in the instance of that of which it is the source.

The information, which, under the denomination of *evidence*, is received or extracted by the judge, belongs not to this head: the character in which it comes under consideration is that of ordinary, not preappointed, evidence.

In respect of evidence of this description, the office is the *receptacle*, and, in so far as such is the usage of the office, the *repository*, but is not the *source*.

Of the evidence furnished, or capable of being furnished, by the judicial office, that which comes under the notion and denomination of preappointed evidence, is that by which the operations performed by the several *dramatis personæ* in the theatre of judicature, are, or may be, brought to view, and consigned to remembrance.

Among the operations in question, the principal class consists in the delivery of the various ready-written *instruments* which in the course of the cause come to be delivered; and where the delivery of an instrument to a certain effect is performed and commemorated, a natural course is, that the instrument itself, or a transcript of it, be preserved.

Instruments, in so far as received into the office, and kept there, record themselves: *operations*, if the remembrance of them is to be preserved in the office, require an official hand to record them. The instrument will show its own existence, but will not show of itself the performance of any operation performed in relation to it; for example, the time when, or the persons by whom, it was delivered or received.

The different uses to which it may happen to the same lot or article of judicial official evidence (*i. e.* of preappointed official evidence, having for its source an office of the judicial kind) to be applicable,—these different uses, as characterized by the different descriptions of persons by whom the use may be made—the service, the benefit, received—may be thus distinguished:—

1. Uses to the parties or their representatives; viz. in respect of their respective interests in the suit supposed to be in hand, the suit which gave occasion to the reception or recordation of the article of evidence in question,—or, if an *instrument*, the framing of it in the office, or the reception of it from without,—if an *operation*, the recordation of it. Here the judicial uses coincide with those which, in the case of an office other than judicial, have been designated under the denomination of the *administrative* uses.

2. Uses which respect the interests of the same or other parties in respect of future contingent suits, in which, if instituted, the evidence in question may eventually be found applicable.*

* These uses may, both of them, in a certain sense, be termed uses to the judge, the adminis-

3. Uses to the sovereign and legislator: consisting in the furnishing such information as may serve as a basis for any such ulterior regulations as from time to time may serve to render the proceedings of the several judicatories, as well as the several portions of substantive law to which it is their duty to give execution and effect, more and more effectually subservient to the several ends of justice: these may be distinguished by the term *statistic* uses.

I. Uses to the parties in respect of the suit in hand: —

Each operation requires to be consigned to remembrance for three purposes — 1. That it may serve as a basis for the next operation which it may render necessary or advisable to be performed, whether on the same side of the cause or on the opposite side;* 2. That it may be seen whether the operation thus performed was proper in itself, and performed in a proper manner; 3. That, in case of any impropriety, it may serve as a ground for satisfaction to be rendered for any such wrong as may have been produced by the impropriety — satisfaction, or even punishment, if the wrong be of such nature as to create a proper demand for punishment.

Under a system of which justice is the object, the operation which, in the ordinary course of things, will naturally come to be registered at or near the outset of the cause, will be the appearance of both the parties in the face of each other and the judge: the next, saving such memoranda as it may have occurred to the legislator to prescribe to be made and preserved for his own use (of which presently,) will be either the decision pronounced by the judge, or the existence of some circumstance which, creating a natural and just demand for delay, would have rendered such immediate decision repugnant to one or other of the direct ends of justice.

Under a system of which the object is injustice, in the shape of factitious delay, vexation, and expense, for the sake of the profit extracted to the use of Judge and Co. out of the expense,—the operations that come to be registered will be those needless and useless operations which serve as pretences for enhancement of the expense, or for the creation of that delay and vexation, the faculty of inflicting which, with the chance of consequent misdecision, constitutes the encouragement afforded to the *malâ fide* litigant on either side to drag along with himself his injured adversary through the kennel of litigation: and of these there is no end.

II. Uses to future contingent parties, in respect of future contingent causes: —

In regard to contingencies of this description, the desirable effect (the door to the temple of justice not being shut by factitious delay, vexation, and expense, or exclusion of instructive evidence,) the best possible effect is, that they come not into existence: the next most desirable effect is, that, coming into existence, they receive a decision as conformable as possible to the direct ends of justice, and at the same time as clear as possible from collateral inconvenience in the shape of delay, vexation, or expense.

To these purposes taken together, the knowledge of the following facts, of the number of those which have actually had place on the occasion of the several causes already instituted, is manifestly subservient:

1. Knowledge of the several facts, ignorance of which, or misconception or uncertainty in regard to them, may, on one side or other, give birth to ulterior suits either between the same parties or between other parties: for instance, that Titius, by his last will, declared it to be his desire, that, upon and after his decease, Sempronius should be proprietor of the field therein described.

2. Application that has been made of the law (viz. by a decision pronounced on the occasion of the past cause) to the fact or facts that were deemed established by sufficient proof on the occasion of that same suit: for instance, that the desire so expressed by Titius was by a judicatory adjudged to be valid, and conformable to law.

III. Uses that bear reference to the legislator, as the functionary by whom the application of the information thus obtained comes to be made, — bear reference to the several ends of justice so often spoken of as the objects to which the operations grounded on such information should be directed: —

If the system of judicial procedure has been already framed by him and established by law, his direct object in the collection of the information under this head will be to see in what particulars it is subservient in the utmost possible degree to the ends of justice, and in what particulars (if in any) it fails of being so: to the end that, in so far as it fails of being so, the failure may be obviated.

If the system of procedure has, in the whole or in any part, been the work not of himself but of the judge, acting according to rules expressed *in terminis*, or not so expressed; then, over and above the correction of any such failures as may in this way pre-

trator of the department to which these offices belong: but, in this instance, the uses derived from them by the administrator do not come altogether so close to him as in other instances.

* Thus, where the altercation is carried on in writing, the delivery of an instrument of demand on the plaintiff's side will naturally have the effect of imposing on the defendant's side the obligation of delivering an instrument of defence. On the other side, the having given to the other party notice of an intention to deliver in an instrument to this or that effect, will naturally have the effect of imposing on that same side the obligation of performing the operation in question in pursuance of such notice.

sent themselves to view in the system thus established by an improper hand, is the giving it its establishment by his own the only proper hand — giving, in determinate words of his own choosing, expression to those rules, where as yet they had none; where it has already received such expression, and that an expression conformable to his views, giving to it the sanction of his authority in express words.

Under a great variety of subordinate heads, information — useful information, may, by the skill and probity of the legislator, be drawn from this source. But, in each instance, its title to the reputation of utility will depend upon its subservience to some one or more of the ends of justice. Hence, under whatever such head information is sought, the propriety of seeking it will find its test and demonstration in the designation of that one or more of those ends to which it is subservient; and, if not sufficiently obvious, of the *means* by which — the *way* in which, its tendency to such subservience manifests itself.

To give a complete list of the several heads of information thus capable of being made subservient to the ends of justice, would be a difficult, and in the present work a misplaced, task. For illustration, the following examples may serve, arranged under those ends of justice to which they may respectively be found subservient:—

I. Prevention of misdecision to the prejudice of either side of the cause.

1. Total number of causes in which the decision turned on the question of fact.

2. With this total, to compare the number of the causes in which evidence of an inferior quality was received, distinguishing between the several causes of inferiority: noting whether the inferior evidence was or was not the only evidence on that side; and whether the decision was in favour or disfavour of the side on which the inferior evidence was produced.

The number of causes individually taken, in which (choosing any given period) the decision was in favour of the inferior evidence, will show the utmost possible amount of the mischief resulting, within that period, from the admission of such inferior evidence.

Comparing period with period, say year with year, — if the number of such cases, individually taken, were constantly upon the increase, it would afford a ground for suspecting, that, by the admission of such inferior evidence, wilful falsehood, deception, misdecision, and thence encouragement to injustice, on the part of individuals, had been produced. Supposing no such increase, or none but what might be satisfactorily accounted for by accident or other causes; it would then be made manifest, that by such admission no such evil consequences had been produced.

3. Number of the appeals from decisions grounded on the question of fact: distinguishing between the cases in which the decision of the subordinate judicatory was, by the superordinate, affirmed purely and simply, and those in which it was either reversed or modified; and — in case of divers appeals grounded on the same original decision, and presented to different judicatories, taking cognizance one after another of the same fact — showing the number of such successive appeals.

If, in each instance, the evidence be exactly the same, and presented in the same shape; then, upon the supposition of consummate wisdom and probity on the part of the judicatory ultimately resorted to in each case, together with sufficient ability in each instance, on the part of the losing side, to carry the cause before an ulterior judicatory,—all these assumptions being made, the proportion between affirmed and reversed or modified, would exhibit the degree of aptitude, in all shapes taken together, on the part of the respective subordinate judicatories.

II. Prevention of preponderant or superfluous delay, vexation, and expense. Showing, in and for each suit, the quantity of delay, vexation, and expense, on both sides of the cause; distinguishing, in the case of each of those three modifications of collateral inconvenience, the portion which was natural and unavoidable, from the portion, if any, which was fictitious and avoidable: and, in regard to that fictitious part, distinguishing between the several portions which were respectively the work and the fault of the system (the established system of procedure,) the party or parties, or the judge. And — in case of different judicatories, to the cognizance of either or any of which the same individual cause might, at the option of a party, on the one or the other side of the cause, have been presented, whether acting under the same or a different system of procedure — serving to show, in respect of the quantity of delay, vexation, and expense in each, the difference between judicatory and judicatory: and thence, in these several shapes, the quantity of fictitious injustice, which, in the instance of those judicatories in which it has been greatest, presents itself as chargeable either on the system or on the judge.

III. Prevention of contraventions against the remote ends of justice. Showing for each period, on the part of the several judicatories, the number of contraventions, if any, against the unimmediate or remote ends of justice; viz. 1. Against obedience to the several manifestations of the will of the legislator — judicial non-conformity at large, and judicial disobedience manifesting itself in the particular shape of usurpation of jurisdiction, to the prejudice of the authority of other judicatories (whether superordinate, co-ordinate, or subordinate to the judicatory so usurping;) 2. Against uniformity of decision as between judicatory and judicatory — mutual discrepancy of decision.

IV. Prevention of judicial injustice in all shapes together. Showing, for each period, the number of causes of the several species, non-penal and penal: and therein and thence, the aggregate amount of the delay, vexation, and expense actually produced; together with the utmost possible number of the instances of misdecision, which, to the prejudice of either side, can have been produced: showing thereby, as between period and period, the increase or decrease of injustice and delinquency in its several shapes, with a view to the demand, if any, for ulterior exertions in the line of legislation.

V. Melioration of the law, whether in respect of *matter*, or *form*: *i. e.* showing the demand for fresh law, or fresh *expression* to be given to this or that portion of already existing law.

The ways in which recordation might be made subservient to this purpose are —

1. Exhibiting the several cases in which a question of law (grounded in this case on statute law) had any place in the dispute between the parties; and in each instance showing the point or points in dispute, reference being made to the several portions of law relied upon on each side, together with the considerations brought forward in the way of argument on all sides.

2. In cases of appeal, exhibiting the ground of the appeal, and the number of stages of appeal, if more than one, in the instance of each cause; and, on each occasion, the treatment given, whether in the way of affirmance, reversal, or modification, by the superordinate judicatory, to the decision of the subordinate.

From the point or points in dispute, compared with the words of the portion of law which formed the ground of the dispute, it would be in each case apparent whether any demand had presented itself for fresh law (viz. law fresh in substance,) or only for fresh expression to be given (viz. for removal of ambiguity or obscurity) to this or that portion of existing law: the melioration being in each case to be made by defalcation, addition, substitution, or transposition, as the nature of the exigence requires.

In so far as, by incapacity, indolence, negligence, or corruption, on the part of the legislator of the day, the rule of action is left in the barbarous state of the species of imposition called *unwritten law*, — the people, in their character of suitors, being (such of them as are honest) habitually, for the benefit of that partnership of which the judge is at the head, and of which the legislator is the accomplice or the dupe, punished for nonconformity to rules which, lest they should be conformed to, are not permitted to be known; — in such case, the number and place of such appeals will, to the legislator of some happier time, afford useful indications, pointing out to him the particular portions of the field of law, in and by which the demand for real and genuine law has thus rendered itself manifest.

The demand for a really existing and accessible standard of obedience, co-extensive with the whole field of law, can be no secret to any one who on this head will permit himself to listen to the most obvious dictates of common sense. The light reflected on this subject by recordation, consists in nothing more than a distinct indication of the particular instances in which this undeniable truth will thus have been brought to view.

There remain two masses of injustice, the quantity or limits of which cannot be shown for any period, in a direct way, by any such documents as the above; — viz. 1. The number of instances in which, in the shape of oppression or extortion, injustice has been produced by an opulent individual in the character of plaintiff; to the prejudice of one who should have been defendant, but was debarred by the load of vexation and expense from the faculty of defending himself. 2. The number of instances in which injustice was committed, and with success, for want of litigation; the wrong-doer trusting to the inability of the party wronged to take upon himself the character of plaintiff with effect.

In a direct way, and in the several particular instances in which injustice thus produced has taken effect, no particular documents can show its amount: but a conception of the aggregate mass may be deduced from the computation of the quantity of money necessary to defray the expense of a suit on both sides, compared with the quantity which it is possible for a father of a family, in the condition of the most numerous class, to have at command for this purpose.

§ 2. *Neglect of English judges and legislators in regard to this kind of preappointed evidence.*

If such as stand above exhibited are indeed the duties of the legislator and the judge, — negligent in the extreme — culpable, and at the same time cruel in the extreme, on this important ground, has been the conduct of English judges and legislators. Were an inquiring mind to turn its eye on this occasion to Westminster Hall, what would it see? A correct, a clear, an all-comprehensive, an easily and cheaply accessible, body of evidence, adapted to the exigencies of all suitors, in all sorts of causes? Alas, no! but instead of it, a parcel of disjointed fragments, composing an imperfect and confused and shapeless mass, stained throughout with mendacity, and drowned in nonsense. What, then, has been the conduct of these high-seated possessors of delegated power? Like savages waiting for a wreck, or rather like insurers making secret preparations for the manufacturing of a wreck, instead of making provision by their own industry for the requisite supply of evidence for their own use, they have lain by, and punished suitors for the deficiency—punished them for the not having produced that precise sort or individual lot of evidence, which, to the exclusion of whatever was attainable, they were, by an unpromulgated resolution of their own, predetermined (or rather, in the way of an *ex post facto* law, such as are all decisions of common law in new cases, these ministers of justice were *post-determined)* not to accept. They leave undone the things they ought to have done; and from this negative trespass it is, that they derive the faculty of doing those things which they ought not to have done — of denying justice, of working injustice, of producing delay, vexation, and expense. If, in the mouths of such exalted and privileged sinners, the established and commanded confession had any useful meaning, how copious might it not be when pointed to this quarter of the official decalogue!

Confounding everything that requires to be distinguished, the nomenclature of English jurisprudence includes under the same general name (records,) and without any names of specific distinction under it, instruments exhibiting judicial transactions, and instruments exhibiting public official contracts, public contractual writings of the more important kinds, king's grants (conveyances in which the king is grantor,) &c.

Distinguishing, on the other hand, by an arbitrary and shifting line, two classes of objects between which there is neither any natural, nor so much as any promulgated or perceptibly instituted difference,—it has divided courts into courts of record, and courts not of record. And what are the courts not of record? Any inferior courts, on the proceedings of which, the two superior purely law courts at Westminister Hall bestow but an inferior degree of credit. And, among those inferior courts, which stands first upon the list? The Court of Chancery, of which the daily functions are to impede and overrule the decisions of them both.*

The Court of Chancery not a court of record? Why so, any more than the two great common-law courts under the same roof—the King's Bench, and Common Pleas? Is it that it keeps no records, or that its records are framed or kept with less care? Let him answer, who has occasion and power to know. One thing I will venture to say: that, in the memorials of the instruments and acts ascribed to the court, or to any member of it, of whatsoever class, there is at any rate less mendacity and nonsense in the court that proceeds upon the Roman model, the court not of record, than in the courts which proceed upon the Anglo-Gallo-Norman model, the courts of record.

On this head, the effrontery and imposture of English judges, and of one in particular, who is in possession of serving as an oracle to the rest,† presents a lesson which will not be deemed undeserving of regard, unless where the bosom is by sinister interest fortified against it.

Geometrical propositions he had heard spoken of, as composing a class of propositions to which men's assent was wont to be engaged by arguments or evidences universally regarded as irresistible, and on the truth of which, without danger of error, the most confident reliance might be placed. Under the name of diagrams, he had heard spoken of a species of figures or graphical representations, employed for the expression of those propositions, and of the arguments from which the verity of them is inferred.

From the first month of his application to the study of the English laws, what from first to last is known to every man who applies himself to the study of that most corrupt of all systems of law, must have been known to this oracle of English law; viz. that, of the sort of instrument or document called by English lawyers a *record*, so far as concerns the judicial class of records, a considerable part is in every instance a tissue of falsehood—unworthy of all credit, in fact not meant to be believed, and which would therefore be as innoxious as it is absurd, were it not for the obscurity and ambiguity, uncertainty, deception, and misdecision, which is the result of the entanglement in which truth and falsehood together have so studiously and effectually been involved. What could not have been unknown to this projector, and in part executor, of a complete abridgment of English law, was, that the falsehoods contained in those pretended repositories of truth had from first to last been habitually applied, as they continue to be applied, to the purposes of depredation for the profit of the judges.

But the more abundant and mischievous and profitable the falsehood was—mischievous to the people, profitable to the authors and their confederates—the more urgent the

* As to the Court of Exchequer, being a sort of motley court—one side of it a law side, the other an equity side,—it must, according to principle, be neither a court of record only, nor a court not of record only, but both together.

† Lord Chief Baron Gilbert, in his Treatise on Evidence.

need of straining every nerve, of heaping falsehood upon falsehood, for the purpose of rendering incurable the blindness of the people, and causing them to venerate this tissue of pernicious falsehood, as if it were a body of pure and spotless truth.

Accordingly, at the outset of his treatise on evidence, these repositories of notorious falsehoods are without limitation spoken of under the rhetorical and sophistical denomination of *diagrams* (diagrams for the *demonstration of right,)* and as composing a species of evidence, in comparison with which all other evidence is weak and unsatisfactory — a species of evidence possessing the attributes of certainty and infallibility, — those attributes which in truth are radically incapable of entering into anything that ever went by the name of evidence.

CHAPTER IX.

OF PREAPPOINTED EVIDENCE, CONSIDERED AS APPLIED TO LEGALLY-OPERATIVE FACTS AT LARGE.

§ 1. *Use of registration, as applied to legally-operative facts.*

By the denomination thus assigned, the facts in question are distinguished from all others, and at the same time the reason why they ought to be had in remembrance, and placed upon the rank of preappointed evidence, is brought to view.

If, in the instance of any given right or obligation undertaken by law to be established, it be necessary to justice and the general welfare of the community that it be established and carried into effect, — it will be equally necessary that the existence of that evidence, without which such effect cannot take place, should be secured. But, even although in any such instance the effectuation or frustration of such right or obligation were in itself a matter of indifference, still the existence of preappointed evidence, of a nature to secure the effectuation of such right or obligation, would not be matter of indifference: for, of such evidence, when by means of it the fact evidenced by it is known to have had place, the effect is to prevent litigation, by rendering it on one side hopeless: while, of the want of such evidence, a natural and frequent effect is, the rendering it matter of doubt whether the fact had place or no; of which doubt, litigation, with the vexation and expense attending it on both sides, and the disappointment on one or both sides, is the bitter fruit.

But, in many instances, such registration, howsoever desirable, will be found unattainable: and in particular, in every instance in which the effect of such registration would (whether on a non-penal or on a penal account) be unfavourable to the only individual or individuals from whom the information of the fact could for that purpose be obtained.

Moreover, in many instances, such registration, though of itself desirable, might be upon the whole prudentially or even physically impracticable: physically, because there exists no person by whom the process of recordation could be performed; prudentially, because, if any person exist by whom it could by possibility be performed, there exists no person by whom it could be performed in a proper manner — *i. e.* in such manner as to render it more likely to be preventive than promotive of consequent misdecision, and at the same time without being productive of preponderant collateral inconvenience in the shape of vexation and expense.

The cases in which, as above, such recordation is impracticable (physically impracticable,) require to be noted, were it only for the purpose of bringing to view the limits opposed by necessity to the exertions of legislative providence in this line: to the end that the legislator may not be subjected to the imputation of negligence, for not aiming to overleap the boundaries of possibility; and at the same time, that he may not seek, in the impossibility of making provision to this effect in some instances, an excuse for omitting it in cases to which the natural and inseparable bar does not extend itself.

From what is above stated, five rules present themselves as proper on the part of the legislator to be kept in remembrance:—

1. To look out for such different descriptions of legally-operative facts as may be found susceptible of recordation, — viz. without preponderant inconvenience, as above.

2. To look out for such persons as, being fit in point of qualifications (intellectual as well as moral,) may, on each respective occasion, either be found, or without preponderant inconvenience rendered, in each case, willing to undertake the charge.

3. On each occasion, to make provision such as the case admits of for the verity, for the correctness and completeness, of the statement so recorded.

4. To consider with himself and determine what legal effect shall be given to the preappointed evidence thus collected and preserved.

5. To make due provision for adapting to his own use, in every practicable shape, the information which has for its more immediate object the giving effect to the rights established for the benefit of the particular individuals, on each respective occasion particularly considered: in a word, to apply it in the aggregate to the *statistic uses* of which it is susceptible.

§ 2. *Facts calling for registration, what?*

I. Facts of a regularly occurring nature; — viz. such as — though, individually taken, not — yet, taken in specie, their recurrence may be considered as certain.

1. Facts affecting *condition in life*. Take for example, the articles of principal importance, which appear as follows — 1. Deaths; 2. Births; 3. Marriages:* to which may be added, though comparatively casual — 4. Arrivals at majority; 5. Declarations of insanity; 6. Declarations of dissolution of marriage, otherwise than by death; 7. Entrance into contracts of apprenticeship; 8. Dissolution of such contracts, otherwise than by expiration of the term; 9. Entrance into partnership contracts; 10. Dissolution of partnership contracts; 11. Appointments to official situations; 12. Removals from official situations.

2. Facts collative and ablative with relation to *contracts* taken in the largest sense: including the making of wills, and other conveyances.

1. Entrance into any contracts other than the above.†

2. Dissolutions or modifications of contracts: in the several ways, by which the several sorts of contracts, according to their respective natures, are capable of being dissolved or modified, — such as expiration, performance, receipt of money, &c.

In regard to entrances into contracts, and dissolutions of contracts, — whether it be eligible upon the whole that registration should take place, will depend upon the joint consideration of the importance of the contract, — the probability of non-notoriety when notoriety is requisite, and of oblivion when remembrance is requisite, — and the vexation and expense attached to the operation of recordation: taking into the account of vexation, whatsoever unpleasant circumstances may be the result of disclosure. See above, Ch. II. *On Contracts.*

* Since the first edition of the work was published, a general legislative system for the registration of births, deaths, and marriages in England, has been made by 6 & 7 W. IV. c. 86, amended by 7 Will. IV. & 1 Vict. c. 22. At the same time, a bill to establish a system somewhat similar in Scotland was laid before Parliament, but has not yet (August 1839) been carried through. — *Ed.*

† In regard to contracts in general, and marriage-contracts in particular, distinguish between the registration of the contract itself (*i. e.* the instrument of contract, when there is one,) and the recordation of the naked fact of the entrance into a contract of the species in question, by or between the party or parties in question. One sort of office may be fittest for the one purpose, another for the other. In practice, the one incident may be constantly the subject of registration, the other seldom or never. In England, for twenty instances of marriages entered into and registered, there is not perhaps more than one, of a marriage-settlement (*i. e.* a marriage instrument of contract) entered into: nor, except in two or three counties, any one of a marriage-settlement registered.

II. Facts of casual occurrence: *casualties*, taken in the largest sense.

1. Deaths; — viz. when by means of marks of violence or other extraordinary appearances, a suspicion is afforded that human agency (positive or negative) may have been contributory to the effect.

2. State and condition of persons or things, in consequence of deterioration supposed to be the result of delinquency:‡ together with any other circumstances, the remembrance of which may, for want of speedy recordation, stand exposed to deperition.

3. So, where supposed to be the result of physical calamity, — in so far as, in consequence of such result, fresh rights and obligations, at the charge of this or that individual, may come into existence. Thus, by the calamity of fire, a right may accrue to the proprietor of a house, attended with a correspondent obligation at the charge of an occupier or an insurance office.

4. To the list of facts of casual occurrence may be added (in the character of facts the recordation of which, in the same mode and by the same hands, may be subservient to the purposes of justice) any facts so circumstanced, that the means of presenting them to the cognizance of the judge may be wanting, unless the testimony of such persons as (from the having stood in relation to them in the character of percipient witnesses) are competent to speak to them in the character of deposing witnesses, be collected at a time in which the collection of it in the ordinary and regular mode is impracticable: the percipient witness, for example, on the point of leaving the country, and the stopping of him either *physically*, or, in respect of preponderant inconvenience in the shape of vexation or expense, *prudentially*, impracticable.

§ 3. *Registration, by whom performable?*

In each case, the propriety of the choice will depend upon two circumstances: — 1. The *trustworthiness* of the person, regard being had to the particular species of *fact* in question; 2. The vexation and expense, if any, attached to the employment of such person in such case.

The trustworthiness of the functionary (meaning the relative trustworthiness, as above) will again depend on the importance of the fact, coupled with the nature of the securities thought fit to be employed for securing the verity (*i. e.* the correctness and completeness) of the evidence necessary to enable the recordation to fulfil the purposes for which it is intended: of which in the next section.

If the form of the entry be reduced to a

‡ This belongs to the head of *real evidence.* See Book V. *Circumstantial.*

certain degree of simplicity—and if, in a form thus simple, the mode of recordation be adequate to the fulfilment of all its purposes,—mere moral trustworthiness, including in that view responsibility in both its senses, may be the sole object of regard: but if intellectual aptitude, and this of so peculiar a nature as to come under the denomination of scientific, be moreover requisite, a proportionable degree of nicety and difficulty will of course be attendant on the choice.

For the registration of facts of a *regularly* occurring nature, as above exemplified, provision has commonly enough been made in practice. Hands competent to the task have accordingly been found for it: nor has the finding of them been attended with any considerable difficulty. What difficulty there may be, seems confined, accordingly, to the finding of hands competent to the registration of facts of *casual* occurrence.

In the species of judge styled a justice of the peace, the official establishment of the British constitution possesses a species of public functionary well adapted for this purpose.

No ulterior functions of this nature can by their importance present a demand for a greater degree of trustworthiness, intellectual as well as moral, than is presented by several of those functions of which he is possessed already.*

From the class of attorneys, persons are taken without the plea of necessity, and at the choice of parties litigant (and without other restriction or condition than that of having two such functionaries named, one on each side,) for the exercise, and even the definitive exercise, of that part of the judicial function which consists in the collection of evidence.†

To prevent deperition, or at any rate deterioration of evidence, is the only (but it should seem the just) ground, on which a departure of this sort from the ordinary mode of collecting evidence can be defended: and, in a case of such necessity, the recurrence to hands of this description might, it should seem, be justified upon at least as good grounds, as when the same hands are employed without any such plea of necessity, as above.

In regard to testimony having for its subject legally-operative facts taken at large (of which facts collative or ablative in relation to property may serve for example;) by what sort of registrator they shall be collected — viz. whether by the judge of the competent judicatory, by a functionary of the judicial class, or by a functionary of the notarial class — will depend upon the probable absence or presence of a sufficient length of time. If there be no want of time, the sort of functionary who on other occasions is regarded as best qualified to the reception and extraction of testimony destined to be applied to a judicial purpose, is the sort of functionary to be employed in this as in other cases. If there be a certain or a probable want of time, if the occasion be so fugitive that it will not be within the power of a functionary so seated, and in a manner fixed to a spot, to arrest it in its flight, — then comes the necessity of admitting the service of a functionary of the other class, whose seat is of a more pliant and ambulatory nature. Under the head of want of time, is in effect included, on the part of such magistrates as can be applied to within the hour, want of inclination to undertake the business. Not only in respect of the time of doing the business, but in respect of the choosing whether he will do it all, — the magistrate, serving justice upon those gratuitous terms on which justice, by this species of judge, is always served, is not nor could easily be subjected to any inflexible obligation. The functionary of the notarial class, in the present instance, is so far in the same case: but, in the assurance of professional emolument, he beholds an inducement over and above any that applies in the other case.‡

* Examples: — 1. Recordation of a riot committed in his presence; and this evidence rendered sufficient of itself to ground a conviction pronounced by himself as judge.

2. Examination of a poor person, for the purpose of ascertaining his settlement; *i. e.* the district on which, in case of indigence on his part, the obligation of providing him with subsistence shall be charged.

3. Examinations preparatory to decision, in the vast variety of other cases, penal and non-penal, which have been committed to his cognizance.

4. Examinations preparatory to provisional incarceration, in penal cases deemed of too high a nature to be committed definitively to his cognizance.

† Viz. in the character of commissioners for the taking depositions to be employed in a court of equity. The occasion on which the examiner (such is the denomination given to the collecting judge) is a permanent officer, is confined to the case where the place of examination lies within a small distance of the metropolis.

‡ Of preappointed evidence of the description here in question, — viz. evidence of miscellaneous facts, received and extracted either antecedently to litigation, or antecedently to the time regularly appointed for the collection of the evidence, — the practice of the English equity courts affords two modifications.

1. One is, the examination *in perpetuam rei memoriam*, used for the establishment of a title to a certain subject-matter of property (suppose an estate in land,) without any particular expectation of any particular occasion on which, in the way of litigation, such evidence will come to be employed; and under circumstances in which it is not regarded as in any immediate danger o perishing.

2. The other is, the examination *de bene esse:* when, for the purpose of some suit, either ac-

§ 4. *How to secure the verity of the evidence thus provided.*

Evidence being subservient to justice no otherwise than in so far as it is undeceptitious, —evidence that, by reason either of incorrectness or incompleteness, proves deceptitious, being worse than no evidence at all, — the attention bestowed on the securing the existence of the evidence, would, if produced by a steady and comprehensive regard to the ends of justice, be accompanied with an attention equally solicitous to secure the verity of such evidence.

As to the instrumental arrangements best adapted to this latter purpose, they have over and over again been brought to view. And in particular, under the head of preappointed evidence, the eventual necessity of employing them has been brought to view in the instance of judicial and other official evidence.

In the case of this species of preappointed evidence, as in the case of every other species of evidence, justice, for the reasons so often given, requires that on each occasion, unless in case of preponderant inconvenience, it be presented in the best shape possible: the verity of it provided for, not merely by eventual punishment and by interrogation, but by counter-interrogation by or in behalf of each individual party whose interest, in case of incorrectness or material incompleteness on the part of the evidence, is liable to be impaired by it.

When, merely in contemplation of future contingent suits, and therefore antecedently to any such suit, evidence for the establishment of any such legally-operative fact as is here in question is (as above) collected, — interrogation by or in behalf of any such party so interested is impossible: no such party being as yet in existence. Therefore, in the best of all shapes, the collection of preappointed evidence is not possible. What remains to be done, is to collect it in the next best shape; that is, the deposing witness speaking under the check of eventual punishment, and subject to interrogation, to be performed by the evidence-collecting judge.

Say that in every case the testimony shall be presented in the best shape in which it can be presented—say but this, and the legal effect proper to be given to preappointed evidence collected as above, is determined. Presented, in the first instance, in the best shape of which preappointed evidence is susceptible; if that interrogation or counter-interrogation which is necessary to the putting it in the very best shape be capable of being applied to it, and the party concerned in interest calls for the faculty of applying it, let that additional security be applied accordingly. But if, by any circumstance, such counter-interrogation have been rendered impracticable, —rendered so, for example, by death, insanity, or expatriation coupled with non-justiciability, on the part of such deposing witness, — then let it, in such its next best form, be received for what it is worth. Evidence thus imperfectly subjected to interrogation will always be more trustworthy than evidence altogether uninterrogated; more trustworthy, therefore, than affidavit evidence, upon which alone causes to any pecuniary amount are in such vast numbers determined in English practice; much more than evidence, the verity of which has not for its security either the scrutiny of interrogation or the fear of eventual punishment, as in the case of hearsay and casually-written evidence.

Suppose, for example, a witness whose testimony is necessary to the proof of some important legally-operative fact — a marriage, the execution of a last will, or other instrument of contract: — suppose him embarked, and on the point of sailing for a country subject to a foreign state, but visited on board, and his testimony collected, the vessel being detained for that purpose, by a functionary armed with the necessary power (in England, suppose a justice of the peace, or, in default of a justice of the peace, an attorney,

tually begun or in contemplation to be begun (the forms of procedure not admitting of the collection of the articles in question by the ordinary collecting judge, at the regularly appointed stage of the cause,) it is allowed to be collected by a party on one side of the cause, without the participation of any party on the other side; but on the terms of not being admitted, if the testimony of the same person be capable of being collected at the regular time in the regular mode,—the parties on the other side having the opportunity of applying to the witness that sort of interrogation which, in the mode of collecting and extracting employed by the equity courts, is called *cross-examination*, but which is widely different in its nature and effects from that which under the same name is employed in the common-law courts. This, in a word, is the mode employed for stopping fugitive evidence, in the case in which it is regarded as being in immediate danger of perishing.

If, in either case, the preservation of the evidence had really been the end for the accomplishment of which the institution was framed, the mode of collection appointed, including the designation of the species of functionary to be employed, would have been adapted to the fugitiveness and urgency of the occasion. But, neither in this instance nor in any other, has the English technical mode of procedure, under any of its modifications, been really directed to any such end. The real end being to catch, not *evidence*, but *money*, the previous drawing and filing of an instrument called a *bill* has been rendered necessary. What the bill does do, is, the putting money into the pocket of the judge, and other lawyers of various sorts and sizes: what the bill does not do, is, contributing to the collection of the evidence. While the bill is going through its forms, the evidence perishes: the fees are collected, and the evidence which should have been collected is not collected.

to whom, under the conditions above mentioned,* a permanent commission for that purpose has been thought fit to be entrusted.) Whatever additional security for the correctness and completeness of the evidence so collected can be given, should, in the event of a suit grounded on such evidence, and at the instance of a party interested, be afforded. Not only the *witness* should, in the event of his being afterwards forthcoming, or by any other means justiciable and interrogable, be subject to interrogation; but so ought the justice of peace or the attorney.

In the case of the justice of peace or of the attorney, what is possible, just possible, is, that—in confidence that the evidence will not come to be made use of, and subjected to judicial scrutiny, till after he has, by death or expatriation, been placed out of the reach of interrogation—he may, for the purpose of favouring some individual, whose probable interest in the matter of the testimony is in his view, collect it in a manner partially and purposely incomplete.

But the existence of such a plan of improbity cannot reasonably be considered as in a preponderant degree probable. It is not probable, that, in consequence of the corruption in question on the part of the judge, the number of instances in which evidence not only false but deceptitious shall have been collected, will be anything like so great as the number of instances in which, for want of it, evidence necessary to the support of a just right will have perished, and the right have been thus defeated.

At any rate, no such danger can consistently be considered as preponderant, by a master of the rolls or a chancellor by whom an attorney is, under the name of examining clerk, or clerk in the examiner's office, appointed and employed to collect the whole body of the evidence for pecuniary causes of the highest magnitude, sitting with the deposing witness in a closet with locked doors, free from all apprehension of being subjected to any such interrogation as here proposed.

In a code drawn up for this purpose, several provisions present themselves, which, if given in the character of *instructions*, and not of regulations sanctioned by pain of nullity, might contribute with advantage to the prevention of abuse.

Instructions stating circumstances by which the trustworthiness of provisional evidence, thus collected, would be regarded as increased:—

1. On the occasion of the examination, use your endeavours to collect impartial bystanders and auditors, the more the better, especially the more important the eventual effect of the evidence; inviting them to attest, if they think fit, by their signatures, the accuracy of the report made of the testimony, and the propriety of the mode in which it was collected: for example, if on board of a ship, the commander, with officers and passengers as many as think fit.

2. Wherever the examination is performed, the trustworthiness of the evidence will be increased, and your own conduct in the collection of it guarded against suspicion, if, at the indication of the party applicant, or at your own motion, you can engage some other trustworthy and intelligent person (professional or non-professional) to sit with you in the business.

By any precaution of this nature, if rendered obligatory on pain of nullity, the effect produced would in many instances be, to defeat the purpose. Rendered optional, whatsoever good effect they produce is pure from mischief. When the checks in question are called in, the evidence will command the confidence which it is thus made to deserve: where no such ground for confidence is formed, the eye of suspicion will be pointed to the transaction by its deficiency; and, from the persons employed in the transaction, an account of the causes of the deficiency will naturally be expected. In a case where evidence for establishing the circumstances attendant on a case of corporal suffering, whether from injury or calamity, is to be recorded, a medical practitioner would be an obviously proper assessor and assistant to the judicial functionary.

CHAPTER X.

OF THE REGISTRATION OF GENEALOGICAL FACTS, VIZ. DEATHS, BIRTHS, AND MARRIAGES.

§ 1. *Uses of registration, as applied to genealogical facts.*

Taken together, these three intimately-connected species of legally-operative events have already been characterized by the appellation of *genealogical* events. Taken together, the uses derivable from the registration of this class of legally-operative events, make a distinguishing figure when viewed in comparison with legally-operative events at large. Taken separately, the uses of each in some points coincide with, but in others are prominently distinct from, the uses of the other two.

I. Uses of registration as applied to deaths.

(1.) Uses having relation to the *non penal* (called civil) branch of law; and for which evidence of the naked fact suffices:—

1. To afford evidence of title by succession, in favour of natural or specially-appointed representatives.

2. To afford evidence of cessation of title, in the case of persons entitled to money or money's-worth during the life of the deceased.

* Section 3.

3. The deceased being under the tie of a matrimonial contract, — to afford evidence of the dissolution of such contract, in behalf of the surviving spouse.

4. The deceased leaving children under age, — to afford in their favour evidence of title to the services of some one in quality of guardian.

5. The deceased leaving a widow or descendants destitute of the means of subsistence, — to afford in their favour evidence of title to relief, at the charge of this or that individual, or of any public fund.

6. In any instance in which the testimony of the deceased would have been exigible, but on condition of its being delivered in the best shape, — to afford to the party who stands in need of it, the opportunity, if allowed by law, of producing it in any inferior shape in which it happens to be obtainable; such as hearsay, extrajudicially and casually-written, &c.

(2.) Uses having relation to the *penal* branch of law; and for which information concerning causes and circumstances is necessary.

These uses consist in the discovering or detecting, and, by fear of discovery and consequent punishment, preventing, death, in so far as it is liable to have for its cause human delinquency, whether *malâ fide* (*i. e.* accompanied with criminative consciousness,) or simply culpable, as being the result of temerity or negligence. Instance, among others, the case where a person not dead is interred on the supposition of his being dead.

The facts or circumstances necessary or proper to be taken for the subjects of registration will vary, according to the nature of the uses, as above distinguished, considered in the character of objects or ends to be aimed at.

Are the civil objects the only ones thought fit to be provided for? The fact of the extinction of life, and the sufficient description of the person, the identity of the deceased, may be the sole objects of attestation, and subjects of registration.

If the prevention or detection of delinquency in this line be also worth providing for, many other circumstances will be to be comprised in the inquiry, and in the declarations made in consequence.

1. Supposed manner of the death, whether gradual or sudden.

2. Supposed cause, — natural decay, or any external application, violent or otherwise: and in either case, whether human agency appeared to be in any way concerned in it.

3. The body, where, and how, and by whom, found.

4. Medical assistant, whether any, and who, called in; and if not, why not.*

II. Uses of registration as applied to births.

1. To ascertain and put out of dispute the fact of legitimacy or illegitimacy.

---

* Over and above making provision for the extraction and recordation of answers to questions such as the above, regulations to the following effect present themselves as conducive to the end in view: —

1. The death happening in the view of any person or persons, — obligation on them all to give notice of it to one or other of a set of functionaries appointed for the purpose; but so that the obligation shall be discharged for all, by performance made by one. The death happening, as in the ordinary state of things it does, in a house, — obligation on the housekeeper; but, in his default, on the several persons present.

2. Penalty on disposing of a body in any manner without notice as above: declaration, that from such clandestine disposal, suspicion of criminality will be induced.[a]

3. On receipt of such notice, a view to be taken, if practicable, antecedently to interment, or other mode of disposal, by, or by appointment of, the functionary to whom such notice has been communicated. The use of such view, not merely to prevent or detect criminal homicide, but to prevent sham interment where no death has taken place. Motive to such delinquency conceivable as follows: — persons next in succession to moveable property, or skilled in the art of forging last wills, have, for example, driven a man into a long voyage, by fears of accusation of an imaginary crime, or a crime of imaginary mischief, such as the law of most countries furnishes in sufficient abundance: then, pretending to bury him, have taken out letters of administration, or probate of his pretended will, as the case may be.

5. Immediately before interment, by the hand or under the inspection of the officiating functionary, require that a spike of appointed length, kept for the purpose, be run either through the heart, or into the brain, through the socket of the eye.

This precaution was suggested by a paragraph in *The Times* newspaper for 7th November 1808, in which it is mentioned as having been employed in a particular instance.

Delayed till the last moment preceding the interment, it may do good, and cannot possibly do harm. It can never produce death, but in a case in which, instead of an immediate, a horrible and lingering death would have been produced for want of it.

Putridity should not be regarded as a cause of dispensation. Putrid matter might be inserted into a coffin inclosing a pretended corpse. Putridity, if real, must have been already encountered by others: nor does it produce its noisome effects if the nose be but stopped, or if a man avoids to draw his breath through it.

Respecting these several precautions, and others that might be suggested, whether upon the whole it be, in any given country, eligible to render the employment of them obligatory, will depend, here as elsewhere, on the aggregate quantity of inconvenience in the shape of vexation and expense on the one hand, compared with the probable amount of delinquency and calamity in

---

[a] By the act above noticed (6 & 7 W. IV. c. 86) there is a penalty, not exceeding £10, exigible from any one who buries, or performs funeral service over a dead body, without a certificate of registry, unless he give information to the registrar within seven days (§ 27.) — *Ed.*

2. In either case, to establish, in favour of the child, title to maintenance at the charge of the proper person or persons.

3. In case of legitimacy, to establish, in favour of the child, its eventual title by succession to property left vacant by the death of its parents and other natural relatives.

4. In the meantime, to establish its title to the rights, and subject it to the obligations, attached to the condition in life into which it is introduced by its birth.

5. To establish the point of time at which it will have arrived at full age.

6. In the meantime, to establish its right to the services of the proper person in the character of guardian, and its correspondent obligation of submitting to the authority of that same person in that same character.

7. To prevent the wrongs that have sometimes been done to third persons by usurpation of sex. Example, the case of a female taking or giving possession of property intended by legal disposition to be confined to males.

8. In case of illegitimacy on the part of the child, — to prevent the wrong that would be done to legitimate children born of the same parents, or either of them, or to other more distant relatives, by an usurped participation of their rights.

9. By indication of its genealogy, to establish its incapacity of marrying within the prohibited degrees.

Measures subservient to the uses derivable from registration in the case of births:—

In ordinary cases —

1. Presentation of the infant to some public officer, by or on the part of the mother, within a certain time after the birth. Penalty, in case of omission. *Ex. gr.* as, in England, among members of the established church, presentation of the child by the sponsors to the minister, for the purpose of baptism.

2. Account thereupon given of the parents.

3. Mention and description thereupon of the midwife or midwifes, male included. If no professional midwife, mention accordingly: mention of any other person or persons assisting or present at the birth, or that there was no such assistant.

4. Register book to be kept by every professional midwife, according to a preappointed form: form for description of the parents included. Penalty on every person acting for hire without a licence.

In extraordinary cases —

1. Case of foundlings. Indication of some public officer, by whom the infant shall be taken care of, that maintenance may be afforded to it at the expense of some public fund, unless and until discovery shall have been made of some individual on whom the obligation have been imposed by law. *Ex. gr.* in English law, an overseer of the poor, by whom the infant is to be provided for at the expense of the parish.

2. Case of bastards born out of marriage. Provision for the examination of the mother, before or after the delivery, for the discovery of the putative father, to the end that the obligation of maintenance may be imposed on him according to law; or, in case of his inability, as well as that of the mother, on some subsidiary fund.

3. Case of bastards begotten in adultery. Provision for the examination of the mother, before the delivery, for the discovery of the putative father (as above,) in cases where the impossibility that the infant should have had the husband for its father is notorious; for example, by absence or impotence. In case of doubt, provision for establishing the fact by other evidence.

III. Uses of registration as applied to marriages.

1. In favour of each spouse, to establish his or her rights at the charge of the other: the husband's title to authority over the wife; the wife's title to charge the husband with debts contracted by her for her subsistence, and so forth.

2. In favour of the wife, to establish her title to the condition in life in which she is placed by her alliance with the husband.

3. In case of adultery on the part of either of them, — to establish the fact of marriage, for the purpose of any satisfaction which the law may have thought fit to afford to the other, and of any punishment which it may have thought fit to inflict upon the transgressing parties or either of them.

4. In case of misbehaviour in any other shape on the part of either to the prejudice of the other, — to establish, in favour of the party wronged, his or her title to whatever satisfaction may have been ordained by law, according to the nature of the case.

5. In case of a second marraige contracted or meditated on the part of either spouse, before any legal dissolution of the existing contract, — to contribute to establish, in favour of any party injured by such second marriage,

---

the various shapes in question prevented on the other.

It will therefore depend perhaps on the state of morality in the given country at the given time. But the aggregate of vexation and expense thus usefully employed, can hardly equal the aggregate quantity of vexation and expense habitually lavished on the occasion of interments, under the dominion of prejudice, and to no useful purpose, except in so far as the gratification of any popular affection, so long as it subsists, may, whatsoever be the cause of it, be considered as being of use.

Here, as in other ceremonies to which religion has attached itself, unfortunately, by the intolerance of some, with pain of disrepute in its hand, the vexation and expense is forced upon others by whom no gratification is derived from it.

his or her title to satisfaction for the injury; and likewise the obligation of the delinquent to undergo any punishment that may in that case have been provided by law.

6. At the death of either spouse, to establish, in favour of the survivor, his or her title, by succession or testament, to whatsoever portion of the property of the deceased may have been destined for him or her by law or legalized contract.

7. To establish, in favour and at the charge of children born under the marriage, their respective titles to the condition in life correspondent to that of the parents, together with such other rights and obligations as are above brought to view in the case of births.

8. In favour of third persons,—to prevent their being subjected to loss by purchase of immoveable or other property unalienably secured, by the marriage-contract, to either spouse, or to the issue of the marriage.

9. In a word,—in favour of third persons, to prevent their being subjected to loss in consequence of contracts entered into by either, on the supposition of his or her being single, or wedded to another.*

IV. Statistic uses derivable by the legislator from the conjunct registration of deaths, births, and marriages.

In general, the collateral uses, derivable in this shape from the registration of these genealogical events, are pretty well understood. In English practice, in particular, the discovery and publication of political facts finds men much less averse to it, than to the making a proper and consistent use of them. Many agree in making the ground, who would not agree about the superstructure.

In the account-books of the legislator, the number of the people is entered on both sides: on the side of profit, and on the side of loss: on the *plus* side, by the resources it affords; on the *minus* side, by the resources it stands in need of: on the side of profit, by what it produces and supplies; on the side of loss, by what it consumes. It produces food, and it produces mouths that are to be fed: it produces men for defenders, and women and children that require to be defended: it produces arms and men that ward off the depredator, and it produces the precious matter that invites him.

The quantities ascertained,—by comparisons made of them, various other indications, pregnant with inferences and regulations, are obtained.

1. By comparison of deaths with births, due allowance being at the same time made for immigration and emigration, the healthiness of each spot, as compared with every other at any given period, and as compared with itself at different periods, is ascertained.

2. Hence, in case of measures taken by the legislator for the increase of salubrity, the degree of success (if any) with which they are attended, may become discernible.

3. Hence, the individual whose situation admits of choice, and in whose eyes health and longevity obtain the preference to rival blessings, sees how and where to choose.

4. Here, too, the forecast of individuals finds a basis for its calculations, and the transactions grounded on them. Provision for a man's self during his life, or for persons dear to him, to take place after his death, is thus secured against uncertainty and disappointment.

But, unless due allowance be made for the difference in point of longevity between different modes of life, severe deception and disappointment will be apt to ensue.

§ 2. *Aberrations of English law in regard to the registration of genealogical facts.*

In most civilized states, and in England among the rest, religious policy has interposed; and, in the pursuit of its own objects, has, as well in respect of correctness as of completeness, deteriorated the whole mass of genealogical preappointed evidence.

In the instance of each species of genealogical event, it has substituted to the fact or event intrinsically material, a fact extraneous to it, and, though most commonly, yet not in its nature necessarily, nor in practice invariably, connected with it.

1. To registration of the fact of death, it has substituted registration of the ceremony of interment, and that only in the case where accompanied with certain formalities; one of which is, the presence and operation of an ecclesiastical functionary of a certain order: so that, if the body is disposed of in any other manner, or by a priest of another order, or without the assistance of a priest, no registration is to take place.

2. To registration of birth, it has substituted registration of *baptism*:† a ceremony which consists in the sprinkling the new-born child with water; on the occasion of which operation, certain words are to be pronounced, viz. in the form of a dialogue, in which one of the interlocutors must have been a priest, of the same order, as above: so that, if the child remains unsprinkled, or the sprinkling be performed without the accompaniment of the recently invented dialogue, or with the intervention of a priest of a different order,

* Securing the legality of the marriage is a collateral end, that might easily be attained by appropriate arrangements, whereof interrogation would be the principal instrument. But we are now considering, not what formalities ought to be observed on the occasion of entering into the contract, but what are the advantages derivable from the registration of it when concluded.

† The statute above noticed (6 & 7 W. IV. c. 86) appoints the *births*, and *deaths*, as the facts for registration.—*Ed.*

or without the intervention of any priest, no registration is to take place.

3. To registration of an instrument of marriage-contract, or of the fact of its having been executed, it has substituted the registration of the performance of a certain ceremony; on the occasion of which ceremony, certain other words are to be pronounced, viz. in the form of a dialogue, in which one of the interlocutors must again have been a priest, of the same order, as above: so that, if the ceremony be performed without the accompaniment of this recently-invented dialogue, or with the intervention of a priest of a wrong order, or without the intervention of any priest, no registration is to take place; or, if any registration happens anywhere to be made of the transaction, no care is taken on the part of government to preserve it, or put it to use.

On this occasion, had it happened to these all-powerful functionaries to join in taking for their object or end in view the welfare and good behaviour of the parties to this contract, care would have been taken (as already intimated) that, on the occasion and by means of this ceremony, a correct and complete conception, and (without which it can neither be correct nor complete) a *particular* conception, should be formed by the parties to this most important of all contracts, of the obligations with which they are respectively about to charge themselves, and of the rights which they are about to acquire. But to the priest, whose interest centres in the obtaining of worship with the fruits of it for himself, and to whom the temporal welfare of ever-sinning mortals is an object beneath, oftentimes even avowedly beneath, his care, their good behaviour in respect of the contract is at best a matter of indifference; while to the lawyer, whose prosperity rises with the unhappiness and misconduct of mankind, it is matter of advantage, that obligations and rights of this class, as of every other, should float in perpetual uncertainty; and that, in this as in every other part of the field of action, the rule of action should remain for ever as completely unknown, and as incapable of being known, as possible. An awe-inspiring formulary — composed of vague generalities and historical allusions, and (by the careful exclusion of all specific delineation of rights and obligations) rendered as barren of useful and applicable instruction as possible — was therefore unexceptionably conformable to both their interests: and hence, on this as on so many other occasions, on the spurious and usual pretence of warming and guiding the *heart*, a composition is framed and employed from which the *head* can derive no use.

It is on pretence of fulfilling the will of Christ Jesus, that the mode of recording this most important modification of preappointed evidence has been rendered to so great an extent inapplicable to the purposes to which it has been, or ought to have been, directed; and in not so much as one of the cases is Christ Jesus so much as pretended to have ever said anything about the matter.

Religion is thus planted and kept on foot by force, under the notion of its indispensable necessity to the well-being of the present life: yet, when opportunity presents itself for rendering it so, the opportunity is, with an uniformity too constant not to be the work of design, suffered to slip by unimproved.

Under the old French law, matters were so arranged, that, with or without the assistance of the mother, it depended on any person or persons having possession of a new-born child, if not absolutely to give to it what parentage they thought fit, at any rate to render its real parentage absolutely unascertainable. The nurse (so for strictness be it said,) in producing the child to the officiating functionary, the parish priest, spoke of it as having such and such persons for its parents: no oath administered, no interrogation proposed, no means provided for subjecting the deponent to eventual punishment in case of falsity: on this naked assertion, was the fact entered upon the register as certain. To prove the falsity of a declaration of this sort, no evidence whatever, not the testimony of any number of witnesses, testifying upon oath, and upon interrogation administered in the ordinary mode, was admitted.* Hearsay evidence was thus not only admitted, but admitted to the exclusion of original evidence.

The fraud thus practiceable had its good effects as well as its bad ones. In the case of a child born in adultery, in circumstances which rendered it notoriously impossible that the husband should have been the father, the reputation of the mother, the peace and honour of the family, was saved from blemish: and so in the case of a birth without marriage.

Upon the whole, was it eligible or not eligible, that transgressions of this sort should be concealed? If eligible, the purpose might have as effectually been provided for without, as by, the falsity. In this case, the proper subject for registration would have been the *fact* that a declaration to such an effect was made — made by individuals styling themselves so and so; not the *inference*, which, as above, was surreptitiously substituted to it.

Among the advantages resulting from the substitution of the plan of honest reserve to that of connivance at fraud, would have been the information of a statistic nature which in that case it would have been in the power of the legislator to derive. The cases of concealed parentage being on this plan distinguished from the ordinary class of cases, the proportion between the one and the other at different periods would thus have been open to observation.

---

* Causes Célèbres.

CHAPTER XI.

OF OFFICES FOR CONSERVATION OF TRANSCRIPTS OF CONTRACTS.*

§ 1. *Uses of transcriptitious registration as applied to contracts.*

WHAT it may be of use to bring to view on the subject of this application of the principle of preappointed evidence, seems referable to one or other of two heads:—viz. 1. Uses to which offices of this description may be applied; 2. Means of adapting them to such their respective uses; 3. Limits to be set to the employment of the principle, *i. e.* to the application of it to its respective uses.

First, in regard to *uses.*

1. Of the uses to which a conservatory of the kind in question may be applied, the simplest and most obvious is that of serving to whatsoever uses the original instrument, be it what it may, was designed to serve. The first use of transcription is that which is identical with that of *scription.* For every fresh transcript, a fresh security against the evils, for the prevention of which, the original script was designed. Preservation—simple preservation—is the name by which this use may be designated.

The description of persons by whom, and by whom alone, to the extent of this use, the benefit is reaped, are the parties to the contract, together with (in case of death) their natural representatives.

2. Next to this comes the sort of use, the benefit of which is designed for third persons—persons other than the parties to the contract and their natural representatives. *Notification*, or *promulgation*, or, when considered in another point of view, *reference*, are the names by which this use may be expressed.

If, with relation to any such third persons, notification of the contract be regarded as prescribed by justice and good faith,—omission of such notification, where performance is regarded as practicable, may be considered as a species of fraud, viz. fraud in the shape of *undue reticence.*†

The particular cases in which this collateral benefit is reaped, may be thus exemplified:—

I. Conditional dispositions made of particular subjects of property (most commonly in the shape of immoveable property,) for the purpose of securing the repayment of money lent; possession, or apparent proprietorship (as by receipt of rent,) remaining unchanged: as in the case of mortgages.

Persons liable in this case to be injured by the non-notification are—

1. Subsequent mortgagees: other persons to whom the like disposition for the like purpose might, for want of notice, come to be made of the same subject.

2. Subsequent creditors at large: persons to whom—in virtue of debts owing to them by the proprietor of the subject, the mortgager—a right is acquired to property to a correspondent amount, in whatever shape, belonging to such their debtor; and who would not have trusted him with the monies respectively in question, had it been known to them that the property thus in appearance free, was in reality charged with the incumbrance.

3. Subsequent purchasers: persons by whom the subject-matter in question might, for want of such notice, come to be purchased, at a price proportioned to the value which it appeared to have—viz. the value which it would have had, had it not been subject to this charge.

II. Absolute dispositions made of a particular subject of property, or of the whole mass of a man's property; possession or apparent proprietorship, as before, remaining unchanged: as in the case of the instrument called in English practice a *bill of sale*, conveying the property of a mass of moveable goods; or in the case of a settlement made, for example on the occasion of marriage, conveying a mass of immoveable property, but in such sort as not to take effect till after the proprietor's death, or at some other future point of time, determinate or indeterminate.

Persons liable to be injured by non-notification, are in this case the same as in the case just mentioned.

III. Long leases: dispositions made of a particular subject of property (most commonly in the shape of immoveable property,) to take effect and continue for a long portion of time, but with intent that, at the expiration of that length of time, it should revert to the disposer or his representatives.

Persons liable in this case to be injured by the non-notification, are by possibility the alienor himself, but much more probably his representatives: as in the case of a house let according to the English custom, for a term of 60 or 99 years,—a disposition which in some instances has been made for a peppercorn, or other small rent—so small as not to be demanded: whence oblivion of the

* An establishment of this sort has place in Scotland. Even in England, however inadequate the footing upon which it has been placed, it has had place, and for near a century, in the two most populous counties;—it has had place in Middlesex and Yorkshire: everywhere (though under the great disadvantages resulting from the form given to the originals) with universally acknowledged good effect. Scotchmen would accordingly not be wanting who would stand up—stand up in Middlesex, and, in the instance of this as of any other obstacle attempted to be opposed to high-seated improbity, pronounce it mischievous, and certify it to be impracticable.

† See Chap. II. § 1.

contract, and loss of the property to the representatives.

§ 2. *Mode of adapting the system of transcriptitious registration to its uses.**

Under this head, five subjects of consideration present themselves:—

1. Contracts registrable, contracts fit to be included in the system of registration, what.

2. How much to be registered? — the whole, or what part?

3. Means of enforcement, what.

4. Mode of reference and notification, what.

5. Mode of designation, in case of land, what.

I. What are the sorts of contracts that shall be registered?

1. For the benefit of parties — at the instance of any party, any contract whatsoever; he paying for the advantage such reasonable price as shall be fixed by law.

2. For the benefit of third persons — for prevention of fraud to the prejudice of third persons, — all contracts, from the non-notification of which, fraud to the prejudice of any third person is with reason to be apprehended.

3. For the security of persons who mean to purchase land, or to accept of a charge upon it as a security for money lent, — all contracts (for instance) by which the title to property in the land in question is capable of being affected.

II. Of each contract, individually taken, how much shall be consigned to the register? Shall it be entered *in toto*, in abridgment, or in extract?

Expense apart, there can be but one answer: enter the whole. By a complete transcript, you are quite sure that every purpose will be answered: that exactly the same effect will be produced by anything less than the whole, cannot be asserted with equal confidence.

So far as the interest of parties alone is concerned, omission of any part will hardly be regarded as desirable. In the transcript, is there any part that would be superfluous? So would it then be in the original: and it is from the original, and by that means from the transcript, not from the transcript alone, that the defalcation ought to be made.

It is only with a view to the interests of third persons, that any reason can present itself for preferring either an abridgment or an extract to an entire transcript; and that with no other view than that of avoiding expense.

For the benefit of third persons, consign to the register (it will naturally be said) so much, and so much only, of the mass, as it can be of use to third persons, as such, to be informed of.

Indications beyond comparison less bulky than the whole instrument, might, it is true, to third persons, be in some respects preferable to the whole; and that not merely on the score of the expense, but even on the score of information: since, by a slight and concise intimation given of the purport of such parts in which alone the individual third person in question is interested, the labour of perusing the entire instrument may be saved.

The truth of the observation is beyond dispute: but, expense apart, the practical inference is, not that the partial indication should be substituted, but that it should be added, to the whole.

By the substitution of an abridgment or an extract to a complete transcript, danger of error would moreover to a certain degree be introduced: whereas in a transcript, all danger, all possibility, of error, may be avoided.†

* See "*Outline of a Plan for a General Register of Real Property*," communicated by the author to the Real Property Commissioners, *supra*, Vol. V. p. 417.

† By the exertions of modern ingenuity, three or four different inventions have been produced, by any one of which, error, as between exemplar and exemplar of the same script, is rendered impossible.

1. Paper little different from the ordinary having been written upon with an ordinary pen, and with ink little different from the ordinary, — copies, one, or (according to the care and skill of the operator) even two or three, all legible, are taken by means of a press. Inventors, Messrs. Bolton and Watt.

2. Paper, ink, and pen, in every respect the same as the ordinary, — two or more pens are, by a simple mechanism upon the principle of the pentagraph, connected in such manner that, one of them being held and put in motion by the hand, another, with a separate sheet of paper under it, is put in motion at the same time. Inventor, Mr. Brunel.

A recent improvement made upon this principle is effected by such a disposition of the apparatus as places the pen which is not in the hand, much nearer to the hand and eye than according to the original plan: at the distance, say, of an inch instead of a foot.

3. Instead of a pen with ink in it, a metallic style or pencil is employed. Between two sheets of paper little different from the ordinary, a leaf of paper impregnated with a black pigment is interposed. The pencil, in pressing upon all three, imprints on the two white sheets (viz. that which is over, and that which is under, the black one,) the characters composed of the matter thus pressed off from the blank one. Inventor, Mr. Wedgwood, of Oxford-street, London.[a]

To pronounce which of these different productions of human ingenuity is upon the whole best adapted to the purpose here in question, belongs not to the competence of the author, any more than to the design of the present work. Thus much however I can take upon me to pronounce, that there is not one of them but is to such a degree adapted to the purpose of legally-operative

[a] See this subject further discussed, *supra*, Vol. V. p. 406.

Making an abridgment or an extract is work for the head—work to which all heads may not be equal: making a transcript is, or may be made, work for the hand only.

III. Mode of enforcing observance.

Supposing no notary employed, this is a point that may be attended with difficulty. But everywhere, with the exception of the few species of contract by the simplicity of which, be the importance of the value at stake ever so considerable, such assistance is generally regarded as unnecessary,—everywhere, and in English practice in particular, such assistance is called in.

For cases of necessity, in which the recurrence to that assistance is by the pressure of the exigency rendered impracticable, provision might be made by giving to the contract a temporary validity, to the end of a length of time within which the practicability of obtaining such assistance may be regarded as certain. Due provision having thus been made for these cases, the intervention of a notary may without danger of injustice be regarded as necessary to the validity of the contract.*

Owing to the imperishable nature of the subject-matter, contracts having relation to

---

the ordinary mode of writing in present use, would, if the interest of the community at large were the end in view, be superseded and laid aside.

The principle of the many-penned instrument (be it observed) is capable of being connected with, and applied to either of the other two: insomuch that, either by the second and first together, or by the second and third together, four exemplars, all of them incapable of erring from each other, may be obtained at once; and, in the case of that in which a style is employed, without the employment of any greater force than what in English practice is employed in writing, with pen and ink, on parchment, the sort of handwriting called *engrossing*.

The ink employed in the first invention, being in this respect not materially different from ordinary ink, is, like that, liable to be obliterated by acid menstrua. The pigment employed in the invention last mentioned, having carbon for its colouring matter, is proof against the agency of acid menstrua at any rate, and, as far as yet known, against all others that are capable of being applied to paper without destroying it, or betraying themselves.

Here, then, is a peculiar security against forgery in the way of *falsification*. But, when compared with the two other inventions, the advantage, so far as concerns registration, has no place; inasmuch as, different exemplars being lodged in different hands, and some of them official, falsification could not be performed upon any one with any prospect of success.

Here, then, without any time, labour, or expense, bestowed on transcription—or, after the first moderate cost of the instruments, any other than that of the paper—is a set of transcripts, one, two, three, or more, produced; whereof one or more applicable to the purpose of official registration.

Here, although there should be three different parties concerned in the contract in point of interest, and so concerned as to require to have each of them a distinct exemplar in his custody,—here is one for each, besides one for the registration office.

It might even so be ordered, that, besides one for the office, there should be one for each of four or five private hands; for an exemplar expressed by characters too faint to be legible with the rapidity required by convenience in ordinary use, might answer the purpose of the registration office. Suppose even here and there a word not legible, the deficiency might be supplied by the context: and, forasmuch as it would be impossible to divine to what word or words (if to any) the failure would attach, falsification would be rendered as effectually hopeless by an imperfect exemplar, as by a perfect one.

So, again, as to the use of registration in the prevention of fraud to the prejudice of third persons for want of notice. The official exemplar must be imperfect indeed, if it failed of giving such intimation of the contents as would be abundantly sufficient for this purpose.

The exemplars, more or fewer, would not any of them be on parchment: and, for instruments which aim at permanence, under English law, parchment is the substratum in present use. But paper possesses permanence to a degree altogether sufficient for the purpose: and it was not by superiority to paper, but by non-existence of paper, that parchment was brought into use.

From a slip of no more than two fingers breadth, parchment for instruments of contract has, together with the tenor of the instruments themselves, swelled to the largest size which the bulk of the animal will afford: and, in the article of breadth, that size is eminently inconvenient: when the eye has reached the end of one line, to find the next to it is a problem, which, to an unpractised eye, is in no small degree difficult to solve.

The use of promulgation paper, provided with a printed border, presenting, in tenor or in the way of reference, such dispositions of law as are applicable to the subject, has been already brought to view. But, by having the margin thus furnished out by the operations of the printing-press, the body of the sheet need not be rendered the less susceptible of being applied to the inventions above mentioned.

In the eye of the minister of finance, in comparison with any the slightest degree of supposed facility in the collection of revenue, all other objects put together, justice and every security it is capable of affording, are of no value. Had they any, it would not become the object of so many sincere and effective though indirect prohibitions, while injustice is combated by so many direct and ineffectual ones.

But, on this occasion as on others, that arbiter of human destiny would as little be in want of the means, as of the desire, of taking care of himself.

* Provided always (as was observed in Chap. III.) that sufficient means have been taken for making it perfectly certain, that no person who can ever have occasion to enter into any of the sorts of contract in question, shall be unapprized of the necessity of obtaining the assistance of a notary.

immoveable property will be regarded as constituting a class in relation to which the demand for registration is in a particular degree manifest and incontestable: but these are the cases in which the scientific assistance of a professional man is most apt to be needed, and the certainty of obtaining it within time most entire.

The intervention of an assistant of this description being then supposed,—in his person the legislator has a security for the observance of this, as of all other, formalities, which it shall have been thought fit to prescribe.

The exemplar being reserved in his hands for the purpose,—to him, under a penalty, it belongs to transmit to the proper register office such exemplar within the space of time prescribed.

To him it might belong to keep an appropriate book, or set of books, in which, under a set of heads prescribed by the legislator (prescribed with a view to the *uses*, as above indicated,) entry shall be made of each contract in which he has been concerned.

The office of each such notary becomes thus, to the extent of the business of this sort done by him, a sort of register office: and, of every such book, an exemplar might be periodically transmitted to the register office belonging to the county or other district within which his residence is situated.

Such seem to be the means which *justice* and *reason* recommend for ensuring the observance of this as of other formalities. Under the influence of the partnership interest begotten by the fee-gathering system, *custom* has established a very different one. In this case, as in the case of operations and instruments of procedure, *nullity* is the consequence of non-observance: without any tolerable ground for supposing that notice of such consequence will uniformly be received—that the party will be apprized of the sword hung by a hair over his head— without any thing done by the legislator towards rendering it probable. For the neglect committed by one man, punishment, and without regard to proportion, inflicted on another;—for the misbehaviour of the inferior member of the law-partnership, the *attorney*, punishment inflicted by the superior members of the same partnership, the judges, on the attorney's *client*, the party who had no share in the blame.

IV. Mode of notification and reference.

To the first clause or paragraph of a scheme for registration grounded on the current principles, I read a marginal content in these words:—" No deed, will, or codicil affecting land, to be valid, unless enrolled within six months; or three years, if the deed or will be executed without the kingdom." And then, to a second clause or paragraph—" The enrolment to be notice to all persons." And afterwards another:—" No land to be affected by a judgment, unless notice left at the reference office."

If, in the instance of every " deed, will, and codicil affecting land," on the margin of the paper on which the instrument was written, the text of a portion of law were printed, denouncing invalidity (as above) as the penal consequence of the neglect in question, viz. the non-enrolment within the appointed time, —the injustice of the provision would, in part at least, be done away: the client would be punished for neglect which would be the act of his lawyer; but the act required to be performed would not be altogether out of the power of him on whom the obligation of performing it was imposed.

If, in the instance of every deed serving for the purchase of land, or for the lending of money on the security of land, on the margin of the paper were to be found in like manner an intimation of the existence of a system of *register offices*, adapted to the purpose in question,—together with a recommendation to search the proper register office, for the purpose of ascertaining whether the land in question had been the subject of any such disposition remaining still in force;—in this way (supposing moreover the practical observance of the provision prescribing registration,) notice of the enrolment— real notice, not merely constructive, *i. e.* sham notice— would be given, if not to all persons, at any rate to all persons concerned in point of interest in the receipt of it.

Six months are, on the above plan, allowed for the operation of enrolment. Within the six months, in confidence of the non-existence of any such contract affecting the land in question, a man purchases the land, and pays the money to the seller, who goes off with it. The money gone, then comes the enrolment; the sole professed object of which is to prevent the payment which has been made.

Should any real desire of opposing effectual prevention to such mischief be entertained the course pursued will be somewhat different. A set of heads, adapted as above, being preappointed by the legislator (and a very short and simple one will be adequate for the purpose;) the notary, having prepared, along with the instrument of contract, a letter of advice addressed to the register office, in which letter of advice is contained a memorandum of the contract, containing an intimation of the matter belonging to those several heads (viz. names of the parties, situation and quantity of the land, general nature of the disposition made of it, whether sale, settlement, lease, or mortgage,) brings it, together with the instrument of contract, to the place appointed for the execution of the instrument of contract; and, as soon as the ceremony has been performed, delivers in at the next post-office such letter of advice; obtaining from the postmaster or his substitute, his signature to a receipt, also ready prepared, and in which the direction inscribed on the letter of advice is transcribed.

In the memorandum of which the substance of this letter of advice is composed, notice sufficient to answer at least the temporary purpose would be already given; as the *caveat* preparatory to an invention-patent answers for the time the purpose of the patent itself. But the very body of the instrument of contract itself,—why need it wait longer? An exemplar for the collateral purpose being already brought into existence along with the other exemplars allotted to the direct purpose of the contract, there will be no more difficulty in sending by the same conveyance, and at the same time, this complete exemplar, than the compressed and imperfect minute of it.

The *letter of advice* so transmitted (as above) to the register office, and deposited, or *filed* (to use the lawyer's word) in that office, serves, from the instant at which it is so deposited, for the information of *searchers: i. e.* of persons having occasion to learn whether any contract has been entered into, whereby the state of the property of the land in question is affected.

Thus, then, the purpose of searchers is answered. But the security and tranquillity of the notary by whom the memorandum or exemplar of the contract was transmitted, remains to be provided for.

For this purpose, instead of one exemplar of the memorandum (as above,) he sends two to the register office.* Of these two, one remains in the office (as above;) the other is re-transmitted to him by the same conveyance, having first received, besides the direction, an acknowledgment of receipt, dated and signed by one of the clerks belonging to the office; to whose onomastic signature may be added, and (for expedition) by a stamp, the words by which a designation is given of the office.

If, besides the memorandum of the contract, it be a case in which an exemplar of the same contract is to be deposited at the office, whether on that same day or a subsequent one;—in this case, instead of *two* exemplars of the memorandum, the notary sends to the office *three*. One remains at the office (as above;) another is re-transmitted to him with the mark of acknowledgment (as above;) the third, being re-transmitted to him on the day on which the instrument of contract is received at the office, serves, by the addition of a few words, for the acknowledgment of the receipt of the instrument of contract so received:—"*Received this day, the deed of which the above is the memorandum.*"†

V. Mode of designation, in case of land.

A short hint on this subject may not be without its uses.

A geometrical survey of the island of Great Britain by order of government has for many years been in hand. Among the purposes to which that important work will be found applicable, that of serving for the designation of portions of land, for the purpose of conveyances and other contracts, may, it should seem, be numbered.

In the vestry-room, or any other more convenient place, in the custody of the minister, or minister and churchwardens, of each parish, might be deposited a copy of that part of the map which exhibits so much of the land as is contained within the precincts of that parish. The map may be divided into squares, and, in deeds, the portion of land in question described by reference to the squares.

In, and in the near neighbourhood of, a town or village, such part of the ground as is already covered, or likely to be soon covered, by buildings, might require to be exhibited by a separate map constructed upon a larger scale.‡

Each parish being thus provided with its authoritative map, here would a standard of reference, to which, in all suits in which situation and quantity of a portion of land came in question, reference should be made: made, in the first place in the instrument of demand, then in the instrument of defence, and lastly, in the judgment.‖

* The produce of the copying apparatus already spoken of.

† In Scotland, enrolment in the register of sasines constitutes a title to land, with which no unenrolled title can interfere; and enrolled or recorded titles have precedence according to the date of their presentation to the registrar. The person who first produces his instrument of sasine for enrolment, is thus preferable to a prior purchaser. The instrument of sasine is the notarial record of the act of taking sasine or infeftment on the land, which is ineffectual unless the instrument be presented to the registrar within sixty days after the ceremony.—*Ed.*

‡ By the convexity and inequality of the earth's surface, difficulties will be produced respecting the adjustment of the mensuration of the minute portions liable to become the subject of legal contracts, to the mensuration of the whole. But, by geometricians, by whom the nature of these difficulties is understood, the means of obviating and surmounting them to a degree sufficient for practice will also be understood.[a]

‖ Under the fee-gathering system, in English practice,—uncertainty, not certainty, being the real end of judicature,—in the instrument of demand (the *declaration* in the action of *ejectment*,) not so much as an approximation towards the description of the quantity really in dispute is attempted. The judgment having no other basis than the instrument of demand, no information respecting quantity is afforded by what is called

[a] See above, Vol. V. p. 428.

§ 3. *Limits to the application of the practice of transcriptitious registration.*

As in case of collection of evidence, and other judicial operations, so in the case of contracts, — notification, though in some respects purely beneficial, will in other respects be, in some cases, and with reference to some description of persons, pernicious.

From this consideration, two objects of solicitude are imposed upon the legislator; viz.

1. Not to require or permit divulgation, where the mischief of it, when carried to the necessary extent, is deemed preponderant over the good.

2. Where the good is preponderant over the mischief, still not to cause or suffer the communication to be made or received by any persons, in relation to whom either no benefit accrues, or, if any, not to such an amount as to outweigh that of the mischief done to others.

So far as the act of registration is purely optional — not performable but at the instance of the only party or parties interested, and, in case of divers parties, of all the parties interested, — the practice can have no need of limitation.

But, by the very act of registration, the existence of the contract is exposed in some sort to disclosure.

If, in such cases, non-disclosure, so far as practicable, be upon the whole desirable, — then comes the question, what, consistently with the act of registration, shall be the arrangements taken to prevent it?

This case is in a manner confined to last wills: under which denomination may be included, if there be any difference, gratuitous dispositions of property made by a single person, not to take effect till his death, and revocable by him at any time during his life.

A contract of this sort it may happen to a man to be desirous of depositing in a public register office for safe custody. In such a case, a desire natural to every man is to conceal the particular terms of it. This object may, in such a place, be effectually secured, by the universally known expedients of folding up and sealing. But in such a case it is not always enough to a man that the particular terms of the disposition made by him should be unknown: it is frequently of essential importance to him that the fact of his having made any disposition of that nature should remain equally unknown and undiscoverable. This object may with little danger of failure be accomplished, by the equally obvious expedient of a solemn engagement to that effect entered into, and universally known to be entered into, by the several officers belonging to the office.

On the mode of correspondence between the individual and the office in this particular case, no separate observation need here be made. Of what has been said on that subject in a former section, the application to the present case is sufficiently obvious.

In the case of a last will, concealment cannot operate to the injury of anybody: property is not bound by it till the death of the party takes place, and then the concealment may be, ought to be, and naturally will be, at an end.

It is only where the interests of third persons of a particular description are liable to be affected by the contract, if concealed from third persons of that description, — in which case, on that consideration, it is proposed to render registration compulsory, — that any question can arise concerning the degree of secrecy, if any, which is proper, and the arrangements fit to be taken in the view of securing it.

Taken in its totality, the subject of contracts is to such a degree multifarious as well as extensive, that, in treating of it, to give to conception a determinate object, here as elsewhere, it will be of use to take, in the first instance at least, a particular class of contracts: say, for instance, in consideration of their superior importance, those which affect property in immoveables.

In this instance, is it of use upon the whole that secrecy in any degree, secrecy as against anybody, should be preserved?

Those who contend for the affirmative, will, on these occasions, be apt to deal in generals. All families have their secrets; from the divulgation of which, great mortification and inconvenience may arise. The state of a man's property is universally regarded as being of the number. In the case of commercial men, when revenue has been the object, particular arrangements, having for their professed object the preservation of secrecy, have, under the British government, with much anxiety been established by law.

Answer: — By the communications necessary to the collection of the property taxes, — by these communications, if divulged, or made public, or rendered generally accessible, the totality of a man's property would be made known. But, by no such registration as it could be proposed to apply to contracts, would the whole of his property be made known or knowable.

The only case in which it could be supposed that, by the registration of contracts, the state of a man's property would be dis-

the *record*, in which the declaration and judgment are compared. When the judgment is in favour of the plaintiff, possession is given — not by the judge to the plaintiff — but by the plaintiff, with the privity and assistance of the sheriff (who on this occasion acts under the authority of, but without any directions from the judge,) — by the plaintiff, at his own peril, to himself.

closed, is that of a contract affecting land (say a mortgage, or a marriage-settlement,) in the instance of a man, the bulk of whose property consists in land.

By a marriage-settlement, if known, no property is pointed out as departed out of the family. The property indeed, to the extent of that which is the subject of the settlement, is shown not to be liable to be disposed of, beyond the lifetime of the present possessor, in discharge of debts. But that is the very thing which individuals in general are in point of interest concerned, and in point of justice intitled, to know;—viz. lest, by trusting their money or money's-worth to one who, knowing he has not wherewithal, intends not to reimburse them, they should be defrauded.

Even by a mortgage — taking the state of the family on the footing of that transaction alone — it can never be known that any diminution of property has taken place. To make improvements, by which the property may be augmented, or provide for incumbrances, the existence of which is already matter of notoriety, such as the payment of younger children's fortunes, may have been the object.

But — in so far as the effect of the mortgage is to place property out of the reach of creditors, out of the reach of justice — in so far is it matter of justice that the transaction should be generally known; lest, as in the former case, fraud should take place.*

The defraudment of creditors, for want of knowledge of the contract, is a mischief (it may be said) that will only have place in here and there an instance: in no case but in the case of prodigality, which, according to the well known and practically useful observation of Adam Smith, is a case comparatively rare; whereas, by the divulgation of such contracts, a mischief is produced which extends to everybody.

Be it so. But this supposed mischief, the result of the disclosure of mortgages, when it does take place, — what, after all, does it amount to?

When everything is distinctly explained, it amounts to neither more nor less than this; viz. that a man is prevented from causing his neighbours and acquaintance to suppose his property to be greater than it is. But of this prevention, where is the real mischief? What harm, even if he should be prevented from obtaining, if not money, at least reputation, on false pretences — that sort of reputation which consists in the opinion of a man's being possessed of money?

To obtain money, or money's-worth, upon false pretences, is made punishable — is treated as a crime next to capital. To obtain advantage in any other shape — in any of those shapes in which it is (as in most shapes it is) transmutable into money, need not certainly be punished in the same degree; but to what good end of morality or policy can it be protected and encouraged?

Supposing it a settled point, that, in relation to contracts affecting land, indiscriminate publicity ought to be granted, the channels and the means are sufficiently obvious. Newspapers are employed for giving publicity to declarations of bankruptcy and to dissolutions of partnerships: newspapers, and in particular the local newspapers of each county, or correspondent territorial district, might be employed for giving publicity to all contracts by which land in that district is affected.

Not that, even for the purpose of limited and appropriate notification, this indiscriminate but momentary mode of divulgation would be sufficient: the day past, the newspaper of the day is forgotten. For search to be performed at any time, a register office would not the less be necessary.

§ 4. *Importance of reducing within compass the matter to be transcribed. — Aberrations of English practice in this respect.*

If improving in point of extent and utility the practice of transcriptitious registration, be among the ends which the legislator ought to propose to himself, two main objects, in the character of means, call for his regard: 1. The giving facility to the operation, viz. that of transcription itself; 2. The reducing within compass the matter to be transcribed.

Everywhere, under the influence of the fee-gathering system, the business of penning instruments of contract (the business of conveyancing as it is called) having been the work of the fee-gathering partnership, Judge and Co., executed under the impulse and direction of the interest of the firm — an interest acting in a direction diametrically opposite to that of the community at large, and thereby directly repugnant to the ends of justice, — the object, in the case of these legalized expressions of private will, as in the case of the expressions of public will, has been, — what? To render, to the extent of the patience of a deluded people, every discourse belonging to this class, as ill-adapted as possible to the common purposes of discourse — to the purposes which, in every discourse, of this most important class in particular, ought to be aimed at with more especial care: — in a word, to render it as obscure, as ambiguous, and, for the joint purposes of obscurity and ambiguousness, as unnatural, and absurd, and voluminous, as possible: to add to the natural obscurity of the subject, as much factitious obscurity and impenetrability as could be given to it by the

* In Scotland by the system of registration above alluded to (p. 579, note +,) no mortgage or heritable burden can be made real without registration. — *Ed.*

boundless accumulation of excrementitious matter, as disgusting and repulsive as it could be made to the taste, as well as impenetrable to the understanding, of the non-lawyer; that is, of every individual who is not paid for wading through it.

On this as on other parts of the field of legal lucre, there has been of course a perpetual contest, and trial of skill, as between the lawyers of the several civilized nations: but by the English lawyer (unless, in this part of the race, the exertions of the Scotch lawyer should be found to afford, in some respects, an exception,) all competitors of all other nations have been left far behind. So far as concerns the mere heaping of words upon words, his exertions, or the fruit of them, may perhaps have been equalled or exceeded. But in the practice of what is called *fiction*, legal fiction, — the most pernicious and basest sort of lying — lying by or with the concurrence and support, as well as for the profit, of the judge, — he has found an implement, in the use of which he has in a manner stood alone. By the help of this instrument of fraud and extortion, he has contrived to make the individual pay, as if it were the plain and honest expression of his will, for a tissue of absurdities, which have no more natural connexion with it than a chapter out of the adventures of Baron Munchausen, or the tales of Mother Goose.*

In a marriage-settlement drawn by a French or a German lawyer, there may possibly be (though it is difficult to conceive how there should be) as many useless and thence pernicious words, as in the non-mendacious parts of the composition of his brother of the trade in England: but, in so far as morality is concerned, if veracity be considered as a branch of it, the most dishonest composition of the Frenchman or the German, is, in comparison with that of the English attorney and his associates (for the work for which a single hand suffices on the continent is in England the work of legion,) the language of sincerity and truth.

To substitute truth to falsehood, common sense to absurdity, would require nothing new but *will* on the part of the English legislator. Of the exertion and ingenuity which is lavished in the service of injustice, a small portion would suffice for the purposes of justice.

Already the legislator is in use to give formularies for judgments of conviction: let him extend the application of the same incontestably useful principle and honest practice to instruments of contract, to conveyances.

Not a fiction but is capable of being translated, and occasionally is translated, into the language of truth. Burn the original, by the hands by which so many less noxious nuisances have been burnt, — burn the original, and employ the translation in its stead. Fiction is no more necessary to justice, than poison is to sustenance.

To the mass of judicial lying called a *fine* — to the other mass of judicial lying called a *recovery*, substitute the plain truth, by which the legal operation of either might be declared in half a dozen lines. To the lease and release, substitute the *feoffment*, to which these two correspondent masses of falsehood and absurdity have themselves been substituted. In the case of the mortgage, declare that right of possession to be *eventual*, which neither is nor is meant to be anything more.

All these instruments of fraud, and receptacles of falsehood and absurdity, teem with fees; in comparison with which, all else is, in the eye of a fee-fed lawyer, without value. But fraud, howsoever necessary to the creation, would not be necessary to the preservation, of the fees.

CHAPTER XII.

OF THE PRINCIPLE OF PREAPPOINTED EVIDENCE AS EXEMPLIFIED IN THE CASE OF REAL EVIDENCE (EVIDENCE FROM THINGS.)

THE subject of *real* evidence will be fully considered in the next book.† There will, however, be no inconvenience in saying here what seems fit to be said with respect to the application of the principle of preappointed evidence to the field of real evidence.

The demand for instruction on this subject is not very considerable. But conception may be assisted, and the purpose of illustration answered, by bringing to view some of the most remarkable instances in which this application has been, and continues to be, generally made.

In the case of immoveable property, the *fences* of various kinds, by which intrusion from various sources is, with a degree of success more or less complete, endeavoured to be guarded against, serve at any rate for the delineation of *boundaries*, and thence of the dimensions of the space contained within them. In the case of landmarks, the purpose is confined to the mere delineation, or rather indication, of boundaries.

The function, which, in the case of boundaries, is permanently performed in relation to portions of *immoveable* property — to quantities carved out, as it were, of the surface of the globe which we inhabit — is performed occasionally in relation to masses of moveable

* Fines, recoveries,[a] lease and release, mortgage, &c., terms assignable *ad infinitum*, have nothing to match them out of England.

[a] Fines and recoveries are abolished by 3 & 4 W. IV. c. 74.—*Ed.*

† Book V. *Circumstantial*, Chap. III.

property, by the several standards of weight and measure: chiefly on the occasion of their changing owners, or on the occasion of their consumption, or change of form, in the hands of the same owner.

Proprietary marks—marks of ownership—may be considered as articles of preappointed real evidence; unless they be considered as constituting so many symbolic modes of signature, indicative of the proprietor, by being significative of his name. At any rate, and whether of real or written, they are so many articles of preappointed evidence.

Imprinted upon any subject-matter of property, the proprietor's name at length would be unquestionably an article of written evidence: no less so the initials, as in the case of G. R. for George Rex. But when, instead of the G. R., come the *broad arrow* on timber, or the *strand* in sail-cloth, then comes the doubt (happily altogether an immaterial one) as between written and real evidence.

Hydrometers, thermometers, and electrometers, are so many other standards of quality, confined, each of them, in its application, to a particular species of body.

As standards or indexes of *quantity*, so may standards or indexes of *quality*, be considered as so many articles or sources of real evidence. Where quality depends upon proportions as between the elements of the same compound body, standards of quantity serve in this way in the character of standards of quality.

Thus, different species of hydrometers serve for indicating the proportional quantities as between alcohol and water, and thence the strength of the ardent spirits composed of the two ingredients. Applied to infusions of malt, or other fermentable matters, a similar instrument, under the name of saccharometer, serves for indication of the proportions between the quantity of sugar and other fermentable matters mixed with the water, and thence the strength and value of the wort.

Touchstones serve as standards of quality, by indicating proportions as between the noble and ignoble metals.

Mint marks applied in the same view, wear an ambiguous aspect; being referable either to the head of *real* or *written*, *circumstantial* or *direct official* evidence.

The following are other examples of preappointed real evidence:—

In the hands of the importer or manufacturer, taxes are imposed upon various sorts of goods; that is, previously to the distribution made of each article in the way of sale, he is subjected to the obligation of paying to the officers of the public revenue a sum of money proportioned to the quantity and quality of the article. Upon the outside of each packet containing a determinate quantity of the article, a stamp or other mark is appointed to be impressed by the officer of the revenue, on receipt of the sum assessed upon it. The existence of any such article, in a certain quantity, not provided with such a stamp or mark, is at the same time directed to be received as sufficient evidence of the species of delinquency consisting in the non-payment of the appointed tax.

For reasons, the policy of which is a question foreign to the present purpose, the exportation of sheep and sheep's wool was for a long time thought fit to be prohibited. For the enforcement of this prohibition, a provision is inserted, prohibiting the packing of this species of commodity in masses exceeding a certain quantity (14lb.) unless it be in packages of a certain description, bearing on the outside the word 'Wool' in conspicuous letters of not less than a certain length (3 inches.*) Thus it is that the existence of a quantity above the small quantity so allowed — otherwise than in one of the sorts of packages so expressly allowed, and bearing on the outside of it the above-mentioned positive evidence of its contents — is, in any place of the description in that behalf specified, *preappointed* to be received as an article of negative evidence sufficient to warrant a decision convicting the proprietor (or other person having the article in his possession) of an individual act, belonging to the species of acts which the law has on this occasion thought fit to insert in the catalogue of punishable offences.

Standards of quality have already been mentioned as among the already established applications of the principle of preappointed to *real* evidence.

But, in many instances, an indication of the *maker* of the article is either the best or the only evidence of its quality that can be presented to the cognizance of a person whose interest, in the character of an owner or occupier, it is, to possess a just conception of it.

Compared with the instances already brought to view, such evidence of quality may be considered as belonging rather to the head of circumstantial than of direct evidence. Perhaps even those others might be considered in the same character: but be this as it may, how satisfactory a species of evidence it is in many cases, scarce any person but has had occasion to observe.

Where a manufacturer has obtained a reputation on the score of the quality of his goods, he is not apt to be insensible to the value of it, or to fail of taking measures, so far as depends upon himself, for availing himself of it: viz. by exhibiting, according to the nature of the goods, either upon the face of the goods themselves, or of the receptacles in

* 38 Geo. III. c. 38, § 28.

which they are kept, an intimation of the hand from which they came.

Unfortunately, — by the same interest by which the real maker of superior goods is excited to make known to individuals in general, in the quality of possible customers, the hand of the real maker from whom they received their quality, and from whom accordingly other goods of equal quality may naturally be expected for the same price, — other manufacturers of goods, of the same denomination but of inferior quality, are excited to have recourse to that species of fraud which consists in causing these inferior goods to be considered as having been the work of the same hand.

A practice of this kind is neither more nor less than a species of fraud — a species of forgery: possessing, if not in equal degree, in the same kind (to a considerable extent at least) the characters of that crime.

The injury, of which it is the instrument, falls in three distinguishable shapes, and on two different descriptions of persons: —

1. On the purchaser, who — the inferior goods being imposed on him for the superior — is defrauded to the amount of the difference in value.

2. On the maker of the superior goods, the rival manufacturer, who — the inferior goods being purchased instead of his superior ones, is thus injured in his property, defrauded to the amount of the profit upon the goods purchased, — in consequence of the deception and consequent mistake.

3. On the superior maker again, who, besides losing the credit attached to the authorship of the superior goods which he really made, is saddled with the discredit attached to the inferior goods which he did not make, — and is thus injured in respect of his professional reputation: and, reputation being in this sort of case a main source of property, he is thus, though in a remote and contingent way, injured in his property to an undefinable amount.

In his character of guardian of the public morals, as well as in that of protector of individual property, it seems incumbent on the legislator to do what depends on him towards the suppression of fraud in this shape. Happily — notwithstanding the names of *fraud* and *forgery*, which with so indisputable a propriety may be attributed to it — measures attended with little rigour, with rigour far inferior to that which is practised in the case of the most common and most formidable of the offences characterized by that name, promise to be sufficient.

Of the measures that seem requisite in this view, intimation may be made under four heads: — viz. 1. Prohibition; 2. Registration; 3. Procedure (summary;) 4. Penalty. Under each, a very slight and general designation is all that room can be found for in this place.

1. Prohibition. If, on goods of all sorts without exception, names and descriptions sufficient in all cases for distinction could be delineated, — prohibition, under a slight penalty, and without registration, might suffice. But the contrary is beyond dispute.

2. Registration. Offices for this purpose would need to be instituted: number and situation depending on local circumstances. But, how dissimilar soever the nature of the goods, one office at a place might serve for all.

Subjects of registration, the mark which each manufacturer might think fit to employ, according to the nature of the goods. The use of the register is, that, a manufacturer having made choice of his mark, no other manufacturer in the same line shall be at liberty to employ either that same mark, or a mark likely to be mistaken for it. To secure a sufficient degree of diversity, a previous licence would, if not absolutely necessary, be at any rate of use. On the other hand, the danger of arbitrary power, and of consequent oppression or extortion, would require to be taken into the account.

For the establishment of the office, compulsion applied to any purpose would neither be necessary nor proper. No compulsion applied to persons not sharing in the benefit, to force them to share in the burthen: in other words, no salary at the public charge. No compulsion to force any manufacturer to register his marks. By each individual in whose eyes the security is worth purchasing, it will be purchased.

The danger would be — where the assignment of the marks required judgment, time, and attention — lest, if the fee for the licence were not left to be adjusted to the quantity of time and attention that might eventually be necessary, assignments should be rashly made or refused: in the opposite case, lest here, as in the judicial offices, the opportunity of increasing official profit by unnecessary consumption or pretended consumption of official time, should become a source of factitious delay, vexation, and expense — of a sort of secret *litigation*, though without the name.*

3. Procedure summary. A topic over and over again insisted on † is, that, except in the comparatively rare cases in which, by

* By the act which gives a copyright in designs for manufacture for a year, and in designs of castings, embossments, &c. for three years (2 & 3. Vict. c. 17,) a system of registration is appointed, and each article of manufacture, to entitle it to the protection of the act must have on it the name of the registered proprietor, the number on the register, and the date of registration. — *Ed.*

† See Scotch Reform, Letter 2 (Vol. V.); and Book VIII. of the present work.

special causes, delay is rendered necessary, all judicature is unjust, that is not summary. But on this occasion, a special demand for summary procedure is created by divers circumstances. To trace out, and secure for the purpose of justiciability, the forthcomingness of the forgerer,—investigation, a process not performable under any other than summary (*i. e.* natural) procedure, will frequently be necessary.

Regular or technical procedure being (in nine out of ten cases individually taken) as inapplicable to the purpose of honest litigants, as it is, and was intended to be, favourable to the purpose of dishonest ones,—so in particular is it in this. A suit in equity is as inapposite in the character of a remedy for an honest plaintiff, as it is infallible in the character of an instrument for crushing an honest defendant, whose pecuniary circumstances are such as to disable him from resisting it.

4. Certainty and facility of conviction being afforded (as above) by the nature of the mode of procedure,—here, as elsewhere, the magnitude of the penalty might be rendered trifling in comparison with what it becomes necessary to make it where factitious uncertainty, combined with the burthen of factitious delay and expense imposed on injured prosecutors, holds out invitation to delinquency.

The shame of conviction, with the addition of the expense necessary to give it adequate publicity (the expense of prosecution having nothing factitious added to it, and the prosecutor being indemnified for his share of it,) would be sufficient. Ordinary forgerers are almost always, in respect of pecuniary circumstances, irresponsible: hence the pretence, and in some measure the necessity, for the rigour of the punishment in that case. Forgerers of this description are scarce ever, in the same respect, otherwise than responsible: sufficiently responsible, in respect of costs and penalty, as above.

Forgerer. " But my wares are in fact nothing inferior to the goods made by that man whose name gives him a monopoly as against me. This artifice is therefore an innocent one, and without which I could never hope to give myself a fair and equal chance."

Legislator. " If your goods are no better than his, no injury is done to you: the same chance which has befriended him, might have befriended, and may at any time befriend, you.

" If you goods become better, or, under the same goo ess, cheaper, sooner or later customers will find out your superiority as they found out his: an' then the tables will be turned in your favour, and you will be the monopolist. Bestir yourself.

" Your wares, *you say*, are as good as his: but how am I to be satisfied of their being so? The evidence of customers — an impartial lot of evidence — is, by your own showing, against you: what have you to oppose to it?

" In *your* instance (you say) the forgerer's wares are as good as the wares of the man of established skill and reputation, whose name, or what is equivalent, forges. Be it so. But how many will there not be whose wares are inferior! and the worse the wares, the greater the profit; — the stronger, therefore, the inducement to the forgery, and therefore the probable number of the forgerers.

" You and your more successful rival have, in my regard, no higher place the one than the other: my favour would lean rather on the side of customers, as being more numerous than makers. By favouring that state of things which holds out to each of you the best chance of a reward proportioned to his real merits, I excite each of you to exert his utmost to win the prize: and the greater your merits — the better the goods at the same price — thence the greater the advantage, the ever increasing advantage, to the people at large, in quality of customers."*

* By the Letters-Patent amendment act, 5 & 6 Wil. IV. c. 83, a person forging the name of a patentee, for the purpose of making goods pass off as his patent commodity, is liable to a penalty of £50 (§ 7.)—*Ed.*

END OF VOLUME VI

STEREOTYPED AND PRINTED BY STEVENSON AND CO.
THISTLE STREET, EDINBURGH

Printed in Great Britain
by Amazon.co.uk, Ltd.,
Marston Gate.